W9-DIE-952

CASES AND MATERIALS

Tort Law and Alternatives

SEVENTH EDITION

by

MARC A. FRANKLIN
Frederick I. Richman Professor of Law
Stanford University

ROBERT L. RABIN
A. Calder Mackay Professor of Law
Stanford University

NEW YORK, NEW YORK
FOUNDATION PRESS
2001

COPYRIGHT © 1971, 1979, 1983, 1987, 1992, 1996 FOUNDATION PRESS
COPYRIGHT © 2001 By FOUNDATION PRESS

11 Penn Plaza, Tenth Floor
New York, NY 10001
Phone Toll Free 1–877–888–1330
Fax (212) 760–8705
fdpress.com

ISBN 1–58778–059–3

TEXT IS PRINTED ON 10% POST
CONSUMER RECYCLED PAPER

IN MEMORY OF

RUTH K. FRANKLIN

*

PREFACE TO THE SEVENTH EDITION

Tort law remains such a dynamic area that we find it a continuing challenge to explore the interplay of doctrinal issues and the import of new case law developments in preparing each new edition. As a consequence we have added a considerable amount of new material, in some instances because it reflects recent developments, but in other instances because we think that the new material offers better pedagogical approaches for reflecting our understanding of the current state of tort law and alternative systems.

To highlight some particulars, we offer an expanded subsection on vicarious liability in the introductory chapter, and we have updated the principal case coverage and notes in the products liability area to focus on new developments in design defect and duty to warn case law, including the new Restatement. The products liability chapter also offers a new sub-section on work-related claims against product manufacturers. In addition, we provide comprehensive treatment of recent innovations in causation, featuring expanded coverage of the role of scientific and other technical evidence in the courtroom. Throughout, we have attempted to provide more focused attention in a variety of contexts to the interplay between tort and contract law.

As in the last edition, we have continued to revise and expand the intentional tort chapter, adding principal cases, notes and questions on defenses. In addition, we have updated the coverage of defamation, and thoroughly revised and updated the materials on privacy and intentional economic harm.

These are some of the highlights of the changes in the new edition. At the same time, we have attempted to integrate these new developments with the landmark cases and doctrinal principles that give torts its distinctive character. We hope you will find that our efforts to revise and reshape the book capture the continuing intellectual vitality of the area.

MARC A. FRANKLIN
ROBERT L. RABIN

Stanford, California
February 2001

*

ACKNOWLEDGMENTS

This revision has been substantially aided by the assistance of William Boyd, Jorey Else, Marc Fuller, Bernadette Meyler, Matthew Ploeger, Derrick Robinson, and Christian Weideman—all present or former students at the Stanford Law School. Our colleagues, William Cohen and Thomas Grey, have made helpful comments at various points during the revision. Pat Adan, Judy Dearing, and Mary Westphal provided technical assistance in preparing the manuscript. The revision received support from the Dorothy Redwine Estate, and from the Stanford Legal Research Fund, made possible by a bequest from Ira S. Lillick and by gifts from other friends of the Stanford Law School.

We would also like to thank the authors and copyright holders of the following works, who permitted their inclusion in this book:

American Law Institute. Restatement of Torts, Restatement (Second) of Torts, copyright © 1938, 1965, 1977, 1979 by the American Law Institute. Reprinted with the permission of the American Law Institute;

American Law Institute. Report to the American Law Institute, Enterprise Responsibility for Personal Injury, Volume II, pp.187-92, copyright 1991 by the American Law Institute. Reprinted with permission of the American Law Institute;

Fleming, John, The Collateral Source Rule and Loss Allocation in Tort Law, 54 California Law Review, 1478, 1546-49 (1966) copyright © 1966, California Law Review, Inc. Reprinted by permission;

Harper, Fowler, Fleming James, Jr., and Oscar Gray, The Law of Torts, 2d. ed.1986, reprinted by permission of Little, Brown & Co. (Inc.)

King, Joseph H., Jr., A Goals-Oriented Approach to Strict Liability for Abnormally Dangerous Activities, 48 Baylor L.Rev. 341, 349-61 (1996);

Kramer, Orin and Briffault, Richard, Workers Compensation: Strengthening the Social Compact, pp. 13-27, 73-75 (1991), reprinted by permission of Insurance Information Institute;

National Conference of Commissioners on Uniform State Laws, Uniform Comparative Fault Act, Sections 1-6. Reprinted by permission;

Posner, Richard A., Economic Analysis of Law, 5th ed. 1998, pp. 192-97, reprinted with the permission of Aspen Law & Business;

Posner, Richard A., A Theory of Negligence, Journal of Legal Studies, Vol. 1, pp. 29, 32-33 (1972), reprinted with the permission of the University of Chicago Press;

Rabin, Robert L., The Ideology of Enterprise Liability, 55 Maryland L.Rev. 1190, 1194-99 (1996);

Rabin, Robert L., Some Thoughts on the Efficacy of a Mass Toxics Administrative Compensation Scheme, 52 Maryland L.Rev. 951, 955-62 (1993);

Rabin, Robert L., Environmental Liability and the Tort System, 24 Houston L.Rev. 27, 28-32 (1987);

Rabin, Robert L., The Historical Development of the Fault Principle: A Reinterpretation, 15 Ga.L.Rev. 925, 950 (1981);

Ross, H. Laurence, Settled out of Court (1980 ed.), reprinted with permission, Aldine de Gruyter, New York, copyright © 1980 by H. Laurence Ross;

Schwartz, Gary, T., Tort Law and the Economy in Nineteenth Century America: A Reinterpretation, reprinted by permission of The Yale Law Journal Company and Fred B. Rothman & Company from the Yale Law Journal, Vol. 90, pp.1717-27.

SUMMARY OF CONTENTS

PREFACE TO THE SEVENTH EDITION v

ACKNOWLEDGMENTS vii

TABLE OF CASES xxi

CHAPTER I.   INTRODUCTION TO TORT LIABILITY 1

A. Prologue 1
B. When Should Unintended Injury Result in Liability? 2
C. The Litigation Process 9
D. The Parties and Vicarious Liability 17

CHAPTER II.   THE NEGLIGENCE PRINCIPLE 29

A. Historical Development of Fault Liability 29
B. The Central Concept 37
    1. The Standard of Care 37
    2. The Reasonable Person 47
C. The Roles of Judge and Jury 58
    1. In General 58
    2. The Role of Custom 67
    3. The Role of Statutes 73
D. Proof of Negligence 85
E. The Special Case of Medical Malpractice 109

CHAPTER III.   THE DUTY REQUIREMENT: PHYSICAL INJURIES 130

A. Introduction 130
B. Obligations to Others 131
C. Obligations to Protect a Third Party 158
D. Landowners and Occupiers 190
E. Intrafamily Duties 214
F. Governmental Entities 225
    1. Municipal and State Liability 226
    2. The Federal Tort Claims Act 249

CHAPTER IV.   THE DUTY REQUIREMENT: NONPHYSICAL HARM 261

A. Emotional Harm 261
B. Economic Harm 301
C. Interference With Procreation and End-of-Life Decisions 325

CHAPTER V. CAUSATION -- 341

A. Cause in Fact -- 341
   1. Basic Doctrine --- 341
   2. Introduction to Joint and Several Liability ------------------------ 368
   3. Multiple Defendants --- 374
   4. The Special Case of Toxic Harms ----------------------------------- 391
B. Proximate Cause -- 399
   1. Unexpected Harm --- 399
   2. Unexpected Manner --- 412
   3. Unexpected Victim --- 419

CHAPTER VI. DEFENSES --- 435

A. The Plaintiff's Fault -- 435
   1. Contributory Negligence --- 435
   2. Comparative Negligence -- 440
   3. Avoidable Consequences -- 457
B. Assumption of Risk --- 460
   1. Express Agreements -- 460
   2. Implied Assumption of Risk -- 469
C. Preemption --- 489

CHAPTER VII. STRICT LIABILITY -- 498

A. Doctrinal Development --- 498
B. Theoretical Perspectives --- 520

CHAPTER VIII. LIABILITY FOR DEFECTIVE PRODUCTS --------------------------- 540

A. Introduction --- 540
B. Manufacturing Defects -- 556
C. Design Defects --- 558
D. Safety Instructions and Warnings --------------------------------------- 581
E. Defenses --- 605
F. Work–Related Injuries -- 614
G. Beyond Products? --- 632
H. The Intersection of Tort and the Uniform Commercial Code --------------- 639

CHAPTER IX. TRESPASS AND NUISANCE -- 652

A. Trespass --- 652
B. Nuisance --- 658
   1. Public Nuisance -- 659
   2. Private Nuisance --- 661

CHAPTER X. DAMAGES AND INSURANCE --- 679

A. Damages -- 679
   1. Compensatory Damages --- 679
   2. Punitive Damages --- 717

B. Introduction to Insurance --- 739
    1. Loss Insurance, Collateral Sources and Subrogation -------------- 747
    2. Liability Insurance -- 761
    3. The Impact of Insurance on Tort Litigation --------------------- 767

CHAPTER XI.   A SURVEY OF ALTERNATIVES------------------------------ 785

A. Incremental Tort Reform --- 787
B. Occupational Injuries—Workers' Compensation ---------------------- 793
C. Motor Vehicle Injuries --- 816
    1. The Past -- 816
    2. The New York Experience ------------------------------------- 819
D. Focused No–Fault Schemes --- 841
E. Comprehensive No–Fault and Beyond---------------------------------- 858

CHAPTER XII.   INTENTIONAL HARM -- 864

A. Basic Doctrine --- 865
    1. Intent --- 865
    2. Assault and Battery --- 872
    3. False Imprisonment-- 882
    4. Intentional Infliction of Emotional Distress --------------------- 888
    5. Defenses and Privileges-- 910
B. Government Liability -- 928
    1. The Federal Civil Rights Action --------------------------------- 928
    2. Liability of Federal Officials------------------------------------- 944

CHAPTER XIII.   DEFAMATION --- 948

A. Common Law Background --- 948
    1. What Is Defamatory? --- 948
    2. "Of and Concerning" Plaintiff ----------------------------------- 963
    3. Strict Liability -- 966
    4. Damages: Libel and Slander------------------------------------- 967
    5. Defenses --- 974
B. Public Plaintiffs and the Constitution ------------------------------- 1000
    1. Public Officials--- 1000
    2. Public Figures-- 1013
    3. The "Actual Malice" Standard ---------------------------------- 1015
C. Private Plaintiffs and the Constitution------------------------------- 1024
D. The Public–Private Distinction -------------------------------------- 1043
    1. Identifying a "Public Official"---------------------------------- 1043
    2. Identifying a "Public Figure"----------------------------------- 1048
E. The Defendant as Commentator ------------------------------------- 1061
F. The Press as Repeater -- 1081
G. Reform Proposals--- 1091
    1. Need for Reform? -- 1091
    2. Proposed Reforms --- 1094

CHAPTER XIV.   PROTECTING PRIVACY ------------------------------------ 1098

A. Public Disclosure of Private Facts ------------------------------- 1100
    1. State Tort Analysis --- 1100
    2. Constitutional Privilege -------------------------------------- 1114
B. False–Light Privacy --- 1140
C. Intrusion -- 1151
D. Appropriation -- 1186

CHAPTER XV.   INTENTIONAL ECONOMIC HARM ----------------------------- 1216

A. Misrepresentation --- 1216
    1. Introduction --- 1216
    2. Deceit --- 1218
    3. Strict Liability --- 1239
B. Interference With Contract -------------------------------------- 1240
C. Interference With Prospective Economic Advantage ---------------- 1246
D. Contract and Tort in the Economic Sphere ------------------------ 1263

INDEX --- 1273

TABLE OF CONTENTS

Preface to the Seventh Edition --- v
Acknowledgments --- vii
Table of Cases -- xxi

Chapter I. Introduction to Tort Liability ----------------------------------- 1

A. Prologue -- 1
B. When Should Unintended Injury Result in Liability? ------------------------ 2
    Hammontree v. Jenner --- 3
C. The Litigation Process -- 9
D. The Parties and Vicarious Liability --------------------------------------- 17
    Christensen v. Swenson et al --- 18
    Baptist Memorial Hospital System v. Sampson ----------------------------- 24

Chapter II. The Negligence Principle -- 29

A. Historical Development of Fault Liability --------------------------------- 29
    Schwartz, Tort Law and the Economy in Nineteenth Century
      America: A Reinterpretation -- 30
    Brown v. Kendall --- 33
B. The Central Concept --- 37
    1. The Standard of Care -- 37
        Adams v. Bullock --- 38
        United States v. Carroll Towing Co. ---------------------------------- 41
    2. The Reasonable Person --- 47
        Bethel v. New York City Transit Authority ---------------------------- 47
C. The Roles of Judge and Jury --- 58
    1. In General -- 58
        Baltimore & Ohio Railroad Co. v. Goodman ----------------------------- 58
        Pokora v. Wabash Railway Co. --- 60
        Andrews v. United Airlines, Inc. ------------------------------------- 64
    2. The Role of Custom -- 67
        Trimarco v. Klein -- 67
    3. The Role of Statutes -- 73
        Martin v. Herzog --- 73
        Tedla v. Ellman -- 76
D. Proof of Negligence --- 85
    Negri v. Stop and Shop, Inc. --- 86
    Gordon v. American Museum of Natural History ----------------------------- 87
    Byrne v. Boadle -- 91
    McDougald v. Perry --- 94
    Ybarra v. Spangard --- 101
E. The Special Case of Medical Malpractice --------------------------------- 109
    Sheeley v. Memorial Hospital --- 109
    Connors v. University Associates in Obstetrics & Gynecology, Inc. 117
    Matthies v. Mastromonaco --- 122

CHAPTER III.   THE DUTY REQUIREMENT: PHYSICAL INJURIES ---------------- 130

A. Introduction --- 130
B. Obligations to Others --- 131
    Harper v. Herman --- 131
    Farwell v. Keaton -- 137
    Strauss v. Belle Realty Co. -------------------------------------- 144
    Uhr v. East Greenbush Central School District -------------------- 151
C. Obligations to Protect a Third Party ----------------------------- 158
    Tarasoff v. Regents of the Univ. of California ------------------- 158
    Randi W. v. Muroc Joint Unified School District ------------------ 170
    Vince v. Wilson -- 179
    Reynolds v. Hicks -- 185
D. Landowners and Occupiers -- 190
    Carter v. Kinney --- 190
    Heins v. Webster County -- 197
    Posecai v. Wal–Mart Stores, Inc. --------------------------------- 206
E. Intrafamily Duties -- 214
    Broadbent v. Broadbent --- 214
F. Governmental Entities --- 225
    1. Municipal and State Liability -------------------------------- 226
        Riss v. City of New York ------------------------------------- 226
        Lauer v. City of New York ------------------------------------ 237
        Friedman v. State of New York -------------------------------- 244
    2. The Federal Tort Claims Act ---------------------------------- 249
        Cope v. Scott -- 250

CHAPTER IV.   THE DUTY REQUIREMENT: NONPHYSICAL HARM --------------- 261

A. Emotional Harm --- 261
    Falzone v. Busch --- 261
    Metro–North Commuter Railroad Company v. Buckley ----------------- 270
    Gammon v. Osteopathic Hospital of Maine, Inc. -------------------- 278
    Portee v. Jaffee --- 282
    Johnson v. Jamaica Hospital -------------------------------------- 291
B. Economic Harm --- 301
    Nycal Corporation v. KPMG Peat Marwick LLP. ---------------------- 302
    People Express Airlines, Inc. v. Consolidated Rail Corp. --------- 313
C. Interference With Procreation and End-of-Life Decisions ---------- 325
    Emerson v. Magendantz -- 326

CHAPTER V.   CAUSATION --- 341

A. Cause in Fact -- 341
    1. Basic Doctrine --- 341
        Stubbs v. City of Rochester ---------------------------------- 342
        Zuchowicz v. United States ----------------------------------- 349
        Alberts v. Schultz --- 359
    2. Introduction to Joint and Several Liability ------------------ 368

A. Cause in Fact—Continued
    3. Multiple Defendants ---------- 374
       Summers v. Tice --------- 374
       Hymowitz v. Eli Lilly & Co. --------- 378
    4. The Special Case of Toxic Harms ---------- 391
       Rabin, Environmental Liability and the Tort System ---------- 391
B. Proximate Cause ---------- 399
    1. Unexpected Harm ---------- 399
       Benn v. Thomas ---------- 399
       Overseas Tankship (U.K.) Ltd. v. Morts Dock & Engineering
         Co., Ltd. (The Wagon Mound) ---------- 405
    2. Unexpected Manner ---------- 412
       McLaughlin v. Mine Safety Appliances Co. ---------- 412
    3. Unexpected Victim ---------- 419
       Palsgraf v. Long Island Railroad Co. ---------- 419

CHAPTER VI. DEFENSES ---------- 435

A. The Plaintiff's Fault ---------- 435
    1. Contributory Negligence ---------- 435
    2. Comparative Negligence ---------- 440
       Uniform Comparative Fault Act ---------- 441
       Fritts v. McKinne ---------- 452
    3. Avoidable Consequences ---------- 457
B. Assumption of Risk ---------- 460
    1. Express Agreements ---------- 460
       Dalury v. S–K–I, Ltd. ---------- 461
    2. Implied Assumption of Risk ---------- 469
       Murphy v. Steeplechase Amusement Co. ---------- 469
       Davenport v. Cotton Hope Plantation Horizontal Property
         Regime ---------- 476
       Roberts v. Vaughn ---------- 484
C. Preemption ---------- 489
    Geier v. American Honda Motor Company, Inc., et al. ---------- 489

CHAPTER VII. STRICT LIABILITY ---------- 498

A. Doctrinal Development ---------- 498
    Fletcher v. Rylands ---------- 498
    Rylands v. Fletcher ---------- 503
    Sullivan v. Dunham ---------- 506
    Indiana Harbor Belt Railroad Co. v. American Cyanamid Co. ---------- 511
B. Theoretical Perspectives ---------- 520
    Rabin, The Ideology of Enterprise Liability ---------- 520
    King, A Goals–Oriented Approach to Strict Tort Liability for
       Abnormally Dangerous Activities ---------- 525
    Posner, Economic Analysis of Law ---------- 535
    MacPherson v. Buick Motor Co. ---------- 540

CHAPTER VIII. LIABILITY FOR DEFECTIVE PRODUCTS ----------- 540
A. Introduction --- 540
    Escola v. Coca Cola Bottling Co. of Fresno ----------------- 546
B. Manufacturing Defects -------------------------------------- 556
C. Design Defects --- 558
    Soule v. General Motors Corporation ----------------------- 559
    Camacho v. Honda Motor Co., Ltd. -------------------------- 572
D. Safety Instructions and Warnings --------------------------- 581
    Hood v. Ryobi America Corporation ------------------------- 582
    Edwards v. Basel Pharmaceuticals -------------------------- 592
    Vassallo v. Baxter Healthcare Corporation ----------------- 597
E. Defenses --- 605
    General Motors Corporation v. Sanchez --------------------- 605
F. Work–Related Injuries -------------------------------------- 614
    Jones v. Ryobi, Ltd. -------------------------------------- 614
    Liriano v. Hobart Corp. ----------------------------------- 619
    Enterprise Responsibility for Personal Injury Vol. II, Approaches
       to Legal and Institutional Change ----------------------- 629
G. Beyond Products? --- 632
    Royer v. Catholic Medical Center -------------------------- 632
H. The Intersection of Tort and the Uniform Commercial Code --- 639
    East River Steamship Corp. v. Transamerica Delaval Inc. ---- 639

CHAPTER IX. TRESPASS AND NUISANCE ---------------------------- 652
A. Trespass -- 652
    Martin v. Reynolds Metals Co. ----------------------------- 653
B. Nuisance -- 658
    1. Public Nuisance -- 659
    2. Private Nuisance --------------------------------------- 661
       Boomer v. Atlantic Cement Co. -------------------------- 663

CHAPTER X. DAMAGES AND INSURANCE ----------------------------- 679
A. Damages --- 679
    1. Compensatory Damages ----------------------------------- 679
       Seffert v. Los Angeles Transit Lines ------------------- 680
       McDougald v. Garber ------------------------------------ 697
       Arambula v. Wells -------------------------------------- 710
    2. Punitive Damages --------------------------------------- 717
       Taylor v. Superior Court ------------------------------- 718
       BMW of North America, Inc. v. Gore --------------------- 726
B. Introduction to Insurance --------------------------------- 739
    1. Loss Insurance, Collateral Sources and Subrogation ----- 747
       Frost v. Porter Leasing Corp. -------------------------- 747
       Fleming, The Collateral Source Rule and Loss Allocation in
          Tort Law --- 755
    2. Liability Insurance ------------------------------------ 761
    3. The Impact of Insurance on Tort Litigation ------------- 767
       a. The Impact on Substantive Rulings ------------------- 767
       b. The Impact of Insurance on Procedure and Settlement - 767
       Lalomia v. Bankers & Shippers Ins. Co. ----------------- 767
       c. Suing the Insurer ----------------------------------- 774
       Pavia v. State Farm Mutual Automobile Ins. Co. --------- 774

CHAPTER XI.   A SURVEY OF ALTERNATIVES ------------------------------ 785

A. Incremental Tort Reform -- 787
B. Occupational Injuries—Workers' Compensation --------------------- 793
   Kramer & Briffault, Workers' Compensation: Strengthening the
      Social Compact --- 793
   New York Workers' Compensation Law -------------------------------- 810
C. Motor Vehicle Injuries --- 816
   1. The Past --- 816
   2. The New York Experience -------------------------------------- 819
      a. Background -- 819
      b. The New York Statute ------------------------------------- 821
         New York Insurance Law ----------------------------------- 822
D. Focused No–Fault Schemes -- 841
   Rabin, Some Thoughts on the Efficacy of a Mass Toxics Adminis-
      trative Compensation Scheme ---------------------------------- 842
E. Comprehensive No–Fault and Beyond ------------------------------- 858

CHAPTER XII.   INTENTIONAL HARM ------------------------------------ 864

A. Basic Doctrine -- 865
   1. Intent --- 865
      Garratt v. Dailey --- 865
   2. Assault and Battery -- 872
      Picard v. Barry Pontiac–Buick, Inc. ------------------------- 872
      Wishnatsky v. Huey -- 876
   3. False Imprisonment --- 882
      Lopez v. Winchell's Donut House ----------------------------- 882
   4. Intentional Infliction of Emotional Distress ---------------- 888
      Womack v. Eldridge -- 889
      McDermott v. Reynolds --------------------------------------- 901
      Hustler Magazine, Inc. v. Falwell --------------------------- 905
   5. Defenses and Privileges -------------------------------------- 910
      a. Consent -- 911
         Hart v. Geysel -- 911
      b. Self Defense --- 914
         Courvoisier v. Raymond ----------------------------------- 914
      c. Protection of Property ----------------------------------- 917
         Katko v. Briney -- 917
      d. Private Necessity -- 922
         Vincent v. Lake Erie Transportation Co. ------------------ 923
B. Government Liability -- 928
   1. The Federal Civil Rights Action ----------------------------- 928
      Wilson v. Layne --- 934
   2. Liability of Federal Officials ------------------------------ 944

CHAPTER XIII.   DEFAMATION --- 948

A. Common Law Background --- 948
    1. What Is Defamatory? ------------------------------------- 948
        Romaine v. Kallinger ----------------------------------- 949
        Matherson v. Marchello --------------------------------- 959
    2. "Of and Concerning" Plaintiff -------------------------- 963
    3. Strict Liability --------------------------------------- 966
    4. Damages: Libel and Slander ----------------------------- 967
        Matherson v. Marchello --------------------------------- 968
        Liberman v. Gelstein ----------------------------------- 970
    5. Defenses --- 974
        a. Truth -- 974
        b. Privileges --- 976
            Liberman v. Gelstein ------------------------------- 978
        c. Fair and Accurate Report --------------------------- 985
            Medico v. Time, Inc. ------------------------------- 985
        d. Retraction and Other Defenses ---------------------- 995
            Burnett v. National Enquirer, Inc. ----------------- 995
B. Public Plaintiffs and the Constitution --------------------- 1000
    1. Public Officials -------------------------------------- 1000
        New York Times Co. v. Sullivan ------------------------ 1000
    2. Public Figures -- 1013
    3. The "Actual Malice" Standard -------------------------- 1015
        a. Substantive issues --------------------------------- 1015
        b. Procedural Issues ---------------------------------- 1022
C. Private Plaintiffs and the Constitution -------------------- 1024
    Gertz v. Robert Welch, Inc. ------------------------------- 1025
D. The Public–Private Distinction ----------------------------- 1043
    1. Identifying a "Public Official" ----------------------- 1043
    2. Identifying a "Public Figure" ------------------------- 1048
        Wells v. Liddy -- 1049
E. The Defendant as Commentator ------------------------------- 1061
    Milkovich v. Lorain Journal Co. --------------------------- 1063
    Flamm v. American Association of University Women --------- 1067
F. The Press as Repeater -------------------------------------- 1081
    Khawar v. Globe International, Inc. ----------------------- 1081
G. Reform Proposals --- 1091
    1. Need for Reform? -------------------------------------- 1091
    2. Proposed Reforms -------------------------------------- 1094

CHAPTER XIV.   PROTECTING PRIVACY ------------------------------ 1098

A. Public Disclosure of Private Facts ------------------------- 1100
    1. State Tort Analysis ----------------------------------- 1100
        Haynes v. Alfred A. Knopf, Inc. ----------------------- 1101
    2. Constitutional Privilege ------------------------------ 1114
        The Florida Star v. B.J.F. ---------------------------- 1116
        Breach of Confidence? --------------------------------- 1131
        Humphers v. First Interstate Bank of Oregon ----------- 1131
B. False–Light Privacy -- 1140
    Cantrell v. Forest City Publishing Co. -------------------- 1141

C. Intrusion -- 1151
   Nader v. General Motors Corp. --------------------------------------- 1151
   Galella v. Onassis--- 1163
   Desnick v. American Broadcasting Companies, Inc.-------------- 1167
   Shulman v. Group W Productions, Inc., et al. --------------------- 1174
D. Appropriation--- 1186
   Zacchini v. Scripps–Howard Broadcasting Co. ------------------- 1187
   Cardtoons, L.C. v. Major League Baseball Players Association ------- 1194

CHAPTER XV. INTENTIONAL ECONOMIC HARM---------------------------------- 1216

A. Misrepresentation -- 1216
   1. Introduction --- 1216
   2. Deceit--- 1218
      Ollerman v. O'Rourke Co., Inc.------------------------------------ 1223
   3. Strict Liability --- 1239
B. Interference With Contract --- 1240
   Imperial Ice Co. v. Rossier--- 1240
C. Interference With Prospective Economic Advantage----------------- 1246
   Della Penna v. Toyota Motor Sales, U.S.A., Inc. ----------------- 1246
D. Contract and Tort in the Economic Sphere ------------------------- 1263
   All–Tech Telecom, Inc. v. Amway Corporation ------------------- 1263

INDEX -- 1273

*

TABLE OF CASES

Principal cases are in bold type. Non-principal cases are in roman type. References are to Pages.

Aas v. Superior Court, 646
ABB Combustion Engineering Services, Inc., Warnek v., 1271
Abbott Laboratories, Martin v., 381, 388
Abbott Laboratories, Sindell v., 381, 386, 387, 388, 389, 390
Abbott v. Page Airways, Inc., 98
Abdulai v. Roy, 835
Abebe–Jira v. Negewo, 880
A.B. Leach & Co., Seneca Wire & Mfg. Co. v., 1217
ACF Industries, Inc., Carrillo v., 496
Ackerman Inv. Co., Tanberg v., 458
Ackley, Stambovsky v., 1233
ACS Investors, Inc. v. McLaughlin, 1244
Acuar v. Letourneau, 717
Adams v. Bullock, 38, 39, 40, 41, 44, 47, 62
Adams v. Government Emp. Ins. Co., 838
Adams v. Murakami, 736
Adams v. Star Enterprise, 673
Adams v. Union Carbide Corp., 625
Adams, Wagenmann v., 310
Adcox v. Children's Orthopedic Hosp. and Medical Center, 300
Addis v. Steele, 417
Adickes v. S.H. Kress & Co., 931, 932
Adkins v. Thomas Solvent Co., 673, 674
Adler, H. Rosenblum, Inc. v., 307, 320
Adolf Philipp Co. v. New Yorker Staats–Zeitung, 983
Aesoph v. Kusser, 1234
Aetna Casualty & Surety Co. v. Safeco Ins. Co., 771
Affiliated Publications, Phantom Touring, Inc. v., 1074, 1075
Afton, Inc., Duncan v., 312
Agnant v. Shakur, 962
Agoado Realty Corp. v. United Intern. Ins. Co., 742
Air Disaster at Lockerbie, Scotland on Dec. 21, 1988, In re, 851
Airport Rent–A–Car, Inc. v. Prevost Car, Inc., 646
A.J. Const. Corp., Egan v., 456
Akins v. Glens Falls City School Dist., 62
Alameda–Contra Costa Medical Ass'n, Bernstein v., 116
Albala v. City of New York, 166, 167, 430
Albany Urology Clinic, P.C. v. Cleveland, 128
Alberts v. Schultz, 359, 367
Albright v. Oliver, 933

Albritton v. Neighborhood Centers Ass'n for Child Development, 225
Alcorn v. Anbro Engineering, Inc., 893
Alcorn v. Mitchell, 875
Alfred A. Knopf, Inc., Haynes v., 1101, 1106, 1108, 1110, 1114, 1127, 1131, 1193
Alfred H. Mayer Co., Jones v., 944
Algee, Munn v., 458
Alibrandi v. Helmsley, 439
Allan v. Levy, 129
Allegheny Airlines, Inc., Nader v., 1236
Allen v. Southern Pac. Co., 468
Allen County Community Jr. College, Britt v., 195
Allen, Goss v., 57
Alliance Resources Corp., TXO Production Corp. v., 736
Allied News Co., Carson v., 1059
Allied Products Corp., Carrel v., 628
Allore v. Flower Hosp., 339
Alloway v. General Marine Industries, L.P., 645
Allred, Sorensen v., 445
Allright, Inc. v. Schroeder, 468
Allstate Ins. Co. v. Batacan, 764
Allstate Ins. Co. v. Mugavero, 741, 743, 745
Allstate Ins. Co., Black v., 225
All–Tech Telecom, Inc. v. Amway Corp., 1263, 1269
Almaraz, Faya v., 277
Alter, Schleier for and on Behalf of Alter v., 217
Aluminium Limited Sales, Inc., Channel Master Corp. v., 1216, 1217, 1219, 1269
Alvarado v. J.C. Penney Co., Inc., 84
Alvarez v. New Haven Register, Inc., 23
Amazing Products, Inc., Briscoe v., 592
Ambassador Ins. Co. v. Montes, 745
Ambrosio, New York City Transit Authority v., 832
Amchem Products, Inc. v. Windsor, 395
AmClyde, McDermott, Inc. v., 448
America Online, Inc., Zeran v., 966
American Airlines, Inc., Borer v., 300
American Airlines, Inc., Harris v., 497
American Ass'n of University Women, Flamm v., 1067, 1076
American Bank & Trust Co. v. Federal Reserve Bank of Atlanta, 1263
American Broadcasting Companies, Inc., Clark v., 963

American Broadcasting Companies, Inc., Desnick v., 975, **1167**, 1172, 1173, 1186

American Broadcasting Companies, Inc., Sanders v., 1185, 1186

American Broadcasting Companies, Inc., Silvester v., 1060

American College of Emergency Physicians, Schwartz v., 975

American Cyanamid Co., Indiana Harbor Belt R. Co. v., 511, 518

American Cyanamid Co., McGrath v., 482

American Employer's Ins. Co. v. Smith, 745

American Family Mut. Ins. Co., Gould v., 488

American Family Service Corp. v. Michelfelder, 1238

American Heritage Products, Inc., Martin Luther King, Jr., Center for Social Change, Inc. v., 1187

American Home Products Corp., Home Ins. Co. v., 744

American Honda Motor Co., Inc., Bittner by Bittner v., 569

American Honda Motor Co., Inc., Geier v., 489, 496, 614

American Motors Corp., Elmore v., 552

American Museum of Natural History, Gordon v., 87, 88

American Nat. Property and Cas. Co., Neiman v., 707

American Policyholders' Ins. Co., Carriers Ins. Co. v., 782

American Safety Equipment Corp. v. Winkler, 604

American Smelting & Refining Co. v. W.C.A.B., 810

American Smelting and Refining Co., Bradley v., 658

American Tobacco Co., Castano v., 394

AMF Harley-Davidson, Kutzler v., 579

A & M Karagheusian, Inc., Santor v., 645

Amway Corp., All-Tech Telecom, Inc. v., 1263, 1269

Amyot v. Luchini, 1239

Anaya v. Superior Court, 404

Anbro Engineering, Inc., Alcorn v., 893

Anderson v. Fisher Broadcasting Companies, Inc., 1111

Anderson v. Liberty Lobby, Inc., 1023

Anderson v. Nissei ASB Mach. Co., Ltd., 623

Anderson v. Owens-Corning Fiberglas Corp., 602

Anderson v. St. Francis-St. George Hosp., Inc., 339

Anderson, Georgia Soc. of Plastic Surgeons, Inc. v., 1060

Anderson, Haben v., 142

Anderson, Liberty Lobby, Inc. v., 999

Andre v. Pomeroy, 64, 214

Andrews v. Reynolds Memorial Hosp., Inc., 709

Andrews v. United Airlines, Inc., 64, 67, 72

Angrand v. Key, 710

Anguiano v. E.I. Du Pont De Nemours & Co., Inc., 496

Animal Quarantine Station, Division of Animal Industry, Dept. of Agriculture, State of Hawaii, Bd. of Agriculture, Campbell v., 296, 297

Ann & Hope of Rhode Island, Inc., Soares v., 886

Ann M. v. Pacific Plaza Shopping Center, 209, 211

Antablin, Cheong v., 474

A.P. Green Industries, Inc., Bourgeois v., 398

Aqueduct Realty Corp., Burgos v., 348, 349

Arambula v. Wells, 710, 715, 747

Arato v. Avedon, 312

Arcadian Corp., Port Authority of New York and New Jersey v., 592

Arcand v. Evening Call Pub. Co., 965

Arcell, Long v., 1022

Arctic Co., Ltd. v. Loudoun Times Mirror, 1061

Ard v. Ard, 224

Ard, Ard v., 224

Argentina v. Emery World Wide Delivery Corp., 832

Ariens Co., Hayes v., 599

Arizona Republic, Crane v., 1048

Arman, Ltd., Sharon P. v., 211

Armstrong Rubber Co., Berry v., 674

Armstrong v. Simon & Schuster, Inc., 957

Arnot-Ogden Memorial Hosp., Karney by Karney v., 689

Arrowwood By and Through Loeb, Estate of v. State, 248

Arsenault v. Pa-Ted Spring Co., Inc., 789

Arthur Young & Co., Bily v., 308

Arthur Young & Co., Mattco Forge, Inc. v., 447

Ash, Cort v., 157

Ashe v. Radiation Oncology Associates, 129

Ashmore v. Cleanweld Products, Inc., 445

Aspen Highlands Skiing Corp., Bauer v., 613

Associated Milk Producers, Inc., Ossenfort v., 299

Associated Press v. Walker, 1013, 1014, 1015

Associated Press, Bufalino v., 991

Associated Press, International News Service v., 1258

Atlantic Cement Co., Boomer v., 309 N.Y.S.2d 312, 257 N.E.2d 870 (N.Y.1970), **663,** 669, 670, 671, 672, 673, 675, 676, 677

Atlantic Cement Co., Inc., Boomer v., 72 Misc.2d 834, 340 N.Y.S.2d 97 (N.Y.Sup. 1972), 673

Atlantic Cement Co., Kinley v., 673

Atlantic Coast Line R. Co., Tiller v., 815

Atlantic Mut. Ins. Co., Locascio v., 832

Atlantic Richfield Co., Tameny v., 1271

Aufrichtig v. Lowell, 312

Augsburger, Commerce Bank v., 222

Austin, Letter Carriers v., 1062, 1074

Autery v. United States, 259

Auto-Owners Ins. Co. v. Churchman, 741

Auvil v. CBS 60 Minutes, 1259

Avco Corp., Hillrichs v., 723

Avedon, Arato v., 312
Avery, General Acc. Fire and Life Assur. Corp., Ltd. v., 834
Aves v. Shah, 696

Bachenberg, Petrillo v., 311
Bader v. Johnson, 334
Baer, Rosenblatt v., 1043, 1044, 1045, 1046, 1048
Bagley, Wheeler v., 451
Bahr v. Statesman Journal Co., 975
Bailey, Summers v., 1167
Baker v. Bhajan, 974
Baker v. David Alan Dorfman, 281
Baker v. Shymkiv, 869
Baker, Moore v., 127
Baldinger v. Consolidated Mut. Ins. Co., 870
Ballard v. Uribe, 172, 177, 212
Ballard, Owens–Corning Fiberglas Corp. v., 738
Baltimore & O.R. Co. v. Goodman, 58, 59, 60, 63
Baltimore & O.R. Co., Holland v., 196
Bamond v. Nationwide Mut. Ins. Co., 831
Bandel v. Friedrich, 715, 717
Bandila Shipping, Inc., Ghotra by Ghotra v., 269
Bangor Hydro–Electric Co., Staples v., 952, 983, 1022, 1076
Bank of New York v. Berisford Intern., 1243
Bank of Oregon v. Independent News, Inc., 1061
Bankers & Shippers Ins. Co., Lalomia v., 740, 764, **767,** 769, 770, 771, 870
Banks v. ICI Americas, Inc., 567, 570
Banner v. Lyon & Healy, 1222
Baptist Memorial Hosp. System v. Sampson, 24, 27, 28
Baptist Memorial Hosp., Sullivan v., 953, 1012
Barcelo v. Elliott, 311
Bardere v. Zafir, 813
Barke, Tresemer v., 136
Barker v. Kallash, 445
Barker v. Lull Engineering Co., 558, 559, 566, 571, 579
Barnes v. Dungan, 142
Barnes v. Geiger, 287
Barnes v. Outlaw, 299
Barnes Hosp., Washington by Washington v., 716
Barnhill v. Davis, 286
Barnstable County Mut. Fire Ins. Co. v. Lally, 771
Barr v. Matteo, 976
Barrera v. State Farm Mut. Auto. Ins. Co., 766
Barrett v. Emanuel Hosp., 108
Barry Pontiac–Buick, Inc., Picard v., 872, 875
Barter v. Wilson, 955
Bartnicki v. Vopper, 1185
Bartolone v. Jeckovich, 402, 458
Bartow v. Smith, 888

Basel Pharmaceuticals, Edwards v., 83, 84, **592,** 596, 614
Bashi v. Wodarz, 54, 55
Baskerville v. Culligan Intern. Co., 896
Basko v. Sterling Drug, Inc., 377
Bassey v. Mistrough, 79
Bast v. Prudential Ins. Co. of America, 497
Batacan, Allstate Ins. Co. v., 764
Batavia Atomic Horseshoes, Inc., Stiles v., 554
Battalla v. State, 266
Bauer v. Aspen Highlands Skiing Corp., 613
Bauer v. J.B. Hunt Transport, Inc., 100
Baughn v. Honda Motor Co., Ltd., 571
Baxter, Biette v., 836
Baxter Healthcare Corp., Vassallo v., 597, 600, 602, 614, 627
Beacon Journal Pub. Co., Lansdowne v., 1042
Bean v. BIC Corp., 588
Bear Stearns & Co., Pacific Gas & Electric Co. v., 1246
Beardsley v. Kilmer, 1262, 1263
Beauharnais v. Illinois, 965, 1000
Bed, Bath & Beyond of La Jolla, Inc. v. La Jolla Village Square Venture Partners, 1245
Belcher Oil Co., Freeman & Mills, Inc. v., 1270
Bell v. Burson, 764
Bellah v. Greenson, 167
Belle Realty Co., Strauss v., 144, 149, 151, 321
Benn v. Thomas, 399, 402
Bennett v. Lembo), 704
Bennett v. Napolitano, 194, 202
Bennington School Dist., Inc., Palmer v., 1047
Ben–Oliel v. Press Pub. Co., 959
Bergen Record Corp., Turf Lawnmower Repair, Inc. v., 1037
Berisford Intern., Bank of New York v., 1243
Berkeley Publishers, Doe v., 1108
Bernstein v. Alameda–Contra Costa Medical Ass'n, 116
Berry v. Armstrong Rubber Co., 674
Berry v. Sugar Notch Borough, 411
Berschauer/Phillips Const. Co. v. Seattle School Dist. No. 1, 324
Berthiaume's Estate v. Pratt, 1162
Berube, Luoni v., 189
Beshada v. Johns–Manville Products Corp., 600, 601
Bessemer Processing Co., Inc., James v., 601, 602
Best v. Taylor Mach. Works, 792
Best Cellars Inc. v. Grape Finds at Dupont, Inc., 1257
Betancourt v. Manhattan Ford Lincoln Mercury, Inc., 412
Beth Israel Hospital, Kallenberg v., 366
Bethel v. New York City Transit Authority, 47, 50, 51, 56, 67
Betty M., Eric J. v., 178
Betty, Seppi v., 450
Bevan v. Vassar Farms, Inc., 449

Beynon v. Montgomery Cablevision Ltd. Partnership, 269
BF Goodrich Co., Douglas–Hanson Co., Inc. v., 1269
Bhajan, Baker v., 974
Biakanja v. Irving, 310, 311
BIC Corp., Bean v., 588
BIC Corp., Ray by Holman v., 567
Bice v. Leslie's Poolmart, Inc., 497
Bicron Corp., Kewanee Oil Co. v., 1258
Biddle v. Warren Gen. Hosp., 1138
Biette v. Baxter, 836
Big Lake Oil Co., Turner v., 82, 505
Billings Mutual Ins. Co., Overcast v., 953
Bilotto, H.E. Butt Grocery Co. v., 450
Bily v. Arthur Young & Co., 308
Binakonsky v. Ford Motor Co., 591, 611
Bio–Science Laboratories, Curlender v., 337
Bird & Son, Inc., Stockdale v., 289
Birdsong, Curtis Pub. Co. v., 1062
Birkner v. Salt Lake County, 23
Bishop v. Nielsen, 222
Bittner by Bittner v. American Honda Motor Co., Inc., 569
Bittner, Green v., 708
Bivens v. Six Unknown Named Agents of Federal Bureau of Narcotics, 260, 945, 946, 947
B.J.F., The Florida Star v.,, 1116, 1125, 1127, 1128, 1184
Black v. Allstate Ins. Co., 225
Black Clawson Co., Gebo v., 554
Black Industries, Inc. v. Emco Helicopters, Inc., 488
Black, Inouye v., 107
Blagg v. Illinois F.W.D. Truck and Equipment Co., 448
Blaine Kern Artista, Inc., Price v., 572
Blair, Principal Cas. Ins. Co. v., 224
Blakely v. Camp Ondessonk, 194
Bland v. Hill, 900
Blankenship v. General Motors Corp., 789
Bloomfield Motors, Inc., Henningsen v., 550
Blue Earth County, Sandborg v., 446
BMW of North America, Inc. v. Gore,, 726, 736, 737, 738
Boadle, Byrne v., 91, 93, 97, 101, 121
Board of County Com'rs of Bryan County, Okl. v. Brown, 930
Board of Ed. of City of New York, Hoffman v., 236, 237
Board of Educ. of City of New York, Chainani by Chainani v., 436
Bob Penkhus Volvo–Mazda, Inc., Liebelt v., 183
Bocre Leasing Corp. v. General Motors Corp. (Allison Gas Turbine Div., 645
Boddie v. Scott, 481
Boehner v. McDermott, 1184, 1185
Boget, Rovira v., 955
Bojarski, Reed v., 165
Bolden v. PRC Inc., 894
Bolton v. Department of Human Services, 969
Bolton v. Stone, 46, 410

Bolubasz, Kaczkowski v., 689
Bomb Disaster At Roseville, California, On April 28, 1973, In re, 519
Bonney, Kelley v., 1047
Bonte, Bonte for Bonte v., 222
Bonte for Bonte v. Bonte, 222
Boomer v. Atlantic Cement Co., 309 N.Y.S.2d 312, 257 N.E.2d 870 (N.Y.1970), **663,** 669, 670, 671, 672, 673, 675, 676, 677
Boomer v. Atlantic Cement Co., Inc., 72 Misc.2d 834, 340 N.Y.S.2d 97 (N.Y.Sup. 1972), 673
Boon v. Rivera, 177, 178
Booth v. Curtis Pub. Co., 1212
Booth v. Mary Carter Paint Co., 448
Booth v. Rome, W. & O.T.R. Co., 509, 510
Borer v. American Airlines, Inc., 300
Borland v. Sanders Lead Co., Inc., 658
Borquez, Ozer v., 1110, 1131
Borrelli, Ochs v., 331
Bortz v. Noon, 1239
Bose Corp. v. Consumers Union of United States, Inc., 1022, 1023
Boss & Phelps, Inc., Remeikis v., 1235
Boston Gas Co., Sullivan v., 282
Boston Herald, Inc., Peckham v., 1109
Boston & W.R. Corp., Farwell v., 37
Boswell v. Phoenix Newspapers, Inc., 998
Boucher By and Through Boucher v. Dixie Medical Center, a Div. of IHC Hospitals, Inc., 299
Bourgeois v. A.P. Green Industries, Inc., 398
Bovsun v. Sanperi, 288, 291, 294, 295
Bower v. Peate, 502
Bower v. Westinghouse Elec. Corp., 396, 397
Bower, Kahn v., 1047
Bowers v. Ottenad, 195
Bowley, Firemen's Ins. Co. of Newark, N.J. v., 836
Bowline, Ferroggiaro v., 430
Bowman v. United States, 257
Boyd v. Nationwide Mut. Ins. Co., 982
Boyd v. Racine Currency Exchange, Inc., 212, 213
Boyer Co., L.C., Field v., 372
Boyle v. United Technologies Corp., 554
Boyle Drug Co., Conley v., 387, 388
Boyles v. Kerr, 745
Bozek, Long Beach, City of v., 886
Bradley v. American Smelting and Refining Co., 658
Bradshaw v. Swagerty, 893
Brady v. Ottaway Newspapers, Inc., 965
Brady, Ellison v., 895
Bragg v. Genesee County Agr. Soc., 197
Bragg v. Owens–Corning Fiberglas Corp., 601
Brahm v. Hatch, 170
Brannigan v. Usitalo, 695
Braun v. Buffalo General Electric Co., 39, 40, 44
Braun v. Flynt, 1148, 1149
Breckenridge, Griffin v., 943, 944
Brennan, Farmer v., 931
Bresee, Santy v., 137

Bresler, Greenbelt Co-op. Pub. Ass'n v., 1061, 1074
Bright, Williams v., 458
Brimelow v. Casson, 1244
Brinckerhoff, Jacoby v., 301
Briney, Katko v., 917
Briscoe v. Amazing Products, Inc., 592
Briscoe v. Reader's Digest Association, Inc., 1112, 1125, 1126, 1127
Britt v. Allen County Community Jr. College, 195
Broadbent, Broadbent by Broadbent v., 214, 221, 224
Broadbent by Broadbent v. Broadbent,, 214, 221, 224
Brooks, Harrison v., 944
Brosnahan v. Western Air Lines, Inc., 67
Brotman, Kumaran v., 1060
Brown v. Collins, 505
Brown v. Kelly Broadcasting Co., 982, 1038
Brown v. Kendall, 33, 36, 37, 435, 510
Brown v. Shyne, 83
Brown v. Superior Court, 382
Brown v. Wal–Mart Discount Cities, 372
Brown, Board of County Com'rs of Bryan County, Okl. v., 930
Brown Forman Corp. v. Brune, 582
Brown, Manning v., 445
Bruce Templeton ex rel. Templeton, Estate of v. Daffern, 189
Brune, Brown Forman Corp. v., 582
Bruno & Stillman, Inc. v. Globe Newspaper Co., 1061
Bruzga v. PMR Architects, P.C., 633
Bryan R. v. Watchtower Bible and Tract Soc. of New York, Inc., 281
Bryant v. Glastetter, 488
Bryant v. United States, 233
Buchanan, Losee v., 504, 509, 658, 758
Buck, Tuttle v., 1261, 1262
Buckeye Gas Products Co., Cotton v., 588
Buckley v. Fitzsimmons, 815, 941
Buckley v. Littell, 1059, 1062
Buckley, Metro–North Commuter R. Co. v., 270, 398
Buckman Co. v. Plaintiffs' Legal Committee, 496
Buettner v. R.W. Martin & Sons, Inc., 627
Bufalino v. Associated Press, 991
Buffalo & Erie County Private Industry Council, Johnson v., 837
Buffalo General Electric Co., Braun v., 39, 40, 44
Buick Motor Co., MacPherson v., 130, 540, 544, 545, 550, 614
Bulger, Welsh v., 115
Bullock, Adams v., 38, 39, 40, 41, 44, 47, 62
Bunge Corp., Tharp v., 195
Buracker, Wilt v., 705
Burger King Corp., Iannelli v., 212
Burgess v. Superior Court, 294
Burgos v. Aqueduct Realty Corp., 348, 349
Burling, Melvin v., 1163
Burlington Industries, Inc. v. Ellerth, 895, 897

Burnett v. National Enquirer, Inc., 995, 998, 1207
Burson, Bell v., 764
Busch, Falzone v., 261, 266, 268, 270, 276, 281, 289, 295
Bush v. Lucas, 946
Butts, Curtis Pub. Co. v., 1013, 1014, 1015
Butz v. Economou, 946
Buyea, Carney v., 436
Byrd v. English, 320
Byrne v. Boadle,, 91, 93, 97, 101, 121

Cain v. Hearst Corp., 1145
Calder v. Jones, 1000
Caldwell v. Haynes, 687
California v. Greenwood, 1166
California Conserving Co. v. D'Avanzo, 1220
California Newspapers, Inc., Hendrickson v., 1113
Caltex, United States v., 928
Calvanese v. Calvanese, 754
Calvanese, Calvanese v., 754
Camacho v. Honda Motor Co., Ltd., 572, 579, 580, 589, 591, 614
Camenisch v. Superior Court, 310
Camp Ondessonk, Blakely v., 194
Campbell v. Animal Quarantine Station, Division of Animal Industry, Dept. of Agriculture, 296, 297
Campbell v. General Motors Corp., 566
Campbell v. Parker–Hannifin Corp., 391
Campbell, Continental Auto Lease Corp. v., 438
Campbell, Perez v., 765
Campo, Crawn v., 473
Campos v. Firestone Tire & Rubber Co., 587
Canton, Ohio, City of v. Harris, 930, 931
Cantrell v. Forest City Pub. Co., 1141, 1145, 1147, 1149, 1150
Cantrell, Clark v., 724, 864
Canuso, Strawn v., 1232
Capital Cities/ABC, Inc., Food Lion, Inc. v., 1186
Capital Cities Communications, Inc., Park v., 1060
Capital Cities Communications, Inc., Prozeralik v., 1092
Capital Co., Herzog v., 1223
Capizzi v. Southern Dist. Reporters, Inc., 808
Cappier, Union Pac. Ry. Co. v., 135
Caraway, Gibbons v., 488
Carbone v. Visco, 833, 837
Carchidi v. Rodenhiser, 693, 694
Carde, Ouellette v., 451
Cardtoons, L.C. v. Major League Baseball Players Ass'n, 1194
Carey v. Lovett, 294
Carey v. Piphus, 943
Carlin v. Superior Court, 602
Carlson v. Green, 945
Carmichael, Kumho Tire Co., Ltd. v., 356
Carney v. Buyea, 436
Carolina Cas. Ins. Co., Warner Trucking, Inc. v., 21

Carr v. Hood, 983

Carradine v. State, 976

Carrel v. Allied Products Corp., 628

Carriers Ins. Co. v. American Policyholders' Ins. Co., 782

Carrillo v. ACF Industries, Inc., 496

Carroll v. Gava, 1237

Carroll v. Whitney, 372, 374

Carroll Mill Co., Inc., Gain v., 286

Carroll, Roman v., 296

Carroll Towing Co., United States v., 41, 43, 44, 45, 70

Carson v. Allied News Co., 1059

Carter v. Kinney, 190, 197, 203, 204

Caruso v. Hall, 835

Carver, Clinkscales v., 75

Casablanca Records, Hicks v., 1214

Casebolt v. Cowan, 183

Casey v. Russell, 79

Casey, Planned Parenthood of Southeastern Pennsylvania v., 333, 1139

Cash & Carry Bldg. Center, Inc., Pridham v., 404

Casson, Brimelow v., 1244

Castano v. American Tobacco Co., 394

Castro v. QVC Network, Inc., 605

Caterpillar Tractor Co., Inc., West v., 649

Catholic Medical Center, Royer v., 632

Catlin v. Union Oil Co. of California, 417

C.B.S., Inc., Valentine v., 955

CBS Inc., Westmoreland v., 1019

CBS 60 Minutes, Auvil v., 964, 1259

Cedar Bldg. Corp., National Conversion Corp. v., 1222

Cedarapids, Inc., Meade v., 1222

Cedars–Sinai Medical Center v. Superior Court, 100

Celli, Pleasant v., 309

Central Arkansas Broadcasting Co., Inc., Holman v., 1113

Cestonaro v. United States, 257, 259

Chainani by Chainani v. Board of Educ. of City of New York, 436

Chamberlain, McNary v., 1245

Champagne v. Raybestos–Manhattan, Inc., 460

Channel Master Corp. v. Aluminium Limited Sales, Inc., 1216, 1217, 1219, 1269

Chapadeau v. Utica Observer–Dispatch, 1039, 1041

Chapin v. Knight–Ridder, Inc., 957, 1091

Chaplinsky v. New Hampshire, 1000

Chapman, Richardson v., 696

Chappell v. Wallace, 946

Charles, Rice v., 708

Chatham Furnace Co. v. Moffatt, 1218

Chavez v. Southern Pac. Transp. Co., 518

Cheatham, Newing v., 108

Chemical Laboratories, Inc., Dundee Cement Co. v., 323

Cheong v. Antablin, 474

Cher v. Forum Intern., Ltd., 7 Med.L.Rptr. 2593 (C.D.Cal.1982), 1212

Cher v. Forum Intern., Ltd., 692 F.2d 634 (9th Cir.1982), 1212

Cherry v. Des Moines Leader, 983

Chesebrough–Pond's, Inc., Harold F. Ritchie, Inc. v., 1257

Cheung v. Ryder Truck Rental, Inc., 96

Chevrolet Division of General Motors, Sandford v., 610

Chevron Chemical Co., Ferebee v., 394

Chiara v. Fry's Food Stores of Arizona, Inc., 90

Chicago, B. & Q.R. Co. v. Krayenbuhl, 44, 196

Chicago Osteopathic Hosp., Jones v., 706, 707

Children's Orthopedic Hosp. and Medical Center, Adcox v., 300

Chilicky, Schweiker v., 946

Chin ex rel. Chin, Estate of v. St. Barnabas Medical Center, 107

Chizmar v. Mackie, 277, 281

Christensen v. Swenson, 18, 22

Christian, Rowland v., 197, 203, 204

Chronicle Publishing Co., Lafayette Morehouse, Inc. v., 1024

Chronicle Publishing Co., Sipple v., 1112

Chrysler Corp., Dawson v., 580

Churchman, Auto–Owners Ins. Co. v., 741

Chuy v. Philadelphia Eagles Football Club, 1059

Cianci v. New Times Pub. Co., 1064, 1090

Cincinnati Bengals, Inc., Hackbart v., 913

Cipollone v. Liggett Group, Inc., 495, 496

Circus Circus Hotels, Inc., Wilson v., 348

Citicorp Mortg., Inc., Gibb v., 1235, 1237

Cities Service Co. v. State, 506

Citizens First Nat. Bank of Princeton, Lovgren v., 1150

City and County of (see name of city)

City Exp., Inc. v. Express Partners, 324

City of Boca Raton, Faragher v., 895, 897

City of Cincinnati, Pembaur v., 930

City of Cohoes, Platz v., 80

City of Des Moines, Meyer v., 459, 460

City of Harker Heights, Tex., Collins v., 931

City of Independence, Mo., Owen v., 942

City of Jamestown, Kircher v., 233

City of Kingston, Parvi v., 142

City of Knoxville, Wright v., 444

City of Los Angeles, Golden State Transit Corp. v., 933

City of Los Angeles, Lubner v., 295, 296

City of New York, Albala v., 166, 167, 430

City of New York, Cuffy v., 155, 231, 232, 243

City of New York, Lanzano v., 687

City of New York, Lauer v., 237, 243, 244

City of New York, Markus v., 12

City of New York, Merced v., 233

City of New York, Riss v., 226, 230, 231, 232, 234, 243, 248, 932

City of New York, Schuster v., 230, 234

City of New York, Sorichetti by Sorichetti v., 230

City of New York, Tucker v., 13

City of Phoenix, Hutcherson v., 371

City of Phoenix, Wiggs v., 372

City of Reno, Posadas v., 974

City of Roanoke Redevelopment and Housing Authority, Wright v., 933

City of Rochester, Stubbs v., 342, 349

City of Rolling Meadows, Poole v., 446

City of St. Paul, Minn., R.A.V. v., 966

City of Westminster, Davidson v., 230, 244

Claiborne Hardware Co., N. A. A. C. P. v., 1260

Clark v. American Broadcasting Companies, Inc., 963

Clark v. Cantrell, 724, 864

Clark v. Pangan, 23

Clark v. Rowe, 452

Clark–Aiken Co. v. Cromwell–Wright Co., Inc., 505

Clark, Ribas v., 1174

Clarke v. Hoek, 165

Clark Equipment Co., Tabieros v., 580

Clarke, Reynolds v., 29

Clayborne, Vereen v., 962

Cleanweld Products, Inc., Ashmore v., 445

Cleveland, Albany Urology Clinic, P.C. v., 128

Clinger v. New York City Transit Authority, 232

Clinkscales v. Carver, 75

Clyburn v. News World Communications, Inc., 1059

C.M. v. J.M., 904

CMP Publications, Inc., Levine v., 1042

Coca Cola Bottling Co. of Fresno, Escola v., 525, 546, 550, 551, 555, 638, 639

Cocking, Farmers Ins. Exchange v., 746

Coclin v. Lane Press, Inc., 980

Coffman v. Keene Corp., 586

Cohen v. Illinois Institute of Technology, 944

Cohen v. Petty, 55

Cohen v. St. Regis Paper Co., 416

Cohen, Junius Const. Co. v., 1235

Cohn, Cox Broadcasting Corp. v., 1114, 1115, 1125, 1126, 1127, 1128, 1149, 1193

Cohoes Co., Hay v., 508, 509

Cole v. Fair Oaks Fire Protection Dist., 813

Cole v. Taylor, 168

Coleman v. MacLennan, 984, 985, 1011

Collins v. City of Harker Heights, Tex., 931

Collins v. Eli Lilly Co., 381, 724

Collins, Brown v., 505

Columbia Broadcasting System, Le Mistral, Inc. v., 1172, 1173

Combs, Cooperative Fire Ins. Ass'n v., 741

Commerce Bank v. Augsburger, 222

Commercial Union Assurance Companies v. Safeway Stores, Inc., 782

Commonwealth Edison Co., Epping v., 691

Commonwealth Highland Theatres, Inc., Malloy v., 99

Compco Corp. v. Day–Brite Lighting, Inc., 1258, 1259

Conboy v. Mogeloff, 167

Cone v. Nationwide Mut. Fire Ins. Co., 771

Conley v. Boyle Drug Co., 387, 388

Connall, Hoffman v., 1239

Connaughton, Harte–Hanks Communications, Inc. v., 1017, 1020, 1023

Connecticut Mut. Life Ins. Co. v. New York & N.H.R. Co., 323

Connelly v. Mammoth Mountain Ski Area, 474

Connes v. Molalla Transport System, Inc., 185

Connolly v. Nicollet Hotel, 93

Connors v. University Associates In Obstetrics and Gynecology, Inc., 117, 121, 122

Consolidated Edison Co., Inc., Food Pageant, Inc. v., 149

Consolidated Edison Co. of New York, Inc., Koch v., 320

Consolidated Edison Co. of New York, Inc., Milliken & Co. v., 321

Consolidated Mut. Ins. Co., Baldinger v., 870

Consolidated Rail Corp. v. Gottshall, 276

Consolidated Rail Corp., People Exp. Airlines, Inc. v., 313, 320, 321, 322, 323, 433, 646, 759

Consolidation Coal Co., Delloma v., 981

Consumers Union of United States, Inc., Bose Corp. v., 1022, 1023

Consumers Union of United States, Inc., Simmons Ford, Inc. v., 999

Continental Auto Lease Corp. v. Campbell, 438

Continental Cas. Co. v. Kinsey, 745

Continental Casualty Co. v. Pacific Indemnity Co., 782

Continental Telephone Co. of Vt., Staruski v., 1215

Conway v. Pacific University, 1234

Conway, Sullivan v., 1075

Cooper v. Parker–Hughey, 1263

Cooper Industries, Inc., Leatherman Tool Group, Inc. v., 738

Cooperative Fire Ins. Ass'n v. Combs, 741

Cope v. Scott, 250, 257, 259

Copiague Union Free School Dist., Donohue v., 235, 236, 237

Copley v. Putter, 377

Coprich v. Superior Court, 100

Corcoran v. United HealthCare, Inc., 497

Cordas v. Peerless Transp. Co., 927

Corey v. Havener, 378

Corning Hospital Dist., Muskopf v., 928

Correctional Healthcare Solutions, Inc., Fleming v., 1271

Cort v. Ash, 157

Costello v. Ocean County Observer, 1019

Cotton v. Buckeye Gas Products Co., 588

Cotton Hope Plantation Horizontal Property Regime, Davenport v., 476, 481, 483

Coty v. Ramsey Associates, Inc., 672

Counseling Service of Addison County, Inc., Peck v., 168

Country–Wide Ins. Co. v. Harnett, 829

County of Alameda, Thompson v., 168

County of Los Angeles, Scott v., 371

County of San Diego, Wiley v., 309

County of Suffolk, Mastroianni v., 231

Courshon, Wiggs v., 893

Courvoisier v. Raymond, 914, 917
Cowan, Casebolt v., 183
Cox v. Spangler, 377
Cox Aircraft Co. of Washington, Crosby v., 518
Cox Broadcasting Corp. v. Cohn, 1114, 1115, 1125, 1126, 1127, 1128, 1149, 1193
Crabtree v. Dawson, 916
Crandall Corp. v. Navistar Intern. Transp. Corp., 1243
Crane v. Arizona Republic, 994, 1048
Crawn v. Campo, 473
Creative Housing Ltd., Mount Vernon Fire Ins. Co. v., 742, 771
Cremeans v. Willmar Henderson Mfg. Co., a Div. of Waycrosse, Inc., 627, 628
Cromwell–Wright Co., Inc., Clark–Aiken Co. v., 505
Cronin v. J.B.E. Olson Corp., 558
Crosby v. Cox Aircraft Co. of Washington, 518
Crosland v. New York City Transit Authority, 232, 243
Crown Center Redevelopment Corp., Firestone v., 696
Cruzan by Cruzan v. Director, Missouri Dept. of Health, 338, 340
C & S Car Service, Friedman v., 693, 694
CSC Credit Services, Henson v., 982
CSX Transp., Inc. v. Palank, 737
CSX Transp. Inc., Lacy v., 451
CSX Transp., Inc., Jenkins v., 674
Cuffy v. City of New York, 155, 231, 232, 243
Culligan Intern. Co., Baskerville v., 896
Cunard S.S. Co., Ltd., O'Brien v., 913
Cunningham Drug Stores, Inc., Williams v., 212
Curlender v. Bio–Science Laboratories, 337
Currier v. Western Newspapers, Inc., 1020
Curtis v. General Motors Corp., 568
Curtis Pub. Co. v. Birdsong, 1062
Curtis Pub. Co. v. Butts, 1013, 1014, 1015
Curtis Pub. Co., Booth v., 1212
Cutter Biological, Inc., a Div. of Miles Inc., Smith v., 389

Dabdoub v. Ochsner Clinic, 429
Daffern, Bruce Templeton ex rel. Templeton, Estate of v., 189
Dailey, Garratt v., 49 Wash.2d 499, 304 P.2d 681 (Wash.1956), 867
Dailey, Garratt v., 46 Wash.2d 197, 279 P.2d 1091 (Wash.1955), **865,** 872, 875, 916, 925
Daily Gazette Co., Inc., Hinerman v., 1060
Daily Mail Pub. Co., Smith v., 1115, 1125
Dairy Stores, Inc. v. Sentinel Pub. Co., Inc., 1037
Dairyland Power Co-op., Jost v., 669, 672, 673
Dalehite v. United States, 250
Dalury v. S–K–I, Ltd., 461, 465, 466, 468, 475, 911
Daly v. General Motors Corp., 610, 611

Daly, Reliance Insurance Companies v., 766
Dameron v. Washington Magazine, Inc., 1059
Damon, Feliberty v., 774
Damron, Ocala Star–Banner Co. v., 1044, 1045
D'Angelo, Ellis v., 56
Daniel O'Connell's Sons, Inc., Ferriter v., 300
Daniels v. GNB, Inc., 558
Daniels, Montgomery v., 828, 829
Daubert v. Merrell Dow Pharmaceuticals, Inc., 355, 356, 357, 358
Daugert v. Pappas, 367
D'Avanzo, California Conserving Co. v., 1220
Davenport v. Cotton Hope Plantation Horizontal Property Regime, 476, 481, 483
David Alan Dorfman, P.L.L.C., Baker v., 281
Davidoff by Davidoff v. Metropolitan Baseball Club, Inc., 475
Davidson v. City of Westminster, 230, 244
Davies v. Mann, 437
Davis v. Monroe County Bd. of Educ., 898
Davis, Barnhill v., 286
Davis, Kaeo v., 451
Dawson v. Chrysler Corp., 580
Dawson, Crabtree v., 916
Day–Brite Lighting, Inc., Compco Corp. v., 1258, 1259
Deaner, Steaks Unlimited, Inc. v., 1061
Decker v. Princeton Packet, Inc., 956
Deffenbaugh–Williams v. Wal–Mart Stores, Inc., 895
DeFoor, State v., 696
De Haen v. Rockwood Sprinkler Co. of Massachusetts, 80, 82, 412
DeHanes v. Rothman, 365
Deiss, Harding v., 455
Delacruz, Savage v., 835
Del E. Webb Development Co., Spur Industries, Inc. v., 675, 676
Della Penna v. Toyota Motor Sales, U.S.A., Inc., 1246, 1256
Delloma v. Consolidation Coal Co., 981
Dellwo v. Pearson, 57
De Long v. Erie County, 232, 708
Delta Air Lines, Inc. v. Douglas Aircraft Co., 646, 647, 1269
Delta Airlines, Inc., Hodges v., 497
Delta Air Lines, Inc., Stagl v., 72
Delta Air Lines, Inc., Sullivan v., 706
Delta Airlines, Inc., Taj Mahal Travel, Inc. v., 963
Delta Intern. Machinery Corp., Williams v., 440
Democratic Nat. Committee v. McCord, 1223
Dempsey v. National Enquirer, 702 F.Supp. 934 (D.Me.1989), 1148, 1150
Dempsey v. National Enquirer, 702 F.Supp. 927 (D.Me.1988), 1149
DeNardo, Levey v., 58, 78
Dennis v. Higgins, 648, 933
Denny v. Ford Motor Co., 604, 605
DEP Corp. v. Interstate Cigar Co., Inc., 1245
Department of Human Services, Bolton v., 969

Department of Industry, Labor and Human Relations, RTE Corp. v., 810

Department of Motor Vehicles, Waschek v., 8

Department of Social Services of City of New York, Monell v., 930

dePasse, Ruffin–Steinback v., 1215

Derdiarian v. Felix Contracting Corp., 412

Dermatossian v. New York City Transit Authority, 94

Derry v. Peek, 1218, 1219

Des Moines Leader, Cherry v., 983

DeSantis v. Frick Co., 604

DeShaney v. Winnebago County Dept. of Social Services, 260, 932

Desnick v. American Broadcasting Companies, Inc., 975, **1167,** 1172, 1173, 1186

Dewey, Ballantine, Bushby, Palmer & Wood, Prudential Ins. Co. of America v., 311

Di Ponzio v. Riordan, 81

Diaz v. Eli Lilly & Co., 297

Diaz v. Oakland Tribune, Inc., 1130

Diaz, Machleder v., 801 F.2d 46 (2nd Cir. 1986) 1147

Diaz, Machleder v., 618 F.Supp. 1367 (S.D.N.Y.1985), 1147

Didner v. Keene Corp., 448

Dietemann v. Time, Inc., 1172, 1173, 1174, 1185, 1186, 1269

DiFranco v. Klein, 109

Dilallo By and Through Dilallo v. Riding Safely, Inc., 467

Dillon v. Legg, 286, 287, 288, 289, 290

Dillon v. Twin State Gas & Electric Co., 402

Dimond v. District of Columbia, 829

Dinger, Weinberg v., 759

Director, Missouri Dept. of Health, Cruzan by Cruzan v., 338, 340

District Court In and For Oklahoma County, Oklahoma Pub. Co. v., 1115

District of Columbia, Dimond v., 829

District of Columbia, Robinson v., 80

Ditto v. McCurdy, 128

Dixie Medical Center, a Div. of IHC Hospitals, Inc., Boucher By and Through Boucher v., 299

Dixon v. Four Seasons Bowling Alley, Inc., 636

Dixon v. Superior Court, 1024

Dobbs Houses, Inc., Mixon v., 137

Dodd, Pearson v., 1159, 1160

Dodson, Polk County v., 931

Doe v. Berkeley Publishers, 1108

Doe v. Mills, 1113

Doe v. Roe, 1131

Doe v. Sundquist, 106 F.3d 702 (6th Cir. 1997), 1140

Doe v. Sundquist, 2 S.W.3d 919 (Tenn.1999), 1140

Doe, Roe v., 1131

Does 1, 2, 3, 4, 5, 6, and 7 v. State, 1139

Dong–A Ilbo, Lee v., 992

Donohue v. Copiague Union Free School Dist., 235, 236, 237

Dorosz v. Green & Seifter, 808

Dorsey v. National Enquirer, Inc., 992

Doubleday & Co., Inc., McManus v., 1090

Dougherty, Watch Tower Bible & Tract Soc. v., 1259

Douglas Aircraft Co., Delta Air Lines, Inc. v., 646, 647, 1269

Douglas–Hanson Co., Inc. v. BF Goodrich Co., 1269

Douglass v. Hustler Magazine, Inc., 1148, 1149

Doupnik, General Motors Corp. v., 299

Dow Jones, Inc., Gutter v., 312

Doyle v. Metropolitan Property & Cas. Ins. Co., 764

Dreisonstok v. Volkswagenwerk, A. G., 568, 571

Drews v. Gobel Freight Lines, Inc., 708

Dumitru, Hall v., 457

Dun & Bradstreet, Inc. v. Greenmoss Builders, Inc., 909, 1076, 1078, 1079, 1080, 1094

Dun & Bradstreet, Inc., Stationers Corp. v., 981, 1074

Dunbar Medical Systems Inc. v. Gammex Inc., 1238

Duncan v. Afton, Inc., 312

Dundee Cement Co. v. Chemical Laboratories, Inc., 323

Dungan, Barnes v., 142

Dungee, Virginia Elec. and Power Co. v., 695

Dunham, Sullivan v., 506, 509

Dunlop, Harvey v., 36

Dunlop, Rochester Gas & Elec. Corp. v., 518

Dunn v. HOVIC, 738

Dunning v. Simmons Airlines, Inc., 896

Dunphy v. Gregor, 290

Duprey, Mihalik v., 1020

Duran v. Heller, 836

Dworkin v. Hustler Magazine Inc., 1079

Dykstra v. United States Bureau of Prisons, 259

Dyson v. General Motors Corp., 568

East Greenbush Cent. School Dist., Uhr ex rel. Uhr v., 151, 154, 155, 157, 189, 242, 1137

East, Hergenrether v., 184

East Ohio Gas Co., Stevenson v., 320

East River S.S. Corp. v. Transamerica Delaval, Inc., 639, 644, 645, 646, 650

Eastern Airlines, Inc. v. Floyd, 851

Eastern Ohio Paving Co., GBJ Corp. v., 1217

Eastwood v. Superior Court, 1211

Eaves Brooks Costume Co., Inc. v. Y.B.H. Realty Corp., 760

Ecole Secondaire Macdonald–Cartier, Rocci v., 1037

Economou, Butz v., 946

Economy Preferred Ins. Co. v. Mass, 870

Edelman, Pulka v., 150, 151

Edro Motel Corp., Ranalli v., 637

Ed's Beach Service, Inc., Kendrick v., 482

Edwards v. Basel Pharmaceuticals, 83, 84, **592,** 596, 614

Edwards v. National Audubon Soc., Inc., 1089, 1090

Egan v. A.J. Const. Corp., 456

Eggert v. Working, 449

Ehrlich, Michelman v., 337

E.I. Du Pont De Nemours & Co., Inc., Anguiano v., 496

E.I. Du Pont De Nemours & Co., Inc., Hall v., 387

E.I. Du Pont de Nemours & Co., Setliff v., 389

E. & J. Trucking Corp., Wilson v., 837

El Al Israel Airlines, Ltd. v. Tsui Yuan Tseng, 852

Elbaor v. Smith, 448

Elden v. Sheldon, 289, 290

Eldridge, Womack v., 889, 893

Elgin, Joliet and Eastern Ry. Co., Espinoza v., 84

Eli Lilly and Co., Hymowitz v., 378, 387, 388, 390, 430

Eli Lilly Co., Collins v., 381, 724

Eli Lilly & Co., Diaz v., 297

Eli Lilly & Co., Smith v., 388

Ellerbee v. Mills, 1047

Ellerth, Burlington Industries, Inc. v., 895, 897

Elliott, Barcelo v., 311

Elliott, Licari v., 835

Elliott, Rogers v., 674

Ellis v. D'Angelo, 56

Ellis v. Peter, 167

Ellison v. Brady, 895

Ellman, Tedla v., 76, 79, 83

Elmore v. American Motors Corp., 552

El Mundo, Inc., Torres-Silva v., 1040

Elmwood Plantation Associates, Ltd., Veazey v., 370

Ely–Norris Safe Co., Mosler Safe Co. v., 1257

Emanuel Hosp., Barrett v., 108

Emco Helicopters, Inc., Black Industries, Inc. v., 488

Emerson v. Magendantz, 326, 332, 333, 334, 335, 337

Emery v. Federated Foods, Inc., 582

Emery World Wide Delivery Corp., Argentina v., 832

Encore of Hicksville, Inc., Heller v., 64

England, McCormick v., 1136, 1138

Engle, R.J. Reynolds Tobacco Co. v., 394

English, Byrd v., 320

Enquirer & News of Battle Creek Michigan, Rouch v., 487 N.W.2d 205 (Mich.1992), 975

Enquirer & News of Battle Creek, Rouch v., 398 N.W.2d 245 (Mich.1986), 991, 993

Epping v. Commonwealth Edison Co., 691

Equifax Services, Inc., Weir v., 981

Erdman v. Johnson Bros. Radio & Television Co., 648

Eric J. v. Betty M., 178

Erickson v. Marsh & McLennan Co., Inc., 980, 983, 1022

Erie County, De Long v., 232, 708

Erlich v. Menezes, 296, 1270

Ernest v. Red Creek Cent. School Dist., 234

Ernst, Gibbs v., 1235

E.R. Squibb & Sons, Inc., Murphy v., 636

Escola v. Coca Cola Bottling Co. of Fresno, 525, 546, 550, 551, 555, 638, 639

Espinoza v. Elgin, Joliet and Eastern Ry. Co., 84

Estate of (see name of party)

Estate of Kollstedt, Nationwide Ins. Co. v., 871

Estate of Pack, Safer v., 165

Etkind v. Suarez, 333

Evans Furniture, Inc., Mastland, Inc. v., 56

Evans, Ollman v., 1062

Evening Call Pub. Co., Arcand v., 965

Ewen v. McLean Trucking Co., 579

Express Partners, City Exp., Inc. v., 324

Exxon Co., U.S.A. v. Sofec, Inc., 457

Ezzy v. Workers' Comp. Appeals Bd., 809

Faberge, Inc., Moran v., 587

Fact Concerts, Inc., Newport, City of v., 943

Fairchild Publications, Inc., Waldbaum v., 1059, 1060

Fairfax Hosp. System, Inc. v. Nevitt, 696

Fair Oaks Fire Protection Dist., Cole v., 813

Falcon v. Memorial Hosp., 366

Falin, Kelly By and Through Kelly, Estate of v., 452

Falls v. Superior Court, 243, 244

Faloona v. Hustler Magazine, Inc., 1149

Falwell, Hustler Magazine v., 905

Falzone v. Busch, 261, 266, 268, 270, 276, 281, 289, 295

Family Fitness Center (No. 107), Inc., Leon v., 466

Fantozzi v. Sandusky Cement Prod. Co., 704

Faragher v. City of Boca Raton, 895, 897

Faricelli v. TSS Seedman's, Inc., 88

Farina v. Pan American World Airlines, Inc., 98

Farmer v. Brennan, 931

Farmer, Pamela L. v., 178

Farmers Educational and Co-op. Union of America v. WDAY, Inc., 977

Farmers Ins. Exchange v. Cocking, 746

Farwell v. Boston & W.R. Corp., 37

Farwell v. Keaton, 137, 141, 142, 367

Fassoulas v. Ramey, 329

Faya v. Almaraz, 277

F.C.C. v. Pacifica Foundation, 909

F.D.I.C., O'Melveny & Myers v., 308

Federal Reserve Bank of Atlanta, American Bank & Trust Co. v., 1263

Federal Signal Corp., Sommer v., 466

Federated Foods, Inc., Emery v., 582

Federated Publications, Inc., Uranga v., 1126

Feisthamel v. State, 436

Feldman v. Lederle Laboratories, 600, 601

Feliberty v. Damon, 774

Felix Contracting Corp., Derdiarian v., 412

Fellows v. National Enquirer, Inc., 1146

Fennell v. Southern Maryland Hosp. Center, Inc., 367

Ferayorni v. Hyundai Motor Co., 601, 602

Ferdinand Marcos, Human Rights Litigation, In re Estate of, 880

Ferebee v. Chevron Chemical Co., 394

Feres v. United States, 259

Ferragamo v. Massachusetts Bay Transp. Authority, 627

Ferriter v. Daniel O'Connell's Sons, Inc., 300

Ferroggiaro v. Bowline, 430

Fetterhoff v. Western Block Co., Division of Am. Hoist & Derrick Co., 814

Fibreboard Corp., Ortiz v., 395

Fibreboard Corp., Sofie v., 695

Fidelity and Cas. Co. of New York, Jansen v., 149

Fiedler Roofing, Inc., Richardson v., 808

Field v. Boyer Co., L.C., 372

Field Clinic, Sherman v., 898

1500 Massachusetts Ave. Apartment Corp., Kline v., 206, 212

5th Ave. Chocolatiere, Ltd. v. 540 Acquisition Co., L.L.C., 321

Filartiga v. Pena–Irala, 880

Filler, Goepfert v., 483

Finlandia Center, Inc., 532 Madison Ave. Gourmet Foods, Inc. v., 321

Fire Ins. Exchange v. Hammond, 782

Fireman's Fund American Ins. Companies v. Knobbe, 108

Fireman's Fund Ins. Companies, Moradi–Shalal v., 779

Fireman's Fund Ins. Co., Yukon Equipment, Inc. v., 517

Firemen's Ins. Co. of Newark, N. J. v. Bowley, 836

Firemen's Ins. Co., Smith v., 831

Firestone v. Crown Center Redevelopment Corp., 696

Firestone, Time, Inc. v., 1042, 1043, 1048

Firestone Tire & Rubber Co., Campos v., 587

Firestone Tire & Rubber Co., Potter v., 276, 278, 397

Firman v. Sacia, 430

First Interstate Bank of Oregon, Humphers v., 1131, 1137, 1138, 1139

First Manhattan Bank, Rosen v., 808

First Western Loan Co., South County, Inc. v., 1233

Fischer v. Hooper, 1159

Fischer v. Johns–Manville Corp., 726

Fischl v. Paller & Goldstein, 324

Fisel v. Wynns, 502

Fisher Broadcasting Companies, Inc., Anderson v., 1111

Fisher Bros. Sales, Inc. v. United States, 259

Fisher, Stop & Shop Companies, Inc. v., 660

Fisher, Torchia v., 518

Fitzgerald, Harlow v., 947

Fitzgerald, Nixon v., 947

Fitzsimmons, Buckley v., 815, 941

540 Acquisition Co., L.L.C., 5th Ave. Chocolatiere, Ltd. v., 321

532 Madison Ave. Gourmet Foods, Inc. v. Finlandia Center, Inc., 321

Flagship Nat. Bank v. Gray Distribution Systems, Inc., 1270

Flaig, Heyer v., 311

Flamm v. American Ass'n of University Women, 1067, 1076

Flanagan v. Wesselhoeft, 116

Flechter, Powell v., 1222

Fleet/Norstar Financial Group, Inc., NBT Bancorp Inc. v., 1245

Fleming v. Correctional Healthcare Solutions, Inc., 1271

Fletcher v. Rylands, 498

Fletcher, Kalina v., 941

Fletcher, Rylands v., 498, 503, 504, 505, 506, 510, 532, 652, 658, 670, 671

Flint, Robins Dry Dock & Repair Co. v., 322

Flohr, Weisbart v., 867, 870

Florence v. Goldberg, 233

Florenzano v. Olson, 1237

Florida Wildlife Federation v. State Dept. of Environmental Regulation, 660

Flower Hosp., Allore v., 339

Floyd, Eastern Airlines, Inc. v., 851

Flynt, Braun v., 1148, 1149

Fontainebleau Hotel Corp. v. Forty–Five Twenty–Five, Inc., 671

Food Lion, Inc. v. Capital Cities/ABC, Inc., 1186

Food Pageant, Inc. v. Consolidated Edison Co., Inc., 149

Footer, Robbins v., 109, 114

Forbes, Inc., Morrell v., 963

Ford v. Herman, 737

Ford Motor Co., Binakonsky v., 591, 611

Ford Motor Co., Denny v., 604, 605

Ford Motor Co., Largosa v., 179, 205

Ford Motor Co., Vandermark v., 551, 553, 635

Ford Motor Co., Zuern By and Through Zuern v., 612

Ford Motor Land Development Corp., Ron Greenspan Volkswagen, Inc. v., 1237

Forest City Pub. Co., Cantrell v., 1141, 1145, 1147, 1149, 1150

Forest Park Baptist Church, Helton v., 99

Forklift Systems, Inc., Harris v., 895, 897

Forrester v. White, 941

Forty–Five Twenty–Five, Inc., Fontainebleau Hotel Corp. v., 671

Forum Intern., Ltd., Cher v., 7 Med.L.Rptr. 2593 (C.D.Cal.1982), 1212

Forum Intern., Ltd., Cher v., 692 F.2d 634 (9th Cir.1982), 1212

Foster v. Loft, Inc., 23, 185

Fote, Weiss v., 247, 248

Four Seasons Bowling Alley, Inc., Dixon v., 636

Fowler v. Seaton, 99

Fox & Lazo Realtors, Hopkins v., 178

Frame v. Kothari, 289

Franklin v. Gwinnett County Public Schools, 897

Franklin Mint Corp., Trans World Airlines, Inc. v., 851

Freeman & Mills, Inc. v. Belcher Oil Co., 1270

Freeman v. Hale, 474

Freeman v. Hoffman–La Roche, Inc., 597

Freightliner Corp. v. Myrick, 496

Freihofer v. Hearst Corp., 1099

Frick Co., DeSantis v., 604

Friedman v. C & S Car Service, 693, 694

Friedman v. Israel Labour Party, 992

Friedman v. State, 244, 248

Friedrich, Bandel v., 715, 717

Friend, Hansen v., 189

Fritts v. McKinne, 452, 455, 460

Fritz Companies, Inc., Greenfield v., 1237

Frost v. Porter Leasing Corp., 747, 752, 754

F–R Pub. Corporation, Sidis v., 1106, 1113, 1127

Fry v. Ionia Sentinel–Standard, 1113

Frye v. United States, 356, 358

Fry's Food Stores of Arizona, Inc., Chiara v., 90

Fuller v. Preis, 403

Gaertner v. Holcka, 460

Gain v. Carroll Mill Co., Inc., 286

Gaines–Tabb v. ICI Explosives, USA, Inc., 579

Gala v. Hamilton, 115

Galella v. Onassis, 533 F.Supp. 1076 (S.D.N.Y.1982), 1166

Galella v. Onassis, 487 F.2d 986 (2nd Cir. 1973), **1163,** 1167

Galen of Virginia, Inc., Roberts v., 157

Gambuzza v. Time, Inc., 954

Gammex Inc., Dunbar Medical Systems Inc. v., 1238

Gammon v. Osteopathic Hosp. of Maine, Inc., 278, 280, 281, 403

Gannett Co., Inc., Kassel v., 1045, 1046, 1058

Gannett Co., Inc., Meisler v., 1020

Garber, McDougald v., 697, 704, 705

Garcia v. Joseph Vince Co., 376

Garcia v. Lifemark Hospitals of Florida, 177

Garcia, Gibson v., 412

Garcia, Gonzalez v., 482

Gardner v. Loomis Armored Inc., 1271

Garratt v. Dailey, 49 Wash.2d 499, 304 P.2d 681 (Wash.1956), 867

Garratt v. Dailey, 46 Wash.2d 197, 279 P.2d 1091 (Wash.1955), **865,** 872, 875, 916, 925

Garrett, Greenlaw v., 497

Garrett, Hines v., 417

Garrison v. State of Louisiana, 1012, 1022, 1080

Garthe v. Ruppert, 71

Gava, Carroll v., 1237

GBJ Corp. v. Eastern Ohio Paving Co., 1217

Geary, Surocco v., 927, 928

Gebo v. Black Clawson Co., 554

Gebser v. Lago Vista Independent School Dist., 897, 898

Geernaert v. Mitchell, 1219

Gehret, Griffin v., 449

Geib, Elston, Frost Professional Ass'n, Sander v., 269, 706, 708

Geier v. American Honda Motor Co., Inc., 489, 496, 614

Geiger, Barnes v., 287

Geiger, Kawaauhau v., 864

Gelstein, Liberman v., 970, 978, 980, 982, 983

Geltman, United Truck Leasing Corp. v., 1243

General Acc. Fire and Life Assur. Corp., Ltd. v. Avery, 834

General Acc., Fire & Life Ins. Co. v. Viruet, 834

General Acc. Ins. Co., Smith v., 780

General Elec. Co. v. Joiner, 356

General Elec. Co., Lionarons v., 482

General Hosp. of City of Syracuse, Kalina v., 295

General Marine Industries, L.P., Alloway v., 645

General Motors Corp. v. Doupnik, 299

General Motors Corp. v. Saenz on Behalf of Saenz, 587

General Motors Corp. v. Sanchez, 605, 613

General Motors Corp. (Allison Gas Turbine Div.), Bocre Leasing Corp. v., 645

General Motors Corp., Blankenship v., 789

General Motors Corp., Campbell v., 566

General Motors Corp., Curtis v., 568

General Motors Corp., Daly v., 610, 611

General Motors Corp., Dyson v., 568

General Motors Corp., LaHue v., 459

General Motors Corp., Maneely v., 582

General Motors Corp., Masaki v., 297

General Motors Corp., Nader v., 1151, 1157, 1159, 1161, 1162, 1183

General Motors Corp., Price v., 557

General Motors Corp., Pruitt v., 566

General Motors Corp., Soule v., 559, 566, 568, 570, 580, 591, 614

General Motors Corp., Swajian v., 459

General Motors Corp., Tacket v., 953

General Motors Corp., Voilas v., 1222

General Motors Corp., Waterson v., 460

General Petroleum Corp., Green v., 518, 522

Genesee County Agr. Soc., Bragg v., 197

Genesee Management, Inc., LaTorre v., 222

George, Hewellette v., 215

George, Orser v., 386

Georgia Soc. of Plastic Surgeons, Inc. v. Anderson, 1060

Gersheimer, Rushink v., 82

Gertz v. Robert Welch, Inc., 680 F.2d 527 (7th Cir.1982), 1036

Gertz v. Robert Welch, Inc., 418 U.S. 323, 94 S.Ct. 2997, 41 L.Ed.2d 789 (1974), 943, **1025,** 1036, 1037, 1039, 1042, 1043, 1045, 1046, 1048, 1059, 1061, 1076, 1077, 1078, 1079, 1080, 1089, 1094, 1095, 1130, 1147, 1149

Getting Organized, Inc., Trepanier v., 1243, 1246

Geysel, Hart v., 911, 912, 917

Ghotra by Ghotra v. Bandila Shipping, Inc., 269

Giant Powder Co., Judson v., 108

Gibb v. Citicorp Mortg., Inc., 1235, 1237

Gibbons v. Caraway, 488

Gibbons, National Steel Service Center, Inc. v., 519

Gibbs v. Ernst, 1235

Gibson v. Garcia, 412

Gibson v. Gibson, 221

Gibson, Gibson v., 221

Gilbert v. Medical Economics Co., 1108

Gilchrist Timber Co. v. ITT Rayonier, Inc., 1237

Gilger v. Hernandez, 189

Gilley, Siegert v., 946

Gimbel's Inc., Newmark v., 636

G.J.D. by G.J.D. v. Johnson, 725

G.J. Leasing Co., Inc. v. Union Elec. Co., 517

Glanzer v. Shepard, 143, 145, 147, 312

Glastetter, Bryant v., 488

Glens Falls City School Dist., Akins v., 62

Globe Communications Corp., State v., 1128

Globe Intern., Inc., Khawar v., 1081, 1089

Globe Intern. Pub., Inc., Mitchell v., 817 F.Supp. 72 (W.D.Ark.1993), 1147

Globe Intern. Pub., Inc., Mitchell v., 773 F.Supp. 1235 (W.D.Ark.1991), 962, 963

Globe Intern. Pub., Inc., Peoples Bank and Trust Co. of Mountain Home v., 1147

Globe Newspaper Co., Bruno & Stillman, Inc. v., 1061

Globe Pub. Co., Gobin v., 232 Kan. 1, 649 P.2d 1239 (Kan.1982), 1043

Globe Pub. Co., Gobin v., 216 Kan. 223, 531 P.2d 76 (Kan.1975), 1041

GNB, Inc., Daniels v., 558

Gobel Freight Lines, Inc., Drews v., 708

Gobin v. Globe Pub. Co., 232 Kan. 1, 649 P.2d 1239 (Kan.1982), 1043

Gobin v. Globe Pub. Co., 216 Kan. 223, 531 P.2d 76 (Kan.1975), 1041

Goepfert v. Filler, 483

Goff v. Harold Ives Trucking Co., Inc., 100

Goff, Yaselli v., 244

Goldberg, Florence v., 233

Goldberg Weprin & Ustin, LLP v. Tishman Const. Corp., 322

Golden State Transit Corp. v. City of Los Angeles, 933

Goldfarb, Public Service Mut. Ins. Co. v., 769

Goldfarb, Weiss v., 451

Goldman v. Johns–Manville Sales Corp., 388

Goldstein Bros. Amusement Co., Tantillo v., 471

Gonzales v. Times Herald Printing Co., 1012

Gonzalez v. Garcia, 482

Goode, Rizzo v., 932

Goodman, Baltimore & O.R. Co. v., 58, 59, 60, 63

Gordon v. American Museum of Natural History, 87, 88

Gordon, Montgomery Elevator Co. v., 451

Gore, BMW of North America, Inc. v., 726, 736, 737, 738

Gorris v. Scott, 82

Goss v. Allen, 57

Gottshall, Consolidated Rail Corp. v., 276

Gould v. American Family Mut. Ins. Co., 488

Government Emp. Ins. Co., Adams v., 838

Graham, Kentucky v., 942

Gramajo, Xuncax v., 880

Grant v. Reader's Digest Ass'n, Inc., 961

Grant–Lafayette Elec. Co-op., Vogel v., 672

Granville, Troxel v., 1139

Grape Finds at Dupont, Inc., Best Cellars Inc. v., 1257

Gray Distribution Systems, Inc., Flagship Nat. Bank v., 1270

Graybar Elec. Co., Washington Water Power Co. v., 646

Grayson v. Wofsey, Rosen, Kweskin and Kuriansky, 309

Green v. Bittner, 708

Green v. General Petroleum Corp., 518, 522

Green v. Ralee Engineering Co., 1271

Green, Carlson v., 945

Green & Seifter, Dorosz v., 808

Greenbelt Co-op. Pub. Ass'n v. Bresler, 1061, 1074

Greene v. Sibley, Lindsay & Curr Co., 40, 44, 62

Greenfield v. Fritz Companies, Inc., 1237

Greenlaw v. Garrett, 497

Greenman v. Yuba Power Products, Inc., 551, 558, 638

Greenmoss Builders, Inc., Dun & Bradstreet, Inc. v., 909, 1076, 1078, 1079, 1080, 1094

Greenson, Bellah v., 167

Greenwood, California v., 1166

Gregor, Dunphy v., 290

Greinke v. Keese, 312

Gretchen v. United States, 694

Greycas, Inc. v. Proud, 1237

Greyhound Lines, Inc. v. Sutton, 709

Griffin v. Breckenridge, 943, 944

Griffin v. Gehret, 449

Grimaldi, Rogers v., 1194

Gritzner v. Michael R., 178

Groh, Wood v., 50, 184

Gross v. Lyons, 377

Gross v. Sweet, 467

Grossman, Tobin v., 288

Group W Productions, Inc., Shulman v., 1110, 1127, 1128, **1174,** 1185, 1186, 1215

Grove Sun Newspaper Co., Inc., Wright v., 993

Gruner & Jahr Printing and Pub., Messenger ex rel. Messenger v., 1100, 1141

Guajardo, Guzman v., 706

Guardianship and Conservatorship of Bloomquist, In re, 755

Guard–Life Corp. v. S. Parker Hardware Mfg. Corp., 1244, 1245

Guille v. Swan, 518

Guillory v. Interstate Gas Station, 808

Guimond v. Trans Union Credit Information Co., 981

Gulf & Western Corp., Harlequin Enterprises Ltd. v., 1257
Gunduz v. New York Post Co., Inc., 975
Gutter v. Dow Jones, Inc., 312
Guzman v. Guajardo, 706
Gwinnett County Public Schools, Franklin v., 897
Gye, Lumley v., 1242, 1243

Haben v. Anderson, 142
Hackbart v. Cincinnati Bengals, Inc., 913
Hacker, Martin v., 586
Hackett v. Perron, 27, 28
Haelan Laboratories, Inc. v. Topps Chewing Gum, Inc., 1187
Haff v. Hettich, 452
Halas, Wernke v., 672
Halberstam v. Welch, 869
Hale, Freeman v., 474
Hall v. Dumitru, 457
Hall v. E.I. Du Pont De Nemours & Co., Inc., 387
Hall v. Post, 1111
Hall v. Wal–Mart Stores, Inc., 736
Hall, Caruso v., 835
Hall, Lester ex rel. Mavrogenis v., 166
Hallam, Post Pub. Co. v., 984, 985, 1000, 1011
Halsted, Peterson v., 182
Hamelin v. Simpson Paper (Vermont) Co., 466
Hamilton, Gala v., 115
Hamm, Lucas v., 310, 311
Hammond, Fire Ins. Exchange v., 782
Hammontree v. Jenner, 3, 6, 7, 8, 13, 14, 15, 17, 54, 121, 441
Hampton Water Works Co., Inc., Libbey v., 149
Hanes Corp. of North Carolina, Kirk v., 588
Hanover Ins. Co. v. Talhouni, 741
Hansen v. Friend, 189
Hansen v. Sunnyside Products, Inc., 590, 591
Hanson, Meredith v., 449, 450
Harbeson v. Parke–Davis, Inc., 336
Harcourt, Brace, Jovanovich, Inc., Johnson v., 1113
Harding v. Deiss, 455
Hardy v. Southwestern Bell Telephone Co., 367
Harlequin Enterprises Ltd. v. Gulf & Western Corp., 1257
Harlow v. Fitzgerald, 947
Harnett, Country–Wide Ins. Co. v., 829
Harold F. Ritchie, Inc. v. Chesebrough–Pond's, Inc., 1257
Harold Ives Trucking Co., Inc., Goff v., 100
Harper v. Herman, 131, 135, 137, 141
Harris v. American Airlines, Inc., 497
Harris v. Forklift Systems, Inc., 895, 897
Harris v. Kissling, 278
Harris v. Soley, 737
Harris, Canton, Ohio, City of v., 930, 931
Harrison v. Brooks, 944
Harrison v. Wisdom, 927

Hart v. Geysel, 911, 912, 917
Hart v. United States, 259
Harte–Hanks Communications, Inc. v. Connaughton, 1017, 1020, 1023
Harte–Hanks Communications, Inc., Villarreal v., 1047
Hartford Accident and Indemnity Co., Reichhold Chemicals, Inc. v., 743
Hartford Courant Co., Williams Ford, Inc. v., 1234
Hartke v. McKelway, 336
Harvey v. Dunlop, 36
Harvey ex rel. Harvey v. Mid–Coast Hosp., 456
Harvey, Smith–Hunter v., 886
Harwood Pharmacal Co. v. National Broadcasting Co., 1256
Haslip, Pacific Mut. Life Ins. Co. v., 727
Hatch, Brahm v., 170
Hatten v. Union Oil Co. of California, Inc., 1243
Haugen, Proctor & Gamble Co. v., 1256
Hauter v. Zogarts, 604
Havener, Corey v., 378
Hawaiian Scenic Tours, Ltd., Wong v., 447
Hawkins v. Pizarro, 165
Hawkins By and Through Hawkins v. Multimedia, Inc., 1130
Hay v. Cohoes Co., 508, 509
Hayes v. Ariens Co., 599
Haymarket Associates, Moody v., 88
Haynes v. Alfred A. Knopf, Inc., 974, 1101, 1106, 1108, 1110, 1114, 1127, 1131, 1193
Haynes, Caldwell v., 687
H.B. Fuller Co., McCullock v., 625
Healey v. New England Newspapers, Inc., 958
Hearst Corp. v. Hughes, 1043
Hearst Corp., Cain v., 1145
Hearst Corp., Freihofer v., 1099
Heathman, Moransais v., 325
Heaven v. Pender, 131
H.E. Butt Grocery Co. v. Bilotto, 450
Heck v. Humphrey, 933
Hedlund v. Superior Court, 168
Heidelberg North America, Inc., Tanges v., 390
Heins v. Webster County, 197, 202, 204, 266
Helfend v. Southern Cal. Rapid Transit Dist., 714, 715, 716
Helinski, Rosenberg v., 994
Heller v. Encore of Hicksville, Inc., 64
Heller, Duran v., 836
Helmsley, Alibrandi v., 439
Helton v. Forest Park Baptist Church, 99
Henchey, Vitale v., 875
Henderson v. Milobsky, 129
Henderson v. Woolley, 214
Hendrickson v. California Newspapers, Inc., 1113
Henning v. Thomas, 115
Henningsen v. Bloomfield Motors, Inc., 550

Henry Mayo Newhall Memorial Hospital, Lisa M. v., 22
Henson v. CSC Credit Services, 982
Hepps, Philadelphia Newspapers, Inc. v., 1041
Herbert v. Lando, 596 F.Supp. 1178 (S.D.N.Y.1984), 1017
Herbert v. Lando, 441 U.S. 153, 99 S.Ct. 1635, 60 L.Ed.2d 115 (1979), 1016
Herdrich, Pegram v., 497
Hergenrether v. East, 184
Heritage Newspapers, Inc., Koniak v., 993
Herman v. Sunshine Chemical Specialties, Inc.,736
Herman, Ford v., 737
Herman, Harper v., 131, 135, 137, 141
Hernandez v. Martin Chevrolet, Inc., 83
Hernandez v. Tokai Corp., 580, 588, 589
Hernandez, Gilger v., 189
Herrmann, Jess v., 447
Herschensohn v. Weisman, 763
Hertz Corp., Lindstrom v., 183
Hertz Corp., Osborn v., 183
Hertz Corp., Steinhauser v., 402, 767
Herzog v. Capital Co., 1223
Herzog, Martin v., 73, 76, 78, 79, 154, 359
Hettich, Haff v., 452
Hewellette v. George, 215
Heyer v. Flaig, 311
Heyward, Spivak v., 100
Hickey v. Zezulka, 446
Hicks v. Casablanca Records, 1214
Hicks v. United States, 366
Hicks, Reynolds v., 185, 189, 370
Higgins, Dennis v., 648, 933
Hightower v. Paulson Truck Lines, Inc., 435
Hill, Bland v., 900
Hill, Time, Inc. v., 1140, 1141, 1149, 1150
Hillrichs v. Avco Corp., 723
Hilton Hotels Corp., Scherr v., 286
Hinerman v. Daily Gazette Co., Inc., 1060
Hines v. Garrett, 417
Hinish v. Meier & Frank Co., 1140
Hinman v. Sobocienski, 358
Hirase–Doi v. United States West Communications, Inc., 896
Hirmer, Phoenix Professional Hockey Club, Inc. v., 323
Hobart Corp., Liriano v., 170 F.3d 264 (2nd Cir.1999), 624
Hobart Corp., Liriano v., 677 N.Y.S.2d 764, 700 N.E.2d 303 (N.Y.1998), **619,** 624
Hocks, Nees v., 1270
Hodges v. Delta Airlines, Inc., 497
Hodges v. Superior Court, 765
Hoek, Clarke v., 165
Hoffman v. Board of Ed. of City of New York, 236, 237
Hoffman v. Connall, 1239
Hoffman–La Roche, Inc., Freeman v., 597
Holcka, Gaertner v., 460
Holden v. Pioneer Broadcasting Co., 998
Holland v. Baltimore & O. R. Co., 196
Holland Abundant Life Fellowship, Stitt v., 193

Holliday v. Jones, 310
Holman v. Central Arkansas Broadcasting Co., Inc., 1113
Holodook v. Spencer, 221, 222
Holy Spirit Ass'n for Unification of World Christianity v. New York Times Co., 993
Home Box Office, Inc., Personal Preference Video, Inc. v., 1244
Home Depot, Inc., Michalski v., 195
Home Ins. Co. v. American Home Products Corp., 744
Honda Motor Co., Ltd., Baughn v., 571
Honda Motor Co., Ltd., Camacho v., 572, 579, 580, 589, 591, 614
Honda Motor Co., Satcher v., 589
Hood v. Ryobi America Corp., 582, 585, 586, 587, 588, 589, 591, 596, 614
Hood, Carr v., 983
Hooks SuperX, Inc. v. McLaughlin, 636
Hooper, Fischer v., 1159
Hopkins v. Fox & Lazo Realtors, 178
Horesh v. State Farm Fire & Cas. Co., 224
Horton, Lydia v., 452
Horwich v. Superior Court, 765
Host Intern., Inc., Wendt v., 1211
Hoven v. Kelble, 636, 637
Hovey, Huber v., 449, 466
HOVIC, Dunn v., 738
Howard v. Wal–Mart Stores, Inc., 90, 91
Howard, Miksis v., 692
Howard, Perkins v., 158
Howard University, Inc., Jones v., 277
Hoyem v. Manhattan Beach City Sch. Dist., 233, 234
H.R. Moch Co. v. Rensselaer Water Co., 143, 144, 149, 321, 651, 759
H. Rosenblum, Inc. v. Adler, 307, 320
Hubbard–Hall Chemical Co. v. Silverman, 84
Huber v. Hovey, 449, 466
Huey, Wishnatsky v., 876, 879, 913
Huggins v. Longs Drug Stores California, Inc., 295
Huggins v. Moore, 1039
Hughes, Hearst Corp. v., 1043
Humana of Florida, Inc., R.J. v., 266
Humphers v. First Interstate Bank of Oregon, 1131, 1137, 1138, 1139
Humphrey, Heck v., 933
Hunnings v. Texaco, Inc., 625
Hustler Magazine v. Falwell, 905
Hustler Magazine, Inc., Douglass v., 1148, 1149
Hustler Magazine Inc., Dworkin v., 1079
Hustler Magazine, Inc., Faloona v., 1149
Hustler Magazine, Inc., Keeton v., 1000
Hutcherson v. City of Phoenix, 371
Hutchinson v. Proxmire, 1045, 1049, 1059
Hutchinson Wil–Rich Mfg. Co., Patton v., 603, 604
Hyde v. North River Ins. Co., 836
Hymowitz v. Eli Lilly and Co., 378, 387, 388, 390, 430
Hyundai Motor Co., Ferayorni v., 601, 602

Iannelli v. Burger King Corp., 212
ICI Americas, Inc., Banks v., 567, 570
ICI Explosives, USA, Inc., Gaines–Tabb v., 579
I.C.U. Investigations v. Jones, 1158
I. de S. v. W. de S., 874
I.J. Weinrot & Son, Inc. v. Jackson, 324
Illinois, Beauharnais v., 965, 1000
Illinois F.W.D. Truck and Equipment Co., Blagg v., 448
Illinois Institute of Technology, Cohen v., 944
Imbler v. Pachtman, 941
Imperial Ice Co. v. Rossier, 1240, 1243, 1244, 1246, 1256
In re (see name of party)
Independent News, Inc., Bank of Oregon v., 1061
Indiana Harbor Belt R. Co. v. American Cyanamid Co., 511, 518
Inouye v. Black, 107
Interlake Steel Co., Wilson v., 658
International News Service v. Associated Press, 1258
International Paper Co. v. Ouellette, 677
International Ry. Co., Wagner v., 428, 429
International Union, United Auto., Aircraft and Agr. Implement Workers of America (UAW–CIO) v. Russell, 1244
Interstate Cigar Co., Inc., DEP Corp. v., 1245
Interstate Gas Station, Guillory v., 808
Ionia Sentinel–Standard, Fry v., 1113
Irving, Biakanja v., 310, 311
Irving Trust Co., K.M.C. Co., Inc. v., 1270
Israel Labour Party, Friedman v., 992
i–Stat Corp., Kaufman v., 1237
Item Publishers, Nichols v., 956
ITT Rayonier, Inc., Gilchrist Timber Co. v., 1237
Ives v. South Buffalo Ry. Co., 805, 829

Jackson v. Longcope, 999
Jackson v. State, 178
Jackson, I.J. Weinrot & Son, Inc. v., 324
Jackson, Rothman v., 977
Jacobson Products Co., Inc., Qualitex Co. v., 1257
Jacoby v. Brinckerhoff, 301
Jacques v. Sears, Roebuck & Co., Inc., 888
Jadwin v. Minneapolis Star and Tribune Co., 1061
Jaffee, Portee v., 282, 286, 287, 288, 289, 290, 450
J.A.H. ex rel. R.M.H. v. Wadle & Associates, P.C., 301
Jamaica Hosp., Johnson v., 291, 294
James v. Bessemer Processing Co., Inc., 601, 602
Jansen v. Fidelity and Cas. Co. of New York, 149
Jason v. Parks, 296
Jaworski v. Kiernan, 179
J.B.E. Olson Corp., Cronin v., 558
J.B. Hunt Transport, Inc., Bauer v., 100
J.C. Penney Casualty Ins. Co. v. M. K., 744

J.C. Penney Co., Inc., Alvarado v., 84
Jean W. v. Commonwealth, 243
Jeckovich, Bartolone v., 402, 458
Jenkins v. CSX Transp., Inc., 674
Jenner, Hammontree v., 3, 6, 7, 8, 13, 14, 15, 17, 54, 121, 441
Jess v. Herrmann, 447
Jewell v. NYP Holdings, Inc., 999
Jewett, Knight v., 472, 474, 481
J.L. v. Kienenberger, 169
J.M., C.M. v., 904
Johannesen v. New York City Dept. of Housing Preservation and Development, 809
Johns Hopkins Health Systems Corp., Wright v., 340
Johnson v. Buffalo & Erie County Private Industry Council, 837
Johnson v. Harcourt, Brace, Jovanovich, Inc., 1113
Johnson v. Jamaica Hosp., 291, 294
Johnson v. Johnson Chemical Co., Inc., 586
Johnson v. Johnson, 1079
Johnson v. Kosmos Portland Cement Co., 417
Johnson v. State, 281
Johnson, Bader v., 334
Johnson Bros. Radio & Television Co., Erdman v., 648
Johnson Chemical Co., Inc., Johnson v., 586
Johnson, G.J.D. by G.J.D. v., 725
Johnson, Johnson v., 1079
Johnson, National County Mut. Fire Ins. Co. v., 224
Johnson, Nelson v., 762
Johnson, United States v., 259
Johnson, Washington Metropolitan Area Transit Authority v., 438
Johns–Manville Corp., Fischer v., 726
Johns–Manville Products Corp., Beshada v., 600, 601
Johns–Manville Sales Corp., Goldman v., 388
Joiner, General Elec. Co. v., 356
Jones v. Alfred H. Mayer Co., 944
Jones v. Chicago Osteopathic Hosp., 706, 707
Jones v. Howard University, Inc., 277
Jones v. Palmer Communications, Inc., 1047
Jones v. Ryobi, Ltd., 614, 618, 624
Jones, Calder v., 1000
Jones, Holliday v., 310
Jones, I.C.U. Investigations v., 1158
Jones & Laughlin Steel Corp. v. Pfeifer, 690, 708
Jordan, Quern v., 942
Joseph Vince Co., Garcia v., 376
Jost v. Dairyland Power Co-op., 669, 672, 673
J.S. v. R.T.H., 156
J.S. Alberici Const. Co., Inc. v. Mid–West Conveyor Co., Inc., 466
Judson v. Giant Powder Co., 108
Julian Messner, Inc. v. Spahn, 1131
Julius Blum, Inc., Spurgeon v., 624
Junius Const. Co. v. Cohen, 1235

Kaczkowski v. Bolubasz, 689
Kadic v. Karadzic, 880

Kaeo v. Davis, 451

Kahn v. Bower, 1047

Kalina v. Fletcher, 941

Kalina v. General Hosp. of City of Syracuse, 295

Kallash, Barker v., 445

Kallenberg v. Beth Israel Hospital, 366

Kallinger, Romaine v., 949, 953, 954, 955, 956, 958, 1125, 1126

Kalman, Petriello v., 347

Kansas City Southern Ry. Co., Rushing v., 678

Kansas State Bank & Trust Co. v. Specialized Transp. Services, Inc., 371

Karadzic, Kadic v., 880

Karney by Karney v. Arnot–Ogden Memorial Hosp., 689

Kassel v. Gannett Co., Inc., 1045, 1046, 1058

Katko v. Briney, 917

Kaufman v. i–Stat Corp., 1237

Kaufmann, Wolf v., 358

Kavanaugh by Gonzales v. Nussbaum, 185

Kawaauhau v. Geiger, 864

Kawananakoa v. Polyblank, 225

Kawasaki Motors Corp. U.S.A., Zygmaniak v., 403

Kearbey, Williams v., 871

Keaton, Farwell v., 137, 141, 142, 367

Keen, Ream v., 658

Keene Corp., Coffman v., 586

Keene Corp., Didner v., 448

Keese, Greinke v., 312

Keeton v. Hustler Magazine, Inc., 1000

Kelble, Hoven v., 636, 637

Kelley v. Bonney, 1047

Kelley v. Kokua Sales and Supply, Ltd., 297

Kelley, Estate of v. Moguls, Inc., 451

Kelly Broadcasting Co., Brown v., 982, 1038

Kelly By and Through Kelly, Estate of v. Falin, 452

Kemezy v. Peters, 736

Kendall, Brown v., 33, 36, 37, 435, 510

Kendall/Hunt Pub. Co. v. Rowe, 1244

Kendrick v. Ed's Beach Service, Inc., 482

Kennedy v. Zimmermann, 977

Kennedy, Veeder v., 900

Kentucky v. Graham, 942

Kentucky Fried Chicken of Cal., Inc. v. Superior Court, 213

Kenty v. Transamerica Premium Ins. Co., 1243

Kerr, Boyles v., 745

Kesick v. Ulster County Self Ins. Plan, 837

Kewanee Oil Co. v. Bicron Corp., 1258

Key, Angrand v., 710

Khawar v. Globe Intern., Inc., 1081, 1089

Kienenberger, J.L. v., 169

Kiernan, Jaworski v., 179

Killington, Ltd., Spencer v., 465

Kilmer, Beardsley v., 1262, 1263

King, Reed v., 1233

Kinley v. Atlantic Cement Co., 673

Kinney, Carter v., 190, 197, 203, 204

Kinney System Rent A Car, Inc., Ventricelli v., 411, 412

Kinsey, Continental Cas. Co. v., 745

Kinsman Transit Co.(Kinsman I), Petition of, 338 F.2d 708 (2d Cir.1964), 431, 767

Kinsman Transit Co. (Kinsman II), Petition of, 388 F.2d 821 (2d Cir.1968), 433, 650

Kirby Co., a Div. of Scott Fetzer Co., McLean v., 185

Kircher v. City of Jamestown, 233

Kirk v. Hanes Corp. of North Carolina, 588

Kirk v. Koch, 899

Kirk v. United States Sugar Corp., 660

Kish v. Nursing and Home Care, Inc., 808

Kissick v. Schmierer, 468

Kissling, Harris v., 278

Kitchen v. K–Mart Corp., 184

Kitsap Transit, Price v., 56

Kline v. 1500 Massachusetts Ave. Apartment Corp., 206, 212

Klein, DiFranco v., 109

Klein, Trimarco v., 67, 70, 71

K.M.C. Co., Inc. v. Irving Trust Co., 1270

KNB Enterprises v. Matthews, 1211

Knight v. Jewett, 472, 474, 481

Knight–Ridder, Inc., Chapin v., 957, 1091

Knight, Shaheen v., 334

Knobbe, Fireman's Fund American Ins. Companies v., 108

Koch v. Consolidated Edison Co. of New York, Inc., 320

Koch, Kirk v., 899

Kohl, State Farm Fire & Cas. Co. v., 771

Kohn v. Schiappa, 310

Kokua Sales and Supply, Ltd., Kelley v., 297

Koniak v. Heritage Newspapers, Inc., 993

Korean Air Lines Disaster of Sept. 1, 1983, In re, 851

Kosmos Portland Cement Co., Johnson v., 417

Kosters v. Seven–Up Co., 553

Kothari, Frame v., 289

Koubek, Scheer v., 835

KPMG Peat Marwick LLP., Nycal Corp. v., 302, 307, 313, 324

Krasnica, Magrine v., 636

Kraus v. New Rochelle Hosp. Medical Center, 1271

Krayenbuhl, Chicago, B. & Q.R. Co. v., 44, 196

Krazek v. Mountain River Tours, Inc., 467

Kresin v. Sears, Roebuck and Co., 705

Kronengold v. Kronengold, 221

Kronengold, Kronengold v., 221

Kuhlman, Siegler v., 514

Kumaran v. Brotman, 1060

Kumho Tire Co., Ltd. v. Carmichael, 356

Kunst v. New York World Telegram Corp., 954

Kurcsics v. Merchants Mut. Ins. Co., 833

Kush v. Lloyd, 337

Kusser, Aesoph v., 1234

Kutzler v. AMF Harley–Davidson, 579

Kwasny v. United States, 691

K–Mart Corp. v. Washington, 969

K–Mart Corp., Kitchen v., 184

K–Mart Corp., Randall v., 89, 90, 91, 93

LaBier v. Pelletier, 439
La Chusa, Thing v., 287
Lacy v. CSX Transp. Inc., 451
Lafayette Morehouse, Inc. v. Chronicle Publishing Co., 1024
Lago Vista Independent School Dist., Gebser v., 897, 898
LaHue v. General Motors Corp., 459
Laird v. Nelms, 519
Lait, Neiman–Marcus v., 965
La Jolla Village Square Venture Partners, Bed, Bath & Beyond of La Jolla, Inc. v., 1245
Lake v. Wal–Mart Stores, Inc., 1146
Lake Erie Transp. Co., Vincent v., 532, **923,** 925, 926, 927
Lakin v. Senco Products, Inc., 792
Lally, Barnstable County Mut. Fire Ins. Co. v., 771
Lalomia v. Bankers & Shippers Ins. Co., 740, 764, **767,** 769, 770, 771, 870
Lancet, Woods v., 17
Landmark Communications, Inc. v. Virginia, 1115
Lando, Herbert v., 596 F.Supp. 1178 (S.D.N.Y.1984), 1017
Lando, Herbert v., 441 U.S. 153, 99 S.Ct. 1635, 60 L.Ed.2d 115 (1979), 1016
Landry v. Leonard, 745
Lane Press, Inc., Coclin v., 980
Langs, Sternemann v., 693
Lanier, United States v., 940
Lansdowne v. Beacon Journal Pub. Co., 1042
Lanzano v. City of New York, 687
Lapez, Montalvo v., 705
Largosa v. Ford Motor Co., 179, 205
Larson v. St. Francis Hotel, 93, 94
LaTorre v. Genesee Management, Inc., 222
Lauer v. City of New York, 237, 243, 244
LaVallee v. Vermont Motor Inns, Inc., 71
Law v. Superior Court In and For Maricopa County, 459
Lawson v. Management Activities, Inc., 266, 267, 268
Layne, Wilson v., 934, 940, 945
Le Mistral, Inc. v. Columbia Broadcasting System, 1172, 1173
Leadfree Enterprises, Inc. v. United States Steel Corp., 323
Leatherman Tool Group, Inc. v. Cooper Industries, Inc., 738
Lederle Laboratories, a Div. of American Cyanamid Co., Shackil v., 389
Lederle Laboratories, Div. of American Cyanamid Co., Tenuto v., 167, 294
Lederle Laboratories, Feldman v., 600, 601
Lee v. Dong–A Ilbo, 992
Leech Brain & Co, Smith v., 409
LeFleur v. Vergilia, 488
Legg, Dillon v., 286, 287, 288, 289, 290
Lego v. Schmidt, 164
Lembo, Bennett v., 704

Leo A. Daly Co., Shen v., 885
Leon v. Family Fitness Center (No. 107), Inc., 466
Leonard v. Watsonville Community Hospital, 98, 116
Leonard, Landry v., 745
Leong v. Takasaki, 297
Leslie's Poolmart, Inc., Bice v., 497
Lester v. Sayles, 300
Lester ex rel. Mavrogenis v. Hall, 166
Lestina v. West Bend Mut. Ins. Co., 473
Letourneau, Acuar v., 717
Letter Carriers v. Austin, 1062, 1074
Levey v. DeNardo, 58, 78
Levine v. CMP Publications, Inc., 1042
Levine v. Russell Blaine Co., 71
Levy, Allan v., 129
Lew v. Superior Court, 661
Lewis v. Miller, 446
Lewis, Sacramento, County of v., 940
Li v. Yellow Cab Co., 440
Libbey v. Hampton Water Works Co., Inc., 149
Liberman v. Gelstein, 970, 978, 980, 982, 983
Liberty Lobby, Inc. v. Anderson, 999
Liberty Lobby, Inc., Anderson v., 1023
Liberty Nat. Life Ins. Co. v. Weldon, 744
Libyan Arab Republic, Tel–Oren v., 880
Licari v. Elliott, 835
Liddy, Wells v., 1049
Liebelt v. Bob Penkhus Volvo–Mazda, Inc., 183
Lifemark Hospitals of Florida, Garcia v., 177
Liggett Group, Inc., Cipollone v., 495, 496
Likes, Tyler, City of v., 296
Lindstrom v. Hertz Corp., 183
Liodas v. Sahadi, 1219
Lionarons v. General Elec. Co., 482
Liriano v. Hobart Corp., 170 F.3d 264 (2nd Cir.1999), 624
Liriano v. Hobart Corp., 677 N.Y.S.2d 764, 700 N.E.2d 303 (N.Y.1998), **619,** 624
Lisa M. v. Henry Mayo Newhall Memorial Hospital, 22
Littell, Buckley v., 1059, 1062
Little Flower Children's Services, Torres v., 237
Little Joseph Realty, Inc. v. Town of Babylon, 671
Livingston v. Marie Callender's, Inc., 605
LJN Toys, Ltd., Lugo by Lopez v., 591
Lloyd, Kush v., 337
Local Union 20, Teamsters, Chauffeurs, Warehousemen, & Helpers of America, Yeager v., 888
Locascio v. Atlantic Mut. Ins. Co., 832
Loft, Inc., Foster v., 23, 185
Loftus, Moisan v., 45
Logerquist v. McVey, 358
Lohr, Medtronic, Inc. v., 491
Lompoc Unified School Dist. v. Superior Court, 205
Long Beach, City of v. Bozek, 886

Long Island Jewish Hillside Medical Center, Martinez v., 337
Long Island R. Co., Palsgraf v., 306, 419, 428, 429, 431
Long v. Arcell, 1022
Longcope, Jackson v., 999
Longs Drug Stores California, Inc., Huggins v., 295
Look Sports, Inc., Westlye v., 613
Loomis Armored Inc., Gardner v., 1271
Lopez v. Precision Papers, Inc., 620, 623
Lopez v. Southern Cal. Rapid Transit Dist., 232
Lopez v. Winchell's Donut House, 882, 885, 888
Lorain Journal Co., Milkovich v., 1063, 1067, 1075, 1076
L'Orange v. Medical Protective Co., 116
Los Angeles Dodgers, Inc., Neinstein v., 475
Los Angeles Transit Lines, Seffert v., 680, 687, 690, 691, 694, 695, 697
Losee v. Buchanan, 504, 509, 658, 758
Lou Bachrodt Chevrolet Co., Peterson v., 715
Loudoun Times Mirror, Arctic Co., Ltd. v., 1061
Lough by Lough v. Rolla Women's Clinic, Inc., 167
Loui v. Oakley, 377
Lovett, Carey v., 294
Lovgren v. Citizens First Nat. Bank of Princeton, 1150
Lovick v. Wil–Rich, 603
Lowell, Aufrichtig v., 312
Lubner v. City of Los Angeles, 295, 296
Lucas v. Hamm, 310, 311
Lucas v. South Carolina Coastal Council, 670
Lucas, Bush v., 946
Luchini, Amyot v., 1239
Lugo by Lopez v. LJN Toys, Ltd., 591
Lukson, Whiteside v., 128
Lull Engineering Co., Barker v., 558, 559, 566, 571, 579
Lumbermens Mut. Cas. Co., Walton v., 832, 833
Lumley v. Gye, 1242, 1243
Lumley v. Wagner, 1242
Lund, Reida v., 870
Lundborg, Marciniak v., 334, 335
Lundman v. McKown, 223
Luoni v. Berube, 189
Luque v. McLean, 579
Lydia v. Horton, 452
Lynch, Schaefer v., 1021
Lyon & Healy, Banner v., 1222
Lyons v. Midnight Sun Transp. Services, Inc., 58
Lyons, Gross v., 377

MacDonald v. Ortho Pharmaceutical Corp., 596
Machleder v. Diaz, 801 F.2d 46 (2nd Cir. 1986), 1147
Machleder v. Diaz, 618 F.Supp. 1367 (S.D.N.Y.1985), 1147

Mackie, Chizmar v., 277, 281
Mackowick v. Westinghouse Elec. Corp., 586
MacLennan, Coleman v., 984, 985, 1011
MacPhail, Morgan v., 126
MacPherson v. Buick Motor Co., 130, 540, 544, 545, 550, 614
Madison v. Yunker, 998
Magendantz, Emerson v., 326, 332, 333, 334, 335, 337
Magiulo v. Superior Court, 813
Magrine v. Krasnica, 636
Maine v. Thiboutot, 933
Maine, Taber v., 259
Major League Baseball Players Ass'n, Cardtoons, L.C. v., 1194
Maldonado v. Southern Pac. Transp. Co., 135, 142
Malloy v. Commonwealth Highland Theatres, Inc., 99
Maloney v. Rath, 8, 27, 767
Maltman v. Sauer, 488
Mammoth Mountain Ski Area, Connelly v., 474
Management Activities, Inc., Lawson v., 266, 267, 268
Maneely v. General Motors Corp., 582
Mangini v. McClurg, 468, 771
Mangus, Municipal Mut. Ins. Co. of West Virginia v., 741
Manhattan Beach City Sch. Dist., Hoyem v., 233, 234
Manhattan & Bronx Surface Transit Operating Authority (Gholson), Matter of, 832
Manhattan Ford Lincoln Mercury, Inc., Betancourt v., 412
Mann, Davies v., 437
Manning v. Brown, 445
Marathon Oil Co., Sterner v., 1244, 1245
Marchello, Matherson v., 959, 968
Marciniak v. Lundborg, 334, 335
Maretti, Prah v., 672
Marie Callender's, Inc., Livingston v., 605
Markus v. City of New York, 12
Marsh & McLennan Co., Inc., Erickson v., 980, 983, 1022
Martin v. Abbott Laboratories, 381, 388
Martin v. Hacker, 586
Martin v. Herzog, 73, 76, 78, 79, 154, 359
Martin v. Reynolds Metals Co., 653, 658, 670
Martin v. Wilson Pub. Co., 1090
Martin Chevrolet, Inc., Hernandez v., 83
Martin Luther King, Jr., Center for Social Change, Inc. v. American Heritage Products, Inc., 1187
Martinez v. Long Island Jewish Hillside Medical Center, 337
Martinez, Uniroyal Goodrich Tire Co. v., 591
Mary Carter Paint Co., Booth v., 448
Mary Lanning Memorial Hosp. Ass'n, Sell v., 287
Marzolf v. Stone, 281, 289
Marzolf, Smith v., 752
Masaki v. General Motors Corp., 297
Mass, Economy Preferred Ins. Co. v., 870

Massachusetts Bay Transp. Authority, Ferra-
gamo v., 627
Massachusetts, Wiseman v., 1131
Masson v. New Yorker Magazine, Inc., 960
F.2d 896 (9th Cir.1992), 1019
Masson v. New Yorker Magazine, Inc., 501
U.S. 496, 111 S.Ct. 2419, 115 L.Ed.2d 447
(1991), 974, 1018, 1148
Mastland, Inc. v. Evans Furniture, Inc., 56
Mastroianni v. County of Suffolk, 231
Mastromonaco, Matthies v., 122, 126,
127, 914
Matherson v. Marchello, 959, 968
Mattco Forge, Inc. v. Arthur Young & Co.,
447
Matteo, Barr v., 976
Matter of (see name of party)
Matthews, KNB Enterprises v., 1211
Matthies v. Mastromonaco, 122, 126, 127,
914
Mauri v. Smith, 1162
Mauro v. Raymark Industries, Inc., 347
Maxwell v. State Farm Mut. Auto. Ins. Co.,
831
Mayo, Symington v., 688
McCarty v. Pheasant Run, Inc., 45
McCloskey, Robertson v., 956
McClurg, Mangini v., 468, 771
McCord, Democratic Nat. Committee v., 1223
McCormick v. England, 1136, 1138
McCullock v. H.B. Fuller Co., 625
McCurdy, Ditto v., 128
McDermott v. Reynolds, 901
McDermott, Boehner v., 1184, 1185
McDermott, Inc. v. AmClyde, 448
McDonnell Douglas Corp., Philippine Air-
lines, Inc. v., 647
McDonnell Douglas Corp., Shatkin v., 268
McDonnell Douglas Corp., Shu–Tao Lin v.,
268
McDougald v. Garber, 697, 704, 705
McDougald v. Perry, 94, 98, 99, 101
McEachern, Muldovan v., 483
McGovern, Rinaldo v., 341
McGrath v. American Cyanamid Co., 482
McIntosh v. Melroe Co., a Div. of Clark
Equipment Co., Inc., 792
McKelvey v. McKelvey, 216
McKelvey, McKelvey v., 216
McKelway, Hartke v., 336
McKichan v. St. Louis Hockey Club, L.P., 474
McKinne, Fritts v., 452, 455, 460
McKinney v. Nash, 127
McKnight, Richardson v., 932
McKown, Lundman v., 223
**McLaughlin v. Mine Safety Appliances
Co., 412,** 416, 417
McLaughlin, ACS Investors, Inc. v., 1244
McLaughlin, Hooks SuperX, Inc. v., 636
McLean v. Kirby Co., a Div. of Scott Fetzer
Co., 185
McLean Credit Union, Patterson v., 894
McLean, Luque v., 579
McLean, Renko v., 224
McLean Trucking Co., Ewen v., 579

McManus v. Doubleday & Co., Inc., 1090
McNally v. Pulitzer Pub. Co., 944
McNary v. Chamberlain, 1245
McPeake v. William T. Cannon, Esquire,
P.C., 310
McVey, Logerquist v., 358
Meade v. Cedarapids, Inc., 1222
Meaney v. Rubega, 100
Medical Economics Co., Gilbert v., 1108
Medical Protective Co., L'Orange v., 116
Medico v. Time, Inc., 977, **985,** 991, 992,
993
Medtronic, Inc. v. Lohr, 491
Meeropol v. Nizer, 1059
Meier & Frank Co., Hinish v., 1140
Meisler v. Gannett Co., Inc., 1020
Melroe Co., a Div. of Clark Equipment Co.,
Inc., McIntosh v., 792
Melvin v. Burling, 1163
Melvin v. Reid, 1106, 1127
Memorial Hosp., Falcon v., 366
Memorial Hosp., Sheeley v., 109, 116
Menezes, Erlich v., 296, 1270
Menlove, Vaughan v., 53
Mennonite Hospital, Renslow v., 166
Mentor Soccer Club, Inc., Zivich v., 467
Menu v. Minor, 136
Merced v. City of New York, 233
Mercer v. Rockwell Intern. Corp., 658
Merchants Mut. Ins. Co., Kurcsics v., 833
Meredith v. Hanson, 449, 450
Meritor Sav. Bank, FSB v. Vinson, 895
Merrell Dow Pharmaceuticals, Inc., Daubert
v., 355, 356, 357, 358
Mertens v. Wolfeboro Nat. Bank, 1217
Messenger ex rel. Messenger v. Gruner &
Jahr Printing and Pub., 1100, 1141
Metro-Goldwyn-Mayer Pictures, Ltd., Yous-
soupoff v., 961
Metromedia, Inc., Rosenbloom v., 1024, 1036,
1039
**Metro–North Commuter R. Co. v. Buck-
ley, 270,** 398
Metropolitan Baseball Club, Inc., Davidoff by
Davidoff v., 475
Metropolitan Property & Cas. Ins. Co., Doyle
v., 764
Metropolitan Transp. Authority, Weiner v.,
232
Metzger, Taylor v., 893
Mexicali Rose v. Superior Court, 637
Meyer v. City of Des Moines, 459, 460
Michael, Plaxico v., 1158
Michael R., Gritzner v., 178
Michalski v. Home Depot, Inc., 195
Michelfelder, American Family Service Corp.
v., 1238
Michelman v. Ehrlich, 337
Middlesex County Sewerage Authority v. Na-
tional Sea Clammers Ass'n, 933
Midnight Sun Transp. Services, Inc., Lyons
v., 58
Mid-America Motorsports, Inc., Wolfgang v.,
456

Mid–Coast Hosp., Harvey ex rel. Harvey v., 456
Midwest Communications, Inc., Ross v., 1108
Mid–West Conveyor Co., Inc., J.S. Alberici Const. Co., Inc. v., 466
Mihalik v. Duprey, 1020
Miksis v. Howard, 692
Milford Radio Corp., Pacella v., 1091
Milgroom v. News Group Boston, Inc., 1047
Milkovich v. Lorain Journal Co., 1063, 1067, 1075, 1076
Millan v. Yan Yee Lau, 837
Miller v. Miller, 835
Miller, Lewis v., 446
Miller, Miller v., 835
Miller Steamship Co. Pty. Ltd. (The Wagon Mound) (No.2), Overseas Tankship (UK) Ltd. v., 428
Milliken & Co. v. Consolidated Edison Co. of New York, Inc., 321
Mills, Doe v., 1113
Mills, Ellerbee v., 1047
Milobsky, Henderson v., 129
Mine Safety Appliances Co., McLaughlin v., 412, 416, 417
Minneapolis Star and Tribune Co., Jadwin v., 1061
Minor, Menu v., 136
Mireles v. Waco, 941
Miriam Collins–Palm Beach Laboratories Co., Ragans v., 587
Miriam Hosp., Schloss v., 334
Missouri Pac. R. Co., Rogers v., 815
Missouri, State of v. National Organization for Women, Inc., 1260
Missouri Valley College, Nazeri v., 973
Mistrough, Bassey v., 79
Mitchell v. Globe Intern. Pub., Inc., 817 F.Supp. 72 (W.D.Ark.1993), 1147
Mitchell v. Globe Intern. Pub., Inc., 773 F.Supp. 1235 (W.D.Ark.1991), 962, 963
Mitchell v. Pearson Enterprises, 348
Mitchell v. Rochester Ry. Co., 265, 266
Mitchell v. Trawler Racer, Inc., 815
Mitchell, Alcorn v., 875
Mitchell, Geernaert v., 1219
Mitchell, Roman v., 769
Mittendorf, Wagner v., 404
Mixon v. Dobbs Houses, Inc., 137
M.K., J.C. Penney Casualty Ins. Co. v., 744
Moffat, Waschak v., 670
Moffatt, Chatham Furnace Co. v., 1218
Mogeloff, Conboy v., 167
Moguls, Inc., Kelley, Estate of v., 451
Mohney v. USA Hockey, Inc., 613
Mohr v. Commonwealth, 1234
Moisan v. Loftus, 45
Molalla Transport System, Inc., Connes v., 185
Moldea v. New York Times Co., 1074
Monell v. Department of Social Services of City of New York, 930
Monitor Patriot Co. v. Roy, 1044
Monroe v. Pape, 929, 931, 943
Monroe County Bd. of Educ., Davis v., 898

Montalvo v. Lapez, 705
Montana v. San Jose Mercury News, Inc., 1213
Montes, Ambassador Ins. Co. v., 745
Montgomery v. Daniels, 828, 829
Montgomery Cablevision Ltd. Partnership, Beynon v., 269
Montgomery Elevator Co. v. Gordon, 451
Montgomery Ward v. Shope, 1158
Moody v. Haymarket Associates, 88
Moore v. Baker, 127
Moore v. Shah, 429, 481
Moore, Huggins v., 1039
Moore, Travis v., 671
Moradi–Shalal v. Fireman's Fund Ins. Companies, 779
Moran v. Faberge, Inc., 587
Moransais v. Heathman, 325
Morgan v. MacPhail, 126
Morgan v. Yuba County, 137, 177
Morrell v. Forbes, Inc., 963
Morris v. Platt, 917
Morrison, Sears v., 436
Morrison, United States v., 897
Morrocco v. Piccardi, 483
Morton v. Owens–Corning Fiberglas Corp., 566
Morts Dock & Engineering Co (The Wagon Mound) (No.1), Overseas Tankship (UK) Ltd v., 405, 409, 410, 428, 432
Mosler Safe Co. v. Ely–Norris Safe Co., 1257
Moss v. Southern Excavation, Inc., 814
Motts, Stewart v., 49
Mount Vernon Fire Ins. Co. v. Creative Housing Ltd., 742, 771
Mountain River Tours, Inc., Krazek v., 467
Mugavero, Allstate Ins. Co. v., 741, 743, 745
Muldovan v. McEachern, 483
Multimedia, Inc., Hawkins By and Through Hawkins v., 1130
Muncie Medical Investors, L.P., Taylor v., 339
Municipal Mut. Ins. Co. of West Virginia v. Mangus, 741
Munn v. Algee, 458
Murakami, Adams v., 736
Muroc Joint Unified School Dist., Randi W. v., 170, 177, 178, 197, 306, 981
Murphy v. E.R. Squibb & Sons, Inc., 636
Murphy v. Steeplechase Amusement Co., 469, 471, 472, 911
Muskin Corp., O'Brien v., 570, 571, 590
Muskopf v. Corning Hospital Dist., 928
Myrick, Freightliner Corp. v., 496

N.A.A.C.P. v. Claiborne Hardware Co., 1260
Nadel v. Regents of University of California, 1080
Nader v. Allegheny Airlines, Inc., 1236
Nader v. General Motors Corp., 1151, 1157, 1159, 1161, 1162, 1183
Nakamura v. Superior Court, 765
Namath v. Sports Illustrated, 1213
Napolitano, Bennett v., 194, 202

Nash, McKinney v., 127

Nasser v. Parker, 168

Nath v. National Equipment Leasing Corp., 553

National Audubon Soc., Inc., Edwards v., 1089, 1090

National Bond & Inv. Co. v. Whithorn, 885

National Broadcasting Co., Harwood Pharmacal Co. v., 1256

National Broadcasting Co., Olivia N. v., 190

National Broadcasting Co., Street v., 1059

National Broadcasting Co., Taylor v., 1215

National Conversion Corp. v. Cedar Bldg. Corp., 1222

National County Mut. Fire Ins. Co. v. Johnson, 224

National Enquirer, Dempsey v., 702 F.Supp. 934 (D.Me.1989),1148, 1150

National Enquirer, Dempsey v., 702 F.Supp. 927 (D.Me.1988), 1149

National Enquirer, Inc., Burnett v., 995, 998, 1207

National Enquirer, Inc., Dorsey v., 992

National Enquirer, Inc., Fellows v., 1146

National Equipment Leasing Corp., Nath v., 553

National Organization for Women, Inc., Missouri, State of v., 1260

National Sea Clammers Ass'n, Middlesex County Sewerage Authority v., 933

National Steel Service Center, Inc. v. Gibbons, 519

National Union Fire Ins. Co. of Pittsburgh, Pa., Northville Industries Corp. v., 743

Nationwide Ins. Co. v. Estate of Kollstedt, 871

Nationwide Mut. Fire Ins. Co., Cone v., 771

Nationwide Mut. Ins. Co., Bamond v., 831

Nationwide Mut. Ins. Co., Boyd v., 982

Nautilus Marine, Inc. v. Niemela, 322

Navistar Intern. Transp. Corp., Crandall Corp. v., 1243

Navistar Intern. Transp. Corp., Webb v., 611

Nazeri v. Missouri Valley College, 973

NBT Bancorp Inc. v. Fleet/Norstar Financial Group, Inc., 1245

Neacosia v. New York Power Authority, 809

Neal v. Neal, 899

Neal, Neal v., 899

Near v. State of Minnesota ex rel. Olson, 1000

Nees v. Hocks, 1270

Neff v. Time, Inc., 1112

Negewo, Abebe–Jira v., 880

Negri v. Stop and Shop, Inc., 86, 88

Neighborhood Centers Ass'n for Child Development, Albritton v., 225

Neiman v. American Nat. Property and Cas. Co., 707

Neiman–Marcus v. Lait, 965

Neinstein v. Los Angeles Dodgers, Inc., 475

Nelms, Laird v., 519

Nelson v. Johnson, 762

Nelson v. Wiggs, 1233

NET Properties Management, Inc., Valenti v., 28

Neurological Medicine, Inc., Stafford v., 403

Nevitt, Fairfax Hosp. System, Inc. v., 696

New England Newspapers, Inc., Healey v., 958

New Hampshire, Chaplinsky v., 1000

New Haven Register, Inc., Alvarez v., 23

New Rochelle Hosp. Medical Center, Kraus v., 1271

New Times Pub. Co., Cianci v., 1064, 1090

New York Cent. R. Co. v. White, 806

New York Cent. R. Co., Ryan v., 430, 757, 758, 759

New York City Dept. of Housing Preservation and Development, Johannesen v., 809

New York City Housing Authority, Price ex rel. Price v., 349

New York City Transit Authority v. Ambrosio, 832

New York City Transit Authority, Bethel v., 47, 50, 51, 56, 67

New York City Transit Authority, Clinger v., 232

New York City Transit Authority, Crosland v., 232, 243

New York City Transit Authority, Dermatossian v., 94

New York & N.H.R. Co., Connecticut Mut. Life Ins. Co. v., 323

New York Post Co., Inc., Gunduz v., 975

New York Post Corp., Wildstein v., 953

New York Power Authority, Neacosia v., 809

New York Times Co. v. Sullivan, 905, 910, **1000,** 1012, 1013, 1020, 1022, 1044, 1048, 1078, 1080, 1094, 1095, 1096, 1097, 1101

New York Times Co. v. United States, 1130, 1141, 1149

New York Times Co., Holy Spirit Ass'n for Unification of World Christianity v., 993

New York Times Co., Moldea v., 1074

New York World Telegram Corp., Kunst v., 954

New Yorker Magazine, Inc., Masson v., 960 F.2d 896 (9th Cir.1992), 1019

New Yorker Magazine, Inc., Masson v., 501 U.S. 496, 111 S.Ct. 2419, 115 L.Ed.2d 447 (1991), 974, 1018, 1148

New Yorker Staats–Zeitung, Adolf Philipp Co. v., 983

Newing v. Cheatham, 108

Newmark v. Gimbel's Inc., 636

Newport, City of v. Fact Concerts, Inc., 943

News and Observer Pub. Co., Renwick v., 1145

News Group Boston, Inc., Milgroom v., 1047

News Group Publications, Inc., Stephano v., 1099

News World Communications, Inc., Clyburn v., 1059

Newton, Urbaniak v., 725

Nichols v. Item Publishers, 956

Nichols v. State Farm Fire and Cas. Co., 100

Nicollet Hotel, Connolly v., 93

Niedert v. Rieger, 1263

Nielsen, Bishop v., 222
Nieman v. Upper Queens Medical Group, 281
Niemela, Nautilus Marine, Inc. v., 322
Nissei ASB Mach. Co., Ltd., Anderson v., 623
Nixon v. Fitzgerald, 947
Nizer, Meeropol v., 1059
NKC Hospitals, Inc., Sword v., 28
Noon, Bortz v., 1239
Nora Beverages, Inc. v. Perrier Group of America, Inc., 1257
Norcal Mutual Ins. Co., Schimmel v., 1270
Norplant Contraceptive Products Litigation, In re, 596
North River Ins. Co., Hyde v., 836
Northville Industries Corp. v. National Union Fire Ins. Co. of Pittsburgh, Pa., 743
Nursing and Home Care, Inc., Kish v., 808
Nussbaum, Kavanaugh by Gonzales v., 185
Nycal Corp. v. KPMG Peat Marwick LLP., 302, 307, 313, 324
NYP Holdings, Inc., Jewell v., 999

Oakland Tribune, Inc., Diaz v., 1130
Oakley, Loui v., 377
O'Brien v. Cunard S.S. Co., Ltd., 913
O'Brien v. Muskin Corp., 570, 571, 590
O'Brien v. Pabst Sales Co., 1207
Ocala Star–Banner Co. v. Damron, 1044, 1045
Ocean County Observer, Costello v., 1019
Ochoa v. Superior Court, 287
Ochs v. Borrelli, 331
Ochsner Clinic, Dabdoub v., 429
O'Daniels, Soldano v., 142
Ohio Academy of Trial Lawyers, State ex rel. v. Sheward, 792
Oklahoma Pub. Co. v. District Court In and For Oklahoma County, 1115
Oliver v. Stimson Lumber Co., 100
Oliver, Albright v., 933
Oliver, Salem Group v., 771
Olivia N. v. National Broadcasting Co., 190
Ollerman v. O'Rourke Co., Inc., 1223, 1237
Ollman v. Evans, 1062
Olson, Florenzano v., 1237
Omega Chemical Co., Inc. v. United Seeds, Inc., 674
O'Melveny & Myers v. F.D.I.C., 308
On Target, Inc., Valentine v., 184
Onassis, Galella v., 533 F.Supp. 1076 (S.D.N.Y.1982), 1166
Onassis, Galella v., 487 F.2d 986 (2nd Cir. 1973), **1163,** 1167
Oncale v. Sundowner Offshore Services, Inc., 896
Onita Pacific Corp. v. Trustees of Bronson, 1233, 1234
Oppen, Union Oil Co. v., 320
Orcutt Union Sch. Dist., Wynne v., 1137
Oresky v. Scharf, 295
O'Rourke Co., Inc., Ollerman v., 1223, 1237
Orser v. George, 386

Ortho Pharmaceutical Corp., MacDonald v., 596
Orthopedic Bone Screw Liability Litigation, In re, 496
Ortiz v. Fibreboard Corp., 395
Osborn v. Hertz Corp., 183
Osceola Refining Co., a Div. of Texas–American Petrochemicals, Inc., Rabidue v., 895
Ossenfort v. Associated Milk Producers, Inc., 299
Osteopathic Hosp. of Maine, Inc., Gammon v., 278, 280, 281, 403
O'Sullivan v. Shaw, 482
Otolaryngology Clinic, Spannaus v., 109
Ottaway Newspapers, Inc., Brady v., 965
Ottenad, Bowers v., 195
Ouellette v. Carde, 451
Ouellette, International Paper Co. v., 677
Outlaw, Barnes v., 299
Overcast v. Billings Mutual Ins. Co., 953
Overseas Tankship (UK) Ltd. v. Miller Steamship Co. Pty. Ltd. (The Wagon Mound) (No.2), 410
Overseas Tankship (UK) Ltd. v. Morts Dock & Engineering Co. (The Wagon Mound) (No.1), 405, 409, 410, 428, 432
Owen v. City of Independence, Mo., 942
Owens–Corning Fiberglas Corp. v. Ballard, 738
Owens–Corning Fiberglas Corp., Anderson v., 602
Owens–Corning Fiberglas Corp., Bragg v., 601
Owens–Corning Fiberglas Corp., Morton v., 566
Owens–Corning Fiberglas Corp., Spaur v., 299
Ozer v. Borquez, 1110, 1131

Pabst Sales Co., O'Brien v., 1207
Pacella v. Milford Radio Corp., 1091
Pachtman, Imbler v., 941
Pacific Coast Borax Co., Scott v., 813
Pacific Gas & Electric Co. v. Bear Stearns & Co., 1246
Pacific Indemnity Co., Continental Casualty Co. v., 782
Pacific Mut. Life Ins. Co. v. Haslip, 727
Pacific Plaza Shopping Center, Ann M. v., 209, 211
Pacific University, Conway v., 1234
Pacific West Mountain Resort, Scott By and Through Scott v., 466
Pacifica Foundation, F.C.C. v., 909
Pacor, Inc., Simmons v., 347, 348
Page Airways, Inc., Abbott v., 98
Paladin Enterprises, Inc., Rice v., 190
Palank, CSX Transp., Inc. v., 737
Palka v. Servicemaster Management Services Corp., 149
Paller & Goldstein, Fischl v., 324
Palma v. United States Industrial Fasteners, Inc., 184
Palmer v. Bennington School Dist., Inc., 1047

Palmer Communications, Inc., Jones v., 1047
Palsgraf v. Long Island R. Co., 306, **419,** 428, 429, 431
Pamela L. v. Farmer, 178
Pan American World Airlines, Inc., Farina v., 98
Pangan, Clark v., 23
Pape, Monroe v., 929, 931, 943
Pappas, Daugert v., 367
Parich v. State Farm Mut. Auto. Ins. Co., 780
Park v. Capital Cities Communications, Inc., 1060
Parker–Hannifin Corp., Campbell v., 391
Parker–Hughey, Cooper v., 1263
Parker, Nasser v., 168
Parke–Davis, Inc., Harbeson v., 336
Parks, Jason v., 296
Parvi v. City of Kingston, 142
Pascagoula Public School Dist., Rodgers v., 611 So.2d 942 (Miss.1992), 770
Pate v. Threlkel, 165
Patterson v. McLean Credit Union, 894
Patterson, Sweeney v., 1000
Patton v. Hutchinson Wil–Rich Mfg. Co., 603, 604
Paulson Truck Lines, Inc., Hightower v., 435
Pavia v. State Farm Mut. Auto. Ins. Co., **774,** 780, 781
Pa–Ted Spring Co., Inc., Arsenault v., 789
Pearson v. Dodd, 1159, 1160
Pearson v. Reed, 244
Pearson, Dellwo v., 57
Pearson Enterprises, Mitchell v., 348
Peate, Bower v., 502
Peat Marwick Main & Co., Security Pacific Business Credit, Inc. v., 307
Pebble Beach Co. v. Tour 18 I Ltd., 1257
Peck v. Counseling Service of Addison County, Inc., 168
Peckham v. Boston Herald, Inc., 1109
Peckham v. Peckham Materials Corp., 813
Peckham Materials Corp., Peckham v., 813
Peek, Derry v., 1218, 1219
Peerless Glass Co., Smith v., 545
Peerless Transp. Co., Cordas v., 927
Pegler, Reynolds v., 973
Pegram v. Herdrich, 497
Pelletier, LaBier v., 439
Pembaur v. City of Cincinnati, 930
Pena–Irala, Filartiga v., 880
Pena, Phan Son Van v., 419
Pender, Heaven v., 131
Pennzoil, Co., Texaco, Inc. v., 1246
People Exp. Airlines, Inc. v. Consolidated Rail Corp., **313,** 320, 321, 322, 323, 433, 646, 759
Peoples Bank and Trust Co. of Mountain Home v. Globe Intern. Pub., Inc., 1147
Perez v. Campbell, 765
Perez v. Wyeth Laboratories Inc., 596
Perez v. Z Frank Oldsmobile, Inc., 1239
Perini Corp., Spano v., 510
Perkins v. Howard, 158
Perrier Group of America, Inc., Nora Beverages, Inc. v., 1257

Perron, Hackett v., 27, 28
Perry v. S.N., 156
Perry, McDougald v., 94, 98, 99, 101
Perry Memorial Hosp. Trust Authority, Strubhart v., 106
Personal Preference Video, Inc. v. Home Box Office, Inc., 1244
Peter, Ellis v., 167
Peters, Kemezy v., 736
Peterson v. Halsted, 182
Peterson v. Lou Bachrodt Chevrolet Co., 715
Peter W. v. San Francisco Unified Sch. Dist., 234
Petition of (see name of party)
Petition of Kinsman Transit Co. (Kinsman I), 338 F.2d 708 (2d Cir.1964), 431, 767
Petition of Kinsman Transit Co. (Kinsman II), 388 F.2d 821 (2d Cir.1968), 433, 650
Petriello v. Kalman, 347
Petrillo v. Bachenberg, 311
Petty, Cohen v., 55
Pfeifer, Jones & Laughlin Steel Corp. v., 690, 708
Phan Son Van v. Pena, 419
Phantom Touring, Inc. v. Affiliated Publications, 1074, 1075
Pheasant Run, Inc., McCarty v., 45
Philadelphia Eagles Football Club, Chuy v., 1059
Philadelphia Newspapers, Inc. v. Hepps, 1041
Philippine Airlines, Inc. v. McDonnell Douglas Corp., 647
Phoenix Newspapers, Inc., Boswell v., 998
Phoenix Professional Hockey Club, Inc. v. Hirmer, 323
Physicians Ins. Co. of Wisconsin, Schreiber v., 127
Piasecki Trucking, Inc., Sutton v., 444
Picard v. Barry Pontiac–Buick, Inc., 872, 875
Piccardi, Morrocco v., 483
Picillo, Wood v., 670
Pierce v. Utica Mut. Ins. Co., 832
Pinkerton Nat. Detective Agency, Inc. v. Stevens, 1157
Pioneer Broadcasting Co., Holden v., 998
Piphus, Carey v., 943
Piro, Tavoulareas v., 1019
Pittman v. Upjohn Co., 585, 586
Pizarro, Hawkins v., 165
Plain v. Plain, 299
Plain, Plain v., 299
Plaintiffs' Legal Committee, Buckman Co. v., 496
Planned Parenthood of Southeastern Pennsylvania v. Casey, 333, 1139
Plant Insulation Co., Williamson v., 706
Planters Lifesavers Co., Welge v., 557
Platt, Morris v., 917
Plattsburgh Pub. Co., Div. of Ottaway Newspapers Inc., Robare v., 1041
Platz v. City of Cohoes, 80
Plaxico v. Michael, 1158
Playboy Enterprises, Inc., Saenz v., 1021
Pleasant v. Celli, 309

Ploof v. Putnam, 922, 926
PMR Architects, P.C., Bruzga v., 633
Pokora v. Wabash Ry. Co., 60, 62, 435
Polemis, In re, 404, 405, 428, 432
Polk County v. Dodson, 931
Polyblank, Kawananakoa v., 225
Pomeroy, Andre v., 64, 214
Poole v. City of Rolling Meadows, 446
Port Authority of New York and New Jersey v. Arcadian Corp., 592
Portee v. Jaffee, 282, 286, 287, 288, 289, 290, 450
Porter Leasing Corp., Frost v., 747, 752, 754
Posadas v. City of Reno, 974
Posecai v. Wal–Mart Stores, Inc., 206, 211, 212
Post, Hall v., 1111
Post Newsweek Stations–Connecticut, Inc. v. Travelers Ins. Co., 1193
Post Pub. Co. v. Hallam, 984, 985, 1000, 1011
Potter v. Firestone Tire & Rubber Co., 276, 278, 397
Powell v. Flechter, 1222
Pozzuoli, Truck Ins. Exchange v., 743
PPG Industries, Inc. v. Transamerica Ins. Co., 781
Prah v. Maretti, 672
Pratt v. Robinson, 234
Pratt, Berthiaume's Estate v., 1162
PRC Inc., Bolden v., 894
Precision Papers, Inc., Lopez v., 620, 623
Preis, Fuller v., 403
Press Pub. Co., Ben–Oliel v., 959
Prevost Car, Inc., Airport Rent–A–Car, Inc. v., 646
Price v. Blaine Kern Artista, Inc., 572
Price v. General Motors Corp., 557
Price v. Kitsap Transit, 56
Price v. Price, 214
Price v. Shell Oil Co., 553
Price v. Workers' Comp. Appeals Bd., 809
Price ex rel. Price v. New York City Housing Authority, 349
Price, Price v., 214
Pridham v. Cash & Carry Bldg. Center, Inc., 404
Princeton Packet, Inc., Decker v., 956
Principal Cas. Ins. Co. v. Blair, 224
Prisoners' Legal Services of New York, Inc., Sweeney v., 1020
Proctor & Gamble Co. v. Haugen, 1256
Progressive Grocery Stores, Ryan v., 545, 546, 600, 635, 648
Proud, Greycas, Inc. v., 313, 1219, 1237
Proxmire, Hutchinson v., 1045, 1049, 1059
Prozeralik v. Capital Cities Communications, Inc., 1092
Prudential Ins. Co. of America v. Dewey, Ballantine, Bushby, Palmer & Wood, 311
Prudential Ins. Co. of America, Bast v., 497
Prudential Property and Cas. Co. v. Szeli, 764
Prudential Property & Cas. Ins. Co., Richardson v., 834

Pruitt v. General Motors Corp., 566
Public Service Mut. Ins. Co. v. Goldfarb, 769
Pulitzer Pub. Co., McNally v., 944
Pulka v. Edelman, 150, 151
Putnam v. Stout, 204
Putnam, Ploof v., 922, 926
Putney, Vosburg v., 868, 869, 879, 913
Putter, Copley v., 377

Quackenbush v. Superior Court (Congress of California Seniors), 765
Qualitex Co. v. Jacobson Products Co., Inc., 1257
Quern v. Jordan, 942
Quill v. Trans World Airlines, Inc., 268
QVC Network, Inc., Castro v., 605

Raber v. Tumin, 108
Rabidue v. Osceola Refining Co., 895
Racine Currency Exchange, Inc., Boyd v., 212, 213
Radiation Oncology Associates, Ashe v., 129
Raftery v. Scott, 903
Ragans v. Miriam Collins–Palm Beach Laboratories Co., 587
Ralee Engineering Co., Green v., 1271
Ramey, Fassoulas v., 329
Ramsey Associates, Inc., Coty v., 672
Ramsbottom, Roberts v., 54
Ranalli v. Edro Motel Corp., 637
Randall v. K–Mart Corp., 89, 90, 91, 93
Randall, Speiser v., 1011
Randi W. v. Muroc Joint Unified School Dist., 170, 177, 178, 197, 306, 981
Rardin v. T & D Mach. Handling, Inc., 649, 1269
Rath, Maloney v., 8, 27, 767
R.A.V. v. City of St. Paul, Minn., 966
Raveling, Wooden v., 266, 268
Ravo by Ravo v. Rogatnick, 368
Ray by Holman v. BIC Corp., 567
Raybestos–Manhattan, Inc., Champagne v., 460
Raybestos–Manhattan, Wheeler v., 388
Raymark Industries, Inc., Mauro v., 347
Raymond, Courvoisier v., 914, 917
Reader's Digest Ass'n, Inc., Grant v., 961
Reader's Digest Ass'n, Inc., Wolston v., 1048, 1049, 1059
Reader's Digest Association, Inc., Briscoe v., 1112, 1125, 1126, 1127
Ream v. Keen, 658
Red Creek Cent. School Dist., Ernest v., 234
Redland Aggregates Ltd., Snead v., 1079
Reed v. Bojarski, 165
Reed v. King, 1233
Reed, Pearson v., 244
Reed–Prentice Division of Package Machinery Co., Robinson v., 623, 624
Regardie, Wolf v., 1113
Regents of University of California, Nadel v., 1080
Regents of University of California, Reisner v., 164, 169

Regents of University of California, Tarasoff v., 158, 163, 164, 165, 167, 168, 169, 177, 197, 212, 234, 370, 1138

Regents of University of California, Zavala v., 445

Regents of University of Cal., Tunkl v., 465, 466

Reichhold Chemicals, Inc. v. Hartford Accident and Indemnity Co., 743

Reid, Melvin v., 1106, 1127

Reida v. Lund, 870

Reisner v. Regents of University of California, 164, 169

Reliance Insurance Companies v. Daly, 766

Remeikis v. Boss & Phelps, Inc., 1235

Renko v. McLean, 224

Renslow v. Mennonite Hospital, 166

Rensselaer Water Co., H.R. Moch Co. v., 143, 144, 149, 321, 651, 759

Renwick v. News and Observer Pub. Co., 1145

Republic Automotive Parts, Inc., Taylor v., 770

Reyes v. Wyeth Laboratories, 849

Reynolds v. Clark, 29

Reynolds v. Hicks, 185, 189, 370

Reynolds v. Pegler, 973

Reynolds, McDermott v., 901

Reynolds Memorial Hosp., Inc., Andrews v., 709

Reynolds Metals Co., Martin v., 653, 658, 670

Rhone–Poulenc Rorer Inc., 394

Ribas v. Clark, 1174

Rice v. Charles, 708

Rice v. Paladin Enterprises, Inc., 190

Richardson v. Chapman, 696

Richardson v. Fiedler Roofing, Inc., 808

Richardson v. McKnight, 932

Richardson v. Prudential Property & Cas. Ins. Co., 834

Rickards v. Sun Oil Co., 323

Riding Safely, Inc., Dilallo By and Through Dilallo v., 467

Rieger, Niedert v., 1263

Riggins, Town & Country Properties, Inc. v., 1213

Rinaldo v. McGovern, 341

Riordan, Di Ponzio v., 81

Riss v. City of New York, 226, 230, 231, 232, 234, 243, 248, 932

Rivera, Boon v., 177, 178

Rizzo v. Goode, 932

R.J. v. Humana of Florida, Inc., 266

R.J. Reynolds Tobacco Co. v. Engle, 394

RKO General, Inc., Weirum v., 190

Robare v. Plattsburgh Pub. Co., Div. of Ottaway Newspapers Inc., 1041

Robbins v. Footer, 109, 114

Roberson v. Rochester Folding Box Co., 1098, 1215

Robert Welch, Inc., Gertz v., 680 F.2d 527 (7th Cir.1982), 1036

Robert Welch, Inc., Gertz v., 418 U.S. 323, 94 S.Ct. 2997, 41 L.Ed.2d 789 (1974), 943,

1025, 1036, 1037, 1039, 1042, 1043, 1045, 1046, 1048, 1059, 1061, 1076, 1077, 1078, 1079, 1080, 1089, 1094, 1095, 1130, 1147, 1149

Roberts v. Galen of Virginia, Inc., 157

Roberts v. Ramsbottom, 54

Roberts v. Vaughn, 484, 487, 488

Robertson v. McCloskey, 956

Robins Dry Dock & Repair Co. v. Flint, 322

Robinson v. District of Columbia, 80

Robinson v. Reed–Prentice Division of Package Machinery Co., 623, 624

Robinson, Pratt v., 234

Rocci v. Ecole Secondaire Macdonald–Cartier, 1037

Rochester Folding Box Co., Roberson v., 1098, 1215

Rochester Gas & Elec. Corp. v. Dunlop, 518

Rochester Ry. Co., Mitchell v., 265, 266

Rockwell Intern. Corp., Mercer v., 658

Rockwood Sprinkler Co., De Haen v., 80, 82, 412

Rodenhiser, Carchidi v., 693, 694

Rodgers v. Pascagoula Public School Dist., 770

Rodrigues v. State, 296, 297

Roe v. Doe, 1131

Roe, Doe v., 1131

Rogatnick, Ravo by Ravo v., 368

Rogers v. Elliott, 674

Rogers v. Grimaldi, 1194

Rogers v. Missouri Pac. R. Co., 815

Rolla Women's Clinic, Inc., Lough by Lough v., 167

Romaine v. Kallinger, 949, 953, 954, 955, 956, 958, 1125, 1126

Roman v. Carroll, 296

Roman v. Mitchell, 769

Roman Catholic Archdiocese of Newark, Schultz v., 225

Rome, W. & O.T.R. Co., Booth v., 509, 510

Ronald M. v. White, 141

Ron Greenspan Volkswagen, Inc. v. Ford Motor Land Development Corp., 1237

Rosen v. First Manhattan Bank, 808

Rosenberg v. Helinski, 994

Rosenblatt v. Baer, 1043, 1044, 1045, 1046, 1048

Rosenbloom v. Metromedia, Inc., 1024, 1036, 1039

Ross v. Midwest Communications, Inc., 1108

Ross, Sargent v., 204, 205

Rossier, Imperial Ice Co. v., 1240, 1243, 1244, 1246, 1256

Rothman v. Jackson, 977

Rothman, DeHanes v., 365

Rotkiewicz v. Sadowsky, 1046

Rouch v. Enquirer & News of Battle Creek, 427 Mich. 157, 398 N.W.2d 245 (Mich. 1986), 991, 993

Rouch v. Enquirer & News of Battle Creek Michigan, 440 Mich. 238, 487 N.W.2d 205 (Mich.1992), 975

Rovira v. Boget, 955

Rowe, Clark v., 452

Rowe, Kendall/Hunt Pub. Co. v., 1244

Rowland v. Christian, 197, 203, 204

Roy, Abdulai v., 835

Roy, Monitor Patriot Co. v., 1044

Royal Dutch Petroleum Co., Wiwa v., 879

Royal Globe Ins. Co. v. Superior Court, 780

Royer v. Catholic Medical Center, 632

RTE Corp. v. Department of Industry, Labor and Human Relations, 810

R.T.H., J.S. v., 156

Rubega, Meaney v., 100

Ruffin–Steinback v. dePasse, 1215

Rufo v. Simpson, 736

Ruppert, Garthe v., 71

Rushing v. Kansas City Southern Ry. Co., 678

Rushink v. Gerstheimer, 82

Russell Blaine Co., Levine v., 71

Russell, Casey v., 79

Russell, International Union, United Auto., Aircraft and Agr. Implement Workers of America (UAW–CIO) v., 1244

Russo v. White, 892

Ruttger Hotel Corp. v. Wagner, 266

R.W. v. T.F., 871

R.W. Martin & Sons, Inc., Buettner v., 627

Ryan v. New York Cent. R. Co., 430, 757, 758, 759

Ryan v. Progressive Grocery Stores, 545, 546, 600, 635, 648

Ryder Truck Rental, Inc., Cheung v., 96

Rylands v. Fletcher, 498, 503, 504, 505, 506, 510, 532, 652, 658, 670, 671

Rylands, Fletcher v., 498

Ryobi America Corp., Hood v., 582, 585, 586, 587, 588, 589, 591, 596, 614

Ryobi, Ltd., Jones v., 614, 618, 624

Sacia, Firman v., 430

Sacramento, County of v. Lewis, 940

Sadowsky, Rotkiewicz v., 1046

Saenz v. Playboy Enterprises, Inc., 1021

Saenz on Behalf of Saenz, General Motors Corp. v., 587

Safeco Ins. Co., Aetna Casualty & Surety Co. v., 771

Safer v. Estate of Pack, 165

Safeway Stores, Inc., Commercial Union Assurance Companies v., 782

Sahadi, Liodas v., 1219

Salem Group v. Oliver, 771

Salima v. Scherwood South, Inc., 488

Salt Lake County, Birkner v., 23

Salter, Underwager v., 1079

Sami v. Varn, 115

Sampson, Baptist Memorial Hosp. System v., 24, 27, 28

Samsung Electronics America, Inc., White v., 1207, 1211

San Diego Gas & Electric Co. v. Superior Court, 658, 677

San Francisco Bay Guardian, Inc. v. Superior Court, 963

San Francisco, City and County of v. Sweet, 754

San Francisco Unified Sch. Dist., Peter W. v., 234

San Jose Mercury News, Inc., Montana v., 1213

Sanchez, General Motors Corp. v., 605, 613

Sandbak By and Through Tully v. Sandbak, 217

Sandbak, Sandbak By and Through Tully v., 217

Sandborg v. Blue Earth County, 446

Sander v. Geib, Elston, Frost Professional Ass'n, 269, 706, 708

Sanders v. American Broadcasting Companies, Inc., 1185, 1186

Sanders Lead Co., Inc., Borland v., 658

Sandford v. Chevrolet Division of General Motors, 610

Sandford, Whittaker v., 885

Sandoval v. Sandoval, 216

Sandoval, Sandoval v., 216

Sandusky Cement Prod. Co., Fantozzi v., 704

Sanger, City of v. Superior Court, 725

Sanperi, Bovsun v., 288, 291, 294, 295

Santa Rosa Junior College v. Workers' Comp. Appeals Bd., 809

Santiago v. Sherwin Williams Co., 389

Santor v. A & M Karagheusian, Inc., 645

Santy v. Bresee, 137

Sargent v. Ross, 204, 205

Saro Corp. v. Waterman Broadcasting Corp., 1061

Satcher v. Honda Motor Co., 589

Sauer, Maltman v., 488

Savage v. Delacruz, 835

Savage Arms, Inc. v. Western Auto Supply Co., 553

Savage, Tuberville v., 875

Sayles, Lester v., 300

Scarangella v. Thomas Built Buses, Inc., 626, 627, 628

Schaefer v. Lynch, 1021

Scharf, Oresky v., 295

Scheer v. Koubek, 835

Schenectady Chemicals, Inc., State v., 659

Schenectady Union Pub. Co., Sweeney v., 1000

Schenectady Union Publishing Company v. Sweeney, 1000

Scherr v. Hilton Hotels Corp., 286

Scherwood South, Inc., Salima v., 488

Schiappa, Kohn v., 310

Schiavone Const. Co. v. Time, Inc., 619 F.Supp. 684 (D.N.J.1985), 964, 1061

Schiavone Const. Co. v. Time, Inc., 735 F.2d 94 (3rd Cir.1984), 994

Schimmel v. Norcal Mutual Ins. Co., 1270

Schleier for and on Behalf of Alter v. Alter, 217

Schloss v. Miriam Hosp., 334

Schmidt, Lego v., 164

Schmierer, Kissick v., 468

Schreiber v. Physicians Ins. Co. of Wisconsin, 127

Schroeder, Allright, Inc. v., 468

Schultz v. Roman Catholic Archdiocese of Newark, 225

Schultz, Alberts v., 359, 367

Schuster v. City of New York, 230, 234

Schwartz v. American College of Emergency Physicians, 975

Schweiker v. Chilicky, 946

Scientific Games Development Corp., System Operations, Inc. v., 1256

Scott v. County of Los Angeles, 371

Scott v. Pacific Coast Borax Co., 813

Scott, Boddie v., 481

Scott By and Through Scott v. Pacific West Mountain Resort, 466

Scott, Cope v., 250, 257, 259

Scott, Gorris v., 82

Scott, Raftery v., 903

Scribner v. Summers, 658

Scripps–Howard Broadcasting Co., Zacchini v., 54 Ohio St.2d 286, 376 N.E.2d 582, 8 O.O.3d 265 (Ohio 1978), 1193

Scripps–Howard Broadcasting Co., Zacchini v., 433 U.S. 562, 97 S.Ct. 2849, 53 L.Ed.2d 965, 5 O.O.3d 215 (1977), 1145, **1187,** 1193, 1194, 1207

Seaman's Direct Buying Service, Inc. v. Standard Oil Co., 1269, 1270

Sears v. Morrison, 436

Sears, Roebuck and Co., Kresin v., 705

Sears, Roebuck & Co. v. Stiffel Co., 1258, 1259

Sears, Roebuck & Co., Inc., Jacques v., 888

Sears, Roebuck & Co., Wellborn v., 706

Seaton, Fowler v., 99

Seattle School Dist. No. 1, Berschauer/Phillips Const. Co. v., 324

Security Pacific Business Credit, Inc. v. Peat Marwick Main & Co., 307

Seely v. White Motor Co., 644, 646

Seffert v. Los Angeles Transit Lines, 680, 687, 690, 691, 694, 695, 697

Sell v. Mary Lanning Memorial Hosp. Ass'n, 287

Senco Products, Inc., Lakin v., 792

Seneca Wire & Mfg. Co. v. A.B. Leach & Co., 1217

Sentinel Pub. Co., Inc., Dairy Stores, Inc. v., 1037

Seppi v. Betty, 450

Servicemaster Management Services Corp., Palka v., 149

Setliff v. E.I. Du Pont de Nemours & Co., 389

Seven–Up Co., Kosters v., 553

Shackil v. Lederle Laboratories, a Div. of American Cyanamid Co., 389

Shaffer v. Victoria Station, Inc., 637

Shah, Aves v., 696

Shah, Moore v., 429, 481

Shaheen v. Knight, 334

Shahvar v. Superior Court, 977

Shakur, Agnant v., 962

Shannon v. Shannon, 746

Shannon, Shannon v., 746

Shansky v. United States, 258, 259

Sharon P. v. Arman, Ltd., 211

Shatkin v. McDonnell Douglas Corp., 268

Shaw, O'Sullivan v., 482

Sheeley v. Memorial Hosp., 109, 116

Shelby v. Sun Printing & Publishing Ass'n, 962

Sheldon, Elden v., 289, 290

Sheldon, Walker v., 1238, 1239

Shell Oil Co., Price v., 553

Shen v. Leo A. Daly Co., 885

Shepard, Glanzer v., 143, 145, 147, 312

Sherman v. Field Clinic, 898

Sherwin Williams Co., Santiago v., 389

Shevin v. Sunbeam Television Corp., 1174

Sheward, Ohio Academy of Trial Lawyers, State ex rel. v., 792

Sheward, State ex rel. Ohio Academy of Trial Lawyers v., 792

Shick v. Shirey, 1271

Shine v. Vega, 128, 338

Shirey, Shick v., 1271

S.H. Kress & Co., Adickes v., 931, 932

Shope, Montgomery Ward v., 1158

Shulman v. Group W Productions, Inc., 1110, 1127, 1128, **1174,** 1185, 1186, 1215

Shuta, Waldorf v., 693

Shu–Tao Lin v. McDonnell Douglas Corp., 268

Shymkiv, Baker v., 869

Shyne, Brown v., 83

Sibley, Lindsay & Curr Co., Greene v., 40, 44, 62

Sidis v. F–R Pub. Corporation, 1106, 1113, 1127

Siegert v. Gilley, 946

Siegler v. Kuhlman, 514

Siliznoff, State Rubbish Collectors Ass'n v., 888, 893

Silva v. Stevens, 1233, 1235, 1237

Silverman, Hubbard–Hall Chemical Co. v., 84

Silvester v. American Broadcasting Companies, Inc., 1060

Simmons v. Pacor, Inc., 347, 348

Simmons Airlines, Inc., Dunning v., 896

Simmons Ford, Inc. v. Consumers Union of United States, Inc., 999

Simmons Mfg. Co., Vulcan Metals Co. v., 1220

Simon & Schuster, Inc., Armstrong v., 957

Simonsen v. Thorin, 136

Simpson Paper (Vermont) Co., Hamelin v., 466

Simpson, Rufo v., 736

Sindell v. Abbott Laboratories, 381, 386, 387, 388, 389, 390

Singleton, Vermont Mut. Ins. Co. v., 871

Sinicropi v. State Farm Ins. Co., 838

Sipple v. Chronicle Publishing Co., 1112

Sisters of Providence in Washington, Sweet v., 76

Six Unknown Named Agents of Federal Bureau of Narcotics, Bivens v., 260, 945, 946, 947

S–K–I, Ltd., Dalury v., 461, 465, 466, 468, 475, 911

Smith v. Cutter Biological, Inc., a Div. of Miles Inc., 389

Smith v. Daily Mail Pub. Co., 1115, 1125

Smith v. Eli Lilly & Co., 388

Smith v. Firemen's Ins. Co., 831

Smith v. General Acc. Ins. Co., 780

Smith v. Leech Brain & Co., 409

Smith v. Marzolf, 752

Smith v. Peerless Glass Co., 545

Smith, American Employer's Ins. Co. v., 745

Smith, Bartow v., 888

Smith, Elbaor v., 448

Smith–Hunter v. Harvey, 886

Smith, Mauri v., 1162

Snead v. Redland Aggregates Ltd., 1079

Snow v. Villacci, 688

S.N., Perry v., 156

Soares v. Ann & Hope of Rhode Island, Inc., 886

Sobocienski, Hinman v., 358

Sofec, Inc., Exxon Co., U.S.A. v., 457

Sofie v. Fibreboard Corp., 695

Soldano v. O'Daniels, 142

Soley, Harris v., 737

Solsrud, Tatur v., 956

Sommer v. Federal Signal Corp., 466

Sorensen v. Allred, 445

Soriano, Wooster v., 831

Sorichetti by Sorichetti v. City of New York, 230

Sortini, Turpin v., 336

Soto v. State Farm Ins. Co., 780, 781

Soule v. General Motors Corp., 559, 566, 568, 570, 580, 591, 614

South Buffalo Ry. Co., Ives v., 805, 829

South Carolina Coastal Council, Lucas v., 670

South County, Inc. v. First Western Loan Co., 1233

Southern Bulk Industries, Inc., Union Camp Corp. v., 1246

Southern Cal. Associated Newspapers, Werner v., 998

Southern Cal. Rapid Transit Dist., Helfend v., 714, 715, 716

Southern Cal. Rapid Transit Dist., Lopez v., 232

Southern Dist. Reporters, Inc., Capizzi v., 808

Southern Excavation, Inc., Moss v., 814

Southern Maryland Hosp. Center, Inc., Fennell v., 367

Southern Pac. Co., Allen v., 468

Southern Pac. Transp. Co., Chavez v., 518

Southern Pac. Transp. Co., Maldonado v., 135, 142

Southwestern Bell Telephone Co., Hardy v., 367

Spahn, Julian Messner, Inc. v., 1131

Spangard, Ybarra v., 93 Cal.App.2d 43, 208 P.2d 445 (Cal.App. 2 Dist.1949), 107

Spangard, Ybarra v., 25 Cal.2d 486, 154 P.2d 687 (Cal.1944), **101,** 107, 108, 109, 376

Spangler, Cox v., 377

Spannaus v. Otolaryngology Clinic, 109

Spano v. Perini Corp., 510

S. Parker Hardware Mfg. Corp., Guard–Life Corp. v., 1244, 1245

Spaur v. Owens–Corning Fiberglas Corp., 299

Specialized Transp. Services, Inc., Kansas State Bank & Trust Co. v., 371

Speiser v. Randall, 1011

Spencer v. Killington, Ltd., 465

Spencer, Holodook v., 221, 222

Spivak v. Heyward, 248 A.D.2d 58, 679 N.Y.S.2d 156 (N.Y.A.D. 2 Dept.1998), 100

Sports Illustrated, Namath v., 1213

Sports Illustrated, Virgil v., 1109

Sprague v. Walter, 1092

Spurgeon v. Julius Blum, Inc., 624

Spur Industries, Inc. v. Del E. Webb Development Co., 675, 676

Staff Jennings, Inc., Wights v., 535, 638

Stafford v. Neurological Medicine, Inc., 403

Stagl v. Delta Air Lines, Inc., 72

St. Amant v. Thompson, 1015, 1017

Stambovsky v. Ackley, 1233

Standard Oil Co., Seaman's Direct Buying Service, Inc. 1269, 1270

Staples v. Bangor Hydro–Electric Co., 952, 983, 1022, 1076

Star Enterprise, Adams v., 673

Staruski v. Continental Telephone Co. of Vt., 1215

State v. _____ (see opposing party)

State, Arrowwood By and Through Loeb, Estate of v., 248

State, Battalla v., 266

State, Carradine v., 976

State, Cities Service Co. v., 506

State, DeFoor v., 696

State, Dept. of Environmental Protection v. Ventron Corp., 506

State Dept. of Environmental Regulation, Florida Wildlife Federation v., 660

State, Does 1, 2, 3, 4, 5, 6, and 7 v., 1139

State ex rel. v. _____ (see opposing party and relator)

State Farm Fire and Cas. Co., Nichols v., 100

State Farm Fire & Cas. Co. v. Kohl, 771

State Farm Fire & Cas. Co., Horesh v., 224

State Farm Ins. Co., Sinicropi v., 838

State Farm Ins. Co., Soto v., 780, 781

State Farm Mut. Auto. Ins. Co., Barrera v., 766

State Farm Mut. Auto. Ins. Co., Maxwell v., 831

State Farm Mut. Auto. Ins. Co., Parich v., 780

State Farm Mut. Auto. Ins. Co., Pavia v., 774, 780, 781

State, Feisthamel v., 436

State, Friedman v., 244, 248

State, Jackson v., 178

State, Johnson v., 281

State of (see name of state)

State of California, Williams v., 237

State of Louisiana, Garrison v., 1012, 1022, 1080
State of Minnesota ex rel. Olson, Near v., 1000
State Rubbish Collectors Ass'n v. Siliznoff, 888, 893
State, Rodrigues v., 296, 297
State, Sun v., 203
State, Tollison v., 342
State, Waschek v., 8
Statesman Journal Co., Bahr v., 975
Stationers Corp. v. Dun & Bradstreet, Inc., 981, 1074
St. Barnabas Medical Center, Chin ex rel. Chin, Estate of v., 107
Steaks Unlimited, Inc. v. Deaner, 1061
Steele, Addis v., 417
Steeplechase Amusement Co., Murphy v., 469, 471, 472, 911
Steinhauser v. Hertz Corp., 402, 767
Stencel Aero Engineering Corp. v. United States, 259
Stephano v. News Group Publications, Inc., 1099
Sterling Drug, Inc., Basko v., 377
Sternemann v. Langs, 693
Sterner v. Marathon Oil Co., 1244, 1245
Stevens v. Tillman, 958, 1075
Stevens v. Veenstra, 57
Stevens, Pinkerton Nat. Detective Agency, Inc. v., 1157
Stevens, Silva v., 1233, 1235, 1237
Stevenson v. East Ohio Gas Co., 320
Stewart v. Motts, 49
St. Francis Hotel, Larson v., 93, 94
St. Francis–St. George Hosp., Inc., Anderson v., 339
Stiffel Co., Sears, Roebuck & Co. v., 1258, 1259
Stiles v. Batavia Atomic Horseshoes, Inc., 554
Stimson Lumber Co., Oliver v., 100
Stitt v. Holland Abundant Life Fellowship, 193
St. Louis County, Tousignant v., 117
St. Louis Hockey Club, L.P., McKichan v., 474
Stockdale v. Bird & Son, Inc., 289
Stockton Newspapers, Inc. v. Superior Court, 1089, 1091
Stoleson v. United States, 403
Stone v. Wall, 900
Stone, Bolton v., 46, 410
Stone, Marzolf v., 281, 289
Stop & Shop Companies, Inc. v. Fisher, 660
Stop and Shop, Inc., Negri v., 86, 88
Stout, Putnam v., 204
Strauss v. Belle Realty Co., 144, 149, 151, 321
Strawn v. Canuso, 1232
Streenz v. Streenz, 216
Streenz, Streenz v., 216
Street v. National Broadcasting Co., 1059
St. Regis Paper Co., Cohen v., 416
Strubhart v. Perry Memorial Hosp. Trust Authority, 106

Stubbs v. City of Rochester, 342, 349
Suarez, Etkind v., 333
Sugar Notch Borough, Berry v., 411
Sullivan v. Baptist Memorial Hosp., 953, 1012
Sullivan v. Boston Gas Co., 282
Sullivan v. Conway, 1075
Sullivan v. Delta Air Lines, Inc., 706
Sullivan v. Dunham, 506, 509
Sullivan, New York Times Co. v., 905, 910, **1000,** 1012, 1013, 1020, 1022, 1044, 1048, 1078, 1080, 1094, 1095, 1096, 1097, 1101
Summers v. Bailey, 1167
Summers v. Tice, 374, 376, 377, 386
Summers, Scribner v., 658
Sun v. State, 203
Sun Oil Co., Rickards v., 323
Sun Printing & Publishing Ass'n, Shelby v., 962
Sun Printing & Publishing Ass'n, Triggs v., 983
Sunbeam Television Corp., Shevin v., 1174
Sundowner Offshore Services, Inc., Oncale v., 896
Sundquist, Doe v., 2 S.W.3d 919 (Tenn.1999), 1140
Sundquist, Doe v., 106 F.3d 702 (6th Cir. 1997), 1140
Sunnyside Products, Inc., Hansen v., 590, 591
Sunshine Chemical Specialties, Inc., Herman v., 736
Superior Court, Aas v., 646
Superior Court, Anaya v., 404
Superior Court, Brown v., 382
Superior Court, Burgess v., 294
Superior Court, Camenisch v., 310
Superior Court, Carlin v., 602
Superior Court, Cedars–Sinai Medical Center v., 100
Superior Court (Congress of California Seniors), Quackenbush v., 765
Superior Court, Coprich v., 100
Superior Court, Dixon v., 1024
Superior Court, Eastwood v., 1211
Superior Court, Falls v., 243, 244
Superior Court, Hedlund v., 168
Superior Court, Hodges v., 765
Superior Court, Horwich v., 765
Superior Court In and For Maricopa County, Law v., 459
Superior Court, Kentucky Fried Chicken of Cal., Inc. v., 213
Superior Court, Lew v., 661
Superior Court, Lompoc Unified School Dist. v., 205
Superior Court, Magliulo v., 813
Superior Court, Mexicali Rose v., 637
Superior Court, Nakamura v., 765
Superior Court, Ochoa v., 287
Superior Court, Royal Globe Ins. Co. v., 780
Superior Court, San Diego Gas & Electric Co. v., 658, 677
Superior Court, San Francisco Bay Guardian, Inc. v., 963

Superior Court, Sanger, City of v., 725
Superior Court, Shahvar v., 977
Superior Court, Stockton Newspapers, Inc. v., 1089, 1091
Superior Court, Taylor v., 718, 723, 744
Superior Court, Temple Community Hospital v., 100
Superior Court, Wilcox v., 1024
Surocco v. Geary, 927, 928
Sutton v. Piasecki Trucking, Inc., 444
Sutton, Greyhound Lines, Inc. v., 709
Swagerty, Bradshaw v., 893
Swajian v. General Motors Corp., 459
Swan, Guille v., 518
Sweeney v. Patterson, 1000
Sweeney v. Prisoners' Legal Services of New York, Inc., 1020
Sweeney v. Schenectady Union Pub. Co., 1000
Sweeney, Schenectady Union Publishing Company v., 1000
Sweet v. Sisters of Providence in Washington, 76
Sweet, Gross v., 467
Sweet, San Francisco, City and County of v., 754
Swenson, Christensen v., 18, 22
Sword v. NKC Hospitals, Inc., 28
Symington v. Mayo, 688
System Operations, Inc. v. Scientific Games Development Corp., 1256
Szeli, Prudential Property and Cas. Co. v., 764

Taber v. Maine, 259
Tabieros v. Clark Equipment Co., 580
Tacket v. General Motors Corp., 953
Taj Mahal Travel, Inc. v. Delta Airlines, Inc., 963
Takasaki, Leong v., 297
Talhouni, Hanover Ins. Co. v., 741
Tameny v. Atlantic Richfield Co., 1271
Tanberg v. Ackerman Inv. Co., 458
Tanges v. Heidelberg North America, Inc., 390
Tantillo v. Goldstein Bros. Amusement Co., 471
Tarasoff v. Regents of University of California, 158, 163, 164, 165, 167, 168, 169, 177, 197, 212, 234, 370, 1138
Tatur v. Solsrud, 956
Tavoulareas v. Piro, 1019
Taylor v. Metzger, 893
Taylor v. Muncie Medical Investors, L.P., 339
Taylor v. National Broadcasting Co., 1215
Taylor v. Republic Automotive Parts, Inc., 770
Taylor v. Superior Court, 718, 723, 744
Taylor, Cole v., 168
Taylor Mach. Works, Best v., 792
T & D Mach. Handling, Inc., Rardin v., 649, 1269
Tedla v. Ellman, 76, 79, 83
Tel–Oren v. Libyan Arab Republic, 880

Temple Community Hospital v. Superior Court, 100
Tenuto v. Lederle Laboratories, Div. of American Cyanamid Co., 167, 294
Texaco, Inc. v. Pennzoil, Co., 1246
Texaco, Inc., Hunnings v., 625
Texas Beef Group v. Winfrey, 1259
T.F., R.W. v., 871
Tharp v. Bunge Corp., 195
The Florida Star v. B.J.F., 1116, 1125, 1127, 1128, 1184
The T.J. Hooper, 70
Thiboutot, Maine v., 933
Thing v. La Chusa, 287
Thomas Built Buses, Inc., Scarangella v., 626, 627, 628
Thomas Solvent Co., Adkins v., 673, 674
Thomas, Benn v., 399, 402
Thomas, Henning v., 115
Thompson v. County of Alameda, 168
Thompson, St. Amant v., 1015, 1017
Thomson Newspapers, West v., 957, 1076
Thorin, Simonsen v., 136
Threlkel, Pate v., 165
Tice, Summers v., 374, 376, 377, 386
Tiller v. Atlantic Coast Line R. Co., 815
Tillman v. Vance Equipment Co., 553
Tillman, Stevens v., 958, 1075
Time, Inc. v. Firestone, 1042, 1043, 1048
Time, Inc. v. Hill, 1140, 1141, 1149, 1150
Time, Inc., Dietemann v., 1172, 1173, 1174, 1185, 1186, 1269
Time, Inc., Gambuzza v., 954
Time, Inc., Medico v., 977, 985, 991, 992, 993
Time, Inc., Neff v., 1112
Time, Inc., Schiavone Const. Co. v., 619 F.Supp. 684 (D.N.J.1985), 964, 1061
Time, Inc., Schiavone Const. Co. v., 735 F.2d 94 (3rd Cir.1984), 994
Time, Inc., Virgil v., 1109, 1129
Times Herald Printing Co., Gonzales v., 1012
Tishman Const. Corp., Goldberg Weprin & Ustin, LLP v., 322
Tobin v. Grossman, 288
Tokai Corp., Hernandez v., 580, 588, 589
Tollison v. State, 342
Topps Chewing Gum, Inc., Haelan Laboratories, Inc. v., 1187
Torchia v. Fisher, 518
Torres v. Little Flower Children's Services, 237
Torres-Silva v. El Mundo, Inc., 1040
Touche, Ultramares Corporation v., 306
Tour 18 I Ltd., Pebble Beach Co. v., 1257
Tousignant v. St. Louis County, 117
Town & Country Properties, Inc. v. Riggins, 1213
Town of Babylon, Little Joseph Realty, Inc. v., 671
Toyota Motor Corp., Whitehead v., 612
Toyota Motor Sales, U.S.A., Inc., Della Penna v., 1246, 1256
Trans Union Credit Information Co., Guimond v., 981

Trans World Airlines, Inc. v. Franklin Mint Corp., 851
Trans World Airlines, Inc., Quill v., 268
Transamerica Delaval, Inc., East River S.S. Corp. v., 639, 644, 645, 646, 650
Transamerica Ins. Co., PPG Industries, Inc. v., 781
Transamerica Ins. Co., Weinberg v., 836
Transamerica Premium Ins. Co., Kenty v., 1243
Travelers Ins. Co., Post Newsweek Stations–Connecticut, Inc. v., 1193
Travis v. Moore, 671
Trawler Racer, Inc., Mitchell v., 815
Trepanier v. Getting Organized, Inc., 1243, 1246
Tresemer v. Barke, 136
Triggs v. Sun Printing & Publishing Ass'n, 983
Trimarco v. Klein, 67, 70, 71
Troman v. Wood, 1041
Troxel v. Granville, 1139
Truck Ins. Exchange v. Pozzuoli, 743
Trull v. Volkswagen of America, Inc., 555
Trustees of Bronson, Onita Pacific Corp. v., 1233, 1234
TSP Newspapers, Inc., Zerangue v., 1047
TSS Seedman's, Inc., Faricelli v., 88
Tsui Yuan Tseng, El Al Israel Airlines, Ltd. v., 852
Tuberville v. Savage, 875
Tucker v. City of New York, 13
Tumin, Raber v., 108
Tunkl v. Regents of University of Cal., 465, 466
Turf Lawnmower Repair, Inc. v. Bergen Record Corp., 1037
Turner v. Big Lake Oil Co., 82, 505
Turpin v. Sortini, 336
Tusla, Vajda v., 694
Tuttle v. Buck, 1261, 1262
Twin State Gas & Electric Co., Dillon v., 402
TXO Production Corp. v. Alliance Resources Corp., 736
Tyler, City of v. Likes, 296

Uhr ex rel. Uhr v. East Greenbush Cent. School Dist., 151, 154, 155, 157, 189, 242, 1137
Ulster County Self Ins. Plan, Kesick v., 837
Ultramar, Inc., White v., 725
Ultramares Corporation v. Touche, 306
Underwager v. Salter, 1079
Union Bag & Paper Co., Whalen v., 677
Union Camp Corp. v. Southern Bulk Industries, Inc., 1246
Union Carbide Corp., Adams v., 625
Union Elec. Co., G.J. Leasing Co., Inc. v., 517
Union Oil Co. v. Oppen, 320
Union Oil Co. of California, Catlin v., 417
Union Oil Co. of California, Inc., Hatten v., 1243
Union Pac. Ry. Co. v. Cappier, 135
Uniroyal Goodrich Tire Co. v. Martinez, 591

United Airlines, Inc., Andrews v., 64, 67, 72
United Air Lines, Inc., Wood v., 518
United HealthCare, Inc., Corcoran v., 497
United Intern. Ins. Co., Agoado Realty Corp. v., 742
United Seeds, Inc., Omega Chemical Co., Inc. v., 674
United States v. _____ (see opposing party)
United States Underwriters Ins. Co. v. Val-Blue Corp., 742, 771
United States West Communications, Inc., Hirase–Doi v., 896
United States, Autery v., 259
United States, Bowman v., 257
United States, Bryant v., 233
United States Bureau of Prisons, Dykstra v., 259
United States, Cestonaro v., 257, 259
United States, Dalehite v., 250
United States Dept. of Navy, United States-Air Inc. v., 67
United States, Feres v., 259
United States, Fisher Bros. Sales, Inc. v., 259
United States, Frye v., 356, 358
United States, Gretchen v., 694
United States, Hart v., 259
United States, Hicks v., 366
United States Industrial Fasteners, Inc., Palma v., 184
United States, Kwasny v., 691
United States, New York Times Co. v., 1130, 1141, 1149
United States, Shansky v., 258, 259
United States Steel Corp., Leadfree Enterprises, Inc. v., 323
United States, Stencel Aero Engineering Corp. v., 259
United States, Stoleson v., 403
United States Sugar Corp., Kirk v., 660
United States, Unthank v., 849
United States, Zuchowicz v., 349, 356, 359, 411
United States, Zumwalt v., 257
United Technologies Corp., Boyle v., 554
United Truck Leasing Corp. v. Geltman, 1243
University Associates In Obstetrics and Gynecology, Inc., Connors v., 117, 121, 122
University of Chicago Hospitals, Williams v., 336
Unthank v. United States, 849
Upjohn Co., Pittman v., 585, 586
Upper Queens Medical Group, Nieman v., 281
Uranga v. Federated Publications, Inc., 1126
Urbaniak v. Newton, 725
Uribe, Ballard v., 172, 177, 212
USA Hockey, Inc., Mohney v., 613
USAir Inc. v. United States Dept. of Navy, 67
Usitalo, Brannigan v., 695
Utica Mut. Ins. Co., Pierce v., 832

Utica Observer–Dispatch, Chapadeau v., 1039, 1041

Vajda v. Tusla, 694
Valenti v. NET Properties Management, Inc., 28
Valentine v. C.B.S., Inc., 955
Valentine v. On Target, Inc., 184
Val–Blue Corp., United States Underwriters Ins. Co. v., 742, 771
Vance Equipment Co., Tillman v., 553
Vandermark v. Ford Motor Co., 551, 553, 635
Varn, Sami v., 115
Vassallo v. Baxter Healthcare Corp., 597, 600, 602, 614, 627
Vassar Farms, Inc., Bevan v., 449
Vaughan v. Menlove, 53
Vaughn, Roberts v., 484, 487, 488
Veazey v. Elmwood Plantation Associates, Ltd., 370
Veeder v. Kennedy, 900
Veenstra, Stevens v., 57
Vega, Shine v., 128, 338
Ventricelli v. Kinney System Rent A Car, Inc., 411, 412
Ventron Corp., State, Dept. of Environmental Protection v., 506
Vereen v. Clayborne, 962
Vergilia, LeFleur v., 488
Vermont Motor Inns, Inc., LaVallee v., 71
Vermont Mut. Ins. Co. v. Singleton, 871
Vernars v. Young, 1161
Victoria Station, Inc., Shaffer v., 637
Villacci, Snow v., 688
Villarreal v. Harte–Hanks Communications, Inc., 1047
Vince v. Wilson, 179, 370, 762
Vincent v. Lake Erie Transp. Co., 532, 923, 925, 926, 927
Vincent, Williams v., 932
Vinson, Meritor Sav. Bank, FSB v., 895
Virgil v. Sports Illustrated, 1109
Virgil v. Time, Inc., 1109, 1129
Virginia Citizens Consumer Council, Inc., Virginia State Bd. of Pharmacy v., 1256
Virginia Elec. and Power Co. v. Dungee, 695
Virginia Hosp. Ass'n, Wilder v., 933
Virginia, Landmark Communications, Inc. v., 1115
Virginia State Bd. of Pharmacy v. Virginia Citizens Consumer Council, Inc., 1256
Viruet, General Acc., Fire & Life Ins. Co. v., 834
Visco, Carbone v., 833, 837
Vitale v. Henchey, 875
Vogel v. Grant–Lafayette Elec. Co-op., 672
Voilas v. General Motors Corp., 1222
Volkswagen of America, Inc., Trull v., 555
Volkswagenwerk, A. G., Dreisonstok v., 568, 571
Vopper, Bartnicki v., 1185
Vosburg v. Putney, 868, 869, 879, 913
Vulcan Metals Co. v. Simmons Mfg. Co., 1220

Vultaggio v. Yasko, 977

Wabash Ry. Co., Pokora v., 60, 62, 435
Waco, Mireles v., 941
Wadle & Associates, P.C., J.A.H. ex rel. R.M.H. v., 301
Wagenmann v. Adams, 310
Wagner v. International Ry. Co., 428, 429
Wagner v. Mittendorf, 404
Wagner, Lumley v., 1242
Wagner, Ruttger Hotel Corp. v., 266
Waite v. Waite, 214
Waite, Waite v., 214
Waldbaum v. Fairchild Publications, Inc., 1059, 1060
Waldman, Williamson v., 277
Waldorf v. Shuta, 693
Walker v. Sheldon, 1238, 1239
Walker, Associated Press v., 1013, 1014, 1015
Wall, Stone v., 900
Wallace, Chappell v., 946
Walter, Sprague v., 1092
Walton v. Lumbermens Mut. Cas. Co., 832, 833
Wal–Mart Discount Cities, Brown v., 372
Wal–Mart Stores, Inc., Deffenbaugh-Williams v., 895
Wal–Mart Stores, Inc., Hall v., 736
Wal–Mart Stores, Inc., Howard v., 90, 91
Wal–Mart Stores, Inc., Lake v., 1146
Wal–Mart Stores, Inc., Posecai v., 206, 211, 212
Ward v. West Jersey & S.R. Co., 265
Ward v. Zelikovsky, 957, 973, 1076
Warnek v. ABB Combustion Engineering Services, Inc., 1271
Warner Trucking, Inc. v. Carolina Cas. Ins. Co., 21
Warren Gen. Hosp., Biddle v., 1138
Waschak v. Moffat, 670
Waschek v. State, 8
Washington by Washington v. Barnes Hosp., 716
Washington, K–Mart Corp. v., 969
Washington Magazine, Inc., Dameron v., 1059
Washington Metropolitan Area Transit Authority v. Johnson, 438
Washington Water Power Co. v. Graybar Elec. Co., 646
Watchtower Bible and Tract Soc. of New York, Inc., Bryan R. v., 281
Watch Tower Bible & Tract Soc. v. Dougherty, 1259
Waterman Broadcasting Corp., Saro Corp. v., 1061
Waters, W.R. Grace & Company--Conn. v., 737, 738
Waterson v. General Motors Corp., 460
Watsonville Community Hospital, Leonard v., 98, 116
Wayne Steffner Productions, Inc., Woodall v., 488

W.C.A.B., American Smelting & Refining Co. v., 810

WDAY, Inc., Farmers Educational and Co-op. Union of America v., 977

W. de S., I. de S. v., 874

Webb v. Navistar Intern. Transp. Corp., 611

Webster County, Heins v., 197, 202, 204, 266

Weinberg v. Dinger, 759

Weinberg v. Transamerica Ins. Co., 836

Weiner v. Metropolitan Transp. Authority, 232

Weinhold v. Wolff, 671

Weir v. Equifax Services, Inc., 981

Weirum v. RKO General, Inc., 190

Weisbart v. Flohr, 867, 870

Weisman, Herschensohn v., 763

Weiss v. Fote, 247, 248

Weiss v. Goldfarb, 451

Welch, Halberstam v., 869

Weldon, Liberty Nat. Life Ins. Co. v., 744

Welge v. Planters Lifesavers Co., 557

Wellborn v. Sears, Roebuck & Co., 706

Wells v. Liddy, 1049

Wells, Arambula v., 710, 715, 747

Welsh v. Bulger, 115

Wendt v. Host Intern., 1211

Werner v. Southern Cal. Associated Newspapers, 998

Wernke v. Halas, 672

Wesselhoeft, Flanagan v., 116

West v. Caterpillar Tractor Co., Inc., 649

West v. Thomson Newspapers, 957, 1076

West Bend Mut. Ins. Co., Lestina v., 473

West Jersey & S. R. Co., Ward v., 265

Western Air Lines, Inc., Brosnahan v., 67

Western Auto Supply Co., Savage Arms, Inc. v., 553

Western Block Co., Division of Am. Hoist & Derrick Co., Fetterhoff v., 885

Western Newspapers, Inc., Currier v., 1020

Westinghouse Elec. Corp., Bower v., 396, 397

Westinghouse Elec. Corp., Mackowick v., 586

Westlye v. Look Sports, Inc., 613

Westmoreland v. CBS Inc., 1019

Whalen v. Union Bag & Paper Co., 677

Wheeler v. Bagley, 451

Wheeler v. Raybestos–Manhattan, 388

White v. Samsung Electronics America, Inc., 1207, 1211

White v. Ultramar, Inc., 725

White, Forrester v., 941

White Motor Co., Seely v., 644, 646

White, New York Cent. R. Co. v., 806

White, Ronald M. v., 141

White, Russo v., 892

Whitehead v. Toyota Motor Corp., 612

Whiteside v. Lukson, 128

Whithorn, National Bond & Inv. Co. v., 885

Whitney, Carroll v., 372, 374

Whittaker v. Sandford, 885

Wiggs v. City of Phoenix, 372

Wiggs v. Courshon, 893

Wiggs, Nelson v., 1233

Wights v. Staff Jennings, Inc., 535, 638

Wilcox v. Superior Court, 1024

Wilder v. Virginia Hosp. Ass'n, 933

Wildstein v. New York Post Corp., 953

Wiley v. County of San Diego,, 309

Williams v. Bright, 458

Williams v. Cunningham Drug Stores, Inc., 212

Williams v. Delta Intern. Machinery Corp., 440

Williams v. Kearbey, 871

Williams v. State of California, 237

Williams v. University of Chicago Hospitals, 336

Williams v. Vincent, 932

Williams Ford, Inc. v. Hartford Courant Co., 1234

William T. Cannon, Esquire, P.C., McPeake v., 310

Williamson v. Plant Insulation Co., 706

Williamson v. Waldman, 277

Willmar Henderson Mfg. Co., a Div. of Waycrosse, Inc., Cremeans v., 627, 628

Wilson v. Circus Circus Hotels, Inc., 348

Wilson v. E. & J. Trucking Corp., 837

Wilson v. Interlake Steel Co., 658

Wilson v. Layne, 934, 940, 945

Wilson, Barter v., 955

Wilson Pub. Co., Martin v., 1090

Wilson, Vince v., 179, 370, 762

Wilt v. Buracker, 705

Wil–Rich, Lovick v., 603

Winchell's Donut House, Lopez v., 882, 885, 888

Windsor, Amchem Products, Inc. v., 395

Winfrey, Texas Beef Group v., 1259

Winkler, American Safety Equipment Corp. v., 604

Winnebago County Dept. of Social Services, DeShaney v., 260, 932

Winterbottom v. Wright, 502

Wisdom, Harrison v., 927

Wiseman v. Massachusetts, 1131

Wishnatsky v. Huey, 876, 879, 913

Wiwa v. Royal Dutch Petroleum Co., 879

Wodarz, Bashi v., 54, 55

Wofsey, Rosen, Kweskin and Kuriansky, Grayson v., 309

Wolf v. Kaufmann, 358

Wolf v. Regardie, 1113

Wolfeboro Nat. Bank, Mertens v., 1217

Wolff, Weinhold v., 671

Wolfgang v. Mid–America Motorsports, Inc., 456

Wolston v. Reader's Digest Ass'n, Inc., 1048, 1049, 1059

Womack v. Eldridge, 889, 893

Wong v. Hawaiian Scenic Tours, Ltd., 447

Wood v. Groh, 50, 184

Wood v. Picillo, 670

Wood v. United Air Lines, Inc., 518

Wood, Troman v., 1041

Woodall v. Wayne Steffner Productions, Inc., 488

Wooden v. Raveling, 266, 268

Woods v. Lancet, 17

Woolley, Henderson v., 214
Wooster v. Soriano, 831
Workers' Comp. Appeals Bd., Ezzy v., 809
Workers' Comp. Appeals Bd., Price v., 809
Workers' Comp. Appeals Bd., Santa Rosa Junior College v., 809
Working, Eggert v., 449
W.R. Grace & Company--Conn. v. Waters, 737, 738
Wright v. City of Knoxville, 444
Wright v. City of Roanoke Redevelopment and Housing Authority, 933
Wright v. Grove Sun Newspaper Co., Inc., 993
Wright v. Johns Hopkins Health Systems Corp., 340
Wright, Winterbottom v., 502
Wyeth Laboratories Inc., Perez v., 596
Wyeth Laboratories, Reyes v., 849
Wynne v. Orcutt Union Sch. Dist., 1137
Wynns, Fisel v., 502

Xuncax v. Gramajo, 880

Yan Yee Lau, Millan v., 837
Yaselli v. Goff, 244
Yasko, Vultaggio v., 977
Ybarra v. Spangard, 93 Cal.App.2d 43, 208 P.2d 445 (Cal.App. 2 Dist.1949), 107
Ybarra v. Spangard, 25 Cal.2d 486, 154 P.2d 687 (Cal.1944), **101,** 107, 108, 109, 376
Y.B.H. Realty Corp., Eaves Brooks Costume Co., Inc. v., 760
Yeager v. Local Union 20, Teamsters, Chauffeurs, Warehousemen, & Helpers of America, 888
Yellow Cab Co., Li v., 440

Young, Vernars v., 1161
Youssoupoff v. Metro-Goldwyn-Mayer Pictures, Ltd., 961
Yuba County, Morgan v., 137, 177
Yuba Power Products, Inc., Greenman v., 551, 558, 638
Yukon Equipment, Inc. v. Fireman's Fund Ins. Co., 517
Yunker, Madison v., 998

Zacchini v. Scripps–Howard Broadcasting Co., 54 Ohio St.2d 286, 376 N.E.2d 582, 8 O.O.3d 265 (Ohio 1978), 1193
Zacchini v. Scripps–Howard Broadcasting Co., 433 U.S. 562, 97 S.Ct. 2849, 53 L.Ed.2d 965, 5 O.O.3d 215 (1977), 1145, **1187,** 1193, 1194, 1207
Zafir, Bardere v., 813
Zavala v. Regents of University of California, 445
Zelikovsky, Ward v., 957, 973, 1076
Zeran v. America Online, Inc., 966
Zerangue v. TSP Newspapers, Inc., 1047
Zezulka, Hickey v., 446
Z Frank Oldsmobile, Inc., Perez v., 1239
Zikely v. Zikely, 221
Zikely, Zikely v., 221
Zimmermann, Kennedy v., 977
Zivich v. Mentor Soccer Club, Inc., 467
Zogarts, Hauter v., 604
Zuchowicz v. United States, 349, 356, 359, 411
Zuern By and Through Zuern v. Ford Motor Co., 612
Zumwalt v. United States, 257
Zygmaniak v. Kawasaki Motors Corp. U.S.A., 403

*

CASES AND MATERIALS

TORT LAW AND ALTERNATIVES

*

CHAPTER I

INTRODUCTION TO TORT LIABILITY

A. PROLOGUE

This book is concerned with the array of injuries that are by-products of a complex society, and with how the legal system responds to the diverse problems raised by such injuries. We will consider a broad range of situations including automobile collisions, airplane crashes, medical mishaps, consumer product injuries, industrial accidents, toxic exposures, fist fights, false accusations of misconduct, invasions of privacy, and false statements to competitors' prospective customers. In each situation, someone claims that another has caused harm and looks to the law for relief. We will not consider how the criminal law might react, but deal only with civil redress. Among civil harms our focus will be on those that do not arise out of disputes over contractual interpretation. The primary concern of tort law has been whether one whose actions harm another should be required to pay compensation for the harm done.

For several centuries tort law was the one outlet through which the legal system did provide such redress. Other sources of compensation have grown dramatically; indeed, a study by the Institute for Civil Justice found that tort liability payments comprised only 7 percent of the total compensation for economic loss in nonfatal accidents in the United States—11 percent when tort payments for intangible loss were added in. (The figures rose to 22 percent and 33 percent, respectively, in the category of motor vehicle accident victims.) See D. Hensler, et al., Compensation for Accidental Injuries in the United States, pp. 107–08 (1991). Nonetheless, as another study of the tort system underscored, the role of tort as a compensation scheme remains pivotal:

> . . . the situation in this country leaves many Americans at risk of suffering sizable uninsured medical expenses and income loss as a result of illness or injury. Perhaps one-fourth of the non-elderly population has no medical insurance and must depend on savings or charity if they need expensive care. A significant percentage of workers have little or no protection against short-term, non-employment-related disability. Again, only savings, charity, or, for some, a state welfare payment will be available if they are unable to work for a period up to six months. For long-term disability Social Security offers protection, but only if the inability to work meets a stringent standard of *totality,* and only for a portion of the disabled person's lost wages. The majority of workers have no insurance for long-term disability except for the

1

partial coverage supplied through the Social Security system or, if the disability is employment-related, the workers' compensation system.

Currently the tort system partially fills some of these gaps by compensating many persons who would not otherwise receive reimbursement for the medical expenses and wage losses occasioned by an illness or injury. Without tort damages many of these accident victims would be uncompensated or undercompensated for their out-of-pocket losses.

Report to the American Law Institute, Enterprise Responsibility for Personal Injury, Vol. II, pp. 555–56 (1991).

We will first consider physical harm to one's person—commonly called the "personal injury"—because it raises serious legal, economic, social and political issues. Although we will discuss intentional harm, we will stress unintentional physical harm, which is far more common and presents great analytical and philosophical dilemmas. During that exploration we will also consider the emotional distress and economic harm that frequently accompany fatal injury, broken bones and destroyed property. The last part of the book will introduce other interests in personality and economic security that the law seeks to protect, such as reputation, privacy and commercial fair dealing.

B.   WHEN SHOULD UNINTENDED INJURY RESULT IN LIABILITY?

The fundamental issue addressed by a system of tort liability for unintended injury is when losses should be shifted from an injury victim to an injurer or some other source of compensation. Of course, no tort system would be required in the first place if losses were simply allowed to remain where they fall. (Is it clear that such a "no-liability" system would be objectionable?) On the other hand, a system of social insurance could be established that provided full compensation in every instance of harm to the individual. Again, choosing this option would obviate the need for judicial fashioning and administration of a body of tort principles.

Because considerations of injury prevention and fairness have been thought to dictate rejection of the no-liability option, and limited resources (and perhaps injury prevention and fairness, as well?) have been thought to preclude the social insurance approach, the courts have developed a complex network of liability rules for determining the allocation of losses in cases of unintended harm. These rules, located in an intermediate zone between no-liability and universal compensation, reflect not only the influence of those polar positions, but perhaps even more importantly, a tension between two court-fashioned liability principles—strict liability and negligence—that will be a pervasive concern of ours in this course. The following case provides an opportunity for a first look at the issue. We will also use it to introduce the basic procedural aspects of tort litigation.

Hammontree v. Jenner*

Court of Appeal of California, 1971.
20 Cal.App.3d 528, 97 Cal.Rptr. 739.

LILLIE, J. Plaintiffs Maxine Hammontree and her husband sued defendant for personal injuries and property damage arising out of an automobile accident. The cause was tried to a jury. Plaintiffs appeal from judgment entered on a jury verdict returned against them and in favor of defendant.

The evidence shows that on the afternoon of April 25, 1967, defendant was driving his 1959 Chevrolet home from work; at the same time plaintiff Maxine Hammontree was working in a bicycle shop owned and operated by her and her husband; without warning defendant's car crashed through the wall of the shop, struck Maxine and caused personal injuries and damage to the shop.

Defendant claimed he became unconscious during an epileptic seizure losing control of his car. He did not recall the accident but his last recollection before it, was leaving a stop light after his last stop, and his first recollection after the accident was being taken out of his car in plaintiffs' shop. Defendant testified he has a medical history of epilepsy and knows of no other reason for his loss of consciousness except an epileptic seizure; prior to 1952 he had been examined by several neurologists whose conclusion was that the condition could be controlled and who placed him on medication; in 1952 he suffered a seizure while fishing; several days later he went to Dr. Benson Hyatt who diagnosed his condition as petit mal seizure and kept him on the same medication; thereafter he saw Dr. Hyatt every six months and then on a yearly basis several years prior to 1967; in 1953 he had another seizure, was told he was an epileptic and continued his medication; in 1954 Dr. Kershner prescribed dilantin and in 1955 Dr. Hyatt prescribed phelantin; from 1955 until the accident occurred (1967) defendant had used phelantin on a regular basis which controlled his condition; defendant has continued to take medication as prescribed by his physician and has done everything his doctors told him to do to avoid a seizure; he had no inkling or warning that he was about to have a seizure prior to the occurrence of the accident.

In 1955 or 1956 the Department of Motor Vehicles was advised that defendant was an epileptic and placed him on probation under which every six months he had to report to the doctor who was required to advise it in writing of defendant's condition. In 1960 his probation was changed to a once-a-year report.

Dr. Hyatt testified that during the times he saw defendant, and according to his history, defendant "was doing normally" and that he continued to take phelantin; that "[t]he purpose of the [phelantin] would be to react on the nervous system in such a way that where, without the medication, I would say to raise the threshold so that he would not be as

---

* Text omissions are indicated by three dots. Omitted citations are indicated by [ ]. There is no indication when footnotes are omitted. When they do appear, footnotes are numbered as in the material quoted.—Eds.

subject to these episodes without the medication, so as not to have the seizures. He would not be having the seizures with the medication as he would without the medication compared to taking medication''; in a seizure it would be impossible for a person to drive and control an automobile; he believed it was safe for defendant to drive.

Appellants' contentions that the trial court erred in refusing to grant their motion for summary judgment on the issue of liability and their motion for directed verdict on the pleadings and counsel's opening argument are answered by the disposition of their third claim that the trial court committed prejudicial error in refusing to give their jury instruction on absolute liability.[1]

Under the present state of the law found in appellate authorities beginning with Waters v. Pacific Coast Dairy, Inc., [131 P.2d 588 (Cal.App. 1942)] (driver rendered unconscious from sharp pain in left arm and shoulder) through Ford v. Carew & English, [200 P.2d 828 (Cal.App.1948)] (fainting spells from strained heart muscles), Zabunoff v. Walker, [13 Cal.Rptr. 463 (App. 1961)] (sudden sneeze), and Tannyhill v. Pacific Motor Trans. Co., [38 Cal.Rptr. 774 (App. 1964)] (heart attack), the trial judge properly refused the instruction. The foregoing cases generally hold that liability of a driver, suddenly stricken by an illness rendering him unconscious, for injury resulting from an accident occurring during that time rests on principles of negligence. However, herein during the trial plaintiffs withdrew their claim of negligence and, after both parties rested and before jury argument, objected to the giving of any instructions on negligence electing to stand solely on the theory of absolute liability. The objection was overruled and the court refused plaintiffs' requested instruction after which plaintiffs waived both opening and closing jury arguments. Defendant argued the cause to the jury after which the judge read a series of negligence instructions and, on his own motion, BAJI 4.02 (res ipsa loquitur).

Appellants seek to have this court override the established law of this state which is dispositive of the issue before us as outmoded in today's social and economic structure, particularly in the light of the now recognized principles imposing liability upon the manufacturer, retailer and all distributive and vending elements and activities which bring a product to the consumer to his injury, on the basis of strict liability in tort expressed first in Justice Traynor's concurring opinion in Escola v. Coca Cola Bottling Co., [150 P.2d 436 (Cal.1944)]; and then in Greenman v. Yuba Power Products, Inc., [377 P.2d 897 (Cal.1963)]; Vandermark v. Ford Motor Co., [391 P.2d 168 (Cal.1964)]; and Elmore v. American Motors Corp., [451 P.2d

---

1. "When the evidence shows that a driver of a motor vehicle on a public street or highway loses his ability to safely operate and control such vehicle because of some seizure or health failure, that driver is nevertheless legally liable for all injuries and property damage which an innocent person may suffer as a proximate result of the defendant's inability to so control or operate his motor vehicle.

"This is true even if you find the defendant driver had no warning of any such impending seizure or health failure." [This is the instruction plaintiffs requested.—Eds.]

84 (Cal.1969)]. These authorities hold that "A manufacturer [or retailer] is strictly liable in tort when an article he places on the market, knowing that it is to be used without inspection for defects, proves to have a defect that causes injury to a human being." [*Greenman* and *Vandermark*]. Drawing a parallel with these products liability cases, appellants argue, with some degree of logic, that only the driver affected by a physical condition which could suddenly render him unconscious and who is aware of that condition can anticipate the hazards and foresee the dangers involved in his operation of a motor vehicle, and that the liability of those who by reason of seizure or heart failure or some other physical condition lose the ability to safely operate and control a motor vehicle resulting in injury to an innocent person should be predicated on strict liability.

We decline to superimpose the absolute liability of products liability cases upon drivers under the circumstances here. The theory on which those cases are predicated is that manufacturers, retailers and distributors of products are engaged in the business of distributing goods to the public and are an integral part of the over-all producing and marketing enterprise that should bear the cost of injuries from defective parts. [*Vandermark* and *Greenman*]. This policy hardly applies here and it is not enough to simply say, as do appellants, that the insurance carriers should be the ones to bear the cost of injuries to innocent victims on a strict liability basis. In Maloney v. Rath, [445 P.2d 513 (Cal.1968)], followed by Clark v. Dziabas, [445 P.2d 517 (Cal.1968)], appellant urged that defendant's violation of a safety provision (defective brakes) of the Vehicle Code makes the violator strictly liable for damages caused by the violation. While reversing the judgment for defendant upon another ground, the California Supreme Court refused to apply the doctrine of strict liability to automobile drivers. The situation involved two users of the highway but the problems of fixing responsibility under a system of strict liability are as complicated in the instant case as those in [*Maloney v. Rath*], and could only create uncertainty in the area of its concern. As stated in *Maloney*: "To invoke a rule of strict liability on users of the streets and highways, however, without also establishing in substantial detail how the new rule should operate would only contribute confusion to the automobile accident problem. Settlement and claims adjustment procedures would become chaotic until the new rules were worked out on a case-by-case basis, and the hardships of delayed compensation would be seriously intensified. Only the Legislature, if it deems it wise to do so, can avoid such difficulties by enacting a comprehensive plan for the compensation of automobile accident victims in place of or in addition to the law of negligence."

The instruction tendered by appellants was properly refused for still another reason. Even assuming the merit of appellants' position under the facts of this case in which defendant knew he had a history of epilepsy, previously had suffered seizures and at the time of the accident was attempting to control the condition by medication, the instruction does not except from its ambit the driver who suddenly is stricken by an illness or physical condition which he had no reason whatever to anticipate and of which he had no prior knowledge.

The judgment is affirmed.

WOOD, P.J., and THOMPSON, J., concurred.

Appellants' petition for a hearing by the Supreme Court of California was denied December 16, 1971.

Notes and Questions

1. In *Hammontree,* there is no indication that plaintiff was in any way to blame for her injuries. Defendant's loss of control of his automobile appears to have been the precipitating event that caused the harm to her. Why should it make any difference whether he had reason to believe that he might suffer a seizure? Why shouldn't it suffice that he caused the harm? Consider the following criticism of strict liability from O. W. Holmes, The Common Law, pp. 94–96 (1881):

> The general principle of our law is that loss from accident must lie where it falls, and this principle is not affected by the fact that a human being is the instrument of misfortune. . . . If this were not so, any act would be sufficient, however remote, which set in motion or opened the door for a series of physical sequences ending in damage; such as riding the horse, in the case of the runaway, or even coming to a place where one is seized with a fit and strikes the plaintiff in an unconscious spasm. Nay, why need the defendant have acted at all, and why is it not enough that his existence has been at the expense of the plaintiff? The requirement of an act is the requirement that the defendant should have made a choice. But the only possible purpose of introducing this moral element is to make the power of avoiding the evil complained of a condition of liability. There is no such power where the evil cannot be foreseen. . . .

> A man need not, it is true, do this or that act,—the term *act* implies a choice,—but he must act somehow. Furthermore, the public generally profits by individual activity. As action cannot be avoided, and tends to the public good, there is obviously no policy in throwing the hazard of what is at once desirable and inevitable upon the actor.

> The state might conceivably make itself a mutual insurance company against accidents, and distribute the burden of its citizens' mishaps among all its members. There might be a pension for paralytics, and state aid for those who suffered in person or estate from tempest or wild beasts. As between individuals it might adopt the mutual insurance principle *pro tanto,* and divide damages when both were in fault, as in the *rusticum judicium* of the admiralty, or it might throw all loss upon the actor irrespective of fault. The state does none of these things, however, and the prevailing view is that its cumbrous and expensive machinery ought not to be set in motion unless some clear benefit is to be derived from disturbing the *status quo.* State interference is an evil, where it cannot be shown to be a good. Universal insurance, if desired, can be better and more cheaply accom-

plished by private enterprise. The undertaking to redistribute losses simply on the ground that they resulted from the defendant's act would not only be open to these objections, but, as it is hoped the preceding discussion has shown, to the still graver one of offending the sense of justice. Unless my act is of a nature to threaten others, unless under the circumstances a prudent man would have foreseen the possibility of harm, it is no more justifiable to make me indemnify my neighbor against the consequences, than to make me do the same thing if I had fallen upon him in a fit, or to compel me to insure him against lightning.

Is Holmes persuasive?

2. Suppose that defendant made his living as a driver and argued that the social benefits derived from his engaging in the activity outweighed the very small likelihood of injury. Would that be a reason to reject strict liability in favor of holding defendant liable only for negligent acts? Consider the following economic perspective on the issue in Posner, A Theory of Negligence, 1 J.Legal Stud. 29, 33 (1972):

> Perhaps, then, the dominant function of the fault system is to generate rules of liability that if followed will bring about, at least approximately, the efficient—the cost-justified—level of accidents and safety. Under this view, damages are assessed against the defendant as a way of measuring the costs of accidents, and the damages so assessed are paid over to the plaintiff (to be divided with his lawyer) as the price of enlisting their participation in the operation of the system. Because we do not like to see resources squandered, a judgment of negligence has inescapable overtones of moral disapproval, for it implies that there was a cheaper alternative to the accident. Conversely, there is no moral indignation in the case in which the cost of prevention would have exceeded the cost of the accident. Where the measures necessary to avert the accident would have consumed excessive resources, there is no occasion to condemn the defendant for not having taken them.

3. The grounds for rejecting strict liability in favor of negligence referred to in the two preceding notes, as well as the counter-arguments, will be explored in much greater detail throughout this book. Why does the court refuse to adopt a strict liability approach in *Hammontree?*

4. Is there a distinctive argument for strict liability here because plaintiff was on her own property when the accident occurred? Commentators seem to agree that in most cases a trespass is not established where the harm is unintended and non-negligently caused. See Restatement (Second) of Torts § 166. Nevertheless, as we shall see, a party's status as land occupier has strongly influenced the character of tort liability rules.

5. Recall that the court did give an instruction on "res ipsa loquitur" that would have permitted the jury to return a verdict for the plaintiff. We return to this subject in Chapter II.

6. As the court indicates, strict liability in tort is now recognized for some aspects of defective product injuries. We will examine the products liability area in great detail in Chapter VIII. For now, however, consider briefly the analogy to auto accidents. On initial consideration, do you find the court's distinction between liability of an enterprise for its product-related injuries and liability of drivers for auto accidents convincing? Would you be more disposed to hold defendant strictly liable if he had been a taxi driver engaged in his business?

7. Why is it "not enough to simply say . . . that the insurance carriers should be the ones to bear the cost of injuries to innocent victims on a strict liability basis"? The influence of insurance on tort liability will be another recurrent theme in this course. The institutional aspects of insurance are covered in Chapter X.

8. Consider the prospect of establishing strict liability against defendant on the basis of a statutory violation of the Vehicle Code. In the cited case of *Maloney v. Rath*, the court refused to hold defendant strictly liable for her non-negligent violation of the traffic law (brake failure due to her garage mechanic's negligence), stating that:

> In few cases, however, are the facts likely to be as simple as they are here. In the next case an accident might be caused by the combination of a brake failure and a stoplight failure under circumstances that would have permitted effective use of an emergency handbrake had the following motorist been properly alerted by the stoplight required by the Vehicle Code. (Veh.Code § 24603.) In another case, a pedestrian might stumble and fall on a dangerous and defective pavement causing a motorist having the right of way to drive across the center line of the highway and strike a speeding oncoming car. Who is to be strictly liable to whom in such cases? However imperfectly it operates, the law of negligence allocates the risks and determines who shall or shall not be compensated when persons simultaneously engaged in the common enterprise of using the streets and highways have accidents.

Would the determination of who was to be held strictly liable in such cases be markedly more difficult than deciding who would be liable for negligence?

Assume that, irrespective of negligence, the defendant in *Maloney* would be *criminally* liable for violation of Vehicle Code § 24603 (note that defendant in *Hammontree* had complied with a reporting requirement to the Department of Motor Vehicles). Should that affect liability in tort? Again, this issue will be explored in greater depth in Chapter II, as will the potential legislative solutions to the accident problem referred to toward the end of the *Hammontree* opinion, see Chapter XI.

9. As to the possibility of suing the DMV, consider Waschek v. State, 69 Cal.Rptr.2d 296 (App.1997). An experienced DMV driving inspector gave a 96-year-old driver a driving test, on which he scored 94 out of 100. The inspector concluded that the driver was able to operate a car safely on the highway and authorized reissue of the driver's license. Twenty months later, the driver struck a pedestrian—who sued the DMV for issuing the license. Under statute, the DMV would be liable only if it negligently performed a "mandatory duty." The court decided that this would have occurred only if the DMV had concluded that the driver was unqualified but had nonetheless issued the license. That did not occur here, and the DMV was immune for its discretionary decision to issue the license. The subject of government liability is considered at length in Chapter III.

10. The court uses the terms "strict liability" and "absolute liability" interchangeably in the course of its opinion. Treating the two terms as synonymous is likely to cause confusion. As we will see, the various forms of strict liability that have been recognized are virtually never "absolute." Consider a single example. In no case of product-related injuries, is liability "absolute" in the sense that plaintiff need only establish that defendant's product "caused" the injury. Typically, plaintiff must also establish a defect in the product, and under certain conditions, plaintiff's own conduct will bar recovery. We will explore a number of other limitations on the "absolute" character of strict liability. For present purposes, we simply note that you should keep strict liability distinct from absolute liability.

C.   THE LITIGATION PROCESS

1.   *Procedure.* In personal injury cases, as in litigation generally, the aggrieved party must initiate the claim and pursue it until she gains redress or has exhausted her legal remedies. Why should she bear this burden? What are the alternatives? In this case, Maxine Hammontree and her husband's first step would be to consult and then retain an attorney, whose first step would be to try to obtain a settlement from those charged with causing her harm. If that fails, the claimant becomes a plaintiff before the courts by filing a complaint stating what occurred and the relief sought. The "complaint" will allege "facts" that plaintiff contends justify granting relief. The legal theory under which the plaintiff is proceeding will usually be apparent from the nature of the facts that the plaintiff contends to be material to her case.

The person sued, the defendant, will retain an attorney who will consider several options available at this early stage of the proceedings. If the plaintiff has sued the defendant on what the attorney believes to be a novel—and unsound—legal theory, the defendant may make a motion to dismiss the complaint—also called a demurrer—on the ground that even if the allegations of fact in the complaint are true, there is no sound legal theory upon which plaintiff is entitled to relief. The defendant will support this motion with legal arguments. When the plaintiff's attorney responds by arguing that the legal theory is sound, the issue will be posed for the judge. For example, assume a complaint that alleged that the defendant failed to invite the plaintiff to a social event, knowing that such a snub would hurt the plaintiff, and that plaintiff suffered emotional distress. The defendant might move to dismiss that complaint on the ground that even if all the facts are true, there is no valid legal reason for the defendant to pay for the plaintiff's distress. This raises a legal question for the judge to decide under the relevant law.

If the judge decides for the defendant, the plaintiff's case will be dismissed and the litigation will be at an end unless the plaintiff decides to appeal. (Sometimes the judge will grant the plaintiff permission to amend the allegations to add essential facts to invoke a sound theory where one was lacking before. A defendant who still believes the complaint to be inadequate will make another motion and the case will proceed as before.)

If the judge denies the defendant's motion to dismiss the complaint, the judge will be saying in effect that the plaintiff's complaint states a good legal theory and the plaintiff will be entitled to recover damages from the defendant if the plaintiff can prove that the essential facts alleged in the complaint are true. At this stage procedures diverge. In some states a defendant may appeal the judge's ruling immediately; in other states the defendant must usually wait until the trial is completed before appealing from unfavorable rulings. Under the latter view the defendant must now contest the plaintiff's allegations of fact or admit them and be held legally liable.

The defendant may meet the plaintiff's fact allegations by a pleading called an "answer" in which the defendant denies some or all of the plaintiff's allegations of fact and perhaps adds some new ones of his own that will destroy the plaintiff's case. Although we traditionally resolve fact disputes at a trial, that process is used only for genuine disputes of fact. Some apparent disputes can be decided without a trial because one of the parties has conclusive evidence that it is telling the truth. Thus, for example, if a merchant sues a customer for not paying a bill and the customer asserts payment we have an apparent dispute of fact. If, in addition, the customer can present a cancelled check and the merchant does not claim that the check was forged or is in some other way irrelevant to this transaction, we will not need a trial because the dispute is so one-sided that reasonable jurors could resolve it only in favor of the customer. There is no need to hold a trial because the conclusion is foreordained. The customer would make a motion for "summary judgment" and attach a sworn statement and copies of the check and bill of sale. If the plaintiff does not respond with evidence that restores a genuine fact dispute, the judge will grant buyer's motion for summary judgment and enter an order dismissing the case—not on the ground that the plaintiff's legal theory was inadequate but rather on the ground that the plaintiff's facts cannot possibly be proven to be true and that a trial would be unnecessary.

It is no coincidence that the foregoing example involved contracts, in which documentary evidence is usually available. In tort cases, on the other hand, the situation is usually quite different because many of the episodes that concern us happen suddenly and rarely lend themselves to documentation. We are more likely to encounter disputes between eyewitnesses as to whether the defendant went through the intersection on a green light or on a red light, or whether a particular product was being used properly at the time plaintiff was hurt. We will often be at the mercy of recollection without being able to reconstruct or to document the actual event. The question of which witnesses are telling the truth is classically reserved for trial and for the decision of the trier of fact, usually a jury of six to twelve persons chosen from the community. Occasionally, we shall see cases in which the facts are determined by the trial judge who, in addition to deciding legal questions, doubles as fact finder as well.

At the trial the plaintiff has the burden of proving the essential facts of her case. That is to say, she must persuade the jury that her version of the facts is "more likely than not" what occurred. In other states, she must persuade the jury of her version by a "preponderance of the evidence." However formulated, plaintiff's burden in a civil case is less onerous than the requirement in criminal trials that the state must prove its case "beyond a reasonable doubt." Why? The jury will also be told that if after all of their deliberations they are in equipoise—they cannot decide which side presented the stronger case—they are to return a verdict against the party who had the burden of persuading them, generally the plaintiff.

Sometimes, however, the trial may not reach the jury stage. If, after plaintiff has presented her evidence, the defendant believes that an essential fact has not been proven, the defendant may make a motion for a "directed verdict," sometimes called "judgment as a matter of law." This, in effect, asks the judge to rule that the plaintiff's evidence is so lacking on at least one essential fact that no jury could reasonably find in the plaintiff's favor and thus it is pointless to continue the trial. The plaintiff will argue against the motion by trying to show that she has presented enough evidence on each essential point so that a jury could find that her version is more likely than not to have occurred. The judge again will be called upon to rule. A judge who rules in favor of the defendant will dismiss the case and the litigation will be over unless the plaintiff appeals successfully. A judge who denies the motion is essentially saying that the plaintiff has presented sufficient facts from which a jury could reasonably find in the plaintiff's favor at this stage of the case—and the trial will continue.

If the defendant should rest without presenting any evidence, the case then proceeds to the closing arguments. Each attorney will summarize the case and will try to persuade the jury to accept a favorable version of the facts. The jury will then be "charged" by the judge. The charge will tell the jurors about burdens of proof and the legal rules they should apply to the facts they find. After deliberation, the jury reports its "verdict" to the judge.

A defendant who does present evidence will proceed much as did the plaintiff—by calling witnesses and introducing documents to bolster the defendant's contentions about what happened in the case. At the end of the defendant's evidence, defendant may again move for a directed verdict on the ground that his presentation has been such a powerful refutation of the plaintiff's claims that no jury could reasonably decide for the plaintiff.* Again, the judge will grant or deny the motion. Or, the judge may "reserve

---

* After all evidence is in, the plaintiff may also move for a directed verdict if the evidence will permit only that outcome. Similarly, plaintiffs may move for summary judg- ment on the question of the defendant's liability if no triable question of fact appears to remain in the case.

decision''—delay deciding it until learning how the jury has reacted to the case. If the jury decides the same way the judge would have, the result is clear. If the jury decides for the plaintiff, but the judge thinks the defendant should have received a directed verdict, the judge may now dismiss the case. The advantage of waiting for the jury is that if an appellate court thinks the jury verdict should stand, it can reverse the trial judge's decision and reinstate the jury's verdict. If the judge had granted the directed verdict without waiting for the jury's verdict, and the appellate court disagreed, the only recourse would be to order a complete new trial.

After a verdict for the plaintiff, an unresigned defendant has several choices. He may move for judgment notwithstanding the verdict (judgment n.o.v.—non obstante veredicto) on essentially those grounds involved in seeking a directed verdict: that the jury has reached a verdict that no jury could reasonably have reached on the evidence in this case. (Rule 50 of the Federal Rules of Civil Procedure has dissolved the difference between a directed verdict and a judgment n.o.v., and now uses the term "judgment as a matter of law" for both of these.)

In some cases, the plaintiff's case is so lacking that no jury could reasonably find in plaintiff's favor; in other cases the plaintiff has presented evidence that would justify a jury believing her side but the defendant has presented an overwhelming amount of conflicting evidence. In the first situation, the judge will properly grant a directed verdict (or judgment n.o.v.) since there is nothing to support the plaintiff's case. In the second situation, however, some evidence supports the plaintiff's contention. This might arise, for example, when the issue is whether the defendant drove through a red light. The plaintiff and an admittedly intoxicated bystander swear that the light was red but ten sober disinterested bystanders swear that it was green. If the jury believes the plaintiff and her witness it could reasonably find that the light was red. This would mean that the judge could not properly grant a directed verdict for the defendant because there is evidence that a jury could reasonably believe to support the plaintiff's case. On the other hand, what about the ten disinterested bystanders who swear that the light was green? If the jury finds that the light was green that verdict would also be supported by the evidence.

Although we have said the judge could not grant a directed verdict when there is a conflict between sets of witnesses, the judge may have an abiding sense that the party who prevailed before the jury did not have the preponderant case, and that the jury may have been swayed by some other factor such as the severity of the plaintiff's injury. This may lead the judge to order a new trial to see whether a second jury will respond to this evidence as did the first jury.

A good example of this situation occurred in Markus v. City of New York, 344 N.Y.S.2d 761 (App.Div.1973), in which the critical question was whether a curve in the road was marked with a warning sign. Plaintiff testified that there were no signs warning of the curve. "On the other hand, several patrolmen and two employees of the Department of Parks testified that there were such signs. The alleged failure on the part of the

City to give adequate warnings is a question for the triers of the fact." The jury found for the plaintiff. The quoted passage indicates that it would have been error for the trial judge to have granted a directed verdict against the plaintiff. Here, however, the appellate court concluded that the verdict was "against the weight of the credible evidence" and directed a new trial. If the second jury reaches the same result as the first, the judges may conclude that the jurors are correct in accepting the plaintiff's view of the facts rather than those of the several defense witnesses. (Note that here the trial judge, playing the role of "thirteenth juror," thought the dispute one for the jury. The appellate court, though not seeing the witnesses, thought that plaintiff's testimony alone was overwhelmed by the contrary testimony and wanted to have the reactions of another jury.)

On occasion the jury can persuade the court. In one case a jury awarded $25,000 for the pain and suffering of a 70-year-old man for 29 days before he died. The appellate court ordered a new trial unless plaintiff agreed to a reduced award of $5,000. Plaintiff refused and the case was tried a second time. The second jury awarded $20,000 for the same item and the trial judge refused to reduce it. This time, the appellate court upheld the award even though it had previously said that $5,000 was appropriate. "In doing so, we are influenced by the fact that a second jury has indicated its belief that such an amount is not excessive." Tucker v. City of New York, 388 N.Y.S.2d 133 (App.Div.1976).

Both of these motions are used largely by the defense, but they are also available to the plaintiff if the jury returns a verdict for the defendant. The plaintiff's most likely recourse, however, is to try to obtain a new trial by asserting that the trial judge committed errors in the admission or exclusion of evidence or the charge to the jury, and that these errors were "prejudicial."

After reaching a conclusive disposition of the case, the judge will enter judgment in favor of the successful party. As we have seen, this may occur at any of several stages. It may be at the outset, if the judge grants defendant's motion to dismiss the plaintiff's complaint on the ground that it asks for relief in a situation in which the law does not provide relief. It may happen on a directed verdict at the end of the plaintiff's case or following all the evidence. It may happen after the verdict, when the trial judge accepts what the jury has done, rejects the defense motions, and enters a judgment for the plaintiff for the amount awarded by the jury.

These motions all occur at the trial court level, but virtually all the cases in this book are appellate cases, and we now turn to the issues presented by an appeal. In general, "the trial judge tries the case and the appellate court tries the trial judge." The party against whom judgment has been entered will seek to persuade the appellate court that the trial judge committed prejudicial error in making rulings in the case. Note that the plaintiffs in *Hammontree* did not challenge the sufficiency of the evidence on appeal; they conceded that there was enough evidence from which the jury could reasonably have accepted defendant's version, and did not contend that the trial judge should have found the defendant's evidence absolutely or relatively insufficient.

They did, however, claim that the judge committed a specific legal error in failing to charge that the jury could find defendant liable irrespective of negligence on his part. This is a question of law, and the appellate court will decide whether the ruling was erroneous and, if so, whether the error was prejudicial to appellants' case.

2. *Hammontree reconsidered.* In view of this brief look at the procedural aspects of tort litigation, consider the following questions about *Hammontree:*

a. How do you think the jury instruction on liability tendered by the judge differed from the plaintiffs' rejected instruction? A version of the negligence charge frequently used by California judges may be found at p. 41, infra.

b. According to the court, plaintiffs withdrew their claim of negligence during the trial, and apparently sought to proceed exclusively on a strict liability theory. Why might plaintiffs have adopted this strategy?

c. If plaintiffs' theory of the case had been adopted, would they have been entitled to summary judgment on liability, as they requested? Summary judgments and directed verdicts in favor of plaintiffs are rare as compared to successful motions by defendants on these grounds. Why do you think this is the case?

d. In view of the trial court's rejection of plaintiffs' theory, might defendant have been entitled to a directed verdict? At what stage in the trial might defendant have tendered the motion? Might summary judgment in his favor have been warranted?

3. *Damages.* Once a plaintiff has brought herself within the rules allowing recovery for personal injury, the traditional goal of tort law has been to restore her to the equivalent of her condition prior to the harm. Most plaintiffs seek money damages, though other remedies exist: sometimes a plaintiff would prefer an injunction to prevent conduct that threatens harm, and in a defamation case the plaintiff may prefer a retraction. In personal injury cases, money damages are viewed as the best solution. Can you think of anything better?

The categories of personal injury damages available to a plaintiff are meant to compensate for both tangible and intangible loss. Tangible losses may already have been incurred or be predictable. The former includes such easily proven items as doctors' bills, hospital bills, and other actual medical expenses. Loss of income is proven almost as easily, especially if the plaintiff is salaried. The projection of such loss, especially for self-employed victims, is speculative, but may be facilitated by effective use of expert testimony. Experts also assist in the projection of medical costs.

The common law provides that plaintiff sue only once for the harm she has suffered, and statutes of limitations establish time limits within which she must do so. Plaintiff generally has no further legal recourse after she recovers a judgment, even if she sustains unanticipated harm that is related to the defendant's tortious conduct. Might this explain why plaintiffs who suffer potentially serious harm may wait a long time before suing? What should the law do if the plaintiff makes an unexpected recovery shortly after winning an award that anticipated a continuing disability? Instead of accepting projections and predictions, the law might have required plaintiff to sue at regular intervals for damages incurred since the last suit. Might the opportunity for recurring access to the court delay plaintiff's recuperation? What other arguments would support a single lump sum judgment? What arguments would weigh against it?

The intangible element of pain and suffering, which plays a central role in most cases of serious personal injury, presents problems of valuation as to both past and future losses. Through this item the law recognizes that the impact of the injury is more than financial. Suppose Maxine Hammontree had suffered serious injuries that left her crippled and disfigured. It is difficult to put price tags on such consequences, but if the law seeks to restore the plaintiff to her prior condition or its equivalent, the continuing pain and embarrassment she suffers must be assessed and translated into monetary terms.

Note that plaintiffs in *Hammontree* also sued for property loss because of the damage to the shop caused by defendant's loss of control of his auto. This is another common category of damage in personal injury cases, particularly in auto accident situations. (The subject of damages is discussed in detail in Chapter X.)

4. *Attorneys and fees.* The attorney's fee presents two questions: who pays and how much.

In most countries losing litigants pay the attorney's fees and other litigation costs of the prevailing party, as well as their own. In the United States it was feared that such a rule would deny persons of limited means access to the courts in close cases. When the courts were used mainly to settle vast estates or large commercial disputes and poor people had few claims, it may have been appropriate for a losing party to pay for both attorneys, but with the industrial revolution, the railroad, and later the automobile, wider access to the courts was essential. Requiring a party to pay even her own attorney presents serious problems for the poor, and tort litigation in this country has come to be handled by what is called the contingent fee system: the injured person pays a fee only if her case is concluded successfully—and the fee is a previously set percentage of the amount recovered. Many other legal systems consider this system unethical or illegal. What might cause this view of the contingent fee? What may be said in its defense? What are the alternatives?

Most personal injury cases in this country are handled for the plaintiff's side by a specialized group of lawyers who accept cases on a contingent fee basis. Lawyers for the defense are also specialized and represent either insurance companies or large commercial and industrial enterprises. Some are permanent employees of their client; others work in independent law firms that are compensated according to the time devoted to a particular case.

5. *Appellate decisions.* During much of this course we will read and discuss appellate opinions. You should know from the outset that these opinions are only a fraction of the yield of the legal process; in personal injury law, for example, perhaps only three percent of all claims actually go to trial and far fewer are appealed. The few appellate decisions, of course, shape the evolution of the law; cases are dropped and settlements are made on the basis of predictions of how the trial and appellate courts will view the controversy. Thus our appellate focus means that instead of seeing a cross-section of typical personal injury cases, we shall consider a small group of particularly significant cases.

Notice that tort problems are more likely to reach litigation than are contract problems. Parties to a contract are seeking an agreement that will provide specific foreseeable benefits. Even if a dispute arises, they have strong incentives to reach an accord that will preserve their mutually advantageous relationship. In tort situations, however, most claims arise from unintended harms. Prior legal counseling is rare. The attorney usually enters after the harm has occurred, and with litigation in mind if settlement negotiations fail. Often, the parties initially become aware of one another when at least one of them is hurt—and probably angry. There is no continuing relationship between the parties encouraging them to settle, and tort suits are hotly disputed because the critical events—as in a car crash—may have taken place within a few seconds.

6. *Court structure.* The California court system is fairly typical of state judicial organization—with its trial court of general jurisdiction (the superior court), a group of regional intermediate appellate courts (the court of appeal) and a single highest court (the supreme court). The major aberration in naming courts is the important state of New York. There the trial level court is called, "the supreme court," the regional intermediate appellate court is the "appellate division of the supreme court," or simply the "appellate division," and the state's highest court is called the "court of appeals."

7. Suggestions for further reading appear throughout this book. Four general books on tort law will be helpful on the doctrinal issues discussed. D. Dobbs, The Law of Torts (2000); K. Abraham, The Forms and Functions of Tort Law (1997); F. Harper, F. James, Jr. and O. Gray, The Law of Torts (2d ed. 1986)(6 vols.); and Prosser and Keeton on Torts (5th ed. 1984). Throughout the book, cases and notes will refer to relevant sections of the Restatement of the Law of Torts (4 vols. 1934–39) and the Second Restatement (4 vols. 1965–79). A Restatement (Third) of Torts: Products Liability was promulgated in 1998. A Restatement (Third) of Torts: Apportionment of Liability was published in 2000. The Restatement is an unofficial effort to summarize the decisional law on a subject. It is prepared by the American Law Institute, a group of lawyers, judges, and scholars. The intellectual foundations of tort law are explored in J. Davies, L. Levine, and E. Kionka, A Torts Anthology (2d ed. 1999); R. Rabin, Perspectives on Tort

Law (4th ed. 1995); and S. Levmore, Foundations of Tort Law (1994). The litigation process is explored in L. Grossman and R. Vaughn, A Documentary Companion to A Civil Action (1999).

D. THE PARTIES AND VICARIOUS LIABILITY

1. *Plaintiffs. Hammontree* involved an adult plaintiff. Her age, physical condition, and occupation would have been relevant to her damage recovery. In other situations it may be more difficult to find the proper plaintiff and to measure the recoverable loss. If a minor is hurt, suit generally will be brought on her behalf by her parent or guardian, and a damage award will be divided so that the minor will recover for any permanent physical harm (though the money will be placed in trust for her) and her parent will recover medical expenses borne on the child's behalf. It is now generally held that an infant who is born alive may sue through a legal guardian for harm suffered before birth. This problem is well discussed in Woods v. Lancet, 102 N.E.2d 691 (N.Y.1951).

Recoveries in cases of death are regulated by statute because under early common law the death of either the plaintiff or the defendant terminated the lawsuit. The death of the defendant now rarely causes the abatement of otherwise valid lawsuits. As for a deceased victim, two separate interests are involved: the victim's interest in her own bodily security and her dependents' interest in continued economic support and in other factors we shall consider later. The first is protected by "survival" statutes that allow the estate of the deceased to bring suit for any harm for which the deceased could have sued had she survived. This would include such items as medical expenses, lost wages, and pain and suffering up to her death. The second interest is generally recognized through "wrongful death" statutes. One common pattern provides that an action may be brought by and on behalf of legally designated beneficiaries, usually close family members or next of kin, to recover for the pecuniary loss that the death has caused. Generically these statutes are called Lord Campbell's Acts, after the first such statute adopted in 1846 in England. The survival and wrongful death interests may be vindicated in a single action.

In a lawsuit on behalf of a dead victim the actual plaintiff is usually an administrator (administratrix) or executor (executrix). An administrator is named by the court to handle the affairs of one who died intestate (with no will). If the deceased has left a will, it usually names an executor to handle the settling of estate matters, including bringing and defending lawsuits. In these cases the deceased may be referred to as the decedent, as plaintiff's intestate, or as plaintiff's testator (testatrix).

Why is Maxine Hammontree's husband a co-plaintiff? Although the property damage to their jointly owned business is one reason, it may be that his principal claim is for loss of consortium—loss of his wife's companionship—due to the injuries she suffered. The various aspects of "relational harm" in cases of death and injury are discussed in Chapters IV and X.

2. *Defendants.* We will see throughout the course that defendants are being held vicariously liable for the torts of another person. This is certainly true when a corporation is held liable for the torts of its employees whether they are lower, middle or upper level employees. It is also true when any person in business is held liable for the torts of his or her employees. These forms of vicarious liability, called "respondeat superior," are the most common. We briefly explore that concept at the outset.

Christensen v. Swenson et al

Supreme Court of Utah, 1994.
874 P.2d 125.

DURHAM, JUSTICE:

[Swenson, a Burns employee, was assigned to guard Gate 4 at Geneva Steel Plant. Guards worked eight-hour continuous shifts, with no scheduled breaks. However, employees were permitted to take ten- to fifteen-minute unscheduled lunch and restroom breaks. Gate 4 guards generally ate a bag lunch but occasionally ordered take-out food from the sole restaurant within close physical proximity to Gate 4, the Frontier Cafe. The Frontier Cafe was located directly across the street from the Geneva plant, approximately 150 to 250 yards from Gate 4. The cafe's menu was posted near the telephone at Gate 4. Aside from vending machines located within a nearby Geneva office building, the Frontier Cafe provided the sole source of food accessible to Gate 4 guards within their breaks. Whether they brought their lunches or ordered from the cafe, Gate 4 guards were expected to eat at their posts.

Shortly after 11 a.m. on the day of the accident, Swenson noticed a lull in the traffic at Gate 4 and decided to get a cup of soup from the Frontier Cafe. She placed a telephone order for the soup from Gate 4 and then drove her automobile to the cafe. She intended to pick up the soup and return to Gate 4 to eat at her post. She expected the round trip to take approximately ten to fifteen minutes, as permitted by Burns' unscheduled break policy. On her return trip, however, she collided with plaintiffs' motorcycle at a public intersection just outside Geneva's property. Several people were injured.

When suit was brought against Swenson and Burns, claiming that Swenson had driven negligently, Burns moved for summary judgment on the ground that Swenson was not acting in the scope of her employment at the time of the accident. The trial court granted the motion and the court of appeals affirmed.]

Summary judgment is appropriate when the record indicates that there is no genuine issue as to any material fact and the moving party is entitled to judgment as a matter of law. . . . [W]e view all relevant facts and all inferences arising from those facts in the light most favorable to the party opposing the motion. . . .

Under the doctrine of respondeat superior, employers are vicariously liable for torts committed by employees while acting within the scope of their employment. [ ] Whether an employee is acting within the scope of her employment is ordinarily a question of fact. [ ] The question must be submitted to the jury " 'whenever reasonable minds may differ as to whether the [employee] was at a certain time involved wholly or partly in the performance of [the employer's] business or within the scope of employment.' " [ ] However, when the employee's activity is so clearly within or outside the scope of employment that reasonable minds cannot differ, the court may decide the issue as a matter of law. [ ]; Birkner v. Salt Lake County, 771 P.2d 1053, 1057 (Utah 1989).

In *Birkner*, we stated that acts falling within the scope of employment are " 'those acts which are so closely connected with what the servant is employed to do, and so fairly and reasonably incidental to it, that they may be regarded as methods, even though quite improper ones, of carrying out the objectives of employment.' " [ ] We articulated three criteria helpful in determining whether an employee is acting within or outside the scope of her employment. First, the employee's conduct must be of the general kind the employee is hired to perform, that is, "the employee must be about the employer's business and the duties assigned by the employer, as opposed to being wholly involved in a personal endeavor." [ ] Second, the employee's conduct must occur substantially within the hours and ordinary spatial boundaries of the employment. [ ] Finally, "the employee's conduct must be motivated, at least in part, by the purpose of serving the employer's interest." [ ]

The court of appeals held that Swenson was not substantially within the ordinary spatial boundaries of her employment because the accident did not occur on Geneva property. . . .

Because the court of appeals concluded that Swenson failed to satisfy the second *Birkner* criterion, it did not address the first and third criteria. [ ] However, our review of the record indicates that reasonable minds could differ on all three criteria. Thus, to avoid a second summary judgment on remand, we address all three of the *Birkner* criteria.

The first *Birkner* criterion requires that the employee's conduct be of the general kind the employee is hired to perform, that is, "the employee must be about the employer's business and the duties assigned by the employer, as opposed to being wholly involved in a personal endeavor." [ ] Reasonable minds could differ as to whether Swenson was about Burns' business when she was involved in the traffic accident between Gate 4 and the Frontier Cafe.

We base this conclusion on two disputed issues of material fact. First, Swenson claims that Burns employed her as a security guard to "see and be seen" on and around the Geneva plant. Thus, traveling the short distance to the Frontier Cafe in uniform arguably heightened the secure atmosphere that Burns sought to project. Burns, on the other hand, claims that Swenson was not hired to perform that function. Burns' position is supported by the deposition of another security guard who stated that he considered lunch trips to the Frontier Cafe to be entirely personal in nature.

A second material issue of fact remains as to whether Burns tacitly sanctioned Gate 4 guards' practice of obtaining lunch from the Frontier Cafe. Burns expected its Gate 4 guards to work eight-hour continuous shifts and to remain at their posts as much as possible. However, because Burns also recognized that the guards must at times eat meals and use the restroom, the company permitted them to take ten- to fifteen-minute paid breaks. The record indicates that Burns was aware that its employees occasionally traveled to the Frontier Cafe during these unscheduled breaks but had never disciplined them for doing so. Indeed, Swenson asserts that a menu from the Frontier Cafe was posted in plain view at Gate 4. Thus, reasonable minds could differ as to whether Burns tacitly sanctioned, or at least contemplated, that its guards would satisfy their need for nourishment by obtaining meals from the Frontier Cafe.

The second *Birkner* criterion states that the employee's conduct must occur substantially within the hours and ordinary spatial boundaries of the employment. [ ] It is undisputed that Swenson's action occurred within the hours of her employment. She was at her post and in uniform when she decided to take advantage of a lull in plant traffic to eat lunch.

With respect to spatial boundaries, we find that reasonable minds might differ as to whether Swenson was substantially within the ordinary spatial boundaries of her employment when traveling to and from the Frontier Cafe. . . . While it is true that Swenson was not on Geneva property when the accident occurred, she was attempting to obtain lunch from a restaurant within the geographic area accessible during her ten- to fifteen-minute break. Given the other facts of this case, reasonable minds could differ as to whether Swenson's trip to the Frontier Cafe fell substantially within the ordinary spatial boundaries of her employment.

Furthermore, Burns could not point to specific orders barring guards from leaving the facility in their own vehicles to go to the Frontier Cafe on break, although two managers opined that such behavior was prohibited. This dispute alone presents a genuine issue of material fact. If guards were expressly forbidden to drive to the Frontier Cafe to pick up lunch during their break, a jury could find that Swenson was substantially outside the ordinary spatial boundaries of her employment; if they were not so forbidden, a jury might find her to have been acting substantially within the ordinary spatial boundaries of her employment.

Under the third criterion of the *Birkner* test, "the employee's conduct must be motivated, at least in part, by the purpose of serving the employer's interest." [ ] Applying this criterion to the instant case poses the question of whether Swenson's trip to the Frontier Cafe was motivated, at least in part, by the purpose of serving Burns' interest. Reasonable minds might also differ on this question.

First, two Burns managers admitted in their depositions that employee breaks benefit both the employee and the employer. Employees must occasionally eat meals and use the restroom, and employers receive the corresponding benefit of productive, satisfied employees. Reasonable minds could differ as to whether Swenson's particular break fell into this mutual-benefit category.

Second, given the continuous-shift nature of the job and the comparatively brief breaks permitted, Burns' break policy obviously placed a premium on speed and efficiency. Swenson claimed that traveling to the Frontier Cafe enabled her to obtain lunch within the allotted period and thus maximize the time spent at her post. In this respect, reasonable minds might conclude that Swenson's conduct was motivated, at least in part, by the purpose of serving Burns' interest. Evidence indicating that Swenson tried to save time on her lunch break by phoning her order ahead, driving instead of walking, and attempting to return immediately to her post is also relevant in this regard.

In sum, we hold that reasonable minds could differ as to whether Swenson was acting within or outside the scope of her employment when she collided with plaintiffs' motorcycle. Thus, summary judgment is inappropriate. We reverse and remand for further proceedings.

ZIMMERMAN, C.J., STEWART, ASSOCIATE C.J., AND GREENWOOD, COURT OF APPEALS JUDGE, concur.

HOWE, JUSTICE, concurring. . . .

Notes and Questions

1. The court suggests that if Burns had ordered guards not to go off the premises for food that might make a difference. What if a master orders a servant trucker not to run red lights or not to drive drunk and the servant causes an accident by doing just that? See Warner Trucking, Inc. v. Carolina Casualty Ins. Co., 686 N.E.2d 102 (Ind.1997)(master may be liable for actions of driver who violated company rule against driving after having consumed alcohol).

2. How would the case be analyzed under section 228 of the Restatement (Second) of Agency:

(1) Conduct of a servant is within the scope of employment if, but only if:

   (a) it is of the kind he is employed to perform;

   (b) it occurs substantially within the authorized time and space limits;

   (c) it is actuated, at least in part, by a purpose to serve the master; and

   (d) if force is intentionally used by the servant against another, the use of force is not unexpectable by the master.

(2) Conduct of a servant is not within the scope of employment if it is different in kind from that authorized, far beyond the authorized

time or space limits, or too little actuated by a purpose to serve the master.

See also Restatement (Second) of Agency § 229(2), which offers ten factors to be considered in deciding whether an employee's conduct has occurred within the scope of the employment.

3. Why do courts and the Restatement frame their inquiries as they do? What is the underlying justification for respondeat superior? Consider the conclusion in Lisa M. v. Henry Mayo Newhall Memorial Hospital, 907 P.2d 358 (Cal.1995), in which a hospital technician sexually assaulted a patient under his care. The court, 4–3, stated that it had "identified policy goals of the respondeat superior doctrine—preventing future injuries, assuring compensation to victims, and spreading the losses caused by an enterprise equitably—for additional guidance as to whether the doctrine should be applied in these circumstances." The majority concluded that the assault was "not a risk predictably created by or fairly attributed to the nature of the technician's employment." Is that the right question? Are these three policy goals helpful in resolving the questions raised in *Swenson*?

4. In a review article, Prof. Gary Schwartz observes that "employer vicarious liability is a doctrine that is embedded in the American tort system." He then identifies justifications for the doctrine starting with "fairness" (about which he is skeptical)—quoting a prominent judge in 1968 who stated that the doctrine is based "in a deeply rooted sentiment that business enterprise cannot justly disclaim responsibility for accidents which may fairly be said to be characteristic of its activities." Turning to economic justifications, Schwartz summarizes three:

> First, vicarious liability gives employers strong incentives to shrewdly select employees and effectively supervise employees; sound and shrewd employer practices should reduce the rate of employee negligence. Secondly, vicarious liability gives employers an incentive to discipline employees who have committed negligence and thereby exposed the employer to liability. This discipline can take the form either of a demotion or an outright discharge; effective disciplinary programs can both remove employees capable of causing future harm and give employees an ongoing incentive to abstain from negligence. Third, insofar as the prospect of employee negligence cannot be fully eliminated by ambitious selection, training, supervision, and disciplining of employees, vicarious liability gives employers incentives to consider alternatives to employee efforts. One such alternative might be the mechanization of particular tasks; another might be simply the reduction in the overall scale of the employer's activities.

After further consideration, Schwartz concludes that these economically based justifications "are promising, yet incomplete." G. Schwartz, The Hidden and Fundamental Issue of Employer Vicarious Liability, 69 S.Cal. L.Rev. 1739 (1996). Do they seem incomplete? Despite the skepticism of some commentators the judicial doctrine is firmly established.

5. Although most issues involve negligent conduct by the servant, recall that Restatement Section 228 contemplated situations involving intentional force. Section 245 expands on that notion: "A master is subject to liability for intended tortious harm by a servant . . . by an act done in connection with the servant's employment, although the act was unauthorized, if the act was not unexpectable in view of the duties of the servant." Does "not unexpectable" mean something different from "expectable"?

In Clark v. Pangan, 998 P.2d 268 (Utah 2000), a postal supervisor allegedly struck a subordinate in a dispute that arose over "how to conduct an inspection and complete the required paperwork." The court rejected the view held by some states that intentional harm can never be within the scope of employment. Rather, it held that the three *Birkner* factors should apply. In *Birkner,* which had involved a "sexual battery," the court had noted that "if the employee acts 'from purely personal motives . . . in no way connected with the employer's interests' or if the conduct is 'unprovoked, highly unusual, and quite outrageous,'" it could be considered outside the scope. Should the result depend on whether the altercation is over business matters or over last night's televised sporting event?

6. The theory of vicarious liability includes the idea that the person held liable may recover indemnity from the person whose negligence or other tort created the liability. There is serious doubt about how often this could occur and does occur. See the discussion in Alvarez v. New Haven Register, Inc., 735 A.2d 306 (Conn.1999). Do considerations about indemnity affect your conclusions about the basic doctrine?

7. What should happen if it were to turn out that the negligent or criminal employee had a record of such behavior in the past? In Foster v. The Loft, Inc., 526 N.E.2d 1309 (Mass.App.1988), plaintiff customer at defendant's bar was punched by a bartender in a melee that broke out after the customer's friend complained that his drink had been improperly mixed. The claim against the defendant bar owner was not that the bartender was functioning within the scope of his employment, but that the owner had hired someone to deal with the public in a hectic environment (a large complex of five bars) who had previously pleaded guilty to assault and battery with a knife and to related charges. Although refusing to hold that an employer can never hire a person with a criminal record, the court did conclude that the jury could reasonably find that the owner failed to take reasonable steps to screen the employees who would be dealing most closely with the public in an atmosphere that was "volatile" and in which "there was a high potential for violence." How does this analysis differ from that of respondeat superior?

8. So far we have been discussing situations in which the employee's status was unquestioned—the only issue being whether the servant was in the scope of employment. Another important aspect of respondeat superior is raised by the following case. It is suggested by the question of whether respondeat superior should apply if Christensen had sued the owners of the Geneva Steel Plant for the negligence of Swenson.

Baptist Memorial Hospital System v. Sampson

Supreme Court of Texas, 1998.
969 S.W.2d 945.

PHILLIPS, CHIEF JUSTICE, delivered the opinion of the Court.

In this case, we decide whether the plaintiff raised a genuine issue of material fact that defendant Hospital was vicariously liable under the theory of ostensible agency for an emergency room physician's negligence. . . . We hold that the plaintiff has not met her burden to raise a fact issue on each element of this theory. Accordingly, we reverse the judgment of the court of appeals, and render judgment that the plaintiff take nothing.

I

[Plaintiff was bitten on the arm by a brown recluse spider. She claims that emergency room treatment by Dr. Zakula at defendant hospital was negligent and led to permanent injuries. Although plaintiff sued several defendants and asserted other theories, they are not important to this part of the case. The trial court granted the hospital summary judgment on plaintiff's claim that it was responsible for the negligence of Dr. Zakula. The court of appeals reversed.]

Both parties agree that BMHS [the hospital's parent] established as a matter of law that Dr. Zakula was not its agent or employee. Thus the burden shifted to Sampson to raise a fact issue on each element of her ostensible agency theory. . . . In our review, we must first determine the proper elements of ostensible agency, then decide whether Sampson raised a genuine issue of material fact on each of these elements.

II

Under the doctrine of respondeat superior, an employer is vicariously liable for the negligence of an agent or employee acting within the scope of his or her agency or employment, although the principal or employer has not personally committed a wrong. [ ] The most frequently proffered justification for imposing such liability is that the principal or employer has the right to control the means and methods of the agent or employee's work. [ ] Because an independent contractor has sole control over the means and methods of the work to be accomplished, however, the individual or entity that hires the independent contractor is generally not vicariously liable for the tort or negligence of that person. [ ] Nevertheless, an individual or entity may act in a manner that makes it liable for the conduct of one who is not its agent at all or who, although an agent, has acted outside the scope of his or her authority. Liability may be imposed in this manner under the doctrine of ostensible agency in circumstances when the principal's conduct should equitably prevent it from denying the existence of an agency.[2] [ ] Ostensible agency in Texas is based on the

2.   Many courts use the terms ostensible agency, apparent agency, apparent authority, and agency by estoppel interchangeably. As a practical matter, there is no distinction

notion of estoppel, that is, a representation by the principal causing justifiable reliance and resulting harm. [   ]

Texas courts have applied these basic agency concepts to many kinds of principals, including hospitals. [   ] A hospital is ordinarily not liable for the negligence of a physician who is an independent contractor. [   ] On the other hand, a hospital may be vicariously liable for the medical malpractice of independent contractor physicians when plaintiffs can establish the elements of ostensible agency. [   ]

III

In this case, the court of appeals held that two distinct theories of vicarious liability with different elements are available in Texas to impose liability on a hospital for emergency room physician negligence: agency by estoppel (referred to in this opinion as ostensible agency), based on the Restatement (Second) of Agency section 267, and apparent agency, based on the Restatement (Second) of Torts section 429. [   ] Under section 267, the party asserting ostensible agency must demonstrate that (1) the principal, by its conduct, (2) caused him or her to reasonably believe that the putative agent was an employee or agent of the principal, and (3) that he or she justifiably relied on the appearance of agency. Restatement (Second) of Agency § 267 (1958).   .   .   .

We first reject the court of appeals' conclusion that there are two methods, one "more difficult to prove" than the other, to establish the liability of a hospital for the malpractice of an emergency room physician. [   ] Our courts have uniformly required proof of all three elements of section 267 to invoke the fiction that one should be responsible for the acts of another who is not in fact an agent acting within his or her scope of authority.   .   .   .

Next, we reject the suggestion of the court of appeals .   .   . that we disregard the traditional rules and take "the full leap" of imposing a nondelegable duty on Texas hospitals for the malpractice of emergency room physicians. [   ] Imposing such a duty is not necessary to safeguard patients in hospital emergency rooms. A patient injured by a physician's malpractice is not without a remedy. The injured patient ordinarily has a cause of action against the negligent physician, and may retain a direct cause of action against the hospital if the hospital was negligent in the performance of a duty owed directly to the patient. [   ]

IV

We now examine the record below in light of the appropriate standard.   .   .   .

As summary judgment evidence, BMHS offered the affidavit of Dr. Potyka, an emergency room physician, which established that the emergen-

among them. [   ] Regardless of the term used, the purpose of the doctrine is to prevent injustice and protect those who have been misled.

cy room doctors are not the actual agents, servants, or employees of the Hospital, and are not subject to the supervision, management, direction, or control of the Hospital when treating patients. Dr. Potyka further stated that when Dr. Zakula treated Sampson, signs were posted in the emergency room notifying patients that the emergency room physicians were independent contractors. Dr. Potyka's affidavit also established that the Hospital did not collect any fees for emergency room physician services and that the physicians billed the patients directly. BMHS presented copies of signed consent forms as additional summary judgment evidence. During both of Sampson's visits to the Hospital emergency room, before being examined or treated, Sampson signed a "Consent for Diagnosis, Treatment and Hospital Care" form explaining that all physicians at the Hospital are independent contractors who exercise their own professional judgment without control by the Hospital. The consent forms read in part:

> I acknowledge and agree that . . ., Southeast Baptist Hospital, . . . and any Hospital operated as a part of Baptist Memorial Hospital System, is not responsible for the judgment or conduct of any physician who treats or provides a professional service to me, but rather each physician is an independent contractor who is self-employed and is not the agent, servant or employee of the hospital.

To establish her claim of ostensible agency, Sampson offered her own affidavits. In her original affidavit, she stated that although the Hospital directed her to sign several pieces of paper before she was examined, she did not read them and no one explained their contents to her. Her supplemental affidavit stated that she did not recall signing the documents and that she did not, at any time during her visit to the emergency room, see any signs stating that the doctors who work in the emergency room are not employees of the Hospital. Both affidavits state that she did not choose which doctor would treat her and that, at all times, she believed that a physician employed by the hospital was treating her. Based on this record we must determine if Sampson produced sufficient summary judgment evidence to raise a genuine issue of material fact on each element of ostensible agency, thereby defeating BMHS's summary judgment motion.

Even if Sampson's belief that Dr. Zakula was a hospital employee were reasonable, that belief, as we have seen, must be based on or generated by some conduct on the part of the Hospital. "No one should be denied the right to set up the truth unless it is in plain contradiction of his former allegations or acts." [   ] The summary judgment proof establishes that the Hospital took no affirmative act to make actual or prospective patients think the emergency room physicians were its agents or employees, and did not fail to make reasonable efforts to disabuse them of such a notion. As a matter of law, on this record, no conduct by the Hospital would lead a reasonable patient to believe that the treating emergency room physicians were hospital employees.

Sampson has failed to raise a fact issue on at least one essential element of her claim. Accordingly, we reverse the judgment of the court of appeals and render judgment that Sampson take nothing.

Notes and Questions

1.   Section 409 of the Restatement (Second) of Torts provides that:

Except as stated in §§ 410–429, the employer of an independent contractor is not liable for physical harm caused to another by an act or omission of the contractor or his servants.

One of those exceptions, § 429, relied upon by the court of appeals in *Sampson*, provides:

One who employs an independent contractor to perform services for another which are accepted in the reasonable belief that the services are being rendered by the employer or by his servants, is subject to liability for physical harm caused by the negligence of the contractor in supplying such services, to the same extent as though the employer were supplying them himself or by his servants.

Is this different from § 267 of the Restatement of Agency? If so, which is preferable? Why is a party generally not liable for the conduct of an independent contractor?

2.   The court of appeals also asserted that the state should make a "full leap" and create a nondelegable duty on a hospital for the conduct of those in its emergency room. Why? Why does the Supreme Court decline?

3.   In *Maloney v. Rath*, p. 8, supra, involving the brake failure, the court concluded that the owner of the car should be held liable for the negligence of the garage mechanic who worked on the brakes, even though the owner had chosen a reputable mechanic and had no reason to suspect that the job had been badly done. The court stressed two statutory requirements that car brakes be in working order. These were said to show that the legislature recognized that improperly maintained motor vehicles threaten "a grave risk of serious bodily harm or death." Responsibility for proper maintenance of such potentially dangerous property "properly rests with the person who owns and operates the vehicle." That person "selects the contractor and is free to insist upon one who is financially responsible and to demand indemnity from him." Is it sound to "require" car owners to learn the solvency of their mechanics before entrusting their cars to them?

The *Maloney* result was rejected in Hackett v. Perron, 402 A.2d 193 (N.H.1979):

Garage mechanics are not employees or agents of their customers. To charge owners with their negligence would be tantamount to imposing absolute liability. . . . It is true that plaintiff may have been faultless, but defendant also was without fault. We do not live in a riskless society and it is no part of the judicial function to fashion the law so that every injured person can find someone to hold liable. We refuse to decide which of two innocent co-users of our highways should be held liable. The fault system provides a fair method of apportioning the risk of co-users of our highways and we will not depart from it.

4. In Valenti v. NET Properties Management, Inc., 710 A.2d 399 (N.H.1998), a patron sued the owner of a shopping mall after falling on snow that covered an entryway. The entryway was supposed to be maintained by an independent contractor. The court held the owner vicariously liable for the negligence of the contractor under the exception of Torts Restatement (Second) section 425, which spoke directly to the situation in which the property owner had delegated the maintenance of grounds. The court concluded that when "these entities invite the public onto their premises for business purposes, policy concerns counsel against allowing them to shield themselves from liability by hiring independent contractors. . . . Moreover, those who own or operate business premises are in the best position to protect against the risk of personal injury on their premises and can seek indemnification or contribution from their independent contractors." Would this analysis apply to *Sampson*? The same court decided both *Valenti* and *Hackett*, in the prior note. Are the cases consistent?

5. Although the supreme court did not mention the point in *Sampson*, the court of appeals had noted in passing that the hospital had referred to itself as a "full service hospital." Should that matter? In Sword v. NKC Hospitals, Inc., 714 N.E.2d 142 (Ind.1999), on facts similar to those of *Sampson*, the court emphasized that the hospital had advertised itself to be a full service hospital. This conveyed the idea that its doctors were its employees. Using § 429, the court concluded that whether the hospital's efforts to negate that impression had succeeded was a question for the jury.

CHAPTER II

THE NEGLIGENCE PRINCIPLE

A.   HISTORICAL DEVELOPMENT OF FAULT LIABILITY

The law of negligence is of relatively recent origin. As late as 1850, one finds only a handful of isolated cases that refer to liability based on negligence. In A History of American Law (2d ed. 1985), Lawrence Friedman observes (at p. 467) that prior to the nineteenth century:

> The common law had little to say about personal injuries brought about by carelessness—the area of life and law that underwent most rapid growth in the [nineteenth] century. The modern law of torts must be laid at the door of the industrial revolution, whose machines had a marvelous capacity for smashing the human body.

[handwritten margin note: indus. rev. brought neg.?]

Was the pre-industrial era characterized by strict liability? Some commentators have thought so. Others have argued that fault considerations always tempered the strictness of tort doctrine in cases of unintended harm. The debate is complicated by the fact that tort law, as Friedman points out, only ripened into a field during the latter part of the nineteenth century. Before the industrial revolution, the infrequent cases of accidental harm that occurred were filtered through the Anglo–American writ system—a procedural system requiring that tort-like wrongs be pleaded as actions in "trespass" or "trespass on the case," rather than the substantive categories we now employ. The flavor of the writ system is well captured in the classic distinction put forward by Fortescue, J., in Reynolds v. Clarke, 1 Strange 634, 92 Eng.Rep. 410 (1726):

> [I]f a man throws a log into the highway, and in that act it hits me; I may maintain trespass, because it is an immediate wrong; but if as it lies there I tumble over it, and receive an injury, I must bring an action upon the case; because it is only prejudicial in consequence, for which originally I could have no action at all.

We begin our consideration of negligence with a closer look at the English common law approach that laid the foundations for the American treatment of unintended harm. In the following excerpt, Gary Schwartz draws upon the leading historical accounts in addressing the question of whether pre-industrial injury law was dominated by a strict liability approach.

Tort Law and the Economy in Nineteenth Century America: A Reinterpretation
Gary T. Schwartz.
90 Yale Law Journal 1717, 1722–27 (1981).

Research into pre-1800 English tort doctrine is fraught with hazards. One can look at judges' remarks ventured in the course of what amounted to oral argument. But as has been observed, "[t]o ransack the Year Books for large statements of doctrine made in irrelevant circumstances by judges barely conscious of their significance is neither a pleasing nor a profitable task." One can also study the pleadings and trial verdicts available in the mostly unpublished plea rolls and rely on them in attempting to infer the pertinent liability standards. But the process of drawing "believable inferences" from raw documents of this sort is frequently "perilous." And whether one turns to the Year Books or the plea rolls, questions of substantive law frequently are obscured or confounded by the demands of the English writ system.

Despite these inadequacies of evidence,[35] many scholars have confidently found huge portions of strict liability in traditional English law. Professor Gregory finds strict liability inherent in the English writ of trespass.[36] But this alignment of English trespass with strict liability is misleading. As developed in the late twelfth century, the early writ of trespass—far from entailing strict liability—seems to have been primarily addressed to intentional harm-causing conduct, conduct that would now be identified as basically criminal. To be sure, by a process we now may be barely able to reconstruct, trespass began to extend to conduct that involved "*vi et armis*" (the trespass formula) only in the loose sense of harm that was forcibly, even if accidentally, inflicted. The propriety of this extension was confirmed, and the standard of liability in trespass explicitly—though ambiguously—discussed, in Weaver v. Ward,[41] a 1616 case concerning the accidental discharge of firearms. Although *Weaver* did suggest that the trespass-plaintiff's proof of immediately caused harm established a prima facie case, it also indicated that the defendant could refute liability by showing that what happened had been an "inevitable accident"—that the defendant had been "utterly without fault" or had "committed no negligence." While these various formulations clearly rule out the idea of unqualified strict liability, their precise meaning is far from clear.[42]

35. Even if medieval law *had* been subject to a significant strict liability rule, that rule would require interpretation. Perhaps medieval thinking imputed a motive (whether conscious or unconscious) to every action in a way that just about eliminated the concept of unintended harm. See A. Ehrenzweig, Psychoanalytic Jurisprudence 244 (1971). Perhaps in a simple medieval world, almost every serious injury was the result of intentional or at least negligent conduct. See J. Fleming, An Introduction to the Law of Torts 3 (3d ed. 1967); [   ].

36. . . . A semantic point: "strict liability" was not a phrase that courts employed during the periods under review. On those occasions when strict liability was considered, the idea was conveyed in a variety of indirect ways.

41. Hobart 134, 80 Eng.Rep. 284 (1616). . . .

42. Related to the "inevitable accident" defense was the idea that trespass would not lie if the object immediately causing the inju-

The question of the liability standard in trespass was further complicated by what was then routine trespass procedure. A trespass writ generally took the form of a "stark uninformative declaration." In answering the writ the defendant could offer a "blank plea of Not Guilty," and then present to the jury whatever extenuating evidence he thought relevant. The standard of liability in trespass thus was left to the effective discretion of the individual jury, and we simply lack information as to how juries exercised this discretion; jury verdicts of guilty and not guilty remain largely "inscrutable."

Professor Malone emphasizes the strict liability he finds in the English fire cases. Though the judicial statements in question contain certain strict liability phrases, they also avail themselves of the language of negligence. Whether these negligence references were mere rhetorical flourishes or were instead intended to posit an actual liability standard is a question that has provoked disagreement. No one contends, however, that a strict liability rule applied to fires that were accidentally set. Rather, the rule is said to have covered deliberately started fires that accidentally spread to a neighbor's property. Even these fires were subject to strict liability only to the extent that they remained "within the control" of the defendant. And since, for example, an unexpectedly strong wind tended to negate control, the control requirement can easily be regarded as a correlate or proxy for fault.

The fire cases were pleaded in trespass on the case. As a general matter, the case variation on the trespass writ provided a remedy for English victims who could not make any plausible claim of forcible injury. In the absence of such a claim, however, the case plaintiff needed to explain in his writ why the imposition of liability was appropriate in his situation. Since it appears that a number of situations were found sufficient in this respect, case possessed from the start a catch-all or "miscellaneous" quality that makes it difficult to generalize about its standard of liability. Traditionally, however, case has been affiliated with negligence, and overall this affiliation seems fair. The earliest instances of case involved suits against professionals like blacksmiths, physicians, and veterinarians who were held liable for negligence in their undertakings. In the fifteenth and sixteenth centuries, a limited number of claims were litigated in case between parties not in any preexisting contractual relation; for these claims, a liability standard approaching negligence was applied. By the late seventeenth century, collision suits began to come before the courts—collisions of vessels at sea, of horse-drawn carriages on highways, and of carriages with pedestrians. Since these collisions involved forceful contacts, they raised a clear trespass possibility. Yet, for several possible reasons,[61] these suits were frequently pleaded in case, with liability depending on proof of the defendant's negligence. Even when the facts of a particular collision led to its being presented in trespass, it appears that negligence was recognized as

---

ry—a ship or a horse, for example—had escaped the defendant's control. . . .

61. One reason was loss of control. See note 42 supra. Another reason was vicarious liability. [ ]

the liability pivot. Of course, collisions of one sort or another—often involving railroads—came to typify tort litigation in the nineteenth century.

One early fire opinion, in vacillating between strict liability and negligence, indicates that an employer could be held strictly liable for the within-the-employment negligence of his employee in allowing a fire to spread. In general, any claim of vicarious liability relegated a plaintiff to case, and as late as 1685 the law was willing—the fire cases apart—to hold employers liable only for torts they had actually commanded. In its sixteenth-century form, moreover, the command rule evidently required the employer to have "commanded the very act in which the wrong consisted (unless the command had been to do a thing in itself unlawful)." Gradually, however, in eighteenth-century England the modern notion developed that the employer could be held liable for any of his employee's scope-of-employment torts;[68] but in personal injury cases this notion seems to have been associated with the assumption of some negligent conduct on the employee's part.

Therefore, whatever the strict liability possibilities that may have harbored in the writ of trespass, these possibilities evidently were connected to or at least contained by a narrow rule of employer vicarious liability, a rule that, as it eventually expanded, acquired a noticeable negligence orientation. Negligence, moreover, was all along the accepted standard of liability in the malpractice and the collision cases. Indeed, if one searches traditional English tort law for clear instances of strict liability, one winds up mainly with the animal cases. Even these cases reveal an uncertain prior history. Cattle owners originally were held liable for those cattle trespasses that their owners deliberately incited; and the early suits over animals attacking humans may well have involved plain negligence on the part of the animals' custodians. To be sure, over time each of these animal doctrines inclined in the direction of strict liability. But the explanations for these evolutions remain very much in doubt; and in any event the modest animal rules posed no particular threat to nineteenth-century industrialization.

To sum up, then, the strict liability strands in traditional English law seem ambivalent and confused; the negligence strands, both more distinct and more capable of extended application.

Notes and Questions

1. The leading historical sources analyzed by Schwartz are J. Baker, An Introduction to English Legal History (1979); C. Fifoot, History and Sources of the Common Law (1949); A. Harari, The Place of Negligence in the Law of Torts (1962); S. Milsom, Historical Foundations of the Common Law (2d ed. 1981); T. Plucknett, A Concise History of the Common Law

---

68. The account afforded here is in opposition to the common assumption that the scope-of-employment test is of "ancient" origin. [   ]

(1956); M. Pritchard, Scott v. Shepherd (1773) and the Emergence of the Tort of Negligence (1976); Arnold, Accident, Mistake and the Rules of Liability in the Fourteenth Century Law of Torts, 128 U.Pa.L.Rev. 361 (1979); Gregory, Trespass to Negligence to Absolute Liability, 37 Va.L.Rev. 359 (1951); and Malone, Ruminations on the Role of Fault in the History of the Common Law of Torts, 31 La.L.Rev. 1 (1970).

2. Virtually all of these sources take as their starting point the question of whether strict liability was dominant at early common law, or whether it was tempered to some extent by fault considerations. As we trace the modern development of negligence and strict liability in the materials that follow, keep in mind the possibility of another perspective: that the pre-industrial era was in fact substantially committed to a "no-liability" approach based on court-imposed immunities, limited duties and restrictive notions of what constituted an actionable claim in the first instance. This thesis is developed in Rabin, The Historical Development of the Fault Principle: A Reinterpretation, 15 Ga.L.Rev. 925 (1981), arguing that "no-liability" thinking continued to influence tort law well into the negligence era.

See also Gilles, Inevitable Accident in Classical English Tort Law, 43 Emory L.J. 575 (1994), arguing that English precedents in the pre-industrial era established a liability regime falling between strict causal-based liability and negligence. That regime was identified as one in which "the question was not whether actors had behaved unreasonably—whether they *should* have avoided the accident—but whether they *could* have avoided it by greater practical care."

3. Undoubtedly, the leading English precedents played a role in shaping early American tort law. In the early nineteenth century, however, the states began to develop their own accident law. Again, there is scholarly disagreement over the role of strict liability in the early post-Revolutionary period. Compare M. Horwitz, The Transformation of American Law, 1780–1860 (1977), pp. 67–108, and Gregory, cited in note 1 supra, with Schwartz at pp. 1727–34, and Schwartz, The Character of Early American Tort Law, 36 UCLA L.Rev. 641 (1989). Whatever the situation might have been before 1850, the universality of the negligence principle was an open question in this country when the following landmark case was decided.

Brown v. Kendall

Supreme Judicial Court of Massachusetts, 1850
6 Cush. (60 Mass.) 292.

This was an action of trespass for assault and battery, originally commenced against George K. Kendall, the defendant, who died pending the suit, and his executrix was summoned in.

It appeared in evidence, on the trial .   .   . that two dogs, belonging to the plaintiff and the defendant, respectively, were fighting in the presence of their masters; that the defendant took a stick about four feet long, and commenced beating the dogs in order to separate them; that the plaintiff was looking on, at the distance of about a rod, and that he advanced a step or two towards the dogs. In their struggle, the dogs approached the place where the plaintiff was standing. The defendant retreated backwards from before the dogs, striking them as he retreated; and as he approached the plaintiff, with his back towards him, in raising his stick over his shoulder, in order to strike the dogs, he accidentally hit the plaintiff in the eye, inflicting upon him a severe injury.

Whether it was necessary or proper for the defendant to interfere in the fight between the dogs; whether the interference, if called for, was in a proper manner, and what degree of care was exercised by each party on the occasion; were the subject of controversy between the parties, upon all the evidence in the case, of which the foregoing is an outline.

[Under instructions from the trial judge, which are reviewed in the opinion, the jury returned a verdict for the plaintiff and the trial judge entered judgment.]

SHAW, C.J.   .   .   .

The facts set forth in the bill of exceptions preclude the supposition, that the blow, inflicted by the hand of the defendant upon the person of the plaintiff, was intentional. The whole case proceeds on the assumption, that the damage sustained by the plaintiff, from the stick held by the defendant, was inadvertent and unintentional; and the case involves the question how far, and under what qualifications, the party by whose unconscious act the damage was done is responsible for it. We use the term "unintentional" rather than involuntary, because in some of the cases, it is stated, that the act of holding and using a weapon or instrument, the movement of which is the immediate cause of hurt to another, is a voluntary act, although its particular effect in hitting and hurting another is not within the purpose or intention of the party doing the act.

It appears to us, that some of the confusion in the cases on this subject has grown out of the long-vexed question, under the rule of the common law, whether a party's remedy, where he has one, should be sought in an action of the case, or of trespass. This is very distinguishable from the question, whether in a given case, any action will lie. The result of these cases is, that if the damage complained of is the immediate effect of the act of the defendant, trespass *vi et armis* lies; if consequential only, and not immediate, case is the proper remedy. [   ]

In these discussions, it is frequently stated by judges, that when one receives injury from the direct act of another, trespass will lie. But we think this is said in reference to the question, whether trespass and not case will lie, assuming that the facts are such, that some action will lie. These *dicta* are no authority, we think, for holding, that damage received by a direct act of force from another will be sufficient to maintain an action of trespass, whether the act was lawful or unlawful, and neither wilful, intentional, or careless.   .   .   .

We think, as the result of all the authorities, the rule is correctly stated by Mr. Greenleaf, that the plaintiff must come prepared with evidence to show either that the *intention* was unlawful, or that the defendant was *in fault;* for if the injury was unavoidable, and the conduct of the defendant was free from blame, he will not be liable. 2 Greenl.Ev. §§ 85 to 92; [   ]. If, in the prosecution of a lawful act, a casualty purely accidental arises, no action can be supported for an injury arising therefrom. [   ] In applying these rules to the present case, we can perceive no reason why the instructions asked for by the defendant ought not to have been given; to this effect, that if both plaintiff and defendant at the time of the blow were using ordinary care, or if at that time the defendant was using ordinary care, and the plaintiff was not, or if at that time, both the plaintiff and defendant were not using ordinary care, then the plaintiff could not recover.

In using this term, ordinary care, it may be proper to state, that what constitutes ordinary care will vary with the circumstances of cases. In general, it means that kind and degree of care, which prudent and cautious men would use, such as is required by the exigency of the case, and such as is necessary to guard against probable danger. A man, who should have occasion to discharge a gun, on an open and extensive marsh, or in a forest, would be required to use less circumspection and care, than if he were to do the same thing in an inhabited town, village, or city. To make an accident, or casualty, or as the law sometimes states it, inevitable accident, it must be such an accident as the defendant could not have avoided by the use of the kind and degree of care necessary to the exigency, and in the circumstances in which he was placed.

    .   .   .   . We can have no doubt that the act of the defendant in attempting to part the fighting dogs, one of which was his own, and for the injurious acts of which he might be responsible, was a lawful and proper act, which he might do by proper and safe means. If, then, in doing this act, using due care and all proper precautions necessary to the exigency of the case, to avoid hurt to others, in raising his stick for that purpose, he accidentally hit the plaintiff in his eye, and wounded him, this was the result of pure accident, or was involuntary and unavoidable, and therefore the action would not lie.   .   .   .

The court instructed the jury, that if it was not a necessary act, and the defendant was not in duty bound to part the dogs, but might with propriety interfere or not as he chose, the defendant was responsible for the consequences of the blow, unless it appeared that he was in the exercise of extraordinary care, so that the accident was inevitable, using the word not in a strict but a popular sense. This is to be taken in connection with the charge afterwards given, that if the jury believed, that the act of interference in the fight was unnecessary, (that is, as before explained, not a duty incumbent on the defendant), then the burden of proving extraordinary care on the part of the defendant, or want of ordinary care on the part of plaintiff, was on the defendant.

The court are of opinion that these directions were not conformable to law. If the act of hitting the plaintiff was unintentional, on the part of the defendant, and done in the doing of a lawful act, then the defendant was not liable, unless it was done in the want of exercise of due care, adapted to the exigency of the case, and therefore such want of due care became part of the plaintiff's case, and the burden of proof was on the plaintiff to establish it. 2 Greenl.Ev. § 85; [   ].

Perhaps the learned judge, by the use of the term extraordinary care, in the above charge, explained as it is by the context, may have intended nothing more than that increased degree of care and diligence, which the exigency of particular circumstances might require, and which men of ordinary care and prudence would use under like circumstances, to guard against danger. If such was the meaning of this part of the charge, then it does not differ from our views, as above explained. But we are of opinion, that the other part of the charge, that the burden of proof was on the defendant, was incorrect. Those facts which are essential to enable the plaintiff to recover, he takes the burden of proving. The evidence may be offered by the plaintiff or by the defendant; the question of due care, or want of care, may be essentially connected with the main facts, and arise from the same proof; but the effect of the rule, as to the burden of proof, is this, that when the proof is all in, and before the jury, from whatever side it comes, and whether directly proved, or inferred from circumstances, if it appears that the defendant was doing a lawful act, and unintentionally hit and hurt the plaintiff, then unless it also appears to the satisfaction of the jury, that the defendant is chargeable with some fault, negligence, carelessness, or want of prudence, the plaintiff fails to sustain the burden of proof, and is not entitled to recover.

New trial ordered.

Notes and Questions

1.   How does Chief Justice Shaw resolve the issue of whether the pre-existing common law recognized strict liability for unintended harm? Was plaintiff arguing for a strict liability standard? What might the trial court have intended by recognizing a distinct standard of care when defendant's conduct "was not a necessary act"?

2.   Apart from the trial court's erroneous reference to necessary acts, how did the jury instruction misstate the law? What, precisely, were the unsettled questions before *Brown v. Kendall* that Shaw resolved in the opinion?

3.   Although *Brown v. Kendall* is generally regarded as a landmark opinion in establishing the fault principle, a handful of state courts had already reached the same conclusion with relatively little difficulty. See, e.g. Harvey v. Dunlop, Lalor Supp. to Hill & Dennis 193 (N.Y.1843), in which one child appears to have unintentionally put out the eye of another in a stone-throwing incident. The court concluded (at p. 194):

No case or principle can be found, or if found can be maintained, subjecting an individual to liability for an act done without fault on his part. . . . All the cases concede that an injury arising from accident, or, which in law or reason is the same thing, from an act that ordinary human care and foresight are unable to guard against, is but the misfortune of the sufferer, and lays no foundation for legal responsibility.

4. Does Shaw indicate *why* the fault principle establishes the appropriate standard of liability? We have already given brief consideration to two scholarly efforts to justify liability based on negligence. Recall the excerpts from Holmes and Posner in Chapter I. Compare their positions with the following interpretation of *Brown v. Kendall* in Gregory, Trespass to Negligence to Absolute Liability, 37 Va.L.Rev. 359, 368 (1951):

> While it is pure speculation, one of Chief Justice Shaw's motives underlying his opinion appears to have been a desire to make risk-creating enterprise less hazardous to investors and entrepreneurs than it had been previously at common law. Certainly that interpretation is consistent with his having furthered the establishment of the fellow servant doctrine and the expansion of the assumption-of-risk defense in actions arising out of industrial injuries. Judicial subsidies of this sort to youthful enterprise removed pressure from the pocket-books of investors and gave incipient industry a chance to experiment on low-cost operations without the risk of losing its reserve in actions by injured employees. Such a policy no doubt seems ruthless; but in a small way it probably helped to establish industry, which in turn was essential to the good society as Shaw envisaged it.

Gregory's mention of the fellow servant doctrine refers to Shaw's famous opinion in Farwell v. Boston & Worcester Railroad Corp., 4 Metc. (45 Mass.) 49 (1842), in which an injured worker's suit against his employer was dismissed on the grounds that a master was not vicariously liable for injuries suffered because of a fellow worker's negligence. More broadly, under nineteenth century negligence law the carelessness of a fellow servant was one of many risks that an employee was taken to assume, and which prevented suit against the employer. See Friedman & Ladinsky, Social Change and the Law of Industrial Accidents, 67 Colum.L.Rev. 50 (1967).

Is Gregory's thesis distinctively different from the views of Holmes and Posner? In what sense could the fault principle be viewed as providing a "subsidy" to industry? Why should a dog-fight case involving two neighbors be regarded as relevant to protection of industrial enterprises, whatever Shaw might have decided in other cases? As you study the materials that follow, ask yourself what rationale for the fault principle seems most convincing. Is it likely that a single rationale will be applicable to every type of unintentional harm?

B. THE CENTRAL CONCEPT

1. THE STANDARD OF CARE

Until now, we have discussed fault liability without making any effort to give content to the central concept of negligence—apart from referring to it as "unreasonable" conduct. Although we have given brief consideration to moral and economic justifications for the fault principle, we have yet to examine how the system actually operates. What standard does a court utilize in deciding whether the defendant's behavior was "negligent"? We begin by exploring the concept of unreasonable risk.

Adams v. Bullock
Court of Appeals of New York, 1919.
227 N.Y. 208, 125 N.E. 93.

CARDOZO, J. The defendant runs a trolley line in the city of Dunkirk, employing the overhead wire system. At one point, the road is crossed by a bridge or culvert which carries the tracks of the Nickle Plate and Pennsylvania railroads. Pedestrians often use the bridge as a short cut between streets, and children play on it. On April 21, 1916, the plaintiff, a boy of twelve years, came across the bridge, swinging a wire about eight feet long. In swinging it, he brought it in contact with the defendant's trolley wire, which ran beneath the structure. The side of the bridge was protected by a parapet eighteen inches wide. Four feet seven and three-fourths inches below the top of the parapet, the trolley wire was strung. The plaintiff was shocked and burned when the wires came together. He had a verdict at Trial Term, which has been affirmed at the Appellate Division by a divided court.

We think the verdict cannot stand. The defendant in using an overhead trolley was in the lawful exercise of its franchise. Negligence, therefore, cannot be imputed to it because it used that system and not another [   ]. There was, of course, a duty to adopt all reasonable precautions to minimize the resulting perils. We think there is no evidence that this duty was ignored. The trolley wire was so placed that no one standing on the bridge or even bending over the parapet could reach it. Only some extraordinary casualty, not fairly within the area of ordinary prevision, could make it a thing of danger. Reasonable care in the use of a destructive agency imports a high degree of vigilance (Nelson v. Branford L. & W. Co., 75 Conn. 548, 551 [1903]; Braun v. Buffalo Gen. El. Co., 200 N.Y. 484 [1911]). But no vigilance, however alert, unless fortified by the gift of prophecy, could have predicted the point upon the route where such an accident would occur. It might with equal reason have been expected anywhere else. At any point upon the route, a mischievous or thoughtless boy might touch the wire with a metal pole, or fling another wire across it [   ]. If unable to reach it from the walk, he might stand upon a wagon or climb upon a tree. No special danger at this bridge warned the defendant that there was need of special measures of precaution. No like accident had occurred before. No custom had been disregarded. We think that ordinary caution did not involve forethought of this extraordinary peril. It has been so ruled in like circumstances by courts in other jurisdictions. [   ] Nothing to the contrary was held in [Braun]; [   ]. In those cases, the accidents were well within the range of prudent foresight [   ]. That was also the basis of the ruling in

[*Nelson*]. There is, we may add, a distinction, not to be ignored, between electric light and trolley wires. The distinction is that the former may be insulated. Chance of harm, though remote, may betoken negligence, if needless. Facility of protection may impose a duty to protect. With trolley wires, the case is different. Insulation is impossible. Guards here and there are of little value. To avert the possibility of this accident and others like it at one point or another on the route, the defendant must have abandoned the overhead system, and put the wires underground. Neither its power nor its duty to make the change is shown. To hold it liable upon the facts exhibited in this record would be to charge it as an insurer.

Impossible to insulate trolley wires

The judgment should be reversed. . . .

HISCOCK, CH. J., CHASE, COLLIN, HOGAN, CRANE and ANDREWS, JJ., concur.

Notes and Questions

no forethought no warning sign

1. What negligence might the jury have found? That in turn will depend on how the trial proceeded and what evidence was introduced. Consider the following observation in Grady, Untaken Precautions, 18 J.Legal Stud. 139, 144 (1989):

> Events do not define what negligence analysis will be the case, and the court does not define it either. Instead, by selecting an untaken precaution on which to rely, the plaintiff defines the analysis that everyone else will use—including the defendant, the court that will try the case, and any court that may hear an appeal. . . . The plaintiff makes his choice from among a group of possible contenders and frequently alleges several untaken precautions in the alternative. . . .

What untaken precautions might have avoided the injury in *Adams*? What about insulating the wires? Building some sort of umbrella over the wires when they pass under bridges? Posting signs on the approaches to bridges, in language that children would understand, warning of the danger of twirling long wires? Are some of these more promising than others?

2. In *Braun*, cited by Judge Cardozo, defendant had strung electric wires some 25 feet above a vacant lot. The wires had been strung around 1890 with insulation that was expected to last three years. They were never inspected. Fifteen years later, a building was begun on the lot. When joists reached over 20 feet from the ground, it would be "natural for one desiring to go from one side of the building to the other to raise the wires so that he could pass under or bear down on them so that he could step over." The decedent, a carpenter, came in contact with the now-exposed wires and was electrocuted. After the lower courts dismissed the complaint, the court of appeals reversed and remanded for trial. Discussing negligence, the court observed:

> Little need or can be said about the condition of the wires, for if the respondent owed any obligation whatever of making them safe it would scarcely have been more negligent if, instead of allowing them to

remain uninspected and unrepaired as it did, it had strung and maintained absolutely naked wires. The only question which is at all close is whether the respondent in the exercise of the reasonable care and foresight should have apprehended that the premises over which the wires were strung might be so used as to bring people in contact with them, and whether, therefore, it should have guarded against such a contingency. As indicated, I think this was fairly a question for the jury. Here was a vacant lot in the midst of a thickly built-up section of a large city. It was no remote or country lot where no buildings could be expected. The neighboring land was covered with buildings. It was the only vacant lot in the vicinity. It fronted on a street and there was plenty of space for a building. Now, what was reasonably to be anticipated—that this lot would be allowed indefinitely to lie unimproved and unproductive, or that it, like other surrounding lots, would be improved by additions to the old building or by the erection of new and independent ones? Was it to be anticipated that its use would be an exception to the rule prevailing in the entire neighborhood or that it would be in conformity therewith? It seems to me that the answer to these questions should have been made by the jury, and that the latter would be justified in saying that the respondent was bound to anticipate what was usual rather than that which was exceptional and act accordingly. It does not appear how much this neighborhood may have changed since the wires were first strung, but assuming that it had materially changed in respect of the use of lots for buildings, such a change in a neighborhood for aught that appears in this case requires some time, and as a basis for responsibility it is not too much to charge a company stringing such wires with notice of gradual changes in the locality through which the wires pass.

Is *Braun* distinguishable from *Adams*?

3. In Greene v. Sibley, Lindsay & Curr Co., 177 N.E. 416 (N.Y.1931), plaintiff was waiting for her change after making a purchase in defendant's store. She noticed, to her right, a mechanic and a floorwalker repairing a cash register. She turned left to get her change and then moved to her right and stumbled over the protruding foot of the mechanic who had just knelt to look at the underside of the register. Plaintiff testified that she had meant to go around the spot where she had seen the mechanic. Judge Cardozo, writing for the five-member majority, ruled that she had failed to establish negligence on the mechanic's part, despite a trial court judgment in her favor and an affirmance by the appellate division:

Looking back at the mishap with the wisdom born of the event, we can see that the mechanic would have done better if he had given warning of the change of pose. Extraordinary prevision might have whispered to him at the moment that the warning would be helpful. What the law exacted of him, however, was only the ordinary prevision to be looked for in a busy world. He was doing a common and simple act in the plain sight of those around him. The act did not involve a continuing obstruction with the indefinite possibilities of mischief that permanence implies. [   ] It was a matter of minutes or perhaps seconds. A saleswoman who had knocked a package off a counter or a customer dropping a handbag or a glove might have done the same thing. If the kneeling mechanic gave any thought to the plaintiff standing at his side, he must have known that she had seen him at work upon his job. Was he to suppose that she would act as if he were still standing there erect when to his knowledge a mere glance would have told her something else?

How might the judge respond to the claim that a warning from the mechanic would have taken almost no effort? Why not call this a "needless" risk of harm created by the mechanic?

4. What result in *Adams v. Bullock* if the same thing had happened twice in recent years? How important is it that "no like accident had occurred before"?

5. How is the concept of "ordinary caution" or "reasonable care" referred to in *Adams* and the note cases, conveyed to the jury? Consider the following version recommended for use in California (BAJI 8th ed., 1994, § 3.10): *instructions given to jury:*

> Negligence is the doing of something which a reasonably prudent person would not do, or the failure to do something which a reasonably prudent person would do, under circumstances similar to those shown by the evidence.

> It is the failure to use ordinary or reasonable care.

> Ordinary or reasonable care is that care which persons of ordinary prudence would use in order to avoid injury to themselves or others under circumstances similar to those shown by the evidence.

Does this formulation capture the spirit of these cases?

The formulation suggests two questions that need to be pursued in greater detail. First, is the concept too general to be used effectively by courts and juries? Second, how do the courts construct the "reasonably prudent person" referred to in the charge? We turn to these questions in order.

First, is it feasible to establish a calculus of risk—a more structured approach to the due care inquiry? Consider the approach to defining unreasonable risk suggested by Judge Learned Hand in the following case.

United States v. Carroll Towing Co.
United States Court of Appeals, Second Circuit, 1947.
159 F.2d 169.

[The harbormaster and a deckhand aboard the Carroll, a tug, readjusted the lines holding fast the Anna C, a barge owned by plaintiff Connors, in the course of their efforts to "drill out" another barge in New York Harbor. Because of their negligence in securing the Anna C, it later broke loose and rammed against a tanker, whose propeller broke a hole near the bottom of the barge. The Anna C soon filled with water and sank, with loss of cargo (owned by the United States) as well as the vessel itself. In this part of the case, Connors was trying to recover the value of its barge from Carroll. Carroll sought to reduce damages pursuant to admiralty law because the plaintiff's bargee was absent from the Anna C. The evidence indicated that siphoning efforts by other boats present in the area would have kept the barge afloat if the bargee had been aboard to sound a warning. The trial judge, as fact finder, reduced the damage recovery of Connors.]

Before L. HAND, CHASE and FRANK, CIRCUIT JUDGES.

L. HAND, CIRCUIT JUDGE.

.   .   .

It appears from the foregoing review that there is no general rule to determine when the absence of a bargee or other attendant will make the owner of the barge liable for injuries to other vessels if she breaks away from her moorings.   .   .   . It becomes apparent why there can be no such general rule, when we consider the grounds for such a liability. Since there are occasions when every vessel will break from her moorings, and since, if she does, she becomes a menace to those about her, the owner's duty, as in other similar situations, to provide against resulting injuries is a function of three variables: (1) The probability that she will break away; (2) the gravity of the resulting injury, if she does; (3) the burden of adequate precautions. Possibly it serves to bring this notion into relief to state it in algebraic terms: if the probability be called P; the injury, L; and the burden, B; liability depends upon whether B is less than L multiplied by P: i.e., whether $B < PL$. Applied to the situation at bar, the likelihood that a barge will break from her fasts and the damage she will do, vary with the place and time; for example, if a storm threatens, the danger is greater; so it is, if she is in a crowded harbor where moored barges are constantly being shifted about. On the other hand, the barge must not be the bargee's prison, even though he lives aboard; he must go ashore at times. We need not say whether, even in such crowded waters as New York Harbor a bargee must be aboard at night at all, it may be that the custom is otherwise .   .   . and that, if so, the situation is one where custom should control. We leave that question open; but we hold that it is not in all cases a sufficient answer to a bargee's absence without excuse, during working hours, that he has properly made fast his barge to a pier, when he leaves her. In the case at bar the bargee left at five o'clock in the afternoon of January 3rd, and the flotilla broke away at about two o'clock in the afternoon of the following day, twenty-one hours afterwards. The bargee had been away all the time, and we hold that his fabricated story was affirmative evidence that he had no excuse for his absence. At the locus in quo—especially during the short January days and in the full tide of war activity—barges were being constantly "drilled" in and out. Certainly it was not beyond reasonable expectation that, with the inevitable haste and bustle, the work might not be done with adequate care. In such circumstances we hold—and it is all that we do hold—that it was a fair requirement that the Conners Company should have a bargee aboard (unless he had some excuse for his absence), during the working hours of daylight.

[The court affirmed the reduction of damages.]

Notes and Questions

1. Consider the following comments by Richard Posner on the *Carroll Towing* formula in A Theory of Negligence, 1 J.Legal Stud. 29, 32–33 (1972):

It is time to take a fresh look at the social function of liability for negligent acts. The essential clue, I believe, is provided by Judge Learned Hand's famous formulation of the negligence standard—one of the few attempts to give content to the deceptively simple concept of ordinary care. . . . [The formulation] never purported to be original but was an attempt to make explicit the standard that the courts had long applied. In a negligence case, Hand said, the judge (or jury) should attempt to measure three things: the magnitude of the loss if an accident occurs; the probability of the accident's occurring; and the burden of taking precautions that would avert it. If the product of the first two terms exceeds the burden of precautions, the failure to take those precautions is negligence. Hand was adumbrating, perhaps unwittingly, an economic meaning of negligence. Discounting (multiplying) the cost of an accident if it occurs by the probability of occurrence yields a measure of the economic benefit to be anticipated from incurring the costs necessary to prevent the accident. The cost of prevention is what Hand meant by the burden of taking precautions against the accident. It may be the cost of installing safety equipment or otherwise making the activity safer, or the benefit forgone by curtailing or eliminating the activity. If the cost of safety measures or of curtailment—whichever cost is lower—exceeds the benefit in accident avoidance to be gained by incurring that cost, society would be better off, in economic terms, to forgo accident prevention. A rule making the enterprise liable for the accidents that occur in such cases cannot be justified on the ground that it will induce the enterprise to increase the safety of its operations. When the cost of accidents is less than the cost of prevention, a rational profit-maximizing enterprise will pay tort judgments to the accident victims rather than incur the larger cost of avoiding liability. Furthermore, overall economic value or welfare would be diminished rather than increased by incurring a higher accident-prevention cost in order to avoid a lower accident cost. If, on the other hand, the benefits in accident avoidance exceed the costs of prevention, society is better off if those costs are incurred and the accident averted, and so in this case the enterprise is made liable, in the expectation that self-interest will lead it to adopt the precautions in order to avoid a greater cost in tort judgments.

Is Posner correct in attributing a strictly economic definition of negligence to Hand? On this score, why does Hand consider it relevant that the bargee must be expected to go ashore at times? Why isn't the question simply how much it would cost the barge owner to hire a second bargee? Similarly, why should the "customary" night-time hours of bargees be relevant? Again, isn't the cost of adequate precaution—hiring a second bargee—the only relevant consideration from an economic standpoint? The role of custom in negligence cases is considered in greater detail later in this Chapter.

2. Is the *Carroll Towing* formula useful in determining whether particular conduct is negligent? How would the formulation apply to *Adams?* To *Braun?* To *Greene?* Does *Greene* (the kneeling mechanic case) present distinct difficulties in applying the *Carroll Towing* formula because it involves a claim of careless *personal behavior,* rather than an allegation of unreasonable business judgment—as in the other cases? Is this a meaningful distinction? Which type of case is *Carroll Towing?* Even in a "business judgment" case such as *Adams,* how would Cardozo have responded to the argument that a warning notice on the bridge would have involved a trivial expense? Should a court assess the cost of such a warning—let alone the kneeling mechanic's "cost"—in purely economic terms? As far as the usefulness of the formula is concerned, should it make a difference that *Carroll Towing* involved property damage and all the other cases involved personal harm?

3. Note Posner's comment that the Hand test was not meant to state a new principle for deciding negligence cases. Compare Chicago, Burlington & Quincy R. Co. v. Krayenbuhl, 91 N.W. 880 (Neb.1902), in which a group of children were playing on the railroad's unlocked turntable. As other children were rotating the turntable, plaintiff's leg got caught and was severed. The court discussed due care in the following terms:

> The business of life is better carried forward by the use of dangerous machinery; hence the public good demands its use, although occasionally such use results in the loss of life or limb. It does so because the danger is insignificant, when weighed against the benefits resulting from the use of such machinery, and for the same reason demands its reasonable, most effective and unrestricted use, up to the point where the benefits resulting from such use no longer outweigh the danger to be anticipated from it. At that point the public good demands restrictions. For example, a turntable is a dangerous contrivance, which facilitates railroading; the general benefits resulting from its use outweigh the exceptional injuries inflicted by it: hence the public good demands its use. We may conceive of means by which it might be rendered absolutely safe, but such means would so interfere with its beneficial use that the danger to be anticipated would not justify their adoption; therefore the public good demands its use without them. But the danger incident to its use may be lessened by the use of a lock which would prevent children, attracted to it, from moving it; the interference with the proper use of the turntable occasioned by the use of such a lock is so slight that it is outweighed by

[handwritten margin note: a lock would do public good]

the danger to be anticipated from an omission to use it; therefore the public good, we think, demands the use of the lock.

4. In McCarty v. Pheasant Run, Inc., 826 F.2d 1554 (7th Cir.1987), plaintiff guest was assaulted in her room at defendant's resort by an intruder who entered by a sliding glass door. The door, which opened onto a walkway, had not been locked but the security chain had been fastened. The plaintiff's theories of negligence included that the defendant should have made sure the door was locked before renting the room, or should have warned her to keep the door locked; or should have equipped the door with a better lock; or should have had more security guards on duty; or should have made the walkway inaccessible to the rooms; or some combination of these things.

After a jury verdict for defendant, plaintiff moved for judgment notwithstanding the verdict. The trial court's denial of the motion was affirmed on appeal. The court, in an opinion by Judge Posner, observed that:

> Ordinarily, and here, the parties do not give the jury the information required to quantify the variables that the Hand Formula picks out as relevant. That is why the formula has greater analytic than operational significance. Conceptual as well as practical difficulties in monetizing personal injuries may continue to frustrate efforts to measure expected accident costs with the precision that is possible, in principle at least, in measuring the other side of the equation—the cost or burden of precaution. [ ] For many years to come juries may be forced to make rough judgments of reasonableness, intuiting rather than measuring the factors in the Hand Formula; and so long as their judgment is reasonable, the trial judge has no right to set it aside, let alone substitute his own judgment.

Judge Hand was even less sanguine about ever knowing or valuing the factors. In Moisan v. Loftus, 178 F.2d 148 (2d Cir.1949), observed, in a case in which a car ran off the road, that of the three factors,

> care is the only one ever susceptible of quantitative estimate, and often that is not. The injuries are always a variable within limits, which do not admit of even approximate ascertainment; and, although probability might theoretically be estimated, if any statistics were available, they never are; and, besides, probability varies with the severity of the injuries. It follows that all such attempts are illusory; and, if serviceable at all, are so only to center attention upon which one of the factors may be determinative in any given situation.

Is this observation sound? Is it significant that this case, unlike *Carroll Towing*, involved personal injury? Does the growing availability of statistics since 1949 change matters?

5. Why not charge the jury in Learned Hand terms? In Gilles, The Invisible Hand Formula, 80 Va.L.Rev. 1016 (1994), the author argues that the Hand formula is "to a significant extent, an unjustifiably underenforced norm." He suggests that the formula can be utilized—without the need for explicit reference—by "comparison between the value the average injurer would assign to precaution costs and the value the average victim would assign to the expected accident costs eliminated by the precaution. Because the average injurer and the average victim, taken together, constitute the average person, the inquiry reduces to whether the average person would take the precaution if he or she bore both the costs and benefits in full." Would this be a useful aid to decisionmaking by the jury?

6. Mark Grady has identified what he refers to as a pocket of strict liability within the negligence rule, based on the fact that "people face a cost of consistent performance that is higher than the sum of the cost of all individual trials." He offers the following illustration:

> It is impossible to drive a car for any period of time without missing a required precaution. There is evidently a special cost of consistent performance, and people respond to this cost by trying to establish for themselves an efficient rate of error which is (hopefully) low. Nevertheless, in most situations judges do not recognize the special cost of consistency. They assess a penalty for every miss, even for those that must be efficient judging from the way reasonable people behave.

Grady refers to this type of negligence, linked to the impossibility of driving—or engaging in any high-repetition precautionary behavior—without an occasional lapse as "compliance error," which he distinguishes from the Learned Hand formula negligence that tends to involve the quality of performance rather than high-repetition situations. Does the distinction make sense? Does it in fact appear to reflect a "pocket of strict liability" within the negligence concept? See Grady, Res Ipsa Loquitur and Compliance Error, 142 U.Pa.L.Rev. 887 (1994).

7. Another perspective on defining reasonable care is suggested in the following excerpt from the concurring opinion of Lord Reid in Bolton v. Stone, [1951] A.C. 850. A visiting team member drove the ball out of the defendant's cricket field on to a relatively untraveled road that had a few houses on the far side. Plaintiff happened to be standing in that road near her house and was injured when the ball hit her. In 28 years six balls had been driven over the field's fence, but no one had been hurt before. The House of Lords unanimously held that the risk was so small that the defendant club might reasonably disregard it. In his response to plaintiff's claim that at least after a ball had once gone over the fence defendants had a duty to prevent a recurrence, Lord Reid observed:

> Once a ball has been driven on to a road without there being anything extraordinary to account for the fact, there is clearly a risk that another will follow, and if it does there is clearly a chance, small though it may be, that someone may be injured. On the theory that it is foreseeability alone that matters it would be irrelevant to consider how often a ball might be expected to land in the road and it would not matter whether the road was the busiest street, or the quietest country lane; the only difference between these cases is in the degree of risk.

It would take a good deal to make me believe that the law has departed so far from the standards which guide ordinary careful people in ordinary life. In the crowded conditions of modern life even the most careful person cannot avoid creating some risks and accepting others. What a man must not do, and what I think a careful man tries not to do, is to create a risk which is substantial.   .   .   . In my judgment the test to be applied here is whether the risk of damage to a person on the road was so small that a reasonable man in the position of the appellants, considering the matter from the point of view of safety, would have thought it right to refrain from taking steps to prevent the danger.

In considering that matter I think that it would be right to take into account not only how remote is the chance that a person might be struck but also how serious the consequences are likely to be if a person is struck; but I do not think that it would be right to take into account the difficulty of remedial measures. If cricket cannot be played on a ground without creating a substantial risk, then it should not be played there at all.

Is Lord Reid's argument persuasive? Why isn't the risk a "needless" one as that term was used in *Adams?* On the other hand, why does he say that in cases of "substantial risk" it would not be "right to take into account the difficulty of remedial measures?" Is he suggesting that one who exposes another to a substantial risk is always negligent for doing so? Do either the Cardozo opinions or Judge Hand's formula suggest any such threshold of harm?

We turn now to the second matter noted above—the construction of the "reasonably prudent person."

2.   THE REASONABLE PERSON

Bethel v. New York City Transit Authority

Court of Appeals of New York, 1998.
92 N.Y.2d 348, 703 N.E.2d 1214, 681 N.Y.S.2d 201.

LEVINE, Judge.

Over a century ago this Court adopted its version of the rule which came to prevail at the time in almost all state jurisdictions, imposing the duty upon common carriers of "the exercise of the *utmost* care, *so far as human skill and foresight can go*," for the safety of their passengers in transit (Kelly v. Manhattan Ry. Co., 112 N.Y. 443, 450 [1889] [emphasis supplied]).   .   .   .

.   .   .

We granted leave to appeal in this case to confront directly whether a duty of highest care should continue to be applied, as a matter of law, to common carriers and conclude that it should not. We thus realign the standard of care required of common carriers with the traditional, basic negligence standard of reasonable care under the circumstances. Under that standard, there is no stratification of degrees of care as a matter of law [   ]. Rather, "there are only different amounts of care as a matter of fact" [   ].

Facts: [Plaintiff was hurt on defendant's bus when the "wheelchair accessible seat" collapsed under him. Plaintiff could not prove that defendant actually knew of the defect but relied on a theory of constructive notice "evidenced by a computer printout repair record of Bus No. 2209, containing two notations that, 11 days before the accident, repairs (adjustment and alignment) were made to a 'Lift Wheelchair.' Plaintiff contended that the repairs to the 'Lift Wheelchair' were to the seat in question, and that a proper inspection during those repairs would have revealed the defect causing the seat to collapse 11 days later."]

The court charged the jury that, as a common carrier, "[t]he bus company here . . . had a duty to use the highest degree of care that human prudence and foresight can suggest in the maintenance of its vehicles and equipment for the safety of its passengers" [   ]. On the issue of constructive notice, arising out of the earlier inspection and repair, the trial court submitted to the jury the question of whether "considering *the duty of care that is imposed on common carriers with respect to this equipment,* a reasonable inspection would have led to the discovery of the condition and its repair" before the accident (emphasis supplied). *Issue*

[The jury found for plaintiff on the constructive notice theory and the Appellate Division affirmed without addressing the issue of standard of care. The court of appeals concluded that the instruction was the "dispositive issue" on appeal.]

History: The duty of common carriers to exercise the highest degree of care . . . was widely adopted at the advent of the age of steam railroads in 19th century America. Their primitive safety features resulted in a phenomenal growth in railroad accident injuries and with them, an explosion in personal injury litigation, significantly affecting the American tort system [   ]. In this century, however, through technological advances and intense governmental regulation, "public conveyances . . . have become at least as safe as private modes of travel" [   ].

Time has also disclosed the inconsistency of the carrier's duty of extraordinary care with the fundamental concept of negligence in tort doctrine.

> "The whole theory of negligence presupposes some uniform standard of behavior. Yet the infinite variety of situations which arise makes it impossible to fix definite rules in advance for all conceivable human conduct. . . . The standard of conduct which the community demands must be an external and objective one, rather than the individual judgment, good or bad, of the particular actor. . . . The courts have dealt with this very difficult problem by creating a fictional person . . . the 'reasonable [person] of ordinary prudence' " (Prosser and Keeton, Torts § 32, at 173–174 [5th ed]).

. . .

The objective, reasonable person standard in basic traditional negligence theory, however, necessarily takes into account the circumstances with which the actor was actually confronted when the accident occurred, including the reasonably perceivable risk and gravity of harm to others and any special relationship of dependency between the victim and the actor.

"The [reasonable person] standard provides sufficient flexibility, and leeway, to permit due allowance to be made . . . for all of the particular circumstances of the case which may reasonably affect the conduct required" (Restatement [Second] of Torts § 283, comment *c*; [ ]).

[The court traced criticisms of the carrier's duty of extraordinary care through a case in 1919, a law review article in 1928, and its own decision in 1950, and concluded that the "single, reasonable person standard is sufficiently flexible by itself to permit courts and juries fully to take into account the ultrahazardous nature of a tortfeasor's activity."]

. . .

For all of the foregoing reasons, we conclude that the rule of a common carrier's duty of extraordinary care is no longer viable. Rather, a common carrier is subject to the same duty of care as any other potential tortfeasor—reasonable care under all of the circumstances of the particular case. Here, because the jury was specifically charged that the defendant carrier was required to exercise "the highest degree of care that human prudence and foresight can suggest" in connection with the issue of its constructive notice of the defective seat, the error cannot be deemed merely harmless.

[The case was remanded for a new trial.]

KAYE, C.J., and BELLACOSA, SMITH, CIPARICK and WESLEY, JJ., concur.

Notes and Questions

1. What was the original justification for the carrier rule? Was it never valid or did it cease to be valid? If the history of steam railroads is the explanation, why was the same rule extended to buses? Is it relevant that passengers have contract relationships with carriers? Is it relevant that passengers still do not know what goes on in bus repair shops? We return to this issue later in the section on proof of negligence. If you were a juror how would the court's change in the law be likely to affect your consideration of whether the Transit Authority was negligent?

2. Are safety concerns satisfied in Stewart v. Motts, 654 A.2d 535 (Pa.1995), involving an accident at an automobile repair shop? Plaintiff appealed an adverse jury verdict on the ground that since the case involved the handling of gasoline the judge should have told the jury that the defendants owed a "high degree of care." The court disagreed, and concluded that the state recognized "only one standard of care in negligence actions involving dangerous instrumentalities—the standard of reasonable

care under the circumstances. It is well established by our case law that the reasonable man must exercise care in proportion to the danger involved in his act. [ ] Thus, when a reasonable man is presented with circumstances involving the use of dangerous instrumentalities, he must necessarily exercise a 'higher' degree of care proportionate to the danger.'' Since the trial judge had told the jury that the care required had to be "in keeping with the degree of danger involved," the charge given was adequate.

Compare Wood v. Groh, 7 P.3d 1163, 269 Kan. 436 (Kans. 2000), in which plaintiff was accidentally shot with defendant's gun fired by his 15-year-old son. The son had used a screwdriver to open his father's locked gun cabinet and had removed the unloaded gun as well as ammunition. The claim was that defendant was responsible for the removal and injury. The trial judge gave an ordinary negligence charge and the jury found for the defendant. Plaintiff appealed on the ground that the judge should have charged that defendant owed "the highest degree of care in safekeeping the handgun." The court agreed:

> We have concluded that the parents in this case owed the highest duty to protect the public from the misuse of the gun, a dangerous instrumentality, stored in their home. The fact that the gun was not loaded is insignificant, for the ammunition was kept in the same locked cabinet. Once access to the gun was obtained, access to the ammunition immediately followed. Storage of the ammunition in the same location as the gun in this case resulted in the gun being easily loaded and made it a dangerous instrumentality.

Although the father kept the cabinet locked, retained the key on his person at all times, and told the son not to take the gun without supervision, the court noted that the son needed only a screwdriver to obtain the gun and the ammunition. On the question of prejudice, the court stated that there was "a real possibility that the jury would have returned a different verdict had the correct standard been given." Why was the original charge erroneous? What reason is there to think that the jury would have reached a different result if given a different charge? Under the due care standard would the jury, in connection with the father's behavior, consider different factors than under the "highest degree" standard?

3. As *Bethel* indicates, courts traditionally have utilized a hypothetical person whose conduct is taken to measure what is reasonable under the circumstances—recall the court's use of an "external and objective" standard. Consider the following description from 3 F. Harper, F. James, Jr. and O. Gray, The Law of Torts, pp. 389–90 (2d ed. 1986):

> § 16.2. General formula: Reasonable person; The external as against the subjective standard. We come next to inquire into the nature of the standard below which conduct must not fall if it is to avoid being negligence. This is ordinarily measured by what the reasonably prudent person would do in the circumstances. As everyone knows, this reasonable person is a creature of the law's imagination. He is an abstraction. He has long been the subject of homely phrase and witty epigram. He is no man who has ever lived and is not to be identified

with any of the parties nor with any member of the jury. Greer, L.J., has described him as " 'the man in the street,' or 'the man in the Clapham omnibus,' or, as I recently read in an American author, 'the man who takes the magazines at home, and in the evening pushes the lawn mower in his shirt sleeves.' "

Now this reasonably prudent person is not infallible or perfect. In foresight, caution, courage, judgment, self-control, altruism and the like he represents, and does not excel, the general average of the community. He is capable of making mistakes and errors of judgment, of being selfish, of being afraid—but only to the extent that any such shortcoming embodies the normal standard of community behavior. On the other hand the general practice of the community, in any given particular, does not necessarily reflect what is careful. The practice itself may be negligent. "Neglect of duty does not cease by repetition to be neglect of duty." Thus the standard represents the general level of moral judgment of the community, what it feels ought ordinarily to be done, and not necessarily what is ordinarily done, although in practice the two would very often come to the same thing.

Is "the general level of moral judgment of the community" necessarily the same as "the general average of the community"?

4. As the section heading from Harper, James and Gray suggests, the authors subsequently discuss the question whether reasonable care should be based on an external standard or the defendant's own capacity for care. In fact, the reasonable care inquiry raises two threshold questions. The first is whether the salient measuring stick of due care is the conduct or the state of mind of the defendant. The second—if defendant's conduct is the determining factor—is whether it is to be measured against the defendant's own capacity or against an external standard. Employing a reasonable person test suggests, of course, that defendant's conduct is the critical determinant, and that the conduct is to be measured against external, "objective" norms, rather than "subjective" ability. In adopting this two-fold external standard, the legal system adheres to a definition of "fault" that is arguably at odds with our everyday usage of the term. Is the approach justifiable?

5. Might the content of the reasonable person influence views on the wisdom of the court's approach in *Bethel*? Consider the approach that Justice Holmes explored in an excerpt from The Common Law 108–110 (1881):

The standards of the law are standards of general application. The law takes no account of the infinite varieties of temperament, intellect, and education which make the internal character of a given act so different in different men. It does not attempt to see men as God sees them, for more than one sufficient reason. In the first place, the impossibility of nicely measuring a man's powers and limitations is far clearer than that of ascertaining his knowledge of law, which has been thought to account for what is called the presumption that every man knows the law. But a more satisfactory explanation is that, when men live in society, a certain average of conduct, a sacrifice of individual peculiarities going beyond a certain point, is necessary to the general welfare. If, for instance, a man is born hasty and awkward, is always having accidents and hurting himself or his neighbors, no doubt his congenital defects will be allowed for in the courts of Heaven, but his slips are no less troublesome to his neighbors than if they sprang from guilty neglect. His neighbors accordingly require him, at his proper peril, to come up to their standard, and the courts which they establish decline to take his personal equation into account.

The rule that the law does, in general, determine liability by blameworthiness, is subject to the limitation that minute differences of character are not allowed for. The law considers, in other words, what would be blameworthy in the average man, the man of ordinary intelligence and prudence, and determines liability by that. If we fall below the level in those gifts, it is our misfortune; so much as that we must have at our peril, for the reasons just given. But he who is intelligent and prudent does not act at his peril, in theory of law. On the contrary, it is only when he fails to exercise the foresight of which he is capable, or exercises it with evil intent, that he is answerable for the consequences.

There are exceptions to the principle that every man is presumed to possess ordinary capacity to avoid harm to his neighbors, which illustrate the rule, and also the moral basis of liability in general. When a man has a distinct defect of such a nature that all can recognize it as making certain precautions impossible, he will not be held answerable for not taking them. A blind man is not required to see at his peril; and although he is, no doubt, bound to consider his infirmity in regulating his actions, yet if he properly finds himself in a certain situation, the neglect of precautions requiring eyesight would not prevent his recovering for an injury to himself, and, it may be presumed, would not make him liable for injuring another. So it is held that, in cases where he is the plaintiff, an infant of very tender years is only bound to take the precautions of which an infant is capable; the same principle may be cautiously applied where he is defendant. Insanity is a more difficult matter to deal with, and no general rule can be laid down about it. There is no doubt that in many cases a man may be insane, and yet perfectly capable of taking the precautions, and of being influenced by the motives, which the circumstances demand. But if insanity of a pronounced type exists, manifestly incapacitating the sufferer from complying with the rule which he has broken, good sense would require it to be admitted as an excuse.

Taking the qualification last established in connection with the general proposition previously laid down, it will now be assumed that, on the one hand, the law presumes or requires a man to possess ordinary capacity to avoid harming his neighbors, unless a clear and manifest incapacity be shown; but that, on the other, it does not in general hold him liable for unintentional injury, unless, possessing such capacity, he might and ought to have foreseen the danger, or, in other words, unless a man of ordinary intelligence and forethought would have been to blame for acting as he did.   .   .   .

Notwithstanding the fact that the grounds of legal liability are moral to the extent above explained, it must be borne in mind that law only works within the sphere of the senses. If the external phenomena, the manifest acts and omissions, are such as it requires, it is wholly indifferent to the internal phenomena of conscience. A man may have as bad a heart as he chooses, if his conduct is within the rules. In other words, the standards of the law are external standards, and, however much it may take moral considerations into account, it does so only for the purpose of drawing a line between such bodily motions and rests as it permits, and such as it does not. What the law really forbids, and the only thing it forbids, is the act on the wrong side of the line, be that act blameworthy or otherwise.   .   .   .

6. *Gender.* In the preceding passages from both Harper, James and Gray, and Holmes, as in tort discourse generally until recent years, gender references regarding reasonable conduct, among other issues, were pervasively male in content; indeed, the "reasonable man" standard was the established reference point. Whether this masculine orientation translated into favorable or unfavorable treatment of female litigants in tort cases is, of course, a separate question. References to the gender/tort literature can be found in M. Schlanger, Injured Women Before Common Law Courts, 1860–1930, 21 Harvard Women's L.J. 79 (1998), a study of the judicial treatment of female litigants in three categories of transportation injury cases. In an earlier study of fright-based claims, Chamallas and Kerber, Women, Mothers, and the Law of Fright: A History, 88 Mich. L.Rev. 814 (1990), the authors remarked, "[t]hat recognizing difference may lead to marginalization, while ignoring difference may lead to inequitable results, has long been the Scylla and Charybdis of feminist theory. A major goal of feminist theory is to find a route past these monsters: first, by being skeptical of conceptual dualisms enshrined in familiar cultural and legal practice, and second, by unmasking claims of difference to reveal unstated norms against which difference is judged."

In the following notes we explore several of the themes raised by the Holmes excerpt.

7. *Mentalability.* In the leading case of Vaughan v. Menlove, 3 Bing. N.C. 468, 132 Eng.Rep. 490 (1837), the defendant landowner piled hay in a way that created a fire hazard to neighbors, including plaintiff. A fire occurred and plaintiff sued and won. Defendant's attorney sought a new trial on the ground that instead of charging the standard of ordinary prudence, the judge should have asked the jury to decide whether defendant had acted to the best of his judgment. He emphasized that since the "measure of prudence varies so with the varying faculties of men," it was impossible to say what was negligence "with reference to the standard of what is called ordinary prudence." Perhaps alluding delicately to his client's limitation, the attorney urged that if the defendant had acted to the best of his judgment "he ought not to be responsible for the misfortune of not possessing the highest order of intelligence." The court unanimously rejected the argument on the ground that "it would leave so vague a line as to afford no rule at all, the degree of judgment belonging to each individual being infinitely various."

Is the court's position persuasive? Should cases of distinctive physical handicap—such as blindness, the example used by Holmes—be measured by a standard that takes defendant's disability into account (presumably the reasonable blind person)? Is the problem of degree likely to be manageable in the physical handicap situation?

8. In Roberts v. Ramsbottom, [1980] 1 All E.R. 7 (Q.B.1979), the judge found that the 73-year-old defendant had suffered a stroke a few minutes before setting out on a drive; that he had experienced no previous warnings or symptoms; that though his consciousness was impaired he was in sufficient possession of his faculties "(i) to have some, though an impaired, awareness of his surroundings and the traffic conditions and (ii) to make a series of deliberate and voluntary though inefficient movements of his hands and legs to manipulate the controls of his car;" and that the defendant "was at no time aware of the fact that he was unfit to drive; accordingly no moral blame can be attached to him for continuing to do so." After reviewing the English case law, the judge concluded:

> The driver will escape liability if his actions at the relevant time were wholly beyond his control. The most obvious case is sudden unconsciousness. But if he retained some control, albeit imperfect control, and his driving, judged objectively, was below the required standard, he remains liable. His position is the same as a driver who is old or infirm. In my judgment unless the facts establish what the law recognizes as automatism the driver cannot avoid liability on the basis that owing to some malfunction of the brain his consciousness was impaired. Counsel for the plaintiff put the matter accurately, as I see it, when he said "One cannot accept as exculpation anything less than total loss of consciousness."

The judge also accepted the alternative ground of liability based on defendant's failure to realize, after one or two misadventures on the road, that he was unfit to continue driving that day. Had he recognized his condition, he would have stopped driving before he hit the plaintiff's car. Although not morally to blame for failing to realize his inadequacy, the defendant was nonetheless responsible for failing to "appreciate [the] proper significance" of his prior mishaps.

Does *Ramsbottom* suggest that the reasonable person standard applies without considering the deficiencies of the elderly or those with relatively minor handicaps? Should it be otherwise? Is the holding consistent with *Hammontree v. Jenner*, p. 3 supra?

9. In Bashi v. Wodarz, 53 Cal.Rptr.2d 635 (App.1996), defendant rear-ended a car, left the scene without stopping, and shortly thereafter collided with plaintiffs. Defendant claimed to have little recall of the events. The traffic report stated: ". . . Somewhere, shortly after making the turn, she stated, 'I wigged out.' She stated that all she could remember was ramming into the back of someone's vehicle and then continuing east. She had no control of her actions at that time and then she remembered being involved in a second collision at an unknown location on White Lane. She also stated, 'My family has a history of mental problems and I guess I just freaked out.' " Apparently concluding that the ~~plaintiff~~ *defendant* had a "sudden, unanticipated onset of mental illness," the trial judge granted summary judgment for defendants. The court of appeal reversed, noting that California "has approved the rule of Cohen v. Petty (D.C.Cir.1933) 65 F.2d 820, that as between an innocent passenger and an innocent fainting driver, the former must suffer. . . . Under a line of appellate authorities beginning in 1942, these cases generally hold that a driver, suddenly stricken by an illness rendering the driver unconscious, is not chargeable with negligence [citing several cases, including *Hammontree v. Jenner*]."

The defendant argued that California should extend *Cohen* to "sudden and unanticipated mental illness as well as to physical illness." The court declined. In addition to a statute that it thought favored plaintiff, the court noted that Restatement § 283B was in accord: "Unless the actor is a child, his insanity or other mental deficiency does not relieve the actor from liability for conduct which does not conform to the standard of a reasonable man under like circumstances." The court extracted four justifications for the position from a comment to the section:

(1) the "difficulty of drawing any satisfactory line between mental deficiency and those variations of temperament, intellect, and emotional balance which cannot" be considered in imposing liability; (2) the "unsatisfactory character of the evidence of mental deficiency in many cases, together with the ease with which it can be feigned"; (3) "if mental defectives are to live in the world they should pay for the damage they do, and that it is better that their wealth, if any, should be used to compensate innocent victims than that it should remain in their hands"; and (4) the expectation that liability will stimulate "those who have charge of them or their estates . . . to look after them, keep them in order, and see that they do not do harm."

Section 283C of the Second Restatement provides that "[i]f the actor is ill or otherwise physically disabled, the standard of conduct to which he must conform to avoid being negligent is that of a reasonable man under like disability."

A comment notes that "a heart attack, or a temporary dizziness due to fever or nausea, as well as a transitory delirium, are regarded merely as circumstances to be taken into account in determining what the reasonable man would do. The explanation for the distinction between such physical illness and the mental illness dealt with in § 283B probably lies in the greater public familiarity with the former, and the comparative ease and certainty with which it can be proved."

On the facts of *Bashi* which Restatement section applies: 283B or 283C?

10. *Superior attributes.* Section 289(b) provides that the defendant, in addition to exercising the "attention, perception of the circumstances, memory, knowledge of other pertinent matters, intelligence, and judgment" as would a reasonable person, must also exercise such "superior" attributes on the listed items as the "actor himself has." Is this asymmetry fair? Is it sound? Is it consistent with *Bethel*?

11. *Children.* Apart from statutes making parents vicariously liable for malicious mischief committed by their children, usually up to a modest amount, parents are rarely vicariously liable for their children. Parents may, however, be liable for their own negligence in permitting children to do something beyond their ability or in failing to exercise control over a dangerous child.

The narrow scope of vicarious liability has meant that plaintiffs must often sue the child directly. Traditionally, children have been held to the standard of conduct reasonable for persons of their actual age, intelligence, and experience. How might such a standard be applied to a child riding a bicycle or throwing a ball? How should we analyze a case involving a child who is unusually rash? Unusually dull? Unusually forgetful? Why should children be treated differently from adults in applying the standard of reasonableness?

In Mastland, Inc. v. Evans Furniture, Inc., 498 N.W.2d 682 (Iowa 1993), the court identified the following role for the jury in judging acts by children:

> [T]he jury's first inquiry is a subjective one: What was the capacity of this particular child—given what the evidence shows about his age, intelligence and experience—to perceive and avoid the particular risk involved in this case? Once this has been determined, the focus becomes objective: How would a reasonable child of like capacity have acted under similar circumstances? The particular child in question can be found negligent only if his actions fall short of what may reasonably be expected of children of similar capacity.

Is this an intelligible standard? The issue was to be taken from the jury "only if the child is so young or evidence of incapacity so overwhelming that reasonable minds could not differ on that issue." This was such a case because the child was under three years old.

In Ellis v. D'Angelo, 253 P.2d 675 (Cal.App.1953), a four-year-old boy was charged with negligently shoving a babysitter to the floor. The court stated that it was "satisfied from our own common knowledge of the mental development of 4-year-old children that it is proper to hold that they have not at that age developed the mental capacity for foreseeing the possibilities of their inadvertent conduct which would rationally support a finding that they were negligent."

A few states hold that children below the age of 6 or 7 are conclusively presumed to be unable to comprehend risk sufficiently to be held negligent. These states also use a rebuttable presumption for children between 7 and 14. See Price v. Kitsap Transit, 886 P.2d 556 (Wash.1994).

When children engage in adult activities, courts have applied adult standards. In Dellwo v. Pearson, 107 N.W.2d 859 (Minn.1961), involving a twelve-year-old driving a motor boat, the court said:

> While minors are entitled to be judged by standards commensurate with age, experience, and wisdom when engaged in activities appropriate to their age, experience, and wisdom, it would be unfair to the public to permit a minor in the operation of a motor vehicle to observe any other standards of care and conduct than those expected of all others. A person observing children at play with toys, throwing balls, operating tricycles or velocipedes, or engaged in other childhood activities may anticipate conduct that does not reach an adult standard of care or prudence. However, one cannot know whether the operator of an approaching automobile, airplane, or powerboat is a minor or an adult, and usually cannot protect himself against youthful imprudence even if warned. Accordingly, we hold that in the operation of an automobile, airplane, or powerboat, a minor is to be held to the same standard of care as an adult.

Is this sound? *Dellwo* has been especially influential in automobile cases. There is dispute about what activities should be categorized as "adult." In Goss v. Allen, 360 A.2d 388 (N.J.1976), a 17-year-old beginning skier, while attempting to negotiate a turn, collided with plaintiff. The court held that skiing was an activity for persons of all ages and did not qualify as an activity for which minors should be held to an adult standard. The court thought that 18, the age of legal majority, was the appropriate age for holding persons to the adult standard. Although the difference between 17 and 18 was hard to define, the court recognized that no matter what age was selected for adult responsibility the line would seem arbitrary.

What about the fact that defendant was a beginner in *Goss v. Allen*? Should inexperienced persons, regardless of age, be held to a less demanding standard? Apart from other considerations, are the line-drawing problems insurmountable?

In Stevens v. Veenstra, 573 N.W.2d 341 (Mich.App.1997), the court held a 14-year-old student driver taking a driver's education course in the public school system to an adult standard for conduct during his first driving lesson (with an instructor). The court rejected the claim that since this education class was a minor-oriented activity it should not be judged by the adult standard:

> While the process of learning involves unique dangers, for which some allowance may be justified for beginners undertaking some activities, when the probability of, or potential harm associated with, a particular activity is great, anyone engaged in the activity must be held to a certain minimum level of competence, even though that level may lie beyond the capability of a beginner. [ ] In other words, some activities are so dangerous that the risk must be borne by the beginner rather than the innocent victims, and lack of competence is no excuse.

12. *Emergency doctrine.* In Levey v. DeNardo, 725 A.2d 733 (Pa. 1999), defendant rear-ended plaintiff who had to stop suddenly when a car came across her path. Over defendant's objection, the trial judge refused to instruct the jury to judge defendant's conduct under the emergency doctrine—that a person confronting an emergency not of his or her own making, "is required to exhibit only an honest exercise of judgment." Plaintiff's verdict and judgment was reversed because it was reversible error not to give the charge in these circumstances. The purpose of the rule was that a "person confronted with a sudden and unforeseeable occurrence, because of the shortness of time in which to react, should not be held to the same standard of care as someone confronted with a foreseeable occurrence."

An increasing number of states refuse to give an emergency charge in any negligence case. As explained in Lyons v. Midnight Sun Transportation Services, Inc., 928 P.2d 1202 (Alaska 1996):

> We believe that the sudden emergency instruction is a generally useless appendage to the law of negligence. With or without an emergency, the standard of care a person must exercise is still that of a reasonable person under the circumstances. With or without the instruction, parties are still entitled to present evidence at trial which will establish what the circumstances were, and are also entitled to argue to the jury that they acted as a reasonable person would have in light of those circumstances. Thus, barring circumstances that we cannot at the moment hypothesize, a sudden emergency instruction serves no positive function.

Does the defendant have enough ways to show the jury the exigencies of the situation without needing the emergency charge?

———

We turn now to a consideration of factors that sometimes circumscribe the role of juries in determining what constitutes due care. After an initial look at the interplay between judge and jury, we examine the roles of custom and statute.

C. THE ROLES OF JUDGE AND JURY

1. IN GENERAL

Baltimore & Ohio Railroad Co. v. Goodman

Supreme Court of the United States, 1927.
275 U.S. 66, 48 S.Ct. 24, 72 L.Ed. 167.

MR. JUSTICE HOLMES delivered the opinion of the Court.

This is a suit brought by the widow and administratrix of Nathan Goodman against the petitioner for causing his death by running him down at a grade crossing. The defense is that Goodman's own negligence caused the death. At the trial, the defendant asked the Court to direct a verdict for it, but the request, and others looking to the same direction, were refused, and the plaintiff got a verdict and a judgment which was affirmed by the Circuit Court of Appeals. 10 F.2d 58.

Goodman was driving an automobile truck in an easterly direction and was killed by a train running southwesterly across the road at a rate of not less than sixty miles an hour. The line was straight, but it is said by the respondent that Goodman "had no practical view" beyond a section house two hundred and forty-three feet north of the crossing until he was about twenty feet from the first rail, or, as the respondent argues, twelve feet from danger, and that then the engine was still obscured by the section house. He had been driving at the rate of ten or twelve miles an hour, but had cut down his rate to five or six miles at about forty feet from the crossing. It is thought that there was an emergency in which, so far as appears, Goodman did all that he could.

We do not go into further details as to Goodman's precise situation, beyond mentioning that it was daylight and that he was familiar with the crossing, for it appears to us plain that nothing is suggested by the evidence to relieve Goodman from responsibility for his own death. When a man goes upon a railroad track he knows that he goes to a place where he will be killed if a train comes upon him before he is clear of the track. He knows that he must stop for the train, not the train stop for him. In such circumstances it seems to us that if a driver cannot be sure otherwise whether a train is dangerously near he must stop and get out of his vehicle, although obviously he will not often be required to do more than to stop and look. It seems to us that if he relies upon not hearing the train or any signal and takes no further precaution he does so at his own risk. If at the last moment Goodman found himself in an emergency it was his own fault that he did not reduce his speed earlier or come to a stop. It is true as said in Flannelly v. Delaware & Hudson Co., 225 U.S. 597, 603, that the question of due care very generally is left to the jury. But we are dealing with a standard of conduct, and when the standard is clear it should be laid down once for all by the Courts. [   ]

Judgment reversed.

Notes and Questions

1.   Under the *Goodman* view, when would plaintiffs win grade crossing cases?

2.   Almost a half-century before *Goodman*, Holmes stated his position on the role of the jury in negligence cases in The Common Law (at pp. 123–24):

> When a case arises in which the standard of conduct, pure and simple, is submitted to the jury, the explanation is plain. It is that the court, not entertaining any clear views of public policy applicable to the

matter, derives the rule to be applied from daily experience, as it has been agreed that the great body of the law of tort has been derived. But the court further feels that it is not itself possessed of sufficient practical experience to lay down the rule intelligently. It conceives that twelve men taken from the practical part of the community can aid its judgment. Therefore it aids its conscience by taking the opinion of the jury.

But supposing a state of facts often repeated in practice, is it to be imagined that the court is to go on leaving the standard to the jury forever? Is it not manifest, on the contrary, that if the jury is, on the whole, as fair a tribunal as it is represented to be, the lesson which can be got from that source will be learned? Either the court will find that the fair teaching of experience is that the conduct complained of usually is or is not blameworthy, and therefore, unless explained, is or is not a ground of liability; or it will find the jury oscillating to and fro, and will see the necessity of making up its mind for itself. . . .

If this be the proper conclusion in plain cases, further consequences ensue. Facts do not often exactly repeat themselves in practice; but cases with comparatively small variations from each other do. A judge who has long sat at *nisi prius* ought gradually to acquire a fund of experience which enables him to represent the common sense of the community in ordinary instances far better than an average jury. He should be able to lead and to instruct them in detail, even where he thinks it desirable, on the whole, to take their opinion. Furthermore, the sphere in which he is able to rule without taking their opinion at all should be continually growing.

Do these arguments justify his position in *Goodman*?

Pokora v. Wabash Railway Co.

Supreme Court of the United States, 1934.
292 U.S. 98, 54 S.Ct. 580, 78 L.Ed. 1149.

[Pokora was driving his truck west across four tracks of defendant's railroad. The easternmost track was a switch track and the one next to that was the main track. A string of boxcars standing on the switch track 5–10 feet north of the crossing cut off plaintiff's view of the track north. As he moved past that track he listened but heard no bell or whistle. As he reached the main track he was struck by a train coming from the north at 25–30 miles per hour. The distance between the western rail of the switch track and the eastern rail of the main track was 8 feet, but 2–3 feet were lost to the overhang of the boxcars. Although there was no showing how far from the front of the truck Pokora was sitting, the opinion suggests "perhaps five feet or even more." Although a view 130 feet north may have been available from a nearby point, the opinion notes that this would not protect plaintiff if the train was 150 feet away when Pokora looked. "For all that appears, he had no view of the main track northward, or none for a substantial distance, till the train was so near that escape had been cut off." Relying on *Goodman,* the court of appeals had upheld a directed verdict for the railroad.]

MR. JUSTICE CARDOZO delivered the opinion of the Court.

. . .

In such circumstances the question, we think, was for the jury whether reasonable caution forbade his going forward in reliance on the sense of hearing, unaided by that of sight. No doubt it was his duty to look along the track from his seat, if looking would avail to warn him of the danger. This does not mean, however, that if vision was cut off by obstacles, there was negligence in going on, any more than there would have been in trusting to his ears if vision had been cut off by the darkness of the night. [ ] Pokora made his crossing in the day time, but like the traveler by night he used the faculties available to one in his position. [ ] A jury, but not the court, might say that with faculties thus limited, he should have found some other means of assuring himself of safety before venturing to cross. The crossing was a frequented highway in a populous city. Behind him was a line of other cars, making ready to follow him. To some extent, at least, there was assurance in the thought that the defendant would not run its train at such a time and place without sounding bell or whistle. . . .

The argument is made, however, that our decision in [*Goodman*], is a barrier in the plaintiff's path, irrespective of the conclusion that might commend itself if the question were at large. There is no doubt that the opinion in that case is correct in its result. Goodman, the driver, traveling only five or six miles an hour, had, before reaching the track, a clear space of eighteen feet within which the train was plainly visible.[2] With that opportunity, he fell short of the legal standard of duty established for a traveler when he failed to look and see. This was decisive of the case. But the court did not stop there. It added a remark, unnecessary upon the facts before it, which has been a fertile source of controversy. "In such circumstances it seems to us that if a driver cannot be sure otherwise whether a train is dangerously near he must stop and get out of his vehicle, although obviously he will not often be required to do more than to stop and look."

. . .

Standards of prudent conduct are declared at times by courts, but they are taken over from the facts of life. To get out of a vehicle and reconnoitre is an uncommon precaution, as everyday experience informs us. Besides being uncommon, it is very likely to be futile, and sometimes even dangerous. If the driver leaves his vehicle when he nears a cut or curve, he will learn nothing by getting out about the perils that lurk beyond. By the time he regains his seat and sets his car in motion, the hidden train may be upon him. [ ] Often the added safeguard will be dubious though the track happens to be straight, as it seems that this one was, at all events as far as

---

2. For a full statement of the facts, see the opinion of the Circuit Court of Appeals,   10 F.2d 58, 59.

the station, about five blocks to the north. A train traveling at a speed of thirty miles an hour will cover a quarter of a mile in the space of thirty seconds. It may thus emerge out of obscurity as the driver turns his back to regain the waiting car, and may then descend upon him suddenly when his car is on the track. Instead of helping himself by getting out, he might do better to press forward with all his faculties alert. So a train at a neighboring station, apparently at rest and harmless, may be transformed in a few seconds into an instrument of destruction. At times the course of safety may be different. One can figure to oneself a roadbed so level and unbroken that getting out will be a gain. Even then the balance of advantage depends on many circumstances and can be easily disturbed. Where was Pokora to leave his truck after getting out to reconnoitre? If he was to leave it on the switch, there was the possibility that the box cars would be shunted down upon him before he could regain his seat. The defendant did not show whether there was a locomotive at the forward end, or whether the cars were so few that a locomotive could be seen. If he was to leave his vehicle near the curb, there was even stronger reason to believe that the space to be covered in going back and forth would make his observations worthless. One must remember that while the traveler turns his eyes in one direction, a train or a loose engine may be approaching from the other.

Illustrations such as these bear witness to the need for caution in framing standards of behavior that amount to rules of law. The need is the more urgent when there is no background of experience out of which the standards have emerged. They are then, not the natural flowerings of behavior in its customary forms, but rules artificially developed, and imposed from without. Extraordinary situations may not wisely or fairly be subjected to tests or regulations that are fitting for the common-place or normal. In default of the guide of customary conduct, what is suitable for the traveler caught in a mesh where the ordinary safeguards fail him is for the judgment of a jury. [   ] The opinion in Goodman's case has been a source of confusion in the federal courts to the extent that it imposes a standard for application by the judge, and has had only wavering support in the courts of the states. We limit it accordingly.

The judgment should be reversed and the cause remanded for further proceedings in accordance with this opinion.

Notes and Questions

1. Under the *Pokora* view, is it ever proper to take cases from the jury on the issues of negligence and contributory negligence? Is Justice Cardozo's opinion consistent with his opinions in *Adams* and *Greene?*

2. Plaintiff was hit in the eye by a foul ball while watching a high school baseball game. Her suit against the school district, which owned the field, was dismissed, 4–3. Akins v. Glens Falls City School District, 424 N.E.2d 531 (N.Y.1981). The majority noted that the field was equipped with a backstop 24 feet high and 50 feet wide located 60 feet behind home plate. Seats for 120 adults and standing room for others were behind the backstop. In addition, two chain link fences, three feet high, ran from each end of the backstop along the baselines to a point 60 feet behind first and third bases. Plaintiff, who arrived while the game was in progress, stood along the third base line, 10 to 15 feet past the end of the backstop. She was hit ten minutes after arriving.

The majority held that there was no basis for a jury to find defendant negligent. Although "what constitutes reasonable care under the circumstances ordinarily is a question for the jury," not every case is for the jury. On the record here, "the school district fulfilled its duty of reasonable care to plaintiff as a matter of law and, therefore, no question of negligence remained for the jury's consideration."

The dissenters argued that the majority had engaged in "an unfortunate exercise in judicial rule making in an area that should be left to the jury. This attempt to precisely prescribe what steps the proprietor of a baseball field must take to fulfill its duty of reasonable care is unwarranted and unwise." They found the majority's opinion "reminiscent" of the effort in *Goodman* to impose a specific duty on drivers at grade crossings:

> The wisdom of eschewing such blanket rules where negligence is concerned is obvious. In the present context, the majority has held as a matter of law that the proprietor of the baseball field has fulfilled his duty of reasonable care by erecting a backstop that was 24 feet high and 50 feet wide. The court issues this rule with no more expertise available to it than Justice Holmes had in 1927. . . . It has selected one of a variety of forms of protection currently in use . . . and has designated it as sufficient protection as a matter of law.

The dissent thought it "would make as much sense for the court to decree, as a matter of law, what sort of batting helmet or catcher's mask a school district should supply to its baseball team. Baseball . . . is hardly immune from technological change and shifts in public perception of what constitute reasonable safety measures. It has traditionally been the jury that reflects these shifts and changes."

3. Plaintiff was getting her hair bleached in defendant's hairdressing salon. During a break, while plaintiff had absorbent cotton in her hair, she lit a cigarette. The cotton caught fire and she was injured. Her suit claimed that the hairdresser should have warned her about the danger of smoking. The trial court entered judgment on a jury verdict for plaintiff. The appellate division unanimously reversed. The Court of Appeals, in turn, reversed, 4–3. The majority stated:

> It cannot be said, as a matter of law, that [the hairdresser] was not negligent in failing to warn the plaintiff of the dangers of smoking while she was undergoing the complicated hair treatment which he had applied. It was within the province of the jury to determine that he had failed to act upon a risk which was foreseeable to him.

As to contributory negligence, "it was also within the province of the jury, taking into account the positions of the respective parties, to determine that the risk was unforeseeable to her.'' Heller v. Encore of Hicksville, Inc., 421 N.E.2d 824 (N.Y.1981).

Does the fact that the judges disagree necessarily indicate, in itself, that a jury question exists? What about the fact that eight judges (five in the appellate division and three in the Court of Appeals) voted that no liability exists, while only five (the trial judge and four in the Court of Appeals) found a jury question?

If the jury had returned a verdict for the defendant which was upheld by the trial judge, what arguments would plaintiff have had to make on appeal?

4. Although motions for summary judgment and for directed verdicts are usually made by defendants in negligence cases, plaintiffs occasionally make such motions. In Andre v. Pomeroy, 320 N.E.2d 853 (N.Y.1974), plaintiff daughter was a passenger in a car driven by defendant mother. Defendant, who ran into the car in front of her, admitted that she was driving in heavy traffic, that she knew a car was in front of her, but that she nonetheless took her eyes off the road to look down into her purse. When she looked back at the road, she found that she was too close to the car in front, which had either stopped or slowed significantly, and she could not avoid it.

The court approved granting plaintiff summary judgment as to liability, 4–3. The majority stated that plaintiffs are entitled to such relief ''only in cases in which there is no conflict at all in the evidence [and] the defendant's conduct fell far below any permissible standard of due care. . . .''

When the negligence is so clear, why would plaintiff risk appeal and reversal of a motion for summary judgment instead of relying on the jury?

Andrews v. United Airlines, Inc.

United States Court of Appeals, Ninth Circuit, 1994.
24 F.3d 39.

Before: FLETCHER, KOZINSKI and TROTT, CIRCUIT JUDGES.

KOZINSKI, CIRCUIT JUDGE.

We are called upon to determine whether United Airlines took adequate measures to deal with that elementary notion of physics—what goes up, must come down. For, while the skies are friendly enough, the ground can be a mighty dangerous place when heavy objects tumble from overhead compartments.

I

During the mad scramble that usually follows hard upon an airplane's arrival at the gate, a briefcase fell from an overhead compartment and seriously injured plaintiff Billie Jean Andrews. No one knows who opened the compartment or what caused the briefcase to fall, and Andrews doesn't claim that airline personnel were involved in stowing the object or opening the bin. Her claim, rather, is that the injury was foreseeable and the airline didn't prevent it.

The district court dismissed the suit on summary judgment, and we review de novo. [   ] This is a diversity action brought in California, whose tort law applies. [   ]

II

The parties agree that United Airlines is a common carrier and as such "owe[s] both a duty of utmost care and the vigilance of a very cautious person towards [its] passengers." Acosta v. Southern Cal. Rapid Transit Dist., 2 Cal. 3d 19, 27 (1970); [   ]. Though United is "responsible for any, even the slightest, negligence and [is] required to do all that human care, vigilance, and foresight reasonably can do under all the circumstances," [   ], it is not an insurer of its passengers' safety, [   ]. "[T]he degree of care and diligence which [it] must exercise is only such as can reasonably be exercised consistent with the character and mode of conveyance adopted and the practical operation of [its] business.   .   .   ." [   ]

To show that United did not satisfy its duty of care toward its passengers, Ms. Andrews presented the testimony of two witnesses. The first was Janice Northcott, United's Manager of Inflight Safety, who disclosed that in 1987 the airline had received 135 reports of items falling from overhead bins. As a result of these incidents, Ms. Northcott testified, United decided to add a warning to its arrival announcements, to wit, that items stored overhead might have shifted during flight and passengers should use caution in opening the bins. This announcement later became the industry standard.

Ms. Andrews's second witness was safety and human factors expert Dr. David Thompson, who testified that United's announcement was ineffective because passengers opening overhead bins couldn't see objects poised to fall until the bins were opened, by which time it was too late. Dr. Thompson also testified that United could have taken additional steps to prevent the hazard, such as retrofitting its overhead bins with baggage nets, as some airlines had already done, or by requiring passengers to store only light-weight items overhead [though—as the court noted in a footnote—Dr. Thompson "recognized that this was not a very practical solution from either the airlines' or the passengers' point of view"].

United argues that Andrews presented too little proof to satisfy her burden [   ]. One hundred thirty-five reported incidents, United points out, are trivial when spread over the millions of passengers travelling on its 175,000 flights every year. Even that number overstates the problem, according to United, because it includes events where passengers merely observed items falling from overhead bins but no one was struck or injured. Indeed, United sees the low incidence of injuries as incontrovertible proof that the safety measures suggested by plaintiff's expert would not merit the additional cost and inconvenience to airline passengers.

III

It is a close question, but we conclude that plaintiff has made a sufficient case to overcome summary judgment. United is hard-pressed to dispute that its passengers are subject to a hazard from objects falling out of overhead bins, considering the warning its flight crews give hundreds of times each day. The case then turns on whether the hazard is serious enough to warrant more than a warning. Given the heightened duty of a common carrier, [   ], even a small risk of serious injury to passengers may form the basis of liability if that risk could be eliminated "consistent with the character and mode of [airline travel] and the practical operation of [that] business. . . ." [   ] United has demonstrated neither that retro-fitting overhead bins with netting (or other means) would be prohibitively expensive, nor that such steps would grossly interfere with the convenience of its passengers. Thus, a jury could find United has failed to do "all that human care, vigilance, and foresight reasonably can do under all the circumstances." [   ]

The reality, with which airline passengers are only too familiar, is that airline travel has changed significantly in recent years. As harried travelers try to avoid the agonizing ritual of checked baggage, they hand-carry more and larger items—computers, musical instruments, an occasional deceased relative. [   ] The airlines have coped with this trend, but perhaps not well enough. Given its awareness of the hazard, United may not have done everything technology permits and prudence dictates to eliminate it. See Treadwell v. Whittier, 80 Cal. 574, 600 (1889)("common carriers . . . must keep pace with science, art, and modern improvement"); Valente v. Sierra Ry., 151 Cal. 534, 543 (1907)(common carriers must use the best precautions in practical use "known to any company exercising the utmost care and diligence in keeping abreast with modern improvement in . . . such precautions").

Jurors, many of whom will have been airline passengers, will be well equipped to decide whether United had a duty to do more than warn passengers about the possibility of falling baggage. A reasonable jury might conclude United should have done more; it might also find that United did enough. Either decision would be rational on the record presented to the district court which, of course, means summary judgment was not appropriate.

Reversed and Remanded.

Notes and Questions

1. On occasion, legislatures have enacted statutes using such terms as gross negligence, recklessness, or wilfulness—and courts have occasionally developed such notions themselves. One legislative example is the "guest statute"—a once-common provision that required guests in cars to prove that their drivers were more than negligent in order to recover any damages. We consider recklessness and wilfulness at p. 437, infra. Until then, we shall concern ourselves with the basic negligence formulation of reasonable care. In this regard, can the phrase "utmost care," used in *Andrews,* be squared with *Bethel?*

2. How would the analysis differ if an airline employee had stowed the bag in the compartment or had opened the compartment at the end of the trip? See Brosnahan v. Western Air Lines, Inc., 892 F.2d 730 (8th Cir.1989), holding that a jury might find airline personnel negligent in failing to adequately supervise the boarding process during which a passenger dropped his carry-on bag on another passenger's head while attempting to stow it in the overhead compartment. See also USAir, Inc. v. United States Dept. of the Navy, 14 F.3d 1410 (9th Cir.1994), holding that a passenger (and his employer) might be held liable for negligently stowing in the overhead compartment a briefcase that fell and hurt another passenger.

3. Why does the court demand that United demonstrate that "retrofitting overhead bins with netting . . . would be prohibitively expensive" or that such steps "would grossly interfere with the convenience of its passengers"? If we assume that 35 of the 135 incidents in 1987 involved no harm whatever and that the other 100 involved 60 bruised bodies, 30 broken bones and 10 serious brain damage cases, might that affect the analysis?

4. How would the case differ if the plaintiff's claim had been that the bottom part of the baggage compartment should have been made of transparent material?

5. One quoted passage demands that carriers "must keep pace with science, art, and modern improvement." How does that obligation differ from what is expected of any reasonable company? Another quotation states the duty in terms of what practical steps are "known to any company." Does that imply that if no company knew of a practical step to avoid the harm there would be no liability? These matters are addressed in the next section.

2. THE ROLE OF CUSTOM

Trimarco v. Klein

Court of Appeals of New York, 1982.
56 N.Y.2d 98, 436 N.E.2d 502, 451 N.Y.S.2d 52.

[Plaintiff tenant was very badly cut when he fell through the glass door that enclosed his tub in defendant's apartment building. The door turned out to be ordinary thin glass that looked the same as the tempered glass that plaintiff thought it was. The building had been built, and the shower installed, in 1953.

Plaintiff presented expert evidence that at least since the 1950s a practice of using shatterproof glass in bathroom enclosures had come into common use, so that by 1976, the date of the accident, "the glass door here no longer conformed to accepted safety standards." Defendant's managing agent admitted that, at least since 1965, it had been "customary for landlords who had occasion to install glass for shower enclosures, whether to replace broken glass or to comply with the request of a tenant or otherwise, to do so with 'some material such as plastic or safety glass.' "

The jury awarded plaintiff damages. A divided appellate division reversed the plaintiff's judgment. Even if there was "a custom and usage at the time to substitute shatterproof glass" and even if that was a "better way or a safer method of enclosing showers," there was no common-law duty on the defendant to replace the glass unless prior notice of the danger had come to the defendants either from the plaintiff or by reason of a similar accident in the building. Since plaintiff had made no such showing, the appellate division majority reversed and dismissed the case.

The dissenters in the appellate division observed that in the 1,000-page trial record there was ample showing that landlords generally had known of the danger of ordinary glass for more than ten years before this accident. The dissenters saw no need for specific notice to this landlord either by prior accident in the building or by personal request from the plaintiff.]

FUCHSBERG, JUDGE.

. . .

Which brings us to the well-recognized and pragmatic proposition that when "certain dangers have been removed by a customary way of doing things safely, this custom may be proved to show that [the one charged with the dereliction] has fallen below the required standard" (Garthe v. Ruppert, 264 N.Y. 290, 296 [1934]). Such proof, of course, is not admitted in the abstract. It must bear on what is reasonable conduct under all the circumstances, the quintessential test of negligence.

It follows that, when proof of an accepted practice is accompanied by evidence that the defendant conformed to it, this may establish due care (Bennett v. Long Is. R.R. Co., 163 N.Y. 1, 4 [1900] [custom not to lock switch on temporary railroad siding during construction]), and, contrariwise, when proof of a customary practice is coupled with a showing that it was ignored and that this departure was a proximate cause of the accident, it may serve to establish liability (Levine v. Russell Blaine Co., 273 N.Y. 386, 389 [1937] [custom to equip dumbwaiter with rope which does not splinter]). Put more conceptually, proof of a common practice aids in "formulat[ing] the general expectation of society as to how individuals will act in the course of their undertakings, and thus to guide the common sense or expert intuition of a jury or commission when called on to judge particular conduct under particular circumstances" (Pound, Administrative Application of Legal Standards, 44 ABA Rep. 445, 456–457).

The source of the probative power of proof of custom and usage is described differently by various authorities, but all agree on its potency. Chief among the rationales offered is, of course, the fact that it reflects the judgment and experience and conduct of many [   ]. Support for its relevancy and reliability comes too from the direct bearing it has on feasibility, for its focusing is on the practicality of a precaution in actual operation and the readiness with which it can be employed (Morris, Custom and Negligence,

42 Col.L.Rev. 1147, 1148). Following in the train of both of these boons is the custom's exemplification of the opportunities it provides to others to learn of the safe way, if that the customary one be. [   ].

From all this it is not to be assumed customary practice and usage need be universal. It suffices that it be fairly well defined and in the same calling or business so that "the actor may be charged with knowledge of it or negligent ignorance" [   ].

However, once its existence is credited, a common practice or usage is still not necessarily a conclusive or even a compelling test of negligence [   ]. Before it can be, the jury must be satisfied with its reasonableness, just as the jury must be satisfied with the reasonableness of the behavior which adhered to the custom or the unreasonableness of that which did not (see Shannahan v. Empire Eng. Corp., 204 N.Y. 543, 550 [1912]). After all, customs and usages run the gamut of merit like everything else. That is why the question in each instance is whether it meets the test of reasonableness. As Holmes' now classic statement on this subject expresses it, "[w]hat usually is done may be evidence of what ought to be done, but what ought to be done is fixed by a standard of reasonable prudence, whether it usually is complied with or not" (Texas & Pacific Ry. Co. v. Behymer, 189 U.S. 468, 470 [1903]).

So measured, the case the plaintiff presented . . . was enough to send it to the jury and to sustain the verdict reached. The expert testimony, the admissions of the defendant's manager, the data on which the professional and governmental bulletins were based, the evidence of how replacements were handled by at least the local building industry for the better part of two decades, these in the aggregate easily filled that bill. Moreover, it was also for the jury to decide whether, at the point in time when the accident occurred, the modest cost and ready availability of safety glass and the dynamics of the growing custom to use it for shower enclosures had transformed what once may have been considered a reasonably safe part of the apartment into one which, in the light of later developments, no longer could be so regarded.

Furthermore, the charge on this subject was correct. The Trial Judge placed the evidence of custom and usage "by others engaged in the same business" in proper perspective, when, among other things, he told the jury that the issue on which it was received was "the reasonableness of the defendant's conduct under all the circumstances." He also emphasized that the testimony on this score was not conclusive, not only by saying so but by explaining that "the mere fact that another person or landlord may have used a better or safer practice does not establish a standard" and that it was for the jurors "to determine whether or not the evidence in this case does establish a general custom or practice."

[The court reversed the dismissal but ordered a new trial because the trial judge had erroneously admitted certain evidence that had hurt the defense.]

CHIEF JUDGE COOKE and JUDGES JASEN, GABRIELLI, JONES, WACHTLER and MEYER concur.

Notes and Questions

1. How did the proof of custom affect the plaintiff's case in *Trimarco?*

2. Recall that in *Carroll Towing*, p. 41 supra, Judge Hand observed that it "may be that the custom" in New York Harbor was not to have bargees on board ships at night and that, if so, it may be that "the situation is one where custom should control." Why might custom establish the standard of care? Although the court did not reach that question, Judge Hand had stated the basic proposition about the role of custom in an earlier case, The T.J. Hooper, 60 F.2d 737 (2d Cir.), cert. denied 287 U.S. 662 (1932). In that case, a tug plying the Atlantic coast sank in a storm, causing the loss of barges it was towing and their cargoes. If the tug had had a radio it would have learned about the storm in time to avoid it. The tug owner sought to make the alleged lack of radios on most tugs the standard of care. Judge Hand observed that some court pronouncements might be read to say that general practice sets the standard. He continued:

> Indeed in most cases reasonable prudence is in fact common prudence; but strictly it is never its measure; a whole calling may have unduly lagged in the adoption of new and available devices. It never may set its own tests, however persuasive be its usages. Courts must in the end say what is required; there are precautions so imperative that even their universal disregard will not excuse their omission. But here there was no custom at all as to receiving sets; some had them; some did not; the most that can be urged is that they had not yet become general. Certainly in such a case we need not pause; when some have thought a device necessary, at least we may say that they were right, and the others too slack.

Except in malpractice cases, courts have rejected the argument that a prevailing custom defines the standard of care. The malpractice situation is discussed at p. 109, infra.

3. Even if prevailing custom does not set the standard of care, adherence to, and deviation from, custom may be important in deciding whether the actor has behaved reasonably.

A defendant who can prove that it has adhered to a prevailing custom may eliminate what might otherwise be a jury question. In a classic article, Morris, Custom and Negligence, 42 Colum.L.Rev. 1147 (1942), the author suggested that such proof alerts the trial court to three main points. First, if an industry adheres to a single way of doing something, the court may be wary of plaintiff's assertion that there are safer ways to do that thing—and may insist that plaintiff clearly demonstrate the feasibility of the asserted alternative. Second, even if the plaintiff can show a feasible alternative, the fact that it may not have been in use anywhere may suggest that it was not unreasonable for the defendant to be unaware of the possibility. Third, the existence of a custom that involves large fixed costs may warn the court of the social impact of a jury or court decision that determines the custom to be unreasonable.

4.   In LaVallee v. Vermont Motor Inns, Inc., 569 A.2d 1073 (Vt.1989), plaintiff guest fell in his room during a power outage at defendant's motel. He claimed that the motel was negligent in that it knew about past power failures, had flashlights at the front desk, had emergency lighting in the hallways, and that "inexpensive battery-powered lighting fixtures were available at the time of the accident and could have been installed in the motel rooms. The trial court concluded that this evidence, even if true, was insufficient as a matter of law to show that the motel owner had failed to exercise ordinary care to the plaintiff." The grant of a directed verdict was upheld on appeal. Even though power failures had occurred in the past, no guest had been hurt during an outage. The defendant's general manager had testified, without contradiction, that in his ten years in the industry "I've never seen emergency lighting in a motel room." The court's total discussion of custom was as follows:

> In [directing a verdict] the trial court appropriately considered evi-
> dence of the motel industry's practice and custom [   ], noting that no
> witness knew of any motel or hotel that provided the sort of emergency
> lighting that plaintiff claims defendant had a duty to provide.   .   .   .
> While industry custom is not conclusive in any given case, it is a useful
> guide, unless it is apparent that under the particular circumstances of
> the case a reasonable person would not conform to the industry-wide
> custom.

What if the cost were $1 per unit?

5.   On the other hand, as Professor Morris pointed out, a plaintiff will find it useful to prove that the defendant fell below the industry custom because it tends to show that others, usually competitors, found it feasible to do something in a safer manner than did the defendant; that the defendant had ample opportunity to learn about the alternative; and that no great social upheaval will follow a judicial determination that the defendant's failure to follow custom was negligence.

In *Levine v. Russell Blaine Co.*, cited in *Trimarco*, plaintiff cut her hand on a rough rope while operating a dumbwaiter. Infection led to amputation of her arm. She sought to show that the defendant building owner had failed to follow the custom of using smooth ropes in dumbwait-ers. The court held that if plaintiff could show that the purpose of the customary use of smooth rope was to avoid such injuries, the evidence of custom was admissible.

6.   Note that the plaintiff can achieve some of these goals simply by proving that others in the industry, although not establishing a custom, have developed safer techniques than did defendant. In *Garthe v. Ruppert*, cited in *Trimarco*, plaintiff slipped on a wet brewery floor. In an effort to show that it was feasible to keep the floors dry, plaintiff sought to show that, although most breweries had slippery floors, one local brewery had a technique that kept floors from getting slippery. The court held that such evidence was inadmissible because it had never "been permitted to take one or two instances as a gauge or guide in place of the custom of the trade." But this evidence might have been relevant if the defendant had tried to argue that it had no way of learning about the techniques that plaintiff claimed it should have used.

In *Andrews*, p. 64 supra, plaintiff's evidence showed that British Airways had begun using restraining netting the year before plaintiff was hurt. What is the significance of the fact that one other airline used baggage nets? Would the plaintiff necessarily have lost if she had been hurt the month before British Airways began using the baggage nets—even if she had proven that such nets were economically and technically feasible? How might the analysis have changed if the plaintiff had proven that more than two thirds of all American carriers used baggage nets at the time of the accident?

7. Should evidence of deviation from custom be usable against a company that is barely profitable—and which would have been unable to continue operations had it made the expenditures necessary to bring it into conformity? If the larger members of an industry follow a custom, should evidence be admitted showing that smaller companies engaged in the same line of business deviate from that custom?

8. Stagl v. Delta Air Lines, Inc., 117 F.3d 76 (2d Cir.1997), involved a passenger hurt at defendant's baggage carousel. At the trial, the judge excluded testimony from a mechanical engineer who was prepared to testify for plaintiff about appropriate conditions at baggage carousels. On appeal from a defense verdict and judgment, the court reversed. After noting that liability may exist even if plaintiff can point to no previous similar accident, the court turned to the admissibility of the expert's testimony:

> In determining whether an expert is sufficiently knowledgeable to be admitted to testify, one of the factors that the district court ought to consider is whether other experts exist who are more specifically qualified and who are nonetheless not in the employ of the company or industry whose practices are being challenged. If the only experts permitted to testify inevitably represent the same side of a civil case, those who possess these experts can, for all practical purposes, set their own standards. And allowing an industry to do this is improper because it is very similar to what has long since been held inappropriate, namely, letting the custom of an industry or trade define what is reasonable in that trade.

The court then reviewed the engineer's qualifications and his admission that he had no expertise in the design of baggage claim areas. He was however, an expert in "the interaction between machines and people." Testimony about that interaction was "directly relevant to Delta's possible negligence in this case. Moreover, such testimony would most likely be beyond the knowledge of an average juror" and thus be helpful. "It is hard to imagine an expert in airport terminal design or baggage claim systems who developed that expertise in any way other than by working for the airline industry. Accordingly, to require the degree of specificity the [trial] court imposed came perilously close to letting that industry indirectly set its own standards. At times this cannot be avoided. But where, as here, well-trained people with somewhat more general qualifications are available, it is error to exclude them.''

9. We consider the role of expert witnesses on scientific and technical questions in greater detail in Chapter V.

3. THE ROLE OF STATUTES

Martin v. Herzog

Court of Appeals of New York, 1920.
228 N.Y. 164, 126 N.E. 814.

CARDOZO, J. The action is one to recover damages for injuries resulting in death.

Plaintiff and her husband, while driving toward Tarrytown in a buggy on the night of August 21, 1915, were struck by the defendant's automobile coming in the opposite direction. They were thrown to the ground, and the man was killed. At the point of the collision the highway makes a curve. The car was rounding the curve when suddenly it came upon the buggy, emerging, the defendant tells us, from the gloom. Negligence is charged against the defendant, the driver of the car, in that he did not keep to the right of the center of the highway (Highway Law, sec. 286, subd. 3; sec. 332; Consol.Laws, ch. 25). Negligence is charged against the plaintiff's intestate, the driver of the wagon, in that he was traveling without lights (Highway Law, sec. 329a, as amended by L.1915, ch. 367). There is no evidence that the defendant was moving at an excessive speed. There is none of any defect in the equipment of his car. The beam of light from his lamps pointed to the right as the wheels of his car turned along the curve toward the left; and looking in the direction of the plaintiff's approach, he was peering into the shadow. The case against him must stand therefore, if at all, upon the divergence of his course from the center of the highway. The jury found him delinquent and his victim blameless. The Appellate Division reversed, and ordered a new trial.

We agree with the Appellate Division that the charge to the jury was erroneous and misleading. The case was tried on the assumption that the hour had arrived when lights were due. It was argued on the same assumption in this court. In such circumstances, it is not important whether the hour might have been made a question for the jury [ ]. A controversy put out of the case by the parties is not to be put into it by us. We say this by way of preface to our review of the contested rulings. In the body of the charge the trial judge said that the jury could consider the absence of light "in determining whether the plaintiff's intestate was guilty of contributory negligence in failing to have a light upon the buggy as provided by law. I do not mean to say that the absence of light necessarily makes him negligent, but it is a fact for your consideration." The defendant requested a ruling that the absence of a light on the plaintiff's vehicle was "*prima facie* evidence of contributory negligence." This request was refused, and the jury were again instructed that they might consider the absence of lights as some evidence of negligence, but that it was not conclusive evidence. The plaintiff then requested a charge that "the fact that the plaintiff's intestate was driving without a light is not negligence in itself," and to this the court acceded. The defendant saved his rights by appropriate exceptions.

We think the unexcused omission of the statutory signals is more than some evidence of negligence. It *is* negligence in itself. Lights are intended for the guidance and protection of other travelers on the highway (Highway Law, sec. 329a). By the very terms of the hypothesis, to omit, willfully or heedlessly, the safeguards prescribed by law for the benefit of another that he may be preserved in life or limb, is to fall short of the standard of diligence to which those who live in organized society are under a duty to conform. That, we think, is now the established rule in this state. [   ] Whether the omission of an absolute duty, not willfully or heedlessly, but through unavoidable accident, is also to be characterized as negligence, is a question of nomenclature into which we need not enter, for it does not touch the case before us. There may be times, when if jural niceties are to be preserved, the two wrongs, negligence and breach of statutory duty, must be kept distinct in speech and thought [   ]. In the conditions here present they come together and coalesce .   .   .

In the case at hand, we have an instance of the admitted violation of a statute intended for the protection of travelers on the highway, of whom the defendant at the time was one. Yet the jurors were instructed in effect that they were at liberty in their discretion to treat the omission of lights either as innocent or as culpable. They were allowed to "consider the default as lightly or gravely" as they would (Thomas, J., in the court below). They might as well have been told that they could use a like discretion in holding a master at fault for the omission of a safety appliance prescribed by positive law for the protection of a workman [   ]. Jurors have no dispensing power by which they may relax the duty that one traveler on the highway owes under the statute to another. It is error to tell them that they have. The omission of these lights was a wrong, and being wholly unexcused was also a negligent wrong. No license should have been conceded to the triers of the facts to find it anything else.

[At this point Judge Cardozo concluded that the jury could well have found that the absence of the light was causally related to the accident. This portion of the case is reprinted at p. 359, infra.]

We are persuaded that the tendency of the charge and of all the rulings following it, was to minimize unduly, in the minds of the triers of the facts, the gravity of the decedent's fault. Errors may not be ignored as unsubstantial when they tend to such an outcome. A statute designed for the protection of human life is not to be brushed aside as a form of words, its commands reduced to the level of cautions, and the duty to obey attenuated into an option to conform.

The order of the Appellate Division should be affirmed, and judgment absolute directed on the stipulation in favor of the defendant, with costs in all courts.

HISCOCK, CH. J., POUND, MCLAUGHLIN, ANDREWS and ELKUS, JJ., concur with CARDOZO, J.; HOGAN, J., reads dissenting opinion [in which he viewed the record as indicating no causal relation between the plaintiff's violation and the crash.—Eds.]

Notes and Questions

1. Plaintiff's stipulation for judgment absolute, mentioned in the final paragraph, meant that if the appellate court found that the plaintiff's judgment could not be reinstated she would not pursue the case. Plaintiff stipulated because the court of appeals would generally review only final judgments. This stipulation made it possible for plaintiff to get a definitive ruling on the critical issue without first having another trial and appeal.

2. On the question of the husband's negligence what did the trial judge charge? What did the defendant ask the trial judge to charge? What does Judge Cardozo say the trial judge should have charged? What distinguishes these formulations? What are the respective roles of the judge and the jury under each view?

3. What kind of penalties do you think the legislature provided for crossing the center line and traveling without lights after dark? Should it matter whether they linked the violation of such requirements to civil liability in personal injury cases? If the legislature failed to do so, why does the court get involved with these statutes at all?

4. In Clinkscales v. Carver, 136 P.2d 777 (Cal.1943), defendant ran a stop sign and crashed into plaintiff. The stop sign had been erected under an ordinance that had never become effective because it had not been properly published, which meant that defendant could not be punished criminally for his action. He argued that this made it improper for the trial judge to use the ordinance in his charge. Justice Traynor, writing for the majority, upheld the charge and the plaintiff's judgment:

Whatever the effect of the irregularity on defendant's criminal liability, it cannot be assumed that the conditions that limit it also limit civil liability. The propriety of taking from the jury the determination of negligence does not turn on defendant's criminal liability. A statute that provides for a criminal proceeding only does not create a civil liability; if there is no provision for a remedy by civil action to persons injured by a breach of the statute it is because the Legislature did not contemplate one. A suit for damages is based on the theory that the conduct inflicting the injuries is a common-law tort. . . . The decision as to what the civil standard should be still rests with the court, and the standard formulated by a legislative body in a police regulation or criminal statute becomes the standard to determine civil liability only because the court accepts it. In the absence of such a standard the case goes to the jury, which must determine whether the defendant has acted as a reasonably prudent man would act in similar circumstances. The jury then has the burden of deciding not only what the facts are but what the unformulated standard is of reasonable conduct. When a legislative body has generalized a standard from the experience of the community and prohibits conduct that is likely to cause harm, the court accepts the formulated standards and applies them [   ] except where they would serve to impose liability without fault. [   ]

Is this consistent with *Martin v. Herzog*?

5.   Section 286 of the Second Restatement provides:

The court may adopt as the standard of conduct of a reasonable man the requirements of a legislative enactment or an administrative regulation whose purpose is found to be exclusively or in part (a) to protect a class of persons which includes the one whose interest is invaded, and (b) to protect the particular interest which is being invaded, and (c) to protect that interest against the kind of harm which has resulted, and (d) to protect that interest against the particular hazard from which the harm results.

In Sweet v. Sisters of Providence in Washington, 895 P.2d 484 (Alaska 1995), the court noted that even if the criteria of § 286 are met, the trial judge "retains discretion to refuse to adopt the law as the standard of care. [   ] For example, rejection of the legislative enactment is appropriate when the law is so obscure, unknown, outdated, or arbitrary as to make its adoption as a standard of reasonable care inequitable." Why should this be so? Are all four reasons equally persuasive?

Tedla v. Ellman

Court of Appeals of New York, 1939.
280 N.Y. 124, 19 N.E.2d 987.

[Two junk collectors, brother and sister, were walking eastward along Sunrise Highway, a major route connecting New York City and Long Island. There were no sidewalks and they could not use the grass center strip because they were transporting junk in baby carriages that would have gotten mired in the soft ground. A 1933 statute provided:

Pedestrians walking or remaining on the paved portion, or traveled part of a roadway shall be subject to, and comply with, the rules governing vehicles, with respect to meeting and turning out, except that such pedestrians shall keep to the left of the center line thereof, and turn to their left instead of right side thereof, so as to permit all vehicles passing them in either direction to pass on their right. Such pedestrians shall not be subject to the rules governing vehicles as to giving signals.

It was Sunday night and "very heavy traffic" was heading westbound back to New York City but there were "very few cars going east." The two were

walking eastward on the edge of the eastbound lane when they were hit
from behind by defendant's car. The trial judge entered judgment on a
plaintiffs' verdict and the appellate division affirmed. On this appeal the
defendant does not contest his negligence, but argues that both pedestrians
were contributorily negligent as a matter of law.]

LEHMAN, J.

. . .

. . . The appellants lean heavily upon [*Martin v. Herzog*] and kin-
dred cases and the principle established by them.

The analogy is, however, incomplete. The "established rule" should
not be weakened either by subtle distinctions or by extension beyond its
letter or spirit into a field where "by the very terms of the hypothesis" it
can have no proper application. At times the indefinite and flexible standard of care of the traditional reasonably prudent man may be, in the
opinion of the Legislature, an insufficient measure of the care which should
be exercised to guard against a recognized danger; at times, the duty,
imposed by custom, that no man shall use what is his to the harm of others
provides insufficient safeguard for the preservation of the life or limb or
property of others. Then the Legislature may by statute prescribe additional safeguards and may define duty and standard of care in rigid terms; and
when the Legislature has spoken, the standard of the care required is no
longer what the reasonably prudent man would do under the circumstances
but what the Legislature has commanded. That is the rule established by
the courts and "by the very terms of the hypothesis" the rule applies where
the Legislature has prescribed safeguards "for the benefit of another that
he may be preserved in life or limb." In that field debate as to whether the
safeguards so prescribed are reasonably necessary is ended by the legislative fiat. Obedience to that fiat cannot add to the danger, even assuming
that the prescribed safeguards are not reasonably necessary and where the
legislative anticipation of dangers is realized and harm results through
heedless or willful omission of the prescribed safeguard, injury flows from
wrong and the wrongdoer is properly held responsible for the consequent
damages.

The statute upon which the defendants rely is of different character. It
does not prescribe additional safeguards which pedestrians must provide
for the preservation of the life or limb or property of others, or even of
themselves, nor does it impose upon pedestrians a higher standard of care.
What the statute does provide is rules of the road to be observed by
pedestrians and by vehicles, so that all those who use the road may know
how they and others should proceed, at least under usual circumstances. A
general rule of conduct—and, specifically, a rule of the road—may accomplish its intended purpose under usual conditions, but, when the unusual
occurs, strict observance may defeat the purpose of the rule and produce
catastrophic results.

Negligence is failure to exercise the care required by law. Where a
statute defines the standard of care and the safeguards required to meet a

recognized danger, then, as we have said, no other measure may be applied in determining whether a person has carried out the duty of care imposed by law. Failure to observe the standard imposed by statute is negligence, as matter of law. On the other hand, where a statutory general rule of conduct fixes no definite standard of care which would under all circumstances tend to protect life, limb or property, but merely codifies or supplements a common-law rule which has always been subject to limitations and exceptions; or where the statutory rule of conduct regulates conflicting rights and obligations in a manner calculated to promote public convenience and safety, then the statute, in the absence of clear language to the contrary, should not be construed as intended to wipe out the limitations and exceptions which judicial decisions have attached to the common-law duty; nor should it be construed as an inflexible command that the general rule of conduct intended to prevent accidents must be followed even under conditions when observance might cause accidents. We may assume reasonably that the Legislature directed pedestrians to keep to the left of the center of the road because that would cause them to face traffic approaching in that lane and would enable them to care for their own safety better than if the traffic approached them from the rear. We cannot assume reasonably that the Legislature intended that a statute enacted for the preservation of the life and limb of pedestrians must be observed when observance would subject them to more imminent danger.

      .   .   .

Even under that construction of the statute, a pedestrian is, of course, at fault if he fails without good reason to observe the statutory rule of conduct. The general duty is established by the statute, and deviation from it without good cause is a wrong and the wrongdoer is responsible for the damages resulting from his wrong. [   ]

      .   .   .

In each action, the judgment should be affirmed, with costs.

CRANE, CH. J., HUBBS, LOUGHRAN and RIPPEY, JJ., concur; O'BRIEN and FINCH, JJ., dissent on the authority of *Martin v. Herzog* [   ].

Notes and Questions

1. How does Judge Lehman distinguish *Martin v. Herzog*? Would his analysis be compromised if in a criminal proceeding against the two pedestrians, the court were to construe the statute as categorical and therefore find them guilty? What if the statute had stated the following at the end: "Pedestrians who violate this provision shall not be permitted to justify their conduct in any judicial proceeding"?

Compare *Levey v. DeNardo*, p. 58 supra, in which plaintiff had claimed that defendant was negligent for violating the "assured clear distance ahead" statute. That statute provided that "[n]o person shall drive a vehicle . . . at a speed greater than will permit the driver to bring his vehicle to a stop within the assured clear distance ahead." The court held that reliance on the statute was misguided. Both cars faced an emergency when the intruding car came across into their lane. The statute "means only what it says: a clear distance that is assured," that is, one that can reasonably be depended on. The rule does not mean that the motorist must carry in his mind every possible series of combinations which could conspire against him, and that he must transport ready-made solutions to overcome all fortuitous hazards which suddenly confront him. Assured does not mean guaranteed." Is it possible that the court's interpretation of the statute is incorrect but that its refusal to use the statute in the civil case is sound?

2. Might the situation in *Tedla* be one in which, as Judge Cardozo said in *Martin v. Herzog,* "the two wrongs, negligence and breach of statutory duty, must be kept distinct in speech and thought"?

3. In Bassey v. Mistrough, 450 N.Y.S.2d 604 (App.Div.1982), a vehicle "came to a stop partially on the highway, and the entire electrical system of the car failed to function." While plaintiff was standing in front of his car searching for the source of the electrical trouble, his car was hit from behind and he was hurt. The judge read the jury the statute requiring the illumination of vehicles on the highway. He refused a request to tell the jury about the possibility of an excuse. Judgment was entered on a jury verdict for the defendant. On appeal, the court reversed. The jury should have been advised that if they found plaintiff "unable to avoid temporarily leaving his stalled, unlighted vehicle on the highway" the violation would be excused.

What if a driver testified that the car's lights failed ten minutes earlier, but that the driver continued on while looking for a store to buy a replacement switch and had not passed one? What if plaintiff testified that although the lights failed ten minutes earlier, the driver continued on and passed a store with the needed switch in order to take a child to the hospital for emergency treatment? Is there a difference between the type of excuse that Tedla offered and an excuse by the plaintiff in *Martin* that the light had just gone out?

4. Tedla's brother, Bachek, was deaf. If he had been walking alone might the case have been different?

5. In Casey v. Russell, 188 Cal.Rptr. 18 (App. 1982), two cars collided head-on as they came around a curve on a narrow winding mountain dirt road. Plaintiff passenger in one of the cars sued both drivers, claiming that the drivers had violated a statute that said to stay to the right of the middle, or a statute that said to blow horns on blind curves where the road is too narrow for two cars to pass. The judge told the jury to find that a violation of either statute would be negligence unless the apparent violator "proves by a preponderance of the evidence that he did what might reasonably be expected of a person of ordinary prudence, acting under similar circumstances, who desired to comply with the law." The jury returned a verdict for both defendants.

On appeal, the court rejected the charge because it did "not adequately convey that there must be some special circumstances which justify violating the statute. The phrase 'who desired to comply with the law' does not mean one who in general is a law-abiding person, but rather refers to one who, although he desired to comply with the particular statute in issue, was faced with other circumstances which prevented compliance or justified noncompliance." Some examples included the "driver who inspected the tail light and found it in good order a short time before it went out;" a heavy blizzard that prevents a railroad from meeting its statutory duty to keep fences clear of snow; and a driver confronted with an emergency not due to his own misconduct—such as the need to swerve into a lane of oncoming traffic to avoid a child "suddenly darting into the road."

In cases in which excuses are offered for violations of the literal terms of criminal statutes, what should be the respective functions of judge and jury in deciding the validity of these excuses?

6. Consider the potential interplay between the role of custom and statutory violations. In Robinson v. District of Columbia, 580 A.2d 1255 (D.C.App.1990), plaintiff, who had been hit by a police van, was held contributorily negligent for violating a traffic regulation by crossing the street outside of a marked cross walk. She argued that her behavior was reasonable because it was "the common practice of pedestrians at the location of the accident." The court disagreed: there was no basis to "excuse violations of the law where such violations are common practice."

7. *Statutory purpose.* Courts have long been unwilling to use statutory violations in cases in which the harm that occurred was different from the harm that the legislature apparently was seeking to prevent.

In Platz v. City of Cohoes, 89 N.Y. 219 (1882), an obstruction in the road, negligently left by the city, led to plaintiffs' injuries while they were violating a statute by riding on Sunday. The only defense was that the plaintiffs would not have been hurt if they had been obeying that statute. After noting several states in which that argument had been upheld, the court rejected it on the ground that the statute was designed to promote public order and not safety.

In De Haen v. Rockwood Sprinkler Co., 179 N.E. 764 (N.Y.1932), a radiator placed about a foot from the edge of an unprotected hoistway on a construction project fell down the shaft and killed a man below. The court, in an opinion by Judge Cardozo, first upheld the liability of Rockwood because its employees had negligently struck the radiator and brought about its fall. The court next upheld liability against LeBeau, whose employees negligently placed the radiator dangerously near the open shaft. The fact that it took the act of another to cause the fall did not exculpate LeBeau. "One may not place an engine of destruction in a position where a heedless touch by someone else will awaken its destructive power." At least, "a jury may so find."

The court then turned to the liability of Turner, the general contractor. Turner had violated a statute by failing to erect a barrier around the hoistway. Two sides were to be rigid. The other two, "which may be used for taking off and putting on materials . . . shall be guarded by an adjustable barrier not less than three nor more than four feet from the floor and not less than two feet from the edges of such shafts or openings."

Although the statute had been violated, that violation "does not establish liability if the statute is intended to protect against a particular hazard, and a hazard of a different kind is the occasion of the injury." Why should that requirement be imposed? The court then sought the purpose of the statute:

> The chief object of this statute is to protect workmen from the hazard of falling into a shaft. We cannot say, however, that no other hazard was within the zone of apprehension. On two sides of the shaft there must be a solid or comparatively solid fence. Only on the other sides where material is taken on or off may there be a single bar. If there was no thought to give protection against falling missiles or debris, the lawmakers might well have stopped with a requirement that there be a single bar on every side. The fact that they did not stop there is evidence of a broader purpose. True, indeed, it is that on two of the four sides the security is only partial and imperfect. A barrier set in place at a height of four feet will often be of little avail in holding back material or rubbish collected on the floor. Even so, security against the hazard of falling objects will not be lacking altogether. One of the requirements of the statute is that the guard shall be placed at least two feet from the edge. In a barrier so fixed there is warning, if no more. Workmen, who may otherwise be tempted to store material in dangerous proximity to the edge of an open shaft will be reminded of the danger and will tend to stand afar. The thoughtless will be checked, though the recklessly indifferent will be free to go their way.

> The potencies of protection that reside in such a barrier have illustration in the case before us. If the hoistway had been guarded, it is unlikely that the radiators thirty-eight inches high would have been placed as they were within falling distance of the edge. It is still less likely that a worker would heedlessly have brushed against them and so brought about the fall. We do not mean to say that these considerations are decisive. Liability is not established by a showing that as chance would have it a statutory safeguard might have avoided the particular hazard out of which an accident ensued. The hazard out of which the accident ensued must have been the particular hazard or class of hazards that the statutory safeguard in the thought and purpose of the Legislature was intended to correct [   ]. Nonetheless, the sequence of events may help to fix the limits of a purpose that would be obscure if viewed alone. A safeguard has been commanded, but without distinct enumeration of the hazards to be avoided. In the revealing light of experience the hazards to be avoided are disclosed to us as the hazards that ensued.

Compare Di Ponzio v. Riordan, 679 N.E.2d 616 (N.Y.1997), in which defendant gas station, in violation of an ordinance requiring that car engines be turned off while the car is being filled with gas, permitted a customer to leave his engine running while he pumped gasoline and then went inside to pay for it. After about five minutes on a level surface, the vehicle inexplicably rolled backward and pinned plaintiff, another customer, between two cars. The court held that the violation of the ordinance, which was in the city's fire prevention code, was irrelevant because its apparent purpose was to prevent fires and not to avoid injuries from moving vehicles. The court analogized the situation to a Restatement example involving a defendant who gives a loaded pistol to a child, who then drops it on a playmate's toe—but it does not fire a bullet.

8. If the court in *De Haen* had concluded that the only purpose of the statute was to keep workers from falling into the open shaft and had refused to use the statute in the case, would Turner necessarily have won the case?

When defendant driver parked outside the pharmacy on the grounds of the Middletown Psychiatric Center, she left her keys in the ignition. "Moments later," a patient drove away in the vehicle and "met his death soon thereafter when it left the road and struck a tree." Plaintiff, the patient's administrator, moved for summary judgment based on violation of the state statute against leaving keys in the ignition of an unattended car. The majority concluded that the statute was enacted to "deter theft and injury from the operation of motor vehicles by unauthorized persons" and was "plainly not designed to protect such unauthorized users from the consequences of their own conduct." Two judges thought the purpose was "to protect the public generally from the consequences that foreseeably flow from unauthorized use of motor vehicles." It was "patently unfair to deny to plaintiff the evidentiary weight of such violation and leave him to the more vigorous burden of establishing common law negligence."

The court unanimously concluded that plaintiff could proceed under common law negligence. Rushink v. Gerstheimer, 440 N.Y.S.2d 738 (App. Div.1981). Why the difference?

Several state courts have concluded that the purpose of the "key-in-the-ignition" statutes is to reduce thefts, and thus reduce both the time police must spend tracking down stolen cars and the payments insurers must make to owners of such cars. In this view there is no safety purpose, and the statute is not invoked in personal injury cases. See Peck, An Exercise Based Upon Empirical Data: Liability for Harm Caused by Stolen Automobiles, 1969 Wis.L.Rev. 909.

9. In violation of the Contagious Diseases Act, defendant shipowner failed to build pens on the deck in order to keep groups of sheep separated. During the voyage, some sheep were washed overboard. A suit by the owners of the sheep failed. Gorris v. Scott, L.R. 9 Ex. 125 (1874). The court observed that "the damage is of such a nature as was not contemplated at all by the statute, and as to which it was not intended to confer any benefit on the plaintiffs."

10. *Licensing.* Licensing statutes have generally not been used to set standards of care. The explanation has been that the purpose of such a statute is to protect the public from actions performed by unskilled persons. If that is the purpose, then plaintiff must prove that the defendant lacked the required skill—in effect proving negligence.

The most common example is a motor vehicle accident involving an unlicensed driver. The lack of a license is irrelevant to the tort claim—whether the unlicensed driver is the plaintiff or the defendant.

Another example occurred in Brown v. Shyne, 151 N.E. 197 (N.Y. 1926), in which a chiropractor allegedly hurt plaintiff by undertaking a treatment only licensed physicians could perform. The court held the defendant to the standard of a physician but ruled that the jury should not be told about defendant's violation of the licensing statute.

Are the driving and medical cases comparable? Should a distinction be drawn between a driver who inadvertently allowed a driving license to expire and one who never took the driving test? Should it matter whether a person's medical license was revoked for income tax evasion or for performing an illegal abortion? Or if the person never had a license?

In 1971, the rule of *Brown v. Shyne* was changed by statute. CPLR § 4504(d) provides that in any action for personal injuries against a person not authorized to practice medicine "the fact that such person practiced medicine without being so authorized shall be deemed prima facie evidence of negligence."

11. Some statutes are interpreted as barring their use in civil cases. Violations of the Occupational Safety and Health Act (OSHA) were held to fall into this category in Hernandez v. Martin Chevrolet, Inc., 649 N.E.2d 1215 (Ohio 1995). The court relied on the statute's preamble in 29 U.S.C.A. § 653(b)(4):

> Nothing in this chapter shall be construed to supersede or in any manner affect any workmen's compensation law or to enlarge or diminish or affect in any other manner the common law or statutory rights, duties, or liabilities of employers and employees under any law with respect to injuries, diseases, or death of employees arising out of, or in the course of, employment.

12. *Compliance.* In *Tedla,* is it conceivable that plaintiffs might have been contributorily negligent if they had been walking in compliance with the statute and had been hit by an oncoming car? More generally, should compliance with a safety statute necessarily satisfy the standard of due care? The question often poses a federalism issue; in particular, whether compliance with federal regulations should, as a matter of judicial deference, insulate the defendant from common law tort liability. Thus, in Edwards v. Basel Pharmaceuticals, 933 P.2d 298 (Okla.1997), suit was brought on behalf of a smoker who had died of a nicotine-induced heart attack while smoking and wearing two nicotine patches. Defendant argued that its compliance with FDA warning requirements should serve as a defense to liability. Although a relatively comprehensive warning was given to prescribing physicians, the package insert cautioned only that an "over-dose might cause you to faint." (We take up in Chapter VIII whether a warning to the physician in itself should suffice, a question that the court in *Edwards* answered in the negative). Regarding the defendant's compliance with the requirement of warning the user in this case, the court concluded:

> [T]he manufacturer's duty to warn the consumer is not necessarily satisfied by compliance with FDA minimum warning requirements. The required warnings must not be misleading, and must be adequate to explain to the user the possible dangers associated with the product. Whether that duty has been satisfied is governed by the common law of the state, not the regulations of the FDA.

In Hubbard-Hall Chemical Co. v. Silverman, 340 F.2d 402 (1st Cir. 1965), plaintiffs were the administrators of the estates of two migrant farm workers who were killed by contact with an insecticide manufactured and distributed by defendant. The Department of Agriculture had found that danger warnings on the sacks conformed to Congressional requirements. Judgments entered for plaintiffs on a jury verdict were affirmed: the "jury could reasonably have believed that defendant should have foreseen that its admittedly dangerous product would be used by, among others, persons like plaintiffs' intestates, who were farm laborers, of limited education and reading ability, and that a warning even if it were in the precise form of the label submitted to the Department of Agriculture would not, because of its lack of a skull and bones or other comparable symbols" be adequate warning. The court found no reason to believe that Congress intended conformity with its requirements to mean that the defendant had "met the possibly higher standard of due care imposed by the common law . . . in actions of tort for negligence."

In Espinoza v. Elgin, Joliet and Eastern Ry. Co., 649 N.E.2d 1323 (Ill.1995), the plaintiff in a grade-crossing accident claimed, among other things, that the defendant railroad should have had better warning devices at the intersection. The relevant state commission had inspected the crossing before the accident and had approved the existing devices. A state statute said in part that "[l]uminous flashing signal or crossing gate devices installed at grade crossings, which have been approved by the Commission, shall be deemed adequate and appropriate." The court interpreted this to mean that once such approval has been given "a conclusive legal presumption is created which prevents plaintiffs from arguing that the railroad should have installed other warning devices." The railroad was entitled to summary judgment on that issue. Can this case be reconciled with *Hubbard-Hall*?

The question can also arise in the context of compliance with a state regulatory scheme. See Alvarado v. J.C. Penney Co., 735 F.Supp. 371 (D.Kan.1990), in which the defendant claimed compliance with the Kansas Product Liability Act. Plaintiff was burned when the nightgown and the robe she wore were both ignited by an open flame gas heater. The court held that compliance with the regulatory standard was not conclusive. See generally, Dieffert, The Role of Regulatory Compliance in Tort Actions, 26 Harv.J.Legis. 175 (1989).

The question of whether and when courts should defer to legislative and administrative decisions about safety is an important and controversial question, to which we return—in the context of whether federal legislation preempts state tort remedies—in Chapter VI. In the meantime, evaluate this excerpt from the conclusion of Huber, Safety and the Second Best: The Hazards of Public Risk Management in the Courts, 85 Colum.L.Rev. 277, 334–35 (1985):

> [J]udicial nondeference may make some sense when the administrative regulatory regime is casual or sporadic, as with consumer products. But it is wholly unpersuasive for comprehensively regulated industries. Vaccines, pesticides, aircraft, electric power plants and the like all entail potentially enormous mass-exposure hazards. Precisely because they can create public risks of this nature, these products and services are also subject to the most searching and complete state and federal safety regulation. Administrative agencies may find it politically convenient to disclaim final responsibility for the public risk choices that inhere in such licensing decisions. But the simple fact is that an agency cannot intelligently issue a license for such public-risk activities without comparing the licensee's risks to those of the competition and determining that the new offering represents some measure of progress or, at worst, no measure of regression in the risk market in question.
>
> Once that determination has been made by an expert licensing agency, the courts should respect it. Regulatory agencies are equipped to make the risk comparisons on which all progressive transformation of the risk environment must be based. The courts are simply not qualified to second-guess such decisions; when they choose to do so they routinely make regressive risk choices. Requiring—or at least strongly encouraging—the courts to respect the comparative risk choices made by competent, expert agencies would inject a first, small measure of rationality into a judicial regulatory system that currently runs quite wild.

For a critique of this view, discussing both the claims for and against judicial deference to regulatory compliance, and concluding that there should be no general presumption in favor of deference, see Rabin, Reassessing Regulatory Compliance, 88 Geo. L.J. 2049 (2000).

D. PROOF OF NEGLIGENCE

Problems of proof occur at virtually every stage of the negligence action. In this section, we focus on the plaintiff's burden of proving that the defendant's conduct fell below the standard of reasonable care. This, in turn, involves proving what the defendant actually did or did not do and, at times, the unreasonableness of such behavior.

The <u>most convincing type of proof</u> is usually documentary or "real" <u>evidence:</u> the broken bottle, the flight recorder in an airplane accident, or a videotape of an automobile crash. In few personal injury accidents, however, is such evidence available. A "lucky" plaintiff will be able to present photographs of skid marks or other <u>visible evidence</u> that might serve almost as well as "real" evidence. The plaintiff may also use "direct" evidence: <u>eyewitnesses may testify.</u> Whether the witness describes skid marks or the crash itself, the party hurt by such testimony may seek to undermine it by cross examination in an effort to show erroneous recall of the facts or to cast doubt on the witness's credibility. When documentary and photographic proof are used, accuracy and credibility are less readily challenged. In fact, however, most evidence is circumstantial.

Negri v. Stop and Shop, Inc.

Court of Appeals of New York, 1985.
65 N.Y.2d 625, 480 N.E.2d 740, 491 N.Y.S.2d 151.

[After a plaintiff's verdict, the trial court entered judgment for the plaintiff in a slip and fall case. The Appellate Division reversed and dismissed the complaint.]

MEMORANDUM.

The order of the Appellate Division, [   ] should be reversed, with costs, and remitted to that court for consideration of the facts and of other issues not previously addressed.

The record contains some evidence tending to show that defendant had constructive notice of a dangerous condition which allegedly caused injuries to its customer. There was testimony that the injured plaintiff, while shopping in defendant's store, fell backward, did not come into contact with the shelves, but hit her head directly on the floor where "a lot of broken jars" of baby food lay; that the baby food was "dirty and messy"; that a witness in the immediate vicinity of the accident did not hear any jars falling from the shelves or otherwise breaking during the 15 or 20 minutes prior to the accident; and that the aisle had not been cleaned or inspected for at least 50 minutes prior to the accident—indeed, some evidence was adduced that it was at least two hours.

Viewing the evidence in a light most favorable to the plaintiffs and according plaintiffs the benefit of every reasonable inference [   ], it cannot be said, as a matter of law, that the circumstantial evidence was insufficient to permit the jury to draw the necessary inference that a slippery condition was created by jars of baby food which had fallen and broken a sufficient length of time prior to the accident to permit defendant's employees to discover and remedy the condition. [   ] Plaintiffs having made out a prima facie case, it was error to dismiss the complaint. If the jury verdict be deemed by the Appellate Division to be against the weight of the evidence, that court's power is limited to ordering a new trial. [   ]

WACHTLER, C.J., and JASEN, MEYER, SIMONS, KAYE and ALEXANDER, JJ., concur.

Gordon v. American Museum of Natural History

Court of Appeals of New York, 1986.
67 N.Y.2d 836, 492 N.E.2d 774, 501 N.Y.S.2d 646.

MEMORANDUM.

The order of the Appellate Division, [ ], should be reversed, with costs, the complaint dismissed and the certified question answered in the negative.

Plaintiff was injured when he fell on defendant's front entrance steps. He testified that as he descended the upper level of steps he slipped on the third step and that while he was in midair he observed a piece of white, waxy paper next to his left foot. He alleges that this paper came from the concession stand that defendant had contracted to have present and which was located on the plaza separating the two tiers of steps and that defendant was negligent insofar as its employees failed to discover and remove the paper before he fell on it. The case was submitted to the jury on the theory that defendant had either actual or constructive notice of the dangerous condition presented by the paper on the steps. The jury found against defendant on the issue of liability. A divided Appellate Division affirmed and granted defendant leave to appeal on a certified question.

There is no evidence in the record that defendant had actual notice of the paper and the case should not have gone to the jury on that theory. To constitute constructive notice, a defect must be visible and apparent and it must exist for a sufficient length of time prior to the accident to permit defendant's employees to discover and remedy it (Negri v. Stop & Shop [ ]). The record contains no evidence that anyone, including plaintiff, observed the piece of white paper prior to the accident. Nor did he describe the paper as being dirty or worn, which would have provided some indication that it had been present for some period of time (cf. [*Negri*] (broken baby food jars were dirty)). Thus, on the evidence presented, the piece of paper that caused plaintiff's fall could have been deposited there only minutes or seconds before the accident and any other conclusion would be pure speculation.

Contrary to plaintiff's contentions, neither a general awareness that litter or some other dangerous condition may be present [ ] nor the fact that plaintiff observed other papers on another portion of the steps approximately 10 minutes before his fall is legally sufficient to charge defendant with constructive notice of the paper he fell on. [Two cited cases] are not to the contrary. In both cases constructive notice was established by other evidence and the issue was whether plaintiffs had presented sufficient evidence on the issue of causation insofar as both plaintiffs failed to specify which step they had fallen on and what condition—wear, wetness or litter—had caused them to slip. In each case, the court concluded that plaintiff had presented a prima facie case because a fall was a natural and probable consequence of the conditions present on the stairs. The defect in plaintiff's case here, however, is not an inability to prove the causation element of his fall but the lack of evidence establishing constructive notice of the particular condition that caused his fall.

WACHTLER, C.J., and MEYER, SIMONS, KAYE, ALEXANDER, TITONE and HANCOCK, JJ., concur in memorandum.

Notes and Questions

1. Are *Negri* and *Gordon* distinguishable?

2. What more might plaintiff have done in *Gordon*? Does the court suggest that the judgment below would have been affirmed if Gordon had testified that the paper looked dirty?

3. Recall the difference, noted in *Negri,* between dismissing the complaint (or granting summary judgment) and ordering a new trial. What controls the appropriate appellate response?

4. In Faricelli v. TSS Seedman's Inc., 720 N.E.2d 864 (N.Y.1999), plaintiff slipped on a banana peel in the housewares section of defendant's department store. "Plaintiff contended that, because the peel was blackened, defendant must have had notice of a dangerous condition on the premises." The court held that there was insufficient proof of notice in a two-sentence opinion: "There was no evidence that defendant knew about the banana peel, or that it had been on the floor long enough prior to the accident that notice might be inferred. [ ] The simple fact that the peel was blackened did not establish constructive notice." Is this consistent with *Negri*?

5. Should plaintiff be able to show that the week before she fell a broken baby food jar had been on the floor in that aisle for more than two hours before being cleaned up? In Moody v. Haymarket Associates, 723 A.2d 874 (Maine 1999), plaintiff who slipped on a wet floor in an office building sued the owner of the building for the negligence of its janitor in not drying the floor or warning about the wetness. The trial judge admitted evidence showing that defendant's premises had been free of accidents for ten years prior to trial (four before the accident and six afterward). The jury found no negligence. The supreme court reversed the defendant's judgment because the judge erred in admitting that evidence:

> We review the court's evidentiary ruling for an abuse of discretion. [ ] In a negligence action, evidence of similar accidents or occurrences, or the absence thereof, may be relevant circumstantially to determine whether a defective or dangerous condition, notice thereof, or causation existed on the occasion in question. [ ] Initially, however, the court must determine whether the evidence is relevant: [the court cited the state's evidence code that requires the judge to "determine the relevance of the evidence on the basis of whether there is a substantial similarity in the operative circumstances between the proffer and the case at bar and whether the evidence is probative on a material issue in the case."] Second, even if the evidence is relevant, the court "must then consider whether the probative value of such evidence is substan-

tially outweighed by the countervailing considerations [of the state's evidence code]," that is, the danger of unfair prejudice, confusion of the issue, or undue delay.

The court concluded that the evidence here "was not relevant to the very narrow issue of whether the janitor acted in a particular way on the day in question. Simply put, because of the narrow issue before the jury, the absence of other accidents in the lobby did not present information about substantially similar circumstances." Is the court's conclusion consistent with the evidence code? Might the same evidence be relevant on a different theory: that defendant had negligently hired and retained an incompetent janitor?

6. In Randall v. K–Mart Corp., 150 F.3d 210 (2d Cir.1998), the plaintiff slipped on loose birdseed in an aisle in defendant's store. After being unable to establish constructive notice, plaintiff sought to invoke the "business practice" rule. As the federal court understood that rule, Vermont does not require constructive notice "for 'business practices' that create a reasonably foreseeable risk of harm to invitees." The court discussed a 1970 Vermont case that "involved a plaintiff who slipped on a small piece of banana in the produce section of a supermarket. Although the plaintiff failed to establish actual or constructive knowledge of the dangerous condition, the court observed that the case involved a 'self-service method of displaying . . . fruits and vegetables' whereby produce was stored in open bins and was handled by both customers and employees." The Vermont court had concluded that under these circumstances the merchant was obligated to anticipate dangerous conditions. As the Vermont court put it:

> This self-service method . . . carried with it a corresponding duty of care by the store to use reasonable measures to discover and remove from the floor debris which may have been dropped or knocked to the floor by persons at the counter. Debris on the floor is to be anticipated in a self-service operation. The fact can reasonably be concluded that such hazard to business invitees constituted a risk of harm within the reasonable foresight of the defendant and that it should have taken reasonable steps to obviate the danger.

The court of appeals in *Randall* concluded that a "merchant that uses such a self-service method of sale must bear the burden of showing what steps were taken to avoid the foreseeable risk of harm." The court then noted that Vermont had applied the same idea in a 1993 case in which a pallet of boxes fell on a customer. The evidence showed that the merchant's practice was to bring pallets stacked with merchandise into the aisle for restocking purposes during business hours. There the Vermont court had observed that "[t]he risk of floor debris from an ordinary self-serve produce display is no greater than the risk of pallets loaded with heavy boxes waiting for shelf stocking throughout the aisles."

Nonetheless, the court refused to apply the "business practice" rule when Randall claimed that Kmart's "self-service method of selling merchandise" relieved him of the burden of showing how long the birdseed was on the floor. The court held:

The business practice exception was created to address the hazard associated with customers who handpick produce from open bins, [ ], but the exception in Vermont has been broadened considerably. [ ] Even so, it is insufficient for Randall to characterize Kmart's merchandising method generally as "self-service," without explaining how Kmart's merchandising of birdseed posed a hazard. Otherwise, every retailer that is not a full-service boutique would be subject to the exception, and the exception would thereby become the rule. Randall relies on Chiara v. Fry's Food Stores, 733 P.2d 283 (Ariz.1987) (extending Arizona's "business practice" exception to bottled "creme rinse"), but we see no reason to assume that Vermont would extend the exception so far.

The court could find "no evidence (and Randall cites none) that indicates how Kmart sold birdseed: in bags of paper or plastic or burlap, or in boxes, or in canisters, or loose and in bulk. On this record, a reasonable jury could not find that Kmart's method of selling birdseed created a foreseeable risk."

7. In *Chiara,* cited in the preceding note, the court stated that the rule "looks to a business's choice of a particular mode of operation and not events surrounding the plaintiff's accident. Under the rule, the plaintiff is not required to prove notice if the proprietor could reasonably anticipate that hazardous conditions would regularly arise. [ ] In other words, a third person's independent negligence is no longer the source of liability, and the plaintiff is freed from the burden of discovering and proving a third person's actions." The court saw no reason to limit the rule to "produce or pizza." The issue was whether defendant "could reasonably anticipate that creme rinse would be spilled on a regular basis." Here, employee depositions showed that spills regularly occurred in the store. From these, it was for a jury to determine if "Fry's reasonably could have anticipated that sealed bottles regularly were opened and spilled." If so, the question would be whether Fry's had exercised reasonable care under these circumstances.

See generally, Comment, Reapportioning the Burden of Uncertainty: Storekeeper Liability in the Self-Service Slip-and-Fall Case, 41 UCLA L.Rev. 861 (1994). Are the "business practice" and "mode of operation" rules consistent with a negligence approach or are they a form of strict liability? What if a store kept a clerk at the produce counter who mopped the area every five minutes?

8. The *Randall* court noted that the plaintiff presented no evidence about such matters as how the product was packaged. Might that warrant some inferences against the plaintiff? In Howard v. Wal–Mart Stores, Inc., 160 F.3d 358 (7th Cir.1998), the question was whether plaintiff had presented enough from which a jury could find that the puddle of liquid soap on which she slipped had been caused by an employee rather than another customer. (Why might plaintiff have pursued that theory in the absence of any direct proof of such facts?) After concluding that the balance of probabilities tipped in plaintiff's favor "though surely only by a hair's breadth," Judge Posner proceeded:

Is a hair's breadth enough, though? Judges, and commentators on the law of evidence, have been troubled by cases in which the plaintiff has established a probability that only minutely exceeds 50 percent that his version of what happened is correct. The concern is illuminated by the much-discussed bus hypothetical. Suppose that the plaintiff is hit by a bus, and it is known that 51 percent of the buses on the road where the plaintiff was hit are owned by Bus Company A and 49 percent by Company B. The plaintiff sues A and asks for judgment on the basis of this statistic alone (we can ignore the other elements of liability besides causation by assuming they have all been satisfied, as in this case); he tenders no other evidence. If the defendant also puts in no evidence, should a jury be allowed to award judgment to the plaintiff? The law's answer is "no." [ ] Our hypothetical case is a variant of Smith v. Rapid Transit, [58 N.E.2d 754 (Mass.1945)], where the court held that it "was not enough" "that perhaps the mathematical chances somewhat favor the proposition that a bus of the defendant caused the accident." . . .

Judge Posner suggested that two reasons for a plaintiff not to present apparently available evidence were (1) that it was known but not favorable and (2) that plaintiff "simply has not bothered to conduct an investigation." Might there be other reasons? The first warranted rejection of the claim and the second might also depending on the monetary value of the claim. The claim in *Howard* was "so tiny that it would make no sense to try to coerce the parties to produce more evidence, when, as we have said, no inference can be drawn from the paucity of evidence that the plaintiff was afraid to look harder for fear that she would discover that a customer and not an employee of Wal–Mart had spilled the soap." In *Howard* the jury found damages to be under $20,000. In *Randall* the damages were $275,000. Are these figures relevant to this inquiry?

9. Warehouse operations such as Home Depot raise other novel questions. See Maharaj, "Sky Shelves" Can Be Lethal for Shoppers, L.A.Times Aug, 16, 2000 at A–1, reporting on the dangers from merchandise that is stacked up to 20 feet above the ground: "Wal-Mart has acknowledged in court filings that during a six-year period ending in 1995, falling merchandise was responsible for about 26,000 customer claims and 7,000 employee injuries." A Wal-Mart spokesman observed that "When you consider we have 100 million customers a week, the number of falling-merchandise cases is very small." The article also reported that court records showed that "accidents had cost Wal-Mart alone $410 million in 1994, up from $275 million in 1992."

Byrne v. Boadle

Court of Exchequer, 1863.
2 H. & C. 722, 159 Eng.Rep. 299.

At the trial before the learned Assessor of the Court of Passage at Liverpool, the evidence adduced on the part of the plaintiff was as follows:—A witness named Critchley said: "On the 18th July, I was in Scotland Road, on the right side going north, defendant's shop is on that side. When I was opposite to his shop, a barrel of flour fell from a window above in defendant's house and shop, and knocked the plaintiff down. He was carried into an adjoining shop. A horse and cart came opposite the defendant's door. Barrels of flour were in the cart. I do not think the barrel was being lowered by a rope. I cannot say: I did not see the barrel until it struck the plaintiff. It was not swinging when it struck the plaintiff. It struck him on the shoulder and knocked him towards the shop. No one called out until after the accident." The plaintiff said: "On approaching Scotland Place and defendant's shop, I lost all recollection. I felt no blow. I saw nothing to warn me of danger. I was taken home in a cab. I was helpless for a fortnight." (He then described his sufferings.) "I saw the path clear. I did not see any cart opposite defendant's shop." Another witness said: "I saw a barrel falling. I don't know how, but from defendant's." The only other witness was a surgeon, who described the injury which the plaintiff had received. It was admitted that the defendant was a dealer in flour.

It was submitted, on the part of the defendant, that there was no evidence of negligence for the jury. The learned Assessor was of that opinion, and nonsuited the plaintiff, reserving leave to him to move the Court of Exchequer to enter the verdict for him with £50 damages, the amount assessed by the jury.

Littler, in the present Term, obtained a rule nisi to enter the verdict for the plaintiff, on the ground of misdirection of the learned Assessor in ruling that there was no evidence of negligence on the part of the defendant. . . .

POLLOCK, C.B. We are all of opinion that the rule must be absolute to enter the verdict for the plaintiff. The learned counsel was quite right in saying that there are many accidents from which no presumption of negligence can arise, but I think it would be wrong to lay down as a rule that in no case can presumption of negligence arise from the fact of an accident. Suppose in this case the barrel had rolled out of the warehouse and fallen on the plaintiff, how could he possibly ascertain from what cause it occurred? It is the duty of persons who keep barrels in a warehouse to take care that they do not roll out, and I think that such a case would, beyond all doubt, afford prima facie evidence of negligence. A barrel could not roll out of a warehouse without some negligence, and to say that a plaintiff who is injured by it must call witnesses from the warehouse to prove negligence seems to me preposterous. So in the building or repairing of a house, or putting pots on the chimneys, if a person passing along the road is injured by something falling upon him, I think the accident alone would be prima facie evidence of negligence. Or if an article calculated to cause damage is put in a wrong place and does mischief, I think that those whose duty it was to put it in the right place are prima facie responsible, and if there is any state of facts to rebut the presumption of negligence, they must prove them. The present case upon the evidence comes to this, a man is passing in front of the premises of a dealer in flour, and there falls down upon him a barrel of flour. I think it apparent that the barrel was in the custody of the defendant who occupied the premises, and who is responsible for the acts of his servants who had the control of it; and in my opinion the fact of its falling is prima facie evidence of negligence, and the plaintiff who was injured by it is not bound to show that it could not fall without negligence, but if there are any facts inconsistent with negligence it is for the defendant to prove them.

[The concurring opinion of BARON CHANNELL is omitted. BRAMWELL, B., and PIGOTT, B., concurred without opinion.]

Notes and Questions

1.   In the midst of the defendant's argument, Pollock, C.B., interrupted to observe, "There are certain cases of which it may be said res ipsa loquitur, and this seems one of them. In some cases the Courts have held that the mere fact of the accident having occurred is evidence of negligence, as, for instance, in the case of railway collisions." This was apparently the first use of a term that was to become central to negligence litigation. Defense counsel sought to distinguish railway cases as limited to collisions involving two trains of the same railroad company. He then argued that in one case the suit was by a passenger and that there was an implicit contract of safe carriage between the passenger and the railroad. What difference would it have made, Pollock inquired, if the case cited had been brought by a bystander instead of a passenger? Defense counsel responded that because of the contract, "The fact of the accident might be evidence of negligence in the one case, though not in the other." What is the relevance of this exchange to the decision in *Byrne?*

2.   Is *Randall* consistent with *Byrne?*

3.   In Larson v. St. Francis Hotel, 188 P.2d 513 (Cal.App.1948), plaintiff pedestrian was struck by a chair thrown out of the window of one of defendant's rooms on V-J Day, August 14, 1945. Plaintiff proved this and her injuries and rested. Defendant's motion for a nonsuit at the end of plaintiff's case was granted.

Compare Connolly v. Nicollet Hotel, 95 N.W.2d 657 (Minn.1959), in which the hotel had been taken over by a convention of the National Junior Chamber of Commerce. In the days before plaintiff's injury, the hotel management had learned that objects were being thrown from windows and that vandalism was occurring throughout the hotel. The day before the incident, the general manager sent a memo to the hotel staff saying in part, "We have almost arrived at the end of the most harrowing experience we have had in the way of conventions, at least in my experience. . . . We had no alternative but to proceed and 'turn the other cheek.' . . ." The following night, plaintiff pedestrian lost an eye when hit by an object thrown from a room.

The majority held that the hotel could have been found to have behaved negligently after knowing of the dangers. Management decided not to try to find out who had thrown the earlier objects, because the convention was "out of control." No increased patrolling was instituted, no new guards were hired, and no appeal was made to responsible officers of the convention. Perhaps the most significant step taken was to cut holes in the corners of the hotel's laundry bags to prevent their use as water containers.

The dissenters argued that it was not reasonable to expect the management to enter every room, or make random entries, or to remain in them to prevent possible misconduct. They relied on *Larson*.

Is the majority relying on a res ipsa argument? Is negligence inferred from the accident itself?

4. In Dermatossian v. New York City Transit Authority, 492 N.E.2d 1200 (N.Y.1986), the plaintiff passenger testified that he struck his head on a defective grab handle as he stood up to leave defendant's bus. The claim was that the handle projected straight down from the ceiling instead of "at the customary angle of about 45 degrees." Although the plaintiff presented no evidence of negligence, the trial court held the case sufficient for a jury. A plaintiff's verdict and judgment followed. On appeal, the court of appeals reversed.

The plaintiff "did not establish control of the grab handle by defendant with sufficient exclusivity to fairly rule out the chance that the defect in the handle was caused by some agency other than defendant's negligence. The proof did not adequately exclude the chance that the handle had been damaged by one or more of defendant's passengers who were invited to use it."

McDougald v. Perry

Supreme Court of Florida, 1998.
716 So.2d 783.

WELLS, JUSTICE.

[In 1990, plaintiff was driving behind a tractor-trailer being driven by Perry. As the tractor-trailer went over some railroad tracks the 130-pound spare tire came out of its cradle underneath the trailer and fell to the ground. The trailer's rear tires then ran over the spare, causing the spare to bounce into the air and crash into the windshield of plaintiff's Jeep Wagoneer.]

The spare tire was housed in an angled cradle underneath the trailer and was held in place by its own weight. Additionally, the tire was secured by a four to six-foot long chain with one-inch links, which was wrapped around the tire. Perry testified that he believed the chain to be the original chain that came with the trailer in 1969. Perry also stated that, as originally designed, the chain was secured to the body of the trailer by a latch device. At the time of the accident, however, the chain was attached to the body of the trailer with a nut and bolt.

Perry testified that he performed a pre-trip inspection of the trailer on the day of the accident. This included an inspection of the chain, although Perry admitted that he did not check every link in the chain. After the accident, Perry noticed that the chain was dragging under the trailer. Perry opined that one of the links had stretched and slipped from the nut which secured it to the trailer. [The chain could not be located at the time of trial.] The judge instructed the jury on the doctrine of res ipsa loquitur. The jury subsequently returned a verdict in McDougald's favor.

On appeal, the district court reversed with instructions that the trial court direct a verdict in respondents' favor. The district court concluded that the trial court erred by: (1) not directing a verdict on the issue of negligence; (2) instructing the jury on res ipsa loquitur. . . . We granted McDougald's petition for review. . . .

This Court discussed the applicability of the doctrine of res ipsa loquitur in Marrero v. Goldsmith, 486 So.2d 530 (Fla.1986); [ ]. In *Marrero*, we stated:

Res ipsa loquitur is a Latin phrase that translates "the thing speaks for itself." Prosser and Keeton, Law of Torts § 39 (5th ed.1984). It is a rule of evidence that permits, but does not compel, an inference of negligence under certain circumstances. "[T]he doctrine of res ipsa loquitur is merely a rule of evidence. Under it an inference may arise in aid of the proof." [ ] In Goodyear Tire & Rubber Co. v. Hughes Supply, Inc., 358 So.2d 1339 (Fla.1978), we explained the doctrine as follows:

It provides an injured plaintiff with a common-sense inference of negligence where direct proof of negligence is wanting, provided certain elements consistent with negligent behavior are present. Essentially the injured plaintiff must establish that the instrumentality causing his or her injury was under the exclusive control of the defendant, and that the accident is one that would not, in the ordinary course of events, have occurred without negligence on the part of the one in control. [ ]

In concluding that it was reversible error for the trial court to give the res ipsa loquitur instruction, the Second District determined that "McDougald failed to prove that this accident would not, in the ordinary course of events, have occurred without negligence by the defendants." . . .

The Second and Third Districts misread and interpret too narrowly what we stated in *Goodyear*. We did not say, as those courts conclude, that "the mere fact that an accident occurs does not support the application of the doctrine." Rather, we stated:

An *injury standing alone, of course, ordinarily does not indicate negligence. The doctrine of res ipsa loquitur simply recognizes that in rare instances an injury may permit an inference of negligence if coupled with a sufficient showing of its immediate, precipitating cause.* [ ]. (emphasis added). *Goodyear* and our other cases permit latitude in the application of this common-sense inference when the facts of an accident in and of themselves establish that but for the failure of reasonable care by the person or entity in control of the injury producing object or instrumentality the accident would not have occurred. On the other hand, our present statement is not to be considered an expansion of the doctrine's applicability. We continue our prior recognition that res ipsa loquitur applies only in "rare instances."

The following comments in section 328D of Restatement (Second) of Torts (1965) capture the essence of a proper analysis of this issue:

c. Type of event. The first requirement for the application of the rule stated in this Section is a basis of past experience which reasonably permits the conclusion that such events do not ordinarily occur unless someone has been negligent. There are many types of accidents which commonly occur without the fault of anyone. The fact that a tire blows out, or that a man falls down stairs is not, in the absence of anything more, enough to permit the conclusion that there was negligence in inspecting the tire, or in the construction of the stairs, because it is common human experience that such events all too frequently occur without such negligence. On the other hand there are many events, such as those of objects falling from the defendant's premises, the fall of an elevator, the escape of gas or water from mains or of electricity from wires or appliances, the derailment of trains or the explosion of boilers, where the conclusion is at least permissible that such things do not usually happen unless someone has been negligent. To such events res ipsa loquitur may apply.

d. Basis of conclusion. In the usual case the basis of past experience from which this conclusion may be drawn is common to the community, and is a matter of general knowledge, which the court recognizes on much the same basis as when it takes judicial notice of facts which everyone knows. It may, however, be supplied by the evidence of the parties; and expert testimony that such an event usually does not occur without negligence may afford a sufficient basis for the inference. . . .

Restatement (Second) of Torts § 328D cmts. *c-d* (1965).

We conclude that the spare tire escaping from the cradle underneath the truck, resulting in the tire ultimately becoming airborne and crashing into McDougald's vehicle, is the type of accident which, on the basis of common experience and as a matter of general knowledge, would not occur but for the failure to exercise reasonable care by the person who had control of the spare tire. As the Fifth District noted, the doctrine of res ipsa loquitur is particularly applicable in wayward wheel cases. [Cheung v. Ryder Truck Rental, Inc., 595 So.2d 82 (Fla.App.1992)]; see also [   ]; Wilson v. Spencer, 127 A.2d 840, 841 (D.C.1956) ("Thousands of automobiles are using our streets, but no one expects the air to be filled with flying hubcaps."). We do not agree with respondent that *Cheung* can be properly distinguished on the basis that in *Cheung* the escaped tire was attached to the axle, whereas in this case the escaped tire was a spare cradled underneath the truck. Rather, common sense dictates an inference that both a spare tire carried on a truck and a wheel on a truck's axle will stay with the truck unless there is a failure of reasonable care by the person or entity in control of the truck. Thus an inference of negligence comes from proof of the circumstances of the accident.

Furthermore, we do not agree with the Second District that McDougald failed to establish this element because "[o]ther possible explanations exist to explain the failure of the chain." [ ] Such speculation does not defeat the applicability of the doctrine in this case. As [a treatise] has noted:

> The plaintiff is not required to eliminate with certainty all other possible causes or inferences. . . . All that is required is evidence from which reasonable persons can say that on the whole it is more likely that there was negligence associated with the cause of the event than that there was not.

Respondents also contend that the res ipsa instruction was inapplicable because McDougald failed to prove that direct evidence of negligence was unavailable. Respondents cite to *Goodyear* for the proposition that res ipsa is not applicable where "the facts surrounding the incident were discoverable and provable." This statement from *Goodyear* was made in a products liability tire blow-out case in which the plaintiff was in possession and control of the injury-causing device. In that case, the plaintiff, who was in possession of the product alleged to have been negligently manufactured, was in the best position to determine the alleged cause of the accident. Thus, the res ipsa inference was not applicable. Here, unlike *Goodyear*, we find that there was insufficient evidence available to McDougald. The likely cause of this accident, the chain and securing device, were in the exclusive possession of respondents and were not preserved. Moreover, this was not the basis upon which the Second District held res ipsa loquitur to be inapplicable.

[The district court's decision was reversed and the case remanded for consideration of remaining issues.]

HARDING, C.J., and OVERTON, SHAW, KOGAN and PARIENTE, JJ., concur.

[ANSTEAD, J., concurred in an opinion that quoted *Byrne* v. *Boadle* in its entirety and observed that "we can hardly improve upon this explanation for our decision today. The common law tradition is alive and well."]

Notes and Questions

1. Might any negligence have been that of the chain maker and not of the driver? Would res ipsa apply against the driver if the accident had occurred in 1970? What about six months after the installation of the nut and bolt by an auto repairer?

2. Is there a difference between a tire that falls onto the road from its restraining cradle and a tire that blows out during driving?

3. Is the principal case as strong for the plaintiff as *Byrne v. Boadle*?

4. At various points in *McDougald* such terms as "inference" and "presumption" are used. What weight should res ipsa loquitur have in the trial? If the judge has concluded that a jury could find that the barrel came out of the defendant's window, should the judge tell the jury (a) that it may but need not find the defendant negligent, (b) that it must find the defendant negligent unless the defendant presents plausible rebutting evidence, or (c) that it must find the defendant negligent unless persuaded that defendant was not negligent?

Some states purport to adopt the inference view; some a stronger view. But even in a state that purports to follow the inference view a fact situation may arise that is so strong that the jury is instructed that it must find negligence in the absence of a persuasive exculpation. For example, in New York, which purports to follow the inference view, an airplane passenger was injured when the plane went off the runway while landing at Kennedy Airport. This showing was "so convincing that the inference of negligence arising therefrom is inescapable if not rebutted by other evidence." In the absence of such counter evidence the plaintiff was entitled to summary judgment on the question of liability. Farina v. Pan American World Airlines, Inc., 497 N.Y.S.2d 706 (App.Div.1986).

In some states if res ipsa applies it is treated as a "presumption affecting the burden of producing evidence." This means that if the defendant offers no plausible rebutting evidence the plaintiff is entitled to a directed verdict on liability. If, however, the defendant offers such evidence the jury is to be informed that the plaintiff still bears the burden of persuading the jury that defendant was negligent. See, e.g., Calif. Evidence Code § 646.

5. Can the defendant ever so "conclusively rebut" the plaintiff's case as to obtain judgment as a matter of law? In Leonard v. Watsonville Community Hospital, 305 P.2d 36 (Cal.1956), a Kelly clamp, about six inches long, was left inside plaintiff after an abdominal operation. The court held initially that res ipsa loquitur applied against all three participating physicians, the surgical nurse, and the hospital. It then considered the testimony of the physicians in deciding whether judgment had been properly granted to MD3. MD1 and MD2 worked on the upper abdomen, where the Kelly clamp was left, and also on the lower abdomen. MD3 testified that he had worked only on the lower abdomen, had left before the incision was closed, and had used only curved clamps—while Kelly clamps were uncurved. The testimony of MD1 and MD2 corroborated MD3. The court held that since this testimony increased the possibility that MD1 and MD2 would be held liable, the "record indicates no rational ground for disbelieving their testimony." The case against MD3 "was dispelled as a matter of law." The court found testimony of another witness less persuasive because it was consistent with her self-interest to shield her employer and associates from liability. Ordinarily, may juries disbelieve witnesses even though there is no "rational ground" for doing so?

6. Is it appropriate to give the benefit of res ipsa loquitur to a plaintiff who also seeks to prove specific acts of negligence? In Abbott v.

Page Airways, Inc., 245 N.E.2d 388 (N.Y.1969), plaintiff's husband was killed in the crash of a helicopter owned by defendant and operated by its employee. In addition to relying on res ipsa loquitur, plaintiff presented witnesses who testified that the pilot waved to someone on the ground just before the crash, had flown too low and too slowly, and had taken several drinks before the flight. The trial judge charged that the jury could properly find negligence in the specific acts charged or they "could infer negligence from the happening of the accident." The charge was upheld on appeal. A few courts disagree. See, e.g., Malloy v. Commonwealth Highland Theatres, Inc., 375 N.W.2d 631 (S.D.1985).

7. In a state with well-developed pretrial discovery procedures, is there still a place for res ipsa loquitur? In Fowler v. Seaton, 394 P.2d 697 (Cal.1964), the plaintiff was a four-year-old child who went to nursery school one morning in good health but returned that evening with a bump on her forehead, a concussion and crossed eyes. Is this enough for res ipsa loquitur? Having these and other facts, the majority thought it was. Two justices dissented on the ground that plaintiff had an obligation "to present such facts as were available to show that the accident was more probably than not the result of the alleged inadequate supervision by defendant." The dissent then listed several omissions from plaintiff's case and observed that they were "undoubtedly obtainable by discovery." Should it suffice for plaintiff to prove the minimum required to permit the critical inference? Do the facts already stated here suffice? Should all facts available by discovery but not presented be taken as adverse to plaintiff?

In Helton v. Forest Park Baptist Church, 589 S.W.2d 217 (Ky.App. 1979), plaintiffs left their two-and-one-half-year-old daughter with about a dozen other children at the nursery room of their church while they attended services. During the service, the daughter suffered a serious eye injury. The two adults who were supervising the children could not explain what had happened. All toys and furniture were inspected, but "no one could find any object which could have caused such an injury." It could not be determined whether she had been struck in the eye by a thrown object or had fallen on some object.

The court denied plaintiffs the benefit of res ipsa loquitur and upheld a summary judgment for the defense. Res ipsa was "inapplicable where the instrumentality producing the injury or damage is unknown or is not in the exclusive control of the defendant." A jury could "only speculate, surmise or guess as to how Melissa's injury occurred, and for this reason the case is one to be decided by the court as a matter of law."

8. *Spoliation of evidence.* The *McDougald* court noted that the chain could not be located at the time of trial. The disappearance of evidence is a common phenomenon in torts cases—usually because the object has been misplaced or lost over time. But another line of cases involves claims alleging that the defendant or the defendant's insurer destroyed important evidence to prevent plaintiff from gaining access to it. Most courts that have considered the question have recognized a tort called "spoliation of evidence" with complex issues about whether the claim covers both intentional and negligent destruction. E.g., Oliver v. Stimson Lumber Co., 993 P.2d 11 (Mont.1999).

California has rejected the action on the grounds that procedural sanctions may be imposed during the original trial and because of a concern about endless litigation. See Cedars-Sinai Medical Center v. Superior Court, 954 P.2d 511 (Cal.1998) (rejecting action against party for intentional destruction) and Temple Community Hospital v. Superior Court, 976 P.2d 223 (Cal.1999) (no action against third party for intentional destruction). In Coprich v. Superior Court, 95 Cal.Rptr.2d 884 (App. 2000), the court understood the logic of the two earlier cases to bar actions for negligent spoliation as well. The same concerns—endless litigation, the difficulty of telling what impact the missing evidence might have had on the original case, costs of preserving evidence after all accidents—existed in both. The court did, however, uphold an action for breach of contract to preserve evidence. For overviews, see Goff v. Harold Ives Trucking Co. Inc., 27 S.W.3d 387, 342 Ark. 143 (Ark. 2000) (concluding that non-tort remedies justify rejecting the tort action) and Nichols v. State Farm Fire & Casualty Co., 6 P.3d 300 (Alaska 2000) (holding that litigation sanctions are adequate against both the defendant and his liability insurer). See also, Wilhoit, Spoliation of Evidence: The Viability of Four Emerging Torts, 46 UCLA L.Rev. 631 (1998).

9. *Automobile cases.* Auto accidents are common and have given rise to suggestions of simple rules, such as that one who rear-ends another is automatically liable. The cases in this note suggest even such apparently simple fact situations require more complex analyses. In Bauer v. J.B. Hunt Transport, Inc., 150 F.3d 759 (7th Cir.1998), defendant's truck veered over onto the plaintiff's side of the road and rolled over onto plaintiff's vehicle during a storm. There was some testimony about a sudden strong wind. A jury verdict for defendant was upheld. The court, using Illinois law, concluded that the plaintiff had the ultimate burden of persuasion even if the defendant had a burden to produce some explanation for his being on plaintiff's side. After defendant offered an explanation, the burden of persuasion remained on the plaintiff. The jury might have found that the sudden strong wind was the reason for the collision.

In Meaney v. Rubega, 703 A.2d 1384 (N.H.1997), the defendant's car rear-ended the plaintiff's car. In responding to plaintiff's suit, defendant alleged that his brakes had failed without warning. The trial judge placed the burden of persuading the jury that defendant was negligent on the plaintiff. The jury returned a defense verdict. The court, 4–1, agreed that defendant was in effect denying negligence rather than raising an affirmative defense as to which he would bear the burden of persuasion. The dissenter argued that the relevant evidence was more accessible to the defendant than the plaintiff and thus the defendant should bear the burden of persuasion. Should accessibility of evidence affect the burden here?

Sometimes the plaintiff may receive procedural help in establishing negligence. In Spivak v. Heyward, 679 N.Y.S.2d 156 (App.Div. 1998), defendant driver admitted that he fell asleep at the wheel and rear-ended the plaintiffs' decedent. In the ensuing suit, the plaintiffs moved for summary judgment as to liability after defendant's admission. The trial court's denial of the motion was reversed on appeal. Faced with two conflicting lines of lower court authority in New York, this court chose the "more plausible view that sleep does not come on without warning, and that the operation of a motor vehicle requires the vigilance of a sentinel on watch." On the other hand, falling asleep at the wheel is not negligent as a matter of law either. A "showing that a defendant fell asleep while driving raises a rebuttable presumption of negligence, since the onerous burden of establishing the circumstances under which the defendant fell asleep would be a difficult, if not an insurmountable, burden for the plaintiff to overcome. [ ] It is logical, therefore, that the burden should fall to a defendant, who is in the best position to know the circumstances of his or her falling asleep, to offer an explanation creating a triable issue of fact." Since defendant had offered no such explanation summary judgment should have been granted against him—and the case should have moved to the damage phase.

Is this a res ipsa case? Is it consistent to force the defendant to come forward with evidence when he says he fell asleep but not when he says that he experienced sudden brake failure?

10. In the last paragraph of the majority opinion in *MacDougald* the court discusses who had access to relevant evidence. Is that issue part of the court's earlier analysis? Part of its discussion of section 328D? Should it be relevant to the applicability of res ipsa loquitur? Was this issue of accessibility relevant in *Byrne* v. *Boadle*? Consider these questions in connection with the following case.

Ybarra v. Spangard

Supreme Court of California, 1944.
25 Cal.2d 486, 154 P.2d 687.

GIBSON, C.J. This is an action for damages for personal injuries alleged to have been inflicted on plaintiff by defendants during the course of a surgical operation. The trial court entered judgments of nonsuit as to all defendants and plaintiff appealed.

On October 28, 1939, plaintiff consulted defendant Dr. Tilley, who diagnosed his ailment as appendicitis, and made arrangements for an appendectomy to be performed by defendant Dr. Spangard at a hospital owned and managed by defendant Dr. Swift. Plaintiff entered the hospital, was given a hypodermic injection, slept, and later was awakened by Doctors Tilley and Spangard and wheeled into the operating room by a nurse whom he believed to be defendant Gisler, an employee of Dr. Swift. Defendant Dr. Reser, the anesthetist, also an employee of Dr. Swift, adjusted plaintiff for the operation, pulling his body to the head of the operating table and, according to plaintiff's testimony, laying him back against two hard objects at the top of his shoulders, about an inch below his neck. Dr. Reser then administered the anesthetic and plaintiff lost consciousness. When he awoke early the following morning he was in his hospital room attended by defendant Thompson, the special nurse, and another nurse who was not made a defendant.

Plaintiff testified that prior to the operation he had never had any pain in, or injury to, his right arm or shoulder, but that when he awakened he felt a sharp pain about half way between the neck and the point of the right shoulder. He complained to the nurse, and then to Dr. Tilley, who gave him diathermy treatments while he remained in the hospital. The pain did not cease, but spread down to the lower part of his arm, and after his release from the hospital the condition grew worse. He was unable to rotate or lift his arm, and developed paralysis and atrophy of the muscles around the shoulder. He received further treatments from Dr. Tilley until March, 1940, and then returned to work, wearing his arm in a splint on the advice of Dr. Spangard.

Plaintiff also consulted Dr. Wilfred Sterling Clark, who had X-ray pictures taken which showed an area of diminished sensation below the shoulder and atrophy and wasting away of the muscles around the shoulder. In the opinion of Dr. Clark, plaintiff's condition was due to trauma or injury by pressure or strain, applied between his right shoulder and neck.

Plaintiff was also examined by Dr. Fernando Garduno, who expressed the opinion that plaintiff's injury was a paralysis of traumatic origin, not arising from pathological causes, and not systemic, and that the injury resulted in atrophy, loss of use and restriction of motion of the right arm and shoulder.

Plaintiff's theory is that the foregoing evidence presents a proper case for the application of the doctrine of res ipsa loquitur, and that the inference of negligence arising therefrom makes the granting of a nonsuit improper. Defendants take the position that, assuming that plaintiff's condition was in fact the result of an injury, there is no showing that the act of any particular defendant, nor any particular instrumentality, was the cause thereof. They attack plaintiff's action as an attempt to fix liability "en masse" on various defendants, some of whom were not responsible for the acts of others; and they further point to the failure to show which defendants had control of the instrumentalities that may have been involved. Their main defense may be briefly stated in two propositions: (1) that where there are several defendants, and there is a division of responsibility in the use of an instrumentality causing the injury, and the injury might have resulted from the separate act of either one of two or more persons, the rule of res ipsa loquitur cannot be invoked against any one of them; and (2) that where there are several instrumentalities, and no showing is made as to which caused the injury or as to the particular defendant in control of it, the doctrine cannot apply. We are satisfied, however, that these objections are not well taken in the circumstances of this case.

The doctrine of res ipsa loquitur has three conditions: "(1) the accident must be of a kind which ordinarily does not occur in the absence of someone's negligence; (2) it must be caused by an agency or instrumentality within the exclusive control of the defendant; (3) it must not have been due to any voluntary action or contribution on the part of the plaintiff." (Prosser, Torts, p. 295.) It is applied in a wide variety of situations, including cases of medical or dental treatment and hospital care. [   ]

There is, however, some uncertainty as to the extent to which res ipsa loquitur may be invoked in cases of injury from medical treatment. This is in part due to the tendency, in some decisions, to lay undue emphasis on the limitations of the doctrine, and to give too little attention to its basic underlying purpose. The result has been that a simple, understandable rule of circumstantial evidence, with a sound background of common sense and human experience, has occasionally been transformed into a rigid legal formula, which arbitrarily precludes its application in many cases where it is most important that it should be applied. If the doctrine is to continue to serve a useful purpose, we should not forget that "the particular force and justice of the rule, regarded as a presumption throwing upon the party charged the duty of producing evidence, consists in the circumstance that the chief evidence of the true cause, whether culpable or innocent, is practically accessible to him but inaccessible to the injured person." (9 Wigmore, Evidence [3d ed.], § 2509, p. 382; [   ]; Maki v. Murray Hospital, [7 P.2d 228 (Mont.)]). In the last-named case, where an unconscious patient in a hospital received injuries from a fall, the court declared that without the doctrine the maxim that for every wrong there is a remedy would be rendered nugatory, "by denying one, patently entitled to damages, satisfaction merely because he is ignorant of facts, peculiarly within the knowledge of the party who should, in all justice, pay them."

The present case is of a type which comes within the reason and spirit of the doctrine more fully perhaps than any other. The passenger sitting awake in a railroad car at the time of a collision, the pedestrian walking along the street and struck by a falling object or the debris of an explosion, are surely not more entitled to an explanation than the unconscious patient on the operating table. Viewed from this aspect, it is difficult to see how the doctrine can, with any justification, be so restricted in its statement as to become inapplicable to a patient who submits himself to the care and custody of doctors and nurses, is rendered unconscious, and receives some injury from instrumentalities used in his treatment. Without the aid of the doctrine a patient who received permanent injuries of a serious character, obviously the result of someone's negligence, would be entirely unable to recover unless the doctors and nurses in attendance voluntarily chose to disclose the identity of the negligent person and the facts establishing liability. [   ] If this were the state of the law of negligence, the courts, to avoid gross injustice, would be forced to invoke the principles of absolute liability, irrespective of negligence, in actions by persons suffering injuries during the course of treatment under anesthesia. But we think this juncture has not yet been reached, and that the doctrine of res ipsa loquitur is properly applicable to the case before us.

The condition that the injury must not have been due to the plaintiff's voluntary action is of course fully satisfied under the evidence produced herein; and the same is true of the condition that the accident must be one which ordinarily does not occur unless someone was negligent. We have here no problem of negligence in treatment, but of distinct injury to a healthy part of the body not the subject of treatment, nor within the area covered by the operation. The decisions in this state make it clear that such circumstances raise the inference of negligence, and call upon the defendant to explain the unusual result. [   ]

The argument of defendants is simply that plaintiff has not shown an injury caused by an instrumentality under a defendant's control, because he has not shown which of the several instrumentalities that he came in contact with while in the hospital caused the injury; and he has not shown that any one defendant or his servants had exclusive control over any particular instrumentality. Defendants assert that some of them were not the employees of other defendants, that some did not stand in any permanent relationship from which liability in tort would follow, and that in view of the nature of the injury, the number of defendants and the different functions performed by each, they could not all be liable for the wrong, if any.

We have no doubt that in a modern hospital a patient is quite likely to come under the care of a number of persons in different types of contractual and other relationships with each other. For example, in the present case it appears that Doctors Swift, Spangard and Tilley were physicians or surgeons commonly placed in the legal category of independent contractors; and Dr. Reser, the anesthetist, and defendant Thompson, the special nurse, were employees of Dr. Swift and not of the other doctors. But we do not believe that either the number or relationship of the defendants alone determines whether the doctrine of res ipsa loquitur applies. Every defendant in whose custody the plaintiff was placed for any period was bound to exercise ordinary care to see that no unnecessary harm came to him and each would be liable for failure in this regard. Any defendant who negligently injured him, and any defendant charged with his care who so neglected him as to allow injury to occur, would be liable. The defendant employers would be liable for the neglect of their employees; and the doctor in charge of the operation would be liable for the negligence of those who became his temporary servants for the purpose of assisting in the operation.

In this connection, it should be noted that while the assisting physicians and nurses may be employed by the hospital, or engaged by the patient, they normally become the temporary servants or agents of the surgeon in charge while the operation is in progress, and liability may be imposed upon him for their negligent acts under the doctrine of *respondeat superior*. Thus a surgeon has been held liable for the negligence of an assisting nurse who leaves a sponge or other object inside a patient, and the fact that the duty of seeing that such mistakes do not occur is delegated to others does not absolve the doctor from responsibility for their negligence.

It may appear at the trial that, consistent with the principles outlined above, one or more defendants will be found liable and others absolved, but this should not preclude the application of the rule of res ipsa loquitur. The control, at one time or another, of one or more of the various agencies or instrumentalities which might have harmed the plaintiff was in the hands of every defendant or of his employees or temporary servants. This, we think, places upon them the burden of initial explanation. Plaintiff was rendered unconscious for the purpose of undergoing surgical treatment by the defendants; it is manifestly unreasonable for them to insist that he identify any one of them as the person who did the alleged negligent act.

The other aspect of the case which defendants so strongly emphasize is that plaintiff has not identified the instrumentality any more than he has the particular guilty defendant. Here, again, there is a misconception which, if carried to the extreme for which defendants contend, would unreasonably limit the application of the res ipsa loquitur rule. It should be enough that the plaintiff can show an injury resulting from an external force applied while he lay unconscious in the hospital; this is as clear a case of identification of the instrumentality as the plaintiff may ever be able to make.

An examination of the recent cases, particularly in this state, discloses that the test of actual exclusive control of an instrumentality has not been strictly followed, but exceptions have been recognized where the purpose of the doctrine of res ipsa loquitur would otherwise be defeated. Thus, the test has become one of right of control rather than actual control. [   ] In the bursting bottle cases where the bottler has delivered the instrumentality to a retailer and thus has given up actual control, he will nevertheless be subject to the doctrine where it is shown that no change in the condition of the bottle occurred after it left the bottler's possession, and it can accordingly be said that he was in constructive control. [   ] Moreover, this court departed from the single instrumentality theory in the colliding vehicle cases, where two defendants were involved, each in control of a separate vehicle. (See Smith v. O'Donnell, [12 P.2d 933 (Cal.1932)]; Godfrey v. Brown, [29 P.2d 165 (Cal.1934)]; Carpenter, 10 So.Cal.L.Rev. 170.) Finally, it has been suggested that the hospital cases may properly be considered exceptional, and that the doctrine of res ipsa loquitur "should apply with equal force in cases wherein medical and nursing staffs take the place of machinery and may, through carelessness or lack of skill, inflict, or permit the infliction of injury upon a patient who is thereafter in no position to say how he received his injuries." ([*Maki v. Murray Hospital*]; see, also, Whetstine v. Moravec, [291 N.W. 425, 435 (Iowa 1940)], where the court refers to the "instrumentalities" as including "the unconscious body of the plaintiff.")

In the face of these examples of liberalization of the tests for res ipsa loquitur, there can be no justification for the rejection of the doctrine in the instant case. As pointed out above, if we accept the contention of defendants herein, there will rarely be any compensation for patients injured while unconscious. A hospital today conducts a highly integrated system of activities, with many persons contributing their efforts. There may be, e.g., preparation for surgery by nurses and interns who are employees of the hospital; administering of an anesthetic by a doctor who may be an employee of the hospital, an employee of the operating surgeon, or an independent contractor; performance of an operation by a surgeon and assistants who may be his employees, employees of the hospital, or independent contractors; and post surgical care by the surgeon, a hospital physician, and nurses. The number of those in whose care the patient is placed is not a good reason for denying him all reasonable opportunity to recover for negligent harm. It is rather a good reason for reexamination of the statement of legal theories which supposedly compel such a shocking result.

We do not at this time undertake to state the extent to which the reasoning of this case may be applied to other situations in which the doctrine of res ipsa loquitur is invoked. We merely hold that where a plaintiff receives unusual injuries while unconscious and in the course of medical treatment, all those defendants who had any control over his body or the instrumentalities which might have caused the injuries may properly be called upon to meet the inference of negligence by giving an explanation of their conduct.

The judgment is reversed.

SHENK, J., CURTIS, J., EDMONDS, J., CARTER, J., and SCHAUER, J., concurred.

Notes and Questions

1. This opinion quotes Prosser's formulation of res ipsa loquitur that conditions its application upon proof of three factors. In this case how is each of them met? Is that formulation consistent with the passage quoted from Wigmore? Would the plaintiff's case have been stronger, or weaker, under the Prosser approach to res ipsa loquitur if he had sued only Drs. Swift and Spangard?

For an extended discussion about imposing liability on a hospital for negligence in granting staff privileges and in reviewing the competency of its medical staff, see Strubhart v. Perry Mem. Hosp. Trust Auth., 903 P.2d 263 (Okl.1995).

2. In this case is res ipsa loquitur "a simple, understandable rule of circumstantial evidence, with a sound background of common sense and human experience"? The court relies mainly on a case involving an unconscious patient "patently entitled to damages." Is that true here?

3. On remand the trial judge as trier of fact accepted the testimony of plaintiff's experts and of an independent court-appointed expert that the injury was traumatic in origin and did not result from an infection. Except for the hospital owner, who did not personally attend plaintiff, each defendant testified that he or she "saw nothing occur which could have caused the injury." The trial judge found against all defendants and his ruling was affirmed. The court observed that "There is nothing inherent in direct testimony which compels a trial court to accept it over the contrary inferences which may reasonably be drawn from circumstantial evidence," and quoted Justice Holmes to the effect that "law does not always keep step with logic." Ybarra v. Spangard, 208 P.2d 445 (Cal.App.1949). Is this result sensible? Could the trial judge have found some defendants liable and some not liable?

4. It has been suggested that in the *Ybarra* case each participant in the operation who stated exactly what he or she did should be entitled to a directed verdict. "It is something of a mockery to require the defendant in the name of fairness to offer an explanation and then let a jury ignore the explanation on no other basis than its choice not to believe." The author does recognize, however, that if the explanation is evasive or "suggests mendacity" the case should go to the jury. Jaffe, Res Ipsa Loquitur Vindicated, 1 Buffalo L.Rev. 1, 11 (1951). Is this defensible?

5. In Inouye v. Black, 47 Cal.Rptr. 313 (App.1965), the defendant surgeon implanted stainless steel wire in plaintiff's neck to stabilize it. Although the tension was expected to break the wire, it was expected that the wire would remain in the body and cause no physical damage. The wire fragmented into unexpectedly small pieces that migrated downward toward the lower spine, necessitating further surgery to retrieve the pieces. Plaintiff sued only the surgeon. Uncontroverted medical testimony showed that he had selected the right type of wire; that if he was telling the truth, he had properly inspected it visually and manually before using it; and that the fragmentation was unexpected. The trial judge's grant of a nonsuit was affirmed on appeal. Res ipsa loquitur was inapplicable because common experience "reveals defendant's negligence as one of several available speculations, but not as a probability." It might have been that the surgeon failed to do some of the things he said he did; but it might also have been that the hospital left the wire too long in the supply room or that the wire left the manufacturer's plant with hidden flaws.

The court observed that a "group of persons and instrumentalities may combine in the performance of a medical procedure culminating in an unexpected, mysterious and disastrous result. With the sources of disaster personified in a group of defendants, the demand for evidence pointing the finger of probability at any one of them is relaxed; all may be called upon to give the jury evidence of care," citing *Ybarra* and other cases. The court then noted that since only the surgeon was before the court, that principle did not apply. If all three had been before the court, might the surgeon still have received a nonsuit?

In Chin v. St. Barnabas Medical Center, 734 A.2d 778 (N.J.1999), a patient died from an air embolism when gas was introduced into her bloodstream during surgery. It was "certainly the result of the negligent use of a medical instrument, but it was unclear who was at fault. [Suit] was brought against all the defendants who had a possible role in the events leading to the patient's death; the doctor who performed the procedure; the nurses in the operating room; the hospital; [and the manufacturer who was dismissed]." The trial judge directed the jury to return a verdict "against at least one defendant in this case because obviously somebody did something wrong." The jury returned a verdict against every defendant except one of the three nurses. On appeal, the court held that the burden of proof had properly been switched to the defendants. Three conditions had all been met: the plaintiff herself was blameless, the injury was one that "bespoke negligence on the part of one or more of the defendants," and "all the potential defendants must be before the court." The fact that the case had been dismissed against the manufacturer did not bar the burden switch. Rather it showed that the manufacturer had borne its burden of showing that it was not culpable. No party contested the fact that the instrument was misconnected and that this was the fault of at least one defendant. "Each defendant simply insisted that he or she was not the party individually responsible." Would this approach apply to a two-car crash that injured a clearly innocent pedestrian?

6. In Fireman's Fund Amer. Ins. Cos. v. Knobbe, 562 P.2d 825 (Nev.1977), plaintiff, a hotel's fire insurer, sued four guests to recover insurance payments it had made as the result of a fire that started in the room occupied by two of the guests. That couple and another couple, who were occupying a connecting room, had all been smoking in the room shortly before the fire broke out. Plaintiff was unable to prove which defendant had been negligent and sought to invoke res ipsa loquitur. The court upheld a summary judgment granted the defendants and rejected *Ybarra*. In doing so, it agreed with Justice Traynor who, dissenting in Raber v. Tumin, 226 P.2d 574 (Cal.1951), had warned of the danger of extending *Ybarra*. He asserted that under *Ybarra*, a plaintiff "who is struck on the head by a flower pot falling from a multistoried apartment building may recover judgment against all the tenants unless the innocent tenants are able to identify the guilty one."

If you are run over by a negligent hit-and-run driver as you cross the street and all you can tell is the year, make and color of the car, what analysis if you sue jointly all local owners of such cars and rest after your testimony about what happened?

7. In Judson v. Giant Powder Co., 40 P. 1020 (Cal.1895), the defendant's nitroglycerine factory exploded, killing all who could possibly have explained why it happened. In a suit by plaintiff, whose property was damaged, the court held that evidence of the explosion sufficed to withstand a nonsuit. Is this sound in a situation in which rebuttal is impossible? Consider also Newing v. Cheatham, 540 P.2d 33 (Cal.1975), in which a private airplane crashed killing all aboard, including the pilot. A directed verdict on liability for the estate of a passenger was upheld on appeal.

8. *Ybarra* was flatly rejected in Barrett v. Emanuel Hospital, 669 P.2d 835 (Or.App.1983). First, "modern discovery practice" casts doubt on the need for the *Ybarra* approach. Second, the inference of res ipsa "is permitted only when the plaintiff is able to establish . . . the probability that a particular defendant's conduct was the cause of the plaintiff's harm." Finally, special protections for unconscious patients could "be achieved in various direct ways which may warrant societal consideration, e.g., strict liability or some form of *respondeat superior* liability. However, we do not think the objective should be pursued by stretching a permissible inference beyond the point where there are underlying facts other than the result from which it can reasonably be drawn." The complaint was dismissed.

See Spannaus v. Otolaryngology Clinic, 242 N.W.2d 594 (Minn.1976), refusing to apply the *Ybarra* approach to a case with a similar fact pattern except that the anesthesiologist was not sued.

E. THE SPECIAL CASE OF MEDICAL MALPRACTICE

In this section we consider special legal and practical problems involved in medical malpractice cases. In the process we review the standard of care, the role of custom, and questions of proof. Consider the following excerpt from Robbins v. Footer, 553 F.2d 123 (D.C.Cir.1977), involving a claim against an obstetrician:

> The conduct of a defendant in a negligence suit is usually measured against the conduct of a hypothetical reasonably prudent person acting under the same or similar circumstances. [ ] In medical malpractice cases, however, courts have required that the specialized knowledge and skill of the defendant must be taken into account. [ ] Although the law had thus imposed a higher standard of care on doctors, it has tempered the impact of that rule by permitting the profession, as a group, to set its own legal standards of reasonable conduct. Whether a defendant has or has not conformed his conduct to a customary practice is generally only evidence of whether he has acted as a reasonably prudent person. [ ] In a malpractice case, however, the question of whether the defendant acted in conformity with the common practice within his profession is the heart of the suit. [ ] As part of his prima facie case a malpractice plaintiff must affirmatively prove the relevant recognized standard of medical care exercised by other physicians and that the defendant departed from that standard when treating the plaintiff. [ ] In almost all cases the plaintiff must present expert witnesses since the technical complexity of the facts and issues usually prevents the jury itself from determining both the appropriate standard of care and whether the defendant's conduct conformed to that standard. In such cases there can be no finding of negligence without expert testimony to support it. [ ]

Despite the refined standard of care, judges must still be sure to use language in their charges that conveys the objective nature of the inquiry. In DiFranco v. Klein, 657 A.2d 145 (R.I.1995), the court overturned a defense verdict in a malpractice case because the trial judge had probably prejudiced the plaintiff by stating that the defendant was not liable "if in the exercise of . . . good faith judgment she has made a mistake as to the course of treatment taken" and that a physician "is not liable for damages resulting from an honest mistake or error in judgment."

Sheeley v. Memorial Hospital

Supreme Court of Rhode Island, 1998.
710 A.2d 161.

[At the time plaintiff gave birth, in 1987, Dr. Ryder, a second-year family practice resident, performed an episiotomy, which involves cutting into the mother's perineum to facilitate the birth and then stitching the incision after the birth. Plaintiff developed complications at the site of this surgery and sued Dr. Ryder and the hospital.]

GOLDBERG, J.

This case is before the court on the appeal of Joanne Sheeley (Sheeley) from the directed verdict entered against her in the underlying medical malpractice action. Specifically Sheeley asserts that the trial justice erred in excluding the testimony of her expert witness, which exclusion resulted in the entry of the directed verdict. For the reasons set forth below, we hold that the trial justice erred in excluding the testimony and reverse the judgment from which the appeal was taken. Furthermore, we take this opportunity to reexamine the proper standard of care to be applied in medical malpractice cases and, in so doing, abandon the "similar locality" rule, which previously governed the admissibility of expert testimony in such actions. . . .

. . .

At the trial on the malpractice action, Sheeley sought to introduce the expert medical testimony of Stanley D. Leslie, M.D. (Dr. Leslie), a board certified obstetrician/gynecologist (OB/GYN). Doctor Leslie planned to testify about Dr. Ryder's alleged malpractice and the applicable standard of care as it relates to the performance of an episiotomy. The defendants objected and filed a motion in limine to exclude the testimony, arguing that Dr. Leslie, as an OB/GYN, was not qualified under G.L.1956 § 9-19-41[3] to testify against a family practice resident who was performing obstetric and gynecological care. A hearing on the motion was conducted, at which time it was disclosed that Dr. Leslie had been board certified in obstetrics and gynecology since 1961 and recertified in 1979. Doctor Leslie testified that board certification represents a level of achievement of skill and knowledge as established by a national standard in which the standard of care is uniform throughout the medical specialty. Doctor Leslie is currently a clinical professor of obstetrics and gynecology at the Hill-Science Center, State University, College of Medicine in Syracuse. He is a member of the New York Statewide Professional Standards Review Council, which reviews disputes between doctors and hospitals regarding diagnosis and management, and the Credentials and Certification Committee at the Crouse-Irving Hospital, where his responsibilities include drafting standards for family practice physicians. It was further revealed that Dr. Leslie has in the course of his career delivered approximately 4,000 babies and that even though he has been retired from the practice of obstetrics since 1975, he has maintained his familiarity with the standards and practices in the field

---

3. [Section 9-19-41] states:

"In any legal action based upon a cause of action arising on or after January 1, 1987, for personal injury or wrongful death filed against a licensed physician . . . . only those persons who by knowledge, skill, experience, training or education qualify as experts in the field of the alleged malpractice shall be permitted to give expert testimony as to the alleged malpractice."

of obstetrics through weekly conferences, active obstetric work, professorial responsibilities, and continuing education.

Nevertheless, relying on Soares v. Vestal, 632 A.2d 647 (R.I.1993), defendants maintained that § 9–19–41 requires a testifying expert to be in the same medical field as the defendant physician. In *Soares* this court upheld the trial justice's decision to exclude the testimony of the plaintiff's expert witness in a situation in which the expert was board certified in neurology and internal medicine, and the underlying malpractice action involved a family practitioner performing emergency medicine. [ ] Agreeing that *Soares* was determinative, the trial justice here granted defendants' motion. . . . Sheeley did not have any other experts prepared to testify, nor was she able to procure one within the two-day period allowed by the trial justice. Consequently defendants' motion for a directed verdict was granted. This appeal ensued.

. . .

. . . In a medical malpractice case expert testimony is an essential requirement in proving the standard of care applicable to the defendant, "unless the lack of care is so obvious as to be within the layman's common knowledge." . . .

"The determination of the competency of an expert witness to testify is within the discretion of the trial justice." [ ] This court will not disturb that decision in the absence of clear error or abuse. [ ] In fairness to the trial justice, we note that in making her determination with respect to the admissibility of the expert's testimony, she was without the benefit of our decisions in Marshall v. Medical Associates of Rhode Island, Inc., 677 A.2d 425 (R.I.1996), and more importantly Buja v. Morningstar, 688 A.2d 817 (R.I.1997), which have distinguished *Soares* and limited its holding to situations in which the physician-expert lacks knowledge, skill, experience, or education in the same medical field as the alleged malpractice. Nevertheless, after a review of these cases, we find it clear that the trial justice did in fact abuse her discretion and commit reversible error in excluding the testimony of Dr. Leslie.

In *Buja* the plaintiffs brought a medical malpractice action against their family practitioners when their child suffered severe medical complications, including cerebral palsy and mental retardation, after having been deprived of oxygen just prior to birth. [ ] At trial, the plaintiffs sought to introduce testimony of a board certified obstetrician. The trial justice, however, excluded the testimony and stated that testimony concerning the standard of care required of a family practitioner practicing obstetrics had to be introduced by an expert in family medicine, not an expert in OB/GYN. [ ] Relying on our previous holding in *Marshall*, this court reversed the trial justice and stated that even though the proposed expert did not practice in the same specialty as the defendants, he clearly had the prerequisite "knowledge, skill, experience, training or education . . . in the field of the alleged malpractice." [ ] The *Buja* court held that nothing in the language of § 9–19–41 requires the expert to practice in the same specialty as the defendant. [ ] "Such an additional requirement is unnecessary and is in contravention to the General Assembly's clear intentions, as expressed in § 9–19–41." [   ] In view of this holding and the striking factual similarities of the instant matter to *Buja*, there can be little doubt that we must reverse the decision of the trial justice and remand the case for a new trial.

Yet in spite of our holdings in *Buja* and *Marshall*, defendants continue to insist that Dr. Leslie is not qualified to testify. In essence defendants argue that Dr. Leslie is overqualified, stating that a board certified OB/ GYN does not possess the same knowledge, skill, experience, training, or education as a second-year family practice resident performing obstetrics in Rhode Island. Furthermore defendants argue that because Dr. Leslie has not actually practiced obstetrics since 1975, his experience in providing obstetrical care is "clearly outdated" and he is therefore not competent to testify concerning the appropriate standard of care as it applied to the performance of an episiotomy and the repair of the same—even while they acknowledge that the standard of care relative to the procedures involved in the alleged malpractice have changed little over the last thirty years. Finally defendants assert that pursuant to the limitations of the "similar locality" rule, Dr. Leslie must be disqualified because he lacks any direct knowledge about the applicable standard of care for a family practice resident providing obstetric care in Rhode Island.

The defendants suggest that Dr. Leslie, although he has attended national conferences and studied medical journals and treatises in addition to his national certification, is not qualified to testify about the applicable local standard of care. In light of these arguments and with a view toward preventing any further confusion regarding the necessary qualifications of an expert testifying about the proper standard of care in medical malpractice actions, we take this opportunity to revisit our position on the appropriate standard of care.

For over three-quarters of a century this court has subscribed to the principle "that when a physician undertakes to treat or diagnose a patient, he or she is under a duty to exercise 'the same degree of diligence and skill which is commonly possessed by other members of the profession who are engaged in the same type of practice in similar localities having due regard for the state of scientific knowledge at the time of treatment.' " [   ] This "same or similar locality" rule is a somewhat expanded version of the "strict locality" rule, which requires that the expert testifying be from the same community as the defendant. See Shilkret v. Annapolis Emergency Hospital Association, [349 A.2d 245, 248 (Md.1975)]; [   ]. The rationale underlying the development of the "strict locality" rule was a recognition that opportunities, experience, and conditions may differ between densely and sparsely populated communities. [   ]

This restrictive rule, however, soon came under attack in that it legitimized a low standard of care in certain smaller communities and that it also failed to address or to compensate for the potential so-called conspiracy of silence in a plaintiff's locality that would preclude any possibility of obtaining expert testimony. [   ] Furthermore, as this court noted in [   ], the locality rule is somewhat of an anachronism in view of "[m]odern systems of transportation and communication." [   ] Thus many jurisdictions, including our own, adopted the "same or similar locality" rule, which allows for experts from similarly situated communities to testify concerning the appropriate standard of care. [   ] Nevertheless, even with this somewhat expanded view, the medical malpractice bar has continually urged a narrow application of the rule, arguing the need for similar, if not identical, education, training, and experience. . . . This is a consequence that we have never intended.

The appropriate standard of care to be utilized in any given procedure should not be compartmentalized by a physician's area of professional specialization or certification. On the contrary, we believe the focus in any medical malpractice case should be the procedure performed and the question of whether it was executed in conformity with the recognized standard of care, the primary concern being whether the treatment was administered in a reasonable manner. Any doctor with knowledge of or familiarity with the procedure, acquired through experience, observation, association, or education, is competent to testify concerning the requisite standard of care and whether the care in any given case deviated from that standard. The resources available to a physician, his or her specific area of practice, or the length of time he or she has been practicing are all issues that should be considered by the trial justice in making his or her decision regarding the qualification of an expert. No one issue, however, should be determinative. Furthermore, except in extreme cases, a witness who has obtained board certification in a particular specialty related to the procedure in question, especially when that board certification reflects a national standard of training and qualification, should be presumptively qualified to render an opinion. See [*Shilkret*]; [   ].

This court is of the opinion that whatever geographical impediments may previously have justified the need for a "similar locality" analysis are no longer applicable in view of the present-day realities of the medical profession. As the *Shilkret* court observed:

> The modern physician bears little resemblance to his predecessors. As we have indicated at length, the medical schools of yesterday could not possibly compare with the accredited institutions of today, many of which are associated with teaching hospitals. But the contrast merely begins at that point in the medical career: vastly superior postgraduate training, the dynamic impact of modern communications and transportation, the proliferation of medical literature, frequent seminars and conferences on a variety of professional subjects, and the growing availability of modern clinical facilities are but some of the developments in the medical profession which combine to produce contemporary standards that are not only much higher than they were just a few short years ago, but are also national in scope.

In sum, the traditional locality rules no longer fit the present-day medical malpractice case. [   ]

We agree. Furthermore, we note that in enacting § 9–19–41, the Legislature failed to employ any reference to the "similar locality" rule. We conclude that this omission was deliberate and constitutes a recognition of the national approach to the delivery of medical services, especially in the urban centers of this country, of which Rhode Island is certainly one.

Accordingly we join the growing number of jurisdictions that have repudiated the "same or similar" communities test in favor of a national standard and hold that a physician is under a duty to use the degree of care and skill that is expected of a reasonably competent practitioner in the same class to which he or she belongs, acting in the same or similar circumstances. [The court cites cases from 20 states.] In this case the alleged malpractice occurred in the field of obstetrics and involved a procedure and attendant standard of care that has remained constant for over thirty years. Doctor Leslie, as a board certified OB/GYN with over thirty years of experience, a clinical professor of obstetrics and gynecology at a major New York hospital, and a member of the New York Statewide Professional Standards Review Council, is undoubtedly qualified to testify regarding the appropriate standard of care.

[The case was remanded to the lower court for a new trial.]

Notes and Questions

1. What was the trial judge's error? What are the arguments for and against "the same locality"? The "same or similar locality"? How should a court determine whether a locality is "similar" for purpose of qualifying an expert?

2. In some states national standards are more likely to be invoked if the defendant is "board-certified." That fact was central to the resolution of *Robbins*, where the obstetrician was board-certified:

> Modern medical education and postgraduate training has been nationalized. Scientific information flows freely among medical institutions throughout the country. Professional journals and numerous other networks of continuing education are all national in scope. [ ] Several courts have . . . established a national standard of care for all physicians, completely abandoning any locality limitation. . . .

> Even in jurisdictions which have not adopted a national standard for all malpractice issues, if a physician holds himself out as a specialist, [as defendant had done here], he is held to the general standard of care required of all physicians in the same specialty. [ ] In order to become a certified specialist in obstetrics, a physician must meet nationally uniform educational and residency requirements. [ ] The textbooks used are national textbooks and the required examination is a national exam graded by a body of examiners selected so as to eliminate any regional peculiarities. [ ] After certification, specialists keep abreast of developments in their field through medical specialty journals available throughout the nation and medical specialty societies

with national memberships. It seems clear that the medical profession itself has adopted a national standard for membership in one of its certified specialties. If the law remains tied to a locality standard it ignores the reality of modern medicine in favor of an outdated mythology.

Is there any remaining room for a locality-based standard?

3. Some statutes have imposed other types of limits on the admissibility of expert testimony. In Sami v. Varn, 535 S.E.2d 172 (Va. 2000), the statute required that the proposed witness, in addition to having the requisite substantive knowledge, must have had an "active clinical practice in either the defendant's specialty or a related field of medicine within one year of the date of the alleged act or omission." Would that preclude Dr. Leslie? Should it?

4. In Gala v. Hamilton, 715 A.2d 1108 (Pa.1998), defendants used local anesthetic while working on plaintiff's neck tumor. Plaintiff alleged that general anesthetic should have been used. The trial judge charged the jury:

> Where there are two schools of thought in the use of local anesthesia, a physician may rightfully choose to practice under either school of thought. If you the Jury find as a fact that the Defendants followed a procedure recognized by [a] reputable and respected, considerable number of medical experts in the use of local anesthesia, even if in the minority, the Defendants would not be deemed negligent or in violation of the standard of care in the use of local anesthesia in 1988 and you must find for the Defendants on this issue.

On appeal from a verdict and judgment for defendants, the court upheld the charge. It held that a "school" could exist even if it has never given rise to a written literature. Must the school be national in scope? Suppose at the trial plaintiff shows that the "local-anesthetic school" in fact produces a higher rate of bad outcomes than the general-anesthetic school—and that this would have been apparent if anyone in the local school had ever published (or tried to publish) anything on the subject?

5. Hospitals themselves may be negligent for failing to use reasonable care in keeping their facilities safe and in failing to select and retain only competent physicians both to serve on the staff and physicians from the community to exercise staff privileges. In Welsh v. Bulger, 698 A.2d 581 (Pa.1997), Dr. T was not legally qualified to perform cesarean sections. This procedure became necessary during a delivery and the baby died when nobody else could perform the procedure in the time available. T had not arranged for assistance, and the hospital knew that T was not qualified to perform surgery. Given that knowledge, a jury could find the hospital negligent for failing to require that a qualified surgeon be available during T's deliveries.

6. How are experts retained and compensated? If witnesses to auto accidents are not paid why should medical experts be paid? In Henning v. Thomas, 366 S.E.2d 109 (Va.1988), the court held that the trial judge committed reversible error by not permitting defendants to try to persuade the jury that the plaintiff's expert was a " 'doctor for hire' who was part of a nationwide group that offered themselves as witnesses, on behalf of medical malpractice plaintiffs. Once the jury was made aware of this information it was for the jury to decide what weight, if any, to give to [the expert's] testimony. This was a classic case of an effort to establish bias, prejudice, or relationship." Is it relevant if an expert retained by one side has never rendered an opinion on behalf of the other side? Is it relevant if an expert has testified in 20 cases during the past year—and has seen patients only three weeks during that period?

7. *Sheeley's* reference to the conspiracy of silence probably alluded to the assertion that the requirement of expert testimony in malpractice cases has been difficult for some plaintiffs to meet for reasons unrelated to the merits of the case. In 1961, a survey of surgeons indicated that only 30 percent would be willing to testify against another surgeon who had removed the wrong kidney. Medical Economics, Aug. 28, 1961. Physicians who criticized colleagues might face expulsion from the local medical society. Bernstein v. Alameda–Contra Costa Medical Ass'n, 293 P.2d 862 (Cal.App.1956). See also L'Orange v. Medical Protective Co., 394 F.2d 57 (6th Cir.1968), in which plaintiff alleged that defendant insurer had cancelled his malpractice policy because he had testified in court against a dentist also insured by the defendant. The potential for concern has not been eliminated by the passage of time or by changes in the organization of medical services. After *Sheeley,* the same court confronted a case in which, as of 1990, all three of the state's pediatric surgeons were associated in the same office. Flanagan v. Wesselhoeft, 712 A.2d 365 (R.I.1998). The case went off on other grounds.

These concerns undoubtedly induced courts to devise techniques for avoiding the need for experts in certain kinds of cases. One change permitted a plaintiff to call the defendant physician and try to use that testimony to fill gaps in plaintiff's case. Some courts permitted the plaintiff to read treatises to educate the jury.

8. At one point, the *Sheeley* court refers to situations "within the layman's common knowledge." As that suggests, on such occasions plaintiffs in malpractice cases do not need experts. For example, it might be shown that without any need for hasty termination of a surgical procedure, a sponge or a surgical instrument was inadvertently left in the plaintiff's abdomen. Or it might be shown that the surgeon operated on the left leg when it was the right leg that needed the treatment. In such cases, it would necessarily follow that even if an expert testified for the defense that the relevant segment of the medical profession normally behaved as the defendant did, the jury would not be required to accept that as the proper standard.

Recall Leonard v. Watsonville Community Hospital, p. 98, supra, involving a clamp that was left inside the plaintiff. The court stated that even if the defendants were trying to assert that there was a custom in the relevant community not to count instruments before closing an incision,

that would not control the case: "It is a matter of common knowledge . . . that no special skill is required in counting instruments.
Although under such circumstances proof of practice or custom is some
evidence of what should be done and may assist in the determination of
what constitutes due care, it does not conclusively establish the standard of
care."

See also Tousignant v. St. Louis County, 615 N.W.2d 53 (Minn.2000),
in which the elderly plaintiff was transferred to defendant's nursing home
with instructions that called for her to be restrained. She was not restrained on her arrival, and fell soon thereafter, breaking her hip. The
court held that no expert testimony was needed. The claim was not that
defendant had "failed to appropriately assess her condition and take
appropriate action; rather, she claims that the standard of care for their
acts was their compliance with the instructions on the referral form itself—
that Tousignant was to wear the vest restraint 'at all times.'" That was
not a question involving "complex scientific or technological issues and is
within the general knowledge and experience of lay persons."

9. Although aspects of the standard of care may be special to medical
malpractice, the need for experts is not. When buildings collapse, when
factories catch fire, when chemicals escape, the plaintiff will often need an
expert to explain the underlying mechanics or technology to the jury so
that the judge can be confident that the jury will understand the facts
sufficiently to be able to make a rational determination of whether or not
there was negligence. In cases involving claims that a complex product is
defective an expert is often required to explain why it was dangerous and
how it might have been made less so. We return to expert testimony in
Chapter V.

10. For comprehensive treatment of the medical malpractice area, see
P. Weiler, Medical Malpractice on Trial (1991); F. Sloan and R. Bovbjerg,
Medical Malpractice: Crisis, Response and Effects (1989); Symposium,
Medical Malpractice: Can the Private Sector Find Relief? 49 Law & Con-
temp.Probs. 1–348 (1986). In Chapter XI we consider recent developments
and proposals for changing the handling of medical malpractice litigation.

Connors v. University Associates in Obstetrics & Gynecology, Inc.

United States Court of Appeals, Second Circuit, 1993.
4 F.3d 123.

[In an effort to become pregnant, plaintiff underwent surgery. After
the surgery she lost all function in her left leg. In this diversity action
brought by plaintiff and her husband, the theory of plaintiff's experts was
that a retractor used to keep the incision open had impinged on a nerve
leading to plaintiff's left leg. Plaintiff's expert testified that the requisite
care with this retractor required (1) caution in opening the blades so as not
to exert too much force; (2) assuring that the blades not impinge on the
muscle, the pelvic wall or various nerves; (3) releasing the retractor during

surgery to reduce pressure on these areas; and (4) altering the position of the retractor blades to avoid prolonged pressure on these areas. Plaintiff tried to show that these had not been done carefully. Experts on both sides agreed that the retractors had to be used carefully. They disagreed, however, over whether the injury could still have occurred even if the defendants had been careful with the retractor. Plaintiff's experts testified that the injury would not have occurred in such a case even if plaintiff's nerve had been abnormally situated. Defense experts testified that plaintiff's nerve was "abnormally positioned, an anatomical rarity that the performing physicians could not have anticipated. These experts also testified that nerve injuries in operations of this type were sometimes unavoidable complications not attributable to negligence."

At the first trial the judge refused to charge res ipsa loquitur. After a defense verdict, the judge granted a new trial on the ground that he had erred in refusing to charge res ipsa. More facts are stated in the opinion.]

Before: NEWMAN, CHIEF JUDGE, VAN GRAAFEILAND, and ALTIMARI, CIRCUIT JUDGES.

ALTIMARI, CIRCUIT JUDGE.

. . .

. . . . At the close of the second trial, the district court, over University Associates' objection, issued the following instruction to the jury:

> In ordinary cases, the mere fact that an accident or injury happened does not furnish evidence that it was caused by any person's negligence. And the plaintiff must prove some negligent act or omission on the part of the defendant. This is the method of finding negligence that I have just described to you.
>
> Nevertheless, I instruct you in this case that you may find the defendant, University Associates, negligent if you find that the plaintiff has proved each of the following elements by a preponderance of the evidence: first, that an injury to the plaintiff [was caused] by the self-retaining retractor used during her surgery; [second], that at the time of the accident or injury, the self-retaining retractor was under the exclusive control or management of Dr. John Brumsted and/or his surgical assistants . . .; and, third, that in the normal course of events this type of injury would not have occurred without the negligence of the person having control and management of the self-retaining retractor.
>
> I say that you may so find. You are not compelled to so find. You should consider all the facts and circumstances in evidence and also the defendant's explanation. You are reminded that the plaintiff has the burden of proving the defendant's negligence by a preponderance of the evidence.

At the close of the second trial, the jury returned a verdict for the plaintiffs in the amount of $800,000. University Associates moved for a new trial, arguing that the res ipsa instruction was error. That motion was denied.

University Associates now appeals the result of the second trial, arguing that the district court erred in instructing the jury on res ipsa loquitur where: (1) expert testimony on causation was given; and (2) Connors introduced direct evidence on the cause of the injury. The appeal brings up for review both the correctness of giving a res ipsa loquitur charge at the second trial and the order granting a new trial for lack of a res ipsa loquitur charge at the first trial.

. . .

University Associates has not challenged the district court's ruling that Vermont law would allow a res ipsa instruction in medical malpractice cases generally. However, the defendants-appellees contend that res ipsa should not apply to medical malpractice cases in which expert testimony is presented. The basis for this contention is that res ipsa is a doctrine traditionally grounded on the theory that jurors share a common experience that allows them to make certain inferences of negligence. If expert testimony is needed to support the inference, then the inference does not come from common experience but from uncommon experience (i.e., specialized medical knowledge).

University Associates has raised an issue that has divided jurisdictions across the country. Unless a medical malpractice case is factually simple (i.e., leaving a sponge in the patient), jurors' common experience will not provide them with the requisite insight to determine whether certain injuries can only be the result of negligence. In such non-obvious cases, courts are presented with a choice of either allowing a res ipsa loquitur instruction and permitting the plaintiff to educate the jury through the use of experts, or of disallowing the application of res ipsa loquitur and leaving the plaintiff to demonstrate negligence solely through the opinions of experts.

Although no Vermont court has ruled on the issue, there is a clear split between states in their treatment of res ipsa loquitur charges in medical malpractice cases. Some states allow the plaintiff to come forward with expert testimony to support a res ipsa theory, while others preclude the use of a res ipsa instruction in non-obvious cases and permit its use only in cases where the plaintiff's injury is one that the average citizen can perceive to be a function of negligence based on everyday experience. . . .

We conclude . . . that the district court was correct in predicting that Vermont would permit a plaintiff to utilize expert testimony to "bridge the gap" between the jury's common knowledge and the uncommon knowledge of experts. The Restatement explicitly encourages the use of expert testimony in medical malpractice cases involving res ipsa loquitur:

> In the usual case the basis of past experience from which this conclusion may be drawn is common to the community, and is a matter of general knowledge, which the court recognizes on much the same basis as when it takes judicial notice of facts which everyone knows. It may, however, be supplied by the evidence of the parties; and expert

testimony that such an event usually does not occur without negligence may afford a sufficient basis for the inference. Such testimony may be essential to the plaintiff's case where, as for example in some actions for medical malpractice, there is no fund of common knowledge which may permit laymen reasonably to draw the conclusion.

Restatement, § 328D, comment *d*. Moreover, states have increasingly chosen to follow the modern trend in permitting expert testimony, [ ].

The restrictive view of res ipsa loquitur, barring expert testimony, erroneously overstates the importance of the traditional "common knowledge" requirement. Whether the knowledge required to evaluate the likelihood of negligent conduct inferred from an accident comes from common or specialized knowledge, the key question is still whether that accident would normally occur in the ordinary course of events. As the district court stated:

> [I]n this era of constantly developing medical science, cases in which injuries bespeak negligence to the average person occur less and less and complex cases predominate. If courts refuse to allow experts to testify to what is common knowledge within their fields, then they are not being responsive to new conditions nor are they keeping abreast of changes in society.

[ ]. Experts within a field share a common knowledge about whether a certain type of injury could only occur through negligence, just as average citizens can share a common knowledge about whether barrels of flour normally roll out of warehouse windows. [ ] These experts can educate the jurors, essentially training them to be twelve new initiates into a different, higher level of common knowledge. The jurors can then determine for themselves whether the expert opinion is credible, after also considering the defendant's experts' opinions that res ipsa does not apply. . . .

This is clearly the type of case in which expert testimony was appropriate and necessary. To find otherwise would place Connors in a "Catch–22," presenting her with a choice of either introducing expert testimony or forgoing a res ipsa instruction. . . . If the res ipsa instruction were to be given without the expert testimony, the jury would be given the opportunity to find the defendants negligent without proof, but the jury would lack the acumen to be able to determine whether the injury was truly the type that could not occur but for the defendant's negligence.

Alternatively, Connors could introduce the expert testimony but do without the res ipsa charge, as in the first trial. This would give the jurors the ability to evaluate the injury, but would not instruct them that they can make the leap to inferring negligence from the fact of the injury. Expert testimony in this case was not able to prove conclusively that negligence caused Connors' injury. Rather, Connors' experts opined that there was nothing unusual about Connors' anatomy, contrary to the defendant-appellant's suggestion, and that the injury could only have occurred if the doctors had negligently used the retractor. This does not, by itself, support a finding of negligence. A res ipsa instruction was needed to allow the jury to make the inference. The res ipsa loquitur instruction in this case was important guidance to the jurors, informing them that, if they credited the testimony of Connors' experts, they could infer that the physicians were negligent simply because the injury occurred.

A res ipsa loquitur instruction is given in order to allow a plaintiff with no ability to show actual negligence the opportunity to prove negligence through inference. It is especially necessary in medical malpractice cases, since the unconscious plaintiff is in no position to be able to testify about what happened to her in surgery. . . .

[On the second issue the court agreed with the district court that plaintiffs had not "proved themselves out of" res ipsa loquitur by trying to prove specific negligence. The court cited Vermont cases that "comport with the majority rule" that a plaintiff can "couple a res ipsa argument with evidence of specific acts of negligence by the defendant."

The judgment was affirmed.]

Notes and Questions

1. Assume the following evidence. Expert evidence shows that custom and good practice require that retractor pressure be released every 15 minutes. The nurse testifies—and the record supports this—that until near the end of the operation she told the surgeon every time 15 minutes had passed and the surgeon stopped working for a minute or two so that the nurse could release the pressure on the retractor. The last time the nurse informed the surgeon that 15 minutes had passed, the surgeon said that he was almost finished with the surgery and rather than take time to release the pressure he told the nurse to do nothing. This meant that the last time the nurse released the pressure was 23 minutes before the end of the surgery. The plaintiff's expert testifies that the extra eight minutes of pressure probably caused the harm that plaintiff suffered. Does this case involve res ipsa loquitur?

2. Why is there general agreement that res ipsa loquitur is available in the "sponge" cases?

3. Why is there disagreement in cases like *Connors*? Is it realistic to suggest that "experts can educate the jurors, essentially training them to be twelve new initiates into a different, higher level of common knowledge"? What are juries likely to discuss after receiving a res ipsa instruction—that is, after being told that an inference of negligence is permissible—in the following cases:

  a.   Byrne v. Boadle.

  b.   Hammontree v. Jenner.

  c.   Sponge left in a surgery patient—no expert testimony.

  d.   The Connors case.

4. If experts testify that out of every 100 operations of a particular type five fail, has plaintiff made out a res ipsa case? What if the testimony is that of those five failures on average three are due to malpractice? Is either of these situations similar to what plaintiff's expert in *Connors* was saying when, based on his experience, he testified that the defendants' use of the retractor was probably negligent—in some undetermined and undeterminable way?

5.   What role might experts play in a case brought by home owners who were hurt when their recently built house collapsed in an earthquake? Might their role extend to helping plaintiff develop a res ipsa case against the contractor?

Matthies v. Mastromonaco

Supreme Court of New Jersey, 1999.
160 N.J. 26, 733 A.2d 456.

POLLOCK, J.

This appeal presents the question whether the doctrine of informed consent requires a physician to obtain the patient's consent before implementing a nonsurgical course of treatment. It questions also whether a physician, in addition to discussing with the patient treatment alternatives that the physician recommends, should discuss medically reasonable alternative courses of treatment that the physician does not recommend. We hold that to obtain a patient's informed consent to one of several alternative courses of treatment, the physician should explain medically reasonable invasive and noninvasive alternatives, including the risks and likely outcomes of those alternatives, even when the chosen course is noninvasive.

[In 1990, the 81-year-old plaintiff fell in her apartment and broke her right hip. When she was discovered two days later she was transported to emergency care. Defendant orthopedic surgeon prescribed bed rest rather than surgery. Further facts are reported in the opinion. The trial court refused to permit an informed consent claim to go to the jury because (1) the doctrine did not apply where the recommendation was noninvasive and (2) the claim was subsumed within the malpractice claim. The jury found that defendant had not committed malpractice by failing to perform surgery on plaintiff. The Appellate Division reversed because of the failure to charge on informed consent.]

.   .   . . Dr. Mastromonaco reviewed Matthies's medical history, condition, and X-rays. He decided against pinning her hip, a procedure that would have involved the insertion of four steel screws, each approximately one-quarter inch thick and four inches long.

Dr. Mastromonaco reached that decision for several reasons. First, Matthies was elderly, frail, and in a weakened condition. Surgery involving the installation of screws would be risky. Second, Matthies suffered from osteoporosis, which led Dr. Mastromonaco to conclude that her bones were too porous to hold the screws. He anticipated that the screws probably would loosen, causing severe pain, and necessitating a partial or total hip replacement. Third, forty years earlier, Matthies had suffered a stroke from a mismatched blood transfusion during surgery. The stroke had left her partially paralyzed on her right side. Consequently she had worn a brace and essentially used her right leg as a post while propelling herself forward with her left leg. After considering these factors, Dr. Mastromonaco decided that with bed rest, a course of treatment that he recognized as "controversial," Matthies's fracture could heal sufficiently to restore her right leg to its limited function. . . .

Before her fall, Matthies had maintained an independent lifestyle. She had done her own grocery shopping, cooking, housework, and laundry. Her dentist of many years, Dr. Arthur Massarsky, testified that he often had observed Matthies climbing unassisted the two flights of stairs to his office. Matthies is now confined to a nursing home.

Matthies's expert, Dr. Hervey Sicherman, a board-certified orthopedic surgeon, testified that under the circumstances, bed rest was an inappropriate treatment. He maintained that bed rest alone is not advisable for a hip fracture unless the patient does not expect to regain the ability to walk. Essentially, he rejects bed rest except when the patient is terminally ill or in a vegetative state. Dr. Sicherman explained that unless accompanied by traction, the danger of treating a hip fracture with bed rest is that the fracture could dislocate. In fact, shortly after Matthies began her bed-rest treatment, the head of her right femur displaced. Her right leg shortened, and she has never regained the ability to walk. According to Dr. Sicherman, the weakness and porosity of Matthies's bones increased the likelihood of this bad outcome. Even defendant's expert, Dr. Ira Rochelle, a board-certified orthopedic surgeon, admitted that pinning Matthies's hip would have decreased the risk of displacement. He nonetheless agreed with Dr. Mastromonaco that Matthies's bones were probably too brittle to withstand insertion of the pins.

Dr. Mastromonaco's goal in conservatively treating Matthies was to help her "get through this with the least complication as possible and to maintain a lifestyle conducive to her disability." He believed that rather than continue living on her own, Matthies should live in a long-term care facility. He explained, "I'm not going to give her that leg she wanted. She wanted to live alone, but she couldn't live alone. . . . I wanted her to be at peace with herself in the confines of professional care, somebody to care for her. She could not live alone."

Matthies asserts that she would not have consented to bed rest if Dr. Mastromonaco had told her of the probable effect of the treatment on the quality of her life. . . .

A jury question existed whether Dr. Mastromonaco consulted either with plaintiff or her family about the possibility of surgery. [There were conflicting recollections on this issue.]

. . . [Plaintiff was transferred to a residential nursing home where she received physical therapy. She] also saw psychiatrists and was treated . . . for depression because she grew increasingly despondent over her continued inability to walk.

. . .

Choosing among medically reasonable treatment alternatives is a shared responsibility of physicians and patients. To discharge their responsibilities, patients should provide their physicians with the information necessary for them to make diagnoses and determine courses of treatment. Physicians, in turn, have a duty to evaluate the relevant information and disclose all courses of treatment that are medically reasonable under the circumstances. Generally, a physician will recommend a course of treatment. As a practical matter, a patient often decides to adopt the physician's recommendation. Still, the ultimate decision is for the patient.

We reject defendant's contention that informed consent applies only to invasive procedures. Historically, the failure to obtain a patient's informed consent to an invasive procedure, such as surgery, was treated as a battery. The physician's need to obtain the consent of the patient to surgery derived from the patient's right to reject a nonconsensual touching. Eventually, courts recognized that the need for the patient's consent is better understood as deriving from the right of self-determination. . . .

The rationale for basing an informed consent action on negligence rather than battery principles is that the physician's failure is better viewed as a breach of a professional responsibility than as a nonconsensual touching. . . . Analysis based on the principle of battery is generally restricted to cases in which a physician has not obtained any consent or has exceeded the scope of consent. [   ] The essential difference in analyzing informed consent claims under negligence, rather than battery principles, is that the analysis focuses not on an unauthorized touching or invasion of the patient's body, but on the physician's deviation from a standard of care.

In informed consent analysis, the decisive factor is not whether a treatment alternative is invasive or noninvasive, but whether the physician adequately presents the material facts so that the patient can make an informed decision. That conclusion does not imply that a physician must explain in detail all treatment options in every case. For example, a physician need not recite all the risks and benefits of each potential appropriate antibiotic when writing a prescription for treatment of an upper respiratory infection. Conversely, a physician could be obligated, depending on the circumstances, to discuss a variety of treatment alternatives, such as chemotherapy, radiation, or surgery, with a patient diagnosed with cancer. Distinguishing the two situations are the limitations of the reasonable patient standard, which need not unduly burden the physician-patient relationship. The standard obligates the physician to disclose only that information material to a reasonable patient's informed decision. [   ] Physicians thus remain obligated to inform patients of medically reasonable treatment alternatives and their attendant probable risks and outcomes. Otherwise, the patient, in selecting one alternative rather than another, cannot make a decision that is informed.

. . . In sum, physicians do not adequately discharge their responsibility by disclosing only treatment alternatives that they recommend.

To assure that the patient's consent is informed, the physician should describe, among other things, the material risks inherent in a procedure or course of treatment. [ ] The test for measuring the materiality of a risk is whether a reasonable patient in the patient's position would have considered the risk material. [ ] Although the test of materiality is objective, a "patient obviously has no complaint if he would have submitted to the therapy notwithstanding awareness that the risk was one of its perils." Canterbury v. Spence, 464 F.2d 772, 790 (D.C.Cir.), cert. denied, 409 U.S. 1064 (1972) (citation omitted). As the court stated in *Canterbury*:

> We think a technique which ties the factual conclusion on causation simply to the assessment of the patient's credibility is unsatisfactory. . . . [W]hen causality is explored at a postinjury trial with a professedly uninformed patient, the question whether he actually would have turned the treatment down if he had known the risks is purely hypothetical. . . . And the answer which the patient supplies hardly represents more than a guess, perhaps tinged by the circumstance that the uncommunicated hazard has in fact materialized. In our view, this method of dealing with the issue on causation comes in second-best. . . . Better it is, we believe, to resolve the causality issue on an objective basis: in terms of what a prudent person in the patient's position would have decided if suitably informed of all perils bearing significance. If adequate disclosure could reasonably be expected to have caused that person to decline the treatment because of the revelation of the kind of risk or danger that resulted in harm, causation is shown, but otherwise not. The patient's testimony is relevant on that score of course but it would not threaten to dominate the findings. And since that testimony would probably be appraised congruently with the factfinder's belief in its reasonableness, the case for a wholly objective standard for passing on causation is strengthened. [ ]

For consent to be informed, the patient must know not only of alternatives that the physician recommends, but of medically reasonable alternatives that the physician does not recommend. [The court found support for this in the regulations of the state's Department of Health and in the Code of Medical Ethics of the American Medical Association.]

[The court rejected the argument that the patient was adequately protected by the negligence charge that was given to the jury.] A physician may select a method of treatment that is medically reasonable, but not the one that the patient would have selected if informed of alternative methods. Like the deviation from a standard of care, the physician's failure to obtain informed consent is a form of medical negligence. . . . Physicians may neither impose their values on their patients nor substitute their level of risk aversion for that of their patients. One patient may prefer to undergo a potentially risky procedure, such as surgery, to enjoy a better quality of life. Another patient may choose a more conservative course of treatment to secure reduced risk at the cost of a diminished lifestyle. The choice is not for the physician, but the patient in consultation with the physician. By not telling the patient of all medically reasonable alternatives, the physician breaches the patient's right to make an informed choice.

The physician's duty to inform the patient of alternatives is especially important when the alternatives are mutually exclusive. If, as a practical matter, the choice of one alternative precludes the choice of others, or even if it increases appreciably the risks attendant on the other alternatives, the patient's need for relevant information is critical. That need intensifies when the choice turns not so much on purely medical considerations as on the choice of one lifestyle or set of values over another.

.   .   .

The issue of informed consent often intertwines with that of medical malpractice. [   ] Because of the interrelationship between the malpractice and informed consent issues in the present case, the jury should consider both issues at the retrial.

The judgment of the Appellate Division is affirmed.

CHIEF JUSTICE PORITZ and JUSTICES HANDLER, O'HERN, GARIBALDI, STEIN, and COLEMAN join in JUSTICE POLLOCK's opinion.

Notes and Questions

1. What standard does the court use for determining how much the defendant should have told the patient? Does an expert have a role in that determination? What was Dr. Sicherman's role in *Matthies*?

Some states require that plaintiff produce an expert in cases claiming a consent based on inadequate information. In New York, for example, the disclosure standard is framed as that which would be made by "a reasonable medical or dental practitioner under similar circumstances." This standard requires the introduction of expert testimony to show that the alleged conduct fell short of that standard. N.Y. Pub.Health Law § 2805–d and N.Y.C.P.L.R. § 4401–a. What would the expert testify about? Other states, such as New Jersey, use the "reasonable patient" standard under which the physician's obligation is to provide the information that a reasonable patient would want.

2. The *Matthies* court rejected the view of states like Pennsylvania in which the essence of the claim is one of battery. See Morgan v. MacPhail, 704 A.2d 617 (Pa.1997), involving two consolidated cases. In one, a local anesthetic was injected into the area around the ribs. In the second, a steroid was injected into an area behind the Achilles tendon. The majority explained that neither injection involved a battery:

It is the invasive nature of the surgical or operative procedure involving a surgical cut and the use of surgical instruments that gives rise to the need to inform the patient of risks prior to surgery. [   ] Neither of the procedures performed in the instant appeals were invasive in nature as both involved the injection of medication which does not rise to the same level of bodily invasion as surgery.

Would the Pennsylvania plaintiffs have prevailed in New Jersey?

3. In most consent cases the physician or surgeon has undertaken an invasive procedure and the patient complains that the risk—which came to pass—was insufficiently explained. In McKinney v. Nash, 174 Cal.Rptr. 642 (App. 1981), for example, the plaintiff underwent surgery to repair a bilateral inguinal hernia. Both his testicles atrophied—a 1 in 1000 risk of the surgery even if the surgery is carefully done. The atrophy was said to have had a psychological effect that caused impotency. The court thought a jury question was presented on the consent issue. Does that kind of case raise different issues from those raised in *Matthies*?

Is it negligent not to inform a patient about an experimental alternative to surgery? What if it is not recognized by professors at the state's medical schools as a "practical alternative" to the surgery and is opposed openly by a number of professional associations, though some unorganized physicians publicly argue that it ought to be accepted? In Moore v. Baker, 989 F.2d 1129 (11th Cir.1993), the court read Georgia law as requiring disclosure only of alternatives that are "generally recognized and accepted by reasonably prudent physicians."

4. When may consent be revoked—and what happens then? In Schreiber v. Physicians Ins. Co. of Wisconsin, 588 N.W.2d 26 (Wis.), cert. denied 528 U.S. 869 (1999), the court held that an earlier consent may be withdrawn while there is still time to adopt an alternative course of action. In this case, while experiencing difficulty in giving birth, plaintiff wanted a cesarean section instead of the previously agreed-upon vaginal delivery. The court asserted that the "function of withdrawal, in effect, places [the parties] in their original position—a physician, a patient, and a series of options for treatment. It creates a blank slate on which the parties must again diagram their plan." The court declined "to view the informed consent doctrine as a solitary and blanketing event, a point on a timeline after which such discussions are no longer needed because they are 'covered' by some articulable occurrence in the past. Rather, a substantial change in circumstances, be it medical or legal, requires a new informed consent discussion."

5. The consent issue is also raised by assertions that health care provider D should not have done the procedure but should have referred the patient to provider T because the collected statistics show that provider D has a 15% rate of adverse outcomes, compared to provider T's rate of 10%. Note that the providers might be hospitals or surgeons. Should the duty to obtain informed consent require that D tell the patient the different statistics (and provide a reasonable and honestly believed explanation for any disparity)? See Twerski & Cohen, Comparing Medical Providers: A First Look at the New Era of Medical Statistics, 58 Brooklyn L.Rev. 15 (1992). The authors suggest that the patient might be awarded 5/15 of the damages sustained in the cited example. Other articles in the same issue address such questions as whether comparative statistics benefit the health care delivery system and whether they should be admissible in malpractice cases. Proposals to create a national registry that would list a physician's malpractice awards, license suspensions and criminal convictions are discussed in Barringer, Seeking Access to Data on Doctors, N.Y.Times, Sept. 18, 2000 at C 15.

6. What must an inexperienced physician tell a patient? In Whiteside v. Lukson, 947 P.2d 1263 (Wash.App.1997), the defendant surgeon did not tell plaintiff patient that he had never before done the procedure he was recommending. By the time he performed the surgery he had done two of them. The procedure in plaintiff's case failed. The court held that the surgeon was not obligated to reveal his inexperience. Consent need be obtained only for the underlying procedure. Should a surgeon be required to reveal less than stellar college or medical school grades?

In Ditto v. McCurdy, 947 P.2d 952 (Haw.1997), plaintiff, whose breast augmentation procedure led to numerous complications, sued defendant who was qualified as, among other things, a facial surgeon and a cosmetic surgeon, but not as a plastic surgeon. Among the claims was one for fraud for failing to advise plaintiff that he was not a plastic surgeon. There was dispute about whether cosmetic surgeons were less fully trained than plastic surgeons. The court concluded that since defendant had accurately held himself out as what he was and did not claim to be more than he was, there was no duty to disclose anything more.

Must physicians volunteer information that is not directly related to the procedure? See Albany Urology Clinic, P.C. v. Cleveland, 528 S.E.2d 777 (Ga.2000), holding, 4–3, that a urologist was not obligated to tell patients of his illegal use of cocaine. The majority was concerned about requiring physicians to tell patients that they were "binge drinkers" or had just received "bad news." The dissenters argued that the cocaine use was different because it was criminal. Should a surgeon be required to volunteer that a child has just committed suicide?

7. Consider the physician's obligation if the patient says "Don't tell me the options or the risks. I'll get frightened. Do what you think is best." Alternatively, consider the physician's response if the patient says "Tell me everything even the most minimal risks." Or, "I am very nervous about my eyes. I want to know every risk—no matter how unlikely—that each option might mean for my eyes."

8. Some patients adopt an active role in their treatment, which may produce other disputes. In Shine v. Vega, 709 N.E.2d 58 (Mass.1999), a 29-year-old woman went to the hospital during a bad asthmatic attack. Over her vehement objections she was intubated. (The result was an intense fear of hospitals such that, two years later, when she really did need emergency help, she delayed so long that she died.) On the consent issue, the trial judge charged that in a life-threatening case consent was not needed—and that the jury should decide whether the situation was life-threatening. The resulting defense judgment was unanimously reversed on appeal. The defendant argued that he should be able to "override [the patient's] wishes as long as he acted 'appropriately and consistent with the standard of accepted medical practice.'" Relying in part on § 892D of the Second Restatement, the court held that a competent adult may refuse life-saving treatment. "If, and only if, the patient is unconscious or otherwise incapable of giving consent, and either time or circumstances do not permit the physician to obtain the consent of a family member, may the physician presume that the patient, if competent, would consent to life-saving medical treatment." Even that intervention was permissible only "if the actor has no reason to believe that the other, if he had the opportunity to consent, would decline."

9.   Where the patient has not been given a choice or expressed one, why does it not suffice for such patients to testify that if given the necessary information they would have made a different choice?

In Henderson v. Milobsky, 595 F.2d 654 (D.C.Cir.1978), plaintiff who was to undergo removal of a wisdom tooth was not told of a 1 in 100,000 risk of permanent loss of sensation in an area a half-inch square just below the lower lip. The court concluded that the risk was "undoubtedly troublesome but hardly disabling." No "prudent juror could reasonably have concluded" that the risk was material.

In Ashe v. Radiation Oncology Associates, 9 S.W.3d 119 (Tenn.1999), the court reviewed the conflict between the objective and subjective standards for determining consent. The subjective standard is consistent with the view that individuals, no matter how misguided, should be able to make their own treatment decisions. The objection to that approach is "the unfairness of allowing the issue of causation to turn on the credibility of the hindsight of a person seeking recovery after experiencing a most undesirable result." The argument for the objective standard was "that neither the plaintiff nor the fact-finder can provide a definitive answer as to what the patient would have done had the patient known of the particular risk prior to consenting to the procedure or treatment." The court chose the objective standard. Can you think of other arguments for each position? How does this causation question differ from the issue of whether the physician was negligent in failing to obtain informed consent?

10.   For a case revolving around the use of written consents and the statutory requirements for such consents, see Allan v. Levy, 846 P.2d 274 (Nev.1993), in which the state's consent statute that provided in its entirety:

A physician .   .   . has conclusively obtained the consent of a patient for a medical or surgical procedure if he has done the following:

1.   Explained to the patient in general terms without specific details, the procedure to be undertaken;

2.   Explained to the patient alternative methods of treatment, if any, and their general nature;

3.   Explained to the patient that there may be risks, together with the general nature and extent of the risks involved, without enumerating such risks; and

4.   Obtained the signature of the patient to a statement containing an explanation of the procedure, alternative methods of treatment and risks involved, as provided in this section.

11.   For comprehensive discussion of the informed consent issue, see Schuck, Rethinking Informed Consent, 103 Yale L.J. 899 (1994).

CHAPTER III

THE DUTY REQUIREMENT: PHYSICAL INJURIES

A. INTRODUCTION

In Chapter II we considered a wide variety of cases in which we explored the basic characteristics of the negligence concept. Typically, the defendant did not deny an obligation to behave reasonably toward the plaintiff. We turn now to cases in which the defendant makes precisely that contention—that defendant had no duty to exercise due care in the particular situation. The purpose of this chapter is to explore situations in which such claims are asserted and to determine how they should be analyzed. The connection between the "negligence" question of Chapter II and the "duty" question of Chapter III is demonstrated by the fact that "negligence" is often referred to as "breach of duty"—a clear indication that some duty must exist before a defendant can be said to have committed actionable negligence. Although pedagogical reasons favored initial exploration of the negligence issue, it should be evident that, logically, the duty question is an antecedent issue.

An appropriate starting point is the question whether a plaintiff must show that a specific duty governs the context in which the case arose—or whether a general duty of due care exists unless the defendant can invoke an exception. As the materials in this chapter will indicate, there seems to be a clear long-term movement towards recognizing a general duty of due care. But the early historical picture is hazy. In many early cases, specific relationships appeared to be the bases for imposing duties of care. These were the classic relationships, such as innkeeper-guest, carrier-passenger, and the like. Yet, during this period, one also finds highway collision cases in which the courts appear to recognize a general obligation of care to others.

The view that duties arose in specific contexts is supported by the fact that *failure* to establish a relational setting was often fatal to the claim that defendant should be held responsible for a lack of due care. A noteworthy example of this restrictive view is the privity doctrine. Under one aspect of that doctrine, courts held that the manufacturer of a product generally owed a duty of due care in its manufacture only to the person who acquired the product from the maker. No general duty of care was owed to remote buyers or users. The survival of the privity doctrine into the twentieth century and its eventual demise are traced in MacPherson v. Buick Motor Co., 111 N.E. 1050 (N.Y.1916), reprinted at p. 540, infra. In *MacPherson*,

Judge Cardozo, concluding that a car manufacturer owed a duty of due care to someone who bought a car from an intermediate dealer, asserted:

> If the nature of a thing is such that it is reasonably certain to place life and limb in peril when negligently made, it is then a thing of danger. Its nature gives warning of the consequences to be expected. If to the element of danger is added knowledge that the thing will be used by persons other than the purchaser, and used without new tests, then, irrespective of contract, the manufacturer of this thing of danger is under a duty to make it carefully. . . . We have put aside the notion that the duty to safeguard life and limb, when the consequences of negligence may be foreseen, grows out of contract and nothing else. We have put the source of the obligation where it ought to be. We have put its source in the law.

As early as 1883, Brett, M.R., in Heaven v. Pender, 11 Q.B.D. 503 (1883), offered a general approach, though one that failed to convey how uneven the landscape remained:

> The proposition which these recognized cases suggest, and which is, therefore, to be deduced from them, is that whenever one person is by circumstances placed in such a position with regard to another that everyone of ordinary sense who did think would at once recognize that if he did not use ordinary care and skill in his own conduct with regard to those circumstances he would cause danger of injury to the person or property of the other, a duty arises to use ordinary care and skill to avoid such danger.

In this chapter, we will examine a number of discrete categories of cases in which Brett's straightforward proposition has been tested by moral and economic considerations—usually of long-standing acceptance—that established limitations on the duty to act reasonably. Related problems, involving the invasion of non-physical interests, will be considered in Chapter IV.

B. OBLIGATIONS TO OTHERS

We begin with a most fundamental inquiry. If an individual is in a situation of danger, should the law impose a duty on others to assist that person? Is there a meaningful distinction between harm arising from action and inaction? Consider the following case.

Harper v. Herman
Supreme Court of Minnesota, 1993.
499 N.W.2d 472.

PAGE, JUSTICE.

This case arises upon a reversal by the court of appeals of summary judgment in favor of the defendant. The court of appeals held that defendant, the owner and operator of a private boat on Lake Minnetonka, had a duty to warn plaintiff, a guest on the boat, that water surrounding the boat was too shallow for diving. We reverse and reinstate judgment in favor of defendant.

The facts are undisputed for the purpose of this appeal. On Sunday, August 9, 1986, Jeffrey Harper ("Harper") was one of four guests on Theodor Herman's ("Herman") 26-foot boat, sailing on Lake Minnetonka. Harper was invited on the boat outing by Cindy Alberg Palmer, another guest on Herman's boat. Herman and Harper did not know each other prior to this boat outing. At the time Herman was 64 years old, and Harper was 20 years old. Herman was an experienced boat owner having spent hundreds of hours operating boats on Lake Minnetonka similar to the one involved in this action. As owner of the boat, Herman considered himself to be in charge of the boat and his passengers. Harper had some experience swimming in lakes and rivers, but had no formal training in diving.

After a few hours of boating, the group decided to go swimming and, at Herman's suggestion, went to Big Island, a popular recreation spot. Herman was familiar with Big Island, and he was aware that the water remains shallow for a good distance away from its shore. Harper had been to Big Island on one previous occasion. Herman positioned the boat somewhere between 100 to 200 yards from the island with the bow facing away from the island in an area shallow enough for his guests to use the boat ladder to enter the water, but still deep enough so they could swim. The bottom of the lake was not visible from the boat. After positioning the boat Herman proceeded to set the anchor and lower the boat's ladder which was at its stern.

While Herman was lowering the ladder, Harper asked him if he was "going in." When Herman responded yes, Harper, without warning, stepped onto the side of the middle of the boat and dove into approximately two or three feet of water. As a result of the dive, Harper struck the bottom of the lake, severed his spinal cord, and was rendered a C6 quadriplegic.

Harper then brought suit, alleging that Herman owed him a duty of care to warn him that the water was too shallow for diving. [The trial court granted defendant's motion for summary judgment on the ground that defendant owed plaintiff no duty to warn. The court of appeals held that defendant voluntarily assumed such a duty when he allowed Harper onto his boat.]

The sole issue on appeal is whether a boat owner who is a social host owes a duty of care to warn a guest on the boat that the water is too shallow for diving.

Harper alleges that Herman owed him a duty to warn of the shallowness of the water because he was an inexperienced swimmer and diver, whereas Herman was a veteran boater. Under those circumstances, Harper argues, Herman should have realized that Harper needed his protection.

We have previously stated that an affirmative duty to act only arises when a special relationship exists between the parties. "The fact that an actor realizes or should realize that action on his part is necessary for another's aid or protection does not of itself impose upon him a duty to take such action . . . unless a special relationship exists . . . between the actor and the other which gives the other the right to protection." Delgado v. Lohmar, 289 N.W.2d 479, 483 (Minn.1979), [ ]. Accepting, *arguendo*, that Herman should have realized that Harper needed protection, Harper must still prove that a special relationship existed between them that placed an affirmative duty to act on the part of Herman.

Harper argues that a special relationship requiring Herman to act for *[P's arg. for spec. relation.]* his protection was created when Herman, as a social host, allowed an inexperienced diver on his boat. Generally, a special relationship giving rise to a duty to warn is only found on the part of common carriers, innkeepers, *[Rest. II definition]* possessors of land who hold it open to the public, and persons who have *[of spec. relation.]* custody of another person under circumstances in which that other person is deprived of normal opportunities of self-protection. Restatement (Second) of Torts § 314A (1965). Under this rule, a special relationship could be *[Application of]* found to exist between the parties only if Herman had custody of Harper *[Rest. II definition]* under circumstances in which Harper was deprived of normal opportunities *[to case]* to protect himself.[2] These elements are not present here.

The record before this court does not establish that Harper was either *[No spec. relat.]* particularly vulnerable or that he lacked the ability to protect himself. *[reasoning]* Further, the record does not establish that Herman held considerable power over Harper's welfare, or that Herman was receiving a financial gain by hosting Harper on his boat. Finally, there is nothing in the record which would suggest that Harper expected any protection from Herman; indeed, no such allegation has been made.

The court of appeals found that Herman owed Harper a duty to warn him of the shallowness of the water because Herman knew that it was "dangerously shallow." We have previously stated that "[a]ctual knowledge *[knowledge ≠]* of a dangerous condition tends to impose a special duty to do something *[duty]* about that condition." Andrade v. Ellefson, 391 N.W.2d 836, 841 (Minn.1986)(holding that county was not immune to charge of improper supervision of day care center where children were abused when county knew about overcrowding at the center). However, superior knowledge of a dangerous condition by itself, in the absence of a duty to provide protection, is insufficient to establish liability in negligence. Thus, Herman's knowl- *[Application]* edge that the water was "dangerously shallow" without more does not create liability. *Andrade* involved a group of plaintiffs who had little opportunity to protect themselves, children in day care, and a defendant to whom the plaintiffs looked for protection. In this case, Harper was not deprived of opportunities to protect himself, and Herman was not expected to provide protection.

2. Prosser describes a circumstance in which one party would be liable in negligence because another party was deprived of normal opportunities for self-protection as occurring when the plaintiff is typically in some respect particularly vulnerable and dependent upon the defendant who, correspondingly, holds considerable power over the plain- tiff's welfare. In addition, such relations have often involved some existing or potential economic advantage to the defendant. Fairness in such cases thus may require the defendant to use his power to help the plaintiff, based upon the plaintiff's expectation of protection, which itself may be based upon the defendant's expectation of financial gain. [ ]

[margin handwritten note: ordinary dangers should be understood by 20-yr-old]

"There are many dangers, such as those of fire and water, . . . which under ordinary conditions may reasonably be expected to be fully understood and appreciated by any child. . . ." Restatement (Second) of Torts § 339 cmt. *j* (1965). If a child is expected to understand the inherent dangers of water, so should a 20-year-old adult. Harper had no reasonable expectation to look to Herman for protection, and we hold that Herman had no duty to warn Harper that the water was shallow.

Reversed and judgment in favor of defendant reinstated.

Notes and Questions

1. What are the arguments in favor of imposing a duty on the defendant? What are the arguments against such an imposition? When it would be virtually costless for defendant to offer assistance, should there be a distinction between moral and legal obligations? Certainly, moral and legal obligations are not *always* distinct. Is it self-evident why they should diverge in a situation involving, say, a helpless infant lying on a railroad track who could easily be rescued before a train arrives? Consider Epstein, A Theory of Strict Liability, 2 J.Legal Stud. 151, 197–98 (1973):

> The common law position on the good Samaritan question does not appeal to our highest sense of benevolence and charity, and it is not at all surprising that there have been many proposals for its alteration or abolition. Let us here examine but one of these proposals. After concluding that the then (1908) current position of the law led to intolerable results, James Barr Ames argued [in Law and Morals, 22 Harv.L.Rev. 97 (1908)], that the appropriate rule should be that:

> > One who fails to interfere to save another from impending death or great bodily harm, when he might do so with little or no inconvenience to himself, and the death or great bodily harm follows as a consequence of his inaction, shall be punished criminally and shall make compensation to the party injured or to his widow and children in case of death.

> Even this solution, however, does not satisfy the *Carroll Towing* formula. The general use of the cost-benefit analysis required under the economic interpretation of negligence does not permit a person to act on the assumption that he may as of right attach special weight and importance to his own welfare. Under Ames' good Samaritan rule, a defendant in cases of affirmative acts would be required to take only those steps that can be done "with little or no inconvenience." But if the distinction between causing harm and not preventing harm is to be disregarded, why should the difference in standards between the two cases survive the reform of the law? The only explanation is that the two situations are regarded at bottom as raising totally different issues, even for those who insist upon the immateriality of this distinction. Even those who argue, as Ames does, that the law is utilitarian must in the end find some special place for the claims of egoism which are an inseparable byproduct of the belief that individual

autonomy—individual liberty—is a good in itself not explainable in terms of its purported social worth. It is one thing to *allow* people to act as they please in the belief that the "invisible hand" will provide the happy congruence of the individual and the social good. Such a theory, however, at bottom must regard individual autonomy as but a means to some social end. It takes a great deal more to assert that men are *entitled* to act as they choose . . . even though it is certain that there will be cases where individual welfare will be in conflict with the social good. Only then is it clear that even freedom has its costs.

. . .

For an article proposing a duty of "easy rescue" and providing a detailed criticism of Epstein's views, see Weinrib, The Case for a Duty to Rescue, 90 Yale L.J. 247 (1980). For a range of other perspectives, see Heyman, Foundations of the Duty to Rescue, 47 Vand.L.Rev. 673 (1994); Adler, Relying Upon the Reasonableness of Strangers: Some Observations about the Current State of Common Law Affirmative Duties to Aid or Protect Others, 1991 Wis.L.Rev. 867; Levmore, Waiting for Rescue: An Essay on the Evolution and Incentive Structure of the Law of Affirmative Obligations, 72 Va.L.Rev. 879 (1986).

2. What if the plaintiff had been ten years old? What if defendant had met Harper at a party a week earlier and had invited him to join other guests for this trip?

If one were to find that the boat owner owed a duty would the rationale extend to the person who invited plaintiff onto the boat? What about his office mate from work who happens to be passing by on another boat and sees disaster about to happen? What if his swimming teacher, who knew plaintiff was a novice, was on the passing boat?

Does the rationale of *Harper* necessarily extend to the case of the infant on the railroad tracks?

3. As *Harper* and the previous note suggest, "special relationships" have led courts to impose duties to act in this type of case. Do the relationships listed by the court suggest a unifying principle for an affirmative obligation? What criteria did the court use to guide its decision on whether a special relationship existed?

4. *Non-negligent injury*. At common law, one who innocently injured another had no duty to exercise due care to ensure the other's subsequent wellbeing. See, e.g., Union Pacific Railway v. Cappier, 72 P. 281 (Kan. 1903), in which the court held that there was no duty to do anything to help a victim who was non-tortiously run over while trespassing on defendant's railroad tracks.

That attitude is fading. In Maldonado v. Southern Pacific Transp. Co., 629 P.2d 1001 (Ariz.App.1981), plaintiff claimed that as he was attempting to board one of defendant's freight trains, it jerked or bumped and he fell off—and under the wheels, suffering a severed arm and other serious injuries. Alleging that defendant's employees knew about his plight but did nothing to help him, he sued for aggravation of his injuries. The court imposed a duty recognized by § 322 of the Second Restatement:

> If the actor knows or has reason to know that by his conduct, whether tortious or innocent, he has caused such bodily harm to another as to make him helpless and in danger of further harm, the actor is under a duty to exercise reasonable care to prevent such further harm.

5. With respect to motor vehicles, one common reaction to the traditional no-duty view in these situations has been the adoption of criminal statutes. California, for example, provides that "the driver of any vehicle involved in an accident resulting in injury .   . . shall render to any person injured in the accident reasonable assistance, including transporting, or making arrangements for transporting, any injured person to a physician, surgeon, or hospital for medical or surgical treatment if it is apparent that treatment is necessary or if that transportation is requested by any injured person." Cal.Vehicle Code § 20003. This statute has been held applicable regardless of whose negligence, if any, caused the accident in the first place. In this situation in which the common law had imposed no affirmative duty, should the existence of the criminal statute persuade a court to create an analogous common law duty? We consider this issue later in this section. If the driver was not negligent, why should that driver's duty be any different from that of a bystander?

6. *Non-negligent creation of risk.* In Simonsen v. Thorin, 234 N.W. 628 (Neb.1931), defendant motorist without fault knocked a utility pole into the street and drove on. In a suit by a motorist who ran into the pole the court held that the defendant had an affirmative duty to use due care to remove the hazard or to warn others of it, though he was not liable for creating the hazard. Why should his duty be any different from that of a bystander who watched the episode?

In Menu v. Minor, 745 P.2d 680 (Colo.App.1987), a driver lost control of his car. It hit the median and came to rest, disabled, blocking a lane of an interstate highway. What might the driver's duties be? A taxicab picked up the driver and drove him away. Some time later, plaintiffs crashed into the disabled car. In a suit against the cab company, plaintiffs contended that the cab should have either stayed at the scene to warn, removed the car, or called the police. The court held that the cab driver had no affirmative duty to do any of these things. The cab driver had not "voluntarily assumed a duty to plaintiffs by acting affirmatively to induce" them to rely on him. Nor had he "created a peril or changed the nature of the existing risk" to them. Transporting the driver from the scene did not change the already existing risk. The knowledge of the danger alone did not create a special relationship.

In Tresemer v. Barke, 150 Cal.Rptr. 384 (App. 1978), plaintiff was seriously injured from use of the Dalkon Shield intrauterine device. She never consulted defendant physician after he inserted the device. Within two years, there was medical information about the dangers of using the device, but the plaintiff was unaware of the risk for another year afterwards and suffered injury because of the delay. The court held that she stated a cause of action against the defendant for failure to warn her about the newly-discovered dangers.

Section 321 of the Second Restatement states that one who has done an act and "subsequently realizes or should realize that it has created an unreasonable risk of causing physical harm to another," is under a duty to exercise due care to prevent the risk from occurring even though at the time the actor had no reason to believe that his act would create such a risk.

7. At one point, the *Harper* court notes that plaintiff did not show that he "expected any protection" from defendant. How might Harper have shown that? What if defendant had charged each guest $10 for the trip?

If plaintiff, when coming on board, says to defendant that he knows little about boating and that "I expect you to let me know if you see me doing anything foolish while on board," would that suffice if defendant did not respond? If defendant responded "OK"?

In Morgan v. County of Yuba, 41 Cal.Rptr. 508 (Cal.App.1964), the plaintiff's decedent expressed fear of the consequences if the sheriff were to release a man he had arrested for threatening her. Although under no duty to do so, the sheriff's office promised to warn her before any release. They failed to do so and the man, upon his release, killed her. After deciding that the county should be treated as a private person, the court held that liability should exist if the plaintiff could establish that the decedent relied on the promise—and would have acted differently without it. What relationship is this?

Other courts have employed similar reasoning. In Mixon v. Dobbs Houses, Inc., 254 S.E.2d 864 (Ga.App.1979), husband informed the manager of the restaurant where he worked that his wife was pregnant and might call at any time to ask for a ride to the hospital. Since husband did not have access to a phone, the manager promised to tell him if his wife called. When the wife went into labor, she called the restaurant three times, and although the manager received the message that the wife had called, he failed to deliver the message to the husband. When husband returned home, his wife had already given birth to a baby girl, "all alone, unassisted and unmedicated, experiencing total fear and excruciating pain." The court held that the manager was obligated to exercise due care in performing his promise. The lower court's dismissal was reversed.

Some courts reject this entire line of cases. See, e.g., Santy v. Bresee, 473 N.E.2d 69 (Ill.App.1984)(rejecting *Morgan* on very similar facts).

Farwell v. Keaton

Supreme Court of Michigan, 1976.
396 Mich. 281, 240 N.W.2d 217.

LEVIN, J. There is ample evidence to support the jury determination that David Siegrist failed to exercise reasonable care after voluntarily coming to the aid of Richard Farwell and that his negligence was the proximate cause of Farwell's death. We are also of the opinion that Siegrist, who was with Farwell the evening he was fatally injured and, as the jury found, knew or should have known of his peril, had an affirmative duty to come to Farwell's aid.

I

On the evening of August 26, 1966, Siegrist and Farwell drove to a trailer rental lot to return an automobile which Siegrist had borrowed from a friend who worked there. While waiting for the friend to finish work, Siegrist and Farwell consumed some beer.

Two girls walked by the entrance to the lot. Siegrist and Farwell attempted to engage them in conversation; they left Farwell's car and followed the girls to a drive-in restaurant down the street.

The girls complained to their friends in the restaurant that they were being followed. Six boys chased Siegrist and Farwell back to the lot. Siegrist escaped unharmed, but Farwell was severely beaten. Siegrist found Farwell underneath his automobile in the lot. Ice was applied to Farwell's head. Siegrist then drove Farwell around for approximately two hours, stopping at a number of drive-in restaurants. Farwell went to sleep in the back seat of his car. Around midnight Siegrist drove the car to the home of Farwell's grandparents, parked it in the driveway, unsuccessfully attempted to rouse Farwell, and left. Farwell's grandparents discovered him in the car the next morning and took him to the hospital. He died three days later of an epidural hematoma.

At trial, plaintiff [Farwell's father, in this wrongful death action] contended that had Siegrist taken Farwell to the hospital, or had he notified someone of Farwell's condition and whereabouts, Farwell would not have died. A neurosurgeon testified that if a person in Farwell's condition is taken to a doctor before, or within half an hour after, consciousness is lost, there is an 85 to 88 percent chance of survival. Plaintiff testified that Siegrist told him that he knew Farwell was badly injured and that he should have done something.

The jury returned a verdict for plaintiff and awarded $15,000 in damages. The Court of Appeals reversed, finding that Siegrist had not assumed the duty of obtaining aid for Farwell and that he neither knew nor should have known of the need for medical treatment.

II

. . .

The existence of a duty is ordinarily a question of law. However, there are factual circumstances which give rise to a duty. The existence of those facts must be determined by a jury. . . .

. . .

Without regard to whether there is a general duty to aid a person in distress, there is a clearly recognized legal duty of every person to avoid any affirmative acts which may make a situation worse. "[I]f the defendant does attempt to aid him, and takes charge and control of the situation, he is regarded as entering voluntarily into a relation which is attended with responsibility. Such a defendant will then be liable for a failure to use reasonable care for the protection of the plaintiff's interests." [ ] "Where performance clearly has begun, there is no doubt that there is a duty of care." [ ]

if person comes to aid of injured voluntarily, enters into spec. relat.

In a case such as the one at bar, the jury must determine, after considering all the evidence, whether the defendant attempted to aid the victim. If he did, a duty arose which required defendant to act as a reasonable person.

. . .

There was ample evidence to show that Siegrist breached a legal duty owed Farwell. Siegrist knew that Farwell had been in a fight, and he attempted to relieve Farwell's pain by applying an ice pack to his head. While Farwell and Siegrist were riding around, Farwell crawled into the back seat and laid down. The testimony showed that Siegrist attempted to rouse Farwell after driving him home but was unable to do so.

[The court summarized the testimony of Farwell's father that when he asked Siegrist why he didn't tell someone when he knew that Farwell was badly hurt, Siegrist replied: "I know I should have, I don't know."]

. . .

III

Siegrist contends that he is not liable for failure to obtain medical assistance for Farwell because he had no duty to do so.

D's arg!

Courts have been slow to recognize a duty to render aid to a person in peril. Where such a duty has been found, it has been predicated upon the existence of a special relationship between the parties; in such a case, if defendant knew or should have known of the other person's peril, he is required to render reasonable care under all the circumstances.

. . .

Farwell and Siegrist were companions on a social venture. Implicit in such a common undertaking is the understanding that one will render assistance to the other when he is in peril if he can do so without endangering himself. Siegrist knew or should have known when he left Farwell, who was badly beaten and unconscious, in the back seat of his car that no one would find him before morning. Under these circumstances, to say that Siegrist had no duty to obtain medical assistance or at least to notify someone of Farwell's condition and whereabouts would be "shocking to humanitarian considerations" and fly in the face of "the commonly accepted code of social conduct." "[C]ourts will find a duty where, in general, reasonable men would recognize it and agree that it exists." [Prosser, *Torts*]

Farwell and Siegrist were companions engaged in a common undertaking; there was a special relationship between the parties. Because Siegrist knew or should have known of the peril Farwell was in and could render assistance without endangering himself he had an affirmative duty to come to Farwell's aid.

The Court of Appeals is reversed and the verdict of the jury reinstated.

KAVANAGH, C.J., and WILLIAMS, J., concurred with LEVIN, J.

LINDEMER and RYAN, JJ., took no part in the decision of this case.

FITZGERALD, J. (dissenting).

.   .   .

The close relationship between defendant and the decedent is said to establish a legal duty upon defendant to obtain assistance for the decedent. No authority is cited for this proposition other than the public policy observation that the interest of society would be benefited if its members were required to assist one another. This is not the appropriate case to establish a standard of conduct requiring one to legally assume the duty of insuring the safety of another.   .   .   .[4]

Plaintiff believes that a legal duty to aid others should exist where such assistance greatly benefits society and only a reasonable burden is imposed upon those in a position to help. He contends further that the determination of the existence of a duty must rest with the jury where questions of foreseeability and the relationship of the parties are primary considerations.

It is clear that defendant's nonfeasance, or the "passive inaction or a failure to take steps to protect [the decedent] from harm" is urged as being the proximate cause of Farwell's death. We must reject plaintiff's proposition which elevates a moral obligation to the level of a legal duty where, as here, the facts within defendant's knowledge in no way indicated that immediate medical attention was necessary and the relationship between the parties imposes no affirmative duty to render assistance.   .   .   .

The relationship of the parties and the question of foreseeability does not require that the jury, rather than the court, determine whether a legal duty exists. We are in agreement with the general principle advanced by plaintiff that the question of negligence is one of law for the court only when the facts are such that all reasonable men must draw the same conclusion. However, this principle becomes operative only after the court establishes that a legal duty is owed by one party to another. Prosser's analysis of the role of the court and jury on questions of legal duty bears repeating:

"The existence of a duty. In other words, whether, upon the facts in evidence, such a relation exists between the parties that the commu-

---

4. Were a special relationship to be the basis of imposing a legal duty upon one to insure the safety of another, it would most probably take the form of "co-adventurers" who embark upon a hazardous undertaking with the understanding that each is mutually dependent upon the other for his own safety. There is no evidence to support plaintiff's position that decedent relied upon defendant to provide any assistance whatsoever.   .   .   .

nity will impose a legal obligation upon one for the benefit of the other—or, more simply, whether the interest of the plaintiff which has suffered invasion was entitled to legal protection at the hands of the defendant. This is entirely a question of law, to be determined by reference to the body of statutes, rules, principles and precedents which make up the law; and it must be determined only by the court. . . . A decision by the court that, upon any version of the facts, there is no duty, must necessarily result in judgment for the defendant." Prosser, Torts (4th ed.), § 37, p. 206.

. . .

The Court of Appeals properly decided as a matter of law that defendant owed no duty to the deceased.

We would affirm.

COLEMAN, J., concurred with FITZGERALD, J.

Notes and Questions

1. As the first paragraph of the opinion indicates, the majority recognizes an obligation of due care on two independent grounds: (1) that Siegrist voluntarily came to the assistance of Farwell and (2) that Siegrist, in any event, had an affirmative duty to aid Farwell on the basis of their pre-existing relationship. We have already examined the second ground in the *Harper* case. How does that apply in *Farwell*? What if Siegrist had never returned, but knew that Farwell had been physically attacked? Would the dissent find a duty on one member of a two-person mountain-climbing team to aid the other? Is *Farwell* different?

2. Compare Ronald M. v. White, 169 Cal.Rptr. 370 (App. 1980), plaintiff was one of a group of ten minors who had been cruising around in an auto during the day, some of whom were drinking and taking drugs. Suit was brought against the members of the group who had not been drinking or taken drugs—or furnished or paid for any—for their alleged failure to restrain the driver before his negligence injured others in the group. The court affirmed the granting of summary judgment for defendants. Is *Farwell* distinguishable?

3. We return now to the court's first ground of recovery in *Farwell*— the duty Siegrist assumed by voluntarily attempting to aid Farwell. Should a voluntary actor assume the same duty of due care as an actor bound by a pre-existing relationship to the plaintiff? Suppose a passerby had discovered Farwell and "voluntarily acted" by trying to revive him, but then decided not to get further involved and left the scene. Should that passerby be held liable for failing to exercise the due care that might be expected of a close relative?

Section 324 of the Second Restatement provides that one who, being under no duty to do so, takes charge of another who is helpless is subject to liability caused by "(a) the failure of the actor to exercise reasonable care to secure the safety of the other while within the actor's charge, or (b) the actor's discontinuing his aid or protection, if by so doing he leaves the other in a worse position than when the actor took charge of him." The Restatement expresses no opinion as to whether "an actor who has taken charge of a helpless person may be subject to liability for harm resulting from his discontinuance of the aid or protection, where by doing so he leaves the other in no worse position than when the actor took charge of him." A comment states that although "A, who has taken B from a trench filled with poisonous gas, does not thereby obligate himself to pay for B's treatment in a hospital, he cannot throw B back into the same trench, or leave him lying in the street where he may be run over." What about leaving him on the nearby sidewalk? See Parvi v. City of Kingston, 362 N.E.2d 960 (N.Y.1977), discussing § 324.

4. In Haben v. Anderson, 597 N.E.2d 655 (Ill.App.1992), a university student died from acute alcohol intoxication after participating in an initiation into a club. Part of the case involved a claim against one member of the club. That member had allegedly participated as one of twelve in the initiation; he then allowed other members to place the unconscious decedent on the floor of the member's room; checked on decedent periodically during the night; and heard him gurgling but did nothing. The court held that the trier of fact could find that the member had assumed a duty to care for the decedent and that he did not act reasonably to prevent harm to the decedent after decedent's placement in his room. Is the member's participation in the initiation essential to sustaining the suit?

5. Referring back to *Farwell*, what role should the jury play in deciding these issues? Is the threshold question of whether a special relationship exists for the jury? What about the question of whether there has been a voluntary undertaking? Or should the jury be limited to determining whether there has been a breach of duty?

6. The *Maldonado* court, p. 135, supra, in which the train ran over the trespasser, also held that plaintiff stated an independent claim under Restatement § 326, in that defendant's employees attempted to dissuade and impede would-be rescuers: "One who intentionally prevents a third person from giving to another aid necessary to prevent physical harm to him, is subject to liability. . . ." Section 327 creates a basis for liability against one who negligently prevents aid.

Consider in this connection Soldano v. O'Daniels, 190 Cal.Rptr. 310 (App.1983), in which a bartender refused to allow a third party to make an emergency phone call to the police on behalf of a person who had been threatened at another bar across the street. Although the court acknowledged that there was no pre-existing relationship between defendant bartender and the deceased, it asserted that the defendant had interfered with the third party's rescue efforts. The court limited its holding to a request made to deal with an emergency by using a telephone in the public portion of a business establishment.

In Barnes v. Dungan, 690 N.Y.S.2d 338 (App.Div. 1999), the suit claimed that a worker suffered a heart attack at work and that a co-worker, trained in CPR, who wanted to help, was ordered not to do so by their supervisor. In a suit against the supervisor and the organization for the victim's death, the court held that the supervisor could be found to have violated his duty not to interfere with a rescue.

The Moch case. In H.R. Moch Co. v. Rensselaer Water Co., 159 N.E. 896 (N.Y.1928), defendant water works had a contract with the City of Rensselaer to supply water for various purposes, including service at fire hydrants. A building caught fire and the flames spread to plaintiff's warehouse, destroying it. Plaintiff alleged that the water company's failure to supply adequate water permitted the spread of the fire to the warehouse. The court of appeals, in an opinion by Judge Cardozo, held that the complaint should be dismissed. Among other grounds discussed, Cardozo held that there was no common law tort action available to users of the water supplied to the city:

> "It is ancient learning that one who assumes to act, even though gratuitously, may thereby become subject to the duty of acting carefully, if he acts at all" (Glanzer v. Shepard, [135 N.E. 275 (N.Y.1922)]; [   ]). The plaintiff would bring its case within the orbit of that principle. The hand once set to a task may not always be withdrawn with impunity though liability would fail if it had never been applied at all. A time-honored formula often phrases the distinction as one between misfeasance and nonfeasance. Incomplete the formula is, and so at times misleading. Given a relation involving in its existence a duty of care irrespective of a contract, a tort may result as well from acts of omission as of commission in the fulfillment of the duty thus recognized by law [   ]. What we need to know is not so much the conduct to be avoided when the relation and its attendant duty are established as existing. What we need to know is the conduct that engenders the relation. It is here that the formula, however incomplete, has its value and significance. If conduct has gone forward to such a stage that inaction would commonly result, not negatively merely in withholding a benefit, but positively or actively in working an injury, there exists a relation out of which arises a duty to go forward (Bohlen, Studies in the Law of Torts, p. 87). So the surgeon who operates without pay, is liable though his negligence is in the omission to sterilize his instruments (cf. *Glanzer v. Shepard*, supra); the engineer, though his fault is in the failure to shut off steam [   ]; the maker of automobiles, at the suit of some one other than the buyer, though his negligence is merely in inadequate inspection (*Mac-Pherson v. Buick Motor Co.*, [   ]). The query always is whether the putative wrongdoer has advanced to such a point as to have launched a force or instrument of harm, or has stopped where inaction is at most a refusal to become an instrument for good [   ].

The plaintiff would have us hold that the defendant, when once it entered upon the performance of its contract with the city, was brought into such a relation with every one who might potentially be benefited through the supply of water at the hydrants as to give to negligent performance, without reasonable notice of a refusal to continue, the quality of a tort. . . . We are satisfied that liability would be unduly and indeed indefinitely extended by this enlargement of the zone of duty. . . . What we are dealing with at this time is a mere negligent omission, unaccompanied by malice or other aggravating elements. The failure in such circumstances to furnish an adequate supply of water is at most the denial of a benefit. It is not the commission of a wrong.

How is this case different from the cited examples of the negligent surgeon and the engineer? Note Cardozo's conclusion that the defendant's behavior was "at most the denial of a benefit. It is not the commission of a wrong." How is the distinction between misfeasance and nonfeasance being used here? Is there a danger that the result in *Moch* will reduce incentives toward safety?

Your house catches on fire. Your neighbor, who has a swimming pool with a pump to allow the water to be drawn from the pool to fight fires, refuses to allow you to use any of that water to fight your fire. Is this like *Moch*?

Is there a relationship between the misfeasance-nonfeasance point and the existence of the contract relationship with the city? Is the existence of the contract relevant to the question of whether the defendant has denied a benefit or committed a wrong? Does the existence of the contract help or hurt the plaintiff's case?

Strauss v. Belle Realty Co.

Court of Appeals, New York, 1985.
65 N.Y.2d 399, 482 N.E.2d 34, 492 N.Y.S.2d 555.

KAYE, J.

On July 13, 1977, a failure of defendant Consolidated Edison's power system left most of New York City in darkness. In this action for damages allegedly resulting from the power failure, we are asked to determine whether Con Edison owed a duty of care to a tenant who suffered personal injuries in a common area of an apartment building, where his landlord—but not he—had a contractual relationship with the utility. We conclude that in the case of a blackout of a metropolis of several million residents and visitors, each in some manner necessarily affected by a 25-hour power failure, liability for injuries in a building's common areas should, as a matter of public policy, be limited by the contractual relationship.

This court has twice before confronted legal questions concerning the 1977 blackout (see, Koch v. Consolidated Edison Co., 62 N.Y.2d 548 [1984], cert. denied 469 U.S. 1210 [1985]; Food Pageant v. Consolidated Edison Co., 54 N.Y.2d 167 [1981]).

Plaintiff, Julius Strauss, then 77 years old, resided in an apartment building in Queens. Con Edison provided electricity to his apartment pursuant to agreement with him, and to the common areas of the building under a separate agreement with his landlord, defendant Belle Realty

Company. As water to the apartment was supplied by electric pump, plaintiff had no running water for the duration of the blackout. Consequently, on the second day of the power failure, he set out for the basement to obtain water, but fell on the darkened, defective basement stairs, sustaining injuries. In this action against Belle Realty and Con Edison, plaintiff alleged negligence against the landlord, in failing to maintain the stairs or warn of their dangerous condition, and negligence against the utility in the performance of its duty to provide electricity.

Plaintiff moved for partial summary judgment against Con Edison (1) to estop it from contesting the charge of gross negligence in connection with the blackout, and (2) to establish that Con Edison owed a duty of care to plaintiff. He argued that Con Edison . . . owed plaintiff a duty even though he was "not a customer of Consolidated Edison in a place where the accident occurred." Con Edison cross-moved for summary judgment dismissing the complaint, maintaining it had no duty to a noncustomer.

The court granted the motion insofar as it sought collateral estoppel regarding gross negligence,[1] and denied Con Edison's cross motion to dismiss the complaint, finding a question of fact as to whether it owed plaintiff a duty of care. The Appellate Division reversed and dismissed the complaint against Con Edison. Citing *Moch Co. v. Rensselaer Water Co.* [ ], the plurality concluded that "Con Ed did not owe a duty to plaintiff in any compensable legal sense" [ ]. Justice Gibbons dissented, finding extension of the duty tolerable here because "[t]he tenants of the building in question constitute a defined, limited and known group of people" [ ]. On public policy grounds, we now affirm the Appellate Division order dismissing the complaint against Con Edison.

A defendant may be held liable for negligence only when it breaches a duty owed to the plaintiff (Pulka v. Edelman, 40 N.Y.2d 781, 782 [1976]). The essential question here is whether Con Edison owed a duty to plaintiff, whose injuries from a fall on a darkened staircase may have conceivably been foreseeable, but with whom there was no contractual relationship for lighting in the building's common areas.

Duty in negligence cases is defined neither by foreseeability of injury [ ] nor by privity of contract. As this court has long recognized, an obligation rooted in contract may engender a duty owed to those not in privity, for "[t]here is nothing anomalous in a rule which imposes upon A, who has contracted with B, a duty to C and D and others according as he knows or does not know that the subject-matter of the contract is intended for their use" (*MacPherson v. Buick Motor Co.*, [ ]). In Fish v. Waverly Elec. Light & Power Co. (189 N.Y. 336 [1907]), for example, an electric company which had contracted with the plaintiff's employer to install ceiling lights had a duty to the plaintiff to exercise reasonable care. And in [*Glanzer v. Shepard* (1922)], a public weigher, hired by a seller of beans to certify the weight of a particular shipment, was found liable in negligence to the buyer. [ ]

---

1. The collateral estoppel question was decided against Con Edison in [*Koch*].

But while the absence of privity does not foreclose recognition of a duty, it is still the responsibility of courts, in fixing the orbit of duty, "to limit the legal consequences of wrongs to a controllable degree" [   ], and to protect against crushing exposure to liability [   ]. "In fixing the bounds of that duty, not only logic and science, but policy play an important role" [   ]. The courts' definition of an orbit of duty based on public policy may at times result in the exclusion of some who might otherwise have recovered for losses or injuries if traditional tort principles had been applied.

Considerations of privity are not entirely irrelevant in implementing policy. Indeed, in determining the liability of utilities for consequential damages for failure to provide service—a liability which could obviously be "enormous," and has been described as *"sui generis,"* rather than strictly governed by tort or contract law principles (see, Prosser and Keeton, Torts § 92, at 663 [5th ed.])—courts have declined to extend the duty of care to noncustomers. For example, in *Moch Co. v. Rensselaer Water Co.* [   ], a water works company contracted with the City of Rensselaer to satisfy its water requirements. Plaintiff's warehouse burned and plaintiff brought an action against the water company in part based on its alleged negligence in failing to supply sufficient water pressure to the city's hydrants. The court denied recovery, concluding that the proposed enlargement of the zone of duty would unduly extend liability. Similarly, in Beck v. FMC Corp. (42 N.Y.2d 1027 [1977], *affg.* 53 A.D.2d 118 [1976]), an explosion interrupted a utility's electrical service, which in turn resulted in the loss of a day's pay for hourly workers at a nearby automobile plant. In an action brought by the workers, the court denied recovery on the basis of controlling the unwarranted extension of liability [   ].

Moch involved ordinary negligence, while Con Edison was guilty of gross negligence, but the cases cannot be distinguished on that basis. In reserving the question of what remedy would lie in the case of "reckless and wanton indifference to consequences measured and foreseen," the court in *Moch* contemplated a level of misconduct greater than the gross negligence involved here [   ]. The court in [*Food Pageant v. Consolidated Edison Co.*], in upholding the jury's verdict against Con Edison, noted as instances of Con Edison's misconduct its employee's failure to follow instructions to reduce voltage by "shedding load" after lightning had hit the electrical system, and its staffing decisions [   ]. Though found by the jury to constitute gross negligence, this behavior was not so consciously culpable as to fall into the category of conduct contemplated as "reckless and wanton" by the court in *Moch* [   ].

In the view of the Appellate Division dissenter, *Moch* does not control because the injuries here were foreseeable and plaintiff was a member of a specific, limited, circumscribed class with a close relationship with Con Edison. The situation was thought to be akin to White v. Guarente (43 N.Y.2d 356 [1977]), where an accounting firm was retained by a limited partnership to perform an audit and prepare its tax returns. As the court noted there, the parties to the agreement contemplated that individual limited partners would rely on the tax returns and audit. Refusing to dismiss a negligence action brought by a limited partner against the accounting firm, the court said, "the services of the accountant were not extended to a faceless or unresolved class of persons, but rather to a known group possessed of vested rights, marked by a definable limit and made up of certain components"; see also, [*Glanzer v. Shepard*].

Central to these decisions was an ability to extend the defendant's duty to cover specifically foreseeable parties but at the same time to contain liability to manageable levels. In *White*, for instance, liability stemmed from a single isolated transaction where the parties to the agreement contemplated the protection of identified individuals. Here, insofar as revealed by the record, the arrangement between Con Edison and Belle Realty was no different from those existing between Con Edison and the millions of other customers it serves. . . . When plaintiff's relationship with Con Edison is viewed from this perspective, it is no answer to say that a duty is owed because, as a tenant in an apartment building, plaintiff belongs to a narrowly defined class.[2]

Additionally, we deal here with a system-wide power failure occasioned by what has already been determined to be the utility's gross negligence. If liability could be found here, then in logic and fairness the same result must follow in many similar situations. For example, a tenant's guests and invitees, as well as persons making deliveries or repairing equipment in the building, are equally persons who must use the common areas, and for whom they are maintained. Customers of a store and occupants of an office building stand in much the same position with respect to Con Edison as tenants of an apartment building. In all cases the numbers are to a certain extent limited and defined, and while identities may change, so do those of apartment dwellers (compare, *White v. Guarente*, [ ] ["situation did not involve prospective limited partners, unknown at the time"]). While limiting recovery to customers in this instance can hardly be said to confer immunity from negligence on Con Edison (see, [*Koch*]) permitting recovery to those in plaintiff's circumstances would, in our view, violate the court's responsibility to define an orbit of duty that places controllable limits on liability.

. . .

In sum, Con Edison is not answerable to the tenant of an apartment building injured in a common area as a result of Con Edison's negligent failure to provide electric service as required by its agreement with the building owner. Accordingly, the order of the Appellate Division should be affirmed, with costs.

---

2. In deciding that public policy precludes liability to a noncustomer injured in the common areas of an apartment building, we need not decide whether recovery would necessarily also be precluded where a person injured in the home is not the family bill payer but the spouse. In another context, where this court has defined the duty of a public accounting firm for negligent financial statements, we have recognized that the duty runs both to those in contractual privity with the accountant and to those whose bond is so close as to be, in practical effect, indistinguishable from privity, and we have on public policy grounds precluded wider liability to persons damaged by the accountant's negligence. (See, Credit Alliance Corp. v. Arthur Andersen & Co., 65 N.Y.2d 536 [1985].)

MEYER, J. (dissenting). My disagreement with the majority results not from its consideration of public policy as a factor in determining the scope of Con Ed's duty, but from the fact that in reaching its public policy conclusion it has considered only one side of the equation and based its conclusion on nothing more than assumption. I, therefore, respectfully dissent.

.   .   .

The majority's blind acceptance of the notion that Consolidated Edison will be crushed if held liable to the present plaintiff and others like him ignores the possibility that through application to the Public Service Commission Con Ed can seek such reduction of the return on stockholders' equity [   ] or increase in its rates, or both, as may be necessary to pay the judgments obtained against it. It ignores as well the burden imposed upon the persons physically injured by Con Ed's gross negligence or, as to those forced to seek welfare assistance because their savings have been wiped out by the injury, the State. Doing so in the name of public policy seems particularly perverse, for what it says, in essence, is the more persons injured through a tort-feasor's gross negligence, the less the responsibility for injuries incurred.

.   .   . There simply is no basis other than the majority's say so for its assumptions [   ], that the impact of a city-wide deprivation of electric power upon the utility is entitled to greater consideration than the impact upon those injured; that a rational boundary cannot be fixed that will include some (apartment tenants injured in common areas, for example), if not all of the injured; that the consequence of imposing some bystander liability will be more adverse to societal interests than will follow from blindly limiting liability for tort to those with whom the tort-feasor has a contractual relationship. Before we grant Con Ed's motion to dismiss, therefore, we should require that a rational basis for such assumptions be established.

Con Ed may well be able to do so, but before its motion is granted at the expense of an unknown number of victims who have suffered injuries the extent and effects of which are also unknown, it should be required to establish that the catastrophic probabilities are great enough to warrant the limitation of duty it seeks [   ].

I would, therefore, deny the summary judgment motions of both sides and remit to Supreme Court for determination of the preliminary fact issues involved.

CHIEF JUDGE WACHTLER and JUDGES SIMONS, ALEXANDER and TITONE concur with JUDGE KAYE; JUDGE MEYER dissents and votes to reverse in a separate opinion in which JUDGE JASEN concurs.

Notes and Questions

1. Public Service Commission approval of Con Edison's rate schedule included a proviso that the utility would be liable only for "willful misconduct or gross negligence." See discussion in *Food Pageant v. Consolidated Edison Co.*, cited in the principal case, involving an action by a grocery chain for food spoilage and loss of business due to the blackout. Why was this limitation alone not a sufficient concession to the court's concern about crushing liability?

2. Presumably if, during the blackout, Strauss had fallen, without fault on his part, in a personal residence that he owned, he would have been able to collect as a ratepayer of Con Edison. Is the *Belle Realty* result nonetheless a substantial assurance against crushing liability?

3. Does the dissent persuasively deal with the majority's concern about crushing liability?

4. Noting that only four states then allowed recovery against water companies in fire cases, Libbey v. Hampton Water Works Co., 389 A.2d 434 (N.H.1978), adopted the majority view of *Moch*. Among other reasons, the court noted that water companies do not charge higher rates in areas of high fire risk. If they did, "water would no longer be a cheap, easily procurable commodity. In areas of high risk, water could become prohibitively expensive." Also, the defendant "cannot be said to have dissuaded the homeowner from selecting another method of protecting his home."

We return to the water company cases from an insurance perspective in Chapter X.

5. In Palka v. Servicemaster Management Services Corp., 634 N.E.2d 189 (N.Y.1994), plaintiff nurse was hurt when a wall-mounted fan in a patient's room fell. Defendant had contracted with the hospital to perform all maintenance functions. The defendant argued that its only duty was owed to the hospital with which it had contracted. The court disagreed. The unanimous court rejected "an open-ended range of tort duty arising out of contractual breaches." To find a duty, the relationship between the defendant's contract obligation and the "injured noncontracting party's reliance and injury must be direct and demonstrable, not incidental or merely collateral [citing *Strauss* and other cases]."

> Here, the functions to be performed by Servicemaster were not directed to a faceless or unlimited universe of persons. Rather, a known and identifiable group—hospital employees, patients and visitors—was to benefit and be protected by safety maintenance protocols assumed and acquired exclusively by Servicemaster. It cannot reasonably claim that it was unaware or that it was entitled to be unaware that individuals would expect some entity's direct responsibility to perform maintenance services with ordinary prudence and care. [ ] In fact, the very "end and aim" of the service contract was that Servicemaster was to become the sole privatized provider for a safe and clean hospital premises (see [*Glanzer*]).

How is *Strauss* different?

6. In Jansen v. Fidelity & Casualty Co., 589 N.E.2d 379 (N.Y.1992), defendant was the workers' compensation insurance carrier for plaintiff's employer. Defendant under the contract had the right to—and did—carry out regular inspections of the premises in an effort to reduce the occurrence of worker injuries. Plaintiff worker, who was injured in an accident on the premises, alleged that the defendant had "performed its inspection negligently" and that he had been hurt as a result. The court rejected a duty because it was "apparent that the safety inspections were undertaken solely for defendant's own underwriting purposes—to reduce the risks that might give rise to liability under the policy."

7. In the cited *Pulka v. Edelman*, plaintiff pedestrian was struck by a car while it was being driven out of the defendant's garage and across an adjacent sidewalk by a patron of the garage. A statute required the driver to stop before entering the sidewalk and to yield to any pedestrian. The trial judge entered judgment against both the driver and the garage after a jury verdict. The court of appeals held, 4–3, that the claim against the garage should be dismissed.

The majority stated the issue to be whether a garage "has a duty to control the conduct of its patrons for the protection of off-premises pedestrians." No such duty arose from the relationship between the garage and the driver because the garage had no reasonable opportunity to control the conduct of the driver. Although the garage may have taken precautions, it could not be said that it had "a reasonable opportunity to stop drivers from disregarding their own sense of danger to pedestrians." To build a duty on this relationship would place "an unreasonable burden on the garage."

Nor could a duty be based on the relationship between garage and pedestrian, which was "at best somewhat tenuous." It "would be most unfair" to impose a duty on the garage with respect to its patrons because it did not "control the tortfeasor." Providing an action against the garage "would be to create an unnecessary extension of a duty beyond the limits required under the law of negligence as we know it." The court continued:

> If a rule of law were established so that liability would be imposed in an instance such as this, it is difficult to conceive of the bounds to which liability logically would flow. The liability potential would be all but limitless and the outside boundaries of that liability, both in respect to space and the extent of care to be exercised, particularly in the absence of control, would be difficult of definition. Consider a city like New York with its almost countless parking garages and lots. Think especially of those in the theatre districts and around sporting stadiums and convention halls with the mass exoduses that occur upon cessation of the events which draw the crowds. Think also of the parking facilities at some hotels, office buildings and shopping centers. The burden cast on the operators of these parking establishments in order to discharge their responsibilities in respect to patron-operated vehicles beyond the confines of their properties would be an impractical and unbearable one.

The dissenters responded:

> [A garage operator] cannot close his eyes to the duty to pedestrians who are thereby imperiled. The obligation of due care might have been

discharged by restricting operation of departing vehicles to garage employees, by cautioning patron drivers of the possible presence of sidewalk pedestrians, by warning the pedestrians themselves, or by some combination of such methods, or by resort to some other means of protecting against injury to passersby. Liability would not necessarily be predicated on an obligation of the garage to control the conduct of its patrons; the responsibility of due care might otherwise have been discharged by the expenditure of some effort and attention. In the present instance there was no evidence that any attempt was made to protect users of the sidewalk.

How might the lack of a sign affect the majority, given its focus on control? Who has the better of the dispute? Is *Pulka* helpful in analyzing *Strauss*?

Uhr v. East Greenbush Central School District
Court of Appeals of New York, 1999.
94 N.Y.2d 32, 720 N.E.2d 886, 698 N.Y.S.2d 609.

ROSENBLATT, J.

[Plaintiff parents sued defendant school district alleging that defendant, in violation of state statute, had failed to test the infant plaintiff annually for scoliosis, and that this failure necessitated surgery that could have been avoided if the statute had been obeyed. Education Law § 905(1) required testing of all students between 8 and 16 years of age for scoliosis at least once in each school year. "Plaintiffs assert, in essence, that the District was negligent in failing to examine the minor plaintiff for scoliosis during the 1993–1994 school year, as a result of which her ailment was allowed to progress undetected, to her detriment. Supreme Court granted the District's motion for summary judgment, holding that Education Law § 905(1) does not create a private right of action, and that plaintiffs had otherwise failed to state a claim for common-law negligence." The Appellate Division affirmed.]

We first address plaintiffs' claim that Education Law § 905(1) may be enforced by a private right of action. Three provisions of the Education Law are relevant to our inquiry. Education Law § 905(1) states that "[m]edical inspectors or principals and teachers in charge of schools in this state shall . . . examine all . . . pupils between eight and sixteen years of age for scoliosis, at least once in each school year." Education Law § 905(2) provides that "[n]ot withstanding any other provisions of any general, special or local law, the school authorities charged with the duty of making such tests or examinations of pupils for the presence of scoliosis pursuant to this section shall not suffer any liability to any person as a result of making such test or examination, which liability would not have existed by any provision of law, statutory or otherwise, in the absence of this section." Finally, Education Law § 911 charges the Commissioner of Education with the duty of enforcing the provisions of sections 901 through 910 of the Education Law and authorizes the Commissioner to "adopt rules and regulations" for such purpose.

The Test for the Availability of a Private Right of Action

As plaintiffs point out, the District's obligation to examine for scoliosis is plain enough. A statutory command, however, does not necessarily carry with it a right of private enforcement by means of tort litigation (see, e.g., Mark G. v. Sabol, 93 N.Y.2d 710 [1999]).

The availability of a private right of action for the violation of a statutory duty—as opposed to one grounded in common-law negligence—is not a new concept. [   ] When a statute itself expressly authorizes a private right of action (e.g., Social Services Law § 420[2] [civil liability for "knowingly and willfully" failing to "report a case of suspected child abuse or maltreatment"]; General Obligations Law § 11–100[1] [civil liability for serving alcohol to a minor who gets intoxicated and then hurts others]; [   ]), there is no need for further analysis. When a statute is silent, as it is here, courts have had to determine whether a private right of action may be fairly implied. In [   ], this Court articulated the standards that were synthesized into a three-part test in Sheehy v. Big Flats Community Day, 73 N.Y.2d 629 [1989]. In making the determination, we ask:

(1) whether the plaintiff is one of the class for whose particular benefit the statute was enacted;

(2) whether recognition of a private right of action would promote the legislative purpose; and

(3) whether creation of such a right would be consistent with the legislative scheme [   ].

There is no doubt that the infant plaintiff is a member of the class for whose particular benefit Education Law § 905(1) was enacted. The first prong is satisfied.

The second prong is itself a two-part inquiry. We must first discern what the Legislature was seeking to accomplish when it enacted the statute, and then determine whether a private right of action would promote that objective [   ].

Here, the purpose of the statute is obvious. Scoliosis is a curvature of the spine which, if left undetected in children, can be crippling [   ]. Upon early detection, scoliosis can be treated successfully, often without the need for surgery. In 1978 the Legislature amended Education Law § 905(1) to add scoliosis screening to the then existing obligations to test children's vision and hearing [   ].

It is apparent that the Legislature was seeking to benefit the population as a whole by creating broad-based screening examinations for scoliosis, recognizing that early detection could serve the entire public in both its health and its purse. A main proponent of the legislation stated that: "The Bill will help reduce the cost of medical care to the general public as well as to the State in the case of indigent consumers. It will reduce hospital utilization as those cases which are detected in their early stage can be medically managed without hospitalization" [   ].

Early detection of the condition serves the dual legislative purpose of promoting public health and avoiding costly hospitalization.

In arguing that a private right of action would promote these objectives, plaintiffs assert that the risk of liability for failure to screen will encourage compliance with Education Law § 905(1), and thereby further the statute's purpose of providing broad-based screenings that benefit the public. In response, the District argues that the risk of liability will prompt school districts to seek waivers of the requirement to screen and thus defeat the statute's purpose.

. . .

In all, we conclude that a private right of action would promote the legislative purpose and, therefore, the second prong is satisfied.

We turn next to the third *Sheehy* prong—whether a private right of action is consistent with the legislative scheme. It is not always easy to distinguish this "consistency" prong from the second *Sheehy* prong, which centers on "promotion" of the legislative goal. The two prongs may overlap and to that extent may resist pigeon-holing. A private right of action may at times further a legislative goal and coalesce smoothly with the existing statutory scheme [   ]. Conversely, a statute's goal may not necessarily be enhanced by adding a private enforcement mechanism. In assessing the "consistency" prong, public and private avenues of enforcement do not always harmonize with one another. A private enforcement mechanism may be consistent with one statutory scheme, but in another the prospect may disserve the goal of consistency—like having two drivers at the wheel. Both may ultimately, at least in theory, promote statutory compliance, but they are born of different motivations and may produce a different allocation of benefits owing to differences in approach [   ].

Plaintiffs argue that a private right of action is not only consistent with Education Law § 905(1) but also necessary for its operation. They assert that the statute offers no other practical means of enforcement and that a private right of action is imperative, in order to give it life. We disagree and conclude that a private right of action would not be consistent with the statutory scheme. To begin with, the statute carries its own potent official enforcement mechanism. The Legislature has expressly charged the Commissioner of Education with the duty to implement Education Law § 905(1) and has equipped the Commissioner with authority to adopt rules and regulations for such purpose [   ]. Moreover, the Legislature has vested the Commissioner with power to withhold public funding from noncompliant school districts. Thus, the Legislature clearly contemplated administrative enforcement of this statute.

The question then becomes whether, in addition to administrative enforcement, an implied private right of action would be consistent with the legislative scheme. It would not. The evolution of Education Law § 905(2) is compelling evidence of the Legislature's intent to immunize the school districts from any liability that might arise out of the scoliosis screening program. By the language of Education Law § 905(2) the Legislature deemed that the school district "shall not suffer any liability to any person as a result of *making* such test or examination" (emphasis added). Plaintiffs contend that by implication, the District is denied immunity for failing to perform the examination. In effect, plaintiffs would interpret the statute as conferring immunity for misfeasance but not nonfeasance. On the other hand, the District contends that it would be incongruous for the Legislature to accord immunity for one circumstance but not the other.

[The court accepted the defendant's contention. It found "persuasive evidence" of legislative desire to immunize school districts in its overturning of one related appellate court ruling together with its failure to overrule two others that barred tort relief. The court also noted that statements antedating the legislation at issue in this case had stated that the program "would have minimal financial impact on school districts."]

In sum, we conclude that a private right of action to enforce Education Law § 905(1) is inconsistent with the statute's legislative scheme and therefore cannot be fairly implied [   ].

Common-Law Negligence

Plaintiffs contend that the lower courts erred in holding that they failed to state a claim for common-law negligence. Essentially, plaintiffs argue that the District assumed a duty to the infant plaintiff and her parents by creating a special relationship with them in connection with the Education Law § 905(1) program and that it breached its duty by failing to perform the examination during the 1993–1994 school year. We agree with the courts below that plaintiffs have failed as a matter of law to state a claim for common-law negligence (see, Cuffy v. City of New York, 69 N.Y.2d 255, 261 [1987]).

Accordingly, the order of the Appellate Division should be affirmed, with costs.

CHIEF JUDGE KAYE and JUDGES BELLACOSA, SMITH, LEVINE, CIPARICK and WESLEY concur.

Notes and Questions

1. Why isn't the school nurse's failure to examine plaintiff, in violation of the statute, negligence per se as that concept was used in Martin v. Herzog, p. 73 supra? How is the issue different here?

2. Is the court persuasive in arguing that an implied private right of action can promote the legislative purpose, but nonetheless be inconsistent with the legislative scheme?

3. The opinion in *Uhr* analyzes whether a duty may arise from a particular statute when neither a special relationship between the parties nor an affirmative obligation to act would create a duty under the common law. The Second Restatement § 874A, "Tort Liability for Violation of Legislative Provision," addresses the same issue:

When a legislative provision protects a class of persons by proscribing or requiring certain conduct but does not provide a civil remedy for the violation, the court may, if it determines that the remedy is appropriate in furtherance of the purpose of the legislation and needed to assure the effectiveness of the provision, accord to an injured member of the class a right of action, using a suitable existing tort action or a new cause of action analogous to an existing tort action.

Are the approaches of § 874A and *Uhr* consistent?

Although the Second Restatement insists that the judiciary must determine whether or not a right of action should be imposed, some courts instead ask if a state legislature, in creating a new statutory duty, either explicitly or implicitly "intended" to create civil liability. How does discussing the intent of the legislature differ from the approach in § 874A?

4. Is the court's reference to the problem of "two drivers" supportable? Would the case be different if the statute were criminal—with the only sanction being a fine imposed on the principal of any school that did not perform the scoliosis tests?

5. In the last paragraph of *Uhr* the court rejects a claim that was understood to be unrelated to the statute. We return to this issue and to the cited *Cuffy* case in the section on government liability.

6. *Duty to rescue.* We have seen that common law will not generally require rescue. What should happen in a state that has made it a crime not to rescue? In the early 1970s, Vermont adopted such a statute. The history of this legislation is traced in Franklin, Vermont Requires Rescue: A Comment, 25 Stan.L.Rev. 51 (1972). The statute, Vt.Stat.Ann., tit. 12, § 519 (1967), provides:

(a) A person who knows that another is exposed to grave physical harm shall, to the extent that the same can be rendered without danger or peril to himself or without interference with important duties owed to others, give reasonable assistance to the exposed person unless that assistance or care is being provided by others.

(b) A person who provides reasonable assistance in compliance with subsection (a) of this section shall not be liable in civil damages unless his acts constitute gross negligence or unless he will receive or expects to receive remuneration. Nothing contained in this subsection shall alter existing law with respect to tort liability of a practitioner of the healing arts for acts committed in the ordinary course of his practice.

(c) A person who wilfully violates subsection (a) of this section shall be fined not more than $100.00.

Only a handful of states have followed Vermont's lead. See Note, Justifications for State Bystander Intervention Statutes: Why Crime Witnesses Should Be Required to Call for Help, 33 Ind.L.Rev. 571, 574–75 (2000). Would providing statutory incentives be a more effective way to encourage rescue than creating criminal duties or duties in tort? In earlier years, some states reacted to the problem of rescue by giving awards to persons hurt while attempting rescues. The object was to indemnify for loss rather than to "reward." See, e.g., Calif.Govt.Code §§ 13970–74.

If Vermont had adopted only sections (a) and (c), should a court create a civil duty to rescue? See the extended discussion in Franklin and Ploeger, Of Rescue and Report: Should Tort Law Impose a Duty to Help Endangered Persons or Abused Children? 40 Santa Clara L.Rev. 991 (2000). See Morris on Torts 146–51 (2d ed. 1980), arguing that the existence of a criminal statute removes judicial concerns about lack of notice and lack of feasibility. Are separate questions introduced by the existence of section (b)?

7. *Duty to report child abuse.* Every state has now adopted some form of law requiring reports by those who have knowledge of or reason to suspect child abuse. Some statutes explicitly impose civil liability. There may also be compelling policy reasons for courts to recognize private causes of action even when state laws do not mandate civil liability. Franklin and Ploeger suggest several distinctions between duties to rescue and duties to report, including: (a) "the need for child abuse reporting seems to be far more pressing than the need for easy rescue" since child abuse "is done in secret and is much harder to ferret out"; (b) "victims of child abuse are unable to articulate their harm or even to contact police or other officials"; (c) "a duty to report child abuse—or just keeping the child away from an abusive person—may infringe less on personal freedom than a duty of easy rescue"; (d) "the harm occurs slowly and over a period of time, allowing the legal system a better chance to measure the harm done by the delay." Do these considerations justify different tort treatment for the two areas?

For differing approaches to child abuse statutes, compare Perry v. S.N., 973 S.W.2d 301 (Tex.1998) (refusing to imply a tort action from the state criminal statute and noting that the plaintiff had not pursued an earlier common-law claim) with J.S. v. R.T.H., 714 A.2d 924 (N.J.1998) (denying summary judgment to the wife of a man who sexually abused his neighbors' two daughters when they visited daily to ride his horses; if the wife suspected or should have suspected her husband, she had a duty "to take reasonable steps to prevent or warn of the harm"). In the latter case, the court relied in part on the existence of the state's criminal reporting statute and § 874A, note 2, supra. Is it easier (or harder) to impose this kind of duty on a spouse than on a stranger who violates a reporting statute?

8. *Duty to report crime.* More recently, several legislatures have penalized those who fail to report crimes that they witness. The most recent stimulus was the 1997 murder of seven-year-old Sherrice Iverson in a Las Vegas casino bathroom while David Cash, the 17-year-old murderer's friend, did not intervene. See Ziegler, Comment, Nonfeasance and the Duty to Assist: The American Seinfeld Syndrome, 104 Dick.L.Rev. 525, 527 (2000). Should courts create civil actions based on these statutes? Should it matter whether Cash stood outside the bathroom the entire time; entered the bathroom and saw the event unfolding before he left; or saw the start of the event, verbally urged the killer to stop—and then left the bathroom?

California's response to the Iverson murder is contained in Penal Code 152.3, adopted in 2000. The statute, to be known as the "Sherrice Iverson Victim Protection Act," provides that "any person who reasonably believes he or she has observed the commission" of murder, rape or other listed sex crimes "where the victim is under the age of 14 years shall notify a peace officer." That duty is satisfied if "the notification or an attempt to provide notice is made by telephone or any other means." Failure to comply is a misdemeanor punishable by a fine of up to $1,500, imprisonment for six months, or both. Three groups of people are relieved of the duty to report: (1) a relative of either the victim or the offender; (2) one who fails to report because of a "reasonable mistake of fact"; and (3) those in reasonable fear of their safety or that of their family. How does this differ from the Vermont statute?

Compare the Hawaii statute: "Any person at the scene of a crime who knows that a victim of the crime is suffering from serious physical harm shall obtain or attempt to obtain aid from law enforcement or medical personnel." Haw.Rev.Stat. § 663–1.6(a). Might this provide a stronger justification for creating a tort action than does the California type of statute? In fact, the Hawaii statute bars civil liability against those who fail to comply as well as those who try to comply. Why might that be?

9. *Federal statutes.* In the absence of a federal common law, the federal courts cannot create civil liability independent of Congressional enactments. In the absence of express statutory provisions, they must decide whether to imply private rights of action. See Cort v. Ash, 422 U.S. 66 (1975). For comprehensive discussion of the subject, see Stewart and Sunstein, Public Programs and Private Rights, 95 Harv.L.Rev. 1195 (1982). See also Stabile, "The Role of Congressional Intent in Determining the Existence of Implied Private Rights of Action," 71 Notre Dame L. Rev. 861 (1996).

Of course, as *Uhr* noted, states may enact statutory torts. Congress, too, may sometimes explicitly create a federal tort action. The recent Emergency Medical Treatment and Active Labor Act (EMTALA) requires that hospitals with emergency facilities accept patients in an "emergency medical condition" and treat them until they are stabilized and can be moved safely. Congress provided a statutory damage action for anyone injured by violations of the Act. See Roberts v. Galen of Virginia, Inc., 525 U.S. 249 (1999), in which a guardian sued for damages alleging that the transfer of his ward from defendant hospital to another while the ward was in unstable condition harmed the ward and violated EMTALA. The Supreme Court rejected the hospital's argument that the statute required a showing that the hospital had acted from an improper motive. There was no reason to read such a requirement into the statute.

10. *Statutory limitations on liability.* In addition to being used to create civil liability, statutes may restrict or preclude common law duties. See the discussion of preemption in Chapter VI. Here we consider statutory efforts to encourage conduct by using immunity as a carrot. In 1959, California provided that no physician licensed in the state "who in good faith renders emergency care at the scene of the emergency, shall be liable for any civil damages as a result of any acts or omissions by such person in rendering the emergency care." Bus. & Prof. Code § 2395. Provisions of this kind are customarily known as "Good Samaritan" statutes. If fear that victims aided in an emergency will sue for malpractice is a major factor in the alleged reluctance of physicians to volunteer, how effective are statutes like California's? How about a statute that protects physicians against liability for negligence but not for gross negligence? How about a total bar on suits against those who try to help at the scenes of accidents? Should these statutes be limited to physicians or should all volunteers be similarly protected? See generally Mason, Comment, Good Samaritan Laws—Legal Disarray: An Update, 38 Mercer L. Rev. 1439 (1987) (analyzing Good Samaritan statutes and case law). Since then, virtually every state has adopted some version of the Good Samaritan statute. The Vermont duty to rescue, discussed earlier, evolved from a lobbying effort to exempt physicians who stopped and assisted at emergency scenes from liability for negligence. For a list of more than a dozen statutory extensions of the protection given physicians, see Perkins v. Howard, 283 Cal.Rptr. 764, 767 n. 2 (App. 1991).

In general, do some situations lend themselves better to "carrots" and others to "sticks"?

C.   Obligations to Protect a Third Party

Tarasoff v. Regents of the Univ. of California

Supreme Court of California, 1976.
17 Cal.3d 425, 551 P.2d 334, 131 Cal.Rptr. 14.

[Dr. Moore, a psychologist employed by the University of California, was treating one Poddar. Poddar killed Tatiana Tarasoff. Plaintiffs, the parents of Tatiana Tarasoff, allege that Poddar had confided his intention to kill Tarasoff to Dr. Moore; that after an abortive effort to detain Poddar, he was released; and that no one warned Tarasoff or plaintiffs of Tarasoff's peril. The trial judge dismissed the suit that was brought against several therapists and others.]

Tobriner, J.

.   .   .

The second cause of action can be amended to allege that Tatiana's death proximately resulted from defendants' negligent failure to warn Tatiana or others likely to apprise her of her danger. Plaintiffs contend that as amended, such allegations of negligence and proximate causation, with resulting damages, establish a cause of action. Defendants, however, contend that in the circumstances of the present case they owed no duty of care to Tatiana or her parents and that, in the absence of such duty, they were free to act in careless disregard of Tatiana's life and safety.

In analyzing this issue, we bear in mind that legal duties are not discoverable facts of nature, but merely conclusory expressions that, in cases of a particular type, liability should be imposed for damage done.

. . .

In the landmark case of *Rowland v. Christian* [   ], Justice Peters recognized that liability should be imposed "for injury occasioned to another by his want of ordinary care or skill" as expressed in § 1714 of the Civil Code. Thus, Justice Peters, quoting from Heaven v. Pender (1883) 11 Q.B.D. 503, 509 stated: " 'whenever one person is by circumstances placed in such a position with regard to another . . . that if he did not use ordinary care and skill in his own conduct . . . he would cause danger of injury to the person or property of the other, a duty arises to use ordinary care and skill to avoid such danger.' "

We depart from "this fundamental principle" only upon the "balancing of a number of considerations"; major ones "are the foreseeability of harm to the plaintiff, the degree of certainty that the plaintiff suffered injury, the closeness of the connection between the defendant's conduct and the injury suffered, the moral blame attached to the defendant's conduct, the policy of preventing future harm, the extent of the burden to the defendant and consequences to the community of imposing a duty to exercise care with resulting liability for breach, and the availability, cost and prevalence of insurance for the risk involved." [citing several cases]

The most important of these considerations in establishing duty is foreseeability. As a general principle, a "defendant owes a duty of care to all persons who are foreseeably endangered by his conduct, with respect to all risks which make the conduct unreasonably dangerous." [   ] As we shall explain, however, when the avoidance of foreseeable harm requires a defendant to control the conduct of another person, or to warn of such conduct, the common law has traditionally imposed liability only if the defendant bears some special relationship to the dangerous person or to the potential victim. Since the relationship between a therapist and his patient satisfies this requirement, we need not here decide whether foreseeability alone is sufficient to create a duty to exercise reasonable care to protect a potential victim of another's conduct.

Although, as we have stated above, under the common law, as a general rule, one person owed no duty to control the conduct of another[5] [   ], nor to warn those endangered by such conduct [   ], the courts have carved out an exception to this rule in cases in which the defendant stands

---

5. This rule derives from the common law's distinction between misfeasance and nonfeasance, and its reluctance to impose liability for the latter. (See Harper & Kime, The Duty to Control the Conduct of Another (1934) 43 Yale L.J. 886, 887.) Morally questionable, the rule owes its survival to "the difficulties of setting any standards of unselfish service to fellow men, and of making any workable rule to cover possible situations where fifty people might fail to rescue. . . ." (Prosser, Torts (4th ed. 1971) § 56, p. 341.) Because of these practical difficulties, the courts have increased the number of instances in which affirmative duties are imposed not by direct rejection of the common law rule, but by expanding the list of special relationships which will justify departure from that rule. [   ]

in some special relationship to either the person whose conduct needs to be controlled or in a relationship to the foreseeable victim of that conduct (see Restatement, Second, Torts, supra, §§ 315–320). Applying this exception to the present case, we note that a relationship of defendant therapists to either Tatiana or Poddar will suffice to establish a duty of care; as explained in section 315 of the Restatement Second of Torts, a duty of care may arise from either "(a) a special relation . . . between the actor and the third person which imposes a duty upon the actor to control the third person's conduct, or (b) a special relation . . . between the actor and the other which gives to the other a right of protection."

Although plaintiffs' pleadings assert no special relation between Tatiana and defendant therapists, they establish as between Poddar and defendant therapists the special relation that arises between a patient and his doctor or psychotherapist. Such a relationship may support affirmative duties for the benefit of third persons. Thus, for example, a hospital must exercise reasonable care to control the behavior of a patient which may endanger other persons. A doctor must also warn a patient if the patient's condition or medication renders certain conduct, such as driving a car, dangerous to others.

Although the California decisions that recognize this duty have involved cases in which the defendant stood in a special relationship *both* to the victim and to the person whose conduct created the danger,[9] we do not think that the duty should logically be constricted to such situations. Decisions of other jurisdictions hold that the single relationship of a doctor to his patient is sufficient to support the duty to exercise reasonable care to protect others against dangers emanating from the patient's illness. The courts hold that a doctor is liable to persons infected by his patient if he negligently fails to diagnose a contagious disease [   ], or having diagnosed the illness, fails to warn members of the patient's family [   ].

. . .

Defendants contend, however, that imposition of a duty to exercise reasonable care to protect third persons is unworkable because therapists cannot accurately predict whether or not a patient will resort to violence. In support of this argument amicus representing the American Psychiatric Association and other professional societies cites numerous articles which indicate that therapists, in the present state of the art, are unable reliably to predict violent acts; their forecasts, amicus claims, tend consistently to overpredict violence, and indeed are more often wrong than right. Since predictions of violence are often erroneous, amicus concludes, the courts should not render rulings that predicate the liability of therapists upon the validity of such predictions.

---

9. Ellis v. D'Angelo [253 P.2d 675 (App. 1953)], upheld a cause of action against parents who failed to warn a babysitter of the violent proclivities of their child; Johnson v. State of California [447 P.2d 352 (Cal.1968)], upheld a suit against the state for failure to warn foster parents of the dangerous tendencies of their ward; Morgan v. County of Yuba [41 Cal.Rptr. 508 App. (1964)], sustained a cause of action against a sheriff who had promised to warn decedent before releasing a dangerous prisoner, but failed to do so.

. . .

We recognize the difficulty that a therapist encounters in attempting to forecast whether a patient presents a serious danger of violence. . . . Within the broad range of reasonable practice and treatment in which professional opinion and judgment may differ, the therapist is free to exercise his or her own best judgment without liability; proof, aided by hindsight, that he or she judged wrongly is insufficient to establish negligence.

In the instant case, however, the pleadings do not raise any questions as to failure of defendant therapists to predict that Poddar presented a serious danger of violence. On the contrary, the present complaints allege that defendant therapists did in fact predict that Poddar would kill, but were negligent in failing to warn.

Amicus contends, however, that even when a therapist does in fact predict that a patient poses a serious danger of violence to others, the therapist should be absolved of any responsibility for failing to act to protect the potential victim. In our view, however, once a therapist does in fact determine, or under applicable professional standards reasonably should have determined, that a patient poses a serious danger of violence to others, he bears a duty to exercise reasonable care to protect the foreseeable victim of that danger. While the discharge of this duty of due care will necessarily vary with the facts of each case, in each instance the adequacy of the therapist's conduct must be measured against the traditional negligence standard of the rendition of reasonable care under the circumstances. . . .

. . . Weighing the uncertain and conjectural character of the alleged damage done the patient by such a warning against the peril to the victim's life, we conclude that professional inaccuracy in predicting violence cannot negate the therapist's duty to protect the threatened victim.

The risk that unnecessary warnings may be given is a reasonable price to pay for the lives of possible victims that may be saved. We would hesitate to hold that the therapist who is aware that his patient expects to attempt to assassinate the President of the United States would not be obligated to warn the authorities because the therapist cannot predict with accuracy that his patient will commit the crime.

Defendants further argue that free and open communication is essential to psychotherapy. . . . The giving of a warning, defendants contend, constitutes a breach of trust which entails the revelation of confidential communications.

We recognize the public interest in supporting effective treatment of mental illness and in protecting the rights of patients to privacy [ ], and the consequent public importance of safeguarding the confidential character of psychotherapeutic communication. Against this interest, however, we must weigh the public interest in safety from violent assault. The Legislature has undertaken the difficult task of balancing the countervailing concerns. In Evidence Code section 1014, it established a broad rule of privilege to protect confidential communications between patient and psychotherapist. In Evidence Code section 1024, the Legislature created a specific and limited exception to the psychotherapist-patient privilege: "There is no privilege . . . if the psychotherapist has reasonable cause to believe that the patient is in such mental or emotional condition as to be dangerous to himself or to the person or property of another and that disclosure of the communication is necessary to prevent the threatened danger."

We realize that the open and confidential character of psychotherapeutic dialogue encourages patients to express threats of violence, few of which are ever executed. Certainly a therapist should not be encouraged routinely to reveal such threats; such disclosures could seriously disrupt the patient's relationship with his therapist and with the persons threatened. To the contrary, the therapist's obligations to his patient require that he not disclose a confidence unless such disclosure is necessary to avert danger to others, and even then that he do so discreetly, and in a fashion that would preserve the privacy of his patient to the fullest extent compatible with the prevention of the threatened danger. [   ]

The revelation of a communication under the above circumstances is not a breach of trust or a violation of professional ethics; as stated in the Principles of Medical Ethics of the American Medical Association (1957), section 9: "A physician may not reveal the confidence entrusted to him in the course of medical attendance . . . *unless he is required to do so by law or unless it becomes necessary in order to protect the welfare of the individual or of the community.*" (Italics added.) We conclude that the public policy favoring protection of the confidential character of patient-psychotherapist communications must yield to the extent to which disclosure is essential to avert danger to others. The protective privilege ends where the public peril begins.

Our current crowded and computerized society compels the interdependence of its members. In this risk-infested society we can hardly tolerate the further exposure to danger that would result from a concealed knowledge of the therapist that his patient was lethal. If the exercise of reasonable care to protect the threatened victim requires the therapist to warn the endangered party or those who can reasonably be expected to notify him, we see no sufficient societal interest that would protect and justify concealment. The containment of such risks lies in the public interest. . . .

. . .

For the reasons stated, we conclude that plaintiffs can amend their complaints to state a cause of action against defendant therapists by asserting that the therapists in fact determined that Poddar presented a serious danger of violence to Tatiana, or pursuant to the standards of their profession should have so determined, but nevertheless failed to exercise reasonable care to protect her from that danger.

. . .

WRIGHT, C.J., SULLIVAN, J., and RICHARDSON, J., concurred.

MOSK, J., Concurring and Dissenting.—I concur in the result in this instance only because the complaints allege that defendant therapists did in fact predict that Poddar would kill and were therefore negligent in failing to warn of that danger.   .   .   .

.   .   .

I cannot concur, however, in the majority's rule that a therapist may be held liable for failing to predict his patient's tendency to violence if other practitioners, pursuant to the "standards of the profession," would have done so. The question is, what standards? Defendants and a responsible amicus curiae, supported by an impressive body of literature discussed at length in our recent opinion in [   ], demonstrate that psychiatric predictions of violence are inherently unreliable.

.   .   .

[JUSTICE CLARK, joined by JUSTICE MCCOMB, dissented. First, he argued that certain legislation indicated an intention that therapists not disclose this information. Entirely apart from the statute, he believed that general tort principles favored nondisclosure. He considered confidentiality critical for three reasons: without such assurances those requiring treatment would be deterred; confidentiality encouraged the full disclosure necessary for effective treatment; and even with full disclosure, confidentiality is necessary to allow the patient to maintain his trust in his psychiatrist. Given the lack of precision in predicting violence, psychiatrists will be tempted either to issue excessive warnings or to commit patients—a practice already used to excess. "We should accept legislative and medical judgment, relying upon effective treatment rather than on indiscriminate warning."]

Notes and Questions

1. The court's citation to § 315 of the Second Restatement raises several questions. The section itself indicates that the relationship must be one that "imposes a duty upon the actor to control the third person's conduct." The comment declares that these relations "are stated in §§ 316–319." Those sections provide that an actor who knows or should know that he or she has the ability to control the third person and knows or should know of the need for the action, comes under a duty to do so as to parent-child (§ 316); master-servant (§ 317); and possessor of land or chattels—user of the land or chattels (§ 318). Section 319 provides: "One who takes charge of a third person whom he knows or should know to be likely to cause bodily harm to others if not controlled is under a duty to exercise reasonable care to control the third person to prevent him from doing such harm." The illustrations deal with an escape of a homicidal maniac and the negligent release of patients who have contagious diseases. Do any of these sections support *Tarasoff?*

2. In Lego v. Schmidt, 805 P.2d 1119 (Colo.App.1990), the court rejected a duty on a passenger to warn the driver about an impending danger to a pedestrian that the driver, moving at five miles per hour, did not appear to recognize. The court quoted comment *b* of § 315 of the Restatement, which states that in the absence of a special relationship between the actor and either the third person or the person hurt:

> [T]he actor is not subject to liability if he fails, either intentionally or through inadvertence, to exercise his ability so to control the actions of the third persons as to protect another from even the most serious harm. This is true although the actor realizes that he has the ability to control the conduct of a third person, and could do so with only the most trivial of efforts and without any inconvenience to himself. Thus if the actor is riding in a third person's car merely as a guest, he is not subject to liability to another run over by the car even though he knows of the other's danger and knows that the driver is not aware of it, and knows that by a mere word, recalling the driver's attention to the road, he would give the driver an opportunity to stop the car before the other is run over.

The passenger, who saw the danger, "rather than shouting or pulling the emergency brake," was said to have "looked away." The court noted that any "attempt on the part of a passenger to direct the driver or to take over control of the brake or wheel could well become negligence itself, and the passenger is trapped into an instantaneous Hobson's choice between action and inaction." The court concluded that there was no duty "to interfere with the driver's control of the car, by either word or deed" and cited other cases including one that it summarized as holding that "passengers had no duty to warn driver that fellow passenger had been thrown from car and was in danger of being run over." The Restatement comment also notes that if the guest is hurt in such a situation the guest's silence may constitute contributory negligence because of the guest's violation of the duty of self-protection.

3. Does the line of cases referred to in the opinion in which a physician failed to warn a patient's family or friends of the patient's contagious condition provide a closer analogy to *Tarasoff* than the Restatement sections? The courts differ in their analyses.

a. *Imposing duty beyond the physician-patient relationship.* In Reisner v. Regents of the University of California, 37 Cal.Rptr.2d 518 (App. 1995), a day after 12-year-old T received a transfusion, her doctor discovered that the blood had been contaminated with HIV antibodies. Although the same doctor continued treating T, he never told her about the situation. Three years later, T became intimate with plaintiff. Two years after that the doctor told T, who died a month later. Shortly thereafter, plaintiff was tested and learned that he was HIV seropositive. The court, relying largely on *Tarasoff*, held that defendant doctor owed a duty to plaintiff despite the lack of a physician-patient relationship. Might the passage of time distinguish the cases? (Note the causal part of plaintiff's case—that if T had been told when she should have been told, she would have warned plaintiff and he would not have been infected.)

In Pate v. Threlkel, 661 So.2d 278 (Fla.1995), defendant surgeon who operated on patient knew or should have known of the likelihood that her adult children would contract the carcinoma involved because it was genetically transferrable. The court imposed a duty to the patient's child who alleged that her cancer would have been discovered sooner and been treatable if her mother had been told about the genetic situation. Since the obligation here was "obviously for the benefit of certain identified third parties and the physician knows of the existence of those third parties, then the physician's duty runs to those third parties."

In a later case, defendant physician incorrectly and negligently told his patient that she had tested negative for hepatitis C. Some months later, she met, and married, a man who later tested positive for hepatitis C. A physician's affidavit asserted that it was "foreseeable that a single, attractive, thirty-nine year old woman [such as this patient] would be dating and engaging in sexual relations." The court rejected the husband's suit because *Pate* required that the third party's existence or identity be known at the time of the negligence, and here the patient "had not yet met [her husband] at the time of the incorrect diagnosis." Hawkins v. Pizarro, 713 So.2d 1036 (Fla.App. 1998).

Although the court in Safer v. Estate of Pack, 677 A.2d 1188 (N.J.App. 1996), refused, because of *Pate*, to dismiss a case, it observed that it "may be necessary, at some stage, to resolve a conflict between the physician's broader duty to warn and his fidelity to an expressed preference of the patient that nothing be said to family members about the details of the disease."

b. *No duty.* In Clarke v. Hoek, 219 Cal.Rptr. 845 (App.1985), plaintiff argued that defendant doctor was negligent in failing to intervene to prevent malpractice by a surgical team while he was proctoring an operation. Defendant was observing the operation as part of the hospital's determination of whether to grant staff privileges to the operating surgeon. The court affirmed summary judgment for the defendant on the ground that the proctoring physician's role was limited to observing and reporting on the operation and that he had no special relationship to the patient. Is this consistent with *Tarasoff*?

It has also been widely, though not uniformly, held that physicians who are employed by companies (or insurers) to give prospective employees (or insureds) physical examinations owe no duty to tell the person being examined if they find signs of trouble. The cases are reviewed in Reed v. Bojarski, 166 N.J. 89, 764 A.2d 433 (2001), which adopted the minority position. The court held that when, during a pre-employment physical exam paid for by the prospective employer, the physician determines that the person being examined has a potentially serious medical condition, the physician has a duty to inform the patient and that obligation may not be delegated to the referring agency. Does this case raise the same issues as the *Jansen* case at p. 149, supra?

The subject of a physician's duties to a third party stranger is explored in detail in Lester by Mavrogenis v. Hall, 970 P.2d 590 (N.M.1998). The court, in a suit by a motorist hurt by defendant's patient, held that the physician had no duty to the motorist to warn the patient about the dangers of driving while taking lithium or to monitor his condition where the accident occurred five days after the last visit. The court distinguished a case in which it had held that a duty was owed "when the patient has just been injected with drugs known to affect judgment and driving ability."

c. *The New York situation.* In Albala v. City of New York, 429 N.E.2d 786 (N.Y.1981), plaintiff alleged that a negligently performed abortion on his mother-to-be in 1971 perforated her uterus and caused him to be born with brain damage in 1975. The court, 5–1, concluded that to recognize this action "would require the extension of traditional tort concepts beyond manageable bounds." The court observed:

> We are not unmindful . . . that at the time Ruth Albala underwent an abortion in 1971 it was foreseeable that she would again conceive and that the health of children born thereafter could be adversely affected by damage to her uterus. We disagree, however, that this foreseeability alone established a duty to plaintiff on the part of defendants. We determined long ago in a case involving policy issues as sensitive as the ones at bar that foreseeability alone is not the hallmark of legal duty for if foreseeability were the sole test we could not logically confine the extension of liability. (*Tobin v. Grossman* [   ]; see *Pulka v. Edelman* [p. 150, supra]).

The majority also expressed concern that extended liability would lead to "defensive medicine" in which a physician might have to choose between a treatment more likely to save the patient, but with risks to possible offspring, and another treatment somewhat less beneficial to the patient but with no dangers to future generations. If liability ran to future generations "society as a whole would bear the cost of our placing physicians in a direct conflict between their moral duty to patients and the proposed legal duty to those hypothetical future generations outside the immediate zone of danger."

The *Albala* approach was rejected in Renslow v. Mennonite Hospital, 367 N.E.2d 1250 (Ill.1977), in which plaintiff alleged that when her mother was 13 years old, the defendant hospital and its director of laboratories negligently transfused her mother with Rh-positive blood. The 13-year-old's Rh-negative blood was incompatible with, and was sensitized by, the new blood. The problem did not become apparent until several years later when the mother became pregnant with plaintiff. As a result of the incompatibility, plaintiff alleged, she needed blood transfusions immediately after birth and suffered severe permanent damage. The court, 4–3, upheld the complaint, with five opinions that explored the appropriate judicial response to claims based on acts alleged to have been committed many years earlier.

Albala was also rejected in Lough v. Rolla Women's Clinic, Inc., 866 S.W.2d 851 (Mo.1993) involving allegations about negligent reporting of a mother's Rh status in an earlier pregnancy.

Until recently, New York has typified states that have kept duty narrowly delimited. In Conboy v. Mogeloff, 567 N.Y.S.2d 960 (App.Div. 1991), defendant prescribed a drug for his patient and told her she could drive a car while taking it. A few days later, while using the drug, she lost consciousness and the car crashed hurting her children passengers. The court rejected a duty to the children, observing that "there are no allegations . . . of the children's reliance on defendant's conduct or of knowledge by the defendant of any such reliance." Would that have changed matters? See Ellis v. Peter, 627 N.Y.S.2d 707 (App.Div.1995) (physician who failed to diagnose tuberculosis in patient husband owed no duty to plaintiff wife who contracted the disease from husband). In *Ellis*, the majority feared that no line could be drawn to prevent such a duty from extending to "children, co-workers, or even fellow commuters."

On the other hand, in Tenuto v. Lederle Laboratories, 687 N.E.2d 1300 (N.Y.1997), the court imposed a duty when a father sued his infant's physician for failure to warn about the danger of getting polio from allowing an open wound to come in contact with the excrement of an infant recently immunized against polio. The absence of a doctor-patient relationship between the parents and the defendant doctor was not controlling: "Courts resolve legal duty questions by resort to common concepts of morality, logic and consideration of the social consequences of imposing the duty." The court identified a "special relationship-based expanded duty of care:"

> Plaintiffs fall within a determinate and identified class—immediate family members—whose relationships to the person acted upon have traditionally been recognized as a means of extending yet limiting the scope of liability for injuries caused by a party's negligent acts or omissions.

The duty was also supported where the physician was a pediatrician because in such cases "the special relationship factor is triangulated here, involving interconnections of reliance running directly between plaintiffs and [the doctor], and indirectly from their status and responsibility as the primary caretakers of his infant patient." What analysis in *Tenuto* if a babysitter changing the diaper gets polio? Is *Tenuto* consistent with *Albala*? With *Conboy*?

4. The *Tarasoff* court lists a number of factors that are said to play a role in the determination whether to impose a duty. Which of these factors are most important?

5. Later California cases have adhered to *Tarasoff* with caution. See Bellah v. Greenson, 146 Cal.Rptr. 535 (App. 1978), in which a patient of the defendant psychiatrist committed suicide. The patient's parents claimed that defendant negligently failed to take sufficient measures to prevent the suicide; that he failed to warn plaintiffs, who were out of state, of the seriousness of their daughter's condition; and that she was consorting with heroin addicts. All claims failed. *Tarasoff* does not apply where the risk is "self-inflicted harm or mere property damage."

In Thompson v. County of Alameda, 614 P.2d 728 (Cal.1980), the county released James, a violent juvenile offender, into his mother's custody although the county knew that he had threatened to kill some unidentified child in the neighborhood. Within 24 hours, James killed plaintiff's son, a boy in his neighborhood. The plaintiffs claimed that the county had been negligent in failing to warn the public, the police, and James's mother.

The trial court's dismissal of the complaint was affirmed, 5–2. There was no identified potential victim. Warnings to the general public were unlikely to do much good because the public is already conditioned to protecting itself against crime and violence and a specific warning might negate the rehabilitative purposes of the probation and parole systems. Nor was a warning to the juvenile's mother likely to be effective. She would not be likely to "inform other neighborhood parents or children that her son posed a general threat to their welfare, thereby perhaps thwarting any rehabilitative effort, and also effectively stigmatizing both the mother and son in the community."

In Hedlund v. Superior Court, 669 P.2d 41 (Cal.1983), a young child harmed during a violent assault on his mother was given an action when threats of violence against the mother had been communicated to defendant psychotherapists. Injuries to a child were foreseeable in an assault upon the mother, and consequently fell within the *Tarasoff* principle.

6. After *Tarasoff*, Cal. Civil Code § 43.92 was enacted to provide that therapists are immune from liability for failure to warn "except when the patient has communicated to the psychotherapist a serious threat of physical violence against a reasonably identifiable victim or victims." If there is a duty to warn, it "shall be discharged by the psychotherapist making reasonable efforts to communicate the threat to the victim or victims and to a law enforcement agency."

7. Some states have accepted and extended *Tarasoff*. E.g., Peck v. Counseling Service of Addison County, 499 A.2d 422 (Vt.1985) (extending the duty in favor of the patient's parents, whose barn was burned down); but see Cole v. Taylor, 301 N.W.2d 766 (Iowa 1981)(no duty owed to the patient herself who claimed that her psychiatrist had not prevented her from committing a murder for which she was imprisoned). A few states have rejected *Tarasoff*. See, e.g., Nasser v. Parker, 455 S.E.2d 502 (Va. 1995)(no duty to warn potential victim of danger from person who had voluntarily committed himself and then checked himself out; psychiatrist had not "taken charge" of the patient). For a review of the case developments and an empirical study of how the cases have shaped professional behavior, see Buckner & Firestone, Where the Public Peril Begins: 25 Years after *Tarasoff*, 21 J.Legal Med. 187 (2000).

8.   After *Tarasoff,* does a physician who knows that a patient has tested positive for the AIDS virus have a duty to notify the sexual partners of the patient if they are known? In Cal.Health & Safety Code § 199.25(c), California, as amended, provided: "No physician has a duty to notify any person of the fact that a patient is reasonably believed to be infected by the probable causative agent of acquired immune deficiency syndrome." Subsections (a) and (b) provide that, subject to some limitations, no physician shall be held liable for "disclosing to a person reasonably believed to be the [spouse, sexual partner, hypodermic needle sharer, or county health officer] that the patient has tested positive on a test to detect infection by the probable causative agent of" AIDS. The physician must first discuss the matter with the patient and attempt to obtain "voluntary consent for notification of his or her contacts." All persons so notified are to be referred for "appropriate care, counseling, and follow up." In *Reisner,* note 3, supra, plaintiff did not claim to be entitled to direct warning from the defendant.

9.   What if a regular patron of Joe's Tavern tells the bartender that he has "had it" with his wife's behavior and is going home to kill her? What if he told his dentist explicitly what he was going to do? Are these stronger or weaker cases for imposing a duty than the facts in *Tarasoff?*

10.   In an omitted part of the *Tarasoff* opinion, Justice Tobriner concluded that the campus police, who detained Poddar for a short while but released him when he appeared rational, and did not warn Tatiana or her parents of any danger, did not owe a duty to the plaintiffs. (Dr. Moore had brought in the police and had then asked them to desist. Do these details suggest a different approach to the case against Dr. Moore?) No special relationship was found between the police and Tatiana or Poddar sufficient to impose a duty to warn upon the police. The affirmative duties of the police and other governmental entities are considered in Section F.

11.   Note that these extended duty cases arise primarily in situations in which the immediately responsible party is unlikely to be a solvent defendant. In the *Tarasoff* sequence of cases, for example, doctors and clinics are generally more promising defendants than homicidal psychopaths. This consideration affects others types of cases as well.

In J.L. v. Kienenberger, 257 Mont. 113, 848 P.2d 472 (1993), suit was brought against the parents of a 13-year-old who was alleged to have raped the plaintiff. Section 316 of the Restatement asserts that a "parent is under a duty to exercise reasonable care so to control his minor child as to prevent it from intentionally harming others or from so conducting itself as to create an unreasonable risk of bodily harm to them, if the parent (a) knows or has reason to know that he has the ability to control his child, and (b) knows or should know of the necessity and opportunity for exercising such control." According to § 12 of the Restatement, "has reason to know" means that the person has information from which a "person of reasonable intelligence or of the superior intelligence of the actor would infer that the fact in question exists" or behave as though it exists; "should know" is used to "denote the fact that a person of reasonable prudence and intelligence or of the superior intelligence of the actor would ascertain the fact in question in the performance of his duty to another'' or would behave as though the fact exists.

The court rejected the section, 5–2, stating that it did not "find it necessary" to expand the existing limited statutory exceptions to the common law rule of nonliability. The dissenters would have imposed such a duty upon a showing that a parent was "aware" of the dangerous propensity which "caused the harm complained of." See also Brahm v. Hatch, 609 N.Y.S.2d 956 (App.Div. 1994), in which a 17-year-old shot and killed his father and others. A suit brought by the estates of the others against the estate of the father was rejected in the absence of a showing that the father was aware of a need to control the son.

Randi W. v. Muroc Joint Unified School District

Supreme Court of California, 1997.
14 Cal.4th 1066, 929 P.2d 582, 60 Cal.Rptr.2d 263.

[Plaintiff, a 13-year-old student at the time, alleged that four school districts, former employers of Robert Gadams, placed unreservedly affirmative references in a placement file for Gadams despite knowing that prior charges or complaints of sexual misconduct and impropriety had been leveled against Gadams during the period he worked in each district; that plaintiff student's school district (Livingston) relied on defendants' letters in hiring Gadams as vice-principal, and that Gadams then sexually assaulted plaintiff. Although plaintiff pressed several theories, the only ones before this court are negligent misrepresentation, fraud, and negligence per se brought against the referring districts. The superior court granted demurrers on all three of these claims, but the court of appeal reversed on all three. Further facts are set forth in the opinion.]

CHIN, ASSOCIATE JUSTICE.

In this case, we must decide under what circumstances courts may impose tort liability on employers who fail to use reasonable care in recommending former employees for employment without disclosing material information bearing on their fitness.   .   .   .

.   .   . Although policy considerations dictate that ordinarily a recommending employer should not be held accountable to third persons for failing to disclose negative information regarding a former employee, nonetheless liability may be imposed if, as alleged here, the recommendation letter amounts to an affirmative misrepresentation presenting a foreseeable and substantial risk of physical harm to a third person.

We also conclude, contrary to the Court of Appeal judgment in this case, that defendants' alleged failure to report the charges of Gadams's improper activities to the appropriate authorities pursuant to state statutory law fails to afford an alternate basis for tort liability in this case, and that the trial court properly sustained defendants' demurrers to the count in the complaint relying on this theory of liability.

.   .   .

II. DISCUSSION

A. *Fraud and Negligent Misrepresentation*

.   .   .

Section 311 of the Restatement Second of Torts, involving negligent conduct, provides that:

"(1) One who negligently gives *false information* to another is subject to liability for physical harm caused by action taken by the other *in reasonable reliance upon such information*, where such harm results

(a) to the other, or

(b) *to such third persons as the actor should reasonably expect to be put in peril by the action taken.*

(2) Such negligence may consist of failure to exercise reasonable care

(a) in ascertaining the accuracy of the information, or

(b) in the manner in which it is communicated." (Italics added.)

.   .   . [W]e consider whether plaintiff has sufficiently pleaded that defendants owed her a duty of care, that they breached that duty by making misrepresentations or giving false information, and that Livingston's reasonable reliance on their statements proximately caused plaintiff's injury. [   ] We examine each element separately.

1. *Duty to Plaintiff*

Did defendants owe plaintiff a duty of care? In defendants' view, absent some special relationship between the parties, or some specific and known threat of harm to plaintiff, defendants had no duty of care toward her, and no obligation to disclose in their letters any facts regarding the charges against Gadams. (See Rest.2d Torts, § 315 [generally no duty to warn those threatened by third person's conduct]; [   ]; *Thompson v. County of Alameda* [supra] [duty to warn "readily identifiable" victim]; *Tarasoff v. Regents of University of California* [supra] ["special relationship" creates duty to warn or control another's conduct]; [   ].)

Plaintiff does not argue that a special relationship existed between defendants and her or Gadams. Instead, she relies on [Garcia v. Superior Court, 789 P.2d 960 (Cal.1990)], where we held that, under section 311 of the Restatement Second of Torts, a parole officer had a duty to exercise reasonable care in giving the victim information regarding the parolee who ultimately killed her. We noted that although the parole officer had no duty to volunteer information regarding the released criminals he supervised, " .   .   . the absence of a duty to speak does not entitle one to speak falsely." [   ] We concluded that the parole officer, "having chosen to communicate information about [the parolee] to [the victim], had a duty to use reasonable care in doing so," and that the officer either knew or should have known that the victim's safety might depend on the accuracy of the information imparted. [   ]

Plaintiff acknowledges that *Garcia* is distinguishable, and that no California case has yet held that one who intentionally or negligently provides false information to another owes a duty of care to a third person who did not receive the information and who has no special relationship with the provider. Accordingly, the issue before us is one of first impression, and we apply the general analytical principles used to determine the existence of duty in particular cases.

In this state, the general rule is that all persons have a duty to use ordinary care to prevent others from being injured as the result of their conduct. [The court here quoted the same California factors quoted in *Tarasoff*. It then quoted a passage from Ballard v. Uribe, 715 P.2d 624 (Cal.1986) discussing the role of the factors: "The foreseeability of a particular kind of harm plays a very significant role in this calculus [citation], but a court's task—in determining 'duty'—is not to decide whether a *particular* plaintiff's injury was reasonably foreseeable in light of a *particular* defendant's conduct, but rather to evaluate more generally whether the category of negligent conduct at issue is sufficiently likely to result in the kind of harm experienced that liability may appropriately be imposed on the negligent party."]

a. Foreseeability and causality

Applying these factors here, we first examine whether plaintiff's injuries were a *foreseeable* result of defendants' representations regarding Gadams's qualifications and character, coupled with their failure to disclose to the Fresno Pacific College placement office information regarding charges or complaints of Gadams's sexual misconduct. Could defendants reasonably have foreseen that the representations and omissions in their reference letters would result in physical injury to someone? Although the chain of causation leading from defendants' statements and omissions to Gadams's alleged assault on plaintiff is somewhat attenuated, we think the assault was reasonably foreseeable. Based on the facts alleged in the complaint, defendants could foresee that Livingston's officers would read and rely on defendants' letters in deciding to hire Gadams. Likewise, defendants could foresee that, had they not unqualifiedly recommended Gadams, Livingston would not have hired him. And, finally, defendants could foresee that Gadams, after being hired by Livingston, might molest or injure a Livingston student such as plaintiff. We must assume, for purposes of demurrer, that plaintiff was indeed *injured* in the manner she alleges, and that a *causal connection exists between defendants' conduct and the injury suffered.* As plaintiff's complaint alleges, her injury was a "direct and proximate result" of defendants' fraud and misrepresentations.

b. Moral blame

Whether defendants were guilty of any *moral blame* would depend on the proof adduced at trial, although it is certainly arguable that their unreserved recommendations of Gadams, together with their failure to disclose facts reasonably necessary to avoid or minimize the risk of further child molestations or abuse, could be characterized as morally blameworthy.

c.   Availability of insurance or alternative courses of conduct

Next, we may assume that standard business liability *insurance* is available to cover instances of *negligent* misrepresentation or nondisclosure as alleged in count three of the complaint, but is not available for the fraud or intentional misconduct alleged in count four. [   ] Perhaps more significantly, defendants had *alternative courses of conduct* to avoid tort liability, namely, (1) writing a "full disclosure" letter revealing all relevant facts regarding Gadams's background, or (2) writing a "no comment" letter omitting any affirmative representations regarding Gadams's qualifications, or merely verifying basic employment dates and details. The parties cite no case or Restatement provision suggesting that a former employer has an affirmative duty of disclosure that would preclude such a no comment letter. As we have previously indicated, liability may not be imposed for mere nondisclosure or other failure to act, at least in the absence of some special relationship not alleged here. [   ]

d.   Public policy considerations

As for public policy, the law certainly recognizes a *policy of preventing future harm* of the kind alleged here. One of society's highest priorities is to protect children from sexual or physical abuse. [   ]; Pen.Code, § 11166 [duty to report suspected child abuse].

Defendants urge that *competing social or economic policies* may disfavor the imposition of liability for misrepresentation or nondisclosure in employment references. They observe that a rule imposing liability in these situations could greatly inhibit the preparation and distribution of reference letters, to the general detriment of employers and employees alike.

· · ·

In defendants' view, rather than prepare a recommendation letter stating all "material" facts, positive and negative, an employer would be better advised to decline to write a reference letter or, at most, merely to confirm the former employee's position, salary, and dates of employment. According to defendants, apart from the former employer's difficulty in deciding how much "negative" information to divulge, an employer who disclosed more than minimal employment data would risk a defamation, breach of privacy, or wrongful interference suit from a rejected job seeker. (See, e.g., Jensen v. Hewlett–Packard Co. [18 Cal.Rptr.2d 83 (App. 1993)][libel action may be based on false accusations in employee evaluation form of criminal conduct, dishonesty, incompetence, or reprehensible personal characteristics or behavior]; [   ]).

· · ·

In response, plaintiff asserts it is unlikely that employers will decline to write reference letters for fear of tort liability, at least in situations involving no foreseeable risks of physical injury to someone. Plaintiff observes that an employer would be protected from a defamation suit by the statutory qualified privilege for nonmalicious communications regarding a job applicant's qualifications. [   ] This provision was amended in 1994 to provide that the qualified privilege available for communications to and by "interested" persons "applies to and includes a communication concerning the job performance or qualifications of an applicant for employment, based upon credible evidence, made without malice, by a current or former employer of the applicant to, and upon request of, the prospective employer." (Civ.Code, § 47, subd. (c).) As plaintiff suggests, the existence of this privilege may encourage more open disclosure of relevant information regarding former employees. [   ] (See also [*Jensen v. Hewlett–Packard Co.,*] [acknowledging public policy disfavoring libel suits based on comments in employee evaluation forms].)

. . .

In light of these factors and policy considerations, we hold, consistent with Restatement Second of Torts sections 310 [intentional misrepresentation] and 311, that the writer of a letter of recommendation owes to third persons a duty not to misrepresent the facts in describing the qualifications and character of a former employee, if making these misrepresentations would present a substantial, foreseeable risk of physical injury to the third persons. In the absence, however, of resulting physical injury, or some special relationship between the parties, the writer of a letter of recommendation should have no duty of care extending to third persons for misrepresentations made concerning former employees. In those cases, the policy favoring free and open communication with prospective employers should prevail.

Having concluded that defendants owed plaintiff a duty not to misrepresent Gadams's qualifications or character in their letters of recommendation, we next must determine whether defendants' letters indeed contained "misrepresentations" or "false information" within the meaning of Restatement Second of Torts sections 310 or 311. If defendants made no misrepresentations, then as a matter of law they could not be found liable under those provisions.

2.   *Misleading Misrepresentation or Mere Nondisclosure?*

The Court of Appeal majority determined that plaintiff adequately alleged defendants committed actual misrepresentation rather than mere nondisclosure, because their letters of recommendation amounted to "misleading half-truths," containing incomplete information regarding Gadams's character and reliability. According to the Court of Appeal, defendants' unqualified recommendation of Gadams, coupled with their failure to disclose that Gadams had been in "sexual situations" with female students and had made "sexual overtures" to them, or that defendants knew complaints regarding Gadams's conduct had resulted in his resignation, amounted to affirmative misrepresentations.

Defendants join the Court of Appeal dissent in asserting that their letters of recommendation contained no misrepresentations that would invoke either Restatement Second of Torts section 310 or 311. As defendants observe, their letters neither discussed nor denied prior complaints of sexual misconduct or impropriety against Gadams.

Like the Court of Appeal majority, we view this case as a "misleading half-truths" situation in which defendants, having undertaken to provide some information regarding Gadams's teaching credentials and character, were obliged to disclose all other facts which "materially qualify" the limited facts disclosed. [   ]; Civ.Code, § 1710, subd. 3 [deceit is the suppression of a material fact by one who gives misleading information of other facts]; [   ].

As the Court of Appeal observed, defendants' letters offered general and unreserved praise for Gadams's character and personality (e.g., "dependable [and] reliable," "pleasant personality," "high standards," "relates well to the students"). According to the Court of Appeal, having volunteered this information, defendants were obliged to complete the picture by disclosing material facts regarding charges and complaints of Gadams's sexual improprieties.

Defendants suggest that a letter noting only a candidate's favorable qualities cannot reasonably be deemed misleading as to any unfavorable ones, and the recipient of such a letter cannot reasonably rely on any implication that the candidate lacks unfavorable qualities. [   ] As one commentator observes, " . . . half of the truth may obviously amount to a lie, *if it is understood to be the whole*." [   ] (Prosser & Keeton, The Law of Torts (5th ed. 1984) [§ 106], italics added.) According to defendants, no reasonable person would assume a letter of recommendation purports to state the whole truth about a candidate's background and character.

In defendants' view, we should characterize letters of recommendation stating only the favorable aspects of an applicant's background or character as a *permissible* variety of "half-truth," which misleads no one, and which, for that reason alone, should not form the basis for liability on a theory of negligent misrepresentation or fraud. (See [   ] [failure of church officers to disclose pastor's history of pedophilia not actionable in absence of affirmative representation denying that history, because "[t]he tort of negligent misrepresentation requires a 'positive assertion' and does not apply to implied misrepresentations"]; [   ] [county officers' failure to notify former district attorney of threats posed by vindictive probationer not actionable despite implied representation to warn]; [   ] [auto club tourbook endorsing motel's accommodations contained no "positive assertion concerning neighborhood safety," precluding negligent misrepresentation suit]; [   ] [failure to disclose sexual misconduct charges against former employee/teacher not actionable because "[t]he mere recommendation of a person for potential employment is not a proper basis for asserting a claim of negligence where another party is responsible for the actual hiring"]; [   ]; cf. [   ] [liability of employment agency based on positive misrepresentation that job seeker's innocent explanation for his rape conviction "had been verified by military officials"].)

But plaintiff argues convincingly that, under the facts pleaded in this case, defendants indeed made "positive assertion[s]" regarding Gadams's character, assertions deceptively incomplete because defendants knowingly concealed material facts regarding Gadams's sexual misconduct with students. Thus, defendant Mendota, through its officer Rossette, allegedly extolled Gadams's "genuine concern" for and "outstanding rapport" with students, knowing that Gadams had engaged in inappropriate physical contact with them. Rossette declared in the letter that he "wouldn't hesitate to recommend Mr. Gadams for any position!"

Defendant Golden Plains, through its officer Cole, stated it would recommend Gadams for "any administrative position," despite its knowledge of Gadams's prior inappropriate conduct while an employee of Golden Plains, conduct that had allegedly led to Gadams's "resigning under pressure from Golden Plains due to sexual misconduct charges. . . ."

Finally, defendant Muroc, through its officers Rice and Malcolm, allegedly recommended Gadams "for an assistant principalship or equivalent position without reservation," describing Gadams as "an upbeat, enthusiastic administrator who relates well to the students," despite its knowledge of disciplinary actions taken against him regarding sexual harassment allegations made during his employment with Muroc, allegations that induced Muroc to force Gadams to resign.

We conclude that these letters, essentially recommending Gadams for any position without reservation or qualification, constituted affirmative representations that strongly implied Gadams was fit to interact appropriately and safely with female students. These representations were false and misleading in light of defendants' alleged knowledge of charges of Gadams's repeated sexual improprieties. We also conclude that plaintiff's complaint adequately alleged misleading half-truths that could invoke an exception to the general rule excluding liability for mere nondisclosure or other failure to act. [   ]

3. Reliance

[The court concluded that the allegations of Livingston's reliance were sufficient under both § 310 and § 311. The court also concluded that sufficient causal connection was alleged between the misrepresentation and the harm.

The majority rejected the claim of negligence per se based on violation of the statute requiring the reporting of child physical abuse. The reporting language required a "child care custodian" to report in various situations. The majority concluded that plaintiff was not a member of the class for whose protection that statute was enacted because the recommending defendant school districts were never the custodians of plaintiff.]

[The court affirmed on negligent misrepresentation and fraud, but reversed as to negligence per se.]

GEORGE, C.J., MOSK and BROWN, JJ., concur.

[Justices Kennard, Baxter and Werdegar dissented on the negligence per se issue. They would have accepted "at face value the Legislature's simple, unqualified statement that the Reporting Act is meant 'to protect children from abuse,' and [the court] should construe the intended protected class broadly to include all children who foreseeably could be protected from abuse by compliance with its provisions."]

Notes and Questions

1.   How does this case differ from *Tarasoff*?

2.   The court's quotation from the *Ballard* footnote explored the relative roles of judge and jury in the California approach. In another part of that footnote, the *Ballard* court stated that the jury considers the "likelihood or foreseeability of injury in determining whether, in fact, the particular defendant's conduct was negligent in the first place." How does *Ballard* suggest distinguishing between the role of the court and the role of the jury? How does the distinction work in *Randi W.*? In *Tarasoff*?

3.   In the cited *Garcia* case, a woman was worried about a violent man with whom she had been living (but who had since moved out). He was on parole from a prior offense and defendant was his parole officer. In response to the woman's expression of concern, the officer told her, "I don't think you have anything to worry about. He's not going to come looking for you." Also, the officer assured her of her safety by emphasizing to her that "[the man] had told him that he was still in love with plaintiff, and repeatedly asking if she really wanted to end the relationship." The man killed her. Why does *Garcia* not control this case? How does *Garcia* differ from *Morgan v. County of Yuba*, p. 137, supra?

4.   Assume that in their letters the districts had hidden the fact that Gadams was habitually unable to process important papers before the deadlines. Assume that Gadams failed to process documents for the Livingston district in time for its superintendent to get a raise that would have been automatic if the filing had been timely. Does the principal case suggest the analysis for that situation? Cases involving economic loss are discussed in greater detail in Chapter IV.

Assume that Gadams's laxity about deadlines resulted in his failure to file school transcripts before the deadline—as a result of which five students were rejected by colleges to which it was clear they would otherwise have been admitted. Although the students can show no economic harm they are greatly distressed by this turn of events. Does the principal case suggest the analysis for this situation? Cases involving emotional distress are discussed in greater detail in Chapter IV.

5.   In Boon v. Rivera, 96 Cal.Rptr.2d 276 (App. 2000), a police officer alleged that when he responded to a 911 call, the defendant wife assured him that her husband, whose behavior had provoked the 911 call, was "not dangerous." The husband shot the officer, who then sued the wife, claiming that if he had been told the truth he would have taken the time to don a

bullet-proof vest. The court acknowledged that if the wife had said nothing or had told the truth there would be no case. But her false statement exposed her to liability. Is this situation covered by *Randi W.*?

Boon cited Pamela L. v. Farmer, 169 Cal.Rptr. 282 (App. 1980), in which plaintiffs alleged that defendant wife frequently left her house knowing that her husband, who had a record as a sexual offender, planned to molest the minor plaintiffs when they visited to use the swimming pool. The wife allegedly also knew that these acts would occur unless she warned the children, their parents or the police. "Furthermore, according to plaintiffs, the wife invited the children into the premises," and told the parents that it was safe to permit their children to be there during her absence. The allegations of invitation and reassurance were held sufficient to create a special relationship with the children and to sustain an action against the wife. What if the only allegation had been that defendant knew that when she left home her husband would use the opportunity to molest minors?

Compare Eric J. v. Betty M., 90 Cal.Rptr.2d 549 (App. 1999). T was a twice-convicted child molester who was living at home with his family. He struck up a relationship with a woman who had a young son and invited her to live at the family home. There he molested the boy. When the mother learned of the situation, she sued the family members for not warning her or the boy about the danger. The court held that no duty existed here: the members did not know that T still behaved that way—indeed they hoped that he had changed. The court distinguished *Pamela L*, because of the misrepresentations in that case. The *Eric J.* court did note that the predator's mother, who owned the family home, had been held liable for leaving the house at times when she knew that only T and the boy remained inside. She did not appeal the judgment. This obligation of a land occupier to those on the premises is explored in more detail later in this chapter. See also Gritzner v. Michael R., 611 N.W.2d 906 (Wis.2000), in which a child molested a young playmate. The court imposed a duty of control on the live-in boyfriend of the child's mother when he was left in charge of the child and also held that the allegations might support a duty to warn playmates' parents based on defendant's knowledge of the danger.

6. In several recent cases parents who have adopted children have sued the agencies involved for failing to reveal negative information about the child before the adoption. In Jackson v. State, 956 P.2d 35 (Mont.1998), the state did not tell the plaintiffs known information, including the results of "psychological evaluations performed on [the adoptee's] biological parents." The court noted that several courts had based a duty on the adopting agencies' "voluntary dissemination of health information concerning the child to potential adopting parents." What is the harm involved in this type of case? Is it feasible for an adoption agency to say nothing whatsoever about the child's health?

7. Several courts have attempted to list duty factors in the California fashion. In Hopkins v. Fox & Lazo Realtors, 625 A.2d 1110 (N.J.1993), the court analyzed a duty question by reviewing New Jersey cases and then concluded:

> Whether a person owes a duty of reasonable care toward another turns on whether the imposition of such a duty satisfies an abiding sense of basic fairness under all of the circumstances in light of considerations of public policy. [   ] That inquiry involves identifying, weighing, and balancing several factors—the relationship of the parties, the nature of the attendant risk, the opportunity and ability to exercise care, and the public interest in the proposed solution. [   ] The analysis is both very fact-specific and principled; it must lead to solutions that properly and fairly resolve the specific case and generate intelligible and sensible rules to govern future conduct.

How does this list compare with the California approach? Compare the Connecticut approach to duty in Jaworski v. Kiernan, 696 A.2d 332 (Conn.1997). After discussing foreseeability, the court observed "While it may seem that there should be a remedy for every wrong, this is an ideal limited perforce by the realities of this world. Every injury has ramifying consequences, like the ripplings of the waters, without end. The problem for the law is to limit the legal consequences of wrongs to a controllable degree."

In Illinois the courts use four elements: "(1) the foreseeability of the injury, (2) the likelihood of the injury, (3) the magnitude of the burden of guarding against the injury, and (4) the consequences of placing the burden upon the defendant." Largosa v. Ford Motor Co., 708 N.E.2d 1219 (Ill.App. 1999). How does this list differ from the factors used by the other states? How does it differ from Judge Hand's approach to the breach of duty issue that was discussed at p. 41 supra?

8.   The insurance question alluded to by the court is discussed in detail in Chapter X.

9.   Is the court correct to minimize concern about the willingness of employers to write recommendation letters for former employees? Possible remedies available to a former employee who thinks that a former employer has written an unhelpful recommendation letter are explored in Chapters XIII, XIV and XV. The general subject of intentional misrepresentation is considered in Chapter XV.

As the following case suggests, the duty to control the conduct of others is not necessarily limited to business and professional relationships.

Vince v. Wilson

Supreme Court of Vermont, 1989.
151 Vt. 425, 561 A.2d 103.

Before ALLEN, C.J., and PECK, GIBSON, DOOLEY and MAHADY, JJ.

MAHADY, JUSTICE.

This personal injury action requires us to further refine our definition of the tort of negligent entrustment. Plaintiff, seriously injured in an automobile accident, brought suit against defendant Wilson, who had provided funding for her grandnephew, the driver of the car in which plaintiff was a passenger at the time of the accident, to purchase the vehicle. Subsequently Ace Auto Sales, Inc. and its president Gary Gardner were added as defendants. Ace sold the vehicle to the driver; Gardner was the salesman of the vehicle.

At the close of plaintiff's case, the trial court directed verdicts in favor of defendants Ace and Gardner. Plaintiff appeals from this ruling. The claim against Wilson, on the other hand, was submitted to the jury, which returned a substantial verdict in favor of plaintiff. Wilson appeals from the judgment entered against her on the jury verdict. For the reasons stated below, we hold that the trial court erred in directing verdicts in favor of Ace and Gardner. As to the judgment against Wilson, we affirm the court's decision to submit the question to the jury, and remand for proceedings consistent with this opinion.

I.

The tort of negligent entrustment has long been recognized in Vermont. [   ] In Dicranian v. Foster, [45 A.2d 650 (Vt.1946)], we noted that such "liability . . . arises out of the combined negligence of both, the negligence of one in entrusting the automobile to an incompetent driver and of the other in its operation." [   ]

Plaintiff argues that the rule should be applied to a person who knowingly provides funding to an incompetent driver to purchase a vehicle and to a person who knowingly sells a vehicle to an incompetent driver. We have not previously had an opportunity to address this issue. In [an earlier case], the defendant negligently entrusted a firearm and ammunition to his child, who negligently discharged the firearm resulting in the death of the plaintiff's intestate. In *Dicranian,* the defendant negligently entrusted his motor vehicle to an incompetent operator whose negligent operation of the vehicle caused injury to the plaintiff.

Defendants urge us to follow those courts which have limited recovery under a claim of negligent entrustment to situations where the defendant "is the owner or has the right to control" the instrumentality entrusted. [   ] These courts have denied liability where a father sold a car to his son who was known to have a drinking problem but not a driver's license, [   ]; where a vehicle was given to an incompetent operator, [   ]; or where a bailee automobile dealer returned an automobile after repair to its obviously intoxicated owner, [   ].

Other courts have applied the rule more broadly. For example, courts have allowed recovery against an automobile dealer who sold a vehicle to an inexperienced and incompetent driver whose driving injured several people when the seller knew or should have known of the incompetency. [   ]

These courts hold that the fact that a defendant had ownership and control over the instrumentality at the time it was turned over to an incompetent individual is sufficient. [   ] Thus, a father was held liable for funding the purchase of an automobile by a son whom the father knew to be an irresponsible driver, [   ], and a complaint against a father who purchased a vehicle for his epileptic son was held to state a cause of action. Golembe v. Blumberg, [27 N.Y.S.2d 692 (App.Div.1941)].

Both lines of cases derive their rule from the Restatement of Torts, which provides:

> One who supplies directly or through a third person a chattel for the use of another whom the supplier knows or has reason to know to be likely because of his youth, inexperience, or otherwise, to use it in a manner involving unreasonable risk of physical harm to himself and others whom the supplier should expect to share in or be endangered by its use, is subject to liability for physical harm resulting to them.

Restatement (Second) of Torts § 390 (1965). The comments to the Restatement support those decisions which extend the rule to individuals such as sellers:

> The rule stated applies to anyone who supplies a chattel for the use of another. It applies to sellers, lessors, donors or lenders, and to all kinds of bailors, irrespective of whether the bailment is gratuitous or for a consideration.

Id., comment *a*.

The cases noted above which restrict the rule to situations where the defendant is the owner or has the right to control the instrumentality have been severely criticized. See [law review comments].

Indeed, the leading commentators on the law of torts have said that such decisions "look definitely wrong," explaining:

> It is the negligent entrusting which creates the unreasonable risk; and this is none the less when the goods are conveyed.

Prosser and Keeton on Torts § 104, at 718 (5th ed. 1984). Seen in this light, the issue is clearly one of negligence to be determined by the jury under proper instruction; the relationship of the defendant to the particular instrumentality is but one factor to be considered. The key factor is that "[t]he negligent entrustment theory requires a showing that the entrustor knew or should have known some reason why entrusting the item to another was foolish or negligent." [   ] This approach, based upon traditional negligence analysis, is consistent with our prior decisions.   .   .   .

II.

With regard to plaintiff's claim against defendant Wilson, we must view the evidence in the light most favorable to plaintiff because of the jury's verdict in plaintiff's favor. [   ] With regard to plaintiff's claims against defendants Ace and Gardner, the trial court directed a verdict in favor of the defendants; as such, we must view the evidence in the light most favorable to plaintiff, excluding the effect of any modifying evidence. [   ]

So viewed, the evidence indicates that Wilson knew that the operator for whom she provided funding to purchase the vehicle had no driver's license and had failed the driver's test several times. Indeed, she communicated this fact to defendant Gardner, an agent of defendant Ace, prior to the sale of the vehicle. Defendant Wilson was also aware of the fact that her grandnephew abused alcohol and other drugs. The evidence also tended to show that the operator's inexperience and lack of training contributed to the accident which caused plaintiff's injuries. The evidence was sufficient to make out a prima facie case of negligent entrustment, and the trial court properly submitted the question to the jury.

Verdicts should not have been directed in favor of defendants Ace and Gardner, however. There was evidence which, if believed by the jury, would establish that they knew the operator had no operator's license and that he had failed the driver's test several times. Viewed in the light most favorable to plaintiff, the evidence tends to demonstrate negligence on the part of Ace and Gardner, and the issue should have been determined by the jury. [   ]

.   .   .

Cause remanded for further proceedings not inconsistent with this opinion [which, for procedural reasons, might include a new trial for Wilson].

Notes and Questions

1.   Does liability in this case result from a straightforward application of "negligent entrustment" principles under section 390? Is it broader? Are there persuasive arguments supporting the notion that lending should produce a different result from selling? From giving? From providing funds for purchase? (Some states impose vicarious liability on car owners who lend their cars even to the best of drivers. Why might these states do this? The subject is considered in Chapter X.)

2.   In Peterson v. Halsted, 829 P.2d 373 (Colo.1992), defendant father in 1985 co-signed a financial note so that his adult daughter could get financing for a car. She made all the payments. She caused an accident due to her drunk driving—which plaintiffs alleged defendant knew about all along. The court declined to impose a duty on a co-signer. Because of the large number of variables in financing arrangements, the court thought it "unwise and destructive of flexibility of analysis to classify suppliers of money or credit categorically as suppliers of chattels . . . even though the loan or credit may be essential to the borrower in obtaining possession of the chattel." The court then turned to the question of whether the parents had a general common law duty to refrain from helping their daughter get a car because they knew of her drinking problems. The court held that a duty in this case would not "comport with fairness under contemporary standards." The court emphasized that the accident occurred three years after the co-signing.

3. The court suggests that the theory requires the combined negligence of two or more persons. In the case cited by the court in which an adult had entrusted a firearm and ammunition to his child, what if the child had been too young to have behaved negligently? Or if the child was eight years old and acted reasonably for a child that age?

4. In Osborn v. Hertz Corp., 252 Cal.Rptr. 613 (App.1988), the court rejected the claim that a car rental company had a duty to investigate the driving record of a sober customer who had a valid driver's license before entrusting a car to that customer—who later had an accident while drunk. A search would have shown two prior convictions for drunk driving and one related six-month license suspension. The court cited cases imposing liability for renting a car to a customer who did not hold a valid driver's license.

Lindstrom v. Hertz Corp., 96 Cal.Rptr.2d 874 (App. 2000), involved a defendant who rented a car to a licensed foreign driver, who later made an allegedly illegal U-turn that led to harm to plaintiff. The claim was that defendant had a duty to give the renter a copy of the rules of the road. The court concluded that the only statutory obligation was to check for a valid driver's license from a state or foreign country. Relying on *Osborn*, the court refused to impose any further obligations. The facts known to Hertz at the time did not suggest incompetence—even though plaintiff presented statistics showing that "foreign drivers are four times more likely than domestic drivers to be involved in serious automobile accidents." The court responded that "[i]nexperience alone, however, does not necessarily indicate incompetency."

In Liebelt v. Bob Penkhus Volvo-Mazda, Inc., 961 P.2d 1147 (Colo.App. 1998), the court refused to impose a duty on a car dealer to assure that the licensed buyer also had the liability insurance required by state law. There was no duty to inquire into such matters. Might it be different if that information came to the dealer's attention? The court observed that the risk of harm was "at least in some ways more attenuated when selling a vehicle to an uninsured but competent driver than to an insured driver known to be incompetent."

5. If D allows a friend who has a spotless record as a driver to use her car overnight—and then coincidentally sees the friend drinking heavily that evening in a restaurant, does D now have a duty to use due care to retrieve the car? See Casebolt v. Cowan, 829 P.2d 352 (Colo.1992)(suggesting a duty in this situation).

6. *Keys in the ignition.* A related issue occurs when the defendant has permitted a third party to acquire a chattel and cause harm. The most common scenario involves the "key in the ignition" case. A car owner leaves an auto unlocked with the key in the ignition, and a thief takes the opportunity to steal it. The thief negligently runs into the plaintiff causing injuries for which a claim is brought against the only solvent party, the car owner, alleging negligence in leaving the car vulnerable to theft. In some states courts derive liability from the violation of a statute. Others reject that approach on the ground that the goal of the statute is not safety but the avoidance of time-consuming and expensive police searches for cars and payments by insurers for their loss. Recall p. 82, supra, involving key-in-the-ignition statutes.

In Palma v. U.S. Industrial Fasteners, 681 P.2d 893 (Cal.1984), defendant's driver left a truck unlocked overnight with the key in the ignition in a highly dangerous neighborhood. The court reviewed the leading California cases, which require "special circumstances" in order to find a duty owed by car owners to the general public, and then observed:

> Factors which distinguished the conduct in [Hergenrether v. East, 393 P.2d 164 (Cal. 1964)] and were held sufficient to establish a duty, are also present here. They included the area in which the truck had been parked—one frequented by persons who had little respect for the rights of others, and populated by alcoholics; the intent that the truck remain in the location for a relatively long period of time—overnight; the size of the vehicle—rendering it capable of inflicting more serious injury or damage if not properly controlled; and the fact that safe operation of a half-loaded two-ton truck was not a matter of common experience. These factors together led to a conclusion there, as similar factors may here, that a foreseeable risk of harm was posed by the truck left with its keys in the ignition or cab warranting imposition of a duty on the owner or operator to refrain from exposing third persons to the risk.

What rationale would limit the duty to "special circumstances"?

7. *Guns.* Compare *Wood v. Groh*, p. 50, supra, involving liability for a son's theft of guns from his father's inadequately secured cabinet, with Valentine v. On Target, Inc., 727 A.2d 947 (Md.1999), rejecting, 4–3, liability against a gun retailer to those injured by bullets fired from guns stolen from its store. The majority observed that "one cannot be expected to owe a duty to the world at large to protect it against the actions of third parties." If "we would hold today that gun merchants owe an indefinite duty to the general public effectively we would be regulating the merchants. This type of regulation is the realm of the legislature and is not appropriate as a judicial enactment."

In Kitchen v. K–Mart Corp., 697 So.2d 1200 (Fla.1997), T, who had been drinking all day, bought a gun and ammunition at defendant's retail store and immediately sought out the plaintiff (his ex-girlfriend) and shot her. The claim was that T was so drunk that he was unable to fill out the required forms to buy the gun because his handwriting was not legible. The clerk filled out the forms and had T initial each of the yes/no answers and sign his name at the bottom. The jury's verdict against K–Mart was upheld on appeal. The court relied upon the part of § 390 providing that one who supplies chattels to another is not entitled to assume that it will be used carefully if the supplier "knows or has reason to know that the other is likely to use it dangerously, as where the other belongs to a class which is notoriously incompetent to use the chattel safely, or lacks the training and experience necessary for such use."

8. Related to the idea of negligent entrustment is negligent hiring, retention or supervision. These involve claims that employers were negligent either in initially hiring or in retaining or in supervising an employee who has committed a tort—usually a violent one. Recall *Foster v. The Loft, Inc.*, p. 23, supra, involving the aggressive bartender. Compare McLean v. Kirby Co., 490 N.W.2d 229 (N.D.1992)(duty on vacuum cleaner manufacturer to investigate backgrounds of salesmen hired to enter homes and demonstrate product) with Connes v. Molalla Transport System, Inc., 831 P.2d 1316 (Colo.1992)(no duty owed by trucking company to assaulted hotel clerk to investigate prospective truck driver's nonvehicular criminal background).

A physician who asks another physician to "cover" on occasion is not vicariously liable for the negligence of the covering physician—but may be liable for negligence in choosing the covering physician. Kavanaugh v. Nussbaum, 523 N.E.2d 284 (N.Y.1988).

9. How great is the difference between lending or giving a car to someone known to drink while driving and serving drinks to a social guest who drove to the house and will be driving away? That issue is raised in the next case.

Reynolds v. Hicks

Supreme Court of Washington, 1998.
134 Wash.2d 491, 951 P.2d 761.

MADSEN, JUSTICE.

Plaintiffs appeal a trial court decision dismissing their personal injury action on summary judgment against the Defendants. At issue is whether the Defendant social hosts who furnished alcohol to a minor owe a duty of care to third persons injured by the intoxicated minor. We affirm the trial court's dismissal finding that the Defendant social hosts owed no duty to third persons injured by the intoxicated minor.

Jamie and Anna Hicks were married on September 10, 1988, at St. Bernadette Church in Seattle. Three hundred people attended the wedding, including Jamie Hicks' under-age nephew, Steven Hicks. The wedding was followed by a dinner reception where wine and champagne were served. After dinner, drinks were available at a hosted bar.

[A jury could have found that Steven Hicks consumed alcohol at the reception, despite claims that the bar was "hosted at all times." At approximately midnight, Steven Hicks left the reception in his sister Dianne's car. At 1:00 A.M. he was involved in an automobile accident with the plaintiff Reynolds. Reynolds and his family alleged that Jamie and Anna Hicks were "negligent in serving alcoholic beverages to Defendant [Steven] with knowledge and/or reason to believe that [he] was below the age of 21 years and/or became intoxicated." Plaintiffs settled with Steven and Dianne Hicks. Defendants sought summary judgment arguing, among other claims, that "Washington law does not extend social host liability for furnishing alcohol to a minor to third persons injured by the intoxicated minor." The superior court granted the motion and the court of appeals certified the case directly to the supreme court.]

Plaintiffs contend that RCW 66.44.270 creates a duty of care owed by the Defendants to the Plaintiffs. RCW 66.44.270(1) makes it unlawful for any person [except a parent] to

> give, or otherwise supply liquor to any person under the age of twenty-one years or permit any person under that age to consume liquor on his or her premises or on any premises under his or her control. [Other sections exempt medicinal and religious uses.]

.   .   .

In Hansen v. Friend, [824 P.2d 483 (Wash.1992)], this court recognized that a minor who is injured as a result of alcohol intoxication has a cause of action against the social host who supplied the alcohol based on RCW 66.44.270. [   ] Plaintiffs ask this court to extend the ruling of *Hansen* to allow a cause of action for third persons who are injured by an intoxicated minor against the social host. We find that such an expansion is not warranted by the statute or Washington case law.

.   .   .

Because of the inherent differences between social hosts and commercial vendors, we have indicated our reluctance to allow a cause of action against a social host to the same extent that we have recognized commercial vendor liability. We have explained:

> There is good reason to withhold common law liability for social hosts even though such liability already exists for commercial and quasi-commercial hosts. Social hosts are not as capable of handling the responsibilities of monitoring their guests' alcohol consumption as are their commercial and quasi-commercial counterparts.   .   .   .
>
> [T]he commercial proprietor has a proprietary interest and profit motive, and should be expected to exercise greater supervision than in the (non-commercial) social setting. Moreover, a person in the business of selling and serving alcohol is usually better organized to control patrons, and has the financial wherewithal to do so.   .   .   .
>
> Additionally, the implications of social host liability are so much more wide sweeping and unpredictable in nature than are the implications of commercial host liability. While liability for commercial providers affects only a narrow slice of our populations, social host liability would touch most adults in the state on a frequent basis. Because social hosts are generally unaccustomed to the pressures involved in taking responsibility for the intoxication of their guests, we cannot predict how well social hosts would respond when the scope of their duties would be so ill defined.

Burkhart v. Harrod, [755 P.2d 759 (Wash.1988)].

Because of these important concerns, this court does not recognize a cause of action in negligence for a third person injured by an intoxicated adult against the social host that served the person while in an obviously intoxicated state, [ ], but does recognize a cause of action against a commercial vendor in the same situation, [ ]. This case dramatically highlights the concerns expressed above. To expect Jamie and Anna Hicks, on their wedding day, to monitor their minor guests' alcohol consumption in the same manner as we expect of an alcohol vendor is unrealistic and has far reaching social implications.

Recognizing an expanded duty to protect third persons raises problematic questions for social hosts in all contexts. Is the host required to card persons at social and family gatherings? Must the host hire a bartender to control and monitor the alcohol in the home so that a minor cannot obtain alcohol at a party? Must the host assure that a minor has not brought outside alcohol to the gathering? Must the host obtain a breathalyzer to check all minor guests before leaving the premises? The differences between the ability of commercial vendors and social hosts in regulating the consumption of alcohol along with the far-reaching implications of social host liability are persuasive reasons for not expanding liability in this case. As Justice Dolliver noted in his dissent in *Hansen*, the " 'judiciary is ill equipped' to impose social host liability." [ ]

[The court discussed two decisions of the court of appeals.]

We agree with the Court of Appeals that the exceptions to liability in RCW 66.44.270 lend weight to the argument that the statute was not enacted to protect third persons. . . . Because the statute allows a parent or guardian to legally give alcohol to a minor who may then injure a third person it is apparent that the statute was not enacted to protect third persons injured by intoxicated minors. . . .

. . .

In conclusion, we decline to extend social host liability to third persons injured by intoxicated minors. We have long recognized that social hosts are ill-equipped to handle the responsibilities of their guests' alcohol consumption, unlike commercial vendors who are in the business of serving and selling alcohol. Thus, we have not allowed a cause of action against social hosts to the extent that we have recognized commercial vendor liability. Washington courts have also recognized that RCW 66.44.270 does not protect third persons injured by an intoxicated minor but, rather, protects minors from their own injuries as a result of their intoxication. We agree and affirm the trial court's dismissal of the Plaintiff's cause of action.

GUY and ALEXANDER, JJ., concur.

DURHAM, CHIEF JUSTICE, concurring.

I agree with the majority that the Defendants, as social host, should not be liable for injuries to third parties caused by an intoxicated minor guest. I am not persuaded, however, by the majority's suggestion that the parental exception to the otherwise criminal prohibition against furnishing alcohol to minors somehow indicates that third parties are not within the statutory protected class. Instead, I would hold that the Defendants are not liable for the reasons expressed in the dissent in Hansen v. Friend, [824 P.2d 483 (Wash.1992)] (Dolliver, J., dissenting).

DOLLIVER and SANDERS, JJ., concur.

JOHNSON, JUSTICE, dissenting.

The majority holds a social host who furnishes alcohol to a minor, in violation of a criminal statute, does not owe a duty of care to third persons injured by that intoxicated minor. I disagree with the majority's shielding from possible civil liability persons who commit a criminal act. I also disagree with the majority's analysis, which confuses the issues of duty and ultimate liability. For these reasons, I respectfully dissent.

This court has clearly recognized where the Legislature has made it a criminal offense to furnish alcohol to a minor, that minor has a civil cause of action. [*Hansen*] This court has also clearly recognized where the Legislature has made it a criminal offense to sell alcohol to a minor, third parties foreseeably injured by that minor have a civil cause of action. [   ] The majority draws an insupportable distinction between social hosts and commercial vendors by ignoring that both are committing criminal acts when they furnish alcohol to a minor.   .   .   .

The Legislature, in criminalizing the act of furnishing or selling alcohol to a minor, has declared that act as the point on which to focus in the causal chain of underage drunk driving. The Legislature has directed us to view the point at which a minor is furnished or sold alcohol as the significant event from which consequences flow. If the minor never obtains the alcohol, the causal chain is stopped.

.   The majority, however, leaves us with the rule that a person commits a crime by furnishing alcohol to a minor, and yet avoids all civil liability for the consequences of that same act. This contradicts common sense.   .   .   . The list of concerns for social hosts expressed by the majority places more emphasis on the possible difficulties posed for social hosts than on a potential remedy for victims of underage drunk driving. However, it is the social hosts that are in the best position to know the ages of the guest they are serving and to regulate their own conduct so as to avoid committing a crime. Should social hosts have to "card" guests before serving them alcohol? Yes, if that's what it takes. Social hosts already have a responsibility to avoid criminal conduct. Nothing changes regarding the actions necessary to meet this responsibility upon imposition of a duty of care.

Under the majority, we are also left with the strained result of different standards for commercial vendors than for social hosts who furnish alcohol to minors. A vendor owes a duty to third parties, whereas a social host does not.   .   .   . I find no justification exists for applying different standards to vendors than to social hosts who furnish alcohol to minors. Both commit crimes.   .   .   . The source of the alcohol should not dictate whether a remedy is available.

.   .   .   .

SMITH AND TALMADGE, JJ., concur.

Notes and Questions

1.   Justice Dolliver's dissent in *Hansen*, relied on by the three concurring justices in *Reynolds*, thought the judiciary "ill equipped to impose social host liability." It also argued that there should be no liability of any sort on commercial vendors or social hosts "without legislative mandate" because of the pervasive legislative regulation of alcohol. Can that position be defended?

2.   How do the three opinions differ?

3.   Why might the statute have exempted parents? Even if the statute is found not to be relevant in a parent case, what about an action based on common law? Recall *Uhr*, p. 151 supra. If parents in Washington serve their child alcohol, and the child then goes out and hurts third parties because of intoxication, should a duty of due care be imposed on the parents? Do the concerns expressed by the lead opinion for social hosts apply to such a situation? In Estate of Templeton v. Daffern, 990 P.2d 968 (Wash.App.2000), the court refused to impose a duty of due care on social hosts where a minor brought his own alcohol to a party and the defendants observed the minor drinking. He was killed in an auto accident while driving away from the party.

4.   If a duty of due care had been imposed in *Reynolds* how would you analyze the due care question?

5.   In the very few states in which courts have found a duty on the part of a social host to a person hurt by the drinker, the legislatures have quickly reinstated either complete immunity (plus more in California) or granted the social host very strong protection (e.g., New Jersey). State developments are recounted in Comment, The Continuing Search for Solutions to the Drinking Driver Tragedy and the Problem of Social Host Liability, 82 Nw.U.L.Rev. 403 (1988).

6.   In Gilger v. Hernandez, 997 P.2d 305 (Utah 2000), the court refused to impose a duty on a social host to protect guests from another guest who had become drunk at a party on the premises. The court understood that "[r]equiring a social host either to control a belligerent guest or to protect her guests from the threat of injury by another guest would impose a duty 'that is realistically incapable of performance' in the usual circumstances." There was no element of dependency and the other guests were able to protect themselves. A duty did arise, however, after the guest was injured. See also Luoni v. Berube, 729 N.E.2d 1108 (Mass.2000) (rejecting a duty on the host where one guest's actions with fireworks injured another guest). Do these cases follow easily from the principal case?

7.   *Some broader implications.* Is there any reason to limit the duty to control the actions of third parties to defendants who bear a particularized relationship—such as host or parent—to the dangerous actor? Suppose, instead, that the defendant is responsible for a situation in which dangerous conduct is generally encouraged or facilitated, without reference to any specific risky individual? For a discussion of broader implications, see generally, Rabin, Enabling Torts, 49 DePaul L.Rev. 435 (1999).

In Weirum v. RKO General, Inc., 539 P.2d 36 (Cal.1975), defendant radio station, which commanded the largest teenage audience in the Los Angeles area, conducted a contest in which the driver who reached a peripatetic disk jockey first would win a prize. The disk jockey was traveling freeways of the area and stopping at various spots for short times. The station was broadcasting clues that identified specific or general destinations, such as "The Real Don Steele is back on his feet again with some money and he is headed for the Valley." In their efforts to be the first to reach him when he stopped, two minor drivers in separate vehicles were following the disc jockey on a freeway. During the course of their pursuit, one of the drivers negligently forced a car off the highway killing its driver. In a suit against the station, the court unanimously upheld a plaintiff's judgment.

In Olivia N. v. National Broadcasting Co., 178 Cal.Rptr. 888 (App. 1981), cert. denied 458 U.S. 1108 (1982), a television network was sued on the claim that it had broadcast a program that contained a particularly vivid scene in which a teenager in a girls' juvenile detention home was "raped" by a group of inmates using a "plumber's helper." Plaintiff, a nine-year-old girl, alleged that some youths who had seen the program had been prompted to reenact the scene a few days later by attacking her with a soda bottle. The defendant's contention that it should not be judged on a negligence standard was upheld on appeal. The analysis stressed the protection of speech and press found in the First and Fourteenth Amendments, which overrode what might otherwise be an appropriate tort duty. See Crump, Camouflaged Incitement: Freedom of Speech, Communicative Torts, and the Borderland of the *Brandenburg* Test, 29 Ga.L.Rev. 1 (1994). See also Rice v. Paladin Enterprises, Inc., 128 F.3d 233, cert. denied 523 U.S. 1074 (1998), involving murders allegedly accomplished by following defendant's book entitled "Hit Man: A Technical Manual for Independent Contractors."

D.   LANDOWNERS AND OCCUPIERS

This section deals with duties owed to entrants by those who own, or are in possession of, land. Although the area showed signs of great change some years ago, the situation appears to have stabilized, with two distinct views emerging. We begin with the traditional view.

Appellant
Carter v. Kinney   Appellee

Supreme Court of Missouri, 1995.
896 S.W.2d 926.

ROBERTSON, JUDGE.

.   .   .

Ronald and Mary Kinney hosted a Bible study at their home for members of the Northwest Bible Church. Appellant Jonathan Carter, a member of the Northwest Bible Church, attended the early morning Bible study at the Kinneys' home on February 3, 1990. Mr. Kinney had shoveled snow from his driveway the previous evening, but was not aware that ice had formed overnight. Mr. Carter arrived shortly after 7:00 a.m., slipped on a patch of ice in the Kinneys' driveway, and broke his leg. The Carters filed suit against the Kinneys.

The parties agree that the Kinneys offered their home for the Bible study as part of a series sponsored by their church; that some Bible studies took place at the church and others were held at the homes of church members; that interested church members signed up for the studies on a sheet at the church, which actively encouraged enrollment but did not solicit contributions through the classes or issue an invitation to the general public to attend the studies; that the Kinneys and the Carters had not engaged in any social interaction outside of church prior to Mr. Carter's injury, and that Mr. Carter had no social relationship with the other participants in the class. Finally, the parties agree that the Kinneys received neither a financial nor other tangible benefit from Mr. Carter in connection with the Bible study class.

They disagree, however, as to Mr. Carter's status. Mr. Carter claims he was an invitee; the Kinneys say he was a licensee. And the parties dispute certain facts bearing on the purpose of his visit, specifically, whether the parties intended a future social relationship, and whether the Kinneys held the Bible study class in order to confer some intangible benefit on themselves and others.

On the basis of these facts, the Kinneys moved for summary judgment. The trial court sustained the Kinneys' summary judgment motion on the ground that Mr. Carter was a licensee and that the Kinneys did not have a duty to a licensee with respect to a dangerous condition of which they had no knowledge. This appeal followed.

. . .

As to premises liability, "the particular standard of care that society recognizes as applicable under a given set of facts is a question of law for the courts." Harris v. Niehaus, 857 S.W.2d 222, 225 (Mo.banc 1993). Thus, whether Mr. Carter was an invitee, as he claims, or a licensee is a question of law and summary judgment is appropriate if the defendants' conduct conforms to the standard of care Mr. Carter's status imposes on them.

. . .

Historically, premises liability cases recognize three broad classes of plaintiffs: trespassers, licensees and invitees. All entrants to land are trespassers until the possessor of the land gives them permission to enter. All persons who enter a premises with permission are licensees until the possessor has an interest in the visit such that the visitor "has reason to believe that the premises have been made safe to receive him." [ ] That makes the visitor an invitee. The possessor's intention in offering the invitation determines the status of the visitor and establishes the duty of care the possessor owes the visitor. Generally, the possessor owes a trespasser no duty of care, [ ]; the possessor owes a licensee the duty to make safe dangers of which the possessor is aware, [ ]; and the possessor owes invitees the duty to exercise reasonable care to protect them against both known dangers and those that would be revealed by inspection. [ ] The exceptions to these general rules are myriad, but not germane here.

A social guest is a person who has received a social invitation. [ ] Though the parties seem to believe otherwise, Missouri does not recognize social guests as a fourth class of entrant. [ ] In Missouri, social guests are but a subclass of licensees. The fact that an invitation underlies a visit does not render the visitor an invitee for purposes of premises liability law. This is because "[t]he invitation was not tendered with any material benefit motive" . . . and "[t]he invitation was not extended to the public generally or to some undefined portion of the public from which invitation, . . . entrants might reasonably expect precautions have been taken, in the exercise of ordinary care, to protect them from danger." [ ] Thus, this Court held that there "is no reason for concluding it is unjust to the parties . . . to put a social guest in the legal category of licensee." [ ]

It does not follow from this that a person invited for purposes not strictly social is perforce an invitee. As [cited case] clearly indicates, an entrant becomes an invitee when the possessor invites with the expectation of a material benefit from the visit or extends an invitation to the public generally. See also Restatement (Second) of Torts, § 332[2] (defining an invitee for business purposes) and 65 C.J.S. Negligence, § 63(41)(A person is an invitee "if the premises are thrown open to the public and [the person] enters pursuant to the purposes for which they are thrown open."). Absent the sort of invitation from the possessor that lifts a licensee to invitee status, the visitor remains a licensee as a matter of law.

The record shows beyond cavil that Mr. Carter did not enter the Kinneys' land to afford the Kinneys any material benefit. He is therefore not an invitee under the definition of ["business visitor"] contained in Section 332 of the Restatement. The record also demonstrates that the Kinneys did not "throw open" their premises to the public in such a way as would imply a warranty of safety. The Kinneys took no steps to encourage general attendance by some undefined portion of the public; they invited only church members who signed up at church. They did nothing more than give permission to a limited class of persons—church members—to enter their property.

Mr. Carter's response to the Kinneys' motion for summary judgment includes Mr. Carter's affidavit in which he says that he did not intend to socialize with the Kinneys and that the Kinneys would obtain an intangible

---

2. Section 332 [provides that an invitee is either "a public invitee or a business visitor." A public invitee is defined as a "person who is invited to enter or remain on land as a member of the public for a purpose for which the land is held open to the public." "A business visitor" is one who is invited to enter or remain on land "for a purpose directly or indirectly connected with business dealings with the possessor of the land."]

benefit, albeit mutual, from Mr. Carter's participation in the class. Mr. Carter's affidavit attempts to create an issue of fact for the purpose of defeating summary judgment. But taking Mr. Carter's statement of the facts as true in all respects, he argues a factual distinction that has no meaning under Missouri law. Human intercourse and the intangible benefits of sharing one's property with others for a mutual purpose are hallmarks of a licensee's permission to enter. Mr. Carter's factual argument makes the legal point he wishes to avoid: his invitation is not of the sort that makes an invitee. He is a licensee.

The trial court concluded as a matter of law that Mr. Carter was a licensee, that the Kinneys had no duty to protect him from unknown dangerous conditions, and that the defendants were entitled to summary judgment as a matter of law. In that conclusion, the trial court was eminently correct.

. . .

The judgment of the trial court is affirmed.

COVINGTON, C.J., and HOLSTEIN, BENTON, THOMAS, and LIMBAUGH, JJ., concur.

PRICE, J., concurs in result.

Notes and Questions

1. What is the justification for treating a social guest as a licensee? Why not an invitee? Consider comment *h* (3) to § 330:

> The explanation usually given by the courts for the classification of social guests as licensees is that there is a common understanding that the guest is expected to take the premises as the possessor himself uses them, and does not expect and is not entitled to expect that they will be prepared for his reception, or that precautions will be taken for his safety, in any manner in which the possessor does not prepare or take precautions for his own safety, or that of the members of his family.

Is this persuasive?

invitees . . .
business
customers?

2. Might the categorization change if Mr. Carter regularly gave Mr. Kinney a lift to work in his car after the class? If Mr. Carter regularly brought pastries to the class (and others brought instant coffee or napkins)? What if the list in the church had asked each person signing up to bring the Kinneys "a small token of appreciation for the use of their house"?

In Stitt v. Holland Abundant Life Fellowship, 614 N.W.2d 88 (Mich. 2000), plaintiff, who was not a church member, went with a friend to attend a bible study class at defendant church. She tripped over a concrete tire stop in the parking lot and claimed that the lighting was inadequate. The court, 5–2, held that she should be treated as a licensee. It recognized that most states to consider the issue had adopted the "public invitee" stance of § 332 extending invitee status to a person who is "invited to enter or remain on land as a member of the public for a purpose for which the land is held open to the public." Nevertheless, the majority decided that "the imposition of additional expense and effort by the landowner, requiring the landowner to inspect the premises and make them safe for visitors, must be directly tied to the owner's commercial business interests. It is the owner's desire to foster a commercial advantage by inviting persons to visit the premises that justifies imposition of a higher duty. In short, we conclude that the prospect of pecuniary gain is a sort of quid pro quo for the higher duty of care owed to invitees."

3. It is one thing to put the plaintiff into one of the three boxes—though the court notes that there are "myriad" exceptions. It is another to determine what duty is owed to each category. For example, the duty to trespassers is stated in § 333:

> Except as stated in §§ 334–339, a possessor of land is not liable to trespassers for physical harm caused by his failure to exercise reasonable care
>
>> (a) to put the land in a condition reasonably safe for their reception, or
>>
>> (b) to carry on his activities so as not to endanger them.

The listed exceptions create obligations to warn, for example, where the possessor knows that persons "constantly intrude upon a limited area" of the land and may encounter a hidden danger, or when the possessor fails to exercise reasonable care for the safety of a known trespasser. Generally, though, the duty is simply not to willfully or wantonly harm trespassers. In Bennett v. Napolitano, 746 A.2d 138 (R.I.2000), plaintiff was walking his dogs in a city park at 2 a.m. when a tree limb fell on him. The court held him a trespasser because the park was legally closed every night at 9 p.m. Since the only duty owed plaintiff was to avoid willful or wanton conduct, defendant had not breached its duty. There was no evidence that the limb's weakness was known and disregarded. What would happen if the limb had fallen on plaintiff while taking an afternoon walk with his dog? For a broad discussion of the category of trespasser and the duty owed to trespassers, see Blakely v. Camp Ondessonk, 38 F.3d 325 (7th Cir.1994)(discussing Illinois law).

4. What duty did the Kinneys owe Mr. Carter? Why does the court hold that they met that duty as a matter of law? *Danger was unknown*

Make safe dangers they were aware of

5. If Mr. Carter had been categorized as an invitee, what duty would the Kinneys have owed? Section 342 provides so far as the condition of the premises is concerned, an occupier is subject to liability to invitees if the occupier:

Protection against known dangers + those could be revealed upon inspection

> (a) knows or by the exercise of reasonable care would discover the condition, and should realize that it involves an unreasonable risk of harm to such invitees, and

(b) should expect that they will not discover or realize the danger, or will fail to protect themselves against it, and

(c) fails to exercise reasonable care to protect them against the danger.

How does this general obligation differ from what the court found was owed to licensees?

6. *Open and obvious dangers.* One issue that has long divided courts involves the duty owed invitees where the danger is "open and obvious." Some courts have concluded that no duty is owed since the danger was apparent to the invitee. Recently, courts have focused more on whether such notice was enough to make the premises reasonably safe. In Tharp v. Bunge Corp., 641 So.2d 20 (Miss.1994), plaintiff was a government grain inspector whose work on defendant's premises involved his having to step from a landing onto sloping ground between 29 and 39 inches below. Plaintiff stood 5 feet 8 inches with a stride of 30 inches.

The court, 5–4, overruled its earlier position that open and obvious dangers did not give rise to liability, and followed § 343 (1), stating in part that a possessor was not liable to invitees for harm from obvious dangers "unless the possessor should anticipate the harm despite such knowledge or obviousness." The court thought it "should discourage unreasonably dangerous conditions rather than fostering them in their obvious form. It is anomalous to find that a defendant has a duty to provide reasonably safe premises and at the same time deny a plaintiff recovery from a breach of that same duty." In the court's view, if the jury finds that both parties behaved unreasonably, comparative negligence would apply.

See also Michalski v. Home Depot, Inc., 225 F.3d 113 (2d Cir. 2000), imposing a duty where a customer tripped over a pallet extending from a forklift in defendant's working warehouse.

7. *Activities.* The foregoing discussion has focused on the condition of the premises. Another set of questions involves *activities* taking place on the premises. The traditional rule was that licensees and trespassers could not recover for active negligence while they were on the premises. Thus, in Britt v. Allen County Community Junior College, 638 P.2d 914 (Kan.1982), the plaintiff, a Shaklee sales representative, was using defendant's auditorium solely to promote sales. Before the session, she asked the custodian to move a piano from the center of the room to a wall. While he was doing this, he lost control of the piano and it tipped over onto plaintiff's foot. The court first held that plaintiff was a licensee because the entry was solely for Shaklee's benefit. It rejected the claim that the purpose of the meeting was to educate the community. The court then held that she could not establish wilful or wanton injury, refused to adopt a distinction between active and passive negligence, and dismissed the case.

Britt was overruled in Bowers v. Ottenad, 729 P.2d 1103 (Kan.1986), involving a social guest who was burned during the preparation of "flaming Irish coffee":

We hold . . . that when a licensee, whose presence is known or should be known, is injured or damaged by some affirmative activity conducted upon the property by the occupier of the property the duty owed to such person is one of reasonable care under the circumstances.

Section 341 of the Second Restatement extends liability to licensees for failure to carry on activities with due care if, but only if, the occupier should expect that the licensee will not discover or realize the danger, and the licensee does not know or have reason to know of the activities and the risk involved.

Assume that a burglar, discovered lurking outside the auditorium of a junior college, is brought into the auditorium by the police for investigation. Should the burglar have an action if the custodian carelessly loses control of a piano that he is moving nearby so that it tips over on the burglar's foot?

8. *Child trespassers.* In Holland v. Baltimore & O. R. Co., 431 A.2d 597 (D.C.App.1981), a nine-year-old boy was injured by a freight train. The court invoked one of the most influential sections of the Restatement, § 339:

A possessor of land is subject to liability for physical harm to children trespassing thereon caused by an artificial condition upon the land if

(a) the place where the condition exists is one upon which the possessor knows or has reason to know that children are likely to trespass, and

(b) the condition is one of which the possessor knows or has reason to know and which he realizes or should realize will involve an unreasonable risk of death or serious bodily harm to such children, and

(c) the children because of their youth do not discover the condition or realize the risk involved in intermeddling with it or in coming within the area made dangerous by it, and

(d) the utility to the possessor of maintaining the condition and the burden of eliminating the danger are slight as compared with the risk to children involved, and

(e) the possessor fails to exercise reasonable care to eliminate the danger or otherwise to protect the children.

The judge found the section inapplicable because "a moving train is a danger so obvious that any nine-year-old child allowed at large would readily discover it and realize the risk involved in coming within the area made dangerous by it."

The special treatment of children dates to the "turntable" cases, involving injuries to children tampering with railroad track-switching devices. Recall the *Krayenbuhl* case, p. 44, supra. These cases evolved into a broader "attractive nuisance" doctrine that covered injuries to children who were unaware, because of their immaturity, of risks associated with a land occupier's property. Most courts did not require that the child have been enticed onto the land by the sight of the danger. The evolution of the doctrine is discussed in Prosser, Trespassing Children, 47 Calif.L.Rev. 427 (1959).

9. *Recreational use of land.* Almost all states have enacted statutes that limit the liability of owners of land used for recreational purposes. The goal is to prevent persons on open land from suing for natural dangers on such land or demanding that warnings be posted of such dangers. Willful misconduct is generally required for liability. See generally Comment, Wisconsin's Recreational Use Statute: Towards Sharpening the Picture at the Edges, 1991 Wis.L.Rev. 491. For a good summary of the considerations behind this type of legislation, see Bragg v. Genesee County Agricultural Society, 644 N.E.2d 1013 (N.Y.1994). Similar statutes in some states now protect landowners who permit others to enter their land to pick their own fruits and vegetables. Centner, The New "Pick-Your-Own" Statutes: Delineating Limited Immunity from Tort Liability, 30 U.Mich.J.L.Reform 743 (1997).

10. The *Carter* court acknowledged that the categories and the respective duties owed to each had "myriad" exceptions. Challenges to the categorization arose first in England, which, by statute, abolished the distinction between invitee and licensee in 1957. In this country the first state case to reject the categories was Rowland v. Christian, 443 P.2d 561 (Cal.1968). The court in *Rowland* speculated that the categories had developed "due to historical considerations stemming from the high place which land has traditionally held in English and American thought, the dominance and prestige of the landowning class in England during the formative period of the rules governing the possessor's liability, and the heritage of feudalism." This passage implies that other areas of tort law were already using a general duty of due care and that the land cases developed later and differently. The history is not at all clear. It may be more appropriate to think of the area as developing from a no-duty context and then asking why it did not evolve earlier into a fully developed duty of due care as other areas around it did so. In any event, the *Rowland* court, using the California duty factors we have already seen in *Tarasoff* and *Randi W.,* moved to a general duty of due care for premises cases.

Heins v. Webster County

Supreme Court of Nebraska, 1996.
250 Neb. 750, 552 N.W.2d 51.

WHITE, C.J., and CAPORALE, FAHRNBRUCH, LANPHIER, WRIGHT, CONNOLLY, and GERRARD, JJ.

CONNOLLY, JUSTICE.

The question presented is whether this court should abolish the common-law classifications of licensee and invitee and require a duty of reasonable care to all nontrespassers.

. . . .

[After a heavy snowfall, plaintiff Roger Heins, accompanied by his wife, visited the defendant's hospital.] The evidence is disputed concerning the nature of this trip. Webster County claims that Heins was merely paying a social visit to his daughter Julie Heins, who was the director of nursing for the hospital. Heins claims that his visit was not only social, but also to coordinate plans for him to play Santa Claus for the hospital staff during the upcoming Christmas season. During their visit with Julie, [Heins] made plans to have lunch with Julie and a friend at a local restaurant.

While . . . exiting the hospital through the main entrance, Roger fell. At trial, Roger testified that [after he held the front door open for his wife and started to exit, he slipped and fell to the ground, allegedly because of the accumulation of ice and snow, and injured his hip.]

Heins [claimed] that Webster County was negligent (1) in failing to properly inspect the above-described entrance prior to inviting the public to use the entrance, (2) in failing to warn Heins of the existence of a dangerous condition, (3) in allowing the ice and snow to accumulate, and (4) in failing to remove the ice and snow.

Following a bench trial, the district court found that Heins "went to the Webster County Hospital to visit his daughter who was an employee of the hospital." Furthermore, the court concluded that Heins was a licensee at the time of his fall and that the county did not act willfully or wantonly or fail to warn of known hidden dangers unobservable by Heins. Thus, the court entered judgment in favor of Webster County. Heins appeals.

Summarized, Heins assigns that the district court erred in not generally holding the hospital to a duty of reasonable care to Heins. In the alternative, he argues the hospital should be held to a duty of reasonable care for one of the following reasons: (1) he was a public invitee, (2) he was a social guest on the hospital premises, or (3) hospital personnel knew he was on the premises.

. . . .

[Plaintiff] calls into question the continued usefulness of the licensee and invitee classifications. In fact, a number of jurisdictions have decided that the common-law classifications have outlived their usefulness, and have either partially or completely abandoned the common-law classifications.

In 1957, England statutorily abolished the common-law distinction between licensees and invitees and imposed upon the occupier a "common duty of care" toward all persons who lawfully enter the premises. [ ] Shortly thereafter, in 1959, the U.S. Supreme Court decided that the classifications would not apply in admiralty law, stating that the classifications created a "semantic morass." See, Kermarec v. Compagnie Generale, 358 U.S. 625, 631 (1959); [ ]. In 1968, the Supreme Court of California decided the landmark case Rowland v. Christian, 443 P.2d 561 (Cal.1968), which abolished the traditional duty classification scheme for licensees, invitees, and trespassers and replaced it with ordinary negligence principles.

.   .   .

Policy Reasons for and Against Abolishing Classifications

A number of policy reasons have been asserted for either abandoning or retaining the common-law classifications. Among the jurisdictions retaining the categories, most find value in the predictability of the common law. Some courts rejecting change have reasoned that replacement of a stable and established system of loss allocation results in the establishment of a system devoid of standards for liability. [   ] It also has been suggested that the harshness of the common-law rules has been ameliorated by the judicial grafting of exceptions and that creation of sub-classifications ameliorated the distinctions between active and passive negligence. [   ] These states have concluded that abandoning the established system of liability in favor of a standard of reasonable care would decrease predictability and ensure that each case would be decided on its facts. Therefore, these states claim that landowners would be less able to guard against risks.   .   .   .

The most common reason asserted for abandoning the categories is that an entrant's status should not determine the duty that the landowner owes to him or her. As the California Supreme Court stated in *Rowland v. Christian* [   ]:

A man's life or limb does not become less worthy of protection by the law nor a loss less worthy of compensation under the law because he has come upon the land of another without permission or with permission but without a business purpose. Reasonable people do not ordinarily vary their conduct depending upon such matters, and to focus upon the status of the injured party as a trespasser, licensee, or invitee in order to determine the question whether the landowner has a duty of care, is contrary to our modern social mores and humanitarian values. The common law rules obscure rather than illuminate the proper considerations which should govern determination of the question of duty.

In abolishing the invitee-licensee distinction, the Massachusetts Supreme Judicial Court recognized:

It no longer makes any sense to predicate the landowner's duty solely on the status of the injured party as either a licensee or invitee. Perhaps, in a rural society with sparse land settlements and large estates, it would have been unduly burdensome to obligate the owner to inspect and maintain distant holdings for a class of entrants who were using the property "for their own convenience" .   .   . but the special immunity which the licensee rule affords landowners cannot be justified in an urban industrial society.

Mounsey v. Ellard, 297 N.E.2d 43, 51 (Mass.1973).

Another justification for abandoning the classifications is to eliminate the complex and unpredictable state of the law necessitated by the harsh nature of the common-law rules. [   ] As the U.S. Supreme Court proclaimed, courts have found it necessary to formulate increasingly subtle verbal refinements, to create subclassifications among traditional common-law categories, and to delineate fine gradations in the standards of care which the landowner owes to each. Yet even within a single jurisdiction, the classifications and subclassifications bred by the common law have produced confusion and conflict.

Kermarec v. Compagnie Generale, [   ]. The Court recognized that the "distinctions which the common law draws between licensee and invitee were inherited from a culture deeply rooted to the land, a culture which traced many of its standards to a heritage of feudalism." [   ] Referring to the judicial interpretation of the common-law distinctions as a "semantic morass," the Court declined to adopt them into admiralty law. [   ]

Those states abandoning the distinctions argue that instead of the entrant's status, the foreseeability of the injury should be the controlling factor in determining the liability of the landowner. [   ] Many jurisdictions that have abandoned the common-law classifications as determinants of liability have found that they remain relevant in determining the foreseeability of the harm under ordinary negligence principles. [   ]

Application of the Law to Heins

The present case illustrates the frustration inherent in the classification scheme. In many instances, recovery by an entrant has become largely a matter of chance, dependent upon the pigeonhole in which the law has put him, e.g., "trespasser," "licensee," or "invitee." [   ] When he was injured, Heins was exiting a county hospital, using the main entrance to the hospital, over the lunch hour. If Heins had been on the hospital premises to visit a patient or purchase a soft drink from a vending machine, he could have been classified as an invitee. [   ] However, he came to visit his daughter and was denied recovery as a matter of law.

Thus, Heins was denied the possibility of recovering under present law, merely because on this trip to the hospital he happened to be a licensee rather than an invitee. In the instant case, the hospital would undergo no additional burden in exercising reasonable care for a social visitor such as Heins, because it had the duty to exercise reasonable care for its invitees. A patient visitor could have used the same front entrance at which Heins fell and would have been able to maintain a negligence action; however, Heins has been denied the opportunity to recover merely because of his status at the time of the fall.

Modern commercial society creates relationships between persons not contemplated by the traditional classifications. [   ] Yet we have continued to pigeonhole individuals as licensees or invitees as a convenient way to ascertain the duty owed by the landowner. For instance, in Presho v. J.M. McDonald Co., 151 N.W.2d 451 (Neb.1967), a customer of a retail store was injured when she entered a back room of the store with the permission of the store manager, in order to retrieve an empty box. We held the customer to be a licensee rather than an invitee because "[s]he was on an errand personal to herself, not in any way connected with the business of the defendant.'' We recognized that while she was in the store proper, she was an invitee. However, we found her to be a licensee when she entered the back room, despite the fact that the ladies' restroom was located in this back room area and was used by customers to the store.

The common-law status classifications should not be able to shield those who would otherwise be held to a standard of reasonable care but for the arbitrary classification of the visitor as a licensee. We find no merit in the argument that the duty of reasonable care is difficult for a fact finder to understand or apply, because it has been used successfully with regard to invitees and is the standard used in almost all other tort actions.

We conclude that we should eliminate the distinction between licensees and invitees by requiring a standard of reasonable care for all lawful visitors. We retain a separate classification for trespassers because we conclude that one should not owe a duty to exercise reasonable care to those not lawfully on one's property. Adopting this rule places the focus where it should be, on the foreseeability of the injury, rather than on allowing the duty in a particular case to be determined by the status of the person who enters upon the property.

Our holding does not mean that owners and occupiers of land are now insurers of their premises, nor do we intend for them to undergo burdens in maintaining such premises. We impose upon owners and occupiers only the duty to exercise reasonable care in the maintenance of their premises for the protection of lawful visitors. Among the factors to be considered in evaluating whether a landowner or occupier has exercised reasonable care for the protection of lawful visitors will be (1) the foreseeability or possibility of harm; (2) the purpose for which the entrant entered the premises; (3) the time, manner, and circumstances under which the entrant entered the premises; (4) the use to which the premises are put or are expected to be put; (5) the reasonableness of the inspection, repair, or warning; (6) the opportunity and ease of repair or correction or giving of the warning; and (7) the burden on the land occupier and/or community in terms of inconvenience or cost in providing adequate protection.

Although we have set forth some of the factors to be considered in determining whether a landowner or occupier has exercised reasonable care for the protection of lawful visitors, it is for the fact finder to determine, on the facts of each individual case, whether or not such factors establish a breach of the duty of reasonable care.

Conclusion

We determine that the invitee-licensee distinction should be abandoned and the new rule applied in the instant case. Considering that other litigants may have relied on our previous rule and incurred time and expense in prosecuting or defending their claims, we conclude, with the exception of the instant case, that the rule announced today shall be applied only to all causes of action arising after this date. We reverse, and remand for a new trial.

FAHRNBRUCH, JUSTICE, dissenting.

.   .   .

The majority opinion dismantles longstanding common law by eliminating the concept of licensee, thereby forcing a landowner to treat a person who is allowed to enter or remain upon premises with the same standard of care as a person who is invited onto the premises for the mutual benefit of both landowner and invitee.

Under the majority opinion, a landowner owes a duty of reasonable care to an individual who becomes injured by conducting activities on the premises without the landowner's express permission or knowledge. From this moment on, public and private institutions, as well as residential homeowners, must be especially aware of unknown, uninvited individuals who take advantage of their land and facilities.

In McCurry v. Young Men's Christian Assn., 313 N.W.2d 689 (Neb. 1981), an individual brought an action against a Young Men's Christian Association (YMCA) as a result of an injury which arose from a fall while the individual was playing basketball on an outdoor asphalt playground owned by the YMCA. The plaintiff was not a member of the YMCA and had not obtained any express permission to use the playground. This court held that the plaintiff was a licensee and affirmed the trial court's directed verdict in favor of the YMCA. Under the majority's opinion, the YMCA and similar institutions will be subject to lawsuits which hold them to a duty to treat such uninvited users of their facilities with the same standard of care as the paying members of the institution.

This court should not enact public policy which, in effect, socializes the use of privately owned property to the extent that the landowner owes the same duty to all, except trespassers, who enter the owner's land. It is not the function of the court to create a liability where the law creates none.
[   ]

Under the majority's opinion, a homeowner would have potential liability for any number of not only uninvited but unwanted solicitors or visitors coming to the homeowner's door.

CAPORALE, J., joins in this dissent.

Notes and Questions

he was a licensee
been an invitee?

1.   Under the traditional categories why does Mr. Heins lose? How might playing Santa Claus have been relevant?

2.   In rejecting the use of the categories, why does the court exclude trespassers? Recall the *Bennett* case involving the dog walker who was hit by a falling tree limb after the park closed, p. 202, supra. Under the approach of the court in *Heins* would Mr. Bennett still lose? *Yes*

3.   What if a shoplifter, who had just stolen something from the hospital gift shop, slipped while carefully leaving the hospital and fell for the same reasons that Mr. Heins fell? Would the court's factors help in

analyzing this case? How would the factors work in deciding the case of the woman who went into the back of the store? How would they work in the case of the basketball player raised by the dissent?

4. Even though *Rowland* abolished separate treatment of trespassers, trespassers rarely brought cases. In the early 1980s, however, concern about potential liability to trespassers and burglars induced the California legislature to adopt a provision that protected landowners against liability to persons hurt on premises while committing or attempting to commit one of 25 enumerated offenses. The bar applies only upon a charge of a felony and the conviction for that felony or a lesser included felony or misdemeanor. The civil action is to be delayed until the conclusion of the criminal action. Calif.Civil Code § 847. For discussion of a similar approach, see Sun v. State of Alaska, 830 P.2d 772 (Alaska 1992).

5. The dissent is concerned about liability to licensees. How might the majority analyze the case of an uninvited solicitor coming to the front door who slips on a defective stair? Is the case different if the solicitor was hurt while going down the stairs after talking with the occupier?

6. The court concludes that its decision should operate prospectively only—except for this case. What are the arguments for and against prospective overruling generally? What are the arguments for and against making only the decision in the case before the court retroactive? Why have we not previously encountered prospective rulings in this course?

7. For a time after *Rowland*, it appeared that the case would signal a massive shift among the states. After a handful of states quickly followed California, the movement lost momentum. In *Carter v. Kinney*, supra, after failing to persuade the court to categorize Mr. Carter as an invitee, the Carters asked the court to overturn the categorical approach and follow California's lead. The court refused to abandon the categories:

> The contours of the legal relationship that results from the possessor's invitation reflect a careful and patient effort by courts over time to balance the interests of persons injured by conditions of land against the interests of possessors of land to enjoy and employ their land for the purposes they wish. Moreover, and despite the exceptions courts have developed to the general rules, the maintenance of the distinction between licensee and invitee creates fairly predictable rules within which entrants and possessors can determine appropriate conduct and juries can assess liability. To abandon the careful work of generations for an amorphous "reasonable care under the circumstances" standard seems—to put it kindly—improvident.

The court quoted a passage from Prosser & Keeton that speculated that the failure of more states to join the "trend"

> may reflect a more fundamental dissatisfaction with certain developments in accident law that accelerated during the 1960's—reduction of whole systems of legal principles to a single, perhaps simplistic, standard of reasonable care, the sometimes blind subordination of other legitimate social objectives to the goals of accident prevention and

compensation, and the commensurate shifting of the balance of power to the jury from the judge. At least it appears that the courts are . . . acquiring a more healthy skepticism toward invitations to jettison years of developed jurisprudence in favor of beguiling legal panacea.

The *Carter* court concluded that the "experience of the states that have abolished the distinction between licensee and invitee does not convince us that their idea is a better one. Indeed, we are convinced that they have chosen wrongly."

The *Rowland* trend seemed strong in the 1970s, weakened in the 1980s, but may have regained strength in the late 1990s. *Heins* reports that of the 37 states to reconsider their positions after *Rowland*, 23 have abolished some or all of the categories; 14 have retained them. The rest have not reconsidered their positions.

8. *Landlord and tenant.* What affirmative obligations, if any, does a landlord owe a tenant to protect the latter from harm? The traditional rules of liability for defective conditions have insulated landlords from liability except in a few situations. As summarized in Sargent v. Ross, 308 A.2d 528 (N.H.1973), a landlord was liable in tort only "if the injury is attributable to (1) a hidden danger in the premises of which the landlord but not the tenant is aware, (2) premises leased for public use, (3) premises retained under the landlord's control, such as common stairways, or (4) premises negligently repaired by the landlord."

Liability was much less likely if the landlord had promised to repair but had failed to take any steps to do so. That distinction between bad repairs and no repairs at all is disappearing. In Putnam v. Stout, 345 N.E.2d 319 (N.Y.1976), the court overturned its earlier view and imposed a duty where a promise had been made:

> First, the lessor has agreed, for a consideration, to keep the premises in repair; secondly, the likelihood that the landlord's promise to make repairs will induce the tenant to forgo repair efforts which he otherwise might have made; thirdly, the lessor retains a reversionary interest in the land and by his contract may be regarded as retaining and assuming the responsibility of keeping his premises in safe condition; finally, various social policy factors must be considered: (a) tenants may often be financially unable to make repairs; (b) their possession is for a limited term and thus the incentive to make repairs is significantly less than that of a landlord; and (c) in return for his pecuniary benefit from the relationship, the landlord could properly be expected to assume certain obligations with respect to the safety of the others. [   ]

In the cited *Sargent v. Ross*, the court took a much more dramatic step to increase the liability of landlords. A child visiting a tenant in defendant's residential building fell to her death from a stairway. The claim was that the stairway was too steep and the railing inadequate. (The stairway was not common premises because it went only to the tenant's apartment.) On appeal, the court adopted the following position:

[A] landlord must act as a reasonable person under all of the circumstances, including the likelihood of injury to others, the probable seriousness of such injuries, and the burden of reducing or avoiding the risk. . . . The questions of control, hidden defects and common or public use, which formerly had to be established as a prerequisite to even considering the negligence of a landlord, will now be relevant only inasmuch as they bear on the basic tort issues such as the foreseeability and unreasonableness of the particular risk of harm.

How does this new approach differ from the *Sargent* court's summary of earlier law?

9. *Liability for harm outside the premises.* On occasion, pedestrians and others outside the premises claim to have been hurt by conditions or activities within the premises. As a recent example, consider *Largosa v. Ford Motor Co.*, p. 179, supra. One defendant was conducting a bungee-jumping business close to a busy highway. Plaintiff claimed to have been "cut off by an unknown vehicle whose driver was gaping at bungee-jumpers adjacent to and over [the interstate highway]" forcing plaintiff to swerve and hit the divider. The court reviewed its cases involving duties to people on adjacent highways and concluded that the focus was "on the reasonable foreseeability of the injury." The court quoted Restatement § 368 that imposed liability on possessors who create artificial conditions "so near an existing highway" that they realize or should realize that it involves an "unreasonable risk" of harm to travelers using due care on that highway. The court denied liability because the defendant's business "did not pose a foreseeable danger directly to plaintiffs on the highway. None of the bungee jumpers launched themselves out onto the highway or even over it. Therefore, we will not impose a duty that would unnecessarily expose defendant to extensive liability for unforeseen negligence."

The court was unclear what measures defendant could "reasonably have taken to avoid distracting motorists." A warning sign would have been a small burden but might only have increased the number of gaping motorists. A wall or curtain would have been impractical since the jumping platform was 180 feet high. The motorists on the highway "were in the best position to avoid accidents by operating their vehicles with care." The court noted that the highways coming into and out of Chicago offered several distractions, including airplanes and occasional fireworks from a baseball stadium. Also, Lake Shore Drive furnished sights of people flying kites, playing golf, roller skating and sun bathing. What about an accident caused by motorists looking at a high school football game being played alongside the road? See Lompoc Unified School District v. Superior Court, 26 Cal.Rptr.2d 122 (App. 1993) (denying liability).

Criminal Activity

During the long development of the category-based approach, most cases involved physical conditions of the premises or the negligent conduct of others. Later, plaintiffs began to sue for harms caused them by criminal conduct occurring on the premises. Most commonly, tenants began suing landlords for providing inadequate protection against criminal activity. The major early case was Kline v. 1500 Massachusetts Ave. Apartment Corp., 439 F.2d 477 (D.C.Cir.1970), in which the court imposed a duty of care on the landlord of a large apartment building toward a tenant who had been assaulted in a common hallway of the building. Crime had been occurring on the premises with mounting frequency. Although the owner could take some steps, such as extra heavy locks or guards, "no individual tenant had it within his power to take measures to guard" against these same perils:

> Not only as between landlord and tenant is the landlord best equipped to guard against the predictable risk of intruders, but even as between landlord and the police power of government, the landlord is in the best position to take the necessary protective measures. Municipal police cannot patrol the entryways and the hallways, the garages and the basements of private multiple unit apartment dwellings. They are neither equipped, manned, nor empowered to do so. In the area of the predictable risk which materialized in this case, only the landlord could have taken measures which might have prevented the injuries suffered by appellant.

>   . . .

>   . . . We do not hold that the landlord is an insurer of the safety of his tenants. His duty is to take those measures of protection which are within his power and capacity to take, and which can reasonably be expected to mitigate the risk of intruders assaulting and robbing tenants. The landlord is not expected to provide protection commonly owed by a municipal police department; but as illustrated in this case, he is obligated to protect those parts of his premises which are not usually subject to periodic patrol and inspection by the municipal police.

The court recognized that the discharge of this duty might often cause "the expenditure of large sums" and that these costs "will be ultimately passed on to the tenant in the form of increased rents. This prospect, in itself, however, is no deterrent to our acknowledging and giving force to the duty, since without protection the tenant already pays in losses from theft, physical assault and increased insurance premiums." The landlord "is entirely justified in passing on the cost of increased protective measures to his tenant, but the rationale of compelling the landlord to do it in the first place is that he is the only one who is in a position to take the necessary protective measures for overall protection of the premises."

Posecai v. Wal–Mart Stores, Inc.

Supreme Court of Louisiana, 1999.
752 So.2d 762.

MARCUS, JUSTICE.

Shirley Posecai brought suit against Sam's Wholesale Club ("Sam's") in Kenner after she was robbed at gunpoint in the store's parking lot. On

July 20, 1995, Mrs. Posecai went to Sam's to make an exchange and to do some shopping. She exited the store and returned to her parked car at approximately 7:20 p.m. It was not dark at the time. As Mrs. Posecai was placing her purchases in the trunk, a man who was hiding under her car grabbed her ankle and pointed a gun at her. The unknown assailant instructed her to hand over her jewelry and her wallet. While begging the robber to spare her life, she gave him her purse and all her jewelry. Mrs. Posecai was wearing her most valuable jewelry at the time of the robbery because she had attended a downtown luncheon earlier in the day. She lost a two and a half carat diamond ring given to her by her husband for their twenty-fifth wedding anniversary, a diamond and ruby bracelet and a diamond and gold watch, all valued at close to $19,000.

When the robber released Mrs. Posecai, she ran back to the store for help. The Kenner Police Department was called and two officers came out to investigate the incident. The perpetrator was never apprehended and Mrs. Posecai never recovered her jewelry despite searching several pawn shops.

At the time of this armed robbery, a security guard was stationed inside the store to protect the cash office from 5:00 p.m. until the store closed at 8:00 p.m. He could not see outside and Sam's did not have security guards patrolling the parking lot. At trial, the security guard on duty, Kenner Police Officer Emile Sanchez, testified that he had worked security detail at Sam's since 1986 and was not aware of any similar criminal incidents occurring in Sam's parking lot during the nine years prior to the robbery of Mrs. Posecai. He further testified that he did not consider Sam's parking lot to be a high crime area, but admitted that he had not conducted a study on the issue.

The plaintiff presented the testimony of two other Kenner police officers. Officer Russell Moran testified that he had patrolled the area around Sam's from 1993 to 1995. He stated that the subdivision behind Sam's, Lincoln Manor, is generally known as a high crime area, but that the Kenner Police were rarely called out to Sam's. Officer George Ansardi, the investigating officer, similarly testified that Lincoln Manor is a high crime area but explained that Sam's is not considered a high crime location. He further stated that to his knowledge none of the other businesses in the area employed security guards at the time of this robbery.

An expert on crime risk assessment and premises security, David Kent, was qualified and testified on behalf of the plaintiff. It was his opinion that the robbery of Mrs. Posecai could have been prevented by an exterior security presence. He presented crime data from the Kenner Police Department indicating that between 1989 and June of 1995 there were three robberies or "predatory offenses" [defined by the court as crimes against the person] on Sam's premises, and provided details from the police reports on each of these crimes. The first offense occurred at 12:45 a.m. on March 20, 1989, when a delivery man sleeping in his truck parked in back of the store was robbed. In May of 1992, a person was mugged in the store's parking lot. Finally, on February 7, 1994, an employee of the store was the victim of a purse snatching, but she indicated to the police that the crime was related to a domestic dispute.

In order to broaden the geographic scope of his crime data analysis, Mr. Kent looked at the crime statistics at thirteen businesses on the same block as Sam's, all of which were either fast food restaurants, convenience stores or gas stations. He found a total of eighty-three predatory offenses in the six and a half years before Mrs. Posecai was robbed. Mr. Kent concluded that the area around Sam's was "heavily crime impacted," although he did not compare the crime statistics he found around Sam's to any other area in Kenner or the New Orleans metro area.

Mrs. Posecai contends that Sam's was negligent in failing to provide adequate security in the parking lot considering the high level of crime in the surrounding area. Seeking to recover for mental anguish as well as for her property loss, she alleged that after this incident she had trouble sleeping and was afraid to go out by herself at night. After a bench trial, the trial judge held that Sam's owed a duty to provide security in the parking lot because the robbery of the plaintiff was foreseeable and could have been prevented by the use of security. A judgment was rendered in favor of Mrs. Posecai, awarding $18,968 for her lost jewelry and $10,000 in general damages for her mental anguish. [The court of appeals affirmed the defendant's liability but modified the allocation of damages.]

The sole issue presented for our review is whether Sam's owed a duty to protect Mrs. Posecai from the criminal acts of third parties under the facts and circumstances of this case.

. . .

This court has never squarely decided whether business owners owe a duty to protect their patrons from crimes perpetrated by third parties. It is therefore helpful to look to the way in which other jurisdictions have resolved this question. Most state supreme courts that have considered the issue agree that business owners do have a duty to take reasonable precautions to protect invitees from foreseeable criminal attacks.

We now join other states in adopting the rule that although business owners are not the insurers of their patrons' safety, they do have a duty to implement reasonable measures to protect their patrons from criminal acts when those acts are foreseeable. We emphasize, however, that there is generally no duty to protect others from the criminal activities of third persons. [ ] This duty only arises under limited circumstances, when the criminal act in question was reasonably foreseeable to the owner of the business. Determining when a crime is foreseeable is therefore a critical inquiry.

Other jurisdictions have resolved the foreseeability issue in a variety of ways, but four basic approaches have emerged. [ ] The first approach, although somewhat outdated, is known as the specific harm rule. [ ] According to this rule, a landowner does not owe a duty to protect patrons from the violent acts of third parties unless he is aware of specific, imminent harm about to befall them. [ ] Courts have generally agreed that this rule is too restrictive in limiting the duty of protection that business owners owe their invitees. [   ]

More recently, some courts have adopted a prior similar incidents test. [   ] Under this test, foreseeability is established by evidence of previous crimes on or near the premises. [   ] The idea is that a past history of criminal conduct will put the landowner on notice of a future risk. Therefore, courts consider the nature and extent of the previous crimes, as well as their recency, frequency, and similarity to the crime in question. [   ] This approach can lead to arbitrary results because it is applied with different standards regarding the number of previous crimes and the degree of similarity required to give rise to a duty. [   ]

The third and most common approach used in other jurisdictions is known as the totality of the circumstances test. [   ] This test takes additional factors into account, such as the nature, condition, and location of the land, as well as any other relevant factual circumstances bearing on foreseeability. [   ] As the Indiana Supreme Court explained, "[a] substantial factor in the determination of duty is the number, nature, and location of prior similar incidents, but the lack of prior similar incidents will not preclude a claim where the landowner knew or should have known that the criminal act was foreseeable." [   ] The application of this test often focuses on the level of crime in the surrounding area and courts that apply this test are more willing to see property crimes or minor offenses as precursors to more violent crimes. [   ] In general, the totality of the circumstances test tends to place a greater duty on business owners to foresee the risk of criminal attacks on their property and has been criticized "as being too broad a standard, effectively imposing an unqualified duty to protect customers in areas experiencing any significant level of criminal activity." [   ]

The final standard that has been used to determine foreseeability is a balancing test, an approach which has been adopted in California [in Ann M. v. Pacific Plaza Shopping Center, 863 P.2d 207 (Cal.1993)] and Tennessee. . . . . The balancing test seeks to address the interests of both business proprietors and their customers by balancing the foreseeability of harm against the burden of imposing a duty to protect against the criminal acts of third persons. [   ] The Tennessee Supreme Court formulated the test as follows: "In determining the duty that exists, the foreseeability of harm and the gravity of harm must be balanced against the commensurate burden imposed on the business to protect against that harm. In cases in which there is a high degree of foreseeability of harm and the probable harm is great, the burden imposed upon defendant may be substantial. Alternatively, in cases in which a lesser degree of foreseeability is present or the potential harm is slight, less onerous burdens may be imposed." McClung v. Delta Square Ltd. Partnership, 937 S.W.2d 891, 902 [Tenn. 1996]. Under this test, the high degree of foreseeability necessary to impose a duty to provide security, will rarely, if ever, be proven in the absence of prior similar incidents of crime on the property. [   ]

We agree that a balancing test is the best method for determining when business owners owe a duty to provide security for their patrons. The economic and social impact of requiring businesses to provide security on their premises is an important factor. Security is a significant monetary expense for any business and further increases the cost of doing business in high crime areas that are already economically depressed. Moreover, businesses are generally not responsible for the endemic crime that plagues our communities, a societal problem that even our law enforcement and other government agencies have been unable to solve. At the same time, business owners are in the best position to appreciate the crime risks that are posed on their premises and to take reasonable precautions to counteract those risks.

With the foregoing considerations in mind, we adopt the following balancing test to be used in deciding whether a business owes a duty of care to protect its customers from the criminal acts of third parties. The foreseeability of the crime risk on the defendant's property and the gravity of the risk determine the existence and the extent of the defendant's duty. The greater the foreseeability and gravity of the harm, the greater the duty of care that will be imposed on the business. A very high degree of foreseeability is required to give rise to a duty to post security guards, but a lower degree of foreseeability may support a duty to implement lesser security measures such as using surveillance cameras, installing improved lighting or fencing, or trimming shrubbery. The plaintiff has the burden of establishing the duty the defendant owed under the circumstances.

The foreseeability and gravity of the harm are to be determined by the facts and circumstances of the case. The most important factor to be considered is the existence, frequency and similarity of prior incidents of crime on the premises, but the location, nature and condition of the property should also be taken into account. It is highly unlikely that a crime risk will be sufficiently foreseeable for the imposition of a duty to provide security guards if there have not been previous instances of crime on the business' premises.

In the instant case, there were only three predatory offenses on Sam's premises in the six and a half years prior to the robbery of Mrs. Posecai. The first of these offenses occurred well after store hours, at almost one o'clock in the morning, and involved the robbery of a delivery man who was caught unaware as he slept near Sam's loading dock behind the store. In 1992, a person was mugged while walking through the parking lot. Two years later, an employee of the store was attacked in the parking lot and her purse was taken, apparently by her husband. A careful consideration of the previous incidents of predatory offenses on the property reveals that there was only one other crime in Sam's parking lot, the mugging in 1992, that was perpetrated against a Sam's customer and that bears any similarity to the crime that occurred in this case. Given the large number of customers that used Sam's parking lot, the previous robbery of only one customer in all those years indicates a very low crime risk. It is also relevant that Sam's only operates during daylight hours and must provide an accessible parking lot to the multitude of customers that shop at its store each year. Although the neighborhood bordering Sam's is considered a high crime area by local law enforcement, the foreseeability and gravity of harm in Sam's parking lot remained slight.

We conclude that Sam's did not possess the requisite degree of foreseeability for the imposition of a duty to provide security patrols in its parking lot. Nor was the degree of foreseeability sufficient to support a duty to implement lesser security measures. [At this point, in a footnote, the court rejected a lower court conclusion that defendant had assumed a duty to protect its patrons from crime when it hired security guards.] Accordingly, Sam's owed no duty to protect Mrs. Posecai from the criminal acts of third parties under the facts and circumstances of this case. . . .

LEMMON, J., concurring.

. . .

JOHNSON, J., concurring.

[The concurrer noted that the majority discusses "four approaches to determine the duty owed by a business owner to an invitee, then selects the more narrow balancing test because of the economic and social impact of requiring business owners to provide security in high crime areas. Only California and Tennessee have adopted the balancing test."]

The totality of circumstances test is best suited for resolving this question. The totality of the circumstances test takes all factors of an incident into account when evaluating the issue of duty. [   ] It incorporates the specific harm and prior similar incidents tests as factors to consider when determining whether a business owes a duty to an invitee without arbitrarily limiting the inquiry to a limited set of factors. [   ] It additionally takes into account the physical characteristics of the premises (i.e. lighting, fencing), other security measures, the location of the premises, the nature of the operation of business, and the owner's observations regarding criminal activity. [   ] While this approach does not require a business to ensure an invitee's safety, it does require that reasonable measures be taken to prevent foreseeable criminal acts against an invitee.

While I agree with the majority's conclusion that the defendant, Sam's Wholesale Club, did not have a duty to provide security patrols in its parking lot under the facts of this case, the majority's analysis, using the balancing test to arrive at this conclusion, is flawed. I would adopt the totality of circumstances test to determine defendant's duty.

Notes and Questions

1. What is the difference between the "totality of the circumstances" test and the "balancing" test? In what kinds of cases will the two tests lead to different results?

2. In *Posecai* is it crucial what type of security the plaintiff sought? Recall the discussion of "untaken precautions" at p. 211, supra.

3. After the cited *Ann M.* case, California decided another important case, Sharon P. v. Arman, Ltd., 989 P.2d 121 (Cal.1999) cert. denied 120

S.Ct.2689 (2000), in which plaintiff was attacked in a commercial parking garage. Since no assaults had been recorded there in the preceding ten years, the court, 6–1, concluded that the occurrence "was not sufficiently foreseeable to support [a requirement that defendant secure the garage]." One judge, although concurring, observed that "a landlord is not, as the prior similar incidents rule would have it, entitled to one free assault before the failure to take appropriate security measures subjects him or her to the risk of civil liability."

4. Under the approach in *Posecai* what issue is left for the jury in determining breach that has not already been decided by the court under duty? Does the excerpt from *Ballard* quoted at p. 172, supra, help on this issue? In Williams v. Cunningham Drug Stores, Inc., 418 N.W.2d 381 (Mich.1988), the court held that defendant drug store owed no duty of care to a customer who was hurt during a robbery. Although juries normally decide what constitutes reasonable care, "in cases in which overriding public policy concerns arise, the court determines what constitutes reasonable care." Is that what happened in *Posecai*?

5. Is the *Posecai* court suggesting that it would apply its analysis to cases of residential harm, as in *Kline*, p. 206, supra? Are the two situations different?

6. In Iannelli v. Burger King Corp., 761 A.2d 417 (N.H. 2000), the court held that defendant owed a duty of due care for the safety of one set of customers, plaintiff and his family, which was attacked by a second group of (rowdy) customers. Is this a case in which the defendant has a special relationship with both sets of customers of the sort discussed in *Tarasoff*, p. 158 supra? Does *Iannelli*'s holding depend on what view the state takes in *Posecai* situations?

Resisting the Robbery and Apprehending Perpetrators

The foregoing cases dealt with the duty to anticipate and try to avert robberies and other criminal conduct. In a case where the proprietor is present, might there be liability for trying to thwart the robbers once the robbery has begun?

In Boyd v. Racine Currency Exchange, Inc., 306 N.E.2d 39 (Ill.1973), a robber approached the currency exchange's bulletproof window, held a gun to a customer's head, and demanded that the access door be opened. The teller refused to comply and dropped to the floor, and the robber killed the customer. His widow's wrongful death claim asserted that the teller had a duty to obey the robber's demands. The court dismissed her action, concluding that robbery victims need not accede to criminal demands:

> If a duty to comply exists, the occupier of the premises would have little choice in determining whether to comply with the criminal demand and surrender the money or to refuse the demand and be held liable in a civil action for damages brought by or on behalf of the hostage. The existence of this dilemma and knowledge of it by those who are disposed to commit such crimes will only grant to them

disagree

additional leverage to enforce their criminal demands. . . . In this particular case the result may appear to be harsh and unjust, but, for the protection of future business invitees, we cannot afford to extend to the criminal another weapon in his arsenal.

In Kentucky Fried Chicken of California, Inc. v. Superior Court, 927 P.2d 1260 (Cal.1997), defendant restaurant cashier did not comply immediately with a robber's demand. A customer who was taken hostage feared being killed—but was not physically harmed. In denying summary judgment, the lower court stressed that it was foreseeable that if the cashier did not comply the robber would hurt the patron and that this created a duty to comply. It also cited police pamphlets that urged citizens to comply with robbers' demands. On appeal, the court, 4–3, reversed the denial of summary judgment. The majority framed the issue as "whether a shopkeeper owes a duty to a patron to comply with an armed robber's demand for money in order to avoid increasing the risk of harm to patrons." The answer was that the shopkeeper "never" owed such a duty.

The majority, finding few cases on point, approved *Boyd*, and also concluded that compliance was not required because of other provisions of state law, including a statute that recognized the right to defend property with reasonable force. Moreover, the majority doubted the benefits of compliance because "robbers are unpredictable and often injure victims and others even though there has been no resistance." A duty to comply would only encourage hostage-taking without assured benefit. (The court declined to consider cases involving "active resistance" to the robber.)

One dissenter objected to the absolute nature of the holding: "a harsh and unjust rule that a business proprietor is never under a duty to accede to the demands of a robber when his customers are present," so that the proprietor "is never required to subordinate any of his own property interests—no matter how insignificant the object and no matter how slightly it is jeopardized—to his customers' safety—no matter how many there are and no matter how gravely they are threatened."

The other two dissenters argued at length that the reasonableness of the proprietor's response to the attack was a jury question, asserting three arguments for not foreclosing the jury's role in this type of case. The first arose "from the irreducible variety of circumstances which may surround an event that causes harm to someone." The "greater accuracy" that results from fact-based decisions "advances the economic function of tort law." An "individualized determination of reasonableness increases efficiency because it allows for the optimal level of care to be determined under the circumstances of each case; it asks not whether in general the cost of additional precautions would be greater than the cost of additional injuries but whether, under the specific circumstances of the case at hand, additional precautions would have been cost effective."

Second, the use of juries allows "successive juries to reassess what precautions are reasonable as social, economic, and technological conditions change over time. . . . By contrast, locking defendants forever into a straitjacket of prescribed conduct removes the incentive for them to lower the costs and increase the level of precautions they provide."

Third, in deciding reasonableness, jurors "bring a wider array of practical experience and knowledge to that task than could a single individual such as a judge."

E. INTRAFAMILY DUTIES

In this section we consider the impact on duty when the plaintiff and the defendant are part of the same family unit, an area that has generated much confusion.

Spousal suits. At common law, courts quite commonly barred spouses from suing one another for personal injury. The common law view was that husband and wife were a unity for legal purposes—and suits between them were a logical impossibility. But in the 19th century, legislatures began adopting so-called "Married Women's Acts" that gave wives the right to own property and to sue over property and contract disputes. With this destruction of the "unity," state courts slowly began eliminating the immunity from tort liability that spouses had enjoyed against being sued by one another.

Initially, abrogation occurred in suits for intentional torts because these claims showed that any spousal harmony sought to be preserved had probably already dissipated. It was harder to abrogate the immunity in suits for negligence because the courts feared not marital disharmony, but rather fraud and collusion against insurers as one spouse readily admitted negligence in hurting the other spouse. Virtually all remnants of spousal immunity have disappeared as to both intentional and negligent harms. See the discussions in Waite v. Waite, 618 So.2d 1360 (Fla.1993) and Price v. Price, 732 S.W.2d 316 (Tex.1987).

Parent-child suits. The parent-child relationship was never treated as a unity. The origin of the immunity of parents to suits by their children can be traced to the late nineteenth century. The ban was very widely adopted, and has recently been an active area of litigation. We have already considered suits within the family, though they did not address the ability of the child to sue. Recall *Andre v. Pomeroy*, p. 64, supra, involving the child's claim against her mother for negligent driving.

Claims by children against parents for intentional harm are almost universally permitted today. For an extended discussion of an "issue of first impression," concluding that a child should be permitted to sue her father for sexual abuse, see Henderson v. Woolley, 644 A.2d 1303 (Conn.1994). The major battleground in parent-child injuries has involved negligently inflicted harms.

Broadbent v. Broadbent
Supreme Court of Arizona, 1995.
184 Ariz. 74, 907 P.2d 43.

CORCORAN, JUSTICE.

We must determine whether the doctrine of parental immunity bars Christopher Broadbent's action against his mother for negligence. . . .

[While defendant mother was watching her 2-1/2-year-old son swimming at the family residence, the phone rang. Defendant went inside to answer it. When she looked out and could not see her son she ran out and found him at the bottom of the pool. Although he was ultimately revived, he "suffered severe brain damage because of lack of oxygen. He has lost his motor skills and has no voluntary movement." The action was brought by the father as conservator of his son. The trial court dismissed the case based on state precedents and the court of appeals affirmed, 2–1. The parties have "stipulated that: (1) the real party in interest was Northbrook Indemnity Company, who provided personal umbrella liability insurance coverage for Laura Broadbent on the date of the accident; (2) Laura may be entitled to indemnity from Northbrook if Laura is liable for the injuries to Christopher; (3) Laura did not want to defend the action but agreed that Northbrook should be permitted to defend; and (4) the only issue in the case was whether the doctrine of parental immunity applied. The court of appeals ordered that Northbrook be permitted to appear and defend the case."]

I.   History and Purpose of the Parental Immunity Doctrine

A.   The Origins of Parental Immunity

We begin by stating a few basic facts about the treatment of children under the law and family immunities. Under common law, a child has traditionally been considered a separate legal entity from his or her parent. [   ] Children have generally been allowed to sue their parents in property and contract actions. Goller v. White, [122 N.W.2d 193, 197 (Wis.1963)]; [   ]. In contrast, at common law the courts merged the identity of husband and wife; therefore, spousal immunity prohibited any action by a wife against her husband because to do so would have been to sue herself. [   ] The doctrine of spousal immunity has been abolished and there has not been a prohibition against siblings suing each other [in Arizona].

The doctrine of parental immunity is an American phenomenon unknown in the English common law. See Gibson v. Gibson, [479 P.2d 648, 649 (Cal.1971)]; [   ]. Courts in Canada and Scotland have held that children may sue their parents in tort. [   ]

In early American history, children were viewed as "evil and in need of strict discipline," and the courts recognized wide parental discretion. [   ]. See, e.g., S.C.Code Ann. § 16–3–40 (Law.Co-op. 1976) (statute originating from 1712 that provided a defense to "[k]illing by stabbing or thrusting" if done while chastising or correcting your child). Only recently has the state intervened to protect children. [   ] Viewed against this backdrop, it is not surprising that no American child had sought recovery against a parent for tortious conduct until the late nineteenth century.

[The court reviewed three famous early cases. In Hewlett v. George, 9 So. 885, 887 (Miss.1891), the court held "without citation to legal authority, that a child could not sue her parent for being falsely imprisoned in an insane asylum because of parental immunity, a doctrine which that court created from whole cloth." The basic ground was that the "peace of society, and of the families composing society, and a sound public policy, designed to subserve the repose of families and the best interests of society, forbid to the minor child a right to appear in court in the assertion of a claim to civil redress for personal injuries suffered at the hands of the parent."

In McKelvey v. McKelvey, 77 S.W. 664 (Tenn.1903), the court held that a minor child could not sue her father for "cruel and inhuman treatment" allegedly inflicted by her stepmother with the consent of her father. In Roller v. Roller, 79 P. 788 (Wash.1905), the court "held that a minor child could not sue her father for rape, even though he had been convicted of the criminal violation, because of the doctrine of parental immunity."]

This "great trilogy" was the inauspicious beginning of the doctrine of parental immunity, which was soon embraced by almost every state. [   ] However, the courts soon began fashioning several exceptions to the doctrine, and in several states the doctrine has been abolished. See [*Gibson*]; Glaskox v. Glaskox, 614 So.2d 906, 909–11 (Miss.1992) (abolishing parental immunity where minor injured as result of parents' negligence in car accident). In several situations, parental immunity does not apply: if the parent is acting outside his parental role and within the scope of his employment; if the parent acts willfully, wantonly, or recklessly; if the child is emancipated; if the child or parent dies; if a third party is liable for the tort, then the immunity of the parent does not protect that third party; and if the tortfeasor is standing in loco parentis, such as a grandparent, foster parent, or teacher, then the immunity does not apply [   ].

B.   Parental Immunity in Arizona

[The state first recognized parental immunity in 1967. In 1970, an unemancipated minor was allowed to sue her parents for injuries resulting from a car accident. Streenz v. Streenz, 471 P.2d 282 (Ariz.1970).] In *Streenz*, this court adopted [*Goller*]. Under the *Goller* standard, parental immunity is abrogated except:

> "(1) where the alleged negligent act involves an exercise of parental authority over the child; and
>
> (2) where the alleged negligent act involves an exercise of ordinary parental discretion with respect to the provision of food, clothing, housing, medical and dental services, and other care."

[   ] The cases following *Streenz* show the difficulty in applying this ambiguous standard.

[In 1981, a child sued his father for leaving the front yard gate open so that the child could ride his tricycle into traffic. The court held that "the parent would not be immune if the parent had a duty to the world at large." Sandoval v. Sandoval, 623 P.2d 800, 802 (Ariz.1981). If the parent's duty was "owed to the child alone and a part of the parental 'care and control' or 'other care' to be provided by the parents," then the parent was immune from liability. The suit failed. In Schleier v. Alter, 767 P.2d 1187 (Ariz.App.1989), the family dog, which had a history of attacking children, bit the Alters' 11-month-old child. The court "held that the parents had a duty to the world at large and therefore were not immune from liability." In Sandbak v. Sandbak, 800 P.2d 8 (Ariz.App.1990), the child wandered onto the next door neighbors' property where the neighbors' pit bull terrier severely mauled her. Her parents "knew that the next door neighbors owned pit bull terriers and that their daughter had a habit of wandering onto the neighbors' property." The court barred the child's claim.]

C. Analysis of the Policy Reasons Advanced in Support of Parental Immunity

Courts and commentators have postulated many policy reasons for the parental immunity doctrine. The primary justifications for this immunity are:

(1) Suing one's parents would disturb domestic tranquility;

(2) Suing one's parents would create a danger of fraud and collusion;

(3) Awarding damages to the child would deplete family resources;

(4) Awarding damages to the child could benefit the parent if the child predeceases the parent and the parent inherits the child's damages; and

(5) Suing one's parents would interfere with parental care, discipline, and control.

[   ] We believe that all of these justifications provide weak support for the parental immunity doctrine.

The injury to the child, more than the lawsuit, disrupts the family tranquility. In fact, if the child is not compensated for the tortious injury, then peace in the family is even less likely. In the seminal Arizona case on parental immunity, the court recognized that family tranquility would not be disturbed if the parents had liability insurance. [   ]

This fear of upsetting the family tranquility also seems unrealistic when we consider how such a lawsuit is initiated. The parent most often makes the decision to sue himself, and the parent is in effect prepared to say that he was negligent. [   ]

The danger of fraud and collusion is present in all lawsuits. We should not deny recovery to an entire class of litigants because some litigants might try to deceive the judicial system. The system can ferret out fraudulent and collusive behavior in suits brought by children against their parents just as the system detects such behavior in other contexts.

.   .   .

A damage award for the child will not deplete, or unfairly redistribute, the family's financial resources. These cases will generally not be brought if no insurance coverage is available, and therefore the worry that the family's resources will be depleted for the benefit of one child is illusory.

The opposite is true. If a child has been seriously injured and needs expensive medical care, then a successful lawsuit against the parent and subsequent recovery from the insurance company could ease the financial burden on the family. It would not be a viable rule to say that liability only exists where insurance exists, but we recognize that lawsuits generally will be brought when there is potential insurance coverage.

The possibility that the parent might inherit money recovered by the child is remote. This becomes a concern only if the parent inherits as a beneficiary under intestate succession laws. This is a concern for the probate courts and the laws of intestate succession, not tort law. The remedy would be to prohibit inheritance by the parent—not to deny recovery to the injured child. See Parent-Child Immunity, at 497–98.

The Arizona courts have embraced the rationale that allowing a child to sue a parent would interfere with parental care, discipline, and control. See [*Streenz*]. We have [in *Sandoval*] cited with approval the Wisconsin Supreme Court's statement that:

> [a] new and heavy burden would be added to the responsibility and privilege of parenthood, if within the wide scope of daily experiences common to the upbringing of children a parent could be subjected to a suit for damages for each failure to exercise care and judgment commensurate with the risk.

The justification that allowing children to sue their parents would undercut parental authority and discretion has more appeal than the other rationales. However, if a child were seriously injured as a result of the exercise of parental authority, such as by a beating, then it would constitute an injury willfully inflicted, and parents are generally not immune for willful, wanton, or malicious conduct. [ ] Furthermore, such a willful beating would probably constitute child abuse and could be criminally prosecuted. [ ]

We want to protect the right of parents to raise their children by their own methods and in accordance with their own attitudes and beliefs. The New York Court of Appeals aptly stated this concern:

> Considering the different economic, educational, cultural, ethnic and religious backgrounds which must prevail, there are so many combinations and permutations of parent-child relationships that may result that the search for a standard would necessarily be in vain. . . .
> For this reason parents have always had the right to determine how much independence, supervision and control a child should have, and to best judge the character and extent of development of their child.

Holodook v. Spencer, [324 N.E.2d 338, 346 (N.Y.1974)]. Though we recognize the importance of allowing parental discretion, we disagree that our searching for a standard would be "in vain." Parents do not possess unfettered discretion in raising their children.

II. The Abolishment of Parental Immunity and Adoption of the "Reasonable Parent" Standard for Parent-Child Suits

Although the above concerns make it difficult to draft a proper standard for the type of action a child may maintain against a parent, we will attempt to do so. We need to "fashion an objective standard that does not result in second-guessing parents in the management of their family affairs." [ ] First, we should make clear what the standard is not. We reject and hereby overrule *Sandoval*, which created the "duty to the world at large versus duty to the child alone" distinction. [ ] This distinction is not capable of uniform application and has no connection with the rationale for parental immunity. This is especially evident when we compare the facts of *Schleier* and *Sandbak*.

In *Schleier*, the negligent act was failure to restrain a dog, and the court found that this was a duty to the world; therefore, parental immunity did not apply. [ ] In *Sandbak*, the negligent act was failure to supervise a child who was bitten by a neighbor's dog, and the court found this was a duty to the child alone; therefore, parental immunity applied. [ ] The children in *Schleier* and *Sandbak* suffered similar injuries; neither case involved parental discipline, and neither case involved the "provision of food, clothing, housing, medical and dental services, and other care," unless "other care" is broadly defined. Both cases involved the negligent supervision of children. If we were to hold that parents are immune for negligent supervision of children, then the issue of liability would revolve around whether an activity could be described as "supervision" and whether lack of supervision was the cause of the injury. This would not involve a consideration of whether the activity infringed on the parents' discretionary decisions regarding care, custody, and control. Almost everything a parent does in relation to his child involves "care, custody, and control."

We add that parents always owe a parental duty to their minor child. The issue of liability should revolve around whether the parents have breached this duty and, if so, whether the breach of duty caused the injury.

In accord with the California Supreme Court, "we reject the implication of *Goller* [which this court approved in *Streenz*] that within certain aspects of the parent-child relationship, the parent has carte blanche to act negligently toward his child. . . . [A]lthough a parent has the prerogative and the duty to exercise authority over his minor child, this prerogative must be exercised within reasonable limits." [*Gibson*]. We hereby reject the *Goller* test as set forth in *Streenz*, and we approve of the "reasonable parent test," in which a parent's conduct is judged by whether that parent's conduct comported with that of a reasonable and prudent parent in a similar situation. [ ]

A parent is not immune from liability for tortious conduct directed toward his child solely by reason of that relationship. [ ] And, a parent is not liable for an act or omission that injured his child if the parent acted as a reasonable and prudent parent in the situation would.

III. Application to the Present Case

In this case, the trier of fact may find that the mother, Laura Broadbent, did not act as a reasonable and prudent parent would have in this situation. The finder of fact must determine whether leaving a two-

and-a-half year old child unattended next to a swimming pool is reasonable or prudent.   .   .   .

The paradox of parental immunity can be seen if we assume that a neighbor child from across the street was a guest and was injured at the same time and under the same circumstances as Christopher. Should the neighbor child be permitted to sue and recover damages from Laura but Christopher be denied the same opportunity?

A parent may avoid liability because there is no negligence, but not merely because of the status as parent. Children are certainly accident prone, and oftentimes those accidents are not due to the negligence of any party. The same rules of summary judgment apply to these cases as to others, and trial courts should feel free to dismiss frivolous cases on the ground that the parent has acted as a reasonable and prudent parent in a similar situation would. [   ]

[The court vacated the decision below and remanded to the trial court for further proceedings.]

MOELLER, V.C.J., and ZLAKET and MARTONE, JJ., concur.

FELDMAN, CHIEF JUSTICE, specially concurring.

I join in the abrogation of parental immunity and the court's adoption of the reasonable and prudent parent test but write separately to sound a note of caution. Although we abolish a rule of tort immunity, we must bear in mind that "difficult problems" remain in "determining when a physical harm should be regarded as actionable." Restatement (Second) of Torts § 895G cmt. *k*. If the alleged tortious conduct does not grow out of the family relationship, the question of negligence "may be determined as if the parties were not related." [   ] However, there are areas of broad discretion in which only parents have authority to make decisions. In these areas, I agree with the Restatement's view that "the standard of a reasonable prudent parent .   .   . recognize[s] the existence of that discretion and thus .   .   . require[s] that the [parent's] conduct be palpably unreasonable in order to impose liability." .   .   .

[Here the opinion distinguishes between enrolling "a two-year-old child in swimming lessons at a neighborhood pool"—where the standard would be "palpably unreasonable"—and "leaving an unsupervised two-year-old child, who was unable to swim, at the side of a swimming pool."]

Notes and Questions

1. Evaluate the five reasons the court offers for the immunity. The majority asserts that "virtually everything a parent does in relation to his child involves 'care, custody and control.'" Is that correct? What about automobile driving?

2. How does the concurrer disagree with the majority? How different is the standard of "palpably unreasonable" from the majority's standard of a "reasonably prudent parent in a similar situation"?

3. The implications of the New York view, affording protection to parents charged with negligent supervision, were spelled out in Zikely v. Zikely, 470 N.Y.S.2d 33 (App.Div. 1983) aff'd on the opinion below, 467 N.E.2d 892 (N.Y.1984). The "infant plaintiff was injured when the defendant parent turned on a hot water faucet in a tub to prepare a bath and then left the room. The child, left unsupervised, wandered into the bathroom and fell into or otherwise entered the tub, suffering severe burns." The majority understood *Holodook* to protect parents who created dangers as well as those who failed to protect children against dangers:

> [T]o at least some degree the parents in *Holodook* took some affirmative action in creating a danger. Bringing a young child to a neighbor and letting the child loose in a yard where an eight-year old is playing with a power mower or bringing a child to a playground containing an 11-foot-high slide involves some affirmative behavior on the part of the parent in creating a danger that the child, if left unsupervised, will suffer injury. [To read *Holodook* to allow suits in such cases would mean that] [e]very time a parent plugged in an iron, started a toaster, or boiled a pot of water on the stove, he would be subjected to potential liability if an unsupervised child came in contact with these common, daily household hazards in a manner which resulted in injury. To accept such a position would be to strip *Holodook* of a significant part of its meaning.

Does the New York view justify protecting a mother who crossed a busy street against a red light while carrying plaintiff child in her arms? See Kronengold v. Kronengold, 598 N.Y.S.2d 698 (App.Div. 1993) (barring suit). How would the facts of *Broadbent* be analyzed in New York? Is the court correct to reject the New York view that in this type of case "the search for a standard would necessarily be in vain"?

4. As the court notes, California, in *Gibson*, rejected the Wisconsin view:

> [W]e reject the implication of *Goller* that within certain aspects of the parent-child relationship, the parent has carte blanche to act negligently toward his child. . . . In short, although a parent has the prerogative and the duty to exercise authority over his minor child, this prerogative must be exercised within reasonable limits. The standard to be applied is the traditional one of reasonableness, but viewed in the light of the parental role. Thus, we think the proper test of a parent's conduct is this: what would an ordinarily reasonable and prudent *parent* have done in similar circumstances?

Does that approach permit taking into account the various kinds of diversity that the New York court deems necessary?

5. Was the limitation of parental liability justifiable at the time it was developed at the end of the nineteenth century? If so, what has changed? Would it be defensible to impose a duty of care and eliminate the immunity only in automobile accident cases? Is it indefensible to allow a child's friends to sue the child's mother for negligent driving but bar the child from such a suit?

If some immunity is sound, should it extend to siblings? Foster parents? The latter is the subject of a spirited debate in *Commercial Bank v. Augsburger*, 680 N.E.2d 822 (Ill.App.1997).

6. Many of these issues arise in a third party context—in which the child (through a guardian) has sued a third person, who seeks contribution from a careless parent. What new issues are raised by adding the third party? In *La Torre v. Genesee Management, Inc.*, 687 N.E.2d 1284 (N.Y. 1997), plaintiff, a 20-year-old developmentally disabled man, was left by his mother at an amusement center in a shopping mall while she went shopping. He got into an altercation with another person. Security guards physically subdued and handcuffed him. When he sued the mall over the episode, the mall filed a third party action against the mother. The court rejected the third party action. Since the plaintiff could not have sued his mother directly because of *Holodook*, that result should not be permitted indirectly. *Holodook*'s concerns of burdensome liability and family stress applied here. Moreover "the fear of ultimate boomerang liability might well present parents with the conflicted choice of seeking legal redress on their child's behalf or anticipatorily avoiding having to defend their own caretaking conduct and actions in courts."

Very few states dissent from this position. For a case that permits contribution even though a direct action against the parent would not lie, see *Bishop v. Nielsen*, 632 P.2d 864 (Utah 1981). The court viewed "the equities in favor of contribution as far outweighing the benefits to be achieved by a strict application of the doctrine [of family immunity]." Given parental immunity, what are the merits of the *Bishop* approach to contribution? We explore contribution further in Chapters V and VI.

7. *Harm to the fetus.* In *Bonte v. Bonte*, 616 A.2d 464 (N.H.1992), a child born alive was allowed to sue her mother for "catastrophic" injuries sustained when her mother failed "to use reasonable care in crossing the street and fail[ed] to use a designated crosswalk." The court, 3–2, held that since a fetus born alive could sue a third party for harm sustained before birth, and since the court had abolished parental immunity, "it follows" that this action should lie. The majority rejected the notion that fetal injury warranted different treatment from claims brought by a child already born. One of the three justices, urging case-by-case development in this area, concluded that the negligence alleged here was actionable "because a breach of the duty owed to [the] fetus could foreseeably cause serious harm to an unborn child." (The majority noted in passing that the defendant mother was "represented by counsel provided by her insurance company," but made nothing of that fact in its decision.)

The dissenters thought that the majority had "failed to fully appreciate the extent of the intrusion into the privacy and physical autonomy rights of women." They drew a sharp distinction between a child suing third persons for what happened in the womb and suing the mother. "Third parties . . . are able to continue to act much as they did before the cause of action was recognized." But extending this duty to a pregnant woman "could govern such details of a woman's life as her diet, sleep, exercise, sexual activity, work and living environment, and, of course, nearly every aspect of her health care." The dissenters had "serious doubts" that it was possible to "subject a woman's judgment, action, and behavior as they related to the well-being of her fetus to a judicial determination of reasonableness in a manner that is consistent and free from arbitrary results."

Should a child be permitted to sue a parent for smoking-related harm suffered prior to birth? What about a suit for respiratory harm caused to a child by a smoking parent after birth?

8. Should parental duties be modified by religious beliefs? In Lundman v. McKown, 530 N.W.2d 807 (Minn.App.1995), cert. denied 516 U.S. 1099 (1996), an 11-year-old boy became ill and died after four days without medical attention. During that period, his condition was easily diagnosable and was treatable by doctors up to two hours before his death. When he first became ill, his mother and his stepfather, who were Christian Scientists, called a local church source and were referred to a practitioner who was "specially trained to provide spiritual treatment through prayer." The mother hired the practitioner to pray for the boy. As the illness worsened a Christian Science nurse was hired who tried to keep the boy clean and comfortable, read hymnals to him, and kept the practitioner informed of the boy's deteriorating condition.

A wrongful death judgment obtained by the boy's father was affirmed against the mother, stepfather, practitioner and nurse. The mother's duty was clear: a "custodial parent has a special relationship to a dependent and vulnerable child that gives rise to duty to protect the child from harm." The stepfather was held to have assumed a duty by his conduct in participating in the treatment. As to the standard of care, the court rejected any formulation that would "insulate Christian Scientists from tort liability in cases involving children." Then, adopting a standard that took account of " 'good-faith Christian Scientist' beliefs, rather than an unqualified 'reasonable person standard,' " the court held that "reasonable Christian Science care is circumscribed by an obligation to take the state's (and child's) side in the tension between the child's welfare and the parents' freedom to rely on spiritual care." A parent's religious belief "must yield when—judged by accepted medical practice—it jeopardizes the life of a child." Was it correct to adopt a mixed standard? Does the mixed standard offer any special protection for exercise of religious beliefs?

The nurse and the practitioner argued that the mother had retained them only to provide services consistent with the mother's religious preferences—that the mother controlled the treatment. The court disagreed: this was "an instance where Christian Science professionals should have been aware of the requirement that they yield to the law of the community." They had a "responsibility on these facts to acknowledge that Christian Science care was not succeeding and to persuade the mother to call in providers of conventional medicine or, persuasion failing, to override her and personally call for either a doctor or the authorities."

9. *The impact of insurance. Broadbent* appears influenced by the institution of insurance. (An umbrella policy protects the insured for sums greater than those afforded by other more common insurance coverages, such as automobile liability or homeowner's liability insurance. We discuss insurance further in Chapter X.) Yet, the court asserts that it "would not be a viable rule to say that liability only exists where insurance exists." Why not? See Ard v. Ard, 414 So.2d 1066 (Fla.1982), allowing intrafamily suits up to the limit of any insurance coverage. (Of course, this may be so attractive to the family that it creates concerns about collusion that must be addressed.)

A few states have preserved total immunity in the face of insurance. See the discussion in Renko v. McLean, 697 A.2d 468 (Md.1997), an automobile accident case in which the court unanimously rejected any liability. The court noted that it had permitted some exceptions, such as a suit against a father's business partner for the negligence of the partnership, and one where "within the span of one week, the father both murdered the child's mother and committed suicide in the child's presence." But an exception for automobile accidents "would effectively negate the rule and open courthouse doors to every conceivable dispute between parent and child."

The court saw several "infirmities" in the limited abrogation, including the concern that insurers were placed in the "unenviable position of attempting to defend a suit that its insured has every incentive to lose." Moreover, the court was concerned that "a jury's generosity is proportionate to the amount of available insurance." Maryland and most states bar telling the jury that insurance is involved in a case. Is this type of case more likely to lead to jury speculation about insurance than the typical auto accident? Finally, the court was concerned about judgments that exceeded the available liability insurance. In such a case the feared intrafamily rancor would reappear. If the court were to try to limit the child's recovery to the amount of available insurance, "the argument that his or her recovery should be no different than that of any person negligently injured once again takes center stage." Further, "many families carry medical insurance that would necessarily compensate the injured child, and therefore, his or her family, for injury-related expenses." How might *Broadbent* answer each of these concerns?

When states have permitted intrafamily suits for auto accidents or other types of harm, insurers have frequently responded by excluding that coverage from the policy. See, e.g., Principal Casualty Ins. Co. v. Blair, 500 N.W.2d 67 (Iowa 1993) (upholding exclusion of coverage of suit for father's negligence in assembling a bicycle where policy explicitly excluded coverage of any claim brought by one member of the family against another).

Some courts permit insurers to exclude coverage of intrafamily claims in non-auto suits but refuse to allow it in auto suits especially where such insurance is compulsory or strongly encouraged. See the discussion in Horesh v. State Farm Fire & Cas. Co., 625 A.2d 541 (App.Div.1993) and the three-way split in National County Mut. Fire Ins. Co. v. Johnson, 879

S.W.2d 1 (Tex.1993). See also Black v. Allstate Insurance Co., 711 N.Y.S.2d 15 (App.Div. 2000) (discussing a statute that bars liability insurance coverage of negligence actions between spouses unless such coverage is expressly written into the policy—and urging the legislature to reconsider the matter). We return to insurance in more detail in Chapter X.

F. GOVERNMENTAL ENTITIES

The doctrine of sovereign immunity, based on the precept that "the King can do no wrong," was a part of the English common law heritage. Despite the absence of a monarch in this country, governmental immunity to tort liability was imported and became firmly established here. Shortly after the turn of the century, in Kawananakoa v. Polyblank, 205 U.S. 349 (1907), Justice Holmes summed up the received wisdom in his characteristically concise fashion: "A sovereign is exempt from suit, not because of any formal conception or obsolete theory, but on the logical and practical ground that there can be no legal right as against the authority that makes the law on which the right depends." See generally, Prosser & Keeton on Torts, § 131 (5th ed. 1984).

If the Holmes position sounds suspiciously conclusory, so too did the public policy rationale stating that tax funds ought not to be diverted from the public purposes for which they were collected.† Nonetheless, the protective embrace of governmental immunity to suit encompassed federal, state and municipal entities until the end of World War II.*

In the two succeeding decades, judicial abrogation and legislative refinement went hand-in-hand in reversing the earlier state of affairs: immunity became the exception rather than the rule.

The abrogation of blanket immunity, however, did not lead to uniform treatment of public and private acts causing unintentional harm. This section explores the ramifications of governmental liability from a duty perspective, because duty limitations have in fact been the principal tech-

---

† For hundreds of years courts protected charities by giving them immunity from liability for the negligent actions of their employees. This limit on respondeat superior was justified on the ground that benefactors gave money to these organizations to further their charitable work and not to be given to those harmed by the work. This protection has virtually disappeared at common law. See, e.g., Albritton v. Neighborhood Centers Ass'n for Child Development, 466 N.E.2d 867 (Ohio 1984). In some states legislative limits have been placed on the amount for which a charity might be held liable and some states condition liability on whether the charity carries liability insurance to cover the risk. See, e.g., Schultz v. Roman Catholic Archdiocese of Newark, 472 A.2d 531 (N.J.1984).

* Not without scholarly criticism, however. In the 1920s, Professor Edwin Borchard wrote a series of articles vigorously attacking governmental immunity. See Borchard, Governmental Liability in Tort, 34 Yale L.J. 1, 129, 229 (1924); 36 Yale L.J. 1, 757, 1029 (1926); and Governmental Responsibility in Tort, 28 Colum.L.Rev. 577, 734 (1928).

Another classic article from this period, attacking the feasibility of distinguishing between "governmental" and "proprietary" functions—a distinction under which municipal entities were held responsible when engaged in activities that had a private ("proprietary") counterpart—is Fuller & Casner, Municipal Tort Liability in Operation, 54 Harv.L.Rev. 437 (1941).

nique for continued recognition of the special character of certain public functions.

1.   MUNICIPAL AND STATE LIABILITY

Riss v. City of New York

Court of Appeals of New York, 1968.
22 N.Y.2d 579, 240 N.E.2d 860, 293 N.Y.S.2d 897.

[The facts are taken from the dissenting opinion. Linda Riss was terrorized for six months by one Pugach who had formerly dated her. He warned that if he could not have her, "no one else will have you, and when I get through with you, no one else will want you." She sought police protection unsuccessfully. She then became engaged to another man and at a celebration party she received a call saying that this was her last chance. She again sought police help but was refused. The next day a thug hired by Pugach threw lye in plaintiff's face, leaving her permanently scarred, blind in one eye, and with little vision in the other.]

BREITEL, J. This appeal presents, in a very sympathetic framework, the issue of the liability of a municipality for failure to provide special protection to a member of the public who was repeatedly threatened with personal harm and eventually suffered dire personal injuries for lack of such protection. The facts are amply described in the dissenting opinion and no useful purpose would be served by repetition. The issue arises upon the affirmance by a divided Appellate Division of a dismissal of the complaint, after both sides had rested but before submission to the jury.

It is necessary immediately to distinguish those liabilities attendant upon governmental activities which have displaced or supplemented traditionally private enterprises, such as are involved in the operation of rapid transit systems, hospitals, and places of public assembly. Once sovereign immunity was abolished by statute the extension of liability on ordinary principles of tort law logically followed. To be equally distinguished are certain activities of government which provide services and facilities for the use of the public, such as highways, public buildings and the like, in the performance of which the municipality or the State may be liable under ordinary principles of tort law. The ground for liability is the provision of the services or facilities for the direct use by members of the public.

In contrast, this case involves the provision of a governmental service to protect the public generally from external hazards and particularly to control the activities of criminal wrongdoers. [   ] The amount of protection that may be provided is limited by the resources of the community and by a considered legislative-executive decision as to how those resources may be deployed. For the courts to proclaim a new and general duty of protection in the law of tort, even to those who may be the particular seekers of protection based on specific hazards, could and would inevitably determine how the limited police resources of the community should be allocated and without predictable limits. This is quite different from the predictable allocation of resources and liabilities when public hospitals, rapid transit systems, or even highways are provided.

Before such extension of responsibilities should be dictated by the indirect imposition of tort liabilities, there should be a legislative determination that that should be the scope of public responsibility [   ].

It is notable that the removal of sovereign immunity for tort liability was accomplished after legislative enactment and not by any judicial arrogation of power (Court of Claims Act, § 8). It is equally notable that for many years, since as far back as 1909 in this State, there was by statute municipal liability for losses sustained as a result of riot (General Municipal Law, § 71). Yet even this class of liability has for some years been suspended by legislative action [   ], a factor of considerable significance.

When one considers the greatly increased amount of crime committed throughout the cities, but especially in certain portions of them, with a repetitive and predictable pattern, it is easy to see the consequences of fixing municipal liability upon a showing of probable need for and request for protection. To be sure these are grave problems at the present time, exciting high priority activity on the part of the national, State and local governments, to which the answers are neither simple, known, or presently within reasonable controls. To foist a presumed cure for these problems by judicial innovation of a new kind of liability in tort would be foolhardy indeed and an assumption of judicial wisdom and power not possessed by the courts.

Nor is the analysis progressed by the analogy to compensation for losses sustained. It is instructive that the Crime Victims Compensation and "Good Samaritan" statutes, compensating limited classes of victims of crime, were enacted only after the most careful study of conditions and the impact of such a scheme upon governmental operations and the public fisc [   ]. And then the limitations were particular and narrow.

For all of these reasons, there is no warrant in judicial tradition or in the proper allocation of the powers of government for the courts, in the absence of legislation, to carve out an area of tort liability for police protection to members of the public. Quite distinguishable, of course, is the situation where the police authorities undertake responsibilities to particular members of the public and expose them, without adequate protection, to the risks which then materialize into actual losses (Schuster v. City of New York, 5 N.Y.2d 75 [1958]).

Accordingly, the order of the Appellate Division affirming the judgment of dismissal should be affirmed.

KEATING, J. (dissenting).   .   .   .

.   .   .

It is not a distortion to summarize the essence of the city's case here in the following language: "Because we owe a duty to everybody, we owe it to nobody." Were it not for the fact that this position has been hallowed by much ancient and revered precedent, we would surely dismiss it as preposterous. To say that there is no duty is, of course, to start with the conclusion. The question is whether or not there should be liability for the negligent failure to provide adequate police protection.

. . .

The fear of financial disaster is a myth. The same argument was made a generation ago in opposition to proposals that the State waive its defense of "sovereign immunity." The prophecy proved false then, and it would now. The supposed astronomical financial burden does not and would not exist. No municipality has gone bankrupt because it has had to respond in damages when a policeman causes injury through carelessly driving a police car or in the thousands of other situations where, by judicial fiat or legislative enactment, the State and its subdivisions have been held liable for the tortious conduct of their employees. . . . [Judge Keating then observed that less than two-tenths of 1% of the city's annual budget was being allocated to payment of tort claims.] That Linda Riss should be asked to bear the loss, which should properly fall on the city if we assume, as we must, in the present posture of the case, that her injuries resulted from the city's failure to provide sufficient police to protect Linda is contrary to the most elementary notions of justice.

The statement in the majority opinion that there are no predictable limits to the potential liability for failure to provide adequate police protection as compared to other areas of municipal liability is, of course, untenable. When immunity in other areas of governmental activity was removed, the same lack of predictable limits existed. Yet, disaster did not ensue.

Another variation of the "crushing burden" argument is the contention that, every time a crime is committed, the city will be sued and the claim will be made that it resulted from inadequate police protection. . . . The argument is . . . made as if there were no such legal principles as fault, proximate cause or foreseeability, all of which operate to keep liability within reasonable bounds. No one is contending that the police must be at the scene of every potential crime or must provide a personal bodyguard to every person who walks into a police station and claims to have been threatened. They need only act as a reasonable man would under the circumstances. At first there would be a duty to inquire. If the inquiry indicates nothing to substantiate the alleged threat, the matter may be put aside and other matters attended to. If, however, the claims prove to have some basis, appropriate steps would be necessary.

. . .

More significant, however, is the fundamental flaw in the reasoning behind the argument alleging judicial interference. It is a complete over-simplification of the problem of municipal tort liability. What it ignores is the fact that indirectly courts are reviewing administrative practices in almost every tort case against the State or a municipality, including even decisions of the Police Commissioner. Every time a municipal hospital is held liable for malpractice resulting from inadequate record-keeping, the courts are in effect making a determination that the municipality should have hired or assigned more clerical help or more competent help to medical records or should have done something to improve its record-keeping procedures so that the particular injury would not have occurred. Every time a municipality is held liable for a defective sidewalk, it is as if the courts are saying that more money and resources should have been allocated to sidewalk repair, instead of to other public services.

. . .

The truth of the matter, however, is that the courts are not making policy decisions for public officials. In all these municipal negligence cases, the courts are doing two things. First, they apply the principles of vicarious liability to the operations of government. Courts would not insulate the city from liability for the ordinary negligence of members of the highway department. There is no basis for treating the members of the police department differently.

Second, and most important, to the extent that the injury results from the failure to allocate sufficient funds and resources to meet a minimum standard of public administration, public officials are presented with two alternatives: either improve public administration or accept the cost of compensating injured persons. Thus, if we were to hold the city liable here for the negligence of the police, courts would no more be interfering with the operations of the police department than they "meddle" in the affairs of the highway department when they hold the municipality liable for personal injuries resulting from defective sidewalks, or a private employer for the negligence of his employees. In other words, all the courts do in these municipal negligence cases is require officials to weigh the consequences of their decisions. If Linda Riss' injury resulted from the failure of the city to pay sufficient salaries to attract qualified and sufficient personnel, the full cost of that choice should become acknowledged in the same way as it has in other areas of municipal tort liability. Perhaps officials will find it less costly to choose the alternative of paying damages than changing their existing practices. That may be well and good, but the price for the refusal to provide for an adequate police force should not be borne by Linda Riss and all the other innocent victims of such decisions.

. . .

No doubt in the future we shall have to draw limitations just as we have done in the area of private litigation, and no doubt some of these limitations will be unique to municipal liability because the problems will not have any counterpart in private tort law. But if the lines are to be drawn, let them be delineated on candid considerations of policy and fairness and not on the fictions or relics of the doctrine of "sovereign immunity." Before reaching such questions, however, we must resolve the fundamental issue raised here and recognize that, having undertaken to provide professional police and fire protection, municipalities cannot escape liability for damages caused by their failure to do even a minimally adequate job of it.

. . .

CHIEF JUDGE FULD and JUDGES BURKE, SCILEPPI, BERGAN and JASEN concur with JUDGE BREITEL; JUDGE KEATING dissents and votes to reverse in a separate opinion.

Notes and Questions

1. Safeguarding the personal security of the community is, of course, one of the traditional functions of government. *Riss* has been a pivotal case because it raises fundamental issues about police responsibility to the public at large. Consider the following cases that arguably pose more focused questions of government responsibility for personal security.

In the earlier case of *Schuster v. City of New York*, cited by Judge Breitel, Schuster provided information to the police that led to the capture of a noted criminal, Willie Sutton. Schuster recognized Sutton from an FBI flyer that had been posted in his father's store. Shortly after he supplied the information to the police his life was threatened, and three weeks later he was killed. The court, 4–3, sustained plaintiff's claim that the police were under a legal duty to respond reasonably to Schuster's request for protection. The court remarked:

> In a situation like the present, government is not merely passive; it is active in calling upon persons "in possession of any information regarding the whereabouts of" Sutton, quoting from the FBI flyer, to communicate such information in aid of law enforcement. Where that has happened, as here, or where the public authorities have made active use of a private citizen in some other capacity in the arrest or prosecution of a criminal, it would be a misuse of language to say that the law enforcement authorities are merely passive. They are active in calling upon the citizen for help, and in utilizing his help when it is rendered.

Is there a satisfying distinction between *Schuster* and *Riss*?

Consider Davidson v. City of Westminster, 649 P.2d 894 (Cal.1982), refusing to find the requisite relationship in a case in which police were keeping a laundromat under surveillance to catch a man who had attacked several women earlier in this and other nearby laundromats. He had escaped a trap the night before. This time, police saw someone they thought was the attacker enter and leave the laundromat several times. Then he returned and stabbed plaintiff. The police, who had hoped to be able to arrest the man after he did something criminal but before he hurt anyone, had not warned the plaintiff before the attack. The court refused to find a special relationship involving either defendant and plaintiff or defendant and attacker. Is the case more closely aligned to *Riss* or to *Schuster*?

2. Sorichetti v. City of New York, 482 N.E.2d 70 (N.Y.1985), involved a suit on behalf of a young child who was badly mutilated by her father while he was exercising his visitation rights. The father had a long history of violent and abusive behavior towards his ex-wife, the child's mother, which had led the Family Court to issue a series of protective orders (which, by statute, gave the police broad discretion to take Sorichetti into custody at the petition of his ex-wife). On the weekend in question when Sorichetti picked up his daughter he threatened to kill his wife, and as for the child, he shouted, "You see Dina; you better do the sign of the cross before this weekend is up." His ex-wife made repeated efforts to initiate police intervention to get the child, but the officers refused to take action on the basis of Sorichetti's verbal threats, and told her to go home. An hour after Sorichetti was to have returned the child on Sunday evening, he severely injured her in a drunken rage.

In imposing a duty based on the police inaction, the court distinguished *Riss* on the basis of the protective orders, Sorichetti's history of violent behavior, and the front-desk officer's assurance that at some point the police would take action. Is *Riss* distinguishable?

3. In Cuffy v. City of New York, 505 N.E.2d 937 (N.Y.1987), the court attempted to establish guidelines for its continuing line of police protection cases. On a number of occasions, the Cuffys sought police protection from their downstairs neighbors (and tenants) the Aitkins, with whom they had had a number of skirmishes. After Mr. Aitkins physically attacked Ms. Cuffy, Mr. Cuffy finally received assurance from the police that something would be done—possibly an arrest—"first thing in the morning." The next evening, when Ralston Cuffy, a son, came to visit, Aitkins attacked him with a baseball bat, and Ms. Aitkins slashed Ms. Cuffy and Cyril Cuffy, another son who lived at home, with a knife. In the interim, the police had done nothing, and the three Cuffys subsequently sued the city for their injuries.

The court stated the general rule to be no tort duty to provide police protection, but recognized an exception in cases of "special relationship"— the elements of which were stated to be: "1) an assumption by the municipality through promises or action, of an affirmative duty to act on behalf of the party who was injured; 2) knowledge on the part of the municipality's agents that inaction could lead to harm; 3) some form of direct contact between the municipality's agents and the injured party; and 4) that party's justifiable reliance on the municipality's undertaking."

Under these principles, Ralston Cuffy was denied recovery because he could establish neither direct contact nor reliance on the police promise— indeed he apparently didn't even know about the promise when he came to visit—and the other Cuffys were denied recovery because by the evening, when the harm occurred, they were no longer relying on a police promise to respond that morning.

Do the four "elements" seem a fair summary of the standards used in deciding the cases in this section? Are they sound? Do they seem to have been properly applied in *Cuffy*? In Mastroianni v. County of Suffolk, 691 N.E.2d 613 (N.Y.1997), a husband fatally stabbed his wife shortly after police officers, who had been called to investigate his presence at her residence and allegedly disorderly conduct in violation of a protective order, left without making an arrest although the husband was still there. The court held that under these circumstances the first two *Cuffy* elements were satisfied by the protective order itself, and that the latter two elements were satisfied by the officers' direct contact with the decedent and their promise to "do whatever they could" if she had any further problems with her husband.

Keep the elements in mind as you read on.

4. *Municipal transport.* The court followed *Riss* in Weiner v. Metropolitan Transportation Authority, 433 N.E.2d 124 (N.Y.1982), involving a subway assault as plaintiff was descending the stairway to train level in a station where no attendant or guard was present. The court ruled that a public transportation authority "owes no duty to protect a person on its premises from assault by a third person, absent facts establishing a special relationship between the authority and the person assaulted. That a nongovernmental common carrier would be liable under the same factual circumstances is not determinative of the authority's liability." The difference was that imposing a duty on the public authority would necessarily have an impact upon the utilization of the transit authority's resources. *Riss* made clear that "the allocation of police resources to protection from criminal wrongdoing is a legislative-executive decision for which there is no liability." Why is *Riss* more compelling than the analogy of the nongovernmental common carrier?

Weiner is distinguished in Crosland v. New York City Transit Authority, 498 N.E.2d 143 (N.Y.1986), in which a Transit Authority employee allegedly witnessed the attack on the plaintiff and failed to summon assistance even though he could have done so without personal risk. Compare Clinger v. New York City Transit Authority, 650 N.E.2d 855 (N.Y.1995), in which plaintiff was raped behind construction materials, including a large metal plate, in a city subway pedestrian tunnel. The court characterized plaintiff's claim as involving "a proprietary act (the location of the metal plate) [that] intersected with a governmental act (the failure either to close the tunnel or to properly police it), to create the conditions under which she was attacked." Summary judgment for defendant was proper because the act was "overwhelmingly governmental." Is this a logical extension of *Weiner*? *Riss*?

Compare Lopez v. Southern California Rapid Transit District, 710 P.2d 907 (Cal.1985), in which a bus driver for the public transit system failed to take any action to assist plaintiffs when a fight broke out on the bus. The court refused to distinguish between public and private carriers in the application of a statute requiring "the utmost care and diligence." Moreover, the court held that cases involving the police were inapposite because a "special relationship" existed here. Finally, the court swept aside resource allocation arguments, asserting that bus companies can adopt reasonable precautionary measures that involve minimal resource expenditures. Is bus safety different from subway safety?

5. *The 911 call.* As municipalities set up emergency phone numbers, the question of liability followed quickly. In De Long v. County of Erie, 457

N.E.2d 717 (N.Y.1983), a woman called 911 to report a burglar outside. The court treated a 911 operator's assurance that help was being sent "right away" as the assumption of a duty to respond with due care to the victim's call for help.

But both direct communication and reliance by the caller are needed to create the special relationship that New York requires for that duty. In Merced v. City of New York, 551 N.E.2d 589 (N.Y.1990), a 911 case in which the caller apparently was not the victim, the court held that the required relationship "cannot be established without proof that the injured party had direct contact with the municipality's agents and justifiably relied to his or her detriment on the municipality's assurances that it would act on that party's behalf."

In Kircher v. City of Jamestown, 543 N.E.2d 443 (N.Y.1989), witnesses who saw the victim being abducted, got the license number and tried to follow the car. They lost it in traffic but gave all the information to a police officer who promised to report it. He did not and the victim sued for the ensuing assault. The court, 5–2, concluded that no special relationship had been established because the victim had not been in direct communication with the police and had not relied on a promise that help was forthcoming.

6. *Other custodial relationships.* The police department undertook to provide school crossing guards whenever the regular crossing guard was ill. The child's mother took the child both ways across one busy street every day during the first two weeks of school. She noticed the guard, decided that further effort was unnecessary, and took a job. The first day she did not accompany the child the guard was absent and the police, though notified, did not guard the crossing. The child was run down crossing the street. In a suit against the city, the court held that the undertaking to provide a substitute guard was enough to impose a duty of care for the safety of children crossing that street. Florence v. Goldberg, 375 N.E.2d 763 (N.Y.1978). What if the parent had sent the child alone each day and had taken her job without knowing that there usually was a guard at the corner?

7. In Hoyem v. Manhattan Beach City School Dist., 585 P.2d 851 (Cal.1978), a ten-year-old student slipped away from school during the day and was run over by a motorcyclist four blocks from the school. The court, 4–3, reversed dismissal of the complaint and held that the defendant school district owed a duty of due care in supervising the plaintiff.

Justice Tobriner's opinion for the majority stressed that the alleged negligence occurred on the school premises even though the injury occurred elsewhere. The decision did not require "truant-proof" schools: "We require ordinary care, not fortresses; schools must be reasonably supervised, not truant-proof." The majority relied on Bryant v. United States, 565 F.2d 650 (10th Cir.1977), in which three boys slipped away from a New Mexico boarding school and later were trapped in a snowstorm. They suffered extreme frostbite and each student had to have both legs amputated. The court, applying state law, imposed a duty to use due care to supervise the students. Are the cases comparable?

The dissenters in *Hoyem* thought it odd that a truant had a lawsuit when a student who had attended all day and was run over after school did not. Using the array of California duty factors discussed in *Tarasoff*, p. 158, supra, two of the dissenters argued against a duty: "These 'considerations of policy' . . . include the fundamental function, purpose, and role of a school and its staff, the nature and probable degree of supervision required to prevent truancy, the physical variables of entrances and exits to school grounds, the financial costs of adequate supervision to prevent truancy, the relative moral culpability of pupil, parent and school administration, the historical experience of schools in the supervision of pupils, truant and nontruant, the expense of adequate insurance to cover the extension of liability herein, and other factors." They wanted to limit the district's liability to students injured on school property or in school-related activities off the premises.

8. Compare Pratt v. Robinson, 349 N.E.2d 849 (N.Y.1976), in which the seven-year-old plaintiff was run over by a truck while crossing a street after having been left off at the school bus stop about five blocks from her house—the closest designated stop. The accident occurred at a busy intersection three blocks from the stop. The complaint against the school district was dismissed, 4–3, on the grounds that the duty terminated when the child left the bus at a designated stop. The district did not have to run a door-to-door service.

Is the majority view in *Pratt* fundamentally at odds with *Hoyem,* or are the two cases distinguishable? The Court of Appeals distinguished *Pratt* in Ernest v. Red Creek Central School District, 717 N.E.2d 690 (N.Y.1999), involving the injury to a child released from school on foot before all the school buses had left—in express contravention of the school's own long-standing policy. According to the opinion, "although a school district's duty of care toward a student generally ends when it relinquishes custody of the student, the duty continues when the student is released into a potentially hazardous situation, particularly when the hazard is partly of the school district's own making." Unlike the situation in *Pratt*, the child in this case "was not released to a safe spot but to a foreseeably hazardous setting partly of the School District's making."

Do the school cases raise a distinctive issue because of concern about interfering with "the discretionary nature of the functions of planning and allocation of resources" in governmental activities? On this score, reconsider *Schuster* and *Riss*.

9. *Educational malpractice.* A graduate of a San Francisco public high school sued the school district for, among other things, its negligent failure to teach him to read above fifth-grade level. Peter W. v. San Francisco Unified School Dist., 131 Cal.Rptr. 854 (App. 1976). After noting that the district had no governmental immunity, the court stated that the problem was one of duty, but cases involving the duty of a school to exercise due care for the physical safety of the students did not control this situation:

> On occasions when the Supreme Court has opened or sanctioned new areas of tort liability, it has noted that the wrongs and injuries

involved were both comprehensible and assessable within the existing judicial framework. [ ] This is simply not true of wrongful conduct and injuries allegedly involved in educational malfeasance. Unlike the activity of the highway or the market place, classroom methodology affords no readily acceptable standards of care, or cause, or injury. The science of pedagogy itself is fraught with different and conflicting theories of how or what a child should be taught, and any layman might—and commonly does—have his own emphatic views on the subject. The "injury" claimed here is plaintiff's inability to read and write. Substantial professional authority attests that the achievement of literacy in the schools, or its failure, are influenced by a host of factors which affect the pupil subjectively, from outside the formal teaching process, and beyond the control of its ministers. They may be physical, neurological, emotional, cultural, environmental; they may be present but not perceived, recognized but not identified.

We find in this situation no conceivable "workability of a rule of care" against which defendants' alleged conduct may be measured, [ ], no reasonable "degree of certainty that . . . plaintiff suffered injury" within the meaning of the law of negligence (see Rest.2d Torts, § 281), and no such perceptible "connection between the defendant's conduct and the injury suffered," as alleged, which would establish a causal link between them within the same meaning. [ ]

These recognized policy considerations alone negate an actionable "duty of care" in persons and agencies who administer the academic phases of the public educational process. Others, which are even more important in practical terms, command the same result. Few of our institutions, if any, have aroused the controversies, or incurred the public dissatisfaction, which have attended the operation of the public schools during the last few decades. Rightly or wrongly, but widely, they are charged with outright failure in the achievement of their educational objectives; according to some critics, they bear responsibility for many of the social and moral problems of our society at large. Their public plight in these respects is attested in the daily media, in bitter governing board elections, in wholesale rejections of school bond proposals, and in survey upon survey. To hold them to an actionable "duty of care," in the discharge of their academic functions, would expose them to the tort claims—real or imagined—of disaffected students and parents in countless numbers. They are already beset by social and financial problems which have gone to major litigation, but for which no permanent solution has yet appeared. [ ] The ultimate consequences, in terms of public time and money, would burden them—and society—beyond calculation.

How might the damages be measured?

New York took a different path to the same result. In Donohue v. Copiague Union Free School District, 391 N.E.2d 1352 (N.Y.1979), the plaintiff alleged that although he attended the defendant's high school for four years and was graduated, he lacks the ability to comprehend written English sufficiently to enable him to complete applications for employment.

The court concluded that if other professionals are held to a duty to the public they serve, nothing precludes similar treatment of professional educators. Creating a standard for judging such performance did not pose an insurmountable problem. Even if proximate causation might be difficult to establish "it perhaps assumes too much to conclude that it could never be established." Damages were clear. Despite this, the court concluded that public policy dictated that courts not entertain such claims. To entertain an action for educational malpractice "would require the courts not merely to make judgments as to the validity of broad educational policies—a course we have unalteringly eschewed in the past—but, more importantly, to sit in review of the day-to-day implementation of these policies. Recognition in the courts of this cause of action would constitute blatant interference with the responsibility for the administration of the public school system lodged by Constitution and statute in school administrative agencies." The court noted that it was holding open the possibility of recourse in cases of "gross violations of defined public policy." Finally, the court noted that administrative procedures were available to any person aggrieved by any "official act or decision" of any school official or board.

Two judges concurred on the ground that the practical problems of administration are so great as to justify concluding that the complaint did not state a cognizable cause of action. The main point was the difficulty of showing causal relation because factors such as "the student's attitude, motivation, temperament, past experience and home environment may all play an essential and immeasurable role in learning."

In Hoffman v. Board of Education, 400 N.E.2d 317 (N.Y.1979), plaintiff alleged that at age five he was negligently determined by defendant's psychologist to be retarded because plaintiff had a serious speech defect. Although the psychologist was sufficiently unsure of his diagnosis to recommend that plaintiff be retested in two years, plaintiff spent 12 years in classes for the retarded before defendant recognized that he was not retarded.

A judgment of $500,000 was reversed, 4–3. The majority followed *Donohue*. The lower courts had distinguished *Donohue* on the ground that it had involved nonfeasance while *Hoffman* involved misfeasance. The court of appeals thought both cases involved negligent acts and omissions. The principle of judicial non-interference in school administration controlled in both cases. The court refused to substitute its judgment for that of the board as to the type of tests to be given and their frequency. "Such a decision would allow a court or jury to second-guess the determinations of each of plaintiff's teachers. To do so would open the door to an examination of the propriety of each of the procedures used in the education of every student in our school system." Again, recourse was available through the administrative process.

The dissenters found "discernible affirmative negligence on the part of the board of education in failing to carry out the recommendation for re-evaluation within a period of two years."

The Court adhered to *Donohue* and *Hoffman* in Torres v. Little Flower Children's Services, 474 N.E.2d 223 (N.Y.1984), involving a Spanish-speaking child whose inability to understand English was misdiagnosed as borderline retardation with educational consequences that allegedly left him functionally illiterate.

10. In Williams v. State, 664 P.2d 137 (Cal.1983), the plaintiff was injured when a piece of the brake drum from a passing truck was propelled through the window of the car in which she was riding. Defendant police officers came to the scene of the accident and investigated, but failed to identify other witnesses, injured parties, or the driver responsible for her injuries. Plaintiff claimed that the alleged negligence of the police deprived her of the opportunity to sue the party primarily responsible for her harm.

A majority of the court refused to recognize an affirmative duty on the part of the police to secure information or preserve evidence for civil litigation, remarking that:

> The officers did not create the peril in which plaintiff found herself; they took no affirmative action which contributed to, increased, or changed the risk which would have otherwise existed; there is no indication that they voluntarily assumed any responsibility to protect plaintiff's prospects for recovery by civil litigation; and there are no allegations of the requisite factors to a finding of special relationship, namely detrimental reliance by the plaintiff on the officers' conduct, statements made by them which induced a false sense of security and thereby worsened her position.

Do these circumstances adequately distinguish the case from the protective relationships discussed in the preceding notes?

Lauer v. City of New York

Court of Appeals of New York, 2000.
95 N.Y.2d 95, 733 N.E.2d 184, 711 N.Y.S.2d 112.

KAYE, CHIEF JUDGE.

On this appeal we revisit a familiar subject: whether a member of the public can recover damages against a municipality for its employee's negligence. Here we answer that question in the negative.

The Facts

Three-year-old Andrew Lauer died on August 7, 1993. That same day, Dr. Eddy Lilavois, a New York City Medical Examiner, performed an autopsy and prepared a report stating that the child's death was a homicide caused by "blunt injuries" to the neck and brain. Although the report indicated that the brain was being preserved for further examination, the following day a death certificate was issued stating that Andrew's death was a homicide. Based on the Medical Examiner's conclusion, the police began investigating what they thought was a homicide, focusing primarily on plaintiff, Andrew's father. Weeks later, on August 31, 1993, the Medical Examiner and a neuropathologist conducted a more detailed study of Andrew's brain. The report, prepared in October 1993, indicated that a ruptured brain aneurysm caused the child's death, thus contradicting the earlier conclusion. The Medical Examiner, however, failed to correct the autopsy report or death certificate, and failed to notify law enforcement authorities.

Meanwhile, the police department's investigation into Andrew's death continued. Some 17 months later, in March 1995, after a newspaper exposé the autopsy findings were revised, the police investigation ceased and an amended death certificate was prepared. As a result of this incident, the City Medical Examiner who had conducted the examination resigned.

[Plaintiff brought a number of claims against the City of New York all of which were dismissed by the trial court. On appeal, the Appellate Division affirmed the dismissals, except for the claim of negligent infliction of emotional distress, which it reinstated by a divided court. "Viability of that single remaining claim is the issue now before us on this appeal." It should be noted that only emotional distress, and not physical injury formed the basis for the plaintiff's claims, but the opinions in the case make no special mention of this fact—focusing instead on the municipal liability issue. We consider the topic of claims for emotional distress absent physical injury in detail in the next chapter.]

The Law as Applied to the Facts

Analysis begins with several undisputed propositions. Municipalities long ago surrendered common law tort immunity for the negligence of their employees. A distinction is drawn, however, between "discretionary" and "ministerial" governmental acts. A public employee's discretionary acts—meaning conduct involving the exercise of reasoned judgment—may not result in the municipality's liability even when the conduct is negligent. By contrast, ministerial acts—meaning conduct requiring adherence to a governing rule, with a compulsory result—may subject the municipal employer to liability for negligence [   ]. No one disputes that the Medical Examiner's misconduct here in failing to correct the record and deliver it to the authorities was ministerial.

There agreement ends. Plaintiff contends that the City should be liable for the Medical Examiner's "ministerial negligence," while defendant urges that the complaint be dismissed.

We do not agree with plaintiff that a ministerial breach by a governmental employee necessarily gives rise to municipal liability. Rather, a ministerial wrong "merely removes the issue of governmental immunity from a given case" [   ]. Ministerial negligence may not be immunized, but it is not necessarily tortious (See [   ]). There must still be a basis to hold the municipality liable for negligence (see, *Florence v. Goldberg,* [p. 233, supra] ["Absent the existence and breach of .   . . a duty, the abrogation of governmental immunity, in itself, affords little aid to a plaintiff seeking to cast a municipality in damages"]; see also, *De Long v. County of Erie*, [p. 232, supra] [liability for ministerial failure to process "911" call rested on County employee's affirmative assurances of assistance made to victim]; [ ]).

This brings us directly to an essential element of any negligence case: duty. Without a duty running directly to the injured person there can be no liability in damages, however careless the conduct or foreseeable the harm (see, *Pulka v. Edelman* p. 150, [supra]). . . . While the Legislature can create a duty by statute, in most cases duty is defined by the courts, as a matter of policy.

Fixing the orbit of duty may be a difficult task. Despite often sympathetic facts in a particular case before them, courts must be mindful of the precedential, and consequential, future effects of their rulings, and "limit the legal consequences of wrongs to a controllable degree" (*Tobin v. Grossman*, [p. 288, infra]; *Strauss v. Belle Realty Co.*, [p. 144, supra]). Time and again we have required "that the equation be balanced; that the damaged plaintiff be able to point the finger of responsibility at a defendant owing, not a general duty to society, but a specific duty to him" (*Johnson v. Jamaica Hosp.*, [p. 291, infra]; see also, *Palsgraf v. Long Is. R.R. Co.*, [p. 419, infra]).

This is especially so where an individual seeks recovery out of the public purse. To sustain liability against a municipality, the duty breached must be more than that owed the public generally (see, *Florence v. Goldberg*, [ ]; [ ]). Indeed, we have consistently refused to impose liability for a municipality in performing a public function absent "a duty to use due care for the benefit of particular persons or classes of persons" ([ ]). Here, because plaintiff cannot point to a duty owed to him by the Office of the Chief Medical Examiner, his negligence claim must fail.

Pointing to New York City Charter § 557, plaintiff argues that the Office of the Chief Medical Examiner owed him a duty to communicate accurate information to authorities pertaining to his son's death. Section 557 charges the Chief Medical Examiner with examining "bodies of persons dying from criminal violence" or other suspicious circumstances, keeping "full and complete records in such form as may be provided by law," and promptly delivering "to the appropriate district attorney copies of all records relating to every death as to which there is, in the judgment of the medical examiner in charge, any indication of criminality."

Violation of a statute resulting in injury gives rise to a tort action only if the intent of the statute is to protect an individual against an invasion of a property or personal interest [ ].

In [ ], for example, plaintiff sought to recover damages suffered as a result of a fire, relying on a City Charter provision requiring maintenance of a fire department. We concluded that liability could not be predicated on the Charter provision, which was not designed to protect the personal interest of any individual, but rather was "designed to secure the benefits of well ordered municipal government enjoyed by all as members of the community" [   ]. We explained that:

> An intention to impose upon the city the crushing burden of such an obligation should not be imputed to the Legislature in the absence of language clearly designed to have that effect.
>
>   .   .   .
>
> Such [City Charter] enactments do not import intention to protect the interests of any individual except as they secure to all members of the community the enjoyment of rights and privileges to which they are entitled only as members of the public. Neglect in the performance of such requirements creates no civil liability to individuals [   ].

New York City Charter § 557 similarly defines one of the municipality's governmental functions. It establishes the Office of the Chief Medical Examiner as part of the City's Department of Health, and requires performance of autopsies and preparation of reports for the benefit of the public at large. Significantly, the only individual to whom the Medical Examiner must by statute report is "the appropriate district attorney" (see, New York City Charter § 557[g]). Neither plaintiff, nor other members of the general public who may become criminal suspects upon the death of a person, are persons "for whose especial benefit the statute was enacted" (see, [   ]). Permitting recovery here would rewrite section 557, radically enlarging both the responsibility of the Office of the Chief Medical Examiner and the potential liability of the City.

Nor do we find any duty to plaintiff derived from a "special relationship" with him. [The court then recited the *Cuffy* factors, p. 231, supra.]

Those requirements are not met here. The Medical Examiner never undertook to act on plaintiff's behalf. He made no promises or assurances to plaintiff, and assumed no affirmative duty upon which plaintiff might have justifiably relied. Plaintiff alleges no personal contact with the Medical Examiner, and therefore also fails to satisfy the "direct contact" requirement of the test. There is, moreover, no indication that the Medical Examiner knew that plaintiff, or anyone else, had become a suspect in the case. Nor do Medical Examiners generally owe a "special duty" to potential homicide suspects. Their function in this context is not as a law enforcement agency but solely to impart objective information to the appropriate authorities for the benefit of the public at large [   ].

As we explained in De Angelis v. Lutheran Med. Ctr. [449 N.E.2d 406 (N.Y.1983)]:

> A line must be drawn between the competing policy considerations of providing a remedy to everyone who is injured and of extending exposure to tort liability almost without limit. It is always tempting, especially when symmetry and sympathy would so seem to be best served, to impose new duties, and, concomitantly, liabilities, regardless of the economic and social burden. But, absent legislative intervention, the fixing of the "orbit" of duty, as here, in the end is the responsibility of the courts.

Here, in order for plaintiff's claim for negligent infliction of emotional distress to be successful, we would have to impose a new duty on the Office of the Chief Medical Examiner, which for the future would run to members of the public who may become subjects of a criminal investigation into a death. This we refuse to do.

. . .

In the end, plaintiff's claim is not supported by existing law, and we cannot agree that the proposed enlargement of the orbit of duty, resting largely on the foreseeability of harm, is a sound one.

Accordingly, the order of the Appellate Division should be reversed, without costs, the complaint dismissed and the certified question answered in the negative.

SMITH, J., dissenting.

Because I believe that plaintiff Edward G. Lauer has adequately pleaded a prima facie case for negligent infliction of emotional distress, I dissent.

. . .

BELLACOSA, J., dissenting.

I agree with Judge Smith's lead dissenting opinion, and add this expression to augment my vote for affirmance of the Appellate Division order.

. . .

The ruling I propose is especially warranted when the public servant, who precipitated the investigation of plaintiff as the suspect in the wrongfully certified homicide of his three-year-old son, fails to remove or at least mitigate the risk and harm that enveloped the life of that one knowable person. Time, circumstance, and place make the Medical Examiner's matter-of-course intervention a reasonable and feasible obligation. The care would, in balanced and controllable theory, extend only to this plaintiff. Indeed, the theoretical, foreseeable class would be a relatively self-defined, small circle of potential suspects, in any event, ... Moreover, a mathematical process of elimination naturally reduces the operational reach of this rule, and would not result in some open-ended potential drain on the public purse.

Next, the juridical norm I proffer is particularly appropriate—arguably, at an *a fortiori* level—when the culpable employee unilaterally possesses the exclusive knowledge and singular power to right the wrong. He should be legally accountable for failing to act reasonably at the time when complete innocence became medically known and certain to him. It should not be overlooked that the public at large was never potentially a suspect in the infant's death; as it turned out and from the outset, only plaintiff was a beleaguered suspect from the moment the mistaken notice of a "homicide" by "blunt injuries to the neck and brain" was reported by the Medical Examiner to the District Attorney of Queens County. Death actually occurred from a natural cause—a ruptured aneurysm within the young-ster's brain.

This duty theorem should be as much the legal canon, as it is the humanistic intuition and moral duty of anyone with such official control over another human being—indeed, someone in a unique and proximate position to "rescue" the very person he spliced onto the investigatory slide. This corollary to standard tort duty propositions involving the general governmental responsibility to the public evolves as an inevitably narrowed obligation, directed toward the unmistakably sole identifiable object of the Medical Examiner's series of actions and subsequent inactions (see [   ]).

. . .

To immunize the kind of alleged misconduct described by the pleading of this case would reward government agents who hide the truth and sweep wrongdoings under a rug of tort impunity. In such instances, truly respon-sible public employees have little to no incentive to own up to wrongdoings, since their official information is usually their secret (especially so in this case), and aggrieved parties will be barred from even entering a courthouse, no less reaching a trial airing of the truth.

The danger to the public purse and public tort policy is not sufficient or proportionate enough to block any chance of accountability and redress here. The zone of the proposed duty, as paradigmed through this case for future guidance, would be prudently limited by the exceptional quality and quantum of factors in this hard, and yes sympathetic, case. The sympathy feature, I must emphasize, does not drive my analysis; nor should it, on the other hand, disqualify the plaintiff and his case from common law evolve-ment. . . .

. . .

Plaintiff has sought only a day in court that is now foreclosed, thus immunizing the government's alleged wrongdoing against a concededly innocent citizen.

Opinion by CHIEF JUDGE KAYE. JUDGES LEVINE, CIPARIK, WESLEY and ROSENBLATT concur. JUDGES BELLACOSA and SMITH dissent and vote to affirm in separate opinions in which each concurs.

Notes and Questions

1.   According to the majority, what is the connection between the duty and immunity analyses?

2.   How does the court distinguish between discretionary and ministe-rial functions? Why does the determination that the Medical Examiner's failure was ministerial not control the outcome of the case?

3.   What use does the majority make of the statute? Compare the discussion of the role of statutes with that in *Uhr*, p. 151, supra.

4.   How might the principle that one who injures another non-negli-gently has the duty to exercise reasonable care to prevent further harm apply to this case? Can it be used to argue effectively for a government duty in such situations?

5. Is the majority's fear of unlimited liability justifiable? How would it affect the criminal justice system if the court's judgment had been different? Is the Bellacosa dissent persuasive on these points?

6. Does *Crosland*, p. 232, supra, support a duty here? Both the majority and the dissents discuss the case in omitted portions of the opinion.

7. *"Public duty."* The "special relationship" requirement that the *Lauer* majority adopts from the *Cuffy* factors, see p. 231, supra, is not universally followed. See, e.g., Jean W. v. Commonwealth, 610 N.E.2d 305 (Mass.1993), in which a clerical error caused the defendant parole authority to mistakenly release a prisoner serving a life term, who subsequently raped the plaintiff. The defendant's motion to dismiss was rejected on the ground that the existing tort claims act was inconsistent with a broad "public duty" limitation on recovery. How would New York courts analyze this situation? The opinions in *Jean W.* cite a number of other jurisdictions that similarly reject a "public duty" limitation on recovery. (The Massachusetts act was soon amended to establish explicitly, among other governmental entity protections, police immunity for *Riss*-type claims).

8. *Official immunities.* What considerations, if any, adduced by the court apply specifically to the Medical Examiner? Traditionally, special immunities have been granted to judges and prosecutors. In Falls v. Superior Court, 49 Cal.Rptr.2d 908 (App. 1996), plaintiffs were parents of Eduardo Samaniego, a 14-year-old youth who witnessed the gang murder of his friend and gave evidence at the preliminary hearing. Although the gang had threatened another witness, a deputy district attorney told the witnesses that he had never heard of non-gang-member witnesses to a gang crime being injured or killed in retaliation for testifying. Before trial, however, the gang killed Samaniego. Plaintiffs brought a wrongful death claim against, among others, the prosecutors.

In its opinion, the court first stated that it would analyze duty as "only a threshold issue, beyond which remain the immunity barriers;" then distinguished judicial immunity from that of the police, analogizing prosecutorial immunity to the former rather than the latter. Explaining that judicial immunity was entrenched in the common law tradition, the court asserted that "[j]udicial immunity is absolute, not qualified;" therefore, even if the judge has acted maliciously or corruptly, or in excess of his jurisdiction, he will remain immune. The rationale is that the judge must be able to exercise his judgment "fully, freely and without favor," and must not be impeded by a plaintiff who would "call in question his official action in a suit for damages." According to the court, "when exercising judicial functions, a judge who has a duty, breaches that duty, and causes injury—however intentionally, maliciously, and corruptly—is immune from civil suit."

By contrast, police did not, at common law, have immunity from civil suit, but simply a "good-faith defense." Thus, the court acknowledged, citing *Davidson,* p. 230, supra, and other cases, that police may be liable if a special relationship can be established. It then contrasted the nature of prosecutorial immunity against police immunity. Citing Yaselli v. Goff, 275 U.S. 503 (1927) and Pearson v. Reed, 44 P.2d 592 (Cal.App.1935), the court explained that prosecutors, since performing a quasi-judicial function, have been held to enjoy absolute immunity in both federal and state contexts. This immunity shields a prosecutor only when he "acts within his official capacity," or, in other words, "when his conduct is an 'integral part of the judicial process' or 'intimately associated with the judicial phase of the criminal process.'" In this case, interviewing Samaniego and persuading him to testify was essential to the prosecutors' role—and, therefore, they were immune from civil suit.

How would the *Falls* court analyze *Lauer?*

Friedman v. State of New York

Court of Appeals of New York, 1986.
67 N.Y.2d 271, 493 N.E.2d 893, 502 N.Y.S.2d 669.

[Three personal injury actions involving crossover collisions were consolidated in this appeal. All were brought under the Court of Claims Act, which provides for court hearing without a jury. In *Friedman v. State of New York,* plaintiff's car was sideswiped on a viaduct causing her to swerve into the oncoming traffic where she was hit head-on. She claimed that the state was negligent in failing to construct a median barrier. The state Department of Transportation (DOT) had studied the question five years earlier and decided that a median barrier should be constructed. But at the time of the accident no action had been taken. Although the state attempted to justify its non-action by pointing to funding priorities and project revisions, it did not offer concrete evidence in support of its claims. The Appellate Division affirmed a judgment for plaintiff.

Both *Cataldo v. New York State Thruway Authority* and *Muller v. State of New York* involved accidents on the Tappan Zee bridge. Once again, the plaintiffs claimed negligence in failing to construct a median barrier that would have prevented the crossover accidents. In these cases, however, departmental studies between 1962 and 1972 had determined that the risks of rear-end collisions from "bounce-back" occurrences and stranded autos if a barrier were constructed exceeded the dangers of crossover collisions without a barrier. Cataldo's accident occurred shortly after the last of these studies. Her claim that the studies reached the wrong conclusion was rejected by the Appellate Division on the ground that the agency decision "was premised on a reasonable public safety plan." By the time Muller was injured, however, the department had changed its mind and decided to construct a barrier. More than three years had passed with no further action taken. Nonetheless, the Appellate Division held that the delay was not unreasonable and dismissed Muller's claim.]

ALEXANDER, J.

.   .   .

We now affirm the orders of the Appellate Division in *Friedman* and *Cataldo,* and reverse the order appealed from in *Muller.*

It has long been held that a municipality " 'owe[s] to the public the absolute duty of keeping its streets in a reasonably safe condition' " (Weiss v. Fote, 7 N.Y.2d 579, 584 [1960]). While this duty is nondelegable, it is measured by the courts with consideration given to the proper limits on intrusion into the municipality's planning and decision-making functions. Thus, in the field of traffic design engineering, the State is accorded a qualified immunity from liability arising out of a highway planning decision [   ]. In the seminal *Weiss* case, we recognized that "[t]o accept a jury's verdict as to the reasonableness and safety of a plan of governmental services and prefer it over the judgment of the governmental body which originally considered and passed on the matter would be to obstruct normal governmental operations and to place in inexpert hands what the Legislature has seen fit to entrust to experts" [   ]. The *Weiss* court examined a municipality's decision to design a traffic light with a four-second interval between changing signals, and concluded that there was no indication that "due care was not exercised in the preparation of the design or that no reasonable official could have adopted it" [   ]. We went on to note that "something more than a mere choice between conflicting opinions of experts is required before the State or one of its subdivisions may be charged with a failure to discharge its duty to plan highways for the safety of the traveling public" [   ].

Under this doctrine of qualified immunity, a governmental body may be held liable when its study of a traffic condition is plainly inadequate or there is no reasonable basis for its traffic plan (Alexander v. Eldred, 63 N.Y.2d 460, 466 [1984] [municipality's traffic engineer's mistaken belief that the city had no authority to place a stop sign on a private road]). Once the State is made aware of a dangerous traffic condition it must undertake reasonable study thereof with an eye toward alleviating the danger [   ]. Moreover, after the State implements a traffic plan it is "under a continuing duty to review its plan in the light of its actual operation" [   ].

Before analyzing the cases before us in light of these principles, it is pertinent to discuss the procedural posture in which they are presented. In *Friedman v. State of New York*, there is an affirmed finding of fact that the State breached its duty by its unreasonable delay in acting to remedy a known dangerous highway condition once the decision to do so had been made. This finding must be upheld if supported by evidence in the record [   ]. In both *Cataldo v. New York State Thruway Auth.* and *Muller v. State of New York*, however, the intermediate appellate courts reached the factual conclusion, contrary to the respective trial courts, that the duty to the claimants was not breached. Thus, the scope of our review is limited to determining whether the evidence of record in each of these cases more nearly comports with the trial court's findings or with those of the Appellate Division [   ].

In *Cataldo* and *Muller* it is clear that no liability can flow from the Authority's initial decision in 1962 not to construct median barriers on the tangent section of the bridge. This decision was consistent with the opinions that were expressed by experts in the Authority's employ and was a rational response to valid safety concerns. The claimants argue, however, that by failing to reevaluate the barrier issue between 1962 and 1972 the Authority breached its "continuing duty to review its plan in the light of its actual operation" (*Weiss v. Fote*, [ ]). They contend that this inactivity was inexcusable given the changes in the state of the art of highway design occurring during that time. While this position might have some force if urged with respect to an accident occurring during the 10-year period of inactivity, such is not the case at bar. Here, both accidents occurred after the Authority reviewed its plan in 1972 and again reached the conclusion that the public's safety would be better served by not installing median barriers.

Claimants argue, however, that the 1972 engineer's reports upon which the Authority's decision was made were the product of inadequate study of the issue [see *Alexander*]. The gravamen of this assertion is that the reports failed to consider the history of the west curve barrier since its installation in 1962 and attached inordinate importance to operational difficulties that would be incurred while downplaying safety concerns to an inappropriate degree.

Strong policy considerations underpin the qualified immunity doctrine set forth in *Weiss* (*supra*), and, in cases such as these where a governmental body has invoked the expertise of qualified employees, the *Weiss* directive should not be lightly discounted. Appellants would have us examine the criteria that were considered by the State's professional staff, emphasize factors allegedly overlooked, and, with the benefit of hindsight, rule that the studies were inadequate as a matter of law. We decline this invitation, for to do so, as the Appellate Division correctly concluded, "would constitute the type of judgment substitution that *Weiss v. Fote* (*supra*) prohibits" [ ].

Because the Authority's decisions prior to the *Cataldo* accident in 1973 not to install median barriers were based on reasonable public safety considerations the Appellate Division properly dismissed the claim in that case. The Authority fulfilled its duty under *Weiss* by studying the dangerous condition, determining that design changes were not advisable and later reaching the same conclusion upon reevaluation of its decision.

In *Friedman* and *Muller*, however, a further basis upon which the defendants may be held liable is tendered: that once a decision has been reached to go forward with a plan intended to remedy a dangerous condition, liability may result from a failure to effectuate the plan within a reasonable period of time. Although this precise question has not been specifically addressed by this court, several Appellate Division decisions have held that when the State is made aware of a dangerous highway condition and does not take action to remedy it, the State can be held liable for resulting injuries [ ]. This conclusion flows logically from the premise that the State has a nondelegable duty to maintain its roads in a reasonably safe condition [ ], and it applies even if the design in question complied with reasonable safety standards at the time of construction. Of course as we have said, when a municipality studies a dangerous condition and determines as part of a reasonable plan of governmental services that certain steps need not be taken, that decision may not form the basis of liability [ ]. When, however, as in *Friedman* and *Muller,* analysis of a hazardous condition by the municipality results in the formulation of a remedial plan, an unjustifiable delay in implementing the plan constitutes a breach of the municipality's duty to the public just as surely as if it had totally failed to study the known condition in the first instance.

In *Friedman,* there is evidence to support the affirmed finding that the State unreasonably delayed its remedial action. The State failed to demonstrate at trial either that the five-year delay between DOT's recognition of the hazardous condition on the viaduct and its project proposal and the Friedman accident was necessary in order to study and formulate a reasonable safety plan, that the delay was itself part of a considered plan of action taken on the advice of experts, or that the delay stemmed from a legitimate ordering of priorities with other projects based on the availability of funding [ ].

Similarly, in *Muller,* we conclude that the record evidence more nearly comports with the trial court's finding that the three-year delay between the Authority's decision in 1974 to construct median barriers and the Muller accident in 1977 was unreasonable. This is not to say that the study and resolution of issues surrounding the concurrent installation of a traffic control system and the optimum location of the barrier, the ostensible cause of the delay, was not warranted. Indeed, a reasonable delay justified by design considerations, as with one resulting from a legitimate claim of funding priorities, would not be actionable. Our review of the evidence, however, reveals that the period of consideration in this case was marked by only intermittent spurts of study and evaluation and long gaps of inactivity, wholly inconsistent with the project's designation in an Authority press release as one having a "high priority" for which "[n]o significant delay [wa]s expected."

.   .   .

We conclude, therefore, that the order of the Appellate Division in *Cataldo* should be affirmed, with costs. The order appealed from in *Muller* should be reversed, with costs, and the judgment of the Court of Claims reinstated. In *Friedman,* the order of the Appellate Division should be affirmed.   .   .   .

CHIEF JUDGE WACHTLER and JUDGES MEYER, SIMONS, KAYE, TITONE and HANCOCK, JR., concur.

Notes and Questions

1. The court quotes the leading case of *Weiss v. Fote* for the proposition that government liability turns on whether "due care was not exercised in the preparation of the design or that no reasonable official could have adopted it." How does this standard, or the court's more detailed discussion of governmental immunity, differ from the ordinary test of negligence applicable to private parties? In what sense does the state transportation agency have a "qualified immunity"?

2. Suppose the plaintiff's injury resulted from a large pothole in the road that was known to the highway department but which had been designated for repair six months later because of funding shortages. Does the nature of the risk bear on the legal obligation to repair?

3. Do these planning and maintenance cases raise different issues, so far as government immunity is concerned, from the police protection and custodial cases considered in conjunction with *Riss*?

4. The *Friedman* case consolidates two distinct types of claims. Should a court exercise a different degree of oversight when an agency has allegedly delayed action inordinately as opposed to a situation in which the agency has purportedly made the wrong decision?

5. Should it matter that municipal negligence cases are ordinarily tried to a jury? Consider the following passage from *Weiss v. Fote*:

> To accept a jury's verdict as to the reasonableness and safety of a plan of governmental services and prefer it over the judgment of the governmental body which originally considered and passed on the matter would be to obstruct normal governmental operations and to place in inexpert hands what the Legislature has seen fit to entrust to experts. Acceptance of this conclusion, far from effecting revival of the ancient shibboleth that "the king can do no wrong," serves only to give expression to the important and continuing need to preserve the pattern of distribution of governmental functions prescribed by constitution and statute.

Is the separation of powers argument of lesser force in cases such as *Friedman,* brought against the state and heard by a court of claims without the right to a jury?

6. In abrogating sovereign immunity, state legislatures have created statutory frameworks governing the terms on which the state may be sued. Often, the grant of jurisdiction preserves state immunity for "discretionary functions." Illustrative is Estate of Arrowwood v. State, 894 P.2d 642 (Alaska 1995), in which the claims were based on the state's failure to close a highway after receiving many reports of icy conditions that had made driving very dangerous—and that caused plaintiff to lose control of her vehicle leading to serious personal injuries and the death of her son. The court held that the state's decision to keep the highway open was "a planning-level decision which falls within the discretionary function exception [provided in the Alaska Tort Claims Act]." Keep the case in mind as you are reading the next section on the Federal Tort Claims Act.

7. Claims of agency impropriety are most commonly reviewed through direct appeal to the courts from an administrative decision, rather than after personal injury has occurred. The body of statutory and case law that has resulted from these supervisory and oversight functions is the subject of the law school course in Administrative Law.

2. THE FEDERAL TORT CLAIMS ACT

The federal government waived its general tort immunity in 1946 in the Federal Tort Claims Act, 28 U.S.C. §§ 1346(b), 2402, 2671 et seq. The most significant sections follow:

§ 1346(b). [T]he district courts . . . shall have exclusive jurisdiction of civil actions on claims against the United States, for money damages, accruing on and after January 1, 1945, for injury or loss of property, or personal injury or death caused by the negligent or wrongful act or omission of any employee of the Government·while acting within the scope of his office or employment, under circumstances where the United States, if a private person, would be liable to the claimant in accordance with the law of the place where the act or omission occurred.

§ 2402. Any action against the United States under section 1346 shall be tried by the court without a jury. . . .

§ 2674. The United States shall be liable, respecting the provisions of this title relating to tort claims, in the same manner and to the same extent as a private individual under like circumstances, but shall not be liable for interest prior to judgment or for punitive damages.

§ 2678. No attorney shall charge, demand, receive, or collect for services rendered, fees in excess of 25 per centum of any judgment rendered [under § 1346(b)]. . . .

§ 2679(b). The remedy against the United States . . . for injury or loss of property, or personal injury or death, arising or resulting from the negligent or wrongful act or omission of any employee of the Government while acting within the scope of his office or employment is exclusive of any other civil action or proceeding for money damages by reason of the same subject matter against the employee whose act or omission gave rise to the claim or against the estate of such employee. Any other civil action or proceeding for money damages arising out of or relating to the same subject matter against the employee or the employee's estate is precluded without regard to when the act or omission occurred.

§ 2680. The provisions of this chapter and section 1346(b) of this title shall not apply to–

(a) Any claim based upon an act or omission of an employee of the Government, exercising due care, in the execution of a statute or regulation, whether or not such statute or regulation be valid, or based upon the exercise or performance or the failure to exercise or perform a discretionary function or duty on the part of a federal agency or an employee of the Government, whether or not the discretion involved be abused.

(b) Any claim arising out of the loss, miscarriage, or negligent transmission of letters or postal matter.

. . . .

(h) [a list of exceptions for intentional torts, discussed at p. 944, infra].

(i) Any claim for damages caused by the fiscal operations of the Treasury or by the regulation of the monetary system.

(j) Any claim arising out of the combatant activities of the military or naval forces, or the Coast Guard, during time of war.

(k) Any claim arising in a foreign country.

What might justify each of the exceptions listed?

The exception for "discretionary functions" was read broadly in Dalehite v. United States, 346 U.S. 15 (1953), involving hundreds of cases that resulted from an explosion in the loading of a shipment of fertilizer. In denying liability, the Court drew a distinction between "planning decisions," which are policy oriented, and "operational decisions," which are of a nondiscretionary nature. Unfortunately, the distinction between the categories, as used in the cases, has often been less than clear. The following case discusses and applies the framework of analysis developed by the Supreme Court in later cases revisiting the discretionary functions exception.

Cope v. Scott

United States Court of Appeals, District of Columbia Circuit, 1995.
45 F.3d 445.

Before WALD, GINSBURG, and TATEL, CIRCUIT JUDGES.

TATEL, J.

In this negligence case, John R. Cope appeals a grant of summary judgment against him in favor of the government. The District Court concluded that the government's allegedly negligent actions were "discretionary functions" immune from suit under the Federal Tort Claims Act ("FTCA"). 28 U.S.C. §§ 1346(b), 2671–2680 (1988 & Supp. V 1993). With respect to Cope's allegations of negligent road maintenance, we affirm the District Court's decision. We find, however, that any discretion exercised by the government with respect to where and how to post signs warning of dangerous road conditions did not implicate "political, social, or economic" policy choices of the sort that Congress intended to protect from suits under the FTCA. We therefore affirm in part, reverse in part, and remand so that the case may proceed to trial on the allegations of improper warnings.

I

Beach Drive, a two-way, two-lane road, is the main north-south route through Rock Creek Park, an urban park in Washington, D.C. that is maintained by the National Park Service. The road was "originally designed for pleasure driving," [ ], as seems evident given what an engineering study described as its "poor alignment"—which we understand to refer to its many sharp curves. The Park Service alleges that the road is not "intended to provide fast and convenient transportation," but to "enhance visitor experience" in the park. [   ] Commuters in Washington appear to believe otherwise, however, and the Park Service has allowed Beach Drive to become an important commuter route connecting downtown Washington with its northern suburbs. As a result, the road carries heavy traffic throughout the day. National Park Service road standards recommend that a road like Beach Drive carry a maximum of 8,000 vehicles daily, but recent estimates indicate that the average daily traffic on the stretch of road involved in this case was between two and three times that load.

On a rainy spring evening in 1987, Cope was driving north along Beach Drive. As a southbound vehicle driven by Roland Scott rounded a curve, it slid into the northbound lane and hit Cope's car. Cope alleges he suffered neck and back injuries. The Park Service officer who responded to the scene classified the pavement in his accident report as a "worn polished surface" that was "slick when wet." [   ] Cope sued Scott and the Park Service, alleging that the latter was negligent "in failing to appropriately and adequately maintain the roadway of Beach Drive . . . and failing to place and maintain appropriate and adequate warning signs along the roadway." [   ]

While preparing for trial, Cope discovered an engineering study of roads in Rock Creek Park that was conducted between 1986 and 1988. The study identified this stretch of Beach Drive as one of nine "high accident areas" in the park, and noted that sections of Beach Drive, including, apparently, the location of the accident, fell below "acceptable skid-resistance levels" in a test conducted five months after the accident. [   ] The study recommended that future repaving use "polish-resistant coarse aggregate" as an overlay in the most dangerous curves. [   ] As for the stretch of road in question here, the study noted that "[t]he curves should be adequately signed and the skid resistance maintained with an opened graded friction course." [   ] Cope also offers an affidavit from a traffic engineer to the effect that over 50% of the accidents that occurred on that stretch of road over the last five years occurred during wet weather, while only 18% of accidents nationwide occur in wet conditions.

Despite the less-than-perfect road surface, the 1988 study listed this stretch of Beach Drive as 33rd on a maintenance priority list of 80 sections of park road. [   ] Maintenance work on this section of road was preceded on the list by at least 15 other projects estimated to be of equal or less cost.

As for the presence of relevant warning signs, the record does not reflect precisely where such signs were located as of the date of the accident. A 1981 road sign inventory indicated that "slippery when wet" signs were located in two places on the half-mile stretch of road bracketing the curve where the accident occurred, and the Assistant Chief of Maintenance of the park stated that in 1990, a slippery road sign was posted in each direction on the same stretch of road, although there is no indication of how close such signs were to the curve where the accident occurred.

In the District Court, the government moved for summary judgment, arguing that its action (or inaction) with respect to the road was discretionary and therefore exempt from suit under the FTCA. [   ] The District Court agreed, ruling that it had no jurisdiction to hear the case. [   ] Cope settled with Scott and now appeals the District Court's immunity ruling.

II

.   .   .

[The "discretionary function" exception in § 2680(a)] lies at the heart of the dispute in this case. When an individual is injured by an act of the government or a government employee, section 1346(b) allows him or her to bring suit unless the action that allegedly caused the injuries is a discretionary function as defined under the FTCA. This exception was designed to prevent the courts from "second guessing," through decisions in tort actions, the way that government officials choose to balance economic, social, and political factors as they carry out their official duties. See United States v. Varig Airlines, 467 U.S. 797 (1984).

Discretionary function determinations are jurisdictional in nature. While we must review the complaint to determine what actions allegedly caused the injuries, we do so only to determine whether the district court has jurisdiction over those actions, not to prejudge the merits of the case. If the district court has jurisdiction over the suit, the plaintiff must still prove that the government's actions were negligent in order for him to prevail.

The Supreme Court has established a two-step test that we use to determine whether an action is exempt from suit under the discretionary function exemption. See United States v. Gaubert, 499 U.S. 315 (1991); Berkovitz v. United States, 486 U.S. 531 (1988). [The first step asks] whether any "federal statute, regulation, or policy specifically prescribes a course of action for an employee to follow." *Gaubert* (citing *Berkovitz*). If a specific directive exists, then the employee had no "choice." The only issue is whether the employee followed the directive, and is thus exempt under the first clause, or whether the employee did not follow the directive, thus opening the government to suit. See 28 U.S.C. § 2680(a). Because no choice is involved where a "specific prescription" exists, the discretionary function exception .   .   . is not applicable.

The discretionary function exception *may* be applicable where there is no specific prescription and the government employee has a "choice" regarding how to act in a particular circumstance. This is true more often than one might expect. Despite the pervasiveness of regulation, government policies will almost always leave some room for individual choice. If the choice led to the events being litigated, the exception may apply. But not all actions that require choice—actions that are, in one sense, "discretionary"—are protected as "discretionary functions" under the FTCA.

This brings us to the second step of the test, where the "basic inquiry" is whether the challenged discretionary acts of a government employee "are of the nature and quality that Congress intended to shield from tort liability." [*Varig*] Decisions that require choice are exempt from suit under the FTCA only if they are "susceptible to policy judgment" and involve an exercise of "political, social, [or] economic judgment." [*Gaubert*; *Varig*]; see [*Berkovitz*] (focusing the analysis on whether a decision is "based on considerations of public policy"). The Court recognized in *Gaubert*, for example, that daily decisions regarding the management of a troubled savings and loan "implicate[d] social, economic, or political policies," and were therefore exempt. [*Gaubert*] In contrast, the Court noted that a government employee may cause an automobile accident through the exercise of poor discretion, but that this type of "garden-variety" discretion is not protected. See id., [   ]. Only discretionary actions of greater significance—those grounded in "social, economic, or political goals"—fall within the protection of the statute. See [*Gaubert*].

Determining whether a decision is "essentially political, social, or economic," [   ], is admittedly difficult, since nearly every government action is, at least to some extent, subject to "policy analysis." See, e.g., [*Gaubert*] (Scalia, J., concurring) (noting that even the decisions of a government driver may implicate policy choices). "Budgetary constraints," for example, "underlie virtually all government activity." [   ]. At oral argument, counsel for the government asserted that these underlying fiscal constraints should therefore exempt "virtually all government activity." With the exception of discretion exercised by bad drivers, the government appears to argue that decisions that involve choice and the faintest hint of policy concerns are discretionary and subject to the exception. This approach, however, would not only eviscerate the second step of the analysis set out in *Berkovitz* and *Gaubert*, but it would allow the exception to swallow the FTCA's sweeping waiver of sovereign immunity. [   ]. It was thus not surprising that, when pressed at oral argument, government counsel was unable to provide, under its theory, even one example of a discretionary decision that would not be exempt for failure to implicate policy concerns.

The government reads the exception far too broadly. The question is not whether there is any discretion at all, but whether the discretion is "*grounded* in the policy of the regulatory regime." [*Gaubert*] (emphasis added). The mere association of a decision with regulatory concerns is not enough; exempt decisions are those "fraught with . . . public policy considerations." [   ]. The mere presence of choice—even if that choice involves whether money should be spent—does not trigger the exception.

Just as we reject the government's effort to expand the exception too far, we also reject Cope's efforts to restrict its application. Cope argues, first, that the government cannot claim the exemption unless it is able to demonstrate that there was an "actual, specific decision involving the balancing of competing policy considerations." [   ]. The Supreme Court has emphasized, however, that the issue is not the decision as such, but whether the "nature" of the decision implicates policy analysis. See [   ]. What matters is not what the decisionmaker was thinking, but whether the type of decision being challenged is grounded in social, economic, or political policy. See [*Gaubert*.] Evidence of the actual decision may be helpful in understanding whether the "nature" of the decision implicated policy judgments, but the applicability of the exemption does not turn on whether the challenged decision involved such judgments.

For the same reasons, we reject Cope's argument that the government's acts are not discretionary since they involve the "implementation" of government policy. [   ]. Cope draws this argument from Indian Towing v. United States, 350 U.S. 61 (1955), in which the Supreme Court allowed the plaintiffs to sue the government for negligent failure to maintain a lighthouse. Cope argues that *Indian Towing* means that the "implementation" or "execution" of policy decisions—particularly with respect to warning the public about hazards resulting from negligence—is never protected under the exception. Cope's argument, however, is merely an effort to establish yet another in a long series of "analytical frameworks" that the Supreme Court has rejected as an inappropriate means of addressing the discretionary function exemption. [   ]. The mechanistic application of these frameworks encourages courts to avoid the proper analysis: Whether the nature of the decision involved the exercise of policy judgment. *Gaubert* cautioned against this sort of shortcut when it rejected a lower court decision that relied upon a distinction between exempt "planning" decisions and non-exempt "operational" decisions. *See* [   ]; *see also* [*Indian Towing*] (rejecting, in a similar context, a "governmental"/"nongovernmental" distinction). Recognizing that the focus is on the nature of the decision, not on the semantic pigeonhole into which the action can be put, we decline to follow Cope's reading of the case law, focusing instead, as we are required, on whether the decision is "fraught with" economic, political, or social judgments. No matter the level at which the decision was made, the nature of the decision, or the impact it had on others, we have consistently held that the discretionary function exception applies "only where 'the question is not negligence but social wisdom, not due care but political practicability, not reasonableness but economic expediency.'" [   ]. Using this approach as our touchstone, we proceed to an analysis of this case.

III

Both because the District Court granted a motion for summary judgment, and because the question before us relates to a purely legal issue—the jurisdiction of the District Court—we review the decision below *de novo*. [   ]. As long as the District Court's legal conclusion was correct, its grant of summary judgment was appropriate, for we perceive in the record no genuine issues of fact material to the jurisdictional issue.

In his complaint, Cope makes two allegations regarding the conduct of the United States. He argues, first, that the government failed "to appropriately and adequately maintain the roadway of Beach Drive," and second, that the government failed "to place and maintain appropriate and adequate warning signs along the roadway." [   ]. We address each of his points in turn, again emphasizing that we do not decide the merits of the case, but only whether Cope is entitled to an opportunity to prove his case at trial.

With respect to his allegation regarding the state of the road surface, Cope points to a manual entitled "Park Road Standards," and, applying step one of the analysis, argues that it sets forth "specific prescriptions" regarding skid resistance and surface type. We do not read the manual to set forth such requirements. .   .   .

.   .   .

We turn, then, to the second step of the analysis, in which we ask whether the discretion exercised over the maintenance and reconstruction of Beach Drive is "subject to policy analysis" and thus discretionary in the sense of the FTCA. .   .   .

As we understand the record and the facts as presented by the parties, no regular maintenance would have prevented the road from deteriorating in the way Cope alleges. This case is therefore different from a case involving mundane decisions to fill or not fill potholes, or even the cumulative effect of such decisions. .   .   . The state of Beach Drive alleged by Cope could have been prevented only by reducing the traffic load, initially paving it with a different surface, resurfacing the curve entirely, or at least milling the curve to create grooves in the surface. [   ]. Determining the appropriate course of action would require balancing factors such as Beach Drive's overall purpose, the allocation of funds among significant project demands, the safety of drivers and other park visitors, and the inconvenience of repairs as compared to the risk of safety hazards. These balances are apparent throughout the 1988 study that placed maintenance on this section of Beach Drive in the middle of a priority list of work that needed to be done on eighty different sections of park roads. Park Service decisions regarding the management of Beach Drive are therefore much like the decisions exempted by the Supreme Court in *Varig* [involving the FAA's spot check system for determining the safety of airplanes]: "[S]uch decisions require the agency to establish priorities for the accomplishment of its policy objectives by balancing the objectives sought to be obtained against such practical considerations as staffing and funding." [   ] And, as in *Varig*, we decline to "second guess" those judgments here. [   ]

IV

We reach a different conclusion with respect to Cope's allegation that the government failed to post adequate warning signs about the nature of the road surface. His case rests on the argument that given the "very specific slippery road problem" on Beach Drive, a "permanently displayed static 'slippery when wet' road sign is inadequate to warn" of the hazard. [   ] Cope hints that the failure to post an adequate sign is nondiscretionary, but relies mostly on the second step argument that any discretion does not implicate policy concerns. The government argues that no specific prescriptions regarding the posting of signs exist, that the resulting discretion involves the exercise of "engineering and aesthetic factors" as well as economic considerations, and that the presence of those concerns in the decision making means that the decisions are exempt from suit under the FTCA.

The government admits that it "is the policy of the National Park Service to follow" the Manual on Uniform Traffic Control Devices when posting signs, but argues that the final decision depends on a variety of engineering and aesthetic considerations. [   ]. Our own review of this manual reveals that it is more of a guidebook for the installation of signs than a "specific prescription" relied on by the Park Service. As the manual points out, it is "not a substitute for engineering judgment," [   ], and warning signs should be posted only "when it is deemed necessary." [   ]. We conclude, then, that the posting of signs in Rock Creek Park involves the exercise of discretion.

In contrast to our decision regarding the road surface, however, we find that the discretion regarding where and what type of signs to post is not the kind of discretion protected by the discretionary function exception. While it may be true, as the government claims, that the placement of signs involves judgments because engineering and aesthetic concerns determine where they are placed, such judgments are not necessarily protected from suit; only if they are "fraught with public policy considerations" do they fall within the exception, and we do not think that is the case here. The "engineering judgment" the government relies on is no more a matter of policy than were the "objective scientific principles" that the *Berkovitz* court distinguished from exempt exercises of policy judgment. [   ].

With respect to the aesthetic considerations, while we acknowledge the Park Service's desire to maintain the park in as pristine a state as possible, the government has failed to demonstrate how such a desire affects the placement of traffic signs on Beach Drive. Indeed, the government's argument is difficult for us to accept in view of the fact that, including the "slippery when wet" signs, no less than "twenty-three traffic control, warning, and informational signs" already exist on the half-mile stretch of road bracketing the curve on which the accident occurred—a stretch of road that carries 20,000 vehicles daily. [   ]. We agree that in certain circumstances, decisions will be exempt under the FTCA because they involve difficult policy judgments balancing the preservation of the environment against the blight of excess signs. But this is not one of those circumstances. Beach Drive is not the Grand Canyon's Rim Drive, nor Shenandoah's Skyline Drive. Here, the Park Service has chosen to manage the road in a manner more amenable to commuting through nature than communing with it. Having done so, and having taken steps to warn users of dangers inherent in that use, the Park Service cannot argue that its failure to ensure that those steps are effective involves protected "discretionary" decisions.

. . .

. . . . Beach Drive is a commuter route through an urban park. The Park Service has already posted signs in an effort to alert drivers to safety hazards on the road. In light of these factors, the Park Service has understandably been unable to articulate how the placement of additional or different signs on Beach Drive implicates the type of economic, social, or political concerns that the discretionary function exception protects from suit under the FTCA.

We affirm the District Court's dismissal of Cope's claim regarding negligent maintenance of the road surface. We conclude, however, that the District Court had jurisdiction over the allegations that the Park Service failed adequately to warn of dangers on Beach Drive. To the extent the Court ruled to the contrary, we vacate its order and remand for further proceedings. Cope is entitled to try to persuade a factfinder that the government acted negligently by failing adequately to sign the curve on Beach Drive.

So ordered.

Notes and Questions

1. According to *Cope*, what differentiates situations involving "garden-variety" discretion (which does not implicate "social, economic, or political goals") from those covered by the discretionary function exception? At what point does "regular maintenance" become major roadwork? What if the park service had deliberately allowed the road to decay—by forgoing regular maintenance—to the point at which only a policy decision could renovate it?

2. Why does the court emphasize that there need not be—as Cope argued—an "actual, specific decision involving the balancing of competing policy considerations" for the discretionary function exception to apply? How would it analyze a case in which there was no evidence whatsoever that the action plaintiff argued should be taken had even been considered?

3. Why does the difference between policy decisions and their "implementation"—or between "planning" and "operational" decisions—not determine the outcome in this case? Does the *Cope* court replace these dichotomies with another? Are there any guidelines for case-by-case decisions about whether the exception applies?

4. What is the relationship between the analysis that the court calls "jurisdictional" and the negligence analysis?

5. One of the Park Service's arguments in *Cope* was that aesthetic considerations prevented it from posting warning signs on the stretch of road in question. In other cases, concern for preserving the environment, maintaining a site's historical quality, or ensuring the aesthetic pleasure of visitors has affected courts' determinations about whether particular decisions involve discretion grounded in policy. See Bowman v. United States, 820 F.2d 1393 (4th Cir.1987) and Zumwalt v. United States, 928 F.2d 951 (10th Cir.1991). The *Cope* court, however, held that the Park Service's mere allegation that a decision was based upon aesthetic discretion was not sufficient to avoid liability. What standard should be applied in this area?

In Cestonaro v. United States, 211 F.3d 749 (3d Cir. 2000), a widow brought a wrongful death action after she, her husband, and their daughter—on vacation in St. Croix, Virgin Islands—were accosted at gun point when returning to their car after dinner, and the husband was killed. The (unofficial) parking lot in which the incident occurred was located within the Christiansted National Historic Site, controlled by the National Park Service; it was ill lit and had been the site of prior crime. Plaintiff alleged that the National Park Service "was negligent in failing to provide adequate lighting and correct the known dangerous condition and to warn others about the existence of the dangerous condition."

The Park Service contended that "its decisions (or non-decisions) not to add lighting nor to post warning signs were grounded in its overarching objective of returning the area to its historic appearance," and adduced several documents to support its claim. The court responded, however, that the Park Service should either have entirely eliminated the parking lot (and its minimal lighting) or assumed the duty of providing a safe area. As the court stated, "The National Park Service fails to show how providing some lighting, but not more, is grounded in the policy objectives with respect to the management of the National Historic Site." Eliminating all indicia of parking might have been consistent with the objective of recreating the area's historic appearance, but this had not been done. Therefore, the court was "unable to find a rational nexus between the National Park Service's lighting or warning decisions (or non-decisions) and social, economic and political concerns." What if the Park Service had placed a few gas lamps—and proven that, although they did not provide as much light as would be present in a modern parking lot, they replicated those in a 19th-century parking area precisely?

Contrast the result in Shansky v. United States, 164 F.3d 688 (1st Cir.1999), in which plaintiff brought suit after she tripped over an antique wooden threshold and suffered serious injuries when departing from the Hubbell Trading Post, a national historic site in Ganado, Arizona. She alleged that a handrail and warning sign should have been present, and gave evidence that other safety measures had been taken. The court rejected the claim, holding that discretion had been involved, and that this discretion could be construed as policy-based. The opinion asserted that the "plausible nexus" linking the aesthetic concerns of the Park Service—which had gone to great lengths to restore the site to its historic appearance—with the lack of handrails and warning signs should be sufficient:

> Aesthetic considerations, including decisions to preserve the historical accuracy of national landmarks, constitute legitimate policy concerns. . . . At the very least, this means that the Park Service may balance aesthetic concerns with those of visitor safety in reaching planning decisions, and that safety concerns will not automatically eclipse all other policy considerations. [   ]. There is nothing anomalous about this sort of balancing. We live in a world of incommensurable, often conflicting, values. Some might prefer to sacrifice history to prevent even infinitesimal risks, whereas others might accept some hazards in order to preserve historical artifacts in a pristine state. It would be a much more convenient world if we had a single metric with

which to measure, and thereby prioritize, all values—but as long as that luxury eludes us, we must rely upon policymakers to reconcile the ensuing conflicts.

The court did acknowledge, however, that the outcome might have been different if the Park Service had placed handrails elsewhere in the area and simply omitted them in this section. Can *Cope* be reconciled with *Cestonaro*? With *Shansky*?

6. Does the discretionary function exception, as interpreted by the Court in *Cope*, express a different set of policy concerns from those just considered in municipal and state liability cases?

7. The range of cases testing the breadth of the discretionary function exception is suggested by Dykstra v. United States Bureau of Prisons, 140 F.3d 791 (8th Cir.1998) (prison counselor's decision not to explain that youthful-looking prisoner might be at risk in the general prison population and corrections officer's subsequent failure to transfer him to protective custody both fell under the discretionary function exception and precluded government liability for prisoner's rape by another inmate); Fisher Bros. Sales, Inc. v. United States, 46 F.3d 279 (3d Cir.1995)(Chilean fruit growers' and others' claims against the United States for damages arising from the FDA's alleged negligence in finding fruit contaminated dismissed); Autery v. United States, 992 F.2d 1523 (11th Cir.1993)(claims for injuries from falling tree in national park dismissed because agency's design and implementation of tree inspection program falls within exception); and Hart v. United States, 894 F.2d 1539 (11th Cir.1990)(government's efforts to identify American flyer shot down over Laos and the decision as to when to discontinue the search for military personnel are discretionary).

8. *The Feres doctrine.* The Court broadened the armed services exception beyond claims "arising out of the combatant services of the military" in Feres v. United States, 340 U.S. 135 (1950), to encompass *all* injuries that arise out of or in the course of military service. The Court adhered to the doctrine, explained its rationale (including a restatement of the traditional concern about maintaining military discipline and effectiveness), and expanded its reach in United States v. Johnson, 481 U.S. 681 (1987), a case in which *Feres* was invoked to bar a surviving wife's claim against the FAA for negligence in providing guidance to a military helicopter pilot who died in a rescue mission. For a lucid analysis of the history and evolution of the Feres doctrine, see Taber v. Maine, 45 F.3d 598 (2d Cir.1995).

In Stencel Aero Engineering Corp. v. United States, 431 U.S. 666 (1977), the Court decided that a government contractor who was held liable to military personnel for a defective product could not get indemnity from the government. The point was to avoid an end run around *Feres*. A related question is whether the government contractor can claim a defense against primary liability. The government contractor defense is considered in Chapter VIII.

9. Actions against federal officials for violation of constitutional rights generally involve claims of intentional wrongdoing. Although most intentional harms are exempted under the FTCA, a constitutional tort, independent of the act, was recognized in Bivens v. Six Unknown Named Agents, 403 U.S. 388 (1971), discussed in Chapter XII.

10. Similar claims against state and municipal officials, under the Civil Rights Act of 1871, 42 U.S.C. § 1983, are discussed in Chapter XII. The interplay between the issues arising in § 1983 cases and issues considered in this section, as well as the earlier section in this chapter on duties of affirmative action, is illustrated by DeShaney v. Winnebago County Dept. of Social Services, 489 U.S. 189 (1989), in which plaintiff, a young boy, suffered serious permanent brain damage from beatings administered by his father. The § 1983 claim against defendant social services agency was based on a failure to intervene and remove plaintiff from his father's custody despite notice from concerned parties on various occasions. The Court denied the claim of constitutional denial of liberty under the due process clause, holding that there is no affirmative duty on the part of the state to protect individuals against invasion by other private parties.

CHAPTER IV

THE DUTY REQUIREMENT: NONPHYSICAL HARM

In this chapter we deal with protection against nonphysical harms. The focus will be on the *types* of harm that plaintiffs suffer. The common law has distinguished situations in which the only harm suffered was psychic or economic from the classic physical injury, and has developed limited or no-duty rules for reasons that we will explore. We begin with a type of harm generically referred to as "emotional harm." Historically, this type of harm has been far less widely protected than the interest in being free from physical harm. Nonetheless, by the early twentieth century some courts began to protect plaintiffs against intentional extreme and outrageous conduct that produced "only" this type of harm. We explore that subject in Chapter XII. Here, we consider the circumstances in which the courts protect non-physical interests against unintended interference.

A.   EMOTIONAL HARM

Falzone v. Busch

Supreme Court of New Jersey, 1965.
45 N.J. 559, 214 A.2d 12.

PROCTOR, J.

The question before us on this appeal is whether the plaintiff may recover for bodily injury or sickness resulting from fear for her safety caused by a negligent defendant, where the plaintiff was placed in danger by such negligence, although there was no physical impact.

The complaint alleges in the first count that the plaintiff, Charles Falzone, was standing in a field adjacent to the roadway when he was struck and injured by defendant's negligently driven automobile. The second count alleges that the plaintiff, Mabel Falzone, wife of Charles, was seated in his lawfully parked automobile close to the place where her husband was struck and that the defendant's negligently driven automobile "veered across the highway and headed in the direction of this plaintiff," coming "so close to plaintiff as to put her in fear for her safety." As a direct result she became ill and required medical attention. [The trial court granted summary judgment for defendant on the second count,] holding that it was constrained to follow the existing New Jersey rule that where there is no physical impact upon the plaintiff, there can be no recovery for the bodily injury or sickness resulting from negligently induced fright. We certified the plaintiffs' appeal before it was considered by the Appellate Division.

case of first impression to lower cts.

Neither this Court nor the former Court of Errors and Appeals has considered a case directly presenting this question. However, since a decision of our former Supreme Court in 1900, Ward v. West Jersey & Seashore R.R. Co., [ ], it has been considered settled that a physical impact upon the plaintiff is necessary to sustain a negligence action. [ ]

. . . . Three reasons for denying recovery were set forth in [*Ward*]. The first was that physical injury was not the natural and proximate result of the negligent act:

> The doctrine of non-liability . . . rests upon the principle that a person is legally responsible only for the natural and proximate results of his negligent act. Physical suffering is not the probable or natural consequences of fright, in the case of a person of ordinary physical and mental vigor; and in the general conduct of business, and the ordinary affairs of life, although we are bound to anticipate and guard against consequences, which may be injurious to persons who are liable to be affected thereby, we have a right, in doing so, to assume, in the absence of knowledge to the contrary, that such persons are of average strength both of body and of mind. [ ]

Second, the court concluded that since this was the first action of its kind in New Jersey, the consensus of the bar must have been that no liability exists in the absence of impact. [ ] The third reason was "public policy" which the court explained by quoting with approval from Mitchell v. Rochester Ry. Co., [45 N.E. 354 (N.Y.1896)]:

> If the right of recovery in this class of cases should be once established, it would naturally result in a flood of litigation in cases where the injury complained of may be easily feigned without detection, and where the damages must rest upon mere conjecture and speculation. The difficulty which often exists in cases of alleged physical injuries, in determining whether they exist, and, if so, whether they were caused by the negligent act of the defendant, would not only be greatly increased, but a wide field would be opened for [fictitious] or speculative claims. [*Ward*]

We think that the reasons assigned in *Ward* for denying liability are no longer tenable, and it is questionable if they ever were. The court there

"capable of being held"

first stated that it is not "probable or natural" for persons of normal health to suffer physical injuries, when subjected to fright, and that since a person whose acts cause fright alone could not reasonably anticipate that physical harm would follow, such acts cannot constitute negligence as to the frightened party. It appears that the court decided as a matter of law an issue which we believe is properly determinable by medical evidence. . . .

And even in Spade v. Lynn & B.R. Co., [47 N.E. 88, 89 (Mass.1897)] (relied upon in *Ward*), where recovery was denied for the physical consequences of fright, the court recognized that:

> Great emotion, may, and sometimes does, produce physical effects . . . A physical injury may be directly traceable to fright, and so may be caused by it. We cannot say, therefore, that such consequences may not flow proximately from unintentional negligence; . . .

Moreover, medical knowledge on the relationship between emotional disturbance and physical injury has steadily expanded, and such relationship seems no longer open to serious challenge. [   ]

New Jersey courts have not generally adhered to the notion that fright cannot be the proximate cause of substantial physical injury, and three rules of law inconsistent with the *Ward* doctrine have developed. It has been held that where a person is injured attempting to avoid a hazard negligently created by another, he may recover for the physical consequences of fright even though the immediate injury suffered was slight and was not a link in the causal chain. Thus, in Buchanan v. West Jersey R.R. Co., 19 A. 254 (N.J.L.1890), cited with approval in *Ward*, a woman standing in a railroad station threw herself to the platform to avoid being struck by a protruding timber on a passing train. "By reason of the shock to her nervous system occasioned by this peril, her health was seriously impaired." [   ] The court allowed recovery even though her fright, and not the injury, if any, sustained in the fall, caused her physical suffering. [   ] Our courts have also been willing to allow recovery for physical injury traceable directly to fright when there is any impact, however inconsequential or slight. Porter v. Delaware Lackawanna & W.R.R. Co., 63 A. 860 (N.J.L.1906); [   ]. The application of this rule was illustrated in [*Porter*] where a woman became ill as the result of her shock at seeing a railroad bridge fall near the place where she was standing. She testified that something fell on her neck and that dust entered her eyes. In allowing recovery for the physical consequences of her fright, the court said either the small injury to her neck or the dust in her eyes was a sufficient "impact" to distinguish the case from *Ward*. And third, recovery has been permitted where physical suffering resulted from a wilfully caused emotional disturbance. [   ]

The second reason given in *Ward* for denying recovery was that the absence of suits of this nature in New Jersey demonstrated the concurrence of the bar with the rule of no liability. We do not believe the court meant to imply that it would deny recovery because of opinions held by lawyers on the legal question presented. And if the court intended to bar the cause of action because of a lack of precedent in this State, a sufficient answer is that the common law would have atrophied hundreds of years ago if it had continued to deny relief in cases of first impression. [   ]

Public policy was the final reason given in *Ward* for denying liability. The court was of the opinion that proof or disproof of fear-induced physical suffering would be so difficult that recovery would often be based on mere conjecture and speculation, and that the door would be opened to extensive litigation in a class of cases where injury is easily feigned. We realize that there may be difficulties in determining the existence of a causal connection between fright and subsequent physical injury and in measuring the extent of such injury. However, the problem of tracing a causal connection from negligence to injury is not peculiar to cases without impact and occurs in all types of personal injury litigation. [   ] As Judge Burke said for the New York Court of Appeals in dealing with the same problem:

> In many instances, just as in impact cases, there will be no doubt as to the presence and extent of the damage and the fact that it was proximately caused by defendant's negligence. In the difficult cases, we must look to the quality and genuineness of proof, and rely to an extent on the contemporary sophistication of the medical profession and the ability of the court and jury to weed out the dishonest claims. Battalla v. State, [176 N.E.2d 729 (N.Y.1961)].

In any event, difficulty of proof should not bar the plaintiff from the opportunity of attempting to convince the trier of fact of the truth of her claim.

As to the possibility of actions based on fictitious injuries, a court should not deny recovery for a type of wrong which may result in serious harm because some people may institute fraudulent actions. Our trial courts retain sufficient control, through the rules of evidence and the requirements as to the sufficiency of evidence, to safeguard against the danger that juries will find facts without legally adequate proof. [   ] Moreover, the allowance of recovery in cases where there has been an impact, however slight, negates the effectiveness of the no impact rule as a method of preventing fraudulent claims.   .   .   .

Ward also asserts that public policy demands denial of recovery in no impact cases to prevent a "flood of litigations." However, there is no indication of an excessive number of actions of this type in other states which do not require an impact as a basis for recovery. And, of more importance, the fear of an expansion of litigation should not deter courts from granting relief in meritorious cases; the proper remedy is an expansion of the judicial machinery, not a decrease in the availability of justice.

The many eminent legal scholars who have considered the rule denying recovery in the absence of impact are virtually unanimous in condemning it as unjust and contrary to experience and logic. [The court cites several law review articles and also notes that both England and New York have repudiated the requirement of "impact."] A great majority of jurisdictions now hold that where physical injury results from wrongfully caused emotional stress, the injured person may recover for such consequences notwithstanding the absence of any physical impact upon him at the time of the mental shock. [   ] Indeed, Dean Prosser has recently written that the impact requirement "is almost certainly destined for ultimate extinction." Prosser, Torts § 55, p. 351 (3d ed. 1964).

Our conclusion is that *Ward* should no longer be followed in New Jersey. We are not dealing with property law, contract law or other fields where stability and predictability may be crucial. We are dealing with torts where there can be little, if any, justifiable reliance and where the rule of *stare decisis* is admittedly limited. [ ] We hold, therefore, that where *holding* negligence causes fright from a reasonable fear of immediate personal injury, which fright is adequately demonstrated to have resulted in substantial bodily injury or sickness, the injured person may recover if such bodily injury or sickness would be regarded as proper elements of damage had they occurred as a consequence of direct physical injury rather than fright. Of course, where fright does not cause substantial bodily injury or sickness, it is to be regarded as too lacking in seriousness and too speculative to warrant the imposition of liability.

We recognize that where there is no impact a defendant may be unaware of the alleged incident and thus not forewarned to preserve evidence upon which he might base his defense. However, this consideration should not be sufficient to bar a meritorious claim. Rather, it is appropriate that the trial judge charge the jury that an undue delay in notifying the defendant of the incident and the resulting injury may weigh heavily in determining the truth of the plaintiff's claim. It is unnecessary to decide here whether an undue delay short of the statute of limitations would justify a dismissal by the trial court.

The plaintiffs should be given the opportunity of submitting proof that Mrs. Falzone suffered substantial bodily injury or sickness and that such bodily injury or sickness was the proximate result of the defendant's negligence.

For reversal: CHIEF JUSTICE WEINTRAUB and JUSTICES JACOBS, FRANCIS, PROCTOR, HALL, SCHETTINO and HANEMAN—7.

For affirmance: None.

Notes and Questions

1. Notice that two separate questions could be raised here: (1) whether any physical impact is required to recover for emotional distress and (2) whether that emotional distress must produce "physical injury" or "physical consequences" or "physical manifestations." The court does not rule on the second because it is apparently satisfied by the complaint's allegation that the plaintiff became ill and required medical attention as a result of the episode.

2. Are the court's responses to *Ward*'s three justifications persuasive? *yes* To the extent that one of the concerns has been the lack of notice to the defendant that a claim might be forthcoming, how persuasive is the court's resolution? If you walked out of class today and were served with a complaint alleging that you drove carelessly a year ago and caused plaintiff to fear for her safety, how would you defend yourself? *proof of injury?*

3. In the cited *Mitchell* case a team of horses ran out of control and were brought to a halt so that plaintiff pregnant woman was situated between the two horses—but apparently untouched by either of them. She

soon had a miscarriage. The New York Court of Appeals denied recovery. In the cited *Battalla* case, defendant negligently failed to secure plaintiff in her ski chair lift. In allowing an action for her fright engendered by such a situation, the court overruled *Mitchell* on the requirement of impact.

4.   The requirement of impact has virtually disappeared today. For a rare insistence on impact, see R.J. v. Humana of Florida, Inc., 652 So.2d 360 (Fla.1995), in which plaintiff alleged that due to defendants' negligence he was diagnosed as HIV positive and remained under that impression until he was retested 18 months later. The court held that plaintiff would be able to state an actionable claim only if treatments or injections had harmed him: plaintiff's "emotional distress suffered must flow from physical injuries the plaintiff sustained in an impact."

In Ruttger Hotel Corp. v. Wagner, 691 So.2d 1177 (Fla.App.1997), two guests sued defendant motel after being accosted by robbers who forced them into their room by putting a gun into their back, and then pushed them into the bathroom. The court, following *Humana*, rejected emotional distress claims because the plaintiffs "failed to show the requisite physical impact that resulted in the physical or psychological injury."

How might the *Falzone* court analyze *Humana* and *Ruttger*?

5.   Although the *Falzone* court noted that plaintiff's husband was hit by the same car, this event plays no apparent part in the analysis of the wife's claim. As we shall see shortly, at the time of *Falzone* it was not yet possible in New Jersey for a plaintiff to claim damages for suffering emotional distress from witnessing an injury to a family member. How might the wife here meet the defendant's argument that at least a large part of her emotional distress was brought about by concern for her husband's safety and not for her own safety?

6.   Is tort law sufficiently different from contract law to support the court's position that the importance of *stare decisis* differs between the two? Once a court rejects *stare decisis* should it use retrospective overruling? Recall the use of modified prospective overruling in *Heins*, p. 197, supra.

7.   *Car crashes v. airplane crashes*. In Wooden v. Raveling, 71 Cal. Rptr.2d 891 (App.1998), the court allowed plaintiff property owner to recover for her emotional distress when defendant's negligently driven car came up onto her property and nearly hit her. *Wooden* rejected an earlier case that had insisted on a pre-existing relationship and outrageous behavior before permitting a recovery for emotional distress.

Then, in Lawson v. Management Activities, Inc., 81 Cal.Rptr.2d 745 (App. 1999), the plaintiffs were employees of a Honda dealership who feared that a falling plane would crash into them. In fact, the plane "crashed into nearby ground." The *Lawson* court "decline[d] to follow the *Wooden* decision to the degree that its facts—a car crash in which a literal bystander feared for her own safety—might be extrapolated to the airplane crash before us." The court, 2–1, noting that the fear had existed "for a brief moment," concluded that California rejected the "independent tort of negligent infliction of emotional distress:"

> Indeed, civilized life would not be possible if there were such a tort. To borrow a phrase from Blake, if tort damages were available for anything which would foreseeably cause our fellow human beings emotional distress, then "who can stand?" No one, saint or sinner, can go through life without "negligently" inflicting emotional distress on others.

The majority then concluded that most of the California duty factors pointed against an action:

> [It takes] no imagination to realize that people on the ground who are close to an airplane crash are going to be very scared. By the same token, while it is foreseeable that the fright will be intense, it is also foreseeable that the actual fright itself will be short lived. What is not foreseeable is the severity of people's psychological reactions to the crash. Emotional distress is a murky cauldron of actuarial imprecision, inherently limitless. It is also an area of remarkable individual idiosyncrasy, with great extremes at either end.

The court thought that the "certainty" of injury "squarely weighs against liability" because of the "loosey-goosey nature of a pure emotional distress claim. . . . Psychological symptoms are much more susceptible to being faked than more palpable effects." On the factors of preventing future harm and blame, the risk of death in an air crash is a good guard against "moral indifference to the possibility of injury. Nothing is to be gained by extending the liability attendant upon air crashes to the emotional distress of ground spectators." Moreover, "there is the regulatory apparatus devoted to air safety which, in quality and intensity of care, is already disproportionate to the safety apparatus which regulates automotive traffic." The final two factors—the burden on defendant and the social consequences—both cut against liability. The majority quoted another court saying that to "hold airlines responsible for the possible emotional injury for such a large and indeterminate group of people would be to expose airlines to 'virtually limitless . . . tort liability.' " Further, the court stated that the "actual unpredictability of emotional distress damages could add significantly to the cost of insuring air transportation." In sum, the "law can hardly permit a major tort suit for unpredictable emotional distress damages for every near-miss and otherwise uneventful unsafe lane change."

The dissenter in *Lawson* rejected the majority's approach and concluded that the majority justices were simply uncomfortable with the concept of emotional distress; they "are just unimpressed with 'weak' people. . . . If they had their way, we would all be certified war heroes. We certainly would not reward those who succumb to fear as a result of someone else's negligence." The two opinions also disagreed about whether "tort law could countenance" an "eggshell psyche." That term alludes to the "eggshell plaintiff"—one who suffers from an abnormally sensitive physical condition, such as hemophilia or brittle bones. We will explore this subject in

Chapter V. The California Supreme Court did not review either *Wooden* or *Lawson*.

8. *Airplane passengers. Falzone* involved fear of imminent harm that did not occur. Other examples occur in airplane crises. In Quill v. Trans World Airlines, Inc., 361 N.W.2d 438 (Minn.App.1985), the court upheld an award of $50,000 to a passenger in an airplane that plunged 34,000 feet in an uncontrolled tailspin before pilots regained control. The plane then continued to shake and shudder for 40 minutes until it could be brought to a safe emergency landing. The plaintiff's claim for negligent infliction of emotional distress was grounded in the severe anxiety he experienced whenever he took an airplane flight after the accident. The court held that the plaintiff had made out a prima facie case:

> [T]he unusually disturbing experience plaintiff endured combined with his physical symptoms assure that his claim is real. There can be few experiences as terrifying as being pinned to a seat by gravity forces as an airplane twists and screams towards earth at just under the speed of sound.

Five other passengers on the same plane settled with the airline for amounts ranging from $2,000 to $70,000, with the highest awards going to passengers who claimed they were no longer able to fly as a result of the incident. See Leebron, Final Moments: Damages for Pain and Suffering Prior to Death, 64 N.Y.U.L.Rev. 256, 299 (1989).

In 1999 a jury awarded sums between $150,000 and $200,000 to each of 13 plaintiffs who sued for emotional distress after their American Airlines flight hit unannounced turbulence and either they or their children were thrown around the cabin. (Small claims for physical injury were involved in some of the cases but did not cause the claimed psychological harm.) The plaintiffs' attorney is quoted as saying that the case had to go to trial because the airline's settlement offers "were insulting, from $5,000 to $20,000." Benjamin Weiser, Airline Ruled Liable for Distress on Turbulent Flight, N.Y.Times, Oct. 8, 1999 at B1. Is it relevant that the time of the turbulence was somewhere between five and 28 seconds?

9. *Emotional distress of victims who realize they are doomed.* As noted in Chapter I, states have adopted "survival" statutes that generally permit the decedent's estate to proceed with any claims that the decedent might have brought but for the death. (The measurement of lost income and medical expense from the injury to the death and for accompanying pain and suffering will be considered in detail in Chapter X.) Should these fears be compensated in cases where the harm caused death?

Again, airplane and auto crashes have provided the most common situations. Most courts have allowed recovery where plaintiff was aware of impending death or injury even if the period of awareness was very short. These cases are quite fact-specific. Compare Shatkin v. McDonnell Douglas Corp., 727 F.2d 202 (2d Cir.1984)(insufficient evidence to show that passenger on right side of plane was even aware of impending disaster until just before the crash) with Shu–Tao Lin v. McDonnell Douglas Corp., 742 F.2d

45 (2d Cir.1984)(upholding judgment of $10,000 for pre-impact fright for passenger in seat over left wing on same flight where jury might reasonably have found that the passenger saw "the left engine and a portion of the wing break away at the beginning of the flight, which lasted some thirty seconds between takeoff and crash").

The phenomenon of pre-impact fright is not limited to airplane cases. For an extended consideration of the issue, see Beynon v. Montgomery Cablevision Limited Partnership, 718 A.2d 1161 (Md.1998), in which the court, 4–3, upheld an award for decedent's "pre-impact fright" which was shown to exist by 71.5 feet of skid marks. After the jury had awarded $1 million for this item, the trial judge, acting under a statute setting a cap on awards for nonphysical injury, cut the award to the maximum $350,000. Affirming, the majority noted that had decedent survived he would have had an action under state law. Given that fact, it "would be illogical" to deny the item where the feared harm came to pass. As to the very short time frame:

> A jury reasonably could have inferred from that evidence that the decedent was aware of the impending peril, that he was going to crash, and attempted an evasive maneuver to avoid it. The jury equally reasonably could have concluded that the decedent suffered emotional distress or fright during that period before the crash, after he became aware of the imminent danger and began braking. This is not rank speculation.

One dissenter noted that at the speed plaintiff was traveling when he hit the brakes, the fright lasted between 1.5 and 2.5 seconds. Even under the reduced award, that was at least $140,000 "per second of assumed fright." The dissenter agreed that the action should be recognized but saw no evidence of distress in this case. It was "rank speculation to conclude that [decedent] was consciously thinking about anything other than stopping his vehicle, or, indeed, that his mind and body were engaged in anything but an instinctive reaction directed entirely at self-preservation, requiring little or no ideation at all."

But see Ghotra v. Bandila Shipping Co., 113 F.3d 1050 (9th Cir.1997), in which the evidence showed that the victim was conscious and survived for ten seconds after the accident. Earlier cases had said that the court would "not adopt a stop watch" approach to the question but would require "an appreciable length of time." That was not satisfied here. There was no evidence showing that this period of consciousness "differs from the periods of insensibility which sometimes intervene between fatal injuries and death" or that the decedent "experienced a period of 'heightened awareness' following his injuries."

Sometimes the distress extends for far longer periods of time. In Sander v. Geib, Elston, Frost, P.A., 506 N.W.2d 107 (S.D.1993), defendant's negligence in reading a pap smear test led to a failure to detect cervical cancer until it was too late to save decedent. The award for her death included $1 million that the court assumed was for her emotional distress. In rejecting a claim of excessiveness, the court responded:

> [Decedent] greatly suffered many faces of pain during the year follow-
> ing the realization that she would die from the very disease which the
> pap smear was designed to detect. The enormity of [decedent's] knowl-
> edge of her impending, unalterable doom, her confusion, fear, misery,
> depression, helplessness, physical pain and mental terror, her sure
> knowledge that she would never live to witness the adulthood of her
> children or old age with her husband, all were proper considerations
> for the jury and surely had a powerful influence upon it.

If there had been no physical pain whatever before the death how large an
award could be justified? What if the jury had returned a verdict on this
item of $3 million? The defendant's strategy was to focus on denying
liability. As a result it "did not argue damages in closing arguments to the
jury." Was this a mistake?

Whatever your views on emotional distress when the person survives,
when the victim dies, why should this money be paid to the estate and,
ultimately, usually to relatives who did not suffer that distress? In Chapter
X, we explore whether the survivors of a personal injury victim should
recover damages for the victim's pain and suffering. Is there a difference
between recovering for the decedent's emotional distress at forthcoming
death and for the decedent's pain and suffering from the injury that caused
the death?

Some states bar recovery for intangible damages if the victim is not
surviving at the time of the final judgment. California has done this by
statute—a position discussed at p. 706, infra.

10.   After the abrogation of the impact rule, what new criteria should
be developed for imposing liability? Should a new rule allow recovery in
certain types of factual situations and not in others? What are the parameters adopted in *Falzone*? Are they well-designed to ensure proof of injury
and prevent a flood of litigation? These issues are addressed in the next
case and later in the chapter.

Metro–North Commuter Railroad Company v. Buckley

Supreme Court of the United States, 1997.
521 U.S. 424, 117 S.Ct. 2113, 138 L.Ed.2d 560.

JUSTICE BREYER delivered the opinion of the Court.

The basic question in this case is whether a railroad worker negligently
exposed to a carcinogen (here, asbestos) but without symptoms of any
disease can recover under the Federal Employers' Liability Act (FELA or
Act), for negligently inflicted emotional distress. We conclude that the
worker before us here cannot recover unless, and until, he manifests
symptoms of a disease. [In an omitted part, the Court also considered a
claim for medical monitoring costs, which we explore in Chapter V.]

I

Respondent, Michael Buckley, works as a pipefitter for Metro–North, a
railroad. For three years (1985–1988) his job exposed him to asbestos for

about one hour per working day. During that time Buckley would remove insulation from pipes, often covering himself with insulation dust that contained asbestos. Since 1987, when he attended an "asbestos awareness" class, Buckley has feared that he would develop cancer—and with some cause, for his two expert witnesses testified that, even after taking account of his now-discarded 15-year habit of smoking up to a pack of cigarettes per day, the exposure created an added risk of death due to cancer, or to other asbestos-related diseases, of either 1% to 5% (in the view of one of plaintiff's experts), or 1% to 3% (in the view of another). Since 1989, Buckley has received periodic medical checkups for cancer and asbestosis. So far, those check-ups have not revealed any evidence of cancer or any other asbestos-related disease.

Buckley sued Metro–North under the FELA, a statute that permits a railroad worker to recover for an "injury . . . resulting . . . from" his employer's "negligence." 45 U.S.C. § 51. He sought damages for his emotional distress and to cover the cost of future medical checkups. His employer conceded negligence, but it did not concede that Buckley had actually suffered emotional distress, and it argued that the FELA did not permit a worker like Buckley, who had suffered no physical harm, to recover for injuries of either sort. After hearing Buckley's case, the District Court dismissed the action. The court found that Buckley did not "offer sufficient evidence to allow a jury to find that he suffered a real emotional injury." [   ] And, in any event, Buckley suffered no "physical impact"; hence any emotional injury fell outside the limited set of circumstances in which, according to this Court, the FELA permits recovery. [   ]; see Consolidated Rail Corporation v. Gottshall, 512 U.S. 532 (1994). . . . [The Second Circuit reversed.]

Arguments

II

The critical question before us in respect to Buckley's "emotional distress" claim is whether the physical contact with insulation dust that accompanied his emotional distress amounts to a "physical impact" as this Court used that term in *Gottshall*. In *Gottshall*, an emotional distress case, the Court interpreted the word "injury" in FELA § 1, a provision that makes "[e]very common carrier by railroad . . . liable in damages to any person suffering injury while . . . employed" by the carrier if the "injury" results from carrier "negligence." [   ] In doing so, it initially set forth several general legal principles applicable here. . . . It pointed out that the Act expressly abolishes or modifies a host of common-law doctrines that previously had limited recovery. [   ] It added that this Court has interpreted the Act's language "liberally" in light of its humanitarian purposes. [   ] But, at the same time, the Court noted that liability under the Act rests upon "negligence" and that the Act does not make the railroad "the insurer" for all employee injuries. [   ] The Court stated that "common-law principles," where not rejected in the text of the statute, "are entitled to great weight" in interpreting the Act, and that those principles "play a significant role" in determining whether, or when, an

ROL:

Gottshall

employee can recover damages for "negligent infliction of emotional distress." [   ]

RGL

The Court also set forth several more specific legal propositions. It recognized that the common law of torts does not permit recovery for negligently inflicted emotional distress unless the distress falls within certain specific categories that amount to recovery-permitting exceptions. The law, for example, does permit recovery for emotional distress where that distress accompanies a physical injury, see, e.g., Simmons v. Pacor, Inc., [674 A.2d 232, 239 (Pa.1996)]; Restatement (Second) of Torts § 924(a) (1977), and it often permits recovery for distress suffered by a close relative who witnesses the physical injury of a negligence victim, e.g., Dillon v. Legg, [441 P.2d 912 (Cal.1968)—to be discussed shortly]; [   ]. The Court then held that FELA § 1, mirroring the law of many States, sometimes permitted recovery "for damages for negligent infliction of emotional distress," [   ], and, in particular, it does so where a plaintiff seeking such damages satisfies the common law's "zone of danger" test. It defined that test by stating that the law permits "recovery for emotional injury" by

Zone of
Danger Test

"those plaintiffs who *sustain a physical impact* as a result of a defendant's negligent conduct, or who are placed in immediate risk of physical harm by that conduct." (emphasis added).

The case before us, as we have said, focuses on the italicized words "physical impact." The Second Circuit interpreted those words as including a simple physical contact with a substance that might cause a disease at a future time, so long as the contact was of a kind that would "cause fear in a reasonable person." [   ] In our view, however, the "physical impact" to which *Gottshall* referred does not include a simple physical contact with a substance that might cause a disease at a substantially later time—where that substance, or related circumstance, threatens no harm other than that disease-related risk.

First, *Gottshall* cited many state cases in support of its adoption of the "zone of danger" test quoted above. And in each case where recovery for emotional distress was permitted, the case involved a threatened physical contact that caused, or might have caused, immediate traumatic harm [citing cases that involved a car accident, a gas explosion, a train striking a car, clothing caught in an escalator and choking victim, and an intruder assaulting plaintiff's husband].

Second, *Gottshall*'s language, read in light of this precedent, seems similarly limited. [   ]; id., at 547–548 (quoting Pearson, Liability to Bystanders for Negligently Inflicted Emotional Harm—A Comment on the Nature of Arbitrary Rules, 34 U. Fla. L.Rev. 477, 488–489 (1982)) ("[T]hose within the zone of danger of physical impact" should be able to "recover for fright" because "a near miss may be as frightening as a direct hit").

Taken together, language and cited precedent indicate that the words "physical impact" do not encompass every form of "physical contact." And, in particular, they do not include a contact that amounts to no more than an exposure—an exposure, such as that before us, to a substance that poses some future risk of disease and which contact causes emotional distress only because the worker learns that he may become ill after a substantial period of time.

Third, common-law precedent does not favor the plaintiff. Common-law courts do permit a plaintiff who suffers from a disease to recover for related negligently caused emotional distress, [ ], and some courts permit a plaintiff who exhibits a physical symptom of exposure to recover [ ]. But with only a few exceptions, common-law courts have denied recovery to those who, like Buckley, are disease and symptom free. [ ]; [*Simmons v. Pacor, Inc.*]; [ ]; see also Potter v. Firestone Tire & Rubber Co., [863 P.2d 795 (Cal.1993)] (no recovery for fear of cancer in a negligence action unless plaintiff is "more likely than not" to develop cancer).

Fourth, the general policy reasons to which *Gottshall* referred—in its explanation of why common-law courts have restricted recovery for emotional harm to cases falling within rather narrowly defined categories—militate against an expansive definition of "physical impact" here. Those reasons include: (a) special "difficult[y] for judges and juries" in separating valid, important claims from those that are invalid or "trivial," [ ]; (b) a threat of "unlimited and unpredictable liability," [ ]; and (c) the "potential for a flood" of comparatively unimportant, or "trivial," claims, [ ].

To separate meritorious and important claims from invalid or trivial claims does not seem easier here than in other cases in which a plaintiff might seek recovery for typical negligently caused emotional distress. The facts before us illustrate the problem. The District Court, when concluding that Buckley had failed to present "sufficient evidence to allow a jury to find . . . a real emotional injury," pointed out that, apart from Buckley's own testimony, there was virtually no evidence of distress. [ ] Indeed, Buckley continued to work with insulating material "even though . . . he could have transferred" elsewhere, he "continued to smoke cigarettes" despite doctors' warnings, and his doctor did not refer him "either to a psychologist or to a social worker." [ ] The Court of Appeals reversed because it found certain objective corroborating evidence, namely, "workers' complaints to supervisors and investigative bodies." [ ] Both kinds of "objective" evidence—the confirming and disconfirming evidence—seem only indirectly related to the question at issue, the existence and seriousness of Buckley's claimed emotional distress. Yet, given the difficulty of separating valid from invalid emotional injury claims, the evidence before us may typify the kind of evidence to which parties and the courts would have to look.

. . .

More important, the physical contact at issue here—a simple (though extensive) contact with a carcinogenic substance—does not seem to offer much help in separating valid from invalid emotional distress claims. That is because contacts, even extensive contacts, with serious carcinogens are common. [ ] (estimating that 21 million Americans have been exposed to work-related asbestos); [ ] (3 million workers exposed to benzene, a majority of Americans exposed outside the workplace); [ ] (reporting that

43% of American children lived in a home with at least one smoker, and 37% of adult nonsmokers lived in a home with at least one smoker or reported environmental tobacco smoke at work). They may occur without causing serious emotional distress, but sometimes they do cause distress, and reasonably so, for cancer is both an unusually threatening and unusually frightening disease. See [   ] (23.5% of Americans who died in 1994 died of cancer); [   ] (half of all men and one-third of all women will develop cancer). The relevant problem, however, remains one of evaluating a claimed emotional reaction to an increased risk of dying. An external circumstance—exposure—makes some emotional distress more likely. But how can one determine from the external circumstance of exposure whether, or when, a claimed strong emotional reaction to an increased mortality risk (say, from 23% to 28%) is reasonable and genuine, rather than overstated—particularly when the relevant statistics themselves are controversial and uncertain (as is usually the case), and particularly since neither those exposed nor judges or juries are experts in statistics? The evaluation problem seems a serious one.

The large number of those exposed and the uncertainties that may surround recovery also suggest what *Gottshall* called the problem of "unlimited and unpredictable liability." Does such liability mean, for example, that the costs associated with a rule of liability would become so great that, given the nature of the harm, it would seem unreasonable to require the public to pay the higher prices that may result? [   ] The same characteristics further suggest what *Gottshall* called the problem of a "flood" of cases that, if not "trivial," are comparatively less important. In a world of limited resources, would a rule permitting immediate large-scale recoveries for widespread emotional distress caused by fear of future disease diminish the likelihood of recovery by those who later suffer from the disease? [   ]

tobacco litigation

We do not raise these questions to answer them (for we do not have the answers), but rather to show that general policy concerns of a kind that have led common-law courts to deny recovery for certain classes of negligently caused harms are present in this case as well. That being so, we cannot find in *Gottshall*'s underlying rationale any basis for departing from *Gottshall*'s language and precedent or from the current common-law consensus. That is to say, we cannot find in *Gottshall*'s language, cited precedent, other common-law precedent, or related concerns of policy a legal basis for adopting the emotional distress recovery rule adopted by the Court of Appeals.

Buckley raises several important arguments in reply. He points out, for example, that common-law courts do permit recovery for emotional distress where a plaintiff has physical symptoms; and he argues that his evidence of exposure and enhanced mortality risk is as strong a proof as an accompanying physical symptom that his emotional distress is genuine.

This argument, however, while important, overlooks the fact that the common law in this area does not examine the genuineness of emotional harm case by case. Rather, it has developed recovery-permitting categories the contours of which more distantly reflect this, and other, abstract general policy concerns. The point of such categorization is to deny courts the authority to undertake a case-by-case examination. The common law permits emotional distress recovery for that category of plaintiffs who suffer from a disease (or exhibit a physical symptom), for example, thereby finding a special effort to evaluate emotional symptoms warranted in that category of cases—perhaps from a desire to make a physically injured victim whole or because the parties are likely to be in court in any event. In other cases, however, falling outside the special recovery-permitting categories, it has reached a different conclusion. The relevant question here concerns the validity of a rule that seeks to redefine such a category. It would not be easy to redefine "physical impact" in terms of a rule that turned on, say, the "massive, lengthy, [or] tangible" nature of a contact that amounted to an exposure, whether to contaminated water, or to germ-laden air, or to carcinogen-containing substances, such as insulation dust containing asbestos. But, in any event, for the reasons we have stated, we cannot find that the common law has done so.

. . .

[The opinion turned to claims for recovery of medical monitoring costs, discussed in Chapter V. It then reversed the decision of the Second Circuit and remanded the case on that claim.]

Chief Justice Rehnquist, and Justice O'Connor, Kennedy, Scalia, Souter and Thomas concurred.

Justice Ginsburg, with whom Justice Stevens joins, concurring in the judgment in part and dissenting in part.

. . .

Buckley's extensive contact with asbestos particles in Grand Central's tunnels, as I comprehend his situation, constituted "physical impact" as that term was used in *Gottshall*. Nevertheless, I concur in the Court's judgment with respect to Buckley's emotional distress claim. In my view, that claim fails because Buckley did not present objective evidence of severe emotional distress. [   ] Buckley testified at trial that he was angry at Metro–North and fearful of developing an asbestos-related disease. However, he sought no professional help to ease his distress, and presented no medical testimony concerning his mental health. [   ] Under these circumstances, Buckley's emotional distress claim fails as a matter of law. Cf. [*Gottshall*] (Ginsburg, J., dissenting) (describing as "unquestionably genuine and severe" emotional distress suffered by one respondent who had a nervous breakdown, and another who was hospitalized, lost weight, and had, inter alia, suicidal preoccupations, anxiety, insomnia, cold sweats, and nausea).

[Justices Ginsburg and Stevens dissented on the monitoring question.]

Notes and Questions

1. Although the Supreme Court applies the FELA in this case, it draws principles from the common law into the Act, and engages in a lengthy discussion of common law precedent. What does the majority mean by saying that courts must develop categorical liability rules rather than decide on recovery case by case? How does the majority's attitude towards the development of the common law compare with that of the *Falzone* court?

2. The Court enumerates several categories of cases where recovery would be permitted. Among these it included the situation in which the plaintiff was placed in a "zone of danger." The *Gottshall* court explained the "zone of danger" test by suggesting that it involved "immediate risk of physical harm." Did *Falzone* implicitly adopt a "zone of danger" rule?

Is the majority's distinction between immediate harm and exposure convincing? Might it matter if the exposure was sudden rather than gradual?

3. How serious is the concern that a flood of emotional distress litigation might bar recovery by later plaintiffs who had actually contracted a disease? For more discussion of this issue, see the discussion of the increased risk of future harm at p. 346, infra.

4. In *Potter v. Firestone Tire and Rubber Co.*, cited in the majority opinion, defendant's dumping of toxic wastes into a landfill near its plant site exposed plaintiffs to carcinogens over a prolonged period. Although none of the plaintiffs suffered from any current condition they faced "an enhanced but unquantified risk of developing cancer in the future due to the exposure." The court held that:

> . . . in the absence of a present physical injury or illness, damages for fear of cancer may be recovered only if the plaintiff pleads and proves that 1) as a result of the defendant's negligent breach of a duty owed to the plaintiff, the plaintiff is exposed to a toxic substance which threatens cancer, *and* 2) the plaintiff's fear stems from a knowledge, corroborated by reliable medical or scientific opinion, that it is more likely than not that the plaintiff will develop the cancer in the future due to the toxic exposure.

The court went on to add that the plaintiff must further show "a serious fear that the toxic ingestion or exposure was of such magnitude and proportion as to likely result in the feared cancer." Since the claim in these cases is based on emotional distress, not the likelihood of actually contracting cancer, why shouldn't a "serious fear" requirement be the exclusive test for liability?

The *Potter* court also held that if plaintiff could establish "oppression, fraud or malice"—the California standard for punitive damages—then a showing that the plaintiff's fear is "serious, genuine and reasonable," would suffice.

5. *HIV cases.* Litigation over fear of getting HIV has arisen in many state courts. Where the plaintiff is concerned because he or she was given an injection with a dirty needle or was pricked by a needle that should have been sheathed in trash, the courts have tended to require the plaintiff to show that the needle in question actually contained the virus. Most have adopted an actual "zone of danger" analysis that requires that the needle be shown to have been infected.

Even if the needle is infected there remains the question of whether the fear of getting HIV from such a needle is tested by objective or subjective standards. Some courts have required objective criteria, expressing concern about a flood of litigation coming from AIDS paranoia. What should happen if the evidence shows that 1 of every 100 discarded needles is infected with HIV and that only 5 in 100 pricks of an infected needle cause the victim to become HIV-positive?

Williamson v. Waldman, 696 A.2d 14 (N.J.1997), expressed similar concern about promoting AIDS paranoia, but refused to require an actual zone of danger. Plaintiff trash collector was stuck by a used needle that defendant physicians had negligently discarded. The court rejected a requirement of actual exposure to HIV in favor of asking what reasonable well-informed citizens might fear. The court said it wanted to use tort law to help reduce ignorance about AIDS—and thus would not accept the actual level of awareness in the community since that would encourage ignorance. But neither would the court follow actual zone of danger because that denies the reality of the distress caused by negligence without increasing citizen awareness. The court concluded that plaintiff was entitled to recover damages for serious and genuine distress "that would be experienced by a reasonable person of ordinary experience who has a level of knowledge that coincides with the then-current, accurate, and generally available public information about the causes and transmission of AIDS."

Consider these possibilities in analyzing *Williamson*: (1) medical science determines that there is virtually no risk to the public from some substance but the findings have not yet been widely publicized; (2) the findings have been widely publicized but are not accepted by the general public; (3) the findings have been accepted by the mass of the public but some significant pockets of the public remain unconvinced; and (4) the vast majority of the public is persuaded but a jury could reasonably find that the plaintiff honestly and intensely feared the substance.

6. *Windows.* A few courts in HIV cases allow recovery for the "window" between the event that creates the concern and the results of tests showing that infection did not occur. See Faya v. Almaraz, 620 A.2d 327 (Md.1993). But should recovery be limited to the "window"? In Chizmar v. Mackie, 896 P.2d 196 (Alaska 1995), plaintiff alleged that defendant physician incorrectly and negligently informed her that she was HIV positive and that this news had caused severe emotional distress. The court upheld an action in this situation. Is there a risk to plaintiff's safety? The court also concluded that the harm in this type of case may well last past the date on which she learns that she is negative. Is there a difference between being told you are HIV positive and being stuck by a needle that you think is or may be infected with the virus?

Another "window" situation involves fears induced by negligent acts affecting pregnant women. See Jones v. Howard University, Inc., 589 A.2d 419 (D.C.App.1991), upholding a mother's claim for the mental distress she suffered as a result of defendant hospital's negligence in giving her an X-ray exam while she was pregnant. The mother alleged that she suffered emotional distress during her pregnancy term due to the possibility that the radiation had harmed her unborn twins and the chance that she might experience severe pregnancy complications. See also Harris v. Kissling, 721 P.2d 838 (Or.App.1986)(upholding mother's verdict for emotional distress suffered during pregnancy as a result of hospital's negligent failure to conduct Rh blood tests). Does the existence of finite periods of distress make it easier or more difficult to recognize this type of claim?

7. On the variety of issues discussed in the preceding notes, see generally, Wells, The Grin Without a Cat: Claims for Damages from Toxic Exposures, 18 Wm. & Mary J. Envtl. L. 285 (1994). See also, Comment, Curing Cancerphobia: Reasonableness Redefined, 62 U.Chi.L.Rev. 1113 (1995), rejecting judicial requirements of "physical injury," "physical manifestation of cancerphobia," "traditional 'reasonableness,' " and the "more-likely-than-not" standard of *Potter*. With 14 million workers who have been significantly exposed to asbestos, plus other situations giving rise to fear of cancer, some screening device is needed in cancerphobia cases. The author argues that each of the listed traditional approaches is unsatisfying as a screening device, and urges a "substantial probability" standard—one that emphasizes the increased risk to plaintiff "over the societal rate based on general levels of exposure."

Gammon v. Osteopathic Hospital of Maine, Inc.

Supreme Judicial Court of Maine, 1987.
534 A.2d 1282.

[Plaintiff's father, Linwood, died in defendant hospital. Plaintiff asked defendant funeral home to make the arrangements. He alleged that the defendants negligently conducted their operations so that he received a bag that was supposedly personal effects, but which in fact contained "a bloodied leg, severed below the knee, and bluish in color." He yelled "Oh my God, they have taken my father's leg off." He ran into the kitchen where an aunt testified that he "was as white as a ghost." In fact the leg was a pathology specimen removed from another person. Thereafter, plaintiff "began having nightmares for the first time in his life, his personality was affected and his relationship with his wife and children deteriorated." After several months Gammon's emotional state began to improve, although he still had occasional nightmares. He sought no medical or psychiatric attention and offered no medical evidence at trial.

The trial court granted a directed verdict on count I—plaintiff's negligence claim for severe emotional distress. On other counts, not directly relevant here, the judge had charged the jury that "severe emotional distress" was distress "such that no reasonable man should be expected to endure it."]

Before McKusick, C.J., and Nichols, Roberts, Wathen, Scolnik and Clifford, JJ.

ROBERTS, JUSTICE [after stating the facts].

The issue is whether, in these circumstances Gammon has established a claim, in tort, for negligent infliction of severe emotional distress. A person's psychic well-being is as much entitled to legal protection as is his physical well-being. We recognize as much and provide compensation when the emotional distress is intentionally or recklessly inflicted, when the emotional distress results from physical injury negligently inflicted, or when negligently inflicted emotional distress results in physical injury. In order to ensure that a claim for emotional distress without physical injury is not spurious, we have previously required a showing of physical impact, objective manifestation, underlying or accompanying tort, or special circumstances. In the case before us, we conclude that these more or less arbitrary requirements should not bar Gammon's claim for compensation for severe emotional distress.

[At this point the court reviewed eight emotional distress cases that it had decided over a period of 100 years.]

No useful purpose would be served by more detailed analyses of our prior decisions or by consideration of whether the holdings of these cases follow a consistent trend. They demonstrate in a variety of ways the difficulty courts have had dealing with psychic injury.[5] They also demonstrate the frailty of supposed lines of demarcation when they are subjected to judicial scrutiny in the context of varying fact patterns. Moreover, these cases disclose our awareness of the extensive criticism aimed at the artificial devices used by courts to protect against fraudulent claims and against undue burden on the conduct of defendants.

The analyses of commentators and the developing trend in case law encourage us to abandon these artificial devices in this and future tort actions and to rely upon the trial process for protection against fraudulent claims. In addition, the traditional tort principle of foreseeability relied upon in [two earlier cases] provides adequate protection against unduly burdensome liability claims for emotional distress. Jurors or trial judges will be able to evaluate the impact of psychic trauma with no greater difficulty than pertains to assessment of damages for any intangible injury. We do not foresee any great extension of tort liability by our ruling today. We do not provide compensation for the hurt feelings of the supersensitive plaintiff—the eggshell psyche. A defendant is bound to foresee psychic harm only when such harm reasonably could be expected to befall the ordinarily sensitive person.[8]

---

5. When discussing this type of injury, the courts of other jurisdictions and the commentators have used as the adjective either "emotional, mental, nervous or psychic" together with the noun "distress, pain, injury, harm, trauma, disturbance or shock." These phrases have not become words of art although each, with varying degrees of accura-cy, seems to refer to non-tactile trauma resulting in injury to the psyche.

8. We described serious mental distress in [an earlier case] as being "where a reasonable person, normally constituted, would be unable to adequately cope with the mental stress engendered by the circumstances of the event." [ ]

We have previously recognized that courts in other jurisdictions have allowed recovery for mental distress alone for negligent mishandling of corpses. [   ] In recognizing that Gammon has made out a claim in the instant case, we do not find it necessary to rely on an extension of this exception. Instead, we look to the rationale supporting the exception. Courts have concluded that the exceptional vulnerability of the family of recent decedents makes it highly probable that emotional distress will result from mishandling the body. [   ] That high probability is said to provide sufficient trustworthiness to allay the court's fear of fraudulent claims. [   ] This rationale, it seems, is but another way of determining that the defendant reasonably should have foreseen that mental distress would result from his negligence. By the same token, on the record before us, a jury could conclude that the hospital and the mortician reasonably should have foreseen that members of Linwood Gammon's family would be vulnerable to emotional shock at finding a severed leg in what was supposed to be the decedent's personal effects. Despite the defendants' argument to the contrary, we hold that the evidence in this case would support a jury finding that either or both defendants failed to exercise reasonable care to prevent such an occurrence.

Although the analysis in the instant case may impact upon the rationale of our recent cases, we do not find it necessary to overrule those cases. We do not hold that any prior case was wrongly decided. Rather, we recognize that the elimination of some barriers to recovery for negligent infliction of severe emotional distress may compel further evaluation of other policy considerations.   .   .   .

On the facts and circumstances of the case before us, however, we find no sound basis to preclude potential compensation to Gammon. We hold, therefore, that the trial court erred in directing a verdict on Gammon's claim for negligent infliction of severe emotional distress.[9] Accordingly, we vacate the judgment in favor of the defendants on Count I.

Remanded for further proceedings consistent with the opinion herein.

Notes and Questions

1. Is the obligation recognized here limited to situations involving death and the special sensitivity of families after a death? If not, are there any limits to the types of situations that may give rise to a claim for emotional distress from a defendant's negligent conduct?

2. As *Gammon* noted, many courts have permitted recovery for emotional distress alone in cases of mishandled corpses and botched funerals. Another situation that has led a significant number of states to permit recovery without physical injury involves the emotional distress that arises

---

9. By virtue of the pleadings and the jury finding in the case before us, our holding necessarily is limited to negligently inflicted severe emotional distress. We do not decide whether a defendant shall be liable for negligently inflicted emotional distress of any lesser degree.

when a telegram arrives that negligently and incorrectly announces that a family member has died. Is this comparable to the mishandled corpse case?

3. In Baker v. Dorfman, 232 F.3d 121(2d Cir. 2000), the court held that New York law would permit an emotional distress action by a person who, due to negligence, had been incorrectly informed that he had tested positive for HIV. The court relied in part on Johnson v. State, 334 N.E.2d 590 (N.Y.1975), upholding an action for a woman who received a telegram incorrectly telling her that her mother had died. See also Nieman v. Upper Queens Medical Group, 220 N.Y.S.2d 129 (City Ct. 1961), upholding a claim that the defendant negligently reported to plaintiff's physician that plaintiff's sperm count indicated sterility. The physician passed the results on to the plaintiff. After a retest, the plaintiff's count was normal. How might *Gammon* analyze these cases?

4. In Bryan R. v. Watchtower Bible & Tract Society of New York Inc., 738 A.2d 839 (Me.1999), cert. denied 120 S.Ct. 1242 (2000), plaintiff sued the church for abuse alleged to have been inflicted by an adult member of the church. In the course of denying a claim against the church based on "pure foreseeability," the court stated that "[o]nly where a particular duty based upon the unique relationship of the parties has been established may a defendant be held responsible, absent some other wrongdoing, for harming the emotional wellbeing of another. See, e.g., [   ]; [*Gammon*] (holding that a hospital's relationship to the family of deceased gives rise to a duty to avoid emotional harm from handling of remains)." Is the approach in *Bryan R.*, focusing on the relationship, sounder than the approach based on the types of exceptions discussed in these notes?

5. *Falzone* required "reasonable" fear of immediate injury. *Gammon* refers to the "ordinarily sensitive person" as supplemented in footnote 8. Do these formulations help control the expansion of this type of liability?

6. *Physical manifestations.* Throughout this section there has been the underlying question of whether plaintiffs must prove that their emotional distress led to physical manifestations. The *Chizmar* court, p. 277, supra, noted that "examples of serious emotional distress may include 'neuroses, psychoses, chronic depression, phobia, and shock.' [   ] However, temporary fright, disappointment or regret does not suffice. . . ." Although "some jurisdictions have required claims of emotional distress to be 'medically diagnosable or objectifiable,' we do not believe that such a limitation is necessary or desirable." The existence of the required distress was a matter of proof for the trier of fact.

In *Marzolf v. Stone*, p. 289, infra, involving bystanders, the court decided that it would not require physical manifestations since that would "severely and irrationally limit the types of symptoms" that would justify a suit. But the court did require that "a plaintiff's emotional distress must be susceptible to medical diagnosis and proven through medical evidence. This approach calls for objective evidence regarding the severity of the distress, and the causal link between the observation at the scene and the subsequent emotional reaction." In a footnote the court approved an earlier decision that had stated that "Depression, sleeplessness, loss of weight, and social and professional dysfunction impairment are all objective symptoms." It also agreed with other states that "examples of emotional distress would include neuroses, psychoses, chronic depression, phobia, shock, post-traumatic stress disorder, or any other disabling mental condition."

In Sullivan v. Boston Gas Co., 605 N.E.2d 805 (Mass.1993), two plaintiffs stood across the street as their house burned to the ground. In an earlier case the court had said that in emotional distress cases the plaintiff must generally show, in addition to other items, "physical harm manifested by objective symptomatology." The court, paraphrasing Restatement § 436, rejecting the line between physical and mental harm in this area, concluded that "repeated hysterical attacks" are illnesses sufficient to corroborate the existence of the claimed distress; that "headaches or nausea" could qualify if they "lasted for a substantial period of time;" but that "transient symptoms such as vomiting" did not qualify "even though they clearly involve physical functions of the body."

Plaintiff McDonald alleged that she suffered from post-traumatic stress disorder that sometimes occurred as often as once or twice a week, the symptoms of which were diarrhea and heart palpitation. In addition, she asserted that she had experienced "sleeplessness, weeping, depression, and feelings of despair." Sullivan alleged that he had experienced tension headaches, muscle tenderness in the back of his head, and problems with concentration and reading, as well as "sleeplessness, gastrointestinal distress, upset stomach, nightmares, depression, feelings of despair, difficulty in driving and working, and an overall 'lousy' feeling" from the explosion. Both were held to meet the required standard, which was seen as an attempt to strike a balance between "our desire to ferret out fraudulent claims and our duty to grant deserving plaintiffs a chance to present their case to a fact finder."

Is a requirement of physical manifestations likely to serve as a meaningful limitation in these cases?

Portee v. Jaffee

Supreme Court of New Jersey, 1980.
84 N.J. 88, 417 A.2d 521.

[Plaintiff and her seven-year-old son, Guy, lived in an apartment building owned by Jaffee. One afternoon Guy became trapped in the building's elevator between its outer door and the wall of the elevator shaft. The elevator was activated and the boy was dragged up to the third floor. Another child ran to seek help. Plaintiff and police arrived and the police worked for four and one-half hours to free the child. While their efforts continued, plaintiff "watched as her son moaned, cried out and flailed his arms. Much of the time she was restrained from touching him, apparently to prevent interference with the attempted rescue." Guy suffered multiple bone fractures and internal injuries. He died while still trapped, "his mother a helpless observer." Companies involved in designing and maintaining the elevator were also sued.

After Guy's death, plaintiff became severely depressed and self-destructive. She slashed her wrist in a suicide attempt and required physical therapy for her wrist and extensive counseling and psychotherapy. The trial court granted summary judgment for defendants on claims by plaintiff for mental and emotional distress. The dismissal was reviewed directly by the supreme court.]

PASHMAN, J. [after stating the facts].

. . .

On many occasions, the law of negligence needs no other formulation besides the duty of reasonable care. Other cases, however, present circumstances rendering application of that general standard difficult, if not impossible. Without adequate guidance, juries may impose liability that is not commensurate with the culpability of defendant's conduct.

This difficulty has been recognized when courts considered liability for mental and emotional distress. We have noted the traditional argument, rejected by this Court in *Falzone*, that the imposition of such liability unoccasioned by any physical impact would lead to "mere conjecture and speculation." [   ] Even where the causal relationship between conduct and emotional harm was clear, courts would deny liability unless the fault of defendant's conduct could be demonstrated by the occurrence of physical harm to the plaintiff. [   ] Under *Falzone*, it became clear that the creation of a risk of physical harm would be a sufficient indication that defendant's conduct was unreasonable. Without such an indication, it might be argued that a jury could not form a reliable judgment regarding negligence. The question now before us is whether we are left to "mere conjecture and speculation" in assessing the culpability of conduct that creates neither the risk nor the occurrence of physical harm.

The task in the present case involves the refinement of principles of liability to remedy violations of reasonable care while avoiding speculative results or punitive liability. The solution is close scrutiny of the specific personal interests assertedly injured. By this approach, we can determine whether a defendant's freedom of action should be burdened by the imposition of liability. In the present case, the interest assertedly injured is more than a general interest in emotional tranquility. It is the profound and abiding sentiment of parental love. The knowledge that loved ones are safe and whole is the deepest wellspring of emotional welfare. Against that reassuring background, the flashes of anxiety and disappointment that mar our lives take on softer hues. No loss is greater than the loss of a loved one, and no tragedy is more wrenching than the helpless apprehension of the death or serious injury of one whose very existence is a precious treasure. The law should find more than pity for one who is stricken by seeing that a loved one has been critically injured or killed.

Courts in other jurisdictions which have found liability in the circumstances before us have placed limits on this type of negligence liability consistent with their view of the individual interest being injured. In Dillon v. Legg, [441 P.2d 912 (Cal.1968)], the California Supreme Court identified three factors which would determine whether an emotional injury would be compensable because "foreseeable:"

Test

> (1) Whether plaintiff was located near the scene of the accident as contrasted with one who was a distance away from it. (2) Whether the shock resulted from a direct emotional impact upon plaintiff from the sensory and contemporaneous observance of the accident, as contrasted with learning of the accident from others after its occurrence. (3) Whether plaintiff and the victim were closely related, as contrasted with an absence of any relationship or the presence of only a distant relationship. [   ]
>
> . . .

We agree that the three factors described in *Dillon* together create a strong case for negligence liability. In any given case, as physical proximity between plaintiff and the scene of the accident becomes closer, the foreseeable likelihood that plaintiff will suffer emotional distress from apprehending the physical harm of another increases. The second requirement of "direct . . . sensory and contemporaneous observance" appears to reflect a limitation of the liability rule to traumatic distress occasioned by immediate perception. The final criterion, that the plaintiff be "closely related" to the injured person, also embodies the judgment that only the most profound emotional interests should receive vindication for their negligent injury.

Our analysis of the specific emotional interest injured in this case—a fundamental interest in emotional tranquility founded on parental love—reveals where the limits of liability would lie. Addressing the *Dillon* criteria in reverse order, we find the last—the existence of a close relationship—to be the most crucial. It is the presence of deep, intimate, familial ties between the plaintiff and the physically injured person that makes the harm to emotional tranquility so serious and compelling. The genuine suffering which flows from such harm stands in stark contrast to the setbacks and sorrows of everyday life, or even to the apprehension of harm to another, less intimate person. The existence of a marital or intimate familial relationship is therefore an essential element of a cause of action for negligent infliction of emotional distress. In the present case, the instinctive affection of a mother for her seven-year-old son would be a sufficiently intimate bond on which to predicate liability.

Application

The second requirement—that the plaintiff witness the incident which resulted in death or serious injury—is equally essential. We recognize that to deny recovery solely because the plaintiff was not subjected to a risk of physical harm would impose an arbitrary barrier that bears no relation to the injury to his basic emotional stability. [   ] Yet avoiding arbitrary distinctions does not entail that a cause of action should exist for all emotional injuries to all the close relatives of the victim. This expansive view would extend judicial redress far beyond the bounds of the emotional interest entitled to protection. To avoid imposing liability in excess of culpability, the scope of recovery must be circumscribed to negligent conduct which strikes at the plaintiff's basic emotional security.

Discovering the death or serious injury of an intimate family member will always be expected to threaten one's emotional welfare. Ordinarily, however, only a witness at the scene of the accident causing death or serious injury will suffer a traumatic sense of loss that may destroy his sense of security and cause severe emotional distress.   .   .   . Such a risk of severe emotional distress is present when the plaintiff observes the accident at the scene. Without such perception, the threat of emotional injury is lessened and the justification for liability is fatally weakened. The law of negligence, while it redresses suffering wrongfully caused by others, must not itself inflict undue harm by imposing an unreasonably excessive measure of liability. Accordingly, we hold that observing the death or serious injury of another while it occurs is an essential element of a cause of action for the negligent infliction of emotional distress.

The first factor discussed in *Dillon*—that the plaintiff be near the injured person—embodies the same observations made concerning the other requirements of direct perception and close familial relationship. Physical proximity may be of some relevance in demonstrating the closeness of the emotional bond between plaintiff and the injured family member. For example, one would generally suppose that the risk of emotional distress to a brother who is halfway across the country is not as great as to a mother who is at the scene of the accident. The proximity of the plaintiff to the accident scene increases the likelihood that he will witness the event causing the death or serious injury of a loved one. Yet it appears that if the plaintiff must observe the accident that causes death or serious injury, a requirement of proximity is necessarily satisfied. The risk of emotional injury exists by virtue of the plaintiff's perception of the accident, not his proximity to it.

An additional factor yet undiscussed is the severity of the physical injury causing emotional distress. The harm we have determined to be worthy of judicial redress is the trauma accompanying the observation of the death or serious physical injury of a loved one. While any harm to a spouse or a family member causes sorrow, we are here concerned with a more narrowly confined interest in mental and emotional stability. When confronted with accidental death, "the reaction to be expected of normal persons," [   ], is shock and fright. We hold that the observation of either death or this type of serious injury is necessary to permit recovery. Since the sense of loss attendant to death or serious injury is typically not present following lesser accidental harm, perception of less serious harm would not ordinarily result in severe emotional distress. Thus, the risk of an extraordinary reaction to less serious injury is not sufficient to result in liability. To impose liability for any emotional consequence of negligent conduct would be unreasonable; it would also be unnecessary to protect a plaintiff's basic emotional stability. Therefore, a cause of action for emotional distress would require the perception of death or serious physical injury.

The cause of action we approve today for the negligent infliction of emotional distress requires proof of the following elements: (1) the death or serious physical injury of another caused by defendant's negligence; (2) a marital or intimate familial relationship between plaintiff and the injured person; (3) observation of the death or injury at the scene of the accident; and (4) resulting severe emotional distress. We find that a defendant's duty of reasonable care to avoid physical harm to others extends to the avoidance of this type of mental and emotional harm.   .   .   .

.   .   .

[The trial court judgment was reversed.]

For *reversal*—CHIEF JUSTICE WILENTZ, and JUSTICES SULLIVAN, PASHMAN, CLIFFORD, SCHREIBER, HANDLER and POLLOCK—7.

For *affirmance*—none.

Notes and Questions

1.   At several points, the *Portee* court expresses concern that "juries may impose liability that is not commensurate with the culpability of defendant's conduct." Is this more of a concern in cases producing nonphysical harm than in those involving broken bones and death?

2.   The *Dillon–Portee* elements of proximity to the scene and sensory impact are closely related to each other, but are not overlapping. In Scherr v. Hilton Hotels Corp., 214 Cal.Rptr. 393 (App. 1985), plaintiff wife, in California, saw live television coverage of a fire then taking place at the Las Vegas Hilton Hotel. She knew her husband was attending a meeting at that hotel and that he was supposed to be in the hotel at that time. She never saw him on camera and did not discover until later that he had in fact been hurt in the fire. The court found that plaintiff had failed to come within the sensory perception requirement. Her perception "of endangerment, while potentially stressful, is insufficient to cause legally cognizable harm, for the stress has not yet ripened into disabling shock." The court did not reach the television aspect of the case. What if the plaintiff had watched her husband, about to be enveloped by flames, jump from a balcony on a high floor and hit the ground? See also Gain v. Carroll Mill Co., Inc., 787 P.2d 553 (Wash.1990), a case apparently involving a televised viewing of an event, but avoiding decision on that ground.

3.   The *Portee* court adds another element—the death or serious injury to the victim. In Barnhill v. Davis, 300 N.W.2d 104 (Iowa 1981), the plaintiff and his mother were driving one behind the other to the same destination. After plaintiff cleared an intersection, he looked in the rear view mirror and saw his mother's car hit on the driver's side by the defendant's car. In fact, the mother was only slightly injured. Plaintiff alleged serious emotional and physical harm from his concern before he learned how slight the injury was. The court said the proper test was whether a reasonable person would believe, and the plaintiff did believe, that his mother would be seriously injured in the type of accident that occurred.

Compare Barnes v. Geiger, 446 N.E.2d 78 (Mass.App.1983), involving a mother who reasonably but mistakenly thought that her child had been horribly injured in an accident that she had witnessed. The victim of that accident was in fact an unrelated child. The mother died the next day from trauma alleged to have resulted from her experience. The court denied recovery:

> Daily life is too full of momentary perturbation. Injury to a child and the protracted anguish placed upon the witnessing parent is, on the scale of human experience, tangible and predictable. Distress based on mistake as to the circumstances is ephemeral and will vary with the disposition of a person to imagine that the worst has happened. We are unwilling to expand the circle of liability [established in earlier cases] to such an additional dimension, because to do so expands unreasonably the class of person to whom a tortfeasor may be liable.

In Sell v. Mary Lanning Memorial Hospital Assn., 498 N.W.2d 522 (Neb.1993), plaintiff mother had been incorrectly and negligently informed that her son had been killed. After two days of planning the funeral, she learned that there had been a case of mistaken identity. Plaintiff's suit for emotional distress was rejected, 4–3, even though Nebraska has indicated a broader approach than the *Portee-Dillon* line.

The majority held that plaintiff's reactions—continual crying, trouble eating and sleeping, and some medication—were inadequate. "Without minimizing plaintiff's apparent and understandable heartache upon being told of her son's death," she had not met the required standard. According to a concurring judge "we should shed tears for the loss of [the dead youth], empathize with the grief of his family and friends, rejoice in Scott Sell's life, and move on." The dissenters thought no further evidence was needed where a mother thought her child had been killed. "I hope our society has not reached the point where we need a doctor to tell us what emotional impact results from loss of a child."

4.   After a period of expansion, California has narrowed its decisions in this area. Contrast Ochoa v. Superior Court, 703 P.2d 1 (Cal.1985)(mother watched child in juvenile hall deteriorate from apparently serious illness when medical staff would not respond to the emergency; he died after she left for the night) with the denial of recovery in Thing v. La Chusa, 771 P.2d 814 (Cal.1989) (mother, who was nearby, neither heard nor saw accident injuring her child, but was told about it and rushed to the scene to see the child's bloody and unconscious body lying in the roadway). The court in *Thing* concluded that the three factors set forth in *Dillon* were defining elements and not simply guidelines: "Experience has shown that, contrary to the expectation of the *Dillon* majority, . . . there are clear judicial days on which a court can foresee forever and thus determine liability but none on which that foresight alone provides a socially and judicially acceptable limit on recovery of damages for that injury."

In elaborating on the three elements, the *Thing* court stated that "absent exceptional circumstances, recovery should be limited to relatives residing in the same household, or parents, siblings, children, and grandparents of the victim." As to the second element, the viewing of "consequences" of an accident was insufficient—even if they were, as the dissent had argued, "immediate consequences." As to the third element, the court identified the requisite distress as "a reaction beyond that which would be anticipated in a disinterested witness and which is not an abnormal response to the circumstances." Is it superfluous to require that plaintiff be in a close relationship with the victim and then to require a reaction beyond "that which would be anticipated in a disinterested witness"?

5. Many states have not moved as far as the multi-factor tests for bystander recovery adopted in *Dillon* and *Portee.* One of those is New York. Early on, Tobin v. Grossman, 249 N.E.2d 419 (N.Y.1969), rejected *Dillon,* concluding that it would be difficult if not impossible to draw lines limiting the action. No recovery for emotional distress was to be permitted in such cases. In Bovsun v. Sanperi, 461 N.E.2d 843 (N.Y.1984), the court, 4–3, overruled *Tobin*'s total refusal to allow an action, and extended a duty to members of the "immediate family" who were themselves in the zone of physical danger:

> The zone-of-danger rule, which allows one who is himself or herself threatened with bodily harm in consequence of the defendant's negligence to recover for emotional distress resulting from viewing the death or serious physical injury of a member of his or her immediate family, is . . . premised on the traditional negligence concept that by unreasonably endangering the plaintiff's physical safety the defendant has breached a duty owed to him or her for which he or she should recover all damages sustained including those occasioned by witnessing the suffering of an immediate family member who is also injured by the defendant's conduct. Recognition of this right to recover for emotional distress attributable to observation of injuries suffered by a member of the immediate family involves a broadening of the duty concept but—unlike the *Dillon* approach—not the creation of a duty to a plaintiff to whom the defendant is not already recognized as owing a duty to avoid bodily harm. In so doing it permits recovery for an element of damages not heretofore allowed. Use of the zone-of-danger rule thus mitigates the possibility of unlimited recovery, an overriding apprehension expressed in *Tobin,* by restricting liability in a much narrower fashion than does the *Dillon* rule. Additionally, the circumstances in which a plaintiff who is within the zone of danger suffers serious emotional distress from observing severe physical injury or death of a member of the immediate family may not be altogether common.

In addition, the emotional distress had to be "serious and verifiable." The dissenters would have adhered to *Tobin.* Before *Bovsun* how did New York handle cases in which defendant's car veered over onto plaintiff's side of the road and crashed into his car, hurting plaintiff and killing his sister, who had been driving? Do you consider either the *Tobin* or the *Bovsun* approach preferable to the *Dillon–Portee* approach?

6. On the other hand, some states are going beyond *Dillon* and *Portee* in some respects. In Marzolf v. Stone, 960 P.2d 424 (Wash.1998), close relatives came by the scene of an accident shortly after it happened. The court said their claims for emotional distress should be upheld if the distress is "caused by observing an injured relative at the scene of an accident shortly after its occurrence and before there is a substantial change in the relative's condition or location." The "challenge is to create a rule that acknowledges the shock of seeing a victim shortly after an accident, without extending a defendant's liability to every relative who grieves for the victim." A bright line had simplicity but was said to be arbitrary.

In Stockdale v. Bird & Son, Inc., 503 N.E.2d 951 (Mass.1987), plaintiff was the mother of a 21-year-old son who had been killed by the alleged negligence of defendant. She learned of the death from the police four hours after it had occurred. She first saw the body 24 hours later in a funeral home. The plaintiff sustained physical and mental suffering that began shortly after learning of the death. The son had lived at home until his death. A unanimous court rejected the claim for negligently inflicted emotional distress. The two lengths of time distinguished the case from an earlier one in which the family had seen the victim in the hospital immediately after the accident. Does the likelihood of serious emotional harm depend on how soon after the accident the plaintiff learns of the consequences?

7. Were the allegations of wrist slashing necessary to the outcome in *Portee*? A few years after *Portee*, the same court observed that *Falzone* had "allowed recovery for emotional distress resulting in physical injury even in the absence of physical impact." It then noted that in *Portee* it had "allowed recovery, even in the absence of physical injury." Frame v. Kothari, 560 A.2d 675 (N.J.1989). Should that loosening apply only in bystander cases?

8. *Beyond the family.* Consider whether the following event might lead a court to extend liability beyond the family. In 1995, in New York City, as a man held the door of an elevator for an exiting woman on the second floor, a second woman caught her foot. As the man moved to free her, the elevator suddenly lurched upward with its doors still open. The movement decapitated the man sending his body to the hallway floor while the elevator continued up to the ninth floor with other passengers and the decapitated man's head—with his Walkman earphones still attached. S.F. Examiner, Jan. 7, 1995, at 2. How would current law handle suits by the passengers—and their spouses? How should it handle such suits?

9. *Unmarried couples and emotional distress.* In Elden v. Sheldon, 758 P.2d 582 (Cal.1988), Richard was hurt in an auto accident allegedly caused by the defendant's negligence. This case involved claims for his emotional distress from witnessing the death of Linda, who was in Richard's car and with whom Richard alleged he had an "unmarried cohabitation relationship . . . which was both stable and significant and parallel to a marital relationship." The court, 6–1, relying on three "policy reasons," affirmed dismissal of claims for emotional distress.

The first was that "the state has a strong interest in the marriage relationship; to the extent unmarried cohabitants are granted the same rights as married persons, the state's interest in promoting marriage is inhibited. . . . The policy favoring marriage is 'rooted in the necessity of providing an institutional basis for defining the fundamental relational rights and responsibilities of persons in organized society.' [   ] Formally married couples are granted significant rights and bear important responsibilities toward one another which are not shared by those who cohabit without marriage." The court cited property rights and support obligations, among others.

The second justification for rejecting the claim was that acceptance of such claims would impose "a difficult burden on the courts" requiring inquiry into whether the relationship "was stable and significant" and into such matters as "sexual fidelity."

The third justification was the need to "limit the number of persons to whom a negligent defendant owes a duty of care." Since every injury has ramifying consequences "the problem for the law is to limit the legal consequences of wrongs to a controllable degree." Here it was enough to allow recovery to those in close family relationships. A "bright line in this area of the law is essential."

The dissenter, in addition to responding to the three points, noted that the majority would presumably preclude "any gay or lesbian plaintiff from stating a *Dillon* cause of action based on the injury of his or her partner. [   ] Clearly the state's interest in marriage is not advanced by precluding recovery to couples who could not in any case choose marriage."

The *Elden* approach was rejected in Dunphy v. Gregor, 642 A.2d 372 (N.J.1994), involving a claim by a woman who witnessed the death of her fiancé. They had been engaged two years earlier and had set the wedding for four years hence. Plaintiff alleged that at the time of the death they had been living together for two years; had taken out life-insurance policies making each other beneficiaries; maintained a joint checking account from which they paid their bills; and had jointly purchased an automobile. In addition, she alleged that the decedent "had asked her several times to elope with him, and he had introduced her in public as his wife."

The court, 5–1, after reviewing *Portee v. Jaffee* and its progeny at length, was "convinced that the solution to the posed question lies not in a hastily-drawn 'bright line' distinction between married and unmarried persons but in the 'sedulous application' of the principles of tort law." The nature and extent of the harm was to be judged by inquiring into such matters as "the duration of the relationship, the degree of mutual dependence, the extent of common contributions to a life together, the extent and quality of shared experience, and, [quoting the court below] 'whether the plaintiff and the injured person were members of the same household, their emotional reliance on each other, the particulars of their day to day relationship, and the manner in which they related to each other in attending to life's mundane requirements.'" The court said that these inquiries must be made in the case of married couples in emotional distress and in loss of consortium cases to assess the harm done to that relationship.

Very shortly after deciding the *Bovsun* case, discussed in note 5, the New York court decided another emotional distress claim.

Johnson v. Jamaica Hospital

Court of Appeals of New York, 1984.
62 N.Y.2d 523, 467 N.E.2d 502, 478 N.Y.S.2d 838.

[Plaintiffs' daughter, Kawana, was born in defendant hospital. After the plaintiff mother was discharged, Kawana was kept for further treatment. When the mother visited a week later, Kawana was discovered missing. She apparently had been abducted that day—a day on which the hospital received two bomb threats. While she was missing plaintiffs brought suit for the emotional distress brought about by defendant's negligence. Kawana was recovered by the police and returned to plaintiffs after four and one-half months. A separate suit was brought on Kawana's behalf, which is not part of this appeal. The trial court denied defendant's motion to dismiss the parents' action for failure to state a cause of action. The Appellate Division affirmed by a divided vote and certified the question whether it had acted properly.]

KAYE, JUDGE [after stating the facts].

Assuming the allegations of plaintiffs' complaint to be true [ ], no cause of action is stated. Plaintiff parents may not recover damages from defendant hospital for any mental distress or emotional disturbances they may have suffered as a result of the direct injury inflicted upon their daughter by defendant's breach of its duty of care to her. [ ] Although in Bovsun v. Sanperi, [ ], we recently decided that damages may be recovered for such indirect "psychic injuries" in limited circumstances, plaintiffs have stated no basis for recovering under the standard set forth in *Bovsun* in that they have not alleged that they were within the zone of danger and that their injuries resulted from contemporaneous observation of serious physical injury or death caused by defendant's negligence. Plaintiffs contend, and the courts below concluded, that their complaint states a cause of action because the defendant hospital owed a duty directly to them, as parents, to care properly for their child, and that it was or should have been foreseeable to defendant that any injury to Kawana, such as abduction, would cause them mental distress. There is no basis for establishing such a direct duty. This court has refused to recognize such a duty on the part of a hospital to the parents of hospitalized children (Kalina v. General

Hosp., 13 N.Y.2d 1023, 245 N.Y.S.2d 599, 195 N.E.2d 309), and there is no reason to depart from that rule here.

In *Kalina,* the plaintiffs, an observant Jewish couple, gave express instructions to the defendant hospital that their newborn son was to be ritualistically circumcised on his eighth day by a mohel in accordance with the tenets of their religion. Instead, due to the alleged negligence and malpractice of the hospital, the baby was circumcised on his fourth day by a physician. The plaintiff parents sought recovery for their mental pain and suffering caused by the assault and battery upon their son. Special Term granted defendants' motion to dismiss the complaint [   ], and we ultimately affirmed on Special Term's opinion. In that opinion, the parents of the hospitalized child were held to be "interested bystanders" to whom no direct duty was owed.

> Both of the pleadings are insufficient because the plaintiffs as individuals, apart from their status as representatives of their son, do not have a legally protected interest under these circumstances [   ]. To paraphrase the language of [*Palsgraf v. Long Island R. Co.,* reprinted in Chapter V], the conduct of the defendants, if a wrong in relation to the son, was not a wrong in its relation to the plaintiffs, remote from the event. Rights are not abstractions but exist only correlatively with duties. Everyone who has been damaged by an interruption in the expected tenor of his life does not have a cause of action. The law demands that the equation be balanced; that the damaged plaintiff be able to point the finger of responsibility at a defendant owing, not a general duty to society, but a specific duty to him.

> The defendants here in accepting a relationship with the son assumed the risk of liability for a tortious performance to him. They did not assume any risk of liability that their acts might violate the personal sensibilities of others, be they the son's parents, his coreligionists or the community at large. [   ]

Jamaica Hospital owed no more of a direct duty to the plaintiff parents to refrain from causing them psychic injury than did the defendants in *Kalina* [and three other cases]. The direct injury allegedly caused by defendant's negligence—abduction—was sustained by the infant, and plaintiffs' grief and mental torment which resulted from her disappearance are not actionable. The foreseeability that such psychic injuries would result from the injury to Kawana does not serve to establish a duty running from defendant to plaintiffs (*Albala v. City of New York,* [p. 166, supra]; *Pulka v. Edelman,* [p. 150, supra]), and in the absence of such a duty, as a matter of law there can be no liability [   ]. That sound policy reasons support these decisions is evident here, for to permit recovery by the infant's parents for emotional distress would be to invite open-ended liability for indirect emotional injury suffered by families in every instance where the very young, or very elderly, or incapacitated persons experience negligent care or treatment.

[The court rejected duties based on the contractual relationship and on a *loco parentis* relationship.]

Finally, our prior holdings in *Johnson v. State of New York*, [   ], and *Lando v. State of New York*, [   ], provide no basis for recovery. In neither case was liability based upon a hospital's breach of care to its patient causing direct injury to the patient resulting in emotional injury to relatives of the patient. In *Johnson* the defendant hospital negligently sent a telegram to plaintiff notifying her of her mother's death when in fact her mother had not died, and in *Lando* the defendant hospital negligently failed to locate a deceased patient's body for 11 days, when it was found in an advanced state of decomposition. Each case presented exceptional circumstances in which courts long ago recognized liability for resultant emotional injuries: a duty to transmit truthfully information concerning a relative's death or funeral [   ] which the hospital assumed by sending the message [   ], and the mishandling of or failure to deliver a dead body with the consequent denial of access to the family [   ]. Neither exception is applicable here.

In summary, Jamaica Hospital, even if negligent in caring for Kawana and directly liable to her, is not liable for emotional distress suffered by plaintiffs as a consequence of the abduction. This is in accord with the majority rule in this country. [   ] There is no duty owing from defendant to plaintiffs to refrain from negligently causing such injury. To hold otherwise would be to invite the very sort of boundless liability for indirect emotional injury that we have consistently rejected.

[The court rejected a dissent argument that liability here can be circumscribed by limiting any duty owed to those parents whose custodial rights have been interfered with because this was not a common occurrence. The majority responded that "any right to recover for emotional injury sustained by plaintiffs because of defendant's negligence in the 'care, custody and management' of their child cannot rationally be refused to other parents, relatives or custodians of persons to whom caretakers of various types, such as schools and day care centers, are alleged to have breached a similar duty."] Accordingly, the order of the Appellate Division should be reversed, the certified question answered in the negative, and the complaint dismissed.

MEYER, JUDGE (dissenting).

I had thought that the fear of "open-ended liability for indirect emotional injury" [   ], had long ago been laid to rest [*Battalla* p. 266 supra], and that *Bovsun v. Sanperi*, [   ], with its recognition that serious and verifiable emotional disturbance [   ], suffered by an immediate family member [   ], was a compensable injury, marked the beginning of a rationale for determining just when "[f]reedom from mental disturbance is . . . . a protected interest in this State" [   ]. . . .

[In an extended opinion the two dissenters asserted that the burden on the courts was not to be considered because it was, quoting Prosser, "the business of the law to remedy wrongs that deserve it, even at the expense of a 'flood of litigation.'" Moreover, a flood was unlikely here because "interference with the right of custody [was] not a common occurrence." As to fear of disproportionate burden on defendant, this case came to the

[handwritten margin note:] Dissent thought we had got away from fear of lit.

court on a motion to dismiss and there was "nothing before the court to indicate what, if any, change in hospital procedures would be required were there imposed upon it a duty to exercise reasonable care not to permit a newborn baby to be removed from the hospital by someone other than the parents or a person having the parents' permission to do so, or how great a burden in time or cost such a duty would impose. Clearly, however, it cannot simply be presumed that the burden would be so great as to foreclose imposition of liability, the more particularly so in view of the fact that it is a matter of common knowledge that hospitals already have a checkout procedure."

Kalina was said to be distinguishable because the hospital had not assumed "any risk of liability that their acts might violate the personal sensibilities of others." Here, however, the hospital interfered with the custodial rights of the parents. Finally, for courts to deny a duty here "is a pitiful confession of incompetence on the part of courts of justice."]

COOKE, C.J., and JONES, WACHTLER and SIMONS, JJ., concur with KAYE, J.

MEYER, J., dissents and votes to affirm in a separate opinion in which JASEN, J., concurs.

Notes and Questions

1. As the court notes, Kawana's own action is not involved at this time. Does she have a claim if she is returned in good health? Is the court overlooking the deterrence function?

2. Is there a meaningful distinction between "direct" and "indirect" harms in these emotional distress cases? Is *Johnson* consistent with *Tenuto*, p. 167, supra, in which the father got polio?

3. In other contexts, courts have viewed the mother who is claiming negligent infliction of emotional distress resulting from giving birth as a special case. She is not seen as a direct victim since the alleged malpractice was addressed to the fetus; she is not a bystander because she is so close to the event as to be part of it. The mother has an action whether conscious at the time or not. (There was concern that the use of anesthetic might become more common in deliveries if the courts barred suits when the mother was not aware of the negligence at the time it occurred.) In one case, Carey v. Lovett, 622 A.2d 1279 (N.J.1993), the father was said to come under the bystander approach. Another court has said that he would "probably" be treated as a bystander. Burgess v. Superior Court (Gupta), 831 P.2d 1197 (Cal. 1992). How might New York analyze this type of case?

4. How does *Bovsun* apply here? Is this a stronger or weaker case for recovery than a zone-of-danger case in which a child is suddenly hurt before a parent's eyes?

5. The dissent argued, among other points, that the limits of this case could be held. What about a suit by a grandparent? By a seven-year-old sibling of Kawana? By an aunt who had been living with the parents for several years?

6. Is *Kalina* controlling? If the court had recognized a duty in the main case would it have had to overrule *Kalina?*

7. In Oresky v. Scharf, 510 N.Y.S.2d 897 (App.Div. 1987), plaintiffs, who were sisters, placed their mother in defendants' nursing home. Plaintiffs alleged that all parties knew that the mother had Alzheimer's Disease. Six months after her arrival, the mother disappeared from the nursing home and, by the time of this appeal, was still missing.

The court traced the same arguments as those raised in the main case and rejected plaintiffs' claim. *Bovsun* did not apply because plaintiffs had "not alleged that they were in the zone of danger or that their alleged emotional injuries resulted from contemporaneous observation of serious physical injury or death caused by the defendants' negligence." The case of the kidnapped baby was said to be "dispositive." Efforts to obtain further review failed.

Is the case of the kidnapped baby stronger (or weaker) than one involving a disappearing parent? What type of action might be brought on behalf of the missing parent?

8. The consequences of being categorized as either direct or bystander are still being developed. In Huggins v. Longs Drug Stores California Inc., 862 P.2d 148 (Cal.1993), plaintiff parents followed an incorrect label and gave their infant an excessive dose of medicine. The child was not permanently injured. The parents' claim against the pharmacist was rejected, 5–2. The goal of the transaction was to provide medication for the baby: "Because plaintiffs were not the patients for whom defendant dispensed the prescribed medication, they cannot recover as direct victims of defendant's negligence." One dissenter thought plaintiffs were "direct victims," since they were "necessary parties to the administration" of the medicine. The other dissenter emphasized the guilt that parents feel when they are the—even innocent—instruments of harm to their children: "It is this additional injury that renders the parent a direct victim."

9. *Damage to property.* In Lubner v. City of Los Angeles, 53 Cal. Rptr.2d 24 (App. 1996), the plaintiff artists sued for property damage and emotional distress when the city's trash truck crashed into their house, damaging the house, two cars and much of their artwork. The court denied recovery for the distress, refusing categorically to allow recovery for emotional distress caused by loss of property:

> The policy of preventing future harm is served by the sanction of compensation for the economic loss, which also meets the factor of the burden on the defendant to avoid runaway trash trucks in the future. The principal consequences to the community of imposing an incremental liability for these damages are the additional taxes to citizens of the City in exchange for city services. . . . On balance, the factors do not favor permitting the emotional distress damages.

How would *Falzone* analyze *Lubner?* Would it matter whether the Lubners were at home when the truck hit the house?

10.   Several cases have involved claims for damage to the house itself. Perhaps the earliest, Rodrigues v. State, 472 P.2d 509 (Haw.1970), involved a house that plaintiffs had built with their own hands. Due to the state's negligence, water flooded the house to a depth of six inches causing damage. In addition to recovery for property damage, the court, 3–2, held that plaintiffs could recover damages for their emotional distress upon a showing that "a reasonable man normally constituted, would be unable adequately to cope with the mental stress engendered by the circumstances of the case." Two of the five justices dissented on the ground that it was inappropriate to award such damages as a result of harm to property.

Although a few states follow *Rodrigues*, most deny recovery in this situation. See, e.g., City of Tyler v. Likes, 962 S.W.2d 489 (Texas 1997), denying emotional distress damages where defendant's conduct caused 3.5 feet of water to enter plaintiff's house. See also, Erlich v. Menezes, 981 P.2d 978 (Cal.1999), involving a "dream house" that soon needed $400,000 in repairs because of defendant contractor's negligence. The court noted that already-high construction costs would go even higher and that "errors are so likely to occur that few if any homeowners would be justified in resting their peace of mind on [the contract's] timely or correct completion." The court approvingly cited *Lubner*, involving the destroyed art. In addition, it asserted that the contracting parties could have included provisions for such damages if they saw fit. Should it matter whether the house is being constructed—or is one in which plaintiffs have lived happily for years?

11.   *Pets.* In Campbell v. Animal Quarantine Station, 632 P.2d 1066 (Haw.1981), plaintiffs learned over the telephone that their dog had died because of the negligence of defendant, which had occurred on the same island in Hawaii. Recovery of $200 for each of five plaintiffs was upheld after a finding that they had each suffered "severe" emotional distress. But see Roman v. Carroll, 621 P.2d 307 (Ariz.App.1980), in which plaintiff alleged that she sustained emotional distress from "watching defendants' St. Bernard dismember plaintiff's poodle while she was walking the dog near her home." The poodle died two days later. The court rejected plaintiff's effort to use the bystander analysis because a dog "is personal property" and "distress from witnessing injury to property" did not give rise to an action.

See Note, In Defense of Floyd: Appropriately Valuing Companion Animals in Tort, 70 N.Y.U.L.Rev. 1059 (1995), rejecting the treatment of pets as property, as exemplified by New York law. In 1996 New York law was so clear that a court said only: "It is well established that a pet owner in New York cannot recover damages for emotional distress caused by the negligent destruction of a dog." Jason v. Parks, 638 N.Y.S.2d 170 (App.Div. 1996).

12.   Cases from Hawaii have been particularly receptive to claims for emotional distress. In addition to *Rodrigues* and *Campbell*, considered supra, consider the following:

a. Leong v. Takasaki, 520 P.2d 758 (Haw.1974). A ten-year-old boy was walking hand-in-hand with his stepfather's mother. She walked into a crosswalk but plaintiff held back because of an oncoming vehicle. He was allowed to recover for the emotional distress of witnessing the ensuing accident. The lack of a blood relationship was not controlling because "Hawaiian and Asian families of this state have long maintained strong ties among members of the same extended family group." The court also concluded that no physical symptoms were required.

b. Kelley v. Kokua Sales & Supply, Ltd., 532 P.2d 673 (Haw.1975). A man in California suffered emotional distress when he was informed by telephone that his daughter and granddaughter had been killed in an auto accident in Hawaii. The court, 4–1, refused to recognize a duty on the ground that the scene of the accident was too remote for the defendants to have reasonably foreseen these consequences of their conduct.

c. Masaki v. General Motors Corp., 780 P.2d 566 (Haw.1989). Plaintiff parents heard that their son had been hurt in an accident. They resided on the same island and went immediately to the hospital where they saw the consequences of the accident and were told that their son would never again walk. The fact that they did not witness the accident was not a bar to recovery but rather "a factor in determining the degree of mental stress suffered. Whether the degree of stress engendered by the circumstances of this case was beyond that with which a reasonable man can be expected to cope is a question for the jury."

Is the Hawaii approach preferable to others we have considered? Are the results in *Rodrigues* and *Campbell* affected by 1986 legislation in Hawaii, (H.R.S. § 663–8.9), that barred recovery for negligent infliction of emotional distress arising from damage to "property or material objects" unless the distress resulted in "physical injury to or mental illness of the person who experiences the emotional distress or disturbance"?

Negligent Interference with Consortium

A very important aspect of family relationships is the harm to one spouse when the other is seriously injured. The history of a third party's liability to one spouse for seriously injuring the other is traced in the following extended excerpt from the opinion of Justice Kaplan in Diaz v. Eli Lilly & Co., 302 N.E.2d 555 (Mass.1973):

In olden days, when married women were under legal disabilities corresponding to their inferior social status, any action for personal or other injuries to the wife was brought in the names of the husband and wife, and the husband was ordinarily entitled to the avails of the action as of his own property. The husband had, in addition, his own recourse by action without even nominal joinder of the wife against those who invaded the conjugal relationship, for example, by criminal conversation with or abduction of his wife. At one time the gravamen of the latter claims for loss of consortium was the deprivation of the wife's services conceived to be owing by the wife to the husband; the action was similar to that of a master for enticement of his servant. Later the grounds of the consortium action included loss of the society of the wife and impairment of relations with her as a sexual partner, and emphasis shifted away from loss of her services or earning capacity. The defendant, moreover, need not have infringed upon the marital relation by an act of adultery or the like, for he could inflict similar injuries upon the husband in the way of loss of consortium by an assault upon the wife or even a negligent injury. Meanwhile, what of the wife's rights? She had none analogous to the husband's. The husband was of course perfectly competent to sue without joinder of the wife for injuries to himself, and there was no thought that the wife had any legal claim to the husband's services or his sexual or other companionship—any claim, at any rate, in the form of a cause of action for third-party damage to the relationship.

With the coming in of the married women's acts in the mid-nineteenth century, the wife became competent to sue in her own name for injuries to herself and could retain the proceeds of those actions. . . . It was held very widely that husbands still retained their consortium rights, the element of loss of wives' services and earnings, however, being excluded from the husbands' recoveries as belonging to the wives themselves. And it was generally held that the new status of married women implied at least some rights of consortium on their part. If adultery with or alienation of the affections of a wife was a wrong to the husband, similar traffic of another woman with the husband should be actionable by the wife. Wives were readily accorded these rights of action.

However, there was difficulty about wives' recovery for acts of third parties not so plainly attacking the marriage relation, say acts of negligence toward the husband injuring him in such a way as to deprive the wife of his society and sexual comfort. The difficulty was perhaps traceable in the end to the reluctance of judges to accept the women's emancipation acts as introducing a broad general premise for fresh decision. . . .

[After reviewing the course of decisions in Massachusetts, Justice Kaplan turned to the situation in the rest of the country. He noted that the wife's right to an action for lost consortium was recognized in the 1950s, and had been adopted in about half the states as of 1973.]

To a few critics the idea of a right of consortium seems no more than an anachronism harking back to the days when a married woman was a chattel slave, and in a formulation such as that of the new Restatement they would find a potential for indefinite expansion of a questionable liability. But that formulation, reflecting a strong current of recent decisions, is a natural expression of a dominant (and commonplace) theme of our modern law of torts, namely, that presumptively there should be recourse for a definite injury to a legitimate interest due to a lack of the prudence or care appropriate to the occasion. That it would be very difficult to put bounds on an interest and value it is a possible reason for leaving it without protection at least in the form of money damages. But the law is moderately confident about the ability of the trier (subject to the usual checks at the trial and appellate levels) to apply common sense to the question. The marital interest is quite recognizable and its impairment may be definite, serious, and enduring, more so than the pain and suffering or mental or psychic distress for which recovery is now almost routinely allowed in various tort actions. The valuation problem here may be difficult but is not less manageable. Nor does it follow that if the husband-wife relationship is protected as here envisaged, identical protection must be afforded by analogy to other relationships from that of parent-child in a lengthy regress to that of master-servant; courts will rather proceed from case to case with discerning caution.   .   .   .

———

In the years since Justice Kaplan's opinion, virtually all states have come to recognize the loss of consortium action for both spouses. For a rare exception, see Boucher By Boucher v. Dixie Medical Center, 850 P.2d 1179 (Utah 1992)(rejecting the action). Today the questions are those raised by Justice Kaplan at the end of the passage—the extension of similar actions to other relationships and the measurement of damages.

Keep in mind that no claim will lie against a negligent spouse for depriving the other spouse of consortium by negligent conduct, such as driving. See Plain v. Plain, 307 Minn. 399, 240 N.W.2d 330 (1976). See also General Motors Corp. v. Doupnik, 1 F.3d 862 (9th Cir.1993).

In some lost consortium cases courts have upheld jury awards of substantial sums. In Ossenfort v. Associated Milk Producers, Inc., 254 N.W.2d 672 (Minn.1977), the court upheld an award of $500,000 to a wife whose 34-year-old husband suffered severe brain damage and was rendered "a spastic quadriplegic." The award was assumed to be almost all for lost consortium. The court noted proof that the marital relationship had been "one of exceptional harmony and happiness.   .   .   . The jury could find that the companionship that would have been [the wife's] for years to come would have provided her with a life more meaningful than the great majority of people could anticipate or would experience." See also Spaur v. Owns–Corning Fiberglas Corp., 510 N.W.2d 854 (Iowa 1994), upholding an award of $800,000 for lost past and future consortium where the couple had been married 34 years, had three grown children, the husband had been a "devoted" husband, and the husband's life expectancy (he died after suit was brought) was 16 years.

Some courts have extended the consortium action to cover nonphysical injuries to the first spouse. In Barnes v. Outlaw, 964 P.2d 484 (Ariz.1998), defendant minister revealed to others information he had learned about plaintiff during confidential counseling sessions. The court held that damages for loss of consortium are not barred solely because the spouse's injury is purely emotional. The court would rely "on the factfinder to determine the legitimacy, nature, and extent of any alleged damages.   .   .   . Factfinders, usually jurors, can   .   .   . and are frequently called upon to do so.   .   .   . Clearly, a marriage may be damaged by emotional trauma. Since loss of consortium is no longer exclusively based on the deprivation of services theory, we see no reason to require physical injury in one spouse before the other may bring a claim. . . . Whether the marital relationship has been harmed enough to warrant damages in any given case is a matter for the jury to decide." Should damages be measured the same way as in a case in which the spouse has suffered serious physical harm?

Loss of companionship involving injured parents and children. Building on the economic history that Justice Kaplan reviewed, most courts began giving the husband, and then both parents, an action for the loss of the companionship of their seriously injured child.

Large consortium damages have been awarded in parent-child situations. See Lester v. Sayles, 850 S.W.2d 858 (Mo.1993), upholding a lost companionship award of $1.86 million to the mother of a young child who suffered "devastating" injuries and would need full time care for life. The mother was deprived of the enjoyment of the child's company and lost the child's services and companionship. See also Adcox v. Children's Orthopedic Hospital, 864 P.2d 921 (Wash.1993), upholding an award of $1.2 million to a mother for the lost companionship of her child, whose injuries left him with the mental development of a one-year-old child—and who would never be able to speak or to care for himself.

The extension of such an action to the child has encountered substantial resistance. In Borer v. American Airlines, Inc., 563 P.2d 858 (Cal.1977), the court refused to allow a suit for the benefit of nine young children whose mother had been injured to such an extent that she was unable to provide the usual parental care. The financial aspects of this loss were recoverable in the mother's action. The mother could also recover the emotional aspects of this loss of ability to care for her children if she were conscious of that loss. The rejection was reached after taking into account "all considerations which bear on the question, including the inadequacy of monetary compensation to alleviate the tragedy, the difficulty of measuring damages, and the danger of imposing extended and disproportionate liability."

A few states have accepted the action. In Ferriter v. Daniel O'Connell's Sons, Inc., 413 N.E.2d 690 (Mass.1980), the children of a paralyzed accident victim pressed a *Borer* claim. The court was "skeptical" of any suggestion that the children's interests were any less intense than the wife's. The court reviewed and rejected the reasons offered by the majority in *Borer* and held that the children "have a viable claim for loss of parental society if they can show that they are minors dependent on the parent, Michael Ferriter. This dependence must be rooted not only in economic requirements, but also in filial needs for closeness, guidance, and nurture."

In one recent case, the court, 4–3, citing a modern trend including *Ferriter* and others, concluded that children who lost their mother during child birth, could bring a claim for lost companionship, even though the wrongful death claim did not exist at common law:

> Concerns that insurance costs will rise and that double recovery will supposedly occur are unconvincing. The permanent economic loss of the mother and her conscious pain and suffering are entirely indepen-

dent of the claims of the children for loss of parental consortium. Under a proper instruction, we believe that a jury is quite capable of making such a distinction.

Are there similar risks if the mother has been rendered comatose but survives?

The refusal of the alleged "direct" victim to go along with the suit may persuade the court to deny an action. In Jacoby v. Brinckerhoff, 735 A.2d 347 (Conn.1999), plaintiff husband sought to sue defendant psychiatrist for treatment of plaintiff's wife that hurt the marriage and caused his children to lose maternal care. The wife would not cooperate. The court had already decided that lost consortium was a derivative action. In that part of the case it was "not prepared to hold that a derivative cause of action may proceed upon the mere possibility that the plaintiff's spouse may have sustained an injury that resulted from negligent or intentional misconduct on the part of a psychiatrist." (On the direct claims in the case "sound public policy counsels that a psychiatrist's treatment of a troubled spouse should not be burdened by accountability to the other spouse.")

A similar result was reached in a case in which a minor child, through his father, sought damages against mental health care providers for loss of his mother's companionship by causing her to develop false memories. The patient objected to the suit. The court rejected a duty running to nonpatients in this type of case. Plaintiff argued that the patient may be too "emotionally altered to recognize the harm that has taken place." The court rejected "this paternalistic approach." Eliminating "the potential for divided loyalties and maintaining confidentiality will in the end preserve the relationship" and this end will outweigh "any threat of foreseeable harm to nonpatient family members." The court explicitly observed that it was not passing on a "provider's duty to protect an identifiable potential victim from a dangerous patient." J.A.H. ex rel R.M.H. v. Wadle & Associates, P.C., 589 N.W.2d 256 (Iowa 1999).

B. ECONOMIC HARM

In this section, we consider cases in which the defendant has exposed plaintiff only to the risk of economic harm. The defendant's conduct threatens no personal injury or property damage to the plaintiff. Initially, we will look at cases in which no personal injury or property damage is threatened to anyone—situations such as a creditor who makes a loan in reliance on negligently prepared financial statements or a beneficiary who fails to get an inheritance because of a defectively drawn will.

As with emotional distress, the courts have not protected economic interests as extensively as those involving physical security of person and property—even when the harm was inflicted intentionally, by fraud. We consider intentional misrepresentation at length in Chapter XV. In this chapter we continue our focus on identifying the situations in which courts do, or should, impose duties of due care—the obligation to use due care to acquire and communicate information. In Chapter VIII, we explore situations in which defective products cause economic harm but no personal injury or property damage.

After considering cases that threaten only economic harm, we will examine a variety of situations in which threatened or actual personal injury or property damage not directed at the plaintiff nonetheless causes economic loss to the plaintiff (for example, when a negligently caused explosion in the vicinity of plaintiff's business causes a loss of profits because customers can no longer reach the shop).

Nycal Corporation v. KPMG Peat Marwick LLP.

Supreme Judicial Court of Massachusetts, 1998.
426 Mass. 491, 688 N.E.2d 1368.

Before WILKINS, C.J., LYNCH, GREANEY, FRIED and IRELAND, JJ.

GREANEY, JUSTICE.

On May 24, 1991, the plaintiff, allegedly in reliance on an auditors' report of the 1990 financial statements of Gulf Resources & Chemical Corporation (Gulf) prepared by the defendant, entered into a stock purchase agreement with the controlling shareholders of Gulf and, on July 12, 1991, the sale was completed. Gulf filed for bankruptcy protection in October, 1993, rendering the plaintiff's investment worthless. The plaintiff filed a civil complaint against the defendant seeking damages and costs incurred as a result of its alleged reliance on the auditors' report. The plaintiff claimed that the report materially misrepresented the financial condition of Gulf,[1] . . . . After applying the liability standard embodied in § 552 of the Restatement (Second) of Torts (1977), a judge in the Superior Court granted summary judgment for the defendant. We granted the parties' applications for direct appellate review of the final judgment. We conclude that the defendant did not breach any legal duty owed to the plaintiff and, accordingly, we affirm the judgment.

1. The following material facts are undisputed. Gulf retained the defendant to audit its 1990 financial statements. At that time, Gulf was listed on the New York Stock Exchange, and was controlled by several of its officers and directors who held their Gulf shares through two other entities (Inoco P.L.C. and Downshire N.V.). The financial statements were prepared by, and were the responsibility of, Gulf's management.

. . .

The defendant's completed auditors' report was included in Gulf's 1990 annual report, which became publicly available on February 22, 1991. In March, 1991, the plaintiff entered into discussions with Gulf concerning the possible purchase of a large block of Gulf shares, and during the course of

---

1. The plaintiff asserted that the report failed to take into account recurring substantial losses from operations, the extent of liability for environmental clean-up costs, inadequate accruals of pension and retirement obligations, and restrictions on transfers in certain bank covenants.

those discussions, Gulf provided the plaintiff with a copy of its 1990 annual report. Thereafter, the plaintiff purchased 3,626,775 shares of Gulf (approximately 35% of the outstanding shares) in exchange for $16,000,000 in cash and $18,000,000 in the plaintiff's stock. The acquisition gave the plaintiff operating control of Gulf.

The defendant first learned of the transaction between the plaintiff and Gulf a few days prior to the July 12, 1991, closing. Until that time, the defendant did not know that any transaction between the plaintiff and Gulf had been contemplated.

2.   We have not addressed the scope of liability of an accountant to persons with whom the accountant is not in privity. Three tests have generally been applied in other jurisdictions, either by common law or by statute, to determine the duty of care owed by accountants to nonclients. These include the foreseeability test, the near-privity test, and the test contained in § 552 of the Restatement.

The plaintiff urges our adoption of the broad standard of liability encompassed in the foreseeability test. Pursuant to this test, which is derived from traditional tort law concepts as first enunciated in Palsgraf v. Long Island R.R., [162 N.E. 99 (N.Y.1928)] [reprinted in Chapter V], an accountant may be held liable to any person whom the accountant could reasonably have foreseen would obtain and rely on the accountant's opinion, including known and unknown investors. See, e.g., H. Rosenblum, Inc. v. Adler, [461 A.2d 138 (N.J.1983)]. This test is generally disfavored, having been adopted by courts in only two jurisdictions. [   ]

Our cases draw a distinction between the duty owed by a professional to a third party for personal injuries and that owed to a third party for pecuniary loss due to a professional's negligence. While we apply traditional tort law principles in cases involving the former, we have not done so in cases concerning the latter. Such principles are particularly unsuitable for application to accountants where, "regardless of the efforts of the auditor, the client retains effective primary control of the financial reporting process." Bily v. Arthur Young & Co., [834 P.2d 745 (Cal.1992)]. The auditor prepares its report from statements and information supplied by the client, and once the report is completed and provided to the client, the client controls its dissemination. If we were to apply a foreseeability standard in these circumstances, "a thoughtless slip or blunder, the failure to detect a theft or forgery beneath the cover of deceptive entries, may expose accountants to a liability in an indeterminate amount for an indeterminate time to an indeterminate class." Ultramares Corp. v. Touche, [174 N.E. 441 (N.Y.1931)]. We refuse to hold accountants susceptible to such expansive liability, and conclude that Massachusetts law does not protect every reasonably foreseeable user of an inaccurate audit report.

The near-privity test, which originated in Chief Judge Cardozo's decision in [*Ultramares*], and was modified by Credit Alliance Corp. v. Arthur Andersen & Co., [483 N.E.2d 110 (N.Y.1985)], limits an accountant's liability exposure to those with whom the accountant is in privity or in a relationship "sufficiently approaching privity." Under this test, an accountant may be held liable to noncontractual third parties who rely to their detriment on an inaccurate financial report if the accountant was aware that the report was to be used for a particular purpose, in the furtherance of which a known party (or parties) was intended to rely, and if there was some conduct on the part of the accountant creating a link to that party, which evinces the accountant's understanding of the party's reliance. [   ]

The defendant professes that the near-privity test is consistent with the standard we have previously applied to other professionals in the absence of privity. We disagree. A review of the relevant cases demonstrates that the first two elements of the near-privity test—reliance by the third party and knowledge that the party intended to rely—have analogs in our case law, but the third element—conduct by the accountant providing a direct linkage to the third party—does not.

.   .   .

We believe that the third test, taken from § 552 of the Restatement (Second) of Torts (1977), comports most closely with the liability standard we have applied in other professional contexts. Section 552 describes the tort of negligent misrepresentation committed in the process of supplying information for the guidance of others as follows:

> (1) One who, in the course of his business, profession or employment, or in any other transaction in which he has a pecuniary interest, supplies false information for the guidance of others in their business transactions, is subject to liability for pecuniary loss caused to them by their justifiable reliance upon the information, if he fails to exercise reasonable care or competence in obtaining or communicating the information.

That liability is limited [under § 552(2)] to

> loss suffered (a) by the person or one of a limited group of persons for whose benefit and guidance he intends to supply the information or knows that the recipient intends to supply it; and (b) through reliance upon it in a transaction that he intends the information to influence or knows that the recipient so intends or in a substantially similar transaction.

.   .   .

The comments explain with regard to the requirement that the plaintiff be a member of a "limited group of persons for whose benefit and guidance" the information is supplied as follows:

> [I]t is not required that the person who is to become the plaintiff be identified or known to the defendant as an individual when the information is supplied. It is enough that the maker of the representation intends it to reach and influence either a particular person or persons, known to him, or a group or class of persons, distinct from the much larger class who might reasonably be expected sooner or later to have access to the information and foreseeably to take some action in reliance upon it.   .   .   . It is sufficient, in other words, insofar as the

plaintiff's identity is concerned, that the maker supplies the information for repetition to a certain group or class of persons and that the plaintiff proves to be one of them, even though the maker never had heard of him by name when the information was given. It is not enough that the maker merely knows of the ever-present possibility of repetition to anyone, and the possibility of action in reliance upon it, on the part of anyone to whom it may be repeated. [Comment *h*]

We concur with the California Supreme Court's conclusion in [*Bily*] that the Restatement test properly balances the indeterminate liability of the foreseeability test and the restrictiveness of the near-privity rule. Section 552 "recognizes commercial realities by avoiding both unlimited and uncertain liability for economic losses in cases of professional mistake and exoneration of the auditor in situations where it clearly intended to undertake the responsibility of influencing particular business transactions involving third persons." [   ]

Although the Restatement standard has been widely adopted by other jurisdictions, courts differ in their interpretations of the standard. The better reasoned decisions interpret § 552 as limiting the potential liability of an accountant to noncontractual third parties who can demonstrate "actual knowledge on the part of accountants of the limited—though unnamed—group of potential [third parties] that will rely upon the [report], as well as actual knowledge of the particular financial transaction that such information is designed to influence." [   ] The accountant's knowledge is to be measured "at the moment the audit [report] is published, not by the foreseeable path of harm envisioned by [litigants] years following an unfortunate business decision." [   ][5]

The plaintiff argues that, by limiting § 552 to allow recovery only by those persons, or limited group of persons, that an accountant actually knows will receive and rely on an audit report, we will be rewarding an accountant's efforts to "remain blissfully unaware" of the report's proposed distribution and uses. We are unpersuaded by this argument. The axiom we have applied in other contexts applies to accountants as well: the Restatement standard will not excuse an accountant's "wilful ignorance" of information of which the accountant would have been aware had the accountant not consciously disregarded that information. [   ]

The judge correctly concluded under § 552, that the undisputed facts failed to show that the defendant knew (or intended) that the plaintiff, or any limited group of which the plaintiff was a member, would rely on the audit report in connection with an investment in Gulf. To the contrary, the record suggests that the defendant did not prepare the audit report for the plaintiff's benefit and that the plaintiff was not a member of any "limited group of persons" for whose benefit the report was prepared. At the time the audit was being prepared, the plaintiff was an unknown, unidentified

---

5. We reject the plaintiff's argument that § 552 encompasses the foreseeability doctrine of traditional tort law, and we decline to adopt the broad construction some courts have given to § 552 as the plaintiff requests. . . .

potential future investor in Gulf. The defendant was not aware of the existence of the transaction between the plaintiff and Gulf until after the stock purchase agreement had been signed and only a few days before the sale was completed.

The summary judgment record further indicates that the defendant neither intended to influence the transaction entered into by the plaintiff and Gulf nor knew that Gulf intended to influence the transaction by use of the audit report. . . .

Moreover, the record suggests that the defendant's audit report was prepared for inclusion in Gulf's annual report and not for the purpose of assisting Gulf's controlling shareholders in any particular transaction. The record does not exhibit that the defendant knew of any particular use that would be made of its audit report. Cf. Guenther v. Cooper Life Sciences, Inc., 759 F.Supp. 1437, 1443 (N.D.Cal.1990) (accountants knew that audit report would be placed in prospectus for public offering and had expressly consented to its inclusion). "Under the Restatement rule, an auditor retained to conduct an annual audit and to furnish an opinion for no particular purpose generally undertakes no duty to third parties." [*Bily*][6]

The rule we adopt today will preclude accountants from having to ensure the commercial decisions of nonclients where, as here, the accountants did not know that their work product would be relied on by the plaintiff in making its investment decision.

Judgment affirmed.

Notes and Questions

1. As the court notes, *Palsgraf*, which is reprinted in the next chapter, involved personal injury. Why does the court here reject foreseeability as the standard in cases of pecuniary harm? As noted, in *Ultramares*, Judge Cardozo was concerned that "a thoughtless slip or blunder, the failure to detect a theft or forgery beneath the cover of deceptive entries, may expose accountants to a liability in an indeterminate amount for an indeterminate time to an indeterminate class." Are these indeterminacies of equal concern? Are they unique to this type of case?

2. What is gained by protecting professionals, such as accountants from liability to foreseeable users for their negligence? How would the court analyze a case in which the client tells the accountant in advance that it plans to show the results to John Smith?

3. As the court suggests in footnote 6, investors act for a variety of reasons, only one of which may be the actual financial statements prepared by the accountant. Is there a greater problem here showing reliance than in cases like *Randi W.*, p. 170, supra?

---

6. We also note that the plaintiff had had the opportunity to conduct more detailed due diligence prior to its purchase of the Gulf shares, although it apparently did not do so. In addition, although the plaintiff asserts reliance on the defendant's report as the basis for making its investment in Gulf, such decisions typically involve other factors. [*Bily*]

4. *Approaches to accountants' liability.* As noted, states have developed three basic approaches to the question of the duty owed by accountants to those not in privity with them. A very small group of states still requires actual privity. This area is surveyed in Pacini, Martin & Hamilton, At the Interface of Law and Accounting: An Examination of a Trend Toward a Reduction in the Scope of Auditor Liability to Third Parties, 37 Am.Bus.L.J. 171 (2000).

a. Near-privity. The New York approach restricts liability by demanding a "linking" between the accountant and the relying party that requires more than notice from the relying party to the accountant. How *much* more is the question. In Security Pacific Business Credit, Inc. v. Peat Marwick Main & Co., 597 N.E.2d 1080 (N.Y.1992), plaintiff lender claimed that it was owed a duty of due care by defendant auditor based essentially on a "single unsolicited phone call" that plaintiff's vice-president had made to defendant. That call had been made after the defendant had completed the field audit of the client but before the final report had been prepared. The defendant responded to the call by saying, at most, that "nothing untoward had been uncovered in the course of the audit." The court held that a lender could not meet the state's requirements and impose "negligence liability of significant commercial dimension and consequences by merely interposing and announcing its reliance in this fashion." If this single call could suffice,

> "then every lender's due diligence list will in the future mandate such a telephone call. For the small price of a phone call, [the lender's lawyer] would in effect acquire additional loan protection by placing the auditor in the role of an insurer or guarantor of loans extended to its clients." The facile acquisition of deep pocket surety coverage, with no opportunity for actuarial assessment and self-protection, by the party sought to be charged, at the mere cost of a telephone call by the lender, is a bargain premium rate indeed.

What if the plaintiff had made the phone call after the client had requested the audit but before the defendant had agreed to do the work? Is there properly a concern about "blissful ignorance" in states that do not use foreseeability?

b. Modified foreseeability. A few states, exemplified by New Jersey, have adopted an approach close to general foreseeability thereby allowing more expansive liability. Would you expect accountants in New Jersey to exercise greater care in their work than those in New York? If so, would the higher degree of care exercised be desirable? Would it affect fees? In 1995, New Jersey, by N.J.S.A. 2A:53A–25, brought itself closer to the New York position. A few states still follow the cited *Rosenblum* case.

c. The Restatement view. Almost half the states follow the approach developed in section 552 and discussed in *Nycal*. Consider the following examples suggested by comments and illustrations to that section:

1. The client asks D to prepare an audit so that the client can show it to Bank B to get a loan of $50,000. D prepares the requested

statements. Bank B fails and, without telling D, the client shows the statements to Bank A, which lends $50,000 in reliance and loses the money when the client goes bankrupt. D is said to owe no duty to Bank A. Why not?

2. If the client had told D that it intended to seek a loan of $50,000 from an unidentified bank, D would owe a duty to any bank that lends the money—even if the client had Bank X in mind at the time but later goes to Bank Y. Why? What if the loan is for $250,000?

3. The client tells D that the documents are to help get a loan of $50,000 from B. Instead, B decides to buy an interest in the client for $250,000. The client soon collapses and B loses everything. D does not owe a duty to B.

How would each of these examples be analyzed in New York?

d. Federal securities law. Some professional liability is controlled by federal securities law—the Securities Act of 1933 and the Securities Exchange Act of 1934. This regulatory scheme is discussed in *Bily* and applied in O'Melveny & Myers v. Federal Deposit Ins. Corp., 512 U.S. 79 (1994). This subject is pursued in upper class courses.

5. *Bily,* the California case, involved investors who claimed reliance on financial statements defendants prepared for Osborne Computer Corp. The court was skeptical about claims of reliance. It understood that the plaintiffs "perceived an opportunity to make a large sum of money in a very short time by investing in a company they believed would (literally within months) become the dominant force in the new personal computer market. Although hindsight suggests they misjudged a number of major factors (including, at a minimum, the product, the market, the competition, and the company's manufacturing capacity), plaintiffs' litigation-focused attention is now exclusively on the auditor and its report." In addition to the points made in the main case, *Bily* concluded that investors "should be encouraged to rely on their own prudence, diligence, and contracting power, as well as other informational tools. This kind of self-reliance promotes sound investment and credit practices and discourages the careless use of monetary resources." The flip side was a concern that the imposition of a duty might lead accountants to "rationally respond to increased liability by simply reducing audit services in fledgling industries where the business failure rate is high, reasoning that they will inevitably be singled out and sued when their client goes into bankruptcy regardless of the care or detail of their audits."

6. *Attorneys and clients.* After accountants the second largest group involved in these cases is the legal profession. Before analyzing the due care obligations that an attorney may owe to third parties, we consider the duty of due care the attorney owes to the client.

a. Meeting filing deadlines. Questions of legal malpractice tend to arise in two contexts. One involves cases in which attorneys fail to file complaints within the statute of limitations or in some other way fail to perform a nonjudgmental task. In such cases, the client may have a good legal claim for malpractice if it is possible to show that the action, if filed, had a good chance for success.

b. Making strategic choices. The second type of claim arises from judgmental decisions that usually occur during litigation, after a strategic choice turns out badly. Here, the courts are not likely to second-guess the attorney's decision unless it lacked any plausible justification. As in the medical situation, attorneys are not expected to "be perfect or infallible," nor "must they always secure optimum outcomes for their clients." In both situations, an expert is usually needed to show the jury the standard and the deviation.

c. Recommending settlements. The strategy question extends beyond how to conduct litigation—to whether and on what terms to settle pending litigation. Advice to settle a claim for too little may lead to liability for malpractice. See Grayson v. Wofsey, Rosen, Kweskin & Kuriansky, 646 A.2d 195 (Conn.1994)(upholding an action where the attorney was alleged to have negligently valued the marital estate so as to induce his client to settle for too little).

d. Criminal cases. Clients in criminal cases may face an extension of the requirement of a valid case. In Wiley v. County of San Diego, 966 P.2d 983 (Cal.1998), the court held that a plaintiff who had been convicted of a crime could not sue his defense attorney for malpractice without proving that he was innocent of the underlying crime. "Regardless of the attorney's negligence, a guilty defendant's conviction and sentence are the direct consequence of his own perfidy." Then, quoting another case:

> Tort law provides damages only for harms to the plaintiff's legally protected interests, [ ], and the liberty of a guilty criminal is not one of them. The guilty criminal may be able to obtain an acquittal if he is skillfully represented, but he has no right to that result (just as he has no right to have the jury nullify the law, though juries sometimes do that), and the law provides no relief if the "right" is denied him.

Wiley also offered pragmatic reasons for treating criminal and civil malpractice differently. All malpractice cases necessitate a "trial within a trial" to determine if the outcome would have been different if the attorney had behaved differently. But retrying a criminal case in a civil damage action presented especially complex problems. "[Plaintiff] must prove by a preponderance of the evidence that, but for the negligence of his attorney, the jury could not have found him guilty beyond a reasonable doubt.
. . . Moreover, while the plaintiff would be limited to evidence admissible in the criminal trial, the defendant attorney could introduce additional evidence, including 'any and all confidential communications, as well as otherwise suppressible evidence of factual guilt.' "

e. Emotional distress. In these cases it is unusual for the awards to include recovery for the client's emotional distress. In Pleasant v. Celli, 22 Cal.Rptr.2d 663 (App. 1993), an attorney missed the statute of limitations on what the jury could find would have been a successful medical malpractice case. The claim against the attorney properly included economic harm, but an award of $500,000 for emotional distress was reversed. The plaintiff in such a case must show that she sustained "highly foreseeable shock stemming from an abnormal event." Missing the statute of limitations did not suffice.

Other courts have suggested that when the attorney is retained for non-economic purposes, such as criminal defense, adoption proceedings, or marital dissolution, damages for emotional distress may be foreseeable and may be recovered as one item of damages. See, e.g., Holliday v. Jones, 264 Cal.Rptr. 448 (App.1989) (incompetent counsel permits client to be convicted of involuntary manslaughter); Kohn v. Schiappa, 656 A.2d 1322 (N.J.Law Div.1995)(lawyer representing clients seeking to adopt a child improperly reveals their names to the natural mother); Wagenmann v. Adams, 829 F.2d 196 (1st Cir.1987) (malpractice led to client's involuntary incarceration in psychiatric hospital). Is this consistent with the general treatment of negligent infliction of emotional distress that we considered earlier?

In a few cases distraught clients have committed suicide allegedly due to the attorneys' malpractice. In McPeake v. William T. Cannon, 553 A.2d 439 (Pa.Super.1989), a client found guilty of rape, among other charges, jumped through a closed fifth floor courtroom window. The court denied recovery, expressing concern that liability here would discourage attorneys "from representing what may be a sizeable number of depressed or unstable criminal defendants."

In Camenisch v. Superior Court, 52 Cal.Rptr.2d 450 (App. 1996), defendant attorney negligently failed to put the client's tax-saving trusts and estate plans into effect. A claim for emotional distress was denied. Such relief should be preserved for cases in which the negligence interferes with the client's liberty interest (letting client get convicted when innocent) and not for property claims.

7. *Attorneys and third parties.* In Biakanja v. Irving, 320 P.2d 16 (Cal.1958), the defendant notary public drew up plaintiff's brother's will giving plaintiff the entire estate. Because of the notary's negligent failure to have the will properly witnessed, the will failed and the brother's property passed by law to other relatives, so that plaintiff got only one-eighth of the estate. Her recovery against the notary for the difference was affirmed:

> Here, the "end and aim" of the transaction was to provide for the passing of Maroevich's estate to plaintiff. (See [*Glanzer v. Shepard*]). Defendant must have been aware from the terms of the will itself that, if faulty solemnization caused the will to be invalid, plaintiff would suffer the very loss which occurred.

In Lucas v. Hamm, 364 P.2d 685 (Cal.1961), cert. denied 368 U.S. 987 (1962), a will was invalid because it violated the rule against perpetuities. In a malpractice action, the court denied that liability "would impose an undue burden" on the legal profession because "although in some situations liability could be large and unpredictable in amount, this is also true of an attorney's liability to his client." The *Lucas* court ultimately concluded, however, that the legal error did not demonstrate negligence because the rule was so difficult to understand and apply.

The *Biakanja-Lucas* line was continued in Heyer v. Flaig, 449 P.2d 161 (Cal.1969), involving another will failure. The court observed that in "some ways, the beneficiary's interests loom greater than those of the client. After the latter's death, a failure in his testamentary scheme works no practical effect except to deprive his intended beneficiaries of the intended bequests." Also, as *Lucas* recognized, "unless the beneficiary could recover against the attorney in such a case, no one could do so and the social policy of preventing future harm would be frustrated."

Courts appear willing to extend duties to non-clients when the client has asked the attorney to provide information to the other side or to prepare documents for a deal. In Petrillo v. Bachenberg, 655 A.2d 1354 (N.J.1995), the court imposed a duty of due care on a seller's attorney in connection with an arguably misleading percolation-test report given to the prospective buyer. The court extended the opinion-letter line of cases to other kinds of information that the attorney knows or should know will influence a non-client because the "objective purpose of documents such as opinion letters, title reports, or offering statements," is to induce others to rely on them. See also Prudential Ins. Co. v. Dewey, Ballantine, Bushby Palmer & Wood, 605 N.E.2d 318 (N.Y.1992), involving a document prepared by a law firm at its client's direction that the law firm forwarded to the relying party at the request of its client.

A small but firm group of states requires privity in will cases. In Barcelo v. Elliott, 923 S.W.2d 575 (Tex.1996), grandchildren who lost their inheritance because of an invalid will were denied recovery. Recognizing that the majority rule extended liability in this situation, the court, 5–3, preferred the minority view that an attorney owed a duty solely to the client. The court feared cases in which the claim was not invalidity but that the will did not reflect the actual instructions of the testator or in which the testator never signed the will. The court was concerned that it would not be able to tell whether that was because of attorney malpractice or because of the testator's change of mind. Do these concerns exist where the will is invalid? The court was "unable to craft a bright-line rule" that would exclude cases that raised doubt about the testator's intentions. "We believe the greater good is served by preserving a bright-line privity rule which denies a cause of action to all beneficiaries whom the attorney did not represent." One dissent began: "With an obscure reference to 'the greater good,' [ ] the Court unjustifiably insulates an entire class of negligent lawyers from the consequences of their wrongdoing, and unjustly denies legal recourse to the grandchildren for whose benefit Ms. Barcelo hired a lawyer in the first place."

8. *Other professionals.* Many of the issues that appear in the context of accountants and attorneys appear in the cases of other professionals as well.

A very important case in this area involved a public weigher, the defendant, who was asked by the seller to weigh a load of beans and to certify the result to the plaintiff buyer. The weigher negligently certified a weight that was too high. This was discovered when the buyer sought to resell them. In the buyer's successful suit against the weigher, Judge Cardozo noted that, even though the two were not in privity, the weigher knew that the "end and aim of the transaction" was to inform the buyer of the amount to be paid. *Glanzer v. Shepard*, p. 143, supra. Why was it not enough for plaintiff simply to show the negligence?

In Gutter v. Dow Jones, Inc., 490 N.E.2d 898 (Ohio 1986), the *Wall Street Journal* incorrectly omitted the letter "f" from an entry in a bond listing, which indicated that the bond was trading with interest. Plaintiff alleged that relying on that information he bought the bonds in question and suffered a loss. The court held that plaintiff did not come within the limited group that could sue under § 552.

In Duncan v. Afton, Inc., 991 P.2d 739 (Wyo.1999), the employer fired plaintiff after the defendant testing company reported to the employer that plaintiff had tested positive for drugs. Since there was no privity, defendant argued that there could be no duty. The court, using an eight-factor duty test, imposed a duty of due care since the company knew that its actions would affect the group of workers being tested. The court discussed the split among the courts on this issue, which is beginning to arise frequently either because of careless testing or failure to inform employers or workers that eating poppy seeds can create false positives. In fact, the court noted, "two out of every five workers testing positive truly are drug free."

Even physicians may be sued for purely economic harm. In Aufrichtig v. Lowell, 650 N.E.2d 401 (N.Y.1995), the court decided that a physician could be sued for understating the severity of plaintiff patient's medical condition in an affidavit. This led the patient to settle her case against her insurer for less than its value. There is a duty of due care to speak carefully if one speaks at all in this relationship. See also Greinke v. Keese, 371 N.Y.S.2d 58 (Sup.1975)(allowing claim where physician negligently told patient he had only 12–18 months to live, plaintiff relied and took early retirement from his job and sustained substantial financial loss).

In Arato v. Avedon, 858 P.2d 598 (Cal.1993), the widow and children of a patient who died of pancreatic cancer sued treating physicians on the ground that they failed to disclose information regarding the poor life expectancy of patients with this type of cancer. If they had done so, and the patient had realized the odds, he would have put his affairs in better order. One claim was for the economic loss sustained by the survivors due to the condition in which the decedent left his affairs. The court rejected the claim. The main point was that the physicians had met their obligation of obtaining informed consent—and that this did not require the use of statistical life expectancy data. Moreover, there was no duty to disclose information that might be material to the patient's non-medical interests. Why might this be so? Might these cases also involve recoverable emotional distress?

9. Professor Bishop argues that the nonliability of accountants and other providers of information can be justified on the ground that suppliers of information cannot capture the benefit of their "product" once it has entered the stream of commerce. He concludes that liability "should be restricted when (a) the information is of a type that is valuable to many potential users, (b) the producer of the information cannot capture in his prices the benefits flowing to all users of the information, and (c) the imposition of liability to all persons harmed would raise potential costs significantly enough to discourage information production altogether. When these three conditions are met the court should impose liability on the defendant in relation to a limited class only." Bishop, Negligent Misrepresentation Through Economists' Eyes, 96 L.Q.Rev. 360 (1980). Do you agree? Bishop's thesis is discussed in Greycas, Inc. v. Proud, 826 F.2d 1560 (7th Cir.1987), cert. denied 484 U.S. 1043 (1988).

10. As *Nycal* and the note cases indicate, the risk in virtually all of these cases has been exclusively economic. Should the analysis differ where the economic harm results from threatened or actual physical harm? Keep this question in mind while reading the next case and the notes that follow it.

People Express Airlines, Inc. v. Consolidated Rail Corp.

Supreme Court of New Jersey, 1985.
100 N.J. 246, 495 A.2d 107.

HANDLER, J.

This appeal presents a question that has not previously been directly considered: whether a defendant's negligent conduct that interferes with a plaintiff's business resulting in purely economic losses, unaccompanied by property damage or personal injury, is compensable in tort. The appeal poses this issue in the context of the defendants' alleged negligence that caused a dangerous chemical to escape from a railway tank car, resulting in the evacuation from the surrounding area of persons whose safety and health were threatened. The plaintiff, a commercial airline, was forced to evacuate its premises and suffered an interruption of its business operations with resultant economic losses.

I.

Because of the posture of the case—an appeal taken from the grant of summary judgment for the defendant railroad, subsequently reversed by the Appellate Division, [   ]—we must accept plaintiff's version of the facts as alleged. The facts are straight-forward.

On July 22, 1981, a fire began in the Port Newark freight yard of defendant Consolidated Rail Corporation (Conrail) when ethylene oxide manufactured by defendant BASF Wyandotte Company (BASF) escaped from a tank car, punctured during a "coupling" operation with another rail car, and ignited. The tank car was owned by defendant Union Tank Car Company (Union Car) and was leased to defendant BASF.

The plaintiff asserted at oral argument that at least some of the defendants were aware from prior experiences that ethylene oxide is a highly volatile substance; further, that emergency response plans in case of an accident had been prepared. When the fire occurred that gave rise to this lawsuit, some of the defendants' consultants helped determine how much of the surrounding area to evacuate. The municipal authorities then evacuated the area within a one-mile radius surrounding the fire to lessen the risk to persons within the area should the burning tank car explode. The evacuation area included the adjacent North Terminal building of Newark International Airport, where plaintiff People Express Airlines' (People Express) business operations are based. Although the feared explosion never occurred, People Express employees were prohibited from using the North Terminal for twelve hours.

The plaintiff contends that it suffered business-interruption losses as a result of the evacuation. These losses consist of cancelled scheduled flights and lost reservations because employees were unable to answer the telephones to accept bookings; also, certain fixed operating expenses allocable to the evacuation time period were incurred and paid despite the fact that plaintiff's offices were closed. No physical damage to airline property and no personal injury occurred as a result of the fire.

[The trial court granted a motion for summary judgment entered by one of the defendants. On appeal, the Appellate Division reversed, holding that recovery of negligently caused economic loss was not automatically barred by the absence of any property damage or personal injury. The question was certified for consideration by the Supreme Court.]

II.

The single characteristic that distinguishes parties in negligence suits whose claims for economic losses have been regularly denied by American and English courts from those who have recovered economic losses is, with respect to the successful claimants, the fortuitous occurrence of physical harm or property damage, however slight. It is well-accepted that a defendant who negligently injures a plaintiff or his property may be liable for all proximately caused harm, including economic losses. [   ] Nevertheless, a virtually *per se* rule barring recovery for economic loss unless the negligent conduct also caused physical harm has evolved throughout this century, based, in part, on Robins Dry Dock & Repair Co. v. Flint, 275 U.S. 303 (1927), and Cattle v. Stockton Waterworks Co., 10 Q.B. 453 (1875). This has occurred although neither case created a rule absolutely disallowing recovery in such circumstances. See, e.g., Stevenson v. East Ohio Gas Co., 73 N.E.2d 200 (Ohio.Ct.App.1946)(employee who was prohibited from working at his plant, which was closed due to conflagration begun by negligent rupture of stored liquified natural gas at nearby utility, could not recover lost wages); Byrd v. English, [43 S.E. 419 (Ga.1903)] (plaintiff who owned printing plant could not recover lost profits when defendant negligently damaged utility's electrical conduits that supplied power to the plant); see also Restatement (Second) of Torts § 766C (1979)(positing rule of nonrecovery for purely economic losses absent physical harm). But see In re Kinsman Transit Co., 388 F.2d 821, 824 (2d Cir.1968) [*Kinsman II*] (after rejecting an inflexible rule of nonrecovery, court applied traditional proximate cause analysis to claim for purely economic losses).

The reasons that have been advanced to explain the divergent results for litigants seeking economic losses are varied. Some courts have viewed the general rule against recovery as necessary to limit damages to reasonably foreseeable consequences of negligent conduct. This concern in a given case is often manifested as an issue of causation and has led to the requirement of physical harm as an element of proximate cause. In this context, the physical harm requirement functions as part of the definition of the causal relationship between the defendant's negligent act and the plaintiff's economic damages; it acts as a convenient clamp on otherwise boundless liability. [   ] The physical harm rule also reflects certain deep-seated concerns that underlie courts' denial of recovery for purely economic losses occasioned by a defendant's negligence. These concerns include the fear of fraudulent claims, mass litigation, and limitless liability, or liability out of proportion to the defendant's fault. [   ]

The assertion of unbounded liability is not unique to cases involving negligently caused economic loss without physical harm. Even in negligence suits in which plaintiffs have sustained physical harm, the courts have recognized that a tortfeasor is not necessarily liable for *all* consequences of his conduct. While a lone act can cause a finite amount of physical harm, that harm may be great and very remote in its final consequences. A single overturned lantern may burn Chicago. Some limitation is required; that limitation is the rule that a tortfeasor is liable only for that harm that he proximately caused. Proximate or legal cause has traditionally functioned to limit liability for negligent conduct. Duty has also been narrowly defined to limit liability. Compare the majority and dissenting opinions in [*Palsgraf*, discussed in Chapter V]. Thus, we proceed from the premise that principles of duty and proximate cause are instrumental in limiting the amount of litigation and extent of liability in cases in which no physical harm occurs just as they are in cases involving physical injury.

Countervailing considerations of fairness and public policy have led courts to discard the requirement of physical harm as an element in defining proximate cause to overcome the problem of fraudulent or indefinite claims. See *Portee v. Jaffee*.   .   .   .

The troublesome concern reflected in cases denying recovery for negligently-caused economic loss is the alleged potential for infinite liability, or liability out of all proportion to the defendant's fault.   .   .   . The answer to the allegation of unchecked liability is not the judicial obstruction of a fairly grounded claim for redress. Rather, it must be a more sedulous application of traditional concepts of duty and proximate causation to the facts of each case. [   ]

It is understandable that courts, fearing that if even one deserving plaintiff suffering purely economic loss were allowed to recover, all such plaintiffs could recover, have anchored their rulings to the physical harm requirement. While the rationale is understandable, it supports only a limitation on, not a denial of, liability. The physical harm requirement capriciously showers compensation along the path of physical destruction, regardless of the status or circumstances of individual claimants. Purely economic losses are borne by innocent victims, who may not be able to absorb their losses. See Comment, 88 Harv.L.Rev. 444, 449–50 (1974). In the end, the challenge is to fashion a rule that limits liability but permits adjudication of meritorious claims. The asserted inability to fix crystalline formulae for recovery on the differing facts of future cases simply does not justify the wholesale rejection of recovery in all cases.

Further, judicial reluctance to allow recovery for purely economic losses is discordant with contemporary tort doctrine. The torts process, like the law itself, is a human institution designed to accomplish certain social objectives. One objective is to ensure that innocent victims have avenues of legal redress, absent a contrary, overriding public policy. [   ] This reflects the overarching purpose of tort law: that wronged persons should be compensated for their injuries and that those responsible for the wrong should bear the cost of their tortious conduct.

Other policies underlie this fundamental purpose. Imposing liability on defendants for their negligent conduct discourages others from similar tortious behavior, fosters safer products to aid our daily tasks, vindicates reasonable conduct that has regard for the safety of others, and, ultimately, shifts the risk of loss and associated costs of dangerous activities to those who should be and are best able to bear them. Although these policies may be unevenly reflected or imperfectly articulated in any particular case, we strive to ensure that the application of negligence doctrine advances the fundamental purpose of tort law and does not unnecessarily or arbitrarily foreclose redress based on formalisms or technicalisms. Whatever the original common law justifications for the physical harm rule, contemporary tort and negligence doctrine allow—indeed, impel—a more thorough consideration and searching analysis of underlying policies to determine whether a particular defendant may be liable for a plaintiff's economic losses despite the absence of any attendant physical harm. [   ]

III.

We may appropriately consider two relevant avenues of analysis in defining a cause of action for negligently-caused economic loss. The first examines the evolution of various exceptions to the rule of nonrecovery for purely economic losses, and suggests that the exceptions have cast considerable doubt on the validity of the current rule and, indeed, have laid the foundation for a rule that would allow recovery. The second explores the elements of a suitable rule and adopts the traditional approach of foreseeability as it relates to duty and proximate cause molded to circumstances involving a claim only for negligently-caused economic injury.

A.

Judicial discomfiture with the rule of nonrecovery for purely economic loss throughout the last several decades has led to numerous exceptions in the general rule. Although the rationalizations for these exceptions differ among courts and cases, two common threads run throughout the exceptions. The first is that the element of foreseeability emerges as a more appropriate analytical standard to determine the question of liability than a *per se* prohibitory rule. The second is that the extent to which the defendant knew or should have known the particular consequences of his negligence, including the economic loss of a particularly foreseeable plaintiff, is dispositive of the issues of duty and fault.

One group of exceptions is based on the "special relationship" between the tortfeasor and the individual or business deprived of economic expectations. Many of these cases are recognized as involving the tort of negligent misrepresentation, resulting in liability for specially foreseeable economic losses. Importantly, the cases do not involve a breach of contract claim between parties in privity; rather, they involve tort claims by innocent third parties who suffered purely economic losses at the hands of negligent defendants with whom no direct relationship existed. Courts have justified their finding of liability in these negligence cases based on notions of a special relationship between the negligent tortfeasors and the foreseeable plaintiffs who relied on the quality of defendants' work or services, to their detriment. The special relationship, in reality, is an expression of the courts' satisfaction that a duty of care existed because the plaintiffs were particularly foreseeable and the injury was proximately caused by the defendant's negligence.

The special relationship exception has been extended to auditors, see *H. Rosenblum, Inc. v. Adler*, [ ] (independent auditor whose negligence resulted in inaccurate public financial statement held liable to plaintiff who bought stock in company for purposes of sale of business to company; stock subsequently proved to be worthless); surveyors, [ ](surveyor whose negligence resulted in error in depicting boundary of lot held liable to remote purchaser); termite inspectors, [ ] (termite inspectors whose negligence resulted in purchase of infested home liable to out-of-privity buyers); engineers, [ ] (engineers whose negligence resulted in successful bidder's losses in performing construction contract held liable); attorneys, see [*Lucas v. Hamm*] (attorney whose negligence caused intended beneficiary to be deprived of proceeds of the will [owed duty] to beneficiary); notaries public, [citing *Biakanja* among other cases]; architects, [ ] (architects whose negligence resulted in use of defective concrete liable to out-of-privity prime contractor); weighers, see [*Glanzer v. Shepard*]; and telegraph companies, [ ] (telegraph company whose negligent transmission caused plaintiff not to obtain contract was liable); see also [ ].

. . . .

Courts have found it fair and just in all of these exceptional cases to impose liability on defendants who, by virtue of their special activities, professional training or other unique preparation for their work, had particular knowledge or reason to know that others, such as the intended beneficiaries of wills (e.g., *Lucas v. Hamm*, supra) or the purchasers of stock who were expected to rely on the company's financial statement in the prospectus (e.g., *H. Rosenblum, Inc. v. Adler*, supra), would be economically harmed by negligent conduct. In this group of cases, even though the particular plaintiff was not always foreseeable, the particular class of plaintiffs was foreseeable as was the particular type of injury.

A very solid exception allowing recovery for economic losses has also been created in cases akin to private actions for public nuisance. Where a plaintiff's business is based in part upon the exercise of a public right, the plaintiff has been able to recover purely economic losses caused by a defendant's negligence. See, e.g., Louisiana ex rel. Guste v. M/V Testbank, 752 F.2d 1019 (5th Cir.1985)(en banc)(defendants responsible for ship collision held liable to all commercial fishermen, shrimpers, crabbers and oystermen for resulting pollution of Mississippi River); Union Oil Co. v. Oppen, 501 F.2d 558 (9th Cir.1974)(fishermen making known commercial use of public waters may recover economic losses due to defendant's oil spill); [ ]. The theory running throughout these cases, in which the plaintiffs depend on the exercise of the public or riparian right to clean water as a natural resource, is that the pecuniary losses suffered by those who make direct use of the resource are particularly foreseeable because they are so closely linked, through the resource, to the defendants' behavior.

Particular knowledge of the economic consequences has sufficed to establish duty and proximate cause in contexts other than those already considered. In Henry Clay v. Jersey City, 74 N.J.Super. 490 (Ch.Div.1962), aff'd, 84 N.J.Super. 9 (App.Div.1964), for example, a lessee-manufacturer had to vacate the building in which its business was located because of the defendant city's negligent failure to maintain its sewer line while the line was repaired. While there was some property damage, the court treated the tenant's and owner's claims separately; the tenant's claims were purely economic, stemming from the loss of use of its property right, as in the instant case. Further, the city had had notice of the leak since 1957 and should have known about it even earlier. Duty, breach and proximate cause were found to exist; the plaintiff-tenant recovered lost profits and expenses incurred during the shut-down. See also J'Aire Corp. v. Gregory, 598 P.2d 60 (Cal.1979)(contractor who undertook construction work for owner of building had duty to tenants to complete construction on time to avoid resultant economic losses).

These exceptions expose the hopeless artificiality of the *per se* rule against recovery for purely economic losses. When the plaintiffs are reasonably foreseeable, the injury is directly and proximately caused by defendant's negligence, and liability can be limited fairly, courts have endeavored to create exceptions to allow recovery. . . .

      . . .

      . . . The foreseeability standard that may be synthesized from these cases is one that posits liability in terms of where, along a spectrum ranging from the general to the particular, foreseeability is ultimately found. [ ] A broad view of these cases reasonably permits the conclusion that the extent of liability and degree of foreseeability stand in direct proportion to one another. The more particular is the foreseeability that economic loss will be suffered by the plaintiff as a result of defendant's negligence, the more just is it that liability be imposed and recovery allowed.

We hold therefore that a defendant owes a duty of care to take reasonable measures to avoid the risk of causing economic damages, aside from physical injury, to particular plaintiffs or plaintiffs comprising an identifiable class with respect to whom defendant knows or has reason to know are likely to suffer such damages from its conduct. A defendant failing to adhere to this duty of care may be found liable for such economic damages proximately caused by its breach of duty.

We stress that an identifiable class of plaintiffs is not simply a foreseeable class of plaintiffs. For example, members of the general public, or invitees such as sales and service persons at a particular plaintiff's business premises, or persons travelling on a highway near the scene of a negligently-caused accident, such as the one at bar, who are delayed in the conduct of their affairs and suffer varied economic losses, are certainly a foreseeable class of plaintiffs. Yet their presence within the area would be fortuitous, and the particular type of economic injury that could be suffered by such persons would be hopelessly unpredictable and not realistically foreseeable. Thus, the class itself would not be sufficiently ascertainable. An identifiable class of plaintiffs must be particularly foreseeable in terms of the type of persons or entities comprising the class, the certainty or predictability of their presence, the approximate numbers of those in the class, as well as the type of economic expectations disrupted. [   ]

We recognize that some cases will present circumstances that defy the categorization here devised to circumscribe a defendant's orbit of duty, limit otherwise boundless liability and define an identifiable class of plaintiffs that may recover. In these cases, the courts will be required to draw upon notions of fairness, common sense and morality to fix the line limiting liability as a matter of public policy, rather than an uncritical application of the principle of particular foreseeability. [   ]

[The court concluded that plaintiff had shown the requisite proximate causal connection between the negligence and the harm—a discussion we consider in Chapter V at p. 433.]

IV.

We are satisfied that our holding today is fully applicable to the facts that we have considered on this appeal. Plaintiff has set forth a cause of action under our decision, and it is entitled to have the matter proceed to a plenary trial. Among the facts that persuade us that a cause of action has been established is the close proximity of the North Terminal and People Express Airlines to the Conrail freight yard; the obvious nature of the plaintiff's operations and particular foreseeability of economic losses resulting from an accident and evacuation; the defendants' actual or constructive knowledge of the volatile properties of ethylene oxide; and the existence of an emergency response plan prepared by some of the defendants (alluded to in the course of oral argument), which apparently called for the nearby area to be evacuated to avoid the risk of harm in case of an explosion. We do not mean to suggest by our recitation of these facts that actual knowledge of the eventual economic losses is necessary to the cause of action; rather, particular foreseeability will suffice. The plaintiff still faces a difficult task in proving damages, particularly lost profits, to the degree of certainty required in other negligence cases. The trial court's examination of these proofs must be exacting to ensure that damages recovered are those reasonably to have been anticipated in view of the defendants' capacity to have foreseen that this particular plaintiff was within the risk created by their negligence.

. . .

For modification and affirmance—CHIEF JUSTICE WILENTZ, and JUSTICES CLIFFORD, HANDLER, O'HERN, GARIBALDI and STEIN—6.

For reversal—None.

Notes and Questions

1. The court refers to the cases that we have just considered involving third-party loss from the activities of accountants, lawyers and the like, as exceptions to the no-recovery rule based on "special relationships"—citing its *Rosenblum* decision (discussed earlier at p. 303, supra), among others. Is *People Express* similar to the various special relationship cases cited by the court?

2. Does *People Express* appear to raise the same issue as *Union Oil Co. v. Oppen*, cited in the opinion at p. 318, supra, in which commercial fishermen sought to recover lost profits as a consequence of the Santa Barbara oil spill?

3. What is the difference between a foreseeability standard and a "particular foreseeability" standard? Is the latter test likely to be helpful in deciding the limits on recovery for economic loss resulting from threatened or actual physical harm? Does the court's approach apply to any defendant other than the railroad?

4. Would the court now reach a different result on the facts of the landmark no-recovery cases of *Stevenson v. East Ohio Gas Co.* and *Byrd v. English*, cited in the opinion?

5. In Koch v. Consolidated Edison Co. of New York, Inc., 468 N.E.2d 1 (N.Y.1984), cert. denied 469 U.S. 1210 (1985), the City of New York attempted to recover damages for various economic losses suffered as a result of the 1977 blackout discussed at p. 144, supra. The court held that the city stated a cause of action for damages caused by looting and vandalism of its property, but dismissed plaintiff's claims for recovery of emergency wages paid to city personnel such as police and fire officers and municipal revenues lost as a consequence of the blackout. What considerations might have led the New York court to its conclusions about recovery? What recovery might have been allowed under the *People Express* test?

6. In Milliken & Co. v. Consolidated Edison Co., 644 N.E.2d 268 (N.Y.1994), tenants of commercial buildings sued defendant utility for economic losses suffered when power failed in the garment district during a crucial sales week. Although these tenants had no direct contractual relation with the utility, their leases required them to pay their landlords a proportionate share of the landlord's utility bills. The unanimous court thought that was inadequate to ground a duty of due care. Relying heavily on *Strauss v. Belle Realty*, p. 144, supra, and the *Moch* case, p. 143, supra, the court concluded that it followed "a general policy and approach [that] declined to leapfrog duties, over directly juridically related parties, to noncontractually related consumers of a utility's service or product." Tenants as such "are not a sufficiently 'narrowly defined class.' "

The tenants tried to distinguish *Strauss* on the ground that the harm here occurred inside the leased premises rather than in common areas. The court thought the plaintiff in *Strauss* was in an identical situation. The court rejected the location argument "because it would hold regulated utilities liable to every tenant in every one of the countless skyscrapers comprising the urban skyline. This would unwisely subject utilities to loss potentials of uncontrollable and unworkable dimensions."

A third-party beneficiary theory also failed. The court distinguished one case in which it had allowed such a claim on the ground that there the utility "had expressly undertaken a contractual duty to supply electricity for the needs of [the contracting party's] customers."

Consider some recent New York cases that involve *People Express* issues. One pair of cases involved the alleged negligence of the owner of a 39-story building on Madison Avenue in Manhattan and other defendants that caused a section of brick wall to collapse. Because of the collapse, the police closed off 15 blocks of Madison Avenue to vehicular and pedestrian traffic for approximately two weeks. In these cases, merchants who had suffered no physical damage were suing only for economic loss. The court, with the same 3–2 vote in both, refused to dismiss the complaints. The reliance of some cases on "minuscule" property damage to support the claims showed "the irony of a rule that posits the right to recover economic losses, no matter how great, upon the fortuitous occurrence of some concomitant physical damage, no matter how slight." (Is this analogous to the role of impact in emotional distress cases?) The dissenters saw no stopping point along the 15 blocks. Just as in *Milliken*, the locale and time of the year were distinctions "without a legal, public policy-rooted difference because, regardless of situs, the same unlimited, undefined class of potential plaintiffs is implicated." All the opinions offer extended reviews of the area, though the majority opinions do not address *Milliken*. Is it distinguishable? 5th Avenue Chocolatiere, Ltd. v. 540 Acquisition Co., L.L.C., 712 N.Y.S.2d 8 (App.Div. 2000) and 532 Madison Avenue Gourmet Foods, Inc. v. Finlandia Center, Inc., 711 N.Y.S.2d 391 (App.Div. 2000).

A few weeks later, the same court rejected claims arising from the collapse in Times Square of a 700-foot construction elevator tower being used in connection with defendants' construction project. Even though no physical injury resulted, Times Square was ordered closed and some buildings were evacuated. Plaintiff here was a law firm suing (and seeking class certification) for economic damages including temporary relocation of their offices. The court, asserting that the claims were "too tenuous and remote to permit recovery on any tort theory," denied recovery. A concurring justice, noting that she had been in the majority in the Madison Avenue cases, sought to distinguish the two situations. She noted that the Madison Avenue claims had been limited to "lost profits suffered by retail merchants whose livelihoods were dependent upon pedestrian traffic, [rather than] almost all ancillary 'inconvenience' costs" sustained here. She also noted that the negligence pleaded in this case was "not as egregious as that alleged" in the earlier cases. Goldberg, Weprin & Ustin, LLP v. Tishman Construction Corp., 713 N.Y.S.2d 57 (App.Div. 2000). If the Madison Avenue situation had involved recklessness would that justify treating it differently from the Times Square case?

7. The court in *People Express* acknowledges a "troublesome concern" about "liability out of all proportion to the defendant's fault." Does its standard give adequate weight to that concern? See generally, Rabin, Tort Recovery for Negligently Inflicted Economic Loss: A Reassessment, 37 Stan.L.Rev. 1513 (1985).

8. In *Robins Dry Dock & Repair Co. v. Flint*, cited in the main case, the time charterers of a boat were denied recovery for loss of use due to defendant's negligent repairs. Justice Holmes observed that the damage to the ship "was no wrong" to the plaintiffs, whose loss arose only from a contract with the owners:

> It seems to have been thought that perhaps the whole might have been recovered by the owners, that in that event the owners would have been trustees for the respondents to the extent of the respondents' share and that no injustice would be done to allow the respondents to recover their share by direct suit. But justice does not permit that the petitioner be charged with the full value of the loss of use unless there is some one who has a claim to it as against the petitioner. The respondents have no claim either in contract or in tort, and they cannot get standing by the suggestion that if some one else had recovered it he would have been bound to pay over a part by reason of his personal relations with the respondents.

Robins has been challenged—unsuccessfully—for years. See, e.g., Nautilus Marine, Inc. v. Niemela, 170 F.3d 1195 (9th Cir.1999), in which the court rejected a charterer's claim for lost profits despite the allegation that the collision was caused intentionally or by recklessness. The court thought *Robins* controlled and that if *Robins* is to be overturned it must be by the Supreme Court or by Congress.

For a discussion of the thesis that courts have denied liability when the party suffering physical harm might have indemnified the victim of economic loss through a "channeling contract"—a contract that would reduce the amount of litigation by allowing the victim of physical harm to recover economic losses as well, see Rizzo, A Theory of Economic Loss in the Law of Torts, 11 J.Legal Stud. 281 (1982).

9. Can a life insurance company maintain an action against a defendant who negligently caused the premature death of the insured? In the leading case of Connecticut Mutual Life Ins. Co. v. New York & N.H. R.R., 25 Conn. 265 (1856), the court said it could not. Does the holding remain sound?

10. In Rickards v. Sun Oil Co., 41 A.2d 267 (N.J.L.1945), discussed in an omitted portion of *People Express,* defendant's barge negligently destroyed a bridge that was the only means of access to the retail businesses of the six plaintiffs. The court, concerned about disproportionate liability for the negligent act committed, denied recovery. The *People Express* court distinguished *Rickards* as a case of general rather than particular foreseeability. See also Dundee Cement Co. v. Chemical Laboratories, Inc., 712 F.2d 1166 (7th Cir.1983) and Leadfree Enters., Inc. v. United States Steel Corp., 711 F.2d 805 (7th Cir.1983).

In Bishop, Economic Loss in Tort, 2 Oxford J. Legal Studies 1 (1982), the author argues that many economic loss situations involve no net social costs. Although these situations involve private costs to the victims, the net effect is a mere redistribution of wealth with no consequent loss to society. Thus, as long as excess capacity exists, the disappointed vacationers in *Rickards* will simply satisfy their needs elsewhere. Private costs occur, but they are in the nature of transfer payments from the disappointed suppliers of goods and services to others who fill the breach, and, as a consequence, liability is appropriately denied.

Is Bishop's thesis generally applicable to the cases in this chapter? When it is applicable, does it follow that the supplier of goods or services ought to be denied recovery? For a highly critical view, see Rizzo, The Economic Loss Problem: A Comment on Bishop, 2 Oxford J. Legal Stud. 197 (1982). See in response, Bishop, Economic Loss: A Reply to Professor Rizzo, 2 Oxford J. Legal Stud. 207 (1982).

11. At early common law, a master was allowed an action for the damages suffered as the result of injury to a servant. Although based on the philosophy of the era of cottage industry, the action long survived in some states for servants generally, and in others for servants who were members of the master's household. But the general trend is to treat servant cases like other cases. See, e.g., Phoenix Professional Hockey Club, Inc. v. Hirmer, 502 P.2d 164 (Ariz.1972), in which the plaintiff's regular goalie was injured in an automobile accident allegedly due to the defendant's negligence. In an effort to avoid the defense that its claim was too speculative, the plaintiff did not sue for general damages for injuries to the employee or for lost profits. Instead, it sued only for out-of-pocket expenses incurred in "hiring and employing a substitute goalie during the remainder of the term" of the injured goalie's contract. The court agreed that the claim was not unduly speculative, but nonetheless dismissed it. Although a negligent wrongdoer "should be held responsible for the natural and probable consequences of his wrong," to protect contract interests from "negligent interference would place an undue burden on freedom of action and could impose a severe penalty on one guilty of mere negligence."

The same result follows where the injured employee is the president of the company, which suffers losses even though someone else carries out the same tasks. This is true whether the claim is for medical expenses and salary paid to the injured victim, I.J. Weinrot & Son, Inc. v. Jackson, 708 P.2d 682 (Cal.1985), or for increased workers' compensation premiums and lost profits caused by the accident, Fischl v. Paller & Goldstein, 282 Cal.Rptr. 802 (App. 1991). The *Weinrot* court suggested that "the plaintiff corporation was peculiarly able to calculate the [value] of services of a key employee and to protect itself against such a loss by securing key employee insurance."

Does this approach to "negligent interference with contracts" help explain other cases in these notes?

12. *An "Economic Loss Rule"?* Some courts have barred tort actions in situations that may appear to lend themselves better to contract remedies. The underlying justification may have begun in cases involving defective products—in which it was argued that if the defect caused only economic loss the plaintiff buyer should be limited to contract remedies. We consider this development at length in Chapter VIII.

Whatever its justification in the products cases, a variant of the doctrine has spread to the areas of performance contracts and professional services. In City Express, Inc. v. Express Partners, 959 P.2d 836 (Haw. 1998), for example, a building owner, alleging that it was in privity with the defendant architect, sued the architect for misdesigning the building in a way that made it unusable for its intended purpose but not dangerous. Plaintiff sought such damages as lost rent and the cost of remedying the problems. The court denied tort recovery. It noted that in earlier cases it had relied on Restatement Second § 552 (discussed in *Nycal*) to permit a tort recovery where defendant had "made direct representations that its product was appropriate for the construction of a sports stadium." In *City Express* the court retreated from that view and followed other states that refuse to apply § 552 "in the context of construction litigation regarding the alleged negligence of design professionals." The case most relied upon was Berschauer/Phillips Const. Co. v. Seattle School District, 881 P.2d 986 (Wash.1994), from which the Hawaii court quoted the following passages:

> The economic loss rule marks the fundamental boundary between the law of contracts, which is designed to enforce expectations created by agreement, and the law of torts, which is designed to protect citizens and their property by imposing a duty of reasonable care on others. The economic loss rule was designed to prevent disproportionate liability and allow the parties to allocate risk by contract.
>
> . . .
>
> If tort and contract remedies were allowed to overlap, certainty and predictability in allocating risk would decrease and impede future business activity. The construction industry in particular would suffer,

for it is in this industry that we see most clearly the importance of the precise allocation of risk as secured by contract. *The fees charged by architects, engineers, contractors, developers, vendors, and so on are founded on their expected liability exposure as bargained and provided for in the contract.* [emphasis added by the Hawaii court].

The Washington–Hawaii approach was explicitly rejected in Moransais v. Heathman, 744 So.2d 973 (Fla.1999), in which plaintiff home buyer sued defendant engineer for failing to find serious defects during a pre-purchase inspection for which the plaintiff had contracted. The majority, 6–1, sought to limit the "rule" to cases of defective products. After reviewing cases in which it admitted it had been less than clear, the court now asserted that it had "never intended to bar well-established common law causes of action, such as those for neglect in providing professional services." The

> mere existence of a contract between the professional services corporation and a consumer does not eliminate the professional obligation of the professional who actually renders the service to the consumer or the common law action that a consumer may have against the professional provider. While the parties to a contract to provide a product may be able to protect themselves through contract remedies, we do not believe the same may be necessarily true when professional services are sought and provided. Indeed, it is questionable whether a professional, such as a lawyer, could legally or ethically limit a client's remedies by contract in the same way that a manufacturer could do with a purchaser in a purely commercial setting.

Is there an important distinction between cases involving misrepresentations and those involving defective performances? Between cases involving consumers and those involving commercial transactions? Between construction contracts and other types of contracts? Between professional services and other types of transactions? The underlying question is when the nature of the relationship warrants limiting parties in privity to their contractual remedies.

We consider this development again in the context of product liability at p. 639, infra and in the context of intentional economic harm at p. 1263, infra.

C. INTERFERENCE WITH PROCREATION AND END-OF-LIFE DECISIONS

The two previous sections of this chapter have, for the most part, treated emotional distress and economic harm separately. In fact, of course, they frequently occur together, as we saw with the attorney malpractice cases, p. 308, supra.

By far the most frequent joint appearance of the two types of harm has been occurring in the areas of life and death. Spurred by legal and technological developments in contraception, abortion, and genetic counseling, courts have confronted a cluster of tort questions concerning the nature and extent of the legal obligations doctors incur when they assist in procreation decisions. The claims may involve genetic counseling prior to or during pregnancy, medical diagnoses during pregnancy, or surgery aimed at avoiding conception or terminating a pregnancy. Suits by parents are sometimes designated "wrongful conception," "wrongful pregnancy," or "wrongful birth" claims, and those by children are labeled "wrongful life" claims. This terminology is disputed, however, and is not central to analyzing the underlying legal issues. For surveys of these and related issues, see Strasser, Misconceptions and Wrongful Births: A Call for a Principled Jurisprudence, 31 Ariz.St.L.J. 161 (1999) and Strasser, Wrongful Life, Wrongful Birth, Wrongful Death, and the Right to Refuse Treatment: Can Reasonable Jurisdictions Recognize All But One?, 64 Mo.L.Rev. 29 (1999).

At the same time, as courts began to consider more negligence claims in the procreation area, they started to evaluate medical professionals' tort liability for failing to respect patients' end-of-life decisions. Although these suits often took traditional forms of negligence, battery, or lack-of-informed-consent, courts and plaintiffs increasingly describe them as "wrongful prolongation of life" or "wrongful living" cases. More detailed discussion of this topic is contained in Strasser, A Jurisprudence in Disarray: On Battery, Wrongful Living, and the Right to Bodily Integrity, 36 San Diego L.Rev. 997 (1999) and Rodriguez, Suing Health Care Providers for Saving Lives: Liability for Providing Unwanted Life–Sustaining Treatment, 20 J.Legal Med. 1 (1999).

As you read this section, ask yourself what difference it makes—to plaintiffs, to courts, and to the outcomes—to categorize these suits according to the types of harms involved rather than simply analyzing them along traditional medical malpractice lines. Professor Strasser claims that the multiplication of terms in the procreation area needlessly obfuscates the real issues and causes confusion. Nonetheless, he acknowledges that it may prove necessary to recognize a cause of action for "wrongful living"—above and beyond simple negligence—to fully compensate certain patients whose end-of-life decisions have been ignored. Also consider the interplay between constitutional law and tort law.

As the following case suggests, many state courts have addressed the various issues of life and death. Although we will further explore these issues in the notes and questions, no attempt will be made to indicate the varying state positions in this fluid area beyond the analysis in this case itself.

Emerson v. Magendantz

Supreme Court of Rhode Island, 1997.
689 A.2d 409.

WEISBERGER, CHIEF JUSTICE.

[A trial judge certified two questions to the state supreme court:

1. Is there a cause of action under Rhode Island law when a physician negligently performs a sterilization procedure and the patient subse-

quently becomes pregnant and delivers a child from that pregnancy?

2. If so, what is the measure of damages?]

The facts giving rise to these certified questions may be summarized as follows from the pleadings and the documents filed by the parties in the Superior Court and in this court. Following the birth of their first child, the Emersons decided for financial reasons to limit their family to one child. Having made this decision, Diane consulted defendant, who was a gynecological specialist, concerning sterilization procedures. The defendant agreed to perform a surgical tubal ligation and did so upon Diane on January 10, 1991. Subsequently, on or about May 31, 1991, Diane was seen by an obstetrician, who determined that she was pregnant in spite of the preceding tubal ligation. Diane gave birth to a child on January 11, 1992. The child, who was named Kirsten, is alleged to have congenital problems that are only generally described in the complaint. Following Kirsten's birth, Diane underwent a second tubal ligation.

[Plaintiffs husband and wife sued, alleging that the birth "was proximately caused by defendant's negligent performance of the tubal-ligation procedure."]

The Emersons also allege that as a result of defendant's negligence Diane suffered severe physical pain and required additional invasive medical treatment. The Emersons further allege that they have suffered mental anguish and distress and that they have lost wages and earning capacity as a result of Diane's unanticipated pregnancy. The Emersons further complain that as a proximate result of defendant's negligence, they have incurred an obligation to expend monetary resources for the medical care and maintenance of Kirsten and that they will continue to be so obligated for many years to come.

I

Is There a Cause of Action under Rhode Island Law When a Physician
Negligently Performs a Sterilization Procedure and the Patient
Subsequently Becomes Pregnant and Delivers a Child?

This question poses an issue of first impression in this state. Of the numerous courts that have considered this question, only one state court of last resort has declined to recognize a cause of action in tort arising out of the negligent performance of a sterilization procedure. [citing a Nevada case]. Even Nevada has suggested there may be an action for breach of warranty. [ ] All other jurisdictions that have considered this question have determined that the negligent performance of a sterilization procedure is a tort for which recovery would be allowed under state law. [ ] In all, approximately thirty-five jurisdictions recognize a cause of action for negligent performance of sterilization procedures whether performed on the wife or on the husband.

We are persuaded by the overwhelming majority of opinions that recognize negligent performance of a sterilization procedure as a tort for which recovery may be allowed. Therefore, we answer the first question in the affirmative.

II

What Is the Measure of Damages?

Courts that have recognized the cause of action arising out of the negligent performance of sterilization or comparable procedures have adopted three general types of remedies as compensation for negligent procedures resulting in unwanted pregnancies. Thirty jurisdictions have adopted a remedy of limited recovery. [   ]

Under the limited-recovery rule the foregoing jurisdictions frequently grant compensation to the plaintiffs for the medical expenses of the ineffective sterilization procedure, for the medical and hospital costs of the pregnancy, for the expense of a subsequent sterilization procedure, for loss of wages, and sometimes for emotional distress arising out of the unwanted pregnancy and loss of consortium to the spouse arising out of the unwanted pregnancy. They also generally include medical expenses for prenatal care, delivery, and postnatal care.

A number of jurisdictions allow for recovery of the cost of child rearing as an element of damages. These jurisdictions may be divided into two groups. One group allows the cost of child rearing but balances against this cost the benefits derived by the parents, either economic or emotional, from having a healthy child. [citing cases from three states]

Two jurisdictions have adopted a full-recovery rule without offsetting either the economic or the emotional benefits to be derived from having a healthy child. Lovelace Medical Center v. Mendez, [805 P.2d 603 (N.M. 1991)]; Marciniak v. Lundborg, [450 N.W.2d 243 (Wis.1990)]. These two courts apply traditional tort principles in allowing for recovery of all damages that are reasonably foreseeable and that would result from the negligent performance of the sterilization procedure. In analyzing § 920 of the Restatement (Second) Torts (1979), which recommends consideration of benefits conferred in mitigation of damages, the New Mexico Supreme Court concluded that applying emotional benefits to economic loss did not apply similar benefits to similar losses. *Lovelace*, [   ]. Consequently that court denied recovery for emotional distress and also denied any offset of emotional benefits derived from having a healthy child. [   ]

Similarly the Supreme Court of Wisconsin declined to offset emotional benefits against economic loss. *Marciniak*, [   ]. The court also declined to offset economic benefits because the court deemed them to be insignificant. [   ]

After considering with great care the opinions in support of limited recovery, of full recovery with benefit offsets, and of full recovery without benefit offsets, we have decided to adopt the limited-recovery rule as described above, save for the element of emotional distress arising out of an unwanted pregnancy that results in the birth of a healthy child.

The Supreme Court of Washington in *McKernan v. Aasheim* [1984] has made some pertinent comments:

> "We believe that it is impossible to establish with reasonable certainty whether the birth of a particular healthy, normal child damaged its parents. Perhaps the costs of rearing and educating the child could be determined through use of actuarial tables or similar economic information. But whether these costs are outweighed by the emotional benefits which will be conferred by that child cannot be calculated. The child may turn out to be loving, obedient and attentive, or hostile, unruly and callous. The child may grow up to be President of the United States, or to be an infamous criminal. In short, it is impossible to tell, at an early stage in the child's life, whether its parents have sustained a net loss or net gain." [   ]

Similarly, the Delaware Supreme Court, in denying recovery of child-rearing costs, suggested that determining damage from the birth of a child was an "exercise in prophecy." [   ] Such a weighing process might be applied at the end of a life but not at the beginning. Such an undertaking was not felt to be within the specialty of factfinders.   .   .   .

.   .   .

We are of the opinion that the public policy of this state would preclude the granting of rearing costs for a healthy child whose parents have decided to forgo the option of adoption and have decided to retain the child as their own with all the joys and benefits that are derived from parenthood. Their decision to forgo the option of releasing the child for adoption constitutes most persuasive evidence that the parents consider the benefit of retaining the child to outweigh the economic costs of child rearing. [   ]

In implementing the limited-benefit rule, such parents would be entitled to recover the costs that the overwhelming majority of jurisdictions have allowed. Under this rule, plaintiffs would be entitled to recover the medical expenses of the ineffective sterilization procedure, the medical and hospital costs of the pregnancy, the expense of a subsequent sterilization procedure, loss of wages, loss of consortium to the spouse arising out of the unwanted pregnancy, and medical expenses for prenatal care, delivery, and postnatal care. However, no recovery would be allowable for emotional distress arising out of the birth of a healthy child.

In the event of the birth of a child who suffers from congenital defects, which birth is a result of an unwanted pregnancy arising out of a negligently performed sterilization procedure, we would follow the reasoning of the Supreme Court of Florida [in Fassoulas v. Ramey, 450 So.2d 822 (Fla. 1984)]. In [*Fassoulas*], the prospective parents, having had two children both of whom had been born with severe congenital abnormalities, sought to prevent the birth of further children through a vasectomy performed upon the husband. The vasectomy was unsuccessful . . . . The court [answering a certified question denied] child-rearing damages for a normal,

healthy child, [ ], but observed that in the case of a physically or a
mentally handicapped child, special medical and educational expenses [that
went] beyond normal rearing costs should be allowed. [ ] The court
recognized that the " 'financial and emotional drain associated with raising
such a child is often overwhelming to the affected parents.' " [ ] Therefore, the court held that special costs associated with bringing up a
handicapped child would be recoverable. We believe that the reasoning of
the Florida court is sound but would add that when a physician is placed on
notice, in performing a sterilization procedure, that the parents have a
reasonable expectation of giving birth to a physically or a mentally handicapped child or if the physician should be placed on notice, by reason of
statistical information of which he/she is or should be aware in the practice
of his/her profession, then the entire cost of raising such a child would be
within the ambit of recoverable damages. It should also be noted that the
extraordinary costs of maintaining a handicapped child would not end
when the child reached majority. Nor would the physician's liability necessarily end at that point. Offset against such liability would be any economic
benefits derived by the parents from governmental or other agencies that
might contribute to defraying the costs of caring for the child or its support
in adult life. Also in the event of the birth of a physically—or a mentally—
handicapped child, the parents should be entitled to compensation for
emotional distress.

The foregoing determinations are made by this court in answer to the
second certified question submitted by the Superior Court. The papers in
the case may be remanded to the Superior Court for further proceedings.

[Two of the five justices wrote separately.]

BOURCIER, J., with whom FLANDERS, J., joins, concurring in part and
dissenting in part.

I concur with my colleagues' response to the first certified question. . . . I dissent, however, from their response to the second certified
question regarding the measure of damages available to the unfortunate
patient upon whom the doctor's negligence has been visited.

I believe that the true legal nature of the cause of action that we all
recognize and acknowledge in this certification proceeding is nothing more
and nothing less than a medical malpractice cause of action. . . .

     . . .

I acknowledge, as do my colleagues, that appellate courts throughout
this country that have considered this damage question have been sharply
divided with regard to what should be proper compensation for the victim
of medical negligence malpractice in the course of a sterilization procedure.

. . . The most balanced . . . cases, however, follow the Massachusetts and Connecticut rule and the Restatement (Second) Torts § 920
(1979) which both permit full recovery for all damages proximately resulting from the physician's negligence while also permitting the trial jury to
mitigate or reduce any damage award by what may be proven to be the

value of the benefit that is conferred upon the plaintiff parent or parents by the birth of the child.

. . .

That "abort, give away, and get no emotional trauma and child support damages" rule announced by [*McKernan v. Aasheim*] appears, in my opinion, to deny a woman's constitutional right not to have children recognized in [decisions of the United States Supreme Court]. . . . I perceive of no justification for courts to force a Hobson's choice upon the unfortunate victim of a physician's negligence by ordering her to abort her unplanned pregnancy, or to give up her unplanned baby for adoption when born, or to accept in lieu of doing either, the judicially created concept that the "joy" of the unplanned birth will serve as full recompense for the doctor's negligence and for the victim's denial of her constitutional right to choose whether to become pregnant and give birth to a child. That "joy" reasoning concept is in my humble opinion nothing more than delusive reasoning employed to justify conclusion-oriented judicial decisions by certain appellate courts. In addition, it either ignores or refuses to recognize what is considered to be one of life's basic human realities, namely, that any normal woman will be hard-pressed to abort her pregnancy or later to give away her unplanned-for baby for adoption without thereafter incurring some form of resulting emotional trauma.

. . .

The reasoning advanced by my colleagues in support of insulating and absolving the negligent physician from all but minuscule responsibility for his or her patient's unplanned-for-child costs and expenses is that "[w]e are of the opinion that the public policy of this state would preclude the granting of rearing costs for a healthy child whose parents have decided to forgo the option of adoption and have decided to retain the child as their own with all the joys and benefits that are derived from parenthood." I respectfully disagree with that assumed public policy view expressed by my colleagues. I agree instead with the view regarding damage recovery and public policy as expressed by the Connecticut Supreme Court [in Ochs v. Borrelli, 445 A.2d 883 (Conn.1982)]:

> "In our view, the better rule is to allow parents to recover for the expense of rearing an unplanned child to majority when the child's birth results from negligent medical care. The defendants ask us to carve out an exception, grounded in public policy, to the normal duty of a tortfeasor to assume liability for all the damages that he has proximately caused. . . . But public policy cannot support an exception to tort liability when the impact of such an exception would impair the exercise of a constitutionally protected right. It is now clearly established that parents have a constitutionally protected interest located 'within the zone of privacy created by several fundamental constitutional guarantees' . . . to employ contraceptive techniques to limit the size of their family." [   ]

. . .

I respectfully suggest that the so-called unwanted pregnancy that my colleagues believe transforms itself into a total joy or blessing that then serves to absolve the negligent physician from practically all liability to his victim patient is indeed a total joy or blessing, but only for the errant physician and not for the unfortunate victim. The joy or blessing concept emerging from the unplanned birth perhaps superficially, at first blush, would appear reasonable in the case of the happily married couple yearning for a child or children. But that is not what is before us in this certification, and that is not the nature of any of the medical-malpractice claims that are usually made against the errant physician who negligently performs a sterilization procedure. The factual reality in the usual medical malpractice case that is brought not only by women but also by males against the errant physicians who have negligently performed sterilization procedures is that the plaintiffs in those cases have decided for various reasons, economic or otherwise, not to have children. In those case situations I do not believe that the joy or blessing concept should automatically apply and restrict the tort recovery allowable to the married couple who had elected not to have children or to limit their family size for health or economic reasons. Neither should it so apply to the detriment of the unmarried young male or female college student or the professional career man or woman, married or single, who did not want to have a child or did not have the time to care for a child without first giving up his or her college, business, or professional career. To adopt a simple joy or blessing rule and then have it apply automatically to all litigants in those fact situations for purposes of limiting, to the point of practically eliminating, the liability of a negligent physician is neither fair nor in compliance with the age-old general tort-recovery damages rule. The joy or blessing rule in those situations is in my humble opinion nothing more than a judicial mirage, invisible to most ordinary mortals.

. . .

Notes and Questions

1. How does the result in Part I of the court's opinion differ from that in an ordinary medical malpractice claim against the defendant?

If a healthy fetus is harmed by a doctor's negligence, the liability is clear. In the situations we are considering here, however, plaintiffs are not claiming that defendant physician's negligence *caused* the relevant defect in the child, just that it allowed the child to be conceived or born.

In the cases that follow, the issue is no longer whether plaintiff may recover the items that the *Emerson* majority recognized—those connected with the birth and the need for another sterilization. These are almost universally awarded.

2. *The role of the constitution.* Towards the end of its opinion, the majority suggests that, in awarding damages, it would distinguish quite sharply between cases in which the baby that resulted from a physician's negligence was healthy and those in which the baby was handicapped. The dissent instead places priority upon the parents' ability to make autonomous decisions about their family, citing Supreme Court decisions on contraception and abortion. Which approach to the area seems more appropriate? Since most courts tend to differentiate along the lines of whether the child is healthy or unhealthy, the following notes will adhere to that division, but keep in mind the problems it may entail. In Misconceptions and Wrongful Births, supra, Professor Strasser argues that the healthy/unhealthy distinction is unhelpful, and indicates that the relevant issue should be procreative autonomy. He then suggests that there is no reason the decision not to have an unhealthy child should be valued more than the decision not to have a child at all—as courts that agree with *Emerson* majority seem to do. According to each approach, how would you justify compensating the harm of having a handicapped child and not that of having a healthy one when the parents' decision was simply not to procreate?

States must adhere to the Supreme Court's interpretation of the scope of the right to an abortion decision, as articulated most recently in Planned Parenthood of Southeastern Pennsylvania v. Casey, 505 U.S. 833 (1992) (state could not place an "undue burden" upon a woman's right to obtain an abortion). Some states have, however, limited the tort remedy for "wrongful birth" by statute. In Etkind v. Suarez, 519 S.E.2d 210 (Ga. 1999), the court held that the federal constitution did not impose an obligation on states "to recognize a woman's right to bring a civil suit against her obstetrician for the negligent failure to assist her in making an informed abortion decision." Denying a tort remedy was deemed to be different from impeding the woman's right to an abortion. Is this distinction valid? For discussion of these statutes, see Ryan, Wrongful Birth: False Representations of Women's Reproductive Lives, 78 Minn.L.Rev. 857 (1994).

If constitutional law changed to permit states to regulate or ban abortions (at least in the types of cases we have been considering), how many of the results might alter? What about outcomes in a state that enacted a restrictive statute? If an abortion would be illegal, would that mean that a physician would be under no duty to warn a pregnant woman that an already conceived fetus is almost certain to be born with severe birth defects? Would it mean that there was no duty to check for such defects in the first place?

3. *The reasons for the choice.* When a person or a couple decide that they wish no children or no more children there may be several reasons. In *Emerson* it was "financial." Does that necessarily mean that they fear falling into serious poverty? Might it also mean that they wish to preserve a life style to which they have become accustomed or to which they aspire? In other cases they may believe that they would not make good parents. In still other cases, there is concern about the mother's physical and mental well-being during a pregnancy. If the concern is about having a child with a congenital defect, as we have already seen, separate issues arise that are discussed later in these notes.

4. *The nature of the negligence.* Where the parties wanted no children or no more children the claims are usually brought against surgeons whose sterilization surgeries have failed, or against physicians who have negligently failed to diagnose a pregnancy in time for an abortion. In the case of those who wish to avoid an unhealthy child, the claim is usually brought for incorrect medical advice that encouraged a pregnancy—from a physician or a genetic counselor. It may also be brought for conduct during a pregnancy—such as misreading of amniocentesis tests or sonograms. See, e.g., Schloss v. The Miriam Hospital, 1999 WL 41875 (Super. R.I. 1999) (defendant physicians and hospital failed to discern that one parent carried the Tay–Sachs gene) and Bader v. Johnson, 732 N.E.2d 1212 (Ind.2000) (consulting doctor failed to advise the mother that an ultrasound had produced abnormal results, and the resultant child died soon after being born hydrocephalic).

In all of these cases, there is the lurking causation question of what the parents would have done if they had been informed of the risks of defect. Should they have to prove that they would have availed themselves of the opportunity to terminate the pregnancy?

5. *Healthy baby.* Although some have challenged the value of the distinction between healthy and unhealthy babies, *Emerson* shows that the courts do in fact tend to analyze the cases that way. We follow that pattern in the following notes.

Where the plaintiffs have sought to avoid having any more children, the dispute over what damages are recoverable has centered on the parents' emotional distress and on the economic burden of the new child. Why does the majority in *Emerson* deny recovery for the economic costs of raising a healthy child? Why does the dissent disagree? The public policy concerns that the majority invokes are not new. In Shaheen v. Knight, 11 Pa.D. & C.2d 41 (1958), the court rejected a case of failed sterilization: "To allow damages in a suit such as this would mean that the physician would have to pay for the fun, joy and affection which plaintiff . . . will have in the rearing and educating of this, [plaintiff's] fifth child. Many people would be willing to support this child were they given the right of custody and adoption, but according to plaintiff's statement, plaintiff does not want such. He wants to have the child and wants the doctor to support it. In our opinion to allow such damages would be against public policy."

Contrast *Marciniak v. Lundborg,* cited in *Emerson,* holding that awarding damages for the rearing of a healthy child would not violate public policy. The court saw no reason to deviate from the rule that made defendants liable for those damages foreseeably flowing from the tort. In casting aside the argument that such an award would cause psychological harm to the child, the court stated:

> The suit is for the costs of raising the child, not to rid themselves of an unwanted child. They obviously want to keep the child. The love, affection, and emotional support they are prepared to give do not bring with them the economic means that are also necessary to feed, clothe, educate and otherwise raise the child. That is what this suit is about

and we trust the child in the future will be well able to distinguish the two. Relieving the family of the economic costs of raising the child may well add to the emotional well-being of the entire family, including this child, rather than bring damage to it.

Nor did the suit "debase the sanctity of human life." The court did not "perceive that the Marciniaks in bringing this suit are in any way disparaging the value of their child's life. They are, to the contrary, attempting to enhance it." Which court's reasoning is more persuasive?

6. If the costs of raising a healthy baby are to be awarded, should economic setoffs also be considered? If so, what might these be in this sort of case? Can you justify offsetting emotional benefits against economic damages? Section 920 of Second Restatement provides:

> When the defendant's tortious conduct has caused harm to the plaintiff or to his property and in so doing has conferred a special benefit to the interest of the plaintiff that was harmed, the value of the benefit conferred is considered in mitigation of damages, to the extent that this is equitable.

Comment *b* states that damages resulting from "an invasion of one interest are not diminished by showing that another interest has been benefited." Why not? One example offered is that "damages for pain and suffering are not diminished by showing that the earning capacity of the plaintiff has been increased by the defendant's act."

Does that suggest how setoffs should be treated in the *Emerson* case? How do the *Emerson* majority and dissent answer this question? Contrast both of their approaches with the *Marciniak* court's refusal to offset emotional benefits against economic damages:

> When parents make the decision to forgo this opportunity for emotional enrichment, it hardly seems equitable to not only force this benefit upon them but to tell them they must pay for it as well by offsetting it against their proven economic damages. With respect to economic benefits, the same argument prevails. In addition, any economic advantages the child might confer upon the parents are ordinarily insignificant.

Is there a connection between the courts' decisions on offsets and their statements about public policy?

7. As to damages for emotional distress, what are the damages that parents might feel upon becoming parents of an unwanted healthy child? Are any or all of these items avoidable by giving the child up for adoption? What are the emotional benefits for parents of unwanted healthy babies? Are both sides equally clear at this time? Should that matter? Should emotional distress damages be offset by emotional benefits?

8. *The unwanted baby that is unhealthy. Emerson* suggests the unusual situation of plaintiffs, who wanted no children for financial reasons, who became parents of an unwanted and unhealthy child. In that scenario what, if any, economic costs should be awarded? Note that here there are two kinds of economic costs—normal rearing expenses and extraordinary medical expenses.

Should recovery depend on whether the plaintiffs told the surgeon the reason for wanting the sterilization? In Williams v. University of Chicago Hospitals, 688 N.E.2d 130 (Ill.1997), parents sought compensation for the extraordinary expenses of raising a congenitally hyperactive child following a failed tubal ligation. The court denied recovery, stating that the birth of a defective child was not a foreseeable consequence of defendants' negligence, despite the fact that the mother's medical history included several failed pregnancies, and a hyperactive son by another father. In arriving at its decision, the court relied on the fact that the parents did not allege that they "were seeking to avoid a specific risk and that the defendants were aware of that."

9.   *Unhealthy baby.* Where the parents fear an unhealthy child and that concern is conveyed to the defendant, who is then negligent, what, if any, economic damages should the parents recover? Might they extend beyond the child's majority? What, if any, damages should be recoverable for emotional distress? What part might setoffs play?

10.   Where the fear of an unhealthy child or other medical concern leads to a sterilization decision, what should happen if the baby is in fact born healthy? In Hartke v. McKelway, 707 F.2d 1544 (D.C.Cir.1983), the plaintiff sought sterilization for therapeutic reasons—to avoid expected harm to herself. She became pregnant due to defendant's negligence, but the feared consequence did not materialize and a healthy baby was born. The court denied recovery for the cost of child-rearing: "the jury could not rationally have found that the birth of this child was an injury to the plaintiff. Awarding child-rearing expenses would only give Hartke a windfall." What about emotional distress for the "window" during which she feared harm to herself?

11.   *The child's claims.* If the condition is one that will shorten life, or cause great pain, and the child's case seems to be based on the proposition that it would have been better off not being born, the courts have been unanimous in declining to recognize its "wrongful life" claim. The most commonly offered explanation in these cases is that it would be impossible to compare life with the disability to nonexistence. Is the problem an inability to measure one or both of the two items or is it the inability to compare the two even if both were measurable? See Strasser, in Wrongful Life, Wrongful Birth, Wrongful Death, p. 326 supra.

Some courts have recognized an action when the condition is not life-shortening and the child is likely to incur extraordinary medical expenses as an adult, but they limit the damages to economic ones. See, e.g., Harbeson v. Parke–Davis, Inc., 656 P.2d 483 (Wash.1983) (fetal hydantoin syndrome) and Turpin v. Sortini, 643 P.2d 954 (Cal.1982) (congenital deafness). Why might courts distinguish along these lines? Does it matter whether economic damages are recovered by the child or by the parent? Are these cases really "wrongful life" cases? Consider the Florida Supreme Court's reasons for permitting the same damages as part of a "wrongful birth" cause of action when the child suffered from a variety of genetic defects:

> [S]ome jurisdictions have at least suggested that the tort of "wrongful life" can address two separate concerns: (1) the extraordinary expenses associated with caring for the impaired child until its death; and (2) liability for "suffering" caused by the impairment. . . . A lawsuit aimed at recovering the second type of "damages" necessarily would require the finder of fact to weigh the value of impaired life against the value of nonexistence. . . . [The same] does not hold true, however, for the extraordinary expenses that will arise from the impairment of a wrongfully born child. These expenses are not properly an aspect of a wrongful life claim at all, but an aspect of wrongful birth. Such damages are quantifiable with reasonable certainty. . . .

Kush v. Lloyd, 616 So.2d 415 (Fla.1992). Does allowing wrongful life suits for economic damages alone solve all logical problems with the cause of action? Why haven't courts recognized "wrongful life" suits when the child is afflicted with a life-shortening problem?

Should the unhealthy child be able to sue the parents for her conception and birth despite genetic contraindications? In Curlender v. BioScience Laboratories, 165 Cal. Rptr. 477 (App. 1980), the court had suggested in dictum that parents who conceive with knowledge of a high risk of birth defects might be liable to a child born with such defects. The legislature responded with Calif.Civil Code § 43.6(a), providing that "No cause of action arises against a parent of a child based upon the claim that the child should not have been conceived or, if conceived, should not have been allowed to have been born alive."

12. *Claims by other relatives.* In Michelman v. Ehrlich, 709 A.2d 281 (N.J.App.Div.1998), a grandfather sued for negligence that caused his grandson to be born with Tay–Sachs disease, a neurological disease that is usually fatal before the age of five. Actions by the parents were pending. The court thought the duty was owed to parents to "diagnose and inform them of abnormalities to the infant so they can use that information to decide whether the pregnancy should be terminated." The duty was extended to the husband "to promote and encourage family unity in forming decisions on such matters, and in further recognition of the reality that where the duty is breached, both parents share equally in the financial and emotional burdens of the child's illness. The fundamental premise of this cause of action, however, is 'the availability of lawful eugenic abortions.' " Given these premises, it "serves no purpose of tort law to extend the duty to grandparents."

In *Emerson*, the parents already had one child. Has that child sustained damages from the unwanted birth? Would it make a difference to that child's claim whether the baby was healthy or not?

13. *Baby not born.* Suits may also arise when a child is not born because of defendant doctor's negligent counseling. In Martinez v. Long Island Jewish Hillside Medical Center, 512 N.E.2d 538 (N.Y.1987), plaintiff alleged that defendants negligently and incorrectly advised her that her baby would be born either with no brain or a small brain. She submitted to an abortion, believing that it was justified under the extraordinary circumstances. Afterward, she learned that the advice had been incorrect and that no abortion had been necessary. At trial, plaintiff and her psychiatrist testified that plaintiff considered abortion to be a sin except under exceptional circumstances; when she discovered the truth, she suffered mental anguish and depression from her awareness that "she had needlessly committed an act in violation of her deep-seated convictions." The claim was upheld. What kind of emotional damages should such a plaintiff recover? How can parents be compensated for the fact that they will never have the child in question on account of defendant's negligence?

Imagine a case in which plaintiffs claim that they never conceived because a genetic counselor falsely and negligently informed them that their child could be afflicted with a devastating congenital impairment— and now it is too late for them to try. How might a court analyze the situation? What would happen if parents learned after conception of a problem that their genetic counselor was negligent in failing to discover and they aborted the fetus? Would they have an emotional distress claim?

14. *Wrongful living.* As we saw in Chapter II, supra, p. 122, doctors must obtain a patient's informed consent before pursuing a course of treatment. In certain emergency situations, however, the patient may not be sufficiently sentient to provide his or her consent. In these instances, unless there is reason to believe otherwise, consent has traditionally been implied, and the doctor may assume that the patient would want to be resuscitated, intubated, or otherwise assisted. This implication may conflict, though, with the desires of a patient who is terminally ill, or who would prefer not to be revived artificially. See the articles, p. 326, supra. The problem has been treated both federally and in the states. The Supreme Court has articulated a constitutionally protected liberty interest in refusing unwanted medical treatment, but has also recognized that states have an interest in preserving life, and may require a high standard of proof before imputing refusal to an incompetent person. Cruzan v. Director, Missouri Dept. of Health, 497 U.S. 261 (1990). States have emphasized their own regard for the right to refuse treatment by passing legislation; these statutes allow patients to sign various kinds of "advance directives" specifying what types of care they intend to refuse, and under what circumstances. Recall also *Shine*, p. 128, supra.

State statutes, however, do not solve all the dilemmas. Advance directives often delegate decision-making to family or friends in case of the patient's own inability to give informed consent; this may lead to conflicts among relatives in end-of-life situations. Likewise, problems of interpretation plague the directives. As a result, some patients and their representatives have opted to pursue tort actions against those who have—they claim—wrongfully prolonged their lives. These may take the traditional form of lack-of-informed consent suits, or battery claims; they can also emerge as defenses to doctors' or hospitals' attempts to recover medical costs. At this point, claims designated as "wrongful living" or "wrongful prolongation of life" have not been recognized by state courts and, in fact, some courts, interpreting more traditional causes of action in this area as "wrongful living" suits in disguise, have denied plaintiffs recovery. See Strasser, A Jurisprudence in Disarray, supra. In reading the following notes, consider the significance of justifying tort actions in this area by invoking a patient's right to make end-of-life decisions and by appealing to a right to maintain bodily integrity. Does it matter which theory is used?

15. The "wrongful living" cause of action exhibits some similarities to the "wrongful life" one discussed above; in both cases, the plaintiff claims that life is a liability due to the defendant's malpractice. In Allore v. Flower Hospital, 699 N.E.2d 560 (Ohio App. 1997), the court refused to allow damages for defendants' wrongful prolongation of plaintiff's life. In Anderson v. St. Francis–St. George Hospital, Inc., 671 N.E.2d 225 (Ohio 1996), the state's highest court had determined that the alleged " 'harm' that was proximately caused by a medical professional's breach of duty in a prolongation-of-life case was the 'benefit of life,' a harm which courts have repeatedly refused to compensate. [ ]. As a result, the *Anderson* court concluded that there are some breaches of duty that affect the lives of others for which there should be no monetary compensation." Compare this reasoning with that used by courts considering "wrongful life" claims. Might one distinguish the two situations? To what extent does the "wrongful living" patient's pre-existing ability to make a decision matter?

16. *State statutes.* As we have seen, p. 151, supra, courts can use statutes by analogy to create common law rights of action. Thus it might be possible to derive a tort claim from statutes designed to further patients' abilities to make end-of-life medical decisions. In Taylor v. Muncie Medical Investors, L.P., 727 N.E.2d 466 (Ind.App.2000), the court declined to follow plaintiffs' suggestion that it recognize the tort of "wrongful prolongation of life":

> The Estate [of Taylor] argues that, although no Indiana courts have directly addressed the issue, it is logical for Indiana to adopt a tort for wrongful prolongation of life. If Indiana does not do so, then the Estate concludes that there is no enforcement mechanism to protect a patient's right to refuse medical treatment and a family's right to make medical decisions for incapacitated relatives. . . . The estate asserts that the "rights" of families to make health care decisions created by the Health Care Consent Act, and recognized by our supreme court . . . are meaningless without a remedy to enforce them.

The court disagreed. Since the Health Care Consent Act was thought to provide a sufficient remedy for situations in which an intrafamily dispute occurred, as it had here, the court said that relatives could use that process to determine who should be able to make decisions for the patient. That was preferable to subsequently suing healthcare providers. What might be argued on the other side?

Over 20 state statutes expressly provide for some type of penalty if a physician fails to comply with the statute and does not transfer the patient to another physician who would comply with the patient's end-of-life decisions. These penalties range from professional censure to civil liability, but many specify that the failure must be intentional or willful. See Rodriguez, Suing Health Care Providers for Saving Life, supra.

For a recent case indicating at least some tendency towards allowing compensation in this area, although not under the rubric of a "wrongful living" suit, see Wright v. Johns Hopkins Health Systems Corp., 728 A.2d 166 (Md.1999). Plaintiff's decedent, a terminal AIDS patient, was resuscitated against his wishes. The court cited *Cruzan* for the proposition that "a liberty interest under the Fourteenth Amendment gives rise to a constitutionally protected right to refuse life saving hydration and nutrition," and invoked a state law that allowed individuals to make advance directives. It then assumed, arguendo, that the statute or the common law accorded "an individual, and, accordingly, the individual's estate, a cause of action for a health care provider's failure to comply with the individual's advance directive." Ultimately, the court found plaintiff's facts inadequate to support claims for negligence, wrongful death, or battery.

CHAPTER V

CAUSATION

In earlier chapters we asked whether the defendant owed a duty of due care to the plaintiff and whether defendant had violated that duty. In this chapter we ask whether the defendant's negligence "caused" the harm for which the plaintiff is suing. This inquiry involves two quite different questions.

First, we consider whether "cause in fact" ("actual cause") has been established. This inquiry seeks to tie the defendant's conduct to the plaintiff's harm in an almost physical or scientific way.

The second question concerns a very different issue called "proximate" or "legal" causation. Here, the question is whether, granting that defendant's negligence has been an actual cause of the plaintiff's harm, the injury occurred under circumstances that allow the defendant to argue plausibly against being required to compensate the plaintiff for that harm. In our consideration of proximate causation we return to some of the aspects of duty that we explored in Chapters III and IV.

A. CAUSE IN FACT

1. BASIC DOCTRINE

From the outset of the book we have implicitly accepted the notion that a defendant who behaves negligently should not have to compensate an injured plaintiff unless the plaintiff's injury is causally connected to the defendant's negligent conduct. Can you justify a system in which a driver who runs a red light or who drives recklessly (but hits no one) should compensate a person who is struck by lightning that very moment several blocks away?

Judicial decisions have accepted the need for some connection between the plaintiff's harm and the defendant's negligent conduct before imposing tort liability on the defendant. Courts have traditionally denied liability when it is clear that the connection was missing. Consider a situation in which a motorist should have sounded the car's horn when going around a dangerous bend that has a sign requiring that the horn be sounded. The negligence is clear. But the causal connection is missing if the lone motorist coming the other way was deaf and would not have heard the horn even if it had been sounded.

In Rinaldo v. McGovern, 587 N.E.2d 264 (N.Y.1991), involving an errant golf drive, one claim was that the golfer negligently failed to shout "fore" before hitting the ball. On this point, the court concluded that a warning "would have been all but futile." Even if the defendant had shouted, "it is unlikely that plaintiffs, who were driving in a vehicle on a nearby roadway, would have heard, much less had the opportunity to act upon, the shouted warning." The chance was "too 'remote' to justify submission of the case to the jury."

Sometimes the lack of actual cause is shown in a different, but equally clear, way. Defendant may be negligent for not maintaining a dam so that it could withstand an ordinary rainfall. If such a normal rain had fallen, the dam would have given way and the defendant's liability for the downstream flooding would have been clear. In fact, however, the next rainfall is not of the ordinary variety; it is an unprecedented deluge beyond anything that the courts would require dam keepers to anticipate. The dam bursts under conditions that would have caused even a well-constructed dam to burst—and downstream flooding occurs that does roughly the same type and amount of harm to the same plaintiffs as would have been done if the dam had burst under the anticipated rain. What arguments support liability on the dam owner? What arguments cut the other way?

In Tollison v. State of Washington, 950 P.2d 461 (Wash.1998), the court held that an adoption placement agency owed a duty to disclose to prospective adopters information mandated by statute. The negligent failure to do so did not, however, cause harm because the adopters admitted that, despite being aware of other serious problems, they wanted to adopt the child anyway. The jury reasonably found that, given what the adopters knew when they adopted, the legally mandated information would not have altered their decision.

In many situations in which actual cause is an issue, we know all the relevant facts. Sometimes, however, the problem results from uncertainty about what happened.

Stubbs v. City of Rochester

Court of Appeals of New York, 1919.
226 N.Y. 516, 124 N.E. 137.

[Defendant supplied Hemlock system water for drinking and Holly system water for firefighting. The evidence indicated that through the city's negligence in May, 1910, the systems had become intermingled near the Brown Street Bridge. The Hemlock water became contaminated by sewage known to be present in the Holly water, but this was not discovered until October. Plaintiff contracted typhoid fever in September and attributed it to the city's negligence. By a 3–2 vote, without opinion, the Appellate Division affirmed a nonsuit granted by the trial judge at the close of plaintiff's case. Other facts are stated in the opinion.]

HOGAN, J. [after stating the facts].

The important question in this case is—did the plaintiff produce evidence from which inference might reasonably be drawn that the cause of his illness was due to the use of contaminated water furnished by defendant. Counsel for respondent argues that even assuming that the city may be held liable to plaintiff for damages caused by its negligence in furnishing contaminated water for drinking purposes, (a) that the evidence adduced by plaintiff fails to disclose that he contracted typhoid fever by drinking contaminated water; (b) that it was incumbent upon the plaintiff to establish that his illness was not due to any other cause to which typhoid fever may be attributed for which defendant is not liable. The evidence does disclose several causes of typhoid fever which is a germ disease, the germ being known as the typhoid bacillus, which causes may be classified as follows:

First. Drinking of polluted water. *Second.* Raw fruits and vegetables in certain named localities where human excrement is used to fertilize the soil are sometimes sources of typhoid infection. *Third.* The consumption of shell fish, though not a frequent cause. *Fourth.* The consumption of infected milk and vegetables. *Fifth.* The house fly in certain localities. *Sixth.* Personal contact with an infected person by one who has a predilection for typhoid infection and is not objectively sick with the disease. *Seventh.* Ice if affected with typhoid bacilli. *Eighth.* Fruits, vegetables, etc., washed in infected water. *Ninth.* The medical authorities recognize that there are still other causes and means unknown. This fact was developed on cross-examination of physicians called by plaintiff.

[Counsel argues first] that the evidence fails to disclose that plaintiff contracted typhoid fever by drinking contaminated water. The plaintiff having been nonsuited at the close of his case is entitled to the most favorable inference deducible from the evidence. That plaintiff on or about September 6th, 1910, was taken ill and very soon thereafter typhoid fever developed is not disputed. That he was employed in a factory located one block distant from the Brown street bridge in which Hemlock lake water was the only supply of water for potable and other purposes, and that the water drawn from faucets in that neighborhood disclosed that the water was roily and of unusual appearance is not questioned. And no doubt prevails that the Holly system water was confined to the main business part of the city for use for fire purposes and sprinkling streets and is not furnished for domestic or drinking purposes.

The evidence of the superintendent of water works of the city is to the effect that Hemlock lake water is a pure wholesome water free from contamination of any sort at the lake and examinations of the same are made weekly; that the Holly water is not fit for drinking purposes taken as it is from the Genesee river. Further evidence was offered by plaintiff by several witnesses, residents in the locality of Brown street bridge, who discovered the condition of the water at various times during July, August and September and made complaint to the water department of the condition of the same. Dr. Goler, a physician and health officer of the city, was called by plaintiff and testified that in September when complaint was made to him by a resident of the district he went to the locality, visited houses in the immediate neighborhood, found that the water drawn from the faucet of the Hemlock supply looked badly and smelled badly. He took a sample of the water to the laboratory and had it examined by a chemist who found that it contained an increase in solids and very many times, that is twenty to thirty times as much chlorine or common salt as is found in the domestic water supply—the presence of chlorine in excessive quantities indicates contamination in that quantity, bad contamination and usually sewage contamination. Further examination followed in the district. Water was collected from various houses and a large number of samples, perhaps less than one hundred, but over twenty-five. . . . About the following day, the source of contamination having been discovered, the doctor made an investigation as to the reported cases of typhoid fever in the city in the months of August, September and October for the purpose of determining the number of cases, where the cases came from, what gave rise to it, and he stated that in his opinion the outbreak of typhoid was due to polluted water, contaminated as he discovered afterwards by sewage. In answer to a hypothetical question embracing generally the facts asserted by plaintiff the witness testified that he had an opinion as to the cause of the infection of plaintiff and such opinion was that it was due to contaminated water.

Doctor Dodge, of the faculty of the University of Rochester, a professor of biology, also bacteriologist of the city of Rochester, about October first made an analysis of samples of water. . . . While his examination did not disclose any colon bacillus, it did disclose some evidence of the same. Dr. Brady, the physician who attended the plaintiff, and Dr. Culkin both testified that in their opinion the plaintiff contracted typhoid fever from drinking polluted water.

Plaintiff called a witness who resided on Brown street about two minutes' walk from the bridge and proved by her that she drank water from the Hemlock mains in the fall of 1910 and was ill with typhoid fever. Thereupon counsel for defendant stipulated that fifty-seven witnesses which the plaintiff proposed to call will testify that they drank water from the Hemlock taps in the vicinity of the district west of the Genesee river and north of Allen street in the summer and fall of 1910 and during said summer and fall suffered from typhoid fever, that in view of the stipulation such witnesses need not be called by plaintiff and the stipulation shall have the same force and effect as though the witnesses had been called and testified to the facts.

The plaintiff resided with his wife some three miles distant from the factory where he was employed. The water consumed by him at his house outside the infected district was Hemlock water. The only water in the factory was Hemlock water and he had there an individual cup from which he drank. He was not outside of the city during the summer of 1910. Therefore, the only water he drank was in the city of Rochester.

A table of statistics as to typhoid fever in the city of Rochester for the years 1901–1910, inclusive, was produced by the health officer and received in evidence. . . . The statistics disclose that the number of typhoid cases in the city in 1910 was 223, an excess of 50 cases of any year of the nine years preceding. Recalling that complaints as to water commenced in the summer of 1910 and as shown by the evidence that typhoid fever does not develop until two or three weeks after the bacilli have been taken into the system, in connection with the fact that the source of contamination was not discovered until October, the statistics disclose that of the 223 cases of typhoid in the city in the year 1910, 180 cases appear during the months of August, September, October and November as against forty-three cases during the remaining eight months; thirty-five of which were prior to August and eight in the month of December, two months after the source of contamination of the water was discovered.

The evidence on the trial discloses that at least fifty-eight witnesses, residents of the district, drank the contaminated water and suffered from typhoid fever in addition to plaintiff; thus one-third of the 180 cases during the months stated were shown to exist in that district.

Counsel for respondent asserts that there was a failure of proof on the part of plaintiff in that he did not establish that he contracted disease by drinking contaminated water and in support of his argument cites a rule of law, that when there are several possible causes of injury for one or more of which a defendant is not responsible, plaintiff cannot recover without proving that the injury was sustained wholly or in part by a cause for which defendant was responsible. He submits that it was essential for plaintiff to eliminate all other of seven causes from which the disease might have been contracted. If the argument should prevail and the rule of law stated is not subject to any limitation the present case illustrates the impossibility of a recovery in any case based upon like facts. One cause of the disease is stated by counsel to be "personal contact with typhoid carriers or other persons suffering with the disease, whereby bacilli are received and accidentally transferred by the hands or some other portion of the person or clothes to the mouth." Concededly a person is affected with typhoid some weeks before the disease develops. The plaintiff here resided three miles distant from his place of employment and traveled to and from his work upon the street car. To prove the time when he was attacked with typhoid, then find every individual who traveled on the same car with him and establish by each one of them that he or she was free from the disease even to his or her clothing is impossible. Again the evidence disclosed that typhoid fever was caused by sources unknown to medical science. If the word of the rule stated is to prevail plaintiff would be required to eliminate sources which had not yet been determined or ascertained. I do not believe the rule stated to be as inflexible as claimed for. If two or more possible causes exist, for only one of which a defendant may be liable, and a party injured establishes facts from which it can be said with reasonable certainty that the direct cause of the injury was the one for which the defendant was liable the party has complied with the spirit of the rule.

The plaintiff was employed in the immediate locality where the water was contaminated. He drank the water daily. The consumption of contaminated water is a very frequent cause of typhoid fever. In the locality there were a large number of cases of typhoid fever and near to sixty individuals who drank the water and had suffered from typhoid fever in that neighborhood appeared as witnesses on behalf of plaintiff. The plaintiff gave evidence of his habits, his home surroundings and his method of living, and the medical testimony indicated that his illness was caused by drinking contaminated water. Without reiteration of the facts disclosed on the trial I do not believe that the case on the part of plaintiff was so lacking in proof as matter of law that his complaint should be dismissed. On the contrary the most favorable inferences deducible from the plaintiff were such as would justify a submission of the facts to a jury as to the reasonable inferences to be drawn therefrom, and a verdict rendered thereon for either party would rest not in conjecture but upon reasonable possibilities.

The judgment should be reversed and a new trial granted, costs to abide the event.

CARDOZO, POUND and ANDREWS, JJ., concur; HISCOCK, CH. J., CHASE and McLAUGHLIN, JJ., dissent [without opinion].

Notes and Questions

1.   Why is it the plaintiff's burden to show the causal relationship?

2.   Each party pays for its expert witnesses and the preparation of its statistics. Who should pay for these expenses? Is it permissible in asking whether a plaintiff has met the burden of showing causation to ask what more the plaintiff might have done?

3.   Why is it relevant that 58 persons who drank the water got typhoid? Didn't they also sleep and get typhoid, or drink milk and get typhoid? Might they all have been bitten by houseflies and gotten typhoid? What further data would be helpful?

4.   If each of the other 57 victims sued one at a time, would it be possible for 35 juries to hold for the plaintiffs and 22 juries for the defendant if the evidence was essentially the same in each case?

5.   Suppose all 58 residents of the district who contracted typhoid fever sued. Suppose historical studies—from earlier years when there was no intermixing of the water supplies—further suggest that ten residents of the district would have contracted typhoid fever from one of the other causes. All 58 residents might well collect full damages, even though it seems clear that ten should not recover. Liability exceeding its responsibility is thus being assigned to the City of Rochester, creating overdeterrence. Is this an insoluble dilemma?

One solution to this problem that has been suggested in recent years as toxic tort cases have become more prevalent is "proportional recovery." Thus, it would be possible to compensate each of the 58 victims for 48/58 of their damages. Are there problems with this approach? See Farber, Toxic Causation, 71 Minn.L.Rev. 1229 (1987) for references to the literature.

6.   *Probabilistic recovery for harm in the future.* Might a proportionate recovery scheme be employed at the time of exposure, even before actual harm was experienced? This issue arises when the defendant's negligence has created the risk that the plaintiff will suffer either more serious harm

or another type of harm as a result of the initial exposure. This has been a common aspect of asbestos litigation where the first evidence of harm may be relatively minor but the future dangers are great.

The most common response has been to tell the plaintiff to sue for the second disease when it develops. See Simmons v. Pacor, Inc., 674 A.2d 232 (Pa.1996), adopting a two-disease rule, whereby the plaintiff with, for example, asbestosis recovers (if at all) only for that present disease, and recovers for consequent lung cancer or mesothelioma, only when the more serious disease occurs. The court also held that plaintiff could only obtain a recovery for emotional distress related to the prospect of developing the more serous condition at the time of the suit for the second disease.

Several reasons argue against giving someone with a 75% chance of future harm 100% recovery now. One is the possibility that P will not get the second disease and will receive money for nonexistent damages. Apart from the unfairness of such an award, it may also deplete the defendant's coffers in a mass tort context so that there will be no money left for those who ultimately do get the disease. At the same time, there is concern about giving a large sum to someone who does not yet need it—and who may spend it now and not have it when the disease does strike. To allow for future recovery when the disease does in fact strike, the rules on statutes of limitation and on splitting causes of action are altered to target "discovery" rather than (or in addition to) "exposure." If a disease may not develop for 20 years, how can a plaintiff prove now a great likelihood of getting it—and what the likely severity will be?

Several arguments cut in favor of permitting those who can show a better-than-even chance of future disease to sue now. These include the difficulty of proof if one must wait 20 or more years to sue. This goes to any fault requirement and also to causation since many more events have intervened. Also, the deterrent aspect of tort law is being delayed and potentially disregarded.

If arguments for current suit are sound, do they also extend to those who can prove a less-than-even chance of getting the future disease? Various positions are discussed in Mauro v. Raymark Industries, Inc., 561 A.2d 257 (N.J.1989), in which the majority allowed those with better-than-even claims to sue for full future damages, and the dissenter wanted to permit those with less-than-even chances to recover that percentage of their damages.

In Petriello v. Kalman, 576 A.2d 474 (Conn.1990), defendant obstetrician negligently performed a procedure on plaintiff, as the result of which plaintiff suffered some immediate injury and also an 8–16% chance of specific future injury. The court upheld a jury instruction that permitted an award for the increased risk. Does the logic of this view require proportionate—rather than full—recovery in cases in which the plaintiff establishes a greater than 51% likelihood of future harm? Should the court be concerned lest the plaintiff spend the money before the future condition strikes?

Our major concern here is the actual enhanced risk of physical harm. Although the enhanced risk also raises questions of emotional distress, as in *Simmons*, based on the fear of contracting the disease, we addressed that issue in depth at p. 270, supra. Nor do we deal here with claims for current recovery for medical monitoring of the future danger. That issue is discussed at p. 396, infra.

7. In *Wilson v. Circus Circus Hotels, Inc.*, 710 P.2d 77 (Nev.1985), a young boy contracted salmonella poisoning following ingestion of food at defendant's hotel restaurant. The plaintiff's proof included expert testimony that there was an 80% chance that the boy was poisoned by defendant's food if he ate only at the defendant hotel during the 52 hours before the onset of symptoms; if no member of the family ate certain items that the boy ate at the hotel; if no member of the family got ill from non-hotel foods that the boy and other family members had eaten; and if the hotel's cups of tartar sauce had been left unrefrigerated for too long. The court noted the difficulties of proving causation in food cases and cited other cases in which courts had ruled that "mere correlation between ingestion and illness is insufficient as a matter of law to establish causation." Here, however, the court concluded that the plaintiff had presented enough to reach a jury. The showing of almost exclusive ingestion at the hotel during the incubation period and the negation of other causes was sufficient.

8. In *Mitchell v. Pearson Enterprises*, 697 P.2d 240 (Utah 1985), a guest in defendant's hotel was murdered in his room by an unknown person. The motive appeared to be robbery. There were no signs of a forced entry. Local police had several hypotheses. Some centered on a person entering the room with a passkey and then being surprised by the guest. Another suggested a gangland killing in which the guest was accosted in the hallway or elevator. The suit claimed inadequate security measures.

Accepting that the plaintiff had made a sufficient showing of negligence, the court affirmed summary judgment for the defendant on the ground that proof of causation was lacking. It was not known how the murderer first encountered the guest or whether they had a prior relationship. The lack of forced entry "could be probative of entrance by a person using an unauthorized master or room key. However, it could also be probative of entrance, at [the deceased's] invitation, by a friend or colleague. Any supposition, therefore, as to the manner of entrance to [the deceased's] room or the identity of the assailant would be totally speculative. A jury cannot be permitted to engage in such speculation."

9. In *Burgos v. Aqueduct Realty Corp.*, 706 N.E.2d 1163 (N.Y.1998), a tenant sued her landlord for an assault committed in the building and sought to prove that the assault was by an intruder rather than another tenant. The court thought it unreasonable to require the tenant to identify the perpetrator. It was enough to provide evidence to show that it was "more likely or more reasonable than not that the assailant was an intruder who gained access to the premises through a negligently maintained entrance." The two cases before the court met the standard: in one, involving a building of 25 apartments, the plaintiff testified that she was familiar with all the tenants and did not recognize her assailant; in the second, a large apartment building, the plaintiff and eyewitness tenants testified that they did not recognize the assailant who entered and left through a broken rear door. How different are these cases from *Stubbs* itself?

Compare Price v. New York City Housing Authority, 706 N.E.2d 1167 (N.Y.1998), decided the same day as *Burgos*. In *Price*, the defendant landlord presented evidence that the assailant was a serial criminal who would not have been stopped even by a locked front door. The jury accepted that evidence and found no causal connection between the lack of a lock and the crime. The court, 5–1, found no errors in the admission of the evidence and affirmed the defense judgment.

Zuchowicz v. United States

United States Court of Appeals, Second Circuit, 1998.
140 F.3d 381.

Before: NEWMAN, ALTIMARI, and CALABRESI, CIRCUIT JUDGES.

CALABRESI, CIRCUIT JUDGE.

[This is an action under the Federal Tort Claims Act, based on Connecticut law. Defendant admitted that its doctors and/or pharmacists at the naval hospital had been negligent in directing Mrs. Zuchowicz to ingest 1600 milligrams of Danocrine—double the maximum authorized dosage. She took the excessive doses for one month, after which her dosage was reduced to the maximum amount for a little over two months. She was then told to discontinue Danocrine. About four months after stopping, she was diagnosed with primary pulmonary hypertension (PPH), "a rare and fatal disease in which increased pressure in an individual's pulmonary artery causes severe strain on the right side of the heart." Treatments include "calcium channel blockers and heart and lung transplants." While Mrs. Zuchowicz was on the waiting list for a lung transplant she became pregnant, which made her ineligible for a transplant and also "exacerbates PPH." One month after giving birth, Mrs. Zuchowicz died and her husband continued the pending case on behalf of her estate. After a bench trial, the court awarded damages. Further facts are stated in the opinion.]

Did the action for which the defendant is responsible cause, in a legal sense, the harm which the plaintiff suffered?—a question easily put and often very hard to answer.   .   .   .

Over the centuries the courts have struggled to give meaning to this requirement—in the simplest of situations, who hit whom, and in the most complex ones, which polluter's emissions, if any, hurt which plaintiff. It is the question that we must seek to answer today in the context of modern medicine and a very rare disease.

[The court summarized the treatment sequence and then turned to the nature of PPH.]

PPH can be "primary" or "secondary"

2. Primary Pulmonary Hypertension

Pulmonary hypertension is categorized as "primary" when it occurs in the absence of other heart or lung diseases. "Secondary" pulmonary hypertension is diagnosed when the hypertension results from another heart or lung disease, such as emphysema or blood clots. PPH is very rare. A National Institute of Health registry recorded only 197 cases of PPH from the mid-1980s until 1992. It occurs predominantly in young women. Exogenous agents known to be capable of causing PPH include birth control pills, some appetite suppressants, chemotherapy drugs, rapeseed oil, and L–Tryptophan.

According to the district court's findings of fact, the disease involves the interplay of the inner layers of the pulmonary blood vessels known as the endothelium and the vascular smooth muscle. The endothelium releases substances called vasodilators and vasoconstrictors, which dilate and constrict the blood vessels. These substances can also cause growth of the vascular smooth muscle. Experts currently believe that an imbalance in vasodilators and vasoconstrictors plays a part in the development of pulmonary hypertension. If too many vasoconstrictors are released, the blood vessels contract, the endothelial cells die, and the vascular smooth muscle cells proliferate. These actions create increased pulmonary vascular resistance.

[The court reported that much of the original research on Danocrine, which was used to treat endometriosis, was done by Dr. W. Paul D'Mowski, one of plaintiff's witnesses, who testified that it is safe and effective when properly used. He also testified that there had been no formal studies of excess doses and that "very, very, few women have received doses this high in any setting."]

B. The Expert Testimony

The rarity of PPH, combined with the fact that so few human beings have ever received such a high dose of Danocrine, obviously impacted on the manner in which the plaintiff could prove causation. The number of persons who received this type of overdose was simply too small for the plaintiff to be able to provide epidemiological, or even anecdotal, evidence linking PPH to Danocrine overdoses. [Plaintiff], therefore, based his case primarily on the testimony of two expert witnesses, Dr. Richard Matthay, a physician and expert in pulmonary diseases, and Dr. Randall Tackett, a professor of pharmacology who has published widely in the field of the effects of drugs on vascular tissues. In rendering a judgment for the plaintiff, the district court relied heavily on the evidence submitted by these two experts. The defendant challenges both the admissibility and the sufficiency of their testimony.

1. Dr. Matthay

Dr. Richard Matthay is a full professor of medicine at Yale and Associate Director and Training Director of Yale's Pulmonary and Critical Care Section. He is a nationally recognized expert in the field of pulmonary medicine, with extensive experience in the area of drug-induced pulmonary diseases. Dr. Matthay examined and treated Mrs. Zuchowicz. His examination included taking a detailed history of the progression of her disease, her medical history, and the timing of her Danocrine overdose and the onset of her symptoms.

Dr. Matthay testified that he was confident to a reasonable medical certainty that the Danocrine caused Mrs. Zuchowicz's PPH. When pressed, he added that he believed the overdose of Danocrine to have been responsible for the disease. His conclusion was based on the temporal relationship *reactionary period* between the overdose and the start of the disease and the differential etiology method of excluding other possible causes. While Dr. Matthay did not rule out all other possible causes of pulmonary hypertension, he did exclude all the causes of secondary pulmonary hypertension. On the basis of Mrs. Zuchowicz's history, he also ruled out all previously known drug-related causes of primary pulmonary hypertension.

Dr. Matthay further testified that the progression and timing of Mrs. Zuchowicz's disease in relation to her overdose supported a finding of drug-induced PPH. Dr. Matthay emphasized that, prior to the overdose, Mrs. Zuchowicz was a healthy, active young woman with no history of cardiovascular problems, and that, shortly after the overdose, she began experiencing symptoms of PPH such as weight gain, swelling of hands and feet, fatigue, and shortness of breath. He described the similarities between the course of Mrs. Zuchowicz's illness and that of accepted cases of drug-induced PPH, and he went on to discuss cases involving classes of drugs that are known to cause other pulmonary diseases (mainly anti-cancer drugs). He noted that the onset of these diseases, which are recognized to be caused by the particular drugs, was very similar in timing and course to the development of Mrs. Zuchowicz's illness.

2. Dr. Tackett

Dr. Randall Tackett is a tenured, full professor of pharmacology and former department chair from the University of Georgia. He has published widely in the field of the effects of drugs on vascular tissues. Dr. Tackett testified that, to a reasonable degree of scientific certainty, he believed that the overdose of Danocrine, more likely than not, caused PPH in the plaintiff by producing: 1) a decrease in estrogen; 2) hyperinsulinemia, in which abnormally high levels of insulin circulate in the body; and 3) increases in free testosterone and progesterone. Dr. Tackett testified that these hormonal factors, taken together, likely caused a dysfunction of the endothelium leading to PPH. Dr. Tackett relied on a variety of published and unpublished studies that indicated that these hormones could cause endothelial dysfunction and an imbalance of vasoconstrictor effects.

II. Discussion

A. Was the Admission of the Plaintiff's Experts' Testimony Manifestly Erroneous?

The defendant's first argument is that the district court erred in admitting the testimony of Dr. Tackett and Dr. Matthay. We review the district court's decision to admit or exclude expert testimony under a highly deferential abuse of discretion standard. See General Elec. Co. v. Joiner, [522 U.S. 136 (1997)]; McCullock v. H.B. Fuller Co., 61 F.3d 1038, 1042 (2d Cir.1995) ("The decision to admit expert testimony is left to the broad discretion of the trial judge and will be overturned only when manifestly erroneous.").

The Federal Rules of Evidence permit opinion testimony by experts when the witness is "qualified as an expert by knowledge, skill, experience, training, or education," and "[i]f scientific, technical, or other specialized knowledge will assist the trier of fact to understand the evidence or to determine a fact in issue." Fed.R.Evid. 702. And though in Daubert v. Merrell Dow Pharmaceuticals, Inc., 509 U.S. 579, 588–89 (1993), the Supreme Court altered the traditional test for the admissibility of expert testimony, it did not change the standard of appellate review of these decisions, see [Joiner].[5]

Under Daubert, trial judges are charged with ensuring that expert testimony "both rests on a reliable foundation and is relevant to the task at hand." [ ] Thus, while Daubert and the Federal Rules of Evidence "allow district courts to admit a somewhat broader range of scientific testimony than would have been admissible under Frye, they leave in place the 'gatekeeper' role of the trial judge in screening such evidence." [Joiner]. Indeed Daubert strengthens this role, for it requires that judges make a "preliminary assessment of whether the reasoning or methodology underlying the testimony is scientifically valid and of whether that reasoning or methodology properly can be applied to the facts in issue." [ ]

The factors identified by the Supreme Court as relevant to this inquiry are: (1) whether the theory can be (and has been) tested according to the scientific method; (2) whether the theory or technique has been subjected to peer review and publication; (3) in the case of a particular scientific technique, the known or potential rate of error; and (4) whether the theory is generally accepted. [ ] The Court emphasized, however, that these factors were not an exclusive or dispositive list of what should be considered, and that the trial court's inquiry should be a "flexible one." [ ]

The question in this case is whether, in light of these factors, the district court's decision to admit the testimony of Dr. Matthay and Dr. Tackett was an abuse of discretion. We addressed a similar question in [McCullock, supra]. In McCullock, we upheld the district court's decision to admit the testimony of an engineer and a medical doctor in a case involving a worker's exposure to glue fumes and her subsequent development of throat polyps. Applying the "manifestly erroneous" standard, we rejected the defendant's argument that the district court had not properly performed its gatekeeping function as required by Daubert. . . .

---

5. In Daubert, the Supreme Court rejected the traditional Frye rule (which had required that a scientific theory be generally accepted by the scientific community to be admissible, see Frye v. United States, 293 F. 1013, 1014 (D.C.Cir.1923)), concluding that adherence to Frye's "rigid 'general acceptance' requirement would be at odds with the 'liberal thrust' of the Federal Rules [of Evidence]."

McCullock provides strong support for the instant plaintiff's position. In the case before us, as in *McCullock*, the district court carefully undertook and fulfilled its role in making the evaluation required by *Daubert*—a "preliminary assessment of whether the reasoning or methodology underlying the testimony is scientifically valid and of whether that reasoning or methodology properly can be applied to the facts in issue." . . .

The district court rejected [attacks on the validity of the experts' methods] stating that the plaintiff's experts "based their opinions on methods reasonably relied on by experts in their particular fields." We do not believe that the district court's decision in this regard was erroneous, let alone manifestly so.

B. Were the District Court's Factual Findings with Respect to Causation Clearly Erroneous?

We review the district court's factual findings for clear error. [   ]; see also Fed.R.Civ.P. 52(a). The defendant argues that, even assuming that the testimony of the plaintiff's experts was admissible, the district court's finding that the Danocrine overdose more likely than not caused Mrs. Zuchowicz's illness was clearly erroneous. The defendant contends that, since Danocrine has never been previously linked to PPH, the district court's conclusion that the drug caused Mrs. Zuchowicz's illness was impermissible. For the reasons stated below, we reject the defendant's arguments.

[The court accepted that Connecticut law applied. "In addition to proving fault, 'the plaintiff must establish a causal relationship between the physician's negligent actions or failure to act and the resulting injury by showing that the action or omission constituted a substantial factor in producing the injury.' [   ] This 'substantial factor' causation requirement is the crux of the case before us."]

2. The Connecticut Law of Causation

To meet the requirement that defendant's behavior was a substantial factor in bringing about the plaintiff's injury, the plaintiff must generally show: (a) that the defendant's negligent act or omission was a *but for* cause of the injury, (b) that the negligence was causally linked to the harm, and (c) that the defendant's negligent act or omission was proximate to the resulting injury. [We will consider proximate cause in the next section—eds.]

. . .

[The case before us] turns only on the difficulty of showing a *but for* cause. On whether, in other words, the plaintiff has sufficiently demonstrated: (a) that defendant's act in giving Mrs. Zuchowicz Danocrine was the source of her illness and death, and (b) that it was not just the Danocrine, but its negligent overdose that led to Mrs. Zuchowicz's demise.

. . .

4. Was Danocrine a But For Cause of Mrs. Zuchowicz's Illness and Death?

[The court held that the finding that the PPH "was, more likely than not, caused by Danocrine" was not clearly erroneous. The finding was justified exclusively on the testimony of Dr. Matthay that he had excluded all causes of secondary pulmonary hypertension and all the previously known drug-related causes of PPH. In addition, he had testified that the "progression and timing of Mrs. Zuchowicz's illness in relationship to the timing of her overdose [led him to] a finding of *drug-induced* PPH to a reasonable medical certainty."]

5. Was the Overdose a But For Cause of Mrs. Zuchowicz's Illness and Death?

To say that Danocrine caused Mrs. Zuchowicz's injuries is only half the story, however. In order for the causation requirement to be met, a trier of fact must be able to determine, by a preponderance of the evidence, that the defendant's *negligence* was responsible for the injury. In this case, defendant's negligence consisted in prescribing an overdose of Danocrine to Mrs. Zuchowicz. For liability to exist, therefore, it is necessary that the fact finder be able to conclude, more probably than not, that the *overdose* was the cause of Mrs. Zuchowicz's illness and ultimate death. The mere fact that the exposure to Danocrine was likely responsible for the disease does not suffice.

The problem of linking defendant's negligence to the harm that occurred is one that many courts have addressed in the past. A car is speeding and an accident occurs. That the car was involved and was a cause of the crash is readily shown. The accident, moreover, is of the sort that rules prohibiting speeding are designed to prevent. But is this enough to support a finding of fact, in the individual case, that *speeding* was, in fact, more probably than not, the cause of the accident? The same question can be asked when a car that was driving in violation of a minimum speed requirement on a super-highway is rear-ended. . . .

At one time, courts were reluctant to say in such circumstances that the wrong could be deemed to be the cause. They emphasized the logical fallacy of *post hoc, ergo propter hoc*, and demanded some direct evidence connecting the defendant's wrongdoing to the harm. See, e.g., Wolf v. Kaufmann, 237 N.Y.S. 550, 551 (App.Div. 1929) (denying recovery for death of plaintiff's decedent, who was found unconscious at foot of stairway which, in violation of a statute, was unlighted, because the plaintiff had offered no proof of "any causal connection between the accident and the absence of light").

All that has changed, however. And, as is so frequently the case in tort law, Chief Judge Cardozo in New York and Chief Justice Traynor in California led the way. In various opinions, they stated that: if (a) a negligent act was deemed wrongful because that act increased the chances that a particular type of accident would occur, and (b) a mishap of that very sort did happen, this was enough to support a finding by the trier of fact that the negligent behavior caused the harm. Where such a strong causal link exists, it is up to the negligent party to bring in evidence denying *but for* cause and suggesting that in the actual case the wrongful conduct had not been a substantial factor.

Thus, in a case involving a nighttime collision between vehicles, one of which did not have the required lights, Judge Cardozo stated that lights were mandated precisely to reduce the risk of such accidents occurring and that this fact sufficed to show causation unless the negligent party demonstrated, for example, that in the particular instance the presence of very bright street lights or of a full moon rendered the lack of lights on the vehicle an unlikely cause. See Martin v. Herzog, [reprinted at p. 73, supra]; see also Clark v. Gibbons, 426 P.2d 525, 542 (Cal.1967) (Traynor, C.J., concurring in part and dissenting in part on other grounds).

. . .

The case before us is a good example of the above-mentioned principles in their classic form. The reason the FDA does not approve the prescription of new drugs at above the dosages as to which extensive tests have been performed is because all drugs involve risks of untoward side effects in those who take them. Moreover, it is often true that the higher the dosage the greater is the likelihood of such negative effects. At the approved dosages, the benefits of the particular drug have presumably been deemed worth the risks it entails. At greater than approved dosages, not only do the risks of tragic side effects (known and unknown) increase, but there is no basis on the testing that has been performed for supposing that the drug's benefits outweigh these increased risks. See generally 21 U.S.C. § 355(d) (indicating that the FDA should refuse to approve a new drug unless the clinical tests show that the drug is safe and effective for use under the conditions "prescribed, recommended, or suggested in the proposed labeling"). It follows that when a negative side effect is demonstrated to be the result of a drug, and the drug was wrongly prescribed in an unapproved and excessive dosage (i.e. a strong causal link has been shown), the plaintiff who is injured has generally shown enough to permit the finder of fact to conclude that the excessive dosage was a substantial factor in producing the harm.

In fact, plaintiff's showing in the case before us, while relying on the above stated principles, is stronger. For plaintiff introduced some direct evidence of causation as well. On the basis of his long experience with drug-induced pulmonary diseases, one of plaintiff's experts, Dr. Matthay, testified that the timing of Mrs. Zuchowicz's illness led him to conclude that the overdose (and not merely Danocrine) was responsible for her catastrophic reaction.

Under the circumstances, we hold that defendant's attack on the district court's finding of causation is meritless.

[The court rejected challenges to the damage award and affirmed.]

Notes and Questions

1. *Establishing causation through reliance on expert testimony: The Daubert case.* In virtually every case involving a toxic exposure claim, plaintiffs rely on science experts to establish that the exposure was in fact the cause of the plaintiff's harm. As toxic tort litigation has proliferated, there has been great controversy over threshold questions of standards of reliability and relevance that are to guide the trial court in determining expert qualifications. For sharp criticism of the courts, see P. Huber, Galileo's Revenge: Junk Science in the Courtroom (1991). See also M. Angell, Science of Trial: The Clash of Medical Evidence and the Law in the Breast Implant Litigation (1996).

Traditionally, the dominant approach to admissibility, as the court notes, had been the *Frye* test, requiring that scientific evidence be based on techniques generally regarded as reliable in the scientific community. But in *Daubert*, one of the many cases in which Bendectin, a morning-sickness drug, was alleged to have caused limb reduction birth defects, the Court held that Federal Rule of Evidence 702 set a more easily-satisfied standard of qualification. As the court notes, the rule provides:

> If scientific, technical, or other specialized knowledge will assist the trier of fact to understand the evidence or to determine a fact in issue, a witness qualified as an expert by knowledge, skill, experience, training, or education, may testify thereto.   .   .   .

The Court concluded that Rule 702 entailed "a preliminary assessment of whether the reasoning or methodology underlying the testimony is scientifically valid and of whether that reasoning or methodology properly can be applied to the facts in issue." This created a judicial "gatekeeping role" that might take general scientific acceptability into account, but that dictated an inquiry beyond scientific orthodoxy in the search for relevance and reliability.

Note the *Daubert* four-factor test for determining relevance and reliability of proposed expert witnesses, mentioned in *Zuchowicz*. What are the underlying suppositions of the test about the kinds of evidence that experts will rely upon? Can the testimony of Drs. Matthay and Tackett be analyzed under the *Daubert* criteria?

In the cited *General Electric Co. v. Joiner*, the Supreme Court held that the standard for review of trial court decisions to admit or reject expert testimony under *Daubert* should be "abuse of discretion."

Then, in Kumho Tire Co. Ltd. v. Carmichael, 526 U.S. 137 (1999), the Court elaborated further on *Daubert*. Here the trial judge had excluded an expert's testimony about why a tire blew out. On appeal from a defense verdict and judgment, the court of appeals reversed. In turn, the Supreme Court reversed. For the majority, Justice Breyer situated the case as follows:

> This case requires us to decide how *Daubert* applies to the testimony of engineers and other experts who are not scientists. We conclude that *Daubert*'s general holding—setting forth the trial judge's general "gatekeeping" obligation—applies not only to testimony based on "scientific" knowledge, but also to testimony based on "technical" and "other specialized" knowledge. [   ] We also conclude that a trial court

may consider one or more of the more specific factors that *Daubert* mentioned when doing so will help determine that testimony's reliability. But, as the Court stated in *Daubert*, the test of reliability is "flexible," and *Daubert*'s list of specific factors neither necessarily nor exclusively applies to all experts or in every case. Rather, the law grants a district court the same broad latitude when it decides how to determine reliability as it enjoys in respect to its ultimate reliability determination. See [*Joiner*] (courts of appeals are to apply "abuse of discretion" standard when reviewing district court's reliability determination). Applying these standards, we determine that the District Court's decision in this case—not to admit certain expert testimony— was within its discretion and therefore lawful.

The expert sought to identify a set of factors that one must consider in deciding why a tire blew out. If a certain number of those factors are present, the expert would conclude causation. In the actual case, this process led him to attribute the blowout to defective manufacturing even though the tire in question had been worn down to the point that it had no tread at all along parts of it and that at least two prior punctures had been inadequately repaired. Justice Breyer noted:

> The particular issue in this case concerned the use of [expert witness] Carlson's two-factor test and his related use of visual/tactile inspection to draw conclusions on the basis of what seemed small observational differences. We have found no indication in the record that other experts in the industry use Carlson's two-factor test or that tire experts such as Carlson normally make the very fine distinctions about, say, the symmetry of comparatively greater shoulder tread wear that were necessary, on Carlson's own theory, to support his conclusions. Nor, despite the prevalence of tire testing, does anyone refer to any articles or papers that validate Carlson's approach. [   ] Indeed, no one has argued that Carlson himself, were he still working for Michelin, would have concluded in a report to his employer that a similar tire was similarly defective on grounds identical to those upon which he rested his conclusion here. Of course, Carlson himself claimed that his method was accurate, but, as we pointed out in *Joiner* "nothing in either *Daubert* or the Federal Rules of Evidence requires a district court to admit opinion evidence that is connected to existing data only by the *ipse dixit* of the expert." [   ]

Three justices concurred in a short opinion by Justice Scalia:

> I join the opinion of the Court, which makes clear that the discretion it endorses—trial-court discretion in choosing the manner of testing expert reliability—is not discretion to abandon the gatekeeping function. I think it worth adding that it is not discretion to perform the function inadequately. Rather, it is discretion to choose among reasonable means of excluding expertise that is fausse and science that is junky. Though, as the Court makes clear today, the *Daubert* factors are not holy writ, in a particular case the failure to apply one or another of them may be unreasonable, and hence an abuse of discretion.

Does the *Daubert* test, as articulated in these cases, appear to establish a more or less liberal standard than *Frye* for qualifying experts?

2. Since *Daubert* is interpreting a federal rule, state courts may adopt it or continue to adhere to *Frye* or to some other standard. See, e.g., Logerquist v. McVey, 1 P.3d 113 (Ariz.2000) (declining to adopt *Daubert*).

3. How does the court support the claim that Danocrine was a "but for" cause in the death? Would your analysis be affected if it turned out that the "exogenous agents" cited in the opinion taken as a group account-ed for only 50 of the 197 reported cases—with the cause in the remaining 147 cases called "unknown"? Why does the plaintiff have to show that it was the overdose that was causally related to the death?

4. The court observes that plaintiff's case is stronger than in some drug cases because here there was "some direct evidence of causation as well." What does that add to the plaintiff's case?

5. What is the court suggesting when it discusses "the logical fallacy of *post hoc, ergo propter hoc*"? If a person falls down in a darkened hallway who should bear the burden of proving whether darkness was the actual cause of the fall? Compare the cited case of *Wolf v. Kaufmann* with Hinman v. Sobocienski, 808 P.2d 820 (Alaska 1991), in which a tenant who was found injured at the foot of a flight of stairs proved only that the flight was "unreasonably dangerous and that she was found injured at its bottom. She introduced no further evidence, however, tending to show that the condi-tion of the stairway contributed to her injuries." The trial court granted a directed verdict for the defendant landlord because there was no showing that she had fallen due to the condition rather than that she was thrown down the stairs or had jumped—though nothing in the record suggested these possibilities. The supreme court, 4–1, reversed:

> Common experience . . . suggests that the presence in a bar/apartment building of a dangerous, dimly lighted staircase greatly increases the chances that a patron or resident will accidentally fall and suffer injury. When a resident is then found injured at the bottom of those stairs, a reasonable inference is that the dangerous condition more likely than not played a substantial part in the mishap. "The court can scarcely overlook the fact that the injury which has in fact occurred is precisely the sort of thing that proper care on the part of the defendant would be intended to prevent." [   ] The absence of evidence that the plaintiff fell—rather than jumped or was pushed—does not negate the reasonableness of the inference.

Assume a fall down a flight of negligently unlighted interior stairs with no further evidence. Compare two analyses: (a) the proof is sufficient because, although we know that individuals often fall down lighted stairways, falls occur more frequently on unlighted stairways; and (b) since individuals often fall down lighted stairs we have no reason to assume that the darkness had anything to do with this fall in the absence of some showing to that effect by plaintiff.

6. In the cited *Martin v. Herzog*, reprinted at p. 73, supra, discussing the role of statutory violation on common law negligence claims, the court, as noted here, placed on the violator of the statute the burden of showing that the violation was not causally related to the harm. Judge Cardozo observed that a statutory violation also makes a "case, *prima facie* sufficient, of negligence contributing to the result. There may indeed be times when the lights on a highway are so many and so bright that lights on a wagon are superfluous. If that is so, it is for the offender to go forward with the evidence.   .   .   ." Why should the burden be shifted? Should it matter whether the admitted negligence was based on a statutory violation?

7. If the experts in *Zuchowicz* were unanimous that there was a 35% likelihood that the overdose caused the harm, should that suffice? Consider this question in reading the following case.

Alberts v. Schultz

Supreme Court of New Mexico, 1999.
126 N.M. 807, 975 P.2d 1279.

FRANCHINI, CHIEF J.

[Dee and Mildred Alberts sued defendants Schultz and Reddy for medical malpractice that allegedly brought about the amputation of Mr. Albert's right leg below the knee. The majority viewed the facts as showing that on July 14, 1992 Mr. Alberts went to Dr. Schultz with a condition known as "rest pain" in which his right leg hurt in the absence of any exercise or activity. This was "an acknowledged sign of impending gangrene that could lead to the amputation of the affected limb." Dr. Schultz did not order an arteriogram. Nor did he conduct other tests. Mr. Alberts' requested referral to Dr. Reddy did not occur until July 27th. Upon seeing the leg, Dr. Reddy immediately sent Mr. Alberts to the hospital and ordered an arteriogram, followed by several procedures that were performed unsuccessfully. On July 28th, bypass surgery was attempted but the leg showed no improvement and the amputation was performed on August 1st. Plaintiff presented expert testimony that is summarized in the opinion. The trial judge granted partial summary judgment for defendants for failure to establish a causal connection between the alleged negligence and the amputation. The court of appeals certified the case to the supreme court.]

   .   .   . The trial court certified the following question for interlocutory appeal: "Should New Mexico recognize a cause of action for the increased risk of harm to a patient as a result of a physician's negligence, and if so, should this doctrine apply to the facts of this case[?]" [   ] We do not believe this theory of recovery—to which we apply the terms "loss of chance" or "lost chance"—should be deemed, as the trial court implies, a new "cause of action." We conclude, however, that it is appropriate for New Mexico to recognize this claim. Nevertheless, after applying the loss-of-chance theory to the facts of this case, we conclude that the Alberts failed to prove causation.

. . .

The Alberts . . . claimed Dr. Schultz did not advise Dee of the true nature of his condition, neglected to perform the appropriate examinations on his leg, and failed to make a timely referral to a specialist. They further asserted that Dr. Reddy had not properly warned Dee about his condition and had failed to perform the appropriate diagnostic tests and treatments. The Alberts argued that the thirteen-day delay before Dr. Reddy's intervention decreased the probability that the leg could be saved.

The Alberts' case was supported by the testimony of Dr. Max Carlton Hutton, a vascular surgeon. Dr. Hutton, through an affidavit and a deposition, testified that in his opinion Dr. Schultz should have performed motor and sensory exams and should have immediately ordered an arteriogram on Dee when he saw him on July 14, and should not have allowed nearly two weeks to pass before Dee could be seen by a vascular surgeon. Dr. Reddy, according to Dr. Hutton, was negligent in not performing motor and sensory exams, and in not doing a bypass immediately on July 27. Dr. Hutton noted that in cases such as Dee's, even the passage of six hours can make the difference between success and failure.

Dr. Hutton's testimony was based on the presumption Dee's leg could have been saved if specific arteries in his leg were suitable candidates for bypass surgery. However, in his testimony, he could not establish this presumption with certainty because the medical records were incomplete regarding the specific arteries in question. Dr. Hutton testified that "[t]he only thing we know is that at least by the point that Dr. Schultz saw the patient, we had crossed the line in non-limb-threatening ischemia to potentially limb-threatening ischemia." Ischemia is the lack of blood flow through vessels. However, Dr. Hutton could not pinpoint a time when the ischemia became irreversible, nor could he pinpoint a time when earlier intervention would have changed the outcome. In Dr. Hutton's opinion "the probability that Mr. Alberts' leg could have been saved decreased significantly," because of the inaction of both physicians. Nevertheless, Dr. Hutton testified that he could not state to a reasonable degree of medical probability that immediate use of the motor and sensory exams, the arteriogram, and the bypass would have increased the chances of saving Dee's leg.

. . .

Generally, the fact pattern in a lost-chance claim begins when a patient comes to a health giver with a particular medical complaint. We will refer to "[t]he illness, disorder, discomfort, pain, fear, etc. that is the main reason for the patient's seeking medical help" as the "presenting problem." [   ] The problem may be a sudden injury or illness, or it may be a malady that the patient has suffered over a long period of time. [   ] A claim for loss of chance is predicated upon the negligent denial by a healthcare provider of the most effective therapy for a patient's presenting medical problem. The negligence may be found in such misconduct as an incorrect diagnosis, the application of inappropriate treatments, or the failure to timely provide the proper treatment. [   ]

The essence of the patient's claim is that, prior to the negligence, there was a chance that he or she would have been better off with adequate care. [   ] Because of the negligence, this chance has been lost. . . . Every patient has a certain probability that he or she will recover from the presenting medical problem. The probability of recovery may be high—more than fifty percent; or the prognosis may be more bleak—less than fifty percent. Whether great or small, there is *some* chance that the person will recover. Under the loss-of-chance theory, the health provider's malpractice has obliterated or reduced those odds of recovery that existed before the act of malpractice. The patient with a greater-than-fifty-percent chance of recovery is deprived of a more promising outcome. The patient with a slim chance is deprived of the opportunity to beat the odds. Where there was once a chance of a better result, now there is a lesser or no chance. See [   ] (citing Joseph H. King, Jr., Causation, Valuation, and Chance in Personal Injury Torts Involving Preexisting Conditions and Future Consequences, 90 Yale L.J. 1353, 1354 (1981); [   ]).

Ultimately, the patient may suffer the consequences of the presenting medical problem. However, under the lost-chance theory, the patient does not allege that the malpractice caused his or her entire injury. Rather, the claim is that the health care provider's negligence reduced the chance of avoiding the injury actually sustained. [   ] Thus, it is that chance in and of itself—the lost opportunity of avoiding the presenting problem and achieving a better result—that becomes the item of value for which the patient seeks compensation. [   ]

. . .

A.   The Elements of Loss of Chance

The basic test for establishing loss of chance is no different from the elements required in other medical malpractice actions, or in negligence suits in general: duty, breach, loss or damage, and causation. [   ] *Loss of chance differs from other medical malpractice actions only in the nature of the harm for which relief is sought.*

The plaintiff bears the burden of proving each of these elements. [   ] Because the issues raised in lost-chance actions are, in virtually every case, "beyond the province of lay persons," the plaintiff will almost always establish these elements through expert testimony. [   ]

. . .

3.   Loss or damage

As mentioned above, it is the injury alleged, that separates a lost-chance claim from other medical malpractice actions. The injury is the lost opportunity of a better result, not the harm caused by the presenting problem. It is not the physical harm itself, but rather the lost chance of avoiding the physical harm. [   ] As we explain below, the causal connection between the negligence and the resultant injury must be medically probable.

The chance of a better result may be conceptualized as a window of time that existed before the malpractice took place; in that window of time the healthcare provider had an opportunity to timely implement proper medical treatments that would avoid or minimize the occurrence of the injury. [ ] Through negligent misdiagnosis, inappropriate therapy, or unnecessary delay, the window of time was closed. The act of malpractice may have immediately shut the window of time, or it may have caused a delay during which the window of time expired. The claim is not for the subsequent injury, but for the fact that it is now too late to do anything to avoid the injury. Correcting the problem is no longer possible.

It must be emphasized that the injury—the lost chance—is not in any way speculative. It is manifested by actual physical harm. This claim must not be confused with cases in which, as a result of the tortious conduct of one party, another party suffers exposure to something harmful, which may, in the future, lead to an injury. Loss of chance does not involve prognostication about future injury or harm. See [*Perez*] ("Of course, the plaintiff or injured person cannot recover merely on the basis of a decreased chance of survival or of avoiding a debilitating illness or injury; the plaintiff must in fact suffer death or debilitating injury before there can be an award of damages."). Rather, the patient must present evidence that the harm for which he or she originally sought treatment—the presenting medical problem—was in fact made worse by the lost chance. [ ]

Thus, in lost-chance cases, courts must be cognizant of two injuries: the underlying injury caused by the presenting problem and the exacerbation of the presenting problem which evinces the chance that has been lost. [ ] Because the defendant's negligence combined with the patient's presenting problem to produce the adverse medical outcome, the patient may have difficulty distinguishing between the underlying injury and the lost-chance injury. [ ] The deterioration of the presenting problem is evidence that the chance of a better result has been diminished or lost.

We see no reason at this time to limit lost-chance claims to those cases in which the chance of a better result has been utterly lost. Denying compensation for the diminution—as opposed to the loss—of a chance may lead to unreasonable hairsplitting. "Evidence of the physical progression of the patient's disease during a negligent delay in diagnosis or treatment may be sufficient to establish that the plaintiff was 'injured' by the delay." [ ] It is possible that trial courts may conclude in some cases that the diminished chance of a better result is of negligible significance. [ ] (limiting loss-of-chance recovery "to those cases in which the chance of recovery lost was sizeable enough to be material, which must be so found by the jury"). The cost of litigating such actions will no doubt discourage claims that are insignificant. [ ]

4. Cause

If the Alberts had brought a claim under an ordinary medical malpractice negligence theory, the injury alleged would be the loss of Dee's leg below the knee. They cannot sustain such a claim, however, because his preexisting condition—peripheral vascular disease—precludes proof to a reasonable degree of medical probability that the doctors' negligence proximately caused the loss of the leg below the knee. In contrast, Dee can submit evidence that he had a chance—even if it was a small chance—of being cured of the presenting problem of rest pain and possible impending gangrene. He can be compensated if he can demonstrate, to a reasonable degree of medical probability, a causal link between the doctor's negligence and the loss of that chance.

As [ ] notes, "When the injury is defined not as the ultimate injury to the patient, but as the loss of a chance of survival, the standard for [proving cause] does not change." . . . Even when a healthcare provider has negligently treated a presenting problem, the fact that there is no longer a definable chance of a better result does not necessarily establish liability. There must be proof of a causal link between the negligence and the lost chance. [ ]

. . .

. . . . In order to dispel the potential for any confusion, we emphasize that the standard in New Mexico is proof to a reasonable degree of medical probability. [ ] The principle behind this terminology, is that, in proving causation, the plaintiff must introduce evidence that the injury more likely than not was . . . caused by the act of negligence.

Both the "preponderance of evidence" and the "reasonable degree of medical probability" standards connote proof that a causal connection is more probable than not. It is appropriate, in a lost-chance case, that the plaintiff does not have to demonstrate absolute certainty of causation, because the physician's malpractice has made it impossible to know how the patient would have fared in the absence of any negligence. "[T]he physician should not be able to avoid liability on the ground that it is uncertain what that outcome would have been." [ ]

B. Calculation of Damages

There are many theories as to the calculation of pecuniary damages for loss of chance. We conclude that damages should be awarded on a proportional basis as determined by the percentage value of the patient's chance for a better outcome prior to the negligent act. . . .

In loss-of-chance cases, most courts apportion damages by valuing the chance of a better result as a percentage of the value of the entire life or limb. [ ] For example, the value of a patient's fifty-percent chance of survival is fifty percent of the value of their total life. If medical malpractice reduced that chance of survival from fifty to twenty percent, that patient's compensation would be equal to thirty percent of the value of their life. [ ]("percentage probability of loss" applicable whether chance of survival is greater than or less than fifty percent). In another example, the value of a plaintiff's twenty-percent chance of saving a limb is twenty percent of the value of the entire limb. If that plaintiff lost the entire twenty-percent chance of saving the limb, their compensation would be twenty percent of the value of that limb. Thus, the percentage of chance lost is multiplied by the total value of the person's life or limb. [   ]

The valuation of life, limb, and lost chances is necessarily imprecise. Just as causation is proved by probabilities, the value of the loss must be established by fair approximations, based on the kinds of proof that courts commonly use when making such determinations. [   ]

III.   LOSS OF CHANCE AS APPLIED TO THIS CASE

When loss of chance, as set forth in this opinion, is applied to the facts of this case, the Alberts' claim must fail. The Alberts have not established the causation element in their negligence claim. They have not demonstrated, to a reasonable degree of medical probability, that the alleged negligence of Dr. Schultz and Dr. Reddy proximately caused Dee to lose the chance of saving his leg.

As mentioned above, a lost-chance claim may be conceived of as the loss of a window of time. The loss of time is the essence of the Alberts' claim. They argue that there was a brief time, beginning on July 14, 1992, during which the proper medical intervention would have saved Dee's leg. He was showing symptoms of imminent gangrene, a condition that can become deadly with the passage of very little time. He was deprived of this window of time because, while his foot continued to deteriorate, he had to wait to see a specialist who would recognize the need for immediate treatment. Further, the Alberts claim Dee lost time because the proper tests were not performed and Dr. Schultz was thus not aware of the gravity of the situation. Additionally, they argue that the last available hours of the window were wasted by Dr. Reddy when he performed the wrong medical procedures.

Unfortunately, the Alberts cannot demonstrate that there was a window of time during which measures could have been taken to foreclose the need to amputate Dee's leg. They cannot show, to a reasonable degree of medical probability, that timely and proper medical intervention would have saved Dee's leg. Specifically, they cannot show that a bypass on July 14, 1992, would have precluded the amputation; nor can they show that Dee was a suitable candidate for a bypass on that date; nor can they show that Dee was a suitable candidate for a bypass on July 27, 1992, when Dr. Reddy finally saw him, but that he became unsuitable by the next day when the bypass was actually performed.

The evidence the Alberts presented to support their lost-chance claim was based on incomplete medical records and unsupported assumptions. Dr. Hutton, the Alberts' expert, based his opinion on inadequately verified and speculative assumptions concerning Dee's condition. For example, he testified that bypass surgery would have had a strong chance of being successful if Dee's leg had exhibited "a good saphenous vein." However, Dr. Hutton stated no authoritative conclusions about the integrity of Dee's saphenous vein. In fact, he unequivocally stated that the medical records were incomplete, that certain information that would have credibly established Dee's suitability for surgery was not available. Thus Dr. Hutton stated that, *if* he had available "better arteriograms," he "would find *probably*" a particular artery to be suitable for bypass surgery. Without proof that Dee's leg possessed at least one vein or artery that was suitable for bypass surgery, the Alberts cannot validly contend that the failure to timely perform a bypass caused the leg to deteriorate. [   ] The Alberts, through their expert, were thus unable to prove to a reasonable medical probability that the physicians' alleged negligence proximately caused the lost chance to avoid the amputation of Dee's leg below the knee. [   ]

.   .   .

In answer to the second part of the certified question, we conclude that, in terms of the lost-chance theory, the Alberts have failed to demonstrate causation.

.   .   .

BACA and SERNA, JJ., concur.

MAES, J. (dissenting).

[The dissent argued that the expert presented enough to go to a jury on causation when he testified that there was a 90% chance of success for the bypass based on what the X-rays showed, even if they did not show all blood vessels in the leg. The dissent accused the majority of improperly weighing the evidence.]

Notes and Questions

1. What is the difference between asking whether the plaintiff (1) proved to a certainty that because of D's negligence he had lost a 25% chance to save his leg (worth $300,000) and (2) proved to a 25% probability that he had lost the leg due to defendant's negligence?

2. In view of the court's approval of the lost-chance approach, why does plaintiff nonetheless lose?

3. The court states that "at this time" it saw no reason to limit lost-chance claims "to those cases in which the chance of a better result has been utterly lost." What if the defendant's negligence has reduced the plaintiff's chance to save the leg from 30% to 10%, but after waiting six months it has now become clear that the leg has been saved and is as good as it would have been if the defendant had not been negligent?

4. If a court adopts the lost-chance approach and awards proportional damages in less-than-even chance cases, should it also award proportional damages in a case in which the plaintiff can show a 75% probability that the defendant's negligence caused the loss of the leg? See DeHanes v. Rothman, 727 A.2d 8 (N.J.1999), in which the jury found that if defendant physician in the emergency room had exercised due care and diagnosed decedent's heart attack, decedent would have had a 70% chance to survive. Although the case went off on other issues, the court noted in passing that the trial judge reduced the jury's verdict "to reflect the lost chance of seventy percent." Was that correct?

5. According to Hicks v. United States, 368 F.2d 626 (4th Cir.1966), "when a defendant's negligent action or inaction has effectively terminated a person's chance of survival, it does not lie in the defendant's mouth to raise conjectures as to the measure of the chances that he has put beyond the possibility of realization. If there was any substantial possibility of survival and the defendant has destroyed it, he is answerable." Is the court's explanation based on probability or fairness? On the other hand, if fairness or proof questions are at the heart of the problem, why should a court insist that the lost opportunity have been a "substantial possibility"? Might such a court award full damages? A few courts have awarded full damages for loss of life in a case in which the plaintiff showed at most the loss of a 40% chance of survival. E.g., Kallenberg v. Beth Israel Hosp., 357 N.Y.S.2d 508 (App.Div. 1974), aff'd 337 N.E.2d 128 (N.Y.1975). Can this course be justified?

6. Courts are split over the lost-chance approach. Most appear to be adopting the approach but several courts have rejected the lost-chance claim. In Falcon v. Memorial Hospital, 462 N.W.2d 44 (Mich.1990), in which the court, 4–3, adopted loss-of-a-chance analysis, the three dissenters decried the departure from traditional tort principles:

> Professor King aptly characterizes a lost chance as a "raffle ticket" destroyed by the defendant's negligence. [ ] King advocates compensation for "statistically demonstrable losses," [ ], so that a person deprived of a forty percent chance of survival should be compensated for forty percent of the compensable value of his life. [ ] Thus, tort law is transformed from a compensatory system to a payout scheme on the basis of a statistical chance that the defendant caused the plaintiff's death. It is no answer that full compensation based on less than a certainty that a plaintiff would have survived is overcompensation. Professor King criticizes the probability standard of causation because, in his view, it treats the better-than-even chance as a certainty, "as though it had materialized or were certain to do so." [ ] Clearly, causation can never be proven to a certainty; the law settles for less in determining that a defendant should be held liable for damages to a plaintiff. . . .

> . . . . [T]here must be some degree of certainty regarding causation before a jury may determine as fact that a medical defendant did cause the plaintiff's injury and should therefore compensate the plaintiff in damages. To dispense with this requirement is to abandon the truth-seeking function of the law. Professor King is willing to do so in his attempt to compensate for the precise magnitude of any lost chance. Professor King's criticism of the more likely than not standard for causation, like the lost chance theory itself, is based on the erroneous premise that it is the purpose of tort law to compensate for lost chances. But tort law should not operate by the same principles that govern lotteries and insurance policies. If the acts of the defendants did not actually cause plaintiff's injury, then there is no rational

justification for requiring defendants to bear the cost of plaintiff's damages.

A number of specific arguments for rejection are offered in Fennell v. Southern Maryland Hospital Center, Inc., 580 A.2d 206 (Md.1990), in which the court denied all recovery to a plaintiff who had shown that the hospital's negligence deprived the decedent of a 40% chance of survival. First, the court thought that the logic of the loss-of-a-chance theory dictated some recovery if a defendant's negligence reduced a plaintiff's chance of survival from 40% to 10%—even if the plaintiff later survived. Second, the court was concerned about the conduct of trials:

> The use of statistics in trials is subject to criticism as being unreliable, misleading, easily manipulated, and confusing to a jury. When large damage awards will be based on the statistical chance of survival before the negligent treatment, minus the statistical chance of survival after the negligent treatment, times the value of the lost life, we can imagine the bewildering sets of numbers with which the jury will be confronted, as well as the difficulties juries will have in assessing the comparative reliability of the divergent statistical evidence offered by each side.

Third, the court identified a fairness concern: "If a plaintiff whose decedent had a 49% chance of survival, which was lost through negligent treatment, is permitted to recover 49% of the value of the decedent's life, then a plaintiff whose decedent had a 51% chance of survival which was lost through negligent treatment, perhaps ought to have recovery limited to 51% of the value of the life lost." Finally, the court stressed the impact of a change in the law on the costs of the delivery of medical services.

Which concerns are most persuasive?

7. Might the court's analysis extend to retaining a termite contractor to try to save a house from termite damage? See Hardy v. Southwestern Bell Tel. Co., 910 P.2d 1024 (Okla.1996) (refusing to extend lost chance beyond medical situations to case against telephone company alleging that failure of 911 emergency system led to death of heart-attack victim).

Does the logic of *Alberts* support loss-of-chance malpractice against attorneys? In Daugert v. Pappas, 704 P.2d 600 (Wash.1985), the court refused to use that approach in a case in which plaintiff's attorney filed a discretionary appeal too late to get it heard. Plaintiff argued that he need only have shown a chance to prevail on the appeal. The court required plaintiff to prove that the court would have exercised its discretion to hear the appeal and would have decided it for him. The jury could have found only a 20% chance of that sequence.

Should the approach have been available against Siegrist in *Farwell*, p. 137, supra, if there had been expert testimony that, if brought to a hospital immediately, the decedent would have had a 35% chance to survive? A 75% chance?

If the jury in a case involving solely a credibility dispute concludes that it is 80% likely that the plaintiff is the one telling the truth, should it be told to award the plaintiff 80% of the agreed-upon damages? See generally, Levmore, Probabilistic Recoveries, Restitution, and Recurring Wrongs, 19 J.Legal Stud. 691 (1990).

2.   INTRODUCTION TO JOINT AND SEVERAL LIABILITY

The basic doctrine. So far we have been dealing with cases in which the focus was on the causal contribution of a single defendant. We turn now to cases in which more than one relevant cause may be involved in the harm that befell plaintiff. One example would be a case in which two cars collide and one of the cars goes up on the sidewalk and hits a pedestrian. The proof shows that if either driver had been careful the accident would have been averted. In other words, the negligence of each driver was essential to plaintiff's harm.

In this type of case the two drivers were traditionally held subject to "joint and several liability." This meant that the plaintiff might sue them together or separately and recover the full extent of the damages against either one. If plaintiff's harm was $50,000, and both defendants were found negligent, the judgment traditionally provided that the plaintiff was to recover $50,000 against D1 and D2. Plaintiff could then collect the entire $50,000 from whichever defendant plaintiff chose—usually the one from whom it was easier to collect the entire award. The plaintiff did not care whether one of the defendants was insolvent because any solvent defendant was liable for the entire award. Originally, the two defendants were held equally responsible between themselves—so that one of the two defendants who paid the plaintiff the full $50,000 would be entitled to recoup $25,000 from the other. As we shall see, that pattern gave way to a system in which the defendants shared on the basis of their respective percentages of fault.

The doctrine operated in situations beyond those in which multiple defendants combined to cause the same harm. Consider Ravo v. Rogatnick, 514 N.E.2d 1104 (N.Y.1987), a case in which plaintiff suffered severe brain damage at birth. The evidence supported the view that the harm could have come from the obstetrician's negligence in delivery or from the pediatrician's negligence immediately thereafter, or from both causes. The jury found eight acts of malpractice by the obstetrician and three by the pediatrician. The trial judge instructed the jury that if they found both defendants negligent and that both had caused a single injury to the plaintiff that could not be apportioned between the defendants, the jury could find each liable for the whole harm. The jury was also told to apportion the fault in the case on the basis of 100%.

The jury returned a verdict finding for plaintiff against both defendants. It also apportioned the fault 80% to the obstetrician and 20% to the pediatrician. The pediatrician asserted that he should be liable for no more than 20% of the award. The court disagreed:

> When two or more tort-feasors act concurrently or in concert to produce a single injury, they may be held jointly and severally liable.
> [ ] This is so because such concerted wrongdoers are considered "joint

tort-feasors" and in legal contemplation, there is a joint enterprise and a mutual agency, such that the act of one is the act of all and liability for all that is done is visited upon each. [   ] On the other hand, where multiple tort-feasors "neither act in concert nor contribute concurrently to the same wrong, they are not joint tort-feasors; rather their wrongs are independent and successive." [   ] Under successive and independent liability, of course, the initial tort-feasor may well be liable to the plaintiff for the entire damage proximately resulting from his own wrongful acts. [   ] The successive tort-feasor, however, is liable only for the separate injury or the aggravation his conduct has caused. [   ]

It is sometimes the case that tort-feasors who neither act in concert nor concurrently may nevertheless be considered jointly and severally liable. This may occur in the instance of certain injuries which, because of their nature, are incapable of any reasonable or practicable division or allocation among multiple tort-feasors. [   ]

The court thought the same reasoning applied to this case. Although the second defendant is not to be held jointly and severally liable "in every case where it is difficult, because of the nature of the injury, to separate the harm done" by each defendant, the evidence here showed that the brain damage was a single indivisible injury.

The fact that the jury allocated only 20% of the negligence to the second defendant did not alter the analysis. This "aspect of the jury's determination of culpability merely defines the amount of contribution defendants may claim from each other, and does not impinge upon plaintiff's right to collect the entire judgment from either defendant."

Recent changes. Since the advent of comparative negligence two changes have occurred that alter the basic doctrine. The first has already been noted—having the defendants obtain contribution from each other in proportion to their fault in the accident. Thus, if D1 was held 75% at fault and D2 25% at fault for the harm suffered by the pedestrian, the victim could still get full damages from either defendant, but they would ultimately share the loss in a 75–25 ratio if both were solvent.

The second recent change in the traditional pattern has been much more significant—questioning the very idea of "joint and several liability." Joint and several liability has come under fire in recent years because of perceived unfairness in certain situations in which one of the two defendants is unable to bear his or her share of the judgment. The problem is suggested by the situation above in which the jury holds D1 75% to blame for an accident. Under the common law each would be jointly and severally liable for the entire judgment—with contribution to follow—if both defendants were solvent. If both were solvent, there was little sense of unfairness. But if either driver turned out to be insolvent, the entire loss would rest on the other one. Thus, the defendant who was 25% at fault might be out of pocket for 100% of the damages.

The advent of comparative negligence, discussed in detail in Chapter VI, was meant to modify the perceived harshness to plaintiffs of the all-or-nothing aspect of contributory negligence. But once comparisons were permitted between plaintiff and defendant, the argument was put forward that it was as appropriate to make similar comparisons among defendants—and then to have each party to the accident bear only the share attributable to his or her fault. Again, if everyone is solvent, there is little reason for concern. But in reality, insolvency often shapes litigation strategy in tort law. (Recall, e.g., *Tarasoff*, p. 158, supra, *Vince v. Wilson*, p. 179, supra, and *Reynolds v. Hicks*, p. 185, supra).

Since the early 1980s, some 40 states have made major legislative changes in the operation of joint and several liability. It is hard to capture the array of changes but they fit very roughly into the following categories:

1. About a dozen states have abolished the doctrine, leaving a solvent defendant responsible only for his or her percentage of fault.

2. About a dozen have abolished the doctrine in cases in which the defendant is less than a certain percentage at fault. In most of these the threshold is 50%.

3. A few states, including California, have retained joint and several liability for economic damages but have abolished it for non-economic damages.

4. A handful of states have abolished the doctrine when the plaintiff is partially at fault, but have retained it when the plaintiff is not at fault.

5. A handful have abolished the doctrine in many kinds of torts but have retained it in a few areas—most commonly toxic and environmental torts. (New York, for example, retains the doctrine in several listed situations, including motor vehicle and motorcycle cases, recklessness cases, and a variety of environmental cases.)

Which if any of these changes would you favor?

The interplay of intent and negligence. Even the states that have modified or abolished joint and several liability still must decide one crucial question of great practical importance: What should they do when the defendant's negligence is combined with an intentional tort or crime?

Veazey v. Elmwood Plantation Associates, Ltd., 650 So.2d 712 (La. 1994), the plaintiff was raped in her apartment and brought an action against the management company for failure to exercise due care for the safety of residents. After the trial judge refused to permit any allocation of fault to the unidentified nonparty rapist, the supreme court split three ways. The majority concluded that it might be appropriate to compare negligence and intentional fault in some cases but that this case was not one of them. Three reasons motivated the majority. First, the defendant's duty to provide a safe place to live encompassed the very risk that injured plaintiff, and the defendant should not be able to reduce its liability when its failure brought about the very harm feared. Second, any comparison would be against public policy because it would reduce the safety incentives of the management company, especially here since any "rational juror" would apportion most of the fault to the rapist at the "innocent plaintiff's expense." Finally, the court concluded that intentional torts are "fundamentally different" from negligence and the two cannot be compared in many situations, including this one.

The concurring justice asserted that the trial judge reached the right result because the two types of torts could never be compared. The dissenters thought that the two types of harm could be, and should be, compared in this case. One dissenter asserted that this "result—holding the negligent tortfeasor(s) responsible for the entirety of the damages because of the mere happenstance that a co-tortfeasor committed an intentional, as opposed to a negligent wrongdoing—is anomalous." That justice concluded that the fault should be apportioned 90 percent to the rapist and 10 percent to the defendant. Under the state law of joint and several liability this would have made the defendant liable for half the plaintiff's damages. Which of the three views seems most sound? Does your view depend on the state's approach to joint and several liability? See also Kansas State Bank & Trust Co. v. Specialized Transportation Services, Inc., 819 P.2d 587 (Kan.1991) (refusing to apportion where defendant negligently hired a school bus driver who attacked a student).

In a state that allows or requires comparison, is a jury ever justified in allocating more fault to the negligent defendant than to the person who committed an intentional tort? How is the jury to compare the two? In Scott v. County of Los Angeles, 32 Cal.Rptr.2d 643 (App.1994), the trial court entered judgment in favor of an abused child on a jury verdict that apportioned fault 99% to the county and the social worker and 1% to the abusive parent. The appellate court rejected that allocation, referring to another case in which another court had overturned a jury's allocation of 95% of the fault to a landlord who had been negligent in not protecting tenants from assaults and 5% against the two rapists.

Compare Hutcherson v. City of Phoenix, 961 P.2d 449 (Ariz.1998), in which a woman called 911 to report that her former boyfriend had threatened her and her new boyfriend—and that the new boyfriend had threatened to kill the former boyfriend if he showed up. The 911 operator indicated that she would send an officer and told the woman to call again if the boyfriend (who was said to live nearby and know where she was) should appear. The 911 operator gave the call a priority 3. After 22 minutes the former boyfriend appeared and killed the two others and then himself. In this claim against the city, it was shown that the average response time to a priority 1 call was 4.4 minutes; the response time for priority 2, often used for domestic violence incidents, averaged 13.6 minutes; and priority 3, for "service" or "report" calls, averaged 32.6 minutes. The operator also failed to prepare a "supplemental dispatch card to police radio personnel according to departmental policy, further hampering a response."

The jury found the 911 operator negligent and allocated fault 75% to the city and 25% to the killer. The city's appeal from the percentage allocation was rejected. The court first concluded that the state's statute required that negligent and intentional conduct be compared. Then, the court turned to the merits of the 75–25 allocation and affirmed:

> The murderer's culpability is enormous, the operator's is slight. He committed deliberate homicide; she misjudged the severity of the call. And when it comes to contribution to causation, at first blush, the imbalance again weighs heavily toward the murderer. When you add relative timing into the picture, however, the balance starts to shift. The operator has notice of a potentially imminent harm and a chance to avoid it. This is a proper factor for the fact finder to weigh. It is also proper for the fact finder to weigh the operator's responsibility for foresight and avoidance. It enters into the weighing of relative degrees of fault.

The trial judge had accepted the jury's allocation, and the appellate court held that the allocation was "not manifestly unfair or shocking."

Absent tortfeasors. Even states that are willing to apportion fault between intentional and negligent tortfeasors must face certain questions before apportioning. For example, what should courts do when the sued defendant seeks to reduce its share of the fault by laying some or all of the blame at the feet of an absent person? The outcome depends on the wording of the state's statute. Thus, following its statute, one court held that a mall sued for an attack could not have the jury apportion fault to the attacker because he was unidentified, and not a "party." The implication was that if the assailant had been caught and identified, the defendant could join him as a party and then ask the jury to apportion the fault. Field v. Boyer Co., L.C., 952 P.2d 1078 (Utah 1998). See also Brown v. Wal–Mart Discount Cities, 12 S.W.3d 785 (Tenn.2000) (holding that store sued for negligently maintaining its premises could not reduce its fault by blaming unidentified customer who spilled ice on floor near company's drink dispenser).

Immune tortfeasors. The issue also exists with immunity. In Carroll v. Whitney, 29 S.W.3d 14 (Tenn. 2000), plaintiffs sought to establish medical malpractice on several defendants, including two staff physicians at a public hospital who, under statute, were immune from common law tort liability. On their motion, the trial court dismissed them from the case. In the suit against the remaining (non-immune) defendants, the jury allocated 70% and 30% of the fault to the two absent physicians and none to any of the remaining defendants. This result was upheld on appeal. The court, 3–1, noted that because of fairness it was committed to getting "a fair and tight fit" between fault and liability. Since "the nonparty defense is an affirmative defense, a jury can apportion fault to a nonparty only after it is convinced" that defendant has met its burden. The court cited cases and statutes from 20 states to indicate that it was following "the vast majority of comparative fault jurisdictions that broadly permit allocation of fault to all persons involved in an injury-causing event."

Non-delegable duties. In Wiggs v. City of Phoenix, 10 P.3d 625 (Ariz. 2000), the city had a contract with T to keep the city's streetlights in repair. The court held that if T's negligence in not keeping a streetlight functioning led to an accident, the city was liable because its duty was non-delegable. Recall the discussion of such duties at p. 24, supra. Arizona had retained joint liability only for persons "acting in concert or if the other person was acting as an agent or servant of the party." The court held that one who carries out a non-delegable duty is an agent for purposes of the statute. Although the city was thus fully liable to the plaintiff it would be entitled to indemnity from T in such a case.

Contribution and indemnity. Recall that in states that retain joint and several liability in all or some cases, there will be questions about contribution and indemnity where there are at least two liable defendants and one has paid more than its fair share. The classic situation was master-servant, in which the master, who was liable only as a matter of law under respondeat superior, could seek indemnification. Recall Chapter I. That right has been extended to what the courts called "active-passive" negligence situations, in which the party asserted to have been negligent in a "passive" manner can obtain indemnity from the "actively" negligent party.

The Restatement. In 1999, the American Law Institute published a segment of the Restatement of the Law Third, called Apportionment of Liability, that develops guidelines for apportioning tort liability among multiple tortfeasors. Due to the great variation among states, the Institute developed five independent analytical approaches. Each track codifies guidelines for apportioning liability among two or more persons who are a legal cause of an indivisible injury.

Track A utilizes joint and several liability. Under track A, a plaintiff may recover all damages from any liable defendant, and the defendant has the burden of joining additional parties or securing contribution from other liable parties. Track B imposes several liability. The plaintiff has the burden of securing recovery from each responsible party. Track C uses joint and several liability with reallocation. This option adopts the Uniform Comparative Fault Act's approach, p. 441, infra. If one defendant persuades the court that a judgment for contribution cannot be fully collected from another defendant, usually due to insolvency, the court must reapportion the uncollectible portion of damages to all remaining parties, including the plaintiff, according to their proportions of comparative responsibility. Track D creates a hybrid system for allocating liability based on a legal threshold percentage of comparative responsibility. If a defendant's percentage of comparative responsibility falls below the legal threshold, the tortfeasor is only severally liable. Conversely, if the tortfeasor's comparative responsibility is equal to or exceeds the legal threshold, the defendant is jointly and severally liable. In the states that have adopted the legal threshold system, the threshold percentage has been set between 10% and 60%, with 50% being the mode. § D18, Reporter's Note, Comment g. Finally, Track E apportions liability under a system similar to the California approach, under which defendants are jointly and severally liable for economic damages, but only severally liable for non-economic damages.

3. MULTIPLE DEFENDANTS

Summers v. Tice

Supreme Court of California, 1948.
33 Cal.2d 80, 199 P.2d 1.

[Plaintiff and defendants Tice and Simonson were hunting quail when both defendants fired in plaintiff's direction. One shot struck plaintiff's eye and another his lip. Both defendants were using the same gauge shotgun and the same size shot. The trial judge, sitting without a jury, found both defendants negligent and found that plaintiff was in no way at fault. Unable to decide which defendant's shot hit the plaintiff, the judge awarded judgment against both defendants, who appealed.]

CARTER, J. [after stating the facts and upholding the negligence determinations].

The problem presented in this case is whether the judgment against both defendants may stand. It is argued by defendants that they are not joint tort feasors, and thus jointly and severally liable, as they were not acting in concert, and that there is not sufficient evidence to show which defendant was guilty of the negligence which caused the injuries—the shooting by Tice or that by Simonson. Tice argues that there is evidence to show that the shot which struck plaintiff came from Simonson's gun because of admissions allegedly made by him to third persons and no evidence that they came from his gun. Further in connection with the latter contention, the court failed to find on plaintiff's allegation in his complaint that he did not know which one was at fault—did not find which defendant was guilty of the negligence which caused the injuries to plaintiff.

Considering the last argument first, we believe it is clear that the court sufficiently found on the issue that defendants were jointly liable and that thus the negligence of both was the cause of the injury or to that legal effect. It found that both defendants were negligent and "That as a direct and proximate result of the shots fired by *defendants, and each of them,* a birdshot pellet was caused to and did lodge in plaintiff's right eye and that another birdshot pellet was caused to and did lodge in plaintiff's upper lip." In so doing the court evidently did not give credence to the admissions of Simonson to third persons that he fired the shots which it was justified in doing. It thus determined that the negligence of both defendants was the legal cause of the injury—or that both were responsible. Implicit in such finding is the assumption that the court was unable to ascertain whether the shots were from the gun of one defendant or the other or one shot from each of them. The one shot that entered plaintiff's eye was the major factor in assessing damages and that shot could not have come from the gun of both defendants. It was from one or the other only.

It has been held that where a group of persons are on a hunting party, or otherwise engaged in the use of firearms, and two of them are negligent in firing in the direction of a third person who is injured thereby, both of those so firing are liable for the injury suffered by the third person, although the negligence of only one of them could have caused the injury. [ ] Oliver v. Miles, [110 So. 666 (Miss.1926)]; [ ]. The same rule has been applied in criminal cases [ ] and both drivers have been held liable for the negligence of one where they engaged in a racing contest causing an injury to a third person [ ]. These cases speak of the action of defendants as being in concert as the ground of decision, yet it would seem they are straining that concept and the more reasonable basis appears in *Oliver v. Miles*, supra. There two persons were hunting together. Both shot at some partridges and in so doing shot across the highway injuring plaintiff who was traveling on it. The court stated they were acting in concert and thus both were liable. The court then stated: "We think that . . . each is liable for the resulting injury to the boy, although no one can say definitely who actually shot him. *To hold otherwise would be to exonerate both from liability, although each was negligent, and the injury resulted from such negligence.*" [Emphasis added.]

. . .

When we consider the relative position of the parties and the results that would flow if plaintiff was required to pin the injury on one of the defendants only, a requirement that the burden of proof on that subject be shifted to defendants becomes manifest. They are both wrongdoers—both negligent toward plaintiff. They brought about a situation where the negligence of one of them injured the plaintiff, hence it should rest with them each to absolve himself if he can. The injured party has been placed by defendants in the unfair position of pointing to which defendant caused the harm. If one can escape the other may also and plaintiff is remediless. Ordinarily defendants are in a far better position to offer evidence to determine which one caused the injury. This reasoning has recently found favor in this court. In a quite analogous situation this court held that a patient injured while unconscious on an operating table in a hospital could hold all or any of the persons who had any connection with the operation even though he could not select the particular acts by the particular person which led to his disability. *Ybarra v. Spangard*, [ ]. There the court was considering whether the patient could avail himself of res ipsa loquitur, rather than where the burden of proof lay, yet the effect of the decision is that plaintiff has made out a case when he has produced evidence which gives rise to an inference of negligence which was the proximate cause of the injury. It is up to defendants to explain the cause of the injury. It was there said: "If the doctrine is to continue to serve a useful purpose, we should not forget that 'the particular force and justice of the rule, regarded as a presumption throwing upon the party charged the duty of producing evidence, consists in the circumstance that the chief evidence of the true cause, whether culpable or innocent, is practically accessible to him but inaccessible to the injured person.'" [ ] Similarly in the instant case plaintiff is not able to establish which of defendants caused his injury.

. . .

It is urged that plaintiff now has changed the theory of his case in claiming a concert of action; that he did not plead or prove such concert. From what has been said it is clear that there has been no change in theory. The joint liability, as well as the lack of knowledge as to which defendant was liable, was pleaded and the proof developed the case under either theory. We have seen that for the reasons of policy discussed herein, the case is based upon the legal proposition that, under the circumstances here presented, each defendant is liable for the whole damage whether they are deemed to be acting in concert or independently.

No matter acting jointly or independently each Δ is liable.

The judgment is affirmed.

GIBSON, C.J., SHENK, J., EDMONDS, J., TRAYNOR, J., SCHAUER, J., and SPENCE, J., concurred.

Notes and Questions

1. Under the common law before comparative fault, if the damages were $20,000, each defendant would be "jointly and severally liable" for the full amount, though plaintiff could not obtain more than one satisfaction of his judgment. Under today's practice, the fact finder, even if unable to determine causation, would have had to assess fault percentages on the defendants—and then follow the state statute. How might the faults differ here?

2. Is it essential to the analysis that the two defendants were hunting as a team? What if they had been independent negligent hunters who never met one another until after the accident?

3. How should the cause issue be analyzed if the judge found that although either pellet might have hit the plaintiff, only Tice's behavior had been negligent, so that the innocent Simonson could not be liable to plaintiff even if his pellet had done the harm? In Garcia v. Joseph Vince Co., 148 Cal.Rptr. 843 (App. 1978), plaintiff fencer was hurt by a defective saber. Plaintiff could not identify which of two manufacturers was the source of the defective saber because it had been put back into a pile of sabers. His effort to invoke *Summers v. Tice* was rejected and the case was dismissed.

1 saber manufacturer was NOT acting neg.

4. What result would the court reach if Tice had fired two shots and Simonson only one? What if three defendants had fired negligently at the same time? What if only two of the three had been negligent?

5. Are the differences between *Ybarra* and *Summers* significant? Which decision is more justifiable? This question is discussed, and *Ybarra* criticized, in Seavey, Res Ipsa Loquitur: Tabula in Naufragio, 63 Harv. L.Rev. 643 (1950). In a subsequent multiple-shooting case, should a plaintiff who cannot prove anyone's negligence be able to invoke *Ybarra* and then use *Summers*?

6. Suppose P is injured in a highway accident when D1 negligently swerves into P's car and that then D2 negligently piles into the tangled autos. Does it follow from the reasoning of *Summers v. Tice* that the burden shifts to each defendant to show that his collision was not the cause of the plaintiff's injuries? See Copley v. Putter, 207 P.2d 876 (App. 1949), treating virtually simultaneous impacts under the *Summers v. Tice* approach.

7. Is the approach limited to "virtually simultaneous" situations? In Loui v. Oakley, 438 P.2d 393 (Haw.1968), the plaintiff was hurt in an auto accident caused by defendant's negligence in August 1961. Plaintiff hurt the "same area of her body" in three subsequent auto accidents before this case came to trial: February, 1962; November, 1962; January, 1965. At trial the issue was the extent of defendant's liability. Each side argued what the court thought "extreme" positions: P argued that D was liable for the entire loss if P could not allocate the harm among the four episodes. D argued for a rule that barred plaintiff from any relief unless P could show by a preponderance of the evidence "the precise damages attributable to the defendant's negligence." The court concluded that if the jury could not allocate the damages by a preponderance of the evidence it was to "make a rough apportionment." On remand, the trial court "should instruct the jury that if it is unable to make even a rough apportionment, it must apportion the damages equally among the various accidents. We recognize that this resolution is arbitrary. It is, however, no less arbitrary than placing the entire loss on one defendant." The court noted that in the future the desirable procedure would be to litigate all four accidents together. This would guarantee the faultless plaintiff "full damages."

The Hawaii approach was rejected in Gross v. Lyons, 763 So.2d 276 (Fla.2000), in which plaintiff was hurt by two negligent defendants three months apart. In the case against D1, in which P claimed that all her injuries were caused by D1, the jury should have been told that if D1 could not bear the burden of allocating between the two accidents, the jury should have awarded full damages against D1. See also Cox v. Spangler, 5 P.3d 1265 (Wash.2000), requiring D to unravel the harms (or pay for the entire injury) where P was injured in a work-related accident six months before D negligently injured P. These apportionment issues are discussed at length in Robertson, The Common Sense of Cause in Fact, 75 Texas L.Rev. 1765 (1997).

8. In Basko v. Sterling Drug, Inc., 416 F.2d 417 (2d Cir.1969), the plaintiff was allegedly blinded after taking two drugs manufactured by the defendant. Under one view of the case, the defendant would have been liable if the blinding had been caused by its Triquin but not if caused by its Aralen. The blinding was caused either by one drug or a combination of the two. The court noted that ordinarily cause could be analyzed in terms of a "but for" test: "defendant's negligence is a cause in fact of an injury where the injury would not have occurred *but for* defendant's negligent conduct. [   ] The test will not work, however, in the situation where two independent forces concur to produce a result which either of them alone would have produced. In such a situation, either force can be said to be the cause in fact of the harm, despite the fact that the same harm would have resulted from either force acting alone." The causation element could be satisfied by a finding that the defendant's negligence was a "substantial factor" in producing the harm:

> The reason for imposing liability in such a situation, as Harper and James explain, is that the "defendant has committed a wrong and this has been *a* cause of the injury; further, such negligent conduct will be more effectively deterred by imposing liability than by giving the wrongdoer a windfall in cases where an all-sufficient innocent cause happens to concur with his wrong in producing the harm." [ ] Similarly, in Navigazione Libera T. S. A. v. Newtown Creek Towing Co., 98 F.2d 694, 697 (2d Cir.1938), Judge Learned Hand stated that "the single tortfeasor cannot be allowed to escape through the meshes of a logical net. He is a wrongdoer; let him unravel the casuistries resulting from his wrong." See also Malone, Ruminations on Cause-In-Fact, 9 Stan.L.Rev. 60, 88–94 (1956). The contrary arguments have been rejected by the Restatement, and there is good reason to believe that the Connecticut courts would follow the Restatement approach. [ ]

Is the court's resolution persuasive?

9. Analyze a case in which two negligent defendants independently race their motorcycles past plaintiff's horse—which bolts and runs away, hurting plaintiff. The act of either defendant alone would have sufficed to cause the harm. See Corey v. Havener, 65 N.E. 69 (Mass.1902). What if one of the motorcyclists had not been negligent? Compare Peaslee, Multiple Causation and Damage, 47 Harv.L.Rev. 1127 (1934) (use but-for test) with Carpenter, Concurrent Causation, 83 U.Pa.L.Rev. 941 (1935) (negligent defendant must be held liable in this type of case).

Hymowitz v. Eli Lilly & Co.

Court of Appeals of New York, 1989.
73 N.Y.2d 487, 539 N.E.2d 1069, 541 N.Y.S.2d 941.
Cert. denied, 493 U.S. 944 (1989).

WACHTLER, CHIEF JUDGE.

Plaintiffs in these appeals allege that they were injured by the drug diethylstilbestrol (DES) ingested by their mothers during pregnancy. They seek relief against defendant DES manufacturers. While not class actions, these cases are representative of nearly 500 similar actions pending in the courts in this State; the rules articulated by the court here, therefore, must do justice and be administratively feasible in the context of this mass litigation. . . .

I.

The history of the development of DES and its marketing in this country has been repeatedly chronicled [ ]. Briefly, DES is a synthetic substance that mimics the effect of estrogen, the naturally formed female hormone. It was invented in 1937 by British researchers, but never patented.

In 1941, the Food and Drug Administration (FDA) approved the new drug applications (NDA) of 12 manufacturers to market DES for the treatment of various maladies, not directly involving pregnancy. In 1947, the FDA began approving the NDAs of manufacturers to market DES for the purpose of preventing human miscarriages; by 1951, the FDA had concluded that DES was generally safe for pregnancy use, and stopped requiring the filing of NDAs when new manufacturers sought to produce the drug for this purpose. In 1971, however, the FDA banned the use of DES as a miscarriage preventative, when studies established the harmful latent effects of DES upon the offspring of mothers who took the drug. Specifically, tests indicated that DES caused vaginal adenocarcinoma, a form of cancer, and adenosis, a precancerous vaginal or cervical growth.

Although strong evidence links prenatal DES exposure to later develop-ment of serious medical problems, plaintiffs seeking relief in court for their injuries faced two formidable and fundamental barriers to recovery in this State; not only is identification of the manufacturer of the DES ingested in a particular case generally impossible, but, due to the latent nature of DES injuries, many claims were barred by the Statute of Limitations before the injury was discovered.

The identification problem has many causes. All DES was of identical chemical composition. Druggists usually filled prescriptions from whatever was on hand. Approximately 300 manufacturers produced the drug, with companies entering and leaving the market continuously during the 24 years that DES was sold for pregnancy use. The long latency period of a DES injury compounds the identification problem; memories fade, records are lost or destroyed, and witnesses die. Thus the pregnant women who took DES generally never knew who produced the drug they took, and there was no reason to attempt to discover this fact until many years after ingestion, at which time the information is not available.

.   .   .

The second barrier to recovery, involving the Statute of Limitations, arose from the long-standing rule in this State that the limitations period accrued upon exposure in actions alleging personal injury caused by toxic substances. [Following a case in which the court refused to change that rule for DES cases, the legislature provided that the statute began to run upon the discovery of "the latent effects of exposure to any substance," and for one year revived causes of action for exposure to DES that had been barred.]

It is estimated that eventually 800 DES cases will be brought under the revival portion of this recent statute.   .   .   .

The present appeals are before the court in the context of summary judgment motions. In all of the appeals defendants moved for summary judgment dismissing the complaints because plaintiffs could not identify the manufacturer of the drug that allegedly injured them. In three of the appeals defendants also moved on Statute of Limitations grounds, arguing that the revival of the actions was unconstitutional under the State and Federal Constitutions, and that the complaints, therefore, are time barred and should be dismissed. The trial court denied all of these motions. On the Statute of Limitations issue, the trial court also granted plaintiffs' cross motions, dismissing defendants' affirmative defenses that the actions were time barred. The Appellate Division affirmed in all respects and certified to this court the questions of whether the orders of the trial court were properly made. [   ] We answer these questions in the affirmative.

II.

In a products liability action, identification of the exact defendant whose product injured the plaintiff is, of course, generally required [   ]. In DES cases in which such identification is possible, actions may proceed under established principles of products liability [   ]. The record now before us, however, presents the question of whether a DES plaintiff may recover against a DES manufacturer when identification of the producer of the specific drug that caused the injury is impossible.

A.

As we noted [   ], the accepted tort doctrines of alternative liability and concerted action are available in some personal injury cases to permit recovery where the precise identification of a wrongdoer is impossible. However, we agree with the near unanimous views of the high State courts that have considered the matter that these doctrines in their unaltered common-law forms do not permit recovery in DES cases [   ].

The paradigm of alternative liability is found in the case of [*Summers v. Tice*]. In *Summers*, plaintiff and the two defendants were hunting, and defendants carried identical shotguns and ammunition. During the hunt, defendants shot simultaneously at the same bird, and plaintiff was struck by bird shot from one of the defendants' guns. The court held that where two defendants breach a duty to the plaintiff, but there is uncertainty regarding which one caused the injury, "the burden is upon each such actor to prove that he has not caused the harm" [   ]; cf., *Ravo v. Rogatnick*, ([p. 368, supra] [successive tort-feasors may be held jointly and severally liable for an indivisible injury to the plaintiff]). The central rationale for shifting the burden of proof in such a situation is that without this device both defendants will be silent, and plaintiff will not recover; with alternative liability, however, defendants will be forced to speak, and reveal the culpable party, or else be held jointly and severally liable themselves. Consequently, use of the alternative liability doctrine generally requires that the defendants have better access to information than does the plaintiff, and that all possible tort-feasors be before the court [   ]. It is also recognized that alternative liability rests on the notion that where there is a small number of possible wrongdoers, all of whom breached a duty to the plaintiff, the likelihood that any one of them injured the plaintiff is relatively high, so that forcing them to exonerate themselves, or be held liable, is not unfair [   ].

In DES cases, however, there is a great number of possible wrongdoers, who entered and left the market at different times, and some of whom no longer exist. Additionally, in DES cases many years elapse between the ingestion of the drug and injury. Consequently, DES defendants are not in any better position than are plaintiffs to identify the manufacturer of the DES ingested in any given case, nor is there any real prospect of having all the possible producers before the court. Finally, while it may be fair to employ alternative liability in cases involving only a small number of potential wrongdoers, that fairness disappears with the decreasing probability that any one of the defendants actually caused the injury. This is particularly true when applied to DES where the chance that a particular producer caused the injury is often very remote [   ]. Alternative liability, therefore, provides DES plaintiffs no relief.

Nor does the theory of concerted action, in its pure form, supply a basis for recovery. This doctrine, seen in drag racing cases, provides for joint and several liability on the part of all defendants having an understanding, express or tacit, to participate in "a common plan or design to commit a tortious act" [   ]. As . . . the present record reflects, drug companies were engaged in extensive parallel conduct in developing and marketing DES [   ]. There is nothing in the record, however, beyond this similar conduct to show any agreement, tacit or otherwise, to market DES for pregnancy use without taking proper steps to ensure the drug's safety. Parallel activity, without more, is insufficient to establish the agreement element necessary to maintain a concerted action claim [   ]. Thus this theory also fails in supporting an action by DES plaintiffs.

In short, extant common-law doctrines, unmodified, provide no relief for the DES plaintiff unable to identify the manufacturer of the drug that injured her. This is not a novel conclusion; in the last decade a number of courts in other jurisdictions also have concluded that present theories do not support a cause of action in DES cases. Some courts, upon reaching this conclusion, have declined to find any judicial remedy for the DES plaintiffs who cannot identify the particular manufacturer of the DES ingested by their mothers (see, Zafft v. Eli Lilly & Co., 676 S.W.2d 241 [Mo 1984][en banc]; Mulcahy v. Eli Lilly & Co., 386 N.W.2d 67 [Iowa 1986] [stating that any change in the law to allow for recovery in nonidentification DES cases should come from the Legislature]). Other courts, however, have found that some modification of existing doctrine is appropriate to allow for relief for those injured by DES of unknown manufacture (e.g., [Sindell v. Abbott Labs., 607 P.2d 924 (Cal.), cert. denied 449 U.S. 912 (1980); Collins v. Eli Lilly & Co., 342 N.W.2d 37 (Wis.), cert. denied 469 U.S. 826 (1984); Martin v. Abbott Labs., 689 P.2d 368 (Wash.1984)]).

We conclude that the present circumstances call for recognition of a realistic avenue of relief for plaintiffs injured by DES. These appeals present many of the same considerations that have prompted this court in the past to modify the rules of personal injury liability, in order "to achieve the ends of justice in a more modern context" [   ], and we perceive that here judicial action is again required to overcome the " 'inordinately difficult problems of proof' '' caused by contemporary products and marketing techniques [   ].

Indeed, it would be inconsistent with the reasonable expectations of a modern society to say to these plaintiffs that because of the insidious nature of an injury that long remains dormant, and because so many manufacturers, each behind a curtain, contributed to the devastation, the cost of injury should be borne by the innocent and not the wrongdoers. This is particularly so where the Legislature consciously created these expectations by reviving hundreds of DES cases. Consequently, the ever-evolving dictates of justice and fairness, which are the heart of our common-law system, require formation of a remedy for injuries caused by DES [   ].

We stress, however, that the DES situation is a singular case, with manufacturers acting in a parallel manner to produce an identical, generically marketed product, which causes injury many years later, and which has evoked a legislative response reviving previously barred actions. Given this unusual scenario, it is more appropriate that the loss be borne by those that produced the drug for use during pregnancy, rather than by those who were injured by the use, even where the precise manufacturer of the drug cannot be identified in a particular action. We turn then to the question of how to fairly and equitably apportion the loss occasioned by DES, in a case where the exact manufacturer of the drug that caused the injury is unknown.

B.

The past decade of DES litigation has produced a number of alternative approaches to resolve this question. Thus, in a sense, we are now in an enviable position; the efforts of other courts provided examples for contending with this difficult issue, and enough time has passed so that the actual administration and real effects of these solutions now can be observed. With these useful guides in hand, a path may be struck for our own conclusion.

[The court decided to adopt a version of the market share concept. In *Sindell*—the first case to adopt such an approach—the "central justification" was the "belief that limiting a defendant's liability to its market share will result, over the run of cases, in liability on the part of a defendant roughly equal to the injuries the defendant actually caused." After *Sindell*, the California court held, in Brown v. Superior Court, 751 P.2d 470 (Cal.1988), that a manufacturer's liability is several only, and, in cases in which all manufacturers in the market are not joined for any reason, liability will still be limited to market share, resulting in a less than 100% recovery for a plaintiff. The *Hymowitz* court also noted that determining the market shares in the years after *Sindell* "proved difficult and engendered years of litigation. After attempts at using smaller geographical units, it was eventually determined that the national market provided the most feasible and fair solution, and this national market information was compiled."

[The court then traced the variations on *Sindell* developed in Wisconsin and Washington, involving such issues as how to determine market shares; how to handle absent defendants; when to allow named defendants to exculpate themselves; and whether to make liability joint and several or only several.]

Turning to the structure to be adopted in New York, we heed both the lessons learned through experience in other jurisdictions and the realities of the mass litigation of DES claims in this State. Balancing these considerations, we are led to the conclusion that a market share theory, based upon a national market, provides the best solution. As California discovered, the reliable determination of any market smaller than the national one likely is not practicable. Moreover, even if it were possible, of the hundreds of cases in the New York courts, without a doubt there are many in which the DES that allegedly caused injury was ingested in another State. Among the thorny issues this could present, perhaps the most daunting is the spectre that the particular case could require the establishment of a separate market share matrix. We feel that this is an unfair, and perhaps impossible burden to routinely place upon the litigants in individual cases.

[The court rejected approaches that required "individualized and open-ended assessment" in each case because it feared that the large number of cases pending in New York would unduly burden the courts.]

Consequently, for essentially practical reasons, we adopt a market share theory using a national market. We are aware that the adoption of a national market will likely result in a disproportion between the liability of individual manufacturers and the actual injuries each manufacturer caused in this State. Thus our market share theory cannot be founded upon the belief that, over the run of cases, liability will approximate causation in this State [   ]. Nor does the use of a national market provide a reasonable link between liability and the risk created by a defendant to a particular plaintiff [   ]. Instead, we choose to apportion liability so as to correspond to the over-all culpability of each defendant, measured by the amount of risk of injury each defendant created to the public-at-large. Use of a national market is a fair method, we believe, of apportioning defendants' liabilities according to their total culpability in marketing DES for use during pregnancy. Under the circumstances, this is an equitable way to provide plaintiffs with the relief they deserve, while also rationally distributing the responsibility for plaintiffs' injuries among defendants.

To be sure, a defendant cannot be held liable if it did not participate in the marketing of DES for pregnancy use; if a DES producer satisfies its burden of proof of showing that it was not a member of the market of DES sold for pregnancy use, disallowing exculpation would be unfair and unjust. Nevertheless, because liability here is based on the over-all risk produced, and not causation in a single case, there should be no exculpation of a defendant who, although a member of the market producing DES for pregnancy use, appears not to have caused a particular plaintiff's injury. It is merely a windfall for a producer to escape liability solely because it manufactured a more identifiable pill, or sold only to certain drugstores.

These fortuities in no way diminish the culpability of a defendant for marketing the product, which is the basis of liability here.

Finally, we hold that the liability of DES producers is several only, and should not be inflated when all participants in the market are not before the court in a particular case. We understand that, as a practical matter, this will prevent some plaintiffs from recovering 100% of their damages. However, we eschewed exculpation to prevent the fortuitous avoidance of liability, and thus, equitably, we decline to unleash the same forces to increase a defendant's liability beyond its fair share of responsibility.[29]

III.

The constitutionality of the revival statute remains to be considered [   ]. This section revives, for the period of one year, actions for damages caused by the latent effects of DES, tungsten-carbide, asbestos, chlordane, and polyvinylchloride. Defendants argue that the revival of barred DES claims was unconstitutional as a denial of both due process and equal protection, under the State and Federal Constitutions.   . . .

[After extended discussion, the court rejected the constitutional challenges.]

Accordingly, in each case the order of the Appellate Division should be affirmed, with costs, and the certified question answered in the affirmative.

MOLLEN, JUDGE (concurring in *Hymowitz* and *Hanfling;* and dissenting in part in *Tigue* and *Dolan.*)

. . .

. . . . I would adopt a market share theory of liability, based upon a national market, which would provide for the shifting of the burden of proof on the issue of causation to the defendants and would impose liability upon all of the defendants who produced and marketed DES for pregnancy purposes, except those who were able to prove that their product could not have caused the injury. Under this approach, DES plaintiffs, who are

---

29.   . . . We are confronted here with an unprecedented identification problem, and have provided a solution that rationally apportions liability. We have heeded the practical lessons learned by other jurisdictions, resulting in our adoption of a national market theory with full knowledge that it concedes the lack of a logical link between liability and causation in a single case. The dissent ignores these lessons, and, endeavoring to articulate a theory it perceives to be closer to traditional law, sets out a construct in which liability is based upon chance, not upon the fair assessment of the acts of defendants. Under the dissent's theory, a manufacturer with a large market share may avoid liability in many cases just because it manufactured a memorably shaped pill. Conversely, a small manufacturer can be held jointly liable for the full amount of every DES injury in this State simply because the shape of its product was not remarkable, even though the odds, realistically, are exceedingly long that the small manufacturer caused the injury in any one particular case. Therefore, although the dissent's theory based upon a "shifting the burden of proof" and joint and several liability is facially reminiscent of prior law, in the case of DES it is nothing more than advocating that bare fortuity be the test for liability. When faced with the novel identification problem posed by DES cases, it is preferable to adopt a new theory that apportions fault rationally, rather than to contort extant doctrines beyond the point at which they provide a sound premise for determining liability.

unable to identify the actual manufacturer of the pill ingested by their mother, would only be required to establish, (1) that the plaintiff's mother ingested DES during pregnancy; (2) that the plaintiff's injuries were caused by DES; and (3) that the defendant or defendants produced and marketed DES for pregnancy purposes. Thereafter, the burden of proof would shift to the defendants to exculpate themselves by establishing, by a preponderance of the evidence, that the plaintiff's mother could not have ingested their particular pill. Of those defendants who are unable to exculpate themselves from liability, their respective share of the plaintiff's damages would be measured by their share of the national market of DES produced and marketed for pregnancy purposes during the period in question.

I would further note that while, on the one hand, the majority would not permit defendants who produced DES for pregnancy purposes to exculpate themselves, the majority at the same time deprives the plaintiffs of the opportunity to recover fully for their injuries by limiting the defendants' liability for the plaintiff's damages to several liability. In my view, the liability for the plaintiff's damages of those defendants who are unable to exculpate themselves should be joint and several thereby ensuring that the plaintiffs will receive full recovery of their damages, as they are entitled to by any fair standard. . . .

. . . .

. . . . [T]his approach, unlike that taken by the majority, does not represent an unnecessary and radical departure from basic principles of tort law. By characterizing this approach as "nothing more than advocating that bare fortuity be the test for liability" [ ], the majority fails to perceive that this is no more and no less than a basic principle of tort law; i.e., a plaintiff may not recover for his or her injuries from a defendant who could not have caused those injuries. When the majority eliminates this fundamental causative factor as a basis for recovery, it effectively indulges in the act of judicial legislating. . . .

Judged by the aforesaid standard, I conclude that the trial courts' orders in [*Tigue & Margolies v. Squibb & Sons* and in *Dolan v. Lilly & Co.*], to the extent that they denied the summary judgment motions of the defendant The Upjohn Company (Upjohn) in both actions and the defendant Rexall Drug Company (Rexall) in the *Tigue* action, were improper. In *Tigue*, Mrs. Tigue, the plaintiff's mother, testified that the DES pill she ingested while she was pregnant with the plaintiff was a white, round tablet [ ]. Similarly, Myrna Margolies' mother testified that the DES pill she ingested was a dark red, hard, round pill [ ]. Mr. Margolies, the plaintiff's father, also recalled that the pills were a reddish color and Mrs. Margolies' obstetrician stated that the DES pill he prescribed to his patients was not an Upjohn product. Moreover, in the *Dolan* action, Mrs. Dolan, the plaintiff's mother, stated that the DES pill she took was a white, round, hard tablet [ ]. This fact was corroborated by Mr. Dolan's testimony [ ]. Finally, it was established that Upjohn's DES pill which was produced and marketed for pregnancy purposes, was in the form of a "perle" which is a pharmaceutical term for a dose form consisting of a soft elastic capsule containing a liquid center [   ]. Based on the evidence submitted in support of Upjohn's summary judgment motions in these two cases, I would conclude that the plaintiffs have failed to adduce sufficient proof in admissible form to raise a triable issue of fact as to whether their mothers ingested an Upjohn DES pill. Accordingly, Upjohn's motion for summary judgment in those actions should have been granted.

Additionally, in [*Tigue* & *Margolies*], Rexall's motion for summary judgment should have been granted since the plaintiffs failed to raise a triable issue of fact as to whether their mothers could have ingested a Rexall DES product during the pregnancies in question. The evidence submitted in support of Rexall's motion established that until 1978, Rexall sold its products, including its DES pill, exclusively to Rexall Drug Stores [   ]. The testimony of the plaintiffs' parents, Mrs. Tigue and Mr. and Mrs. Margolies established that they had purchased their DES prescriptions from non-Rexall pharmacies during the periods of their respective pregnancies, i.e., 1960 and 1953. Based on this uncontroverted evidence demonstrating Rexall's noninvolvement in these plaintiffs' injuries, Rexall's motion for summary judgment should have been granted.

.   .   .

ALEXANDER, TITONE and HANCOCK, JJ., concur with WACHTLER, C.J.

MOLLEN, J., [concurring and dissenting].

SIMONS, KAYE and BELLACOSA, JJ., taking no part.

Notes and Questions

1. The various state courts have had to consider a market-share analysis because they almost uniformly rejected the traditional theories plaintiffs put forth. In addition to rejecting *Summers v. Tice*, the court, as noted, also refused to adopt the "concert of action" theory. This theory has been used more broadly than in the drag race cases. In Orser v. George, 60 Cal.Rptr. 708 (App. 1967), for example, several men negligently fired in the plaintiff's direction. D1 and D2 alternately fired with the gun that was identified as the one causing the fatal injury. D3 was firing at the same time with a different gun. D3 was held jointly and severally liable with the others—although his bullet could not have caused the injury—because he knew the others were acting tortiously and encouraged them by doing the same thing.

The *Sindell* court, in the influential California DES case, rejected the concert-of-action analogy on the ground that in cases like *Orser* there was an allegation that the defendant knew others were acting tortiously. In *Sindell*, however, there was no allegation that "each defendant knew the other defendants' conduct was tortious toward plaintiff, and that they assisted and encouraged one another to inadequately test DES and to provide inadequate warnings. Indeed, it seems dubious whether liability on the concert of action theory can be predicated upon substantial assistance and encouragement given by one alleged tortfeasor to another pursuant to a tacit understanding to fail to perform an act." All the cases cited by plaintiff had involved "conduct by a small number of individuals whose actions resulted in a tort against a single plaintiff, usually over a short span of time, and the defendant held liable was either a direct participant in the acts which caused damages, or encouraged and assisted the person who directly caused the injuries by participating in a joint activity."

A third theory rejected by the DES cases has been industry-wide liability or "enterprise liability." The plaintiff relied on Hall v. E.I. Du Pont De Nemours & Co., Inc., 345 F.Supp. 353 (E.D.N.Y.1972), in which the defendants were six blasting cap manufacturers "comprising virtually the entire blasting cap industry in the United States" and their trade association. The claim resulted from blasts allegedly due to inadequate warnings and other safety precautions. The *Sindell* court, for example, saw *Hall* as a case in which "there was evidence that defendants, acting independently, had adhered to an industry-wide standard with regard to the safety features of blasting caps, that they had in effect delegated some functions of safety investigation and design, such as labelling, to their trade association, and that there was industry-wide cooperation in the manufacture and design of blasting caps."

Hall itself had cautioned against application of the doctrine to large numbers of producers. The difference between six and 200 was too great. Moreover, there was no showing of delegation in the DES situation. There was one further distinction, according to the *Sindell* court:

> Equally important, the drug industry is closely regulated by the Food and Drug Administration, which actively controls the testing and manufacture of drugs and the methods by which they are marketed, including the contents of warning labels. To a considerable degree, therefore, the standards followed by drug manufacturers are suggested or compelled by the government. Adherence to those standards cannot, of course, absolve a manufacturer of liability to which it would otherwise be subject. [ ] But since the government plays such a pervasive role in formulating the criteria for the testing and marketing of drugs, it would be unfair to impose upon a manufacturer liability for injuries resulting from the use of a drug which it did not supply simply because it followed the standards of the industry.

Do the distinctions recognized by the *Sindell* court require the exploration of a new theory for DES cases?

2. The majority in *Hymowitz* refers to the "reasonable expectations of a modern society" and to "the relief [plaintiffs] deserve." What might these mean in this type of case? The separate opinion seeks to "ensure that these plaintiffs receive full recovery for their damages, as they are properly entitled to by any fair standard." What is the source of that entitlement?

3. The judges agree on using a national market share. What are the benefits of that approach? The drawbacks?

Conley v. Boyle Drug Co., 570 So.2d 275 (Fla.1990), decided that the market "should be as narrowly defined as the evidence in a given case allows. Thus, where it can be determined that the DES ingested by the mother was purchased from a particular pharmacy, that pharmacy should be considered the relevant market." This definition was consistent with allowing exculpation by defendants who did not market in the region in which the DES was purchased. Also, the narrower the market, "the greater the likelihood that liability will be imposed only on those drug companies who could have manufactured the DES which caused the plaintiff's injuries."

Conley demanded that plaintiff show due diligence in trying to find the specific source of the DES before she would be allowed to bring a market share action. Market share liability was a "theory of last resort" to be used only where need could be shown.

How does the *Conley* approach compare with the *Sindell* and *Hymowitz* approaches in terms of fairness? Administrative feasibility? All market-share approaches were rejected in Smith v. Eli Lilly & Co., 560 N.E.2d 324 (Ill.1990), as "too great a deviation from our existing tort principles."

In the cited *Martin* case, the court used a rebuttable presumption that all defendants had an equal (local) market share totaling 100%; each could rebut this by proof of its actual market share; those who could not do so had their shares inflated to return the group total to 100%.

4. The judges in *Hymowitz* disagree over whether each defendant should be permitted to try to exculpate itself. Who has the better of that argument? Is the majority's approach to the case of the identifiable defendant relevant to the treatment of the exculpation question?

5. The judges disagree over whether to use several liability or joint and several liability. Who has the better of that argument?

6. *Other possible applications.* In the wake of the DES cases, plaintiffs have tried to extend market share liability to other products, with mixed success. Is there a common theme?

a. *Asbestos.* In Goldman v. Johns–Manville Sales Corp., 514 N.E.2d 691 (Ohio 1987), the court observed that the essential condition required for market share treatment was "fungibility"—all the products made pursuant to a single formula. "In contrast, asbestos is not a 'product,' but rather a generic name for a family of minerals." Asbestos-containing products "do not create similar risks of harm because there are several varieties of asbestos fibers, and they are used in various quantities, even in the same class of products." In one example, the court noted that a tape made by one company was 95% asbestos by weight, while tapes from another company varied from 80 to 100%, and those made by a third company were 15% asbestos and 85% sodium silicate.

Compare Wheeler v. Raybestos–Manhattan, 11 Cal.Rptr.2d 109 (App. 1992), in which the court extended the market share approach to manufacturers of brake pads that used asbestos fibers because the pads were sufficiently fungible and their asbestos content was similar.

b. *Lead paint.* In Santiago v. Sherwin Williams Co., 3 F.3d 546 (1st Cir.1993), a child who was allegedly harmed by exposure to lead paint sued several manufacturers. He was born in 1972 and lived in the same house until 1978. An expert tied the child's hyperactivity and motor skills problems to lead in the house, which had been painted several times between 1917 (when it was built) and 1970. An expert testified that one layer of lead paint was applied between 1933 and 1939; and another layer between 1956 and 1969. The court thought this evidence was not sufficiently precise for Massachusetts to impose market share liability on this group of paint companies—some were not making lead paint during part of this period. Moreover, there were other sources of lead: airborne, food, water, soil and dust. The neighborhood in question had "heavily contaminated" soil.

c. *Childhood vaccines.* In Shackil v. Lederle Laboratories, 561 A.2d 511 (N.J.1989), the court, 4–2, refused to extend market share liability to manufacturers of diphtheria-typhoid-pertussis vaccine in a personal injury suit in which plaintiff could not identify the producer of the particular dose. The court noted that the pertussis portion of the vaccine causes almost all the adverse reactions. There were then three major types of that part of the vaccine, each with a different risk factor. Although one version was most likely responsible for the child's illness, at least one of the defendants also marketed one of the other vaccines at the same time. Should plaintiff have sought market share liability against only those who marketed the likely cause? One of the cases on which *Shackil* relied concluded that public policy goals would be subverted by allowing market share liability for producers of vital vaccines. A legislative approach to the vaccine injuries is discussed in Chapter XI.

d. *Blood clotting factors.* A blood coagulant used by hemophiliacs may give rise to market share liability even though the product "does not have the constant quality of DES [because] the donor source of the plasma is not a constant." The plasma in question came from donors infected with HIV. If all defendants were negligent in their acquisition and production methods, the court thought it appropriate to develop "new rules of causation, for otherwise innocent plaintiffs would be left without a remedy." The court adopted a national market. Smith v. Cutter Biological, Inc., 823 P.2d 717 (Haw.1991).

e. *Paint shop products.* The doctrine was rejected in Setliff v. E.I. Du Pont de Nemours & Co., 38 Cal.Rptr.2d 763 (App.1995), involving a plaintiff who worked in a paint shop and claimed he was harmed by volatile organic compounds (VOCs). He sued 40 defendants who had supplied products that included VOCs but he could not identify which compound had caused his harm. Market share analysis was rejected because there was no allegation that the products alleged to have caused the harm were fungible in their harmful capacity—only that VOCs were common to paint and other related products.

7. For an extended discussion of the possible justifications for *Sindell* and an exploration of possible extensions, see Robinson, Multiple Causation in Tort Law: Reflections on the DES Cases, 68 Va.L.Rev. 713 (1982). The author suggests that "As long as liability is proportionate to the risks created by a defendant, there is no reason why the *Sindell* liability rule cannot be applied to cases involving multiple and *different* risk-creating activities." He posits a victim who has contracted cancer and three events that contributed to the risk of his developing cancer: he worked as an asbestos installer for 20 years; then he worked 10 years at a chemical plant where he was exposed to chemical wastes; and he took medication that created a risk of cancer. Robinson suggests that if the estimates of these three contributions to cancer were 60/20/20, each might be held liable in those percentages under a modest extension of *Sindell*. Would it be preferable to put all liability on the asbestos company? See Twerski, Market Share—A Tale of Two Centuries, 55 Brook.L.Rev. 869 (1989).

Although other causes might have produced the cancer, Robinson suggests that it is not necessary to bring all, or even most, possible causes before the court. In such cases, the "plaintiff would bear the costs associated with the unidentified causal agenda." The same result would follow for identified but non-actionable causes. Would this pattern be an improvement over the current treatment of causation?

8. *The statute of repose and the statute of limitations.* The *Hymowitz* case involved long lapses of time between the sale and the harm. Indeed, as noted, the legislature adopted special legislation to permit such late filings. In Tanges v. Heidelberg North America, Inc., 710 N.E.2d 250 (N.Y.1999), plaintiff was hurt by defendant's printing press, which had been first sold by defendant ten years and three months before plaintiff was injured while using it. Since the alleged defective manufacturing and the injury both occurred in Connecticut, the court decided to use that state's statute to test whether the suit was timely. The Connecticut statute provided that any claim involving a product had to be brought within three years after the injury and not "later than ten years from the date that the party last parted with possession or control of the product." As the *Tanges* court explained:

> Statutes of repose are theoretically and functionally distinct from typical time limitations. The former are an increasingly common feature of comprehensive products liability codifications. States use the enhanced repose concept as a tool to alleviate the increasing cost burden borne by manufacturers and sellers seeking to obtain products liability insurance. [ ] Unlike the usual limitation provision, which does not begin to run until a cause of action accrues [ ], a statute of repose begins to run when the specific event takes place, regardless of whether a potential claim has accrued or, indeed, whether any injury has occurred.

As the court noted, under Connecticut law this claim was extinguished before it arose. The court concluded that one benefit of using the Connecticut statute in this case was that it "should help to discourage forum shopping, and may improve judicial efficiency and provide fair, even-handed justice to all parties.'' How would using the Connecticut statute achieve that purpose?

Perhaps the most prominent statute of repose is one that takes effect 18 years after the manufacturer of a general aviation aircraft delivers the aircraft ''to its first purchaser or lessee.'' General Aviation Revitalization Act of 1994 (GARA), Pub.Law 103.238, 49 U.S.C.A. § 40101 note. GARA is discussed and applied in Campbell v. Parker–Hannifin Corp., 82 Cal. Rptr.2d 202 (App. 1999). See also Comment, A Critical Evaluation of the General Aviation Revitalization Act of 1994, 63 J.Air L. & Com. 759 (1998).

4.   THE SPECIAL CASE OF TOXIC HARMS

The causal relation issue has been central to a wide variety of extensively publicized concerns about toxics in the environment: among others, claims based on asbestos, Agent Orange, hazardous wastes, and atomic test fallout. These environmental harm controversies, along with silicone breast implants and drug cases such as DES and Bendectin, have posed a number of distinctive issues for the tort system that are discussed in the following excerpt.

Environmental Liability and the Tort System
Robert L. Rabin.
24 Houston Law Review 27, 27–32 (1987).

. . .

. . . . Essentially, environmental liability stands out in bold relief from the generality of everyday risks embraced by tort law because of three critical characteristics that are found, singly or in combination, in every case of harm from toxics or other pollutants. I will refer to these characteristics of environmental liability as problems of *identification, boundaries* and *source.*

(1) *Problems of Identification.* Through the centuries of common law development, the identification of a tortious injury has hardly ever been a problem. At earliest common law, it was the unwanted intrusion on the land of another or the physical violation of a right to bodily integrity. Well into the twentieth century, one finds remarkably little change on this score. Auto accidents and overcharged coke bottles are the modern-day counterpart of trespassers and runaway buggies from the pre-industrial era. The focus is consistently on an accidental injury, the relatively sudden event in which the victim's bodily security or property is violated. If problems of causation exist, they are ordinarily of the ''whodunit'' variety, rather than issues of whether the victim actually suffered identifiable harm that can be isolated from the everyday risks of living.

But it is precisely this latter inquiry which characterizes the case of environmental harm. Toxics of all sorts—impure water, hazardous chemicals, defective synthetics—often breed disease rather than cause immediate injury. As a consequence, the tort system is severely tested. Since diseases do not occur instantaneously, there are serious time-lag issues. And because diseases are frequently a product of the background risks of living (or at least intertwined with those risks), technical information is essential to establish attribution. Thus, *identification*, ordinarily a routine issue of cause in fact at common law, is a costly enterprise that relies on types of evidence and probability judgments which can be regarded as ill-suited to traditional resolution through the adversary process.

(2) *Problems of Boundaries.* Let us assume that through epidemiological studies, laboratory tests or rough mortality data it can be established that a particular widespread incidence of disease was "caused" by the release of an identifiable toxic substance. At first blush, environmental liability may then appear to be similar to a classical mass tort episode— akin to a commercial airline disaster or the collapse of a hotel balcony. But appearances are deceiving; once again, the case of environmental harm frequently creates problems that place special stress on the tort system.

The crux of the matter, again, is the accident/disease distinction. The harm suffered in an airplane crash is extensive but it is also bounded. Most of the victims die, and, apart from derivative loss, there are virtually no post-generational consequences. Contrast the toxic tort scenario. In cases like Agent Orange and hazardous waste dump exposure, the claims are potentially unbounded. Victims of exposure not yet ill fear that it is only a matter of time before they show signs of pathology, *in utero* exposure is an overriding concern, and generations not yet conceived may suffer genetic damage.

Moreover, these are only the most peripheral claims. Even with respect to first-generation, identifiable victims, the *ex ante* assessment of limits on liability is often highly open-ended. Unlike an airplane or public facilities disaster, the aggregate exposure can be hard to define in advance. In addition, the extent of harm may be unpredictable because the need for post-exposure treatment is extensive (degeneration rather than instant death is, by and large, far more common in toxic tort episodes than mass accident cases) and the array of disorders is far more wide-ranging.

By *boundaries,* then, I have in mind an *ex ante* assessment of the magnitude of harm. Mass accident torts are rare at common law, and in fact, put the flexibility of the tort system to the test when they occur. But they pose nothing like the challenge of unconfined liability intrinsic to many environmental harms. In common law terms, valuation of damages is the crux of the matter. Asbestos and the emerging toxic tort cases claim victims in the thousands, not the low hundreds. And, the intrinsic vagaries of chemically-induced diseases introduce bizarre pathologies that are costly to treat and raise intergenerational concerns which vex a torts process designed for more modest purposes. In sum, it is both the two-party structure of traditional tort litigation and the underlying premise of sudden accidental injury that are confounded by environmental harm.

(3) *Problems of Source.* A generation ago, tort lawyers viewed the frontiers of causal responsibility as defined by cases like *Summers v. Tice,* the classic accident situation in which the victim could not identify which

of his two careless hunting companions fired the shotgun pellet which entered his eye. *Summers* seems almost an ancient artifact bearing witness to the practices of an earlier epoch when compared with the source-related issues presented by toxic tort and pollution cases. To venture for a moment into the world of conjecture (or, perhaps, nightmare), suppose at some future date uncertainty over the harmful effects of chlorofluorocarbon emissions is resolved through an extraordinarily sharp rise in the incidence of skin cancer. To continue in a speculative vein, assume that the multitude of victims can properly pursue a class action. Would the action be appropriately brought against the thousands of emitters of chlorofluorocarbons including the producers of aerosols, foams, solvents, freezers and insulation materials? Should the multinational chemical companies producing the constituent products be joined? What about the host governments that approve (or, at least, allow) the processes to be undertaken? The prospects stagger the imagination.

But one need not create a parade of future horribles to illustrate the problem. The vast array of asbestos producers and insurers, or the typical participants in the hazardous waste chain of distribution—generators, transporters and operators of sites—are present-day examples of the singular difficulties in dealing with problems of *source* in environmental liability cases.

Here, too, the long-standing premises of tort law are challenged by the rise of toxic and pollutant harms. Because tort law has traditionally been concerned with accidents, the search for a responsible source has never raised overwhelming difficulties. At most, the classic single-party focus of responsibility is extended slightly along a horizontal axis in cases like *Summers v. Tice* or a multi-car collision. Under other circumstances, the single-party focus may be extended slightly along a vertical (production/distribution) axis in cases where a defective product may be the responsibility of an assembler and manufacturers of component parts. But these modest variations on the two-party tort configuration in which some*one* is responsible for the harm clearly are of small consequence to the system.

By contrast, environmental torts evoke an entirely different perspective on liability, one which is virtually unknown at common law. Frequently, environmental harm is a consequence of the aggregate risk created by a considerable number of independently acting enterprises. It may be that the risk generated by any single source is, in fact, inconsequential. Or, it may be that the risk inherent in the product is substantial, but it soon merges into a common pool. Whatever the case, environmental harm is very often *collective* harm.

Acid rain, chlorofluorocarbons, Agent Orange, and asbestos fibers confound the private law perspective in a dual sense. Not only are they potentially the source of widespread harm, but they are frequently produced by a vast number of discrete enterprises, each making independent decisions about the extent to which they will degrade or endanger the commons. Traditional tests of causal responsibility—the but-for principle, substantial factor causation, *pro rata* joint-and-several liability—are operating in foreign territory when they are employed in such cases. They are premised on a wrongful act that in itself triggers accidental harm, an act that can be isolated and pinned down as consequential.

In view of these distinctive characteristics, it is small wonder that environmental liability has achieved special recognition in discourse about standards of liability and the efficacy of the torts process. Automobiles and power lawnmowers may wreak havoc, but their dangers are readily cognizable. We understand how they work and why they go awry. Toxic substances evoke the special apprehensions of unseen risks. They emanate from sources that are hard to identify. They attack us unawares, planting the seeds of future debilitating disease. They run a course that we cannot discern. Translated into legal terms, they pose unique challenges to a tort system premised on adversary treatment of easily identifiable two-party accidents.

Notes and Questions

1. In a following section, the article points out that not all cases of environmental harm exhibit the same distinctive characteristics. The article discusses three scenarios: (1) individualized harm such as Ferebee v. Chevron Chemical Co., 736 F.2d 1529 (D.C.Cir.1984), in which an agricultural worker claimed toxic poisoning from exposure to a herbicide; (2) multiple party harm in which injuries occurred to residents of a discrete and limited geographical area; and (3) mass tort claims such as the thousands of cases arising from asbestos exposure.

2. *Mass tort claims: aggregation issues.* The latter category, in particular, places singular strains on the tort system—partly because of causation-related issues, but also due to the procedural difficulties created by the enormous volume of cases. The complexities in aggregating mass tort claims are discussed in Matter of Rhone–Poulenc Rorer, Inc., 51 F.3d 1293 (7th Cir.), cert. denied 516 U.S. 867 (1995) (rejecting HIV-infected hemophiliacs' class action against blood solids suppliers) and Coffee, Class Wars: The Dilemma of the Mass Tort Class Action, 95 Colum.L.Rev. 1343 (1995).

In Castano v. American Tobacco Co., 84 F.3d 734 (5th Cir.1996), the court overturned the certification of a nationwide class of nicotine-dependent tobacco plaintiffs. Relying heavily on *Rhone–Poulenc Rorer*, the court pointed out that variations in applicable state law, as well as serious doubts that the Rule 23(b)(3) class action requirements of superiority over individual treatment and predominance of common issues were satisfied, led to the conclusion that the tobacco litigation was not then suited for aggregate treatment.

After the de-certification of a nationwide class action in *Castano*, plaintiffs' attorneys filed a large number of statewide class actions against the tobacco industry with almost no greater success. See Kearns, Decertification of Statewide Tobacco Class Actions, 74 N.Y.U. L.Rev. 1336 (1999). In a notable exception, however, a Florida appellate court upheld certification of a statewide class in R.J. Reynolds Tobacco Co. v. Engle, 672 So.2d 39

(Fla.App.), review denied, 682 So.2d 1100 (Fla.1996). A jury awarded three class representative plaintiffs a total of $12.7 million in compensatory damages. In the punitive phase of the case, the jury in mid-2000, awarded $144.8 billion. The case is on appeal; the next phase would involve mini-trials on compensatory damages for the 300,000–700,000 class members.

In Amchem Products, Inc. v. Windsor, 521 U.S. 591 (1997), the Court affirmed, 6–2, the court of appeals, which had thrown out a major class action settlement of asbestos-related claims—again involving interpretation of the requirements of Rule 23(b)(3). The plaintiff class included both already injured and "exposure-only" victims; claimants presented a wide array of diseases. The majority quoted approvingly from the Third Circuit opinion:

> Class members were exposed to different asbestos-containing products, for different amounts of time, in different ways, and over different periods. Some class members suffer no physical injury or have only asymptomatic pleural changes, while others suffer from lung cancer, disabling asbestosis, or from mesothelioma. . . . Each has a different history of cigarette smoking, a factor that complicates the causation inquiry.

> The [exposure-only] plaintiffs especially share little in common, either with each other or with the presently injured class members. It is unclear whether they will contract asbestos-related disease and, if so, what disease each will suffer. They will also incur different medical expenses because their monitoring and treatment will depend on singular circumstances and individual medical histories.

Although the benefits of settlement were not to be ignored, the majority went on to point out that differences in applicable state law and doubts about adequate representativeness of the named parties compounded its concerns about the settlement—which it proceeded to vacate.

In Ortiz v. Fibreboard Corp., 527 U.S. 815 (1999), the Court rejected the lower courts' approval of a proposed global settlement of another asbestos class action. The majority held that the record before the trial judge did not justify certifying the class because it failed to "support the essential premises of mandatory limited fund actions." The record relied on below "failed to demonstrate that the fund was limited except by the agreement of the parties, and it showed exclusions from the class and allocations of assets at odds with the concept of limited fund treatment and the structural protections of Rule 23(a) explained in *Amchem*."

For a succinct treatment of Rule 23 provisions for class actions in the context of mass tort claims, see J. Eggen, Toxic Torts (2d ed. 2000), Chapter 9. The topic is generally given more detailed consideration in advanced courses.

3. *Future claimants.* For an especially useful survey of the entire range of issues raised by mass torts episodes, see Report of the Advisory Committee on Civil Rules and the Working Group on Mass Torts, Civil

Rules Advisory Committee (1999). With regard to future claimants, the Report comments:

> Particularly troublesome problems arise from injuries that may not become manifest until many years after exposure to the causal event. Injuries from exposure to asbestos, for example, may not occur until decades have passed. The resulting substantive law issues include whether remedies should be awarded to "exposure only" victims for medical monitoring, fear of future injury, and risk of future injury. A related problem is that statutes of limitations may force plaintiffs to file claims before the fact or extent of injury can be known, substantially expanding the number of claims filed. These accelerated filings lead to the problem of finding methods to defer consideration of plaintiffs with no present needs in favor of those who have serious present injuries.

> The mirror image of these questions arises from the desire of defendants to achieve closure—to buy "global peace"—by resolving all present and future claims at once. Any procedure that would purport to bind future claimants would have to provide them with adequate representation and at least some form of notice. Representation problems arise partly from the difficulty of finding lawyers who are experienced, capable of vigorously litigating the claims, and free from disabling conflicts between present and future claimants. It also is difficult, if not impossible, to provide meaningful notice to people who may not be aware of their past exposure. It has been suggested that one means of addressing this problem might be to follow the approach of Rule 23(b)(3) class actions by providing future claimants an opportunity to opt out of a settlement or even a litigated judgment after they become aware of actual injury. But such opt-out provisions raise questions of their own, and could discourage settlement by making global peace difficult, if not impossible, for defendants to obtain.

> Another concern arises when there is a perceptible risk that a defendant lacks sufficient assets to compensate fully all present and future claimants. Inclusion of future claimants becomes a question not merely of achieving peace for the defendant but also of ensuring that future claimants have an opportunity for compensation reasonably equal to that of present claimants.

4. *Medical monitoring.* In Bower v. Westinghouse Electric Corp., 522 S.E.2d 424 (W.Va.1999), the court addressed the question whether "a plaintiff who does not allege a present physical injury can assert a claim for the recovery of future medical monitoring costs where such damages are the proximate result of defendant's tortious conduct." Plaintiffs, who had no then-existing symptoms, alleged that defendant manufacturer of light bulbs had exposed them to a contaminated source containing 30 potentially deleterious substances.

Citing a number of jurisdictions that had recognized such an action, the court first pointed out that claims for future damage are routinely recognized when coupled with present physical harm. The court then refused to treat physical harm as a necessary condition to allowing medical monitoring costs, quoting with approval the policy considerations detailed in Potter v. Firestone Tire and Rubber Co., 863 P.2d 795 (Cal.1993):

> First, there is an important public health interest in fostering access to medical testing for individuals whose exposure to toxic chemicals creates an enhanced risk of disease, particularly in light of the value of early diagnosis and treatment for many cancer patients. [   ] Second, there is a deterrence value in recognizing medical surveillance claims— "[a]llowing plaintiffs to recover the cost of this care deters irresponsible discharge of toxic chemicals by defendants. . . ." [   ] Third, "[t]he availability of a substantial remedy before the consequences of the plaintiffs' exposure are manifest may also have the beneficial effect of preventing or mitigating serious future illnesses and thus reduce the overall costs to the responsible parties." [   ] In this regard, the early detection of cancer may improve the prospects for cure, treatment, prolongation of life and minimization of pain and disability. Finally, societal notions of fairness and elemental justice are better served by allowing recovery of medical monitoring costs. That is, it would be inequitable for an individual wrongfully exposed to dangerous toxins, but unable to prove that cancer or disease is likely, to have to pay the expense of medical monitoring when such intervention is clearly reasonable and necessary. [   ]

The *Bower* court next set out its criteria for recognizing such claims:

> . . . in order to sustain a claim for medical monitoring expenses under West Virginia law, the plaintiff must prove that (1) he or she has, relative to the general population, been significantly exposed; (2) to a proven hazardous substance; (3) through the tortious conduct of the defendant; (4) as a proximate result of the exposure, plaintiff has suffered an increased risk of contracting a serious latent disease; (5) the increased risk of disease makes it reasonably necessary for the plaintiff to undergo periodic diagnostic medical examinations different from what would be prescribed in the absence of the exposure; and (6) monitoring procedures exist that make the early detection of a disease possible.

Assume that the normal risk in a community of 100,000 is that some disease will strike two persons in their lifetimes. After an escape of gas from defendant's plant, the risk is shown to have risen to five in 100,000 for those in a neighborhood of 5,000 downwind from the plant. If there is a monitoring procedure that can detect the onset of the disease before a standard medical examination could do so, does this mean that everyone in that neighborhood will be entitled to medical surveillance costs for the rest of their lives? In the hypothetical, note that the defendant has more than doubled the exposure risk of the neighborhood. Suppose surveillance in such cases involves expensive scanning and laboratory tests? How might the majority in *Bower* analyze this case?

Should it matter if the disease is invariably fatal? The *Bower* court thought not, adopting the position of a concurring judge in Bourgeois v. A.P. Green Indus., Inc., 716 So.2d 355 (La.1998):

> One thing that . . . a plaintiff might gain [even in the absence of available treatment] is certainty as to his fate, whatever it might be. If a plaintiff has been placed at an increased risk for a latent disease through exposure to a hazardous substance, absent medical monitoring, he must live each day with the uncertainty of whether the disease is present in his body. If, however, he is able to take advantage of medical monitoring and the monitoring detects no evidence of disease, then, at least for the time being, the plaintiff can receive the comfort of peace of mind. Moreover, even if medical monitoring did detect evidence of an irreversible and untreatable disease, the plaintiff might still achieve some peace of mind through this knowledge by getting his financial affairs in order, making lifestyle changes, and, even perhaps, making peace with estranged loved ones or with his religion. Certainly, those options should be available to the innocent plaintiff who finds himself at an increased risk for a serious latent disease through no fault of his own.

For a skeptical view of monitoring liability see *Metro-North*, p. 270, supra, in which the Court, after rejecting recovery for emotional distress, barred, 7–2, the recovery of lump-sum medical monitoring costs. The Court concluded that the cases allowing recovery "do not endorse a full-blown traditional tort law cause of action for lump-sum damages—of the sort that the Court of Appeals seems to have endorsed here." Rather, those courts were seen as suggesting court-supervised funds or other limitations on traditional tort damages. The Court noted the "uncertainty among professionals about just which tests are most usefully administered and when. [ ] And in part those difficulties can reflect the fact that scientists will not always see a medical need to provide systematic scientific answers to the relevant legal question, namely, whether an exposure calls for extra monitoring." The court also suggested a concern about a "flood" of "less important cases (potentially absorbing resources better left available to those more seriously harmed [ ]), and the systemic harms that can accompany 'unlimited and unpredictable liability' (for example, vast testing liability adversely affecting the allocation of scarce medical resources.)"

5. *Fear of future injury and risk of future injury.* As the excerpt from the Advisory Committee report, quoted in note 3 supra, indicates, these types of injury claims, like medical monitoring, tend to be characteristic of toxic harm cases. Nonetheless, they raise cross-cutting issues that apply more generally to the conceptual framework of accidental harm cases. We have considered fear of future injury claims, p. 270, supra, in the section on duty to compensate for emotional distress, and we addressed enhanced risk of future injury claims, p. 346, supra, in the section on causation in conjunction with probabilistic harm issues.

6. There have been a number of useful case studies of the range of perplexing issues raised by mass tort episodes. In particular, see J. Sanders,

Bendectin on Trial: A Study of Mass Tort Litigation (1998); M. Green, Bendectin and Birth Defects: The Challenges of Mass Toxic Substances Litigation (1996); M. Angell, Science on Trial: The Clash of Medical Evidence and the Law in the Breast Implant Litigation (1996); and P. Schuck, Agent Orange on Trial: Mass Toxic Disasters in the Courts (1986).

7. Would causation issues be more fairly and efficiently decided under an administrative scheme than through tort litigation? See Rabin, Some Thoughts on the Efficacy of a Mass Toxics Administrative Compensation Scheme, 52 Md.L.Rev.951 (1993). No-fault and social insurance replacements for the tort system are discussed generally in Chapter XI.

B. PROXIMATE CAUSE

In the cases presented in this section, either the plaintiff has made out the elements previously discussed—duty, breach of duty, and cause in fact—or else they are sufficiently in dispute that the defendant cannot establish the absence of any of them as a matter of law. Instead, the defendant will argue that even a negligent defendant who actually caused the harm in question should not be liable for the plaintiff's harm. The legal formulation of the claim is that the defendant's admitted or assumed negligence was not the proximate cause (or "legal cause") of the plaintiff's harm. The cases in which this claim is given serious consideration tend to have one feature in common—something quite unexpected has contributed either to the occurrence of the harm or to its severity.

1. UNEXPECTED HARM

Benn v. Thomas

Supreme Court of Iowa, 1994.
512 N.W.2d 537.

Considered by McGIVERIN, C.J., and HARRIS, LARSON, SNELL, and ANDREASEN, JJ.

McGIVERIN, CHIEF JUSTICE.

The main question here is whether the trial court erred in refusing to instruct the jury on the "eggshell plaintiff" rule in view of the fact that plaintiff's decedent, who had a history of coronary disease, died of a heart attack six days after suffering a bruised chest and fractured ankle in a motor vehicle accident caused by defendant's negligence. The court of appeals concluded that the trial court's refusal constituted reversible error. We agree with the court of appeals and reverse the judgment of the trial court and remand for a new trial.

[Benn's executor sued defendant for Loras Benn's injuries and his death in 1989 after defendant's vehicle rear-ended the van in which decedent was a passenger.]

At trial, the estate's medical expert, Dr. James E. Davia, testified that Loras had a history of coronary disease and insulin-dependent diabetes. Loras had a heart attack in 1985 and was at risk of having another. Dr. Davia testified that he viewed "the accident that [Loras] was in and the attendant problems that it cause[d] in the body as the straw that broke the camel's back" and the cause of Loras's death. Other medical evidence indicated the accident did not cause his death.

Based on Dr. Davia's testimony, the estate requested an instruction to the jury based on the "eggshell plaintiff" rule, which requires the defendant to take his plaintiff as he finds him, even if that means that the defendant must compensate the plaintiff for harm an ordinary person would not have suffered. [Plaintiff requested the following charge:

> If Loras Benn had a prior heart condition making him more susceptible to injury than a person in normal health, then the Defendant is responsible for all injuries and damages which are experienced by Loras Benn, proximately caused by the Defendant's actions, even though the injuries claimed produced a greater injury than those which might have been experienced by a normal person under the same circumstances.

The trial judge denied that request and instead gave the following general charge:

> The conduct of a party is a proximate cause of damage when it is a substantial factor in producing damage and when the damage would not have happened except for the conduct. "Substantial" means the party's conduct has such an effect in producing damage as to lead a reasonable person to regard it as a cause.

Special Verdict Number 4 asked the jury: "Was the negligence of Leland Thomas a proximate cause of Loras Benn's death?" The jury answered this question, "No." The jury returned a verdict for $17,000 for Loras's injuries but nothing for his death. In its special verdict, the jury determined the defendant's negligence in connection with the accident did not proximately cause Loras's death. The court of appeals reversed the trial court's judgment for $17,000 and remanded the case because the charge given to the jury failed to convey the applicable law.]

A tortfeasor whose act, superimposed upon a prior latent condition, results in an injury may be liable in damages for the full disability. [ ] This rule deems the injury, and not the dormant condition, the proximate cause of the plaintiff's harm. [ ] This precept is often referred to as the "eggshell plaintiff" rule, which has its roots in cases such as Dulieu v. White & Sons, [1901] 2 K.B. 669, 679, where the court observed:

> If a man is negligently run over or otherwise negligently injured in his body, it is no answer to the sufferer's claim for damages that he would have suffered less injury, or no injury at all, if he had not had an unusually thin skull or an unusually weak heart. [ ]

. . . .

Defendant contends that plaintiff's proposed instruction was inappropriate because it concerned damages, not proximate cause. Although the eggshell plaintiff rule has been incorporated into the Damages section of the Iowa Uniform Civil Jury Instructions, we believe it is equally a rule of proximate cause. See Christianson v. Chicago, St. Paul, Minneapolis & Omaha Ry. Co., 69 N.W. 640, 641 (Minn.1896) ("Consequences which follow in unbroken sequence, without an intervening efficient cause, from the original negligent act, are natural and proximate; and for such consequences the original wrongdoer is responsible, even though he could not have foreseen the particular results which did follow.").

Defendant further claims that the instructions that the court gave sufficiently conveyed the applicable law. . . .

We agree that the jury might have found the defendant liable for Loras's death as well as his injuries under the instructions as given. But the proximate cause instruction failed to adequately convey the existing law that the jury should have applied to this case. The eggshell plaintiff rule rejects the limit of foreseeability that courts ordinarily require in the determination of proximate cause. [   ] Once the plaintiff establishes that the defendant caused some injury to the plaintiff, the rule imposes liability for the full extent of those injuries, not merely those that were foreseeable to the defendant. Restatement (Second) of Torts § 461 (1965) ("The negligent actor is subject to liability for harm to another although a physical condition of the other . . . makes the injury greater than that which the actor as a reasonable man should have foreseen as a probable result of his conduct.").

The instruction given by the court was appropriate as to the question of whether defendant caused Loras's initial personal injuries, namely, the fractured ankle and the bruised chest. This instruction alone, however, failed to adequately convey to the jury the eggshell plaintiff rule, which the jury reasonably could have applied to the cause of Loras's death.

Defendant maintains "[t]he fact there was extensive heart disease and that Loras Benn was at risk any time is not sufficient" for an instruction on the eggshell plaintiff rule. Yet the plaintiff introduced substantial medical testimony that the stresses of the accident and subsequent treatment were responsible for his heart attack and death. Although the evidence was conflicting, we believe that it was sufficient for the jury to determine whether Loras's heart attack and death were the direct result of the injury fairly chargeable to defendant Thomas's negligence. [   ]

.   .   .

To deprive the plaintiff estate of the requested instruction under this record would fail to convey to the jury a central principle of tort liability.

.   .   .

The record in this case warranted an instruction on the eggshell plaintiff rule. We therefore affirm the decision of the court of appeals. We reverse the judgment of the district court and remand the cause to the district court for a new trial consistent with this opinion.

Notes and Questions

1. Do questions of actual causation exist in this case?

2. What is wrong with the instruction the trial court gave?

3. In the famous case of Dillon v. Twin State Gas & Electric Co., 163 A. 111 (N.H.1932), a boy lost his balance while sitting on the girder of a bridge. In an effort to avoid falling, he grabbed hold of a negligently exposed wire and was electrocuted. The court concluded that if it were found that the boy would have been killed by the fall without regard to the wire, any award against the defendant utility for the exposed wire should be reduced drastically. Is that sound? Can *Dillon* be reconciled with *Benn*?

4. In Steinhauser v. Hertz Corp., 421 F.2d 1169 (2d Cir.1970), although the 14-year-old plaintiff sustained no bodily injury in a minor automobile accident, she began, within minutes, to behave in "an unusual way." In the following days "things went steadily worse." She was institutionalized for a period and diagnosed with a "chronic schizophrenic reaction." The court cited a variety of events in plaintiff's life that occurred shortly before the accident and might have given her "a predisposition to schizophrenia which, however, requires a 'precipitating factor' to produce an outbreak." The court held that the trial judge had committed prejudicial error by failing to charge that plaintiff was entitled to recover for the schizophrenia if the jury concluded that it had been "precipitated" by the accident. At the same time the court observed that the existence of the prior tendencies might greatly affect damages. Defendants were entitled to explore the possibility that plaintiff would have developed schizophrenia in any event. On this point the court concluded that although this kind of prediction may be "taxing" for those "who have devoted their lives to psychiatry, it is one for which a jury is ideally suited."

5. In Bartolone v. Jeckovich, 481 N.Y.S.2d 545 (App.Div. 1984), plaintiff was slightly injured in a four-car chain reaction collision, suffering primarily from whiplash and back strain for which he was treated with muscle relaxants and physical therapy. He was a single 48-year-old man who worked as a carpenter. He was "very proud of his physique and his strength, spending an average of four hours daily . . . engaged in body building." On weekends, he painted, sang, and played music. Since the accident, plaintiff had been withdrawn, hostile, delusional, heard voices, refused to cut his hair, shave or bathe, and no longer participated in any of his former activities.

It appeared at the trial that plaintiff's mother and sister had died of cancer at early ages and that plaintiff had probably acquired a fear and dislike of physicians. His body building was being done to avoid doctors and ward off illness. After the accident, he perceived that his "bodily integrity was impaired and that he was physically deteriorating." This led to psychological and social deterioration as well. The consensus of the plaintiff's experts was that plaintiff had "suffered from a pre-existing schizophrenic illness which had been exacerbated by the accident [and] was now in a chronic paranoid schizophrenic state which is irreversible." The trial judge cut plaintiff's award of $500,000 to $30,000. The appellate court reinstated the verdict. A defendant "must take a plaintiff as he finds him and hence may be liable in damages for aggravation of a preexisting illness." The court noted that the defense had argued that plaintiff's schizophrenia "had not been exacerbated by the accident" and apparently had not argued that the accident only "precipitated" the onset. Was that a wise strategy?

6. *Suicide.* Courts have shown an increasing willingness to allow recoveries where the defendant's negligence has severely injured a person who later commits suicide. In Fuller v. Preis, 322 N.E.2d 263 (N.Y.1974), the victim was a 43-year-old surgeon who sustained injuries in an automobile accident that left him subject to seizures and caused a physical deterioration. Meanwhile, his wife, who had been partially paralyzed by polio, suffered "nervous exhaustion." Seven months after the crash he learned that his mother had cancer. One of his suicide notes warned his family to destroy it because "it would alter the outcome of the 'case'—i.e., it's worth a million dollars to you all." The court held that the required "irresistible impulse" did not necessarily mean a "sudden impulse." The jury could find that the irresistible impulse that "caused decedent to take his life also impelled the acquisition of the gun and the writing of the suicide notes."

See also Zygmaniak v. Kawasaki Motors Corp., 330 A.2d 56 (App. 1974)(defendant liable for the death of a victim who was shot and killed at the victim's request by his brother after defendant's negligence had rendered the victim a quadriplegic); Stafford v. Neurological Medicine, Inc., 811 F.2d 470 (8th Cir.1987)(defendant liable for suicide after negligently permitting patient to receive mail indicating incorrectly that she was suffering from a brain tumor). But recall the reluctance of courts to hold negligent attorneys liable for the suicides of disappointed clients, p. 309, supra.

7. *Emotional distress.* In discussing claims based on emotional distress, courts often say that to be actionable the harm must be such that it would cause distress in the ordinarily sensitive person or the reasonably constituted person. Recall *Gammon,* p. 278, supra. If that standard is met in a case, should the plaintiff's recovery be limited by such a standard or should plaintiff recover the harm that plaintiff actually sustained even if it is greater than what an "ordinarily sensitive person" would have suffered?

8. *Secondary harm.* In Stoleson v. United States, 708 F.2d 1217 (7th Cir.1983), plaintiff worked in a munitions plant and was found to have suffered heart problems from negligently being exposed to nitroglycerine. Although the harm was temporary and should have stopped when plaintiff ceased working at the factory, she developed hypochondria after the episode and was unable to function normally. The court adverted to the possibility that the plaintiff's condition was brought about by medical advice given her after the exposure to nitroglycerine had ended:

> If a pedestrian who has been run down by a car is taken to a hospital and because of the hospital's negligence incurs greater medical ex-

penses or suffers more pain and suffering than he would have if the hospital had not been negligent, he can collect his incremental as well as his original damages from the person who ran him down, since they would have been avoided if that person had used due care.

Is the original wrongdoer liable if the hospital staff reasonably chooses a course of treatment that does not work—if it later appears that another reasonable choice would in fact have done the job? Why?

9. Does the principle from the medical aggravation cases extend to transportation to the hospital for needed attention? In Pridham v. Cash & Carry Bldg. Center, Inc., 359 A.2d 193 (N.H.1976), plaintiff, who had been seriously injured by defendant's negligence, died when the ambulance driver transporting him to a hospital suffered a heart attack and the ambulance swerved into a tree. The trial judge charged that the defendant was liable for further injuries resulting from "normal efforts of third persons in rendering aid . . . which the other's injury reasonably requires irrespective of whether such acts are done in a proper or in a negligent manner." The charge was upheld on appeal from a plaintiff's judgment. If medical services "are rendered negligently, the rule based on questions of policy makes the negligence of the original tortfeasor a proximate cause of the subsequent injuries suffered by the victim." The ambulance trip was a "necessary step in securing medical services required by the accident at Cash & Carry." Should it matter whether the ambulance was racing to the hospital or proceeding in the normal stream of traffic?

In Anaya v. Superior Court, 93 Cal.Rptr.2d 228 (App. 2000), plaintiff's child was injured in an accident with a city garbage truck. As she was being airlifted to a hospital, the helicopter crashed and she was killed. The cases that imposed liability on the original tortfeasor for subsequent malpractice, were authority for imposing liability for aggravation incurred during transportation to the hospital.

10. In Wagner v. Mittendorf, 134 N.E. 539 (N.Y.1922), the defendant negligently broke plaintiff's leg. While plaintiff was recovering, through no fault of his own his crutch slipped and the leg was rebroken. The court held the defendant liable for that aggravation. Why? What if the plaintiff must use crutches permanently and is killed ten years later in a fire because of his inability to run away?

———

The Polemis case. In the English case of *In re Polemis*, [1921] 3 K.B. 560 (Ct.App.1921), while stevedores were moving benzine from one hold to another on the ship Thrasyvoulos, a worker carelessly dropped a wooden board into the hold. Fire broke out and the ship was destroyed. The case centered on whether those responsible for the acts of the careless stevedore were liable for the loss of the ship. A panel of arbitrators, whose fact findings were binding, found "that the fire arose from a spark igniting petrol vapour in the hold; that the spark was caused by the falling board coming into contact with some substance in the hold; . . . . [and] that the causing of the spark could not reasonably have been anticipated from the falling of the board though some damage to the ship might reasonably have been anticipated." The court of appeal affirmed an award of the full loss to the owners. Lord Justice Bankes noted that a split existed:

> According to the one view, the consequences which may reasonably be expected to result from a particular act are material only in reference to the question whether the act is or is not a negligent act; according to the other view, those consequences are the test whether the damages resulting from the act, assuming it to be negligent, are or are not too remote to be recoverable.

He adopted the first view, observing that the "fire appears to me to have been directly caused by the falling of the plank. Under these circumstances I consider that it is immaterial that the causing of the spark by the falling of the plank could not have been reasonably anticipated." Lord Justice Scrutton, in his opinion, stated:

> Once the act is negligent, the fact that its exact operation was not foreseen is immaterial. . . . In the present case it was negligent in discharging cargo to knock down the planks of the temporary staging, for they might easily cause some damage either to workmen, or cargo, or the ship. The fact that they did directly produce an unexpected result, a spark in an atmosphere of petrol vapour which caused a fire, does not relieve the person who was negligent from the damage which his negligent act directly caused.

Polemis played a central role in the following case.

Overseas Tankship (U.K.) Ltd. v. Morts Dock & Engineering Co., Ltd. (The Wagon Mound)

Privy Council, 1961.
[1961] A.C. 388.

[Plaintiffs-respondents, a ship-repairing firm, owned a wharf in Sydney Harbour, Australia, and were refitting the ship Corrimal. At a different wharf, about 600 feet away, the ship Wagon Mound, chartered by defendants, was taking on bunkering oil. A large quantity of bunkering oil spilled into the bay and some of it concentrated near plaintiffs' property. Defendants set sail, making no effort to disperse the oil. When plaintiffs' manager became aware of the condition he stopped all welding and burning until he could assess the danger. Based on discussions with the manager at the Wagon Mound berth and his own understanding about furnace oil in open waters, he felt he could safely order activities to be resumed with all precautions taken to prevent flammable material from falling off the wharf into the oil.

For two days work proceeded and there was no movement of the oil. Then, oil under or near the wharf was ignited and a fire spread, causing extensive damage to the wharf and plaintiffs' equipment. The trial judge found that floating on the oil underneath the wharf was a piece of debris on which lay some cotton waste or rag that had caught fire from molten metal falling from the wharf, and that this set the floating oil afire either directly or by first setting fire to a wooden pile coated with oil.

[The trial judge awarded judgment to the plaintiffs and the Full Court of the Supreme Court of New South Wales dismissed the defendants' appeal.]

Viscount Simonds [after stating the facts].

The trial judge also made the all-important finding, which must be set out in his own words: "The *raison d'être* of furnace oil is, of course, that it shall burn, but I find the defendant did not know and could not reasonably be expected to have known that it was capable of being set afire when spread on water." This finding was reached after a wealth of evidence, which included that of a distinguished scientist, Professor Hunter. It receives strong confirmation from the fact that at the trial the respondents strenuously maintained that the appellants had discharged petrol into the bay on no other ground than that, as the spillage was set alight, it could not be furnace oil. An attempt was made before their Lordships' Board to limit in some way the finding of fact, but it is clear that it was intended to cover precisely the event that happened.

One other finding must be mentioned. The judge held that apart from damage by fire the respondents had suffered some damage from the spillage of oil in that it had got upon their slipways and congealed upon them and interfered with their use of the slips. He said: "The evidence of this damage is slight and no claim for compensation is made in respect of it. Nevertheless it does establish some damage, which may be insignificant in comparison with the magnitude of the damage by fire, but which nevertheless is damage which, beyond question, was a direct result of the escape of the oil." It is upon this footing that their Lordships will consider the question whether the appellants are liable for the fire damage.   .   .   .

.   .   .

There can be no doubt that the decision of the Court of Appeal in *Polemis* plainly asserts that, if the defendant is guilty of negligence he is responsible for all the consequences whether reasonably foreseeable or not. The generality of the proposition is perhaps qualified by the fact that each of the Lords Justices refers to the outbreak of fire as the direct result of the negligent act. There is thus introduced the conception that the negligent actor is not responsible for consequences which are not "direct," whatever that may mean.   .   .   .

.   .   . If the line of relevant authority had stopped with *Polemis*, their Lordships might, whatever their own views as to its unreason, have felt some hesitation about overruling it. But it is far otherwise.   .   .   .

.   .   .

Enough has been said to show that the authority of *Polemis* has been severely shaken though lip-service has from time to time been paid to it. In their Lordships' opinion it should no longer be regarded as good law. It is not probable that many cases will for that reason have a different result, though it is hoped that the law will be thereby simplified, and that in some cases, at least, palpable injustice will be avoided. For it does not seem consonant with current ideas of justice or morality that for an act of negligence, however slight or venial, which results in some trivial foreseeable damage the actor should be liable for all consequences however unforeseeable and however grave, so long as they can be said to be "direct." It is a principle of civil liability, subject only to qualifications which have no present relevance, that a man must be considered to be responsible for the probable consequences of his act. To demand more of him is too harsh a rule, to demand less is to ignore that civilized order requires the observance of a minimum standard of behaviour.

[handwritten margin note: probable = forseeable ; too harsh = unfair]

This concept applied to the slowly developing law of negligence has led to a great variety of expressions which can, as it appears to their Lordships, be harmonized with little difficulty with the single exception of the so-called rule in *Polemis.* For, if it is asked why a man should be responsible for the natural or necessary or probable consequences of his act (or any other similar description of them) the answer is that it is not because they are natural or necessary or probable, but because, since they have this quality, it is judged by the standard of the reasonable man that he ought to have foreseen them. Thus it is that over and over again it has happened that in different judgments in the same case, and sometimes in a single judgment, liability for a consequence has been imposed on the ground that it was reasonably foreseeable or, alternatively, on the ground that it was natural or necessary or probable. The two grounds have been treated as coterminous, and so they largely are. But, where they are not, the question arises to which the wrong answer was given in *Polemis.* For, if some limitation must be imposed upon the consequences for which the negligent actor is to be held responsible—and all are agreed that some limitation there must be—why should that test (reasonable foreseeability) be rejected which, since he is judged by what the reasonable man ought to foresee, corresponds with the common conscience of mankind, and a test (the "direct" consequence) be substituted which leads to nowhere but the never-ending and insoluble problems of causation. . . .

.   .   .

It is, no doubt, proper when considering tortious liability for negligence to analyze its elements and to say that the plaintiff must prove a duty owed to him by the defendant, a breach of that duty by the defendant, and consequent damage. But there can be no liability until the damage has been done. It is not the act but the consequences on which tortious liability is founded. Just as (as it has been said) there is no such thing as negligence in the air, so there is no such thing as liability in the air. Suppose an action brought by A for damage caused by the carelessness (a neutral word) of B, for example, a fire caused by the careless spillage of oil. It may, of course, become relevant to know what duty B owed to A, but the only liability that is in question is the liability for damage by fire. It is vain to isolate the liability from its context and to say that B is or is not liable, and then to ask for what damage he is liable. For his liability is in respect of that damage and no other. If, as admittedly it is, B's liability (culpability) depends on the reasonable foreseeability of the consequent damage, how is that to be determined except by the foreseeability of the damage which in fact happened—the damage in suit? And, if that damage is unforeseeable so as to displace liability at large, how can the liability be restored so as to make compensation payable?

But, it is said, a different position arises if B's careless act has been shown to be negligent and has caused some foreseeable damage to A. Their Lordships have already observed that to hold B liable for consequences however unforeseeable of a careless act, if, but only if, he is at the same time liable for some other damage however trivial, appears to be neither logical nor just. This becomes more clear if it is supposed that similar unforeseeable damage is suffered by A and C but other foreseeable damage, for which B is liable, by A only. A system of law which would hold B liable to A but not to C for the similar damage suffered by each of them could not easily be defended. Fortunately, the attempt is not necessary. For the same fallacy is at the root of the proposition. It is irrelevant to the question whether B is liable for unforeseeable damage that he is liable for foreseeable damage, as irrelevant as would the fact that he had trespassed on Whiteacre be to the question whether he has trespassed on Blackacre. Again, suppose a claim by A for damage by fire by the careless act of B. Of what relevance is it to that claim that he had another claim arising out of the same careless act? It would surely not prejudice his claim if that other claim failed: it cannot assist it if it succeeds. Each of them rests on its own bottom, and will fail if it can be established that the damage could not reasonably be foreseen. . . .

Their Lordships conclude this part of the case with some general observations. They have been concerned primarily to displace the proposition that unforeseeability is irrelevant if damage is "direct." In doing so they have inevitably insisted that the essential factor in determining liability is whether the damage is of such a kind as the reasonable man should have foreseen. This accords with the general view thus stated by Lord Atkin in *Donoghue v. Stevenson*: "The liability for negligence, whether you style it such or treat it as in other systems as a species of 'culpa,' is no doubt based upon a general public sentiment of moral wrongdoing for which the offender must pay." It is a departure from this sovereign principle if liability is made to depend solely on the damage being the "direct" or "natural" consequence of the precedent act. Who knows or can be assumed to know all the processes of nature? But if it would be wrong that a man should be held liable for damage unpredictable by a reasonable man because it was "direct" or "natural," equally it would be wrong that he should escape liability, however "indirect" the damage, if he foresaw or could reasonably foresee the intervening events which led to its being done. . . . <u>Thus foreseeability becomes the effective test</u>. In reasserting this principle their Lordships conceive that they do not depart from, but follow and develop, the law of negligence as laid down by Baron Alderson in *Blyth v. Birmingham Waterworks Co.* [discussed in note 8 infra].

. . .

Their Lordships will humbly advise Her Majesty that this appeal should be allowed, and the respondents' action so far as it related to damage caused by the negligence of the appellants be dismissed with costs. . . . The respondents must pay the costs of the appellants of this appeal and in the courts below.

Notes and Questions

1.   The Judicial Committee of the Privy Council had jurisdiction over appeals from the Commonwealth courts, whereas the House of Lords had jurisdiction over appeals from British courts. In the House of Lords, each judge delivers an opinion, but the Privy Council at the time of this case delivered but one opinion—and no dissents. Since the Privy Council was advising Her Majesty on the disposition, a single opinion was thought more useful. It is rumored that the Privy Council split 3–2 in *Wagon Mound*. See The Foresight Saga 3 (Haldane Society 1962).

2.   The court observes that "all are agreed" that there must be some limitation upon the consequences for which the negligent actor is held responsible. Would setting such a limit be facilitated by ascertaining its purpose?

3.   What is the basis for the court's decision? Is it dictated by logic?

4.   In Smith v. Leech Brain & Co., [1962] 2 Q.B. 405, through the defendant's negligence in providing inadequate shielding, a worker was burned on the lip by a piece of molten metal. The burn was treated but did not heal. It ulcerated, developed into cancer that spread, and the worker died of cancer three years later. The judge found that the worker had probably become pre-disposed to cancer by ten years of work in the gas industry earlier in his life. He held that *Wagon Mound* did not alter the principle that a defendant must take his victim as he finds him:

> The test is not whether these employers could reasonably have foreseen that a burn would cause cancer and he would die. The question is whether these employers could reasonably foresee the type of injury he suffered, namely, the burn. What, in the particular case, is the amount of damage which he suffers as a result of that burn, depends upon the characteristics and constitution of the victim.

Is this approach consistent with *Wagon Mound?*

5.   After *Wagon Mound,* is there room for a distinction between the "type" and the "extent" of harm? Suppose the defendant is driving negligently through skid row and runs down a person who appears to be one of the derelicts on the street. In fact the victim is a successful and highly paid athlete who was posing as a derelict to work among the area's residents. How might Viscount Simonds respond to the defendant's argument that he could reasonably expect to have done only minor harm—and not the great harm suffered by this prosperous athlete and his or her family?

6. Assume that the foreseeable cloggage could be expected to affect 10 feet of slipway and to cause $10,000 worth of damage. What if an unprecedented wind occurs after the negligence with the result that the slipway is clogged for 30 feet with a loss of $30,000? How might Viscount Simonds analyze this? What about $50,000 worth of unforeseeable fire damage? $5,000 worth of unforeseeable fire damage?

7. Viscount Simonds puts the example of A and C who suffer damage at the hands of B. He suggests that a system that allowed A to recover for the negligently inflicted unforeseeable harm but denied such recovery to C "could not easily be defended." Why not? Is the problem allowing A to recover or not allowing C to recover?

8. In Blyth v. Birmingham Waterworks Co., 11 Exch. 781 (1856), cited at the end of *Wagon Mound*, the defendant's water main sprang a leak during an unprecedented frost and the escaping water damaged plaintiff's house. On appeal from a jury verdict for the plaintiff, Baron Alderson concluded: "Such a state of circumstances constitutes a contingency against which no reasonable man can provide. The result was an accident for which the defendants cannot be held liable." How does this opinion support the *Wagon Mound* court?

9. The owners of the Corrimal brought a separate action against the charterers of the Wagon Mound. The trial judge held against plaintiffs on the negligence claim. The Privy Council reversed. Overseas Tankship (U.K.), Ltd. v. Miller Steamship Co. (Wagon Mound No. 2), [1967] 1 A.C. 617. The Privy Council read the trial judge's findings to suggest that the defendants might have foreseen a very slight danger of fire. This contrasted with the finding in No.1 that the defendant "did not know and could not reasonably be expected to have known that [the oil] was capable of being set afire when spread on water." The Privy Council reconciled the two cases by noting that in No.1 if the plaintiffs had tried "to prove that it was foreseeable by the engineers of the Wagon Mound that this oil could be set alight, they might have had difficulty in parrying the reply that then this must also have been foreseeable by their manager. Then there would have been contributory negligence" which would have been a complete defense. Does this suggest something about the nature of the adversary process and the purposes of litigation?

There was no such embarrassment in this case. The Privy Council saw the new finding as raising a question akin to that presented in the cricket case, *Bolton v. Stone*, p. 46, supra, in which the risk was not totally unforeseeable but rather was judged too small to dictate evasive action. "But it does not follow that, no matter what the circumstances may be, it is justifiable to neglect a risk of such a small magnitude. A reasonable man would only neglect such a risk if he had some valid reason for doing so: e.g., that it would involve considerable expense to eliminate the risk." The Council found liability because discharging the oil could not be justified since it also caused a major loss to defendants: "If the ship's engineer had thought about the matter there could have been no question of balancing the advantages and disadvantages. From every point of view it was both his duty and his interest to stop the discharge immediately.''

What might Viscount Simonds have said if the fire had occurred shortly after the discharge of the oil and before the plaintiff had reason to know of any oil in the area?

10. In an omitted footnote in *Zuchowicz*, p. 349, supra, Judge Calabresi addressed the need to "link" defendant's conduct to the plaintiff's harm:

> The effect of the requirement that a defendant's act or omission be causally linked to, or have a causal tendency toward, the harm that occurs is demonstrated most dramatically in cases in which (a) *but for* the defendant's actions the accident would clearly not have occurred, and (b) the defendant's actions are extremely close in time and space to the harm that came about, yet no one can reasonably believe that what the defendant did, though wrong, enhanced (at the time the defendant acted) the chances of the harm occurring or that it would increase the chances of a similar accident in the future if the defendant should repeat the same wrong. In such a situation, the requirement of causal link is not met and the defendant is not held liable.

> The leading case involving this requirement is Berry v. Sugar Notch Borough, 43 A. 240 (Pa.1899). In *Berry*, a tree fell on a trolley car whose excess speed had caused the tram to be at that specific place when the tree fell. The court held that the requirement of causation was not met. This result was correct since, although the accident would not have occurred *but for* the trolley's speeding, speeding does not increase the probability of trees falling on trolleys. Other similar cases (termed "darting out" cases) involve speeders who but for their velocity would not have been at the particular spot when children darted out from behind trees, etc., and were hit. In such cases—assuming that, had the speeders been at the same spot at the same time, they would have been unable to avoid the collision even if they were driving within the speed limit—no liability results. [   ]

> In a sense, the *causal link* requirement and the *but for* requirement are two different but related ways of asking whether a defendant's actions were a substantial factor in causing the injury. Causal link says that, even if defendant's wrong was a *but for* cause of the injury in a given case, no liability ensues unless defendant's wrong increases the chances of such harm occurring in general. *But for* says even if what the defendant did greatly increased the risk of certain injuries occurring, unless it was a *sine qua non* of the specific harm that actually came about, no liability will be assessed w/o which not

Is the result in *Berry* sound?

Does the "linking principle" help analyze Ventricelli v. Kinney System Rent A Car, 383 N.E.2d 1149 (N.Y.1978)? Plaintiff's rented car had a defective rear trunk lid that flew up while plaintiff was driving. Plaintiff pulled the car over into a regular parking space along the city street and was trying to get the lid to stay down when he was hit by a car. The lessor was held not liable. In a later case, the court explained its result in *Ventricelli* by stating that although the lessor's negligence "undoubtedly served to place the injured party at the site of the accident, the intervening act was divorced from and not the foreseeable risk associated with the original negligence. And the injuries were different in kind than those which would have normally been expected from a defective trunk. In short, the negligence of the renter merely furnished the occasion for an unrelated act to cause injuries not ordinarily anticipated." The quotation is from Derdiarian v. Felix Contracting Corp., 414 N.E.2d 666 (N.Y.1980).

The court in Betancourt v. Manhattan Ford Lincoln Mercury Inc., 607 N.Y.S.2d 924 (App.Div. 1994), refused to apply *Ventricelli* where a defective car is forced to pull over to the side of a busy highway—as opposed to stopping in a legal parking space.

11. Recall *DeHaen,* p. 80, supra, in which Judge Cardozo thought it important to identify the purposes behind the statute's requirement of a barrier around an open hole at a construction site. Did that analysis use "linking"? Is the statutory purpose question analogous to the proximate cause question presented in these cases?

2.   UNEXPECTED MANNER

In the previous section, we considered situations in which the defendant claimed that the harm that resulted was unexpected given the nature of the negligent act. In this section, the defendant contends that although the harm that occurred was of the sort that might have been expected, the manner of its occurrence justifies exculpating the defendant. For example, plaintiff alleged that the defendant Los Angeles Transit had negligently allowed a wooden power pole on a main road to deteriorate to such an extent that when a negligent driver crashed into it, it fell over onto the plaintiff who was walking by at the time. Gibson v. Garcia, 216 P.2d 119 (Cal.App.1950). The court rejected the defendant's argument that, although it might be liable if the pole had simply fallen by itself, it should not be liable when the fall was caused by a negligent driver. Do you agree with the court? If so, can you imagine any situation in which you would exculpate the defendant because of what caused the pole to come down?

McLaughlin v. Mine Safety Appliances Co.

Court of Appeals of New York, 1962.
11 N.Y.2d 62, 181 N.E.2d 430, 226 N.Y.S.2d 407.

[Plaintiff was removed unconscious from a lake after nearly drowning. The local fire department brought blankets but more heat was needed and a fireman gave a nurse at the scene heating blocks marketed by defendant. The blocks were covered in "flocking" that resembled flannel. Attached to the flocking was a label containing the block's trade name and the defendant's name and design. On the cardboard container was written, "Always

Ready for Use'' and, in much smaller print, instructions for use—the last one of which said ''Wrap in insulation medium, such as pouch, towel, blanket or folded cloth.''

One fireman at the scene, Traxler, testified that he recalled having been told by defendant's representative at a training session some five years earlier that the block must be insulated before use, that he was fully aware of the need for insulation, and that he had told the nurse to wrap the blocks before using. Then the nurse applied the blocks directly to the plaintiff's body while Traxler, who had activated the blocks, stood next to her and watched. The plaintiff's aunt could recall hearing no warning about insulation from Traxler to the nurse. Plaintiff received third degree burns from the blocks.

On appeal from a judgment for plaintiff, the appellate division affirmed after plaintiff agreed to a reduction in damages.]

FOSTER, J.

. . .

The jury, under the court's instructions, could have found that a hidden or latent danger existed in the use of the product, or at least that the form and design of the product itself, together with the printing on the container, could mislead ultimate users as to the need for further insulation. [ ] The blocks were dressed in ''flocking'' and appeared to be insulated, and the bold lettering on the containers revealed that the blocks were ''ALWAYS READY FOR USE'' and ''ENTIRELY SELF CONTAINED,'' all of which seemed to indicate that nothing extrinsic to the contents of the package was needed. And inasmuch as the blocks were designed for use on the human body, and if improperly used could cause severe injuries, the jury was justified in finding that the final sentence of the instructions, found in small print on the back side of the containers, advising use of a further insulating medium, was totally inadequate as a warning commensurate with the risk; indeed, they were entitled to find that the *instructions,* not particularly stressed, did not amount to a *warning of the risk at all,* and that it was foreseeable that the small print instruction might never be read, and might be disregarded even if read [ ]. It also was foreseeable, and the jury could have found, that the blocks would be reused ultimately by persons without notice of the risks involved in failing to insulate, long after the cardboard containers bearing the so-called ''warning'' had been dispensed with, and that the distributor would be liable to such unwarned ultimate users. The containers themselves encouraged such reuse, and told how new ''charges'' could be obtained.

But the true problem presented in this case is one of proximate causation, and not one concerning the general duty to warn or negligence of the distributor. In this regard the trial court instructed the jury that the defendant would not be liable if ''an actual warning was conveyed to the person or persons applying the blocks that they should be wrapped in insulation of some kind before being placed against the body'' for in that event the ''failure to heed that warning would be a new cause which intervened." Subsequently, and after the jury retired, they returned and asked this question: "Your Honor, if we, the jury, find that the M.S.A. Company was negligent in not making any warning of danger on the heat block itself, but has given proper instructions in its use up to the point of an intervening circumstance (the nurse who was not properly instructed), is the M.S.A. Company liable?"

The trial court answered as follows: "Ladies and gentlemen of the jury, if you find from the evidence that the defendant, as a reasonably prudent person under all of the circumstances should have expected use of the block by some person other than those to whom instruction as to its use had been given, either by the wording on the container or otherwise, and that under those circumstances a reasonably prudent person would have placed warning words on the heat block itself, and if you find in addition to that that the nurse was not warned at the scene and that a reasonably prudent person in the position of the nurse, absent any warning on the block itself, would have proceeded to use it without inquiry as to the proper method of use, then the defendant would be liable." Counsel for the defendant excepted to that statement. The jury then returned its verdict for the plaintiffs.

From the jury's question, it is obvious that they were concerned with the effect of the fireman's knowledge that the blocks should have been wrapped, and his apparent failure to so advise the nurse who applied the blocks in his presence. The court in answering the jury's question instructed, in essence, that the defendant could still be liable even though the fireman had knowledge of the need for further insulation, if it was reasonably foreseeable that the blocks, absent the containers, would find their way from the fireman to unwarned third persons.

We think that the instruction, as applied to the facts of this case, was erroneous. In [cases discussed by the court], the manufacturer or distributor failed to warn the original vendee of the latent danger, and there were no additional acts of negligence intervening between the failure to warn and the resulting injury or damage. This was not such a case, or at least the jury could find that it was not. Nor was this simply a case involving the negligent failure of the vendee to inspect and discover the danger; in such a case the intervening negligence of the immediate vendee does not necessarily insulate the manufacturer from liability to third persons, nor supersede the negligence of the manufacturer in failing to warn of the danger (Rosebrock v. General Elec. Co., 236 N.Y. 227 [1923]; Sider v. General Elec. Co., 203 App.Div. 443 [1922], affd. 238 N.Y. 64 [1924]).

In the case before us, the jury obviously believed that the fireman, Traxler, had actual knowledge of the need for further insulation, and the jury was preoccupied with the effect of his failure to warn the nurse as she applied the blocks to the plaintiff's person. The jury also could have believed that Traxler removed the blocks from the containers, thereby depriving the nurse of *any* opportunity she might have had to read the instructions printed on the containers, and that Traxler actually activated the blocks, turned them over, uninsulated, to the nurse for her use, and stood idly by as they were placed directly on the plaintiff's wet skin.

Under the circumstances, we think the court should have charged that if the fireman did so conduct himself, without warning the nurse, his negligence was so gross as to supersede the negligence of the defendant and to insulate it from liability. This is the rule that prevails when knowledge of the latent danger or defect is *actually* possessed by the original vendee, who then deliberately passes on the product to a third person without warning (see Stultz v. Benson Lbr. Co., 6 Cal.2d 688 [1936]; Catlin v. Union Oil Co., 31 Cal.App. 597 [1916]; [   ]).

In short, whether or not the distributor furnished ample warning on his product to third persons in general was not important here, if the jury believed that Traxler had actual notice of the danger by virtue of his presence at demonstration classes or otherwise, and that he deprived the nurse of her opportunity to read the instructions prior to applying the blocks. While the distributor might have been liable if the blocks had found their way into the hands of the nurse in a more innocent fashion, the distributor could not be expected to foresee that its demonstrations to the firemen would callously be disregarded by a member of the department.   .   .   .

Here, the jury might have found that the fireman not only had the means to warn the nurse, but further that, by his actions, he prevented any warning from reaching her, and, indeed, that he actually had some part in the improper application of the blocks. Such conduct could not have been foreseen by the defendant.

.   .   .

The judgment should be reversed and a new trial granted, with costs to abide the event.

Van Voorhis, J. (dissenting). The recovery by plaintiff should not, as it seems to us, be reversed on account of lack of foreseeability or a break in the chain of causation due to any intervening act of negligence on the part of a volunteer fireman. These heat blocks were dangerous instrumentalities unless wrapped in "insulating" media, "such as pouch, towel, blanket or folded cloth" as the instructions on the container directed. What happened here was that the container, with the instructions on it, was thrown away, and the nurse who applied the heat block was unaware of this safety requirement. In our minds the circumstances that the fireman who knew of the danger failed to warn the nurse, even if negligent, did not affect the fact, as the jury found it, that this was a risk which the manufacturer of the heat block ought to have anticipated in the exercise of reasonable care, nor intercept the chain of causation. The jury found by their verdict that a duty was imposed on the manufacturer to inscribe the warning on the heat block for the reason that in the exercise of reasonable care it should have anticipated that the warning written on the container might be lost or discarded under circumstances similar to those surrounding this injury.

The rule is not absolute that it is not necessary to anticipate the negligence or even the crime of another. It has been said in the Restatement of Torts (§ 449): "If the realizable likelihood that a third person may act in a particular manner is the hazard or one of the hazards which makes the actor negligent, such an act whether innocent, negligent, intentionally tortious or criminal does not prevent the actor from being liable for harm caused thereby." It is further provided by section 447: "The fact that an intervening act of a third person is negligent in itself or is done in a negligent manner does not make it a superseding cause of harm to another which the actor's negligent conduct is a substantial factor in bringing about, if (a) the actor at the time of his negligent conduct should have realized that a third person might so act" [   ].

The judgment appealed from should be affirmed.

JUDGES FULD, FROESSEL and BURKE concur with JUDGE FOSTER; JUDGE VAN VOORHIS dissents in an opinion in which JUDGE DYE concurs; CHIEF JUDGE DESMOND taking no part.

Notes and Questions

1. What negligence on MSA's part might the jury reasonably have found?

2. What if Traxler had testified, and was believed, that:

a. He remembered about the wrapping and warned the nurse.

b. He thought he remembered but wasn't sure and assumed the nurse knew best.

c. He forgot—the course had been many years earlier and had been quite short.

d. He forgot even though the course had been only a short time before.

e. He remembered about the wrapping but stayed silent because the victim was a person who had been bothering him over the years.

In Cohen v. St. Regis Paper Co., 481 N.E.2d 562 (N.Y.1985), a worker was killed by exposure to dry ice. In a claim against the supplier of the ice, the supplier argued that even if it had failed to provide a warning of the dangers involved, it was not liable because the employer knew the danger and did not warn the worker. The court rejected the argument because here there was "no evidence of gross negligence such as there was in *McLaughlin*, where the warnings that might otherwise have been seen were removed and the remover stood idly by while the decedent was exposed to danger." It was for the jury to decide whether the employer's "negligent failure to warn" relieved the supplier of liability.

3. Is it essential to the majority that Traxler may have removed the block from the container? What if the nurse removed the block without reading the container—but a person standing in the crowd knew how to use the block, realized the nurse was misusing it, and said nothing? Is the problem the fireman's possible contribution to the harm or the callousness of a person who watched another get burned?

4. How are the Restatement sections that the dissent quotes relevant to the case? In Hines v. Garrett, 108 S.E. 690 (Va.1921), a train improperly carried the 18-year-old plaintiff a mile past her stop. The conductor told her to walk back to the depot, even though he knew she would have to walk through a disreputable area known as Hoboes' Hollow. In her action against the railroad for damages for rape, the court held that the intervening criminal conduct did not insulate the railroad from liability. Is *Hines* comparable to the principal case?

5. Consider the relevance of Second Restatement § 435, which provides as follows:

(1) If the actor's conduct is a substantial factor in bringing about harm to another, the fact that the actor neither foresaw nor should have foreseen the extent of the harm or the manner in which it occurred does not prevent him from being liable.

(2) The actor's conduct may be held not to be a legal cause of harm to another where after the event and looking back from the harm to the actor's negligent conduct, it appears to the court highly extraordinary that it should have brought about the harm.

How might each opinion have used § 435?

6. In Addis v. Steele, 648 N.E.2d 773 (Mass.App.1995), guests at an inn were injured when forced to jump from a second floor window to escape a late-night fire. Their claim of negligent failure to provide lights or reasonable escape paths withstood defendant's claim that it was not liable because the fire was set by an arsonist. The defendant's obligation was to anticipate fire from whatever source. It had failed in that respect and the actual source of this fire was irrelevant. Would the analysis be the same if the fire was started by the first recorded lightning in the region?

Compare Johnson v. Kosmos Portland Cement Co., 64 F.2d 193 (6th Cir.), cert. denied 290 U.S. 641 (1933), in which the defendant allowed a barge to become and remain full of potentially explosive petroleum gases that exploded, hurting nearby workers. Is such conduct negligent? Should it matter whether the cause of the spark was ordinary lightning? Unprecedented lightning? An arsonist? Should the cause of the explosion be relevant to the defendant's liability?

Why not say that the defendant's obligation in *McLaughlin v. MSA* was to anticipate burns from whatever source?

7. In the cited *Catlin* case, the defendant negligently delivered a mixture of gasoline and kerosene to Riley's store in response to an order for kerosene. Riley sold quantities of the mixture to customers who immediately complained that something was wrong. Riley tested their purchases and the other containers that defendant had delivered and decided that some of the delivered containers had been pure kerosene, some pure gasoline, and some a mixture. He called defendant, who agreed to take back this delivery.

Shortly afterward, Catlin asked for kerosene and Riley sold him a quantity of the liquid from the disputed delivery in the belief that this container was pure kerosene. In fact there was some gasoline mixed in with the kerosene. When Catlin sought to use the liquid at home, it exploded and burned him fatally. Pure kerosene would not have exploded under those conditions. The court held that defendant was not liable because Riley had become aware of the problem.

8.   If foreseeability is to play a role in these cases, we must first decide what it is that needs to be foreseeable. Professor Clarence Morris has addressed this question in considering the role of unusual details in these cases:

> For example, in *Hines v. Morrow*,[17] two men were sent out in a service truck to tow a stalled car out of a mud hole. One of them, the plaintiff, made a tow rope fast and tried to step from between the vehicles as the truck started. His artificial leg slipped into the mud hole in the road, which would not have been there had defendant-railroad not disregarded its statutory duty to maintain this part of the highway. He was unable to pull out his peg-leg and was in danger of being run over by the stalled car. He grabbed the tailgate of the service truck to use its forward force to pull him loose. A loop in the tow rope lassoed his good leg, tightened, and broke his good leg. As long as these details are considered significant facts of the case, the accident is unforeseeable. No doubt some judges would itemize the facts and hold that the railroad's neglect was not the proximate cause of the injury. As a matter of fact, courts have on occasion ruled that much less freakish injuries were unforeseeable. But in the peg-leg case, the court quoted with approval the plaintiff's lawyer's "description" of the "facts," which was couched in these words, "The case, stated in the briefest form, is simply this: Appellee was on the highway, using it in a lawful manner, and slipped into this hole, created by appellant's negligence, and was injured in undertaking to extricate himself." The court also adopted the injured man's answer to the railroad's attempt to stress unusual details: "Appellant contends [that] it could not reasonably have been foreseen that slipping into this hole would have caused the appellee to have become entangled in a rope, and the moving truck, with such dire results. The answer is plain: The exact consequences do not have to be foreseen."
>
> In this . . . class of cases, foreseeability can be determined only after the significant facts of the case have been described. If official description of the facts of the case as formulated by the court is detailed, the accident can be called unforeseeable; if it is general, the accident can be called foreseeable. Since there is no authoritative guide to the proper amount of specificity in describing the facts, the process of holding that a loss is—or is not—foreseeable is fluid and often embarrasses attempts at accurate prediction.

---

17.   236 S.W. 183 (Tex.Civ.App.1921).

Professor Morris cautioned that an advocate who pushes too far hurts rather than helps the cause: "A plaintiff's lawyer who insists on a too-general description appears to be trying to suppress important facts; a defense counsel who insists on a too-specific description appears to be taking advantage of mere technicality." Morris on Torts, 164–66 (2d ed. 1980).

In light of the Morris excerpt, consider Phan Son Van v. Pena, 990 S.W.2d 751 (Tex.1999), in which minor gang members illegally obtained alcohol from defendant and got drunk at an initiation ceremony. As two girls happened to wander past, they were raped and murdered by the gang. The court held that the criminal conduct was not foreseeable. "It is foreseeable, for example, that the sale of alcohol to a minor will result in the minor driving while intoxicated and either causing injury or being injured. [   ] On the other hand, the intentional sexual assault and brutal murder of two teenage girls who happen upon a gang initiation some distance in time and location from the illegal sale of alcohol is not the type of harm that would ordinarily result from such a sale."

3. UNEXPECTED VICTIM

Palsgraf v. Long Island Railroad Co.
Court of Appeals of New York, 1928.
248 N.Y. 339, 162 N.E. 99.

[Appeal from a judgment entered on a plaintiff's verdict. The Appellate Division affirmed, 3–2.]

CARDOZO, CH. J. Plaintiff was standing on a platform of defendant's railroad after buying a ticket to go to Rockaway Beach. A train stopped at the station, bound for another place. Two men ran forward to catch it. One of the men reached the platform of the car without mishap, though the train was already moving. The other man, carrying a package, jumped aboard the car, but seemed unsteady as if about to fall. A guard on the car, who had held the door open, reached forward to help him in, and another guard on the platform pushed him from behind. In this act, the package was dislodged, and fell upon the rails. It was a package of small size, about fifteen inches long, and was covered by a newspaper. In fact it contained fireworks, but there was nothing in its appearance to give notice of its contents. The fireworks when they fell exploded. The shock of the explosion threw down some scales at the other end of the platform, many feet away. The scales struck the plaintiff, causing injuries for which she sues.

The conduct of the defendant's guard, if a wrong in its relation to the holder of the package, was not a wrong in its relation to the plaintiff, standing far away. Relatively to her it was not negligence at all. Nothing in the situation gave notice that the falling package had in it the potency of peril to persons thus removed. Negligence is not actionable unless it involves the invasion of a legally protected interest, the violation of a right. "Proof of negligence in the air, so to speak, will not do" (Pollock, Torts

[11th ed.], p. 455; [   ]). "Negligence is the absence of care, according to the circumstances" (Willes, J., in Vaughan v. Taff Vale Ry. Co., 5 H. & N. 679, 688; [   ]; *Adams v. Bullock*, [p. 38, supra]; Parrot v. Wells, Fargo & Co., 15 Wall. [82 U.S.] 524). The plaintiff as she stood upon the platform of the station might claim to be protected against intentional invasion of her bodily security. Such invasion is not charged. She might claim to be protected against unintentional invasion by conduct involving in the thought of reasonable men an unreasonable hazard that such invasion would ensue. These, from the point of view of the law, were the bounds of her immunity, with perhaps some rare exceptions, survivals for the most part of ancient forms of liability, where conduct is held to be at the peril of the actor (Sullivan v. Dunham, 161 N.Y. 290 [1900]). If no hazard was apparent to the eye of ordinary vigilance, an act innocent and harmless, at least to outward seeming, with reference to her, did not take to itself the quality of a tort because it happened to be a wrong, though apparently not one involving the risk of bodily insecurity, with reference to some one else. "In every instance, before negligence can be predicated on a given act, back of the act must be sought and found a duty to the individual complaining, the observance of which would have averted or avoided the injury" (McSherry, C.J., in West Virginia Central & P. Ry. Co. v. State, 96 Md. 652, 666 [1903]; [   ]). "The ideas of negligence and duty are strictly correlative" (Bowen, L.J., in Thomas v. Quartermaine, 18 Q.B.D. 685, 694). The plaintiff sues in her own right for a wrong personal to her, and not as the vicarious beneficiary of a breach of duty to another.

A different conclusion will involve us, and swiftly too, in a maze of contradictions. A guard stumbles over a package which has been left upon a platform. It seems to be a bundle of newspapers. It turns out to be a can of dynamite. To the eye of ordinary vigilance, the bundle is abandoned waste, which may be kicked or trod on with impunity. Is a passenger at the other end of the platform protected by the law against the unsuspected hazard concealed beneath the waste? If not, is the result to be any different, so far as the distant passenger is concerned, when the guard stumbles over a valise which a truckman or a porter has left upon the walk? The passenger far away, if the victim of a wrong at all, has a cause of action, not derivative, but original and primary. His claim to be protected against invasion of his bodily security is neither greater nor less because the act resulting in the invasion is a wrong to another far removed. In this case, the rights that are said to have been violated, the interests said to have been invaded, are not even of the same order. The man was not injured in his person nor even put in danger. The purpose of the act, as well as its effect, was to make his person safe. If there was a wrong to him at all, which may very well be doubted, it was a wrong to a property interest only, the safety of his package. Out of this wrong to property, which threatened injury to nothing else, there has passed, we are told, to the plaintiff by derivation or succession a right of action for the invasion of an interest of another order, the right to bodily security. The diversity of interests emphasizes the futility of the effort to build the plaintiff's right upon the basis of a wrong to some one else. The gain is one of emphasis, for a like result would follow if the interests were the same. Even then, the orbit of the danger as disclosed to the eye of reasonable vigilance would be the orbit of the duty. One who jostles one's neighbor in a crowd does not invade the rights of others standing at the outer fringe when the unintended contact casts a bomb upon the ground. The wrongdoer as to them is the man who carries the bomb, not the one who explodes it without suspicion of the danger. Life will have to be made over, and human nature transformed, before prevision so extravagant can be accepted as the norm of conduct, the customary standard to which behavior must conform.

The argument for the plaintiff is built upon the shifting meanings of such words as "wrong" and "wrongful," and shares their instability. What the plaintiff must show is "a wrong" to herself, i.e., a violation of her own right, and not merely a wrong to some one else, nor conduct "wrongful" because unsocial, but not "a wrong" to any one. We are told that one who drives at reckless speed through a crowded city street is guilty of a negligent act and, therefore, of a wrongful one irrespective of the consequences. Negligent the act is, and wrongful in the sense that it is unsocial, but wrongful and unsocial in relation to other travelers, only because the eye of vigilance perceives the risk of damage. If the same act were to be committed on a speedway or a race course, it would lose its wrongful quality. The risk reasonably to be perceived defines the duty to be obeyed, and risk imports relation; it is risk to another or to others within the range of apprehension [   ]. This does not mean, of course, that one who launches a destructive force is always relieved of liability if the force, though known to be destructive, pursues an unexpected path. "It was not necessary that the defendant should have had notice of the particular method in which an accident would occur, if the possibility of an accident was clear to the ordinarily prudent eye" (Munsey v. Webb, 231 U.S. 150, 156 [1913]; [   ]). Some acts, such as shooting, are so imminently dangerous to any one who may come within reach of the missile, however unexpectedly, as to impose a duty of prevision not far from that of an insurer. Even today, and much oftener in earlier stages of the law, one acts sometimes at one's peril [   ]. Under this head, it may be, fall certain cases of what is known as transferred intent, an act willfully dangerous to A resulting by misadventure in injury to B (Talmage v. Smith, 101 Mich. 370, 374 [1894]). These cases aside, wrong is defined in terms of the natural or probable, at least when unintentional (Parrot v. Wells, Fargo & Co. [The Nitro–Glycerine Case], 15 Wall. [82 U.S.] 524 [1872]). The range of reasonable apprehension is at times a question for the court, and at times, if varying inferences are possible, a question for the jury. Here, by concession, there was nothing in the situation to suggest to the most cautious mind that the parcel wrapped in newspaper would spread wreckage through the station. If the guard had thrown it down knowingly and willfully, he would not have threatened the plaintiff's safety, so far as appearances could warn him. His conduct would not have involved, even then, an unreasonable probability of invasion of her bodily security. Liability can be no greater where the act is inadvertent.

Negligence, like risk, is thus a term of relation. Negligence in the abstract, apart from things related, is surely not a tort, if indeed it is understandable at all [   ]. Negligence is not a tort unless it results in the commission of a wrong, and the commission of a wrong imports the violation of a right, in this case, we are told, the right to be protected against interference with one's bodily security. But bodily security is protected, not against all forms of interference or aggression, but only against some. One who seeks redress at law does not make out a cause of action by showing without more that there has been damage to his person. If the harm was not willful, he must show that the act as to him had possibilities of danger so many and apparent as to entitle him to be protected against the doing of it though the harm was unintended. Affront to personality is still the keynote of the wrong. Confirmation of this view will be found in the history and development of the action on the case. Negligence as a basis of civil liability was unknown to mediaeval law (8 Holdsworth, History of English Law, p. 449; Street, Foundations of Legal Liability, vol. 1, pp. 189, 190). For damage to the person, the sole remedy was trespass and trespass did not lie in the absence of aggression, and that direct and personal [   ]. Liability for other damage, as where a servant without orders from the master does or omits something to the damage of another, is a plant of later growth [   ]. When it emerged out of the legal soil, it was thought of as a variant of trespass, an offshoot of the parent stock. This appears in the form of action, which was known as trespass on the case [   ]. The victim does not sue derivatively, or by right of subrogation, to vindicate an interest invaded in the person of another. Thus to view his cause of action is to ignore the fundamental difference between tort and crime (Holland, Jurisprudence [12th ed.], p. 328). He sues for breach of a duty owing to himself.

The law of causation, remote or proximate, is thus foreign to the case before us. The question of liability is always anterior to the question of the measure of the consequences that go with liability. If there is no tort to be redressed, there is no occasion to consider what damage might be recovered if there were a finding of a tort. We may assume, without deciding, that negligence, not at large or in the abstract, but in relation to the plaintiff, would entail liability for any and all consequences, however novel or extraordinary ([   ]; Smith v. London & S.W. Ry. Co., L.R. 6 C.P. 14; [   ]; cf. Matter of Polemis, L.R. 1921, 3 K.B. 560; [   ]). There is room for argument that a distinction is to be drawn according to the diversity of interests invaded by the act, as where conduct negligent in that it threatens an insignificant invasion of an interest in property results in an unforeseeable invasion of an interest of another order, as, e.g., one of bodily security. Perhaps other distinctions may be necessary. We do not go into the question now. The consequences to be followed must first be rooted in a wrong.

The judgment of the Appellate Division and that of the Trial Term should be reversed, and the complaint dismissed, with costs in all courts.

ANDREWS, J. (dissenting). Assisting a passenger to board a train, the defendant's servant negligently knocked a package from his arms. It fell between the platform and the cars. Of its contents the servant knew and could know nothing. A violent explosion followed. The concussion broke some scales standing a considerable distance away. In falling they injured the plaintiff, an intending passenger.

Upon these facts may she recover the damages she has suffered in an action brought against the master? The result we shall reach depends upon our theory as to the nature of negligence. Is it a relative concept—the breach of some duty owing to a particular person or to particular persons? Or where there is an act which unreasonably threatens the safety of others, is the doer liable for all its proximate consequences, even where they result in injury to one who would generally be thought to be outside the radius of danger? This is not a mere dispute as to words. We might not believe that to the average mind the dropping of the bundle would seem to involve the probability of harm to the plaintiff standing many feet away whatever might be the case as to the owner or to one so near as to be likely to be struck by its fall. If, however, we adopt the second hypothesis we have to inquire only as to the relation between cause and effect. We deal in terms of proximate cause, not of negligence.

.   .   .

But we are told that "there is no negligence unless there is in the particular case a legal duty to take care, and this duty must be one which is owed to the plaintiff himself and not merely to others." (Salmond, Torts [6th ed.], 24.) This I think too narrow a conception. Where there is the unreasonable act, and some right that may be affected there is negligence whether damage does or does not result. That is immaterial. Should we drive down Broadway at a reckless speed, we are negligent whether we strike an approaching car or miss it by an inch. The act itself is wrongful. It is a wrong not only to those who happen to be within the radius of danger but to all who might have been there—a wrong to the public at large. Such is the language of the street.   .   .   .

It may well be that there is no such thing as negligence in the abstract. "Proof of negligence in the air, so to speak, will not do." In an empty world negligence would not exist. It does involve a relationship between man and his fellows. But not merely a relationship between man and those whom he might reasonably expect his act would injure. Rather, a relationship between him and those whom he does in fact injure. If his act has a tendency to harm some one, it harms him a mile away as surely as it does those on the scene. We now permit children to recover for the negligent killing of the father. It was never prevented on the theory that no duty was owing to them. A husband may be compensated for the loss of his wife's services. To say that the wrongdoer was negligent as to the husband as well as to the wife is merely an attempt to fit facts to theory. An insurance company paying a fire loss recovers its payment of the negligent incendiary. We speak of subrogation—of suing in the right of the insured. Behind the cloud of words is the fact they hide, that the act, wrongful as to the insured, has also injured the company. Even if it be true that the fault of father, wife or insured will prevent recovery, it is because we consider the original negligence not the proximate cause of the injury. [   ]

In the well-known *Polemis* Case [   ], Scrutton, L.J., said that the dropping of a plank was negligent for it might injure "workman or cargo or ship." Because of either possibility the owner of the vessel was to be made good for his loss. The act being wrongful the doer was liable for its proximate results. Criticized and explained as this statement may have been, I think it states the law as it should be and as it is. [   ]

The proposition is this: Every one owes to the world at large the duty of refraining from those acts that may unreasonably threaten the safety of others. Such an act occurs. Not only is he wronged to whom harm might reasonably be expected to result, but he also who is in fact injured, even if he be outside what would generally be thought the danger zone. There needs be duty due the one complaining but this is not a duty to a particular individual because as to him harm might be expected. Harm to some one being the natural result of the act, not only that one alone, but all those in fact injured may complain. We have never, I think, held otherwise.   .   .   .

If this be so, we do not have a plaintiff suing by "derivation or succession." Her action is original and primary. Her claim is for a breach of duty to herself—not that she is subrogated to any right of action of the owner of the parcel or of a passenger standing at the scene of the explosion.

The right to recover damages rests on additional considerations. The plaintiff's rights must be injured, and this injury must be caused by the negligence. We build a dam, but are negligent as to its foundations. Breaking, it injures property down stream. We are not liable if all this happened because of some reason other than the insecure foundation. But when injuries do result from our unlawful act we are liable for the consequences. It does not matter that they are unusual, unexpected, unforeseen and unforeseeable. But there is one limitation. The damages must be so connected with the negligence that the latter may be said to be the proximate cause of the former.

These two words have never been given an inclusive definition. What is a cause in a legal sense, still more what is a proximate cause, depend in each case upon many considerations, as does the existence of negligence itself. Any philosophical doctrine of causation does not help us. A boy throws a stone into a pond. The ripples spread. The water level rises. The history of that pond is altered to all eternity. It will be altered by other causes also. Yet it will be forever the resultant of all causes combined. Each one will have an influence. How great only omniscience can say. You may speak of a chain, or if you please, a net. An analogy is of little aid. Each cause brings about future events. Without each the future would not be the same. Each is proximate in the sense it is essential. But that is not what we mean by the word. Nor on the other hand do we mean sole cause. There is no such thing.

Should analogy be thought helpful, however, I prefer that of a stream. The spring, starting on its journey, is joined by tributary after tributary. The river, reaching the ocean, comes from a hundred sources. No man may say whence any drop of water is derived. Yet for a time distinction may be possible. Into the clear creek, brown swamp water flows from the left.

Later, from the right comes water stained by its clay bed. The three may remain for a space, sharply divided. But at last, inevitably no trace of separation remains. They are so commingled that all distinction is lost.

As we have said, we cannot trace the effect of an act to the end, if end there is. Again, however, we may trace it part of the way. A murder at Sarajevo may be the necessary antecedent to an assassination in London twenty years hence. An overturned lantern may burn all Chicago. We may follow the fire from the shed to the last building. We rightly say the fire started by the lantern caused its destruction.

A cause, but not the proximate cause. What we do mean by the word "proximate" is, that because of convenience, of public policy, of a rough sense of justice, the law arbitrarily declines to trace a series of events beyond a certain point. This is not logic. It is practical politics. Take our rule as to fires. Sparks from my burning haystack set on fire my house and my neighbor's. I may recover from a negligent railroad. He may not. Yet the wrongful act has directly harmed the one as the other. We may regret that the line was drawn just where it was, but drawn somewhere it had to be. We said the act of the railroad was not the proximate cause of our neighbor's fire. Cause it surely was. The words we used were simply indicative of our notions of public policy. Other courts think differently. But somewhere they reach the point where they cannot say the stream comes from any one source.

Take the illustration given in an unpublished manuscript by a distinguished and helpful writer on the law of torts. A chauffeur negligently collides with another car which is filled with dynamite, although he could not know it. An explosion follows. A, walking on the sidewalk nearby, is killed. B, sitting in a window of a building opposite, is cut by flying glass. C, likewise sitting in a window a block away, is similarly injured. And a further illustration. A nursemaid, ten blocks away, startled by the noise, involuntarily drops a baby from her arms to the walk. We are told that C may not recover while A may. As to B it is a question for court or jury. We will all agree that the baby might not. Because, we are again told, the chauffeur had no reason to believe his conduct involved any risk of injuring either C or the baby. As to them he was not negligent.

But the chauffeur, being negligent in risking the collision, his belief that the scope of the harm he might do would be limited is immaterial. His act unreasonably jeopardized the safety of any one who might be affected by it. C's injury and that of the baby were directly traceable to the collision. Without that, the injury would not have happened. C had the right to sit in his office, secure from such dangers. The baby was entitled to use the sidewalk with reasonable safety.

The true theory is, it seems to me, that the injury to C, if in truth he is to be denied recovery, and the injury to the baby is that their several injuries were not the proximate result of the negligence. And here not what the chauffeur had reason to believe would be the result of his conduct, but what the prudent would foresee, may have a bearing. May have some

Hypothetical

bearing, for the problem of proximate cause is not to be solved by any one consideration.

It is all a question of expediency. There are no fixed rules to govern our judgment. There are simply matters of which we may take account. We have in a somewhat different connection spoken of "the stream of events." We have asked whether that stream was deflected—whether it was forced into new and unexpected channels. [   ] This is rather rhetoric than law. There is in truth little to guide us other than common sense.

There are some hints that may help us. The proximate cause, involved as it may be with many other causes, must be, at the least, something without which the event would not happen. The court must ask itself whether there was a natural and continuous sequence between cause and effect. Was the one a substantial factor in producing the other? Was there a direct connection between them, without too many intervening causes? Is the effect of cause on result not too attenuated? Is the cause likely, in the usual judgment of mankind, to produce the result? Or by the exercise of prudent foresight could the result be foreseen? Is the result too remote from the cause, and here we consider remoteness in time and space. (Bird v. St. Paul F. & M. Ins. Co., 224 N.Y. 47 [1918], where we passed upon the construction of a contract—but something was also said on this subject.) Clearly we must so consider, for the greater the distance either in time or space, the more surely do other causes intervene to affect the result. When a lantern is overturned the firing of a shed is a fairly direct consequence. Many things contribute to the spread of the conflagration—the force of the wind, the direction and width of streets, the character of intervening structures, other factors. We draw an uncertain and wavering line, but draw it we must as best we can.

Once again, it is all a question of fair judgment, always keeping in mind the fact that we endeavor to make a rule in each case that will be practical and in keeping with the general understanding of mankind.

Here another question must be answered. In the case supposed it is said, and said correctly, that the chauffeur is liable for the direct effect of the explosion although he had no reason to suppose it would follow a collision. "The fact that the injury occurred in a different manner than that which might have been expected does not prevent the chauffeur's negligence from being in law the cause of the injury." But the natural results of a negligent act—the results which a prudent man would or should foresee—do have a bearing upon the decision as to proximate cause. We have said so repeatedly. What should be foreseen? No human foresight would suggest that a collision itself might injure one a block away. On the contrary, given an explosion, such a possibility might be reasonably expected. I think the direct connection, the foresight of which the courts speak, assumes prevision of the explosion, for the immediate results of which, at least, the chauffeur is responsible.

It may be said this is unjust. Why? In fairness he should make good every injury flowing from his negligence. Not because of tenderness toward him we say he need not answer for all that follows his wrong. We look back to the catastrophe, the fire kindled by the spark, or the explosion. We trace the consequences—not indefinitely, but to a certain point. And to aid us in fixing that point we ask what might ordinarily be expected to follow the fire or the explosion.

This last suggestion is the factor which must determine the case before us. The act upon which defendant's liability rests is knocking an apparently harmless package onto the platform. The act was negligent. For its proximate consequences the defendant is liable. If its contents were broken, to the owner; if it fell upon and crushed a passenger's foot, then to him. If it exploded and injured one in the immediate vicinity, to him also as to A in the illustration. Mrs. Palsgraf was standing some distance away. How far cannot be told from the record—apparently twenty-five or thirty feet. Perhaps less. Except for the explosion, she would not have been injured. We are told by the appellant in his brief "it cannot be denied that the explosion was the direct cause of the plaintiff's injuries." So it was a substantial factor in producing the result—there was here a natural and continuous sequence—direct connection. The only intervening cause was that instead of blowing her to the ground the concussion smashed the weighing machine which in turn fell upon her. There was no remoteness in time, little in space. And surely, given such an explosion as here it needed no great foresight to predict that the natural result would be to injure one on the platform at no greater distance from its scene than was the plaintiff. Just how no one might be able to predict. Whether by flying fragments, by broken glass, by wreckage of machines or structures no one could say. But injury in some form was most probable.

Under these circumstances I cannot say as a matter of law that the plaintiff's injuries were not the proximate result of the negligence. That is all we have before us. The court refused to so charge. No request was made to submit the matter to the jury as a question of fact, even would that have been proper upon the record before us.

The judgment appealed from should be affirmed, with costs.

Pound, Lehman and Kellogg, JJ., concur with Cardozo, Ch. J.; Andrews, J., dissents in opinion in which Crane and O'Brien, JJ., concur.

Notes and Questions

1. Motion for reargument was denied, 164 N.E. 564 (N.Y. 1928), with the following opinion:

> If we assume that the plaintiff was nearer the scene of the explosion than the prevailing opinion would suggest, she was not so near that injury from a falling package, not known to contain explosives, would be within the range of reasonable prevision.

How close would have been close enough for the majority? The three original dissenters concurred in the denial of reargument.

2. In what way do the facts of *Palsgraf* differ from those of *Polemis* and *Wagon Mound?* How might the facts of *Wagon Mound* be altered to resemble *Palsgraf?*

3. Are there differences between the approach taken by Judge Cardozo and that taken by Viscount Simonds in *Wagon Mound?* Compare the reasons for limiting liability for negligence offered by Viscount Simonds and Judge Andrews.

4. How might Judge Cardozo analyze the hypothetical involving A, B, and C that is discussed in the next-to-last paragraph of *Wagon Mound?* How would Judge Andrews analyze it?

5. What is the role of proximate cause in *Wagon Mound?* In the Cardozo analysis?

6. How are the functions of judge and jury allocated under the Cardozo view? Under the Andrews view?

7. In what types of cases are Cardozo and Andrews most likely to reach different results?

8. How might Judge Cardozo's suggested distinction between the risk of an insignificant invasion of property and the occurrence of bodily injury work? He suggests other distinctions might be desirable. Assume plaintiff is standing four feet from the railroad agents. Instead of the package falling on P's foot it hits the ground and explodes, taking out one of P's eyes. Would it make sense to distinguish between a risk to the feet and a risk to the eyes?

9. Toward the end of his opinion, Judge Cardozo says that to permit the plaintiff to sue "derivatively" to "vindicate an interest invaded in the person of another" would be to "ignore the fundamental difference between tort and crime." What does he mean?

10. Do the *Palsgraf* facts suggest any other theory on which plaintiff might have been more successful in a suit against the railroad? How should the case have been analyzed if plaintiff had argued that the railroad's negligence was the failure to secure adequately the weighing scale?

11. *Recurring fact patterns of causation questions.* Even though proximate cause cases individually seem freakish, some fact patterns have emerged with some regularity. Consider the following.

a. *Rescue.* Judge Cardozo had previously decided a case in which plaintiff was hurt while trying to rescue his cousin who had fallen from defendant's train due to the negligence of the crew. Wagner v. International Railway Co., 133 N.E. 437 (N.Y.1921). The trial judge had charged that the negligence toward the cousin would not lead to liability to the rescuer unless the jury found that the train conductor had invited the plaintiff to partake in the rescue and had accompanied him with a lantern. Rejecting that approach, Judge Cardozo wrote:

> Danger invites rescue. The cry of distress is the summons to relief. The law does not ignore these reactions of the mind in tracing conduct to its consequences. It recognizes them as normal. It places their

effects within the range of the natural and probable. The wrong that imperils life is a wrong to the imperilled victim; it is a wrong also to his rescuer.   .   .   . The risk of rescue, if only it be not wanton, is born of the occasion. The emergency begets the man. The wrongdoer may not have foreseen the coming of a deliverer. He is accountable as if he had.

Is this consistent with *Palsgraf?* What about a case in which the area is so desolate that the defendant could not reasonably anticipate anyone around to attempt to rescue someone defendant is negligently harming or threatening? Judge Cardozo then turned to another issue:

> The defendant says that we must stop, in following the chain of causes, when action ceases to be "instinctive." By this, is meant, it seems, that rescue is at the peril of the rescuer, unless spontaneous and immediate. If there has been time to deliberate, if impulse has given way to judgment, one cause, it is said, has spent its force, and another has intervened. In this case, the plaintiff walked more than four hundred feet in going to Herbert's aid. He had time to reflect and weigh; impulse had been followed by choice; and choice, in the defendant's view, intercepts and breaks the sequence. We find no warrant for thus shortening the chain of jural causes. We may assume, though we are not required to decide, that peril and rescue must be in substance one transaction; that the sight of the one must have aroused the impulse to the other; in short, that there must be unbroken continuity between the commission of the wrong and the effort to avert its consequences. If all this be assumed, the defendant is not aided. Continuity in such circumstances is not broken by the exercise of volition.   .   .   . The law does not discriminate between the rescuer oblivious of peril and the one who counts the cost. It is enough that the act, whether impulsive or deliberate, is the child of the occasion.

In his Cogitations on Torts 35 (1954), Seavey doubts "that an airplane pilot who negligently crashes on a mountain, would be liable to an injured and non-negligent member of a rescue party." Is that consistent with *Wagner?* Is it sound? Might it matter whether the rescuer is bitten by a snake, struck by lightning, or hurt in the crash of a helicopter that has joined the search? Injuries to professional rescuers are discussed at p. 484, infra.

In Moore v. Shah, 458 N.Y.S.2d 33 (App.Div. 1982), plaintiff alleged that he was a rescuer entitled to recovery where he donated his kidney to his father who had been hurt by defendant's malpractice. Although it was foreseeable that malpractice might create the need for a kidney and that a child might feel the need to donate a kidney to a parent in need, the court denied recovery. The donor's actions were not spontaneous or instantaneous; rather, the son's action was "deliberate and reflective, not made under the pressures of an emergency situation, and significantly, at a time after defendant's alleged negligent acts." Why should the time frame matter? For a discussion of other kidney donation cases, all of which reach the same outcome as *Moore*, see Dabdoub v. Ochsner Clinic, 760 So.2d 347 (La.App. 2000).

b. *Time.* In Firman v. Sacia, 184 N.Y.S.2d 945 (App.Div. 1959), plaintiff alleged that as the result of defendant's negligent driving, he struck a three-year-old boy named Springstead who sustained serious brain injuries that induced him, seven years later, to shoot the plaintiff. Plaintiff alleged that at the time of the shooting Springstead was "unable to realize the nature and consequences of his act, was not able to resist pulling the trigger of the rifle, and was deprived of capacity to govern his conduct in accordance with reason"—though insanity or incompetency was not claimed. The trial judge's dismissal of the complaint was upheld on appeal:

> Assuming, as we must, that defendant's conduct was negligent as it related to the rights of the Springstead child, the fact of negligence was not, of course, thereby established for all purposes or as necessarily definitive of defendant's relationship to others. If, in his conduct, there was no risk of danger to this infant plaintiff "reasonably to be perceived", there was no breach of duty, or negligence, as to him. [*Palsgraf*] In this case, the order and judgment seem to us sustainable on the grounds that, as in *Palsgraf*, the risk was not "within the range of apprehension." [   ]

Does a long time interval between wrongful act and injury necessarily mean the risk is outside "the range of apprehension?" Recall the discussions in *Albala,* p. 166, supra, involving the negligently performed abortion and in *Hymowitz,* p. 378, supra.

Cases involving long time periods between the act and the harm are not usually barred by the statute of limitations. Tort limitations usually start to run at the time of the plaintiff's injury. They have traditionally been even longer in the case of injuries to minors, sometimes allowing the minor to wait until majority before suing. Recently, several states, especially in medical malpractice cases, have shortened the period for minors (and also for adults). On the other hand, as *Hymowitz* indicates, several states, either by statute or by judicial decision, have lengthened some statutes of limitation to protect plaintiffs who may not realize that they have been injured. This is especially likely to occur with conditions that have long incubation periods, such as asbestosis or slowly developing cancers. For further discussion, see Rheingold, The Hymowitz Decision—Practical Aspects of New York DES Litigation, 55 Bklyn.L.Rev. 883 (1989); Green, The Paradox of Statutes of Limitations in Toxic Standards Litigation, 76 Calif.L.Rev. 965 (1988).

c. *Distance.* Defendant negligently collided with another car and careened off the road, hitting a box that contained the master traffic signal devices for several intersections including one two miles away. The lights at that intersection jammed and in the ensuing confusion, plaintiff was hurt in a collision. Liability was imposed. Ferroggiaro v. Bowline, 315 P.2d 446 (App. 1957).

d. *Fire.* The fire rule to which Judge Andrews referred is unique to New York and originated in Ryan v. New York Central R. Co., 35 N.Y. 210 (1866). Sparks from defendant's negligently maintained engine ignited one of its sheds and the fire spread to other buildings, including plaintiff's. The court denied recovery:

> I prefer to place my opinion upon the ground that, in the one case, to wit, the destruction of the building upon which the sparks were thrown by the negligent act of the party sought to be charged, the result was to have been anticipated the moment the fire was communicated to the building; that its destruction was the ordinary and natural result of its being fired. In the second, third or twenty-fourth case, as supposed, the destruction of the building was not a natural and expected result of the first firing. That a building upon which sparks and cinders fall should be destroyed or seriously injured must be expected, but that the fire should spread and other buildings be consumed, is not a necessary or [a] usual result. That it is possible, and that it is not infrequent, cannot be denied. The result, however, depends, not upon any necessity of a further communication of the fire, but upon a concurrence of accidental circumstances, such as the degree of the heat, the state of the atmosphere, the condition and materials of the adjoining structures and the direction of the wind. These are accidental and varying circumstances. The party has no control over them, and is not responsible for their effects.

Later New York cases have extended the liability somewhat, but the fundamental limitation remains. Does Judge Andrews adequately distinguish this line of cases? Virtually all other states reject this limitation.

For further reading on *Palsgraf*, see J. Noonan, Persons and Masks of the Law, Ch. 4 (1976); R. Posner, Cardozo: A Study in Reputation, Ch. 3 (1990); Green, The Palsgraf Case, 30 Colum.L.Rev. 789 (1930); Prosser, Palsgraf Revisited, 52 Mich.L.Rev. 1 (1953); Seavey, Mr. Justice Cardozo and the Law of Torts, 39 Colum.L.Rev. 20 (1939); 52 Harv.L.Rev. 372 (1939); 48 Yale L.J. 390 (1939).

———

The Kinsman cases. Several of the issues raised in the foregoing proximate cause cases came together in Petition of Kinsman Transit Co., 338 F.2d 708 (2d Cir.1964), cert. denied 380 U.S. 944 (1965). The Buffalo River "with many turns and bends" was full of floating ice in winter. A thaw had begun and two ice jams were moving downstream under strong current. Because its crew responded inadequately to the impending danger, the Shiras, owned by Kinsman, was torn loose from its moorings at the Concrete Elevator dock operated by Continental and began floating downstream. The Shiras crashed into a properly moored ship, the Tewksbury, tearing it loose, and both ships (one 525 feet long and the other 425 feet long) careened down the river (whose channel was 177 feet wide) toward a lift bridge operated by the city, situated three miles from the Continental dock. Because of the city's negligence, the bridge was not raised, and the two ships crashed into it, destroying it and some surrounding property. The wreckage of the ships and the bridge formed a dam that caused the ice and the water to back up causing property to sustain flooding damage as far back upstream as the Continental dock. This case involves claims for the property damage. In a complex group of rulings, the trial judge found liability against Continental, Kinsman, and the City of Buffalo.

The court of appeals, in an opinion by Judge Friendly, affirmed (over a dissent as to the city). As to Kinsman, the timing of the negligence of the crew was such that what followed was foreseeable. (What new question would have been raised if the flooding had damaged property upstream from the dock?) As to the city, the majority once again concluded that the conditions that day made it reasonably foreseeable that a dam might be created at the bridge if the span were not lifted in time and that upriver flooding might result. (How would you analyze a case against the city brought by flooded property owners upstream from the dock?)

The difficult case was Continental, which was negligent because of failure to inspect a "deadman" device at its dock over an extended period of time. The court thought that the negligence in failing to maintain equipment was not time-specific. This raised the question of the liability of a defendant who could have foreseen the ships crashing into property as they made their way down the river, but not the flooding that actually occurred. Although Judge Friendly stated his agreement with the result in *Wagon Mound* because the defendant there "had no reason to believe that the floating furnace oil would burn," his opinion also conveyed the spirit of *Polemis*:

> On that view [*Wagon Mound*] simply applies the principle which excludes liability where the injury sprang from a hazard different from that which was improperly risked, [ ]. Although some language in the judgment goes beyond this, we would find it difficult to understand why one who had failed to use the care required to protect others in the light of expectable forces should be exonerated when the very risks that rendered his conduct negligent produced other and more serious consequences to such persons than were fairly foreseeable when he fell short of what the law demanded. Foreseeability of danger is necessary to render conduct negligent; where as here the damage was caused by just those forces whose existence required the exercise of greater care than was taken—the current, the ice, and the physical mass of the Shiras—the incurring of consequences other and greater than foreseen does not make the conduct less culpable or provide a reasoned basis for insulation.[9]

The weight of authority in this country rejects the limitation of damages to consequences foreseeable at the time of the negligent conduct when the consequences are "direct," and the damage, al-

---

9. The contrasting situation is illustrated by the familiar instances of the running down of a pedestrian by a safely driven but carelessly loaded car, or of the explosion of unlabeled rat poison, inflammable but not known to be, placed near a coffee burner. [ ] Exoneration of the defendant in such cases rests on the basis that a negligent actor is responsible only for harm the risk of which was increased by the *negligent aspect* of his conduct. [ ]

. . .

though other and greater than expectable, is of the same general sort that was risked. . . .

We see no reason why an actor engaging in conduct which entails a large risk of small damage and a small risk of other and greater damage, of the same general sort, from the same forces, and to the same class of persons, should be relieved of responsibility for the latter simply because the chance of its occurrence, if viewed alone, may not have been large enough to require the exercise of care.

Was the harm that occurred due to the crew's negligence of the "same general sort" as might have been reasonably expectable from that negligence? Are you persuaded that the *Kinsman* facts are different from the cases in the court's footnote 9?

After quoting the phrase from Judge Andrews that decisions in these cases were "all a question of expediency . . . of fair judgment," Judge Friendly observed that it "would be pleasant if greater certainty were possible, [   ], but the many efforts that have been made at defining the *locus* of the 'uncertain and wavering line' [Andrews], are not very promising; what courts do in such cases makes better sense than what they, or others, say." Would Judge Cardozo agree? Viscount Simonds?

Kinsman II. Another set of claims arose from the closure of the bridge. 388 F.2d 821 (2d Cir.1968). Here the court rejected claims based on the higher costs of unloading ships due to the inability of tugs to reach them, and the costs of obtaining substitute grain to fulfil contracts when grain could not be moved to elevators above the bridge. The "instant claims occurred only because the downed bridge made it impossible to move traffic along the river. Under all the circumstances of this case, we hold that the connection between the defendants' negligence and the claimants' damages is too tenuous and remote to permit recovery":

In the final analysis, the circumlocution whether posed in terms of "foreseeability," "duty," "proximate cause," "remoteness," etc. seems unavoidable. As we have previously noted [in *Kinsman I*], we return to Justice Andrews' frequently quoted statement [in *Palsgraf*] "It is all a question of expediency . . . of fair judgment, always keeping in mind the fact that we endeavor to make a rule in each case that will be practical and in keeping with the general understanding of mankind."

Kinsman II was distinguished in *People Express*, p. 313, supra. Although tortfeasors "are liable only for the results falling within the foreseeable risks of their negligent conduct," that condition was satisfied in *People Express*. The economic losses in *People Express* were "the natural and probable consequences of a defendant's negligence in the sense that they are reasonably to be anticipated in view of defendant's capacity to have foreseen that the particular plaintiff or identifiable class of plaintiff, is demonstrably within the risk created by defendant's negligence." For the court in *People Express*, proximate causation "is that combination of 'logic, common sense, justice, policy and precedent' that fixes a point in a chain of events, some foreseeable and some unforeseeable, beyond which the law will bar recovery. [   ] The standard of particular foreseeability may be successfully employed to determine whether the economic injury was proximately caused, i.e., whether the particular harm that occurred is compensable, just as it informs the question whether a duty exists." In which types of cases do duty and proximate cause raise substantially the same issue?

For further reading on proximate cause, see Green, Rationale of Proximate Cause (1927); H. Hart and A. Honore, Causation in the Law (1959); C. Morris and C. Robert Morris, Morris on Torts, Ch. VII (2d ed. 1980); Calabresi, Concerning Cause and the Law of Torts: An Essay for Harry Kalven, Jr., 43 U.Chi.L.Rev. 69 (1975); Kelley, Proximate Cause in Negligence Law: History, Theory, and the Present Darkness, 69 Wash. U.L.Q. 49 (1991).

CHAPTER VI

DEFENSES

A. THE PLAINTIFF'S FAULT

The foregoing chapters have explored the prima facie case that the plaintiff must present in order to establish liability for negligence (except for damages, a subject discussed in Chapter X). But the common law has recognized several defenses against the plaintiff's claim. By far the most common is the defendant's contention that even if defendant was negligent toward the plaintiff, the plaintiff was careless about his or her own safety and was "contributorily" negligent. This defense appears as early as 1809 in England and seems to have been well established in this country by 1850—the time of *Brown v. Kendall*, p. 33, supra. We have already encountered the defense in a number of cases, such as the *Goodman–Pokora* sequence, p. 58, supra.

1. CONTRIBUTORY NEGLIGENCE

The common law elements of the defense parallel those of the basic negligence claim—except in the sense that any duty owed is to one's self rather than to others. The trier uses an adapted risk calculus to determine the reasonableness of the plaintiff's conduct. The conduct must be an actual cause of the plaintiff's harm. This is illustrated by Hightower v. Paulson Truck Lines, Inc., 559 P.2d 872 (Or.1977), in which plaintiff's recovery was not affected, despite his having followed too closely on the highway, because defendant "suddenly slowed" without warning. A jury could have found that even if the plaintiff had been following at a reasonably safe distance, he still could not have stopped in time.

Actual cause

The plaintiff's negligence must also be a proximate cause of the plaintiff's harm. For example, assume P is warned not to stand on a high platform because it is shaky and may not hold P's weight. Without justification P disregards the advice, stands on the platform, and is hurt when an adjacent wall collapses as the result of defendant's negligence and knocks P from the platform to the ground below. Assuming P is hurt, his or her negligence may have causally contributed to the injury, but was it a proximate cause or was the unexpected consequence one that absolves plaintiff of the unreasonableness?

prox. cause

Recall the determination in *Brown v. Kendall* that the plaintiff had the burden of proving freedom from contributory negligence. Many states have switched that burden to the defendant. Is one approach more clearly appropriate than the other?

435

When the defense of contributory negligence was established, the effect was a total bar to recovery. Thus, the traditional negligence law operated on an all-or-nothing basis. As we shall soon see, this feature of the system produced a range of legal doctrines to ease the impact of the contributory negligence defense on certain plaintiffs.

Despite the apparent symmetry, courts sometimes appeared to make contributory negligence more difficult to establish than the elements might suggest. Rescuers who were hurt going to the aid of others would often be barred by a straightforward application of the risk calculus because the risks attending the attempted rescue often clearly outweighed the expected gain both to the victim and the rescuer. Nevertheless, the courts usually allowed these cases to reach juries by declaring them to involve issues on which reasonable persons could differ.*

Statutes. In some situations where a statutory command is understood to be an effort to protect some group against its own inability to protect itself the statute may be interpreted as barring a defense of contributory negligence. See, e.g. Chainani v. Board of Education, 663 N.E.2d 283 (N.Y.1995), discussing a statute requiring school bus operators to instruct students in crossing streets, to flash red lights, and to wait until students disembarking from the bus have crossed the street. The court had already decided that the purpose was to protect the school children against their own negligence, and now held that that purpose would be thwarted if a child's contributory negligence were a defense.

Relatively few statutes have been given such effect. In Feisthamel v. State, 453 N.Y.S.2d 904 (App.Div.1982), a nine-year-old girl was badly cut when she tried to walk through the glass drum that was wrapped around a revolving glass door. The girl had mistakenly believed that she had reached an exit point from the revolving door. The state, which had violated a statutory obligation to mark glass revolving doors, asserted contributory negligence. The trial court accepted the defense and reduced damages by half. On appeal, the court, 3–2, affirmed: the statute "was not enacted for the protection of a definite class of persons from a hazard which they themselves are incapable of avoiding." The dissenters argued that the statute's purpose was to protect users of glass doors from colliding with the glass due to their inability to perceive it as such. They would have awarded full damages. See generally, Prosser, Contributory Negligence as Defense to Violation of Statute, 32 Minn.L.Rev. 105 (1948).

---

* Might a lack of due care for one's own safety create liability toward others? In Sears v. Morrison, 90 Cal.Rptr.2d 528 (App. 1999), defendant, while repairing a machine on his premises, tripped over a wire and the machine came down on top of him. A friend, who was reading elsewhere on the premises, came to help and cut himself while trying to lift the machine. The court imposed a duty of due care to the rescuer. To the same effect, see Carney v. Buyea, 65 N.Y.S.2d 902 (App. Div.1946), in which defendant parked her car on an incline, walked about 20 feet in front of the car and bent down to remove something from the road. Her car started downhill and plaintiff, standing nearby, rushed to her rescue, and was struck by the car while pushing her to safety.

Limitations on contributory negligence. Even if contributory negligence was found in a particular case, several rules emerged over the years that limited the applicability of the defense.

a.   Recklessness. Virtually all courts decided that contributory negligence was a defense only in cases of negligence. If the misconduct of the defendant was more serious—recklessness or willful misconduct—the appropriate defense would have been "contributory recklessness" or "contributory willful misconduct." Contributory negligence was totally irrelevant in such cases and the plaintiff recovered all of his or her damages. Why?

Consider Second Restatement § 500, which provides the following approach to the common law aspects of recklessness, usually considered to be synonymous with willful or wanton misconduct:

> The actor's conduct is in reckless disregard of the safety of another if he does an act or intentionally fails to do an act which it is his duty to the other to do, knowing or having reason to know of facts which would lead a reasonable man to realize, not only that his conduct creates an unreasonable risk of physical harm to another, but also that such risk is substantially greater than that which is necessary to make his conduct negligent.

b.   Last clear chance. Contributory negligence was also disregarded under circumstances that came to be called "last clear chance." In these cases the plaintiff behaved carelessly and got into a dangerous situation that led to injury. In response to the defense of contributory negligence, P claimed that even though P was careless for P's own safety, the defendant had, but failed to utilize, the "last clear chance" to avoid the injury to plaintiff. The doctrine is first mentioned in Davies v. Mann, 10 M. & W. 546, 152 Eng.Rep. 588 (1842), in which defendant ran into a donkey that plaintiff had carelessly left tied in the roadway.

Two types of dangerous situations triggered the doctrine of last clear chance. In one, the plaintiff had gotten into a position of "helpless peril" and was no longer able to take protective steps. In that situation most courts invoked last clear chance against a defendant who knew or should have known of the plaintiff's plight while still able to avoid the harm by the exercise of due care. The other type of last clear chance case involved a plaintiff who was oblivious to the danger but who could, if behaving reasonably, become aware of it and avoid harm up to the last minute. Here most courts required that before the doctrine could be applied the defendant driver had to have actual knowledge of plaintiff's danger in time to avoid harm by the exercise of due care.

Generally, the doctrine was regarded as having a chronological aspect. Thus, a claim that the defendant could not stop in time because of brake failure would not have invoked last clear chance because most courts required that the defendant be able to do something in the period after the plaintiff's peril starts. Sections 479 and 480 of the Second Restatement discuss these intricacies.

When last clear chance was held applicable, the fact that the plaintiff was contributorily negligent became totally irrelevant and the plaintiff recovered all appropriate damages with no offset. The doctrine remains important in contributory negligence states. See Washington Metropolitan Area Transit Authority v. Johnson, 726 A.2d 172 (D.C.App. en banc 1999).

c. Refusal to impute contributory negligence. We have already observed that on occasion the law will impute the negligence of one person to another. The most significant example of imputed primary negligence is respondeat superior, the doctrine that has given rise to the imposition of liability on employers. Recall the discussion in Chapter I. On the plaintiff's side, we have also seen examples of cases in which the courts have reached a similar result by calling one action derivative from another, thus giving the person bringing the second action only the rights that the first person had.

These imputation rules do not necessarily reflect a single ethical or economic rationale. Respondeat superior, for example, served the important function of providing a class of defendants who were more likely than their servants to be able to respond to the damage awards that the courts were imposing and might be able to make the entire operation safer. On the other hand, calling an action "derivative" rather than "independent" in the consortium and wrongful death cases appears to spring more from a notion of regarding the cluster of plaintiffs as a group, and then finding it "unfair" for the defendant to owe a greater obligation to some "indirect" plaintiffs than to the original victim.

Many of the rules that impute negligence to persons as defendants do not have the same effect when the person becomes a plaintiff. The most important of these arises in automobile accidents. This is discussed in Continental Auto Lease Corp. v. Campbell, 227 N.E.2d 28 (N.Y.1967), in which Kamman, who rented a car from plaintiff, was involved in an accident with Shepard. Both drivers were negligent. Continental sued Shepard for the property damage to its car. The court rejected the claim that Kamman's negligence should be imputed to Continental. The court noted that the goal of vicarious liability against defendants was to protect the injured plaintiff but that imputing negligence to defeat actions had the effect of leaving innocent victims uncompensated. Nor was it relevant that Continental was benefiting financially from the rental. It had no control or interest in where the car was driven nor did it have a right to control the driver.

Imputation of contributory negligence reached its peak in the late nineteenth century. Its two most significant manifestations were (a) imputing the negligence of a driver or engineer to all the passengers on the vehicle, preventing their suits against other parties whose negligence contributed to the collision; and (b) imputing to the child a parent's negligence in failing to protect that child.

If a child is hurt through the combined negligence of its mother and a stranger, we generally no longer impute the mother's negligence to bar the child's action. Indeed, as we have seen, we may even permit the child to sue the mother as well as the stranger, or we may permit the child to sue the stranger and then—depending on other considerations—are reluctant to allow the stranger to obtain contribution from the mother. Recall p. 222, supra. See the discussion of these various issues in LaBier v. Pelletier, 665 A.2d 1013 (Me.1995)(refusing to impute a mother's negligence to her child in an action against a stranger but noting that the stranger may file a third-party claim against the mother; even if the parents might "realize some incidental benefit from the child's recovery, it is unfair to remedy that problem by shifting the windfall to the nonparental tortfeasor").

The "derivative" questions aside, virtually all imputed contributory negligence has been eliminated over the years. The rigors of the contributory negligence doctrine and the changing perceptions of the relationships involved have undoubtedly played important roles in its demise.

d.   The jury's role. Surely the most modern technique for ameliorating the perceived harshness of the all-or-nothing contributory negligence rule (prior to the adoption of comparative negligence) was the increased frequency with which courts found that reasonable persons could differ over the characterization of the plaintiff's conduct—so that a jury question was presented. Observers asserted that most juries rejected the judge's instruction to return a defense verdict if they found any contributory negligence— even the most minimal contributory fault, so long as it proximately related to the harm. The belief was that the jury simply reduced the plaintiff's damages by some amount rather than returning a defense verdict. Consider the following passage from Alibrandi v. Helmsley, 314 N.Y.S.2d 95 (Sup.Ct. 1970), in which, in a trial to the court, the judge assumed that defendant was negligent and concluded that the plaintiff was contributorily negligent. He then continued:

> Plaintiff's injuries were not trivial. I am as confident as one can be about these matters that, had the case been tried to a jury, the jury would have determined the sum of plaintiff's damages in a substantial amount, deducted a portion equivalent to the degree of his negligence, and returned a verdict for the difference. In short, as every trial lawyer knows, the jury would likely have ignored its instructions on contributory negligence and applied a standard of comparative negligence.

> It would be comfortable for me simply to guess what the jury's verdict would have been and then file a one-sentence decision holding defendants liable in that amount. Comfortable but false. My duty is to apply the law as I understand it, and I do not understand that, no matter what a jury might do, a Judge may pretend to make a decision on the basis of contributory negligence while actually deciding on comparative negligence.

Did the judge reach the right decision? Did the plaintiff's attorney commit malpractice by not demanding a jury in the case? Does the judge's analysis reflect badly on the legal system? The jury system?

From the plaintiff's standpoint, a basic problem was that contributory negligence was sometimes so clear that no self-respecting judge could permit the issue to go to the jury. In other words, the device of sending a close case to the jury worked only when the closeness was in the question of whether plaintiff had been negligent at all—not in cases in which plaintiff's negligence was clear, but relatively minor. Of course, plaintiffs also faced the prospect that some juries might actually follow the judge's instructions.

2.   COMPARATIVE NEGLIGENCE

Until the late 1960s, only a handful of states had abandoned the all-or-nothing contributory negligence approach. These few states adopted a system called "comparative negligence" in which a negligent plaintiff's recovery depended on how serious P's negligence was compared to the defendant's. Three principal versions have developed. In one, called "pure" comparative negligence, the plaintiff who is 90% to blame for an accident can recover 10% of the damages from the defendant who was found to be 10% at fault. (A defendant who was also hurt in that same accident could recover 90% of damages from the plaintiff.) The second and third versions are lumped together as a "modified" system. Under one variant, a plaintiff who is at fault can recover as under the pure system but only so long as that negligence is "not as great as" the defendant's. Under the other variant, plaintiff can recover as under the pure system but only so long as that negligence is "no greater than" the defendant's. When does this distinction matter?

In addition to the states, the federal statute regulating injuries to railroad workers, discussed at p. 814, infra, used a pure system. Still, comparative negligence remained largely a reform proposal at the beginning of the 1970s.

Today, only a handful of states adhere to traditional contributory negligence. In Williams v. Delta Int'l Machinery Corp., 619 So.2d 1330 (Ala.1993), the court concluded that, despite the fact that virtually all states had adopted comparative negligence, it would decline: after "exhaustive study and these lengthy deliberations, the majority of this Court, for various reasons, has decided that we should not abandon the doctrine of contributory negligence, which has been the law in Alabama for approximately 162 years."

Of the states that have adopted comparative negligence, about a dozen use the "pure" version, and almost all the others are divided between those adhering to the "not as great as" and the "no greater than" variants. (A few use "slight" and "gross.") This flood was undoubtedly due in part to growing unhappiness with the harshness of contributory negligence. But it seems to have received a considerable boost from efforts to undermine proponents of no-fault auto insurance, who were arguing that too many auto accident victims were getting no tort compensation because of the contributory negligence rule. We discuss the no-fault approach in Chapter XI.

Although most of the action in the 1970s and early 1980s occurred in state legislatures, some major courts, including those of California, Florida, and Illinois adopted comparative negligence by judicial decision. See, e.g., Li v. Yellow Cab Co., 532 P.2d 1226 (Cal.1975), discussing at length the propriety of judicial action in this area. Those courts willing to change the rule have emphasized the fact that the original doctrine was judicially created and thus was amenable to judicial change. They also stress the power of the common law to grow and develop in response to newly perceived needs. In contrast, those courts that have refused to make the change have emphasized that the doctrine has been such a central part of negligence law for 100 years that legislative consideration should occur before it is changed. Who has the better of this argument?

Recall that in *Hammontree v. Jenner,* p. 3, supra, the court rejected the plaintiff's suggestion that the court abandon the negligence approach in favor of strict liability principles. Is there a distinction between the two situations? Is it possible to generalize from these two cases about the circumstances in which judicial reform of basic tort doctrine—as opposed to legislative reform—is appropriate?

In the states that proceeded by legislation, the statutes were usually quite short and simply announced which version of comparative negligence was being adopted—most frequently a modified, rather than pure, version. No attempt was made to anticipate the many questions that would arise after any such basic change in the system was enacted. By contrast, virtually all the states that proceeded by judicial decision adopted the "pure version"—in large part because the choice of either modified version involved what might have appeared to be an arbitrary selection.

Implementation issues. The courts, though perhaps discussing some of the impending problems more than the legislatures, also did not anticipate many of the complications that have emerged. We will explore the central issues raised by a comparative fault approach through consideration of a model statute and discussion of the judicial issues that have arisen in the area. The statute, which is more elaborate than any state act, is the Uniform Comparative Fault Act promulgated by the National Conference of Commissioners on Uniform State Laws in 1977.

Read the statute to learn the rights of your client C in the following situations (disregard insurance):

a.   There has been an accident in which A has suffered damages of $40,000 and has brought suit against B, C, and D. A trial has established that the relative shares of fault are A–40%; B–30%; C–10%; and D–20%. Assume all are solvent.

b.   At trial it appears that D is insolvent. Now what?

c.   Same as (a) except that C has also been hurt and has sustained damages of $25,000.

Uniform Comparative Fault Act
12 Uniform Laws Annotated 33 (1981 Supp.).

Section 1. [Effect of contributory fault]

(a) In an action based on fault seeking to recover damages for injury or death to person or harm to property, any contributory fault chargeable to

the claimant diminishes proportionately the amount awarded as compensatory damages for an injury attributable to the claimant's contributory fault,
but does not bar recovery. This rule applies whether or not under prior law
the claimant's contributory fault constituted a defense or was disregarded
under applicable legal doctrines, such as last clear chance.

(b) "Fault" includes acts or omissions that are in any measure negligent or reckless toward the person or property of the actor or others, or
that subject a person to strict tort liability. The term also includes breach
of warranty, unreasonable assumption of risk not constituting an enforceable express consent, misuse of a product for which the defendant otherwise would be liable, and unreasonable failure to avoid an injury or to
mitigate damages. Legal requirements of causal relation apply both to fault
as the basis for liability and to contributory fault.

Section 2. [Apportionment of damages]

(a) In all actions involving fault of more than one party to the action,
including third-party defendants and persons who have been released
under Section 6, the court, unless otherwise agreed by all parties, shall
instruct the jury to answer special interrogatories or, if there is no jury,
shall make findings, indicating:

(1) the amount of damages each claimant would be entitled to recover
if contributory fault is disregarded; and

(2) the percentage of the total fault of all of the parties to each claim
that is allocated to each claimant, defendant, third-party defendant, and
person who has been released from liability under Section 6. For this
purpose the court may determine that two or more persons are to be
treated as a single party.

(b) In determining the percentages of fault, the trier of fact shall
consider both the nature of the conduct of each party at fault and the
extent of the causal relation between the conduct and the damages claimed.

(c) The court shall determine the award of damages to each claimant
in accordance with the findings, subject to any reduction under Section 6,
and enter judgment against each party liable on the basis of rules of joint-
and-several liability. For purposes of contribution under Sections 4 and 5,
the court also shall determine and state in the judgment each party's
equitable share of the obligation to each claimant in accordance with the
respective percentages of fault.

(d) Upon motion made not later than [one year] after judgment is
entered, the court shall determine whether all or part of a party's equitable
share of the obligation is uncollectible from that party, and shall reallocate
any uncollectible amount among the other parties, including a claimant at
fault, according to their respective percentages of fault. The party whose
liability is reallocated is nonetheless subject to contribution and to any
continuing liability to the claimant on the judgment.

Section 3. [Set-off]

A claim and counterclaim shall not be set off against each other, except by agreement of both parties. On motion, however, the court, if it finds that the obligation of either party is likely to be uncollectible, may order that both parties make payment into court for distribution. The court shall distribute the funds received and declare obligations discharged as if the payment into court by either party had been a payment to the other party and any distribution of those funds back to the party making payment had been a payment to him by the other party.

Section 4. [Right of contribution]

(a) A right of contribution exists between or among two or more persons who are jointly and severally liable upon the same indivisible claim for the same injury, death, or harm, whether or not judgment has been recovered against all or any of them. It may be enforced either in the original action or by a separate action brought for that purpose. The basis for contribution is each person's equitable share of the obligation, including the equitable share of a claimant at fault, as determined in accordance with the provisions of Section 2.

(b) Contribution is available to a person who enters into a settlement with a claimant only (1) if the liability of the person against whom contribution is sought has been extinguished and (2) to the extent that the amount paid in settlement was reasonable.

Section 5. [Enforcement of contribution]

(a) If the proportionate fault of the parties to a claim for contribution has been established previously by the court, as provided by Section 2, a party paying more than his equitable share of the obligation, upon motion, may recover judgment for contribution.

(b) If the proportionate fault of the parties to the claim for contribution has not been established by the court, contribution may be enforced in a separate action, whether or not a judgment has been rendered against either the person seeking contribution or the person from whom contribution is being sought.

(c) If a judgment has been rendered, the action for contribution must be commenced within [one year] after the judgment becomes final. If no judgment has been rendered, the person bringing the action for contribution either must have (1) discharged by payment the common liability within the period of the statute of limitations applicable to the claimant's right of action against him and commenced the action for contribution within [one year] after payment, or (2) agreed while action was pending to discharge the common liability and, within [one year] after the agreement, have paid the liability and commenced an action for contribution.

Section 6. [Effect of release]

A release, covenant not to sue, or similar agreement entered into by a claimant and a person liable discharges that person from all liability for contribution, but it does not discharge any other persons liable upon the same claim unless it so provides. However, the claim of the releasing person against other persons is reduced by the amount of the released person's equitable share of the obligation, determined in accordance with the provisions of Section 2.

Notes and Questions

1. *Pure or modified version?* The introductory notes by the commissioners make three arguments against the modified version. First, a party more at fault than the other who has to bear his or her own losses and also a share of the other party's losses, is worse off than at common law. Second, if several parties are at fault, the modified version creates chaos—especially if the plaintiff's share of the fault is greater than that of some defendants but less than that of others. This problem is discussed further in note 5, infra. Third, if a plaintiff whose fault is greater than the defendant's is excluded from the benefits of the statute and is relegated to traditional common law, plaintiff might, in some cases, such as last clear chance, recover full damages: "The anomaly therefore arises that he may be better off if his negligence is found to be greater than that of the defendant and he thus recovers full damages. . . ." Are these persuasive attacks on the modified version? What are the problems of the "pure" version?

In Sutton v. Piasecki Trucking, Inc., 451 N.E.2d 481 (N.Y.1983), plaintiff driver disregarded a stop sign and was hit by an approaching truck. Plaintiff was allocated 99% of the fault—and received 1% of his damages. Is such an award repugnant?

2. *What is to be compared?* The comments to § 2 of the UCFA state that in setting fault percentages, the trier of fact should consider:

> such matters as (1) whether the conduct was mere inadvertence or engaged in with an awareness of the danger involved, (2) the magnitude of the risk created by the conduct, including the number of persons endangered and the potential seriousness of the injury, (3) the significance of what the actor was seeking to attain by his conduct, (4) the actor's superior or inferior capacities, and (5) the particular circumstances, such as the existence of an emergency requiring a hasty decision.

Making this comparison sometimes can produce widely varying appraisals. In Wright v. City of Knoxville, 898 S.W.2d 177 (Tenn.1995), for example, plaintiff girlfriend was riding in a car driven by defendant boyfriend. At an extremely busy intersection, the green arrow came on and boyfriend began to make a left turn when he heard a siren. Because he could not locate the siren, he continued making the turn—and he collided with a police car that was driving east in the westbound lane to avoid traffic backed up at the light. The officer, who was responding to a call of "an accident with injuries," was moving at 10–15 miles per hour. Plaintiff sued both her boyfriend and the officer driving the police car. The judge sitting as trier of fact allocated 75% of the fault to the officer and 25% to the boyfriend. The court of appeals found that the boyfriend had violated a number of Tennessee traffic regulations and allocated 100% of the fault to him. The Supreme Court held that the officer should be assigned 25% of the fault because she had driven on the wrong side of the road with full knowledge that drivers would be turning directly at her. Despite the result in the Knoxville case, courts generally are reluctant to reassess the fact finder's allocation of percentages unless they are totally indefensible. Why might this be?

3. *Reckless conduct.* What types of conduct should be compared? Under contributory negligence, the plaintiff's negligence generally was overlooked when the defendant's conduct had been reckless. The Uniform Act's sweep in § 1(b) is quite broad, reaching matters of liability and of damage measurement. Even though few courts have adopted this draft legislation, virtually all states with pure versions have concluded that reckless conduct should be compared with negligence. E.g. Sorensen v. Allred, 169 Cal.Rptr. 441 (App. 1980)(comparing defendant's drunk and speeding driving (55%) with plaintiff's careless left turn in front of defendant (45%)); Zavala v. Regents of the University of California, 178 Cal.Rptr. 185 (App. 1981)(comparing plaintiff's 80% fault with defendant's 20%). In states with modified versions, the comparison cannot be made when the plaintiff has been reckless and the defendant negligent.

Some courts appear reluctant to follow the logic of comparison when the plaintiff's conduct is thought to be socially offensive. See Barker v. Kallash, 468 N.E.2d 39 (N.Y.1984), in which the 15-year-old plaintiff was hurt when a pipe bomb that he was making exploded in his hands. His suit against various defendants was totally barred, 5–2, even though the state had adopted pure comparative negligence: "when the plaintiff has engaged in activities prohibited, as opposed to regulated, by law, the courts will not entertain the suit if the plaintiff's conduct constituted a serious violation of the law and the injuries for which he seeks recovery were the direct result of that violation." Contra, Ashmore v. Cleanweld Products, Inc., 672 P.2d 1230 (Or.App.1983), also involving a 15-year-old bomb maker, in which the court relied on § 889 of the Second Restatement, providing in part that "One is not barred from recovery for an interference with his legally protected interests merely because at the time of the interference he was committing a tort or a crime." The strong public policy against illegal manufacture of explosives "is best effectuated . . . through penal laws."

New York adhered to its *Barker* approach in Manning v. Brown, 689 N.E.2d 1382 (N.Y.1997). The plaintiff and the defendant were teenage friends who took a car for a joy ride, even though neither held a driver's license. As they were returning the car, defendant driver, at plaintiff's suggestion, attempted to reset the radio station to its original position so that the taking might not be detected. As she did so, she took her eyes off the road. The car swerved and plaintiff passenger was hurt in the ensuing crash. The court unanimously barred plaintiff from all recovery because her harm was a "direct result of a serious violation of the law involving hazardous activities which were not justified under the circumstances."

Should one compare when both defendants are negligent but not when they are both reckless? How would the Uniform Act handle this? "Reckless" and "willful and wanton" are of course complex notions. See Poole v. City of Rolling Meadows, 656 N.E.2d 768 (Ill.1995), in which four justices divided willful and wanton misconduct into two categories: the one closer to negligence would bear comparison with negligence, but the one closer to intentional harm would not. The other three justices concluded that all willful and wanton misconduct involved "acts performed in conscious disregard of a known risk or with utter indifference to the consequences" and should not be compared with negligence. See also Lewis v. Miller, 543 A.2d 590 (Pa.Super.1988) (court will not compare claim by one drag racer against another).

4. *The interplay of intent and negligence.* Although the vast majority of states will compare the plaintiff's negligence with the defendant's recklessness, what should they do when the defendant has committed an intentional tort or crime and the plaintiff has been negligent? Recall the related question of what to do when there are two defendants, one of whom has been negligent and the other of whom was an intentional tortfeasor or criminal, p. 370, supra. The comments to § 1 of the Uniform Act state that although the Act does not include intentional torts, courts are not precluded from making comparisons in such cases if they find it appropriate. Of the few states that have addressed the issue, most have refused to compare the negligence of a plaintiff with the intentional tort of a defendant because intentional conduct is different "in kind" from negligent or reckless conduct and therefore may not be compared.

Does it raise different questions to ask whether a court should compare the intentional actions of the plaintiff with the negligence of a defendant? Compare Hickey v. Zezulka, 487 N.W.2d 106 (Mich.1992)(negligent campus police officer, who had failed to remove decedent's belt from holding cell, entitled to comparative fault instruction so jury could compare officer's negligence with decedent's fault in intentionally committing suicide) with Sandborg v. Blue Earth County, 615 N.W.2d 61 (Minn.2000) (comparative negligence not available where jail officials were on notice of the suicidal tendencies of the prisoner).

5. *Should the fault of multiple defendants be combined?* In states following a modified version of comparative negligence, it becomes critical to decide whether to compare the plaintiff's negligence with the aggregated negligence of the defendants (or all negligent actors) or whether it is to be compared with the negligence of each defendant individually. Most states with modified versions compare the plaintiff's fault to the combined fault of the defendants. Consider these two distributions of negligence:

(1) P 30%; D1 60%; D2 10%

(2) P 40%; D1 30%; D2 30%

In a state that imposes joint and several liability, what are the implications of your choice for comparison? What are the implications of your choice in a state that has only several liability? What if all three parties are hurt in the accident and sue each other? These problems are discussed in Wong v. Hawaiian Scenic Tours, Ltd., 642 P.2d 930 (Haw.1982).

Do these cases support the states that have retained joint and several liability in cases in which the plaintiff has not been at fault, but have abolished the doctrine in cases in which the plaintiff has been negligent and invokes comparative negligence? Recall p. 370, supra.

6. *Should the judgments be set off against each other?* The denial of set-offs in the Uniform Act is designed to cover situations in which insurance exists on both sides so that injured parties will maximize their recoveries. The issue arose in Jess v. Herrmann, 604 P.2d 208 (Cal.1979), in which the court, 4–3, denied set-off: if both drivers were adequately insured, the "setoff produces results detrimental to the interests *of both parties* and accords the insurance companies of the parties a fortuitous windfall simply because each insured happens to have an independent claim against the person he has injured."

7. *What if one defendant is insolvent?* Example (b) at the outset of the statute suggests how the Uniform Act handles insolvencies. Since most states, however, do not follow the Uniform Act, their treatment will depend on the state's law on joint and several liability. In states that retain the doctrine of joint and several liability, but do not follow the Uniform Act, the loss due to one defendant's insolvency will be spread among the remaining defendants. With several liability, the plaintiff will bear that loss.

8. *Multiparty disputes in which all do not settle.* It is quite common for cases against two or more defendants to involve settlements with some but not all defendants. This issue is addressed in several UCFA sections. An example identifies several questions. Suppose that P seeks $50,000 from D1 and D2 for negligence in a situation in which they would be jointly and severally liable. P settles with D1 for $10,000. At trial, the jury awards plaintiff $30,000 and determines that D2 was 50% at fault (and that D1 was also 50% at fault). Several possible resolutions are possible. In each consider the pros and cons of that approach.

a.   Under the 1939 Uniform Contribution Act, P would collect $20,000 from D2, who would then be able to recover $5,000 from D1.

b.   Under the 1955 version of the Uniform Contribution Act and California law—the pro tanto—rule P collects $20,000 from D2, who cannot recover anything from D1—so long as it is determined that D1's settlement was a good faith settlement (and did not involve collusion between P and D1). See Mattco Forge, Inc. v. Arthur Young & Co., 45 Cal.Rptr.2d 581 (App. 1995) (rejecting a settlement in which D1 paid less than 1% of the plausible value of P's claim).

c.   Under § 6 of the UCFA, P's recovery against D2 is not reduced by Ps' recovery against D1, but is reduced instead by D1's proportionate share of the liability. D1 "should" have paid $15,000. P can recover from D2 only D2's fair share of $15,000. As a result, P obtains only $25,000 in total. This approach is followed in McDermott, Inc. v. AmClyde, 511 U.S. 202 (1994). The court was not concerned that under this approach P may also recover more than $30,000 if P has obtained a high settlement from D1 based on the fault percentages that the jury assesses. As the Court saw it, "a plaintiff's good fortune in striking a favorable bargain with [D1] gives other defendants no claim to pay less than their proportionate share of the total loss."

d. In New York, the court reduces D2's liability by the larger of (1) D1's equitable share based on the percentages or (2) the actual amount D1 paid in the settlement. See Didner v. Keene Corp., 624 N.E.2d 979 (N.Y. 1993).

When multiple defendants are involved, there are also important litigation issues. One controversial settlement technique is the so-called Mary Carter agreement, which first appeared in Booth v. Mary Carter Paint Co., 202 So.2d 8 (Fla.App.1967). In this type of agreement, the defendant remains in the case and guarantees the plaintiff a certain payment. The size of that payment depends on the plaintiff's success against the other defendants. The danger of this agreement becomes obvious when the settling defendant testifies at the trial in a manner that helps the plaintiff and hurts the remaining defendants, who are now adversaries of the settling defendant. A few bar Mary Carter agreements. E.g., Elbaor v. Smith, 845 S.W.2d 240 (Tex.1992)(voiding such agreements because of a case in which secretly settling defendants sat at defense table and told jury that plaintiff had suffered "devastating" injuries and "astoundingly high" damages, and used their "cross-examination" of the plaintiff to aid her showing of pain and suffering). Most courts conclude that if the jury is told about the situation the danger of misleading the jury is eliminated.

9. *Should the negligence of one plaintiff be imputed to another plaintiff?* Several types of cases raise the question whether the actions of one victim should be imputed to the plaintiff. We review four such situations here. In all three situations the great majority of states have concluded that the actions are "derivative" in the sense that defenses available against the "direct" victim are available against the plaintiff. In each situation, though, a few have decided that the actions are "independent" and thus defenses against one do no apply against the other.

a. Loss of consortium. Does the Act speak to the question of an action for loss of consortium where the injured spouse and the defendant were both at fault? Most states that have addressed this question have treated the claim as derivative and have imputed the negligence of the injured spouse to the other spouse. This rule emerged during the days of contributory negligence and was criticized by commentators. Now that comparative negligence has become virtually universal, these states have retained the rule but now find it easier to defend. In Blagg v. Illinois F.W.D. Truck & Equip. Co., 572 N.E.2d 920 (Ill.1991), the court noted that one reason to treat the action as derivative was that the action of the negligent injured spouse "harms not only the marital interest of the other spouse, but also affects the unity of the familial entity which is in fact an 'economic unit.' " A second reason was that imputation was the "simplest and most efficient way to reach a just result."

In a situation in which the negligent spouse was 15% at fault and the stranger 85%, how might imputation produce a "just result"? With these numbers, the court in Eggert v. Working, 599 P.2d 1389 (Alaska 1979), chose the derivative approach. The goal of pure comparative negligence was that "the loss resulting from an accident is best distributed among those whose negligence caused it in proportion to the fault of each of them." In the "ideal" solution, the wife would recover her full consortium loss, 85% from the defendant and 15% from her negligent husband. Imputing the husband's negligence, though not "ideal," was "very close to the same thing, because the evidence is clear that [the husband and wife] are in effect if not in law, an economic unit. That, it seems to us, is likely to be the case in most instances where substantial loss of consortium damages are suffered." Should it matter whether the wife can sue the husband directly? Whether the state allows the stranger to obtain contribution from the husband?

For the minority approach, see the discussion in Huber v. Hovey, 501 N.W.2d 53 (Iowa 1993), in which the court concluded that from the "vantage point of the negligent defendant, [the plaintiff] is simply a foreseeable plaintiff to whom he owes a separate duty of care." The *Huber* court extended that analysis by refusing to bind an absent wife to the terms of an exculpatory agreement signed by her husband—who was then hurt and held barred from recovery.

b.   Wrongful death. Do the same considerations apply in a wrongful death action? Most courts treat the action as derivative. E.g., Bevan v. Vassar Farms, Inc., 793 P.2d 711 (Idaho 1990). In Griffin v. Gehret, 564 P.2d 332 (Wash.App.1977), the court, in rejecting a parent's argument that his dead child's negligence should not be imputed to his parent, noted that under comparative negligence the parent's claim was not legally barred. But if the decedent's negligence were not imputed, then "the parents of a 17-year-old minor decedent who was 99 percent negligent would be entitled to recover 100 percent from a 17-year-old tortfeasor who was only 1 percent negligent." Why not treat the parents as independent foreseeable plaintiffs who are owed a separate duty?

c.   Bystander emotional distress. How should an action for emotional distress be analyzed? In Meredith v. Hanson, 697 P.2d 602 (Wash.App. 1985), the infant plaintiffs sued for their emotional distress at seeing their stepfather struck and killed by a passing car. The court distinguished the wrongful death case of *Griffin:* "If the present action was a survival action or for wrongful death, the contributory negligence of the decedent would be at issue. [   ] It is neither. The case at bench concerns the emotional distress suffered by the plaintiffs due to [the defendant's] negligence. It makes no difference whether [the stepfather] was negligent so long as his negligence was not the sole proximate cause of the accident. The plaintiffs do not seek compensation for [the stepfather's] death. [His] negligence should not have been imputed to the children." Even if the stepfather's negligence was 99%?

In *Portee v. Jaffee*, p. 282, supra, the court took the contrary position in an omitted part of the opinion: "to allow a plaintiff seeking damages for emotional injuries to recover a greater proportion than the injured party would surely create liability in excess of the defendant's fault." Any award was to be reduced by the negligence of the injured victim "as well as, of course, any contributing negligence of the plaintiff himself."

Should it matter whether the state has pure or modified comparative negligence? What reasons might the *Meredith* court have for distinguishing between wrongful death plaintiffs and emotional distress plaintiffs? Is the distinction sound?

d. Parent-child. Recall that under contributory negligence, later courts refused to impute the negligence of parents to children, p. 438, supra. The emergence of comparative negligence has not changed that approach. Should it?

10. *Should jurors be told the consequences of their verdict?* States disagree over whether juries should know the implications of their decisions. In H.E. Butt Grocery Co. v. Bilotto, 985 S.W.2d 22 (Tex.1998), the question was whether to use special verdicts that tell the jury the legal consequences of any verdict that it might render. The majority, 5–4, approved telling the jury. Justice Gonzalez, concurring at length, asserted that "Most jurisdictions that have addressed the issue in the last twenty-five years have moved away from the rule against informing the jury of the legal effect of its answers." He quoted from Seppi v. Beatty, 579 P.2d 683 (Idaho 1978):

> It would be incredibly naive to believe that jurors, after having listened attentively to testimony of the parties and a parade of witnesses and after having heard the arguments of counsel, will answer questions . . . without giving any thought to the effect those answers will have on the parties and to whether their answers will effectuate a result in accord with their own lay sense of justice. With respect to most questions, the jury would have to be extremely dullwitted not to be able to guess which answers favor which parties. In those instances where the legal effect of their answer is not so obvious, the jurors will nonetheless speculate, often incorrectly, and thus subvert the whole judicial process.

The Idaho court had further observed that "jurors are concerned about the effect of their verdicts on the ultimate outcome of the case and the use of a special verdict or special interrogatories does not magically eliminate that well known trait of American juries."

Justice Gonzalez added that good lawyers "pick a few themes they hope will resonate with the jury. They try to advance their theory at every opportunity, beginning with the pleadings, through opening statements and voir dire, all during the trial itself, and concluding with the charge and final summation. The whole aim of this exercise is to appeal to the conscious and subconscious mind of the jury. Jurors would not be human if they did not give some thought to the effect of their answers."

Some states address the question in their statutes. Nebraska's 1992 version, for example, states that "The jury shall be instructed on the effects of the allocation of negligence." See Wheeler v. Bagley, 575 N.W.2d 616 (Neb.1998).

The question of how much to tell the jury arises in other contexts as well. See, e.g., Weiss v. Goldfarb, 713 A.2d 427 (N.J.1998) (jury not to be told that hospital's statutory maximum liability is $10,000 in case in which outside doctors are also being sued—and noting that statute bars telling jury about cap on punitive damages); Lacy v. CSXT Transp., 520 S.E.2d 418 (W.Va.1999) (jury not to be told about operation of joint and several liability); contra Kaeo v. Davis, 719 P.2d 387 (Haw.1986) (jury to be informed of effect of holding D1 99% at fault and D2 1% at fault in joint-and-several-liability state).

11. *Other changes wrought by comparative negligence.* The introduction of comparative negligence has forced courts to reconsider almost every aspect of the negligence system. Some defenses, such as last clear chance, were eliminated. Some other changes include:

a. Res ipsa loquitur. Under comparative negligence what if the evidence clearly shows undeniable contributory negligence on plaintiff's part? In Montgomery Elevator Co. v. Gordon, 619 P.2d 66 (Colo.1980), the court asserted that res ipsa could be used if the plaintiff's evidence showed only the first two conditions. Then, once "the trial court rules that the doctrine is applicable, the jury must then compare any evidence of negligence of the plaintiff with the inferred negligence of the defendant and decide what percentage of negligence is attributable to each party."

b. Rescue. Since the introduction of comparative negligence, defendants have argued that rescuers—who were not held at fault earlier unless rash or reckless—no longer need special protection. Most courts have agreed. But see Ouellette v. Carde, 612 A.2d 687 (R.I.1992), in which the court held that comparative negligence "does not fully protect the rescue doctrine's underlying policy of promoting rescue." The law "places a premium on human life, and one who voluntarily attempts to save a life of another should not be barred from complete recovery." Since the defendant did not allege that the plaintiff had acted rashly or recklessly, the trial judge should not have charged at all on the issue of plaintiff's negligence.

c. The drinking plaintiff. In Estate of Kelley v. Moguls, Inc., 632 A.2d 360 (Vt.1993), the court held that the estate of a person who has killed himself by driving while drunk may have a common law negligence action against the licensed vendor who supplied the alcohol. The defendant argued that this would encourage drunk driving and allow a wrongdoer to profit from his own wrong. The court responded that under comparative negligence plaintiff would not be made whole and that it was appropriate that both parties in this situation be deterred from their conduct. Contra, Estate of Kelly v. Falin, 896 P.2d 1245 (Wash.1995)(allowing suit by intoxicated adult against vendor of alcohol would foster irresponsibility and reward drunk driving).

States that have adopted comparative negligence also permit negligent entrustment actions by drinking drivers against the persons who lent them the car although they knew that plaintiffs were incapable of driving safely. See cases collected in Lydia v. Horton, 2000 WL 1634185 (S.C.App. 2000). Should the cases against alcohol suppliers and car suppliers differ?

d.   Subsequent harm. The North Dakota legislature replaced joint and several liability with several liability when it adopted modified comparative negligence. The court then confronted a case in which defendant negligently hurt plaintiff in an auto accident and plaintiff's condition was aggravated by some actions of his chiropractors. The court held that the defendant motorist was not responsible for the aggravation because the introduction of several liability showed a legislative desire to hold defendants liable only for their own fault. A majority of the court thought this an unfortunate result because it would encourage suits against the medical profession. But two concurrers thought that result was dictated by the statute. Haff v. Hettich, 593 N.W.2d 383 (N.D.1999). Recall the notes on secondary harm, p. 403, supra.

12.   Further complexities of settlements are explored in the discussion of damages, at p. 771, infra.

13.   *Economic cases.* Although there has been occasional doubt about whether principles of comparative negligence apply to cases of economic loss, the general view applies the doctrine. In Clark v. Rowe, 701 N.E.2d 624 (Mass.1998), plaintiff sued her lawyer and banker over losses sustained in real estate investments. The court noted that, even though the state comparative negligence statute did not cover this type of loss, the court might "apply the public policy considerations underlying [that section] to support a common law rule of comparative negligence in a case such as this." There was no firm argument against applying the doctrine in malpractice cases since it was already used in medical cases. Nor could the court see any other reason not to apply the doctrine in negligence cases generally. The court also noted that the comments to UCFA § 1 stated that the fact that its terms did not cover economic loss cases "is not intended to preclude application of the general principle to them if a court determines that the common law of the state would make the application."

Fritts v. McKinne

Court of Civil Appeals of Oklahoma, 1996.
934 P.2d 371.

STUBBLEFIELD, JUDGE.

.   .   .

David Fritts was seriously injured in a one-vehicle accident, which occurred during the early morning hours of February 20, 1990. David Fritts and his friend, David Manus, had been drinking prior to the accident. There was some dispute about which one of the two men was driving the Fritts pickup truck at the time of the accident. In any event, the vehicle hit a tree at approximately seventy miles per hour and overturned.

David Fritts sustained serious injuries as a result of the accident. He was diagnosed with a Lefort II fracture—literally all of his major facial bones were broken. He was placed in intensive care due to concern over the impact injury to his chest but later moved into a regular room.

[On February 25, 1990, Fritts underwent surgery to repair his facial fractures. During that surgery, defendant was performing a tracheostomy to allow Fritts to breathe during surgery. Fritts began gushing blood, lost a major amount of blood, lost consciousness and died three days later. Plaintiff claimed that defendant negligently failed to identify and isolate the proper artery. Defendant claimed that the artery was anomalous—that it was in the neck area "when normally it should have been in the chest." He also asserted a comparative negligence defense based on the contention that Fritts was injured while driving drunk or was drunk while riding in a vehicle with Manus, who also was drunk. When plaintiff objected to any mention of the use of drugs or alcohol, the defendant argued that such evidence was relevant to comparative negligence because "[his] injury arose in the automobile accident that he caused, because he [either drove] drunk or elected to ride with somebody who was driving drunk." Defendant also argued that the evidence was "relevant to the issue of damages—he would present expert testimony that Fritts had a substantially diminished life expectancy due to his drug and alcohol use." The trial court denied the plaintiff's motion to exclude the evidence. Much of the trial was devoted to evidence about Fritts's drunkenness at the time of the accident as well as his past drug and alcohol abuse.]

. . . Over plaintiff's objection, the trial court instructed the jury on the issue of Fritts' comparative negligence. These instructions included an instruction on "General Duty of Drivers," which stated that "[i]t is the duty of the driver of a motor vehicle to use ordinary care to prevent injury to himself or to other persons."

The jury returned a verdict in favor of Dr. McKinne. . . .

Plaintiff raises two interrelated propositions of error on appeal. She claims that the trial court erred in admitting evidence regarding her deceased husband's history of substance abuse and in allowing the jury to consider comparative negligence—based on the events of the automobile accident—as a basis for reducing or denying recovery on the medical negligence claim. . . .

. . . [Defendant] defended against the allegations of negligence by contending that, due to Fritts's unusual anatomy and the resultant injury to his artery from the high speed impact, the rupture of the artery was inevitable. This was a proper and appropriate defense. However, we conclude that the interjection of the issue of Fritts's possible negligence in the automobile accident, a matter unrelated to the medical procedures, was a substantial error that removed the jury's consideration from the relevant issues and led to an erroneous excursion into irrelevant and highly prejudicial matters.

There are limited circumstances under which reasonableness of patient conduct can be an appropriate consideration in medical negligence cases. For example, evidence of a patient's failure to reveal medical history that would have been helpful to his physician raises the issue of contributory negligence, particularly where the evidence also shows that the patient may have been advised of the importance of this information. [   ] A patient's furnishing of false information about his condition, failure to follow a physician's advice and instructions, or delay or failure to seek further recommended medical attention also are appropriate considerations in determining contributory negligence. . . .

Under the guise of a claim of contributory negligence, a physician simply may not avoid liability for negligent treatment by asserting that the patient's injuries were originally caused by the patient's own negligence. "Those patients who may have negligently injured themselves are nevertheless entitled to subsequent non-negligent medical treatment and to an undiminished recovery if such subsequent non-negligent treatment is not afforded." [   ]

Thus, aside from limited situations, negligence of a party which necessitates medical treatment is simply irrelevant to the issue of possible subsequent medical negligence. Herein, Dr. McKinne testified that, at the time of the surgery, which was five days after the accident, "alcohol was not a problem." Yet, from the time of his opening statement, the principal focus of the doctor's counsel was on the behavior of the decedent before and leading up to the automobile accident . . .

Thus, we conclude that the submission of the issue of comparative negligence—decedent's conduct unrelated to his medical treatment—was error. We also find a strong probability that the erroneously given instructions misled the jurors and caused them to reach a result different from what they would have reached but for the flawed instructions.

. . .

Fritts's history of substance abuse is relevant to the issue of damages where there is evidence of its effect on probable life expectancy, and Plaintiff seeks damages based on loss of future earnings. However, like evidence of Fritts's drinking on the night of the accident, it was not proper for the jury to consider such evidence in regard to the claim of negligence against Dr. McKinne. Where evidence is admissible on a certain point only, the trial court should at least advise the jury to consider it on that point alone in order to assure that the evidence will not be applied improperly. [   ] Here, where the evidence is extremely inflammatory, bifurcation of trial of the liability and damages issues would have avoided completely the possibility of prejudice from the evidence.

We find that evidence of Fritts's intoxication and history of substance abuse, along with repeated references to it by defense counsel, was sufficiently prejudicial to Plaintiff's case as to have prevented a full and fair trial of the issues. Furthermore, the admission of relevant but inflammatory evidence, admissible for only one issue, was reversible error in the absence of limiting instructions or bifurcated trial.

[The judgment was reversed and remanded for a new trial.]

GOODMAN, P.J., and BOUDREAU, J., concur.

Notes and Questions

1.   What are the arguments for and against comparing in this type of situation? Do they involve questions of safety incentives?

2.   Should *Fritts* apply where the plaintiff has consciously created the very danger that required medical attention? In Harding v. Deiss, 3 P.3d 1286 (Mont.2000), 14-year-old Candice went horseback riding although she knew she was allergic to horses. During the ride she had "trouble breathing and eventually collapsed." The stable staff administered CPR and she was transported to a nearby hospital's emergency room, and then to a second hospital, at which she died. Plaintiffs alleged that their daughter's death was due to negligent medical treatment at both hospitals. The trial judge allowed the jury to consider evidence of her conduct before she collapsed and the jury returned a defense verdict. On appeal, the court reversed, following the general rule that pre-treatment conduct should not be considered in the liability phase of this type of case. The alternative would lead to the "absurd result" that in any hospitalization due to the patient's fault, "the treating physician would not be liable for negligent treatment." Is that correct?

Should a physician be able to show that a negligently treated bullet wound had been inflicted while plaintiff robber was trying to escape from the police?

3.   Compare *Fritts* with the comments to § 2 of the UCFA, which provide that in determining fault the fact-finder should consider "the relative closeness of the causal relationship of the negligent conduct of the defendants and the harm to the plaintiff. Degrees of fault and proximity of causation are inextricably mixed, as a study of last clear chance indicates, and that common law doctrine has been absorbed into this Act."

Does the UCFA suggest that a system of comparative negligence leaves no room for proximate cause analysis because a jury can always take into account a party's negligence, no matter how attenuated, in determining fault percentages? Or should the jury compare only negligent conduct that has at least a "minimal" level of causal connection to the harm? A "substantial" level? In other words, should the question of proximate cause be antecedent to the allocation of fault rather than being inextricably mixed with it? Consider this excerpt from Prosser & Keeton, Torts (5th ed. 1984), p. 474–75:

Once causation in fact has been established, however, the determination of proximate or legal cause remains a question of policy that may be susceptible to proportionate division. A court which is able to award an injured plaintiff substantially diminished damages may thus be willing to extend the traditional boundaries of proximate cause and permit a limited recovery against a remotely negligent defendant. . . . In any event, at either end of the fault continuum, where one party's negligence approaches one hundred percent and the other party's approaches zero, the court may rule or the jury find that the conduct of the plaintiff or of the defendant was the "sole proximate cause" of the plaintiff's harm, so that damages will not be awarded—or reduced—at all.

4. For an extended discussion of comparative negligence in the malpractice setting, see Harvey v. Mid–Coast Hospital, 36 F.Supp.2d 32 (D.Me. 1999), refusing to allow a physician to show that the patient was in the hospital because of a drug overdose from an attempted suicide. The condition presented to the physician (lots of pills in the body) could be shown, but not the reason for the condition.

5. Should this reluctance to compare be limited to medical malpractice cases? Consider Wolfgang v. Mid–America Motorsports, Inc., 111 F.3d 1515 (10th Cir.1997), in which plaintiff professional car racer had negligently crashed on defendant racetrack. He sued only for harm due to a subsequent fire that was not extinguished quickly because of the track's alleged negligence. The court, using Kansas law, held that since plaintiff was suing only for the excess harm caused by the late rescue, the defendant could not show how plaintiff had been hurt.

6. *The impact of chronology.* In the principal case and the notes to this point, any plaintiff's negligence has preceded that of the defendant. What new questions appear if the sequence is reversed?

In Egan v. A.J. Construction Corp., 724 N.E.2d 366 (N.Y.1999), defendant's elevator, carrying 25–30 construction workers, negligently stalled six feet above the building's lobby. The operator called for help. After 10–15 minutes, two workers near the door opened the doors and jumped down to the lobby floor. Then others did so until only plaintiff and the operator remained. When plaintiff jumped he landed on his heels and hurt himself. The court unanimously concluded that plaintiff's jump "was not foreseeable in the normal course of events resulting from defendants' alleged negligence." He was not "threatened by injury." He had "only been on the elevator for 10 to 15 minutes when he decided to put his safety at risk by jumping, and there was no indication that the subsequent delay would be inordinately long. Thus, plaintiff's jump superseded defendants' conduct and terminated defendants' liability for his injuries." The court cited its swimming pool cases discussed at p. 482 infra. When plaintiff pointed to the actions of the other workers, the court responded that their actions did not make his own "either less risky or more foreseeable." Is it unforeseeable as a matter of law that 25–30 workers will jump down six feet from an elevator that is stuck?

See also Exxon Co., U.S.A. v. Sofec, Inc., 517 U.S. 830 (1996), an admiralty case, in which defendant negligently created a risk to plaintiff ship and crew during a storm by allowing a connection to break as the ship was pumping oil. After half an hour, an assisting ship removed a broken hose that had been attached to the ship and that had been impairing its maneuverability. For the next half hour the ship's captain maneuvered the ship out to sea—to avoid the dangers of being stranded in shallow water. After that point, the captain was negligent in a variety of ways, leading to hitting a reef with the ship being a total loss. The Court unanimously affirmed the trial judge's decision not to compare the two faults. The trier had found that the decisions of the captain were "made calmly, deliberately and without the pressure of an imminent peril." Does this analysis also mean that an owner of cargo lost when the ship hit the reef would not be able to sue the original defendant?

3. AVOIDABLE CONSEQUENCES

During the era of contributory negligence there existed side by side a related doctrine called "avoidable consequences," which addressed the measure of damages but not issues of liability. Even if the accident was entirely the defendant's fault, the plaintiff's recovery might be reduced by failure to exercise due care to mitigate the harm done.

The clearest form of avoidable consequences issue involved the plaintiff's failure to get medical attention or to follow medical advice. Courts quite generally refused to award damages for complications that could have been avoided by the exercise of due care after the accident. This situation may raise particularly sensitive problems. In Hall v. Dumitru, 620 N.E.2d 668 (Ill.App.1993), the court held a person under no duty to undergo surgery to mitigate the damages caused by defendant's negligence. Refusing to distinguish between major and minor surgery, the court thought the crucial line was between treatments that involved a "recognized risk" and those that did not. The duty to mitigate applied in the latter case, but not in the former:

> [I]f the proposed treatment could result in an aggravation of the existing condition or the development of an additional condition of ill health, or if the prospect for improved health is slight, then there should be no duty to undergo the treatment. If the risk is clearly remote, the exception should not apply. But the risk need not be significant or even probable in order to trigger the exception.

Once the grounds for an exception are established, the plaintiff need not articulate reasons for rejecting the procedure. "It is not the place of the court or the jury to evaluate a patient's reasons for declining surgery or treatment, if the risks are recognized." In the actual case the proposed surgery was a tubal ligation that involved "general anesthetic which alone has attendant risks which can be potentially harmful and life threatening. The procedure itself involves the use of a sharp instrument in close proximity to vital organs necessitating the use of carbon dioxide to inflate the abdomen. It is apparent from the record that a tubal ligation surgery involves risks to a woman's life or member. [   ] Therefore, the plaintiff was under no duty to undergo the surgery to mitigate her damages. . . ."

The reluctance to mitigate by treatment raises special problems when the reasons are based on religious beliefs. In Munn v. Algee, 924 F.2d 568 (5th Cir.1991), the court held that the decedent's religious beliefs would not justify her failure to accept a blood transfusion. The case is criticized in Note, Reason, Religion, and Avoidable Consequences: When Faith and the Duty to Mitigate Collide, 67 N.Y.U.L.Rev. 1111 (1992), which develops a "reasonable believer" notion under which the jury would be "instructed to assess the reasonableness of a plaintiff's mitigation efforts according to the standard of a reasonable, sincere adherent of the plaintiff's religious tenets." The note suggests an analogy to "eggshell skull. . . . From a policy standpoint . . . a victim of another's tortious conduct—whose religion constrains her from taking what others might deem reasonable, ameliorative steps—ought not be forced to choose between being spiritually or financially whole." But see Simons, The Puzzling Doctrine of Contributory Negligence, 16 Cardozo L.Rev. 1693, 1730 (1995), suggesting that the result in *Munn* is better explained on the ground that although "decedent's decision to honor her religious beliefs is *not* unreasonable, defendant has no duty to subsidize her choice to sacrifice her life in the name of religion."

See also Williams v. Bright, 658 N.Y.S.2d 910 (App.Div. 1997), involving a religiously-motivated rejection of a blood transfusion that led to serious permanent injury. The court observed that no one "suggests that the State, or, for that matter, anyone else, has the right to interfere with that religious belief. But the real issue here is whether the consequences of that belief must be fully paid for here on earth by someone other than the injured believer." It promulgated a charge for the retrial in which the jury was to be told that plaintiff's "belief is a factor for you to consider, together with all the other evidence you have heard, in determining whether the plaintiff acted reasonably in caring for her injuries, keeping in mind, however, that the overriding test is whether the plaintiff acted as a reasonably prudent person, under all the circumstances confronting her." A dissenter argued that the "eggshell plaintiff" applied, citing *Bartolone* at p. 402, supra. The dissenter also quoted a commentator who wrote that the occurrence of this type of religious refusal "is sufficiently rare that the hypothetical cost pose[d] to society is negligible."

In Tanberg v. Ackerman Investment Co., 473 N.W.2d 193 (Iowa 1991), plaintiff sustained a back injury due to defendant's negligence. His physician advised him to lose weight to mitigate the back pain. A jury found that plaintiff failed to make a reasonable effort to lose weight, and that plaintiff was 70% at fault for his damage compared to 30% for the tortfeasor. The court held the finding was plausible and affirmed after concluding that under the state's modified comparative negligence rule plaintiff recovered nothing. How would the Uniform Act handle this situation?

One heavily litigated current aspect of the avoidable consequences issue involves the failure to use seat belts or safety belts in automobiles or helmets with motorcycles. Although traditional obligations to mitigate arose only after the original injury, these new cases raise what might be called an issue of "anticipatory avoidable consequences." Under the regime of contributory negligence, efforts by defendants to bar recovery under that doctrine generally failed. With the emergence of comparative fault, the issue has become quite complicated. The problem is posed by assuming some numbers:

a. Defendant was solely to blame for a two-car crash in which the plaintiff, the other driver, was not wearing an available seat belt. Defendant offers unrebutted expert testimony that use of the belt would have kept the damages at $20,000 instead of $200,000.

b. Does anything change if the defendant was a drunk driver?

c. What if the plaintiff was 20% at fault in causing the initial accident? 90%?

The states have responded to these issues in a variety of ways. Some legislatures, when making it a crime not to use a belt or helmet, have added a provision that makes the violation inadmissible in any civil action. Others have provided that the violation, if causally related to the harm, may affect civil damages but by no more than a small percentage. See, e.g., Meyer v. City of Des Moines, 475 N.W.2d 181 (Iowa 1991), discussing the Iowa statute that limits the reduction in the plaintiff's recovery to 5%. See also LaHue v. General Motors Corp., 716 F.Supp. 407 (W.D.Mo.1989)(maximum reduction in Missouri of 1%). When statutes have commanded use of these safety devices but have said nothing about civil consequences, some courts have chosen to treat the failure to use belts or helmets as a species of fault.

Some states, including California and New York, allow the failure to use safety devices to fully reduce recoverable damages, though the defendant is likely to bear the burden of showing what part of plaintiff's harm was due to the failure to use the safety equipment. See the extended discussion in Law v. Superior Court, 755 P.2d 1135 (Ariz.1988). Others reject any reduction. See Swajian v. General Motors Corp., 559 A.2d 1041 (R.I.1989):

> We recognize the safety-belt defense for what it is worth—a manifestation of public policy. This court believes that any attempt at reducing highway fatalities through promoting the increased use of safety belts is best accomplished by legislative action. Recent studies indicate that the vast majority of Rhode Islanders refuse to buckle up. [ ] If we were to impose a duty to wear safety belts, in essence this court would be condemning most motor-vehicle occupants as negligent. Such a determination, if desirable, is properly left to the Legislature. . . . Moreover, should recent safety-belt-use studies prove reliable, it could be argued that manufacturers should design vehicles in a manner safe for those who foreseeably will not wear safety belts. The above discussion smacks of public-policy considerations more appropriately addressed by the Legislature. In any event, we are doubtful that a contrary holding would encourage increased use of safety belts.

In the *Meyer* case, supra, which involved the failure to wear a helmet, the state legislature had not addressed that question. The court noted that under the state's comparative negligence statute a plaintiff who was more than 50% at fault would get nothing. If failure to wear a helmet were treated as fault for this purpose, the plaintiff might get no recovery whatever—and the doctrine of avoidable consequences would be operating as comparative fault. This was one among several reasons for excluding evidence of the failure to use a helmet.

For an attempt to weave an intermediate course in which the plaintiff will lose some portion of the damages attributable to the failure to wear the belt or helmet, but cannot lose more than half the actual damages by such conduct, see Waterson v. General Motors Corp., 544 A.2d 357 (N.J.1988). See also Gaertner v. Holcka, 580 N.W.2d 271 (Wis.1998).

Is the problem one of comparing faults? Is it one of causation—so that the plaintiff should bear the full consequences of allowing what would otherwise have been a relatively minor injury to become a catastrophe? Are the issues in these anticipatory avoidable consequences cases, different from those raised in the *Fritts* case, p. 452, supra?

Another current aspect of the doctrine of avoidable consequences occurs in the world of synergistic interactions. In Champagne v. Raybestos–Manhattan, Inc., 562 A.2d 1100 (Conn.1989), plaintiff's job brought him into contact with asbestos. After being tested in 1975, he was warned that his chest X-ray had shown change and was "strongly advised [to] discontinue cigarette smoking." The jury could have found that plaintiff had continued smoking until his death despite repeated warnings. He left work in 1979, developed lung cancer in late 1984 or early 1985, and died in 1985 at age 60. An expert testified that the most likely cause of the cancer was "asbestos exposure along with the incidence of smoking." His basis for such an opinion was that the incidence of cancer in smokers exposed to asbestos is "from ten to sixty times more than the incidence of cancer in nonsmokers exposed to asbestos." The judge's charge allowed the jury to allocate comparative responsibility. The jury found for plaintiff but reduced the award by 75%. This part of the case was affirmed on appeal. The court held that the jury could reasonably have concluded that the decedent knew or should have known that his conduct was not reasonable and, consequently, there was no basis for upsetting the jury's decision.

B. ASSUMPTION OF RISK

1. EXPRESS AGREEMENTS

Parties sometimes agree in advance that the defendant need not exercise due care for the safety of the plaintiff. This is generally done in a more-or-less formal written contract, usually called an exculpatory or a hold-harmless agreement. If the plaintiff is later hurt by what is claimed to be defendant's negligence, the contract is usually at the center of any ensuing litigation. Such litigation generally raises two types of questions: (1) will the courts enforce even the most clearly drafted contract given the type of activity involved, and (2) if so, is the contract in question sufficiently clear. The following case suggests the nature of the inquiries.

Dalury v. S–K–I, Ltd.

Supreme Court of Vermont, 1995.
670 A.2d 795.

[While skiing at defendants' resort, plaintiff was badly hurt when he collided with a metal pole that formed part of the control maze for a ski lift line. Before the season had started plaintiff had purchased a season pass and signed a form that provided in relevant part:

RELEASE FROM LIABILITY AND CONDITIONS OF USE

1. I accept and understand that Alpine Skiing is a hazardous sport with many dangers and risks and that injuries are a common and ordinary occurrence of the sport. As a condition of being permitted to use the ski area premises, I freely accept and voluntarily assume the risks of injury or property damage and release Killington Ltd., its employees and agents from any and all liability for personal injury or property damage resulting from negligence, conditions of the premises, operations of the ski area, actions or omissions of employees or agents of the ski area or from my participation in skiing at the area, accepting myself the full responsibility for <u>any and all</u> such damage or injury of any kind which may result.

Plaintiff also signed a photo identification card that contained the same language. The trial judge granted defendant summary judgment.]

Before ALLEN, C.J., and GIBSON, DOOLEY, MORSE and JOHNSON, JJ.

JOHNSON, JUDGE.

. . . .

On appeal, plaintiffs contend that the release was ambiguous as to whose liability was waived and that it is unenforceable as a matter of law because it violates public policy. We agree with defendants that the release was quite clear in its terms. Because we hold the agreement is unenforceable, we proceed to a discussion of the public policy that supports our holding.

I.

This is a case of first impression in Vermont. While we have recognized the existence of a public policy exception to the validity of exculpatory agreements, see [ ], in most of our cases, enforceability has turned on whether the language of the agreement was sufficiently clear to reflect the parties' intent. See [ ]; [ ] (broad exculpatory language at end of limited warranty clause insufficient to release defendant for negligent design); [ ] (agreement in entirety sufficiently clear to show experienced, professional freestyle skier intended to hold ski area harmless); [ ] (language of contract sufficiently clear to show parties' intent to hold railroad harmless for its own negligence).

Even well-drafted exculpatory agreements, however, may be void because they violate public policy. Restatement (Second) of Torts Sec. 496B comment *e* (1965). According to the Restatement, an exculpatory agreement should be upheld if it is (1) freely and fairly made, (2) between parties who are in an equal bargaining position, and (3) there is no social interest with which it interferes. Sec. 496B comment *b*. The critical issue here concerns the social interests that are affected.

Courts and commentators have struggled to develop a useful formula for analyzing the public policy issue. The formula has been the "subject of great debate" during "the whole course of the common law," and it had proven impossible to articulate a precise definition because the "social forces that have led to such characterization are volatile and dynamic." Tunkl v. Regents of Univ. of Cal., 383 P.2d 441, 444 (Cal.1963).

The leading judicial formula for determining whether an exculpatory agreement violates public policy was set forth by Justice Tobriner of the California Supreme Court [in *Tunkl*]. An agreement is invalid if it exhibits some or all of the following characteristics:

> [1.] It concerns a business of a type generally thought suitable for public regulation. [2.] The party seeking exculpation is engaged in performing a service of great importance to the public, which is often a matter of practical necessity for some members of the public. [3.] The party holds [it]self out as willing to perform this service for any member of the public who seeks it, or at least for any member coming within certain established standards. [4.] As a result of the essential nature of the service, in the economic setting of the transaction, the party invoking exculpation possesses a decisive advantage of bargaining strength against any member of the public who seeks [the party's] services. [5.] In exercising a superior bargaining power the party confronts the public with a standardized adhesion contract of exculpation, and makes no provision whereby a purchaser may pay additional reasonable fees and obtain protection against negligence. [6.] Finally, as a result of the transaction, the person or property of the purchaser is placed under the control of the seller, subject to the risk of carelessness by the seller or [the seller's] agents.

[ ]. Applying these factors, the court concluded that a release from liability for future negligence imposed as a condition for admission to a charitable research hospital was invalid. [ ] Numerous courts have adopted and applied the *Tunkl* factors. See Wagenblast v. Odessa Sch. Dist., 758 P.2d 968, 971–73 (Wash.1988)(release for school district's interscholastic athletics violated public policy); Kyriazis v. University of W.Va., 450 S.E.2d 649, 654–55 (W.Va.1994)(release for state university-sponsored club rugby was invalid because "[w]hen a state university provides recreational activities to its students, it fulfills its educational mission, and performs a public service").

Other courts have incorporated the *Tunkl* factors into their decisions. The Colorado Supreme Court has developed a four-part inquiry to analyze the validity of exculpatory agreements: (1) existence of a duty to the public, (2) the nature of the service performed, (3) whether the contract was fairly entered into, and (4) whether the intention of the parties is expressed in clear and unambiguous language. Jones v. Dressel, 623 P.2d 370, 376 (Colo.1981). In the *Jones* case, the court concluded, based on the *Tunkl* factors, that no duty to the public was involved in air service for a parachute jump, because that sort of service does not affect the public interest. [   ] Using a similar formula, the Wyoming Supreme Court concluded that a ski resort's sponsorship of an Ironman Decathlon competition did not invoke the public interest. Milligan v. Big Valley Corp., 754 P.2d 1063, 1066–67 (Wyo.1988).

On the other hand, the Virginia Supreme Court recently concluded, in the context of a "Teflon Man Triathlon" competition, that a pre-injury release from liability for negligence is void as against public policy because it is simply wrong to put one party to a contract at the mercy of the other's negligence. Hiett v. Lake Barcroft Community Ass'n, 418 S.E.2d 894, 897 (Va.1992). The court stated: " '[T]o hold that it was competent for one party to put the other parties to the contract at the mercy of its own misconduct . . . can never be lawfully done where an enlightened system of jurisprudence prevails. Public policy forbids it, and contracts against public policy are void.' " [   ]

Having reviewed these various formulations of the public policy exception, we accept them as relevant considerations, but not as rigid factors that, if met, preclude further analysis. Instead, we recognize that no single formula will reach the relevant public policy issues in every factual context. Like the court in Wolf v. Ford, 644 A.2d 522, 527 (Md.1994), we conclude that ultimately, the "determination of what constitutes the public interest must be made considering the totality of the circumstances of any given case against the backdrop of current societal expectations."

II.

Defendants urge us to uphold the exculpatory agreement on the ground that ski resorts do not provide an essential public service. They argue that they owe no duty to plaintiff to permit him to use their private lands for skiing, and that the terms and conditions of entry ought to be left entirely within their control. Because skiing, like other recreational sports, is not a necessity of life, defendants contend that the sale of a lift ticket is a purely private matter, implicating no public interest. See, e.g., *Milligan*, [   ] ("Generally, a private recreational business does not qualify as a service demanding a special duty to the public, nor are its services of a special, highly necessary or essential nature"). We disagree.

Whether or not defendants provide an essential public service does not resolve the public policy question in the recreational sports context. The defendants' area is a facility open to the public. They advertise and invite skiers and nonskiers of every level of skiing ability to their premises for the price of a ticket. At oral argument, defendants conceded that thousands of people buy lift tickets every day throughout the season. Thousands of people ride lifts, buy services, and ski the trails. Each ticket sale may be, for some purposes, a purely private transaction. But ~~when a substantial number of such sales take place as a result of the seller's general invitation to the public to utilize the facilities and services in question, a legitimate public interest arises~~.

The major public policy implications are those underlying the law of premises liability. In Vermont, a business owner has a duty "of active care to make sure that its premises are in safe and suitable condition for its customers." [   ] This duty of care "increases proportionately with the foreseeable risks of the operations involved." [   ] The business invitee "ha[s] a right to assume that the premises, aside from obvious dangers, [are] reasonably safe for the purpose for which he [is] upon them, and that proper precaution [has] been taken to make them so." [   ] We have already held that a ski area owes its customers the same duty as any other business—to keep its premises reasonably safe. [   ]

The policy rationale is to place responsibility for maintenance of the land on those who own or control it, with the ultimate goal of keeping accidents to the minimum level possible. Defendants, not recreational skiers, have the expertise and opportunity to foresee and control hazards, and to guard against the negligence of their agents and employees. They alone can properly maintain and inspect their premises, and train their employees in risk management. They alone can insure against risks and effectively spread the cost of insurance among their thousands of customers. Skiers, on the other hand, are not in a position to discover and correct risks of harm, and they cannot insure against the ski area's negligence.

If defendants were permitted to obtain broad waivers of their liability, an important incentive for ski areas to manage risk would be removed, with the public bearing the cost of the resulting injuries. [   ] It is illogical, in these circumstances, to undermine the public policy underlying business invitee law and allow skiers to bear risks they have no ability or right to control.

. . . . We do not accept the proposition that because ski resorts do not provide an essential public service, such agreements do not affect the public interest. [   ] A recognition of the principles underlying the duty to business invitees makes clear the inadequacy of relying upon the essential public service factor in the analysis of public recreation cases. While interference with an essential public service surely affects the public interest, those services do not represent the universe of activities that implicate public concerns.

Moreover, reliance on the private nature of defendants' property would be inconsistent with societal expectations about privately owned facilities that are open to the general public. Indeed, when a facility becomes a place of public accommodation, it "render[s] a 'service which has become of public interest' in the manner of the innkeepers and common carriers of old." [   ] Defendants are not completely unfettered, as they argue, in their ability to set the terms and conditions of admission. Defendants' facility may be privately owned, but that characteristic no longer overcomes a myriad of legitimate public interests. Public accommodations laws that prohibit discrimination against potential users of the facility are just one example of limitations imposed by law that affect the terms and conditions of entry. See 9 V.S.A. Sec. 4502 (prohibiting discrimination in place of public accommodation).

Defendants argue that the public policy of the state, as expressed in the "Acceptance of inherent risks" statute, 12 V.S.A. 1037 ["a person who takes part in any sport accepts as a matter of law the dangers that inhere therein insofar as they are obvious and necessary"] indicates a willingness on the part of the Legislature to limit ski area liability. Therefore, they contend that public policy favors the use of express releases such as the one signed by plaintiff. On the contrary, defendants' allocation of responsibility for skiers' injuries is at odds with the statute. The statute places responsibility for the "inherent risks" of any sport on the participant, insofar as such risks are obvious and necessary. [   ] A ski area's own negligence, however, is neither an inherent risk nor an obvious and necessary one in the sport of skiing. Thus, a skier's assumption of the inherent risks of skiing does not abrogate the ski area's duty " 'to warn of or correct dangers which in the exercise of reasonable prudence in the circumstances could have been foreseen and corrected.' " [   ]

Reversed and remanded.

Notes and Questions

1.   *Tunkl* involved a release required of all patients entering a hospital. Is the court suggesting that the same analysis should apply to skiing? How do the *Tunkl* factors play out here?

2.   Why is the law of premises liability appropriate here? Is this situation comparable to that of a department store or a park?

3.   The court invokes the "ultimate goal of keeping accidents to the minimum level possible." Does that suggest that the ski resort would be liable here for having slopes that are more than minimal? To require that no skier be allowed to start down a slope until a signal has been received from below that the last skier has safely cleared the slope?

4.   On the other hand, should a ski resort be protected from liability when it places an unpadded metal pole in a skier's path?

5.   What is the role of the statute discussed in the last paragraph of the opinion?

6.   In Spencer v. Killington, Ltd., 702 A.2d 35 (Vt.1997), the court, 3–2, applied *Dalury* to void a release that plaintiff had signed in order to compete in an amateur "Ski Bum" race series held at defendant's ski area. The differences between the two cases were "minor compared to the obvious similarities." In both cases there was reason to be concerned that if "broad waivers of liability" were upheld "an important incentive for ski

areas to manage risk would be removed." The majority stated that the release in the case would have protected defendant "if a racer were injured upon striking a shovel accidentally left on the course by race promoters." Would the release in *Dalury* have had that effect? Should a court bar the release of such liability?

The Vermont court took a different approach when the agreement did not involve the victim. In Hamelin v. Simpson Paper (Vermont) Co., 702 A.2d 86 (Vt.1997), plaintiff security guard employed by T Co. was hurt when a wooden stair gave way under him while he was at work in D's factory. After settling P's claim, D sought indemnity from T under a contract requiring T to reimburse D for any judgments that T's workers have obtained against D. The court, 3–2, upheld the contract despite T's claim that the contract violated public policy by discouraging D's due care. The majority distinguished *Dalury*: the considerations there, "such as unequal bargaining power, fairness, and the benefits of risk-spreading, are not present here. [ ] Moreover, [enforcing the contract] does not significantly undermine [D's] incentives to keep its premises reasonably safe. The contract with [T] does not affect [D's] liability for injures suffered by other individuals at the plant, including [D's] own employees and guests." The contract in this type of case "merely allocated the cost of liability insurance." The dissent argued that the result was undesirable because it created poor safety incentives. How would you assess the agreement's impact on safety? A similar agreement was rejected in J.S. Alberici Const. Co., Inc. v. Mid–West Conveyor Co. Inc., 750 A.2d 518 (Del.Supr.2000), as violating Delaware's public policy.

7. Compare Leon v. Family Fitness Center (No. 107), Inc., 71 Cal. Rptr.2d 923 (App. 1998), in which the plaintiff was hurt when a sauna bench collapsed under him at defendant's health club. Although plaintiff had been required to sign an elaborate release before joining the club, the court found the writing no bar. No patron "can be charged with realistically appreciating the risk of injury from simply reclining on a sauna bench." Since use of a sauna bench is not a "known risk," there could be no assumed risk. Nor was the defendant's negligence reasonably related to the object of the release, which appeared to be the use of equipment. The court likened this case to the falling of a ceiling fan or a collapsing office chair. Further, the release was ineffective since it had been placed between two parts that dealt with the risk of exercise without saying it was meant to insulate against the club's own negligence.

8. No matter what the situation, courts generally agree that gross negligence or recklessness may never be disclaimed by agreement no matter what words are used. Sommer v. Federal Signal Corp., 593 N.E.2d 1365 (N.Y.1992)(alarm company's failure to relay alarm). Why should this be so if the activity is not one that implicates the *Tunkl* factors?

9. Even if the release itself is valid, the ability of adults to sign releases that bind members of their family is in serious doubt. See Scott v. Pacific West Mountain Resort, 834 P.2d 6 (Wash.1992)(refusing to enforce ski release signed by parent against injured child); Huber v. Hovey, 501

N.W.2d 53 (Iowa 1993)(refusing to enforce against wife release signed by husband). See also Dilallo v. Riding Safely, Inc., 687 So.2d 353 (Fla.App. 1997), refusing to enforce a clear release signed by a 14-year-old in order to ride at the stable. The court asserted that the need to protect minors warranted a rule that minors be able to get out of any release.

Other cases are more willing to bar children from suit. See Zivich v. Mentor Soccer Club, Inc., 696 N.E.2d 201 (Ohio 1998), holding that a parent's signature on a release to permit a child's participation in a soccer league bound the child and also barred the parents' derivative action for harm to the child—at least in cases involving non-profit groups. The court cited King, Exculpatory Agreements for Volunteers in Youth Activities— the Alternative to "Nerf (R)" Tiddlywinks, 53 Ohio St.L.J. 683 (1992), which argues that denying immunity will deter volunteers. The "choice for many may be between youth activities without a right to sue and no organized youth activities at all." He suggests that immunity even for acts of gross negligence and recklessness may be appropriate here because it is difficult to predict how actions will be judged in advance and because volunteers are not motivated by greed to endanger others.

10. *Drafting the contract.* Even in jurisdictions that are willing to permit exculpatory agreements in certain situations, the actual form must meet certain criteria. New York, for example, requires that the agreement state "unambiguously" that it involves an exemption from liability for negligence. See Gross v. Sweet, 400 N.E.2d 306 (N.Y.1979).

In Krazek v. Mountain River Tours, Inc., 884 F.2d 163 (4th Cir.1989), the release executed before a river rafting trip stated:

> I am aware that during [the trip] certain substantial risks and dangers may occur, including but not limited to, hazards of traveling on a rubber raft in rough river conditions, hiking in tough terrain, accidents or illnesses in remote places without medical facilities, the forces of nature, and travel by automobile, bus or other conveyance.
>
> In consideration of and as part payment for the right to participate in such river trips or other activities and the services and food, if any, arranged for me by Mountain River Tours, Inc., its agents, employees and associates, I have and do hereby assume all of the above risks, and release, and will hold harmless from any and all liability actions, causes of action, debts, claims and demand of every kind and nature whatso-ever which I now have or which may arise out of or in connection with my trip or participation in any other activity. The terms hereof shall serve as a release, indemnification, and assumption of risk for my heirs, executors and administrators and for all members of my family, including any minors accompanying me.

During plaintiff's trip a severe hail storm began. The rafter guide, an employee of defendant, ordered the rafters into the river to protect them from the hail. "While in the river Ms. Krazek was swept away by the current, thrown up against rocks, and injured." Her claim was that the form did not specifically mention negligence and thus she had not waived her right to pursue that remedy. ~~The court disagreed~~. Applying West Virginia law, it began by noting that ~~exculpatory clauses must be clear and definite and that contracts releasing a party from liability due to his own~~ negligence "~~are looked upon with disfavor, and are strictly construed against the releasee.~~" Additionally, "any ambiguities in a contract will be strictly construed against the preparer."

Nonetheless, ~~the court concluded that this form was clear enough to protect the defendant from negligence liability~~—particularly the phrase waiving any claim "of every kind or nature whatsoever." To fail to bar this action "would create a requirement that to bar negligence claims all releases must include the words 'negligence' or 'negligent act.' We decline, however, to formulate a rule that requires the use of specific 'magic words' in contracts such as this one." The court also enforced the contract's indemnification provision to require plaintiff to reimburse the defendant for its costs in defending this action.

Compare Kissick v. Schmierer, 816 P.2d 188 (Alaska 1991), in which three prospective passengers on a private plane belonging to an aviation club were required to agree that they would not sue for negligence that caused "any loss, damage or injury to my person or my property." The passengers were killed. ~~The court held that the agreement did not bar suits for death~~. A dissenter was "incredulous."

11. Before we turn to cases in which defendants claim that plaintiff's conduct shows an implied assumption of the risk, we should note briefly an intermediate area—cases in which defendants claim that a contract exists by virtue of a sign posted on defendant's land combined with plaintiff's conduct. The typical case involves a bailment at a parking lot with a large sign that announces that all cars are left at owner's risk. When the car is stolen the courts reject the claim that the bailment contract included the disclaimer, in the absence of a showing that the limitation—whether on a sign or on a claim check—was drawn to the plaintiff's attention. See, e.g., Allright, Inc. v. Schroeder, 551 S.W.2d 745 (Tex.Civ.App.1977); Allen v. Southern Pacific Co., 213 P.2d 667 (Utah 1950)(limitation sign in railroad checkroom).

12.   *Post-injury releases.* The *Dalury* court's discussion is limited to pre-injury releases. Those written after injury are essentially settlement agreements and raise typical contract issues. In Mangini v. McClurg, 249 N.E.2d 386 (N.Y.1969), some of plaintiff's injuries did not manifest themselves until after the settlement was signed. In discussing how to analyze the contract, the court observed:

> [There are] many reasons, including doubtful liability, the willingness to take a calculated risk, the desire to obtain an earlier rather than a later settlement, and perhaps others, why releasors may wish to effect a settlement and intend to give the releasee a discharge of liability for any unknown injuries—in short to bargain for general peace. When general peace is the consideration, there can be no mutual mistake as to the extent of the injuries, known or unknown.

Some of these considerations, of course, also explain why some claims are settled for less than even the harm sustained from known injuries. Citing support for the proposition that unknown injuries are not generally within the contemplation of the parties "despite the generality of standardized language in releases," the court concluded that the plaintiffs were entitled to try to prove, "directly or circumstantially, that there was no intention to release a claim for unknown injuries." Settlements are explored in more detail in Chapter X.

2. IMPLIED ASSUMPTION OF RISK

In this section, no express language or agreement indicates the intentions or understandings of the parties. The area is quite controversial, in part because of disagreement over whether the term plays any useful role in negligence litigation. Throughout the materials in this section consider whether the doctrine serves a purpose distinct from other aspects of the negligence framework we have considered up to this point.

Murphy v. Steeplechase Amusement Co.

Court of Appeals of New York, 1929.
250 N.Y. 479, 166 N.E. 173.

Appeal from a judgment of the Appellate Division of the Supreme Court, affirming a judgment in favor of plaintiff entered upon a verdict.

CARDOZO, CH. J. The defendant, Steeplechase Amusement Company, maintains an amusement park at Coney Island, New York.

One of the supposed attractions is known as "The Flopper." It is a moving belt, running upward on an inclined plane, on which passengers sit or stand. Many of them are unable to keep their feet because of the movement of the belt, and are thrown backward or aside. The belt runs in a groove, with padded walls on either side to a height of four feet, and with padded flooring beyond the walls at the same angle as the belt. An electric motor, driven by current furnished by the Brooklyn Edison Company, supplies the needed power.

Plaintiff, a vigorous young man, visited the park with friends. One of them, a young woman, now his wife, stepped upon the moving belt. Plaintiff followed and stepped behind her. As he did so, he felt what he describes as a sudden jerk, and was thrown to the floor. His wife in front and also friends behind him were thrown at the same time. Something more was here, as every one understood, than the slowly-moving escalator that is common in shops and public places. A fall was foreseen as one of the risks of the adventure. There would have been no point to the whole thing, no adventure about it, if the risk had not been there. The very name above the gate, the Flopper, was warning to the timid. If the name was not enough, there was warning more distinct in the experience of others. We are told by the plaintiff's wife that the members of her party stood looking at the sport before joining in it themselves. Some aboard the belt were able, as she viewed them, to sit down with decorum or even to stand and keep their footing; others jumped or fell. The tumbling bodies and the screams and laughter supplied the merriment and fun. "I took a chance," she said when asked whether she thought that a fall might be expected.

Plaintiff took the chance with her, but, less lucky than his companions, suffered a fracture of a knee cap. He states in his complaint that the belt was dangerous to life and limb in that it stopped and started violently and suddenly and was not properly equipped to prevent injuries to persons who were using it without knowledge of its dangers, and in a bill of particulars he adds that it was operated at a fast and dangerous rate of speed and was not supplied with a proper railing, guard or other device to prevent a fall therefrom. No other negligence is charged.

We see no adequate basis for a finding that the belt was out of order. It was already in motion when the plaintiff put his foot on it. He cannot help himself to a verdict in such circumstances by the addition of the facile comment that it threw him with a jerk. One who steps upon a moving belt and finds his heels above his head is in no position to discriminate with nicety between the successive stages of the shock, between the jerk which is a cause and the jerk, accompanying the fall, as an instantaneous effect. There is evidence for the defendant that power was transmitted smoothly, and could not be transmitted otherwise. If the movement was spasmodic, it was an unexplained and, it seems, an inexplicable departure from the normal workings of the mechanism. An aberration so extraordinary, if it is to lay the basis for a verdict, should rest on something firmer than a mere descriptive epithet, a summary of the sensations of a tense and crowded moment [   ]. But the jerk, if it were established, would add little to the case. Whether the movement of the belt was uniform or irregular, the risk at greatest was a fall. This was the very hazard that was invited and foreseen [   ].

Volenti non fit injuria. One who takes part in such a sport accepts the dangers that inhere in it so far as they are obvious and necessary, just as a fencer accepts the risk of a thrust by his antagonist or a spectator at a ball game the chance of contact with the ball [   ]. The antics of the clown are not the paces of the cloistered cleric. The rough and boisterous joke, the horseplay of the crowd, evokes its own guffaws, but they are not the pleasures of tranquillity. The plaintiff was not seeking a retreat for meditation. Visitors were tumbling about the belt to the merriment of onlookers when he made his choice to join them. He took the chance of a like fate, with whatever damage to his body might ensue from such a fall. The timorous may stay at home.

A different case would be here if the dangers inherent in the sport were obscure or unobserved ([   ]; Tantillo v. Goldstein Bros. Amusement Co., 248 N.Y. 286 [1928]), or so serious as to justify the belief that precautions of some kind must have been taken to avert them [   ]. Nothing happened to the plaintiff except what common experience tells us may happen at any time as the consequence of a sudden fall. Many a skater or a horseman can rehearse a tale of equal woe. A different case there would also be if the accidents had been so many as to show that the game in its inherent nature was too dangerous to be continued without change. The president of the amusement company says that there had never been such an accident before. A nurse employed at an emergency hospital maintained in connection with the park contradicts him to some extent. She says that on other occasions she had attended patrons of the park who had been injured at the Flopper, how many she could not say. None, however, had been badly injured or had suffered broken bones. Such testimony is not enough to show that the game was a trap for the unwary, too perilous to be endured. According to the defendant's estimate, two hundred and fifty thousand visitors were at the Flopper in a year. Some quota of accidents was to be looked for in so great a mass. One might as well say that a skating rink should be abandoned because skaters sometimes fall.

There is testimony by the plaintiff that he fell upon wood, and not upon a canvas padding. He is strongly contradicted by the photographs and by the witnesses for the defendant, and is without corroboration in the testimony of his companions who were witnesses in his behalf. If his observation was correct, there was a defect in the equipment, and one not obvious or known. The padding should have been kept in repair to break the force of any fall. The case did not go to the jury, however, upon any such theory of the defendant's liability, nor is the defect fairly suggested by the plaintiff's bill of particulars, which limits his complaint. The case went to the jury upon the theory that negligence was dependent upon a sharp and sudden jerk.

The judgment of the Appellate Division and that of the Trial Term should be reversed. . . .

POUND, CRANE, LEHMAN, KELLOGG and HUBBS, JJ., concur; O'BRIEN, J., dissents on the authority of [*Tantillo v. Goldstein Brothers Amusement Co.*].

Notes and Questions

1. Why does Judge Cardozo say that even if the belt had jerked unexpectedly this would not help plaintiff's case? What might he have said if such a jerk made everyone on the belt fall and suffer broken limbs?

2. In the *Tantillo* case cited, judgment was affirmed in favor of a 14-year-old plaintiff who was admitted to defendant's show without paying in return for his agreement to participate in a vaudeville act. He was hurt when one of the performers failed to catch him as he was tossed through the air. How is *Tantillo* relevant to *Murphy*?

3. What was the defendant's negligence in *Murphy*?

4. Judge Cardozo suggests that *Murphy* might have been different if the Flopper caused so many accidents that its "inherent nature" made it "too dangerous to be continued without change." If one of every three patrons suffered a broken bone and such information was posted conspicuously at the entrance to the Flopper and each prospective customer had to watch for ten minutes before getting on, how would that case differ from *Murphy?*

5. More generally, should the supplier of a product, service or activity be insulated from liability for known risks—no matter how serious—as long as the information is clearly provided to the potential victim? Note that this issue is distinct from the question in the preceding section where the claim was that the victim expressly agreed not to sue. We will reconsider this question in Chapter VIII, when we discuss product liability cases.

6. *Participants.* In the 1990s, there was a spurt of litigation between participants in amateur sports. The first major case was decided in California. In Knight v. Jewett, 834 P.2d 696 (Cal.1992), plaintiff alleged that during halftime of a Super Bowl telecast, she and her friends decided to play an informal game of touch football on an adjoining dirt lot, using a "peewee" football. Each side included both men and women. No rules were explicitly discussed before the game. Plaintiff alleged that defendant, one of her opponents, played aggressively and that on the play before she was hurt she told him to "be careful" or she would stop playing. On the next play, he knocked plaintiff over from behind while defending on a pass play—and stepped on her hand, injuring it. The trial judge granted defendant summary judgment.

On appeal, the court affirmed, 6–1, but split 4–3 on the right way to approach these cases. The majority asserted that the crucial analysis was on the duty defendant owed the plaintiff. If the defendant had met whatever duty was owed the plaintiff, the defendant would not be liable to plaintiff for anything. If, on the other hand, the defendant had violated the duty owed plaintiff, the defendant would be liable, subject to a reduction for whatever contributory negligence might be shown. (The four justices taking this view split over terminology. Three called the analysis focusing on duty "primary assumption of the risk" and the part focusing on possible defenses after breach "secondary assumption of the risk." The fourth judge wanted to eliminate all use of "assumption of risk" in favor of duty and comparative negligence.) For the majority:

> . . . [I]n the heat of an active sporting event like baseball or football, a participant's normal energetic conduct often includes accidentally careless behavior. . . . [V]igorous participation in such sporting events likely would be chilled if legal liability were to be imposed on a participant on the basis of his or her ordinary careless conduct. . . . [E]ven when a participant's conduct violates a rule of the game and may subject the violator to internal sanctions prescribed by the sport itself, imposition of legal liability for such conduct might well alter fundamentally the nature of the sport by deterring participants from vigorously engaging in activity that falls close to, but on the permissible side, of a prescribed rule.

Liability would flow "only if the participant intentionally injures another player or engages in conduct that is so reckless as to be totally outside the range of the ordinary activity involved in the sport." The defendant's behavior here was at most careless and summary judgment was properly granted.

Three justices argued that the proper approach to this type of case centered on the notion of the plaintiff's "consent" to accept specific risks. Two of them found that consent here because plaintiff admitted that she expected to receive contact and "bumps and bruises." The third did not find that consent and dissented.

A different analysis was developed in Lestina v. West Bend Mut. Ins. Co., 501 N.W.2d 28 (Wis.1993), involving a soccer injury. The court, 4–3, held that negligence should be the governing principle. The majority rejected the notion that vigorous participation would be chilled by invocation of negligence:

> To determine whether a player's conduct constitutes actionable negligence (or contributory negligence), the fact finder should consider such material factors as the sport involved, the rules and regulations governing the sport; the generally accepted customs and practices of the sport (including the types of contact and the level of violence generally accepted); the risks inherent in the game and those that are outside the realm of anticipation; the presence of protective equipment or uniforms; and the facts and circumstances of the particular case, including the ages and physical attributes of the participants, the participants' respective skills at the game, and the participants' knowledge of the rules and customs.

The dissenters rejected the idea that "negligence was flexible enough to be applied under any set of circumstances." They were concerned that applying the negligence standard to contact sports would chill vigorous participation. Why might the court's formulation chill participants?

In Crawn v. Campo, 643 A.2d 600 (N.J.1994), arising when a base runner in an informal softball game either ran into or slid into the catcher, the court unanimously held that "the duty of care applicable to participants in informal recreational sports is to avoid the infliction of injury caused by reckless or intentional conduct." Justice Handler cited two "policy reasons" for this result: "One is the promotion of vigorous participation in athletic activities . . . The other is to avoid a flood of litigation." He responded to the lower court's reliance on the Wisconsin case as follows:

> The problem with the court's analysis lies in the extraordinary difficulty in judging conduct that is based on limitless variables with respect to how the same game is played among different groups of people. The relationship among sports participants is derived from a consensual arrangement that involves both articulated and unarticulated rules, obvious and obscure conventions, and clear and not-so-clear expectations. Some rules are broken, yet their transgression is tolerated. Certain practices are customary yet others are followed inconsistently. Some conventions are well understood, others are not always known or appreciated by all participants. Each player's expectations

are often subjective, and may not be shared or experienced by others in the same way.

On the "flood of litigation" point, Justice Handler noted:

> One might well conclude that something is terribly wrong with a society in which the most commonly-accepted aspects of play—a traditional source of a community's conviviality and cohesion—spur litigation. The heightened-recklessness standard recognizes a commonsense distinction between excessively harmful conduct and the more routine rough-and-tumble of sports that should occur freely on the playing fields and should not be second-guessed in courtrooms.

Should fouls in basketball be tolerated even though they are rule violations? What if a player falls and is hurt after being fouled? Is there a legal distinction between "regular" fouls and "flagrant" fouls? As to hockey injuries, see McKichan v. St. Louis Hockey Club, L.P., 967 S.W.2d 209 (Mo.App.1998) (denying an action when a professional hockey player badly hurt an opponent after the whistle had stopped play).

In Freeman v. Hale, 36 Cal.Rptr.2d 418 (App. 1994), plaintiff skier was injured in a collision with defendant drunken skier. In response to defendant's argument that collisions are an inherent risk of skiing, the court relied on *Knight* in upholding actions in situations in which prohibiting the conduct in question "would neither deter vigorous participation in the sport nor otherwise fundamentally alter the nature of the sport." Although defendant "did not have a duty to avoid an inadvertent collision with [plaintiff], he did have a duty to avoid increasing the risk of such a collision. [   ] He did not establish that, by drinking alcohol while he was skiing, he did not increase that risk." In Cheong v. Antablin, 946 P.2d 817 (Cal.1997), the court held that a skier who tried to slow down by turning—and who turned into the path of an oncoming skier—did not owe the other a duty of due care. Should that change the result in the earlier *Freeman?*

Compare Connelly v. Mammoth Mountain Ski Area, 45 Cal.Rptr.2d 855 (App. 1995), in which the plaintiff, an advanced skier, was skiing down an "advanced intermediate" run when his ski bindings released and he fell and slid downhill into a large metal tower that supported the ski lift. The court denied recovery under *Knight v. Jewett,* noting that the tower was visible for 200 yards and that the run was fairly wide at the point at which the tower bisected it. In response to plaintiff's claim that the tower's padding was not at snow level and was inadequate in any event to cushion the blow, the court said that on previous occasions it had identified some of the inherent dangers of skiing to include "variations in terrain, surface or subsurface snow or ice conditions; bare spots; rocks, trees and other forms of natural growth or debris; collision with ski lift towers and their components, with other skiers, or with properly marked or plainly visible snow-making or snow-grooming equipment." The risk in this case was inherent in skiing. Ski operators had no duty to pad their clearly visible towers and it "would be anomalous to hold an operator who padded its towers—as Mammoth did here—more liable than an operator who failed to do so." There was no claim that defendant had done anything that caused plaintiff to collide with the tower: "colliding with a ski lift tower while skiing is an inherent risk within the doctrine of primary assumption of risk, and Mammoth owed no duty to Connelly to protect him from this inherent risk." Recall the *Dalury* case, p. 461, supra, involving express assumption of risk questions in a similar accident.

7. *Baseball spectators*. In Davidoff v. Metropolitan Baseball Club, 463 N.E.2d 1219 (N.Y.1984), the 14-year-old plaintiff was sitting in the first row behind first base during a professional game at Shea Stadium when she was badly injured by a foul ball. The court, 5–2, affirmed defendant stadium owner's summary judgment:

> Claims involving injuries sustained by spectators from misdirected baseballs were traditionally decided—and dismissed—on the ground of assumption of risk. However, with the enactment of [comparative negligence] in 1975, the absolute defense was no longer applicable and it became necessary to define the duty of care owed by a proprietor of a baseball field to its spectators. This we did in [   ]:

>> [W]here a proprietor of a ball park furnishes screening for the area of the field behind home plate where the danger of being struck by a ball is greatest and that screening is of sufficient extent to provide adequate protection for as many spectators as may reasonably be expected to desire such seating in the course of an ordinary game, the proprietor fulfills the duty of care imposed by law and, therefore, cannot be liable in negligence.

> Here, there has been no showing by plaintiff that (1) defendants failed to erect a screen behind home plate providing adequate protection in that area, and (2) there are not sufficient seats behind the screen to accommodate as many spectators as reasonably may be expected to desire such seating. No evidence that the screen was inadequate was presented, and it is undisputed that there were unoccupied seats behind the screen at Shea on the day plaintiff was injured.

The fact that others have been injured in this unscreened area did not matter. Plaintiff's claim that notice of danger should raise a jury question "would require a baseball field proprietor to operate as an insurer of spectators unless there was a protective screen shielding every seat."

The dissenters argued that requiring screening only behind home plate "does nothing more than to artificially limit the liability of ball park owners." Moreover, even if the majority's focus on unoccupied screened seats made sense in a sandlot where spectators may move around, it "is utterly out of place when the setting is a major sports stadium where . . . all seats are individually assigned or allocated to a specific area." A fan who is "unable to secure a seat behind home plate must go home or fully assume responsibility for any consequences of remaining at the ball park no matter how unreasonable the risk of injury."

In Neinstein v. Los Angeles Dodgers, Inc., 229 Cal.Rptr. 612 (App. 1986), the court followed a similar approach, observing that imposing a duty to protect all spectators would require owners either (1) to place "all

~~spectators behind a protective screen~~ thereby reducing the quality of everyone's view" and preventing spectators from catching balls, or ~~(2) to continue the status quo and increase ticket prices to cover the cost of compensating those hurt~~. The latter course would mean that "persons of meager means might be 'priced out' of enjoying the great American pastime." The introduction of comparative fault did not change the court's analysis.

The court also observed that but for the constraint of an earlier decision, "we would not be persuaded that there is a need to impose a duty to provide *any* screened seats. A person who fears injury always has the option of refraining from attending a baseball game or of sitting in a part of the park which is out of reach of balls traveling with sufficient velocity to cause harm." How would prospective spectators learn about the total absence of screening?

Would the result or the analysis in these cases change if the plaintiff had been a foreign tourist who had heard about baseball but did not know about its dangers? Does it matter whether the spectator is hurt during the first two minutes after taking a seat or after one hour?

Legislation. After adverse judgments against both the Chicago Cubs and White Sox, the Illinois legislature adopted protective legislation. Essentially, owners and operators of stadiums are not liable to anyone hit by a ball or bat unless they were sitting behind a negligently defective screen or they were hurt as the result of willful or wanton conduct. 745 I.L.C.S. 38/10. Colorado adopted similar legislation just as it got its first major league team. The legislation, Colo.Rev.Stat. § 13–21–120, asserts that professional baseball is a "wholesome and healthy family activity which should be encouraged," that the "state will derive economic benefit from spectators" who attend the games, and that it is thus in the state's interest to "encourage attendance at professional baseball games." Limiting the civil liability of team owners and stadium owners "will help contain costs, keeping ticket prices more affordable."

Davenport v. Cotton Hope Plantation Horizontal Property Regime

Supreme Court of South Carolina, 1998.
333 S.C. 71, 508 S.E.2d 565.

TOAL, JUSTICE.

This is a comparative negligence case arising out of an accident in which respondent, Alvin Davenport, was injured while descending a stairway near his apartment. We granted certiorari to review the [decision of the court of appeals]. . . .

[Plaintiff rented from its owner a condominium unit on the top floor of a three-floor building within defendant's premises. Three stairways offered access: one at each end and one in the middle of the building. Plaintiff's unit was five feet from the middle stairway. For two months before his fall, plaintiff had been reporting to management that the middle stairway's floodlights were not working, but he continued using that stairway. One night, as plaintiff descended the middle stairway to go to work, he tripped and was hurt in the resulting fall. He testified that what he thought was a step turned out to be a shadow caused by the broken floodlights. The trial court directed a verdict against plaintiff based on assumed risk and also held that even if comparative negligence applied, plaintiff was more negligent than defendant as a matter of law. The court of appeals reversed on both points.]

The threshold question we must answer is whether assumption of risk survives as a complete bar to recovery under South Carolina's [modified] comparative negligence system.   .   .   .

.   .   .

[This court] ultimately extended the defense [of assumption of risk] to negligence cases outside the traditional master-servant context. See, e.g., Smith v. Edwards, [195 S.E. 236 (S.C.1938)]. In *Smith*, the plaintiff died as a result of burns she suffered while receiving a "permanent wave" at a beauty shop. The defendant argued that the plaintiff had diabetes which made her peculiarly susceptible to the injuries, and consequently, she assumed the risk of injury. The plaintiff argued that under these facts, assumption of risk was not available as an affirmative defense. This Court disagreed, stating, "[assumption of risk] applies to any case   .   .   . where the facts proved show that the person against whom the doctrine of assumption of risk is pleaded knew of the danger, appreciated it, and acquiesced therein." [   ]

Currently in South Carolina, there are four requirements to establishing the defense of assumption of risk: (1) the plaintiff must have knowledge of the facts constituting a dangerous condition; (2) the plaintiff must know the condition is dangerous; (3) the plaintiff must appreciate the nature and extent of the danger; and (4) the plaintiff must voluntarily expose himself to the danger.   .   .   .

As noted by the Court of Appeals, an overwhelming majority of jurisdictions that have adopted some form of comparative negligence have essentially abolished assumption of risk as an absolute bar to recovery. [   ] In analyzing the continuing viability of assumption of risk in a comparative negligence system, many courts distinguish between "express" assumption of risk and "implied" assumption of risk. [   ] Implied assumption of risk is further divided into the categories of "primary" and "secondary" implied assumption of risk. [   ] We will discuss each of these concepts below.

Express assumption of risk applies when the parties expressly agree in advance, either in writing or orally, that the plaintiff will relieve the defendant of his or her legal duty toward the plaintiff. See Restatement (Second) of Torts § 496B (1965); [   ]. Thus, being under no legal duty, the defendant cannot be charged with negligence. [   ] Even in those comparative fault jurisdictions that have abrogated assumption of risk, the rule remains that express assumption of risk continues as an absolute defense in an action for negligence. [citing 16 cases and treatises] The reason for this is that express assumption of risk sounds in contract, not tort, and is based upon an express manifestation of consent. [   ]

.   .   .

Express assumption of risk is contrasted with implied assumption of risk which arises when the plaintiff implicitly, rather than expressly, assumes known risks. As noted above, implied assumption of risk is characterized as either primary or secondary. Primary implied assumption of risk arises when the plaintiff impliedly assumes those risks that are inherent in a particular activity. [   ] (student injured in a collision during football drill); [   ] (injured while watching softball game). Primary implied assumption of risk is not a true affirmative defense, but instead goes to the initial determination of whether the defendant's legal duty encompasses the risk encountered by the plaintiff. E.g., Perez v. McConkey, 872 S.W.2d 897 (Tenn.1994); [   ]. In *Perez*, the Tennessee Supreme Court summarized the doctrine in the following way:

> In its primary sense, implied assumption of risk focuses not on the plaintiff's conduct in assuming the risk, but on the defendant's general duty of care.   .   .   . Clearly, primary implied assumption of risk is but another way of stating the conclusion that a plaintiff has failed to establish a prima facie case [of negligence] by failing to establish that a duty exists.

[   ] In this sense, primary implied assumption of risk is simply a part of the initial negligence analysis. [   ]

Secondary implied assumption of risk, on the other hand, arises when the plaintiff knowingly encounters a risk created by the defendant's negligence. [   ] It is a true defense because it is asserted only after the plaintiff establishes a prima facie case of negligence against the defendant. Secondary implied assumption of risk may involve either reasonable or unreasonable conduct on the part of the plaintiff. [The court quoted a lower court case that had discussed "secondary unreasonable implied assumption of the risk" in the context of a person who "dashed into a fire in order to save his hat." Such a risk could be found to be "out of all proportion to the advantage which he is seeking to gain."][4] Since express and primary implied assumption of risk are compatible with comparative negligence, we will refer to secondary implied assumption of risk simply as "assumption of risk."

As alluded to in [   ], assumption of risk and contributory negligence have historically been recognized as separate defenses in South Carolina. [   ] However, other courts have found assumption of risk functionally indistinguishable from contributory negligence and consequently abolished assumption of risk as a complete defense. [   ]

---

4. Reasonable implied assumption of risk exists when the plaintiff is aware of a risk negligently created by the defendant but, nonetheless, voluntarily proceeds to encounter the risk; when weighed against the risk of injury, the plaintiff's action is reasonable. [   ]

To date, the only comparative fault jurisdictions that have retained assumption of risk as an absolute defense are Georgia, Mississippi, Nebraska, Rhode Island, and South Dakota. [ ] Only the Rhode Island Supreme Court has provided a detailed discussion of why it believes the common law form of assumption of risk should survive under comparative negligence. [ ] In Kennedy v. Providence Hockey Club, Inc., [376 A.2d 329 (R.I.1977)], the Rhode Island Supreme Court distinguished between assumption of risk and contributory negligence, emphasizing the former was measured by a subjective standard while the latter was based on an objective, reasonable person standard. The court further noted that it had in the past limited the application of assumption of risk to those situations where the plaintiff had actual knowledge of the hazard. The court then rejected the premise that assumption of risk and contributory negligence overlap:

> [C]ontributory negligence and assumption of the risk do not overlap; the key difference is, of course, the exercise of one's free will in encountering the risk. Negligence analysis, couched in reasonable hypotheses, has no place in the assumption of the risk framework. When one acts knowingly, it is immaterial whether he acts reasonably. [ ]

Rhode Island's conclusions are in sharp contrast with the West Virginia Supreme Court's opinion in King v. Kayak Manufacturing Corp., [387 S.E.2d 511 (W.Va.1989)]. Like Rhode Island, the West Virginia Supreme Court in *King* recognized that assumption of risk was conceptually distinct from contributory negligence. The court specifically noted that West Virginia's doctrine of assumption of risk required actual knowledge of the dangerous condition, which conformed with the general rule elsewhere in the country. [ ] In fact, the court cited Rhode Island's decision in *Kennedy* as evidence of this general rule. [ ] Nevertheless, the West Virginia court concluded that the absolute defense of assumption of risk was incompatible with its comparative fault system. The court therefore adopted a comparative assumption of risk rule, stating, "a plaintiff is not barred from recovery by the doctrine of assumption of risk unless his degree of fault arising therefrom equals or exceeds the combined fault or negligence of the other parties to the accident." [ ] The court explained that the absolute defense of assumption of risk was as repugnant to its fault system as the common law rule of contributory negligence. [ ]

A comparison between the approaches in West Virginia and Rhode Island is informative. Both jurisdictions recognize that assumption of risk is conceptually distinct from contributory negligence. However, Rhode Island focuses on the objective/subjective distinction between the two defenses and, therefore, retains assumption of risk as a complete bar to recovery. On the other hand, West Virginia emphasizes that the main purpose of its comparative negligence system is to apportion fault. Thus, West Virginia rejects assumption of risk as a total bar to recovery and only allows a jury to consider the plaintiff's negligence in assuming the risk. If the plaintiff's total negligence exceeds or equals that of the defendant, only then is the plaintiff completely barred from recovery.

Like Rhode Island and West Virginia, South Carolina has historically maintained a distinction between assumption of risk and contributory negligence, even when the two doctrines appear to overlap. [ ] Thus, the pertinent question is whether a plaintiff should be completely barred from recovery when he voluntarily assumes a known risk, regardless of whether his assumption of that risk was reasonable or unreasonable. Upon considering the purpose of our comparative fault system, we conclude that West Virginia's approach is the most persuasive model.

In [a 1984 South Carolina appellate case], Judge Sanders provided the following justification for adopting a comparative negligence system: "It is contrary to the basic premise of our fault system to allow a defendant, who is at fault in causing an accident, to escape bearing any of its cost, while requiring a plaintiff, who is no more than equally at fault or even less at fault, to bear all of its costs." [ ] By contrast, the main reason for having the defense of assumption of risk is not to determine fault, but to prevent a person who knowingly and voluntarily incurs a risk of harm from holding another person liable. [ ] Cotton Hope argues that the justification behind assumption of risk is not in conflict with South Carolina's comparative fault system. We disagree.

As stated by Judge Sanders, it is contrary to the premise of our comparative fault system to require a plaintiff, who is fifty-percent or less at fault, to bear all of the costs of the injury. In accord with this logic, the defendant's fault in causing an accident is not diminished solely because the plaintiff knowingly assumes a risk. If assumption of risk is retained in its current common law form, a plaintiff would be completely barred from recovery even if his conduct is reasonable or only slightly unreasonable. In our comparative fault system, it would be incongruous to absolve the defendant of all liability based only on whether the plaintiff assumed the risk of injury. Comparative negligence by definition seeks to assess and compare the negligence of both the plaintiff and defendant. This goal would clearly be thwarted by adhering to the common law defense of assumption of risk.

. . .

[The court concluded that] (1) although the absolute defense of assumption of risk has historically been treated as a separate defense from contributory negligence, it is incompatible with our comparative fault system; (2) a plaintiff's conduct in assuming a risk can be compared with the defendant's negligence; (3) a plaintiff's conduct in assuming the risk can be made a part our comparative fault system; (4) by abolishing assumption of risk as an absolute bar to recovery, South Carolina will not be adopting a policy that would encourage people to take unnecessary risks; and (5) even if Davenport assumed the risk of injury, he will not be barred from recovery unless his negligence exceeds the defendant's negligence.

We therefore hold that a plaintiff is not barred from recovery by the doctrine of assumption of risk unless the degree of fault arising therefrom is greater than the negligence of the defendant. . . . Express and primary implied assumption of risk remain unaffected by our decision.

. . .

Cotton Hope finally argues that we should affirm the trial court's ruling that, as a matter of law, Davenport was more than fifty-percent negligent. The trial court based its ruling on the fact that Davenport knew of the danger weeks before his accident, and he had a safe, alternate route. However, there was also evidence suggesting Cotton Hope was negligent in failing to properly maintain the lighting in the exterior stairway. In the light most favorable to Davenport, it could be reasonably concluded that Davenport's negligence in proceeding down the stairway did not exceed Cotton Hope's negligence. Thus, it is properly submitted for jury determination.

[The case was remanded for a new trial.]

FINNEY, C.J., MOORE, WALLER and BURNETT, JJ., concur.

Notes and Questions

1. What were the trial judge's errors? What should happen on remand?

2. Why does "express" assumption of the risk remain compatible with comparative negligence?

3. Why does "primary" assumption of the risk remain compatible with comparative negligence? Does the court's analysis of this issue adequately explain cases like *Knight v. Jewett*, p. 472, supra?

4. With "secondary" implied assumption of the risk does it matter why a person runs into a house that has been set afire by defendant's negligence? Whether to save a child or save his hat?

In Boddie v. Scott, 722 A.2d 407 (Md.App.1999), plaintiff electrician was working in defendant's basement when defendant allowed a grease fire to start on her stove upstairs. When she shouted for help, plaintiff rushed upstairs and grabbed newspapers that he wrapped around the pan handle and ran to the door. Before he got there, flames curled toward him and he tossed the pan toward the open door—but a breeze sent some of the fire back onto him. Defendant argued that plaintiff assumed the risk in that only property was involved and he had no need to risk his life. The jury returned a verdict that plaintiff was not contributorily negligent, and the court affirmed the judgment for plaintiff. It relied in part on Restatement Second § 496E that states, in part, that assumed risk must be voluntary. It is not voluntary if defendant's tortious conduct has left the plaintiff no reasonable alternative way to protect another or to "exercise or protect a right or privilege of which the defendant has no right to deprive him." A plaintiff with a choice of evils will not be found to have assumed the risk.

Recall *Moore v. Shah*, p. 429, supra, involving the donation of the kidney. Might *Moore* be analyzed as assumed risk?

5. If plaintiff in *Davenport* is not barred by assumption of risk, what weight can be given to his continued use of the middle stairway?

6. In Gonzalez v. Garcia, 142 Cal.Rptr. 503 (App. 1977), plaintiff knowingly accepted a ride from defendant with whom plaintiff had been drinking for an extended period. In a suit after an accident, the trial judge treated the case as one of negligence and the jury found that plaintiff had been 20% at fault and defendant 80%. On appeal, defendant argued that the trial judge had committed error by refusing to charge on assumption of the risk. The court disagreed and affirmed. Why not conclude that the defendant met his duty when he effectively warned the plaintiff about the dangers of riding with him? Should it matter why plaintiff was riding with defendant—whether plaintiff wanted to visit a friend and had no other way to get there, or wanted to rush his wife who had just had an accident to the hospital?

7. *Swimming pools.* Several cases have denied recovery (from pool owners, pool manufacturers, property owners and municipalities) to plaintiffs who knowingly dove into shallow water or murky water or who dove from platforms that they had not tested. Sometimes, the diver's reckless behavior is called a "superseding act of negligence absolving defendants." Lionarons v. General Electric Co., 626 N.Y.S.2d 321 (App.Div.), aff'd 658 N.E.2d 214 (N.Y.1995). In O'Sullivan v. Shaw, 726 N.E.2d 951 (Mass.2000), plaintiff alleged that defendant was negligent in permitting visitors to dive into the shallow end of defendant's home swimming pool. The court held that the open and obvious danger of diving into a swimming pool barred recovery. The adoption of comparative negligence and the statutory abolition of the "the defense of assumption of risk" did not change the rule that plaintiff must show that defendant owed a duty to plaintiff that had been breached. Here the obviousness of the risk negated any duty. (Is this analysis comparable to the "open and obvious" danger issue discussed at p. 195, supra?) But see Kendrick v. Ed's Beach Service, Inc., 577 So.2d 936 (Fla.1991)("foolhardy conduct by diving into four feet of water" is to be compared with defendant's negligence in a pure comparative state).

8. New Jersey was the first state clearly to reject the existence of the term assumption of risk—and did so well before comparative negligence became popular. The history is set forth in McGrath v. American Cyanamid Co., 196 A.2d 238 (N.J.1963):

> In *Meistrich v. Casino Arena Attractions, Inc.*, [   ], we pointed out that assumption of the risk was theretofore used in two incongruous senses: in one sense it meant the defendant was not negligent, while in its other sense it meant the plaintiff was contributorily negligent. We said that in truth there are but two issues—negligence and contributory negligence—both to be resolved by the standard of the reasonably prudent man, and that it was erroneous to suggest to the jury that assumption of the risk was still another issue.
>
> . . .
>
> In *Meistrich* we said the terminology of assumption of the risk should not be used when it is projected in its secondary sense, i.e., that of contributory negligence [   ]. We thought, however, that "[p]erhaps a well-guarded charge of assumption of risk in its primary sense will

aid comprehension" [ ]. . . . Experience, however, indicates the term "assumption of risk" is so apt to create mist that it is better banished from the scene. We hope we have heard the last of it. Henceforth let us stay with "negligence" and "contributory negligence."

Does the emergence of comparative negligence affect the analysis?

9. *Minority view.* The states identified in *Davenport* as minority states often begin their analyses with the defense of assumed risk. Consider this example. Some college students were driving to town but were moving slowly because of traffic. The decedent, in the passenger seat, said, "Let us out. Let us out right here." After further words, and while the car was moving at 10–15 miles per hour, the defendant driver said, "If you want to get out, get out." The passenger "without a word, opened the door and jumped out" and was killed. The court held as a matter of law that the defense of assumed risk applied. How might the driver have been negligent—a subject not reached by the court? Goepfert v. Filler, 563 N.W.2d 140 (S.D.1997). How might *Davenport* have analyzed these facts?

For other cases from minority states, see Muldovan v. McEachern, 523 S.E.2d 566 (Ga.1999) (parents of youth killed in variation of "Russian roulette" barred, 5–2, from suing shooter) and Morrocco v. Piccardi, 713 A.2d 250 (R.I.1998) (plaintiff who slipped on the driveway that had been made slippery by the defendant landscape contractor's negligence could sue).

10. *The employment context.* The doctrine of assumed risk was of major significance in nineteenth-century industrial injury cases—before workers' compensation legislation replaced the tort system. In fact, the doctrine proved to be such an effective bar to employee tort suits that it played a key role in triggering the workers' compensation movement. See generally Friedman and Ladinsky, Social Change and the Law of Industrial Accidents, 67 Colum.L.Rev. 50 (1967). Utilization of the doctrine in employment cases has been justified on economic grounds—as a tool in facilitating freedom of contract. See Posner, A Theory of Negligence, 1 J.Legal Stud. 29, 45 (1972). Consider the following response in Rabin, The Historical Development of the Fault Principle: A Reinterpretation, 15 Ga.L.Rev. 925, 940 (1981):*

> With regard to assumed risk, Posner has argued that the courts, by effecting a trade-off between higher wages and an injury premium, were giving explicit recognition to the worker's desire to market his taste for risk. Resting this argument, as he does, on freedom of contract is obviously circular. The empirical question is whether workers in relatively dangerous occupations possessed the autonomy and mobility to effect trade-offs between safety and wages in their negotiations with employers, or whether they simply were impelled by circum-

* This article was originally published in 15 Ga.L.Rev. No. 4 and is reprinted by permission.

stances to confront unwanted hazards. Posner offers no evidence on this score. As Gary Schwartz has indicated, there is some historical documentation to suggest the contrary.[55] In a similar vein, a leading contemporaneous authority on industrial injury law remarked:

> Upon the average man it is certain that the fear of the disagreeable, and it may be, frightful consequences which will almost certainly ensue from the failure to obtain work or from the loss of a position, must always operate as a very strong coercive influence, indeed. To speak of one whom that fear drives into or detains in a dangerous employment as being a voluntary agent is a mere trifling with words.[56]

Moreover, the history of workmen's compensation reform is singularly free of any reference to laborers protesting against the legislation on the grounds that a compulsory safety premium was likely to have a depressing effect on wages. Where were the risk-preferring workers when their wage premiums were under siege? If the historical record is to be believed, they were unappreciatively on the side of unseating their judicial protectors.

Any trace of harmonization between the fault principle and assumed risk is further weakened when one examines the scope of the doctrine closely, for it was by no means limited to well-understood risks of the workplace. To the contrary, Labatt points out that the doctrine was applied to abnormal or transitory risks of the employment as well as "normal" hazards. Moreover, Schwartz, in his study of New Hampshire cases, concludes that the risks assumed were not limited to those immediately apparent in the employment situation.

Workers' compensation legislation is given detailed treatment in Chapter XI.

Roberts v. Vaughn

Supreme Court of Michigan, 1998.
459 Mich. 282, 587 N.W.2d 249.

BRICKLEY, J.

We granted leave in this case to determine whether the firefighter's rule adopted in Kreski v. Modern Wholesale Electric Supply Co., 415 N.W.2d 178 (Mich.1987), applies to bar a suit brought by a volunteer firefighter injured while responding to an emergency. [In a footnote here the court stated that "The firefighter's rule generally bars firefighters' or police officers' recovery for injuries sustained as a result of the negligence that gave rise to their emergency duties."] After considering the public

---

55. See Schwartz, Tort Law and the Economy in Nineteenth Century America: A Reinterpretation, 90 Yale L.J. 1717, 1769 & nn. 389–90 (1981). [   ]

56. 3 C. Labatt, Master and Servant § 963, at 2490 (1913).

policy basis of the firefighter's rule, we conclude that the rule should not be extended to volunteers.

I

The facts are not in dispute. Plaintiff Mark Roberts was a part-time volunteer firefighter and emergency medical technician for Tittabawassee Township. Although the township provided Roberts with protective gear and some training, he received no pay, pension, or medical health benefits for his efforts. On December 21, 1990, plaintiff was dispatched to the scene of an accident involving a collision between a semitruck and an automobile operated by defendant Fizena Vaughn, an unlicensed minor driver. By the time plaintiff and other emergency personnel arrived on the scene, Ms. Vaughn was pinned beneath the dashboard. As plaintiff attempted to extricate Vaughn from the wreckage of her vehicle, she kicked her legs and knocked plaintiff to the pavement, causing his injuries. Plaintiff is now permanently disabled, and unable to return to his regular occupation. [The court, in a footnote, noted that plaintiff receives $15,000 per year in workers' compensation benefits and an unspecified amount in disability payments.]

Plaintiff instituted this suit against defendant Vaughn and defendant Silvia Medina, alleging negligence and gross negligence with respect to Vaughn, and negligent entrustment with respect to Medina, who provided Vaughn with the keys to the vehicle.

[After discovery, the circuit court granted both defendants summary judgment. The court of appeals, relying on *Kreski*, affirmed.]

II

The specific question this case presents is whether, notwithstanding any negligence on the part of defendants that may have caused plaintiff's injuries, plaintiff is barred from recovery because he was a volunteer firefighter responding to an emergency. The firefighter's rule generally waives the duty of care that third parties owe firefighters and police officers. We examine whether the rationale of that rule justifies exonerating private parties from a duty of care toward volunteer safety workers.

In *Kreski*, supra, this Court formally adopted the firefighter's rule, thereby barring a suit brought on behalf of a professional firefighter who was killed when part of a burning building fell on him. Refusing to justify the rule on the doctrine of assumption of risk, we expressly embraced the firefighter's rule on the basis of a number of public policy rationales, thereby precluding recovery by police officers and firefighters for damages in tort for performance of their jobs, which they were already obligated to perform and for which they previously received compensation that was presumably calculated with considerations of the risks faced:

> The public hires, trains, and compensates fire fighters and police officers to deal with dangerous, but inevitable situations. Usually, especially with fires, negligence causes the occasion for the safety officer's presence.

The [firefighter's] rule developed from the notion that taxpayers employ firemen and policemen, at least in part, to deal with future damages that may result from the taxpayers' own negligence. To allow actions by policemen and firemen against negligent taxpayers would subject them to multiple penalties for the protection.

After examining the nature of the service provided by firefighters and police officers, as well as the relationship of the officer to the public, we concluded that the firefighter's rule was "based on practicability and common sense." [   ] We further emphasized that, rather than representing a bright-line rule, the firefighter's rule would be subject to "fine tuning . . . to best balance the underlying rationales with the interest of allowing recovery when those rationales are not implicated." [   ]

More recently, in Gibbons v. Caraway, 565 N.W.2d 663 (Mich.1997), we confirmed the public policy rationale for the firefighter's rule, but circumscribed the scope of the rule, noting that all risks encountered by safety officers do not fall within the ambit of the rule. [*Gibbons* held that "the firefighter's rule does not bar a claim for damages for injuries caused by the subsequent wrongdoing of a third party unconnected to the situation that brought the officer to the scene, where the wrongdoing resulted from wanton, reckless, or grossly negligent behavior."] We also held that a plaintiff's receipt of worker's compensation benefits is "not dispositive of the issue of the applicability of the fireman's rule."

III

Citing this Court's opinion in *Kreski*, along with decisions from two other jurisdictions, the Court of Appeals concluded that the firefighter's rule extends to volunteers:

Although not directly compensated, volunteer fire fighters receive training, access to equipment, and worker's compensation. The relationship of the public with a salaried fire fighter is no different than with a volunteer. [   ]

We cannot agree with the Court of Appeals determination that no valid distinction exists in the application of the rule between professional and volunteer firefighters. We also reject the factors cited by the Court, as they do not rise to the level of societal and professional commitment articulated in *Kreski*.

As we have explained, the firefighter's rule is based on considerations of a public policy derived from the unique relationship between professional safety officers and the public. In accordance with that public policy, we concluded that no duty is owed for ordinary negligence because professional safety officers are presumably extensively trained and specially paid to confront dangerous situations in order to protect the public, and that, therefore, these safety officers undertake their profession with the knowledge that their personal safety is at risk. Because of the unique relationship between the public, the safety officer, and those third parties who require the services of the officer, the otherwise applicable duty of care toward the safety officer is replaced by the third party's contribution to tax-supported compensation for those services: when injury occurs, liberal compensation is provided. [The court noted that volunteer firefighters are specifically excluded from membership in the state retirement system provided for professionals.] This relationship is clearly missing between an uncompensated volunteer firefighter and a third party.

Although defendants urge that they should be excused from the usual duty of care on the basis of the public policy expressed by the firefighter's rule, at the root of defendants' arguments seems to be the presumption that a volunteer firefighter intends to act gratuitously when providing service to the community. Notwithstanding the accuracy or inaccuracy of that statement, implicit in defendants' rationale is the presumption that an individual who acts from altruistic motives is in some way not entitled to recovery for losses incurred during a rescue. [The court here refers to the rescue doctrine and the *Wagner* case, p. 428, supra.] We are unwilling, without the benefit of empirical evidence and other related tools readily available to the Legislature, to deviate from tort principles that otherwise impose a general duty to avoid injuring others, particularly where such a departure is not supported by clear public policy. Moreover, denying volunteers the opportunity to recover on the basis that their undertaking is gratuitous essentially resurrects the doctrine of assumption of risk, which we expressly rejected in *Kreski* as an adequate rationale.

The promotion of mutual aid is clearly a valid ideal; thus, while the firefighter's rule articulated in *Kreski* recognizes that private law remedies sought by professional safety officers are misdirected and therefore barred on the basis of the fact that professionals receive compensation for their efforts, those same concerns and underlying principles are not implicated in the case of volunteers, who are not similarly compensated for the same efforts. We find a common-law rule disallowing recovery for volunteer rescuers to be not only inconsistent with basic restitutionary principles, but also contrary to the considerations of public policy articulated in *Kreski*.

[The case was reversed and remanded.]

MALLETT, C.J., and MICHAEL F. CAVANAGH, BOYLE, WEAVER, MARILYN J. KELLY, and TAYLOR, JJ., concurred with BRICKLEY, J.

Notes and Questions

1. Why does the court suggest that the defense argument "essentially resurrects" assumption of risk?

2. The court refers to the "unique relationship between professional safety officers and the public." What is unique about that relationship and why does it not apply to *Roberts*?

In an omitted footnote near the end, the *Roberts* court notes that "[a]lthough the instant plaintiff qualifies as a volunteer in the real sense of that word, we leave for another day situations involving safety officers who, although styled volunteers, receive more than nominal consideration for their efforts.'' Should that change the result?

3. The court notes that most cases have arisen in the context of a fire. Others have involved defective premises on which the safety officer has slipped. Another group has involved automobile accidents, in which the officer is hurt while directing traffic around the first accident. Do these situations raise different issues for the justification of the firefighter's rule?

4. Why does the rule not operate as a defense for subsequent wrong-doers? In most states that retain the rule it is clear that if D1's negligence brings a safety officer to the scene of an accident and the officer is then hurt by D2, a negligent motorist, the officer may sue D2 but not D1. Is this consistent with *Gibbons,* cited in *Roberts*?

5. Does the principal case shed light on cases involving dangerous private occupations? Consider the following situations.

a. A private tow truck operator was called to the scene of an accident caused by D's drunk driving. While at the scene the operator is hurt by the negligence of a second motorist. See Bryant v. Glastetter, 38 Cal.Rptr.2d 291 (App. 1995) rejecting the claim.

Would it be appropriate to treat the private tow truck driver as a professional rescuer? See Maltman v. Sauer, 530 P.2d 254 (Wash.1975), denying recovery against a negligent motorist when a professional rescue helicopter crashed on its way to rescue him in a remote area. An effort to limit *Maltman* to cases involving public employees failed in Black Industries, Inc. v. Emco Helicopters, Inc., 577 P.2d 610 (Wash.App.1978): "public policy demands that recovery be barred whenever a person, fully aware of a hazard created by another's negligence, voluntarily confronts the risk for compensation." Why?

b. An Alzheimer's patient hurts a nurse who is taking care of him. Gould v. American Family Mut. Ins. Co., 543 N.W.2d 282 (Wis.1996) (no recovery).

c. A student driver crashes the car, hurting the driving instructor. Might it matter whether the student made a mistake that is common among beginners or made one that is most unexpected—even among beginners? See La Fleur v. Vergilia, 117 N.Y.S.2d 244 (App.Div. 1952) (recovery denied 3–2).

d. A homeowner begins to rewire the house. After some work the homeowner gets nervous and calls an electrician and describes what has been done so far. Shortly after beginning work the electrician is electrocuted by a danger that the electrician had failed to take into account. See Salima v. Scherwood South, Inc., 38 F.3d 929 (7th Cir.1994), in which the court rejected a duty on a land occupier to tell a handyman (who was later electrocuted) about what management had learned in its prior unsuccessful attempts to locate the source of an electrical problem.

e. In Woodall v. Wayne Steffens Productions, Inc., 20 Cal.Rptr. 572 (App. 1962), the plaintiff had developed a stunt that involved riding a kite into the air on the power of a boat or a car. He had all the details under his own control except the speed of the vehicle. The speed had to rise to 30 mph and then, when the kite was aloft, had to be reduced. Defendant producer of a television show, "You Asked For It," contracted with plaintiff to present his stunt, called "The Human Kite." Defendant offered to provide an experienced driver. The driver, who was in fact not experienced, was told what to do but raised the speed instead of lowering it at the crucial moment. Plaintiff's kite fell and plaintiff was badly hurt.

At trial, the jury rejected claims both of contributory negligence and of assumed risk. On the former, the court had told the jury that an assurance of safety "may have a bearing on the determination" whether that person behaved reasonably. On the latter, the appellate court said that plaintiff had "assumed any risk growing out of inexpert manipulation of the kite, a sudden windstorm, breaking loose of the tow rope which he had fastened, the kite splitting in the air, or any one of many eventualities that were not properly attributable to [defendants'] own activities." Nonetheless, he did not assume the risk of the inept driving. He had decided not to bring his own driver based on defendant's assurances that Hollywood stunt drivers were very skilled. The plaintiff "does not assume the risk of any negligence which he has no reason to anticipate."

7.   Several states have abolished the firefighter's rule by judicial decision; others by statute; and many have retained it. Is the proper course clear?

8.   For a broad review of the entire subject of assumed risk, see Sugarman, Assumption of Risk, 31 Valp.L.Rev. 833 (1997).

C.   PREEMPTION

Earlier, we discussed the issue of whether courts should recognize a regulatory compliance defense as a matter of common law deference, in situations where a defendant's conduct has satisfied applicable regulatory standards; see p. 83, supra. Here, we consider a related scenario with constitutional dimensions; in particular, a defense claim that the common law tort action is overridden by legislative or regulatory standards intended to preempt tort claims. As we will see, this preclusion claim can arise in the context of federal or state legislative/regulatory standards addressing the subject matter of a tort suit.

Geier v. American Honda Motor Company, Inc., et al.

Supreme Court of the United States, 2000.
529 U.S. 861, 120 S.Ct. 1913, 146 L.Ed.2d 914.

JUSTICE BREYER delivered the opinion of the Court.

This case focuses on the 1984 version of a Federal Motor Vehicle Safety Standard promulgated by the Department of Transportation under the authority of the National Traffic and Motor Vehicle Safety Act of 1966, 15 U.S.C. § 1381 et seq. (1988 ed.). The standard, FMVSS 208, required auto manufacturers to equip some but not all of their 1987 vehicles with passive restraints. We ask whether the Act pre-empts a state common-law tort action in which the plaintiff claims that the defendant auto manufacturer, who was in compliance with the standard, should nonetheless have equipped a 1987 automobile with airbags. We conclude that the Act, taken together with FMVSS 208, pre-empts the lawsuit.

I

In 1992, petitioner Alexis Geier, driving a 1987 Honda Accord, collided with a tree and was seriously injured. The car was equipped with manual shoulder and lap belts which Geier had buckled up at the time. The car was not equipped with airbags or other passive restraint devices.

[In the suit by Geier and her parents against the manufacturer and its affiliates (American Honda), they claimed, "among other things, that American Honda had designed its car negligently and defectively because it lacked a driver's side airbag." The District Court dismissed the lawsuit.] The court noted that FMVSS 208 gave car manufacturers a choice as to whether to install airbags. And the court concluded that petitioners' lawsuit, because it sought to establish a different safety standard—i.e., an airbag requirement—was expressly pre-empted by a provision of the Act which pre-empts "any safety standard" that is not identical to a federal safety standard applicable to the same aspect of performance, 15 U.S.C. § 1392(d) (1988 ed.); [ ] (We, like the courts below and the parties, refer to the pre-1994 version of the statute throughout the opinion; it has been recodified at 49 U.S.C. § 30101 et seq.).

The Court of Appeals agreed with the District Court's conclusion but on somewhat different reasoning. It had doubts, given the existence of the Act's "saving" clause, 15 U.S.C. § 1397(k) (1988 ed.), that petitioners' lawsuit involved the potential creation of the kind of "safety standard" to which the Safety Act's express pre-emption provision refers. But it declined to resolve that question because it found that petitioners' state-law tort claims posed an obstacle to the accomplishment of FMVSS 208's objectives. For that reason, it found that those claims conflicted with FMVSS 208, and that, under ordinary pre-emption principles, the Act consequently pre-empted the lawsuit. The Court of Appeals thus affirmed the District Court's dismissal. [ ]

Several state courts have held to the contrary, namely, that neither the Act's express pre-emption nor FMVSS 208 pre-empts a "no airbag" tort suit. [citing five state high courts]. All of the Federal Circuit Courts that have considered the question, however, have found pre-emption. One rested its conclusion on the Act's express pre-emption provision. [ ] Others, such as the Court of Appeals below, have instead found pre-emption under ordinary pre-emption principles by virtue of the conflict such suits pose to FMVSS 208's objectives, and thus to the Act itself. [ ] We granted certiorari to resolve these differences. We now hold that this kind of "no airbag" lawsuit conflicts with the objectives of FMVSS 208, a standard authorized by the Act, and is therefore pre-empted by the Act.

In reaching our conclusion, we consider three subsidiary questions. First, does the Act's express pre-emption provision pre-empt this lawsuit? We think not. Second, do ordinary pre-emption principles nonetheless apply? We hold that they do. Third, does this lawsuit actually conflict with FMVSS 208, hence with the Act itself? We hold that it does.

II

We first ask whether the Safety Act's express pre-emption provision pre-empts this tort action. The provision reads as follows:

> Whenever a Federal motor vehicle safety standard established under this subchapter is in effect, no State or political subdivision of a State shall have any authority either to establish, or to continue in effect, with respect to any motor vehicle or item of motor vehicle equipment[,] any safety standard applicable to the same aspect of performance of such vehicle or item of equipment which is not identical to the Federal standard. 15 U.S.C. § 1392(d) (1988 ed.).

American Honda points out that a majority of this Court has said that a somewhat similar statutory provision in a different federal statute—a provision that uses the word "requirements"—may well expressly pre-empt similar tort actions. See, e.g., [Medtronic, Inc. v. Lohr, 518 U.S. 470 (1996)]. Petitioners reply that this statute speaks of pre-empting a state-law "safety standard," not a "requirement," and that a tort action does not involve a safety standard. Hence, they conclude, the express pre-emption provision does not apply.

We need not determine the precise significance of the use of the word "standard," rather than "requirement," however, for the Act contains another provision, which resolves the disagreement. That provision, a "saving" clause, says that "[c]ompliance with" a federal safety standard "does not exempt any person from any liability under common law." 15 U.S.C. § 1397(k) (1988 ed.). The saving clause assumes that there are some significant number of common-law liability cases to save. And a reading of the express pre-emption provision that excludes common-law tort actions gives actual meaning to the saving clause's literal language, while leaving adequate room for state tort law to operate—for example, where federal law creates only a floor, i.e., a minimum safety standard. See, e.g., Brief for United States as Amicus Curiae 21 (explaining that common-law claim that a vehicle is defectively designed because it lacks antilock brakes would not be pre-empted by 49 C.F.R. § 571.105 (1999), a safety standard establishing minimum requirements for brake performance). Without the saving clause, a broad reading of the express pre-emption provision arguably might pre-empt those actions, for, as we have just mentioned, it is possible to read the pre-emption provision, standing alone, as applying to standards imposed in common-law tort actions, as well as standards contained in state legislation or regulations. And if so, it would pre-empt all nonidentical state standards established in tort actions covering the same aspect of performance as an applicable federal standard, even if the federal standard merely established a minimum standard. On that broad reading of the pre-emption clause little, if any, potential "liability at common law" would remain. And few, if any, state tort actions would remain for the saving clause to save. We have found no convincing indication that Congress wanted to pre-empt, not only state statutes and regulations, but also common-law tort actions, in such circumstances. Hence the broad reading cannot be correct. The language of the pre-emption provision permits a narrow reading that excludes common-law actions. Given the presence of the saving clause, we conclude that the pre-emption clause must be so read.

III

We have just said that the saving clause at least removes tort actions from the scope of the express pre-emption clause. Does it do more? In particular, does it foreclose or limit the operation of ordinary pre-emption principles insofar as those principles instruct us to read statutes as pre-empting state laws (including common-law rules) that "actually conflict" with the statute or federal standards promulgated thereunder? [   ] Petitioners concede, as they must in light of [   ], that the pre-emption provision, by itself, does not foreclose (through negative implication) "any possibility of implied [conflict] pre-emption." [   ] But they argue that the saving clause has that very effect.

We recognize that, when this Court previously considered the pre-emptive effect of the statute's language, it appeared to leave open the question of how, or the extent to which, the saving clause saves state-law tort actions that conflict with federal regulations promulgated under the Act. [   ] We now conclude that the saving clause (like the express pre-emption provision) does not bar the ordinary working of conflict pre-emption principles.

Nothing in the language of the saving clause suggests an intent to save state-law tort actions that conflict with federal regulations. The words "[c]ompliance" and "does not exempt," 15 U.S.C. § 1397(k) (1988 ed.), sound as if they simply bar a special kind of defense, namely, a defense that compliance with a federal standard automatically exempts a defendant from state law, whether the Federal Government meant that standard to be an absolute requirement or only a minimum one. See Restatement (Third) of Torts: Products Liability § 4(b), Comment e (1997) (distinguishing between state-law compliance defense and a federal claim of pre-emption). It is difficult to understand why Congress would have insisted on a compliance-with-federal-regulation precondition to the provision's applicability had it wished the Act to "save" all state-law tort actions, regardless of their potential threat to the objectives of federal safety standards promulgated under that Act. Nor does our interpretation conflict with the purpose of the saving provision, say by rendering it ineffectual. As we have previously explained, the saving provision still makes clear that the express pre-emption provision does not of its own force pre-empt common-law tort actions. And it thereby preserves those actions that seek to establish greater safety than the minimum safety achieved by a federal regulation intended to provide a floor. [   ]

Moreover, this Court has repeatedly "decline[d] to give broad effect to saving clauses where doing so would upset the careful regulatory scheme established by federal law." [   ] We find this concern applicable in the present case. And we conclude that the saving clause foresees—it does not foreclose—the possibility that a federal safety standard will pre-empt a state common-law tort action with which it conflicts.   .   .   .

Neither do we believe that the pre-emption provision, the saving provision, or both together, create some kind of "special burden" beyond that inherent in ordinary pre-emption principles—which "special burden" would specially disfavor pre-emption here. [   ] The two provisions, read together, reflect a neutral policy, not a specially favorable or unfavorable policy, towards the application of ordinary conflict pre-emption principles. On the one hand, the pre-emption provision itself reflects a desire to subject the industry to a single, uniform set of federal safety standards. Its pre-emption of all state standards, even those that might stand in harmony with federal law, suggests an intent to avoid the conflict, uncertainty, cost, and occasional risk to safety itself that too many different safety-standard cooks might otherwise create. [   ] This policy by itself favors pre-emption of state tort suits, for the rules of law that judges and juries create or apply in such suits may themselves similarly create uncertainty and even conflict, say, when different juries in different States reach different decisions on similar facts.

On the other hand, the saving clause reflects a congressional determination that occasional nonuniformity is a small price to pay for a system in which juries not only create, but also enforce, safety standards, while simultaneously providing necessary compensation to victims. That policy by itself disfavors pre-emption, at least some of the time. But we can find nothing in any natural reading of the two provisions that would favor one set of policies over the other where a jury-imposed safety standard actually conflicts with a federal safety standard.

.   .   .

IV

The basic question, then, is whether a common-law "no airbag" action like the one before us actually conflicts with FMVSS 208. We hold that it does.

In petitioners' and the dissent's view, FMVSS 208 sets a minimum airbag standard. As far as FMVSS 208 is concerned, the more airbags, and the sooner, the better. But that was not the Secretary's view. DOT's comments, which accompanied the promulgation of FMVSS 208, make clear that the standard deliberately provided the manufacturer with a range of choices among different passive restraint devices. Those choices would bring about a mix of different devices introduced gradually over time; and FMVSS 208 would thereby lower costs, overcome technical safety problems, encourage technological development, and win widespread consumer acceptance—all of which would promote FMVSS 208's safety objectives.

A

The history of FMVSS 208 helps explain why and how DOT sought these objectives. [ ] In 1967, DOT, understanding that seatbelts would save many lives, required manufacturers to install manual seat belts in all automobiles. It became apparent, however, that most occupants simply would not buckle up their belts. [ ] DOT then began to investigate the feasibility of requiring "passive restraints," such as airbags and automatic seatbelts.

[The Court then reviewed the history of the 1984 seatbelt regulation and DOT's explanation of the provision, and concluded that the agency had decided, on balance, that it would be better to phase in air bag regulation, rather than to make them mandatory at that time: "In sum, as DOT now tells us through the Solicitor General, the 1984 version of FMVSS 208 'embodies the Secretary's policy judgment that safety would best be promoted if manufacturers installed alternative protection systems in their fleets rather than one particular system in every car.' "]

One final point: We place some weight upon DOT's interpretation of FMVSS 208's objectives and its conclusion, as set forth in the Government's brief, that a tort suit such as this one would " 'stan[d] as an obstacle to the accomplishment and execution' " of those objectives. [ ] Congress has delegated to DOT authority to implement the statute; the subject matter is technical; and the relevant history and background are complex and extensive. The agency is likely to have a thorough understanding of its own regulation and its objectives and is "uniquely qualified" to comprehend the likely impact of state requirements. [ ] And DOT has explained FMVSS 208's objectives, and the interference that "no airbag" suits pose thereto, consistently over time. [ ] In these circumstances, the agency's own views should make a difference. [ ]

. . .

The judgment of the Court of Appeals is affirmed.

JUSTICE STEVENS, with whom JUSTICE SOUTER, JUSTICE THOMAS, and JUSTICE GINSBURG join, dissenting.

Airbag technology has been available to automobile manufacturers for over 30 years. There is now general agreement on the proposition "that, to be safe, a car must have an airbag." [ ] Indeed, current federal law imposes that requirement on all automobile manufacturers. [ ] The question raised by petitioner's common-law tort action is whether that proposition was sufficiently obvious when Honda's 1987 Accord was manufactured to make the failure to install such a safety feature actionable under theories of negligence or defective design. The Court holds that an interim regulation motivated by the Secretary of Transportation's desire to foster gradual development of a variety of passive restraint devices deprives state courts of jurisdiction to answer that question. I respectfully dissent from that holding, and especially from the Court's unprecedented extension of the doctrine of pre-emption. . . .

"This is a case about federalism," [ ], that is, about respect for "the constitutional role of the States as sovereign entities." [ ] It raises important questions concerning the way in which the Federal Government may exercise its undoubted power to oust state courts of their traditional jurisdiction over common-law tort actions. The rule the Court enforces today was not enacted by Congress and is not to be found in the text of any Executive Order or regulation. It has a unique origin: it is the product of the Court's interpretation of the final commentary accompanying an interim administrative regulation and the history of airbag regulation generally. Like many other judge-made rules, its contours are not precisely defined. . . .

. . .

When a state statute, administrative rule, or common-law cause of action conflicts with a federal statute, it is axiomatic that the state law is without effect. U.S. Const., Art. VI, cl. 2; Cipollone v. Liggett Group, Inc., 505 U.S. 504, 516 (1992). On the other hand, it is equally clear that the Supremacy Clause does not give unelected federal judges carte blanche to use federal law as a means of imposing their own ideas of tort reform on the States. Because of the role of States as separate sovereigns in our federal system, we have long presumed that state laws—particularly those, such as the provision of tort remedies to compensate for personal injuries, that are within the scope of the States' historic police powers—are not to be pre-empted by a federal statute unless it is the clear and manifest purpose of Congress to do so. Medtronic, Inc. v. Lohr, 518 U.S. 470, 485 (1996); [   ].

[In view of the conflict between the pre-emption clause and the savings clause, the dissent would have recognized pre-emption of tort actions only if such claims created a "special burden" on the regulatory scheme as envisioned by Congress—and finding no such burden in this instance, would have permitted the state tort action.]

Because neither the text of the statute nor the text of the regulation contains any indication of an intent to pre-empt petitioners' cause of action, and because I cannot agree with the Court's unprecedented use of inferences from regulatory history and commentary as a basis for implied pre-emption, I am convinced that Honda has not overcome the presumption against pre-emption in this case. I therefore respectfully dissent.

Notes and Questions

1.   Virtually every court confronted with the question has read "requirement" in preemption statutes to include common law tort liability. In the cited *Cipollone* case, the Supreme Court faced a similar argument under the 1965 cigarette labeling act. It responded first by noting that the broad language of the statute in question "suggests no distinction between positive enactments and common law." Moreover, it was clear that "regulation can be as effectively exerted through an award of damages as through some form of preventive relief. The obligation to pay compensation can be, indeed is designed to be, a potent method of governing conduct and controlling policy." What is the opposing argument? Does the reference to "safety standards" in the auto safety act suggest any different analysis?

2. What is the relationship between express and implied preemption, as explained by the majority, and how does "conflict" preemption illustrate the latter? Why does the "saving clause," according to the majority, allow tort suits to be preserved, yet at the same time not bar the application of implied preemption?

3. When should a court find that federal regulation is simply intended to "provide a floor" of minimum safety, and thus should not preempt higher state standards? What evidence might it use to differentiate between cases in which state law "stands as an obstacle" to the accomplishment of Congress's purposes, and when it simply supplements a federal enactment?

4. Can you articulate the relationship between preemption analysis and the regulatory compliance doctrine, discussed at p. 83 supra?

5. In the cited *Cipollone* case, involving a claim for lung cancer against a tobacco company, the Court concluded that claims alleging failure to warn were preempted under the federal cigarette warning legislation, but that claims based on express warranty, fraud, and misrepresentation were not preempted. Is there any reason to think that *Geier* would find otherwise?

In *In re* Orthopedic Bone Screw Products Liability Litigation, 159 F.3d 817 (3d Cir.1998), the court held that a state claim that the applicant filed fraudulent documents with the FDA while trying to obtain clearance for a product was not preempted. The Supreme Court has granted certiorari limited to the question "whether federal law preempts state law claims alleging fraud on the Food and Drug Administration during the regulatory process for marketing clearance applicable to certain medical devices." Buckman Co. v. Plaintiffs' Legal Committee, 120 S.Ct. 2739 (2000).

6. In Freightliner Corp. v. Myrick, 514 U.S. 280 (1995), the Court held that a state law claim that a tractor-trailer was defectively designed because it lacked air brakes was not preempted by federal regulation. Although regulations promulgated under the National Highway Traffic Safety Act did not address the subject of air brakes, the defendant manufacturer argued that the absence of regulation was itself indicative of an intent to preclude state regulation. That argument has prevailed where the courts have found that "Congress intended to centralize all authority over the regulated area in one decision-maker: the Federal Government." But in *Myrick*, the Court found no such intent.

For a recent example of field preemption, see Carrillo v. ACF Industries, Inc., 980 P.2d 386 (Cal.1999), cert. denied 528 U.S. 1077 (2000), in which the court held that the Federal Safety Appliance Act barred the plaintiff's state law claim against a manufacturer of railroad cars for lack of a safety device on the top of freight cars to prevent workers from falling off. Although the act had no provisions addressing this issue, uniformity was crucial in switching these cars and states could not add to the cars' design.

7. The preemption battleground covers many areas that had previously been litigated as common-law tort cases, as suggested in the following cases: Anguiano v. E. I. Du Pont De Nemours & Co., 44 F.3d 806 (9th

Cir.1995)(design claim for product to ameliorate problems with temporal mandibular joint is not preempted by the 1976 Medical Devices Amendments to the Food Drug & Cosmetic Act); Harris v. American Airlines, Inc., 55 F.3d 1472 (9th Cir.1995)(claim that airline failed to stop passenger from directing rude and obnoxious racially-motivated remarks toward plaintiff passenger was preempted by the Airline Deregulation Act); Hodges v. Delta Airlines, Inc., 44 F.3d 334 (5th Cir. en banc 1995)(negligence claim by passenger hit by falling case of rum against airline for allowing case to be stored in overhead bin was not preempted by Airline Deregulation Act); Bice v. Leslie's Poolmart, Inc., 39 F.3d 887 (8th Cir.1994)(claim of inadequate labeling on chemical swimming pool maintenance product was preempted by Federal Insecticide, Fungicide, and Rodenticide Act "FIFRA"); Greenlaw v. Garrett, 59 F.3d 994 (9th Cir.1995)(federal employee's state claims against former employer for sex discrimination were preempted by federal Civil Service Reform Act). See generally, Ausness, The Case for a "Strong" Regulatory Compliance Defense, 55 Md.L.Rev. 1210 (1996).

————

ERISA preemption. A recent cluster of federal cases has addressed the subject of when and whether health maintenance organizations can be sued for physical harm or death resulting from decisions wrongly denying medical treatment to their insureds. The cases have uniformly concluded that the 1974 Congressional enactment of the Employee Retirement and Income Security Act (ERISA), 29 U.S.C.A. §§ 1001–1461, does not provide a federal basis for tort actions for damages for health impairments suffered as the result of denial of benefits—and also that the Act bars tort actions under state law. The judges deciding these cases have been unusually outspoken about the need for Congressional action. E.g., Bast v. Prudential Insurance Co. of America, 150 F.3d 1003 (9th Cir.1998), involving the refusal to authorize an autologous bone marrow transplant; the refusal allegedly leading to death from breast cancer. Quoting from another case, the court said "Although moved by the tragic circumstances of this case and the seemingly needless loss of life that resulted, we conclude the law gives us no choice but to affirm." The *Bast* court also noted that "without action by Congress, there is nothing we can do to help the Basts and others who may find themselves in this same unfortunate situation." See also Corcoran v. United Healthcare, Inc., 965 F.2d 1321 (5th Cir.), cert. denied, 506 U.S. 1033 (1992), in which a fetus died after the HMO refused to authorize hospitalization in a high-risk pregnancy ("The Corcorans have no remedy, state or federal, for what may have been a serious mistake"). In these cases, the courts have frequently observed that a statute enacted to protect employees and their families has come to bar them from suing for the harm suffered where benefits are wrongly denied. ERISA does not preempt suits for breach of contract over whether a particular treatment is covered by the contract. See also, Pegram v. Herdrich, 530 U.S. 211 (2000), a non-tort case, holding that, in making decisions involving both eligibility and treatment, an HMO is not acting in a fiduciary capacity for purposes of ERISA.

CHAPTER VII

Strict Liability

In the first part of this chapter, we will consider the doctrinal developments that have led to the concept of strict liability for certain types of activities. In tracing the evolution of this traditional form of strict liability, we will see the courts venturing beyond isolated cases—such as escaping fires, rampaging wild animals and straying cattle—to fashion a more comprehensive principle of liability without fault. It should be said, however, that there is no clear demarcation of the emergence of traditional strict liability. In the late nineteenth century, for instance, continued reference to "the blasting cases" indicates the judicial affinity for narrow categorization. But as the leading case of *Rylands v. Fletcher*, along with the cases that follow, should demonstrate, the courts were quite consciously drawing on a principle that they regarded as contrary to negligence liability when they invoked the doctrine of strict liability for ultrahazardous, or abnormally dangerous, activity.

In the second part of the Chapter, we examine a variety of scholarly efforts to establish the theoretical underpinnings of strict liability. This literature consists of efforts both to identify the strands of strict liability in the case law and to advocate a broader reliance on strict liability for normative reasons. An examination of the theories should serve as a reprise of the tension between strict liability and negligence, as well as providing a bridge to the analysis of defective products cases in the next Chapter.

A. DOCTRINAL DEVELOPMENT

Fletcher v. Rylands

Exchequer Chamber, 1866.
L.R. 1. Ex. 265.

[Plaintiff Fletcher was a tenant mining coal under agreement with the landowner. Defendant Rylands was a tenant operating a cotton mill on nearby land.]

The judgment of the Court (WILLES, BLACKBURN, KEATING, MELLOR, MONTAGUE SMITH, and LUSH, JJ.), was delivered by BLACKBURN, J. This was a special case stated by an arbitrator, under an order of nisi prius, in which the question for the court is stated to be whether the plaintiff is entitled to recover any, and, if any, what damages from the defendants, by reason of the matters therein before stated.

issue

In the Court of Exchequer, the Chief Baron and Martin, B., were of opinion that the plaintiff was not entitled to recover at all, Bramwell, B., being of a different opinion. The judgment in the Exchequer was consequently given for the defendants, in conformity with the opinion of the majority of the court. The only question argued before us was whether this judgment was right, nothing being said about the measure of damages in case the plaintiff should be held entitled to recover. We have come to the conclusion that the opinion of Bramwell, B., was right, and that the answer to the question should be that the plaintiff was entitled to recover damages from the defendants, by reason of the matters stated in the case, and consequently, that the judgment below should be reversed, but we cannot at present say to what damages the plaintiff is entitled.

It appears from the statement in the case, that the plaintiff was damaged by his property being flooded by water, which, without any fault on his part, broke out of a reservoir constructed on the defendants' land by the defendants' orders, and maintained by the defendants.

It appears from the statement in the case that the coal under the defendants' land had, at some remote period, been worked out; but this was unknown at the time when the defendants gave directions to erect the reservoir, and the water in the reservoir would not have escaped from the defendants' land, and no mischief would have been done to the plaintiff, but for this latent defect in the defendants' subsoil. And it further appears, that the defendants selected competent engineers and contractors to make their reservoir, and themselves personally continued in total ignorance of what we have called the latent defect in the subsoil; but that these persons employed by them in the course of the work became aware of the existence of the ancient shafts filled up with soil, though they did not know or suspect that they were shafts communicating with old workings.

It is found that the defendants, personally, were free from all blame, but that in fact proper care and skill was not used by the persons employed by them, to provide for the sufficiency of the reservoir with reference to these shafts. The consequence was, that the reservoir when filled with water burst into the shafts, the water flowed down through them into the old workings, and thence into the plaintiff's mine, and there did the mischief.

The plaintiff, though free from all blame on his part, must bear the loss, unless he can establish that it was the consequence of some default for which the defendants are responsible. The question of law therefore arises, what is the obligation which the law casts on a person who, like the defendants, lawfully brings on his land something which, though harmless whilst it remains there, will naturally do mischief if it escape out of his land. It is agreed on all hands that he must take care to keep in that which he has brought on the land and keeps there, in order that it may not escape and damage his neighbors, but the question arises whether the duty which the law casts upon him, under such circumstances, is an absolute duty to keep it in at his peril, or is, as the majority of the Court of Exchequer have thought, merely a duty to take all reasonable and prudent precautions, in order to keep it in, but no more. If the first be the law, the person who has brought on his land and kept there something dangerous, and failed to keep it in, is responsible for all the natural consequences of its escape. If the second be the limit of his duty, he would not be answerable except on proof of negligence, and consequently would not be answerable for escape arising from any latent defect which ordinary prudence and skill could not detect.

Supposing the second to be the correct view of the law, a further question arises subsidiary to the first, viz., whether the defendants are not so far identified with the contractors whom they employed, as to be responsible for the consequences of their want of care and skill in making the reservoir in fact insufficient with reference to the old shafts, of the existence of which they were aware, though they had not ascertained where the shafts went to.

We think that the true rule of law is, that the person who for his own purposes brings on his lands and collects and keeps there anything likely to do mischief if it escapes, must keep it in at his peril, and, if he does not do so, is prima facie answerable for all the damage which is the natural consequence of its escape. He can excuse himself by showing that the escape was owing to the plaintiff's default; or perhaps that the escape was the consequence of vis major, or the act of God; but as nothing of this sort exists here, it is unnecessary to inquire what excuse would be sufficient. The general rule, as above stated, seems on principle just. The person whose grass or corn is eaten down by the escaping cattle of his neighbor, or whose mine is flooded by the water from his neighbour's reservoir, or whose cellar is invaded by the filth of his neighbour's privy, or whose habitation is made unhealthy by the fumes and noisome vapours of his neighbour's alkali works, is damnified without any fault of his own; and it seems but reasonable and just that the neighbour, who has brought something on his own property which was not naturally there, harmless to others so long as it is confined to his own property, but which he knows to be mischievous if it gets on his neighbour's, should be obliged to make good the damage which ensues if he does not succeed in confining it to his own property. But for his act in bringing it there no mischief could have accrued, and it seems but just that he should at his peril keep it there so that no mischief may accrue, or answer for the natural and anticipated consequences. And upon authority, this we think is established to be the law whether the things so brought be beasts, or water, or filth, or stenches.

The case that has most commonly occurred, and which is most frequently to be found in the books, is as to the obligation of the owner of cattle which he has brought on his land, to prevent their escaping and doing mischief. The law as to them seems to be perfectly settled from early times; the owner must keep them in at his peril, or he will be answerable for the natural consequences of their escape; that is with regard to tame beasts, for the grass they eat and trample upon, though not for any injury to the person of others, for our ancestors have settled that it is not the general nature of horses to kick, or bulls to gore; but if the owner knows

that the beast has a vicious propensity to attack man, he will be answerable
for that too.

. . .

. . . But it was further said by Martin, B., that when damage is done
to personal property, or even to the person, by collision, either upon land or
at sea, there must be negligence in the party doing the damage to render
him legally responsible; and this is no doubt true, and as was pointed out
by Mr. Mellish during his argument before us, this is not confined to cases
of collision, for there are many cases in which proof of negligence is
essential, as for instance, where an unruly horse gets on the footpath of a
public street and kills a passenger [   ]; or where a person in a dock is
struck by the falling of a bale of cotton which the defendant's servants are
lowering [   ]; and many other similar cases may be found. But we think
these cases distinguishable from the present. Traffic on the highways,
whether by land or sea, cannot be conducted without exposing those whose
persons or property are near it to some inevitable risk; and that being so
those who go on the highway, or have their property adjacent to it, may
well be held to do so subject to their taking upon themselves the risk of
injury from that inevitable danger; and persons who by the license of the
owner pass near to warehouses where goods are being raised or lowered,
certainly do so subject to the inevitable risk of accident. In neither case,
therefore, can they recover without proof of want of care or skill occasion-
ing the accident; and it is believed that all the cases in which inevitable
accident has been held an excuse for what prima facie was a trespass, can
be explained on the same principle, viz., that the circumstances were such
as to show that the plaintiff had taken that risk upon himself. But there is
no ground for saying that the plaintiff here took upon himself any risk
arising from the uses to which the defendants should choose to apply their
land. He neither knew what these might be, nor could he in any way
control the defendants, or hinder their building what reservoirs they liked,
and storing up in them what water they pleased, so long as the defendants
succeeded in preventing the water which they there brought from interfering with the plaintiff's property.

The view which we take of the first point renders it unnecessary to
consider whether the defendants would or would not be responsible for the
want of care and skill in the persons employed by them, under the
circumstances stated in the case.

neg. inapplicable?

. . .

Judgment for the plaintiff.

Notes and Questions

1. The independent contractor question was difficult because there
had as yet been no decision holding the employer of an independent
contractor liable for the contractor's negligence. That did not come until

Bower v. Peate, 1 Q.B.D. 321 (1876). Recall the discussion of vicarious liability in Chapter I.

Fletcher did not sue the contractor directly—probably because earlier cases had concluded that in such situations the contractor would be held to owe a duty only to the employer and not to strangers. The leading case was Winterbottom v. Wright, 152 Eng.Rep. 402 (1842), discussed at p. 543, infra.

2. In the Court of Exchequer, the defendant prevailed, 2–1. The majority found that the traditional actions for interference with real property—trespass and nuisance—were inapplicable. Trespass required direct and immediate invasion of the plaintiff's land, while in this case the water flowed down and through intervening shafts and land. If the water had been cast upon plaintiff's land that would have amounted to a trespass. Nuisance, which is an interference with the plaintiff's use and enjoyment of his land, failed because a reservoir was lawful and the defendants had no reason to expect that any damage was likely to ensue. Furthermore, nuisances were usually continuing harm, such as noxious fumes, rather than a single occurrence. Martin, B., emphasized the fault requirement in collision cases and concluded that to "hold the defendant liable without negligence would be to constitute him an insurer, which, in my opinion, would be contrary to legal analogy and principle." Trespass and nuisance are discussed in Chapter IX. Bramwell, B., dissented in an opinion in which he argued that the plaintiff had a "right to be free from what has been called 'foreign' water, that is, water artificially brought or sent to him directly, or indirectly by its being sent to where it would flow to him." It was irrelevant whether defendants knew of the danger.

3. What was the reason for Justice Blackburn's ruling?

4. At one point he emphasizes that "but for" the defendants' act no mischief would have resulted. Is he saying that cause-in-fact suffices for finding liability for any act that harms another's land?

5. If the reservoir had been made exclusively from material on the defendants' land and had been filled only with rain water that fell on the land, would this be covered by Justice Blackburn's opinion?

6. Are the trespassing animal cases relevant to this case? For one state's extended history on the law of straying animals, see Fisel v. Wynns, 667 So.2d 761 (Fla.1996).

7. Is the rule about potentially vicious animals relevant here?

8. Might the analysis have been different if the plaintiff had been working in his mine and had been drowned by the water? What if the drowned man had been an employee of plaintiff?

9. How successful are Justice Blackburn's efforts to distinguish the highway injury cases, in which he admits that negligence must be shown? Recall that the falling barrel case, p. 91, supra, had been decided only three years earlier. What analysis if the flooding had caused part of a public highway to collapse, injuring a traveler? Or destroying a wagon?

10. Defendants appealed to the House of Lords.

Rylands v. Fletcher

House of Lords, 1868.
L.R. 3 H.L. 330.

THE LORD CHANCELLOR (Lord Cairns) [after stating the facts].

My Lords, the principles on which this case must be determined appear to me to be extremely simple. The Defendants treating them as the owners or occupiers of the close on which the reservoir was constructed, might lawfully have used that close for any purpose for which it might in the ordinary course of the enjoyment of land be used; and if, in what I may term the natural user of that land, there had been any accumulation of water, either on the surface or underground, and if, by the operation of the laws of nature, that accumulation of water had passed off into the close occupied by the Plaintiff, the Plaintiff could not have complained that that result had taken place. If he had desired to guard himself against it, it would have lain upon him to have done so, by leaving, or by interposing, some barrier between his close and the close of the Defendants in order to have prevented that operation of the laws of nature.

. . . .

On the other hand if the Defendants, not stopping at the natural use of their close, had desired to use it for any purpose which I may term a non-natural use, for the purpose of introducing into the close that which in its natural condition was not in or upon it, for the purpose of introducing water either above or below ground in quantities and in a manner not the result of any work or operation on or under the land,—and if in consequence of their doing so, or in consequence of any imperfection in the mode of their doing so, the water came to escape and to pass off into the close of the Plaintiff, then it appears to me that that which the Defendants were doing they were doing at their own peril; and, if in the course of their doing it, the evil arose to which I have referred, the evil, namely, of the escape of the water and its passing away to the close of the Plaintiff and injuring the Plaintiff, then for the consequence of that, in my opinion, the Defendants would be liable. . . .

My Lords, these simple principles, if they are well founded, as it appears to me they are, really dispose of this case.

The same result is arrived at on the principles, referred to by Mr. Justice Blackburn. [Lord Cairns here quotes in full the paragraph starting "We think that the true rule of law is. . . ."—Eds.]

My Lords, in that opinion, I must say I entirely concur. Therefore, I have to move your Lordships that the judgment of the Court of Exchequer Chamber be affirmed, and that the present appeal be dismissed with costs.

LORD CRANWORTH:—My Lords, I concur with my noble and learned friend in thinking that the rule of law was correctly stated by Mr. Justice

Blackburn in delivering the opinion of the Exchequer Chamber. ~~If a person brings, or accumulates, on his land anything which, if it should escape, may cause damage to his neighbour, he does so at his peril. If it does escape, and cause damage, he is responsible, however careful he may have been, and whatever precautions he may have taken to prevent the damage.~~

. . .

Judgment of the Court of Exchequer Chamber affirmed.

Notes and Questions

1. *Rylands* has inspired a vast literature, including the following: Bohlen, The Rule in Rylands v. Fletcher, 59 U.Pa.L.Rev. 298, 373, 423 (1911); Goodhart, Rylands v. Fletcher Today, 72 L.Q.Rev. 184 (1956); 3 Harper, James & Gray, The Law of Torts, §§ 14.2–14.5 (2d ed.1986); Molloy, Fletcher v. Rylands—A Reexamination of Juristic Origins, 9 U.Chi. L.Rev. 266 (1941); Prosser, The Principle of Rylands v. Fletcher, in Prosser, Selected Topics in the Law of Torts 134 (1954); Simpson, Legal Liability for Bursting Reservoirs: The Historical Context of Rylands v. Fletcher, 13 J. Legal Stud. 209 (1984). Particularly interesting are the views of Bohlen, arguing that "in England, the dominant class was the landed gentry, whose opinion the judges, who either sprang from this class or hoped to establish themselves and their families within—naturally reflected" (p. 318), and Molloy, reporting social and biographical data on the judges in *Rylands* that contradicts the "landed gentry" thesis.

2. Is there a difference between Justice Blackburn's "not naturally there" and Lord Cairns's "non-natural use"? Does Lord Cranworth agree with Lord Cairns?

3. Where does Justice Blackburn's rationale stand after the decision of the House of Lords?

4. Is *Rylands* limited in time and place to the social conditions in mid-nineteenth century England? From the outset, most American courts were less than enthusiastic about recognizing a broad principle of strict liability, on the basis of *Rylands,* that would apply to cases involving neighboring landowners. Consider the leading case of Losee v. Buchanan, 51 N.Y. 476 (1873), in which defendant's steam boiler—used in connection with a paper manufacturing business—exploded and was catapulted onto plaintiff's land and through several of his buildings. Rejecting *Rylands,* as well as the line of cases recognizing strict liability for harm caused by straying animals, the court extolled the virtues of the fault principle in an industrializing society:

By becoming a member of civilized society, I am compelled to give up many of my natural rights, but I receive more than a compensation from the surrender by every other man of the same rights and the security, advantage and protection which the laws give me. So, too, the general rules that I may have the exclusive and undisturbed use and possession of my real estate, and that I must so use my real estate as not to injure my neighbor, are much modified by the exigencies of the social state. We must have factories, machinery, dams, canals and railroads. They are demanded by the manifold wants of mankind, and lay at the basis of all our civilization. If I have any of these upon my lands, and they are not a nuisance and are not so managed as to become such, I am not responsible for any damage they accidentally and unavoidably do my neighbor. He receives his compensation for such damage by the general good, in which he shares, and the right which he has to place the same things upon his lands. I may not place or keep a nuisance upon my land to the damage of my neighbor, and I have my compensation for the surrender of this right to use my own as I will by the similar restriction imposed upon my neighbor for my benefit. I hold my property subject to the risk that it may be unavoidably or accidentally injured by those who live near me; and as I move about upon the public highways and in all places where other persons may lawfully be, I take the risk of being accidentally injured in my person by them without fault on their part. Most of the rights of property, as well as of person, in the social state, are not absolute but relative, and they must be so arranged and modified, not unnecessarily infringing upon natural rights, as upon the whole to promote the general welfare.

See also Brown v. Collins, 53 N.H. 442 (1873), another leading contemporaneous American decision, similarly rejecting the strict liability rule of *Rylands* because it would "impose a penalty upon efforts, made in a reasonable, skillful, and careful manner, to rise above a condition of barbarism" and would serve as "an obstacle in the way of progress and improvement." But compare the favorable reception in Massachusetts dating back to 1868, which is traced to the present in Clark–Aiken Co. v. Cromwell–Wright Co., Inc., 323 N.E.2d 876 (Mass.1975).

5. More particularly, on the escape of impounded water, contrast the *Rylands* view with Turner v. Big Lake Oil Co., 96 S.W.2d 221 (Tex.1936):

. . . what use of land is or may be a natural use, one within the contemplation of the parties to the original grant of land, necessarily depends upon the attendant circumstances and conditions which obtain in the territory of the original grants, or the initial terms of those grants.

In Texas we have conditions very different from those which obtain in England. A large portion of Texas is an arid or semi-arid region. West of the 98th meridian of longitude, where the rainfall is approximately 30 inches, the rainfall decreases until finally, in the extreme western part of the State, it is only about 10 inches. This land of decreasing rainfall is the great ranch or live stock region of the State, water for which is stored in thousands of ponds, tanks, and lakes on the surface of the ground. The country is almost without streams; and without the storage of water from rainfall in basins constructed for the purpose, or to hold waters pumped from the earth, the great livestock industry of West Texas must perish. No such condition obtains in England. With us the storage of water is a natural or necessary and common use of the land, necessarily within the contemplation of the State and its grantees when grants were made, and obviously the rule announced in *Rylands v. Fletcher*, predicated upon different conditions, can have no application here.

Compare Cities Service Co. v. State, 312 So.2d 799 (Fla.App.1975). Cities Service operated a phosphate rock mine in which it collected phosphate slimes in settling ponds. When a dam broke, one billion gallons of slime escaped into a creek and then into a river "killing countless numbers of fish and inflicting other damage." In this damage action the court concluded that the doctrine of *Rylands v. Fletcher* should be applied in Florida: "In a frontier society there was little likelihood that a dangerous use of land could cause damage to one's neighbor. Today our life has become more complex. Many areas are overcrowded, and even the non-negligent use of one's land can cause extensive damages to a neighbor's property. Though there are still many hazardous activities which are socially desirable, it now seems reasonable that they pay their own way."

6.   As *Cities Service Co.* implies, *Rylands* may have gained new life as an environmental harm principle. In particular, consider State, Dept. of Environmental Protection v. Ventron Corp., 468 A.2d 150 (N.J.1983). The State Department of Environmental Protection brought a damage action against Ventron and others for the cost of cleanup and removal of mercury pollution emanating from a tract of land on which defendants had conducted mercury processing for almost 50 years. The operations had raised the mercury content of a nearby tidal estuary to the highest found in fresh water sediments anywhere in the world. Among other theories, plaintiff argued for liability on the basis of *Rylands*. The court responded affirmatively:

> We believe it is time to recognize expressly that the law of liability has evolved so that a landowner is strictly liable to others for harm caused by toxic wastes that are stored on his property and flow onto the property of others. Therefore, we overrule [an earlier case rejecting *Rylands*] and adopt the principle of liability originally declared in *Rylands v. Fletcher*. The net result is that those who use, or permit others to use, land for the conduct of abnormally dangerous activities are strictly liable for resultant damages.

Is this a logical extension of *Rylands? Rylands* has not fared nearly so well in its land of origin. See Fleming, Comment: The Fall of a Crippled Giant, 3 Tort L. Rev. 56 (1995).

7.   Despite the mixed reception given *Rylands*, the concept of strict liability for harm caused by entrepreneurial activity was not unknown to American courts at the time. The following case provides the context.

Sullivan v. Dunham

Court of Appeals of New York, 1900.
161 N.Y. 290, 55 N.E. 923.

[Defendant land owner employed two men to dynamite a 60-foot tree on the land. The blast hurled a fragment of wood 412 feet onto a highway where it struck plaintiff's decedent and killed her. The two blasters were also sued. The trial judge charged that negligence need not be proven to establish liability. Defendants appealed from a judgment entered on a plaintiff's verdict and affirmed by the appellate division.]

VANN, J. The main question presented by this appeal is whether one who, for a lawful purpose and without negligence or want of skill, explodes a blast upon his own land and thereby causes a piece of wood to fall upon a person lawfully traveling in a public highway, is liable for the injury thus inflicted.

The statute authorizes the personal representative of a decedent to "maintain an action to recover damages for a wrongful act, neglect, or default, by which the decedent's death was caused, against a natural person who, or a corporation which, would have been liable to an action in favor of the decedent, by reason thereof, if death had not ensued." (Code Civ.Pro. § 1902.) It covers any action of trespass upon the person, which the deceased could have maintained if she had survived the accident. Stated in another form, therefore, the question before us is whether the defendants are liable as trespassers.

This is not a new question, for it has been considered, directly or indirectly, so many times by this court that a reference to the earlier authorities is unnecessary. In the leading case upon the subject, the defendant, in order to dig a canal authorized by its charter, necessarily blasted out rocks from its own land with gunpowder, and thus threw fragments against the plaintiff's house, which stood upon the adjoining premises. Although there was no proof of negligence, or want of skill, the defendant was held liable for the injury sustained. All the judges concurred in the opinion of Gardiner, J., who said:

> The defendants had the right to dig the canal. The plaintiff the right to the undisturbed possession of his property. If these rights conflict, the former must yield to the latter, as the more important of the two, since, upon grounds of public policy, it is better that one man should surrender a particular use of his land, than that another should be deprived of the beneficial use of his property altogether, which might be the consequence if the privilege of the former should be wholly unrestricted. The case before us illustrates this principle. For if the defendants in excavating their canal, in itself a lawful use of their land, could, in the manner mentioned by the witnesses, demolish the stoop of the plaintiff with impunity, they might, for the same purpose, on the exercise of reasonable care, demolish his house, and thus deprive him of all use of his property. The use of land by the proprietor is not therefore an absolute right, but qualified and limited by the higher right of others to the lawful possession of their property. To this possession the law prohibits all direct injury, without regard to its extent or the motives of the aggressor. . . . He may excavate a canal, but he cannot cast the dirt or stones upon the land of his neighbor, either by human agency or the force of gunpowder. If he cannot construct the work without the adoption of such means, he

must abandon that mode of using his property, or be held responsible for all damages resulting therefrom. He will not be permitted to accomplish a legal object in an unlawful manner. [Hay v. Cohoes Co., 2 N.Y. 159 (1849)].

This case was followed immediately by Tremain v. Cohoes Co. (2 N.Y. 163), a similar action against the same defendant, which offered to show upon the trial "that the work was done in the best and most careful manner." It was held that the evidence was properly excluded because the manner in which the defendant performed its work was of no consequence, as what it did to the plaintiff's injury was the sole question.

These were cases of trespass upon lands, while the case before us involves trespass upon the person of a human being, when she was where she had the same right to protection from injury as if she had been walking upon her own land. As the safety of the person is more sacred than the safety of property, the cases cited should govern our decision unless they are no longer the law.

The *Hay* case was reviewed by the Commission of Appeals in Losee v. Buchanan (51 N.Y. 476, 479) [1873], where it was held that one who, without negligence and with due care and skill, operates a steam boiler upon his own premises, is not liable to his neighbor for the damages caused by the explosion thereof. That was not a case of intentional but of accidental explosion. A tremendous force escaped, so to speak, from the owner, but was not voluntarily set free. The court, commenting upon the *Hay* case, said: "It was held that the defendant was liable for the injury, although no negligence or want of skill in executing the work was alleged or proved. This decision was well supported by the clearest principles. The acts of the defendant in casting the rocks upon plaintiff's premises were direct and immediate. The damage was the necessary consequence of just what the defendant was doing, and it was just as much liable as if it had caused the rocks to be taken by hand, or any other means, and thrown directly upon plaintiff's land."

The *Hay* case was expressly approved and made the basis of judgment in St. Peter v. Denison (58 N.Y. 416) [1874], where a blast, set off by a contractor with the state in the enlargement of the Erie canal, threw a piece of frozen earth against the plaintiff when he was at work upon the adjoining premises for the owner thereof. . . .

This case is analogous to the one before us, because the person injured did not own the land upon which he stood when struck, but he had a right to stand there the same as the plaintiff's intestate had a right to walk in the highway. We see no distinction in principle between the two cases.

. . .

When the injury is not direct, but consequential, such as is caused by concussion, which, by shaking the earth, injures property, there is no liability in the absence of negligence.

. . .

We think that the *Hay* case has always been recognized by this court as a sound and valuable authority. After standing for fifty years as the law of the state upon the subject it should not be disturbed, and we have no inclination to disturb it. It rests upon the principle, founded in public policy, that the safety of property generally is superior in right to a particular use of a single piece of property by its owner. It renders the enjoyment of all property more secure by preventing such a use of one piece by one man as may injure all his neighbors. It makes human life safer by tending to prevent a landowner from casting, either with or without negligence, a part of his land upon the person of one who is where he has a right to be. It so applies the maxim of *sic utere tuo* as to protect person and property from direct physical violence, which, although accidental, has the same effect as if it were intentional. It lessens the hardship by placing absolute liability upon the one who causes the injury. The accident in question was a misfortune to the defendants, but it was a greater misfortune to the young woman who was killed. The safety of travelers upon the public highway is more important to the state than the improvement of one piece of property, by a special method, is to its owner. . . .

. . .

The judgment is right and should be affirmed, with costs.

All concur, except GRAY, J., not voting.

Notes and Questions

1. Judge Vann states that courts will apply the maxim of *sic utere* so "as to protect person and property from direct physical violence, which, although accidental, has the same effect as if it were intentional." Is this consistent with *Losee?* ~~no~~

2. How might the *Sullivan* facts have been analyzed by Justice Blackburn? By Lord Cairns?   *same, str. liab.*

3. Did the court in *Losee* adequately distinguish the *Hay* case? What analysis in *Losee* if the defendant had been testing this boiler's capacity by increasing the pressure until it exploded? *intentional, not accidental*

4. The difference in treatment accorded harms caused by debris and by concussion was justified by one view of the history of the writ system. Direct harm from debris might give rise to a trespass action, in which intent and fault were once irrelevant; concussion damage was viewed as indirect, or consequential, harm for which only an action on the case would lie—and a fault component developed here earlier than in trespass. Can this distinction be supported on other grounds? In the leading case of Booth v. Rome, W. & O.T.R.R. Co., 35 N.E. 592 (N.Y.1893), the court held the 1849 *Hay* case inapplicable to harm suffered by concussion because there the defendant's act had caused direct harm to the plaintiff's property and was thus a trespass. In *Booth,* the court emphasized that the defendant was engaged in a "lawful act" on its own land. "The immediate act was confined to its own land, but the blasts, by setting the air in motion, or in some other unexplained way, caused an injury to plaintiff's house. . . . The blasting was necessary, was carefully done, and the injury was consequential. There was no technical trespass." The court added that "to exclude the defendant from blasting to adapt its lot to the contemplated uses, at the instance of the plaintiff, would not be a compromise between conflicting rights, but an extinguishment of the right of the one for the benefit of the other." Again, "public policy is sustained by the building up of towns and cities and the improvement of property. Any unnecessary restraint on freedom of action of a property owner hinders this." The New York cases are discussed in detail, along with the roughly contemporaneous decisions in *Brown v. Kendall* and *Rylands v. Fletcher*, in Gregory, Trespass to Negligence to Absolute Liability, 37 Va.L.Rev. 359 (1951).

The distinction between debris and concussion has virtually disappeared. It survived in New York until Spano v. Perini Corp., 250 N.E.2d 31 (N.Y.1969), in which, referring to the second set of reasons in *Booth,* the court said:

> This rationale cannot withstand analysis. The plaintiff in *Booth* was not seeking, as the court implied, to "exclude the defendant from blasting" and thus prevent desirable improvements to the latter's property. Rather, he was merely seeking compensation for the damage which was inflicted upon his own property as a result of that blasting. The question, in other words, was not *whether* it was lawful or proper to engage in blasting but *who* should bear the cost of any resulting damage—the person who engaged in the dangerous activity or the innocent neighbor injured thereby. Viewed in such a light, it clearly appears that *Booth* was wrongly decided and should be forthrightly overruled.

5. The Restatement sought to generalize from these pockets of liability in sections 519 and 520. In the first Restatement the covered activity was described as "ultrahazardous," which was defined as involving a risk that "cannot be eliminated by the exercise of the utmost care" and "is not a matter of common usage." The Second Restatement reframed the approach by providing that one who "carries on an abnormally dangerous activity is subject to liability for harm . . . resulting from the activity, although he has exercised the utmost care to prevent the harm." In determining whether an activity is "abnormally dangerous," section 520 listed six factors for consideration:

(a) existence of a high degree of risk of some harm to the person, land or chattels of others;

(b) likelihood that the harm that results from it will be great;

(c) inability to eliminate the risk by the exercise of reasonable care;

(d) extent to which the activity is not a matter of common usage;

(e) inappropriateness of the activity to the place where it is carried on; and

(f) extent to which its value to the community is outweighed by its dangerous attributes.

This section is central to the case that follows.

Indiana Harbor Belt Railroad Co. v. American Cyanamid Co.* *[handwritten: Abnormally dangerous activity *]*

United States Court of Appeals, Seventh Circuit. 1990.
916 F.2d 1174.

Before POSNER, MANION and KANNE, CIRCUIT JUDGES.

POSNER, CIRCUIT JUDGE.

American Cyanamid Company, the defendant in this diversity tort suit *[handwritten: D is manufactor of chemicals]* governed by Illinois law, is a major manufacturer of chemicals, including acrylonitrile, a chemical used in large quantities in making acrylic fibers, plastics, dyes, pharmaceutical chemicals, and other intermediate and final goods. On January 2, 1979, at its manufacturing plant in Louisiana, Cyanamid loaded 20,000 gallons of liquid acrylonitrile into a railroad tank car that it had leased from the North American Car Corporation. The next day, a train of the Missouri Pacific Railroad picked up the car at Cyanamid's siding. The car's ultimate destination was a Cyanamid plant in New Jersey served by Conrail rather than by Missouri Pacific. The Missouri Pacific train carried the car north to the Blue Island railroad yard of *[handwritten: P is small switching line for RRs.]* Indiana Harbor Belt Railroad, the plaintiff in this case, a small switching line that has a contract with Conrail to switch cars from other lines to Conrail, in this case for travel east. The Blue Island yard is in the Village of Riverdale, which is just south of Chicago and part of the Chicago metropolitan area.

The car arrived in the Blue Island yard on the morning of January 9, 1979. Several hours after it arrived, employees of the switching line noticed fluid gushing from the bottom outlet of the car. The lid on the outlet was broken. After two hours, the line's supervisor of equipment was able to stop the leak by closing a shut-off valve controlled from the top of the car. No one was sure at the time just how much of the contents of the car had leaked, but it was feared that all 20,000 gallons had, and since acrylonitrile is flammable at a temperature of 30 degrees Fahrenheit or above, highly toxic, and possibly carcinogenic [ ], the local authorities ordered the homes near the yard evacuated. The evacuation lasted only a few hours, until the car was moved to a remote part of the yard and it was discovered that only about a quarter of the acrylonitrile had leaked. Concerned nevertheless that there had been some contamination of soil and water, the Illinois Department of Environmental Protection ordered the switching line to take decontamination measures that cost the line $981,022.75, which it sought to recover by this suit.

[After some procedural tangles, the district judge granted plaintiff summary judgment on its strict liability claim and dismissed plaintiff's negligence claim. Defendant appealed and plaintiff cross-appealed.]

issue

The question whether the shipper of a hazardous chemical by rail should be strictly liable for the consequences of a spill or other accident to the shipment en route is a novel one in Illinois [despite earlier confusion that might have suggested otherwise].

The parties agree that the question whether placing acrylonitrile in a rail shipment that will pass through a metropolitan area subjects the shipper to strict liability is, as recommended in Restatement (Second) of Torts § 520, comment *l* (1977), a question of law, so that we owe no particular deference to the conclusion of the district court. They also agree . . . that the Supreme Court of Illinois would treat as authoritative the provisions of the Restatement governing abnormally dangerous activi-

RoL: Rst. 520

ties. The key provision is section 520, which sets forth six factors to be considered in deciding whether an activity is abnormally dangerous and the actor therefore strictly liable.

The roots of section 520 are in nineteenth-century cases. The most famous one is Rylands v. Fletcher, 1 Ex. 265, aff'd, L.R. 3 H.L. 300 (1868), but a more illuminating one in the present context is Guille v. Swan, 19 Johns. (N.Y.) 381 (1822). A man took off in a hot-air balloon and landed, without intending to, in a vegetable garden in New York City. A crowd that had been anxiously watching his involuntary descent trampled the vegetables in their endeavor to rescue him when he landed. The owner of the garden sued the balloonist for the resulting damage, and won. Yet the balloonist had not been careless. In the then state of ballooning it was impossible to make a pinpoint landing.

Application of Guille to sec. 520.

Guille is a paradigmatic case for strict liability. (a) The risk (probability) of harm was great, and (b) the harm that would ensue if the risk materialized could be, although luckily was not, great (the balloonist could have crashed into the crowd rather than into the vegetables). The confluence of these two factors established the urgency of seeking to prevent such accidents. (c) Yet such accidents could not be prevented by the exercise of due care; the technology of care in ballooning was insufficiently developed. (d) The activity was not a matter of common usage, so there was no presumption that it was a highly valuable activity despite its unavoidable riskiness. (e) The activity was inappropriate to the place in which it took place—densely populated New York City. The risk of serious harm to others (other than the balloonist himself, that is) could have been reduced by shifting the activity to the sparsely inhabited areas that surrounded the city in those days. (f) Reinforcing (d), the value to the community of the activity of recreational ballooning did not appear to be great enough to offset its unavoidable risks.

These are, of course, the six factors in section 520. They are related to each other in that each is a different facet of a common quest for a proper legal regime to govern accidents that negligence liability cannot adequately control. The interrelations might be more perspicuous if the six factors were reordered. One might for example start with (c), inability to eliminate the risk of accident by the exercise of due care. [   ] The baseline common law regime of tort liability is negligence. When it is a workable regime, because the hazards of an activity can be avoided by being careful (which is to say, nonnegligent), there is no need to switch to strict liability. Sometimes, however, a particular type of accident cannot be prevented by taking care but can be avoided, or its consequences minimized, by shifting the activity in which the accident occurs to another locale, where the risk or harm of an accident will be less (e), or by reducing the scale of the activity in order to minimize the number of accidents caused by it (f). [ ] By making the actor strictly liable—by denying him in other words an excuse based on his inability to avoid accidents by being more careful—we give him an incentive, missing in a negligence regime, to experiment with methods of preventing accidents that involve not greater exertions of care, assumed to be futile, but instead relocating, changing, or reducing (perhaps to the vanishing point) the activity giving rise to the accident. [ ] The greater the risk of an accident (a) and the costs of an accident if one occurs (b), the more we want the actor to consider the possibility of making accident-reducing activity changes; the stronger, therefore, is the case for strict liability. Finally, if an activity is extremely common (d), like driving an automobile, it is unlikely either that its hazards are perceived as great or that there is no technology of care available to minimize them; so the case for strict liability is weakened.

The largest class of cases in which strict liability has been imposed under the standard codified in the Second Restatement of Torts involves the use of dynamite and other explosives for demolition in residential or urban areas. [ ] Explosives are dangerous even when handled carefully, and we therefore want blasters to choose the location of the activity with care and also to explore the feasibility of using safer substitutes (such as a wrecking ball), as well as to be careful in the blasting itself. Blasting is not a commonplace activity like driving a car, or so superior to substitute methods of demolition that the imposition of liability is unlikely to have any effect except to raise the activity's costs.

Against this background we turn to the particulars of acrylonitrile. Acrylonitrile is one of a large number of chemicals that are hazardous in the sense of being flammable, toxic, or both; acrylonitrile is both, as are many others. A table in the record, [ ], contains a list of the 125 hazardous materials that are shipped in highest volume on the nation's railroads. Acrylonitrile is the fifty-third most hazardous on the list.   .   .   .
The plaintiff's lawyer acknowledged at argument that the logic of the district court's opinion dictated strict liability for all 52 materials that rank higher than acrylonitrile on the list, and quite possibly for the 72 that rank lower as well, since all are hazardous if spilled in quantity while being shipped by rail. Every shipper of any of these materials would therefore be strictly liable for the consequences of a spill or other accident that occurred while the material was being shipped through a metropolitan area. The plaintiff's lawyer further acknowledged the irrelevance, on her view of the case, of the fact that Cyanamid had leased and filled the car that spilled the acrylonitrile; all she thought important is that Cyanamid introduced the product into the stream of commerce that happened to pass through the Chicago metropolitan area. Her concession may have been incautious. One

might want to distinguish between the shipper who merely places his goods on his loading dock to be picked up by the carrier and the shipper who, as in this case, participates actively in the transportation. But the concession is illustrative of the potential scope of the district court's decision.

No cases recognize so sweeping a liability. Several reject it, though none has facts much like those of the present case. .   .

[The court discussed Siegler v. Kuhlman, 502 P.2d 1181 (Wash.1972), in which the trailer of defendant's gasoline truck broke away and rolled down onto a highway on which plaintiff motorist was traveling. Plaintiff's car went into a pool of gasoline spilled from the trailer and the resulting explosion "obliterated the plaintiff's decedent and her car"—and evidence of what happened. Although the *Siegler* court used strict liability, Judge Posner suggested that res ipsa loquitur would have sufficed. He also noted that the suit was against the transporter of the gasoline rather than its manufacturer.]

So we can get little help from precedent, and might as well apply section 520 to the acrylonitrile problem from the ground up. To begin with, we have been given no reason, whether the reason in *Siegler* or any other, for believing that a negligence regime is not perfectly adequate to remedy and deter, at reasonable cost, the accidental spillage of acrylonitrile from rail cars. [   ] Acrylonitrile could explode and destroy evidence, but of course did not here, making imposition of strict liability on the theory of the *Siegler* decision premature. More important, although acrylonitrile is flammable even at relatively low temperatures, and toxic, it is not so corrosive or otherwise destructive that it will eat through or otherwise damage or weaken a tank car's valves although they are maintained with due (which essentially means, with average) care. No one suggests, therefore, that the leak in this case was caused by the inherent properties of acrylonitrile. It was caused by carelessness—whether that of the North American Car Corporation in failing to maintain or inspect the car properly, or that of Cyanamid in failing to maintain or inspect it, or that of the Missouri Pacific when it had custody of the car, or that of the switching line itself in failing to notice the ruptured lid, or some combination of these possible failures of care. Accidents that are due to a lack of care can be prevented by taking care; and when a lack of care can (unlike *Siegler*) be shown in court, such accidents are adequately deterred by the threat of liability for negligence.

.   .   . For all that appears from the record of the case or any other sources of information that we have found, if a tank car is carefully maintained the danger of a spill of acrylonitrile is negligible. If this is right, there is no compelling reason to move to a regime of strict liability, especially one that might embrace all other hazardous materials shipped by rail as well. .   .   . If the vast majority of chemical spills by railroads are preventable by due care, the imposition of strict liability should cause only a slight, not as [amici] argue a substantial, rise in liability insurance rates, because the incremental liability should be slight. The amici have momentarily lost sight of the fact that the feasibility of avoiding accidents simply by being careful is an argument against strict liability.

. . .

The district judge and the plaintiff's lawyer make much of the fact that the spill occurred in a densely inhabited metropolitan area. Only 4,000 gallons spilled; what if all 20,000 had done so? Isn't the risk that this might happen even if everybody were careful sufficient to warrant giving the shipper an incentive to explore alternative routes? Strict liability would supply that incentive. But this argument overlooks the fact that, like other transportation networks, the railroad network is a hub-and-spoke system. And the hubs are in metropolitan areas. Chicago is one of the nation's largest railroad hubs. In 1983, the latest year for which we have figures, Chicago's railroad yards handled the third highest volume of hazardous-material shipments in the nation. East St. Louis, which is also in Illinois, handled the second highest volume. [   ] With most hazardous chemicals (by volume of shipments) being at least as hazardous as acrylonitrile, it is unlikely—and certainly not demonstrated by the plaintiff—that they can be rerouted around all the metropolitan areas in the country, except at prohibitive cost. Even if it were feasible to reroute them one would hardly expect shippers, as distinct from carriers, to be the firms best situated to do the rerouting. Granted, the usual view is that common carriers are not subject to strict liability for the carriage of materials that make the transportation of them abnormally dangerous, because a common carrier cannot refuse service to a shipper of a lawful commodity. Restatement, supra, § 521. Two courts, however, have rejected the common carrier exception. National Steel Service Center, Inc. v. Gibbons, 319 N.W.2d 269 (Iowa 1982); Chavez v. Southern Pacific Transportation Co., 413 F.Supp. 1203, 1213–14 (E.D.Cal.1976). If it were rejected in Illinois, this would weaken still further the case for imposing strict liability on shippers whose goods pass through the densely inhabited portions of the state.

The difference between shipper and carrier points to a deep flaw in the plaintiff's case. Unlike *Guille* and unlike *Siegler*, and unlike the storage cases, beginning with *Rylands* itself, here it is not the actors—that is, the transporters of acrylonitrile and other chemicals—but the manufacturers, who are sought to be held strictly liable. [   ] A shipper can in the bill of lading designate the route of his shipment if he likes, 49 U.S.C. § 11710(a)(1), but is it realistic to suppose that shippers will become students of railroading in order to lay out the safest route by which to ship their goods? Anyway, rerouting is no panacea. Often it will increase the length of the journey, or compel the use of poorer track, or both. When this happens, the probability of an accident is increased, even if the consequences of an accident if one occurs are reduced; so the expected accident cost, being the product of the probability of an accident and the harm if the accident occurs, may rise. [   ] It is easy to see how the accident in this case might have been prevented at reasonable cost by greater care on the part of those who handled the tank car of acrylonitrile. It is difficult to see how it might have been prevented at reasonable cost by a change in the activity of transporting the chemical. This is therefore not an apt case for strict liability.

[Although an argument might have been made that Cyanamid should be treated as a "shipper-transporter" subject to rules more onerous than those imposed on "shippers" the court found it had not been made in this case and was waived.] Which is not to say that had it not been waived it would have changed the outcome of the case. The very fact that Cyanamid participated actively in the transportation of the acrylonitrile imposed upon it a duty of due care and by doing so brought into play a threat of negligence liability that, for all we know, may provide an adequate regime of accident control in the transportation of this particular chemical.

In emphasizing the flammability and toxicity of acrylonitrile rather than the hazards of transporting it, as in failing to distinguish between the active and the passive shipper, the plaintiff overlooks the fact that ultra-hazardousness or abnormal dangerousness is, in the contemplation of the law at least, a property not of substances, but of activities: not of acrylonitrile, but of the transportation of acrylonitrile by rail through populated areas. . . . Whatever the situation under products liability law (section 402A of the Restatement), the manufacturer of a product is not considered to be engaged in an abnormally dangerous activity merely because the product becomes dangerous when it is handled or used in some way after it leaves his premises, even if the danger is foreseeable. [ ] The plaintiff does not suggest that Cyanamid should switch to making some less hazardous chemical that would substitute for acrylonitrile in the textiles and other goods in which acrylonitrile is used. Were this a feasible method of accident avoidance, there would be an argument for making manufacturers strictly liable for accidents that occur during the shipment of their products (how strong an argument we need not decide). Apparently it is not a feasible method.

. . . Brutal though it may seem to say it, the inappropriate use to which land is being put in the Blue Island yard and neighborhood may be, not the transportation of hazardous chemicals, but residential living. The analogy is to building your home between the runways at O'Hare.

The briefs hew closely to the Restatement, whose approach to the issue of strict liability is mainly allocative rather than distributive. By this we mean that the emphasis is on picking a liability regime (negligence or strict liability) that will control the particular class of accidents in question most effectively, rather than on finding the deepest pocket and placing liability there. . . .

The case for strict liability has not been made. Not in this suit in any event. . . .

[Although the improper grant of summary judgment normally requires a remand for trial of that part of the case, this case was different because no new facts were suggested that would warrant strict liability. Defendant conceded that if the strict liability claim fell, the negligence claim had to be remanded for trial.]

The judgment is reversed (with no award of costs in this court) and the case remanded for further proceedings, consistent with this opinion, on the plaintiff's claim for negligence.

Notes and Questions

1. Why might manufacturing, transportation, and storage be treated as different activities for purposes of strict liability?

2. Why is the Restatement section framed in terms of activities rather than "acts," as in negligence? (We will consider liability for defective products shortly.)

Consider the following example offered by Judge Posner in G.J. Leasing Co. v. Union Electric Co., 54 F.3d 379 (7th Cir.1995):

> Keeping a tiger in one's backyard would be an example of an abnormally dangerous activity. The hazard is such, relative to the value of the activity, that we desire not just that the owner take all due care that the tiger not escape, but that he consider seriously the possibility of getting rid of the tiger altogether; and we give him an incentive to consider this course of action by declining to make the exercise of due care a defense to a suit based on an injury caused by the other—in other words, by making him strictly liable for any such injury.

Might strict liability also induce the owner to consider moving the tiger elsewhere? Can one analyze keeping a tiger in terms of negligence?

3. The first Restatement used the term "ultrahazardous" instead of "abnormally dangerous" activity and framed the liability as a rule instead of using a list of factors. According to that version, strict liability was to be imposed if the activity

> (a) necessarily involves a risk of serious harm to the person, land or chattels of others which cannot be eliminated by the exercise of the utmost care, and

> (b) is not a matter of common usage.

How does this version differ from the one used by the court? Would its use have altered the result of the principal case?

4. A few courts have rejected the approach of the Restatement. See e.g., Yukon Equipment, Inc. v. Fireman's Fund Ins. Co., 585 P.2d 1206 (Alaska 1978), involving the explosion of a building used to store explosives. The court insisted that the use and storage of dynamite warranted the imposition of strict liability no matter how valuable the activity might be to the community and even if there were no safer place to store it:

> The reasons for imposing absolute liability on those who have created a grave risk of harm to others by storing or using explosives are largely independent of considerations of locational appropriateness. We see no reason for making a distinction between the right of a homesteader to recover when his property has been damaged by a blast set off in a remote corner of the state, and the right to compensation of

an urban resident whose home is destroyed by an explosion originating in a settled area. In each case, the loss is properly to be regarded as a cost of the business of storing or using explosives. Every incentive remains to conduct such activities in locations which are as safe as possible, because there the damages resulting from an accident will be kept to a minimum.

How might Judge Posner respond?

5. In Torchia v. Fisher, 468 A.2d 1061 (N.J.1983), the court held the owner of a stolen airplane liable for ground damage to plaintiffs under a statute construed to create "absolute liability." The court asserted that "as between an unsuspecting homeowner or person on the ground and the plane's owner, the Legislature could rationally decide to place the loss on the owner, for whom the plane served some purpose."

Contrary to a view taken in the First Restatement, most courts now refuse to hold owners or pilots of falling aircraft strictly liable for harm to land, persons or chattels on the ground. See e.g., Crosby v. Cox Aircraft Co. of Washington, 746 P.2d 1198 (Wash.1987). The framers of the Second Restatement, however, after much debate, adopted a special provision making the owner and operator of any aircraft liable for harm caused to land, persons or chattels on the ground by the aircraft itself or any object falling therefrom "even if he has exercised the utmost care to prevent it." A comment to the section observed that despite great strides the safety records did not indicate "that the ordinary rules of negligence should be applied." The comment also stressed that those on the ground have "no place to hide from falling aircraft and are helpless to select any locality for their residence or business in which they will not be exposed to the risk, however minimized it may be." § 520A. Is this a unique hazard?

For a capsule view of the evolving judicial treatment of aircraft cases in New York, see Guille v. Swan, 19 Johns. (N.Y.) 381 (1822)(discussed in the principal case); Rochester Gas & Elec. Corp. v. Dunlop, 266 N.Y.S. 469 (Sup. 1933); and Wood v. United Air Lines, Inc., 223 N.Y.S.2d 692 (Sup. 1961), affirmed without opinion 226 N.Y.S.2d 1022 (App.Div.), appeal dismissed 184 N.E.2d 180 (N.Y.1962).

6. In 1973, an explosion occurred in the Southern Pacific yards near Roseville, California. Eighteen boxcars laden with bombs, all belonging to the United States, exploded, causing widespread damage and injury, and triggering several lawsuits. In Chavez v. Southern Pacific Transp. Co., 413 F.Supp. 1203 (E.D.Cal.1976), cited in *Harbor Belt*, the railroad argued that where a carrier is required to accept dangerous cargo, it is "unjust" to impose strict liability. The judge concluded that California courts would not create such an exception even though the Second Restatement's § 521 did reject strict liability in such a situation:

If California predicated liability solely upon the "fairness" rationale appearing in [Green v. General Petroleum Corp., 270 P. 952 (Cal. 1928)], it might well find that strict liability was inappropriate. Under the *Green* rationale strict liability is imposed because the ultrahazardous factor intentionally exposes others to a serious danger—an anti-social act is being redressed. Where the carrier has no choice but to accept dangerous cargo and engage in an ultrahazardous activity, it is the public which is requiring the carrier to engage in the anti-social activity. The carrier is innocent.

But, there is no logical reason for creating a "public duty" exception when the rationale for subjecting the carrier to absolute liability is the carrier's ability to distribute the loss to the public. Whether the carrier is free to reject or bound to take the explosive cargo, the plaintiffs are equally defenseless. Bound or not, Southern Pacific is in a position to pass along the loss to the public. Bound or not, the social and economic benefits which are ordinarily derived from strict liability are achieved.   .   .   . A more efficient allocation of resources results. Thus, the reasonable inference to be drawn from the adoption of the risk distribution rationale in Smith v. Lockheed Propulsion Co., [56 Cal.Rptr. 128 (App. 1967)] is that California would .   .   . find carriers engaging in ultrahazardous activity are subject to strict liability.

For an extensive discussion of the carrier issue, see National Steel Service Center, Inc. v. Gibbons, 319 N.W.2d 269 (Iowa 1982), also rejecting the Second Restatement's position.

7. In Laird v. Nelms, 406 U.S. 797 (1972), the Court, 6–2, concluded that "wrongful" as used in 28 U.S.C. § 1346(b) of the Federal Tort Claims Act did not permit recovery against the government on a strict liability theory. See p. 249, supra. That section gives district courts jurisdiction to hear tort claims against the government for harm caused "by a negligent or wrongful act or omission" of a government employee. The *Nelms* case involved property damage caused by sonic booms from military planes. Although state law might recognize an action on a strict liability theory, the statute did not permit imposition of such liability on the government. See Peck, *Laird v. Nelms*: A Call for Review and Revision of the Federal Tort Claims Act, 48 Wash.L.Rev. 391 (1973) and Note, Utility, Fairness and the Takings Clause: Three Perspectives on *Laird v. Nelms*, 59 Va.L.Rev. 1034 (1973).

See also In re Bomb Disaster at Roseville, California, 438 F.Supp. 769 (E.D.Cal.1977), in which the court concluded that *Laird v. Nelms* barred recovery against the United States for the explosions that occurred.

8. *Defenses.* There have been relatively few cases involving defenses in this branch of strict liability. Why might this be? Second Restatement § 523 states that plaintiff's assumption of the risk of harm from the activity "bars his recovery for the harm." An illustration states that a person who drives along the public highway knowing that a magazine of explosives is adjacent to the highway is not barred by assumption of the risk if the magazine explodes as the car is driving past. Why not?

Another illustration asserts that if a flagman warns P about an impending blast down the road and asks P to wait five minutes, P will be barred by assumption of the risk if he refuses to wait the five minutes.

Section 524 states that contributory negligence is not a defense to strict liability except when the plaintiff's conduct involves "knowingly and unreasonably subjecting himself to the risk of harm from the activity. . . ." An illustration to § 524 states that if a driver is so intent on passing the truck ahead that the driver fails to see "Danger, Dynamite" plainly marked on the truck, and collides with the truck causing an explosion, the driver is not barred by contributory negligence. The driver who has read the sign, however, is barred from recovery. Why? What if no explosion follows the collision?

The Restatement sections were prepared before the emergence of comparative negligence. Should a state that has adopted comparative fault for negligence cases extend it to this type of strict liability case? This issue is discussed in the context of liability for defective products at p. 605, infra.

B.   THEORETICAL PERSPECTIVES

Strict liability can be seriously regarded as a comprehensive alternative to the fault principle only if it is grounded in a broader-based foundation than the cases involving abnormally dangerous activities. The various formulations of enterprise liability adopted by the courts, initially in the abnormally dangerous activity cases, but more extensively in defective products litigation, supply the basic elements for such a theory. These elements, along with other insights drawn from economics and moral theory, served as the basis for a substantial body of tort scholarship in recent years aimed at illuminating the principles of strict liability.

This section offers selections from that literature, beginning with a historical perspective arguing that the evolving strict liability case law that has been considered in the preceding section can be seen as reflecting a fundamental shift in focus from a corrective justice to a collective justice perspective—a shift in which enterprise liability emerges as a dominant theme in explaining modern strict liability.

The Ideology of Enterprise Liability

Robert L. Rabin.
55 Maryland Law Review 1190, 1194–99 (1996).

In the nineteenth century, strict liability for accidental harm is generally identified with two sources—*Rylands v. Fletcher*[23] and the blasting cases.[24] Neither reflects a different perspective on the ideological source of rights and duties in tort, as I see it, from the principles of fault liability that were developing contemporaneously. The point is nicely illustrated by the opinion of Justice Blackburn in *Rylands*, as he attempted to reconcile his position that fault was irrelevant in that case with cases involving "traffic on the highways," in which he observed that a showing of fault was a necessary condition to liability. "Traffic on the highways" became a

---

23. [1866] L.R. 1 Ex. 265, aff'd, [1868] L.R. 3 H.L. 330.

24. See, e.g., Hay v. Cohoes Co., 2 N.Y. 159, 162–63 (1849). . . .

metaphor for situations in which individuals are injured while pursuing their daily lives in public rather than enjoying the privacy of their own domicile. To the nineteenth century judicial mind, still dominated by interpersonal notions of neighborliness rooted in property rights, one's domicile remained sacrosanct:

> The person whose grass or corn is eaten down by the escaping cattle of his neighbour, or whose mine is flooded by the water from his neighbour's reservoir, or whose cellar is invaded by the filth of his neighbour's privy, or whose habitation is made unhealthy by the fumes and noisome vapours of his neighbour's alkali works, is damnified without any fault of his own; and it seems but reasonable and just that the neighbour, who has brought something on his own property which was not naturally there, harmless to others so long as it is confined to his own property, but which he knows to be mischievous if it gets on his neighbour's, should be obliged to make good the damage which ensues if he does not succeed in confining it to his own property.

Blackburn's emphasis on "doing right" by one's neighbor is just as focused on moralistic judgment about appropriate private behavior as is the code of personal conduct at the foundation of the fault principle.

The blasting cases reveal similar origins in trespassory notions of protecting private rights in land. As later cases, such as *Sullivan v. Dunham*, shifted the focus to protection of those injured in public by blasting activities, these decisions also blurred the meaning of "trespass," drawing on still other venerable precedents of liability for "direct" acts. But the critical point, in reading turn-of-the-century blasting cases like *Sullivan*, is that there is not the slightest evidence of attention to risk-bearing, creating incentives to safer conduct, or other utilitarian concerns. Instead, in these opinions, norms of interpersonal conduct remain deeply ingrained: "As the safety of the person is more sacred than the safety of property, the cases cited [recognizing that the use of land by the proprietor is not an absolute right, but limited by the higher right of others to lawfully possess their property] should govern our decision. . . ."[30]

Rights qualified and rights absolute, *sic utere tuo*[31] as a guiding principle, trespass as a buffer against invasive conduct—these are the

30. [ ]. But cf. Losee v. Buchanan, 51 N.Y. 476, 479 (1873) (rejecting strict liability in a case involving explosion of a steam boiler on grounds that a growing industrialized society required a more limited foundation for responsibility than strict liability—namely, fault). Cases like *Losee* planted the seed for a collective-based notion of fault, but the ripening of utilitarian considerations in fault cases did not really become evident until the mid-twentieth century. Consider in particular the influence of what came to be known as the Learned Hand test for negligence, United States v. Carroll Towing Co., 159 F.2d 169, 173 (2d Cir.1947) (establishing a calculus in which due care of a barge owner was to be assessed as "a function of three variables: (1) the probability that she will break away; (2) the gravity of the resulting injury if she does, (3) the burden of adequate precautions")—although it is far from clear that Judge Hand had present-day economic efficiency considerations in mind when he spelled out his formula.

31. The complete phrase is "*Sic utere tuo ut alienum non laedas*," or "use your own so as not to injure another's property." Cochran's Law Lexicon 271 (5th ed. 1973).

touchstones of strict liability as traditionally conceived. It is a discourse grounded in ethical norms of interpersonal conduct.[32] It is akin to Oliver Wendell Holmes's contemporaneous account in The Common Law, forging a foreseeability-based rationale for fault liability in a pre-modern society free of industrial injuries, product mishaps, and impulses to view accidental harm as a collective concern.

Flash forward to 1973. A federal district court in California, in *Chavez v. Southern Pacific Transportation Co.*, entertained a number of lawsuits arising out of an explosion of eighteen boxcars filled with bombs in a railroad yard in Roseville, California.[35] The carrier argued a "public duty" defense—that it was required to accept the cargo by the federal government and consequently should not be strictly liable. The court responded in terms revealing the paradigm shift that has occurred:

> If California predicated liability solely upon the "fairness" rationale appearing in . . . [Green v. General Petroleum Corp., 270 P. 952 (Cal.1928)], it might well find that strict liability was inappropriate. Under the *Green* rationale strict liability is imposed because the ultrahazardous actor intentionally exposes others to a serious danger— an anti-social act is being redressed. Where the carrier has no choice but to accept dangerous cargo and engage in an ultrahazardous activity, it is the public which is requiring the carrier to engage in the anti-social activity. The carrier is innocent.
>
> But, there is no logical reason for creating a "public duty" exception when the rationale for subjecting the carrier to absolute liability is the carrier's ability to distribute the loss to the public. Whether the carrier is free to reject or bound to take the explosive cargo, the plaintiffs are equally defenseless. Bound or not, Southern Pacific is in a position to pass along the loss to the public. Bound or not, the social and economic benefits which are ordinarily derived from imposing strict liability are achieved.

The federal district court in *Chavez* relied on *Smith v. Lockheed Propulsion Co.*,[38] a 1967 case involving reverberation damage from rocket testing, that had in turn relied on *Luthringer v. Moore*,[39] a 1948 case involving personal injuries from fumigation in an adjoining building. To complete the strict liability lineage, *Luthringer* relied on *Green*, cited in the passage above. In 1928, as the quote suggests, the *Green* court was still

---

32. The ethical basis for these norms of interpersonal conduct has in fact taken a variety of forms. Compare, e.g., George P. Fletcher, Fairness and Utility in Tort Theory, 85 Harv. L. Rev. 537, 546–51 (1972) [hereinafter Fletcher, Fairness and Utility] as amplified in George P. Fletcher, Corrective Justice for Moderns, 106 Harv. L. Rev. 1658, 1677–78 (1993) [hereinafter Fletcher, Corrective Justice] (reviewing Jules Coleman, Risks and Wrongs (1992)) (emphasizing nonreciprocity of risk posed by intersecting activities) with

Richard A. Epstein, A Theory of Strict Liability, 2 J. Legal Stud. 151, 200–04 (1973) and Richard A. Epstein, Defenses and Subsequent Pleas in a System of Strict Liability, 3 J. Legal Stud. 165, 168–69 (1974) (articulating a causation-based theory).

35. Chavez v. Southern Pac. Transp. Co., 413 F. Supp. 1203, 1205 (E.D.Cal.1976).

38. 56 Cal. Rptr. 128, 132 (App.1967).

39. 190 P.2d 1, 3 (Cal.1948).

operating in a world of interpersonal ethical dictates. Significantly, the *Green* court relied on a California Civil Code provision that read "[o]ne must so use his own rights as not to infringe upon the rights of another."[40] Two decades later, the *Luthringer* court's opinion was wholly opaque, revealing not the slightest clue as to why—beyond the hazardous nature of the fumigant and the uncommon character of fumigation (satisfying the then-existing Restatement standards)—liability was to be strict. Twenty-eight years later, however, *Chavez* clarified the reasoning and firmly anchored strict liability in collective justice/enterprise liability ideology.

Thus we find, well into the twentieth century, that there is no necessary connection between strict liability and an ideology of enterprise liability. That the recent enterprise liability literature suggests otherwise, is explained by the near single-minded preoccupation with the dynamic development of products liability law beginning in the 1960s. That development, of course, explicitly turned on the "revolution" of enthroning strict liability as a replacement for liability based on fault. But, as developments in the more prosaic domain of traditional strict liability reveal, the relational nexus rather is between enterprise liability and a radically different way of thinking about the social function of the tort system—in particular, viewing tort as a redistributive and regulatory mechanism—that has evolved independently of doctrinal change.

In a similar vein, consider that most ancient and ubiquitous form of strict liability—vicarious liability. In earlier times, before vicarious liability came to be taken for granted, scholars debated the origins of this imperfection in the design of responsibility based on fault. Baty, a staunch opponent of the concept, identified nine separate justifications for vicarious liability, which he then proceeded to annihilate with relish.[47] Without reciting his litany, it is interesting to note the singular commitment to corrective justice embodied in the various pre-modern explanations for the concept. To name just a few: a control theory, emphasizing responsibility for close personal supervision over the work of an employee; a retribution theory, an explanation offered by Holmes in The Common Law, based on vicarious liability as a form of payment in place of forfeiting entitlement to the services of a wrongdoing servant; an identification theory, a somewhat mystical (and conclusory) conception of the master and servant as a single entity for legal purposes; an evidentiary theory, serving as a kind of off-shoot of res ipsa loquitur that emphasizes the master's superior ability to identify the wrongful actor responsible for a victim's injury; a profit-based theory, turning on the fairness of linking the burdens of a vagrant employee's labors with the correlative benefits derived from his services; and others.

By contrast, in the more modern writers such as Atiyah and Harper and James, one finds clear reference to the ideology of enterprise liability

40. Green v. General Petroleum Corp., 270 P. 952, 954–55 (Cal.1928) (quoting Cal. Civ. Code § 3514).

47. T. Baty, Vicarious Liability 148–54 (1916).

as the contemporaneous underpinning for vicarious liability.[55] Summarizing the early writing of Guido Calabresi,[56] Atiyah's treatise on vicarious liability, published at the dawn of the modern products liability era, offers both risk-spreading and safety incentives rationales for holding employers responsible for the tortious acts of their employees. In like fashion, Calabresi's mentor, Fleming James, offered an explicitly distributional justification a decade earlier.[58] Old wine, it seems, had been poured into new bottles.

Notes and Questions

1.   The introduction to this article discusses recent contributions to the enterprise liability literature, including Priest, The Invention of Enterprise Liability: A Critical History of the Intellectual Foundations of Modern Tort Law, 14 J. Legal Stud. 461 (1985). In discussing Priest's views, Rabin describes enterprise liability as characterized by "the twin notions that an enterprise should bear the risks of accidents it produces because (1) an enterprise has superior risk-bearing capacity compared to victims who would otherwise bear the costs of accidents, and (2) an enterprise is generally better placed to respond to the safety incentives created by liability rules than is the party suffering harm." In what sense does this rationale better fit strict liability than liability based on negligence? To what extent is it consistent with the doctrine of abnormally dangerous activities in Restatement Second §§ 519–520, p. 510, supra?

2.   The safety incentives rationale was developed into a full-blown theory of general, or optimal, deterrence in the pathbreaking work of Guido Calabresi, The Costs of Accidents (1970), which explored the risk-spreading rationale as well. More recent contributions to the enterprise liability literature include Croley & Hanson, Rescuing the Revolution: The Revived Case for Enterprise Liability, 91 Mich. L.Rev. 683 (1993); V. Nolan & E. Ursin, Understanding Enterprise Liability: Rethinking Tort Reform for the Twenty–First Century (1995); Keating, The Idea of Fairness in the Law of Enterprise Liability, 95 Mich. L.Rev. 1266 (1997); and Geistfeld, Should Enterprise Liability Replace the Rule of Strict Liability for Abnormally Dangerous Activities?, 45 UCLA L.Rev. 611 (1998).

3.   In reading the selection that follows, consider whether the risk-spreading/safety incentives characterization seems to provide a persuasive underpinning for enterprise liability. What, if anything, does it leave out as a satisfying explanation for strict liability more generally? We return to these questions in considering the case law development of strict liability

---

55.   See generally P.S. Atiyah, Vicarious Liability (1967) 22–28; . . .

56.   See, e.g., Guido Calabresi, Some Thoughts on Risk Distribution and the Law of Torts, 70 Yale L.J. 499, 499–500 (1961) (examining the theoretical justifications for loss allocation).

58.   2 Harper & James, [ ] at 1364–74. A collective justice lineage in fact can be traced back still further to the pioneering essay of William O. Douglas, Vicarious Liability and Administration of Risk I, 38 Yale L.J. 584 (1929).

for defective products in Chapter VIII; in particular, consider Justice Traynor's influential concurring opinion in *Escola v. Coca Cola Bottling Co. of Fresno*, reprinted at p. 546, infra.

A Goals–Oriented Approach to Strict Tort Liability for Abnormally Dangerous Activities

Joseph H. King, Jr.
48 Baylor Law Review 341, 349–61 (1996).

B. Goals of Strict Tort Liability

Most authorities would agree that multiple goals have animated and influenced the evolution of strict liability. There is, however, less agreement on what those goals should be and the relative weight they should accord. The absence of a single normative predicate or a meta-prioritization for strict liability has resulted in an uncertain and unstable legal system with courts and commentators oscillating between various goals, when goals are mentioned at all. The uncertainty has been compounded by the failure of both the Restatement and the courts to meaningfully incorporate these goals into the criteria for strict liability. The challenge is to identify the best combination of goals to guide decisions on the question of strict liability for dangerous activities.

1. Loss–Spreading

A central goal of strict liability is to spread losses caused by accidental injuries among a broad class of persons. This loss-spreading or distributive justice goal helps to assure that the effects of otherwise devastating losses are ameliorated by diffusing them among a broad array of appropriate entities and individuals. Fleming James articulated this loss-spreading goal in terms of the marginal utility of money, which he explained with his "bottom dollar" thesis.[54] A person's bottom dollar is that person's most valuable dollar, and each added dollar has decreasing value to that person. In other words, "(a)s one loses wealth, each additional dollar imposes a greater sacrifice." The underlying premise for loss-spreading is that accident costs should be "collectively, not individually, borne," because a loss causes less social and economic disruption if it is shared by many people.

Under the loss-spreading goal, the decision whether to impose strict liability hinges partially on whether the actor engaging in the injurious activity is an appropriate party to incur and then redistribute, or "spread," a loss. This loss-spreading function would thus depend on the extent to which the actor was able to anticipate and evaluate the underlying risk, take appropriate steps to accumulate resources to insure against the loss, and then systematically recapture those outlays by passing them on to suitable consumers. This loss-spreading goal should not, however, be con-

---

54. Fleming James, Jr., Some Reflections on the Bases of Strict Liability, 18 La. L. Rev. 293, 294 n.2 (1958). . . .

sidered in isolation. The fact that other avenues for compensating injuries exist—such as workers' compensation, Social Security disability benefits, and first-party insurance—must also be taken into account. Various institutions too often operate insularly and even at cross purposes. The relative inefficiency of strict tort liability should be compared with other systems. Less than half of each insurance premium dollar reaches accident victims. This is an important factor to keep in mind when considering non-tort loss-spreading alternatives.

As strict liability matured as a discrete liability-producing concept, its primary focus shifted from the deterrent goals central under fault-based liability to the direction of loss-spreading. Although some commentators continue to minimize the centrality of loss-spreading under strict liability, loss-spreading is increasingly regarded as one of the dominant rationales for strict liability. Professor Gregory, an influential commentator on strict liability during the formative years between the two Restatements, noted that perhaps the strongest argument for strict "enterprise" liability stemmed from the fact that industry was the most practical institution to administer a loss-bearing system.[63]

If loss-spreading were the only goal of a tort compensation system, and if a broader distribution of a loss were better, then there would be no stopping point short of government liability for all accidents. This is one reason why other goals should be incorporated into the matrix for determining strict liability. Vindication of other goals not only serves the interests of these other goals, but also provides a manageable "stopping point" that is otherwise absent when loss-spreading is the only goal.

2. Loss Avoidance (or Risk Reduction)

A second goal of strict liability is loss avoidance or reduction. This goal, sometimes referred to as the "primary" reduction of accident costs,[66] aims at imposing liability in a way that reduces the number and severity of accidents.[67] This goal requires appraisal of the actor's ability to systematically evaluate the risks of his activities and make sound cost-benefit decisions about the manner of operations as well as the level and location of the activity, safeguards, and alternatives. Calabresi describes this general deterrence function as seeking to impose accident costs on those engaging in the injurious activities who could "reduce accident costs most cheaply."[68]

---

63. Gregory, [Trespass to Negligence to Absolute Liability, 37 Va. L.Rev. 359 (1951)]. . . .

66. Calabresi, [The Costs of Accidents] at 26–27.

67. Id. at 26. Calabresi and Hirschoff have also articulated the goal more broadly in terms of seeking "minimization of the sum of accident costs and of accident avoidance costs." Guido Calabresi & Jon T. Hirschoff, Toward a Test for Strict Liability in Torts, 81 Yale L.J. 1055, 1084 (1972).

68. Calabresi, [The Costs of Accidents] at 135. Under this formulation, the judge or jury need not evaluate (or second guess) the defendant's conduct in terms of the relative costs of the accident and its avoidance. Instead, the judge or jury would decide which of the parties was the best cost-benefit analyst—the one "in the best position to make the cost-benefit analysis . . . and to act on the decision once it is made." Calabresi & Hirschoff, supra note 67, at 1060.

. . . .

Even commentators who view the loss avoidance goal as central to strict liability would probably agree that it must nevertheless be applied in conjunction with other considerations. Thus, the need and effectiveness of general deterrence should be assessed in the context of other potential means for reducing accidents, such as collective ("specific") deterrence through direct governmental regulation of the activity.[69] Moreover, other goals must inevitably be taken into account when one cannot make, in Calabresi's classic oxymoron, "intelligent intuitive choices"[70] of the best or cheapest cost avoiders (or best cost benefit analysts).

There are several reasons why the loss avoidance goal, albeit entitled to consideration, should be accorded less weight than loss-spreading considerations. First, a contradiction lurks in the goal. On one hand, strict liability may be imposed on a defendant even if that defendant is innocent.[71] Yet, the very existence of loss avoidance goals by definition assumes that some aspect of the defendant's activity could have been changed for the better. Perhaps this apparent contradiction could be finessed by asserting that, under strict liability, the threat of liability operates not as a deterrent, but rather as an incentive to promote safer conduct. This semantic sleight of hand leaves one still wondering. Perhaps strict liability promotes loss reduction and prevention through incentives and disincentives that affect defendants' activities, a sphere that negligence law may not address comprehensively. Nonetheless, how much the threat of strict liability adds to loss reduction beyond the reduction already produced by negligence liability is questionable.

Secondly, serious questions exist about the efficacy of general deterrence. These concerns are relevant in applying strict liability. Deterrence, or loss avoidance incentives, requires an often unattainable knowledge of relevant risks by responsible decisionmakers. Moreover, the message of deterrence is often quite attenuated under the tort system. The extent of the injury will often not coincide with the appropriate level of deterrence in any particular case. Similar injuries are not compensated similarly. There is an absence of predictable outcomes of litigation and standards of behavior are not effectively communicated to appropriate decisionmakers. Furthermore, various theories of disordered behavior suggest that there are inherent psychological limitations on the efficacy of deterrence or rational response to incentives. Thus, according to some theories of disordered behavior, dangerous conduct may be the product of organic brain impairment, genetic factors, biochemical factors, or the product of internalized, often unconscious, determinants. Even behavioral theorists who contend that "people behave as they do because they have learned that behavior" would confront factors in the torts system that may confound deterrence.

---

69. See generally Calabresi, at 95–129.

70. Id. at 157.

71. Some commentators have argued that strict liability is not really a morally neutral concept at all. They argue that the community sense of morality would find ab-normally dangerous activities "blameworthy" if there were not some provision for compensation for the injuries caused by such activities. See generally Robert E. Keeton, Conditional Fault in the Law of Torts, 72 Harv. L. Rev. 401, 427 (1959) . . .

These factors stem from the fact that the torts system lacks the celerity and consistency of outcome so important to reinforce behavior, and relies on punishment rather than more potentially influential positive rewards.

Third, the threat of liability can frequently over-deter, producing negative results. One example is the do-it-yourselfer who chooses a more dangerous alternative to an activity which has been forced out of availability. This idea is sometimes more broadly conceived as the "theory of the second best" under which high prices or unavailability of products or services causes consumers to turn to substitutes that are less safe.[81] Thus, the goal of reducing the incidence or severity of accidental losses, if pursued solely to alter the conduct of the defendant, may be subverted by strict liability. On the other hand, if the availability of alternatives to the activity in question is considered, in the context of the goal of loss allocation, as a means of educating consumers about the true costs so that they might intelligently opt for less costly alternatives, the goal of loss avoidance may be better served. The limitations of the loss avoidance goal underscore the importance of considering an array of goals in applying strict liability.

Notwithstanding reservations about the goal of loss avoidance, it may still make sense to consider this objective when deciding whether to impose strict liability. Strict liability was developed in part because of the difficulties encountered by plaintiffs attempting to prove negligence. If it is true that much of the negligence that occurs cannot be proven, then strict liability may afford significant deterrence against this kind of occult negligence, and thus offer more effective deterrence than traditional negligence law.

Strict liability for dangerous activities may also fill a gap created by the failure of negligence theory, at least in some situations, to adequately address and evaluate the level of a defendant's activity, rather than merely the quality of that activity, in the application of the due care standard. According to Steven Shavell, in order to evaluate the reasonableness of a defendant's activity level, "(c)ourts would, by definition, have to decide on the appropriate level of activity, and their competence to do this is problematic."[85] To the extent that negligence law does not or cannot realistically be expected to evaluate activity levels when assessing due care, then strict liability may operate to fill that void. Thus, even if courts and juries are not appropriate institutions to evaluate the reasonableness of enterprise activity levels, those engaging in such activities may be sufficiently experienced and positioned to systematically consider their own activity level when faced with potential strict liability. Strict liability may therefore create incentives not simply with respect to the manner of the

81. Mark Geistfeld, Implementing Enterprise Liability: A Comment on Henderson and Twerski, 67 N.Y.U. L. Rev. 1157, 1170–71 (1992). "(T)he theory of the second best shows that if individuals make choices from a set of activities, regulations designed to achieve efficient behavior with respect to one activity may lead to greater overall inefficiency if enough people switch from regulated to unregulated activities." Id. at 1170.

85. Shavell, [Strict Liability versus Negligence, 9 Journal of Legal Studies 1 (1980)] at 22.

activity's conduct, but also for relocating, changing, or reducing the activity. Accordingly, a relevant consideration in strict liability is the degree to which the actor responsible for an injury is capable of systematically evaluating the risks and benefits of conducting the underlying enterprise at present levels.

3. Loss Allocation (or Internalization)

A third goal of strict liability is loss allocation. The objective is for a loss to be initially borne (or "internalized") by the enterprise whose activities engendered it and whose activities are sufficiently connected to the loss to make it appropriate to reflect the loss in the cost of the enterprise's services. Such added charges will constitute a signal to interested service consumers, owners or shareholders, managers, and employees of the enterprise, of the true costs of the activities of that enterprise. This will promote better informed choices by these interested parties, thereby encouraging investment in safety and discouraging or moderating consumption and investment in relatively more hazardous products and services (or at least making such consumption and investment more discriminating). Thus, internalization of costs through loss allocation will induce price-mediated adjustments in production and activity levels, with reduction of the incidence of accidents. In turn, society will ideally move closer to an optimal allocation of its limited resources. Liability thus prevents enterprise costs from being externalized and avoids forcing society to unwittingly subsidize the dangerous enterprise.

Loss allocation is inextricably intertwined with other goals. It is essentially the emanation of loss spreading, delineating the route along which spreading must take place. Loss allocation also serves to inform enterprises and consumers of the true costs of an activity so that they may appropriately adjust their activity levels, selection of services and products, and manner of operation in ways that reduce the net cost of accidents.

Notwithstanding the positive effects of the loss allocation goal, if taken too far, loss allocation can have a serious downside. Forcing enterprises to internalize too many costs can inhibit economic development and technological innovation. Also, forcing too many costs on an enterprise may foster efforts to avoid liability by substituting unregulable modes of behavior. These attempts to avoid loss allocation might include sales of goods and services in "black markets" and other "clandestine production and distribution" methods. In addition, as a greater proportion of the costs of accidents are shifted to enterprises, a concomitantly smaller percentage of their resources will be available to entrepreneurs and managers to develop and nurture the enterprise. In this era of fierce international competition and declining profit margins, continued dissipation of the resources available to decisionmakers to manage and develop their enterprises will have a profound rippling effect. Domestic enterprises will be less able to compete against international competitors who are far less burdened by potential liability. It also affects the vitality of the free enterprise system, which depends on managers having a critical mass of resources necessary to animate their entrepreneurial discretion.

4. Administrative Efficiency

A fourth goal of strict liability is to achieve an acceptable level of administrative costs. Sometimes this goal is expressed in terms of reducing the "tertiary" costs of accidents, meaning the systemic transaction costs involved in imposing liability.[93] This tertiary goal "tells us to question constantly whether an attempt to reduce accident costs, either by reducing accidents themselves or by reducing their secondary effects, costs more than it saves."[94]

Strict liability would produce administrative savings with simplified liability determinations by removing the need for proving fault, an expensive exercise often requiring expert testimony. It would also improve the overall administrative integrity of the system by promoting recovery in cases where the evidence was destroyed or unavailable, which sometimes occurs in accidents arising out of abnormally dangerous activities. For strict liability to realize its potential for administrative efficiency, however, the rules for identifying liability-producing activities must be simplified and conformed to the goals of strict liability. Professor Henderson identifies several process norms that must be satisfied in order for liability rules to provide a coherent guide to judges and juries: the rules must be comprehensible, encompass verifiable facts, and lend themselves to common law adjudication.[96]

Even if strict liability cases are more efficiently resolved than their negligence cousins, adoption of strict liability may in some respects increase overall transaction costs. Broadening the reach of strict liability will increase the number of tort claims. That in turn may magnify the overall inefficiencies of the tort system. The challenge is to formulate a standard for strict liability that vindicates its goals while keeping administrative costs at an acceptable level. . . .

5. Fairness

Another goal frequently invoked for strict liability is fairness. One dimension of this goal is embodied in George Fletcher's paradigm of reciprocity.[101] This paradigm represents, according to Fletcher, one of two ways of looking at tort liability, the other being the paradigm of reasonableness,[102] which animates fault-based liability. The paradigm of reciprocity focuses on the relative magnitude and quality of the risks created by the activities of the defendant and those of the victim. According to this paradigm, "a victim has a right to recover for injuries caused by a risk greater in degree and different in order from those created by the victim and imposed on the defendant—in short, for injuries resulting from nonre-

---

93. Calabresi, at 28.

94. Id.

96. Henderson, [Judicial reliance on Public Policy: An Empirical Analysis of Products Liability Decisions, 59 Geo. Wash. L.Rev. 1579 (1971)] at 1580–83.

101. See Fletcher, [Fairness and Utility in Tort Theory, 85 Harv. L. Rev. 537 (1972)] at 540–42. Fletcher apparently views fairness as also encompassing other concerns and thus too broad to be coterminous with his paradigm of reciprocity. Id. at 541.

102. Id. at 542.

ciprocal risks."[103] This fairness rationale is more commonly stated simply as a belief that between two innocent persons, the initiator who benefits from the ultimately injurious activity should be liable.

Strict liability is, however, subject to some serious reservations in terms of fairness. Fletcher's reciprocity paradigm has been criticized as "temporally bound"[106] with a misplaced focus. Instead of tying liability to the goal of cheapest cost avoidance, Fletcher's paradigm is said to advance a "philosophical theory of desert . . . (with) new risks . . . less deserving" than existing ones. There is no clear understanding or consensus on what is meant by "fairness." One might also question the fairness of a rule requiring consumers to pay higher prices so that accident victims can be compensated at levels reflecting their pre-accident physical and economic prospects. Is it really "fair" to charge everyone more for abnormally dangerous services so that economically-advantaged members of society can maintain their economic level in the event the activity harms one of them? And is it fair to compensate victims of abnormally dangerous activities but not victims of accidents arising from more benign or generic sources?

Fairness, whatever that term connotes, probably does not figure centrally among the goals of strict liability, at least as a conceptually distinct rationale. Indeed, fairness may actually embrace other goals. For example, perhaps Fletcher's paradigm of reciprocity is better characterized not in terms of fairness, but as normatively advancing a whole range of strict liability goals. Thus, an imbalance in risk creation between actor and victim may suggest an absence of notice to the victim or lack of a reasonable opportunity or ability to prepare for or endure a loss, a fact relevant to the goals of loss spreading, loss avoidance, and loss allocation.

6. Protection of Individual Autonomy

Protection of individual autonomy is also occasionally mentioned by some writers as a goal of strict liability. . . .

Notes and Questions

1. *Economic theories.* Are the goals that King identifies as loss avoidance and loss allocation distinct? As the author indicates, these goals serve as the foundation for the general deterrence theory, spelled out by Guido Calabresi in The Costs of Accidents, and further explained in the cited Calabresi & Hirschoff. Another seminal contribution to the economic vantage point was Coase, The Problem of Social Cost, 3 J. of Law & Econ. 1 (1960), discussed at p. 676, infra, in the context of nuisance law. Coase addressed issues of causation from the perspective of both intersecting activities resulting in harm to one of the parties and loss allocation under conditions of perfect information about risk. He set the stage for later analysis of appropriate liability rules in situations where costless bargaining and access to information were impaired.

103. Id. . . .

106. Calabresi & Hirschoff, supra note 67, at 1081 & n.84.

2. At one point, King observes that loss allocation is "inextricably intertwined with other goals." Can you think of situation in which the loss allocation goal and the loss-spreading goal would lead to different liability rules? At another point, he asserts that loss avoidance "should be accorded less weight than loss spreading." Are his arguments for this proposition convincing?

3. Gary Schwartz has systematically reviewed the empirical evidence bearing on the economists' claims for the deterrent effect of tort law and their many critics' claims that tort law does not effectively deter. Schwartz, Reality in the Economic Analysis of Tort Law: Does Tort Law Really Deter?, 42 UCLA L. Rev. 377 (1994). He concludes that neither polar position is correct: "tort law, while not as effective as economic models suggest, may still be somewhat successful in achieving its stated deterrence goals." For discussion of the psychological literature on the deterrent effect of tort sanctions, see Shuman, The Psychology of Deterrence in Tort Law, 42 Kans.L.Rev. 115 (1993).

4. The excerpt from Richard Posner, Economic Analysis of Law, which follows, will expand on the economic perspective in the context of a comparison between strict liability and negligence. But first consider some non-economic perspectives.

5. *Moral theories.* Several writers have objected to the focus on economics because other values have been diluted or disregarded. Among the critics of the economic approach to tort liability is Professor George Fletcher, as indicated in the King excerpt. In Fairness and Utility in Tort Theory, 85 Harv.L.Rev. 537 (1972), he objected that "the thrust of the academic literature is to convert the tort system into something other than a mechanism for determining the just distribution of accident losses. . . . Discussed less and less are precisely those questions that make tort law a unique repository of intuitions of corrective justice: What is the relevance of risk-creating conduct to the just distribution of wealth? What is the rationale for an individual's 'right' to recover for his losses? What are the criteria for justly singling out some people and making them, and not their neighbors, bear the costs of accidents?"

Fletcher developed an approach—briefly described by King—that built on a variety of cases, including the *Rylands* case, the ultrahazardous group, and *Vincent v. Lake Erie Transp. Co.*, reprinted at p. 923, infra:

> The general principle expressed in all of these situations governed by diverse doctrinal standards is that a victim has a right to recover for injuries caused by a risk greater in degree and different in order from those created by the victim and imposed on the defendant—in short, for injuries resulting from nonreciprocal risks. . . . For example, a pilot or an airplane owner subjects those beneath the path of flight to nonreciprocal risks of harm. Conversely, cases of nonliability [*i.e.*, in which there is no such "right" to recover] are those of reciprocal risks, namely those in which the victim and the defendant subject each other to roughly the same degree of risk. For example, two airplanes flying in the same vicinity subject each other to reciprocal risks of a mid-air

collision. Of course, there are significant problems in determining when risks are nonreciprocal.   .   .   .

Professor Fletcher then sketched a paradigm of reasonableness opposing the paradigm of reciprocity. The reasonableness paradigm "represents a rejection of non-instrumentalist values and a commitment to the community's welfare as the criterion for determining both who is entitled to receive and who ought to pay compensation. Questions that are distinct under the paradigm of reciprocity—namely, is the risk nonreciprocal and was it unexcused—are collapsed in this paradigm into a single test: was the risk unreasonable?"

Although the paradigm of reciprocity bears resemblance to strict liability and that of reasonableness to negligence, Fletcher asserted that the reciprocity cases cut across these lines and that many cases now handled under negligence lend themselves to analysis under both paradigms—in particular, because liability is warranted between reciprocal risk-creators when one party negligently harms the other. Much of the article was devoted to analyzing groups of cases to suggest how they fit into one or the other of the paradigms.

At one point Fletcher flatly rejected assignments of liability based on access to insurance or the ability to invoke the market mechanism to distribute losses: "This is an argument of distributive rather than corrective justice, for it turns on the defendant's wealth and status, rather than his conduct. Using the tort system to redistribute negative wealth (accident losses) violates the premise of corrective justice, namely that liability should turn on what the defendant has done, rather than on who he is. [   ] What is at stake is keeping the institution of taxation distinct from the institution of tort litigation."

Calabresi responded to Fletcher in Calabresi and Hirschoff, Toward a Test for Strict Liability in Torts, cited supra. Posner responded in Strict Liability: A Comment, 2 J.Legal Stud. 205 (1973).

6. In Fletcher, Corrective Justice for Moderns, 106 Harv. L. Rev. 1658 (1993), he revisits his thesis, now arguing that tort law should be understood as a "middle position" between criminal law and contract law:

> . . . . cases of strict liability reflect criminal law. The influence begins early in the law of torts under the writ of trespass and carries forward in the various situations in which we perceive the defendant's action as aggression that dominates the interests of a plaintiff insulated by her rights. In contrast, the influence of private law thinking breaks through in the collaborative principle underlying the law of negligence. By entering into certain spheres of risk-taking, plaintiff and defendant both come under duties to act with a view to the costs and benefits of their actions. They become a unit, acting under an implicit obligation to optimize the consequences of their actions.

He elaborates on the distinction between dominance and collaboration with three airplane operators' liability examples. In the first two, where harm occurs to passengers or owners of other planes, the parties have entered into a collaborative enterprise and thus fall under a negligence system. In the third, involving homeowners in the path of flight, the situation is one of dominance and strict liability applies. Does the dominance-collaboration perspective seem consistent with Fletcher's earlier non-reciprocity-reciprocity perspective?

7. King's last-mentioned goal, protection of individual autonomy, was perhaps most prominently developed (albeit not referred to in King's discussion) by Richard Epstein. The economic approach (and Fletcher's right-based reciprocity analysis) were rejected by Epstein in favor of a strict liability approach that relied heavily on notions of causation, which he introduced in:

> four distinct paradigm cases covered by the proposition "A caused B harm." These paradigms are not the only way in which we can talk about torts cases. They do, however, provide modes of description which best capture the ordinary use of causal language. Briefly put, they are based upon notions of force, fright, compulsion and dangerous conditions. . . . [D]espite the internal differences, it can, I believe, be demonstrated that each of these paradigms, when understood, exhibits the features that render it relevant to the question of legal responsibility. [2 J.Legal Stud. at 166]

Epstein developed applications of the paradigm cases and defenses in Epstein, A Theory of Strict Liability, 2 J.Legal Stud. 151 (1973), and Defenses and Subsequent Pleas in a System of Strict Liability, 3 J.Legal Stud. 165 (1974). The theory was further elaborated in Epstein, Nuisance Law: Corrective Justice and Its Utilitarian Constraints, 8 J.Legal Stud. 49 (1979).

The theories developed by Epstein and Fletcher are criticized in Schwartz, The Vitality of Negligence and the Ethics of Strict Liability, 15 Ga.L.Rev. 963, 977–1005 (1981). See also Posner, The Concept of Corrective Justice in Recent Theories of Tort Law, 10 J.Legal Stud. 187 (1981) and Borgo, Causal Paradigms in Tort Law, 8 J.Legal Stud. 419 (1979). Epstein responded in Causation and Corrective Justice: A Reply to Two Critics, 8 J.Legal Stud. 477 (1979).

Subsequently, however, Epstein took the position that his theory of strict liability may be excessively formalistic and insufficiently sensitive to the social consequences of liability rules. See, Epstein, Causation—In Context: An Afterword, 63 Chi–Kent L.Rev. 653 (1987), an essay appearing in a wide-ranging collection of papers addressing the role of causation in tort law from many perspectives. See Symposium on Causation in the Law of Torts, 63 Chi–Kent L.Rev. 397–680 (1987).

8. More recent contributions to the corrective justice literature can be found in E. Weinrib, The Idea of Private Law (1995) (positing a formalist theory of corrective justice, which draws principally on Aristotle and Kant, to articulate a foreseeability-based system of negligence liability) and J. Coleman, Risks and Wrongs (1992) (arguing that tort law serves a rectification function in repairing wrongful losses and annulling wrongful gains).

See generally, D. Owen (ed.), Philosophical Foundations of Tort Law (1995) (a collection of wide-ranging essays by law and philosophy scholars interested in the tort system). For extensive readings on economic, moral, historical and other approaches to the analysis of tort law, see the collection of essays in R. Rabin (ed.), Perspectives on Tort Law (4th ed. 1995). See also S. Levmore (ed.), Foundations of Tort Law (1994).

9. Should the choice of theory affect damages? In the final part of King's article he proposes that strict liability for abnormally dangerous activities be limited to the victim's pecuniary loss. See also Nolan & Ursin, cited at p. 524, supra, proposing an extension of strict liability to "business premises enterprise liability" combined with a limitation on recovery of pain and suffering in business premises cases.

Courts considering damages in strict liability cases have thus far failed to draw any distinction. In one of the few explicit references to this problem, the court, in Wights v. Staff Jennings, Inc., 405 P.2d 624 (Or. 1965), was reluctant to adopt a general strict liability approach in a products case in part because

> Although we believe that it is the function of the judiciary to modify the law of torts to fit the changing needs of society, we feel that the judicial extension of the theory of strict liability to all cases where it is convenient for those engaged in commerce to spread the risk would not be advisable. If enterprise liability is to be so extended, there is a strong argument for limiting the victim's measure of recovery to some scheme of compensation similar to that employed in workmen's compensation. The legislature alone has the power to set up such a compensation scheme. The court cannot put a limit upon the jury's verdict.

The subjects of damages and damage reform are discussed in detail in Chapters X and XI.

Why should the measure of recovery change if strict liability replaces negligence as the basis for recovery? Why cannot a court limit the amount of a jury verdict? Why has the award of common law damages in strict liability situations produced little comment? Does this imply that strict liability is still perceived as a species of fault? See R. Keeton, Conditional Fault in the Law of Torts, 72 Harv.L.Rev. 401 (1959). Might one explanation be that until the emergence of a discrete area of strict liability for defective products, activities creating strict liability usually caused property damage alone and did not raise the question of pain and suffering? *Wights* is discussed further at p. 638, infra.

Economic Analysis of Law
Richard A. Posner.
192–97 (5th ed. 1998).

Strict tort liability means that someone who causes an accident is liable for the victim's damages even if the injury could not have been avoided by the exercise of due care (PL might be $150 and B $300). As a first approximation, strict liability has the same effects on safety as negligence liability, provided that there is a defense of contributory negligence, as there usually is though often under a different name. (Why is the defense actually more important for strict liability than for negligence?) If B is smaller than PL, the strictly liable defendant will take precautions to avoid the accident, just as the defendant in a negligence system will, in order to reduce his net costs. Less obviously, if B is larger than PL, the strictly liable defendant will not take precautions, just as under negligence. True, he will have to pay the victim's damages. But those damages, discounted by the probability of the accident, are less than the cost of avoidance; in other words, the expected cost of liability (= PL) is less than the cost of avoidance, so avoidance doesn't pay.

And yet there are significant economic differences between negligence and strict liability. Think back to the distinction between more care and less activity as methods of reducing the probability of an accident. One way to avoid an auto accident is to drive more slowly; another is to drive less. But rarely do courts in a negligence case try to determine the optimal level of the activity that gave rise to the accident; they do not ask, when a driver is in an accident, whether the benefit of the particular trip (maybe he was driving to the grocery store to get some gourmet food for his pet iguana) was equal to or greater than the costs, including the expected accident cost to other users of the road; or whether driving was really cheaper than walking or taking the train when all social costs are reckoned in. Such a judgment is too difficult for a court to make in an ordinary tort case. Only if the benefits of the activity are obviously very slight, as where a man runs into a burning building to retrieve an old hat and does so as carefully as he can in the circumstances but is seriously burned nonetheless, will the court find that engaging in the activity was itself negligence, even though once the decision to engage in the activity was made, the actor (plaintiff or defendant) conducted himself with all possible skill and circumspection.

Judicial inability to determine optimal activity levels except in simple cases is potentially a serious shortcoming of a negligence system. Suppose railroads and canals are good substitutes in transportation but railroads inflict many accidents that cannot be avoided by due care by either the railroad or potential accident victims, and canals none. Were it not for these accident costs, railroads would be 10 percent cheaper than canals, but when these accident costs are figured in, railroads are actually 5 percent more costly. Under a rule of negligence liability, railroads will displace canals even though they are the socially more costly method of transportation.

In contrast, potential injurers subject to a rule of strict liability will automatically take into account possible changes in activity level, as well as possible changes in expenditures on care, in deciding whether to prevent accidents.   .   .   .

.   .   .

The problem with using this analysis to support a general rule of strict liability is that changes in activity level by victims are also a method of accident avoidance, and one that is encouraged by negligence liability but discouraged by strict liability. . . .

So if a class of activities can be identified in which activity-level changes by potential injurers are the most efficient method of accident prevention there is a strong argument for imposing strict liability on the people engaged in those activities. Conversely, if there is a class of activities in which activity-level changes by potential victims are the most efficient method of accident prevention, there is a strong argument for no liability, as by applying the doctrine of assumption of risk to participation in dangerous sports. Through the concept of ultrahazardous activities, tort law imposes strict liability on activities that involve a high degree of danger that cannot feasibly be prevented by the actor's being careful or potential victims' altering their behavior. An example is strict liability for injuries by wild animals. If my neighbor has a pet tiger, there is little I can do (at reasonable cost) to protect myself. And there is only so much the owner can do, in the way of being careful, to keep the tiger under control. The most promising precaution may consist simply of his not having a tiger—an activity-level change. But suppose we are speaking not of a neighbor's tiger but of the zoo's. Is it likely that the best way of controlling accidents to visitors at zoos is not to have dangerous animals in zoos—just gentle ones? The cost of this particular activity change would be prohibitive. So it is no surprise that the courts have made an exception to the rule of strict liability for injuries caused by wild animals in zoos, circuses, and other animal parks and shows.

Another area of strict liability for ultrahazardous activities is blasting with explosives. No matter how careful the construction company is, there will be accidents; and since construction goes on everywhere, it is unlikely that the best way to minimize these accidents is for potential victims to alter their activities. The best way may be for the companies to switch to alternative methods of demolition that are less dangerous; and strict liability creates an incentive to consider such alternatives.

The category of ultrahazardous activities is not fixed; the tendency is to apply the label to new activities (often called nonnatural), such as reservoirs in England or ballooning in early nineteenth-century America. New activities tend to be dangerous because there is little experience with their safety characteristics. For the same reason, the dangers may not be avoidable simply by taking care—yet the fact that the activities are new implies that there are good substitutes for them. Hence the best method of accident control may be to cut back on the scale of the activity—to slow its spread while more is learned about conducting it safely.

The distinction between care and activity is not the only dimension along which negligence and strict liability differ. Another, ... has to do with the costs of administering these different rules. The trial of a strict liability case is simpler than that of a negligence case because there is one less issue, negligence; and the fewer the issues, the easier it should be to settle the case without a trial. On both counts we can expect litigation costs to be lower under strict liability than under negligence—for the same number of claims. But the number may not be the same. In principle, under strict liability, every accident to which there is more than one party gives rise to a claim, not just every accident in which the defendant may have been negligent.[5] This makes it important, before one chooses strict liability, to assess the responsiveness of the accident rate to the incentives that such liability will create. If the accident rate in some activity will fall dramatically if strict liability is imposed, because accident costs exceed the costs of avoiding them through changes in the level of the activity, there may well be fewer claims under strict liability; and since the average cost of processing claims should be lower under strict liability, the substitution of strict liability for negligence will be an unequivocal economic gain. But if most of the accidents that occur in some activity are unavoidable in an economic sense either by taking greater care or by reducing the amount of the activity (because the costs of greater care, or less activity, exceed any savings in reduced accident costs), the main effect of switching from negligence to strict liability will be to increase the number of damages claims.

Another difference is that strict liability operates to insure victims of unavoidable accidents. It is a gain only if the cost of insurance through the tort system is less than the cost to potential victims of buying accident insurance policies in the insurance market; almost certainly it is greater. All sides of the no-fault debate agree that the tort system is a very costly method of providing insurance; the debate is over whether it provides another good, the deterrence of non-cost-justified accidents. A related point is that, . . . the size of, and economic rents earned in, an industry subject to strict liability will be smaller than if the industry were subject to negligence.

Courts make mistakes; which regime—strict liability or negligence—is more robust against mistakes? On the one hand, an erroneous finding that an injurer is not negligent cannot have misallocative consequences under strict liability, because the injurer's negligence is not an issue. On the other hand, the consequences of a mistaken ascription of causation, or an overestimation of damages, are worse under strict liability. Under negligence, a person is sanctioned only for inefficient conduct; under strict liability, he may be sanctioned for efficient conduct, and if the actual costs of that conduct are exaggerated, the conduct may be deterred. Suppose for example that the cost of some precaution is 10, the expected accident cost under an error-free regime of strict liability is 9, but the expected accident cost (really the expected legal-judgment cost) given errors as to causation or damages favoring plaintiffs is 11. Then the conduct will be deterred under strict liability but not under negligence, unless mistakes as to causation and damages infect the determination of the standard of care.

---

5. In addition, strict liability results in higher information costs to potential injurers (as distinct from judicial information costs). Can you see why?

Because of these differences between negligence and strict liability, we would not expect the tort system to opt all for one or all for the other. Nor would we expect the balance between the two regimes to be the same at all times. . . .

It would be a mistake to dichotomize negligence and strict liability. Negligence has a strict liability component. . . . This is a result in part of the reasonable-person rule, which makes persons having above-average costs of taking care strictly liable for their accidents, and in part of the doctrine of respondeat superior, ... Moreover, as we have seen, care has a stochastic (i.e., probabilistic) component. Being careful means having attitudes, acquiring skills and knowledge, etc. that reduce the probability of a careless slip but do not eliminate it; to eliminate it would require an excessive investment in care. The law, though, does not recognize "optimal negligence," and it has been argued that as a result it creates a bias in favor of investing in capital rather than labor methods of avoiding accidents (can you see why?).[6] Does strict liability avoid this problem?

Notes and Questions

1. Can you think of other major differences between strict liability and negligence in addition to those mentioned by Posner?

2. What empirical evidence would be useful in resolving the comparative advantages of each that he discusses?

3. Posner elaborates on the argument made by Steven Shavell in Strict Liability versus Negligence (discussed briefly by King, supra) that the competence of courts to undertake an independent determination of the appropriate level of injurer activity under a negligence regime is "problematic." Is that invariably the case? Why should it generally be true?

4. Posner's defense of strict liability draws heavily on examples of "abnormally dangerous activities." Does his development of the differences between strict liability and negligence suggest that he would favor a more general limitation of strict liability to those situations? Would King's set of goals supporting strict liability suggest a limitation to abnormally dangerous activities?

5. Would Posner subscribe to the enterprise liability rationale for strict liability discussed in the Rabin excerpt and the notes following? Which of the goals discussed by King would Posner regard as appropriate?

6. Mark F. Grady, Why are People Negligent? Technology, Nondurable Precautions, and the Medical Malpractice Explosion, 82 Nw. U.L. Rev. 293 (1988).

CHAPTER VIII

LIABILITY FOR DEFECTIVE PRODUCTS

A. INTRODUCTION

No area of personal injury law has changed as dramatically in this century as the law governing liability for defective products. Nineteenth century products liability law languished in the shadow of the privity doctrine, which required a contractual relationship between the parties as the basis for a duty of due care. As the following landmark case indicates, the privity requirement was eventually undermined by a cluster of categorical exceptions created in response to the growing influence of the negligence principle. But as we shall see, the judicial impulse to refashion the liability rules in this area was not exhausted by consolidation of the negligence principle. Instead, the courts later began to construct a system of strict liability—a process that continues to lend a dynamic, and controversial, character to defective products law. The materials in this section, then, provide an excellent opportunity for exploring the fundamental resource allocation issues underlying competing systems of tort liability. At the same time, products liability is of particular interest because of the interplay between contract and tort law in shaping the approach to the subject.

MacPherson v. Buick Motor Co.
Court of Appeals of New York, 1916.
217 N.Y. 382, 111 N.E. 1050.

Appeal, by permission, from a judgment of the Appellate Division . . . . affirming a judgment in favor of plaintiff entered upon a verdict.

CARDOZO, J. The defendant is a manufacturer of automobiles. It sold an automobile to a retail dealer. The retail dealer resold to the plaintiff. While the plaintiff was in the car, it suddenly collapsed. He was thrown out and injured. One of the wheels was made of defective wood, and its spokes crumbled into fragments. The wheel was not made by the defendant; it was bought from another manufacturer. There is evidence, however, that its defects could have been discovered by reasonable inspection, and that inspection was omitted. There is no claim that the defendant knew of the defect and willfully concealed it. The case, in other words, is not brought within the rule of Kuelling v. Roderick Lean Mfg. Co. (183 N.Y. 78 [1905]).

The charge is one, not of fraud, but of negligence. The question to be determined is whether the defendant owed a duty of care and vigilance to any one but the immediate purchaser.

The foundations of this branch of the law, at least in this state, were laid in Thomas v. Winchester (6 N.Y. 397 [1852]). A poison was falsely labeled. The sale was made to a druggist, who in turn sold to a customer. The customer recovered damages from the seller who affixed the label. "The defendant's negligence," it was said, "put human life in imminent danger." A poison falsely labeled is likely to injure any one who gets it. Because the danger is to be foreseen, there is a duty to avoid the injury. Cases were cited by way of illustration in which manufacturers were not subject to any duty irrespective of contract. The distinction was said to be that their conduct, though negligent, was not likely to result in injury to any one except the purchaser. We are not required to say whether the chance of injury was always as remote as the distinction assumes. Some of the illustrations might be rejected today. The principle of the distinction is for present purposes the important thing.

Thomas v. Winchester became quickly a landmark of the law. In the application of its principle there may at times have been uncertainty or even error. There has never in this state been doubt or disavowal of the principle itself. The chief cases are well known, yet to recall some of them will be helpful. Loop v. Litchfield (42 N.Y. 351 [1870]) is the earliest. It was the case of a defect in a small balance wheel used on a circular saw. The manufacturer pointed out the defect to the buyer, who wished a cheap article and was ready to assume the risk. The risk can hardly have been an imminent one for the wheel lasted five years before it broke. In the meanwhile the buyer had made a lease of the machinery. It was held that the manufacturer was not answerable to the lessee. *Loop v. Litchfield* was followed in Losee v. Clute (51 N.Y. 494 [1873]), the case of the explosion of a steam boiler. That decision has been criticized [   ]; but it must be confined to its special facts. It was put upon the ground that the risk of injury was too remote. The buyer in that case had not only accepted the boiler, but had tested it. The manufacturer knew that his own test was not the final one. The finality of the test has a bearing on the measure of diligence owing to persons other than the purchaser [   ].

These early cases suggest a narrow construction of the rule. Later cases, however, evince a more liberal spirit. First in importance is Devlin v. Smith (89 N.Y. 470 [1882]). The defendant, a contractor, built a scaffold for a painter. The painter's servants were injured. The contractor was held liable. He knew that the scaffold, if improperly constructed, was a most dangerous trap. He knew that it was to be used by the workmen. He was building it for that very purpose. Building it for their use, he owed them a duty, irrespective of his contract with their master, to build it with care.

From *Devlin v. Smith* we pass over intermediate cases and turn to the latest case in this court in which *Thomas v. Winchester* was followed. That case is Statler v. George A. Ray Mfg. Co. (195 N.Y. 478, 480 [1909]). The defendant manufactured a large coffee urn. It was installed in a restaurant.

When heated, the urn exploded and injured the plaintiff. We held that the manufacturer was liable. We said that the urn "was of such a character inherently that, when applied to the purposes for which it was designed, it was liable to become a source of great danger to many people if not carefully and properly constructed."

It may be that *Devlin v. Smith* and *Statler v. George A. Ray Mfg. Co.* have extended the rule of *Thomas v. Winchester*. If so, this court is committed to the extension. The defendant argues that things imminently dangerous to life are poisons, explosives, deadly weapons—things whose normal function it is to injure or destroy. But whatever the rule in *Thomas v. Winchester* may once have been, it has no longer that restricted meaning. A scaffold [*Devlin v. Smith*], is not inherently a destructive instrument. It becomes destructive only if imperfectly constructed. A large coffee urn [*Statler*] may have within itself, if negligently made, the potency of danger, yet no one thinks of it as an implement whose normal function is destruction. What is true of the coffee urn is equally true of bottles of aerated water (Torgesen v. Schultz, 192 N.Y. 156 [1908]).   .   .   .

.   .   .

We hold, then, that the principle of *Thomas v. Winchester* is not limited to poisons, explosives, and things of like nature, to things which in their normal operation are implements of destruction. If the nature of a thing is such that it is reasonably certain to place life and limb in peril when negligently made, it is then a thing of danger. Its nature gives warning of the consequences to be expected. If to the element of danger there is added knowledge that the thing will be used by persons other than the purchaser, and used without new tests, then, irrespective of contract, the manufacturer of this thing of danger is under a duty to make it carefully. That is as far as we are required to go for the decision of this case. There must be knowledge of a danger, not merely possible, but probable. It is possible to use almost anything in a way that will make it dangerous if defective. That is not enough to charge the manufacturer with a duty independent of his contract. Whether a given thing is dangerous may be sometimes a question for the court and sometimes a question for the jury. There must also be knowledge that in the usual course of events the danger will be shared by others than the buyer. Such knowledge may often be inferred from the nature of the transaction. But it is possible that even knowledge of the danger and of the use will not always be enough. The proximity or remoteness of the relation is a factor to be considered. We are dealing now with the liability of the manufacturer of the finished product, who puts it on the market to be used without inspection by his customers. If he is negligent, where danger is to be foreseen, a liability will follow. We are not required at this time to say that it is legitimate to go back of the manufacturer of the finished product and hold the manufacturers of the component parts. To make their negligence a cause of imminent danger, an independent cause must often intervene; the manufacturer of the finished product must also fail in his duty of inspection. It may be that in those circumstances the negligence of the earlier members of the series is too remote to constitute, as to the ultimate user, an actionable wrong [   ]. We leave that question open. We shall have to deal with it when it arises. The difficulty which it suggests is not present in this case. There is here no break in the chain of cause and effect. In such circumstances, the presence of a known danger, attendant upon a known use, makes vigilance a duty. We have put aside the notion that the duty to safeguard life and limb, when the consequences of negligence may be foreseen, grows out of contract and nothing else. We have put the source of the obligation where it ought to be. We have put its source in the law.

From this survey of the decisions, there thus emerges a definition of the duty of a manufacturer which enables us to measure this defendant's liability. Beyond all question, the nature of an automobile gives warning of probable danger if its construction is defective. This automobile was de-signed to go fifty miles an hour. Unless its wheels were sound and strong, injury was almost certain. It was as much a thing of danger as a defective engine for a railroad. The defendant knew the danger. It knew also that the car would be used by persons other than the buyer. This was apparent from its size; there were seats for three persons. It was apparent also from the fact that the buyer was a dealer in cars, who bought to resell. The maker of this car supplied it for the use of purchasers from the dealer just as plainly as the contractor in *Devlin v. Smith* supplied the scaffold for use by the servants of the owner. The dealer was indeed the one person of whom it might be said with some approach to certainty that by him the car would not be used. Yet the defendant would have us say that he was the one person whom it was under a legal duty to protect. The law does not lead us to so inconsequent a conclusion. Precedents drawn from the days of travel by stage coach do not fit the conditions of travel today. The principle that the danger must be imminent does not change, but the things subject to the principle do change. They are whatever the needs of life in a developing civilization require them to be.

. . .

In England the limits of the rule are still unsettled. Winterbottom v. Wright (10 M. & W. 109)[1842] is often cited. The defendant undertook to provide a mail coach to carry the mail bags. The coach broke down from latent defects in its construction. The defendant, however, was not the manufacturer. The court held that he was not liable for injuries to a passenger. . . .

There is nothing anomalous in a rule which imposes upon A, who has contracted with B, a duty to C and D and others according as he knows or does not know that the subject-matter of the contract is intended for their use. We may find an analogy in the law which measures the liability of landlords. If A leases to B a tumble-down house he is not liable, in the absence of fraud, to B's guests who enter it and are injured. This is because B is then under the duty to repair it, the lessor has the right to suppose that he will fulfill that duty, and, if he omits to do so, his guests must look to him (Bohlen, supra, at p. 276). But if A leases a building to be used by the lessee at once as a place of public entertainment, the rule is different.

There injury to persons other than the lessee is to be foreseen, and foresight of the consequences involves the creation of a duty (Junkermann v. Tilyou R. Co., 213 N.Y. 404 [1915], and cases there cited).

. . .

We think the defendant was not absolved from a duty of inspection because it bought the wheels from a reputable manufacturer. It was not merely a dealer in automobiles. It was a manufacturer of automobiles. It was responsible for the finished product. It was not at liberty to put the finished product on the market without subjecting the component parts to ordinary and simple tests [   ]. Under the charge of the trial judge nothing more was required of it. The obligation to inspect must vary with the nature of the thing to be inspected. The more probable the danger, the greater the need of caution. There is little analogy between this case and Carlson v. Phenix Bridge Co. (132 N.Y. 273 [1892]), where the defendant bought a tool for a servant's use. The making of tools was not the business in which the master was engaged. Reliance on the skill of the manufacturer was proper and almost inevitable. But that is not the defendant's situation. Both by its relation to the work and by the nature of its business, it is charged with a stricter duty.

Other rulings complained of have been considered, but no error has been found in them.

The judgment should be affirmed with costs.

HISCOCK, CHASE and CUDDEBACK, JJ., concur with CARDOZO, J., and HOGAN, J., concurs in result; WILLARD BARTLETT, CH. J., reads dissenting opinion; POUND, J., not voting.

[The dissenting opinion stressed that the earlier cases could all be explained by the "inherently dangerous" analysis and that the court should not go beyond that formulation.]

Notes and Questions

1. Earlier analyses had understood the English case of *Winterbottom v. Wright* to stand for the proposition that manufacturers, suppliers, and repairers of chattels could be liable for their negligence only to those with whom they had contracted. In that case, Lord Abinger had stated:

> There is no privity of contract between these parties; and if the plaintiff can sue, every passenger, or even any person passing along the road, who was injured by the upsetting of the coach, might bring a similar action. Unless we confine the operation of such contracts as this to the parties who entered into them, the most absurd and outrageous consequences, to which I can see no limit, would ensue.

How might Judge Cardozo respond to that assertion?

2. What is your understanding of the state of the law before the *MacPherson* decision? What was Judge Cardozo's contribution? Recall the discussion at p. 130, supra.

Duty just those who had contract — Cardozo extended

[handwritten margin notes: probable = forseeable; yes; duty no longer only in contracts; Buick had duty to inspect]

3. What is the meaning of the requirement that there "must be knowledge of a danger, not merely possible, but probable"? Was that met here?

4. Assess the significance of Judge Cardozo's statement that "We have put the source of the obligation where it ought to be. We have put its source in the law."

5. What arguments might justify imposing a duty on Buick but not on the wheel manufacturer? In Smith v. Peerless Glass Co., 181 N.E. 576 (N.Y.1932), a soda bottle exploded and hurt plaintiff. The court treated the bottle maker as the manufacturer of a component part and brought it within the *MacPherson* principle. Might there be proximate cause problems in such cases?

6. Is the rationale of *MacPherson* entirely congruent with the notions of due care we have already developed? The doctrine of *MacPherson* came to be accepted generally throughout the United States. It covered injuries to bystanders including pedestrians hurt by a careening car or tire, property damage, duty of repairers as well as manufacturers, and cases where damage was not "reasonably certain."

Other developments included treating a retailer who sold a product under its own brand name as though it were the manufacturer and thus holding it liable for negligent manufacture. Also, manufacturers who incorporated component parts in the final product were held liable for the negligence of the subcontractors. Eventually, courts began holding architects and builders liable for negligence in construction that hurt patrons or tenants.

7. *Warranty development.* But as these extensions of *MacPherson* were occurring, a new approach to the area was taking shape.

Warranty law had been an integral part of sales law for many years before the common law of sales was codified in the Uniform Sales Act and then in the Uniform Commercial Code. For the most part, sales law dealt with products that did not meet the purposes for which they were bought or were otherwise unsatisfactory, rather than products that caused personal injury. Nevertheless, occasionally the latter were involved and the operation of modern warranty law in such cases can be seen in Ryan v. Progressive Grocery Stores, Inc., 175 N.E. 105 (N.Y.1931), in which Mrs. Ryan asked the defendant storekeeper for a loaf of Ward's bread. Her husband was seriously injured when he swallowed a pin embedded in a slice of the bread. Judge Cardozo held the shopkeeper liable for breach of the implied warranty of merchantability, ruling that a loaf of bread with a pin in it was not of such quality. He noted in imposing such liability on the retailer without any finding of fault that "the burden may be heavy. It is one of the hazards of business." At the same time he rejected plaintiff's claim for breach of an implied warranty of fitness for a particular purpose, in which the buyer relies on the seller's choice of product to meet a need stated by the buyer. Because Mrs. Ryan asked for a specific brand of bread there was no such reliance.

Finally, Judge Cardozo rejected the argument that liability be limited to the difference in value between a good loaf and a bad one. Rather, he used the basic contract rule permitting higher damages where the seller had "notice from the nature of the transaction that the bread was to be eaten." These implied warranties were codified in the Uniform Sales Act, § 15, and remain in its successor, the Uniform Commercial Code, §§ 2–314, 2–315.

Warranties traditionally ran only between parties in contract privity. In *Ryan*, this might have presented a problem because the person hurt was not the person who bought the bread from the retailer. Judge Cardozo resolved this problem in his first sentence by saying that the plaintiff "through his wife, who acted as his agent, bought a loaf of bread." In efforts to permit warranty recoveries courts resorted to many devices to avoid the lack-of-privity barrier. One author catalogued 29 theories used to achieve the result, mostly in food cases. Gillam, Products Liability in a Nutshell, 37 Or.L.Rev. 119, 153–155 (1957).*

8. These developments notwithstanding, a tension between negligence and strict liability in tort became more evident, as the following case suggests.

Escola v. Coca Cola Bottling Co. of Fresno

Supreme Court of California, 1944.
24 Cal.2d 453, 150 P.2d 436.

[Plaintiff, a waitress, was injured when a soda bottle broke in her hand as she moved it from the case to the refrigerator. She testified that she had handled it carefully. The defendant bottler used pressure to bottle carbonated beverages. An engineer from the bottle manufacturer (which was not sued) testified at the trial about how bottles are tested and called these tests "pretty near" infallible. The majority affirmed a plaintiff's judgment and held that plaintiff had properly benefited from res ipsa loquitur in her negligence action. The following three paragraphs give the flavor of the majority opinion.]

It thus appears that there is available to the industry a commonly used method of testing bottles for defects not apparent to the eye, which is almost infallible. Since Coca Cola bottles are subjected to these tests by the

---

* The UCC eliminated the traditional requirement of privity. Its drafters offered three versions of § 2–318 from which the states were to pick one. Under all three versions whatever warranties the seller does extend with the product are statutorily extended to certain classes of people who may reasonably be expected to "use, consume or be affected by the goods." Version A extends the warranties to "any natural person who is in the family or household of his buyer or who is a guest in his home . . . who is injured in person. . . ." Version B extends to "any natural person . . . who is injured in person. . . ." Version C extends to "any person . . . who is injured. . . ."

Most state legislatures adopted Version A, but in some of these states the courts considered themselves free to expand such protection.

manufacturer, it is not likely that they contain defects when delivered to the bottler which are not discoverable by visual inspection. Both new and used bottles are filled and distributed by defendant. The used bottles are not again subjected to the tests referred to above, and it may be inferred that defects not discoverable by visual inspection do not develop in bottles after they are manufactured. Obviously, if such defects do occur in used bottles there is a duty upon the bottler to make appropriate tests before they are refilled, and if such tests are not commercially practicable the bottles should not be re-used. This would seem to be particularly true where a charged liquid is placed in the bottle. It follows that a defect which would make the bottle unsound could be discovered by reasonable and practicable tests.

Although it is not clear in this case whether the explosion was caused by an excessive charge or a defect in the glass, there is a sufficient showing that neither cause would ordinarily have been present if due care had been used. Further, defendant had exclusive control over both the charging and inspection of the bottles. Accordingly, all the requirements necessary to entitle plaintiff to rely on the doctrine of res ipsa loquitur to supply an inference of negligence are present.

[handwritten: 2 elements of res ipsa l. are satisfied.]

It is true that defendant presented evidence tending to show that it exercised considerable precaution by carefully regulating and checking the pressure in the bottles and by making visual inspections for defects in the glass at several stages during the bottling process. It is well settled, however, that when a defendant produces evidence to rebut the inference of negligence which arises upon application of the doctrine of res ipsa loquitur, it is ordinarily a question of fact for the jury to determine whether the inference has been dispelled.

[One justice concurred separately.]

Traynor, J. I concur in the judgment, but I believe the manufacturer's negligence should no longer be singled out as the basis of a plaintiff's right to recover in cases like the present one. In my opinion it should now be recognized that a manufacturer incurs an absolute liability when an article that he has placed on the market, knowing that it is to be used without inspection, proves to have a defect that causes injury to human beings. [*MacPherson v. Buick Motor Co.*] established the principle, recognized by this court, that irrespective of privity of contract, the manufacturer is responsible for an injury caused by such an article to any person who comes in lawful contact with it. [   ] In these cases the source of the manufacturer's liability was his negligence in the manufacturing process or in the inspection of component parts supplied by others. Even if there is no negligence, however, public policy demands that responsibility be fixed wherever it will most effectively reduce the hazards to life and health inherent in defective products that reach the market. It is evident that the manufacturer can anticipate some hazards and guard against the recurrence of others, as the public cannot. Those who suffer injury from defective products are unprepared to meet its consequences. The cost of an injury and the loss of time or health may be an overwhelming misfortune to the person injured, and a needless one, for the risk of injury can be insured by the manufacturer and distributed among the public as a cost of doing business. It is to the public interest to discourage the marketing of products having defects that are a menace to the public. If such products nevertheless find their way into the market it is to the public interest to place the responsibility for whatever injury they may cause upon the manufacturer, who, even if he is not negligent in the manufacture of the product, is responsible for its reaching the market. However intermittently such injuries may occur and however haphazardly they may strike, the risk of their occurrence is a constant risk and a general one. Against such a risk there should be general and constant protection and the manufacturer is best situated to afford such protection.

The injury from a defective product does not become a matter of indifference because the defect arises from causes other than the negligence of the manufacturer, such as negligence of a submanufacturer of a component part whose defects could not be revealed by inspection [ ] or unknown causes that even by the device of res ipsa loquitur cannot be classified as negligence of the manufacturer. The inference of negligence may be dispelled by an affirmative showing of proper care. If the evidence against the fact inferred is "clear, positive, uncontradicted, and of such a nature that it cannot rationally be disbelieved, the court must instruct the jury that the nonexistence of the fact has been established as a matter of law." (Blank v. Coffin, [126 P.2d 868 (Cal.1942)].) An injured person, however, is not ordinarily in a position to refute such evidence or identify the cause of the defect, for he can hardly be familiar with the manufacturing process as the manufacturer himself is. In leaving it to the jury to decide whether the inference has been dispelled, regardless of the evidence against it, the negligence rule approaches the rule of strict liability. It is needlessly circuitous to make negligence the basis of recovery and impose what is in reality liability without negligence. If public policy demands that a manufacturer of goods be responsible for their quality regardless of negligence there is no reason not to fix that responsibility openly.

. . .

The retailer, even though not equipped to test a product, is under an absolute liability to his customer, for the implied warranties of fitness for proposed use and merchantable quality include a warranty of safety of the product. [ ] This warranty is not necessarily a contractual one [ ], for public policy requires that the buyer be insured at the seller's expense against injury. [ ] The courts recognize, however, that the retailer cannot bear the burden of this warranty, and allow him to recoup any losses by means of the warranty of safety attending the wholesaler's or manufacturer's sale to him. [ ] Such a procedure, however, is needlessly circuitous and engenders wasteful litigation. Much would be gained if the injured person could base his action directly on the manufacturer's warranty.

The liability of the manufacturer to an immediate buyer injured by a defective product follows without proof of negligence from the implied warranty of safety attending the sale. Ordinarily, however, the immediate buyer is a dealer who does not intend to use the product himself, and if the warranty of safety is to serve the purpose of protecting health and safety it must give rights to others than the dealer. In the words of Judge Cardozo in the *MacPherson* case: "The dealer was indeed the one person of whom it might be said with some approach to certainty that by him the car would not be used. Yet, the defendant would have us say that he was the one person whom it was under a legal duty to protect. The law does not lead us to so inconsequent a solution." While the defendant's negligence in the *MacPherson* case made it unnecessary for the court to base liability on warranty, Judge Cardozo's reasoning recognized the injured person as the real party in interest and effectively disposed of the theory that the liability of the manufacturer incurred by his warranty should apply only to the immediate purchaser. It thus paves the way for a standard of liability that would make the manufacturer guarantee the safety of his product even when there is no negligence.

This court and many others have extended protection according to such a standard to consumers of food products, taking the view that the right of a consumer injured by unwholesome food does not depend "upon the intricacies of the law of sales" and that the warranty of the manufacturer to the consumer in absence of privity of contract rests on public policy. [   ] Dangers to life and health inhere in other consumers' goods that are defective and there is no reason to differentiate them from the dangers of defective food products. [   ]

In the food products cases the courts have resorted to various fictions to rationalize the extension of the manufacturer's warranty to the consumer: that a warranty runs with the chattel; that the cause of action of the dealer is assigned to the consumer; that the consumer is a third party beneficiary of the manufacturer's contract with the dealer. They have also held the manufacturer liable on a mere fiction of negligence: "Practically he must know it [the product] is fit, or bear the consequences if it proves destructive." [   ] Such fictions are not necessary to fix the manufacturer's liability under a warranty if the warranty is severed from the contract of sale between the dealer and the consumer and based on the law of torts [   ] as a strict liability. [   ] Warranties are not necessarily rights arising under a contract. An action on a warranty "was, in its origin, a pure action of tort," and only late in the historical development of warranties was an action in assumpsit allowed. (Ames, The History of Assumpsit, 2 Harv. L.Rev. 1, 8; 4 Williston on Contracts (1936) § 970.) . . .

As handicrafts have been replaced by mass production with its great markets and transportation facilities, the close relationship between the producer and consumer of a product has been altered. Manufacturing processes, frequently valuable secrets, are ordinarily either inaccessible to or beyond the ken of the general public. The consumer no longer has means or skill enough to investigate for himself the soundness of a product, even when it is not contained in a sealed package, and his erstwhile vigilance has been lulled by the steady efforts of manufacturers to build up confidence by advertising and marketing devices such as trade marks. [   ] Consumers no longer approach products warily but accept them on faith, relying on the reputation of the manufacturer or the trade mark. [ ] Manufacturers have sought to justify that faith by increasingly high standards of inspection and a readiness to make good on defective products by way of replacements and refunds. (See Bogert and Fink, Business Practices Regarding Warranties in the Sale of Goods, 25 Ill.L.Rev. 400.) The manufacturer's obligation to the consumer must keep pace with the changing relationship between them; it cannot be escaped because the marketing of a product has become so complicated as to require one or more intermediaries. Certainly there is greater reason to impose liability on the manufacturer than on the retailer who is but a conduit of a product that he is not himself able to test.

The manufacturer's liability should, of course, be defined in terms of the safety of the product in normal and proper use, and should not extend to injuries that cannot be traced to the product as it reached the market.

Notes and Questions

1. What were the majority's justifications for using res ipsa loquitur? What were Justice Traynor's objections?

2. Consider separately each sentence in the first paragraph of Justice Traynor's opinion. What justifications for strict liability are presented? Are other justifications presented elsewhere in the opinion?

3. How does *MacPherson* support Justice Traynor's theory of liability here?

4. Warranty doctrine as a basis for strict liability recovery in tort remained largely limited to the food cases until the 1960 decision in Henningsen v. Bloomfield Motors, Inc., 161 A.2d 69 (N.J.1960). A defect in the steering mechanism of a recently-acquired Plymouth caused the car to spin out of control, seriously injuring plaintiff driver. Echoing Justice Traynor's language in *Escola*, the court held that

> [u]nder modern marketing conditions, when a manufacturer puts a new automobile in the stream of trade and promotes its purchase by the public, an implied warranty that it is reasonably suitable for use as such accompanies it into the hands of the ultimate purchaser. Absence of agency between the manufacturer and the dealer who makes the ultimate sale is immaterial.

For related reasons, the court struck down express disclaimers limiting liability that were "imposed upon the automobile consumer" in "a standardized form designed for mass use" as contrary to public policy.

For the moment, it appeared that the move beyond negligence to strict liability might be grounded in warranty, rather than the tort theory urged by Traynor. See the classic contemporaneous article, Prosser, The Assault on the Citadel, 69 Yale L.J. 1099 (1960). But Traynor was to have the final word on this issue.

5. *Subsequent California developments.* Beginning in the early 1960s, a series of California decisions foreshadowed similar developments in other jurisdictions that have now become accepted by the overwhelming majority of states.

a. Greenman v. Yuba Power Products, Inc., 377 P.2d 897 (Cal.1963). Plaintiff's wife bought from a retailer a Shopsmith power tool made by defendant. While using the tool as a lathe with the necessary attachment, plaintiff was hurt when the piece of wood flew up and struck him in the forehead. Plaintiff's judgment against the manufacturer, based on negligence and express warranty claims, was affirmed by Justice Traynor writing for a unanimous court. Experts had testified that the lathe was of defective design because the set screws were inadequate to hold the wood given the lathe's normal vibrations, and that better fastening of the machine's parts would have prevented the harm. From this Justice Traynor concluded that the jury could have found negligence as well as breach of the express warranty that included the assertion that "every component has positive locks that hold adjustments through rough or precision work."

Since there was a general verdict, the manufacturer sought a new trial contending that it was not liable for breach of express (or any) warranties because of the plaintiff's failure to comply with a statutory requirement that notice of the alleged breach be given "within a reasonable time" after it is discovered. Justice Traynor disagreed. Warranty notice requirements should not apply when the plaintiff and the manufacturer have not dealt directly with one another because the injured party would probably be unaware of such an obligation. Moreover, echoing his concurrence in *Escola*, Justice Traynor concluded that a "manufacturer is strictly liable in tort when an article he places on the market, knowing that it is to be used without inspection for defects, proves to have a defect that causes injury to a human being." In addition to his other reasons, he noted that the "purpose of such liability is to insure that the costs of injuries resulting from defective products are borne by the manufacturers that put such products on the market rather than by the injured persons who are powerless to protect themselves. Sales warranties serve this purpose fitfully at best."

b. Vandermark v. Ford Motor Co., 391 P.2d 168 (Cal.1964). Plaintiff bought a new Ford from defendant retailer Maywood Bell Ford. The brakes soon locked pulling the car to the right and into a pole, hurting plaintiff and his sister, who also sued. Expert testimony suggested a wrong-sized part or improper assembly or adjustment. The trial judge nonsuited plaintiffs on both negligence and breach of implied warranty against the manufacturer, Ford, and on a warranty count against Maywood Bell. The jury returned a verdict for Maywood Bell on the negligence count.

On appeal Justice Traynor, speaking for a unanimous court, upheld the jury verdict on Maywood Bell's negligence but reversed the other three rulings. Ford could not insulate itself by delegating final inspection and adjustment to Maywood Bell. The "warranty" count against Ford should not have been dismissed because of the evidence of the defect and of its existence at the time of delivery to plaintiff. The negligence count against Ford should stand because the evidence suggested manufacturing negligence.

Maywood Bell's disclaimer in the sales contract limited its liability to replacement "of such parts as shall be returned to the Dealer and as shall be acknowledged by Dealer to be defective. . . . This warranty is expressly in lieu of all other warranties, express or implied, and of all other obligations on the part of Dealer." (The crash occurred within the warranty period.) Since Maywood Bell was "an integral part of the overall producing and marketing enterprise," and the retailer may be able to ensure product safety or to put pressure on the manufacturer toward that end, and was often the one link in the chain that plaintiff could conveniently sue, Justice Traynor concluded that the retailer "is strictly liable in tort for personal injuries caused by defects in cars sold by it." He noted that this provided maximum protection for the plaintiff but did no injustice to the defendants since "they can adjust the costs of such protection between them in the course of their continuing business relationship." Contractual disclaimers were immaterial: "Regardless of the obligations it assumed by contract, it is subject to strict liability in tort because it is in the business of selling automobiles, one of which proved to be defective and caused injury to human beings."

c. *Elmore v. American Motors Corp.*, 451 P.2d 84 (Cal.1969). Plaintiff Elmore purchased a new Rambler manufactured by one defendant and sold by the other. It veered across the road and into the oncoming car of Waters. Occupants of both cars were hurt or killed and suits were brought against both defendants. The cases were consolidated for trial, at which there was testimony that just before the crash the drive shaft had fallen out of Elmore's car, which was almost new. Nonsuits for both defendants were unanimously reversed on appeal in an opinion by Justice Peters. First, the evidence was sufficient to permit a jury to find that the drive shaft did fall out, that this was due to a defect that had been present at the time of sale, and that it caused the crash. He then observed that bystanders such as Waters were entitled to the same strict liability protections as those in the Elmore car:

> If anything, bystanders should be entitled to greater protection than the consumer or user where injury to bystanders from the defect is reasonably foreseeable. Consumers and users, at least, have the opportunity to inspect for defects and to limit their purchases to articles manufactured by reputable manufacturers and sold by reputable retailers, whereas the bystander ordinarily has no such opportunities. . . .

> An automobile with a defectively connected drive shaft constitutes a substantial hazard on the highway not only to the driver and passenger of the car but also to pedestrians and other drivers. The public policy which protects the driver and passenger of the car should also protect the bystander, and where a driver or passenger of another car is injured due to defects in the manufacture of an automobile and

without any fault of their own, they may recover from the manufacturer of the defective automobile.

Finally, for the reasons suggested in *Vandermark*, the court concluded that the retailer was liable to bystanders as well as customers.

6. *Extensions to others*. Strict liability has been extended greatly on the defendant's side to include a wide variety of suppliers and those who aid suppliers, including bailors. Price v. Shell Oil Co., 466 P.2d 722 (Cal.1970). Some courts have extended the doctrine to franchisors who impose quality control upon their franchisees. See Kosters v. Seven–Up Co., 595 F.2d 347 (6th Cir.1979) (imposing strict liability on the franchisor for the franchisee's defective design of a carton for carrying soda bottles where the franchisor had consented to the use of that type of carton). On the other hand, courts have been reluctant to apply the doctrine to companies that finance purchases by others. See, e.g, Nath v. National Equipment Leasing Corp., 439 A.2d 633 (Pa.1981) (refusing to apply strict liability in a suit by a worker whose hand was injured in the machine his employer had financed through defendant).

A question that overlaps the law of torts and of corporations involves the liability of successor corporations for defective products marketed by businesses before they were bought by the successor. The Products Restatement § 12 provides that such successor liability exists if the acquisition "(a) is accompanied by an agreement for the successor to assume such liability; or (b) results from a fraudulent conveyance to escape liability for the debts or liabilities of the predecessor; or (c) constitutes a consolidation or merger with the predecessor; or (d) results in the successor becoming a continuation of the predecessor."

These and three more exceptions to the general rule of non-liability are discussed in **Savage Arms, Inc. v. Western Auto Supply Co.,** 2000 WL 869342 (Alaska 2000) rehearing pending. Rejecting the Restatement's limited position, the court adopted a "continuity of enterprise" exception under which "a successor corporation may be held liable for injuries caused by its predecessor's products where the totality of the transaction between the successor and the predecessor demonstrates a basic continuity of the predecessor enterprise. The successor may be held liable even though the sale of assets is for cash and there is no continuity of shareholders." The court explored and rejected a variety of attacks on this expansion of successor liability.

7. *Used goods*. Most courts have declined to impose strict liability on sellers of used goods—even when the claim is that the product has had the defect in question since it was first marketed. In Tillman v. Vance Equipment Co., 596 P.2d 1299 (Or.1979), the court noted that of its three reasons for strict liability—spreading the risk, satisfying reasonable buyer expectations, and risk reduction—only the first applied to dealers in used products. The second did not apply since these sellers generally make no particular representations about the quality of their goods. The third did not apply since these dealers have no direct relationship to the manufacturers or distributors of the goods. Providing an adequate remedy for the victim "cannot provide the sole justification for imposing liability without fault on a particular class of defendants." The analogy to strict liability for lessors did not apply because lessors offer the same products—repeatedly to different users—as products they have selected and this may amount to a representation as to their quality. Moreover, the lessor may have acquired the goods from someone in the original distribution chain, something that is unlikely for a dealer in used goods. Why should that matter? Occasional sellers of used goods are even less likely to meet these criteria. See Gebo v. Black Clawson Co., 703 N.E.2d 1234 (N.Y.1998); Stiles v. Batavia Atomic Horseshoes, Inc., 613 N.E.2d 572 (N.Y.1993) (refusing to impose strict liability on a defendant who sold a used punch press to plaintiff's employer where defendant's normal business was making horseshoes).

8. *Government contractors.* In Boyle v. United Technologies Corp., 487 U.S. 500 (1988), the Court held, 5–4, that the family of a Marine Corps pilot who died when unable to escape from his downed helicopter before it sank, could not sue the helicopter's manufacturer alleging that the escape hatch was defectively designed. The Court held that a private contractor who followed government specifications in making a product could not be held liable for inadequacies in the design as long as certain requirements were met. The imposition of liability in this type of case would "directly affect the terms of Government contracts: either the contractor will decline to manufacture the design specified by the Government, or it will raise its price. Either way, the interests of the United States will be directly affected." A state's effort to impose a duty of product design conflicted with the duty imposed by the Government contract—to deliver helicopters with the sort of escape mechanisms called for in the specifications. In such a case

> Liability for design defects in military equipment cannot be imposed, pursuant to state law, when (1) the United States approved reasonably precise specifications; (2) the equipment conformed to those specifications; and (3) the supplier warned the United States about the dangers in the use of the equipment that were known to the supplier but not to the United States.

The third element was necessary to remove any incentive contractors might have to withhold such information "since conveying that knowledge might disrupt the contract but withholding it would produce no liability." The dissenters relied heavily on the lack of any action by Congress to legislate such a defense. Should Congress be obliged to enact a government contractor immunity in order to shield the federal government from indirect tort liability? Is this judicially fashioned defense consistent with the thrust of the Federal Tort Claims Act, p. 249, supra?

For a broad discussion of the government contractor problem, see Cass & Gillette, The Government Contractor Defense: Contractual Allocation of Public Risk, 77 Va.L.Rev. 257 (1991). The government contractor defense played a particularly interesting role throughout the mass tort litigation against the manufacturers of Agent Orange. For discussion, see the case study, P. Schuck, Agent Orange on Trial: Mass Toxics Disasters in the Courts (enlarged edition, 1987).

9. *Causation.* In products cases the causation issue is as important as it is in negligence cases. We shall see shortly the difficulty that a litigant faces in showing that the connection between a defect and harm when the product is badly damaged or destroyed. Another example is the "enhanced injury" situation, in which plaintiff usually sues over the lack of safety inside a vehicle that has been in an accident. We consider this on the merits at p. 572 infra. The relevant point here, however, is that courts disagree about who bears the burden of showing that the defect caused harm over and above what was suffered in the original impact. The situation is explored in Trull v. Volkswagen of America, Inc., 761 A.2d 477 (N.H. 2000), a car crash case. Courts agree that when the "injuries are separate and divisible" the plaintiff must show the enhancement. Where they are "indivisible," as the court found here, the court followed the majority view. That view holds that once the plaintiff establishes that the defect was a substantial factor in producing damages over and above those that were probably caused as a result of the original impact, "the burden" shifts to the defendants to show which injuries were attributable to the initial collision and which to the defect. The minority approach was rejected largely because it was seen as implicitly deciding that "it is better that a plaintiff, injured through no fault of his own, take nothing, than that a wrongdoer pay more than his theoretical share of the damages arising out of a situation which his wrong has helped to create."

The Restatements

Early in the development of the modern approach, the American Law Institute promulgated § 402A of the Restatement (Second) of Torts, a most influential section that provided an early black letter formulation of the new approach. The section, published in 1965, provided:

prod. lib.

(1) One who sells any product in a defective condition unreasonably dangerous to the user or consumer or to his property is subject to liability for physical harm thereby caused to the ultimate user or consumer, or to his property, if

(a) the seller is engaged in the business of selling such a product, and

(b) it is expected to and does reach the user or consumer without substantial change in the condition in which it is sold.

(2) The rule stated in Subsection (1) applies although

(a) the seller has exercised all possible care in the preparation and sale of his product, and

(b) the user or consumer has not bought the product from or entered into any contractual relation with the seller.

The mixed contract-tort heritage of strict products liability, suggested in *Escola*, is reflected in the Restatement's definition of a defect. Plaintiff must demonstrate that the product causing the injuries was in a "defective condition unreasonably dangerous" to person or property at the time it left defendant's possession. The Restatement's comments define the requisite defective state in terms of a consumer's expectations—the traditional contract approach. See comment *i*.

Although § 402A has been much quoted and relied upon since 1965, it was promulgated as the area was first developing. In the succeeding years, other approaches began to emerge in cases that either rejected the Second Restatement's approach or elaborated upon issues it had not addressed.

The Restatement Third: Products Liability (sometimes referred to as the Products Restatement or Restatement of Products Liability) came into existence in 1998, after several years of debate. It took a quite different approach. Section 1 provides that "One engaged in the business of selling or otherwise distributing products who sells or distributes a defective product is subject to liability for harm to persons or property caused by the defect." Then section 2 provides that for purposes of determining whether a product is defective, there are three types of defects. A product

Mft defect

(a) contains a manufacturing defect when the product departs from its intended design even though all possible care was exercised in the preparation and marketing of the product;

Dsn defect

(b) is defective in design when the foreseeable risks of harm posed by the product could have been reduced or avoided by the adoption of a reasonable alternative design by the seller or other distributor, or a predecessor in the commercial chain of distribution, and the omission of the alternative design renders the product not reasonably safe;

Wrng defect

(c) is defective because of inadequate instructions or warnings when the foreseeable risks of harm posed by the product could have been reduced or avoided by the provision of reasonable instructions or warnings by the seller or other distributor, or a predecessor in the commercial chain of distribution, and the omission of the instructions or warnings renders the product not reasonably safe.

What appear to be the essential differences between the two approaches? Keep both in mind as we consider recent developments in liability for defective products. Be sure to note in each situation which Restatement—if either—is being analyzed. For extensive discussions of the Products Restatement, see Symposium, 26 Hofstra L. Rev. 567–834 (1998); Symposium, Restatement (Third) of Torts: Products Liability, 8 Kan.J.L. & Pub. Policy 1–124 (1998).

B.   MANUFACTURING DEFECTS

The most common and straightforward cases of defective products involve the aberrational mass-produced item that has come off the assembly line different from (and more dangerous than) the intended product. The defect is generally apparent in the flawed unit by the time of trial, and courts have concluded that strict liability should follow. These dangers are almost always latent. There are not many open and obvious ("patent") manufacturing defect cases, either because modern manufacturing processes can identify incipient problems or because retailers who find them while preparing goods for sale will take them off the shelves. Whatever the reason, patent manufacturing defects have not led to much litigation. The issue is much more complex with design defects, as we shall see shortly.

The issues in manufacturing defect claims are more likely to be practical than theoretical. In Welge v. Planters Lifesavers Co., 17 F.3d 209 (7th Cir.1994), for example, plaintiff was hurt when a glass jar of peanuts smashed as he tried to re-fasten its plastic lid. The fragments of the jar were preserved and the experts agreed that it "must have contained a defect but they could not find the fracture that had precipitated the shattering of the jar and they could not figure out when the defect . . . had come into being." The case revolved around efforts to identify the cause of the failure. Defendants, the jar manufacturer, Planters who filled the jar, and K–Mart, the retailer, argued that actions of plaintiff and the person with whom he boarded had created the weakness; plaintiff's evidence suggested that nothing untoward had occurred to the jar after purchase. Summary judgment against plaintiff was inappropriate:

> The strict liability element in modern products liability law comes precisely from the fact that a seller subject to that law is liable for defects in his product even if those defects were introduced, without the slightest fault of his own for failing to discover them, at some anterior stage of production. [ ] So the fact that K–Mart sold a defective jar of peanuts to Karen Godfrey would be conclusive of K–Mart's liability. . . . In exactly the same way, Planter's liability would be unaffected by the fact, if it is a fact, that the defect was due to [the jar manufacturer] rather than to itself. To repeat an earlier and fundamental point, a seller who is subject to strict products liability is responsible for the consequences of selling a defective product even if the defect was introduced without any fault on his part by his supplier or by his supplier's supplier.

Against which defendant is the plaintiff's case strongest? Would res ipsa loquitur have applied against each of the three defendants? What if the plaintiff had bought defective jam from the country store that made the jam?

As an indication of the practical problems confronting plaintiffs in cases alleging manufacturing defects, consider the causation issue in Price v. General Motors Corp., 931 F.2d 162 (1st Cir.1991). Plaintiffs alleged their car suddenly swerved from the highway into a utility pole. The car had been "inadvertently destroyed" before major investigation could be conducted. The court upheld summary judgment for defendant:

> Even if the Price vehicle leaked power steering fluid, the leak could as well have been due to inadequate maintenance, improper repairs to any of several hoses and seals, or defective non-GM replacement parts, as it could to an original [manufacturing defect]. The Prices purchased their 1981 Citation second-hand in 1983, after it had been driven more than 63,000 miles; they drove it approximately 15,000 additional miles.

Appellants offered no evidence relating to the maintenance and repair history of the vehicle prior to their purchase. . . . Finally, appellants' own expert conceded that he had no way of knowing whether any of the mechanical parts in the power steering mechanism were original.

The failure to preserve the product is not always fatal to plaintiff's case if there is enough evidence of the malfunction to permit an inference of defect. See, e.g., Daniels v. GNB, Inc., 629 So.2d 595 (Miss.1993)(plaintiff's testimony about exploding auto battery together with expert who said that plaintiff's version of the accident, if accurate, was consistent with a product defect, sufficed to withstand summary judgment).

C.   DESIGN DEFECTS

In Cronin v. J.B.E. Olson Corp., 501 P.2d 1153 (Cal.1972), a bakery truck driver was injured when, in a crash, the trays came forward and struck him in the back. Defendant appealed from a judgment for plaintiff on the ground that the trial judge's charge on strict liability omitted the requirement that any defect in the product must be found to be "unreasonably dangerous" as required by § 402A. The court disagreed. It thought the phrase "burdened the injured plaintiff with proof of an element which rings of negligence. . . . A bifurcated standard is of necessity more difficult to prove than a unitary one. But merely proclaiming that the phrase 'defective condition unreasonably dangerous' requires only a single finding would not purge that phrase of its negligence complexion":

> We recognize that the words "unreasonably dangerous" may also serve the beneficial purpose of preventing the seller from being treated as the insurer of its products. However, we think that such protective end is attained by the necessity of proving that there was a defect in the manufacture or design of the product and that such defect was a proximate cause of the injuries.

Although the court assumed that *Greenman* had involved a manufacturing defect, it saw "no difficulty in applying the *Greenman* formulation to the full range of products liability situations, including those involving 'design defects.' A defect may emerge from the mind of the designer as well as from the hand of the workman." Although it may be "easier to see the 'defect' in a single imperfectly fashioned product than in an entire line badly conceived, a distinction between manufacture and design defects is not tenable." It rejected the Restatement's "unreasonably dangerous" standard in both contexts.

A large number of states followed *Cronin* in dropping the "unreasonably dangerous" phrase from the definition of defect. Does the Products Restatement appear to reinstate it?

The *Barker* case. In Barker v. Lull Engineering Co., Inc., 573 P.2d 443 (Cal.1978), plaintiff was hurt when the high-lift loader he was operating overturned on a slope. The court reversed a defense judgment because the trial judge, ruling before *Cronin* had been decided, used the "unreasonably dangerous" language in the charge to the jury. The court also found error in the trial judge's limitation of liability to situations in which the product was used in the "intended" manner. Such a limitation would prevent liability in cases of automobile crashes or in situations in which products are widely used for purposes for which they are not "intended," such as standing on chairs or using a screwdriver to pry up the lid of a tin. The appropriate limiting phrase would require the product to be used in the "intended or a reasonably foreseeable manner."

The court then discussed how plaintiffs might show that a product was defectively designed. "First, our cases establish that a product may be found defective in design if the plaintiff demonstrates that the product failed to perform as safely as an ordinary consumer would expect when used in an intended or reasonably foreseeable manner."

But this could not be the exclusive yardstick because in many situations consumers "have no idea how safe the product could be made." This led to a second formulation: that design defect could be shown "if through hindsight the jury determines that the product's design embodies 'excessive preventable danger,' or, in other words, if the jury finds that the risk of danger inherent in the challenged design outweighs the benefits of such design." The jury was to consider

> [a]mong other relevant factors, the gravity of the danger posed by the challenged design, the likelihood that such danger would occur, the mechanical feasibility of a safer alternative design, the financial cost of an improved design, and the adverse consequences to the product and to the consumer that would result from an alternative design.

On this second prong, the defendant had the burden of persuading the trier of fact that the product should not be judged defective. Plaintiff and amicus argued that this second prong was equivalent to demanding a showing of negligence. The court disagreed. In many cases it is true that a showing of defect "may also demonstrate that the manufacturer was negligent in choosing such a design. As we have indicated, however, in a strict liability case, as contrasted with a negligent design action, the jury's focus is properly directed to the condition of the product itself, and not to the reasonableness of the manufacturer's conduct."

Barker plays a central role in the case that follows and is discussed further in the case.

Soule v. General Motors Corporation

Supreme Court of California, 1994.
8 Cal.4th 548, 882 P.2d 298, 34 Cal.Rptr.2d 607.

BAXTER, JUSTICE.

Plaintiff's ankles were badly injured when her General Motors (GM) car collided with another vehicle. She sued GM, asserting that defects in her automobile allowed its left front wheel to break free, collapse rearward, and smash the floorboard into her feet. GM denied any defect and claimed that the force of the collision itself was the sole cause of the injuries. Expert witnesses debated the issues at length. Plaintiff prevailed at trial, and the Court of Appeal affirmed the judgment.

We granted review to resolve three questions. First, may a product's design be found defective on grounds that the product's performance fell below the safety expectation of the ordinary consumer (see [*Barker*]), if the question of how safely the product should have performed cannot be answered by the common experience of its users? [The second question was whether it was error to deny GM's requested instruction that even if a defect is found it "cannot be a legal cause of injury if the accident would have produced the same injury even without the defect" and the third was whether an erroneous denial of an instruction was always reversible error.]

We reach the following conclusions: The trial court erred by giving an "ordinary consumer expectations" instruction in this complex case. Moreover, the court should have granted GM's request for a special instruction explaining its correct theory of legal cause. However, neither error warrants reversal unless it caused actual prejudice, and both errors were harmless on this record. We will therefore affirm the Court of Appeal's judgment.

[During a slight drizzle one afternoon, plaintiff was driving her Camaro on the street "apparently" not wearing her seat belt. An approaching Datsun suddenly skidded into plaintiff's path. The Datsun's left rear quarter struck plaintiff's car in the area of the left front wheel at a combined closing speed estimated variously at from 30 to 70 miles per hour. "The collision bent the Camaro's frame adjacent to the wheel and tore loose the bracket that attached the wheel assembly (specifically, the lower control arm) to the frame. As a result, the wheel collapsed rearward and inward. The wheel hit the underside of the 'toe pan'—the slanted floorboard area beneath the pedals—causing the toe pan to crumple, or 'deform,' upward into the passenger compartment." In addition to various minor injuries, plaintiff sustained two fractured ankles, including a compound compression fracture of her left ankle, which caused permanent injury.

The "failed bracket" was retrieved but the rest of the Camaro was acquired by a salvage dealer, repaired and resold. In the ensuing suit, plaintiff "asserted a theory of strict tort liability for a defective product. She claimed the severe trauma to her ankles was not a natural consequence of the accident, but occurred when the collapse of the Camaro's wheel caused the toe pan to crush violently upward against her feet. Plaintiff attributed the wheel collapse to a manufacturing defect, the substandard quality of the weld attaching the lower control arm bracket to the frame. She also claimed that the placement of the bracket, and the configuration of the frame, were defective designs because they did not limit the wheel's rearward travel in the event the bracket should fail."

The "available physical and circumstantial evidence left room for debate about the exact angle and force of the impact and the extent to which the toe pan had actually deformed. The issues of defect and causation were addressed through numerous experts produced by both sides in such areas as biomechanics, metallurgy, orthopedics, design engineering, and crash-test simulation.''

Plaintiff presented evidence of improper welding techniques and of a design on Ford Mustangs of comparable years that were said to ''provide protection against unlimited rearward travel of the wheel should a bracket assembly give way.'' GM denied the claims of poor welding and design defect, and argued that the Ford design was ''not distinctly safer for all collision stresses to which the vehicle might be subjected.'' One witness asserted that at least one recent Ford product had adopted the Camaro's design. GM also argued that the force of the collision was the sole cause of the ankle injuries—that plaintiff's unrestrained body went forward and downward at the moment of impact, causing the ankle injury ''before significant deformation of the toe pan occurred.''

The trial court gave a conventional ''ordinary consumer expectations'' charge that required plaintiff to show ''(1) the manufacturer's product failed to perform as safely as an ordinary consumer would expect, (2) the defect existed when the product left the manufacturer's possession, (3) the defect was a 'legal cause' of plaintiff's 'enhanced injury,' and (4) the product was used in a reasonably foreseeable manner.'' As noted earlier, the judge denied GM's requested instruction on causation.

The jury made special findings that the Camaro contained a ''defect (of unspecified nature) which was a 'legal cause' of plaintiff's 'enhanced injury.' '' The jury found that plaintiff was at fault for not wearing a seat belt but that it was not a legal cause of her enhanced injuries. The jury awarded $1.65 million. The court of appeal affirmed.]

DISCUSSION

. . .

In *Barker*, we offered two alternative ways to prove a design defect, each appropriate to its own circumstances. The purposes, behaviors, and dangers of certain products are commonly understood by those who ordinarily use them. By the same token, the ordinary users or consumers of a product may have reasonable, widely accepted minimum expectations about the circumstances under which it should perform safely. Consumers govern their own conduct by these expectations, and products on the market should conform to them.

In some cases, therefore, ''ordinary knowledge . . . as to . . . [the product's] characteristics'' [§ 402A], may permit an inference that the product did not perform as safely as it should. If the facts permit such a conclusion, and if the failure resulted from the product's design, a finding of defect is warranted without any further proof. The manufacturer may not defend a claim that a product's design failed to perform as safely as its ordinary consumers would expect by presenting expert evidence of the design's relative risks and benefits.[3]

---

3. For example, the ordinary consumers of modern automobiles may and do expect that such vehicles will be designed so as not to explode while idling at stoplights, experi-

However, as we noted in *Barker*, a complex product, even when it is being used as intended, may often cause injury in a way that does not engage its ordinary consumers' reasonable minimum assumptions about safe performance. For example, the ordinary consumer of an automobile simply has "no idea" how it should perform in all foreseeable situations, or how safe it should be made against all foreseeable hazards. [*Barker*]

An injured person is not foreclosed from proving a defect in the product's design simply because he cannot show that the reasonable minimum safety expectations of its ordinary consumers were violated. Under *Barker*'s alternative test, a product is still defective if its design embodies "excessive preventable danger" [   ], that is, unless "the benefits of the . . . design outweigh the risk of danger inherent in such design" [   ]. But this determination involves technical issues of feasibility, cost, practicality, risk, and benefit [   ], which are "impossible" to avoid [   ]. In such cases, the jury must consider the manufacturer's evidence of competing design considerations [   ] and the issue of design defect cannot fairly be resolved by standardless reference to the "expectations" of an "ordinary consumer."

As we have seen, the consumer expectations test is reserved for cases in which the everyday experience of the product's users permits a conclusion that the product's design violated minimum safety assumptions, and is thus defective regardless of expert opinion about the merits of the design. It follows that where the minimum safety of a product is within the common knowledge of lay jurors, expert witnesses may not be used to demonstrate what an ordinary consumer would or should expect. Use of expert testimony for that purpose would invade the jury's function [   ], and would invite circumvention of the rule that the risks and benefits of a challenged design must be carefully balanced whenever the issue of design defect goes beyond the common experience of the product's users.[4]

---

ence sudden steering or brake failure as they leave the dealership, or roll over and catch fire in two-mile-per-hour collisions. If the plaintiff in a product liability action proved that a vehicle's design produced such a result, the jury could find forthwith that the car failed to perform as safely as its ordinary consumers would expect, and was therefore defective.

4. Plaintiff insists that manufacturers should be forced to design their products to meet the "objective" safety demands of a "hypothetical" reasonable consumer who is fully informed about what he or she should expect. Hence, plaintiff reasons, the jury may receive expert advice on "reasonable" safety expectations for the product. However, this function is better served by the risk-benefit prong of Barker. There, juries receive expert advice, apply clear guidelines, and decide accordingly whether the product's design is an acceptable compromise of competing considerations. On the other hand, appropriate use of the consumer expectations test is not necessarily foreclosed simply because the product at issue is only in specialized use, so that the general public may not be familiar with its safety characteristics. If the safe performance of the product fell below the reasonable, widely shared minimum expectations of those who do use it, perhaps the injured consumer should not be forced to rely solely on a technical comparison of risks and benefits. By the same token, if the expectations of the product's limited group of ordinary consumers are beyond the lay experience common to all jurors, expert testimony on the limited subject of what the product's actual consumers do expect may be proper. [   ]

By the same token, the jury may not be left free to find a violation of ordinary consumer expectations whenever it chooses. Unless the facts actually permit an inference that the product's performance did not meet the minimum safety expectations of its ordinary users, the jury must engage in the balancing of risks and benefits required by the second prong of *Barker*.

Accordingly, as *Barker* indicated, instructions are misleading and incorrect if they allow a jury to avoid this risk-benefit analysis in a case where it is required. [ ] Instructions based on the ordinary consumer expectations prong of *Barker* are not appropriate where, as a matter of law, the evidence would not support a jury verdict on that theory. Whenever that is so, the jury must be instructed solely on the alternative risk-benefit theory of design defect announced in *Barker*.[5]

GM suggests that the consumer expectations test is improper whenever "crashworthiness," a complex product, or technical questions of causation are at issue. Because the variety of potential product injuries is infinite, the line cannot be drawn as clearly as GM proposes. But the fundamental distinction is not impossible to define. The crucial question in each individual case is whether the circumstances of the product's failure permit an inference that the product's design performed below the legitimate, commonly accepted minimum safety assumptions of its ordinary consumers.

GM argues at length that the consumer expectations test is an "unworkable, amorphic, fleeting standard" which should be entirely abolished as a basis for design defect. In GM's view, the test is deficient and unfair in several respects. First, it defies definition. Second, it focuses not on the objective condition of products, but on the subjective, unstable, and often unreasonable opinions of consumers. Third, it ignores the reality that ordinary consumers know little about how safe the complex products they use can or should be made. Fourth, it invites the jury to isolate the particular consumer, component, accident, and injury before it instead of considering whether the whole product fairly accommodates the competing expectations of all consumers in all situations [ ]. Fifth, it eliminates the careful balancing of risks and benefits which is essential to any design issue.

In its amicus curiae brief, the Product Liability Advisory Council, Inc. (Council) makes similar arguments. The Council proposes that all design defect claims be resolved under a single risk-benefit analysis geared to "reasonable safety."

We fully understand the dangers of improper use of the consumer expectations test. However, we cannot accept GM's insinuation that ordinary consumers lack any legitimate expectations about the minimum safety of the products they use. In particular circumstances, a product's design

---

5. Plaintiff urges that any limitation on use of the consumer expectations test contravenes *Greenman's* purpose to aid hapless consumers. But we have consistently held that manufacturers are not insurers of their products; they are liable in tort only when "defects" in their products cause injury. . . .

may perform so unsafely that the defect is apparent to the common reason, experience, and understanding of its ordinary consumers. In such cases, a lay jury is competent to make that determination.

Nor are we persuaded by the Council's proposal. In essence, it would reinvest product liability claims with the requirement of "unreasonable danger" that we rejected in *Cronin* and *Barker*.

When use of the consumer expectations test is limited as *Barker* intended, the principal concerns raised by GM and the Council are met. Within these limits, the test remains a workable means of determining the existence of design defect. We therefore find no compelling reason to overrule the consumer expectations prong of *Barker* at this late date, and we decline to do so.[7]

Applying our conclusions to the facts of this case, however, we agree that the instant jury should not have been instructed on ordinary consumer expectations. Plaintiff's theory of design defect was one of technical and mechanical detail. It sought to examine the precise behavior of several obscure components of her car under the complex circumstances of a particular accident. The collision's exact speed, angle, and point of impact were disputed. It seems settled, however, that plaintiff's Camaro received a substantial oblique blow near the left front wheel, and that the adjacent frame members and bracket assembly absorbed considerable inertial force.

An ordinary consumer of automobiles cannot reasonably expect that a car's frame, suspension, or interior will be designed to remain intact in any and all accidents. Nor would ordinary experience and understanding inform such a consumer how safely an automobile's design should perform under the esoteric circumstances of the collision at issue here. Indeed, both parties assumed that quite complicated design considerations were at issue, and that expert testimony was necessary to illuminate these matters. Therefore, injection of ordinary consumer expectations into the design defect equation was improper.

We are equally persuaded, however, that the error was harmless, because it is not reasonably probable defendant would have obtained a more favorable result in its absence.   .   .   .

[The court stressed that "the consumer expectations theory was never emphasized at any point." The case was "tried on the assumption that the alleged design defect was a matter of technical debate. Virtually all the evidence and argument on design defect focused on expert evaluation of the strengths, shortcomings, risks, and benefits of the challenged design, as compared with a competitor's approach." Neither "plaintiff's attorney nor

7. GM observes that some other states have rejected the consumer expectations test. (E.g., Prentis v. Yale Mfg. Co. [365 N.W.2d 176, 185–186 (Mich.1984)] [adopting pure negligence theory for product injury]; [ ]). But a substantial number of jurisdictions ex-pressly recognize, consistent with *Barker*, that a product's design is defective if it either violates the minimum safety expectations of an ordinary consumer or contains dangers which outweigh its benefits. [ ]

any expert witness on her behalf told the jury that the Camaro's design violated the safety expectations of the ordinary consumer."]

Under these circumstances, we find it highly unlikely that a reasonable jury took that path. We see no reasonable probability that the jury disregarded the voluminous evidence on the risks and benefits of the Camaro's design, and instead rested its verdict on its independent assessment of what an ordinary consumer would expect. Accordingly, we conclude, the error in presenting that theory to the jury provides no basis for disturbing the trial judgment.[8]

[The court then turned to GM's requested causation instruction, concluding that it should have been given, but that the failure to give it was harmless error. Overruling several cases that had called for automatic reversal when a request to charge was erroneously granted or refused, the court concluded that "there is no rule of automatic reversal or 'inherent' prejudice applicable to any category of civil instructional error, whether of commission or omission."]

Instructional error in a civil case is prejudicial "where it seems probable" that the error "prejudicially affected the verdict." [   ]

. . .

The trial court erred when it instructed on the consumer expectations test for design defect, and when it refused GM's special instruction on causation. However, neither error caused actual prejudice. Accordingly, the judgment of the Court of Appeal, upholding the trial court judgment in favor of plaintiff, is affirmed.

KENNARD, GEORGE, WERDEGAR and BOREN (assigned) JJ., concur.

MOSK, ACTING CHIEF JUSTICE, concurring [addressing the issue of reversals for instructional errors].

ARABIAN, JUSTICE, concurring and dissenting [agreeing with the majority on the first two grounds but concluding that the failure to give GM's requested charge was reversible error].

---

8. In a separate argument . . . both GM and the Council urge us to reconsider *Barker's* holding . . . that under the risk-benefit test, the manufacturer has the burden of proving that the utility of the challenged design outweighs its dangers. [   ] We explained in *Barker* that placement of the risk-benefit burden on the manufacturer is appropriate because the considerations which influenced the design of its product are "peculiarly within . . . [its] knowledge." . . . GM argues that *Barker* unfairly requires the manufacturer to "prove a negative"—i.e., the absence of a safer alternative design. The Council suggests our "peculiar knowledge" rationale is unrealistic under liberal modern discovery rules. We are not persuaded. *Barker* allows the evaluation of competing designs, but it does not require proof that the challenged design is the safest possible alternative. The manufacturer need only show that given the inherent complexities of design, the benefits of its chosen design outweigh the dangers. Moreover, modern discovery practice neither redresses the inherent technical imbalance between manufacturer and consumer nor dictates that the injured consumer should bear the primary burden of evaluating a design developed and chosen by the manufacturer. GM and the Council fail to convince us that Barker was incorrectly decided in this respect.

Notes and Questions

1.   What is the difference in this case between plaintiff's claim based on a manufacturing defect and her claim based on a design defect? Does the distinction affect any of GM's defense arguments?

2.   Consider how the four elements of the consumer expectations test listed by the trial judge would work in a case like Campbell v. General Motors Corp., 649 P.2d 224 (Cal.1982), in which a bus passenger was thrown from her seat and injured during a sharp turn. She claimed a defective design because there was no "grab bar" within easy reach of her seat. Plaintiff presented no expert testimony but did present photographs of the interior of the bus.

The court held that it was enough for Campbell to show "the objective conditions of the product" so that the jurors could employ "[their] own sense of whether the product meets ordinary expectations as to its safety under the circumstances presented by the evidence. Since public transportation is a matter of common experience, no expert testimony was required to enable the jury to reach a decision on this part of the *Barker* inquiry."

How might *Campbell* be analyzed under the second prong of *Barker*?

3.   In Pruitt v. General Motors Corp., 86 Cal.Rptr.2d 4 (App.1999), the plaintiff was hurt when an air bag deployed in a "low impact collision." After a judgment for defendant, the appellate court upheld the trial court's refusal to charge on the consumer expectations test because the "deployment of an air bag is, quite fortunately, not part of the 'everyday experience' of the consuming public. Minimum safety standards for air bags are not within the common knowledge of lay jurors. Jurors are in need of expert testimony to evaluate the risks and benefits of the challenged design." To the examples in *Soule*'s footnote 3, this court added "air bags inflating for no apparent reason while one is cruising down the road at 65 miles per hour." How different is that from what actually happened?

Compare Morton v. Owens Corning Fiberglas Corp., 40 Cal.Rptr.2d 22 (App.1995), in which a former insulation installer sued asbestos suppliers after getting mesothelioma—a cancer of the lining that surrounds the lungs. Plaintiff succeeded before the jury on a consumer expectations approach. On appeal, defendant argued that such a test was inapplicable in an asbestos case because of its complexity. The court held the consumer expectations test applicable, stating that the question was whether "the circumstances of the product's failure permit an inference that the product's design performed below the legitimate, commonly accepted minimum safety assumptions of its ordinary consumers."

4.   What is the basis for GM's argument that the consumer expectations test should be eliminated? Which of the five reasons offered seems strongest?

5.   The court suggests that some car accidents are properly subject to the consumer expectations test. What do they have in common? Why doesn't this case fit within that category?

6. Few states have joined California in shifting the burden of proof to defendants on the issue of "excessive preventable danger." Indeed, in Ray v. BIC Corp., 925 S.W.2d 527 (Tenn.1996) the position was called "aberrant." What are the arguments for and against such a shift?

7. In deciding how the risk-utility factors apply in a particular case, much attention has been given to the feasibility of the alternatives. Consider this passage from Banks v. ICI Americas, Inc., 450 S.E.2d 671 (Ga.1994):

> Numerous lists of factors to be considered by the trier of fact in balancing the risk of the product against the utility or benefit derived from the product have been compiled by various authorities. One factor consistently recognized as integral to the assessment of the utility of a design is the availability of alternative designs, in that the existence and feasibility of a safer and equally efficacious design diminishes the justification for using a challenged design. [   ] The alternative safer design factor reflects the reality that
>
> > [i]t often is not possible to determine whether a safer design would have averted a particular injury without considering whether an alternative design was feasible. The essential inquiry, therefore, is whether the design chosen was a reasonable one from among the feasible choices of which the manufacturer was aware or should have been aware. [   ]
>
> Indeed, the reasonableness of choosing from among various alternative product designs and adopting the safest one if it is feasible is considered the "heart" of design defect cases, [   ], since it is only at their most extreme that design defect cases reflect the position that a product is simply so dangerous that it should not have been made available at all. [   ]

How does a court decide what the "choices" are? Whether they are "feasible"? Why must the choice be the "safest one"?

8. *Reasonable alternative design (RAD).* The approach in *Banks* has been formalized in the Products Restatement § 2 comment *f*, which asserts that the plaintiff "must prove that a reasonable alternative design would have reduced the foreseeable risk of harm." Sometimes "the feasibility of a reasonable alternative design is obvious and understandable to lay persons and therefore expert testimony is unnecessary to support a finding that the product should have been designed differently and more safely." Other products already on the market may serve "a similar function at lower risk and at comparable cost." (One exception to the necessity for a RAD is discussed in note 12 infra.) The comment is explicit about some criteria but recognizes that they will vary from case to case: a "broad range of factors may be considered in determining whether an alternative design is reasonable and whether its omission renders a product not reasonably safe." These factors include "among others" the "magnitude and probability of the foreseeable risks of harm, the instructions and warnings accompanying the product, and the nature and strength of consumer expectations regarding the product, including expectations arising from product portrayal and marketing." In addition, the relative advantages and disadvantages of the product and its proposed alternative must be considered. These include the impact on production costs and on "product longevity, maintenance, repair and esthetics; and the range of consumer choice among products":

> Moreover, the factors interact with one another. For example, evidence of the magnitude and probability of foreseeable harm may be offset by evidence that the proposed alternative design would reduce the efficiency and utility of the product. On the other hand, evidence that a proposed alternative design would increase production costs may be offset by evidence that product portrayal and marketing created substantial expectations of performance or safety, thus increasing the probability of foreseeable harm. . . . On the other hand, it is not a factor under Subsection (b) that the imposition of liability would have negative effect on corporate earnings or would reduce employment in a given industry.

How might the plaintiff in *Soule* go about proving a RAD? From the standpoint of the two Restatements, consider the cases discussed in the following notes. Many that were decided before the Products Restatement raise the same issues.

9. When analyzing risk-utility cases, comparisons among products must consider only comparable products. See Dyson v. General Motors Corp., 298 F.Supp. 1064 (E.D.Pa.1969), refusing to hold a hard-top car defective because it was less protective than a full-frame sedan. But one hard-top car should not be "appreciably less safe" than other hard-tops. See also Curtis v. General Motors Corp., 649 F.2d 808 (10th Cir.1981).

10. In Dreisonstok v. Volkswagenwerk, A.G., 489 F.2d 1066 (4th Cir.1974), plaintiff passengers were hurt when the microbus in which they were riding left the road and ran into a tree. One distinctive feature of the microbus was that its passenger compartment was at the very front of the vehicle. Plaintiffs' negligence claim alleged that the design was defective because it provided less protection than that available in a "standard American made vehicle, which is a configuration with the passengers in the middle and the motor in the front." The court, reversing a plaintiffs' judgment, rejected the claim. After quoting *Dyson* on the need to distinguish types of vehicles, it continued:

> Price is, also, a factor to be considered, for, if a change in design would appreciably add to cost, add little to safety, and take an article out of the price range of the market to which it was intended to appeal, it may be "unreasonable" as well as "impractical" for the courts to require the manufacturer to adopt such change. Of course, if an article can be made safer and the hazard of harm may be mitigated "by an alternate design or device at no substantial increase in price," then the manufacturer has a duty to adopt such a design but a Cadillac may be expected to include more in the way of both conveniences and "crashworthiness" than the economy car. Moreover, in a "crashworthy" case, it is necessary to consider the circumstances of the accident itself. As

Dyson puts it, "it could not reasonably be argued that a car manufacturer should be held liable because its vehicle collapsed when involved in a head-on collision with a large truck, at high speed." In summary, every case such as this involves a delicate balancing of many factors in order to determine whether the manufacturer has used ordinary care in designing a car, which, giving consideration to the market purposes and utility of the vehicle, did not involve unreasonable risk of injury to occupants within the range of its "intended use."

Applying the foregoing principles to the facts of this particular case, it is clear that there was no violation by the defendant of its duty of ordinary care in the design of its vehicle. The defendant's vehicle, described as "a van type multipurpose vehicle," was of a special type and particular design. This design was uniquely developed in order to provide the owner with the maximum amount of either cargo or passenger space in a vehicle inexpensively priced and of such dimensions as to make possible easy maneuverability. To achieve this, it advanced the driver's seat forward, bringing such seat in close proximity to the front of the vehicle, thereby adding to the cargo or passenger space. This, of course, reduced considerably the space between the exact front of the vehicle and the driver's compartment. All of this was readily discernible to any one using the vehicle; in fact, it was, as we have said, the unique feature of the vehicle. The usefulness of the design is vouchsafed by the popularity of the type. It was of special utility as a van for the transportation of light cargo, as a family camper, as a station wagon and for use by passenger groups too large for the average passenger car. It was a design duplicated in the construction of the large trucking tractors, where there was the same purpose of extending the cargo space without unduly lengthening the tractor-trailer coupling. There was no evidence in the record that there was any practical way of improving the "crashability" of the vehicle that would have been consistent with the peculiar purposes of its design.

The court concluded that the microbus was to be compared only with comparable vehicles. Here, the defense had presented unrefuted testimony that the safety of the microbus "was equal to or superior to that of other vehicles of like type."

In Bittner v. American Honda Motor Co., 533 N.W.2d 476 (Wis.1995), plaintiff was hurt when his 3-wheel all-terrain vehicle (ATV) overturned going around a corner on a mowed grass path. Honda was properly permitted to compare safety records of this ATV with other products intended for similar purposes—snowmobiles, minibikes, trailbikes and 4-wheel ATVs—to suggest that the accident in question was more likely attributable to the operator than to the product. But Honda should not have been allowed to introduce evidence about the risks of "dissimilar products and activities"—sky-diving, skiing, bicycle riding, scuba diving, football, and passenger automobiles—to show that ATVs were not unreasonably dangerous. Such evidence could not help the jury decide whether the product at issue was reasonably safe. The manufacturer's obligations "persist whether or not the product has a high rate of injury associated with it."

11. Does *Soule* require, or permit, differentiating between products that may be dangerous only to the users, such as food, drink and microbuses, and those that might be dangerous to bystanders as well, such as snowmobiles and power mowers that toss rocks beyond the lawn? If a manufacturer has achieved a huge cost reduction by the sacrifice of a small amount of safety, should bystanders be subjected to the additional danger without hope of recovering damages under a balancing test, when they receive no direct benefit from the reduced price?

12. *The irreducibly unsafe product.* The "most extreme" case, mentioned in *Banks* supra, and the subject of the Products Restatement's exception to the need for a RAD, involves products whose dangers are known and often great, but for which there are no RADs. O'Brien v. Muskin, 463 A.2d 298 (N.J.1983), sharpened this issue. Plaintiff was hurt when he dove into an above-ground swimming pool that was properly filled with 3-1/2 feet of water. The trial judge submitted a warning claim to the jury, which decided it for defendant. The judge's refusal to submit a design defect claim was reversed on appeal. The court recognized that if there was no reasonable alternative, "recourse to a unique design is more defensible." Nonetheless:

> The evaluation of the utility of a product also involves the relative need for that product; some products are essentials, while others are luxuries. A product that fills a critical need and can be designed only one way should be viewed differently from a luxury item. Still other products, including some for which no alternative exists, are so dangerous and of such little use that under the risk-utility analysis, a manufacturer would bear the cost of liability of harm to others. That cost might dissuade a manufacturer from placing the product on the market, even if the product has been made as safely as possible. Indeed, plaintiff contends that above-ground pools with vinyl liners are such products and that manufacturers who market those pools should bear the cost of injuries they cause to foreseeable users.

> . . . The trial judge should have permitted the jury to consider whether, because of the dimensions of the pool and slipperiness of the bottom, the risks of injury so outweighed the utility of the product as to constitute a defect. . . . Viewing the evidence in the light most favorable to plaintiff, even if there are no alternative methods of making bottoms for above-ground pools, the jury might have found that the risk posed by the pool outweighed its utility.

The majority then turned to emphasize a main difference between them and the dissenter:

> [The dissenter] would find that no matter how dangerous a product may be, if it bears an adequate warning, it is free from design defects if there is no known alternative. Under that hypothesis, manu-

facturers, merely by placing warnings on their products, could insulate themselves from liability regardless of the number of people those products maim or kill. By contrast, the majority concludes that the judicial, not the commercial, system is the appropriate forum for determining whether a product is defective, with the resultant imposition of strict liability upon those in the commercial chain.

What does "defective" mean in this context? What analysis if, after several years of warnings that all reasonable people recognize as more than adequate in substance, size and placement, ten people per year in New Jersey still dive into these pools and are paralyzed? Recall the *Dreisonstok* case, note 10, supra, in which the court refused to compare the microbus design with that of dissimilar—safer—vehicles. Is that case inconsistent with *O'Brien*?

What if 1,000 people accidentally cut themselves badly on sharp knives in New Jersey each year? In the *Barker* case, p. 558, supra, the court noted that it need not consider "whether a product that entails a substantial risk of harm may be found defective even if no safer alternative design is feasible." It cited a law review article in which Justice Traynor suggested that liability might be imposed for products "whose norm is danger." Reconsider Judge Cardozo's analysis of the "Flopper," p. 469, supra. Despite the package warnings and general knowledge, should cigarette manufacturers be liable for design defects?

Other states have rejected *O'Brien*. In Baughn v. Honda Motor Co., Ltd., 727 P.2d 655 (Wash.1986), for example, the court held that a manufacturer of "mini-trail bikes" could not be held liable for injuries suffered when the bikes were used on public roads in disregard of explicit warnings against such usage. Plaintiff relied on *O'Brien* for the proposition that the case should go to the jury to weigh the risk and utility of the bikes. The court insisted that the product was not defective as a matter of law when its warnings (which were found adequate) were followed. Should it matter if 10% of the users of these bikes are killed in highway accidents?

The New Jersey legislature sought to restrict *O'Brien* by providing that there is no liability when there is no "practical and technically feasible alternative design that would have prevented the harm without substantially impairing the reasonably anticipated or intended function of the product." An exception was created where the court found by "clear and convincing evidence" that "(1) the product is egregiously unsafe or ultra-hazardous; (2) the ordinary user or consumer of the product cannot reasonably be expected to have knowledge of the product's risks, or the product poses a risk of serious injury to persons other than the user or consumer; and (3) the product has little or no usefulness." N.J.S.A. 2A:58C–3.

NJ exception to O'Brien

The Products Restatement states that liability may flow even if a product has no RAD if its value is deemed to be minimal. It recognized that some courts had imposed liability for generic products with a "manifestly unreasonable design." Section 2, comments *d* and *e*, accepted this approach as to prank exploding cigars but rejected it for "alcoholic beverages, firearms, and above-ground swimming pools." What about all-terrain vehicles?

13. *Causation.* As with manufacturing defects, the supplier must anticipate uses that were not intended. In Price v. Blaine Kern Artista, Inc., 893 P.2d 367 (Nev.1995), plaintiff entertainer had bought an oversized caricature head mask of then-President George Bush made by defendant. While plaintiff was performing in Las Vegas, he either tripped or was pushed from behind and was hurt by the shifting weight of the mask when he fell. His negligence action claimed a defective design in that the mask did not have a safety harness to support the head and neck in case of a fall. Defendant argued that if plaintiff had been deliberately pushed by a drunk or by a political foe of President Bush that was not a foreseeable use of the mask. The court disagreed: a fact question was presented whether defendant should have foreseen the possibility of some sort of violent reaction by intoxicated or politically volatile persons, "ignited by the oversized caricature of prominent political figures." What if it had been shown that the plaintiff had tripped over a wire? Been bumped into accidentally?

14. Should a consumer expectations test—whether narrowly or broadly defined—be retained? Or should exclusive reliance be placed on risk-utility analysis? Consider the following case.

Risk-Utility

Camacho v. Honda Motor Co., Ltd.

Supreme Court of Colorado, 1987.
741 P.2d 1240, cert. dismissed 485 U.S. 901 (1988).

[In March 1978, plaintiff bought a new Honda Hawk motorcycle. In an intersection accident with a car, plaintiff suffered severe leg injuries. Plaintiff and his wife sued the various parties in the chain of distribution, claiming that the absence of crash bars to protect the legs made the product defective under a strict liability analysis. Negligence and breach-of-warranty claims were not before the court. Two mechanical engineers supplied depositions asserting that "the state of the art in mechanical engineering and motorcycle design was such that effective leg protection devices were available in March 1978 and that several manufacturers other than Honda had made such devices available as optional equipment; that, although room for further improvement of crash bars existed in March 1978, crash bars then available from manufacturers other than Honda provided some protection in low-speed collisions and, in particular, would have reduced or completely avoided the serious leg injuries" that plaintiff suffered. The trial court granted Honda summary judgment. The court of appeals affirmed on the ground that the danger "would have been fully anticipated by or within the contemplation of the ordinary user or consumer."]

KIRSHBAUM, JUSTICE.

. . . .

In Roberts v. May, [583 P.2d 305 (Colo.App.1978)], the Court of Appeals recognized the applicability of the "crashworthiness" doctrine in

Colorado. Under this doctrine, a motor vehicle manufacturer may be liable in negligence or strict liability for injuries sustained in a motor vehicle accident where a manufacturing or design defect, though not the cause of the accident, caused or enhanced the injuries. [   ] The doctrine was first recognized in the landmark case of Larsen v. General Motors Corp., 391 F.2d 495 (8th Cir.1968), in which the court noted that a manufacturer's duty encompassed designing and building a product reasonably fit and safe for its intended use, that automobiles are intended for use on the roadways and that injury-producing collisions are a frequent, foreseeable and statistically expectable result of such normal use. Incumbent upon the automobile manufacturer was a duty of reasonable care in the design and manufacture of its product, including a duty to use reasonable care to minimize the injurious effects of a foreseeable collision by employing commonsense safety features. [   ] The crashworthiness doctrine has been adopted by the vast majority of courts in other jurisdictions which have considered the issue. [   ] We agree with the reasoning of those decisions, as did the Court of Appeals in its consideration of this case, and adopt the crashworthiness doctrine for this jurisdiction.

crashworthiness doctrine

Rule Choice

The crashworthiness doctrine has been applied to accidents involving motorcycles. [   ] Honda argues, however, that motorcycles are inherently dangerous motor vehicles that cannot be made perfectly crashworthy and, therefore, that motorcycle manufacturers should be free of liability for injuries not actually caused by a defect in the design or manufacture of the motorcycle. We find no principled basis to conclude that liability for failure to provide reasonable, cost-acceptable safety features to reduce the severity of injuries suffered in inevitable accidents should be imposed upon automobile manufacturers but not upon motorcycle manufacturers. The use of motorcycles for transportation over roadways is just as foreseeable as the use of automobiles for such purpose. The crashworthiness doctrine does not require a manufacturer to provide absolute safety, but merely to provide some measure of reasonable, cost-effective safety in the foreseeable use of the product. [   ] Honda acknowledges that motorcycle accidents are just as foreseeable as automobile accidents and that motorcycle riders face a much greater risk of injury in the event of an accident than do occupants of automobiles. In view of the important goal of encouraging maximum development of reasonable, cost-efficient safety features in the manufacture of all products, the argument that motorcycle manufacturers should be exempt from liability under the crashworthiness doctrine because serious injury to users of that product is foreseeable must be rejected. [   ]

D's arg

Reason for rejecting

pub. pol. rejects foreseability arg

III.

In determining the extent of liability of a product manufacturer for a defective product, this court has adopted the doctrine of strict products liability as set forth in [§ 402A].

Rule Choice

Honda asserts that as a matter of law a motorcycle designed without leg protection devices cannot be deemed "in a defective condition unreasonably dangerous to the user" because the risk of motorcycle accidents is foreseeable to every ordinary consumer and because it is obvious that motorcycles do not generally offer leg protection devices as a standard item. In support of this argument Honda relies on comment *i* to section 402A, which states in pertinent part:

> i.   Unreasonably dangerous. The rule stated in this Section applies only where the defective condition of the product makes it unreasonably dangerous to the user or consumer. . . . The article sold must be dangerous to an extent beyond that which would be contemplated by the ordinary consumer who purchases it, with the ordinary knowledge common to the community as to its characteristics.

The trial court and the Court of Appeals in essence applied this consumer contemplation test in dismissing the Camachos' claims.

In *Cronin v. J.B.E. Olson Corp.*, [   ], the California Supreme Court declined to require an injured person to establish that a product is unreasonably dangerous as a requisite to recovery for injuries in a strict liability design defect context. In Union Supply Co. v. Pust, [583 P.2d 276 (Colo.1978)], this court rejected the *Cronin* rationale, recognizing that requiring a party who seeks recovery on the basis of an alleged defective product to establish that the product is unreasonably dangerous appropriately places reasonable limits on the potential liability of manufacturers. However, we also held in *Pust* that the fact that the dangers of a product are open and obvious does not constitute a defense to a claim alleging that the product is unreasonably dangerous. We noted that adoption of such a principle would unfairly elevate the assumption of risk defense to a question of law.[6] The obvious and foreseeable consumer contemplation test employed by the trial court and approved by the Court of Appeals is substantially similar to the open and obvious standard specifically rejected in *Pust*. It is not the appropriate standard in Colorado for measuring whether a particular product is in a defective condition unreasonably dangerous to the consumer or user.

A consumer is justified in expecting that a product placed in the stream of commerce is reasonably safe for its intended use, and when a product is not reasonably safe a products liability action may be maintained. [   ] Of course, whether a given product is reasonably safe and, therefore, not unreasonably dangerous, necessarily depends upon many

---

6. Where the obviousness of the danger inherent in the ordinary use of a product is not dispositive of whether the product is unreasonably dangerous, the plaintiff's appreciation of the danger may nonetheless rise to the level of assumption of the risk. Assumption of the risk is an affirmative defense to strict liability, requiring a showing of more than ordinary contributory negligence in that the plaintiff must have voluntarily and un-reasonably proceeded to encounter a known danger the specific hazards of which the plaintiff had actual subjective knowledge. [   ] The question of whether a plaintiff had actual knowledge of the specific hazards comprising the danger is ordinarily a fact question which should be left for the jury and not precluded by the conclusion that the danger should have been obvious. . . . .

circumstances. Any test, therefore, to determine whether a particular product is or is not actionable must consider several factors. While reference to "reasonable" or "unreasonable" standards introduces certain negligence concepts into an area designed to be free from these concepts [   ], that difficulty is much less troublesome than are the problems inherent in attempting to avoid dealing with the competing interests involved in allocating the risk of loss in products liability actions.   .   .   .

These considerations strongly suggest that the consumer contemplation concept embodied in comment *i*, while illustrative of a particular problem, does not provide a satisfactory test for determining whether particular products are in a defective condition unreasonably dangerous to the user or consumer. In the final analysis, the principle of products liability contemplated by section 402A is premised upon the concept of enterprise liability for casting defective products into the stream of commerce. [   ] The primary focus must remain upon the nature of the product under all relevant circumstances rather than upon the conduct of either the consumer or the manufacturer. [   ] Total reliance upon the hypothetical ordinary consumer's contemplation of an obvious danger diverts the appropriate focus and may thereby result in a finding that a product is not defective even though the product may easily have been designed to be much safer at little added expense and no impairment of utility. [   ] Uncritical rejection of design defect claims in all cases wherein the danger may be open and obvious thus contravenes sound public policy by encouraging design strategies which perpetuate the manufacture of dangerous products. [   ]

pub. pol. rationale

In Ortho Pharmaceutical Corp. v. Heath, 722 P.2d 410 (Colo.1986), we recently recognized that exclusive reliance upon consumer expectations is a particularly inappropriate means of determining whether a product is unreasonably dangerous under section 402A where both the unreasonableness of the danger in the design defect and the efficacy of alternative designs in achieving a reasonable degree of safety must be defined primarily by technical, scientific information.[8] Moreover, manufacturers of such complex products as motor vehicles invariably have greater access than do ordinary consumers to the information necessary to reach informed decisions concerning the efficacy of potential safety measures. [   ] The princi-

Consumer expectation is inappropriate to determine unreasonable danger

---

8. Honda asserts that the application of the consumer expectation test is particularly appropriate in the context of motorcycle design defect claims because the motorcycle purchaser who is injured in an accident has bargained for the condition about which he complains and because the element of conscious consumer choice is invariably present in contradistinction to those claims involving accidents occurring in the workplace. We cannot agree that the purchaser of a motorcycle bargains for the risk of serious leg injury; rather, the purchaser bargains for a motorized vehicle the purpose of which is to pro-

vide an economical, open-air, maneuverable form of transportation on the roadways. Cf. Wade, On the Nature of Strict Liability for Products, 44 Miss.L.J. 825, 839–40 (1973)(noting that a plaintiff who has cut his finger on a sharp knife should not be able to maintain a cause of action against the manufacturer of the knife on the theory that the knife was unsafe because it was sharp, because the very purpose of a knife is to cut); Page, Generic Product Risks: The Case Against Comment k and For Strict Tort Liability, 58 N.Y.U.L.Rev. 853, 857 (1983).   .   .   .

ples that have evolved in the law of products liability have in part been developed to encourage manufacturers to use information gleaned from testing, inspection and data analysis to help avoid the "massive problem of product accidents." [   ]

. . . In *Ortho* we noted that the following factors are of value in balancing the attendant risks and benefits of a product to determine whether a product design is unreasonably dangerous:

Test for unreasonable danger (danger-utility test)

(1) The usefulness and desirability of the product—its utility to the user and to the public as a whole.

(2) The safety aspects of the product—the likelihood that it will cause injury and the probable seriousness of the injury.

(3) The availability of a substitute product which would meet the same need and not be as unsafe.

(4) The manufacturer's ability to eliminate the unsafe character of the product without impairing its usefulness or making it too expensive to maintain its utility.

(5) The user's ability to avoid danger by the exercise of care in the use of the product.

(6) The user's anticipated awareness of the dangers inherent in the product and their avoidability because of general public knowledge of the obvious condition of the product, or of the existence of suitable warnings or instructions.

(7) The feasibility, on the part of the manufacturer, of spreading the loss by setting the price of the product or carrying liability insurance.

[*Ortho*] (relying on [Wade's article]). The factors enumerated in *Ortho* are applicable to the determination of what constitutes a product that is in a defective unreasonably dangerous condition. By examining and weighing the various interests represented by these factors, a trial court is much more likely to be fair to the interests of both manufacturers and consumers in determining the status of particular products.

The question of the status of the motorcycle purchased by Camacho involves in part the interpretation of mechanical engineering data derived from research and testing—interpretation which necessarily includes the application of scientific and technical principles. In addition, the question posed under the crashworthiness doctrine is not whether the vehicle was obviously unsafe but rather whether the degree of inherent dangerousness could or should have been significantly reduced. The record contains some evidence to support the conclusion that Honda could have provided crash bars at an acceptable cost without impairing the motorcycle's utility or substantially altering its nature and Honda's failure to do so rendered the vehicle unreasonably dangerous under the applicable danger-utility test. It is far from certain, however, that the ultimate answer to this question can be determined on the basis of the limited facts thus far presented to the trial court.

. . .

The Camachos proffered evidence that the Honda Hawk motorcycle could have been equipped with crash bars which would mitigate injuries in low-speed, angled-impact collisions such as the one in which Camacho was involved. The Camachos' expert witnesses' interpretation of research and testing data indicated that the maneuverability of the motorcycle could be retained by making the crash bars no wider than the handlebars, that the stability of the motorcycle could be retained by mounting the crash bars relatively close to the center of gravity and that the addition of crash bars would not impair the utility of the motorcycle as a fuel efficient, open-air vehicle nor impair the safety of the motorcycle in accidents which varied in kind from the accident involving Camacho. These conclusions are all strenuously disputed by Honda. However, precisely because the factual conclusions reached by expert witnesses are in dispute, summary judgment as to whether the design strategies of Honda were reasonable is improper.

The judgment is reversed, and the case is remanded to the Court of Appeals with directions to remand the case to the trial court for further proceedings consistent with the views expressed in this opinion.

[Three justices concurred in Justice Kirshbaum's opinion.]

VOLLACK, JUSTICE, dissenting

Because I believe that the court of appeals correctly affirmed the trial court's order, I respectfully dissent.

The issue before the court is what test should apply in determining whether a product has a design defect causing it to be in a defective condition that is unreasonably dangerous. After arriving at the appropriate test, we must decide whether the court of appeals correctly affirmed the trial court's summary judgment order. . . .

. . .

II.

We have not before decided what test should apply in determining whether a product is "unreasonably dangerous" in a design defect case. I believe the appropriate test is defined in [comment *i* to § 402A]: "The article sold must be dangerous to an extent beyond that which would be contemplated by the ordinary consumer who purchases it, with the ordinary knowledge common to the community as to its characteristics" [hereinafter the consumer contemplation test].

Some jurisdictions have adopted this test; others have adopted it in part or rejected it. [   ]

. . .

Other jurisdictions have adopted a variation of the consumer expectation test. Dart v. Wiebe Mfg., Inc., [709 P.2d 876 (Ariz.1985)](where consumer expectation test is sufficient to resolve a case, that test is to be used; where that test "fails to provide a complete answer," application of risk/benefit factors is appropriate [   ]); Nichols v. Union Underwear Co.,

602 S.W.2d 429 (Ky.1980)(consumer expectation or knowledge is just one factor to be considered by a jury in determining whether a product is unreasonably dangerous. [   ]); Knitz v. Minster Machine Co., [432 N.E.2d 814 (Ohio 1982)](product is of defective design "if (1) it is more dangerous than an ordinary consumer would expect when used in an intended or reasonably foreseeable manner, or (2) if the benefits of the challenged design do not outweigh the risk inherent in such design." [   ]).

Other states have rejected the consumer expectation test. Prentis v. Yale Mfg. Co., [365 N.W.2d 176 (Mich.1984)]("[W]e adopt, forthrightly, a pure negligence, risk utility test in products liability actions against manufacturers of products, where liability is predicated upon defective design." [   ]); Turner v. General Motors Corp., 584 S.W.2d 844 (Tex.1979)(risk-utility test will be applied "when the considerations of utility and risk are present in the state of the evidence." [   ]).

III.

. . .

The cases discussed demonstrate that states have taken a variety of approaches to resolve this question. Because of the nature of the product here, I believe the appropriate test is the consumer contemplation or consumer expectation test. The facts presented in this case differ from cases which involve the defective condition of products such as automobile brakes, prescription drugs, and gas tanks. With those types of products, the ordinary consumer is not capable of assessing the danger of the product. On the other hand, an ordinary consumer is necessarily aware that motorcycles can be dangerous. The plaintiff had the choice to purchase other motorcycles by other manufacturers which carried additional safety features, and instead elected to purchase this particular motorcycle and ride it without leg protection devices. The conclusion follows that the trial court's ruling and the court of appeals' decision were correct.

. . .

I also believe the majority incorrectly relies on [*Ortho*]. I believe the risk benefit test cited by the majority and applied in *Ortho* is an appropriate test for products such as drugs, because their danger "is defined primarily by technical, scientific information," and because some drugs are unavoidably unsafe in some respect. [ ] A consumer of drugs cannot realistically be expected to foresee dangers in prescribed drugs which even scientists find to be complex and unpredictable. On the other hand, the purchaser of a motorcycle knows that the purchase and use of "an economical, open-air, maneuverable form of transportation," [ ], presents the risk of accidents and resulting injuries due to the open-air nature of the motorcycle.

Because I believe that the correct test under facts such as these is the consumer contemplation test, I would affirm the court of appeals' decision. Accordingly, I respectfully dissent.

I am authorized to state that JUSTICE ERICKSON and JUSTICE ROVIRA join in this dissent.

Notes and Questions

1. On the crashworthiness issue, what is the argument for applying the doctrine in the case of automobiles? Do these considerations justify extending it to motorcycles? – yes

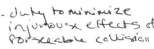

duty to minimize injurious effects of forseeable collision

2. Is it justifiable to use the risk-utility test when the danger is as "open and obvious" as it was in this case? If a state uses the consumer expectation test can the victim ever win a claim based on defective design when hurt by a danger that was "open and obvious"? In Luque v. McLean, 501 P.2d 1163 (Cal.1972), defendant manufactured a power lawnmower that cut grass with a single revolving blade and ejected it through an open, unprotected hole in the front. Printed next to the hole was the word "caution." While mowing, plaintiff stepped in front of the running mower to remove a carton from its path. He slipped on wet grass and, as he fell backward, his hand slid into the unguarded hole and was mangled by the rotary blade spinning at 100 revolutions per second. How might this case be analyzed under the two opinions in *Camacho*?

3. What is the relevance of the discussion in footnote 8 about plaintiff's motivations in buying the model he chose? Courts that use the consumer expectation test in this type of motorcycle case reject plaintiffs' claims in comparable fact situations. See, e.g., Kutzler v. AMF Harley–Davidson, 550 N.E.2d 1236 (Ill.App.), appeal denied 555 N.E.2d 377 (Ill. 1990).

4. The court states that "the record contains some evidence to support the conclusion that Honda could have provided crash bars at an acceptable cost without impairing the motorcycle's utility or substantially altering its nature." If the motorcycle cost $10,000, how much could the crash bars cost and still be an "acceptable cost"? What is the significance of the fact that other manufacturers offered the crash bars? Is it relevant that they offered it as optional equipment?

5. Under the risk-utility test how do the *Barker* factors, p. 558, supra, differ from the seven-factor test used in *Camacho*?

6. Can you imagine a situation in which the absence of leg guards would cause injury to a bystander? If so, should the dissent analyze the case differently? That is, should the consumer expectation test apply to cases in which the harm is suffered not by the buyer or user but by a stranger? Would this apply to a power lawnmower that cast rocks on passersby?

Some courts have focused on the victim. E.g., Ewen v. McLean Trucking Co., 706 P.2d 929 (Or.1985) (consumer expectation test inapplicable where pedestrian is hit by truck claimed to have blind spot when the truck backs up). Other courts, however, focus on the expectations of the buyer or user. Gaines–Tabb v. ICI Explosives, USA, Inc., 160 F.3d 613 (10th Cir.

1998), arose out of the bombing of the federal building in Oklahoma City. The court held that since the ordinary consumers, the farmers who bought ammonium nitrate to use as fertilizer, knew of its explosive dangers, the manufacturer could not be held liable to bombing victims under the state's consumer expectation test. See also Tabieros v. Clark Equipment Co., 944 P.2d 1279 (Haw.1997), in which plaintiff was hurt by a co-worker who backed into him due to a blind spot in the vehicle. The court held that since the blind spot was an open and obvious danger known to everyone working in the area, the plaintiff was barred under the consumer expectation test. (Would the analysis change if the truck had backed into a stranger outside of the work area while being taken for servicing?)

7. In the Products Restatement, the only explicit exception to risk-utility analysis applies in food cases, and draws largely on cases involving customers who choke on chicken bones in chicken salad or on fish bones in chowder. Though plaintiffs in these cases might have claimed a manufacturing defect, it was difficult to tell if this was an aberration from a norm or an intrinsic (albeit unwanted) part of a designed dish. Section 7 provides that "a harm-causing ingredient of the food product constitutes a defect if a reasonable consumer would not expect the food product to contain that ingredient."

8. The significance of the choice between the tests is suggested by Hernandez v. Tokai Corp., 2 S.W.3d 251 (Tex.1999), involving a child who was burned after a sibling gained access to a disposable lighter and started a fire:

> Tokai argues that the weight of authority in other jurisdictions is to reject disposable lighter design-defect claims as a matter of law. This is true, but there is more to it. Courts in jurisdictions that employ a consumer-expectation test for determining defect have mostly held that disposable lighters without childproof features are not defectively designed because they function in the manner expected by the intended adult consumers. But courts in jurisdictions employing a risk-utility analysis have mostly concluded that the determinative considerations are usually matters for the jury. Courts in risk-utility jurisdictions that have rejected disposable lighter design-defect claims as a matter of law have reasoned that the test for liability should apply differently to "simple tools" like disposable lighters.

Does the lighter example suggest that one test is preferable to the other in lighter cases? In all cases?   risk utility

9. Did "strict liability" play a role in the decision in either *Soule* or *Camacho?* Would either be decided differently under a negligence analysis? Recall that section 2b of the Products Restatement, p. 556, supra, does not use either conceptual label.

10. One criticism leveled at case-by-case risk-utility analysis is that it denies products manufacturers the guidance of uniform standards. That concern is discussed in Dawson v. Chrysler Corp., 630 F.2d 950 (3d Cir.1980), cert. denied 450 U.S. 959 (1981). The court, applying New Jersey law, upheld a judgment for $2 million for a driver who was crushed after his car skidded sideways into a pole and wrapped around it. Evidence showed that using a firmer side frame would have added 200–250 pounds to the weight of the car and $300 to the cost. The court went on to point out that:

> The result of such arrangement is that while the jury found Chrysler liable for not producing a rigid enough vehicular frame, a factfinder in another case might well hold the manufacturer liable for producing a frame that is too rigid. Yet, as pointed out at trial, in certain types of accidents—head-on collisions—it is desirable to have a car designed to collapse upon impact because the deformation would absorb much of the shock of the collision, and divert the force of deceleration away from the vehicle's passengers. In effect, this permits individual juries applying varying laws in different jurisdictions to set nationwide automobile safety standards and to impose on automobile manufacturers conflicting requirements. It would be difficult for members of the industry to alter their design and production behavior in response to jury verdicts in such cases, because their response might well be at variance with what some other jury decides is a defective design. Under these circumstances, the law imposes on the industry the responsibility of insuring vast numbers of persons involved in automobile accidents.

conflicting standards

> Equally serious is the impact on other national social and economic goals of the existing case-by-case system of establishing automobile safety requirements. As we have become more dependent on foreign sources of energy, and as the price of that energy has increased, the attention of the federal government has been drawn to a search to find alternative supplies and the means of conserving energy. More recently, the domestic automobile industry has been struggling to compete with foreign manufacturers which have stressed smaller, more fuel-efficient cars. Yet, during this same period, Congress has permitted a system of regulation by ad hoc adjudications under which a jury can hold an automobile manufacturer culpable for not producing a car that is considerably heavier, and likely to have less fuel efficiency.

prob. for auto industry

The court concluded that letting individual juries impose liability for defective designs was neither "fair nor efficient." Since Congress had permitted the common law to continue, and "because Congress is the body best suited to evaluate and, if appropriate, to change that system, we decline today to do anything in this regard except to bring the problem to the attention of the legislative branch."

D.   SAFETY INSTRUCTIONS AND WARNINGS

After having considered the design of the product, we turn to the search for defects in the words—instructions and warnings—that accompany the product whether on the package, on the product or in an insert that comes with the product. These words may reduce risk by instructing users in how to obtain the benefits from the product's intended use and by alerting users to the dangers of using the product in ways unintended by the manufacturer. Words may also alert potential buyers and users to irreducible dangers in the product, dangers that cannot be reasonably reduced by the manufacturer nor avoided by consumers no matter how careful they may be. Warnings of side effects of pharmaceuticals are perhaps the most common examples of the latter. Keep these differing roles of words in mind throughout this section.

A threshold issue: Common knowledge and the duty to warn. The first issue in these cases is whether any words at all are needed to address the risk in question. In Brown Forman Corp. v. Brune, 893 S.W.2d 640 (Tex.App.1994), the court held that no notice was required on a bottle of tequila to warn against the dangers of drinking a large quantity in a short period of time. The underage plaintiff, already intoxicated from other drinking, died after drinking unmixed tequila from a glass, and then the bottle, "heavily and rapidly." The dangers were apparent even to an 18-year-old person. Nor would a warning have averted what happened. Is this a harder case than one based on the lack of warning that a knife was sharp?

Nor is there a duty to warn about the dangers of riding unrestrained in the cargo bed of a pickup truck. In Maneely v. General Motors Corp., 108 F.3d 1176 (9th Cir.1997), the court, using California law, noted the pervasiveness of "buckle-up" campaigns and the "manifest danger" of "being ejected from the vehicle during a crash or being slammed against an unforgiving hard surface of the vehicle itself." From all of this "we conclude that the dangers of riding unrestrained in a moving motor vehicle have become common knowledge and are firmly engraved upon the public consciousness." (As to design defect, the consumer expectation test would yield the same analysis. The truck passed risk-utility analysis because the design outweighed its dangers as a matter of law: to redesign a pickup truck to provide protective seats "and occupant packaging" would "transform the cargo-hauling pickup truck into just another passenger-carrying vehicle and would eliminate its utility in carrying cargo.")

In Emery v. Federated Foods, Inc., 863 P.2d 426 (Mont.1993), 2½-year-old Chad choked on marshmallows. The court held, 5–2, that a jury should decide whether it was common knowledge that young children were at risk in eating marshmallows because marshmallows expand "when they are soaked with liquid secretions that are present in the breathing tubes of the lungs." Further, an "aspirated marshmallow fragment might not be reachable with a finger and could be difficult to dislodge with a Heimlich maneuver."

We turn now to cases in which defendant does not contest the need for a warning. The issue, rather, is the adequacy of the warning from a variety of perspectives.

Hood v. Ryobi America Corporation
United States Court of Appeals, Fourth Circuit, 1999.
181 F.3d 608.

Before WILKINSON, CHIEF JUDGE, and WIDENER and KING, CIRCUIT JUDGES.
WILKINSON, CHIEF JUDGE.

. . .

Hood purchased a Ryobi TS–254 miter saw in Westminster, Maryland on February 25, 1995, for the purpose of performing home repairs. The saw was fully assembled at the time of purchase. It had a ten-inch diameter blade mounted on a rotating spindle controlled by a finger trigger on a handle near the top of the blade. To operate the saw, the consumer would use that handle to lower the blade through the material being cut.

Two blade guards shielded nearly the entire saw blade. A large metal guard, fixed to the frame of the saw, surrounded the upper half of the blade. A transparent plastic lower guard covered the rest of the blade and retracted into the upper guard as the saw came into contact with the work piece.

A number of warnings in the operator's manual and affixed to the saw itself stated that the user should operate the saw only with the blade guards in place. For example, the owner's manual declared that the user should "KEEP GUARDS IN PLACE" and warned: "ALWAYS USE THE SAW BLADE GUARD. Never operate the machine with the guard removed"; "NEVER operate this saw without all guards in place and in good operating condition"; and "WARNING: TO PREVENT POSSIBLE SERIOUS PERSONAL INJURY, NEVER PERFORM ANY CUTTING OPERATION WITH THE UPPER OR LOWER BLADE GUARD REMOVED." The saw itself carried several decals stating "DANGER: DO NOT REMOVE ANY GUARD. USE OF SAW WITHOUT THIS GUARD WILL RESULT IN SERIOUS INJURY"; "OPERATE ONLY WITH GUARDS IN PLACE"; and "WARNING . . . DO NOT operate saw without the upper and lower guards in place."

The day after his purchase, Hood began working with the saw in his driveway. While attempting to cut a piece of wood approximately four inches in height Hood found that the blade guards prevented the saw blade from passing completely through the piece. Disregarding the manufacturer's warnings, Hood decided to remove the blade guards from the saw. Hood first detached the saw blade from its spindle. He then unscrewed the four screws that held the blade guard assembly to the frame of the saw. Finally, he replaced the blade onto the bare spindle and completed his cut.

Rather than replacing the blade guards, Hood continued to work with the saw blade exposed. He worked in this fashion for about twenty minutes longer when, in the middle of another cut, the spinning saw blade flew off the saw and back toward Hood. The blade partially amputated his left thumb and lacerated his right leg.

Hood admits that he read the owner's manual and most of the warning labels on the saw before he began his work. He claims, however, that he believed the blade guards were intended solely to prevent a user's clothing or fingers from coming into contact with the saw blade. He contends that he was unaware that removing the blade guards would permit the spinning blade to detach from the saw. But Ryobi, he claims, was aware of that possibility. In fact, another customer had sued Ryobi after suffering a similar accident in the mid-1980s.

[In Hood's diversity case he] raised claims of failure to warn and defective design under several theories of liability. On cross-motions for summary judgment the district court entered judgment for the defendants on all claims, finding that in the face of adequate warnings Hood had altered the saw and caused his own injury. [   ] Hood appeals.

II.

A manufacturer may be liable for placing a product on the market that bears inadequate instructions and warnings or that is defective in design. Moran v. Fabergé, Inc., [332 A.2d 11 (Md.1975)]; [   ]. Hood asserts that Ryobi failed adequately to warn of the dangers of using the saw without the blade guards in place. Hood also contends that the design of the saw was defective. We disagree on both counts.[1]

A.

Hood first complains that the warnings he received were insufficiently specific. Hood admits that Ryobi provided several clear and conspicuous warnings not to operate the saw without the blade guards. He contends, however, that the warnings affixed to the product and displayed in the operator's manual were inadequate to alert him to the dangers of doing so. In addition to Ryobi's directive "never" to operate a guardless saw, Hood would require the company to inform of the actual consequences of such conduct. Specifically, Hood contends that an adequate warning would have explained that removing the guards would lead to blade detachment.

We disagree. Maryland does not require an encyclopedic warning. Instead, "a warning need only be one that is reasonable under the circumstances." Levin v. Walter Kidde & Co., [248 A.2d 151 (Md.1968)]. A clear and specific warning will normally be sufficient—"the manufacturer need not warn of every mishap or source of injury that the mind can imagine flowing from the product." [   ]; see *Levin*, [   ] (declining to require warning of the danger that a cracked syphon bottle might explode and holding "never use cracked bottle" to be adequate as a matter of law). In deciding whether a warning is adequate, Maryland law asks whether the benefits of a more detailed warning outweigh the costs of requiring the change. [*Moran*].

Hood assumes that the cost of a more detailed warning label is minimal in this case, and he claims that such a warning would have prevented his injury. But the price of more detailed warnings is greater than their additional printing fees alone. Some commentators have observed that the proliferation of label detail threatens to undermine the effectiveness of warnings altogether. See James A. Henderson, Jr. & Aaron

---

1. Hood raises these claims under three theories of recovery: strict liability, negligence, and breach of warranty. The principles of Maryland law governing these three theories, at least as relevant to this case, are virtually identical.

D. Twerski, Doctrinal Collapse in Products Liability: The Empty Shell of Failure to Warn, 65 N.Y.U. L.Rev. 265, 296–97 (1990). As manufacturers append line after line onto product labels in the quest for the best possible warning, it is easy to lose sight of the label's communicative value as a whole. Well-meaning attempts to warn of every possible accident lead over time to voluminous yet impenetrable labels—too prolix to read and too technical to understand.

By contrast, Ryobi's warnings are clear and unequivocal. Three labels on the saw itself and at least four warnings in the owner's manual direct the user not to operate the saw with the blade guards removed. Two declare that "serious injury" could result from doing so. This is not a case where the manufacturer has failed to include any warnings at all with its product. [ ] Ryobi provided warnings sufficient to apprise the ordinary consumer that it is unsafe to operate a guardless saw—warnings which, if followed, would have prevented the injury in this case.

It is apparent, moreover, that the vast majority of consumers do not detach this critical safety feature before using this type of saw. Indeed, although Ryobi claims to have sold thousands of these saws, Hood has identified only one fifteen-year-old incident similar to his. Hood has thus not shown that these clear, unmistakable, and prominent warnings are insufficient to accomplish their purpose. Nor can he prove that increased label clutter would bring any net societal benefit. We hold that the warnings Ryobi provided are adequate as a matter of law.

[The court then rejected plaintiff's claim based on design defect, discussed in the notes that follow.]

Warned never to operate his miter saw without the blade guards in place, Hood nonetheless chose to detach those guards and run the saw in a disassembled condition. We hold that Ryobi is not liable for Hood's resulting injuries under any of the theories of recovery raised here. The judgment of the district court is therefore affirmed.

Notes and Questions

1. *Adequacy.* What are the strongest arguments for inadequacy in *Hood*? What would it take to create a jury question here? Several cases have developed criteria for determining the adequacy of a warning. Consider this summary from Pittman v. Upjohn Co., 890 S.W.2d 425 (Tenn.1994):

> A reasonable warning not only conveys a fair indication of the dangers involved, but also warns with the degree of intensity required by the nature of the risk. [ ] Among the criteria for determining the adequacy of a warning are: 1. the warning must adequately indicate the scope of the danger; 2. the warning must reasonably communicate the extent or seriousness of the harm that could result from misuse of the drug; 3. the physical aspects of the warning must be adequate to alert a reasonably prudent person to the danger; 4. a simple directive warning may be inadequate when it fails to indicate the consequences

that might result from failure to follow it and, . . . 5. the means to convey the warning must be adequate. [ ]

Are these appropriate factors? How does the warning in *Hood* fare under them?

The adequacy of a warning may be a question even where the plaintiff did not read the warning that was given. In Johnson v. Johnson Chemical Co., 588 N.Y.S.2d 607 (App.1992), plaintiff was hurt when an anti-roach fogger exploded while plaintiff was using it in the kitchen—with the pilot light on the stove still lit, despite a warning to shut off pilot lights among other possible sources of flame. When defendant argued that the adequacy of the warning was irrelevant when the warning was not read, the court responded:

> This argument loses its persuasive force, however, once it is understood that the intensity of the language used in the text of a warning is only one of the factors to be considered in deciding whether such warning is adequate. A second factor to be considered is the prominence with which such language is displayed. [ ] For example, the warning "harmful if swallowed" is less intense than the warning, "swallowing will result in death"; however, the former, less intense warning, when displayed prominently in block letters on the front label of a product, may be ultimately more effective than the latter, more intense warning, when [the latter is] displayed unobtrusively in small letters in the middle of a 10-page package insert [ ]. A consumer such as Ms. Kono who, by her own admission, tends to ignore one sort of label, might pay heed to a different, more prominent or more dramatic label.

Although the question of adequacy has generally been held to be a question of fact, courts recognize that in clear cases it may become one of law. See Martin v. Hacker, 628 N.E.2d 1308 (N.Y.1993), involving a warning accompanying the drug reserpine. The court reviewed the text at length and, using the same factors listed in *Pittman*, supra, found no question for a jury. Some courts treat the issue as one of law in the first instance on the ground that the text of the warning is before the court and it can make that decision. See, e.g., Mackowick v. Westinghouse Electric Corp., 575 A.2d 100 (Pa.1990).

2. *Causation and the "heeding presumption."* Several recent cases have invoked a "heeding presumption"—requiring the party responsible for the inadequate warning to show that the user would not have heeded an adequate warning. See Coffman v. Keene Corp., 628 A.2d 710 (N.J.1993), in which the defendant argued that the presumption could not be justified empirically because "it is nearly impossible to go through a day without consciously ignoring warnings designed to protect health and safety." The court accepted that assertion but concluded that the presumption was justified because it would operate as a "powerful incentive" to manufacturers. If they omitted needed warnings they could no longer argue that the plaintiff might not have heeded one even if it had been there. A possible subject for "speculation" was removed from the jury's consideration.

Compare General Motors Corp. v. Saenz, 873 S.W.2d 353 (Tex.1993), in which the court rejected a heeding presumption where plaintiffs claimed that they had not been adequately warned about the dangers of overloading a truck. Although warnings to that effect were placed in the owner's manual and in the door jamb, plaintiffs argued that the wording was inadequate. The court found no reason to conclude that if the wording had been better the accident would not have happened.

3. *Safety instructions.* Words that can help make the product safer might include statements that certain uses should be avoided or more specific directions about how to use or apply a product. Consider the following examples.

a. In *Moran v. Fabergé, Inc.*, cited in *Hood*, two teenagers decided to try to scent a candle by pouring cologne on it somewhat below the flame. As one did this, the cologne, containing 82% alcohol, instantly ignited causing serious burns to the other teenager. After the jury found defendant negligent for failing to warn of the cologne's flammability, the trial judge granted judgment n.o.v. The appellate court reinstated the verdict. Although this particular accident was unforeseeable, other similar accidents, such as a woman accidentally spilling the cologne onto a lighted candle, might warrant a warning. The "cost of giving an adequate warning is usually so minimal, amounting only to the expense of adding some more printing to a label, that this balancing process will almost always weigh in favor of an obligation to warn of latent dangers, if the manufacturer is otherwise required to do so." Is it relevant that the cologne had not caused a known accident in 27 years? What might the safety directions say? Might the defendant also need to warn against ingesting? Against keeping it within reach of infants? Against not cleaning it up after it spills? Can *Hood* be reconciled with *Moran*?

b. Even the most explicit language may not suffice. See Campos v. Firestone Tire & Rubber Co., 485 A.2d 305 (N.J.1984), suggesting that a jury might find that pictorial messages were required if the product was likely to be used by migrant workers who did not speak English.

c. In Ragans v. Miriam Collins–Palm Beach Laboratories Co., 681 So.2d 1173 (Fla.App.1996), plaintiff hairstylist was using a permanent wave kit that she had used 30–50 times before. It contained wave lotion in a clear bottle and neutralizer in a white plastic bottle. The activator came in a tube that said "ADD TO CLEAR BOTTLE ONLY." The instructions also stated that adding the activator "to other than wave lotion can cause serious injury." Plaintiff inadvertently poured a few drops of activator into the neutralizer bottle. "The resulting mixture reacted explosively and shot out of the neutralizer bottle with enough force to hit the ceiling" and cause severe chemical burns and permanent facial injuries. The court concluded that a jury question was presented because the words failed to warn of the dangerous consequences of not following the five-word direction. Neither did a leaflet inside the box which, in step number 5, again simply warned of "serious injury." Is it relevant that plaintiff argued that she understood the instructions to mean that an improper mixture could damage a customer's scalp or hair?

4. Why does the court reject plaintiff's argument that Ryobi should have told him about the precise danger of removing the guard? If a user thinks that a warning is addressed to getting fingers or clothing caught in the machine, and thinks correctly that such a peril can be avoided, and Ryobi knows another (not widely known) reason for keeping the guard on, why shouldn't they have to tell the user about that peril as well? *Hood* suggests that information has costs as well as benefits. Consider Cotton v. Buckeye Gas Prods. Co., 840 F.2d 935 (D.C.Cir.1988), in which plaintiff was hurt when propane tanks on the job site exploded. He argued that the labels were inadequate. In the course of rejecting the claims, the court observed:

[handwritten: Shorter warns. are more effective bc of consumer attention span] The primary cost [of added warning] is, in fact, the increase in time and effort required for the user to grasp the message. The inclusion of each extra item dilutes the punch of every other item. Given short attention spans, items crowd each other out; they get lost in fine print. . . .

[Plaintiff] discounts altogether the warnings in the pamphlet, without even considering what the canister warning would have looked like if Buckeye had supplemented it not only with the special items he is personally interested in—in hindsight—but also with all other equally valuable items (i.e., "equally" in terms of the scope and probability of the danger likely to be averted and the incremental impact of the information on user conduct). If every foreseeable possibility must be covered, "[T]he list of foolish practices warned against would be so long, it would fill a volume." [ ]

Is this analysis relevant to Mr. Hood's claim?

5. *The addressee.* An important question in judging the need for, and adequacy of, warnings is to whom they are addressed. The normal rule is that they must reach the person who is likely to use the product. Sometimes, though, that may not be feasible, as where children may be users. One cluster of cases involves the claim that disposable cigarette lighters are dangerous because they are likely to fall into the hands of very young children who could easily get them to work. In addition to attacks on the design, claims were also made that a warning was needed. Compare Bean v. BIC Corp., 597 So.2d 1350 (Ala.1992)(jury question whether warnings on package and lighter were adequate) with Kirk v. Hanes Corp., 16 F.3d 705 (6th Cir.1994)(Michigan law imposes no duty to warn since danger of lighter is obvious to adult buyers). Recall the *Tokai* case, p. 580, supra and note 8, infra.

6. *Interplay of design and warning.* When, if ever, can the supplier choose to give a safety instruction instead of making the intrinsic product safer? Assume that Honda, rejecting the advice of its marketing department, had placed in large print on every item that lacked leg guards the following conspicuous statement: "WARNING. THIS PRODUCT CON-

TAINS NO LEG GUARDS. ANY ACCIDENT IS LIKELY TO CAUSE THE OCCUPANT SERIOUS LEG INJURIES.'' Might this have affected the result in *Camacho*? Would it have mattered whether the leg guards could have been added for a cost that was lower than the expected benefits?

States that hold that products with open and obvious dangers cannot be defective would follow the dissent in *Camacho* and deny liability using either that rule itself or a consumer expectation test. For a discussion of events that led a state to overturn its "open and obvious" rule in a motorcycle leg guard case, see Satcher v. Honda Motor Co., 52 F.3d 1311 (5th Cir.1995)(Mississippi law).

7. In the design part of its case, the *Hood* court understood plaintiff to be asserting that "Ryobi should have designed its saw to operate equally well with the guards in place or removed." The court responded that Maryland imposed "no duty to predict that a consumer will violate clear, easily understandable safety warnings such as those Ryobi included with this product." Assume that a power lawnmower has a large hole over the place where the blades turn and that it could be covered by a safety screen with minimal impairment of performance at the cost of 75 cents. Can you frame a warning clear enough to protect the manufacturer against liability? The *Hood* court adverted to that question in the following passage on the link between design and warning:

> We are all afflicted with lapses of attention; warnings aimed simply at avoiding consumer carelessness should not absolve a manufacturer of the duty to design reasonable safeguards for its products. [ ] See [Products Restatement] cmt. *l*, illus. 14 (when warning could not eliminate the possibility of accidental contact with a dangerous shear point, decal declaring "keep hands and feet away" does not bar a design defect claim).
>
> The Maryland courts have already made clear, however, that warnings will not inevitably defeat liability for a product's defective design. [ ] (such warnings as "never leave tool running unattended" and "do not place fingers or hands in the path of the saw blade" are too vague to defeat manufacturer's liability for failing to include blade guards on its saws). Maryland has thus sought to encourage manufacturers to rid their products of traps for the unwary, while declining to hold them responsible for affirmative consumer misuse.

Why were the warnings in *Hood* not "too vague"? What kind of a warning could "eliminate the possibility of accidental contact with a dangerous shear point"?

8. In *Tokai*, p. 580, supra, involving disposable cigarette lighters, the opinion noted that a "product intended for adults need not be designed to be safe for children solely because it is possible for the product to come into a child's hands. . . . The risk that adults, for whose use the products were intended, will allow children access to them, resulting in harm, must be balanced against the products' utility to their intended users." If the product design is deemed appropriate for adults, might a warning still be needed?

The court expressed concern lest liability overly restrict consumer choice. It noted that the Products Restatement had stated that small cars were not defective because they were not as crashworthy as large cars. The drafters had also stated that buyers might prefer a bullet-proof vest that had only front-and-back protection but was more flexible and cheaper than a wrap-around model that fully covered the upper body. Do these examples involve warning issues? The court continued:

> Consumers are entitled to consider the risks and benefits of the different designs and choose among them. The briefs in this case suggest other examples: a chemistry set for teenagers that includes a Bunsen burner and chemicals that most younger children should not be allowed to use; a high-power nail gun that should be used only by experienced carpenters; and a sailboat designed for speed rather than stability that is safe only for more experienced sailors. A chemistry set designed for the ordinary teenager is not unreasonably dangerous solely because it is possible that a younger sibling could get into it and harm himself or others. Products liability law does not force experienced carpenters to use only nail guns that are safe for the garage workshop. A sailboat pilot may choose between speed and stability. To make such products safe for the least apt, and unintended, user would hold other users hostage to the lowest common denominator.

If one accepts this line of reasoning for the design defect claim, does it have implications for the warning question?

9. As notes 6, 7 and 8 have indicated, questions of design and warning often overlap. Recall *O'Brien v. Muskin*, p. 570 supra. Recall also the discussion in the Products Restatement that the way a product is portrayed or marketed is relevant to risk-utility analysis, p. 567, supra. We turn now to a more explicit discussion of the interplay between the two.

Although most courts have separated the product's design from the words accompanying the product, that separation has recently begun to be challenged. In Hansen v. Sunnyside Products, Inc., 65 Cal.Rptr.2d 266 (App. 1997), plaintiff was injured when defendant's household cleanser, which contained hydrofluoric acid, came through a tiny hole in a glove she was wearing to protect against contact with the cleanser. The defendant sought to present evidence about the warnings on the package in an effort to show that the warnings had prevented harm in the past. The court agreed that this was permissible since it might help the jury to decide the design question: "The bottom-line issue is whether the product is likely to cause harm. Warnings are appropriately considered in that determination." The two theories differ because "whereas an adequate warning will avoid liability on a failure to warn theory, it is but one factor to be weighed in the balance in a design defect case." Finally:

We do not think that the risk to the consumer of the design of many household products can be rationally evaluated without considering the product's warnings. Thus, for example, what is the risk of the design of a power saw, or other power tools or equipment, without considering the product's directions and warnings? We dare say that the risk would be astronomically, and irrationally high. The same could be said about common garden pesticides, or even the household microwave oven. In our view, were we to ask jurors to evaluate the risks of the design of many household products without considering their directions or warnings, the practical result would be the withdrawal from the market of many useful products that are dangerous in the abstract but safe when used as directed.

Compare Uniroyal Goodrich Tire Co. v. Martinez, 977 S.W.2d 328 (Tex.1998), cert. denied 526 U.S. 1040 (1999), involving a tire that exploded while being mounted on the wrong-sized rim. The court, 5–4, held that if there was a safer way to make a product, the manufacturer could be held liable even though the injury could have been avoided if the user had followed the warnings. The dissenters noted that § 2, comment *f*, of the Products Restatement, citing *Hansen*, included among the factors to be considered in risk-utility analysis "the nature and strength of consumer expectations regarding the product, including expectations arising from product portrayal and marketing." The dissenters asserted that another example of the role of warnings in design cases was the aerosol can: "Such cans are not defective merely because they could be redesigned so as not to explode if punctured or incinerated. A warning against such misuse ought to be sufficient." Is that sound? Is it consistent with the discussion of warning in *Hood*?

10. *Misuse.* As *Camacho* and *Hood* suggest, injuries often result from "unintended" uses of the product. As these cases and *Soule* make clear, this is not a complete defense if the "misuse" or "unintended use" was one that was reasonably foreseeable. At its simplest, a manufacturer of screwdrivers is expected to know that its product is widely used to pry open the lids of tins and other containers. So, too, a supplier of chairs must anticipate that many people use them to stand on instead of using ladders. How wide a range of uses must suppliers anticipate? Consider these examples and whether a warning would have mattered.

a.   In Binakonsky v. Ford Motor Co., 133 F.3d 281 (4th Cir.1998), plaintiff drunk driver was killed when he ran into a tree at 40–47 mph. His death was attributable to a fire caused by defendant's use of plastic pipes in the car's fuel system. The court, 2–1, held that under Maryland law the design defect claim should be submitted to the jury because the defendant must anticipate a variety of ways in which their cars may hit trees or be involved in other high-speed collisions. The dissent disagreed that a manufacturer should be forced to worry about this type of crash.

b.   Sometimes the question of defect is affected by the marketing scheme. In Lugo v. LJN Toys, Ltd., 552 N.E.2d 162 (N.Y.1990), a playmate threw a detachable part of a doll made by defendant into the eye of plaintiff. The claim was that the doll was a replica of a well-known television cartoon character, Voltron, who overcame enemies by hurling his shield at them. The detachable part of the doll that was thrown was variously described as a "shield," "blade," or "star."

The court held that summary judgment was properly denied. Product suppliers had to anticipate uses that were "unintended but reasonably foreseeable." Here, plaintiff "has submitted expert evidence that, based upon customs and standards in the toy safety community, the part was defective because detachable from the doll and that throwing it was foreseeable because of the extensive television exposure in which Voltron did so."

c. Sometimes the notions of misuse and proximate cause are closely connected. In Briscoe v. Amazing Products, Inc., 23 S.W.3d 228 (Ky.App. 2000), a high school student, knowing the danger of the product, threw drain cleaner at her rival. The court held that the defendants in the product chain were not required to anticipate that use of the product. See also Port Authority of New York and New Jersey v. Arcadian Corp., 189 F.3d 305 (3d Cir.1999), holding that fertilizer products used in making the bomb that was used to trigger a terrorist blast at the World Trade Center were not defective. The misuse here was "not objectively foreseeable." No jury "could conclude that one accidental explosion 50 years ago [in Texas City], one terrorist act in this country almost 30 years ago [at the University of Wisconsin], and scattered terrorist incidents throughout the world over the course of the last 30 years would make an incident like [this bombing] anything more than a remote or theoretical possibility." (The court also concluded that proximate cause was lacking.) What if the drain cleaner and the fertilizer could be made as effectively and as cheaply in a safe version?

Are there common themes among all these different claims of misuse?

11. As discussed in note 5, ordinarily warnings must reach the ultimate user who is most affected by the product and who is expected to use the instructions or warnings to avoid harm. That note suggested that with products aimed at children or that might harm children the appropriate addressee is the parent or guardian. The following case suggests another important exception to the supplier's obligation to convey needed warnings to the user.

Edwards v. Basel Pharmaceuticals
Supreme Court of Oklahoma, 1997.
933 P.2d 298.

[The federal court of appeals certified to the state supreme court the question of the scope the state gives to the "learned intermediary" rule.]

SUMMERS, VICE CHIEF JUSTICE:

The facts provided in the Order of Certification are these. Alpha Edwards brought a wrongful death action for the death of her husband. He died of a nicotine-induced heart attack as a result of smoking cigarettes while wearing two Habitrol nicotine patches. Habitrol is manufactured by Basel Pharmaceuticals. Plaintiff's theory of liability was that the warnings given in conjunction with the Habitrol patches were inadequate to warn her husband of the fatal risk associated with smoking and overuse of the product. A relatively thorough warning was given to physicians providing the Habitrol patch, but the insert provided for the user did not mention the possibility of a fatal or cardiac related reaction to a nicotine overdose, cautioning that an "overdose might cause you to faint."

The pamphlet provided to Dr. Howard and other physicians prescribing the patch said:

> Prostration, hypotension and respiratory failure may ensue with large overdoses. Lethal doses produce convulsions quickly and death follows as a result of peripheral or central respiratory paralysis or, less frequently, cardiac failure.

[The court took it "as fact" that defendant complied with the FDA's mandate that specific warnings reach the ultimate consumer.]

Basel contends that the "learned intermediary doctrine" bars liability, because the prescribing physicians were given complete warnings regarding the use of the patches. Basel concedes that consumer warnings were required by the FDA, but argues that by complying with those FDA warning requirements the case again is controlled by the learned intermediary doctrine, with its attendant shield affording protection to the manufacturer. Mrs. Edwards disagrees, stating that the warnings given to her late husband were inadequate, regardless of whether FDA requirements were met.

Our products liability law generally requires a manufacturer to warn consumers of danger associated with the use of its product to the extent the manufacturer knew or should have known of the danger. [   ] Certain products, prescription drugs among them, are incapable of being made safe, but are of benefit to the public despite the risk. Their beneficial dissemination depends on adequate warnings . . . . The user must be adequately warned. [   ]

There is, however, an exception known as the "learned intermediary doctrine", which Oklahoma has recognized as applicable in prescription drug cases, [   ], and prosthetic implant cases, [   ]. The doctrine operates as an exception to the manufacturer's duty to warn the ultimate consumer, and shields manufacturers of prescription drugs from liability if the manufacturer adequately warns the prescribing physicians of the dangers of the drug. [   ] The reasoning behind this rule is that the doctor acts as a learned intermediary between the patient and the prescription drug manufacturer by assessing the medical risks in light of the patient's needs. [   ]

[handwritten margin note: an exception to the "learned intermediary doctrine" is giving doctors warning]

> Where a product is available only on prescription or through the services of a physician, the physician acts as a "learned intermediary" between the manufacturer or seller and the patient. It is his duty to inform himself of the qualities and characteristics of those products

which he prescribes for or administers to or uses on his patients, and to exercise independent judgment, taking into account his knowledge of the patient as well as the product. The patient is expected to and, it can be presumed, does place primary reliance upon that judgment. The physician decides what facts should be told to the patient. Thus, if the product is properly labeled and carries the necessary instructions and warnings to fully apprise the physician of the proper procedures for use and the dangers involved, the manufacturer may reasonably assume that the physician will exercise the informed judgment thereby gained in conjunction with his own independent learning, in the best interest of the patient.

Wooderson v. Ortho Pharmaceutical Corp., [681 P.2d 1038, 1052 (Kan.), cert. denied 469 U.S. 965 (1984)]. The doctrine extends to prescription drugs because, unlike over the counter medications, the patient may obtain the drug only through a physician's prescription, and the use of prescription drugs is generally monitored by a physician. [   ] The learned intermediary doctrine has been held applicable to prescription nicotine gum, because there was a sufficient relationship established between doctor and patient. [   ]

EXCEPTIONS TO THE LEARNED INTERMEDIARY DOCTRINE

Two exceptions have been recognized which operate to remove the manufacturer from behind the shield of the learned intermediary doctrine. The first involves mass immunizations. [   ] Mass immunizations fall outside the contemplated realm of the learned intermediary doctrine because there may be no physician-patient relationship, and the drug is not administered as a prescription drug. [   ] Under these conditions individualized attention may not be given by medical personnel in assessing the needs of the patient. The only warnings the patient may receive are those from the manufacturer. Oklahoma has adopted this exception. [   ]

The second exception, which has been adopted by several jurisdictions including Oklahoma, arises when the Food and Drug Administration mandates that a warning be given directly to the consumer. [   ] By this exception several states have held that the learned intermediary doctrine itself does not protect the manufacturer. MacDonald v. Ortho Pharmaceutical Corp., [475 N.E.2d 65 (Mass.), cert. denied 474 U.S. 920 (1985)]; [plus three federal district court cases]. But see [one Delaware case and two federal district court cases]. Most of the cases adopting this exception have dealt with contraceptives and the FDA's extensive regulation of contraceptive drugs and devices. See 21 C.F.R. § 310.501 and § 310.502 (requirements for patient and physician warnings with regard to intrauterine devices and birth control pills). However, courts have not limited the exception to this arena alone.

We see no reason that this second exception should not apply to nicotine patches available by prescription. When direct warnings to the user of a prescription drug have been mandated by a safety regulation promulgated for the protection of the user, an exception to the learned intermediary doctrine exists, and failure on the part of the manufacturer to warn the consumer can render the drug unreasonably dangerous. According to the material certified by the Federal Court, the FDA has found a need to require that prescriptions for nicotine patches be accompanied by warnings to the ultimate consumer as well as to the physician, as is required in the distribution of oral contraceptives and intrauterine devices.

[The court next rejected the defendant's contention that compliance with the FDA's requirement that it warn users should serve as a defense to plaintiff's state common law tort claim. Recall the earlier discussion of *Edwards* in the context of statutory compliance, p. 83, supra.]

Oklahoma requires that the manufacturer warn of dangers which are foreseeable and known to the manufacturer. [   ] Those warnings must be adequate to inform the user of the dangers associated with the product's use. [   ] The manufacturer is not, however, required to warn of obvious dangers. [   ]

In the present case it appears the manufacturer clearly had knowledge of the dangers associated with the Habitrol patch; it furnished detailed warnings to the prescribing physicians. However, as to the warnings the late Mr. Edwards received in his Habitrol insert, state products liability law must be applied to determine their adequacy.

CONCLUSION

We hold that when the FDA requires warnings be given directly to the patient with a prescribed drug, an exception to the "learned intermediary doctrine" has occurred, and the manufacturer is not automatically shielded from liability by properly warning the prescribing physician. . . . The required warnings must not be misleading, and must be adequate to explain to the user the possible dangers associated with the product. Whether that duty has been satisfied is governed by the common law of the state, not the regulations of the FDA, and necessarily implicates a fact-finding process, something beyond our assignment in response to this certified question.

Question Answered.

[Five justices concurred, one of them adding that compliance was not an issue in the case. One justice dissented in part on the ground that compliance was an issue and one justice dissented without opinion.]

Notes and Questions

1.   What justifies the learned intermediary rule in the first instance? Are the two exceptions consistent with the justification? Should the second exception extend to nicotine patches?

2.   Might the cases under the "second exception" be extended broadly to "well patients"—those who see a physician because they wish to enhance their quality of life, rather than because they "need" help? Should the "well patient" category include patients who seek prescription drugs

for such matters as baldness and erectile dysfunction as well as contraception? Who should be warned about the differences between two uniformly successful baldness treatments, one of which is much faster but carries a 1% risk of total irreversible baldness, the other being much slower but having no known risks? Is the case for the learned intermediary defense stronger or weaker if the 1% risk is of a serious chronic skin condition? Under a well-patient exception, should the plaintiff be informed of differential success rates?

3.   Another exception to the doctrine was articulated in Perez v. Wyeth Laboratories, Inc., 734 A.2d 1245 (N.J.1999), in which the court held, in a Norplant contraceptive implant case, that the doctrine does not apply where the defendant advertises prescription drugs directly to the consumer. In such cases, the manufacturer must discuss the product's risks in its advertisements. *Perez* refused to follow In re Norplant Contraceptive Products Litigation, 165 F.3d 374 (5th Cir.1999), in which the court, predicting Texas law, held that the learned intermediary doctrine applied to prescription drugs even when advertising is directed at the consumer. Is there a difference between the approach in *Perez* and that in the main case?

4.   In learned intermediary cases there may be further variations. In the first, when the physician is given adequate instructions, what claims might the patient have against the physician? In the second, the claim is that the physician was given inadequate information. If the physician testifies that even with an adequate warning, the physician would still have prescribed the medicine in question, what impact might that have on plaintiff's suit against the manufacturer? Against the physician? Is there room here for a heeding presumption?

5.   On the question of adequacy, the *Edwards* court leaves the issue to the federal court in which the trial record is being compiled. Could a trier of fact find the warning that actually reached the patient in *Edwards* inadequate? In the cited *MacDonald* case, the contraceptive user was warned that "[t]he most serious known side effect is abnormal blood clotting which can be fatal," but was not warned of "stroke." The court held that a jury could find that the failure to warn of stroke could render the warning inadequate. Is the inadequacy in *MacDonald* a closer call than that alleged in the main case? Is the *MacDonald* approach to adequacy consistent with that of *Hood*?

6.   *Prescription drugs.* Cases brought by those claiming side effects from prescribed drugs have been troublesome, especially if the side effect could not reasonably have been discovered before it manifested itself. This issue is addressed in the following case and notes. But even if the drug's side effects were known and warned against, might it still be possible to claim that the product was defective because its side effects exceeded its known (and warned-against) side effects? Under the Second Restatement, there was disagreement about the role of risk-benefit analysis—and whether liability was always to be analyzed from a negligence perspective. The Products Restatement sought to resolve this confusion by providing in § 6 (c) that

A prescription drug or medical device is not reasonably safe due to defective design if the foreseeable risks of harm posed by the drug or medical device are sufficiently great in relation to its foreseeable therapeutic benefits that reasonable health-care-providers, knowing of such foreseeable risks and therapeutic benefits, would not prescribe the drug or medical device for any class of patients.

In Freeman v. Hoffman–La Roche, Inc., 618 N.W.2d 827 (Neb.2000), the court found no state cases analyzing this provision. In the case before it the plaintiff alleged that she had suffered serious side effects from Accutane, which had been prescribed for her chronic acne. The court rejected § 6(c) for several reasons. Among other reasons, the court objected to the result that liability for any drug was defeated for all plaintiffs if the drug was suitable for "any class of patients." For critical commentary, see Conk, Is There a Design Defect in the Restatement (Third) of Torts: Products Liability?, 109 Yale L. J. 1087 (2000).

7. *Allergy.* A manufacturer ordinarily has no duty to change a product's design to guard against allergic reactions when the product's benefit to the public outweighs the harm it may cause to the idiosyncratic few. Liability for failure to warn may be imposed, however, where the number of allergic sufferers is substantial. Beyond that, where the potential for serious harm from the reaction is foreseeable, some courts have required warnings even where the reaction occurs in fewer than one in a million users. See generally, Henderson, Process Norms in Products Litigation: Liability for Allergic Reactions, 51 U. Pitt. L. Rev. 761 (1990).

8. Would the differences between strict liability and negligence affect the analysis of safety instruction or warning cases? Note, once again, that the Products Restatement makes no reference to this terminology in section 2(c), p. 556, supra.

The following case discusses the question of liability where the claim is that there was a failure to warn even though the information about the risk that came to pass was unknown at the time the product was distributed. The court uses warranty terminology because of a peculiarity of state law, but the discussion is addressed to tort liability and both Restatements.

Vassallo v. Baxter Healthcare Corporation

Supreme Judicial Court of Massachusetts, 1998.
428 Mass. 1, 696 N.E.2d 909.

Before WILKINS, C.J., and ABRAMS, LYNCH, GREANEY and MARSHALL, JJ.

GREANEY, JUSTICE.

[Plaintiff claimed that silicone breast implants, manufactured by a company since bought by defendant, had been negligently designed, accompanied by negligent product warnings, and that they breached the implied warranty of merchantability, with the consequence that she was injured. Her husband claimed loss of consortium. A jury returned verdicts on the negligence and warranty counts in favor of the plaintiffs. On direct appeal, the court upheld the judgment entered on the negligence verdict.]

Because the plaintiffs' recoveries can be upheld on the jury's findings of negligence, we need not address the defendants' claims of error concerning the breach of warranty count. We take this opportunity, however, to consider the defendants' argument that we should change our products liability law concerning the implied warranty of merchantability from what is stated in Hayes v. Ariens Co., 462 N.E.2d 273 (Mass.1984), and that the law should be reformulated to adopt a "state of the art" standard that conditions a manufacturer's liability on actual or constructive knowledge of the risks.

Our current law, regarding the duty to warn under the implied warranty of merchantability, presumes that a manufacturer was fully informed of all risks associated with the product at issue, regardless of the state of the art at the time of the sale, and amounts to strict liability for failure to warn of these risks. [   ] This rule has been justified by the public policy that a defective product, "unreasonably dangerous due to lack of adequate warning[s], [is] not fit for the ordinary purposes for which [it is] used regardless of the absence of fault on [a defendant's] part." [   ]

At trial, the defendants requested a jury instruction that a manufacturer need only warn of risks "known or reasonably knowable in light of the generally accepted scientific knowledge available at the time of the manufacture and distribution of the device." The judge declined this request, and instead gave an instruction using language taken almost verbatim from that in [Hayes]. While the judge's instruction was a correct statement of our law, we recognize that we are among a distinct minority of States that applies a hindsight analysis to the duty to warn.

The majority of States, either by case law or by statute, follow the principle expressed in Restatement (Second) of Torts § 402A comment *j* (1965), which states that "the seller is required to give warning against [a danger], if he has knowledge, or by the application of reasonable, developed human skill and foresight should have knowledge, of the . . . danger." [   ]; [Products Restatement, Reporters' Note to § 2 comment *m*, at 104 (1998)] ("An overwhelming majority of jurisdictions supports the proposition that a manufacturer has a duty to warn only of risks that were known or should have been known to a reasonable person"). At least three jurisdictions that previously applied strict liability to the duty to warn in a products liability claim have reversed themselves, either by statute or by decision, and now require knowledge, or reasonable knowability as a component of such a claim. [Colorado]; Feldman v. Lederle Labs., [479 A.2d 374 (N.J.1984)]; La.Rev.Stat. Ann. § 9:2800.59(B) (West 1997). The change in the law of New Jersey is particularly relevant, because we relied in part on New Jersey law in formulating the strict liability standard expressed in the *Hayes* decision. See [Hayes] citing Beshada v. Johns–Manville Prods. Corp., [447 A.2d 539 (N.J.1982)].

The thin judicial support for a hindsight approach to the duty to warn is easily explained. The goal of the law is to induce conduct that is capable of being performed. This goal is not advanced by imposing liability for failure to warn of risks that were not capable of being known. [   ]

The [Products Restatement § 2(c)] reaffirms the principle expressed in Restatement (Second) of Torts, at § 402A comment *j*, by stating that a product "is defective because of inadequate instructions or warnings when the foreseeable risks of harm posed by the product could have been reduced or avoided by the provision of reasonable instructions or warnings . . . and the omission of the instructions or warnings renders the product not reasonably safe." The rationale behind the principle is explained by stating that "[u]nforeseeable risks arising from foreseeable product use . . . by definition cannot specifically be warned against." [   ] However, comment *m* also clarifies the manufacturer's duty "to perform reasonable testing prior to marketing a product and to discover risks and risk-avoidance measures that such testing would reveal. A seller is charged with knowledge of what reasonable testing would reveal." [   ]

We have stated that liability under the implied warranty of merchantability in Massachusetts is "congruent in nearly all respects with the principles expressed in Restatement (Second) of Torts § 402A." [   ] The main difference has been our application of a hindsight approach to the duty to warn of (and to provide adequate instructions regarding) risks associated with a product. We recognize that this approach has received substantial criticism in the literature . . .

In recognition of the clear judicial trend regarding the duty to warn in products liability cases, and the principles stated in Restatement (Third) of Torts: Products Liability, supra at § 2(c) and comment *m*, we hereby revise our law to state that a defendant will not be held liable under an implied warranty of merchantability for failure to warn or provide instructions about risks that were not reasonably foreseeable at the time of sale or could not have been discovered by way of reasonable testing prior to marketing the product. A manufacturer will be held to the standard of knowledge of an expert in the appropriate field, and will remain subject to a continuing duty to warn (at least purchasers) of risks discovered following the sale of the product at issue. In accordance with the usual rule governing retroactivity in this type of action, the standard just expressed will apply to all claims on which a final judgment has not been entered, or as to which an appeal is pending or the appeal period has not expired, and to all claims on which an action is commenced after the release of this opinion. [   ]

[The court noted that the jury's sustainable verdict on negligence in failing to warn of known risks precluded the defendant from taking advantage of the change in the law. The judgment was affirmed.]

Notes and Questions

1. Does the use of a warranty theory explain the earlier *Hayes* outcome? Is there any reason to think that the outcome would have been

different if the court had been using tort concepts before *Vassallo*? Recall the *Ryan* case, involving the pin in the loaf of bread, p. 545, supra.

2. What are the arguments for and against a hindsight approach? Consider developments in states whose courts have articulated or followed positions of strict liability and then retreated to at least some extent. In the cited *Beshada* case, workers injured by handling asbestos products before 1960 sued the manufacturers of asbestos. Defendants argued that the medical profession did not recognize these particular health hazards from asbestos until the 1960s. Plaintiffs responded that, even if true, this fact was no defense to a strict liability claim. The New Jersey court agreed: "Strict liability focuses on the product, not the fault of the manufacturer."

This result was said to be consistent with the three main reasons the court had adopted strict liability—risk spreading, accident avoidance, and reducing administrative costs by avoiding "complicated, costly, confusing and time-consuming" trials about the distant past. On the second point, the court asserted that the " 'state of the art' at a given time is partly determined by how much industry invests in safety research. By imposing on manufacturers the costs of failure to discover hazards, we create an incentive for them to invest more actively in safety research." In addition, "fairness" suggested that "manufacturers not be excused from liability because their prior inadequate investment in safety rendered the hazards of their product unknowable."

In the cited *Feldman* case, the New Jersey court reversed course. Plaintiff's teeth were discolored by a drug that was prescribed for respiratory infections. No warning was given about this side effect until late in the course of the plaintiff's use of the product. Defendant claimed that the danger had only then become apparent and could not have been warned about earlier. The court noted that once knowledge of danger is imputed to a supplier "strict liability analysis becomes almost identical to negligence analysis in its focus on the reasonableness of the defendant's conduct." The issue was the imputation. The court concluded that as to design and warning questions, "generally conduct should be measured by knowledge at the time the manufacturer distributed the product." The courts should ask when the manufacturer had "actual or constructive knowledge of the danger." In making this determination the manufacturer should be "held to the standard of an expert in the field." This implied the "notion that at least in some fields, such as those impacting on public health, a manufacturer may be expected to be informed and affirmatively to seek out information concerning the public's use of its own product." The court "restrict[ed] *Beshada* to the circumstances giving rise to its holding."

The *Feldman* court did, however, shift the burden of proof to the defendant on the question of whether and when the relevant technical information became available:

> The defendant is in a superior position to know the technological material or data in the particular field or specialty. The defendant is the expert, often performing self-testing. It is the defendant that injected the product in the stream of commerce for its economic gain.

As a matter of policy the burden of proving the status of knowledge in the field at the time of distribution is properly placed on the defendant.

Does the shift in the burden of proof and the emphasis on the defendant as "an expert in the field" undermine any practical difference between *Beshada* and *Feldman*? See generally, Rabin, Indeterminate Risk and Tort Reform, 14 J.Legal Stud. 633 (1985).

The assumption of the asbestos industry's inability to know of the danger underlying *Beshada* was suspect from the beginning. See generally, P. Brodeur, Outrageous Misconduct: The Asbestos Industry on Trial (1985). See also Bragg v. Owens–Corning Fiberglas Corp., 734 A.2d 643 (D.C.App.1999) (noting that Pliny the Elder "reported a lung disease in slaves weaving asbestos").

In James v. Bessemer Processing Co., Inc., 714 A.2d 898 (N.J.1998), chemical and petroleum manufacturers were sued for failing to warn workers who reconditioned container drums that the drums contained toxic products. The court, after noting that plaintiffs could proceed under either strict liability or negligence, undertook to identify the differences:

> In cases proceeding under a theory of strict liability, knowledge of the harmful effects of a product will be imputed to a manufacturer on a showing that "knowledge of the defect existed within the relevant industry." [   ] Once proof of such knowledge in the industry has been established, triggering the duty to warn, the plaintiff must show that an adequate warning was not provided. When proceeding under a theory of negligence, the plaintiff must demonstrate that the specific defendant knew or should have known of the potential hazards of the product.

Is this an intelligible distinction? After either theory is established, the "heeding presumption" comes into play so that a plaintiff need "introduce evidence that the defendant's failure to warn . . . led to plaintiff's exposure only if it becomes necessary to defeat a defendant's attempt to rebut the heeding presumption with its own proofs."

3. Compare Ferayorni v. Hyundai Motor Co., 711 So.2d 1167 (Fla. App.1998), which concerned the proper jury instructions in a claim of a defective restraint system that hurt a very small driver. The appellate court rejected Hyundai's claim that failure to warn "is nothing more than a negligence case." For the court, the "issue, specifically, is whether a claim of strict liability failure to warn requires, like its counterpart in negligence, proof that the manufacturer knew or should have known of the product's dangerous propensities." The court held that:

> This infusion of knowledge and reasonableness requirements [in comment *j* to § 402A] has led some courts to hold that strict liability failure to warn has merged with negligence. [   ] We reject this view, and specifically hold that a prima facie case of strict liability failure to warn does not require a showing of negligence. In so holding, we note that the policy behind strict products liability is to facilitate a plaintiff's recovery where a manufacturer places on the market a potentially

dangerous product and thereby "undertakes a certain and special responsibility toward the consuming public who may be injured by it."

Yet, the court realized that "[s]trict liability does not make the manufacturer or seller an insurer. [   ] Thus, it may not be appropriate to entirely do away with a requirement that the manufacturer have some actual or constructive knowledge of the risk to which the failure to warn attaches." The court then adopted what it understood to be the California position spelled out in Anderson v. Owens–Corning Fiberglas Corp., 810 P.2d 549 (Cal.1991) and Carlin v. Superior Court, 920 P.2d 1347 (Cal.1996). The Florida court understood these cases to hold "that the required showing of scienter for strict liability is not as burdensome as in the negligence context."

> While we recognize that a required showing of knowledge or constructive knowledge makes strict liability "to some extent a hybrid of traditional strict liability and negligence doctrine," [*Carlin*], we find that this result best serves to promote the countervailing policies underlying strict liability articulated in [an earlier Florida case]. As we construe [*Anderson*], manufacturers are to be held to a higher standard than that imposed under negligence jurisprudence, but are not reduced to insurers; manufacturers are not required to warn of every risk which might be remotely suggested by any obscure tidbit of available knowledge, but only of those risks which are discoverable in light of the "generally recognized and prevailing best" knowledge available.

Is this the same position as that reached by New Jersey in *Bessemer,* supra?

4. *State of the art*. This discussion implicates an often-used phrase in this type of litigation: "state of the art." The Products Restatement states that the term "has been variously defined by a multitude of courts. For some, it refers to industry custom or industry practice; for others, it means the safest existing technology that has been adopted for use; for others it means cutting edge technology." § 2, comment *c*.

Test these various meanings of "state of the art" in several situations: (a) in the months before a product with an unknown risk is marketed in the United States, a small company in Finland had discovered that very risk and, without public announcement, had begun preparing a new product that avoided the risk; (b) a few weeks before defendant's product was marketed, the risk had first been reported in a Finnish scientific journal. Should "negligence principles" and "strict liability principles" lead to different results in these cases? Would *Vassallo* and *Ferayorni* reach different results?

5. *Discovery of danger after distribution*. The *Vassallo* court suggested the existence of a continuing duty to warn after sale. That issue has arisen in several cases: Even if defendants are not liable for the first totally unexpected injuries that occur after their product is marketed, have they an obligation when the first hint of trouble does appear?

In Lovick v. Wil–Rich, 588 N.W.2d 688 (Iowa 1999), an experienced farmer was injured in 1993 when a design defect caused a linkage to break and the wing of a farm cultivator to fall unexpectedly. Defendant began marketing this type of cultivator in 1971. Plaintiff's model was made in 1981 and he bought it in "the late 80s." In 1983, defendant received the first report of a falling wing. Since that time it received eight more. In 1988 it began attaching warnings to new cultivators. In 1994, it began trying to notify owners of existing cultivators of the danger and providing a backup safety kit. Plaintiff introduced evidence that Deere & Co., defendant's competitor, had begun a safety program in 1983 for its similarly designed cultivator after learning of instances of wing malfunction. Deere's efforts included trying to locate owners of previously sold cultivators and equipping them with a safety latch and upgraded warning. The court stated that defendant, although it learned of Deere's 1983 actions in 1987, did not start its campaign until 1994 "essentially due to the practical difficulties of identifying and locating the owners and users of previously sold cultivators." The trial judge submitted to the jury "a general reasonableness standard of care instruction." The jury returned a verdict for compensatory and punitive damages.

On appeal, the court rejected defendant's first argument that it owed no duty as to dangers discovered after the sale. The court noted that most states to address the issue recognized such a duty, and that a state statute implied it. Other courts reject a post-sale duty. See cases cited in Patton v. Hutchinson Wil–Rich Mfg. Co., 861 P.2d 1299 (Kan.1993), noting contrary cases in an opinion in which it upheld a post-sale duty to warn in a case involving the same model cultivator as in *Lovick*.

The *Lovick* court then turned to the nature of that duty. Although the rationale for a duty to warn after the sale was "nearly identical" to those supporting a duty to warn at time of sale, "the parameters of those duties must be separately identified." The court noted that § 10 of the Products Restatement asserted that a reasonable seller would warn if (1) the seller knows or reasonably should know that the product poses a substantial risk of harm to persons or property; (2) those who would benefit from the warning can be identified and are likely unaware of the risk; (3) a warning can effectively be communicated to and acted upon by recipients; and (4) that the "risk of harm is sufficiently great to justify the burden of providing a warning."

The court agreed that negligence was the proper standard in this area. Nonetheless, the general reasonableness charge was inadequate to convey the different considerations that apply to post-sale warnings. In future cases, trial judges should charge on all four factors to help the jury focus on the obligation—even though the Restatement factors were stated as issues for judges to consider.

How different is this question from the case of a physician who acts reasonably at the time, but later discovers that the conduct created an unexpected danger to the patient, p. 136, supra?

Should the duty to warn include the duty to pay for the safety kits that Deere and Wil–Rich were providing? The *Patton* court, supra, though imposing a duty to warn, refused to impose a duty to retrofit or to recall the product. Administrative agencies were "better able to weigh the benefits and costs involved in locating, recalling, and retrofitting products."

6. Is there a difference between after-acquired knowledge of danger and after-acquired knowledge of a technique for reducing a known danger? See DeSantis v. Frick Co., 745 A.2d 624 (Pa.Super.1999), in which plaintiff died from inhaling anhydrous ammonia while working with an industrial freezer. The danger of leaking ammonia was known at the time the freezer was sold but there was no known technique for avoiding the problem. One was developed after the sale but the manufacturer did not alert the buyers of earlier models. (The sale occurred in 1964; the new technique was developed in the mid-1980s, and plaintiff died in 1993.) The court held that there was no duty to inform earlier buyers where the product was not defective at the time it was marketed. The court read section 10's factors to apply to this situation—and then rejected the section. Should the section apply to both situations?

7. *Misrepresentations.* So far the discussion in this section has revolved around cases in which either there was no warning at all or the warning was claimed to be inadequate. What about words that affirmatively mislead? Section 9 of the Products Restatement addresses this issue by providing that a seller or distributor who "makes a fraudulent, negligent, or innocent misrepresentation of fact concerning the product is subject to liability for harm to persons or property caused by the misrepresentation." The comments make clear that this section intended no change in existing law.

The earlier formulation is found in § 402B of the Second Restatement. That section provides that a seller is liable for physical harm to one who justifiably relies on a material misrepresentation even if the maker is not negligent in misrepresenting and even if the person hurt did not buy the product from the seller. How can the failure to require a showing of fault be justified? For an extended consideration of § 402B and its relation to warranty theories, see American Safety Equipment Corp. v. Winkler, 640 P.2d 216 (Colo.1982); Hauter v. Zogarts, 534 P.2d 377 (Cal.1975), involving a plaintiff injured by the operation of the "Golfing Gizmo," a training device intended to help unskilled golfers improve their games.

In Denny v. Ford Motor Co., 662 N.E.2d 730 (N.Y.1995), a jury could have found that an off-road vehicle that had certain advantages off the normal highway had been advertised and sold as appropriate for normal driving. The features that made it useful for off-road driving—high center of gravity, narrow track width, and short wheel base—made it dangerous when drivers took evasive action on paved roads. The court developed a dual-purpose doctrine under which a product that might pass the risk-utility test for one purpose could be defective if offered as suitable for another purpose that might not be appropriate. Could *Denny*, which used a warranty analysis, be analyzed under § 9?

See also Castro v. QVC Network, Inc., 139 F.3d 114 (2d Cir.1998), in which the defendant advertised a pan on television as fit for cooking 25-pound turkeys. In fact, the pan was fit for many other purposes but was allegedly inadequate for this one because its handles were too small. Plaintiff was burned when the pan tipped over due to the small handles. The court, using New York law and following *Denny*, held that a "jury could have found that the roasting pan's overall utility for cooking low-volume foods outweighed the risk of injury when cooking heavier foods, but that the product was nonetheless unsafe for the purpose for which it was marketed and sold—roasting a twenty-five pound turkey—and, as such, was defective under the consumer expectations test." What gave rise to this expectation—the kind of knowledge that comes with everyday experience or the words that defendant used to sell the product?

In Livingston v. Marie Callender's, Inc., 85 Cal.Rptr.2d 528 (App. 1999), plaintiff alleged that he had alerted the server to his severe allergy to monosodium glutamate (MSG) and had asked whether it was used in the soup he was ordering. The server incorrectly assured plaintiff that there was no MSG in the soup. The court held that plaintiff was "entitled to a trial on the theory there was a failure to warn of an ingredient to which a substantial number of the population are allergic." Is misrepresentation a stronger claim here?

E. DEFENSES

Since product cases have raised issues in the prima facie case unlike those we have previously considered, it should not be surprising that differences might appear in the area of defenses, as well. As you read this section, consider whether the crucial lines are (1) those that divide product-derived harms from others, (2) those that separate strict liability from negligence, or (3) those that distinguish among personal injury, property damage and economic harm. State statutes may explicitly cover products liability—as in the case below—or courts may extend either common law or statutory principles of comparative fault to products cases.

Comparative fault or responsibility has been applied in the products liability context in the overwhelming majority of states. In these instances, issues emerge about what it is that should be compared. The following case addresses a common situation that gives rise to comparison and also discusses the treatment of defenses to products liability in the Second Restatement and in the subsequent Products Restatement.

General Motors Corporation v. Sanchez

Supreme Court of Texas, 1999.
997 S.W.2d 584.

JUSTICE GONZALES delivered the opinion for a unanimous Court. The principal question in this case is when does the doctrine of comparative responsibility apply in a products-liability case. . . .

I

Because there were no witnesses, relatively little is known first hand about the circumstances of the accident that is the basis of this litigation. Lee Sanchez, Jr. left his home to feed a pen of heifers in March 1993. The ranch foreman found his lifeless body the next morning and immediately called Sanchez's father. Apparently, Sanchez's 1990 Chevy pickup had rolled backward with the driver's side door open pinning Sanchez to the open corral gate in the angle between the open door and the cab of the truck. Sanchez suffered a broken right arm and damaged right knee where the gate crushed him against the door pillar, the vertical metal column to which the door is hinged. He bled to death from a deep laceration in his right upper arm.

The family, his estate, and his wife sued General Motors Corporation and the dealership that sold the pickup for negligence, products liability, and gross negligence based on a defect in the truck's transmission and transmission-control linkage. The plaintiffs presented circumstantial evidence to support the following theory of how the accident happened. Sanchez drove his truck into the corral and stopped to close the gate. He mis-shifted into what he thought was Park, but what was actually an intermediate, "perched" position between Park and Reverse where the transmission was in "hydraulic neutral." Expert witnesses explained that hydraulic neutral exists at the intermediate positions between the denominated gears, Park, Reverse, Neutral, Drive, and Low, where no gear is actually engaged. Under this scenario, as Sanchez walked toward the gate, the gear shift slipped from the perched position of hydraulic neutral into Reverse and the truck started to roll backwards. It caught Sanchez at or near the gate and slammed him up against it, trapping his right arm and knee. He was pinned between the gate and the door pillar by the pressure the truck exerted while idling in Reverse. Struggling to free himself, Sanchez severed an artery in his right arm and bled to death after 45 to 75 minutes.

[At trial, G.M. presented alternative theories.]

The jury rejected G.M.'s theories and found that G.M. was negligent, the transmission was defectively designed, and G.M.'s warning was [inadequate]. The jury also found that Sanchez was fifty percent responsible for the accident, but the trial court disregarded this finding. The trial court rendered judgment for actual and punitive damages of $8.5 million for the plaintiffs. [The court of appeals, en banc, affirmed.]

G.M. argues that there is no evidence to support liability for negligence or strict liability. Alternatively, G.M. challenges the trial court's refusal to apply the comparative responsibility statute. The plaintiffs respond that evidence supports both the negligence and strict liability findings, and that Sanchez's negligence was nothing more than a failure to discover or guard against a product defect. Thus, they contend, comparative responsibility does not apply here as a defense to strict liability.

Here, G.M. does not dispute that Sanchez's fatal injury was caused when he mis-shifted the truck's transmission into hydraulic neutral, which then migrated into Reverse. The parties agree that all transmissions made today can mis-shift, that no design eliminates the possibility of a mis-shift, and that a mis-shifted car is dangerous. As G.M. puts it, a "[m]is-shift is just physics." G.M. contends that it has no liability, even if its product is defective, because the plaintiffs failed to present evidence of a safer alternative design.

[The court first concluded that an expert's testimony of an alternative design supported the jury's finding of a design defect.]

III

The jury found that Sanchez was fifty percent responsible for his accident. G.M. argues that this finding should be applied to reduce its liability for damages whether in negligence or strict liability. However, the plaintiffs argue that Sanchez's actions amounted to no more than a failure to discover or guard against a product defect and, because of our decision in Keen v. Ashot Ashkelon, Ltd., [748 S.W.2d 91 (1988) (failure to discover or guard against a defect is no defense to a strict liability claim)], such negligence does not constitute a defense to strict liability. To review the plaintiffs' claim, we must first consider the effect of the 1987 revisions to Chapter 33 of the Civil Practice and Remedies Code upon our decision in *Keen*.

[Before 1987, cases were submitted under the statutory comparative negligence system. *Keen* was decided under this law—including "the rule in comment *n* to § 402A of the Restatement (Second) of Torts, that negligent failure to discover or guard against a product defect is not a defense."]

In 1987, the Legislature changed Chapter 33 from comparative negligence to comparative responsibility. Under comparative responsibility, a court reduces a claimant's damages recovery by the "percentage of responsibility" attributed to him by the trier of fact. The new statute expressly included suits based on strict tort liability. It defined "Percentage of responsibility" as the percentage that a party "cause[d] or contribute[d] to cause in any way, whether by *negligent act or omission,* . . . [or] by *other conduct or activity violative of the applicable legal standard*" the harm for which damages are sought. Thus, as the emphasized language indicates, the new statute applies to a claimant's conduct that violated the duty to use ordinary care or some other applicable legal standard.

comparative responsibility

G.M. contends that the 1987 revisions of Chapter 33 effectively over-rule *Keen*. It is not quite that simple. Implicit in this Court's holding in *Keen* was that a consumer has no duty to discover or guard against a product defect. The 1987 changes to Chapter 33, which apportion responsibility based on a breach of a legal duty or other applicable legal standard, do not impose a new duty on plaintiffs. The statute merely says that if a claimant breaches an existing duty, then comparative responsibility shall apply. Accordingly, if a plaintiff's failure to discover or guard against a product defect breaches no duty, the statute does not apply.

Keen = no duty to discover defect

statute does not apply

P has no duty to discover in Str. lb. case

Contrb. neg. is not a defense; Assumption of Risk is 2nd Rest ↑ & Keen

Thus, *Keen*'s viability after the 1987 revisions depends on whether a plaintiff in a strict liability case has a duty to take steps to discover and guard against product defects. [A later court] refused to recognize such a failure as a defense, relying in part on comment *n* to section 402A of the Restatement (Second):

Contributory negligence of the plaintiff is not a defense when such negligence consists merely in a failure to discover the defect in the product, or to guard against the possibility of its existence. On the other hand the form of contributory negligence which consists in voluntarily and unreasonably proceeding to encounter a known danger, and commonly passes under the name of assumption of risk, is a defense under this Section as in other cases of strict liability. If the user or consumer discovers the defect and is aware of the danger, and nevertheless proceeds unreasonably to make use of the product and is injured by it, he is barred from recovery.

We note that comment "*n*" was not carried forward in the Restatement (Third). The position of Restatement (Third), section 17(a), is that a plaintiff's conduct should be considered to reduce a damages recovery if it fails to conform to applicable standards of care, similar to the Texas 1987 statutory scheme. However, comment *d* to Restatement (Third) states:

3rd Rest. ↓ Must be evidence that P's failure to discover defect, failed to meet a standard of reasonable care

[W]hen the defendant claims that the plaintiff failed to discover a defect, there must be evidence that the plaintiff's conduct in failing to discover a defect did, in fact, fail to meet a standard of reasonable care. In general, a plaintiff has no reason to expect that a new product contains a defect and would have little reason to be on guard to discover it.

holding

We believe that a duty to discover defects, and to take precautions in constant anticipation that a product might have a defect, would defeat the purposes of strict liability. Thus, we hold that a consumer has no duty to discover or guard against a product defect, but a consumer's conduct other than the mere failure to discover or guard against a product defect is subject to comparative responsibility. Public policy favors reasonable conduct by consumers regardless of whether a product is defective. A consumer is not relieved of the responsibility to act reasonably nor may a consumer fail to take reasonable precautions regardless of a known or unknown product defect. We therefore disapprove of *Keen* to the extent it suggests that the failure to discover or guard against a product defect is a broad category that includes all conduct except the assumption of a known risk. Because we conclude that a consumer has no duty to discover or guard against a product defect, we next determine whether the decedent's conduct in this case was merely the failure to discover or guard against a product defect or some other negligence unrelated to a product defect.

Evidence

The truck's owner's manual describes safety measures designed to ensure that the truck would not move when parked: (1) set the parking brake; (2) place the truck completely in Park; (3) turn off the engine; (4) remove the key from the ignition; and (5) check that Park is fully engaged by pulling down on the gear shift. Sanchez's father testified that his son probably read the entire owner's manual. The plaintiff's own experts agreed at trial that Sanchez failed to perform any of the safety measures described in the owner's manual and that performing any one of them would have prevented the accident. This evidence is sufficient to support the jury's negligence finding.

Regardless of any danger of a mis-shift, a driver has a duty to take reasonable precautions to secure his vehicle before getting out of it. The danger that it could roll, or move if the engine is running, exists independently of the possibility of a mis-shift. For instance, the driver could inadvertently leave a vehicle in gear or a mechanical problem unrelated to a product defect could prevent Park from fully engaging. A moving vehicle without a driver is a hazard to public safety. The state licenses drivers who have demonstrated the minimum knowledge and skill necessary to safely operate a motor vehicle. Many, perhaps most, consumer products may be operated without a license, including lawn and garden equipment, household appliances, and powered hand tools. It follows then that, because of this licensing requirement, as well as other special duties imposed on drivers, more is expected of an operator of a motor vehicle than of users of most other consumer products. Thus, although we do not expect the average driver to have the engineering background to discover defects in their car's transmission, we do expect the reasonably prudent driver to take safety precautions to prevent a runaway car. Sanchez had a responsibility to operate his truck in a safe manner. The fact that the precautions demanded of a driver generally would have prevented this accident does not make Sanchez's negligence a mere failure to discover or guard against a mis-shift.

P was neg.

We recognize that there may be some tension between how we apply the law to the facts of this case and the *Keen* majority's characterization of the plaintiff's conduct in that case. As discussed previously, the *Keen* analysis was flawed from the outset because it recognized only two categories of plaintiff conduct: mere failure to discover or guard against a defect and assumption of the risk. All conduct that was not assumption of the risk was categorized as failure to discover or guard against a defect and thus no defense. Today, we hold that a plaintiff's conduct other than the mere failure to discover or guard against a product defect is subject to comparative responsibility.

court rejects Keen analysis

Sanchez's actions amounted to conduct other than a mere failure to discover or guard against a product defect. We hold as a matter of law that such conduct must be scrutinized under the duty to use ordinary care or other applicable duty. We conclude that there was legally sufficient evidence to support the jury's verdict that Sanchez breached the duty to use ordinary care and was fifty percent responsible for the accident.

Sanchez 50% responsible

[The court reversed the punitive damage award and remanded for entry of the award for actual damages reduced by 50 percent.]

Notes and Questions

1. Why does the court conclude that "a consumer has no duty to discover or guard against a product defect"?

2. Which of the decedent's actions allowed the court to conclude that a jury could find more than a failure to discover or guard against a product defect?

3. How do the two Restatements differ on this type of defense?

4. How does the jury determine the respective percentages of responsibility? This has been an issue ever since courts began to compare in these situations. In Daly v. General Motors Corp., 575 P.2d 1162 (Cal.1978), an early influential products case involving crashworthiness, the court, 4–3, applied comparative fault (which it thought might better be termed "equitable apportionment of the loss"). The dissent lamented that:

> The majority's assumption that a jury is capable of making a fair apportionment between a plaintiff's negligent conduct and a defendant's defective product is no more logical or convincing than if a jury were to be instructed that it should add a quart of milk (representing plaintiff's negligence) and a metal bar three feet in length (representing defendant's strict liability for a defective product), and that the two added together equal 100 percent—the total fault for plaintiff's injuries; that plaintiff's quart of milk is then to be assigned its percentage of the 100 percent total and defendant's metal bar is to be assigned the remaining percentage of the total. Either the jury or the trial judge will then subtract from the total amount of plaintiff's damages an amount equal to the percentage of total fault allocated to plaintiff.

One author suggested that the way to apportion damages "is to compare the plaintiff's conduct with how he should have conducted himself (the objective standard of the reasonable man) and reduce his recovery according to the extent of his fault." Fischer, Products Liability—Application of Comparative Negligence, 43 Mo.L.Rev. 431 (1978). Does that formula involve comparison? Is it easier for a jury to understand?

Compare the approach taken in Sandford v. Chevrolet Division, 642 P.2d 624 (Or.1982). Plaintiff suffered burns when a pickup truck she was driving caught fire. The defendants alleged that plaintiff's negligence had caused the injuries. In dealing with the question of how to compare the parties' faults, the court suggested that the conduct of each party should be evaluated "against behavior that would have been faultless under the circumstances." The product supplier's norm involved "the magnitude of the defect rather than negligence or moral 'blameworthiness' ":

> In this comparison, the benchmark for assessing a defendant's fault for marketing a product which is dangerously defective in design, manufacture, or warning is what the product should have been without the defect. The benchmark for the injured claimant's fault is conduct which would not be unlawful or careless in any relevant respect.

The deviation from the benchmark could be thought of as a "fault line," with the absence of fault being zero, and deliberate wrongdoing having a value of ten. Each party's deviation would be determined individually. Then they would be compared and apportioned in percentages. For example, if the product defect rated a 3 and the plaintiff's fault a 2, these numbers would be converted to a defendant's "fault" of 60% and plaintiff's of 40%. Would this more substantive account of the different natures of "fault" in the products liability and the negligence contexts allay some of the *Daly* dissent's fears about the impossibility of comparison?

5. Whether in a state with a comparative negligence statute or in a state in which the court created comparative negligence judicially, the courts have extended the underlying principles to products liability cases. Some courts in states with modified comparative negligence statutes have adapted these in products cases to a pure version. Other states have enacted comparative fault or responsibility statutes that cover products liability as well as comparative negligence. For a survey of approaches, see Webb v. Navistar International Transportation Corp., 692 A.2d 343 (Vt. 1996). The relevant parts of the 1987 amendment to the Texas statute read:

(a) In an action to recover damages for negligence resulting in personal injury, property damage, or death or an action for products liability grounded in negligence, a claimant may recover damages only if his percentage of responsibility is less than or equal to 50 percent.

(b) In an action to recover damages for personal injury, property damage, or death in which at least one defendant is found liable on a basis of strict tort liability, strict products liability, or breach of warranty . . . , a claimant may recover damages only if his percentage of responsibility is less than 60 percent.

Why did the legislature decide to implement disparate rules for products liability cases depending upon whether they sounded in negligence or in strict liability? Texas amended its statute yet again in 1995, so that now it reads simply "In an action to which this chapter applies, a claimant may not recover damages if his percentage of responsibility is greater than 50 percent"? Tex. Civ. Prac. and Rem. § 33.001. Why should a plaintiff recover nothing if a defective product caused or enhanced the injuries?

6. In many cases, plaintiffs do not allege that the product defect caused the entirety of their injury, but simply that it aggravated what would otherwise have been a less serious harm.

In Binakonsky v. Ford Motor Co., p. 591, supra, plaintiffs' decedent, driving drunk, had hit an oak tree head on, and his Ford van caught on fire. Plaintiffs, alleging that this fire—and not the crash—had killed him, claimed that a design defect had caused the fire. The majority explained that the defense of contributory negligence did not apply to strict products liability claims under Maryland law. It then explained why assumption of risk should not bar plaintiff's present suit:

Assumption of risk, sometimes called a form of contributory negligence, is a defense to claims based on strict liability. The defense is available against a plaintiff who unreasonably uses a product despite a known risk of danger. . . . Drunk driving is an unreasonable use of a car, and it is common knowledge that a driver who strikes a tree will cause damage. For this reason, a drunk driver, such as Binakonsky, assumes the risk of injury from the initial impact.

It is not generally known however, that plastic lines and connectors and the lack of an anti-siphoning device will cause a vehicle to burst into a devastating post-collision fire. Moreover, Ford gave no warning about the likelihood of such fire. For these reasons the plaintiffs are entitled to the reasonable inference that Binakonsky did not assume the risk of a lethal fire.

The dissent responded that the van could not be considered defective, since an automobile manufacturer did not have "a duty to design its automobiles to withstand risks of injury from a head-on collision with an oak tree at a speed of 40–47 miles per hour." (Does the manufacturer have to anticipate wrong-way drivers hitting the car head-on at similar closing speeds?)

Contrast Whitehead v. Toyota Motor Corp., 897 S.W.2d 684 (Tenn. 1995), in which plaintiff was entirely responsible for a two-car crash in which he was hurt. In a suit for enhanced injuries, the court thought it appropriate that "the fault of the defendant and of the plaintiff should be compared with each other with respect to all damages and injuries for which the conduct of each party is a cause in fact and a proximate cause." Why "all"?

7. Many of these defense cases raise potentially serious causation questions. Assume a faultless driver, wearing a safety belt when negligently rear-ended by driver T, sues her car's manufacturer for enhanced injuries due to a crashworthiness defect. Should the manufacturer be able to reduce its share of the liability (or eliminate part of its liability in a state that no longer uses joint and several liability) by apportioning to T a large part of the blame for the plaintiff's harm?

This was the question in Zuern v. Ford Motor Company, 937 P.2d 676 (Ariz.App.1996), in which T admitted full responsibility for rear-ending plaintiff, and was, in fact, sent to prison for drunk driving. At trial, Ford adduced evidence of T's intoxication and conviction, and, based on that evidence, "Ford's counsel told the jury in closing argument that it should assess 'by far the largest degree of fault' to [T] and urged the jury, as 'the conscience of the community,' to 'figure out what we are going to do with drunk drivers in this community.'" The jury allocated fault 70% to T and 30% to Ford. In explaining why it upheld the trial court's admission of this evidence, the court of appeals explained that a state statute "requires the trier to assess 'degrees of fault,' not just degrees of causation. Although causation (or physical contribution to the injury) is a necessary condition precedent to consideration of a person's fault . . . once causation is found the trier of fact must determine and apportion 'the relative degrees of fault' of all parties and nonparties." Is a defectively designed car that may injure passengers in a crash (from any cause) substantially less "at fault" than a drunk driver?

8. *Disclaimers and contracts.* Would the court's analysis in *Sanchez* have differed if the sale of decedent's Chevy had been accompanied by a disclaimer stating that "The manufacturers retain no responsibility for injury of any kind from this product"?

The Products Restatement addresses the validity of disclaimers in Section 18: "disclaimers and limitations of remedies by product sellers or other distributors, waivers by product purchasers, and other similar contractual exculpations, oral or written, do not bar or reduce otherwise valid products liability claims against sellers or other distributors of new products for harm to persons." This section adopts and extends comment *m* to § 402A of the Second Restatement, which stated that "The consumer's cause of action [in tort] . . . is not affected by any disclaimer or other agreement. . . ." According to the Products Restatement, a clear majority of courts take the same stance as the Second Restatement, though it was not as clear to the drafters whether the majority of courts also refuse to accept express assumption of risk as a defense in the products liability area.

9.   Should the other defenses that we considered in connection with negligence in Chapter VI apply equally to the cases that we have been considering in this chapter? If not, what is the difference? Is it a difference between negligence and strict liability or is it a difference between cases involving defective products and the types of cases we considered under the negligence regime? Consider these questions in the context of the three distinct viewpoints on express assumed risk:

a.   In Westlye v. Look Sports, Inc., 22 Cal.Rptr.2d 781 (App. 1993), the court held that express assumption of the risk would bar plaintiff's negligence action but not her strict liability claim for the failure of her ski boot bindings to release when she fell. The court asserted that "one purpose of strict liability in tort is to prevent a manufacturer from defining the scope of his responsibility for harm caused by his products." Allowing a defense of disclaimer in the products area would contravene this fundamental end of strict liability.

b.   In Bauer v. Aspen Highlands Skiing Corp., 788 F.Supp. 472 (D.Colo.1992), the court, without mentioning products liability, held that there was no public policy objection to an express assumption of risk defense against plaintiff's claims that the bindings on her ski boots had failed to release.

c.   In Mohney v. USA Hockey, Inc., 77 F.Supp.2d 859 (N.D.Ohio 1999), the court held that a release barred a strict liability claim against a hockey equipment manufacturer: "[S]ince strict liability requires a lesser showing of culpability than does negligence, it stands to reason that if a plaintiff can waive a negligence claim, he can also waive a strict liability claim."

See generally, Ausness, "Waive" Goodbye to Tort Liability: A Proposal to Remove Paternalism from Product Sales Transactions, 37 San Diego

L.Rev. 293 (2000), arguing for allowing waivers of liability by consumers in product sales cases involving personal injuries.

10. Where the plaintiff has prevailed against the retailer and the manufacturer in the case of a metal sliver in a can of tuna fish, how should the liability be apportioned? What if the defective product is a car with a loose wheel that should have been found by the retailer during its final check before delivering the car—and the plaintiff has recovered a judgment against both the manufacturer and the retailer?

11. *Preemption.* As we saw in Chapter VI, an increasing number of federal statutes and regulations are reducing the scope of state tort liability. The principal case on the preemption defense, *Geier*, p. 489, supra, involved a defective products claim, although the Court made nothing of that fact. A large number of preemption cases do in fact arise in product contexts, but they are subject to the same sorts of considerations that we addressed earlier. As an example of that sweep, see Note, The Federal Boat Safety Act of 1971 and Propeller Strike Injuries: An Unexpected Exercise in Federal Preemption, 68 Fordham L. Rev. 487 (1999).

F.   Work-Related Injuries

Almost all the main cases in this Chapter have involved claims brought by consumers. Recall *MacPherson* (car), *Soule* (car), *Camacho* (motorcycle), *Hood* (home saw), *Edwards* (nicotine patch) and *Vassallo* (breast implant). In each, the plaintiff has been the person who bought and used the product in question. As we have seen, the victim might also have been a passenger or pedestrian but in each the product was being used at the consumer stage. There is a second important group of cases that sometimes raises special questions: the product-related injury that occurs on the job. In this section we consider these special problems, including the impact of workers' compensation.

Although workers' tort suits against their employers are ordinarily barred, workers covered by compensation are generally able to sue third parties they believe violated tort obligations toward them—as though the compensation system did not exist. (In a few states, suits are barred against any third party contributing to the compensation system.) Moreover, the worker may accept compensation benefits and pursue the tort action simultaneously without waiving one or the other, though, as we shall see, the worker ordinarily must return the duplicative compensation benefits after recovering in tort. This has undoubtedly occurred in many cases that we have considered, especially in the defective product area. The internal operation of the compensation system is explored in detail in Chapter XI.

Jones v. Ryobi, Ltd.

United States Court of Appeals, Eighth Circuit, 1994.
37 F.3d 423.

Before FAGG, CIRCUIT JUDGE, HEANEY, SENIOR CIRCUIT JUDGE, and LOKEN, FAGG, CIRCUIT JUDGE.

Jennifer Jones was employed at Business Cards Tomorrow (BCT) as the operator of a small printing press known as an offset duplicator. Jones seriously injured her left hand when she caught it in the moving parts of the press. Alleging negligence and strict product liability for defective design, Jones brought this diversity lawsuit against Ryobi, Ltd. (the manufacturer) and A.B. Dick Corporation (the distributor). At trial, Jones dropped her negligence claims but she later moved to amend her complaint to reassert her negligence claim against the distributor. The district court denied Jones's motion to amend. At the close of Jones's case, the manufacturer and the distributor moved for judgment as a matter of law (JAML). The district court granted the manufacturer's and the distributor's motions for JAML. Jones appeals and we affirm.

The press involved in Jones's injury operates by passing blank paper through several moving parts, imprinting an image on the paper, and dispensing the printed paper through upper and lower "eject wheels." To avoid streaking the freshly printed image, on each job the operator must adjust the eject wheels to ensure the wheels do not touch the freshly printed area. The press was manufactured and sold to BCT equipped with both a plastic guard that prevented the operator from reaching into the moving parts to adjust the eject wheels, and an electric interlock switch that automatically shut off the press if the guard was opened. Sometime after the press was manufactured and delivered to BCT, the guard was removed and the interlock switch was disabled to allow the press to run without the guard. Because this modification increased production by saving the few seconds required to stop and to restart the press when the operator adjusted the eject wheels, the modification was a common practice in the printing industry.

Jones learned to operate the press by watching other BCT employees. Jones testified she knew the guard was missing and knew it was dangerous to have her hands near the unguarded moving parts, but her supervisor pressured her to save time by adjusting the eject wheels while the press was running. Jones feared she would be fired if she took the time to stop the press. While Jones was adjusting the eject wheels on the running press, a noise startled her. Jones jumped and her left hand was caught in the press's moving parts and crushed.

In granting the manufacturer's and the distributor's motions for JAML, the district court relied on the open and obvious nature of the asserted danger. See Restatement (Second) of Torts § 402A cmt. *i* (1965)(consumer expectation test). The district court did not reach the manufacturer's and the distributor's other grounds for JAML. We review the district court's grant of JAML de novo; thus, we may affirm on another ground. [ ] Because we conclude the district court's grant of JAML was proper on an alternate ground, we need not consider the ground relied on by the district court.

To recover on a theory of strict liability for defective design under Missouri law, Jones must prove she was injured as a direct result of a defect that existed when the press was sold. [   ] Jones had the burden to show the press had not been modified to create a defect that could have proximately caused her injury. [   ] Jones failed to meet this burden because her evidence showed the press had been substantially modified by removing the safety guard and disabling the interlock switch, and showed the modification caused her injury. When a third party's modification makes a safe product unsafe, the seller is relieved of liability even if the modification is foreseeable. [   ] Jones did not show who modified the press, but her evidence clearly showed that a third party, not the manufacturer or the distributor, was responsible for the modification.

Although the manufacturer provided tools for general maintenance of the press that could also be used to remove the guard, we do not believe this made the manufacturer responsible for the guard's removal. Jones produced no evidence that any representative of the manufacturer or the distributor removed the guard or instructed BCT to remove the guard from the press involved in Jones's injury. Indeed, the distributor's service representative testified he told BCT's owner several times the guard should be replaced, but BCT's owner shrugged off the suggestion. Because BCT knew the guard was missing and the interlock switch was disabled, but did not follow the distributor's advice to repair the disabled safety features, the distributor's service work on the press did not extend the distributor's liability to defects that were not present when the press was sold. [   ]

Jones argues the modification rule does not apply because the press was not safe even before the modification. We disagree. The press was safe before the modification because the press would not run without the safety guard covering the moving parts. The fact BCT encouraged Jones to operate the press without the safety features to increase production does not show the press was sold "in a defective condition [and thus] was unreasonably dangerous when put to a reasonably anticipated use." [   ] Although several witnesses testified the press operated more efficiently without the safety guard and interlock switch, other witnesses testified similar presses operated satisfactorily with the designed safety features intact. The press could be operated safely without removing the guard because the eject wheels did not have to be adjusted while the press was running. Jones's expert witness opined the press was unsafe as designed, but the expert based his view on the printing industry's tendency to disable the press's safety features to achieve greater production. Thus, the expert's testimony does not show the press was unreasonably dangerous when used in the same condition as when it was sold. [   ]

Because Jones's evidence showed a third party's modification, not a defect existing when the press was sold, was the sole cause of her injury, her strict product liability claim for defective design fails as a matter of law. [   ] The district court thus properly granted the manufacturer's and the distributor's JAML motions.

Finally, Jones contends the district court committed error in refusing to allow her to amend her complaint to reassert her negligence claim against the distributor. We disagree. The district court did not abuse its discretion to deny the amendment because the evidence presented did not show colorable grounds for Jones's negligence theory. [   ]

Accordingly, we affirm.

HEANEY, SENIOR CIRCUIT JUDGE, dissenting.

Viewing the evidence in the light most favorable to Jones, as we must, I cannot subscribe to the majority's opinion that the offset duplicator was safe as originally manufactured.

The rule to which Missouri adheres, as correctly stated by the majority, is that a manufacturer is not liable where a modification is foreseeable, but the modification renders a safe product unsafe.   .   .   .

.   .   . The critical question, thus, is whether the duplicator as manufactured was unreasonably dangerous.

The testimony of Dr. Creighton, Jones's expert witness, is alone sufficient to support the inference that the offset duplicator was not safe as originally designed.   .   .   . He testified that the duplicator's guard, in addition to not being fail-safe, was made of material "that will break   .   .   . readily," did not allow for proper ventilation of the internal components of the machine, and invited removal. He further testified that the design of the eject wheels, which essentially requires operators to make manual adjustments while the offset duplicator is running, was "absolutely not safe," indeed "the worst of situations from a human factors standpoint." The duplicator could have been equipped, he noted, with external adjustment handles to enable operators to make adjustments to the eject wheels without placing their hands in close proximity to the moving parts of the machine.

Further, although not direct proof that the duplicator was defectively designed, the fact that an overwhelming majority of machines had their guards removed after their delivery is evidence that the duplicator was incapable of operating efficiently according to industry standards. According to [a representative of the former distributor of the product] nearly ninety-eight percent of all machines he came into contact with had their safety covers removed. [   ] Indeed, [he] testified that he told duplicator operators in effect to remove the guard in order to alleviate problems with ink emulsification that occurred as a result of humidity which frequently became trapped inside the plastic shield. [   ]

The majority does not address (nor need it, given the focus of its opinion) the open-and-obvious defense on which the district court relied in granting the defendants' motion for judgment as a matter of law. I touch on it briefly [to show that it will not support affirmance.]

We have held that the obviousness of a defect or danger is material to the issue of whether a product is unreasonably dangerous. [   ] It does not, however, alone constitute a defense to a submissible case of strict liability under section 402A. [The question under Missouri law] is not simply whether the danger was open and obvious, but whether the product was unreasonably dangerous taking into account the obviousness of the danger.

There is no question in my mind that there was sufficient evidence from which a jury, taking into account the obviousness of the conceded danger, could conclude that the offset duplicator was unreasonably dangerous.   .   .   .

In my judgment there was sufficient evidence to support the inference that the offset duplicator was unreasonably dangerous and thus was defectively designed. This case should have met its fate in the hands of the jury members, not the district court's and not now ours.

Notes and Questions

1.   How would you analyze the trial judge's basis for dismissing the case—open and obvious danger?

2.   What is the significance of the fact that defendant distributor knew that BCT had removed the guard and tried "several times" to persuade management to put it back? Even if it did not know about BCT's practices, should it be enough that the manufacturer knew of the "common practice" in the industry to remove the guards? Suppose the distributor's representatives tried to sell the defendant's machine by encouraging buyers to remove the guard? Is it important whether the defendant manufacturer was aware of the distributor's approach?

3.   Is it relevant why the industry removed the guards? Does it matter whether it was to (a) save ten seconds three times a day, (b) increase production by 20%, (c) improve the quality of the end product? What does it mean to say that a guard "invites removal"?

4.   If a manufacturer has no duty to design a product that takes into account foreseeable substantial modifications what is the nature of a duty to market a reasonably safe product? How might the plaintiff show that the duplicator was "not safe" when it left the hands of the manufacturer and the distributor?

5.   Several witnesses testified that the machine operated more efficiently without the safety devices, while other witnesses testified that similar presses operated satisfactorily with the devices intact. Why does this not present a jury question?

6.   *Statutory change.* Although the judicial split may favor the dissent in *Ryobi*, the situation is less clear when statutory developments are considered. As we have noted in connection with joint and several liability, p. 370, supra, and will note more generally in Chapter XI, legislative changes to common law tort decisions have become more common recently. About a quarter of the states have adopted statutes aimed at protecting suppliers of goods that have been altered after the supplier distributed them. Some of these protect suppliers only when the alteration was not foreseeable. But several others apply to any substantial alteration.

7.   We turn now to the role of warnings in alteration cases. We return to questions of modification after the following case.

Liriano v. Hobart Corp.

Court of Appeals of New York, 1998.
92 N.Y.2d 232, 700 N.E.2d 303, 677 N.Y.S.2d 764.

CIPARICK, JUDGE.

In Robinson v. Reed–Prentice Div. of Package Mach. Co., [403 N.E.2d 440 (N.Y.1980)], we held that a manufacturer is not responsible for injuries resulting from substantial alterations or modifications of a product by a third party that render the product defective or otherwise unsafe. The present case certifies the issue of whether a plaintiff, whose design claim is barred by the substantial modification defense stated in *Robinson*, may nevertheless maintain a claim for failure to warn of the consequences of such modification. Finding the issue to be an open one, the United States Court of Appeals for the Second Circuit certified the following question to our Court:

> Can manufacturer liability exist under a failure to warn theory in cases in which the substantial modification defense would preclude liability under a design defect theory, and if so, is such manufacturer liability barred as a matter of law on the facts of this case, viewed in the light most favorable to the plaintiff?

We answer the first part of the certified question in the affirmative and decline to answer the second part .   .   .

[In 1993, Liriano, a 17-year-old recent immigrant, was employed in the meat department of a "Super" grocery store. He lost his right hand and lower forearm when his hand was caught in a meat grinder manufactured and sold by defendant in 1961. The safety guard had been removed from the grinder while it was in Super's possession and there was no warning on the grinder about the danger of using it without a guard. In 1962, after Hobart became aware that a significant number of purchasers of its meat grinders had removed the safety guards, it began issuing warnings on its meat grinders concerning removal of the safety guard.

Liriano sued Hobart under theories of negligence and strict products liability for, among other things, defective product design and failure to warn. Hobart impleaded Super. At trial the jury apportioned liability 5% to Hobart and 95% to Super. It then allocated 33 1/3% of the total responsibility to plaintiff. The trial judge entered a judgment that was conformed to reflect the jury's allocations.]

A manufacturer who places a defective product on the market that causes injury may be liable for the ensuing injuries [   ]. A product may be defective when it contains a manufacturing flaw, is defectively designed or is not accompanied by adequate warnings for the use of the product [   ]. A manufacturer has a duty to warn against latent dangers resulting from foreseeable uses of its product of which it knew or should have known [   ]. A manufacturer also has a duty to warn of the danger of unintended uses of a product provided these uses are reasonably foreseeable [citing among other cases, *Lugo*, p. 591, supra, and *McLaughlin v. Mine Safety Appliances Co.*, p. 412, supra].

A manufacturer is not liable for injuries caused by substantial alterations to the product by a third party that render the product defective or
unsafe [*Robinson*]. Where, however, a product is purposefully manufactured to permit its use without a safety feature, a plaintiff may recover for
injuries suffered as a result of removing the safety feature [Lopez v.
Precision Papers, 492 N.E.2d 1214 (N.Y.1986)].

[Hobart argued that *Robinson* should apply to failure-to-warn claims as
well as design claims.] Several intermediate appellate courts have interpreted *Robinson* to mean that, where a substantial alteration of a product
occurs, an injured party is also precluded from asserting a claim for failure
to warn [   ]. Relying on *Robinson* and these lower court decisions, Hobart
urges that the plaintiff's failure-to-warn claim should be barred as a matter
of law. *Robinson*, however, did not resolve the issue of whether preclusion
of a claim for defective design because of substantial alteration by a third
party should also bar a claim for failure to warn.

This Court's rationale in *Robinson* stemmed from the recognition that
a manufacturer is responsible for a "purposeful design choice" that presents an unreasonable danger to the user [*Robinson*.] This responsibility
derives from the manufacturer's superior position to anticipate reasonable
uses of its product and its obligation to design a product that is not harmful
when used in that manner. However, this duty is not open-ended, and it is
measured as of the time the product leaves the manufacturer's premises.
Thus, a manufacturer is not required to insure that subsequent owners and
users will not adapt the product to their own unique uses. That kind of
obligation is much too broad and would effectively impose liability on
manufacturers for all product-related injuries [   ].

While this Court stated that principles of foreseeability are inapplicable
where there has been a substantial modification of the product, that
discussion was limited to the manufacturer's responsibility for defective
design where there had been a substantial alteration of a product by a third
party [   ]. Thus, this Court stated that a manufacturer's duty "does not
extend to *designing* a product that is impossible to abuse or one whose
safety features may not be circumvented" and the manufacturer need not
trace its "product through every link in the chain of distribution to insure
that users will not adapt the product to suit their own unique purposes"
[   ] [emphasis added].

Hobart and amici argue that the rationale of *Robinson* is equally
applicable to failure-to-warn claims where a substantial modification of the
product occurs and that application of the failure-to-warn doctrine in these
circumstances would undermine *Robinson*'s policy justification and destroy
its purpose. This Court is not persuaded that the existence of a substantial
modification defense precludes, in all cases, a failure-to-warn claim.

The factors militating against imposing a duty to design against
foreseeable post-sale product modifications are either not present or less
cogent with respect to a duty to warn against making such modifications.
The existence of a design defect involves a risk/utility analysis that requires
an assessment of whether "if the design defect were known at the time of

the manufacture, a reasonable person would conclude that the utility of the product did not outweigh the risk inherent in marketing a product designed in that manner" [   ]. Such an analysis would be unreasonably complicated, and may very well be impossible to measure, if a manufacturer has to factor into the design equation all foreseeable post-sale modifications. Imposition of a duty that is incapable of assessment would effectively result in the imposition of absolute liability on manufacturers for all product-related injuries [see *Robinson*]. This Court has drawn a policy line against that eventuality.

These concerns are not as strongly implicated in the context of a duty to warn. Unlike design decisions that involve the consideration of many interdependent factors, the inquiry in a duty to warn case is much more limited, focusing principally on the foreseeability of the risk and the adequacy and effectiveness of any warning. The burden of placing a warning on a product is less costly than designing a perfectly safe, tamper resistant product. Thus, although it is virtually impossible to design a product to forestall all future risk-enhancing modifications that could occur after the sale, it is neither infeasible nor onerous, in some cases, to warn of the dangers of foreseeable modifications that pose the risk of injury.

Furthermore, this Court has held that a manufacturer may be liable for failing to warn against the dangers of foreseeable misuse of its product [   ]. No material distinction between foreseeable misuse and foreseeable alteration of a product is evident in this context. Thus, the rationale of [*Lugo*] should apply to both situations.[2]

This Court has also recognized that, in certain circumstances, a manufacturer may have a duty to warn of dangers associated with the use of its product even after it has been sold. Such a duty will generally arise where a defect or danger is revealed by user operation and brought to the attention of the manufacturer; the existence and scope of such a duty are generally fact-specific (see, Cover v. Cohen, [473 N.Y.S.2d 378 (N.Y.1984)]; [   ].)[3]

The justification for the post-sale duty to warn arises from a manufacturer's unique (and superior) position to follow the use and adaptation of its product by consumers (see, [*Cover*]). Compared to purchasers and users of a product, a manufacturer is best placed to learn about post-sale defects or dangers discovered in use. A manufacturer's superior position to garner information and its corresponding duty to warn is no less with respect to the ability to learn of modifications made to or misuse of a product. Indeed, as in this case, Hobart was the only party likely to learn about the removal

---

2. True, issues of foreseeability, obviousness, proximate cause or the adequacy of warnings can be troublesome in failure-to-warn cases, as has been noted by various commentators [   ]. Those difficulties do not, however, negate the duty to warn against foreseeable product misuse which is well established in this Court's precedents as well as contemporary products liability jurisprudence.

3. As we noted in *Cover*, the post-sale duty of a manufacturer to warn involves the weighing of a number of factors: including the degree of danger the problem involves, the number of reported incidents, the burden of providing the warning, as well as the burden and/or ability to track a product post-sale. [   ]

of the safety guards and, as it ultimately did, pass along warnings to customers.

This Court therefore concludes that manufacturer liability can exist under a failure-to-warn theory in cases in which the substantial modification defense as articulated in *Robinson* might otherwise preclude a design defect claim.

We should emphasize, however, that a safety device built into the integrated final product is often the most effective way to communicate that operation of the product without the device is hazardous. Thus, where the injured party was fully aware of the hazard through general knowledge, observation or common sense, or participated in the removal of the safety device whose purpose is obvious, lack of a warning about that danger may well obviate the failure to warn as a legal cause of an injury resulting from that danger [   ]. Thus, in appropriate cases, courts could as a matter of law decide that a manufacturer's warning would have been superfluous given an injured party's actual knowledge of the specific hazard that caused the injury [   ]. Nevertheless, in cases where reasonable minds might disagree as to the extent of plaintiff's knowledge of the hazard, the question is one for the jury [   ].

Similarly, a limited class of hazards need not be warned of as a matter of law because they are patently dangerous or pose open and obvious risks, [   ]. Where a danger is readily apparent as a matter of common sense, "there should be no liability for failing to warn someone of a risk or hazard which he [or she] appreciated to the same extent as a warning would have provided" [   ]. Put differently, when a warning would have added nothing to the user's appreciation of the danger, no duty to warn exists as no benefit would be gained by requiring a warning. On the other hand, the open and obvious defense generally should not apply when there are aspects of the hazard which are concealed or not reasonably apparent to the user.

This is particularly important because requiring a manufacturer to warn against obvious dangers could greatly increase the number of warnings accompanying certain products. If a manufacturer must warn against even obvious dangers, "[t]he list of foolish practices warned against would be so long, it would fill a volume" [   ]. Requiring too many warnings trivializes and undermines the entire purpose of the rule, drowning out cautions against latent dangers of which a user might not otherwise be aware. Such a requirement would neutralize the effectiveness of warnings as an inexpensive way to allow consumers to adjust their behavior based on knowledge of a product's inherent dangers.

While important to warning law, the open and obvious danger exception is difficult to administer [   ]. The fact-specific nature of the inquiry into whether a particular risk is obvious renders bright-line pronouncements difficult, and in close cases it is easy to disagree about whether a particular risk is obvious. It is hard to set a standard for obviousness that is neither under- nor over-inclusive. Because of the factual nature of the inquiry, whether a danger is open and obvious is most often a jury question

[   ]. Where only one conclusion can be drawn from the established facts, however, the issue of whether the risk was open and obvious may be decided by the court as a matter of law.

[The court declined to answer the second question because failure-to-warn "liability is intensely fact-specific, including but not limited to such issues as feasibility and difficulty of issuing warnings in the circumstances [   ]; obviousness of the risk from actual use of the product; knowledge of the particular product user; and proximate cause." The factual record was being developed in the federal court. Thus, "any remaining question posed is appropriately addressed by the Second Circuit in light of the substantive law question we have now resolved."]

Accordingly, the certified question should be answered as follows: manufacturer liability for failure to warn may exist in cases where the substantial modification defense would preclude liability on a design defect theory.

KAYE, C.J., and TITONE, BELLACOSA, SMITH, LEVINE and WESLEY, JJ., concur.

Notes and Questions

1. Why does *Robinson* bar a design defect claim in this case? Is the court's treatment of the distinction between design and warning in this context persuasive? When the reasons for *Robinson* are considered in warning cases why are they "not present or less cogent?"

2. If "the principles of foreseeability are inapplicable where there has been a substantial modification of the product," what does the court mean when it refers to a product that "is purposefully manufactured to permit its use without a safety feature"?

In the cited *Lopez* case, plaintiff forklift operator was injured when an object fell onto his unprotected head. The overhead guard had been removed in the workplace. In the suit against the manufacturer, the court distinguished *Robinson*, stating in full:

> The record presents triable issues of fact concerning whether the forklift, as marketed with an attached but removable overhead safety guard, was "not reasonably" safe [   ] for the uses intended or reasonably anticipated by the manufacturer.
>
> [*Robinson*] does not compel a different result. In contrast with the detaching of the removable safety guard in this case, *Robinson* involved "[m]aterial alterations [i.e. cutting a 6-inch by 14-inch access hole in the safety gate of a plastic molding machine] which work[ed] a substantial change in the conditions in which the product was sold by destroying the functional utility of a key safety feature" [   ]. There is evidence in this record that the forklift was purposefully manufactured to permit its use without the safety guard.

3. Other courts have responded differently to the alteration problem than have Missouri and New York. Consider Anderson v. Nissei ASB

Machine Co., Ltd., 3 P.3d 1088 (Ariz.App.1999), involving a machine for making plastic bottles. The machine came with safety doors that left a six-inch space through which hands could fit. It also came with "purge guards" that were attached to the safety doors with three small screws (not rivets) and that reduced the open space from six inches to three inches. Opening or jarring the safety doors automatically shut down the machine. Once shut down, the machine took as long as two hours to restart. Workers faced the problem of how to remove "drool"—molten waste material that quickly hardens into rock-like lumps. If it is not removed at least every 15 minutes, the drool will damage the machine and render it inoperable. Defendant's manual did not mention drool or how to remove it. The workers developed their own system: inserting a stick with a long hook into the three-inch gap left by the purge guard and dragging out the drool. If the stick hit or jarred the doors the machine would shut down. As frequently happened with this machine model, someone in the factory (other than plaintiff) removed the purge guards so that it would be easier to get the drool out without jarring the machine. An expert testified that increasing the open space from three to six inches made removal much easier. As plaintiff reached into the six-inch gap of the operating machine his hand and forearm were crushed.

The court, 2–1, upheld a jury finding that the machine was defective as marketed. The court focused on the ease of removal of the purge guards and the defendant's failure to warn or address the issue of drool. Since the modification was essential to keep the machine running and purge-guard removal was common in the industry, a jury could find that the removal was foreseeable, and the product defective. The court distinguished the New York position in *Robinson* on the ground that the modification here was not simply to increase the employer's productivity but to make the machine function adequately for the purpose for which it was sold. Also, in *Robinson* there was no defect in the design of the safety gate. The court disagreed with *Jones v. Ryobi* because Missouri law denied recovery even in cases of foreseeable dangerous modification. (The recovery was reduced because of the worker's contributory responsibility, a subject addressed shortly in these notes.)

See also Spurgeon v. Julius Blum, Inc., 816 F.Supp. 1317 (C.D.Ill. 1993), suggesting that the requisite foreseeability may be established by showing that a machine guard is easily removed, difficult to replace, must be removed frequently for cleaning, or that the guard inhibits the task the machine is to perform.

4. On remand in *Liriano*, on the warning question, the Second Circuit found a jury question. 170 F.3d 264 (2d Cir.1999). Judge Calabresi noted that—taking the facts most favorably to the plaintiff—Liriano, who was 17 years old at the time of the accident, had "recently immigrated" to the United States, had been employed at Super for one week, had not been instructed in the operation of the grinder, and had used it only two or three times previously. In addition, the danger was not visible to the operator. Defendant argued that the danger of grinders was so widely understood that no warning was necessary.

But the court observed that a warning may do more "than exhort its audience to be careful." Beyond showing danger, a warning can also show ways to avoid harm. He used the distinction between two signs: "Danger— Steep Grade" and "Danger—Steep Grade Ahead—Follow Suggested Detour to Avoid Dangerous Areas." Even if New York "would consider the danger of meat grinders to be obvious as a matter of law, that obviousness does not substitute for the warning that a jury could, and indeed did, find that Hobart had a duty to provide." On causation, the court invoked a "heeding presumption."

Concurring, Judge Newman observed that a warning might have spurred the plaintiff to ask others for help. He also noted that it was easier for a driver to avoid a steep grade than for a worker to refuse to work on a dangerous product. Reasonable minds might differ on "avoiding use of a machine from which a safety guard had been removed and requesting a machine with the guard in place." He noted that Hobart had already placed "on its machines a warning against use if the safety guard has been removed." What is likely to happen when the guard is removed from a machine with a warning on it?

5. *The bulk supplier.* As we saw earlier with the exception for learned intermediaries, p. 592 supra, we find here a frequently-encountered exception when one company supplies a product in bulk to a large enterprise where it will be used by many workers. A typical example is Adams v. Union Carbide, 737 F.2d 1453 (6th Cir.), cert. denied 469 U.S. 1062 (1984), in which the plaintiff sued Union Carbide for failing to provide direct warnings of dangers associated with toluene diisocyanate (TDI) that it supplied to her employer, General Motors. Union Carbide had warned GM about the dangers and had relied on GM to communicate these warnings to its employees. The court, using Ohio law, held that no direct warnings were necessary. GM was held to be a sophisticated buyer on whom Union Carbide could rely.

Some states have been reluctant to apply the exception. In McCullock v. H.B. Fuller Co., 981 F.2d 656 (2d Cir.1992), defendant supplied hot melt glue to plaintiff's employer, a book bindery. Plaintiff claimed that fumes from the glue had harmed her. Defendant had warned the employer of the need for adequate ventilation by affixing labels on each box that complied with OSHA regulations and warned of dangers and referred the purchaser to a data sheet that defendant in fact had sent to the employer. Plaintiff claimed that she never saw any warning because she did not transfer the glue from the shipping box to the glue pot. She also claimed that a representative of defendant visited the bindery every few weeks and "knew that the glue pot was unventilated." Applying Vermont law, the court relied on a state case that had asserted that a manufacturer's duty to warn was not "limited to purchasers but extended to employees of purchasers as well."

For a case in which the manufacturer of a dangerous liquid bulk product was held to owe at a minimum a duty to stop supplying downstream repackagers who omitted necessary warnings, see Hunnings v.

Texaco, Inc., 29 F.3d 1480 (11th Cir.1994) (applying Florida law). Plaintiff's claim could also encompass a requirement that defendant instruct "downstream distributors to notify retailers to discontinue the practice of packaging mineral spirits in milk containers, [   ], or curtailing business with customers who were known to distribute the product to errant retailers."

6. *Defenses in the employment setting.* As one might imagine, several unique issues arise in evaluating defenses to products liability claims deriving from the workplace. First, we will examine the question of whether an employer's negotiated agreement with a product supplier can operate as a bar to the employee's suit against the seller. Then we will consider under what conditions an employee can be said to have assumed a risk encountered during the course of employment. Both of these issues address the question of how employers incorporate employees' personal safety into their own calculus of costs. The nature of workers' compensation systems, discussed in Chapter XI, may also affect judicial attitudes in this area.

7. *The employer as buyer.* To what extent should a product supplier be able to transfer responsibility for employees' personal injuries through its negotiations with an employer? This question arises when courts consider whether or not product suppliers should be obliged to evaluate the risks to employees created by the absence of safety features that employer purchasers have bargained away. Should an employer's purchasing decisions be imputed to its employees?

In Scarangella v. Thomas Built Buses, Inc., 717 N.E.2d 679 (N.Y.1999), plaintiff employee of a school bus company (Huntington) was hurt when one of the company's buses, built by defendant, backed into her in the bus yard. The new bus had been bought without the optional backup alarm. Clifford, the chief operating officer of Huntington, testified that he made what the court called "a considered decision" not to purchase the "screaming alarms" because he intended to park the buses at yards in the middle of residential neighborhoods and had been experiencing problems with neighbors concerned with noise pollution. Although there was a "tremendous amount" of backing up in the yard, Clifford ordered drivers to be careful and to use their ordinary horns. Clifford also considered the risk to be minimal because "the only significant incidence of operating buses in reverse was in positioning buses in and backing them out of the yard." Because of the blind spot when buses were moving in reverse, the drivers "were instructed as part of their training not to operate the buses in reverse except in the yard." The trial judge's directed verdict for defendant was affirmed on appeal. The court reviewed its prior cases on when a product without an optional safety device was defective:

> The product is not defective where the evidence and reasonable inferences therefrom show that: (1) the buyer is thoroughly knowledgeable regarding the product and its use and is actually aware that the safety feature is available; (2) there exist normal circumstances of use in which the product is not unreasonably dangerous without the optional equipment; and (3) the buyer is in a position, given the range of uses of

the product, to balance the benefits and the risks of not having the safety device in the specifically contemplated circumstances of the buyer's use of the product. In such a case, the buyer, not the manufacturer is in the superior position to make the risk-utility assessment, and a well-considered decision by the buyer to dispense with the optional safety equipment will excuse the manufacturer from liability.

The court concluded that all three factors had been established as a matter of law and that no jury questions remained. It did observe that had the accident occurred outside of the yard or had the plaintiff submitted evidence of "some incidence of buses backing up outside the yard, at least a triable issue might have been created as to whether there was an actual separate and distinct normal use of the buses without back-up alarms which was reasonably safe." When the court says that the buyer was in a "superior position" to the manufacturer, is the risk to the user/employee relevant?

Should the court have reached the same result if suit had been brought by a student run over by a bus that was backing up? Should it matter whether the school buses had to go in reverse only 1% of the time they were on assignment or 10%?

Is *Scarangella* consistent with the cases on misuse and alteration, supra?

A related defense may arise in cases in which employers or their agents have negotiated waivers and expressly assumed the risks entailed by a product. These sellers may assert that the employer's explicit assumption of risk should apply to an injured employee as well. Courts disagree on this. In Buettner v. R.W. Martin & Sons, Inc., 47 F.3d 116 (4th Cir.1995) (applying Virginia law), plaintiff was a supervisor in the flatwork department of a commercial laundry. One day as she handled a flatwork ironer in preparation for the day's work, her sweater became entangled in the front of the ironer, and her right arm was amputated below the elbow. Both a written sales proposal by the seller and the sales invoice specified that the (used) ironer was sold "as is." The court held that the disclaimer could be enforced against the employee as well as her employer, and that a statutory provision rendering limitations of remedies in personal injury cases prima facie unconscionable applied only to consumer goods. Can disparate outcomes in the consumer and employee areas be justified?

Contrast Ferragamo v. Massachusetts Bay Transportation Authority, 481 N.E.2d 477 (Mass.1985), arising after a worker was killed by inhaling PVCs that suffused the used trolley cars that the Transportation Authority had sold his employer. The buyer had signed a contract of sale containing a comprehensive disclaimer that specified that the buyer would be "solely responsible for all injuries to persons." The employee was held not to be bound by the disclaimer, and, furthermore, the "disclaimer [was] irrelevant in an action which, although framed as one for breach of warranty, [was] based on strict tort liability." Recall *Vassallo*, p. 597, supra.

8. *The employee's behavior.* Some Ohio cases have considered assumption of risk in the workplace context. In Cremeans v. Willmar Henderson Manufacturing Co., 566 N.E.2d 1203 (Ohio 1991), plaintiff's job was to load fertilizer at Sohio's plant. The loader had been designed by defendant Willmar to be sold with a protective cage for the driver, known as a ROPS. Since the loader could not fit into the fertilizer room to scoop the fertilizer if it had the cage, Sohio ordered it without the protective covering. In the bill of sale, the defendant insisted that Sohio assume any liability arising from the removal of the cage. "Cremeans continued to operate the [un-caged] loader in the fertilizer bins even though he was aware of the potential for an avalanche. Cremeans continued to operate the loader because it was his job." If the loader had had its ROPS, plaintiff "would not have sustained his injury." Before considering plaintiff's conduct, how might the *Scarangella* court have analyzed this case?

A divided supreme court refused to apply assumption of risk against Cremeans. The plurality thought that

> The record in this case demonstrates that Cremeans encountered the risks associated with the use of the Willmar loader because he was required to do so in the normal performance of his job duties and responsibilities and that Cremeans was injured during the execution of such duties and responsibilities. Therefore, his assumption of the risk was neither voluntary nor unreasonable and, hence, ... Cremeans is not barred from recovery on his products liability claim based upon strict liability in tort. This is so regardless of the fact that it was Cremeans's employer, and not Willmar, who required Cremeans to perform the particular job duty which resulted in the injury. Given the facts of this case, to wit, that Willmar knew that the loader it was selling to Sohio was not equipped with a necessary safety device and, in fact, demanded indemnity from Sohio before agreeing to make the sale, the issue is even clearer.

> . . . . Thus, Cremeans was put at risk either solely as a result of the product defect, or by the combination of the defect and the conduct of Cremeans's employer, Sohio. In either event, the economic pressures associated with the reality of today's workplace inevitably came to bear on Cremeans's decision to encounter the risk.

For the dissenters "[t]he unbelievably bad result of the majority opinion here is that the manufacturer becomes an insurer of his product whenever an employer coerces his workers into exposing themselves to unconscionable risk of injury." Why is that result "unbelievably bad?" Does the indemnity contract alter that characterization?

Is the plurality's concern with the "economic pressures" placed upon the employee analogous to courts' worries in the consumer situation about customers' bargaining powers?

After *Cremeans*, Ohio adopted legislation providing in part that when plaintiff establishes a strict liability defect, a showing that the victim "expressly or impliedly assumed the risk" is a "complete bar" to recovery of damages. Would that alter the result in *Cremeans*? In any event, could Cremeans have avoided the statute by proving negligence?

In Carrel v. Allied Products Corp., 677 N.E.2d 795 (Ohio 1997), the court held that the common law action of negligent design did survive the legislation, but limited *Cremeans* by asserting that the case had not completely eliminated the assumption of risk defense when an employee is injured by a defective product. Carrel, a long-term employee of Whirlpool Corp., was hurt while assisting a newly-trained co-worker in determining the cause of a misaligned piece on a six-hundred-ton transfer press. He claimed that the absence of barrier guards to prevent the machine from cycling had caused the amputation of several fingers. The court found a role for implied assumption of the risk:

> An employee will be deemed to have voluntarily exposed himself or herself to a risk when he or she has elected to use a defective product. However, the defense of assumption of the risk is not available when the employee is required to encounter the risk while performing normal job duties.

In this instance, Carrel had not assumed the risk since he had not necessarily "appreciated the full danger of the risk." In what kinds of cases would the defense apply? A dissenter argued that the majority should have focused on whether or not Carrel assumed the risk voluntarily, rather than whether or not he "appreciated the full danger of the press." If an experienced worker could not be said to "appreciate the full danger" of a product in his workplace, could the court find that anyone had done so?

Are these cases consistent with the discussion of work-related defenses in negligence cases? Recall, generally, p. 483 supra.

Meshing Compensation and Tort

In our consideration of products liability cases involving work-related injuries, we have not considered a very important aspect—the interplay between tort law and workers' compensation. The following excerpt discusses that relationship. In recent years, along with the increasing number of suits brought by injured workers against third parties, these third parties have sought to recoup all or part of their tort payments from the employer. The question in these cases is whether the exclusivity provision in the typical compensation statute bars actions for contribution or indemnity by defendants who would have been jointly liable with the employer under traditional tort rules, yet who have been held solely liable for the full extent of the injury. To what extent is the latter action simply an indirect suit by the employee that should be barred by the statute? Consider the following discussion of alternative approaches to this problem.

Enterprise Responsibility for Personal Injury Vol. II, Approaches to Legal and Institutional Change
Report to the American Law Institute (1991). 187–92.

III.   The Policy Options

A.   The Dominance of WC Policy

At this time the great majority of states still deny the third-party manufacturer any contribution at all from the negligent employer toward the full tort damages awarded to the injured employee.

The policy rationale for this position is that the employer, which has been promised full immunity from fault-based tort liability in return for financing no-fault WC benefits for its employees, should not face any erosion in that legal protection through the device of the employee's suing a third party and the third party's forcing the employer to foot a share of the resulting tort award. But the practical consequence is that even in cases in which the employer was negligent, the employer will emerge scot-free from any financial contribution to compensate the injuries if tort liability happens to be fixed on a third party and if part of the proceeds are then used to satisfy the employer's lien for its WC payments.

As we noted, from the point of view of compensation policy this result is neutral because the injured worker ends up with full tort damages and no more. From the point of view of administration this position is the most economical because it avoids any need to resolve an often contentious dispute over whether and to what extent the employer was at fault in the accident, as compared with the responsibility of worker and manufacturer. But the price of such administrative saving is a potentially serious gap and distortion in effective prevention. In these kinds of cases the employer faces no legal-financial impact from its misuse of "defective" products; instead, all such incentives are trained on the manufacturer to build costly safeguards into its products in order to avoid the hazards created by a minority of employers who are prepared to disregard the safety and health of their employees.

B.   The Dominance of Tort Policy

In response to that concern, courts in a few jurisdictions have moved to a legal position which effectively ignores the WC exclusivity principle in this context and simply applies a new tort law approach, apportioning burdens among all negligent actors. In effect, these courts are prepared to bear the additional administrative price of establishing and comparing the employer's responsibility for the injury in order to secure the basic tort function of creating a financial incentive for all parties to avoid the legal risk by taking reasonable steps to prevent the injury from occurring in the first place.

The problem in that approach is its focusing on the apparently sensible tort disposition of the immediate case while overlooking the broader policy trade-off within the WC system as a whole. Under tort law the manufacturer will be liable in full for any injuries (in the workplace or otherwise) caused by its products which are defective. . . . By contrast, under WC the employer has immunity from direct tort suit for full damages even where it has been at fault because the same employer is obligated to pay for guaranteed but limited WC benefits to all employees who are hurt on the job, even when the employer was not at fault—indeed, even in cases where the injury was due to the fault of the employee himself or of a judgment-proof outside party. But now, simply because a particular injured employee may happen to have a valid tort claim against a third party, the employer will be required to shoulder an additional financial burden for injuries in its workplace over and above what the community has decided was appropriate under its WC policy.

C.   Substantive Blend of Tort and WC Policy

Recognition of that problem has led a few states to a solution that appeared to mesh more successfully the principles and policies of the WC and tort regimes. The employer would be required to contribute a share of the injured worker's damage award against the third-party manufacturer, but only up to the amount of the employer's financial exposure to pay WC benefits for the injury. In effect, the limited employer contribution to tort damages would offset what otherwise would be the employer's WC lien against the tort award. The simplest legal mechanism for accomplishing that result is to allow the third party to assert the amount of the employer's WC payment as a setoff against the employee's tort claim and to reduce correspondingly the employer's lien against the employee's tort award.

The positive virtue of this substantive policy blend is that the employer continues to bear its expected WC share of the cost of workplace injuries. As a result, the happenstance of third-party tort litigation will not relieve the employer of the normal financial incentive it faces under WC to adopt feasible precautions to avoid injuries to its employees. However, the negative flip side of this new policy is that an additional and expensive contest over the employer's fault in managing its workplace is introduced into what otherwise would be a more straightforward dispute between the employee and the manufacturer about the safety of a particular product. Moreover, complex and often contentious calculations are necessary in order to work out the appropriate reductions and setoffs whenever there is a compromise settlement (rather than an itemized adjudication) of such a tort claim, often involving only partial tort damages where full WC benefits have already been paid.

D.   Administrative Accommodation of WC and Tort

To avoid some of these difficulties we endorse a different tack toward the same objective, an approach contained in the proposed Uniform Product Liability Act.

State WC legislation should be altered by eliminating any subrogation right of the employer against the injured worker's tort award. At the same time, product liability law should be altered by reducing the size of tort damages by the amount of WC benefits payable by the employer to the employee.

Note that there are substantial differences between this resolution of the problem and that embodied in Model C above. Under this proposal the manufacturer's tort liability would be reduced only by the WC benefit actually payable by the employer, rather than by some appropriate measure of the culpable employer's share of the larger tort award. At the same time, all employers, not only culpable employers, would lose their subrogation right against the worker's tort award. The aim is to exclude not simply the contentious issue of the employer's comparative fault, but also the very presence of the employer from the tort contest between injured worker and third-party manufacturer. . . . In contrast with the current offset-lien rule in the vast majority of jurisdictions, we would shift a somewhat greater share of the current burden of compensating workers to the considerably cheaper-to-administer WC insurance regime, away from the increasingly expensive tort litigation/liability insurance system. In the long run such a move would enure to the benefit of employers as well, because the manufacturers' rising expenses for product liability insurance and legal fees are eventually incorporated in the prices firms charge customers for their products; and in the case of workplace products, the customers are those very employers.

———

There is a fifth possibility: barring the tort action—a position rejected by the Report. In O'Connell and Oldfather, A Lost Opportunity: A Review of the American Law Institute's Reporters' Study on Enterprise Responsibility for Personal Injury, 30 San Diego L. Rev. 307 (1993), the authors quote approvingly the proposal of an insurance industry group:

> [R]emove all employee rights to sue product manufacturers in tort for workplace injuries [in third party accidents] in return for significant improvements in [no-fault workers' compensation] benefits available to all workers (in particular the indexing of long term [workers' compensation] disability or survivorship benefits), while preserving the employer's right to sue the product manufacturer to recover [workers' compensation] benefits paid for injuries resulting from the wrongful conduct of the third-party manufacturer.

Which of the various alternatives seems most appealing to you? The level of workers' compensation benefits is considered in Chapter XI.

G. BEYOND PRODUCTS?

Royer v. Catholic Medical Center

Supreme Court of New Hampshire, 1999.
741 A.2d 74.

BROCK, C.J.

[Plaintiff underwent a total knee replacement at defendant CMC, during which a prosthetic knee provided by defendant was surgically implanted. When he complained of pain in the knee, his doctors discovered that the prosthesis was defective. He underwent a second operation during which the defective prosthesis was removed and a second one implanted. Plaintiff alleged that CMC "was strictly liable to [Royer] because it had sold a prosthesis with a design defect that was in an unreasonably dangerous condition." The defendant moved to dismiss, arguing, inter alia, that it was not a "seller of goods" for purposes of strict products liability. The trial court granted CMC's motion to dismiss the complaint.]

In New Hampshire, "[o]ne who sells any product in a defective condition unreasonably dangerous to the user or consumer or to his property is subject to [strict] liability for physical harm thereby caused" if, inter alia, "the seller is engaged in the business of selling such a product." [§ 402A] If the defendant merely provides a service, however, there is no liability absent proof of a violation of a legal duty. [   ] In this case, we are asked to determine whether a health care provider that supplies a defective prosthesis in the course of delivering health care services is a "seller" of prosthetic devices, or is merely providing a professional service.

In deciding this issue of first impression, we are guided by the principles that have supported the development of a cause of action for strict liability in New Hampshire. "Strict liability for damages has traditionally met with disfavor in this jurisdiction." Bruzga v. PMR Architects, [693 A.2d 401, 404–05 (N.H.1997)]. As a general rule,

> strict liability is available only where the Legislature has provided for it or in those situations where the common law of this state has imposed such liability and the Legislature has not seen fit to change it. [   ]

> . . .

> The reasons for the development of strict liability in tort were the lack of privity between the manufacturer and the buyer, the difficulty of proving negligence against a distant manufacturer using mass production techniques, and the better ability of the mass manufacturer to spread the economic risks among consumers.

[*Bruzga*]. Particularly crucial to our adoption of strict liability in the context of defective products was the practical impossibility of proving legal fault in many products liability cases. [   ]

Although we have adopted a cause of action for strict products liability, we have recognized limits to the doctrine. [   ] In *Bruzga*, we rejected an argument that strict liability should extend to architects and building contractors who allegedly designed and "manufactured" a defective building. [   ] After determining that the reasons supporting strict liability did not apply to architects and contractors, we concluded that architects and contractors provide a professional service. [   ] Although we acknowledged that a building contractor "supplies" a structure to the purchaser, we declined to extend strict products liability to contractors because they are "engaged primarily in the rendition of a service." [   ]

A majority of the jurisdictions that have addressed whether a health care provider who supplies a defective prosthesis is subject to strict liability have declined to extend strict liability, similarly reasoning that the health care provider primarily renders a service, and that the provision of a prosthetic device is merely incidental to that service. [The court cited supporting and disagreeing cases.] The defendant urges us to adopt this rationale.

The plaintiffs argue, however, that the distinction between selling products and providing services is a legal fiction. The defendant, according to the plaintiffs, acted both as a seller of the prosthetic knee and as a provider of professional services in the transaction. Because the defendant charged separately for the prosthesis and earned a profit on the "sale," the plaintiffs argue that the defendant should be treated no differently than any other distributor of a defective product. The defendant, according to the plaintiffs, primarily supplied a prosthesis, while the surgeon provided the professional "services."

Although a defendant may both provide a service and sell a product within the same transaction for purposes of strict liability, [   ] the dispositive issue in this case is not whether the defendant "sold" or transferred a prosthetic knee, but whether the defendant was an entity "engaged in the business of selling" prosthetic knees so as to warrant the imposition of liability without proof of legal fault. "[T]he language of 402A, . . . as with other non-statutory declarations, is a common law pronouncement by the court, which always retains the right and the duty to test the reason behind a common law rule in determining the applicability of such a rule to the facts before it." [   ] We find the reasoning of both *Bruzga* and the majority of courts that have declined to extend strict liability to health care providers who supply defective prostheses to be persuasive.

. . .

. . . . "[T]he essence of the transaction between the retail seller and the consumer relates to the article sold. The seller is in the business of supplying the product to the consumer. It is that, and that alone, for which he is paid." [   ] A patient, by contrast, does not enter a hospital to "purchase" a prosthesis, "but to obtain a course of treatment in the hope of being cured of what ails him." [   ] Indeed, "to ignore the ancillary nature of the association of product with activity is to posit surgery, or . . . any medical service requiring the use of a physical object, as a marketing device for the incorporated object." [   ]

We decline to ignore the reality of the relationship between Ira Royer and CMC, and to treat any services provided by CMC as ancillary to a primary purpose of selling a prosthetic knee. Rather, the record indicates that in addition to the prosthesis, Royer was billed for a hospital room, operating room services, physical therapy, a recovery room, pathology laboratory work, an EKG or ECG, X-rays, and anesthesia. Thus, it is evident that Ira Royer entered CMC not to purchase a prosthesis, but to obtain health care services that included the implantation of the knee, with the overall objective of restoring his health. [   ] Necessary to the restoration of his health, in the judgment of his physicians, was the implantation of the prosthesis. We do not find this scenario, as [plaintiff urges], analogous to one in which a plaintiff purchases a defective tire from a retail tire distributor and has the distributor install the tire. [   ]

Moreover, the policy rationale underlying strict liability, as in *Bruzga*, does not support extension of the doctrine under the facts of this case. With respect to the inherent difficulty of proving negligence in many products liability cases, this rationale fails in the context of non-manufacturer cases alleging a design defect. Because "ordinarily there is no possibility that a distributor other than the manufacturer created a design defect[,] . . . strict liability would impose liability when there is no possibility of negligence." [ ] The plaintiffs do not allege in this case that the defendant altered the prosthesis in any way. Further, holding health care providers strictly liable for defects in prosthetic devices necessary to the provision of health care would likely result in higher health care costs borne ultimately by all patients, [ ], and "place an unrealistic burden on the physicians and hospitals of this state to test or guarantee the tens of thousands of products used in hospitals by doctors," [ ]. Additionally, "research and innovation in medical equipment and treatment would be inhibited." [ ] We find that the "peculiar characteristics of medical services[,] . . . [which] include the tendency to be experimental, . . . a dependence on factors beyond the control of the professional[,] and a lack of certainty or assurance of the desired result," [ ], outweigh any reasons that might support the imposition of strict liability in this context.

"In short, medical services are distinguished by factors which make them significantly different in kind from the retail marketing enterprise at which 402A is directed." [ ] We conclude that where, as here, a health care provider in the course of rendering health care services supplies a prosthetic device to be implanted into a patient, the health care provider is not "engaged in the business of selling" prostheses for purposes of strict products liability. Accordingly, the trial court did not err in granting the defendant's motion to dismiss.

. . .

Affirmed.

All concurred.

Notes and Questions

1. Why should it matter that the prosthetic knee was provided as part of a service? (Apparently, the suit was brought against CMC because the prosthesis manufacturer had filed for bankruptcy.) Are there justifications for strict liability that might have produced a different result in this case?

2. What if CMC's EKG or X-ray machines are defective and produce an erroneous diagnosis that leads to mistreatment of the patient? Is this case analogous to a suit against a retail distributor who has installed a defective tire? Can *Vandermark v. Ford Motor Co.*, p. 545, supra, or *Ryan v. Progressive Stores*, p. 551, supra, be reconciled with the court's reluctance to impose strict liability "where there is no possibility of negligence" (on the part of a non-manufacturer in the distribution chain)?

3. Should an action based on strict liability lie against a physician or surgeon who made a reasonable decision that turned out in hindsight to have been wrong and harmful? What if it were shown that the three best surgeons in the world would have made the right choice? See the extensive discussion in Hoven v. Kelble, 256 N.W.2d 379 (Wis.1977), refusing to extend strict liability to diagnoses and decisions made by medical providers.

4. In Murphy v. E.R. Squibb & Sons, Inc., 710 P.2d 247 (Cal.1985), the court, 4–3, rejected a strict liability action against a pharmacist who filled prescriptions for DES. The court had already concluded that doctors who prescribed the drug were not strictly liable: "the doctor prescribed the medication only as an aid to effect a cure and was not in the business of selling the drug." Here, plaintiff asserted that the pharmacist simply reads a prescription, fills the container with the proper dosage, types the label, attaches it to the container, and exchanges the container for payment. The plaintiff concluded that a pharmacist was the functional equivalent of "an experienced clerk at a hardware store." The defense stressed the professional aspects of pharmacists.

The plurality expressed concern that if strict liability were imposed, some pharmacists would refuse to stock drugs that carried even remote risks. Furthermore, a pharmacist who has a choice might stock only the more expensive products of an established manufacturer in order to be able to secure indemnity. Some pharmacies were owned by large chains, but most were not. (Should that matter?) One concurring justice, although recognizing that most customers used pharmacists as retailers, rejected strict liability because drugs are dispensed "only at the direction of a prescriber who is himself exempt from such liability." The dissenters found the focus on professional status "elitist." For them, the sale aspect dominated the transaction and all the policies of strict liability would be furthered by imposing it here.

For an application of negligence against pharmacists, see Hooks SuperX, Inc. v. McLaughlin, 642 N.E.2d 514 (Ind.1994) (imposing a duty not to refill a prescription for a habit-forming drug if the pharmacist should reasonably realize that the patient is using the drug at an improperly fast rate based on what the physician had prescribed).

5. The New Jersey experience with "hybrid" cases involving both products and services is illuminating. It began in Magrine v. Krasnica, 227 A.2d 539 (N.J.Law.Div. 1967), aff'd sub nom. Magrine v. Spector, 241 A.2d 637 (N.J.A.D.1968), aff'd 250 A.2d 129 (N.J.1969), in which the court rejected strict liability against a dentist for a needle that broke in the patient's mouth. A year later, in Newmark v. Gimbel's, Inc., 258 A.2d 697 (N.J.1969), the court imposed strict liability on a beauty salon that applied defective hair solution to a patron's scalp. To distinguish the two, the *Newmark* court explained:

> In our judgment, the nature of the services, the utility of and the need for them, involving as they do, the health and even survival of many people, are so important to the general welfare as to outweigh in the policy scale any need for the imposition on dentists and doctors of the rules of strict liability in tort.

In Dixon v. Four Seasons Bowling Alley, Inc., 424 A.2d 428 (N.J.A.D.1980), an appellate court rejected strict liability when plaintiff fell while bowling and cut her finger on defendant's chipped bowling ball. The use was "incidental to the use of defendant's premises and the supplying of such equipment should not result in imposition of liability on defendant on any basis other than liability for injuries caused by conditions of the premises." In Ranalli v. Edro Motel Corp., 690 A.2d 137 (N.J.A.D. 1997), the court rejected strict liability for a motel guest when the frying pan supplied in the room caught fire while he was cooking. The guest could expect diligence in inspecting the premises for defects but "cannot reasonably expect that the owner will correct defects of which he is unaware and that cannot be discerned by a reasonable inspection." The court declined to "make the owner an insurer for defects in any wire, screw, latch, cabinet door, pipe or other article on and in the premises at the time it is let, despite the fact that owner neither installed the item nor had any knowledge or reason to know of the defect."

6. As noted earlier, p. 580, supra, the consumer expectation test is still widely used when food causes the harm. Although some early cases held that providing food in restaurants was a service that did not produce warranties (or products liability in tort), virtually all courts have now agreed that these cases come within the product notion—but difficulties continue. See, e.g., Mexicali Rose v. Superior Court, 822 P.2d 1292 (Cal. 1992), in which plaintiff was injured when he swallowed a chicken bone while eating a chicken enchilada at defendant's restaurant. The court unanimously agreed that plaintiff should be able to sue in negligence, but rejected, 4–3, defective products and breach of warranty theories. The majority would have permitted all three theories if the harm had been caused by a "foreign" object, such as a piece of glass or wire. Why the difference?

In Shaffer v. Victoria Station, Inc., 588 P.2d 233 (Wash.1978), the court extended strict liability for food to a defective wine glass that shattered in a restaurant patron's hand. Is this distinguishable from the case involving the frying pan in the motel?

7. Early in the development of strict liability for defective products, in a passage quoted in *Hoven v. Kelble*, note 3 supra, Professor Kalven sounded a note of caution:

> The idea of enterprise liability has been in the wind for years, originally in an effort to explain the doctrines of agency. On this view what is important is that the defendant is an enterprise, that is, systematically engaged in generating the risks, and has access to the mechanism of the market. The first characteristic is thought to make him a good target for the deterrence of the tort sanction—liability is imposed in the quest for safety and accident prevention; the second characteristic is thought to make him a superior risk-bearer able to pass on the loss into channels of wide distribution. There is undoubted power in these policy notions and this is not the place to debate them seriously. We would merely note that the premises now have considerable reach, and if we are serious about enterprise liability, a good part of contemporary tort law will need to be revised accordingly, and very

little of its once spacious domain is likely to be left to the negligence principle.

Kalven, Tort Law—Tort Watch, 34 J.Am.Trial Law. 1, 57 (1972).

8. Soon after the movement toward strict liability began, one court hesitated. In Wights v. Staff Jennings, Inc., 405 P.2d 624 (Or.1965), the wife of the purchaser sued the manufacturer for injuries suffered when a pleasure boat exploded. Although reversing a judgment for the defendant, Justice O'Connell declined to follow the approach taken by Justice Traynor in *Escola* and *Greenman*:

> Substantially the same reasons for imposing strict liability upon sellers of defective chattels have been advanced in several other cases and in various texts and articles. Summarized, the thesis is that a loss resulting from the use of defendant's defective goods "is a casualty produced by the hazards of defendant's enterprise, so that the risk of loss is properly a risk of that enterprise,"[9] a view commonly described as the theory of enterprise liability.[10] The theory is a corollary of the broader thesis urged by some writers, particularly Harper and James on Torts, that compensation of the victim rather than fault of the defendant should be the objective in the adjudication of accident cases.[11]

> . . .

> The rationale of risk spreading and compensating the victim has no special relevancy to cases involving injuries resulting from the use of defective goods. The reasoning would seem to apply not only in cases involving personal injuries arising from the sale of defective goods, but equally to any case where an injury results from the risk creating conduct of the seller in any stage of the production and distribution of goods. Thus a manufacturer would be strictly liable even in the absence of fault for an injury to a person struck by one of the manufacturer's trucks being used in transporting his goods to market. It seems to us that the enterprise liability rationale employed in the *Escola* case proves too much and that if adopted would compel us to apply the principle of strict liability in all future cases where the loss could be distributed.

How substantial is this concern? Can it be answered? Recall that the *Wights* court also had reservations about retaining common law damages if

---

9. James, General Products—Should Manufacturers be Liable Without Negligence?, 24 Tenn.L.Rev. 923, 926 (1957).

10. Ehrenzweig, Negligence Without Fault, 4 (1951); [ ].

11. "It is the principal job of tort law today to deal with these [human] losses. They fall initially on people who as a class can ill afford them, and this fact brings great hardship upon the victims themselves and causes unfortunate repercussions to society as a whole. The best and most efficient way to deal with accident loss, therefore, is to assure accident victims of substantial compensation, and to distribute the losses involved over society as a whole or some very large segment of it. Such a basis for administering losses is what we have called social insurance." 2 Harper and James, Law of Torts, § 13.2, pp. 762–63 (1956).

enterprise liability were to be adopted. See p. 535, supra. Are the safety considerations of *Escola* applicable to driving a truck? Oregon soon adopted the emerging law of defective products.

H.   THE INTERSECTION OF TORT AND THE UNIFORM COMMERCIAL CODE

So far we have been focusing on the role of tort law when victims have been hurt by allegedly defective products. By contrast, the course in contracts involves cases in which plaintiffs with disappointed economic expectations seek damages under common law contract or UCC theories. Although these are the two major categories of cases, two smaller but important categories remain: claims in tort by plaintiffs seeking to recover for economic harm, and claims in contract and under the UCC for personal injury. As we turn first to the role of tort law in product-related economic harm cases, recall the discussion of such cases in the negligence context in Chapter IV.

East River Steamship Corp. v. Transamerica Delaval Inc.

Supreme Court of the United States, 1986.
476 U.S. 858, 106 S.Ct. 2295, 90 L.Ed.2d 865.

[Defendant Delaval made turbines, each costing $1.4 million, for four supertankers, each costing $125 million. East River and three other plaintiffs were the separate charterers of each ship for 20–22 years from the owner. Each charterer assumed responsibility for the cost of any repairs. When the first ship made its maiden voyage, the high-pressure turbine malfunctioned, but the ship was able to get to port. Inspection revealed that an essential ring had virtually disintegrated and had caused additional damage to other parts of the turbine. Eventually, the ship was permanently and satisfactorily repaired. As a result of this experience, the second and third ships were inspected. The same condition was discovered and satisfactory repairs were made. These problems are involved in the first three counts of the complaint. (The fourth count, involving another design claim, is not relevant here.)

The problem with the fourth ship was that a valve between the high-pressure and low-pressure turbines was installed backwards. Because of that error, steam entered the low-pressure turbine and damaged it. This condition was repaired. This episode is the subject of the fifth count—which alleged negligence.

The charterers' complaints invoked the admiralty jurisdiction and set forth tort claims for the cost of repairing the ships and for income lost while the ships were out of service. The district court granted Delaval summary judgment and the court of appeals affirmed. The Supreme Court granted certiorari to resolve a conflict among the courts of appeals sitting in admiralty.]

JUSTICE BLACKMUN delivered the opinion of the Court.

In this admiralty case, we must decide whether a cause of action in tort is stated when a defective product purchased in a commercial transaction malfunctions, injuring only the product itself and causing purely economic loss. The case requires us to consider preliminarily whether admiralty law, which already recognizes a general theory of liability for negligence, also incorporates principles of products liability, including strict liability. Then, charting a course between products liability and contract law, we must determine whether injury to a product itself is the kind of harm that should be protected by products liability or left entirely to the law of contracts.

[The Court concluded that the claims fell within the admiralty jurisdiction since the wrongs alleged occurred on or near the high seas or navigable waters. This meant that admiralty substantive law applied. Absent a statute, the general maritime law, as developed by the judiciary from state and federal sources, applied. The Supreme Court joined the courts of appeals in recognizing concepts of products liability based on both negligence and strict liability. But this acceptance of products liability into maritime law "is only the threshold determination to the main issue in this case."]

IV.

Products liability grew out of a public policy judgment that people need more protection from dangerous products than is afforded by the law of warranty. See Seely v. White Motor Co., [403 P.2d 145, 149 (Cal.1965)]. It is clear, however, that if this development were allowed to progress too far, contract law would drown in a sea of tort. See G. Gilmore, The Death of Contract 87–94 (1974). We must determine whether a commercial product injuring itself is the kind of harm against which public policy requires manufacturers to protect, independent of any contractual obligation.

A

The paradigmatic products-liability action is one where a product "reasonably certain to place life and limb in peril," distributed without reinspection, causes bodily injury. See, e.g., [MacPherson]. The manufacturer is liable whether or not it is negligent because "public policy demands that responsibility be fixed wherever it will most effectively reduce the hazards to life and health inherent in defective products that reach the market." [Escola](concurring opinion).

For similar reasons of safety, the manufacturer's duty of care was broadened to include protection against property damage. [   ] Such damage is considered so akin to personal injury that the two are treated alike. See [Seely].

In the traditional "property damage" cases, the defective product damages other property. In this case, there was no damage to "other" property. Rather, the first, second, and third counts allege that each supertanker's defectively designed turbine components damaged only the turbine itself. Since each turbine was supplied by Delaval as an integrated package, each is properly regarded as a single unit. "Since all but the very simplest of machines have component parts, [a contrary] holding would require a finding of 'property damage' in virtually every case where a product damages itself. Such a holding would eliminate the distinction between warranty and strict products liability." Northern Power & Engineering Corp. v. Caterpillar Tractor Co., 623 P.2d 324, 330 (Alaska 1981). The fifth count also alleges injury to the product itself. Before the high-pressure and low-pressure turbines could become an operational propulsion system, they were connected to piping and valves under the supervision of Delaval personnel. [   ] Delaval's supervisory obligations were part of its manufacturing agreement. The fifth count thus can best be read to allege that Delaval's negligent manufacture of the propulsion system—by allowing the installation in reverse of the astern guardian valve—damaged the propulsion system. [   ] Obviously, damage to a product itself has certain attributes of a products-liability claim. But the injury suffered—the failure of the product to function properly—is the essence of a warranty action, through which a contracting party can seek to recoup the benefit of its bargain.

B

The intriguing question whether injury to a product itself may be brought in tort has spawned a variety of answers. At one end of the spectrum, the case that created the majority land-based approach, *Seely* (defective truck), held that preserving a proper role for the law of warranty precludes imposing tort liability if a defective product causes purely monetary harm. [   ]

At the other end of the spectrum is the minority land-based approach, whose progenitor, Santor v. A and M Karagheusian, Inc., [207 A.2d 305, 312–313 (N.J.1965)] (marred carpeting), held that a manufacturer's duty to make nondefective products encompassed injury to the product itself, whether or not the defect created an unreasonable risk of harm. The courts adopting this approach, including the majority of the Courts of Appeals sitting in admiralty that have considered the issue, [   ] find that the safety and insurance rationales behind strict liability apply equally where the losses are purely economic. These courts reject the *Seely* approach because they find it arbitrary that economic losses are recoverable if a plaintiff suffers bodily injury or property damage, but not if a product injures itself. They also find no inherent difference between economic loss and personal injury or property damage, because all are proximately caused by the defendant's conduct. Further, they believe recovery for economic loss would not lead to unlimited liability because they think a manufacturer can predict and insure against product failure. [   ]

Between the two poles fall a number of cases that would permit a products-liability action under certain circumstances when a product injures only itself. These cases attempt to differentiate between "the disappointed users . . . and the endangered ones," Russell v. Ford Motor Co., [575 P.2d 1383, 1387 (Or.1978)], and permit only the latter to sue in tort. The determination has been said to turn on the nature of the defect, the type of risk, and the manner in which the injury arose. [   ] The Alaska Supreme Court allows a tort action if the defective product creates a situation potentially dangerous to persons or other property, and loss occurs as a proximate result of that danger and under dangerous circumstances. [   ]

We find the intermediate and minority land-based positions unsatisfactory. The intermediate positions, which essentially turn on the degree of risk, are too indeterminate to enable manufacturers easily to structure their business behavior. Nor do we find persuasive a distinction that rests on the manner in which the product is injured. We realize that the damage may be qualitative, occurring through gradual deterioration or internal breakage. Or it may be calamitous. [   ] But either way, since by definition no person or other property is damaged, the resulting loss is purely economic. Even when the harm to the product itself occurs through an abrupt, accident-like event, the resulting loss due to repair costs, decreased value, and lost profits is essentially the failure of the purchaser to receive the benefit of its bargain—traditionally the core concern of contract law. See E. Farnsworth, Contracts § 12.8, pp. 839–840 (1982).

We also decline to adopt the minority land-based view espoused by [*Santor* and other cases]. Such cases raise legitimate questions about the theories behind restricting products liability, but we believe that the countervailing arguments are more powerful. The minority view fails to account for the need to keep products liability and contract law in separate spheres and to maintain a realistic limitation on damages.

C

Exercising traditional discretion in admiralty, [   ], we adopt an approach similar to *Seely* and hold that a manufacturer in a commercial relationship has no duty under either a negligence or strict products-liability theory to prevent a product from injuring itself.

"The distinction that the law has drawn between tort recovery for physical injuries and warranty recovery for economic loss is not arbitrary and does not rest on the 'luck' of one plaintiff in having an accident causing physical injury. The distinction rests, rather, on an understanding of the nature of the responsibility a manufacturer must undertake in distributing his products." [*Seely*] When a product injures only itself the reasons for imposing a tort duty are weak and those for leaving the party to its contractual remedies are strong.

The tort concern with safety is reduced when an injury is only to the product itself. When a person is injured, the "cost of an injury and the loss of time or health may be an overwhelming misfortune," and one the person is not prepared to meet. [*Escola*](concurring opinion). In contrast, when a product injures itself, the commercial user stands to lose the value of the product, risks the displeasure of its customers who find that the product does not meet their needs, or, as in this case, experiences increased costs in performing a service. Losses like these can be insured. [   ] Society need not presume that a customer needs special protection. The increased cost to the public that would result from holding a manufacturer liable in tort for injury to the product itself is not justified. Cf. [*United States v. Carroll Towing Co.*]

Damage to a product itself is most naturally understood as a warranty claim. Such damage means simply that the product has not met the customer's expectations, or, in other words, that the customer has received "insufficient product value." [   ] The maintenance of product value and quality is precisely the purpose of express and implied warranties. See UCC § 2–313 (express warranty), § 2–314 (implied warranty of merchantability), and § 2–315 (warranty of fitness for a particular purpose). Therefore, a claim of a nonworking product can be brought as a breach-of-warranty action. Or, if the customer prefers, it can reject the product or revoke its acceptance and sue for breach of contract. See UCC §§ 2–601, 2–608, 2–612.

Contract law, and the law of warranty in particular, is well suited to commercial controversies of the sort involved in this case because the parties may set the terms of their own agreements. The manufacturer can restrict its liability, within limits, by disclaiming warranties or limiting remedies. See UCC §§ 2–316, 2–719. In exchange, the purchaser pays less for the product. Since a commercial situation generally does not involve large disparities in bargaining power, [   ] we see no reason to intrude into the parties' allocation of the risk.

While giving recognition to the manufacturer's bargain, warranty law sufficiently protects the purchaser by allowing it to obtain the benefit of its bargain. [   ] The expectation damages available in warranty for purely economic loss give a plaintiff the full benefit of its bargain by compensating for forgone business opportunities. [   ] Recovery on a warranty theory would give the charterers their repair costs and lost profits, and would place them in the position they would have been in had the turbines functioned properly.[9] [   ] Thus, both the nature of the injury and the resulting damages indicate it is more natural to think of injury to a product itself in terms of warranty.

A warranty action also has a built-in limitation on liability, whereas a tort action could subject the manufacturer to damages of an indefinite amount. The limitation in a contract action comes from the agreement of the parties and the requirement that consequential damages, such as lost profits, be a foreseeable result of the breach. See Hadley v. Baxendale, 9 Ex. 341, 156 Eng.Rep. 145 (1854). In a warranty action where the loss is purely economic, the limitation derives from the requirements of foreseeability and of privity, which is still generally enforced for such claims in a commercial setting. [   ]

9. In contrast, tort damages generally compensate the plaintiff for loss and return him to the position he occupied before the injury. [   ] Tort damages are analogous to reliance damages, which are awarded in contract when there is particular difficulty in measuring the expectation interest. [   ]

In products-liability law, where there is a duty to the public generally, foreseeability is an inadequate brake. Cf. Petitions of Kinsman Transit Co., 388 F.2d 821 (C.A.2 1968). [ ] Permitting recovery for all foreseeable claims for purely economic loss could make a manufacturer liable for vast sums. It would be difficult for a manufacturer to take into account the expectations of persons downstream who may encounter its product. In this case, for example, if the charterers—already one step removed from the transaction—were permitted to recover their economic losses, then the companies that subchartered the ships might claim their economic losses from the delays, and the charterers' customers also might claim their economic losses, and so on. "The law does not spread its protection so far." Robins Dry Dock & Repair Co. v. Flint, 275 U.S. 303, 309 (1927).

And to the extent that courts try to limit purely economic damages in tort, they do so by relying on a far murkier line, one that negates the charterers' contention that permitting such recovery under a products-liability theory enables admiralty courts to avoid difficult linedrawing. Cf. [*Ultramares Corp. v. Touche*]; [ ].

D

For the first three counts, the defective turbine components allegedly injured only the turbines themselves. Therefore, a strict products-liability theory of recovery is unavailable to the charterers. Any warranty claims would be subject to Delaval's limitation, both in time and scope, of its warranty liability.   .   .   .

.   .   .

Similarly, in the fifth count, alleging the reverse installation of the astern guardian valve, the only harm was to the propulsion system itself rather than to persons or other property. Even assuming that Delaval's supervision was negligent, as we must on this summary judgment motion, Delaval owed no duty under a products-liability theory based on negligence to avoid causing purely economic loss. [ ] Thus, whether stated in negligence or strict liability, no products-liability claim lies in admiralty when the only injury claimed is economic loss.

.   .   . [W]e affirm the entry of judgment for Delaval.

Notes and Questions

1. What is the impact of choosing between tort and contract in this type of case? Although it is not binding on state courts, *East River* has been widely accepted.

2. In *Seely*, a dissenting judge said that he found it "hard to understand how one might .   .   . award a traveling salesman lost earnings if a defect in his car causes his leg to break in an accident but deny that salesman his lost earnings if the defect instead disables only his car before any accident occurs." How might Justice Blackmun respond?

3. What are the strengths and weaknesses of the *Santor* approach? Of the "intermediate" approach? Of the Court's approach?

New Jersey largely abandoned its *Santor* approach in Alloway v. General Marine Ind., 695 A.2d 264 (N.J.1997), a case involving an economic loss claim based on a boat that, because of a defective seam in its bottom, sank while docked. After lengthy discussion, the court rejected the applicability of a tort regime to the plaintiff's purchase of a luxury boat, holding that "[b]y providing for express and implied warranties, the U.C.C. amply protects all buyers—commercial purchasers and consumers alike—from economic loss arising out of the purchase of a defective product." The court did, however, reserve judgment on the applicability of warranty to (1) a case in which the product posed a risk of personal injury or property damage, as well as to (2) a case in which "the parties are of unequal bargaining power, the product is a necessity, no alternative source for the product is readily available, and the purchaser cannot reasonably insure against consequential damages." Two justices concurred on the latter score, arguing that a "gross inequality of bargaining power should supplant the U.C.C. remedy with tort."

Is tort liability more justifiable when the buyer is an individual? Consider Jones, Product Defects Causing Commercial Loss: The Ascendancy of Contract over Tort, 44 U.Miami L.Rev. 731 (1990), concluding that when individual consumers are the buyers, "because of limitations on consumer knowledge and because of disparities in consumer wealth, it cannot be said that contractual reallocations of risk are economically efficient and socially acceptable in the general run of manufacturer-consumer transactions." But when the buyer is a commercial enterprise, that economic efficiency exists and any social concerns are minimal. In such cases, the role of tort law is "redundant and perverse. It is used by litigants and courts to undermine allocations of risks agreed to by the parties and to substitute judicial solutions for contractual arrangements that are almost certainly superior in terms of both fairness and efficiency."

4. In Bocre Leasing Corp. v. General Motors Corp., 645 N.E.2d 1195 (N.Y.1995), plaintiff was a "four-times removed downstream purchaser of a helicopter" that defendant had made and sold some 15 years earlier. Plaintiff bought it from a broker "as is." As the result of an alleged engine defect the helicopter experienced a power loss in flight but landed safely, causing damage only to the helicopter itself "with no damage whatsoever to persons or other property." The court rejected a tort claim despite the fact that the alleged defect created a serious risk of personal injury. Plaintiff here could have bargained with its vendor for warranty protections and acquired insurance against harm to the property and lost profits, such as lost rentals and air time. The denial of tort did not undercut safety: since "any product put into the stream of commerce has the theoretical potential to injure persons and property, the incentive to provide safe products is always present." One judge would have allowed a tort action for the property damage to the helicopter but not for the economic loss. How would the case be analyzed under *East River*?

For a strong statement of the economic loss doctrine, see Airport Rent–A–Car, Inc. v. Prevost Car, Inc., 660 So.2d 628 (Fla.1995), in which plaintiff alleged that it owned several buses manufactured by defendant that it had bought from a company that was not a "merchant" under the UCC (and thus against whom no warranty actions would lie). Two buses caught fire and were destroyed—one while transporting school children. The court held that no tort action lay for the loss of the buses because of the "economic loss rule." It was irrelevant that a warranty action might be unavailable or that the losses were sudden calamities.

East River's analysis was rejected in Washington Water Power Co. v. Graybar Electric Co., 774 P.2d 1199 (Wash.1989), on the ground that the "increased certainty [of identifying the line between tort and contract] comes at too high a price." The court preferred the "risk of harm" approach because it encouraged greater attention to product safety.

5. How similar are the problems in cases like *East River* and those raised in the *People Express* case, p. 313, supra?

6. In the cited *Seely* case, plaintiff's truck bounced and did not ride smoothly after many repair attempts. The case came to stand for the proposition that if the truck itself had been damaged—perhaps by over-turning—a tort action would have been possible. But the actual harm in the case was thought to be economic. This limited the plaintiff to a contract claim. Several California courts, relying on a different ground, however, have denied sellers' liability for commercial products even where they have damaged themselves. These courts have held either that the law of products liability did not apply when the buyer was a commercial party, or that a commercial buyer's agreement to assume the risk should be enforced against it.

7. In Aas v. Superior Court, 12 P.3d 1125 (Cal.2000), homeowners brought tort claims for construction defects against the developer, contractor and subcontractors who had built their homes. The court held, 5–2, that since no damage had yet occurred—the only claims being for cost of repairs and diminished value—no tort action would lie.

8. In Delta Air Lines, Inc. v. Douglas Aircraft Co., 47 Cal.Rptr. 518 (App. 1965), Delta claimed that Douglas should be held liable for negligence and breach of express and implied warranties after a plane that Douglas had sold was damaged when the nose wheel malfunctioned during a landing. The court, reversing a trial court judgment for plaintiffs, held that Douglas was insulated from liability by the exculpatory clause in the contract, and that this clause was not void as against public policy. Delta's argument, according to the opinion, was that "modern law, in what is commonly referred to as the field of products liability, has shown a movement away from the traditional doctrine that a manufacturer has an absolute freedom of contract and may disclaim his liability." The court responded:

Unlike [*Greenman*, *Tunkl*, and *Henningsen*], this case involves no element of personal injury; and, also, unlike *Greenman* and *Henningsen*, involves no issue of "privity of contract."

Perhaps more important, the case at bench involves none of the elements of inequality of bargaining on which the cited cases, and other recent cases of the same sort, have laid their stress. Delta, bargaining for the purchase and delivery of an airplane yet to be built, is hardly the pain-wracked sufferer seeking emergency admission to the hospital whose plight secured relief in *Tunkl*; it was not faced, as were *Henningsen* and *Vandermark*, with an industry-wide stock contract not open to negotiation; it is not now faced with a "fine print" clause not known to it when it signed the contract; and it did not stand as a single inexperienced individual purchaser vis-à-vis a large seller relatively indifferent to the making or not making of a single purchase.

It is clear from the record that Delta, one of the major airlines of the nation, with the aid of a staff of experienced executives and attorneys, had negotiated a contract with terms individual to Douglas.

At this time, early in the emergence of products liability, the court distinguished between the consumer's circumscribed freedom of contract and the commercial purchaser's much stronger bargaining powers. The lack of personal injury, although mentioned, provided only a subsidiary ground for accepting defendant's waiver defense. Would the analysis still apply if Douglas refused to eliminate the waiver for a higher price?

The rough equality of the parties' bargaining powers conveyed in *Delta v. Douglas* has been a central aspect of subsequent extensions of its holding—extensions in cases where the harm caused was not only economic. In Philippine Airlines, Inc. v. McDonnell Douglas Corp., 189 Cal.Rptr.3d 423 (App. 1987), plaintiff alleged that the manufacturer's negligence had caused a "rejected take-off," which resulted in injuries to the plane's passengers. Defendant asserted that the limitation of liability clause that the parties had signed protected it from plaintiff's indemnification suit. The court upheld the waiver, finding that it would not be a substantial disincentive to creating safe products, and that the airline would not be more reluctant to settle tort claims if it could not seek reimbursement from the manufacturer.

The "exculpatory clause does not conflict with the public interest, but is, rather the result of a 'private, voluntary transaction in which one party, for a consideration, agrees to shoulder a risk which the law would otherwise have placed upon the other party.' " In sum,

> Although [previous cases] involved property damage only, we find for the reasons we have discussed, that the distinction between property damage and personal injuries is of no legal importance as it relates to the clause at issue. The damage to PAL was economic, and PAL expressly contracted to limit its remedies for economic loss. The injured passengers may still seek recovery from MDC should they so choose.

What rationale for the existence of products liability law supports the court's conclusion that a commercial party's agreement to assume the risk should be upheld—even if the harm caused was physical? How does analyzing these cases according to the type of harm caused (economic, property, or personal) differ from examining them according to the plaintiff involved (consumer, commercial, or employee)?

9.   *Introduction to personal injury litigation outside of tort law.* The remaining category involves suits for personal injury that do not arise as tort claims. These are typically brought under a warranty provision of the UCC.

a.   Implied warranties. The implied warranty sections, §§ 2–314 and 2–315, generally involve aberrationally defective products—so-called manufacturing defects. Recall the *Ryan* case, p. 545, supra, involving a pin in a loaf of bread. Why might a plaintiff prefer to go on a warranty theory rather than tort law—especially where the contract theories may offer privity problems and less attractive damage awards because of limits on punitive damages or on non-pecuniary awards? One answer is the statute of limitations. The Code's statute of limitations is four years from the delivery of the goods, § 2–725. The tort limitation may be shorter but generally runs only from the time of the plaintiff's injury or perhaps discovery of that injury. It is not difficult to imagine situations in which plaintiffs might find one avenue barred while the other is still open. Also, if the claim is for property damage the contract limits on recoverable damages are not a serious impediment.

b.   Express warranty. This is potentially a very important basis for liability under the Code—with a tort analogue. If a manufacturer makes an express warranty about the quality or attributes of the product, anyone hurt if such a representation or warranty turns out to be false may recover damages—even without fault on the maker's part. In some states this may be true even though the victim did not know about the warranty and did not rely on it in using the product. See §§ 2–313, 2–316. See Note, Express Warranties Under the Uniform Commercial Code: Is There a Reliance Requirement?, 66 N.Y.U.L.Rev. 468 (1991). Note that the product need not be defective; it may be perfectly adequate. The claim is based on the failure of the product to live up to what the supplier claimed for it. Recall the discussion earlier of the *Dennis* and *Castro* cases, p. 604, supra.

10.   *Introduction to warranty defenses.* We have seen that courts tend to use a comparative approach to defenses in tort cases. What happens when the case is brought under the Code? The Code nowhere contemplates shared responsibility; it speaks in terms of proximate cause, suggesting that once a buyer discovers a defect or should reasonably have discovered it, there can no longer be reasonable reliance on the warranty, and thus no recovery. See § 2–314 comment 13; § 2–316 comment 8; § 2–715 comment 5.

A few courts have adopted this approach. See Erdman v. Johnson Bros. Radio & Television Co., 271 A.2d 744 (Md.1970)(no warranty liability for fire where plaintiffs continued using a television set after seeing sparks coming from it).

Other courts have developed a comparative fault approach to warranty cases analogous to what the state would do in the tort action. See West v. Caterpillar Tractor Co., 547 F.2d 885 (5th Cir.1977)(developing a partial defense to avoid the anomaly of permitting negligent defendants sued in tort to reduce their liability under comparative negligence, but not permitting innocent defendants sued in warranty a similar reduction where the plaintiff carelessly failed to observe the danger).

11. *The interplay between tort and contract: a reprise.* In Rardin v. T & D Machine Handling, Inc., 890 F.2d 24 (7th Cir.1989), Rardin bought a press from Whiteacre that was sold "as is, where is." The press had to be moved and for that task Whiteacre hired defendant. The contract between Rardin and Whiteacre provided that Whiteacre was liable for damage to the press incurred by fault or negligence of Whiteacre's "employees, agents, contractors or representatives." During the move the press was damaged due to the negligence of defendant. Rardin incurred costs to repair the press, and lost profits during the time it took to put the press in working order. Rardin settled with Whiteacre for the damage to the press. Rardin's negligence action under Illinois law against defendant for lost profits was rejected in an opinion by Judge Posner.

The court analogized the problem to one in which A takes a watch to B retail store for repair and B sends it out to C for the actual repair. Through negligence C damages the watch and it does not always tell time accurately. As a result, A misses an important meeting with his creditors and is thrown into bankruptcy, losing everything. The court assumed that "but for C's negligence A would have made the meeting and averted the bankruptcy, just as but for T & D's negligence the press would have arrived in working condition. The issue is not causation; it is duty."

The court stated that the "basic reason why no court (we believe) would impose liability on C in a suit by A is that C could not estimate the consequences of his carelessness, ignorant as he was of the circumstances of A, who is B's customer." Although in "a perfect world of rational actors and complete information," there would be no negligence, "it is not realistic to assume that every responsible citizen can and will avoid ever being negligent. In fact, all that taking care does is make it less likely that one will commit a careless act. In deciding how much effort to expend on being careful—and therefore how far to reduce the probability of a careless accident—the potential injurer must have at least a rough idea of the extent of liability. C in our example could not form such an idea. He does not know the circumstances of the myriad owners of watches sent him to repair. He cannot know what costs he will impose if through momentary inattention he negligently damages one of the watches in his charge."

The court thought that two further points "argue against liability." The first was that A could have protected himself by a contract with B. "The fact that B would in all likelihood refuse to give such a guaranty for a consideration acceptable to A is evidence that liability for all the consequences of every negligent act is not in fact optimal." Second, A could have taken steps "to reduce his dependency on his watch." He could have left a margin of error for getting to the meeting in time or "consulted another timepiece."

The court thought that the "spirit of *Hadley v. Baxendale . . .* broods over this case." The contract measure of damages in that case did not extend to lost profits from down time. The plaintiff mill owners could have protected themselves from this loss by having a spare shaft available. Although it is "generally true that consequential damages are recoverable in tort law although not in contract law, [a cited case] shows that the classification of a case as a tort case or a contract case is not decisive on this question."

Judge Posner noted that the "economic loss" doctrine followed by Illinois, other states, and *East River* "rests on an insight . . . that contractual-type limitations on liability may make sense in many tort cases that are not contract cases only because there is no privity of contract between the parties." He also noted that the doctrine "is not the only tort doctrine that limits for-want-of-a-nail-the-kingdom-was-lost liability. It is closely related to the doctrine . . . that bars recovery for economic loss even if the loss does not arise from a commercial relationship between the parties—even if for example a negligent accident in the Holland Tunnel backs up traffic for hours, imposing cumulatively enormous and readily monetizable costs of delay"—referring to an example offered by the court in *Kinsman II*, p. 433, supra.

This rejection of liability was "in tension with other doctrines of tort law that appear to expose the tortfeasor to unlimited liability. One is the principle that allows recovery of full tort damages in a personal-injury suit for injury resulting from a defective or unreasonably dangerous product—a form of legal action that arises in a contractual setting and indeed originated in suits for breach of warranty." A second example was the "thin-skull" plaintiff rule. Judge Posner saw three explanations for this tension:

> The first difference is that the potential variance in liability is larger when the victim of a tort is a business, because businesses vary in their financial magnitude more than individuals do; more precisely, physical capital is more variable than human capital. The second is that many business losses are offset elsewhere in the system; Rardin's competitors undoubtedly picked up much or all of the business he lost as a result of the delay in putting the press into operation, so that his loss overstates the social loss caused by T & D's negligence. [ ] Third, tort law is a field largely shaped by the special considerations involved in personal-injury cases, as contract law is not. Tort doctrines are, therefore, prima facie more suitable for the governance of such cases than contract doctrines are.

Judge Posner noted that tort liability might still extend to "purely economic losses" in some cases. Among these he noted "suits against an attorney or accountant for professional malpractice or negligent misrepresentation that causes business losses to the plaintiff. [ ] These cases are distinguishable, however, as ones in which the role of the defendant is, precisely, to guarantee the performance of the other party to the plaintiff's contract, usually a seller. The guaranty would be worth little without a remedy, necessarily in tort (or in an expansive interpretation of the doctrine of third-party beneficiaries) against the guarantor.''

Finally, Judge Posner found support in *H.R. Moch Co. v. Rensselaer Water Co.*, p. 143, supra. "The city was acting as the agent of its residents in negotiating with the water company, and the water company was entitled to assume that, if it was to be the fire insurer for the city's property, the city would compensate it accordingly.'' Similarly, in this case, since Whiteacre was acting as Rardin's agent in dealing with the defendant handler, the defendant was "entitled to assume that, if it was to be an insurer of Rardin's business losses, Whiteacre on behalf of Rardin would compensate it accordingly.''

The extended analysis "underscores the desirability—perhaps urgency—of harmonizing the entire complex and confusing pattern of liability and nonliability for tortious conduct in contractual settings.'' But that was a task for the Supreme Court of Illinois.

CHAPTER IX

Trespass and Nuisance

Trespass and nuisance are related doctrines that protect interests in, respectively, the exclusive possession, and the use and enjoyment, of land. In an earlier era, trespass came to be regarded primarily as a safeguard against physical intrusions on land. By contrast, nuisance actions have a long history of affording protection against offensive uses of neighboring land. As we shall see, however, in modern times the distinctions between the situations in which the cases arise begin to blur.

Because of the special importance that the law traditionally placed on protection of interests in land, strict liability has been a dominant feature of the law in this area. As the mixed reception of *Rylands v. Fletcher*, p. 503, supra, indicated, however, great confusion and debate exist over the "strictness" of liability for harms to interests in land.

The subject is given separate consideration here for two main reasons. Most important, as this brief introduction suggests, the courts have long regarded interests in land as a functionally distinct category. As a consequence, trespass and nuisance actions cut across the boundaries of the intentional and unintentional tort categories that we have been examining. In addition, the modern cases, in particular, provide the common-law foundation for analyzing environmental disputes. For both of these reasons, the judicially-fashioned liability rules in this area deserve special attention.

Our brief treatment of basic doctrine will place considerable emphasis on the Restatement approach, which has brought some semblance of order to a confused body of case law.

A. Trespass

At early common law, every unauthorized entry by a person or object onto another's land that resulted from a voluntary act was subject to liability as a trespass. Obviously, a person who was carried against his will onto the land of another would not have satisfied the requirement of voluntary conduct, and could not therefore be held to have committed a trespass. Such narrow instances aside, however, a person who non-negligently but incorrectly believed that particular property was his own, or that he was authorized to go upon it, would nonetheless be liable for trespass because he intended to enter the property.

As the New York blasting cases, p. 506, supra, indicated, many courts required actual physical entry by a tangible object, since the interest that plaintiff sought to protect was the exclusive possession of his land. Once this requirement was satisfied, however, any technical invasion could serve as the basis for an action, since trespass was the principal method by which lawful possessors of land could vindicate their property rights and ensure that a continuing trespass did not ripen into a prescriptive right. Because the gist of the action was considered to be the intrusion or "breaking of the close," demonstrable harm was not required for at least nominal damages to be assessed.

As plaintiffs came to allege trespassory invasions resulting from objects—such as exploding boilers and flying debris—rather than people, many courts began to distinguish between "direct" and "indirect," or trespassory and non-trespassory harms. This distinction, borrowed from the common-law writ system, where it was not limited to invasions of land, created great confusion. Again, the New York cases, considered earlier, offer examples.

Modern trespass doctrine has largely obliterated the historical distinction between direct and indirect trespassory invasions of land. But a distinction of another kind—a present day differentiation between intentional and unintentional trespasses—has continuing vitality. The Restatement (Second) of Torts § 165 states that unintended intrusions—those resulting from reckless or negligent conduct or from abnormally dangerous activities—will be subjected to liability only if the intrusion causes actual harm.

By contrast, partly because actions for trespass remain an important means of maintaining the integrity of a possessory interest in land, intentional trespasses retain much of their common-law strict liability character. Section 158 states that one is liable to another in trespass for an intentional intrusion, irrespective of harm caused. In this context, "intent" refers to the intent to enter the land, not necessarily to invade another's interest in the exclusive possession of land. Thus, a mistaken, non-negligent entry can result in liability—as at earlier common law—even if no harm occurred.

The strictness of the intentional trespass action is mitigated to some extent through a series of privileges that shield from liability activity that would otherwise constitute a trespass. These privileges may arise out of the consent of the possessor (§§ 167–175), or may be afforded as a matter of law because of the purposes for which the actor enters the premises (§§ 176–211). The scope of these privileges, however, is in general quite narrow and limited to specific types of situations. Thus, despite the increased flexibility these privileges afford to defendants, no overarching principle of reasonableness has yet developed in the area of intentional, as compared to unintentional, trespasses.

With this background in mind, consider the following case.

Martin v. Reynolds Metals Co.

Supreme Court of Oregon, 1959.
221 Or. 86, 342 P.2d 790, cert. denied 362 U.S. 918 (1960).

[Plaintiffs sued for trespass, claiming damage to their farm land from the operation of defendant's nearby aluminum reduction plant. The trial judge awarded plaintiffs $71,500 for damages to their land, which could no longer be used to raise livestock because the cattle were poisoned by ingesting the fluoride compounds that became airborne from the plant and settled on the plaintiffs' land. (The daily emanation of fluorides from the plant averaged 800 pounds.) The judge also awarded $20,000 for the deterioration of the land through growth of brush and weeds resulting from the lack of grazing. The judge rejected punitive damages. The damages covered the period from August 1951 through the end of 1955. If the action were properly brought in trespass, with its six-year statute of limitations, the award was permissible. But if the action were one of nuisance, then damages were recoverable for only 1954 and 1955, because of the two-year statute of limitations.]

O'CONNELL, J.

. . .

The gist of the defendant's argument is as follows: a trespass arises only when there has been a "breaking and entering upon real property," constituting a direct, as distinguished from a consequential, invasion of the possessor's interest in land; and the settling upon the land of fluoride compounds consisting of gases, fumes and particulates is not sufficient to satisfy these requirements.

Before appraising the argument we shall first describe more particularly the physical and chemical nature of the substance which was deposited upon plaintiffs' land. In reducing alumina (the oxide of aluminum) to aluminum the alumina is subjected to an electrolytic process which causes the emanation of fluoridic compounds consisting principally of hydrogen fluoride, calcium fluoride, iron fluoride and silicon tetrafluoride. The individual particulates which form these chemical compounds are not visible to the naked eye. A part of them were captured by a fume collection system which was installed in November, 1950; the remainder became airborne and a part of the uncaptured particles eventually were deposited upon plaintiffs' land.

. . .

Trespass and private nuisance are separate fields of tort liability relating to actionable interference with the possession of land. They may be distinguished by comparing the interest invaded; an actionable invasion of a possessor's interest in the exclusive possession of land is a trespass; an actionable invasion of a possessor's interest in the use and enjoyment of his land is a nuisance. [   ]

The same conduct on the part of a defendant may and often does result in the actionable invasion of both of these interests, in which case the choice between the two remedies is, in most cases, a matter of little consequence. Where the action is brought on the theory of nuisance alone the court ordinarily is not called upon to determine whether the conduct would also result in a trespassory invasion. In such cases the courts' treatment of the invasion solely in terms of the law of nuisance does not mean that the same conduct could not also be regarded as a trespass. Some of the cases relied upon by the defendant are of this type; cases in which the court holds that the interference with the plaintiff's possession through soot, dirt, smoke, cinders, ashes and similar substances constitute a nuisance, but where the court does not discuss the applicability of the law of trespass to the same set of facts. [   ]

However, there are cases which have held that the defendant's interference with plaintiff's possession resulting from the settling upon his land of effluents emanating from defendant's operations is exclusively nontrespassory. [   ] Although in such cases the separate particles which collectively cause the invasion are minute, the deposit of each of the particles constitutes a physical intrusion and, but for the size of the particle, would clearly give rise to an action of trespass. The defendant asks us to take account of the difference in size of the physical agency through which the intrusion occurs and relegate entirely to the field of nuisance law certain invasions which do not meet the dimensional test, whatever that is. In pressing this argument upon us the defendant must admit that there are cases which have held that a trespass results from the movement or deposit of rather small objects over or upon the surface of the possessor's land.

[The court cites examples such as molten lead, soot, and gunshot pellets.]

And liability on the theory of trespass has been recognized where the harm was produced by the vibration of the soil or by the concussion of the air which, of course, is nothing more than the movement of molecules one against the other. . . . The view recognizing a trespassory invasion where there is no "thing" which can be seen with the naked eye undoubtedly runs counter to the definition of trespass expressed in some quarters. [   ] It is quite possible that in an earlier day when science had not yet peered into the molecular and atomic world of small particles, the courts could not fit an invasion through unseen physical instrumentalities into the requirement that a trespass can result only from a *direct* invasion. But in this atomic age even the uneducated know the great and awful force contained in the atom and what it can do to a man's property if it is released. In fact, the now famous equation $E = mc^2$ has taught us that mass and energy are equivalents and that our concept of "things" must be reframed. If these observations on science in relation to the law of trespass should appear theoretical and unreal in the abstract, they become very practical and real to the possessor of land when the unseen force cracks the foundation of his house. The force is just as real if it is chemical in nature and must be awakened by the intervention of another agency before it does harm.

If, then, we must look to the character of the instrumentality which is used in making an intrusion upon another's land we prefer to emphasize the object's energy or force rather than its size. Viewed in this way we may define trespass as any intrusion which invades the possessor's protected interest in exclusive possession, whether that intrusion is by visible or invisible pieces of matter or by energy which can be measured only by the mathematical language of the physicist.

We are of the opinion, therefore, that the intrusion of the fluoride particulates in the present case constituted a trespass.

. . .

. . . The modern law of trespass can be understood only as it is seen against its historical background. Originally all types of trespass, including trespass to land, were punishable under the criminal law because the trespasser's conduct was regarded as a breach of the peace. When the criminal and civil aspect of trespass were separated, the civil action for trespass was colored by its past, and the idea that the peace of the community was put in danger by the trespasser's conduct influenced the courts' ideas of the character of the tort. Therefore, relief was granted to the plaintiff where he was not actually damaged, partly at least as a means of discouraging disruptive influences in the community. Winfield on Torts (4th ed.) p. 305 expresses the idea as follows:

> The law, on the face of it, looks harsh, but trespass was so likely in earlier times to lead to a breach of the peace that even unwitting and trivial deviations on to another person's land were reckoned unlawful. At the present day there is, of course, much greater respect for the law in general and appreciation of the security which it affords, and the theoretical severity of the rules as to land trespass is hardly ever exploited in practice.

. . . If then, we find that an act on the part of the defendant in interfering with the plaintiff's possession, does, or is likely to result in arousing conflict between them, that act will characterize the tort as a trespass, assuming of course that the other elements of the tort are made out. . . .

Probably the most important factor which describes the nature of the interest protected under the law of trespass is nothing more than a feeling which a possessor has with respect to land which he holds. It is a sense of ownership; a feeling that what one owns or possesses should not be interfered with, and that it is entitled to protection through law. This being the nature of the plaintiff's interest, it is understandable why actual damage is not an essential ingredient in the law of trespass. As pointed out in 1 Harper & James, Torts, § 1.8, p. 26, the rule permitting recovery in spite of the absence of actual damages "is probably justified as a vindicatory right to protect the possessor's proprietary or dignitary interest in his land."

We think that a possessor's interest in land as defined by the considerations recited above may, under the appropriate circumstances, be violated by a ray of light, by an atomic particle, or by a particulate of fluoride and, contrariwise, if such interest circumscribed by these considerations is not violated or endangered, the defendant's conduct, even though it may result in a physical intrusion, will not render him liable in an action of trespass.
[   ]

We hold that the defendant's conduct in causing chemical substances to be deposited upon the plaintiffs' land fulfilled all of the requirements under the law of trespass.

The defendant contends that trespass will not lie in this case because the injury was indirect and consequential and that the requirement that the injury must be direct and immediate to constitute a trespass was not met. We have held that the deposit of the particulates upon the plaintiff's land was an intrusion within the definition of trespass. That intrusion was direct. The damages which flowed from it are consequential, but it is well established that such consequential damage may be proven in an action of trespass. [   ] The distinction between direct and indirect invasions where there has been a physical intrusion upon the plaintiff's land has been abandoned by some courts. [   ] Since the invasion in the instant case was direct it is not necessary for us to decide whether the distinction is recognized in this state.

. . .

It is also urged that the trial court erred in failing to enter a special finding requested by the defendant. The requested finding in effect stated that it was impossible in the operation of an aluminum reduction plant to capture all fluorides which are created in the manufacturing process; that the fume collection system was in operation during the period in question; and that it was the most efficient of the systems known in aluminum reduction plants in the United States.

It is argued that since the trial court elected to enter special rather than general findings it was required by ORS 17.430 to enter findings on all material issues which, it is claimed, would include the issue defined in the requested findings. The complaint alleged that the defendant "carelessly, wantonly and willfully continuously caused to be emitted," from its plant the poisonous compounds. This allegation was denied in the defendant's answer. The issue thus raised, as to the character of defendant's conduct in making the intrusion upon plaintiffs' land, would be material only with respect to the claim for punitive damages which, as we have already indicated, was rejected by the trial court. Since we hold that the intrusion in this case constituted a trespass it is immaterial whether the defendant's conduct was careless, wanton and willful or entirely free from fault. Therefore, the refusal to enter the requested finding is not error.

The judgment of the lower court is affirmed.

[The concurring opinion of MCALLISTER, C.J., is omitted.]

Notes and Questions

1. Is aluminum production an ultrahazardous activity? Is the theory of liability here different from that of the New York blasting cases in Chapter VII?

2. Why is it irrelevant whether the defendant's fume collection system constituted a reasonable effort to capture the fluoride particulates? Is the case distinguishable from *Losee v. Buchanan*, p. 508, supra?

3. Can *Martin* be viewed as an application of the doctrine of *Rylands v. Fletcher*?

4. Under the court's expansive view of the trespass action, what types of cases would be exclusively nuisance actions? *Martin* is adopted and the question of overlap between trespass and nuisance discussed at length in Borland v. Sanders Lead Co., Inc., 369 So.2d 523 (Ala.1979)(action in trespass for lead pollution emitted from defendant's smelter). See also Bradley v. American Smelting and Refining Co., 709 P.2d 782 (Wash.1985), adopting *Martin* in a case involving deposit of airborne particles from a copper smelter, but rejecting the Restatement view that an intentional trespass entitles a landowner to damages irrespective of actual harm. The court required a showing of "actual and substantial damage" as a safeguard against mass trivial claims by neighboring landowners. See also Scribner v. Summers, 84 F.3d 554 (2d Cir.1996)(classifying physical contamination of land with barium particles as a trespass as well as a nuisance, where the claim was for actual damages); Mercer v. Rockwell Intern., 24 F.Supp.2d 735 (W.D.Ky.1998)(following *Martin* in holding that invasion by invisible particles (PCBs) could constitute a trespass, but declining to find liability where no "actual" harm).

Is there a meaningful distinction between "exclusive possession" and "use and enjoyment" of land? If the plant in *Martin* had emitted a noxious stench, would the court have regarded the harm as actionable in trespass? In nuisance? What about a continuing abrasive level of noise? See Wilson v. Interlake Steel Co., 649 P.2d 922 (Cal.1982), in which the court asserted that "intangible intrusions, such as noise, odor, or light alone, are dealt with as nuisance cases, not trespass." *Wilson* was re-affirmed in San Diego Gas & Electric Co. v. Superior Court, 920 P.2d 669 (Cal.1996), in which plaintiffs purchased a house near defendant SDG & E's powerlines (which were on adjacent property). Defendant subsequently increased the number of power lines, which plaintiff alleged "dramatically increased the dangerous levels of electromagnetic radiation." On the trespass claim, the court held that electric and magnetic fields are "intangible" as defined in *Wilson*, and thus to bring a trespass action plaintiffs would need to allege physical damage to their property, which they failed to do; as in *Wilson* they alleged only diminution in property value. Compare Ream v. Keen, 838 P.2d 1073 (Or.1992), in which the Oregon court relied on *Martin* to find liability for trespass in a case involving "intrusion of smoke and its lingering odor" from defendant farmer's burning of grass stubble on his field.

B.   NUISANCE

The confusion attending the law of nuisance is indicated by the frequent references to Prosser's comment that "[t]here is no more impenetrable jungle in the entire law than that which surrounds the word 'nuisance.' " Some of this confusion can be avoided by distinguishing at the outset between public and private nuisance. Despite the overlapping terminology, the interests protected by each action and the corresponding elements in establishing a prima facie case are quite different. Although private nuisance is our primary concern, private individuals may, under certain circumstances, employ public nuisance doctrine to protect against harm to person and property. We begin with a brief discussion of the action for public nuisance.

1.   PUBLIC NUISANCE

The historical origins of public nuisance are found in criminal interferences with the rights of the Crown, such as encroachments on the royal domain or on public highways. Subsequently, invasions of the rights of the public—represented by the Crown—became actionable as well. At common law, public nuisance came to cover a broad group of minor criminal offenses that involved unreasonable interferences with some right of the general public. These "included interference with the public health, as in the keeping of diseased animals . . .; with the public safety, as in the case of storage of explosives in the midst of a city . . .; with the public morals, as in houses of prostitution . . .; with the public peace as by loud and disturbing noises; with the public comfort, as in the case of widely disseminated bad odors, dust, and smoke; with the public convenience as by obstruction of a public highway or navigable stream; and with a wide variety of miscellaneous public rights of a similar kind." Restatement (Second) of Torts § 821B comment *b*. Most states, having abolished common law crimes, now have broadly-phrased statutes providing criminal penalties for public nuisances, or have enacted specific statutes declaring certain kinds of conduct to be public nuisances. It does not follow, however, that public nuisance actions have become superfluous. Consider, for example, State v. Schenectady Chemicals, Inc., 479 N.Y.S.2d 1010 (App.Div. 1984), in which the court found that the migration of chemical wastes over a thirty-year period did not constitute a "discharge" within the meaning of a relevant statute, but did constitute the basis for a public nuisance action initiated by the state. See generally, Note, Chemical Discharge: Application of Public Nuisance Theory as a Remedy for Environmental Law Violations, 26 Suffolk L. Rev. 51 (1992).

Traditionally, the tort of public nuisance required the element of criminality to justify private relief. The Second Restatement, however, has eliminated the reference to a "criminal interference." The motivation for the change was concern that the criminality requirement would limit too severely the usefulness of public nuisance doctrine as a means of protecting the environment, which had become of increasing public concern. Instead, § 821B(1) defines public nuisance as "an unreasonable interference with a right common to the general public," and in subsection (2) lists circumstances that could make an interference unreasonable. These include: a significant interference with the public health, safety, peace, comfort, or convenience; the existence of a statute or ordinance proscribing the conduct; or conduct of a continuing nature or of long-lasting effect that the "actor knows or has reason to know has a significant effect upon the public right."

In a novel application, a substantial number of municipalities sued the handgun industry in the late 1990s alleging that the distribution and sales practices of the industry—and the consequent use of handguns for criminal purposes—constituted a public nuisance. As stated by a proponent, "to make out a public nuisance claim, an appropriate governmental entity . . . must establish that the defendant's conduct creates or contributes to a substantial, unreasonable interference with common public rights and that defendant failed to take reasonable measure that would eliminate or ameliorate the harm. The remedy is usually directed at 'abatement' of the nuisance and typically includes injunctive relief and damages." See Kairys, The Governmental Handgun Cases and the Elements and Underlying Policies of Public Nuisance Law, 32 Conn. L.Rev. 1175 (2000). The public nuisance handgun litigation is viewed in a broader context in Developments in the Law—Civil Litigation, 113 Harv. L.Rev. 1752, 1759–83 (2000).

Private litigants attempting to bring public nuisance suits must overcome strict standing requirements. At early common law, a public nuisance action, in keeping with its criminal character, could be maintained only by a public official. Beginning in the sixteenth century, a private individual who could show special harm different in kind, and not just degree, from that suffered by the general public was allowed to bring a private tort suit. The usual justification for this requirement was that a defendant should not be subjected to the numerous actions that could result from a widespread interference with common rights.

Section 821C(1) retains special harm as a prerequisite for recovery of damages in an individual action. According to § 821C(2), standing to bring such an action requires that parties other than public officials either have suffered special harm or "have standing to sue as a representative of the general public, as a citizen in a citizen's action, or as a member of a class in a class action." The requirement may be relaxed, however, in an injunctive action against a public nuisance. Comment *j* explains that the reasons for the special-harm rule are less applicable to injunctive actions and that there are indications of possible change in the courts. Several commentators have suggested that the special-harm requirement be abandoned, again primarily in response to the possibility of using nuisance doctrine as a means of controlling environmental pollution.

The requirement of specific harm to the claimant is reaffirmed and discussed with reference to a variety of illustrative cases in Stop & Shop Companies, Inc. v. Fisher, 444 N.E.2d 368 (Mass.1983). The individualized harm requirement may be overcome in some cases, particularly in the environmental field, by relying upon a statutory special injury requirement. See, e.g., Florida Wildlife Federation v. State Department of Environmental Regulation, 390 So.2d 64 (Fla.1980), relying on the state Environmental Protection Act; Kirk v. United States Sugar Corp., 726 So.2d 822 (Fla.App. 1999)("any citizen who sues in the name of the state to enjoin a public nuisance need not show that he or she has sustained or will sustain special damages or injury different in kind from injury to the public at large").

In some cases, the distinction between public and private nuisance (next to be discussed) may be less than clear. See Lew v. Superior Court, 25 Cal.Rptr.2d 42 (App. 1993), involving successful claims for damages by neighboring residents against the owner of an apartment complex whose tenants were heavily involved in drug dealing activities on the premises. In granting recovery, the court referred to defendant's conduct as both a public and private nuisance.

See generally, Abrams & Washington, The Misunderstood Law of Public Nuisance: A Comparison with Private Nuisance Twenty Years After *Boomer,* 54 Alb.L.Rev. 359 (1990); Hodas, Private Actions for Public Nuisance: Common Law Suits for Relief from Environmental Harm, 16 Ecol.L.Q. 883 (1989); Bryson and MacBeth, Public Nuisance, The Restatement (Second) of Torts and Environmental Law, 2 Ecol.L.Q. 241 (1972).

2. PRIVATE NUISANCE

Section 822 states the general rule that one is subject to liability for conduct that is a legal cause of an invasion of another's interest in the private use and enjoyment of land if the invasion is either: (a) intentional and unreasonable, or (b) unintentional and arising out of negligent or reckless conduct or abnormally dangerous conditions or activities. The latter category, unintentional nuisances, is governed primarily by the rules relating to the underlying negligence, recklessness, or abnormally dangerous activity on which the nuisance is based, with the added requirement that the injury be related to an invasion of interests in the use and enjoyment of land.

By far the more significant category of nuisances is that which the Restatement defines as intentional. Section 825 extends that category to situations in which there is knowledge that the conduct is invading, or is substantially certain to invade, another's interest in the use and enjoyment of land. Virtually all conduct of a continuing nature, then, such as the typical instances of industrial pollution, would be intentional after an initial invasion.

An intentional invasion satisfies the "unreasonableness" requirement, according to § 826, if "(a) the gravity of the harm outweighs the utility of the actor's conduct, or (b) the harm caused by the conduct is serious and the financial burden of compensating for this and similar harm to others would not make the continuation of the conduct not feasible." "Gravity of harm" and the "utility of the conduct" are in turn elaborated as follows:

§ 827 Gravity of Harm—Factors Involved

In defining the gravity of the harm from an intentional invasion of another's interest in the use and enjoyment of land, the following factors are important:

(a) The extent of the harm involved;

(b) the character of the harm involved;

(c) the social value that the law attaches to the type of use or enjoyment invaded;

(d) the suitability of the particular use or enjoyment invaded to the character of the locality; and

(e) the burden on the person harmed of avoiding the harm.

§ 828   Utility of the Conduct—Factors Involved

In determining the utility of conduct that causes an intentional invasion of another's interest in the use and enjoyment of land, the following factors are important:

(a) The social value that the law attaches to the primary purpose of the conduct;

(b) the suitability of the conduct to the character of the locality; and

(c) the impracticability of preventing or avoiding the invasion.

These lists of factors are not intended to be exhaustive, and the relative weight to be given each factor is dependent on the circumstances of the particular case. Obviously, this formulation gives the courts very considerable discretion in determining the final outcome of a balancing test.

The first Restatement of Torts included only the test for unreasonableness contained in Restatement (Second) § 826(a)—whether the gravity of the harm outweighs the utility of the conduct. If this were the sole standard, it could be questioned whether there would be much difference between the tests for intentional and unintentional nuisance—even though "unreasonableness" is to be determined, in the case of intentional nuisances, with reference to the gravity of the harm actually suffered, and in the case of unintended harm, with reference to the likelihood of injury multiplied by the prospective extent of the harm. As comment k to § 822 explains, the negligent, reckless, and abnormally dangerous standards of unintentional nuisances incorporate in some form a balancing of harm against the utility of the conduct, as in the concept of unreasonable risk. And this balancing is made explicit for intentional invasions in § 826.

But § 826(a) is not the sole test in the Second Restatement. An intentional invasion may now be unreasonable under § 826(b) even though the utility of the conduct outweighs the gravity of the harm, if the harm is serious and the defendant could afford to compensate the plaintiff and others similarly harmed while continuing to be engaged in its activity. Similarly, § 829A declares that the gravity of an invasion outweighs its utility (and hence is unreasonable under § 826) whenever the harm caused is both substantial and greater than the plaintiff "should be able to bear without compensation." Thus, an invasion, particularly one causing harm "physical in character," may be so grievous that it outweighs as a matter of law any utility arising from the activity.

At this point it should be evident that substantial similarities exist between the Restatement approach to trespass and nuisance—particularly as the rules governing intentional nuisance come to be strongly influenced by strict liability. Apart from the standards of liability, however, what remedies are available to an aggrieved party? Although trespasses traditionally tended to involve individual instances of harm, equity courts were willing to award injunctive relief when the threat of continued trespassory activity existed. In the nuisance context, the question of remedial alternatives often is critical, since continuing diminution of the plaintiff's use and enjoyment of land is usually present. Should injunctive relief be generally available? The following case deals with this important issue, and also provides the opportunity to go beyond this general introduction and explore in greater detail some fundamental questions about the threshold rules of liability.

Boomer v. Atlantic Cement Co.

Court of Appeals of New York, 1970.
26 N.Y.2d 219, 257 N.E.2d 870, 309 N.Y.S.2d 312.

BERGAN, J. Defendant operates a large cement plant near Albany. These are actions for injunction and damages by neighboring land owners alleging injury to property from dirt, smoke and vibration emanating from the plant. A nuisance has been found after trial, temporary damages have been allowed; but an injunction has been denied.

The public concern with air pollution arising from many sources in industry and in transportation is currently accorded ever wider recognition accompanied by a growing sense of responsibility in State and Federal Governments to control it. Cement plants are obvious sources of air pollution in the neighborhoods where they operate.

But there is now before the court private litigation in which individual property owners have sought specific relief from a single plant operation. The threshold question raised by the division of view on this appeal is whether the court should resolve the litigation between the parties now before it as equitably as seems possible; or whether, seeking promotion of the general public welfare, it should channel private litigation into broad public objectives.

A court performs its essential function when it decides the rights of parties before it. Its decision of private controversies may sometimes greatly affect public issues. Large questions of law are often resolved by the manner in which private litigation is decided. But this is normally an incident to the court's main function to settle controversy. It is a rare exercise of judicial power to use a decision in private litigation as a purposeful mechanism to achieve direct public objectives greatly beyond the rights and interests before the court.

Effective control of air pollution is a problem presently far from solution even with the full public and financial powers of government. In large measure adequate technical procedures are yet to be developed and some that appear possible may be economically impracticable.

It seems apparent that the amelioration of air pollution will depend on technical research in great depth; on a carefully balanced consideration of the economic impact of close regulation; and of the actual effect on public health. It is likely to require massive public expenditure and to demand more than any local community can accomplish and to depend on regional and interstate controls.

A court should not try to do this on its own as a by-product of private litigation and it seems manifest that the judicial establishment is neither equipped in the limited nature of any judgment it can pronounce nor prepared to lay down and implement an effective policy for the elimination of air pollution. This is an area beyond the circumference of one private lawsuit. It is a direct responsibility for government and should not thus be undertaken as an incident to solving a dispute between property owners and a single cement plant—one of many—in the Hudson River valley.

The cement making operations of defendant have been found by the court at Special Term to have damaged the nearby properties of plaintiffs in these two actions. That court, as it has been noted, accordingly found defendant maintained a nuisance and this has been affirmed at the Appellate Division. The total damage to plaintiffs' properties is, however, relatively small in comparison with the value of defendant's operation and with the consequences of the injunction which plaintiffs seek.

The ground for the denial of injunction, notwithstanding the finding both that there is a nuisance and that plaintiffs have been damaged substantially, is the large disparity in economic consequences of the nuisance and of the injunction. This theory cannot, however, be sustained without overruling a doctrine which has been consistently reaffirmed in several leading cases in this court and which has never been disavowed here, namely that where a nuisance has been found and where there has been any substantial damage shown by the party complaining an injunction will be granted.

The rule in New York has been that such a nuisance will be enjoined although marked disparity be shown in economic consequence between the effect of the injunction and the effect of the nuisance.

The problem of disparity in economic consequence was sharply in focus in Whalen v. Union Bag & Paper Co. (208 N.Y. 1 [1913]). A pulp mill entailing an investment of more than a million dollars polluted a stream in which plaintiff, who owned a farm, was "a lower riparian owner." The economic loss to plaintiff from this pollution was small. This court, reversing the Appellate Division, reinstated the injunction granted by the Special Term against the argument of the mill owner that in view of "the slight advantage to plaintiff and the great loss that will be inflicted on defendant" an injunction should not be granted (p. 2). "Such a balancing of injuries cannot be justified by the circumstances of this case," Judge Werner noted (p. 4). He continued: "Although the damage to the plaintiff may be slight as compared with the defendant's expense of abating the condition, that is not a good reason for refusing an injunction" (p. 5).

Thus the unconditional injunction granted at Special Term was reinstated. The rule laid down in that case, then, is that whenever the damage resulting from a nuisance is found not "unsubstantial," viz., $100 a year, injunction would follow. This states a rule that had been followed in this court with marked consistency [ ].

. . .

Although the court at Special Term and the Appellate Division held that injunction should be denied, it was found that plaintiffs had been damaged in various specific amounts up to the time of the trial and damages to the respective plaintiffs were awarded for those amounts. The effect of this was, injunction having been denied, plaintiffs could maintain successive actions at law for damages thereafter as further damage was incurred.

The court at Special Term also found the amount of permanent damage attributable to each plaintiff, for the guidance of the parties in the event both sides stipulated to the payment and acceptance of such permanent damage as a settlement of all the controversies among the parties. The total of permanent damages to all plaintiffs thus found was $185,000. This basis of adjustment has not resulted in any stipulation by the parties.

This result at Special Term and at the Appellate Division is a departure from a rule that has become settled; but to follow the rule literally in these cases would be to close down the plant at once. This court is fully agreed to avoid that immediately drastic remedy: the difference in view is how best to avoid it.*

One alternative is to grant the injunction but postpone its effect to a specified future date to give opportunity for technical advances to permit defendant to eliminate the nuisance; another is to grant the injunction conditioned on the payment of permanent damages to plaintiffs which would compensate them for the total economic loss to their property present and future caused by defendant's operations. For reasons which will be developed the court chooses the latter alternative.

If the injunction were to be granted unless within a short period—e.g., 18 months—the nuisance be abated by improved methods, there would be no assurance that any significant technical improvement would occur.

The parties could settle this private litigation at any time if defendant paid enough money and the imminent threat of closing the plant would build up the pressure on defendant. If there were no improved techniques found, there would inevitably be applications to the court at Special Term for extensions of time to perform on showing of good faith efforts to find such techniques.

---

* Respondent's investment in the plant is in excess of $45,000,000. There are over 300 people employed there.

Moreover, techniques to eliminate dust and other annoying by-products of cement making are unlikely to be developed by any research the defendant can undertake within any short period, but will depend on the total resources of the cement industry nationwide and throughout the world. The problem is universal wherever cement is made.

For obvious reasons the rate of the research is beyond control of defendant. If at the end of 18 months the whole industry has not found a technical solution a court would be hard put to close down this one cement plant if due regard be given to equitable principles.

On the other hand, to grant the injunction unless defendant pays plaintiffs such permanent damages as may be fixed by the court seems to do justice between the contending parties. All of the attributions of economic loss to the properties on which plaintiffs' complaints are based will have been redressed.

The nuisance complained of by these plaintiffs may have other public or private consequences, but these particular parties are the only ones who have sought remedies and the judgment proposed will fully redress them. The limitation of relief granted is a limitation only within the four corners of these actions and does not foreclose public health or other public agencies from seeking proper relief in a proper court.

It seems reasonable to think that the risk of being required to pay permanent damages to injured property owners by cement plant owners would itself be a reasonably effective spur to research for improved techniques to minimize nuisance.

The power of the court to condition on equitable grounds the continuance of an injunction on the payment of permanent damages seems undoubted. [   ]

The damage base here suggested is consistent with the general rule in those nuisance cases where damages are allowed. "Where a nuisance is of such a permanent and unabatable character that a single recovery can be had, including the whole damage past and future resulting therefrom, there can be but one recovery" (66 C.J.S., Nuisances, § 140, p. 947). It has been said that permanent damages are allowed where the loss recoverable would obviously be small as compared with the cost of removal of the nuisance [   ].

. . .

Thus it seems fair to both sides to grant permanent damages to plaintiffs which will terminate this private litigation. The theory of damage is the "servitude on land" of plaintiffs imposed by defendant's nuisance. (See United States v. Causby, 328 U.S. 256, 261, 262, 267 [1946], where the term "servitude" addressed to the land was used by Justice Douglas relating to the effect of airplane noise on property near an airport.)

The judgment, by allowance of permanent damages imposing a servitude on land, which is the basis of the actions, would preclude future recovery by plaintiffs or their grantees.

This should be placed beyond debate by a provision of the judgment that the payment by defendant and the acceptance by plaintiffs of permanent damages found by the court shall be in compensation for a servitude on the land.

Although the Trial Term has found permanent damages as a possible basis of settlement of the litigation, on remission the court should be entirely free to re-examine this subject. It may again find the permanent damage already found; or make new findings.

The orders should be reversed, without costs, and the cases remitted to Supreme Court, Albany County to grant an injunction which shall be vacated upon payment by defendant of such amounts of permanent damage to the respective plaintiffs as shall for this purpose be determined by the court.

JASEN, J. (dissenting). I agree with the majority that a reversal is required here, but I do not subscribe to the newly enunciated doctrine of assessment of permanent damages, in lieu of an injunction, where substantial property rights have been impaired by the creation of a nuisance.

It has long been the rule in this State, as the majority acknowledges, that a nuisance which results in substantial continuing damage to neighbors must be enjoined. [　]

To now change the rule to permit the cement company to continue polluting the air indefinitely upon the payment of permanent damages is, in my opinion, compounding the magnitude of a very serious problem in our State and Nation today.

In recognition of this problem, the Legislature of this State has enacted the Air Pollution Control Act (Public Health Law, §§ 1264–1299-m) declaring that it is the State policy to require the use of all available and reasonable methods to prevent and control air pollution (Public Health Law, § 1265).

The harmful nature and widespread occurrence of air pollution have been extensively documented. Congressional hearings have revealed that air pollution causes substantial property damage, as well as being a contributing factor to a rising incidence of lung cancer, emphysema, bronchitis and asthma.

The specific problem faced here is known as particulate contamination because of the fine dust particles emanating from defendant's cement plant. The particular type of nuisance is not new, having appeared in many cases for at least the past 60 years. [　] It is interesting to note that cement production has recently been identified as a significant source of particulate contamination in the Hudson Valley. This type of pollution, wherein very small particles escape and stay in the atmosphere, has been denominated as the type of air pollution which produces the greatest hazard to human health. We have thus a nuisance which not only is damaging to the plaintiffs, but also is decidedly harmful to the general public.

I see grave dangers in overruling our long-established rule of granting an injunction where a nuisance results in substantial continuing damage. In permitting the injunction to become inoperative upon the payment of permanent damages, the majority is, in effect, licensing a continuing wrong. It is the same as saying to the cement company, you may continue to do harm to your neighbors so long as you pay a fee for it. Furthermore, once such permanent damages are assessed and paid, the incentive to alleviate the wrong would be eliminated, thereby continuing air pollution of an area without abatement.

It is true that some courts have sanctioned the remedy here proposed by the majority in a number of cases, but none of the authorities relied upon by the majority are analogous to the situation before us. In those cases the courts, in denying an injunction and awarding money damages, granted their decision on a showing that the use to which the property was intended to be put was primarily for the public benefit. Here, on the other hand, it is clearly established that the cement company is creating a continuing air pollution nuisance primarily for its own private interest with no public benefit.

This kind of inverse condemnation [   ] may not be invoked by a private person or corporation for private gain or advantage. Inverse condemnation should only be permitted when the public is primarily served in the taking or impairment of property. [   ] The promotion of the interests of the polluting cement company has, in my opinion, no public use or benefit.

Nor is it constitutionally permissible to impose servitude on land, without consent of the owner, by payment of permanent damages where the continuing impairment of the land is for a private use. [   ] This is made clear by the State Constitution (art. I, § 7, subd. [a]) which provides that "[p]rivate property shall not be taken for *public use* without just compensation" (emphasis added). It is, of course, significant that the section makes no mention of taking for a *private* use.

In sum, then, by constitutional mandate as well as by judicial pronouncement, the permanent impairment of private property for private purposes is not authorized in the absence of clearly demonstrated public benefit and use.

I would enjoin the defendant cement company from continuing the discharge of dust particles upon its neighbors' properties unless, within 18 months, the cement company abated this nuisance.

It is not my intention to cause the removal of the cement plant from the Albany area, but to recognize the urgency of the problem stemming from this stationary source of air pollution, and to allow the company a specified period of time to develop a means to alleviate this nuisance.

I am aware that the trial court found that the most modern dust control devices available have been installed in defendant's plant, but, I submit, this does not mean that *better* and more effective dust control devices could not be developed within the time allowed to abate the pollution.

Moreover, I believe it is incumbent upon the defendant to develop such devices, since the cement company, at the time the plant commenced production (1962), was well aware of the plaintiffs' presence in the area, as well as the probable consequences of its contemplated operation. Yet, it still chose to build and operate the plant at this site.

In a day when there is a growing concern for clean air, highly developed industry should not expect acquiescence by the courts, but should, instead, plan its operations to eliminate contamination of our air and damage to its neighbors.

Accordingly, the orders of the Appellate Division, insofar as they denied the injunction, should be reversed, and the actions remitted to Supreme Court, Albany County to grant an injunction to take effect 18 months hence, unless the nuisance is abated by improved techniques prior to said date.

CHIEF JUDGE FULD and JUDGES BURKE and SCILEPPI concur with JUDGE BERGAN; JUDGE JASEN dissents in part and votes to reverse in a separate opinion; JUDGES BREITEL and GIBSON taking no part.

Notes and Questions

1. In *Boomer* the defendant argued at the trial level that it was not committing a nuisance. The trial judge found that the defendant "took every available and possible precaution to protect the plaintiffs from dust." Nonetheless, the court found a nuisance because the "discharge of large quantities of dust upon each of the properties and excessive vibration from blasting deprived each party of the reasonable use of his property and thereby prevented his enjoyment of life and liberty therein." 287 N.Y.S.2d 112 (Albany Cty. 1967). In *Boomer* the defendant knew to a substantial certainty that those nearby would be subjected to dust and vibration, and continued the operation after having actual knowledge of the harm. Notice that by this analysis the overwhelming majority of alleged industrial nuisances are "intentional." In what sense is the harm intended here? Is there a difference between defendant's conduct in this case and that of a product manufacturer who knows to a substantial certainty that one widget out of ten thousand he produces will cause injury?

2. The fact that the vast majority of industrial nuisances are "intentional" makes all the more important the question whether, in addition to being intentional, the activity is also "unreasonable." This problem was explored at length in Jost v. Dairyland Power Cooperative, 172 N.W.2d 647 (Wis.1969), in which sulfur dioxide gas was discharged into the atmosphere by defendant's power plant, damaging nearby crops. The farmers sued and the defendant sought to prove that it had used due care in the construction and operation of its plant and that the "social and economic utility of the Alma plant outweighed the gravity of damage to the plaintiffs." The trial judge's rejection of such proof as to liability was affirmed. The court found crop damage of several hundred dollars and then, turning to liability, concluded:

> that the court properly excluded all evidence that tended to show the utility of the Dairyland Cooperative's enterprise. Whether its economic or social importance dwarfed the claim of a small farmer is of no consequence in this lawsuit. It will not be said that, because a great and socially useful enterprise will be liable in damages, an injury small by comparison should go unredressed. We know of no acceptable rule of jurisprudence that permits those who are engaged in important and desirable enterprises to injure with impunity those who are engaged in enterprises of lesser economic significance. Even the government or other entities, including public utilities, endowed with the power of eminent domain—the power to take private property in order to devote it to a purpose beneficial to the public good—are obliged to pay a fair market value for what is taken or damaged. To contend that a public utility, in the pursuit of its praiseworthy and legitimate enterprise, can, in effect, deprive others of the full use of their property without compensation, poses a theory unknown to the law of Wisconsin, and in our opinion would constitute the taking of property without due process of law.

Is the court's reasoning consistent with the approach taken in the initial Restatement p. 662, supra? In the Second Restatement? In *Boomer*? For a comprehensive discussion of the case law and law review literature on *Boomer* and private nuisance in the succeeding two decades (including a tally of the cases adopting some version of the Second Restatement approach to balancing the utilities), see Lewin, *Boomer* and the American Law of Nuisance: Past, Present, and Future, 54 Alb.L.Rev. 189 (1990). For a case providing the flavor of nuisance controversies—and resolutions—prior to the adoption of strict liability analysis, see Waschak v. Moffat, 109 A.2d 310 (Pa.1954). On the analogue to governmental takings, with particular reference to Lucas v. South Carolina Coastal Council, 505 U.S. 1003 (1992), see Halper, Untangling the Nuisance Knot, 26 B.C. Envtl. Aff. L.Rev. 89 (1998).

3. Recall that the trial court in *Rylands*, p. 503, supra, decided that there was no nuisance because the act was not a continuing harm. Although most nuisances have been accompanied by continuing harm, this is no longer considered an essential element.

4. The *Boomer* case also suggests the overlap between nuisance and trespass. Reconsider *Martin v. Reynolds Metals Co.*, p. 653, supra. Under the *Boomer* approach, does it matter for purposes of liability whether defendant's conduct is characterized as nuisance or trespass? Compare Wood v. Picillo, 443 A.2d 1244 (R.I.1982), in which the court enjoined the further operation of a chemical dump on the defendant's property on nuisance grounds, remarking that "it could well be argued that one who utilizes his land for abnormally dangerous activities or for storage of abnormally dangerous substances may be strictly liable for resultant injuries, even in the absence of a finding of nuisance or negligence," and citing *Rylands v. Fletcher*.

5. The law of private nuisance has occasionally been characterized as a form of judicial zoning. Although the court of appeals in *Boomer* does not mention it, the appellate division opinion notes that the area was zoned. 294 N.Y.S.2d 452 (App.Div. 1968). Apparently before the defendant began operations in 1962, the town zoned the defendant's property to permit quarrying and business, so that defendant's activity was lawful. Should the zoning be relevant to whether the defendant is liable for any nuisance? Is it proper for a court to find a common-law nuisance when the defendant has obeyed legislative zoning requirements? For an extensive discussion of the subject, see Ellickson, Alternatives to Zoning: Covenants, Nuisance Rules, and Fines as Land Use Controls, 40 U.Chi.L.Rev. 681 (1973).

Boomer was held inapplicable in Little Joseph Realty, Inc. v. Town of Babylon, 363 N.E.2d 1163 (N.Y.1977), in which plaintiff sued to enjoin the construction and operation of an asphalt plant on defendant's adjoining property. The lower court determined that the plant, which violated the town's zoning ordinance, was a nuisance, and ordered it enjoined unless certain remedial devices were installed—and they were. On appeal, reversed. New York's long-standing rule that structures built on adjoining or nearby property in violation of zoning ordinances were enjoinable at the demand of a specially-damaged neighbor, was not changed by *Boomer*.

Boomer involved a private dispute between two parties in which it was proper to adjust "competing uses with a view towards maximizing the social value of each." But zoning "is far more comprehensive. Its design is, on a planned basis, to serve as a 'vital tool for maintaining a civilized form of existence' for the benefit and welfare of an entire community. . . . It follows that, when a continuing use flies in the face of a valid zoning restriction, it must, subject to the existence of any appropriate equitable defenses, be enjoined unconditionally." This does not mean that "risk-utility considerations have not entered into the adoption of a zoning law's restriction on use. It is rather that presumptively they have already been weighed and disposed of by the Legislature which enacted them."

6. A considerable body of nuisance law deals with land use disputes that lack the broader environmental aspects of the *Boomer* case. Typically, these cases deal with the loss of commercial value of adjoining property, such as Fontainebleau Hotel Corp. v. Forty–Five Twenty–Five, Inc., 114 So.2d 357 (Fla.App.1959), in which a Miami Beach hotel sought an injunction to prevent a neighboring hotel from building a 14-floor addition that would cut off a considerable amount of sunlight from plaintiff's property, or a loss of economic value of residential property, such as the numerous efforts to enjoin a funeral parlor from locating in a neighborhood. See, e.g., Travis v. Moore, 377 So.2d 609 (Miss.1979). At times, the claims combine allegations of loss of market value with pain and suffering; see Weinhold v. Wolff, 555 N.W.2d 454 (Iowa 1996), involving a successful claim for damages from noxious odors emanating from a neighboring hog feeding and confinement facility. Hard feelings and spiteful behavior are not uncommon in these cases. Consider Coty v. Ramsey Associates, 546 A.2d 196 (Vt.), cert. denied 487 U.S. 1236 (1988), in which defendants were held liable after establishing a pig farm next to the property of neighbors who had success-fully opposed the defendants' effort to build a motel on their land. Contrast Wernke v. Halas, 600 N.E.2d 117 (Ind.App.1992), in which the court held that nailing a toilet seat to a tree and placing offensive graffiti on a fence facing the plaintiffs' property might constitute "unsightliness or lack of aesthetic virtue" but did not rise to the level of a nuisance.

For a case merging the environmental and commercial aspects of nuisance law, see Prah v. Maretti, 321 N.W.2d 182 (Wis.1982), in which the court upheld the claim of the owner of a solar-heated residence against a neighbor's proposed construction that would have interfered with the plaintiff's solar access. See also Vogel v. Grant–Lafayette Elec. Co-op., 548 N.W.2d 829 (Wis.1996), allowing a nuisance claim for stray voltage from defendant's electric power grid that caused plaintiffs' cattle to exhibit "violent or erratic behavior" and to produce less milk. Detailed consider-ation of these dimensions of nuisance law is beyond the scope of a Torts course; the residential and commercial aspects of nuisance law—and zoning law, as well—are taken up in courses in Land Use and Property.

7. In *Boomer,* the defendant came to the area more recently than the plaintiffs. Is this relevant? Sometimes the defendant establishes its facility in an isolated area only to find the nearby town expanding and others moving closer to it. The question raised is whether a plaintiff who has knowingly encountered the nuisance is barred from suing. Restatement (Second) of Torts § 840D says that this is "not in itself sufficient to bar his action, but it is a factor to be considered in determining whether the nuisance is actionable." How might this be a relevant factor? Might there be an underlying concern about first-comers exercising extra-territorial controls over large areas of land? Might the price plaintiff paid for the land be relevant? The issue is discussed in Wittman, First Come, First Served: An Economic Analysis of "Coming to the Nuisance," 9 J.Legal Stud. 557 (1980).

8. Turning now to questions of remedy for private nuisance, what relief did the trial judge award in *Boomer*? How did the court of appeals alter the remedy granted by the lower courts?

9. In the *Jost* case the court also awarded damages:

> We see no basis for the jury's conclusion that the market value of one of the farms was reduced by $500 and the value of the others not at all. Such a result—although there could have been a differential—is completely unsupported by the evidence.

> We conclude that the plaintiffs are entitled to recover for the crops and damage to vegetation for the years complained of—1965 and 1966—as found by the jury, but after those years recovery cannot again be for specific items of damage on a year-by-year basis. Their avenue for compensation is for permanent and continuing nuisance as may be reflected in a diminution of market value. Of course, permitting a

recovery now for a permanent loss of market value presupposes that the degree of nuisance will not increase. If such be the case, an award of damages for loss of market value is final. If, however, the level of nuisance and air pollution should be increased above the level that may now be determined by a jury, with a consequent additional injury the plaintiffs would have the right to seek additional permanent damage to compensate them for the additional diminished market value.

What is the justification for reopening the case if the defendant increases the amount of sulphur dioxide it emits? Is this similar to cases in which after final judgment the plaintiff's injury turns out to be more serious than previously believed?

10. What should happen in *Boomer* and *Jost* if, after paying permanent damages, the defendant reduces the harm being inflicted—either by closing down the operation or by installing newly developed control devices? But what is the defendant's incentive in *Boomer* to install any new devices at all? What if the plaintiff in *Jost* switches to crops that are less profitable but impervious to sulfur dioxide gas?

11. Is the majority persuasive in its reasons for denying an injunction? The appellate division upheld the trial court's denial, relying on "the zoning of the area, the large number of persons employed by the defendant, its extensive business operations and substantial investment in plant and equipment, its use of the most modern and efficient devices to prevent offensive emissions and discharges, and its payment of substantial sums of real property and school taxes." 294 N.Y.S.2d 452 (App.Div. 1968). Are these factors relevant to the remedy question? The liability question?

Further litigation ensued over the damage measurement. The opinions discuss extensively the role of experts in land valuation problems. Boomer v. Atlantic Cement Co., 340 N.Y.S.2d 97 (Albany Cty. 1972), affirmed in Kinley v. Atlantic Cement Co., 349 N.Y.S.2d 199 (App.Div. 1973).

12. In Adams v. Star Enterprise, 51 F.3d 417 (4th Cir.1995), property owners brought suit against defendant oil distribution facility for a major discharge of oil that created a plume extending underground to near their property—although not yet actually contaminating their property. They sought damages for emotional distress and diminished property value on, among other theories, private nuisance. Applying Virginia law, the court held that there could be no recovery on a nuisance theory absent some evidence of physically perceptible harm. Here the plume was "incapable of detection" from plaintiffs' properties.

What are some of the problems associated with allowing such claims to go forward on the grounds of depreciation of property values without "physically perceptible harm?" In Adkins v. Thomas Solvent Co., 487 N.W.2d 715 (Mich.1992), which held that property owners living near a contaminated site could not recover for the diminution of their property values in the absence of evidence demonstrating that contaminants had migrated to their property, the majority reasoned that:

[i]f any property owner in the vicinity of the numerous hazardous-waste sites that have been identified can advance a claim seeking damages when unfounded public fears of exposure cause property depreciation, the ultimate effect might be a reordering of the polluter's resources for the benefit of the persons who have suffered no cognizable harm at the expense of those claimants who have been subjected to a substantial and unreasonable interference in the use and enjoyment of property.

The dissent, however, would have allowed a nuisance action on a showing "that the defendants actually contaminated soil and ground water in the neighborhood of plaintiffs' homes with toxic chemicals and industrial wastes, that the market perception of the value of plaintiffs' homes was actually adversely affected by the contamination of the neighborhood, and thus that plaintiffs' loss was causally related to defendants' conduct." Who has the better argument? For an outcome similar to that in *Adkins*, see Berry v. Armstrong Rubber Co., 989 F.2d 822 (5th Cir.1993), cert. denied, 510 U.S. 1117 (1994) (rejecting nuisance action claiming property depreciation because of "stigma" arising out of a tire manufacturer's dumping in the area where the evidence failed to establish some physical damage to the owners' land caused by tire manufacturer). In contrast, a few courts have been willing to allow a nuisance action without evidence of physical harm. See, e.g., Omega Chemical Co. v. United Seeds, 560 N.W.2d 820 (Neb.1997) (finding a nuisance where accumulated snow on defendant's roof merely threatened harm to the plaintiff). What about situations involving continuing noxious odors, high noise levels, or strong vibrations? Do these meet the threshold requirement of physically perceptible harm? Should they?

13.   Where the exposure leads to an individual claim of personal injury, nuisance law typically holds that the harm suffered should be determined by reference to a "normal" person in the community. Why might this be? For an early case articulating the general approach, see Rogers v. Elliott, 15 N.E. 768 (Mass.1888) (denying relief to plaintiff who suffered harm from ringing of church bells because of his highly nervous condition). For a more recent application, see Jenkins v. CSX Transportation, Inc., 906 S.W.2d 460 (Tenn.App.1995) (holding that the rarity of landowner's allergic condition to creosote fumes from railroad ties, transported through neighboring rail yard, precluded his nuisance claim). Is this approach contrary to the eggshell plaintiff rule considered at p. 399, supra? Compare the treatment of the super-sensitive plaintiff in emotional distress cases, p. 278, supra.

14.   In an influential article, Property Rules, Liability Rules, and Inalienability: One View of the Cathedral, 85 Harv.L.Rev. 1089 (1972), Calabresi and Melamed discuss a framework of rules that the law uses to protect "entitlements" (decisions regarding which of two or more conflicting parties will prevail). These rules yield the traditional results of no liability, damages, or injunctive relief.

An entitlement is protected by a "property" rule when a person who wishes to obtain the entitlement must purchase it at a price determined by the holder. Thus, the New York rule regarding injunctions for nuisances, before *Boomer,* provided an entitlement in cases of "not unsubstantial" damage to the neighbors of a polluter that was protected by a property rule: A polluter who wished to continue operations had to buy the right to do so. Alternatively, an entitlement protected by a property rule could be given to the polluter. This would be the case if the courts adopted a rule of no liability for pollution damage.

Two other results are possible. The entitlement held by the polluter or by the neighbors might be protected only by a "liability" rule, which is the case when one of the parties in conflict can purchase the entitlement at an objectively determined price. This rule corresponds to the imposition of damages by a court. *Boomer* is an example of an entitlement in the plaintiffs protected by a liability rule—defendant polluter can continue operations as long as damages are paid in satisfaction of the entitlement.

The fourth alternative, giving the polluter an entitlement protected by a liability rule, is rarely recognized as a possibility. The leading nuisance case employing this approach, Spur Industries, Inc. v. Del E. Webb Development Co., 494 P.2d 700 (Ariz.1972), involved a conflict between defendant's pre-existing cattle feedlot operation and plaintiff's residential subdivision, which expanded towards the feedlot until the flies and odors drifting onto the development made sale of more units impossible and provoked numerous complaints from existing residents. The court found that the feedlot was an enjoinable nuisance, but held that because of the "coming to the nuisance" aspect of the case, plaintiff developer would be required to indemnify defendant Spur for the cost of "moving or shutting down." The court reasoned:

> It does not seem harsh to require a developer, who has taken advantage of the lesser land values in a rural area as well as the availability of large tracts of land on which to build and develop a new town or city in the area, to indemnify those who are forced to leave as a result.

The court emphasized, however, that:

> this relief to Spur is limited to a case wherein a developer has, with foreseeability, brought into a previously agricultural or industrial area the population which makes necessary the granting of an injunction against a lawful business and for which the business has no adequate relief.

Is the remedy accorded in *Spur* likely to be useful or applicable in many cases? Consider that here the homeowners' individual interests were represented by the development company. If an action were brought by an individual or by a class, how would compensation to the feedlot be apportioned among all the homeowners affected? What about homeowners who failed to join in the action?

What factors should be considered in deciding who gets an entitlement? In deciding whether the entitlement should be protected by a property rule or a liability rule? See generally, E. Rabin, Nuisance Law: Rethinking Fundamental Assumptions, 63 Va.L.Rev. 1299 (1977); Lewin,

Compensated Injunctions and the Evolution of Nuisance Law, 71 Iowa L. Rev. 775 (1986).

15. Is it helpful to analyze these cases in terms of causal responsibility? See Epstein, Nuisance Law: Corrective Justice and Its Utilitarian Constraints, 8 J. Legal Stud. 49 (1979).

Contrast the following two views on assigning causal responsibility. Professor Fletcher, in the 1972 article discussed at p. 532, supra, argues that a victim of harm

> has a right to recover for injuries caused by a risk greater in degree and different in order from those created by the victim and imposed on the defendant—in short, for injuries resulting from nonreciprocal risks.

In Coase, The Problem of Social Cost, 3 J. of Law & Econ. 1 (1960), discussed at p. 531, supra, the author challenges widely-accepted notions of causal direction:

> The question is commonly thought of as one in which A inflicts harm on B and what has to be decided is: how should we restrain A? But this is wrong. We are dealing with a problem of a reciprocal nature. To avoid the harm to B would inflict harm on A. The real question that has to be decided is: should A be allowed to harm B or should B be allowed to harm A? . . . [An] example is afforded by the problem of straying cattle which destroy crops on neighboring land. If it is inevitable that some cattle will stray, an increase in the supply of meat can only be obtained at the expense of a decrease in the supply of crops. The nature of the choice is clear: meat or crops.

Is one of these formulations more helpful than the other in thinking about nuisance cases? Do they address the issue of appropriate remedy as well as initial right (entitlement)? Does *Spur* reflect the idea that the feedlot and the development impose reciprocal costs on each other?

16. In his article Coase goes on to argue that in the absence of transaction costs (i.e., costs associated with striking a bargain) the rule of liability does not matter from an economic efficiency standpoint. In a *Boomer* situation, if the polluter is liable he will invest more in pollution control measures only when doing so is cheaper than paying damages or going out of business. If the polluter is not liable, the victim will "bribe" him to invest in pollution control equipment where doing so costs less than the damage the victim would otherwise suffer. Whatever the liability rule, the choice between pollution control measures and victim harm will result in precisely the same amount of resources being invested in elimination of the harm—although, of course, the distributional consequences will differ.

Since there are almost invariably transaction costs—consider the costs of getting the parties together in *Boomer,* and the potential "holdout" problems if a "property" rule (injunctive relief) were granted—the rights and remedies recognized by nuisance law do generally make a considerable difference. The economic consequences under various assumptions about bargaining behavior are systematically explored in Polinsky, Resolving

Nuisance Disputes: The Simple Economics of Injunctive and Damage Remedies, 32 Stan.L.Rev. 1075 (1980).

17. In the *Union Bag* case, cited in *Boomer*, the plaintiff's harm was assessed at $100 per year. Plaintiff enforced his injunction, and the mill, which represented an investment of $1,000,000, was permanently closed. Why was the pre-*Boomer* New York rule on injunctive relief on its face so favorable to plaintiffs? Did it embody a distinctive view about property rights in land? Is the majority in *Boomer* correct in its assertion that the court's essential function is to decide "the rights of the parties before it"? Does the dissent disagree?

18. One legislative remedy available in New York against air pollution was Public Health Law §§ 1264–98, establishing an administrative body to determine standards for pollution and to promulgate regulations accordingly. The Commissioner of Health was to investigate and determine violations. His conclusions were subject to administrative and judicial review. Failure to take corrective action subjected the offender to penalties not to exceed $1,000 plus $200 for each day of continued violation. The Commissioner could also seek an injunction. The act expressly stated that it was supplementary to any other existing remedies, but at the same time provided that the rules and regulations promulgated under the statute were "not intended to create in any way new or enlarged rights or to enlarge existing rights." Any determination by the Commissioner that pollution existed or that a regulation had been violated "shall not create by reason thereof any presumption of law or finding of fact which shall inure to or be for the benefit of any person other than the state." New York had also entered interstate compacts to combat water and air pollution. (N.Y. Public Health Law §§ 1299–1299s.) Does the existence of these procedures affect your views of the majority decision?

19. *Intersection with environmental regulatory schemes.* Since 1970, the federal government has assumed a major presence in the field of regulatory control of environmental pollution. A wide variety of statutory schemes have been enacted in an effort to develop a more comprehensive approach to many of the environmental harms associated with air and water pollution, hazardous wastes, and toxic substances (among others). For the most part, these enactments have not been interpreted as preempting private nuisance actions under state common law, but there are exceptions. In International Paper Co. v. Ouellette, 479 U.S. 481 (1987), for example, the Supreme Court held that the Clean Water Act preempts state nuisance law when applied to an out-of-state source.

At the state level, most states have enacted pollution control statutes that either specifically preserve nuisance actions or have been interpreted by the courts to preserve such actions. As in the federal system, however, there are exceptions. In *San Diego Gas & Electric Co. v. Superior Court*, discussed at p. 658 supra, on the trespass claim, in which a group of homeowners alleged that electric and magnetic fields (EMF) emitted from the utility's electric power lines had caused them emotional distress, made their homes uninhabitable, and destroyed the market value of their homes, the court rejected their private nuisance action, holding that an award of damages would impermissibly interfere with the Public Utility Commission's policy on power-line electric and magnetic fields. Recall the discussion of the preemption defense at p. 489, supra. Is there reason to think it would play out differently in the nuisance context? For an overview of the preemption issue and an argument that nuisance law should be retained as a supplemental remedy rather than being preempted by pollution control statutes, see Heimert, Keeping Pigs Out of Parlors: Using Nuisance Law to Affect the Location of Pollution, 27 Envtl. L. 403 (1997).

Conversely, consider the prospect of nuisance law being used to enforce regulations. See, e.g., Rushing v. Kansas City Southern Ry. Co., 185 F.3d 496 (5th Cir.1999), cert. denied 528 U.S. 1160 (2000) (holding, among other things, that a plaintiff pressing a common-law private nuisance claim, asserted under Mississippi law against a railroad in connection with alleged excessive noise and vibration from its switching yard operations, could not seek to enforce noise limits stricter than those set forth in regulations implementing the federal Noise Control Act of 1978—but that such an action could be used to enforce the statutory limits).

Although the regulatory approach to environmental pollution cannot be explored in a Torts course, it is important to be aware of the fact that a distinctly different way of dealing with health and safety issues does exist— an approach that has its counterpart in other areas, such as regulation of product safety, occupational safety, and motor vehicle safety.

CHAPTER X

DAMAGES AND INSURANCE

Our emphasis so far has been on the doctrinal development of negligence and strict liability, with principal attention to legal liability in various fact patterns. By and large, tort defendants are less concerned with the concept of liability than with the consequences of that liability—the imposition of damages. The defendant charged with professional malpractice may be quite concerned with liability because a small adverse judgment or even the filing of suit may tarnish a physician's reputation in some communities. More typically, however, corporations and businesses treat tort liability as a cost of doing business and discount its tarnishing effect. They are concerned with the total annual cost of tort liability.

We begin this Chapter with an introduction to the basic items of recoverable damages and highlight the central problems of damage measurement. We then examine the institution of insurance to see how it operates and the critical role it plays in contemporary tort liability and litigation.

A. DAMAGES

1. COMPENSATORY DAMAGES

The fundamental goal of damage awards in the unintentional tort area is to return the plaintiff as closely as possible to his or her condition before the accident. This is achieved by measuring certain items of harm in past and future terms. The total amount of these past and future damages is usually awarded in a single judgment. Since the plaintiff generally may sue no more than once for all items of damage arising from the event in question, to the extent that the plaintiff is not completely healed by the time of trial, some predictions must be made.

It would be possible to have a system in which every few years the plaintiff must sue anew to recover for the damages shown to have been suffered since the last payment. There are obvious advantages and disadvantages to such a procedure. One drawback is the concern that victims of accidents who are told that their award will depend on how quickly or slowly they recover from the original injury may tend to appear not to recover too quickly. This may not be conscious malingering as much as a subconscious fear that they will be found in later hearings to be healthier than they actually are, and thus have their damages unfairly reduced or terminated. In workers' compensation, as we shall see, this may also be a problem, but the danger there is somewhat reduced by the fact that the periodic awards are meant to provide no more than two-thirds of lost wages and many awards do not continue indefinitely. In tort law, the damages are theoretically to compensate fully for both amount and duration of loss. In such a system, the rules should encourage speedy recovery. This may be best achieved by a one-time-only recovery that tells the plaintiff what compensation has been recovered and that there is no more to come.

The best explanation for the single-judgment approach, though, has undoubtedly been the administrative difficulty of handling periodic recoveries. In the early days of the common law, the judiciary was incapable of handling such cases. Today such techniques exist. See generally, Henderson, Designing a Responsible Periodic–Payment System for Tort Awards, 32 Ariz.L.Rev.21 (1990). The principal cases in this Chapter all involve the single-judgment and single-payment approach.

Seffert v. Los Angeles Transit Lines

Supreme Court of California, 1961.
56 Cal.2d 498, 364 P.2d 337, 15 Cal.Rptr. 161.

PETERS, J. Defendants appeal from a judgment for plaintiff for $187,903.75 entered on a jury verdict. Their motion for a new trial for errors of law and excessiveness of damages was denied.

At the trial plaintiff contended that she was properly entering defendants' bus when the doors closed suddenly catching her right hand and left foot. The bus started, dragged her some distance, and then threw her to the pavement. Defendants contended that the injury resulted from plaintiff's own negligence, that she was late for work and either ran into the side of the bus after the doors had closed or ran after the bus and attempted to enter after the doors had nearly closed.

The evidence supports plaintiff's version of the facts. Several eyewitnesses testified that plaintiff started to board the bus while it was standing with the doors wide open. Defendants do not challenge the sufficiency of the evidence. They do contend, however, that prejudicial errors were committed during the trial and that the verdict is excessive.

[Here Justice Peters rejected the defendants' contention that the trial judge had made certain erroneous legal rulings during the trial. He continued:]

One of the major contentions of defendants is that the damages are excessive, as a matter of law. There is no merit to this contention.

The evidence most favorable to the plaintiff shows that prior to the accident plaintiff was in good health, and had suffered no prior serious injuries. She was single, and had been self-supporting for 20 of her 42 years. The accident happened on October 11, 1957. The trial took place in July and August of 1959.

As already pointed out, the injury occurred when plaintiff was caught in the doors of defendants' bus when it started up before she had gained full entry. As a result she was dragged for some distance. The record is uncontradicted that her injuries were serious, painful, disabling and permanent.

The major injuries were to plaintiff's left foot. The main arteries and nerves leading to that foot, and the posterior tibial vessels and nerve of that foot, were completely severed at the ankle. The main blood vessel which supplies blood to that foot had to be tied off, with the result that there is a permanent stoppage of the main blood source. The heel and shin bones were fractured. There were deep lacerations and an avulsion[3] which involved the skin and soft tissue of the entire foot.

These injuries were extremely painful. They have resulted in a permanently raised left heel, which is two inches above the floor level, caused by the contraction of the ankle joint capsule. Plaintiff is crippled and will suffer pain for life.[4] Although this pain could, perhaps, be alleviated by an operative fusion of the ankle, the doctors considered and rejected this procedure because the area has been deprived of its normal blood supply. The foot is not only permanently deformed but has a persistent open ulcer on the heel, there being a continuous drainage from the entire area. Medical care of this foot and ankle is to be reasonably expected for the remainder of plaintiff's life.

Since the accident, and because of it, plaintiff has undergone nine operations and has spent eight months in various hospitals and rehabilitation centers. These operations involved painful skin grafting and other painful procedures. One involved the surgical removal of gangrenous skin leaving painful raw and open flesh exposed from the heel to the toe. Another involved a left lumbar sympathectomy in which plaintiff's abdomen was entered to sever the nerves affecting the remaining blood vessels of the left leg in order to force those blood vessels to remain open at all times to the maximum extent. Still another operation involved a cross leg flap graft of skin and tissue from plaintiff's thigh which required that her left foot be brought up to her right thigh and held at this painful angle, motionless, and in a cast for a month until the flap of skin and fat, partially removed from her thigh, but still nourished there by a skin connection, could be grafted to the bottom of her foot, and until the host site could develop enough blood vessels to support it. Several future operations of this nature may be necessary. One result of this operation was to leave a defective area of the thigh where the normal fat is missing and the muscles exposed, and the local nerves are missing. This condition is permanent and disfiguring.

Another operation called a debridement, was required. This involved removal of many small muscles of the foot, much of the fat beneath the skin, cleaning the end of the severed nerve, and tying off the severed vein and artery.

---

3. Defined in Webster's New International Dictionary (2d ed.) as a "tearing asunder; forcible separation."

4. Her life expectancy was 34.9 years from the time of trial.

The ulcer on the heel is probably permanent, and there is the constant and real danger that osteomyelitis may develop if the infection extends into the bone. If this happens the heel bone would have to be removed surgically and perhaps the entire foot amputated.

Although plaintiff has gone back to work, she testified that she has difficulty standing, walking or even sitting, and must lie down frequently; that the leg is still very painful; that she can, even on her best days, walk not over three blocks and that very slowly; that her back hurts from walking; that she is tired and weak; that her sleep is disturbed; that she has frequent spasms in which the leg shakes uncontrollably; that she feels depressed and unhappy, and suffers humiliation and embarrassment.

Plaintiff claims that there is evidence that her total pecuniary loss, past and future, amounts to $53,903.75. This was the figure used by plaintiff's counsel in his argument to the jury, in which he also claimed $134,000 for pain and suffering, past and future. Since the verdict was exactly the total of these two estimates, it is reasonable to assume that the jury accepted the amount proposed by counsel for each item.

The summary of plaintiff as to pecuniary loss, past and future, is as follows:

Doctor and Hospital Bills	$10,330.50	
Drugs and other medical expenses stipulated to in the amount of	2,273.25	
Loss of earnings from time of accident to time of trial	5,500.00	$18,103.75
Future Medical Expenses:		
$2,000 per year for next 10 years	20,000.00	
$200 per year for the 24 years thereafter	4,800.00	
Drugs for 34 years........................	1,000.00	25,800.00
		43,903.75
Possible future loss of earnings		10,000.00
Total Pecuniary Loss		$53,903.75

There is substantial evidence to support these estimates. The amounts for past doctor and hospital bills, for the cost of drugs, and for a past loss of earnings, were either stipulated to, evidence was offered on, or is a simple matter of calculation. These items totaled $18,103.75. While the amount of $25,800 estimated as the cost of future medical expense, for loss of future earnings and for the future cost of drugs, may seem high, there was substantial evidence that future medical expense is certain to be high. There is also substantial evidence that plaintiff's future earning capacity may be substantially impaired by reason of the injury. The amounts estimated for those various items are not out of line, and find support in the evidence.

This leaves the amount of $134,000 presumably allowed for the nonpecuniary items of damage, including pain and suffering, past and future. It is this allowance that defendants seriously attack as being excessive as a matter of law.

It must be remembered that the jury fixed these damages, and that the trial judge denied a motion for new trial, one ground of which was excessiveness of the award. These determinations are entitled to great weight. The amount of damages is a fact question, first committed to the discretion of the jury and next to the discretion of the trial judge on a motion for new trial. They see and hear the witnesses and frequently, as in this case, see the injury and the impairment that has resulted therefrom. As a result, all presumptions are in favor of the decision of the trial court. [ ] The power of the appellate court differs materially from that of the trial court in passing on this question. An appellate court can interfere on the ground that the judgment is excessive only on the ground that the verdict is so large that, at first blush, it shocks the conscience and suggests passion, prejudice or corruption on the part of the jury. The proper rule was stated in Holmes v. Southern Cal. Edison Co., [177 P.2d 32 (App. 1947)], as follows: "The powers and duties of a trial judge in ruling on a motion for new trial and of an appellate court on an appeal from a judgment are very different when the question of an excessive award of damages arises. The trial judge sits as a thirteenth juror with the power to weigh the evidence and judge the credibility of the witnesses. If he believes the damages awarded by the jury to be excessive and the question is presented it becomes his duty to reduce them. [Citing cases.] When the question is raised his denial of a motion of new trial is an indication that he approves the amount of the award. An appellate court has no such powers. It cannot weigh the evidence and pass on the credibility of the witnesses as a juror does. To hold an award excessive it must be so large as to indicate passion or prejudice on the part of the jurors." . . .

There are no fixed or absolute standards by which an appellate court can measure in monetary terms the extent of the damages suffered by a plaintiff as a result of the wrongful act of the defendant. . . . The amount to be awarded is "a matter on which there legitimately may be a wide difference of opinion" [ ]. . . .

While the appellate court should consider the amounts awarded in prior cases for similar injuries, obviously, each case must be decided on its own facts and circumstances. Such examination demonstrates that such awards vary greatly. (See exhaustive annotations in [ ].) Injuries are seldom identical and the amount of pain and suffering involved in similar physical injuries varies widely. These factors must be considered. [ ] Basically, the question that should be decided by the appellate courts is whether or not the verdict is so out of line with reason that it shocks the conscience and necessarily implies that the verdict must have been the result of passion and prejudice.

In the instant case, the nonpecuniary items of damage include allowances for pain and suffering, past and future, humiliation as a result of being disfigured and being permanently crippled, and constant anxiety and fear that the leg will have to be amputated. While the amount of the award is high, and may be more than we would have awarded were we the trier of the facts, considering the nature of the injury, the great pain and suffering, past and future, and the other items of damage, we cannot say, as a matter of law, that it is so high that it shocks the conscience and gives rise to the presumption that it was the result of passion or prejudice on the part of the jurors.

Defendants next complain that it was prejudicial error for plaintiff's counsel to argue to the jury that damages for pain and suffering could be fixed by means of a mathematical formula predicated upon a per diem allowance for this item of damages. The propriety of such an argument seems never to have been passed upon in this state. In other jurisdictions there is a sharp divergence of opinion on the subject. [ ] It is not necessary to pass on the propriety of such argument in the instant case because, when plaintiff's counsel made the argument in question, defendants' counsel did not object, assign it as misconduct or ask that the jury be admonished to disregard it. Moreover, in his argument to the jury, the defendants' counsel also adopted a mathematical formula type of argument. This being so, even if such argument were error (a point we do not pass upon), the point must be deemed to have been waived, and cannot be raised properly, on appeal. [   ]

The judgment appealed from is affirmed.

GIBSON, C.J., WHITE, J., and DOOLING, J., concurred.

TRAYNOR, J. I dissent.

Although I agree that there was no prejudicial error on the issue of liability, it is my opinion that the award of $134,000 for pain and suffering is so excessive as to indicate that it was prompted by passion, prejudice, whim, or caprice.

Before the accident plaintiff was employed as a file clerk at a salary of $375 a month. At the time of the trial she had returned to her job at the same salary and her foot had healed sufficiently for her to walk. At the time of the accident she was 42 years old with a life expectancy of 34.9 years.

During closing argument plaintiff's counsel summarized the evidence relevant to past and possible future damages and proposed a specific amount for each item. His total of $187,903.75 was the exact amount awarded by the jury.

His proposed amounts were as follows:

.   .   .

Total Pecuniary Loss		$ 53,903.75
Pain and Suffering:		
From time of accident to time of trial (660 days) @ $100 a day	$66,000.00	
For the remainder of her life (34 years) @ $2,000 a year	68,000.00	134,000.00
Total proposed by counsel		$187,903.75

The jury and the trial court have broad discretion in determining the damages in a personal injury case. [   ] A reviewing court, however, has responsibilities not only to the litigants in an action but to future litigants and must reverse or remit when a jury awards either inadequate or excessive damages. [   ]

The crucial question in this case, therefore, is whether the award of $134,000 for pain and suffering is so excessive it must have resulted from passion, prejudice, whim or caprice. "To say that a verdict has been influenced by passion or prejudice is but another way of saying that the verdict exceeds any amount justified by the evidence." (Zibbell v. Southern Pacific Co., [116 P. 513 (Cal.1911)]; [   ].)

There has been forceful criticism of the rationale for awarding damages for pain and suffering in negligence cases. [   ] Such damages originated under primitive law as a means of punishing wrongdoers and assuaging the feelings of those who had been wronged. [   ] They become increasingly anomalous as emphasis shifts in a mechanized society from ad hoc punishment to orderly distribution of losses through insurance and the price of goods or of transportation. Ultimately such losses are borne by a public free of fault as part of the price for the benefits of mechanization. [   ]

Nonetheless, this state has long recognized pain and suffering as elements of damages in negligence cases [   ]; any change in this regard must await reexamination of the problem by the Legislature. Meanwhile, awards for pain and suffering serve to ease plaintiffs' discomfort and to pay for attorney fees for which plaintiffs are not otherwise compensated.

It would hardly be possible ever to compensate a person fully for pain and suffering. "No rational being would change places with the injured man for an amount of gold that would fill the room of the court, yet no lawyer would contend that such is the legal measure of damages." ([*Zibbell*]; see 2 Harper and James, The Law of Torts 1322.) "Translating pain and anguish into dollars can, at best, be only an arbitrary allowance, and not a process of measurement and consequently the judge can, in his instructions give the jury no standard to go by; he can only tell them to allow such amount as in their discretion they may consider reasonable. . . . The chief reliance for reaching reasonable results in attempting to value suffering in terms of money must be the restraint and common sense of the jury. . . ." (McCormick, Damages, § 88, pp. 318–319.) Such restraint and common sense were lacking here.

A review of reported cases involving serious injuries and large pecuniary losses reveals that ordinarily the part of the verdict attributable to pain and suffering does not exceed the part attributable to pecuniary losses. [   ] The award in this case of $134,000 for pain and suffering exceeds not only the pecuniary losses but any such award heretofore sustained in this state even in cases involving injuries more serious by far than those suffered by plaintiff. [   ] In *McNulty v. Southern Pacific Co.* [   ], the court reviewed a large number of cases involving injuries to legs and feet, in each of which the total judgment, including both pecuniary loss and pain and suffering did not exceed $100,000. Although excessive damages is "an issue which is primarily factual and is not therefore a matter which can be decided upon the basis of awards made in other cases" [   ], awards for similar injuries may be considered as one factor to be weighed in determining whether the damages awarded are excessive. [   ].

The excessive award in this case was undoubtedly the result of the improper argument of plaintiff's counsel to the jury. Though no evidence was introduced, though none could possibly be introduced on the monetary value of plaintiff's suffering, counsel urged the jury to award $100 a day for pain and suffering from the time of the accident to the time of trial and $2,000 a year for pain and suffering for the remainder of plaintiff's life.

The propriety of counsel's proposing a specific sum for each day or month of suffering has recently been considered by courts of several jurisdictions. [   ] The reasons for and against permitting "per diem argument for pain and suffering" are reviewed in [   ] [1959 Florida decision holding such argument is permissible] and *Botta v. Brunner*, [1958 New Jersey decision holding such argument to be an "unwarranted intrusion into the domain of the jury"].

The reason usually advanced for not allowing such argument is that since there is no way of translating pain and suffering into monetary terms, counsel's proposal of a particular sum for each day of suffering represents an opinion and a conclusion on matters not disclosed by the evidence, and tends to mislead the jury and result in excessive awards. The reason usually advanced for allowing "per diem argument for pain and suffering" is that it affords the jury as good an arbitrary measure as any for that which cannot be measured.

Counsel may argue all legitimate inferences from the evidence, but he may not employ arguments that tend primarily to mislead the jury. [   ] A specified sum for pain and suffering for any particular period is bound to be conjectural. Positing such a sum for a small period of time and then multiplying that sum by the number of days, minutes or seconds in plaintiff's life expectancy multiplies the hazards of conjecture. Counsel could arrive at any amount he wished by adjusting either the period of time to be taken as a measure or the amount surmised for the pain for that period.

. . .

The misleading effect of the per diem argument was not cured by the use of a similar argument by defense counsel. Truth is not served by a clash of sophistic arguments. (See Michael and Adler, The Trial of an Issue of Fact, 34 Colum.L.Rev. 1224, 1483–1484.) Had defendant objected to the improper argument of plaintiff's counsel this error would be a sufficient ground for reversal whether or not the award was excessive as a matter of law. Defendant's failure to object, however, did not preclude its appeal on the ground that the award was excessive as a matter of law or preclude this court's reversing on that ground and ruling on the impropriety of counsel's argument to guide the court on the retrial. [   ]

I would reverse the judgment and remand the cause for a new trial on the issue of damages.

SCHAUER, J., and McCOMB, J., concurred.

Notes and Questions

1. *Past pecuniary losses.* The clearest category of recoverable damages is past pecuniary losses—in *Seffert* those incurred for doctors, hospitals, drugs, and lost earnings. Most of the medical expenses are documented by bills; the lost earnings may be a bit more complicated to establish, especially for self-employed persons, but can usually be reconstructed without much difficulty.

One recurrent problem in awarding lost earnings is the question of taxation. Although some percentage of the gross wages lost would have been taxed if the plaintiff had in fact earned them, Congress has decided that compensatory damage awards are not taxable. What, if anything, should the judge charge the jury on this question? Some courts say nothing and let the jury think whatever it might on the subject. Others charge the jury that the award of lost earnings is not taxable and that the jury should not worry about being sure that plaintiff gets enough to pay the taxes. See Lanzano v. City of New York, 519 N.E.2d 331 (N.Y.1988). In an effort to remove the ambiguity about when and how the jury should be told about the tax implications, one court has decided that "the measurement of after-tax income is the 'more accurate and therefore proper, measure of damages'" and that the plaintiff has the burden of proving that sum. Caldwell v. Haynes, 643 A.2d 564 (N.J.1994).

2. *Future pecuniary losses.* As *Seffert* shows, these same items may cause losses into the future. To take the easiest case, the evidence shows that the plaintiff will need a specific drug for the next five years. There are of course as yet no bills. But the jury must calculate the cost now. How much will the drug cost over the next five years? What will inflation look like in the prescription drug market? If the plaintiff requires physical therapy or psychological counselling in the future, how long will the course of treatment be needed? If any of these expenses appear likely to be lifelong, life expectancy tables will be used. Should the trier then consider health factors unrelated to the accident, such as smoking, and reduce plaintiff's life expectancy accordingly?

Even more complicated than figuring out future medical expenses is the task of calculating the plaintiff's future earnings. For instance, assume that at the time of her injury, the plaintiff had been earning $30,000 a year and would never be able to work again. (Of course, in some litigation the permanence of plaintiff's disability will be hotly contested, but assume our plaintiff is completely disabled.) In order to decide how large her award should be, the court must first determine how many years she would have worked had she not been injured. The plaintiff might have died in an unrelated accident the next day, in which case she hardly would have worked at all, or she could live into her nineties and have a long, productive career. This question is further complicated by the increasing unpredicta-bility of retirement ages. Given these uncertainties, attorneys may begin with the average work career of an employee in plaintiff's field and present evidence on whether there is reason to believe the plaintiff's career would have varied from the norm.

Once a predicted retirement date has been set, the plaintiff's award cannot be set by multiplying her current wage by the number of years she had left to work. A worker's wages rarely remain stable over the course of a lifetime. What about promotions and merit raises? Even without these personal achievements, the plaintiff's wages could be expected to rise. In the decades after World War II, increases in productivity resulted in an overall rise in wages for workers as a class. Apart from these "real" increases in workers' wages, many workers have contractual "cost of living adjustments" that automatically increase their wages in relation to the consumer price index so that general inflation drives wages up. And what about fringe benefits such as medical coverage, pensions, and retirement plans?

The defense is likely to present countervailing considerations. Shouldn't the plaintiff, who no longer has to commute, or buy business clothes or uniforms, and thus no longer incurs the cost of these expenses, have them deducted from her award for future earnings? Moreover, as mentioned above, the plaintiff's lump-sum award is tax-free, so in figuring her lost future earnings, it can be argued that only after-tax earnings should be considered. Often a court will offset some of these variables, declaring, for instance, that lost fringe benefits will be roughly equal to the decrease in work-related expenses.

Must plaintiff show a net loss in past or future earnings? What if the showing is that plaintiff lost an opportunity for great financial success? In Snow v. Villacci, 754 A.2d 360 (Maine 2000), plaintiff was enrolled in a 25-month program to become a "financial consultant" at a major brokerage house. In the 20th month, his success "was possible but not assured." At that time he was negligently injured by defendant and lost 14 weeks of work. Although the broker gave him extra time, plaintiff alleged that he was unable to complete the program. The alleged consequence was that although the broker retained him in another capacity, he was unable to complete the program and would not be allowed another chance to do so. The court held that if plaintiff could show that he had been deprived of a special opportunity to which he had already been given access, and would have succeeded but for the injury, he might be able to recover for this loss. The court noted that, because the case had come up on summary judgment, it had no occasion to consider how far into the future any recovery might reach.

No matter how old a plaintiff may be there is a future life expectancy. In Symington v. Mayo, 590 N.W.2d 450 (N.D.1999), the 87-year-old woman plaintiff had a life expectancy of 6.4 years. The jury's award of future economic damages of $100,000 was upheld on a "common sense" view of the matter. She had previously been independent and now could walk only with a bad limp. She now needed help in bathing, fixing her hair, and cleaning her home. No improvement was possible. A fall or a harsh winter or any setback would send her to a nursing home—which would cost $27,000 per year. Even though she could return home now, "it's not mere speculation that the length of time that she is going to be able to care for herself has been considerably diminished as a result of the accident."

3. *Discounting to present value.* Assume that after considering all these factors, the trier of fact determines that the plaintiff would have worked for the next five years and that her after-tax salary in those years would be $30,000, $32,000, $34,000, $36,000 and $38,000 for a total of $170,000. Our calculations are not yet done. To award the plaintiff a lump sum of $170,000 would be to overcompensate her, because by investing the total amount at the outset, she could earn interest on the lump sum that, combined with the initial amount of principal, would exceed her lost future earnings. To adjust for this earning potential, the court must reduce the plaintiff's award to its present value. In other words, the trier of fact must determine the amount of money the plaintiff should be awarded today so that, if invested prudently, it will earn interest bringing the total award to $170,000 after five years. Although the original lump-sum award is tax free, the interest earned on it is not, so the original award will have to be high enough to earn interest that will cover the taxes and still provide $30,000 for the first year, $32,000 for the second year, etc., and be exhausted after the last payment.

Thus in order to determine the proper award, the court must decide upon a discount rate, which is in effect the estimated return on prudent investment for the next five years. Each party will present evidence as to why its estimate of this uncertain figure is the better one. Adding to the complexity is the inflation rate. Although the plaintiff may earn additional money through interest, that money may be worth less because of inflation. Plaintiff will argue that her award should not be discounted because the inflation rate and the return on investment cancel each other out. Courts are divided on how to handle this issue. Some accept this "total offset" rationale. See Kaczkowski v. Bolubasz, 421 A.2d 1027 (Pa.1980)("As a matter of law . . . future inflation shall be presumed equal to future interest rates with those factors offsetting").

Other courts adopt the theory that the market interest rate reflects three factors: risk, protection from inflation, and the "real interest rate." The risk element should not be considered in the tort award, because the plaintiff should make only safe investments to ensure compensation. That leaves the real market rate and the inflationary rate. In determining the discount rate for a tort award, these courts believe that the real interest rate is the proper discount rate, letting inflation be offset by the "inflationary interest rate." Otherwise, a total offset would overcompensate the plaintiff.

The impact of choosing a rate is suggested in Karney v. Arnot–Ogden Memorial Hospital, 674 N.Y.S.2d 449 (App.Div. 1998), in which the issue was the expense of housing plaintiff child in a group home for a life expected to last 60.6 years. The court noted that the item would be $3.78 million without taking inflation into account. That figure rose to $8.44 million using an annual 2.6% inflation rate. For more detailed discussions of these issues, see Jones & Laughlin Steel Corp. v. Pfeifer, 462 U.S. 523 (1983) and Brady, Inflation, Productivity, and the Total Offset Method of Calculating Damages for Lost Future Earnings, 49 U.Chi.L.Rev. 1003 (1982).

4. *Pain and suffering.* We turn now to the nonpecuniary losses that formed the core of the *Seffert* case. What is the theoretical justification for awarding damages in this type of case for pain and suffering?

Among the articles cited by Justice Traynor, Jaffe's offered the sharpest attack on pain and suffering awards. Jaffe, Damages for Personal Injury: The Impact of Insurance, 18 Law & Contemporary Probs. 219 (1953). Jaffe recognized that when the defendant's conduct is "reprehensible, damages are an apt instrument of punishment" because criminal law is a clumsy way to handle "unsocial activity. . . . To pay money to one's victim is a salutary humiliation." But justification was harder when the defendant's behavior was negligent rather than willful. The usual justification here is that, although there is no way to measure the loss in question, plaintiff has in fact lost "something" and the wrongdoer should not escape liability because of the difficulty of valuation.

But Jaffe challenged this by asking what justified any award. It could not be returning to plaintiff something that was his or her own for that was an economic notion based on "maintaining the integrity of the economic arrangements which provide the normally expectable basis for livelihood in our society. Pain is a harm, an 'injury,' but neither past pain nor its compensation has any consistent economic significance. The past experience is not a loss except in so far as it produced present deterioration." He continued:

> I am aware, however, that though the premise may elude detection, some deep intuition may claim to validate this process of evaluating the imponderable. One who has suffered a violation of his bodily integrity may feel a sense of continuing outrage. This is particularly true where there has been disfigurement or loss of a member (even though not giving rise to economic loss). Because our society sets a high value on money it uses money or price as a means of recognizing the worth of non-economic as well as economic goods. If, insists the plaintiff, society really values my personality, my bodily integrity, it will signify its sincerity by paying me a sum of money. Damages thus may somewhat reestablish the plaintiff's self-confidence, wipe out his sense of outrage. Furthermore, though money is not an equivalent it may be a consolation, a solatium. These arguments, however, are most valid for disfigurements or loss of member giving rise to a continuing sense of injury. (And in such cases there may be potential economic injury which cannot be established.) It is doubtful that past pain figures strongly as present outrage. And even granting these arguments there must be set over against them the arbitrary indetermi-

nateness of the evaluation. Insurance aside, it is doubtful justice seriously to embarrass a defendant, though negligent, by real economic loss in order to do honor to plaintiff's experience of pain. And insurance present, it is doubtful that the pooled social fund of savings should be charged with sums of indeterminate amount when compensation performs no specific economic function. This consideration becomes the stronger as year after year the amounts set aside for the security account become a larger proportion of the national income.

As to those arguments he discusses, is Jaffe persuasive? Are there other arguments supporting recovery for pain and suffering that are not mentioned here? Is it useful to distinguish between transitory physical pain and permanent disfigurement or loss of function? See Ogus, Damages for Lost Amenities: For a Foot, a Feeling or a Function?, 35 Mod.L.Rev. 1 (1972).

Compare Kwasny v. United States, 823 F.2d 194 (7th Cir.1987), in which the court affirmed an award under the Federal Tort Claims Act. In passing, Judge Posner observed:

> We disagree with those students of tort law who believe that pain and suffering are not real costs and should not be allowable items of damages in a tort suit. No one likes pain and suffering and most people would pay a good deal of money to be free of them. If they were not recoverable in damages, the cost of negligence would be less to the tortfeasors and there would be more negligence, more accidents, more pain and suffering, and hence higher social costs.

Do you agree? Is the deterrence argument more powerful than the compensation argument for retaining pain and suffering? Can pain and suffering be justified on deterrence grounds even if people would not insure, in advance, against the prospect of such losses? For discussion of these issues, see Leebron, Final Moments: Damages for Pain and Suffering Prior to Death, 64 N.Y.U. L.Rev. 256, 270–78 (1989); Schwartz, Proposals for Products Liability Reform: A Theoretical Synthesis, 97 Yale L.J. 353, 362–67 (1988); Croley and Hanson, The Nonpecuniary Costs of Accidents: Pain-and-Suffering Damages in Tort Law, 108 Harv.L.Rev. 1785 (1995).

5. Consider the following very large damage awards for pain and suffering, and the logic that lies behind each.

a. Compare with *Seffert*, Epping v. Commonwealth Edison Co., 734 N.E.2d 916 (Ill.App.2000), in which the only issue was the award of $9 million for non-economic damages. According to the court,

> Epping sustained serious injuries, including: multiple open fractures of the right proximal tibial plateau (in the area of the knee); an open fracture of the right foot; a large wound over the top of the right foot; a closed fracture of the left ankle; a fractured left wrist; and a fractured and dislocated left hip with cracked pelvis. Epping had to be extricated from her car and air-lifted by helicopter to Lutheran General Hospital.

The jury learned that when the accident occurred Epping was 49 years old, had been married for 28 years, was the mother of one daughter and a grandmother of one. Epping was a part-time teacher of anthropology at McHenry County Community College and the executive director of the Elgin Public Museum. She traveled extensively as the president of the Midwest Museum Conference. She had been named the Business Woman of the Year and the YWCA Woman of the Year. She enjoyed sailing and reading.

After the accident, Epping's injuries caused her to undergo 32 operations and procedures between 1996 and 1999. The jury viewed photographs of Epping's severely deformed leg and foot. It saw a video depicting a day in Epping's life.

The jury learned that Epping is unable to walk and needs assistance getting out of bed, getting into a chair, or getting onto the toilet. It learned she requires assistance attending to matters of personal hygiene. She can no longer drive a car and, because her left wrist joint has been "fixed" in place, she has difficulty maneuvering her own wheelchair. Epping's right leg is called "flail leg" and cannot support her weight. Doctors are optimistic that with further reconstructive surgery Epping might have the future ability to independently "ambulate" around the interior of her home with the aid of a walker or by holding on to furniture. But there is still the potential that Epping's right leg will have to be amputated.

Despite a number of surgeries, Epping continues to experience difficulty with her left hip. Epping will never be able to return to work, independently ambulate outside her home, or be able to perform the normal tasks of living—cleaning, cooking, or taking care of household chores. Her life expectancy is 32 years.

The award did not "shock the judicial conscience." The court rejected defendant's characterization of the injuries as "orthopedic injuries—but that is it." The court focused on the potential loss of limbs, the "flail leg," the "severe impairment" of her mobility, and the repeated dislocation of her left hip. Defendant also argued that plaintiff's "disfigurements are not readily visible and, consequently, are less repulsive to public eyes." The court responded that she "must suffer the indignities of these deformities each day—a constant reminder of the pain and suffering she has already suffered and will continue to suffer in the future." The court thought that an inquiry into the return on this money if invested was irrelevant. When defendant argued that a reduction in the award "might assist businessmen or individuals in determining what constitutes adequate insurance coverage," the court responded that its "duty is to decide cases, not to assist in coverage planning."

b. In Miksis v. Howard, 106 F.3d 754 (7th Cir.1997), the 21-year-old plaintiff suffered brain damage, loss of control of both legs, and attention difficulties. His "problem solving skills are impaired and he is less able to adapt to changes in his environment. Additionally, the accident caused deficits in auditory comprehension, memory, and his ability to process information." A jury valued his damages at $10 million. On appeal, the court affirmed. The defense's reliance on other awards "prove[s] nothing except that some plaintiffs have received less money than Miksis; they do not show the current award to be 'monstrously excessive [the applicable standard].' " The district court had cited seven cases that showed the verdict to be in line with awards in similar cases.

On the other hand, in Waldorf v. Shuta, 142 F.3d 601 (3d Cir.1998), the 24-year-old plaintiff claimed that his award of $2.5 million for quadriplegia was inadequate. The court disagreed. Although the award "may have been less than we would have awarded if we made a de novo damages determination in this case, the award was within permissible limits for pain and suffering even for the devastating damages which Waldorf suffered." Citations to other cases in which quadriplegic plaintiffs received as much as $10 million did not establish that this award was inadequate.

c. In Sternemann v. Langs, 460 N.Y.S.2d 614 (App.Div. 1983), the court considered an award for pain and suffering sustained by a 26-year-old mother of three, with a life expectancy of 53 years:

> [Plaintiff] will suffer constant, excruciating and unremitting pain in her right arm for the balance of her life. . . . As a result, the plaintiff has effectively lost much of the use of her right arm, has been deprived of a social life, can no longer properly care for her young children, has great difficulty sleeping, and cannot even sleep lying down. In fact, the only way that the plaintiff can continue to function is by the constant administration of narcotic medication in ever-increasing quantities, which medication not only affects her perception and serves to render her groggy and depressed, but has caused her to become a narcotics addict who will require prolonged institutionalization, on the order of three to six months out of every year, for detoxification the remainder of her life. . . . [I]t simply cannot be said that the award of $1,000,000 in damages for a lifetime of pain and suffering was excessive.

How should the court have reacted to a verdict of $5 million for this item?

d. Can a verdict be so "excessive" as to call for reduction if it does not shock the judicial conscience? In the mid-1980s New York enacted a statute that directed the appellate division to "determine that an award is excessive or inadequate if it deviates materially from what would be reasonable compensation." N.Y. CPLR § 5501(c).

6. *Per diems and other monetary guides.* Courts are divided over the wisdom of giving the jury some monetary guidelines when they consider pain and suffering. Most states permit arguments using monetary guidelines. A few permit the argument but without numbers. E.g., Friedman v. C & S Car Service, 527 A.2d 871 (N.J.1987). On the other hand, in Carchidi v. Rodenhiser, 551 A.2d 1249 (Conn.1989), the court, noting that it had already barred plaintiffs from naming the amount sought in the complaint and did not permit *per diem* arguments, barred the plaintiff's attorney in closing arguments from giving the jury any number that would be an appropriate award for pain and suffering because of the "risk of improper influence upon a jury." *Carchidi* was overturned by a statute providing that in any damage action counsel for any party "shall be entitled to specifically articulate to the trier of fact during closing arguments, in lump sums or by mathematical formulae, the amount of past and future economic and noneconomic damages claimed to be recoverable." The jury is to be told that the numbers are arguments but not evidence. See Vajda v. Tusla, 572 A.2d 998 (Conn.1990).

7. *Discounting awards for intangible losses.* However the sum for intangible awards is arrived at, there is the further question of discounting. The *Friedman* court, note 6, supra, rejected discounting. The "great majority" of courts do not discount these awards because of the "incongruity of discounting to present value damages that are, by their very nature, so speculative and imprecise." The use of time-unit arguments may lend an "aura of rationality" to this type of award but does not convert the award into one for economic loss. To allow discounting here "would add to the time, expense, and complexity of civil trials without any corresponding enhancement of the reliability, accuracy, or fairness of damages awards." But see, Gretchen v. United States, 618 F.2d 177 (2d Cir.1980)(discounting the award). A similar issue regarding loss of society in death cases is discussed shortly.

8. In Blumstein, Bovbjerg, & Sloan, Beyond Tort Reform: Developing Better Tools for Assessing Damages for Personal Injury, 8 Yale J. Regulation 171 (1991), the authors argue that liability decisions rely on precedent to narrow the range of choice, but that with damages we give jurors no guidance from prior results. Prior awards should be collected and analyzed. Information "on the spectrum of prior damage awards should be provided to juries, judges, or both, as an aid to decisionmaking." The jury should be told that if it wants to make an award in the top (or bottom) quartile of past results it must justify that result by pointing to facts in its case that tilt it to the high (or low) side of the range:

> The middle range of prior awards of a similar nature should be given "presumptive" validity. That is, awards that fall in the middle range of the distribution should be deemed presumptively valid. In contrast, where valuations in a case differ significantly from prior results, tort valuations should be subject to both a burden of explanation by the jury and heightened review by the court. . . . An unexplained outlier should constitute a prima facie case for either remittitur or additur by the trial judge or an appellate holding of inadequacy or excessiveness of the judgment.

For a similar approach, using the analogy of prison sentencing guidelines, see Levin, Pain and Suffering Guidelines: A Cure for Damages Measurement "Anomie," 22 J.L.Reform 303 (1989). Do these efforts resemble Justice Traynor's view in *Seffert*?

Should juries be given information gained from surveying people about their willingness to pay to avoid various kinds of disabling injuries? What about studies analyzing wage differentials for hazardous activities in the labor market? For empirical analyses, see Miller, Willingness to Pay Comes of Age: Will the System Survive?, 83 Nw.U.L.Rev. 876 (1989); Viscusi, Pain and Suffering in Product Liability Cases: Systematic Compensation or Capricious Awards?, 8 Int'l.Rev. L. & Econ. 203 (1988).

For a study rethinking the role of pain and suffering, see McCaffery, Kahneman & Spitzer, Framing the Jury: Cognitive Perspectives on Pain and Suffering, 81 Va.L.Rev. 1341 (1995). Using experimental data, the authors compared the implications of thinking about compensating specific injuries from an *ex post* perspective of "making whole" and an *ex ante* perspective of how much money healthy persons would want to sell their good health for the same injuries. Those viewing the matter from the *ex ante* perspective tended to award about twice as much as those viewing the injury from the "making whole" perspective. See also Geistfeld, Placing a Price on Pain and Suffering: A Method for Helping Juries Determine Tort Damages for Nonmonetary Injuries, 83 Calif.L.Rev. 775 (1995).

9. *Statutory change—caps on awards for intangible losses.* In an effort to reduce the size of damage awards, some states set maximum amounts that may be awarded for "pain and suffering." The movement began in the mid-1970s when California enacted Civil Code § 3333.2, which limited pain and suffering awards in cases brought against health care providers to $250,000. Others have followed with limits—some of which are also limited to malpractice cases, but many of which are applicable across tort actions. For example, Colorado enacted a cap of $250,000 for pain and suffering in all cases unless the plaintiff could show by clear and convincing evidence that the award should exceed that sum, in which case it might reach a maximum of $500,000. Colo.Rev.Stat. § 13–21–102.5(3)(a). Maryland adopted a limit of $350,000. Md.Code.Ann. § 11–108. Although many courts have upheld these caps against constitutional challenge, some have not. Sofie v. Fibreboard Corp., 771 P.2d 711 (Wash.1989)(cap on pain and suffering violated the state's constitutional protection for trial by jury); Brannigan v. Usitalo, 587 A.2d 1232 (N.H.1991) (statutory cap of $875,000 on noneconomic loss violates state constitution's equal protection clause). We revisit statutory change in a later discussion of incremental tort reform, at p. 787, infra.

10. *Some large total awards.* The combined damage award in *Seffert* for major suffering was so small as to be almost quaint by today's standards. Although some of the cases involving pain and suffering produce large amounts, the very largest are likely to include major components of both economic and non-economic losses. Still, some awards may be very high from non-economic items alone. See, e.g., Virginia Electric & Power Co. v. Dungee, 520 S.E.2d 164 (Va.1999), upholding an award of $20 million (that included no medical award) to a ten-year-old child who was severely burned while in defendant's substation. In addition to the physical pain and procedures, the court reported that on one occasion when plaintiff asked someone for directions, that person "looked at me and ran." The following are not typical by any means, but they suggest the current high end of awards to surviving plaintiffs. (Keep in mind that these figures are for compensatory damages only; the size of an award may be greatly enhanced if punitive damages are awarded—a topic addressed in the next section.)

In Richardson v. Chapman, 676 N.E.2d 621 (Ill.1997), the court upheld an award totaling $21.35 million to a woman rendered quadriplegic when rear-ended by a truck. Her life expectancy at trial was 54.5 years. The jury award consisted of some $250,000 for past medical expenses; $11 million for future medical expenses; $900,000 for past and future lost earnings; $3.5 million for disability; $2.1 million for irremediable facial disfigurement; and $4.6 million for pain and suffering. After reviewing the facts at length, including the way plaintiff now lived, and addressing claims of excessiveness and of duplication, the court reduced future medical expenses by $1 million and affirmed the remainder of the award. The court rejected defense arguments based on comparisons with other cases because the court did "not believe that such comparisons would be helpful here."

In Aves v. Shah, 997 F.2d 762 (10th Cir.1993), a jury found that defendant physician had committed obstetrical malpractice and was responsible for $21.2 million, 90% of the total damages sustained. The court's short summary indicated that the child "suffers from epilepsy, cerebral palsy, mental retardation, cortical blindness and small head size. Medical and economic experts testified for the plaintiffs concerning the staggering cost of caring for [the child] for the remainder of her life. Such costs will include therapy, prescription drugs, medical testing, education and group home placement." The award was "well within the range" that plaintiff's economist presented. The "constellation of problems, especially her blindness and inclination to suffer seizures, may make future care difficult and expensive. There was testimony that she will experience frustration and that her mobility, as well as her mental capacity, is severely limited. To be sure, the award is large; however, given the record before us, the amount does not shock the conscience of the court."

In Firestone v. Crown Center Redevelopment Corp., 693 S.W.2d 99 (Mo.1985), the plaintiff was hurt in the collapse of suspended skyways in the Hyatt Regency in Kansas City, which killed 114 people. Plaintiff was a 34-year-old unmarried woman who was making $33,000 per year, including fringe benefits, as a computer repairer for IBM. She was rendered quadriplegic as a result of the accident. The court upheld a compensatory award of $15 million.

11. *Statutory change—caps on total awards.* Although most state legislation has been addressed to capping noneconomic loss, a few have capped the total award in certain types of cases. See Fairfax Hosp. Sys., Inc. v. Nevitt, 457 S.E.2d 10 (Va.1995), for a discussion of Virginia's $1 million cap on the total recovery in any medical malpractice case. Colorado capped the total recovery available against governmental units at $150,000 per person and $400,000 per occurrence. The limitation was upheld in State v. DeFoor, 824 P.2d 783 (Colo.), cert. denied 506 U.S. 981 (1992), in which nine bus passengers were killed and 19 injured when a 6.7-ton boulder being moved by a state road crew fell onto a tourist bus passing below. Some of these caps are tied to changes in the consumer price index.

12. *Contingent fees.* The majority in *Seffert* discusses the damage award as though it will go entirely to the plaintiff. In fact, this was almost certainly not the case; plaintiffs' attorneys are retained in tort cases on a contingent fee basis and take a fee ranging from 20%–50% of the final award or settlement amount in the case. Typically, the fee will be one-third of the final award, but a variety of factors may lead to deviance from the informal norm: in an especially high-risk case, or one requiring trial and appellate work, an attorney may charge more than the norm; in certain types of cases—airline crash claims are an example—the fee charged may ordinarily be near the low end of the scale. See J. Kakalik, E. King, M. Traynor, P. Ebener, & L. Picus, Costs and Compensation Paid in Aviation Accident Litigation (1988).

Does the likelihood that Seffert had to pay one-third of the award to her attorney affect your view of the merits of redressing pain and suffering in addition to out-of-pocket loss? Are there arguments for the contingent fee that seem compelling?

As early as the mid-1970s, critics of the tort system aimed their fire at the contingent fee; see the California Medical Injury Compensation Reform Act, which set a sliding scale of decreasing maximum percentages for plaintiffs' contingent fees, linked to the size of the damage award. A dozen states have adopted such proposals. In the mid-1990s, a proposal to create an "early offer" mechanism to limit fees in cases settled at an early stage in the case received considerable attention. See Horowitz, Making Ethics Real, Making Ethics Work: A Proposal for Contingency Fee Reform, 44 Emory L.J. 173 (1995), discussing the proposal which he co-authored with Professors Jeffrey O'Connell and Lester Brickman. The main features of the proposal are: (1) that when defendant makes an offer within 60 days of receipt from plaintiff of a demand for compensation and the offer is accepted, "plaintiffs' counsel fees are limited to hourly rate charges and are capped at 10% of the first $100,000 of the offer and 5% of any greater amount;" (2) that if the early offer is rejected by plaintiff, "contingency fees may only be charged against net recoveries in excess of those offers;" and (3) that if there is no defendant's offer "contingency fee contracts are unaffected by the proposal." Does this seem a sensible reform? For criticism of the proposal, see Silver, Control Fees? No, Let the Market Do Its Job, Natl. L.J., April 18, 1994 at A17. See Brickman, Contingency Fee Abuses: Ethical Mandates, and the Disciplinary System: The Case Against Case-by-Case Enforcement, 53 Wash. & Lee L.Rev. 1339 (1996).

McDougald v. Garber

Court of Appeals of New York, 1989.
73 N.Y.2d 246, 536 N.E.2d 372, 538 N.Y.S.2d 937.

[Defendants' malpractice left plaintiff in a "permanently comatose condition." In her suit for damages the parties agreed that, if liability were established, she would be entitled to the usual pecuniary damage items—past and future loss of earning capacity, and medical expenses, including custodial care. The parties also agreed that plaintiff could not recover damages for conscious pain and suffering unless she were found to have been aware of experiencing them, but they disagreed over whether she had the requisite level of awareness. "At trial, defendants sought to show that Mrs. McDougald's injuries were so severe that she was incapable of either experiencing pain or appreciating her condition. Plaintiffs, on the other hand, introduced proof that Mrs. McDougald responded to certain stimuli to a sufficient extent to indicate that she was aware of her circumstances."

The judge charged that to "experience suffering" there must be "some level of awareness. . . . If, however, you conclude that there is some level of perception or that she is capable of an emotional response at some level, then damages for pain and suffering should be awarded." In addition, the judge charged:

> Damages for the loss of the pleasures and pursuits of life, however, require no awareness of the loss on the part of the injured person. Quite obviously, Emma McDougald is unable to engage in any of the activities which constitute a normal life, the activities she engaged in prior to her injury. . . . Loss of the enjoyment of life may, of course, accompany the physical sensation and emotional responses that we refer to as pain and suffering, and in most cases it does. It is possible, however, for an injured person to lose the enjoyment of life without experiencing any conscious pain and suffering. Damages for this item of injury relate not to what Emma McDougald is aware of, but rather to what she has lost. What her life was prior to her injury and what it has been since September 7, 1978 and what it will be for as long as she lives.

Defendants objected that this item was not a separate recoverable item and, in any event, required awareness of loss.

In addition to pecuniary awards, the jury awarded $1 million for conscious pain and suffering and $3.5 million for loss of enjoyment of life. The judge reduced these amounts to a single award of $2 million. The appellate division affirmed the award as modified. The only issues now before the court on appeal involve "nonpecuniary damages," which the court defined as those damages "awarded to compensate an injured person for the physical and emotional consequences of the injury, such as pain and suffering and the loss of the ability to engage in certain activities."]

WACHTLER, CHIEF JUDGE.

. . .

We begin with the familiar proposition that an award of damages to a person injured by the negligence of another is to compensate the victim, not to punish the wrongdoer [   ]. The goal is to restore the injured party, to the extent possible, to the position that would have been occupied had the wrong not occurred [   ]. To be sure, placing the burden of compensation on the negligent party also serves as a deterrent, but purely punitive damages—that is, those which have no compensatory purpose—are prohibited unless the harmful conduct is intentional, malicious, outrageous, or otherwise aggravated beyond mere negligence [ ].

Damages for nonpecuniary losses are, of course, among those that can be awarded as compensation to the victim. This aspect of damages, however, stands on less certain ground than does an award for pecuniary damages. An economic loss can be compensated in kind by an economic gain; but recovery for noneconomic losses such as pain and suffering and loss of enjoyment of life rests on "the legal fiction that money damages can compensate for a victim's injury" [ ]. We accept this fiction, knowing that although money will neither ease the pain nor restore the victim's abilities, this device is as close as the law can come in its effort to right the wrong. We have no hope of evaluating what has been lost, but a monetary award may provide a measure of solace for the condition created [ ].

Our willingness to indulge this fiction comes to an end, however, when it ceases to serve the compensatory goals of tort recovery. When that limit is met, further indulgence can only result in assessing damages that are punitive. The question posed by this case, then, is whether an award of damages for loss of enjoyment of life to a person whose injuries preclude any awareness of the loss serves a compensatory purpose. We conclude that it does not.

Simply put, an award of money damages in such circumstances has no meaning or utility to the injured person. An award for the loss of enjoyment of life "cannot provide [such a victim] with any consolation or ease any burden resting on him. . . . He cannot spend it upon necessities or pleasures. He cannot experience the pleasure of giving it away" [ ].

We recognize that, as the trial court noted, requiring some cognitive awareness as a prerequisite to recovery for loss of enjoyment of life will result in some cases "in the paradoxical situation that the greater the degree of brain injury inflicted by a negligent defendant, the smaller the award the plaintiff can recover in general damages" [ ]. The force of this argument, however—the temptation to achieve a balance between injury and damages—has nothing to do with meaningful compensation for the victim. Instead, the temptation is rooted in a desire to punish the defendant in proportion to the harm inflicted. However relevant such retributive symmetry may be in the criminal law, it has no place in the law of civil damages, at least in the absence of culpability beyond mere negligence.

Accordingly, we conclude that cognitive awareness is a prerequisite to recovery for loss of enjoyment of life. We do not go so far, however, as to require the fact finder to sort out varying degrees of cognition and determine at what level a particular deprivation can be fully appreciated. With respect to pain and suffering, the trial court charged simply that there must be "some level of awareness" in order for plaintiff to recover. We think that this is an appropriate standard for all aspects of nonpecuniary loss. No doubt the standard ignores analytically relevant levels of cognition, but we resist the desire for analytical purity in favor of simplicity. A more complex instruction might give the appearance of greater precision but, given the limits of our understanding of the human mind, it would in reality lead only to greater speculation.

We turn next to the question whether loss of enjoyment of life should be considered a category of damages separate from pain and suffering.

IV.

There is no dispute here that the fact finder may, in assessing nonpecuniary damages, consider the effect of the injuries on the plaintiff's capacity to lead a normal life. Traditionally, in this State and elsewhere, this aspect of suffering has not been treated as a separate category of damages; instead, the plaintiff's inability to enjoy life to its fullest has been considered one type of suffering to be factored into a general award for nonpecuniary damages, commonly known as pain and suffering.

Recently, however, there has been an attempt to segregate the suffering associated with physical pain from the mental anguish that stems from the inability to engage in certain activities, and to have juries provide a separate award for each. [   ]

Some courts have resisted the effort, primarily on the ground that duplicative and therefore excessive awards would result [   ]. Other courts have allowed separate awards, noting that the types of suffering involved are analytically distinguishable [   ]. Still other courts have questioned the propriety of the practice but held that, in the particular case, separate awards did not constitute reversible error [   ].

In this State, the only appellate decisions to address the question are the decision . . . now under review and the decision of the Second Department in *Nussbaum v. Gibstein* [which the court reverses at the same time it decides *McDougald*]. Those courts were persuaded that the distinctions between the two types of mental anguish justified separate awards and that the potential for duplicative awards could be mitigated by carefully drafted jury instructions. In addition, the courts opined that separate awards would facilitate appellate review concerning the excessiveness of the total damage award.

We do not dispute that distinctions can be found or created between the concepts of pain and suffering and loss of enjoyment of life. If the term "suffering" is limited to the emotional response to the sensation of pain, then the emotional response caused by the limitation of life's activities may be considered qualitatively different [   ]. But suffering need not be so limited—it can easily encompass the frustration and anguish caused by the inability to participate in activities that once brought pleasure. Traditionally, by treating loss of enjoyment of life as a permissible factor in assessing pain and suffering, courts have given the term this broad meaning.

If we are to depart from this traditional approach and approve a separate award for loss of enjoyment of life, it must be on the basis that such an approach will yield a more accurate evaluation of the compensation due to the plaintiff. We have no doubt that, in general, the total award for nonpecuniary damages would increase if we adopted the rule. That separate awards are advocated by plaintiffs and resisted by defendants is sufficient evidence that larger awards are at stake here. But a larger award does not by itself indicate that the goal of compensation has been better served.

The advocates of separate awards contend that because pain and suffering and loss of enjoyment of life can be distinguished, they must be treated separately if the plaintiff is to be compensated fully for each distinct injury suffered. We disagree. Such an analytical approach may have its place when the subject is pecuniary damages, which can be calculated with some precision. But the estimation of nonpecuniary damages is not amenable to such analytical precision and may, in fact, suffer from its application. Translating human suffering into dollars and cents involves no mathematical formula; it rests, as we have said, on a legal fiction. The figure that emerges is unavoidably distorted by the translation. Application of this murky process to the component parts of nonpecuniary injuries (however analytically distinguishable they may be) cannot make it more accurate. If anything, the distortion will be amplified by repetition.

Thus, we are not persuaded that any salutary purpose would be served by having the jury make separate awards for pain and suffering and loss of enjoyment of life. We are confident, furthermore, that the trial advocate's art is a sufficient guarantee that none of the plaintiff's losses will be ignored by the jury.

.   .   .

[A new trial was ordered as to nonpecuniary damages.]

TITONE, JUDGE (dissenting).

The majority's holding represents a compromise position that neither comports with the fundamental principles of tort compensation nor furnishes a satisfactory, logically consistent framework for compensating nonpecuniary loss. Because I conclude that loss of enjoyment of life is an objective damage item, conceptually distinct from conscious pain and suffering, I can find no fault with the trial court's instruction authorizing separate awards and permitting an award for "loss of enjoyment of life" even in the absence of any awareness of that loss on the part of the injured plaintiff. Accordingly, I dissent.

It is elementary that the purpose of awarding tort damages is to compensate the wronged party for the actual loss he or she has sustained [   ]. Personal injury damages are awarded "to restore the injured person to the state of health he had prior to his injuries because that is the only way the law knows how to recompense one for personal injuries suffered" [   ]. Thus, this court has held that "[t]he person responsible for the injury must respond for all damages resulting directly from and as a natural consequence of the wrongful act" [   ].

The capacity to enjoy life—by watching one's children grow, participating in recreational activities, and drinking in the many other pleasures that life has to offer—is unquestionably an attribute of an ordinary healthy individual. The loss of that capacity as a result of another's negligent act is at least as serious an impairment as the permanent destruction of a physical function, which has always been treated as a compensable item under traditional tort principles [   ]. Indeed, I can imagine no physical loss that is more central to the quality of a tort victim's continuing life than the destruction of the capacity to enjoy that life to the fullest.

Unquestionably, recovery of a damage item such as "pain and suffering" requires a showing of some degree of cognitive capacity. Such a requirement exists for the simple reason that pain and suffering are wholly subjective concepts and cannot exist separate and apart from the human consciousness that experiences them. In contrast, the destruction of an individual's capacity to enjoy life as a result of a crippling injury is an objective fact that does not differ in principle from the permanent loss of an eye or limb. As in the case of a lost limb, an essential characteristic of a healthy human life has been wrongfully taken, and, consequently, the injured party is entitled to a monetary award as a substitute, if, as the majority asserts, the goal of tort compensation is "to restore the injured party, to the extent possible, to the position that would have been occupied had the wrong not occurred" [   ].

Significantly, this equation does not suggest a need to establish the injured's awareness of the loss. The victim's ability to comprehend the degree to which his or her life has been impaired is irrelevant, since, unlike "conscious pain and suffering," the impairment exists independent of the victim's ability to apprehend it. Indeed, the majority reaches the conclusion that a degree of awareness must be shown only after injecting a new element into the equation. Under the majority's formulation, the victim must be aware of the loss because, in addition to being compensatory, the award must have "meaning or utility to the injured person." [   ] This additional requirement, however, has no real foundation in law or logic. "Meaning" and "utility" are subjective value judgments that have no place in the law of tort recovery, where the primary goal is to find ways of quantifying, to the extent possible, the worth of various forms of human tragedy.

Moreover, the compensatory nature of a monetary award for loss of enjoyment of life is not altered or rendered punitive by the fact that the unaware injured plaintiff cannot experience the pleasure of having it. The fundamental distinction between punitive and compensatory damages is that the former exceed the amount necessary to replace what the plaintiff lost [   ]. As the Court of Appeals for the Second Circuit has observed, "[t]he fact that the compensation [for loss of enjoyment of life] may inure as a practical matter to third parties in a given case does not transform the nature of the damages" (Rufino v. United States, 2nd Cir., 829 F.2d 354, 362).

·   ·   ·

In the final analysis, the rule that the majority has chosen is an arbitrary one, in that it denies or allows recovery on the basis of a criterion that is not truly related to its stated goal. In my view, it is fundamentally unsound, as well as grossly unfair, to deny recovery to those who are completely without cognitive capacity while permitting it for those with a mere spark of awareness, regardless of the latter's ability to appreciate either the loss sustained or the benefits of the monetary award offered in compensation. In both instances, the injured plaintiff is in essentially the same position, and an award that is punitive as to one is equally punitive as to the other. Of course, since I do not subscribe to the majority's conclusion that an award to an unaware plaintiff is punitive, I would have no difficulty permitting recovery to both classes of plaintiffs.

Having concluded that the injured plaintiff's awareness should not be a necessary precondition to recovery for loss of enjoyment of life, I also have no difficulty going on to conclude that loss of enjoyment of life is a distinct damage item which is recoverable separate and apart from the award for conscious pain and suffering.   .   .   .

In fact, while "pain and suffering compensates the victim for the physical and mental discomfort caused by the injury; .   .   . loss of enjoyment of life compensates the victim for the limitations on the person's life created by the injury," a distinctly objective loss [   ]. In other words, while the victim's "emotional response" and "frustration and anguish" are elements of the award for pain and suffering, the "limitation of life's activities" and the "inability to participate in activities" that the majority identifies are recoverable under the "loss of enjoyment of life" rubric. Thus, there is no real overlap, and no real basis for concern about potentially duplicative awards where, as here, there is a properly instructed jury.

Finally, given the clear distinction between the two categories of nonpecuniary damages, I cannot help but assume that permitting separate awards for conscious pain and suffering and loss of enjoyment of life would contribute to accuracy and precision in thought in the jury's deliberations on the issue of damages. Indeed, the view that itemized awards enhance accuracy by facilitating appellate review has already been expressed by the Legislature in enacting [some special verdict procedures]. In light of the concrete benefit to be gained by compelling the jury to differentiate between the specific objective and subjective elements of the plaintiff's nonpecuniary loss, I find unpersuasive the majority's reliance on vague concerns about potential distortion owing to the inherently difficult task of computing the value of intangible loss. My belief in the jury system, and in the collective wisdom of the deliberating jury, leads me to conclude that we may safely leave that task in the jurors' hands.

.   .   . Accordingly, I would affirm the order below affirming the judgment.

SIMONS, KAYE, HANCOCK and BELLACOSA, JJ., concur with WACHTLER, C.J. TITONE, J., dissents and votes to affirm in a separate opinion in which ALEXANDER, J., concurs.

Notes and Questions

1. At one point the majority talks of efforts to "segregate the suffering associated with physical pain from the mental anguish that stems from the inability to engage in certain activities." This makes clear that New York seeks to compensate both the pain and the loss of the pleasure under the same rubric.

Other states, however, segregate these items, calling the loss of pleasure "loss of enjoyment of life." In Fantozzi v. Sandusky Cement Prod. Co., 597 N.E.2d 474 (Ohio 1992), the court approved a separate charge to the jury addressing "the plaintiff's inability, presently and prospectively, to perform the usual activities of life, such as the basic mechanical bodily movements that accommodate walking, climbing stairs, feeding oneself, driving a car, etc."

> The claim for damages for deprivation or impairment of life's usual activities has, in other jurisdictions, been applied to a wide variety of pleasurable activities shown to have been curtailed by the injuries received by the plaintiff. Such damages include loss of ability to play golf, dance, bowl, play musical instruments, engage in specific outdoor sports, along with other activities. These types of experiences are all positive sensations of pleasure, the loss of which could provide a basis for an award of damages to the plaintiff in varying degrees depending upon his involvement, as shown by the evidence. Such proof differs from the elements of mental suffering occasioned by the plaintiff's injury such as nervousness, grief, shock, anxiety, and so forth. Although the loss of the ability to engage in a usual pleasant activity of life is an emotional experience, it is a loss of a positive experience rather than the infliction of a negative experience.

The court thought that the use of more and smaller categories "would help the jury understand exactly what claimed damages it is addressing. This adds more clarity and objectivity to this part of the jury determination." To avoid double recoveries, the court mandated an elaborate two-paragraph instruction detailing how the jury should avoid double counting. Do you think this separation will create more rational jury discussions of intangible loss? Is it relevant that plaintiffs generally press for recognition of new damage categories while defendants argue against them? See also Bennett v. Lembo, 761 A.2d 494 (N.H. 2000).

How should courts handle the case of a woman with a scar across her face that deters her from playing golf—something she did weekly for 20 years before the accident? Suppose she has no scar but cannot play as well as she did before? Does it matter whether this is because her arm hurts every time she swings or whether her coordination has suffered?

2. How does the compensatory role of tort law fit into the discussion in *McDougald*? Is it a "paradoxical situation" that the worse a person is hurt the less likely that person may be able to recover anything for pain and suffering? Might this also be true in wrongful death cases?

3. The dissent addresses the issue of who is likely to get to spend the pain and suffering award in this type of case. Should that matter? What role does the majority's concern about the "utility" of the award play?

Under the dissent's approach what is recoverable if the victim died instantly?

4. Omitted parts of the dissent raised two other issues:

a. that the majority has compromised its declared goal by allowing any "level of awareness" to suffice for an award. How might this compromise the majority view?

b. that the time frames differ for the two considerations. Damages for pain and suffering are available only during the period of cognitive awareness. But damages for loss of enjoyment of life are to compensate for losses "over a natural life span." With respect to the latter, the dissent asked, is plaintiff "entitled to recover an award representing his entire lifetime's loss notwithstanding that he was conscious of the loss for only a few moments before lapsing into cognitive oblivion?" How might the majority analyze such a case? Might it limit recovery to the period of awareness?

5. For further discussion of issues raised by *McDougald*, see Wilt v. Buracker, 443 S.E.2d 196 (W.Va.1993), cert. denied 511 U.S. 1129 (1994)(discussing at length the nature of expert economic testimony in this type of case that values life by drawing on studies about willingness to pay to avoid injury, and rejecting such testimony in favor of treating hedonic damages as part of general damages); Montalvo v. Lapez, 884 P.2d 345 (Haw.1994)(same); and Note, Hedonic Damages for Wrongful Death: Are Tortfeasors Getting Away with Murder?, 78 Geo.L.J. 1687 (1990).

6. Some cases support the intuition that splitting the non-economic aspects into several compartments may indeed lead to larger verdicts than would otherwise have been returned—or upheld. In Kresin v. Sears, Roebuck & Co., 736 N.E.2d 171 (Ill.App. 2000), the major items in a jury award for a 73-year-old woman were $6 million for present and future pain and suffering; $7 million for disability; and $2 million for disfigurement. All were affirmed on appeal over the claim that the award was excessive. The challenge to the disfigurement award was based on plaintiff's age and injuries. Defendant contrasted similar injuries to a child with a longer life expectancy. The court noted that it had refused to engage in such comparisons. Next, defendant argued that there had been no facial injury. The court responded that the evidence showed that plaintiff "is unable to straighten her left elbow and that her hand is so contorted that it is permanently fixed in a claw-like position" and that her left leg is paralyzed. Those involved disfigurement as well as disability.

7. *Death cases—survival actions.* Much of what we have been discussing is equally applicable to survival cases. The measurement of past lost income and medical expense—that is, loss suffered between the time of injury and the time of death—is similar. The survival action also typically allows recovery for pain and suffering sustained by the decedent. In a case in which the plaintiff is very badly burned as a result of the defendant's negligence, remains conscious in excruciating pain for a day or two, and then dies, why should anyone else receive compensation for that pain? Is there an answer other than deterrence?

In Wellborn v. Sears, Roebuck & Co., 970 F.2d 1420 (5th Cir.1992), a 14-year-old boy was caught under a descending automatic garage door that pinned him to the ground. The evidence showed that he had been alive and probably conscious for as short a time as three to five minutes to as long as "several hours." The coroner's estimate was 30 minutes. The jury's award of $1 million for pre-death pain and suffering was upheld on appeal. See also Guzman v. Guajardo, 761 S.W.2d 506 (Tex.App.1988)(upholding award of $600,000 for 15 minutes of child's severe pain before death).

In Sander v. Geib, Elston, Frost, P.A., 506 N.W.2d 107 (S.D.1993), defendant's negligence in reading a pap smear test led to a failure to detect cervical cancer until it was too late to save decedent, a 34-year-old wife and mother of three children. She underwent some radiation therapy but was found unsuitable for any radical procedures because the cancer was too far advanced. The court does not recount evidence of physical pain in its opinion. In a suit for her death, the jury made an award that was assumed to include $1 million for her pain and suffering. In rejecting a claim of excessiveness, the court responded:

> [Decedent] greatly suffered many faces of pain during the year following the realization that she would die from the very disease which the pap smear was designed to detect. The enormity of [decedent's] knowledge of her impending, unalterable doom, her confusion, fear, misery, depression, helplessness, physical pain and mental terror, her sure knowledge that she would never live to witness the adulthood of her children or old age with her husband, all were proper considerations for the jury and surely had a powerful influence upon it.

Is each of these considerations proper? What if the jury had returned a verdict on this item of $3 million? $300,000? The defendant's strategy was to focus on denying liability. As a result it "did not argue damages in closing arguments to the jury." Was this a mistake?

By statute California has barred the award of pain and suffering in cases in which the victim dies before judgment. See the discussion in Williamson v. Plant Insulation Co., 28 Cal.Rptr.2d 751 (App. 1994), denying such a recovery where the victim died a few days before final judgment was entered. The court suggested that if the statute seemed to be drawing an arbitrary line that harms plaintiffs' estates, they may benefit from that line if a plaintiff who had been awarded future pain and suffering based on a long life expectancy should die one day after obtaining judgment. In Sullivan v. Delta Air Lines, Inc., 935 P.2d 781 (Cal.1997), the plaintiff, after obtaining a judgment that included pain and suffering, died while the case was on appeal. The court held that the judgment was "final" for purposes of the statute. Is there anything unsatisfying about having this type of recovery depend on the precise moment of death?

In Jones v. Chicago Osteopathic Hospital, 738 N.E.2d 542 (Ill.App. 2000), as the result of defendant's negligence, a baby was born with severe brain damage and led a "debilitative life" until he died at the age of 18 months. As the court summarized the situation, "Andrew was blind, deaf, and suffered from spastic quadriparesis—a condition which caused Andrew's body to be very stiff and inflexible. Andrew had no control over the movement of his legs and arms, he could not suck or swallow, had to be tube fed, and required almost constant suctioning of his airway. He required oxygen regularly and at times was placed on a ventilator." The jury awarded the estate over $4 million on the survival claim and the statutory beneficiaries $2.2 million on the wrongful death claim. Both were upheld on appeal: "In light of the nature and extent of Baby Andrew's injuries, which he endured over the 18 months he survived, we cannot say the $4 million awarded Baby Andrew's estate in the survival action was excessive or the product of passion or prejudice." On the other item the court said only that the evidence showed that the mother was a "dedicated and devoted mother to Baby Andrew during his lifetime. Her loss of his future companionship, love and affection can hardly be disputed. The father and siblings, too, were denied the opportunity of ever having a relationship with Andrew normally available to fathers and brothers."

8. *Death cases—wrongful death actions.* As in the *Jones* case, wrongful death and survival actions are often brought together. In wrongful death actions, the major item of damages traditionally has been the economic loss to the beneficiaries, because in many states only "pecuniary" loss is recoverable. Since the beneficiaries were to recover only their loss, however defined, an additional measurement had to be made in the economic loss category—they could not be awarded the decedent's lost wages as such. From that lost income figure the amount the decedent would have spent personally for food, clothing and other habitual items had to be deducted. Until recently, many states imposed small caps on wrongful death awards. These have been eliminated or made more generous. See, e.g., Neiman v. American National Property & Casualty Co., 613 N.W.2d 160 (Wis.2000), noting that in 1995 the state had a cap on wrongful death awards of $150,000. This was raised in 1998 to $500,000 for a deceased minor and to $350,000 for a deceased adult. What justifies any limit in such cases?

New York has been the state most closely identified with a strict interpretation of the statutory requirement that the damages be "pecuniary." The language states in relevant part that the damages awardable in death cases are such sum as the trier "deems to be fair and just compensation for the pecuniary injuries resulting from the decedent's death to the persons for whose benefit the action is brought." A recent case involved expert economic testimony about the value of the life of an 84-year-old woman. The defense expert had testified that the woman's savings level would remain constant, and that during her expected seven years of life, she would consume more of her income than could have been generated through interest. He concluded that the "distributees are actually financially better off as a result of [the decedent's] death." Accepting that testimony, the judge, as trier of fact, awarded funeral expenses as the only recoverable item for her wrongful death. "Crass though it may seem (and if crass it is, it is because of the current state of the law), the Court finds that the only pecuniary loss suffered" was an $8,000 funeral bill. He noted that other states had expanded recovery to include loss of society and urged a change in New York law. See the extended report of Hubbard v. State, in N.Y.L.J., June 29, 2000 at 1.

In DeLong v. County of Erie, 457 N.E.2d 717 (N.Y.1983), a jury could have found that the plaintiff underwent up to 12 minutes of terror before being stabbed to death by an intruder. The county's liability was based on its delayed response to a 911 call caused by the dispatcher's failure to get the right address. After upholding a survival award of $200,000 for conscious pain and suffering due to the victim's "fear and apprehension," the court affirmed a wrongful death award of $600,000 to the beneficiaries of the 28-year-old mother of three, who was not employed outside the home. The court approved the use of an economist to evaluate the replacement cost for cooking, cleaning, housekeeping, and bookkeeping.

Recall *Sander*, supra, involving the wrongful death of the woman whose pap smear was misread. Among the damages that the *Sander* court assumed the jury to have made on the wrongful death part of the case was $388,000 as the pecuniary value of decedent's loss to the family (perhaps such items as housekeeping, buying necessities, bookkeeping, cooking, gardening); $480,000 to each of her three children for lost advice, companionship, moral training, and education (the children were 15, 12, and 8 at the time of death); and $890,000 for the pecuniary value to her husband (perhaps advice, companionship). These sums were not challenged.

See also Drews v. Gobel Freight Lines, Inc., 578 N.E.2d 970 (Ill.1991), upholding, 6–1, an award of $8.3 million for the wrongful death of a 32-year-old insurance salesman. The court emphasized the decedent's professional accomplishments and his strong family commitments. The dissenter argued that an award of $1 million invested at 6% would produce the income he was earning at his death while leaving the principal intact would suffice. The court also rejected the claim that the wrongful death award of $8.3 million was excessive. He would have upheld $1.5 million.

For discussion of a statute that permits non-pecuniary recoveries, see Rice v. Charles, 532 S.E.2d 318 (Va. 2000), including damages for "sorrow, mental anguish, and solace which may include society, companionship, comfort, guidance, kindly offices and advice of the decedent." Recall also the analysis in *Jones* in the last note.

9. *Wrongful death of a child.* The issue involved when children are killed revolves even more clearly around the distinction between the states that limit recovery to pecuniary injuries and those that do not. For an effort to avoid the statutory limitations, see Green v. Bittner, 424 A.2d 210 (N.J.1980), involving the wrongful death of a high school senior. The trial judge told the jury to consider the services the child had performed around the house to date and those that she might have undertaken to provide her parents as she grew older. From this, the jury was to subtract the value of food, clothing, and education that the family would have spent on her until her majority. The jury returned a verdict of no damages. The trial judge upheld the verdict, observing that the "jury in this particular case followed literally the language of the statute." On appeal, the court reversed. The court, though staying within the constraint of the statute, greatly expanded the recoverable damages in such cases:

> We hold that [in addition to the usual items] the jury should be allowed, under appropriate circumstances, to award damages for the parents' loss of their child's companionship as they grow older, when it may be most needed and valuable, as well as the advice and guidance that often accompanies it. As noted later, these other losses will be confined to their pecuniary value, excluding emotional loss. Given this expansion of permissible recovery, a verdict finding no damages for the death of a child should ordinarily be set aside by the trial court and a new trial ordered. To sustain such a verdict "would result in a return to the outmoded doctrine that a child is a liability—not an asset." [ ]

In discussing the nature of the recoverable loss of "guidance, advice and counsel," the court stressed:

> The loss of guidance, advice and counsel is similarly to be confined to its pecuniary element. It is not the loss simply of the exchange of views, no matter how perceptive, when child and parent are together; it is certainly not the loss of the pleasure which accompanies such an exchange. Rather it is the loss of that kind of guidance, advice and counsel which all of us need from time to time in particular situations, for specific purposes, perhaps as an aid in making a business decision, or a decision affecting our lives generally, or even advice and guidance needed to relieve us from unremitting depression. It must be the kind of advice, guidance or counsel that could be purchased from a business adviser, a therapist, or a trained counselor, for instance. That some of us obtain the same benefit without charge from spouses, friends or children does not strip it of pecuniary value.

The court also noted that the proportion of elderly people is growing. "We suspect that there are many more children aged 45 to 55 who are faced with their parents' need for care and guidance than there were in the past. . . . Nursing homes are not the only vehicle for this assistance. The parents' need is real, and when a middle-aged son or daughter is not there because of a wrongful death, a prospective pecuniary advantage of the aged or infirm parent has been lost." The fact that many of these services were likely to be rendered only in the distant future presented no special problem. Ascertaining their present value involves the same discounting process whether the event is two years away or 20.

In Andrews v. Reynolds Memorial Hospital, Inc., 499 S.E.2d 846 (W.Va.1997), the court held a judgment of $1.75 million in lost earnings attributable to the death of a one-day-old baby could be justified. The plaintiffs' expert had used "an average life expectancy, an average work-life expectancy and, in addition, the educational background of [the baby's] parents." The evidence indicated but for the malpractice the baby would have had an average life expectancy. The award was not too speculative.

In Greyhound Lines, Inc. v. Sutton, 765 So.2d 1269 (Miss.2000), three young children of plaintiffs were killed. In cases in which the child has no work experience, the court rejected the lower court's decision to use "an average income for persons of the community in which they lived:"

> Who is say that a child from the most impoverished part of the state or with extremely poor parents has less of a future earnings potential than a child from the wealthiest part of the state or with wealthy parents? Today's society is much more mobile than in the past. Additionally, there are many more educational and job-training opportunities available for children as a whole today. We must not assume that individuals forever remain shackled by the bounds of community or class. The law loves certainty and economy of effort, but the law also respects individual aptitudes and differences.

The court then held that where a child has no earnings record, future income should be calculated on a "rebuttable presumption that the deceased child's income would have been the equivalent of the national average as set forth by the United States Department of Labor." Either side could rebut by presenting relevant evidence that might include such things as "precocity, mental and physical health, intellectual development, and relevant family circumstances."

10.   Should the plaintiff be able to introduce "grief experts" to testify about the impact of wrongful death on the family? See the three-way split in Angrand v. Key, 657 So.2d 1146 (Fla.1995), holding that such an expert may testify if the trial judge concludes that it might help the jury. Two concurring justices observed that the discretion should be reserved for "unusual circumstances" because grief is a "subject generally understood by the average person." Three dissenters thought the evidence should generally be admissible.

We turn now to situations in which the victim has received aid from another source.

Arambula v. Wells

Court of Appeal of California, 1999.
72 Cal.App.4th 1006, 85 Cal.Rptr.2d 584.

CROSBY, J.

[Plaintiff was injured in a rear-end collision. He was employed in a family-owned business in which he owned 15% of the stock. "Despite missing work because of his injuries, he continued to receive his $2,800 weekly salary. He testified that his brother [who held 70% of the stock] 'wished' to be reimbursed, but he had not promised to do so." In the ensuing suit, defendant admitted liability and contested causation and damages. Plaintiff alleged severe brain injury. Defendant denied that claim.]

At the start of trial, Wells moved *in limine* to exclude all evidence and testimony regarding Arambula's lost wages claim of approximately $50,000. Her attorney, relying on dicta in a footnote in Helfend v. Southern Cal. Rapid Transit Dist. [465 P.2d 61 (Cal. 1970)], argued, "Plaintiff is not receiving payment by means of disability insurance, pension or from utilizing [   ] sick time or vacation time. Further, plaintiff has failed to provide any documentation or demand that the monies received from his employer will be required to be reimbursed."

[The trial judge agreed and instructed the jury not to award damages for lost earnings "because his employer paid for the time he was off without any requirement to do so and there was no agreement by plaintiff to refund same." The jury awarded $54,334 to Arambula but nothing for lost wages.]

Under the collateral source rule, plaintiffs in personal injury actions can still recover full damages even though they already have received compensation for their injuries from such "collateral sources" as medical insurance. [   ] The idea is that tortfeasors should not recover a windfall from the thrift and foresight of persons who have actually or constructively secured insurance, pension or disability benefits to provide for themselves and their families. A contrary rule, it is feared, would misallocate liability for tort-caused losses and discourage people from obtaining benefits from independent collateral sources. [   ]

Helfend is the leading case. The court rejected defense efforts to introduce evidence that about 80 percent of an injured motorist's medical bills had been paid by his Blue Cross insurance carrier. Applying a benefit of the bargain rationale, the Supreme Court allowed the motorist to receive the advantage of his investment of "years of insurance premiums to assure his medical care." It stated "[t]he tortfeasor should not garner the benefits of his victim's providence." [   ][1]

Helfend on its face says nothing about gratuitous wage payments. Wells, however, cited *Helfend* to convince the trial court to limit the collateral source rule to situations where plaintiffs incurred an expense, obligation or liability in obtaining the services for which they seek compensation. According to Wells, *Helfend* is "replete with indications that the

---

1. The collateral source rule also recognizes the inadequacies of damage awards for personal injuries. That is because "[l]egal 'compensation' for personal injuries does not actually compensate. Not many people would sell an arm for the average or even the maximum amount that juries award for loss of an arm. Moreover the injured person seldom gets the compensation he 'recovers,' for a substantial attorney's fee usually comes out of it. The Rule helps to remedy these problems inherent in compensating the tort victim." [   ] Since collateral sources only cover economic damages like medical costs and lost earnings, there is no possibility of a double recovery for intangibles like pain and suffering "which can be translated into monetary loss only with great difficulty." [   ] Rather than overcompensating a plaintiff, the collateral source rule "partially provides a somewhat closer approximation to full compensation for his injuries." [   ]

California Supreme Court does not intend for the collateral source rule to apply to gratuitous payments and services.''

[Defendant relied on footnote 5 in *Helfend*, which noted that New York's rule against reimbursing non-insurance gifts was "reasonable." On the other hand, the *Helfend* court elsewhere had said that it was leaving open all questions other than insurance payments.]

We take *Helfend* at its word. Not only do we consider its language at face value, but we construe it in the light of its facts and the issues raised. [   ] While we do not take lightly any of the Supreme Court's statements, we reasonably construe them in the context of the thoroughness of the court's analysis and in light of its prior expressions on the same subject. [   ] There are five specific reasons why footnote five fails to pass these tests.

First, there is the matter of existing California law (prior to *Helfend*), which made no special distinction for purely gratuitous collateral benefits. In [   ], the court stated, "The same rule [as to collateral sources] seems to apply to wages paid an injured person by the employer. The injured employee may still recover the full amount of such wages from the wrongdoer." The Supreme Court repeated similar language in Fifield Manor v. Finston [354 P.2d 1073 (Cal.1960)]: "The fact that *either under contract or gratuitously* such treatment has been paid for by another does not defeat the cause of action of the injured party to recover the reasonable value of such treatment from the tortfeasor." (Italics added.) If the Supreme Court desired to throw into doubt such long-established pronouncements (including its own decision in *Fifield Manor*), we believe it would have done so more directly than through footnote 5's oblique references to New York decisional law.

Second, no subsequent appellate opinion has construed footnote 5 in the highly expansive manner suggested by Wells. To the contrary, several post-*Helfend* decisions have allowed plaintiffs to recover the costs of gratuitous medical care as an element of their damages even without any contractual right to reimbursement. [   ] [parents who cared for minor child can recover special damages for reasonable costs of such care based on prevailing rates for home care nurses, even though services were rendered "without an agreement or expectation of payment"]; [   ] [same with respect to wife who provided 24-hour-a-day attendant care to her injured husband: "Insofar as gratuities are concerned, the rule appears to be in keeping with the collateral source rule rationale."]; see also [   ] [in "California even [gratuitous] benefits are subject to the collateral source rule."]. Wells's proposal would create a conflict in the law with [these three cases].

Third, a majority of jurisdictions and many commentators are in accord. [   ]

In Montgomery Ward & Co., Inc. v. Anderson [976 S.W.2d 382 (Ark. 1998)], a hospital partially forgave a patient's medical bills. The court held the patient was entitled to recover compensation for the full amount of the harm inflicted upon her, notwithstanding the discount, stating "There is no evidence of record showing that [defendant] had anything to do with procuring the discount of [plaintiff's] bill by [the hospital]. The rationale of the rule favors her, just as it would had she been compensated by insurance for which she had arranged." [   ]

Fourth, public policy concerns weigh heavily in favor of application of the collateral source rule to gratuitous payments and services. Just as the Supreme Court in *Helfend* found the rule "expresses a policy judgment in favor of encouraging citizens to purchase and maintain insurance for personal injuries and for other eventualities" [   ], so too we adhere to the rule to promote policy concerns favoring private charitable assistance. Indeed, until recent times, family assistance has been the primary means of coping with a tragedy in this country. Were we to permit a tortfeasor to mitigate damages because of a third party's charitable gift, the plaintiff would be in a worse position than had nothing been done. Why would a family member (or a stranger) freely give of his or her money or time if the wrongdoer would ultimately reap the benefits of such generosity?

.   .   .

This is more than "do-gooderism"; the state's own self-interest is involved as well. To the extent that private generosity steps to the fore, the impact on the state is lightened "by rendering beneficences which the state would otherwise be obliged to furnish or indirectly further the interests of the state by the public benefit they promote." [   ]

.   .   .

[Fifth,] even without an ironclad requirement of reimbursement, the plaintiff may be motivated to repay the donor from any tort recovery, or, inspired by example, to similar acts of generosity on the notion that one good act leads to another. Such reimbursement would avoid any prospects of a double recovery, as if there ever could be a double recovery where pain and suffering is concerned. Moreover, as *Helfend* noted, the injured victim may not have been made whole because generally "plaintiff's attorney will receive a large portion of the plaintiff's recovery in contingent fees.   .   .   . The collateral source rule partially serves to compensate for the attorney's share and does not actually render 'double recovery' for the plaintiff." [   ]

The rationale of the collateral source rule thus favors sheltering gratuitous gifts of money or services intended to benefit tort victims, just as it favors insurance payments from coverage they had arranged. No reason exists in these circumstances to confer a bonanza upon the party causing the injury. As one court noted nearly a century ago in connection with an employer's voluntary wage payment, "[I]f time has been lost as the result of a tort, sound sense, common justice, and, it may be, public policy would demand that the tortfeasor be prohibited from making a defense founded upon the proposition .   .   . that some third person, not only not in sympathy with the wrongdoer, but despising him and his act, has, from some worthy motive, paid to the injured person an amount which, if it had come from the wrongdoer, would have equaled the damages which would have been assessed against him." (Nashville, C. & St. L.Ry. v. Miller [47 S.E. 959, 960 (Ga.1904)].

III

A

While a gift is presumptively intended for the benefit of the donee, the presumption should be a rebuttable one. We can posit examples where a wrongdoer's family or friends might pay the victim's bills out of a sense of moral obligation or atonement. Public policy encourages such expiation. Under these circumstances the tortfeasor may well be entitled to an offset to effectuate the donors' intent and to avoid a double recovery. Put another way, such sources might not be considered as "wholly independent" of the tortfeasor. [ ]

We also do not decide whether the collateral source rule extends to payments from a public source.[4] The question of gratuitous public benefits is not at issue here and invokes a host of other concerns, which must be considered in light of their specific factual contexts. [*Helfend*]

B

The collateral source rule operates both as a substantive rule of damages and as a rule of evidence. As a rule of evidence, it precludes the introduction of evidence of the plaintiff being compensated by a collateral source unless there is a "persuasive showing" that such evidence is of "substantial probative value" for purposes other than reducing damages. [ ][5]

We do not resolve such issues of admissibility here, but leave them to the sound discretion of the trial judge on remand. [ ] We note, however, our decision does not automatically bar evidence that Arambula's wages were paid by his brother during his period of disability. For example, such evidence may be admissible, in the court's reasonable discretion and subject to a limiting instruction, to impeach his claimed inability to work. Evidence of actual wage payments may be persuasive to show that no time was lost, the employee actually performed substantial services during the period of disability, or had a motive to malinger. (See Corsetti v. Stone Co. [483

4. See e.g., Washington by Washington v. Barnes Hospital (Mo.1995) 897 S.W.2d 611 (collateral source rule does not apply to free governmental benefits previously received by plaintiff); 4 Harper, James & Gray, The Law of Torts, supra, § 25.22 at pp. 663–664 ("[u]nless such [a contrary legislative] intent is made fairly clear, however, it seems reasonable to suppose that statutory benefits and free services furnished by government to needy classes of people are meant simply to make sure certain of their needs will be fulfilled and not to confer an additional bounty on the recipient"); but see Ensor v. Wilson (Ala.1987) 519 So.2d 1244 (collateral source rule applies to future special education benefits by governmental entity because of uncertainty of their continued existence).

5. The Legislature, as part of the Medical Injury Compensation Reform Act of 1975 (MICRA), has abrogated the collateral source rule as a rule of evidence in medical malpractice cases. MICRA allows defendants to introduce evidence the plaintiffs had received collateral source benefits, and it prohibits "collateral sources" from obtaining reimbursement from malpractice defendants. (Civ.Code, § 3333.1.)

N.E.2d 793, 802 (Mass.1985)] [evidence of collateral source income relevant to show employee had motive other than physical disability not to work].)

In Pensak v. Peerless Oil Co. [166 A. 792 (Pa.1933)], an employee received salary payments (as a supposed gift) from his father and brother (who were co-owners of the business) during the time of his incapacity. But the court distinguished between making a claim of gift and proving it: "Characterizing as a gift the money paid to him does not make it so. To permit a recovery of money under the guise of wages lost would, with the facts as they here appear, open a wide door to misrepresentation and fraud in this class of cases."

[Other parts of the opinion were not published. The court remanded "for a limited new trial to determine the amount of damages for lost wages (if any) legally caused by defendant's negligence. The judgment for damages in his favor is otherwise affirmed."]

SILLS, P.J., and RYLAARSDAM, J., concur.

Notes and Questions

1. Is there a single underlying explanation for the collateral source rule? Should the rule apply equally to a gift from a brother, a loan from that brother repayable if and when the tort suit succeeds, a reduced hospital bill, and a payment from a health insurer?

In Peterson v. Lou Bachrodt Chevrolet Co., 392 N.E.2d 1 (Ill. 1979), the court, recognizing that it was adopting a minority position, refused to permit plaintiff to recover for the value of medical services he had received at a Shriners' Hospital: "The purpose of compensatory damages is to compensate [ ]; it is not the purpose of such damages to punish defendants or bestow a windfall upon plaintiffs." The dissenters asserted that the donors to the hospital "intended that the plaintiff, not the tortfeasor, be the beneficiary of their largess."

2. In Bandel v. Friedrich, 584 A.2d 800 (N.J.1991), the court applied the rule to prevent an offset for the value of needed gratuitous nursing services provided to the permanently disabled plaintiff by his mother. Does that raise issues different from those raised in *Arambula*?

3. Notice that two distinct questions are involved in these cases. The first is whether the defendant should get the benefit of the payment from the collateral source. If the answer to that question is negative, there is sometimes a further question: should the plaintiff keep any double payment that may result? The issue arises most commonly where the victim is protected by health or medical insurance or by wage protection insurance. Should it matter whether plaintiff paid the premiums himself or whether his employer provided the medical coverage as a fringe benefit? This issue, addressed generally under the framework of "subrogation," is explored at length at p. 747, infra.

4. In *Helfend*, the case that is central to *Arambula*, the court held that public agencies should be subject to the same collateral source rules that apply to private defendants. After noting that the Blue Cross contract contained a subrogation provision, the court continued:

> Hence, the plaintiff receives no double recovery; the collateral source rule simply serves as a means of by-passing the antiquated doctrine of non-assignment of tortious actions and permits a proper transfer of risk from the plaintiff's insurer to the tortfeasor by way of the victim's tort recovery. The double shift from the tortfeasor to the victim and then from the victim to his insurance carrier can normally occur with little cost in that the insurance carrier is often intimately involved in the initial litigation and quite automatically receives its part of the tort settlement or verdict.

> Even in cases in which the contract or the law precludes subrogation or refund of benefits, or in situations in which the collateral source waives such subrogation or refund, the rule performs entirely necessary functions in the computation of damages. For example, the cost of medical care often provides both attorneys and juries in tort cases with an important measure for assessing the plaintiff's general damages. [ ] To permit the defendant to tell the jury that the plaintiff has been recompensed by a collateral source for his medical costs might irretrievably upset the complex, delicate, and somewhat indefinable calculations which result in the normal jury verdict. [ ]

> We also note that generally the jury is not informed that plaintiff's attorney will receive a large portion of the plaintiff's recovery in contingent fees or that personal injury damages are not taxable to the plaintiff and are normally deductible by the defendant. Hence, the plaintiff rarely actually receives full compensation for his injuries as computed by the jury. The collateral source rule partially serves to compensate for the attorney's share and does not actually render "double recovery" for the plaintiff. . . .

A footnote in *Helfend* recognizes that this justification for the collateral source rule applies only to the plaintiffs who benefit from the rule, and is "only an incomplete and haphazard solution to providing all tort victims with full compensation." Do these added justifications for the collateral source rule make a persuasive case for its retention?

5. Should government programs be treated differently? In the cited *Barnes Hospital*, as a result of defendant's malpractice, plaintiffs' brain-damaged child would need special education for life. Plaintiffs proved what such a private education would cost. The court held that the defendant was improperly prevented from arguing that public education was available for that need. Although most courts had sided with the plaintiff, this court disagreed:

> Here plaintiffs need not purchase the public school benefits, nor work for them as an employment benefit, nor contract for them. Hence the "benefit of the bargain" rationale does not apply. Nor are these benefits provided as a gift by a friend or family member to assist plaintiffs specifically, such that it would be inequitable to transfer the

value of the benefit from plaintiffs to defendants. Nor is this a benefit that is dependent upon plaintiffs' indigence or other special status. Instead, public school programming is available to all by law. While to some extent public schools are funded by plaintiffs' tax dollars, they are also funded by defendants' tax dollars and no windfall results to either. We reject the concept that the collateral source rule should be utilized solely to punish the defendant. Damages in our tort system are compensatory not punitive.

On the remand, plaintiffs "of course, may respond to this evidence with arguments of its inadequacy, the risk of its continued availability, etc."

6. The matter is at the center of the changing face of medical care. In Acuar v. Letourneau, 531 S.E.2d 316 (Va.2000), the plaintiff's full medical bills were $41,000. Of that total, $28,000 were written off by the providers because of an arrangement with the plaintiff's medical insurer. In the court's view the test was not what plaintiff had paid but the amount of the liability he incurred. Defendant could not deduct from its liability "any part of the benefits [plaintiff] received from his contractual arrangement with his health insurance carrier, whether those benefits took the form of medical expense payments or amounts written off because of agreements between his health insurance carrier and his health care providers. Those amounts written off are as much of a benefit for which [plaintiff] paid consideration as are the actual cash payments made by his health insurance carrier to the health care providers." The collateral source rule applied.

7. *Statutory change.* The collateral source rule has been the subject of statutory change in about a dozen states. The nature of these changes is considered at p. 787, infra.

8. The court in *Bandel*, discussed in note 2, suggested that giving the defendant the benefit of the mother's nursing care would have a disparate impact on poor victims. Why might that be? In addition, it is often asserted that various damage rules and tort reform efforts affect groups unequally in cases of race and gender. See, e.g., Koenig & Rustad, His and Her Tort Reform: Gender Injustice in Disguise, 70 Wash.L.Rev. 1 (1995); Chamallas, Questioning the Use of Race–Specific and Gender–Specific Economic Data in Tort Litigation: A Constitutional Argument, 63 Fordham L.Rev. 73 (1994); Note, Caps on Noneconomic Damages and the Female Plaintiff: Heeding the Warning Signs, 44 Case W.Res.L.Rev. 197 (1994).

2.   PUNITIVE DAMAGES

Until now we have been exploring the nature of compensatory damages. We turn now to the question of whether damages that do not seek to compensate should also be available in certain kinds of cases. Almost all the states have concluded that sometimes damages may be awarded to punish the defendant or to make an example of that defendant so that others will avoid this very serious kind of misconduct. At the extreme, intentional unjustified conduct would warrant this type of treatment. We consider this when we cover intentional torts in Chapter XII. Many states have expanded the availability of punitive damages to other types of serious misbehavior. For example, under California Civil Code § 3294, "where the defendant has been guilty of oppression, fraud, or malice, express or implied, the plaintiff, in addition to actual damages, may recover damages for the sake of example and by way of punishing the defendant." Even in states that sometimes permit punitive damages, the jury has total discretion about whether or not to award them.

The following case explores generally the nature of punitive damages in the context of drunk driving.

Taylor v. Superior Court

Supreme Court of California, 1979.
24 Cal.3d 890, 598 P.2d 854, 157 Cal.Rptr. 693.

[Taylor sued Stille for compensatory and punitive damages arising from a collision between their cars. Plaintiff alleged that Stille had "acted with a conscious disregard" for plaintiff's safety. Stille moved to dismiss the claim for punitive damages. The trial judge agreed and dismissed that part of the complaint. Plaintiff then sought a writ of mandate to require the judge to reinstate the claim for punitive damages.]

Richardson, J.

.   .   .

.   .   . In pertinent part, the complaint alleged that the car driven by Stille collided with plaintiff's car, causing plaintiff serious injuries; that Stille is, and for a substantial period of time had been, an alcoholic "well aware of the serious nature of his alcoholism" and of his "tendency, habit, history, practice, proclivity, or inclination to drive a motor vehicle while under the influence of alcohol"; and that Stille was also aware of the dangerousness of his driving while intoxicated.

The complaint further alleged that Stille had previously caused a serious automobile accident while driving under the influence of alcohol; that he had been arrested and convicted for drunken driving on numerous prior occasions; that at the time of the accident herein, Stille had recently completed a period of probation which followed a drunk driving conviction; that one of his probation conditions was that he refrain from driving for at least six hours after consuming any alcoholic beverage; and that at the time of the accident in question he was presently facing an additional pending criminal drunk driving charge.

In addition, the complaint averred that notwithstanding his alcoholism, Stille accepted employment which required him both to call on various commercial establishments where alcoholic beverages were sold, and to deliver or transport such beverages in his car. Finally, it is alleged that at the time the accident occurred, Stille was transporting alcoholic beverages, "was simultaneously driving .   .   . while consuming an alcoholic beverage," and was "under the influence of intoxicants."

.   .   .

Although we rarely grant extraordinary relief at the pleading stage of a lawsuit, mandamus will lie when it appears that the trial court has deprived a party of an opportunity to plead his cause of action or defense, and when extraordinary relief may prevent a needless and expensive trial and reversal. (Coulter v. Superior Court [577 P.2d 669 (Cal.1978)]; [   ]). Such a combination of circumstances is herein presented and, accordingly, we examine the propriety of the trial court's ruling in the light of applicable statutory and decisional law.

Section 3294 of the Civil Code authorizes the recovery of punitive damages in noncontract cases "where the defendant has been guilty of oppression, fraud, or malice, express or implied.   .   .   ." As we recently explained, "This has long been interpreted to mean that malice in fact, as opposed to malice implied by law, is required. [Citations.] The malice in fact, referred to .   .   . as *animus malus*, may be proved under section 3294 either expressly (by direct evidence probative on the existence of hatred or ill will) or by implication (by indirect evidence from which the jury may draw inferences). [Citation.]" (Bertero v. National General Corp. [529 P.2d 608 (Cal.1974)].)

Other authorities have amplified the foregoing principle. Thus it has been held that the "malice" required by section 3294 "implies an act conceived in a spirit of mischief or with criminal indifference towards the obligations owed to others." [   ]; see Gombos v. Ashe [322 P.2d 933 (App. 1958)]; [   ]. In Dean Prosser's words: "Where the defendant's wrongdoing has been intentional and deliberate, and has the character of outrage frequently associated with crime, all but a few courts have permitted the jury to award in the tort action 'punitive' or 'exemplary' damages.   .   .   . Something more than the mere commission of a tort is always required for punitive damages. There must be circumstances of aggravation or outrage, such as spite or 'malice,' or a fraudulent or evil motive on the part of the defendant, *or such a conscious and deliberate disregard of the interests of others that his conduct may be called wilful or wanton.*" [   ]

Defendant's successful demurrer to the complaint herein was based upon plaintiff's failure to allege any actual intent of defendant to harm plaintiff or others. Is this an essential element of a claim for punitive damages?   .   .   .

.   .   .

We note that when *Gombos* was decided it was unclear whether, as a general principle, an award of punitive damages could be based upon a finding of defendant's conscious disregard of the safety of others. In the evolution of this area of tort law during the ensuing 20 years it has now become generally accepted that such a finding is sufficient. Examining the pleadings before us, we have no difficulty concluding that they contain sufficient allegations upon which it may reasonably be concluded that defendant consciously disregarded the safety of others. There is a very commonly understood risk which attends every motor vehicle driver who is intoxicated.   .   .   . The effect may be lethal whether or not the driver had a prior history of drunk driving incidents.

The allowance of punitive damages in such cases may well be appropriate because of another reason, namely, to deter similar future conduct, the "incalculable cost" of which is well documented. (E.g., *Coulter*, [   ].) Section 3294 expressly provides that punitive damages may be recovered "for the sake of example." .   .   .

We are not unmindful of the speedy legislative response to our *Coulter* holding as evidenced by the very recent enactment of Business and Professions Code section 25602, subdivisions (a) and (c), which absolve the server of alcoholic beverages, commercial or social, from any civil liability to third persons no matter how dangerous or obvious the condition of the consumer of the alcohol.   .   .   . We discern no valid reason whatever for immunizing the driver himself from the exposure to punitive damages given the demonstrable and almost inevitable risk visited upon the innocent public by his voluntary conduct as alleged in the complaint. Indeed, under another recent amendment enacted following our *Coulter* decision, the Legislature has expressly acknowledged that "the consumption of alcoholic beverages is the proximate cause of injuries inflicted upon another by an intoxicated person." (Civ.Code, § 1714, subd. (b).)

Since the filing of *Coulter* we have had the enactment of section 25602. There also has appeared a graphic illustration of the magnitude of the danger in question. In June 1978, the Secretary of Health, Education, and Welfare filed the Third Special Report to the U.S. Congress on Alcohol and Health. We take judicial notice of, and extract the following from, this extensive and very recent official study: "Traffic accidents are the greatest cause of violent death in the United States, and approximately one-third of the ensuing injuries and *one-half of the fatalities are alcohol related*. In 1975, as many as *22,926 traffic deaths involved alcohol.   .   .   .*"

.   .   .

It is crystal clear to us that courts in the formulation of rules on damage assessment and in weighing the deterrent function must recognize the severe threat to the public safety which is posed by the intoxicated driver. The lesson is self-evident and widely understood. Drunken drivers are extremely dangerous people.

.   .   .

Defendant's final contention is that many instances of simple negligent conduct not involving consumption of alcoholic beverages could also be alleged to involve a conscious disregard of the safety of others. For example, one who wilfully disobeys traffic signals or speed limit laws arguably possesses such a state of mind and culpability. That case is not before us and we express no opinion on it.   .   .   .

.   .   .

Let a peremptory writ of mandate issue directing the trial court to overrule defendant Stille's demurrer.

TOBRINER, J., MOSK, J., and MANUEL, J., concurred.

BIRD, C.J. concurring.—Although I concur in the judgment of the court, I must respectfully dissent from that portion of the majority opinion which allows a cause of action for punitive damages in every case where a person has driven under the influence of alcohol. . . .

In this particular case the defendant is charged with repeatedly driving while intoxicated after his own experience has made him completely aware of the possible consequences of his act. Therefore, in this particular case it may be possible for a jury to conclude that "the second time was no accident."

NEWMAN, J., concurred [with Bird, C.J.]

CLARK, J. dissenting.—I share the majority's dismay at the carnage on our highways. And if today's decision would significantly reduce the number of accidents involving drunk drivers, the majority might be justified in changing the law relating to punitive damage. However, today's decision clearly will not reduce the number of drunk drivers on our highways. . . .

The reasons for hesitancy in awarding punitive damages are obvious. First, the plaintiff is fully compensated for injury by compensatory damages. An additional award or fine from the defendant may constitute unjust enrichment. . . .

Second, civil law is concerned with vindicating rights and compensating persons for harm suffered when those rights are invaded. Criminal law is concerned with punishing wrongdoers. In our tripartite system of government, the Legislature prescribes punishment for criminal conduct. . . .

. . . Moreover, when the defendant's conduct also constitutes a crime for which he has been or will be punished, the punitive award constitutes double punishment—potentially in excess of the maximum punishment specified in the Penal Code and a dubious exception to the prohibition against multiple punishment. (Pen.Code, § 654.)

Third, punitive damage trials interfere with policies governing trial procedures. Punishment ordinarily serves as a deterrent to future conduct. As Justice Peters pointed out, if the plaintiff can place punitive damages in issue, it means "that the plaintiffs can offer evidence of the financial status of the defendant. This would convert personal injury cases where intoxication or wilful misconduct are involved from the trial of a negligence case into a field day in which the financial standing of the defendant would become a major issue." [*Gombos*]

Fourth, although situations do exist where punitive awards have a substantial deterrent effect, others exist in which deterrence is marginal at best. Because restitution only requires a wrongdoer give up his unjustified gains, compensatory damage will not always constitute deterrence. If the conduct while clearly wrongful is not criminal, a punitive award may be necessary to deter. Otherwise persons contemplating the wrongful conduct may feel they are in a no-lose situation, only gaining by the wrongful conduct. [   ]

On the other hand, deterrent effect of a punitive award may be minimal or marginal where the conduct already constitutes a crime and the criminal statute is regularly and effectively enforced. Deterrence by punitive award is also marginal where wrongful conduct is as likely to result in injury to the wrongdoer as to others. [   ]

.   .   .

Fifth, the prevalence of liability insurance in our society, requires that any evaluation of punitive damage in accident cases, especially in the context of deterrence, must consider the insurance factor.

Under the traditional view, an award of punitive damage nullifies all insurance coverage. An insurer is not liable for loss intentionally caused by the insured, and any contract providing for liability is void as being against public policy. (Ins. Code § 533; Civ.Code § 1668; [   ].)[5] .   .   .

.   .   .

Sixth, creation of the new punitive award appears contrary to the solicitude for injured wrongdoers reflected by the recent adoption of comparative fault. [   ] A plaintiff guilty of wilful misconduct may not recover any damages against a negligent defendant [   ]. Because malice imports wilfulness, intoxicated drivers will be barred from any recovery against negligent defendants.

The foregoing six considerations suggest we adhere rigidly to Justice Peters' fundamental principle that punitive damage should be awarded with "the greatest caution" in accident cases.

.   .   .

Notes and Questions

1.   What is the crucial difference between the concurring judges and the majority?

2.   What is the relevance of a showing that half of all traffic deaths are "alcohol related?" Should it depend on the proportion of drunk drivers who are actually involved in traffic accidents? Is it a "windfall" for a plaintiff to recover punitive damages when injured by a drunken driver

---

5.   Insurance Code section 533 provides: "An insurer is not liable for a loss caused by the wilful act of the insured; but he is not exonerated by the negligence of the insured, or of the insured's agents or others." Civil Code section 1668 provides: "All contracts which have for their object, directly or indirectly, to exempt anyone from responsibility for his own fraud, or wilful injury to the person or property of another, or violation of law, whether wilful or negligent, are against the policy of the law."

rather than simply a negligent driver? Are all punitive damage awards "windfalls?"

3.   Since this decision, federal bankruptcy law has been amended to deny discharges for judgments against drunk drivers. 11 U.S.C. § 523(a). Does this support the dissent? When would the dissenter allow punitive damages in drunk driving cases? Note that the dissent's sixth point involving comparative negligence was altered by later cases permitting a reckless plaintiff to obtain partial recovery against a negligent defendant, p. 445, supra. The fifth point, concerning insurance coverage, is addressed at p. 744, infra.

4.   Several years after *Taylor* the text of section 3294 was amended to require that the oppression, fraud or malice be "proven by clear and convincing evidence." In addition those three terms were defined as follows:

> (1) "Malice" means conduct which is intended by a defendant to cause injury to the plaintiff or despicable conduct which is carried on by the defendant with a willful and conscious disregard of the rights or safety of others.

> (2) "Oppression" means despicable conduct that subjects a person to cruel and unjust hardship in conscious disregard of that person's rights.

> (3) "Fraud" means an intentional misrepresentation, deceit, or concealment of a material fact known to the defendant with the intention on the part of the defendant of thereby depriving a person of property or legal rights or otherwise causing injury.

Would these definitions change the analysis of *Taylor?* In addition, the legislature provided in section 3295 that, on request, the court must exclude evidence of defendant's profits or financial condition until "after the trier of fact returns a verdict for plaintiff awarding actual damages" and finding the requisite behavior under section 3294. This type of bifurcation is particularly important when the defendant might be exposed to multiple claims for punitive damages, see p. 737, infra.

5.   In Hillrichs v. Avco Corp., 514 N.W.2d 94 (Iowa 1994), the court upheld a compensatory award against the manufacturer of a corn picking machine in favor of a farmer whose hand was caught in the machine. Evidence showed that the manufacturer had known of the danger and had consciously decided not to install an emergency stop device nearby because of the "so-called 'dependency hypothesis,' the theory that the product as designed would discourage farmers from making contact with the roller bed and that the plaintiff's proposed device would invite farmers to unreasonably depend on it despite the dangerousness of the husking roller bed." A jury might disagree with this judgment but that evidence also shows "that an award of punitive damages is inappropriate when room exists for reasonable disagreement over the relative risks and utilities of the conduct and device at issue." There was no showing that defendant's act was "in disregard of a risk that was so great as to make it highly probable that harm would follow." On liability for punitive damages as the result of consciously-made risk/utility decisions, see Schwartz, The Myth of the Ford Pinto Case, 43 Rutgers L.Rev. 1013 (1991).

6. For an economic account of the rationale for punitive damages, see Polinsky and Shavell, Punitive Damages: An Economic Analysis, 111 Harv. L. Rev. 869 (1998), arguing that punitive damages can be justified from a deterrence perspective when defendant has a significant chance of otherwise escaping liability. See also Craswell, Deterrence and Damages: The Multiplier Principle and Its Alternatives, 97 Mich. L. Rev. 2185 (1999). What other justifications might be offered?

For empirical analysis of the impact of punitive damages, see Eisenberg, et al., The Predictability of Punitive Damages, 26 J. Legal Stud. 623 (1997), reporting a punitive damage award rate of less than 10% of jury trials, with a median award of $50,000 and a mean (because of high end awards) of $534,000. See also Galanter, Real World Torts: An Antidote to Anecdote, 55 Md. L. Rev. 1093 (1996), similarly questioning the significance of punitive awards from a system-wide perspective; and in a contrary vein, see Polinsky, Are Punitive Damages Really Insignificant, Predictable and Rational? A Comment on Eisenberg, et al., 26 J. Legal Stud. 663 (1997), emphasizing the potential effects of large and unpredictable awards of punitive damages on the settlement process. See also Sunstein, Kahneman & Schkade, Assessing Punitive Damages (with Notes on Cognition and Valuation in Law), 107 Yale L.J. 2071 (1998) and Schkade, Sunstein & Kahneman, Deliberating About Dollars: The Severity Shift, 100 Colum. L. Rev. 1139 (2000). For references to recent empirical studies and a review of the literature on punitive damages, see Developments in the Law—The Paths of Civil Litigation, 113 Harv L.Rev. 1753, 1783–1806 (2000).

7. The availability of punitive damages may be affected by some of the other legal questions that we have discussed earlier. Thus, some courts that either permit market share liability in the DES situation or help plaintiffs in other ways when they cannot identify the culpable defendant have concluded that in such cases punitive damages are not recoverable. E.g., Collins v. Eli Lilly Co., 342 N.W.2d 37 (Wis.), cert. denied 469 U.S. 826 (1984)(insisting that punitive damages are not recoverable unless it is "certain that the wrongdoer being punished because of his conduct actually caused the plaintiff's injuries.")

8. The general view is that in a comparative fault state, the plaintiff's compensatory award should be reduced to reflect any fault, but punitive awards should not be reduced. See Clark v. Cantrell, 529 S.E.2d 528 (S.C.2000). Why might that be?

9. *Employer liability for punitive damages.* When plaintiffs seek to impose punitive damages on employers, the states have adopted varying positions. In some states, punitive damages flow with vicarious liability. Other states follow the Second Restatement § 909, which provides:

> Punitive damages can properly be awarded against a master or other principal because of an act by an agent if, but only if,

(a) the principal or a managerial agent authorized the doing and the manner of the act, or

(b) the agent was unfit and the principal or a managerial agent was reckless in employing or retaining him, or

(c) the agent was employed in a managerial capacity and was acting in the scope of employment, or

(d) the principal or a managerial agent of the principal ratified or approved the act.

California's approach in § 3294(b) is that no employer is liable for punitive damages based on an employee's actions "unless the employer had advance knowledge of the unfitness of the employee and employed him or her with a conscious disregard of the rights or safety of others or authorized or ratified the wrongful conduct for which the damages are awarded or was personally guilty of oppression, fraud, or malice." In the case of corporate employers, the advance knowledge and the conscious disregard must be on the "part of an officer, director, or managing agent of the corporation." Which view is preferable? In White v. Ultramar, Inc., 981 P.2d 944 (Cal.1999), the court held that the power to hire and fire was not enough to make the employee a "managing agent" for purposes of the statute.

10. *Liability for punitive damages when tortfeasor or victim dies.* The overwhelming majority of states deny recovery of punitive damages from the estate of a deceased tortfeasor. Comment, Punitive Damages and the Deceased Tortfeasor, 98 Dickinson L.Rev. 329 (1994). Is this view consistent with the theory underlying punitive damages? Recall the discussion of whether a victim's estate should be able to recover for the pain and suffering sustained by the victim before death, p. 705, supra. Are the considerations the same for punitive damages when the victim dies before judgment? See Urbaniak v. Newton, 277 Cal.Rptr. 354 (App. 1991), noting that the same statute that bars pain and suffering where the victim has not survived explicitly permits the recovery of punitive damages in such cases.

In G.J.D. v. Johnson, 713 A.2d 1127 (Pa.1998), defendant committed suicide when sued for distributing sexually explicit photos of plaintiff. The court, recognizing that it was joining a small minority and exploring the situation at length, held that punitive damages might be recovered against the estate.

11. What do the purposes of punitive damages suggest about holding the government liable for such damages? Calif. Govt. Code § 818 provides that "a public entity is not liable for damages awarded under § 3294 of the Civil Code or other damages imposed primarily for the sake of example and by way of punishing the defendant." Why not? But see Calif. Govt. Code § 825 permitting the public entity to indemnify officials held liable for such damages under certain conditions.

Is there any reason why a city should not be able to recover punitive damages? See City of Sanger v. Superior Court, 10 Cal.Rptr.2d 436 (App.

1992)(allowing city to recover punitive damages for contamination of its water system).

12.   In Fischer v. Johns–Manville Corp., 512 A.2d 466 (N.J.1986), the court upheld an award in an asbestos case. The court offered two lists of factors: one for the question whether to award punitive damages and one for measuring the appropriate size of the recovery. Should the long passage of time between act and injury influence the availability of punitive damages? The *Fischer* court focused on asbestos cases. Might one argue that the result should differ in other types of cases? Is it realistic to suggest that investors carefully study the past practices of a corporation before investing in it?

BMW of North America, Inc. v. Gore

Supreme Court of the United States, 1996.
517 U.S. 559, 116 S.Ct. 1589, 134 L.Ed.2d 809.

JUSTICE STEVENS delivered the opinion of the Court.

The Due Process Clause of the Fourteenth Amendment prohibits a State from imposing a " 'grossly excessive' " punishment on a tortfeasor. TXO Production Corp. v. Alliance Resources Corp., 509 U.S. 443, 454 (1993) (and cases cited). The wrongdoing involved in this case was the decision by a national distributor of automobiles not to advise its dealers, and hence their customers, of pre-delivery damage to new cars when the cost of repair amounted to less than 3% of the car's suggested retail price. The question presented is whether a $2 million punitive damages award to the purchaser of one of these cars exceeds the constitutional limit.

[Parts of plaintiff's car had been repainted, at a cost of about $600, or 1.5% of the car's price, due to acid rain during transit. Plaintiff was not told about this. Some 13 other cars were similarly sold in Alabama—and some 983 with repair costs of over $300 were sold as new nationwide without informing either the dealer or the customer. BMW's policy at the time was to advise only if the repairs cost over 3% of the retail price—a policy that at the time conformed with the most stringent state statute on the subject. At trial, the jury concluded that plaintiff had suffered $4,000 in actual damages from loss of market value and awarded $4 million in punitive damages, "based on a determination that the nondisclosure policy constituted 'gross, oppressive or malicious' fraud." A few days after the jury award, BMW instituted a national policy of informing of all repairs no matter how minor. The state supreme court reduced the punitive award to $2 million. Some concern was expressed about the use of out-of-state sales to measure the award. The state court's "discussion of the amount of its remitted award expressly disclaimed any reliance on 'acts that occurred in other jurisdictions;' instead, the court explained that it had used a 'comparative analysis' that considered Alabama cases, 'along with cases from other jurisdictions, involving the sale of an automobile where the seller misrepresented the condition of the vehicle and the jury awarded punitive damages to the purchaser.' "]

. . . . Based on its analysis, the [state supreme] court concluded that BMW's conduct was "reprehensible"; the nondisclosure was profitable for the company; the judgment "would not have a substantial impact upon [BMW's] financial position"; the litigation had been expensive; no criminal sanctions had been imposed on BMW for the same conduct; the award of *no* punitive damages in *Yates* [a similar case brought before *Gore*] reflected "the inherent uncertainty of the trial process"; and the punitive award bore a "reasonable relationship" to "the harm that was likely to occur from [BMW's] conduct as well as . . . the harm that actually occurred." [   ]

. . .

II

Punitive damages may properly be imposed to further a State's legitimate interests in punishing unlawful conduct and deterring its repetition. Gertz v. Robert Welch, Inc., 418 U.S. 323, 350 (1974); [   ]. In our federal system, States necessarily have considerable flexibility in determining the level of punitive damages that they will allow in different classes of cases and in any particular case. Most States that authorize exemplary damages afford the jury similar latitude, requiring only that the damages awarded be reasonably necessary to vindicate the State's legitimate interests in punishment and deterrence. See [*TXO* and Pacific Mutual Life Ins. Co. v. Haslip, 499 U.S. 1 (1991)]. Only when an award can fairly be categorized as "grossly excessive" in relation to these interests does it enter the zone of arbitrariness that violates the Due Process Clause of the Fourteenth Amendment. [   ] For that reason, the federal excessiveness inquiry appropriately begins with an identification of the state interests that a punitive award is designed to serve. We therefore focus our attention first on the scope of Alabama's legitimate interests in punishing BMW and deterring it from future misconduct.

No one doubts that a State may protect its citizens by prohibiting deceptive trade practices and by requiring automobile distributors to disclose presale repairs that affect the value of a new car. But the States need not, and in fact do not, provide such protection in a uniform manner. Some States rely on the judicial process to formulate and enforce an appropriate disclosure requirement by applying principles of contract and tort law. Other States have enacted various forms of legislation that define the disclosure obligations of automobile manufacturers, distributors, and dealers. The result is a patchwork of rules representing the diverse policy judgments of lawmakers in 50 States.

That diversity demonstrates that reasonable people may disagree about the value of a full disclosure requirement. Some legislatures may conclude that affirmative disclosure requirements are unnecessary because the self-interest of those involved in the automobile trade in developing and maintaining the goodwill of their customers will motivate them to make voluntary disclosures or to refrain from selling cars that do not comply with self-imposed standards. Those legislatures that do adopt affirmative disclosure obligations may take into account the cost of government regulation, choosing to draw a line exempting minor repairs from such a requirement. In formulating a disclosure standard, States may also consider other goals, such as providing a "safe harbor" for automobile manufacturers, distributors, and dealers against lawsuits over minor repairs.

We may assume, *arguendo*, that it would be wise for every State to adopt Dr. Gore's preferred rule, requiring full disclosure of every presale repair to a car, no matter how trivial and regardless of its actual impact on the value of the car. But while we do not doubt that Congress has ample authority to enact such a policy for the entire Nation, it is clear that no single State could do so, or even impose its own policy choice on neighboring States. [   ] Similarly, one State's power to impose burdens on the interstate market for automobiles is not only subordinate to the federal power over interstate commerce, [   ], but is also constrained by the need to respect the interests of other States, [   ].

We think it follows from these principles of state sovereignty and comity that a State may not impose economic sanctions on violators of its laws with the intent of changing the tortfeasors' lawful conduct in other States. Before this Court Dr. Gore argued that the large punitive damages award was necessary to induce BMW to change the nationwide policy that it adopted in 1983. But by attempting to alter BMW's nationwide policy, Alabama would be infringing on the policy choices of other States. To avoid such encroachment, the economic penalties that a State such as Alabama inflicts on those who transgress its laws, whether the penalties take the form of legislatively authorized fines or judicially imposed punitive damages, must be supported by the State's interest in protecting its own consumers and its own economy.   .   .   .

[Although the jury award reflected out-of-state conduct, the state court] properly eschewed reliance on BMW's out-of-state conduct, [   ], and based its remitted award solely on conduct that occurred within Alabama. The award must be analyzed in the light of the same conduct, with consideration given only to the interests of Alabama consumers, rather than those of the entire Nation. When the scope of the interest in punishment and deterrence that an Alabama court may appropriately consider is properly limited, it is apparent—for reasons that we shall now address—that this award is grossly excessive.

III

Elementary notions of fairness enshrined in our constitutional jurisprudence dictate that a person receive fair notice not only of the conduct that will subject him to punishment, but also of the severity of the penalty that a State may impose. Three guideposts, each of which indicates that BMW did not receive adequate notice of the magnitude of the sanction that Alabama might impose for adhering to the nondisclosure policy adopted in 1983, lead us to the conclusion that the $2 million award against BMW is grossly excessive: the degree of reprehensibility of the nondisclosure; the disparity between the harm or potential harm suffered by Dr. Gore and his punitive damages award; and the difference between this remedy and the civil penalties authorized or imposed in comparable cases. We discuss these considerations in turn.

Degree of Reprehensibility

Perhaps the most important indicium of the reasonableness of a punitive damages award is the degree of reprehensibility of the defendant's conduct. As the Court stated nearly 150 years ago, exemplary damages imposed on a defendant should reflect "the enormity of his offense." [ ] This principle reflects the accepted view that some wrongs are more blameworthy than others. Thus, we have said that "nonviolent crimes are less serious than crimes marked by violence or the threat of violence." [ ] Similarly, "trickery and deceit," [ ], are more reprehensible than negligence. In *TXO*, both the West Virginia Supreme Court and the Justices of this Court placed special emphasis on the principle that punitive damages may not be "grossly out of proportion to the severity of the offense." . . .

In this case, none of the aggravating factors associated with particularly reprehensible conduct is present. The harm BMW inflicted on Dr. Gore was purely economic in nature. The presale refinishing of the car had no effect on its performance or safety features, or even its appearance for at least nine months after his purchase. BMW's conduct evinced no indifference to or reckless disregard for the health and safety of others. To be sure, infliction of economic injury, especially when done intentionally through affirmative acts of misconduct, [ ], or when the target is financially vulnerable, can warrant a substantial penalty. But this observation does not convert all acts that cause economic harm into torts that are sufficiently reprehensible to justify a significant sanction in addition to compensatory damages.

. . . .

Finally, the record in this case discloses no deliberate false statements, acts of affirmative misconduct, or concealment of evidence of improper motive, such as were present in *Haslip* and *TXO*. [ ] We accept, of course, the jury's finding that BMW suppressed a material fact which Alabama law obligated it to communicate to prospective purchasers of repainted cars in that State. But the omission of a material fact may be less reprehensible than a deliberate false statement, particularly when there is a good-faith basis for believing that no duty to disclose exists.

That conduct is sufficiently reprehensible to give rise to tort liability, and even a modest award of exemplary damages does not establish the high degree of culpability that warrants a substantial punitive damages award. Because this case exhibits none of the circumstances ordinarily associated with egregiously improper conduct, we are persuaded that BMW's conduct was not sufficiently reprehensible to warrant imposition of a $2 million exemplary damages award.

Ratio

The second and perhaps most commonly cited indicium of an unreasonable or excessive punitive damages award is its ratio to the actual harm inflicted on the plaintiff. See [*TXO* and *Haslip*]. The principle that exemplary damages must bear a "reasonable relationship" to compensatory damages has a long pedigree. Scholars have identified a number of early English statutes authorizing the award of multiple damages for particular wrongs. Some 65 different enactments during the period between 1275 and 1753 provided for double, treble, or quadruple damages. Our decisions in both *Haslip* and *TXO* endorsed the proposition that a comparison between the compensatory award and the punitive award is significant.

In *Haslip* we concluded that even though a punitive damages award of "more than 4 times the amount of compensatory damages" might be "close to the line," it did not "cross the line into the area of constitutional impropriety." [   ] *TXO*, following dicta in *Haslip*, refined this analysis by confirming that the proper inquiry is " 'whether there is a reasonable relationship between the punitive damages award and *the harm likely to result* from the defendant's conduct as well as the harm that actually has occurred.' " [*TXO*, (emphasis in original), quoting *Haslip*]. Thus, in upholding the $10 million award in *TXO*, we relied on the difference between that figure and the harm to the victim that would have ensued if the tortious plan had succeeded. That difference suggested that the relevant ratio was not more than 10 to 1.

The $2 million in punitive damages awarded to Dr. Gore by the Alabama Supreme Court is 500 times the amount of his actual harm as determined by the jury. [The Court noted that even if the 13 other Alabama plaintiffs were included at $4,000 each, the award would have been 35 times greater than the total actual damages of the 14 plaintiffs.] Moreover, there is no suggestion that Dr. Gore or any other BMW purchaser was threatened with any additional potential harm by BMW's nondisclosure policy. The disparity in this case is thus dramatically greater than those considered in *Haslip* and *TXO*.

Of course, we have consistently rejected the notion that the constitutional line is marked by a simple mathematical formula, even one that compares actual *and potential* damages to the punitive award. [*TXO*] Indeed, low awards of compensatory damages may properly support a higher ratio than high compensatory awards, if, for example, a particularly egregious act has resulted in only a small amount of economic damages. A higher ratio may also be justified in cases in which the injury is hard to detect or the monetary value of noneconomic harm might have been difficult to determine. It is appropriate, therefore, to reiterate our rejection of a categorical approach. Once again, "we return to what we said . . . in *Haslip*: 'We need not, and indeed we cannot, draw a mathematical bright line between the constitutionally acceptable and the constitutionally unacceptable that would fit every case. We can say, however, that [a] general concer[n] of reasonableness . . . properly enter[s] into the constitutional calculus.' " [   ] In most cases, the ratio will be within a constitutionally acceptable range, and remittitur will not be justified on this basis. When the ratio is a breathtaking 500 to 1, however, the award must surely "raise a suspicious judicial eyebrow." [*TXO*, [   ] (O'CONNOR, J., dissenting)].

Sanctions for Comparable Misconduct

Comparing the punitive damages award and the civil or criminal penalties that could be imposed for comparable misconduct provides a third indicium of excessiveness. As Justice O'CONNOR has correctly observed, a reviewing court engaged in determining whether an award of punitive damages is excessive should "accord 'substantial deference' to legislative judgments concerning appropriate sanctions for the conduct at issue." [   ] In *Haslip*, [   ], the Court noted that although the exemplary award was "much in excess of the fine that could be imposed," imprisonment was also authorized in the criminal context. In this case the $2 million economic sanction imposed on BMW is substantially greater than the statutory fines available in Alabama and elsewhere for similar malfeasance.

The maximum civil penalty authorized by the Alabama Legislature for a violation of its Deceptive Trade Practices Act is $2,000; other States authorize more severe sanctions, with the maxima ranging from $5,000 to $10,000. Significantly, some statutes draw a distinction between first offenders and recidivists; thus, in New York the penalty is $50 for a first offense and $250 for subsequent offenses. None of these statutes would provide an out-of-state distributor with fair notice that the first violation—or, indeed the first 14 violations—of its provisions might subject an offender to a multimillion dollar penalty. Moreover, at the time BMW's policy was first challenged, there does not appear to have been any judicial decision in Alabama or elsewhere indicating that application of that policy might give rise to such severe punishment.

The sanction imposed in this case cannot be justified on the ground that it was necessary to deter future misconduct without considering whether less drastic remedies could be expected to achieve that goal. The fact that a multimillion dollar penalty prompted a change in policy sheds no light on the question whether a lesser deterrent would have adequately protected the interests of Alabama consumers. In the absence of a history of noncompliance with known statutory requirements, there is no basis for assuming that a more modest sanction would not have been sufficient to motivate full compliance with the disclosure requirement imposed by the Alabama Supreme Court in this case.

IV

We assume, as the juries in this case and in the *Yates* case found, that the undisclosed damage to the new BMW's affected their actual value. Notwithstanding the evidence adduced by BMW in an effort to prove that the repainted cars conformed to the same quality standards as its other cars, we also assume that it knew, or should have known, that as time passed the repainted cars would lose their attractive appearance more rapidly than other BMW's. Moreover, we of course accept the Alabama courts' view that the state interest in protecting its citizens from deceptive trade practices justifies a sanction in addition to the recovery of compensatory damages. We cannot, however, accept the conclusion of the Alabama

Supreme Court that BMW's conduct was sufficiently egregious to justify a punitive sanction that is tantamount to a severe criminal penalty.

The fact that BMW is a large corporation rather than an impecunious individual does not diminish its entitlement to fair notice of the demands that the several States impose on the conduct of its business. Indeed, its status as an active participant in the national economy implicates the federal interest in preventing individual States from imposing undue burdens on interstate commerce. While each State has ample power to protect its own consumers, none may use the punitive damages deterrent as a means of imposing its regulatory policies on the entire Nation.

As in *Haslip*, we are not prepared to draw a bright line marking the limits of a constitutionally acceptable punitive damages award. Unlike that case, however, we are fully convinced that the grossly excessive award imposed in this case transcends the constitutional limit. Whether the appropriate remedy requires a new trial or merely an independent determination by the Alabama Supreme Court of the award necessary to vindicate the economic interests of Alabama consumers is a matter that should be addressed by the state court in the first instance.

The judgment is reversed, and the case is remanded for further proceedings not inconsistent with this opinion.

It is so ordered.

JUSTICE BREYER, with whom JUSTICE O'CONNOR and JUSTICE SOUTER join, concurring.

The Alabama state courts have assessed the defendant $2 million in "punitive damages" for having knowingly failed to tell a BMW automobile buyer that, at a cost of $600, it had repainted portions of his new $40,000 car, thereby lowering its potential resale value by about 10%. The Court's opinion, which I join, explains why we have concluded that this award, in this case, was "grossly excessive" in relation to legitimate punitive damages objectives, and hence an arbitrary deprivation of life, liberty, or property in violation of the Due Process Clause. [   ] Members of this Court have generally thought, however, that if "fair procedures were followed, a judgment that is a product of that process is entitled to a strong presumption of validity." [   ] And the Court also has found that punitive damages procedures very similar to those followed here were not, by themselves, fundamentally unfair. [   ] Thus, I believe it important to explain why this presumption of validity is overcome in this instance.

The reason flows from the Court's emphasis in *Haslip* upon the constitutional importance of legal standards that provide "reasonable constraints" within which "discretion is exercised," that assure "meaningful and adequate review by the trial court whenever a jury has fixed the punitive damages," and permit "appellate review [that] makes certain that the punitive damages are reasonable in their amount and rational in light of their purpose to punish what has occurred and to deter its repetition."
[   ]

This constitutional concern, itself harkening back to the Magna Carta, arises out of the basic unfairness of depriving citizens of life, liberty, or property, through the application, not of law and legal processes, but of arbitrary coercion.   .   .   .

Legal standards need not be precise in order to satisfy this constitutional concern. [   ] But they must offer some kind of constraint upon a jury or court's discretion, and thus protection against purely arbitrary behavior. The standards the Alabama courts applied here are vague and open ended to the point where they risk arbitrary results. In my view, although the vagueness of those standards does not, by itself, violate due process, see [*Haslip*], it does invite the kind of scrutiny the Court has given the particular verdict before us. [   ] This is because the standards, as the Alabama Supreme Court authoritatively interpreted them here, provided no significant constraints or protection against arbitrary results.

[After reviewing in detail the Alabama punitive damages statute and the state supreme court's application of its court-fashioned "factors" for determining arbitrariness in the context of this case, Justice Breyer concluded:]

The upshot is that the rules that purport to channel discretion in this kind of case, here did not do so in fact. That means that the award in this case was both (a) the product of a system of standards that did not significantly constrain a court's, and hence a jury's, discretion in making that award; and (b) grossly excessive in light of the State's legitimate punitive damages objectives.

The first of these reasons has special importance where courts review a jury-determined punitive damages award. That is because one cannot expect to direct jurors like legislators through the ballot box; nor can one expect those jurors to interpret law like judges, who work within a discipline and hierarchical organization that normally promotes roughly uniform interpretation and application of the law. Yet here Alabama expects jurors to act, at least a little, like legislators or judges, for it permits them, to a certain extent, to create public policy and to apply that policy, not to compensate a victim, but to achieve a policy-related objective outside the confines of the particular case.

To the extent that neither clear legal principles nor fairly obvious historical or community-based standards (defining, say, especially egregious behavior) significantly constrain punitive damages awards, is there not a substantial risk of outcomes so arbitrary that they become difficult to square with the Constitution's assurance, to every citizen, of the law's protection? The standards here, as authoritatively interpreted, in my view, make this threat real and not theoretical. And, in these unusual circumstances, where legal standards offer virtually no constraint, I believe that this lack of constraining standards warrants this Court's detailed examination of the award.

The second reason—the severe disproportionality between the award and the legitimate punitive damages objectives—reflects a judgment about a matter of degree. I recognize that it is often difficult to determine just when a punitive award exceeds an amount reasonably related to a State's legitimate interests, or when that excess is so great as to amount to a matter of constitutional concern. Yet whatever the difficulties of drawing a precise line, once we examine the award in this case, it is not difficult to say that this award lies on the line's far side. The severe lack of proportionality between the size of the award and the underlying punitive damages objectives shows that the award falls into the category of "gross excessiveness" set forth in this Court's prior cases.

These two reasons *taken together* overcome what would otherwise amount to a "strong presumption of validity." [*TXO*] And, for those two reasons, I conclude that the award in this unusual case violates the basic guarantee of nonarbitrary governmental behavior that the Due Process Clause provides.

JUSTICE SCALIA, with whom JUSTICE THOMAS joins, dissenting.

Today we see the latest manifestation of this Court's recent and increasingly insistent "concern about punitive damages that 'run wild.'" [*Haslip*]. Since the Constitution does not make that concern any of our business, the Court's activities in this area are an unjustified incursion into the province of state governments.

In earlier cases that were the prelude to this decision, I set forth my view that a state trial procedure that commits the decision whether to impose punitive damages, and the amount, to the discretion of the jury, subject to some judicial review for "reasonableness," furnishes a defendant with all the process that is "due." [   ] I do not regard the Fourteenth Amendment's Due Process Clause as a secret repository of substantive guarantees against "unfairness"—neither the unfairness of an excessive civil compensatory award, nor the unfairness of an "unreasonable" punitive award. What the Fourteenth Amendment's procedural guarantee assures is an opportunity to contest the reasonableness of a damages judgment in state court; but there is no federal guarantee a damages award actually *be* reasonable. [   ]

This view, which adheres to the text of the Due Process Clause, has not prevailed in our punitive damages cases. . . . The Constitution provides no warrant for federalizing yet another aspect of our Nation's legal culture (no matter how much in need of correction it may be), and the application of the Court's new rule of constitutional law is constrained by no principle other than the Justices' subjective assessment of the "reasonableness" of the award in relation to the conduct for which it was assessed.

.   .   .

The relationship between judicial application of the new "guideposts" and jury findings poses a real problem for the Court, since as a matter of logic there is no more justification for ignoring the jury's determination as to *how* reprehensible petitioner's conduct was (i.e., how much it deserves to be punished), than there is for ignoring its determination that it was reprehensible *at all* (i.e., that the wrong was willful and punitive damages are therefore recoverable). That the issue has been framed in terms of a constitutional right against unreasonably *excessive* awards should not obscure the fact that the logical and necessary consequence of the Court's approach is the recognition of a constitutional right against unreasonably *imposed* awards as well. The elevation of "fairness" in punishment to a principle of "substantive due process" means that every punitive award unreasonably imposed is unconstitutional; such an award is by definition excessive, since it attaches a penalty to conduct undeserving of punishment. Indeed, if the Court is correct, it must be that every claim that a state jury's award of *compensatory* damages is "unreasonable" (because not supported by the evidence) amounts to an assertion of constitutional injury. [   ] And the same would be true for determinations of liability. By today's logic, *every* dispute as to evidentiary sufficiency in a state civil suit poses a question of constitutional moment, subject to review in this Court. That is a stupefying proposition.

For the foregoing reasons, I respectfully dissent.

JUSTICE GINSBURG, with whom THE CHIEF JUSTICE joins, dissenting.

The Court, I am convinced, unnecessarily and unwisely ventures into territory traditionally within the States' domain, and does so in the face of reform measures recently adopted or currently under consideration in legislative arenas. The Alabama Supreme Court, in this case, endeavored to follow this Court's prior instructions; and, more recently, Alabama's highest court has installed further controls on awards of punitive damages [referring to bifurcation, special verdicts, and—after litigation expenses are paid—the equal division of any award between the plaintiff and the state]. I would therefore leave the state court's judgment undisturbed, and resist unnecessary intrusion into an area dominantly of state concern.

.   .   .

The Court finds Alabama's $2 million award not simply excessive, but grossly so, and therefore unconstitutional. The decision leads us further into territory traditionally within the States' domain, and commits the Court, now and again, to correct "misapplication of a properly stated rule of law." .   .   . The Court is not well equipped for this mission. Tellingly, the Court repeats that it brings to the task no "mathematical formula," [   ], no "categorical approach," [   ], no "bright line," [   ]. It has only a vague concept of substantive due process, a "raised eyebrow" test, [   ], as its ultimate guide. [At the end of a footnote at this point, Justice Ginsburg stated: "What is the Court's measure of too big? Not a cap of the kind a legislature could order, or a mathematical test this Court can divine and impose. Too big is, in the end, the amount at which five Members of the Court bridle." At the end of her opinion, she attached an appendix documenting state legislative actions that either set caps on awards, provide for payment of sums to state agencies, or mandate bifurcated trials as to punitive damages.]

Notes and Questions

1. What does the concurrence add to the majority opinion? How do the dissents differ from each other?

2. In the cited *TXO* case, the Court upheld a West Virginia punitive award of $10 million, 526 times larger than the compensatory award of $19,000. The Court rejected a constitutional challenge based on the disparity. There was no maximum ratio that one part of the award had to bear to the other. The Court quoted approvingly a passage from an earlier West Virginia case:

> For instance, a man wildly fires a gun into a crowd. By sheer chance, no one is injured and the only damage is to a $10 pair of glasses. A jury reasonably could find only $10 in compensatory damages, but thousands of dollars in punitive damages in order to discourage future bad acts.

Might it be "millions" instead of thousands if the defendant was very wealthy and the behavior truly outrageous? Is *BMW* consistent with *TXO*?

3. *Defendant's wealth.* Do the Court's three factors include defendant's wealth? Would that be appropriate? The role of wealth has been important at the state level. Some state courts or statutes appear to require the plaintiff to show that wealth as part of the case for punitive damages. See, e.g., Herman v. Sunshine Chemical Specialties, Inc., 627 A.2d 1081 (N.J.1993) and Adams v. Murakami, 813 P.2d 1348 (Cal.1991). But see Hall v. Wal–Mart, 959 P.2d 109 (Utah 1998) in which the defendant challenged a punitive award of $25,000 for lack of proof of wealth. The court, 3–2, held that this was not necessary in every case. It relied heavily on Kemezy v. Peters, 79 F.3d 33 (7th Cir.1996), in which Judge Posner observed:

> The reprehensibility of a person's conduct is not mitigated by his not being a rich person, and plaintiffs are never required to apologize for seeking damages that if awarded will precipitate the defendant into bankruptcy. A plea of poverty is a classic appeal to the mercy of the judge or jury, and why the plaintiff should be required to make the pleas on behalf of his opponent eludes us. . . . The defendant who cannot pay a large award of punitive damages can point this out to the jury so that they will not waste their time and that of the bankruptcy courts by awarding an amount that exceeds his ability to pay.

The *Hall* court did note, however, that a plaintiff might be well advised to present evidence on this question when requesting a very large punitive award because an award that might otherwise be presumptively excessive under prevailing standards "can be justified by the defendant's relative wealth." The dissenters objected that the majority had read "relative wealth" out of the state's list of seven factors to be used whenever punitive damages were considered.

Although it has sometimes been suggested that punitive awards may not exceed some percentage of the defendant's assets, courts appear to focus more on the conduct in question. See Rufo v. Simpson, 2001 WL

65512 (Cal.App.2001), affirming two punitive damage awards of $12.5 million against a defendant the jury found to have committed two murders.

   4.   Despite *Gore*, large awards may still be upheld. In CSX Transportation, Inc. v. Palank, 743 So.2d 556 (Fla.App.1999), cert. denied 121 S.Ct. 65 (2000), the court upheld awards of $6.14 million in compensatory damages and $50 million in punitive damages in a wrongful death arising from a railroad accident. Plaintiff had asked for a punitive award of between $275 and $550 million. The evidence showed that the accident had been caused by a switch that broke at least seven months before the accident—and which had been installed backwards some ten years earlier—and that the defendant knew about the problem. There was also evidence that required track inspections were not made and that defendant filed false safety reports. Defendant was shown to have saved $2.4 billion over ten years by a "systematic reduction in its maintenance of way employees." The court agreed with the trial court's determination that the conduct in question "not only bespeaks culpable negligence. It is borderline criminal."

   In Ford v. Herman, 737 N.E.2d 332 (Ill.App. 2000), the defendant was held liable for $80,000 in compensatory damages and $6 million in punitive damages for an auto accident caused by his driving while intoxicated. At that time, it was his third such offense. Between then and appeal he was convicted two more times. The claim of disproportion was rejected: "Given the outrageousness of Herman's behavior, the fact that the award clearly serves the punishment and deterrence purposes of a punitive damages award, and the lack of proof of passion, partiality, or corruption, we conclude that the amount in question is not excessive." Does the constitution bar this award—in which the ratio is 75:1? Suppose the compensatory damages had been $8,000?

   See also Harris v. Soley, 756 A.2d 499 (Maine 2000), involving a punitive award to tenants who had to endure very difficult living conditions and who were harassed and threatened by their landlord. The punitive award was $1 million, roughly 16 times the compensatory awards of $62,060. After reviewing the facts and other high ratios, the court upheld the award.

   5.   *Repeated awards.* In W.R. Grace & Co. v. Waters, 638 So.2d 502 (Fla.1994), a mass tort action involving asbestos products, the court refused to bar multiple awards of punitive damages. The court noted that other courts have "unanimously" rejected the idea that such damages be awarded only once—perhaps to the first successful plaintiff:

> We acknowledge the potential for abuse when a defendant may be subjected to repeated punitive damage awards arising out of the same conduct. Yet, like the many other courts which have addressed the problem, we are unable to devise a fair and effective solution. Were we to adopt the position advocated by Grace, our holding would not be binding on other state courts or federal courts. This would place Floridians injured by asbestos on an unequal footing with the citizens of other states with regard to the right to recover damages from

companies who engage in extreme misconduct. Any realistic solution to the problems caused by the asbestos litigation in the United States must be applicable to all fifty states. It is our belief that such a uniform solution can only be effected by federal legislation.

Although the lower court had suggested that Grace could use the fact of prior awards as mitigation before this jury, "advising the jury of previous punitive damage awards would actually hurt its cause" as it tries to argue that it should not be punished at all. The *Grace* court sought to meet this concern by ordering lower courts to bifurcate the proceeding. The first step would permit evidence on (1) liability, (2) the amount of compensatory damages and (3) liability for punitive damages. If the jury determines that punitive damages are appropriate, the second step would permit evidence on the amount of such damages, including any prior awards. This would permit defendant to "build a record for a due process argument based on the cumulative effect of prior awards." More than a dozen states use this type of bifurcation. See also Owens–Corning Fiberglas Corp. v. Ballard, 749 So.2d 483 (Fla.1999), upholding a punitive award of $31 million in an asbestos case.

For an extended consideration of the problem of exposure to repeated punitive awards, see Dunn v. HOVIC, 1 F.3d 1371 (3d Cir. en banc), cert. denied 510 U.S. 1031 (1993), holding, 8–5, that repeated awards are not per se unconstitutional, though repeated awards may be relevant in assessing constitutional attacks on the awards—either on the ground that the total sum is too high or on the ground that the particular defendant cannot afford to pay them. The dissenting opinion of Judge Weis emphasized that even within a single state early punitive awards risked leaving later victims without recovery for even their compensatory damages.

Does the existence of a large number of claims for the same conduct argue against the availability of punitive damages?

6. *Statutory change.* Justice Ginsburg's dissent relied in part on the actions that states were taking to constrain punitive damages. As the end of the excerpt notes, statutory change has occurred in more than half the states. A handful have abolished punitive damages, joining another handful that had long taken that position. A few states require that plaintiffs share their punitive awards with the state; others have increased the burden of proof to "clear and convincing;" and a dozen or so have set maximum dollar amounts or ratios above which punitive damages may not be recovered—such as a cap of $250,000 or three times compensatory damages, whichever is higher. Which of these alternative approaches seems most desirable? In states that have adopted these statutory limitations, do the constitutional constraints of *Gore* add anything?

7. An unresolved issue is what standard should be used for the appellate review of an award of punitive damages. The circuits are split between the "abuse of discretion" and "de novo review" standards. The Supreme Court granted certiorari limited to the question: "What is the standard of review of a trial court's ruling on a challenge to the constitutionality of a punitive damage award?" Leatherman Tool Group, Inc. v.

Cooper Industries, Inc., 205 F.3d 1351 (9th Cir.1999), cert. granted 121 S.Ct. 297 (2000).

8. For general discussions of punitive damages, see Symposium, The Future of Punitive Damages, 1998 Wis. L.Rev. 1–462.

B. INTRODUCTION TO INSURANCE

Inevitably a course on tort law emphasizes accidental injuries caused by others. In the real world, however, we often accidentally hurt ourselves or suffer injury at the hands of natural forces that are not subject to tort law. As society has grown more affluent, many more individuals have sought to insure themselves and their families against the financial burden of these misfortunes. The institution of life insurance, which is several hundred years old, was developed to permit a person to protect others against the insured's premature death. (Since death is inevitable, many view life insurance as a form of savings rather than insurance.) Insurance against loss of property is older than life insurance. The twentieth century saw the emergence of insurance against the expenses of hospitalization, unusual medical expenses, disruption of income as the result of an accident or illness, and disability. In each of these forms of insurance, the insured is seeking protection against the financial consequences of the occurrence of an undesired event—without regard to any legal rules of tort liability. This is called "first-party" insurance: protection of the insured or the insured's family from the direct adverse economic effects of a particular event. Liability insurance, taken out to protect the insured against the economic impact of having to pay damages to another person, is called "third-party" insurance because the insurer pays a third person for a loss the insured has caused. Liability insurance did not appear until the end of the nineteenth century.

Although third-party and first-party insurance come into play in different situations and serve different goals, they may co-exist in the same insurance policy. The conventional automobile insurance policy contains both first-party and third-party provisions.

First-party coverages:

Medical Payments (Med. Pay.) coverage provides protection against specified amounts of hospital and medical costs for each person injured in the policyholder's vehicle (usually a relatively small amount, e.g., $5,000).

Collision insurance covers the cost of repairs to a policyholder's car after an accident, regardless of whether the policyholder is at fault.

Comprehensive (Comp.) coverage protects the policyholder's car against the perils of fire, theft, flood, vandalism or malicious mischief.

Personal Injury Protection (PIP)—available only in no-fault States.

Third-party coverages:

> Bodily Injury Liability (BI) is the coverage that compensates the economic and non-economic bodily losses of third parties resulting from accidents in which the policyholder (or other lawful operator) is found to be at fault. It is usually sold in varying multiples of thousands of dollars of coverage per person and per occurrence. For example, BI coverage of $25,000/$50,000 would provide protection up to $25,000 for each person, and up to $50,000 for all persons, injured in an accident in which the policyholder (or other lawful operator) is at fault. BI coverage also obligates the insurer to defend the policyholder against third-party bodily injury claims.

> Property Damage Liability (PD) coverage compensates third parties for loss of or damage to their property (whether a picket fence or a car) inflicted by the policyholder's vehicle under circumstances in which the policyholder (or other lawful operator) is found to be at fault. Here, too, the insurer is obligated to defend the policyholder against third-party claims.

Some coverages are hybrids that partake of both first and third party coverage:

> Uninsured Motorists (UM) coverage provides specified amounts of protection to the policyholder and occupants of his or her car against bodily injury and property damage losses incurred in an accident in which the other driver is uninsured and is determined to be at fault. [Underinsured motorist coverage operates in a similar fashion.]

First-party coverages are offered with a variety of coverage limitations and deductible amounts. Deductibles are not generally available under third-party coverages.

———

As does auto insurance, homeowner's insurance has both first-party and third-party aspects. Briefly, this coverage is primarily what homeowners buy to protect the value of their property against loss by fire or, in some cases, earthquake. A property owner with a mortgage may be required to purchase such insurance to secure the value of the loan. There is, however, a third-party aspect to the policy—a liability coverage that protects the insured against liability that is incurred in non-vehicular contexts. This aspect is at the center of the *Lalomia* case, p. 767, infra.

Before exploring the impact of first-party and third-party insurance on tort law, we consider some important questions of when and whether it is permissible to buy protection against certain risks. These restrictions may be found either in the insurance contract itself or may be imposed by law.

Contractual restrictions on coverage. The most important contractual restriction on coverage for tort law purposes is the common insurer goal of covering only "accidents." The contract language either limits coverage to "accidents," often defined as a "sudden event . . . neither expected or intended by the insured," or offers broad coverage and then excludes coverage of actions that are "intentional." Two lines of cases have emerged and are summarized in Cooperative Fire Ins. Ass'n v. Combs, 648 A.2d 857 (Vt.1994), involving a shooting death and an insurance policy that excluded coverage of liability resulting from "an intentional act of an insured." It was stipulated that the shooter-insured was "insane." One line of cases holds that "an insane person cannot act intentionally as a matter of law" for insurance purposes and the second holds that "so long as there is evidence that the insured understood the physical nature and consequences of his action, he is capable of intent even though he may not be capable of distinguishing between right and wrong or of controlling his conduct." Even under this second view "there will be coverage if the insured is so mentally ill that he does not, in fact, know what he is doing, as when, for instance, he points a pistol thinking he is peeling a banana." The court adopted the first view. What are the consequences to the victims, the insured, and the insurer of adopting the first view? The second view?

The reasons for the various positions are explored in Hanover Ins. Co. v. Talhouni, 604 N.E.2d 689 (Mass.1992)(coverage for insured who assaulted stranger while on "bad trip" from LSD and who "was completely out of touch with reality, was hallucinating and delusional, and did not know that he was assaulting another human being"); Municipal Mut. Ins. Co. v. Mangus, 443 S.E.2d 455 (W.Va.1994)(no coverage where insured shot neighbor: "he knew he was picking up a gun and not a banana; that when he went outside with that gun, he knew he was pointing the gun at a man and knew that man was Rickey Fields"); Auto–Owners Ins. Co. v. Churchman, 489 N.W.2d 431 (Mich.1992) (holding that even though "an insane or mentally ill insured may be unable to form the criminal intent necessary to be charged with murder, such an individual can still intend or expect the results of the injuries he causes" and insurance coverage is excluded).

Sexual abuse. In Allstate Ins. Co. v. Mugavero, 589 N.E.2d 365 (N.Y. 1992), the insured, who had been sued for damages for sexually molesting two children, wanted the insurer to defend the claims. The victims' complaint alleged (1) that the insured acted with "force and violence, and against the consent" of the children; (2) that the molestation occurred "without intending the resultant serious injuries"; and (3) that the abuse was committed "negligently and carelessly, and with wanton disregard of others." (Claims against the wife are discussed shortly.) The insurer, whose policy stated "We do not cover bodily injury . . . intentionally caused by an insured person," claimed that the policy did not cover the events. The children and the insured joined in arguing for coverage.

The court, 4–3, denied coverage. The insured argued that the exclusion did not apply because "it requires that the harm be intended rather than the act causing it. And they insist that theoretically the perpetrator can lack the subjective intent of causing harm while committing an act of sodomy or sexual abuse on a young child." The court disagreed because sexual abuse usually caused severe damage. To allow coverage here would be to permit the insured "to transfer the responsibility for his deeds onto the shoulders of other homeowners in the form of higher insurance premiums."

"Assault and battery." The question of coverage does not stop with the perpetrator of intentional harm. Issues may arise as well in a negligence context. In U.S. Underwriters Ins. Co. v. Val–Blue Corp., 647 N.E.2d 1342 (N.Y.1995), Val–Blue employed a retired police office as a security guard at its nightclub. One night he shot Hanley, an off-duty police officer. There was dispute about whether Hanley had told the guard that he was an off-duty officer before the two shots were fired. Hanley claimed (1) that the guard "negligently, carelessly and recklessly" shot him, (2) that the club was liable under respondeat superior and (3) that the club was negligent in hiring, supervising and training employees. The insurer declined to defend on the ground that the policy excluded coverage under an "Assault and Battery Exclusion Endorsement" that stated:

> It is agreed that no coverage shall apply under this policy for any claim, demand or suit based on Assault and Battery, and Assault and Battery shall not be deemed an accident, whether or not committed by or at the direction of the insured.

In this declaratory judgment action the court concluded that the exclusion was unambiguous and the insurer need not defend the suit. Plaintiff claimed there was no intentional tort because the guard never intended to shoot a police officer. The court responded that the underlying claim against the guard was for an assault and battery and came within the exclusion. The other claims, such as negligent hiring, "are all 'based on' that assault and battery without which Hanley would have no cause of action."

What if the claim was that the nightclub had insufficient guards as the result of which a patron was assaulted in the rest room by a person other than the insured or an employee of the insured? In Mt. Vernon Fire Ins. Co. v. Creative Housing Ltd., 668 N.E.2d 404 (N.Y.1996), plaintiff sued the owner of her apartment house for negligent supervision and control after she was assaulted by a person identified by the court as a "third party wholly unconnected to the insured." The policy had a clause very similar to that in *Val–Blue*. The court applied *Val–Blue*. The plaintiff's claim was "based on" an assault and battery excluded from coverage by the contract's terms. The insurance coverage did not apply whether the assaulter was a stranger or an employee of the defendant. What are the implications of the court's approach to this type of clause?

But in Agoado Realty Corp. v. United International Ins. Co., 733 N.E.2d 213 (N.Y. 2000), an unknown assailant murdered the tenant, whose estate sued the landlord. In this case the landlord's attempt to get liability insurance coverage succeeded. The policy purported to cover "accidents" and the court understood this occurrence to be an accident from the landlord's vantage point. Nor did the exclusion for injuries "expected or intended from the standpoint of the insured" apply. *Mt. Vernon* was "easily distinguishable" because in that case the policy excluded "any claim . . . based on Assault and Battery, and Assault and Battery shall not be deemed an accident whether or not committed by or at the direction of the insured." No such exception existed here.

When the abuse victims in *Mugavero*, supra, sued the wife (also an insured) for her negligence as a baby sitter in allowing her husband access to the victims, the court denied coverage on the ground that the harm was "caused" by an excluded act—even if it was not one committed by the wife.

"Sudden." Another broad category of cases involves liability for pollution. The standard clauses were involved in Northville Industries Corp. v. National Union Fire Ins. Co., 679 N.E.2d 1044 (N.Y.1997). Insured ran a petroleum storage and distribution business. Its liability policies covered "an occurrence," which was defined as "an accident, including continuous or repeated exposure to conditions, which results in bodily injury or property damage neither expected nor intended from the standpoint of the insured." Each policy also contained a pollution exception that barred coverage for injury or damage "arising out of the discharge, dispersal, release or escape of . . . toxic chemical, liquids . . . or other . . . pollutants into or upon land . . . but this exclusion does not apply if such discharge, dispersal, release or escape is sudden and accidental." Insured discovered that leaks had occurred at two facilities totaling some 2 million gallons.

All parties agreed that the discharge was an "accident" and met the basic definition. The dispute was over whether it was "sudden," which the court held had a temporal meaning and was different from accidental. The focus was "on the initial release of the pollutant, not on the length of time the discharge remains undiscovered, nor the length of time that damage to the environment continued as a result of the discharge, nor on the time span of the eventual dispersal of the discharged pollutant in the environment." Since every dispersal begins with an abrupt entry of pollutant into the environment, the word could not refer to the movement of the first molecule from the container to the environment. Plaintiff's claim failed here, as a matter of law, because the allegations and plaintiff's affidavits suggested leaks that "occurred continuously over a period of many years, suggesting the opposite of suddenness." In one case the affidavits spoke of escape through a "corrosion-based 'pinhole' "; the other leaked from a "failed underground elbow joint" some time ten years before discovery. For a discussion of differing views, see Reichhold Chemicals, Inc. v. Hartford Accident & Indemnity Co., 750 A.2d 1051 (Conn. 2000).

In Truck Ins. Exchange v. Pozzuoli, 21 Cal.Rptr.2d 650 (App. 1993), the court held that liability for a long-term leak of gasoline from a tank on the premises of the insured's gas station was not covered by its policy. That policy used the standard language for "accident," but also contained a standard "pollution exclusion" clause under which coverage was excluded for damage "arising out of the discharge . . . of . . . liquids . . . into or upon the land, . . . but this exclusion does not apply if such discharge . . . is sudden and accidental." "Sudden" was defined as "not continuous or repeated in nature." If the tank had exploded and spewed gasoline over neighboring property, the court asserted that there would have been coverage.

Legal restrictions on insurance. Although the development of insurance took place primarily in the private sector as new kinds of contracts were developed in response to demand, and many cases involve contract interpretation, some coverages and provisions have received legislative attention. We explore two important ones here.

1. Insurable interest. As new first-party coverages developed, some critics saw these as creating temptations: life insurance was a form of gambling, fire insurance was an invitation to arson. Among several safeguards developed to allay such concerns, was the concept of an "insurable interest," which limits what may be insured by whom. A person may insure his or her own life, those closely related to that person may do so, and creditors may protect their loans by taking out life insurance on the debtor. This avoids the "moral hazard" that would exist if, for example, one were permitted to insure a stranger's house against fire or a neighbor's life. Perhaps the dangers are best suggested by Liberty National Life Ins. Co. v. Weldon, 100 So.2d 696 (Ala.1957), in which the defendant issued a life insurance policy on a young child to her aunt who, under state law, did not have the requisite insurable interest in the child. The aunt killed the child in an attempt to recover the insurance proceeds. (The court upheld an award to the child's parents in their wrongful death action against the insurance company for its negligence in issuing the illegal policy to the aunt.)

2. Intentional and criminal conduct. Much third-party (liability) coverage has been written to cover the insured's liability for "all sums" for which the insured is held legally liable. As we have seen, insurers commonly limit coverage to "accidents." Other policies exclude certain types of damage awards. Although these are often overlapping categories, they must be kept distinct. If the policy does not exclude such harm, different legal questions arise.

In California, as we saw in *Taylor*, p. 718, supra, section 533 of the Insurance Code provides that an insurer is not liable for a "wilful act of the insured," which state courts have equated with an intent to harm. The section "reflects a fundamental public policy of denying coverage for willful wrongs. [ ] The parties to an insurance policy therefore cannot contract for such coverage." J.C. Penney Casualty Ins. Co. v. M.K., 804 P.2d 689 (Cal.), cert. denied 502 U.S. 902 (1991) (even if policy is not interpreted to exclude coverage of a claim for sexual molestation, the state's public policy bars insurance coverage of such a claim).

Even if the insurance policy does not exclude coverage of a claim, New York has decided that its "public policy precludes insurance indemnification for punitive damages awards, whether the punitive damages are based on intentional actions or actions which, while not intentional, amount to 'gross negligence, recklessness, or wantonness' [ ] or 'conscious disregard of the rights of others or for conduct so reckless as to amount to such disregard' [ ]." Home Ins. Co. v. American Home Products Corp., 550

N.E.2d 930 (N.Y.1990). If the injury has been "intentionally" caused, the state's policy further forbids the insurer from paying any part of the compensatory award as well. Recall the *Mugavero* case, supra, in which coverage of sexual abuse was analyzed as an issue of contract interpretation. If the court had interpreted the contract to provide coverage of the claims, would New York's public policy have permitted the insurer to cover the husband? The wife?

A few states try to avoid this dilemma by enforcing an insurance contract that is interpreted to cover intentional harm or punitive damages, and then allowing the liability insurer to recover over against the tortfeasor-insured. See Continental Cas. Co. v. Kinsey, 499 N.W.2d 574 (N.D. 1993); Ambassador Ins. Co. v. Montes, 388 A.2d 603 (N.J.1978). Is this an improvement over the alternatives?

Litigants often attempt to shape their complaints to avoid contract and legislative exclusions. See, e.g., American Employer's Ins. Co. v. Smith, 163 Cal.Rptr. 649 (App. 1980), in which an arsonist was sued for negligence. The defense argued that the action should be dismissed since the insured clearly was guilty of intentional wrongdoing. The court concluded that "it is not a defense to negligence to contend that the conduct was willful or the harm intended." But the court left open the question of whether the plaintiff could satisfy any judgment through the defendant's insurance. The tort liability question was separate from the insurability question. But see Landry v. Leonard, 720 A.2d 907 (Me.1998), in which plaintiff cab driver sued a robber for negligence. The court held that the insurer need not defend the suit because the policy excluded coverage of bodily injury "which is expected or intended by the 'insured.' " The court also held that the negligence action failed. Given the "intentional act of robbing Landry with the use of a dangerous weapon, a finding of negligence for that act is excluded." See also Boyles v. Kerr, 855 S.W.2d 593 (Tex.1993) (alleging that defendant, who secretly taped his sexual relations with plaintiff and then showed them to others, had behaved negligently). See Pryor, The Stories We Tell: Intentional Harm and the Quest for Insurance Funding, 75 Tex. L. Rev. 1721 (1997).

Critics have been concerned about two cross-currents that intersect at punitive damages and insurance. Some argue that states have been permitting punitive damages too readily—for such conduct as gross negligence and in vicarious liability situations—and have not been reviewing jury awards sufficiently carefully. Recall the discussion earlier in this chapter.

The second strand, as we have just seen, is that the laws of several states bar the insurability of punitive damages. This view probably developed at a time when a punitive award signified outrageous behavior. But if it is now possible to be held liable for punitive damages for conduct that is not "all that different" from negligence, is noninsurability still justifiable?

See Restivo, Insuring Punitive Damages, Nat'l.L.J., July 24, 1995, at C1, discussing these two strands and listing state positions on these questions. On a related point, is it defensible for an insurer to write a policy that does not exclude either intentional harm or punitive damages, collect the premiums—and then argue that it would be unconscionable to pay out in such a case? Is there a difference between a case of murder and one of drunk driving? See generally Baker, Reconsidering Insurance for Punitive Damages, 1998 Wis.L.Rev. 101.

Permissive exclusions. Sometimes legislation authorizes insurers to write specific exclusions if doubt exists at common law about permissibility of the exclusion. The most important of these involves reluctance to cover intrafamily claims. Pursuant to statutory authorization, an auto policy excluded coverage of any insured for harm to any relative who lived in the same household. The statute's constitutionality was upheld when a wife sued her husband for his alleged negligent driving. Farmers Ins. Exchange v. Cocking, 628 P.2d 1 (Cal.1981). The legislature had several rational bases for passage, including fear of collusion. To require this coverage might lead to "substantial increases" in premiums and might lead to an undesired increase in the number of uninsured motorists. See also Shannon v. Shannon, 442 N.W.2d 25 (Wis.1989) (holding that this exclusion serves a legitimate purpose in protecting insurers "from situations where an insured might not completely cooperate and assist an insurance company's administration of the case"). Recall the discussion of insurance in intrafamily situations at p. 224, supra.

———

Beyond the voluntarily acquired first-party insurance already discussed, compulsory governmental programs protect individuals against certain dangers. These include some coverage of medical costs for those over age 65, benefit programs for disabled persons of whatever age—some stressing long term disabilities and others temporary conditions—and attempts to cushion the financial shocks of unemployment and retirement. Still other government programs help those injured in accidents. We discuss workers' compensation in Chapter XI.

All studies indicate that non-tort first-party sources of aid are already significant and becoming more so as first-party insurance becomes more popular. For example, major medical insurance, which covered 32.6 million persons in 1960, covered over 170 million by the late 1980s. Membership in health maintenance organizations (HMOs) rose from 6 million in 1976 to 50 million by 1995 to 92 million in 2000. A major survey published in 1991 indicated that almost 60% of the 23 million people receiving compensation for accident losses reported some payment from their own health insurance. Only 10% of all accident victims reported receipt of tort payments, which in turn constituted only 7% of the total accident compensation paid for economic loss in nonfatal accidents. The percentages are considerably higher for auto accidents—almost one-third of these victims received some tort compensation, which constituted 22% of total payments. D. Hensler, et al., Compensation for Accidental Injuries in the United States (1991).

In many law schools, a course on Insurance is offered as a regular upper-class elective. Several multi-volume treatises cover the subject. The following pages seek only to introduce students to some of the ways in which insurance may affect tort law. For an extended discussion of some of the most basic questions of insurance, including the roles of efficiency and equity, and practical and theoretical problems of coverage, see K. Abraham, Distributing Risk—Insurance, Legal Theory, and Public Policy (1986).

1.   LOSS INSURANCE, COLLATERAL SOURCES AND SUBROGATION

Our immediate question is what impact, if any, these private and governmental programs do, and should, have on assessing the damages to be awarded in a tort action. The virtually universal common-law rule in this country, as we saw in *Arambula*, p. 710, supra, has been to treat first-party benefits that plaintiff has received as "collateral" to the defendant's responsibility and not relevant to tort law's determination of liability or damages. This extends generally to benefits from insurance that the plaintiff has purchased, such as reimbursement of hospitalization and doctors' bills, to gifts made to the plaintiff from rich aunts or uncles, or from an employer in the form of payment of wages not earned. It also extends to the benefits of collective bargaining agreements between the union and the company, for such things as sick leave or accident disability payments, as well as to government benefits.

One concern raised by the collateral source rule is that holding the defendant liable for particular items might allow plaintiff to recover twice for these items. In order to know whether the plaintiff will keep a double recovery we must know more than simply whether the defendant is to be given credit for money or services plaintiff has already received. If the defendant is given that credit, then of course the plaintiff will not be paid twice. But if the defendant is not given credit the result will depend on matters explored in the following case.

Frost v. Porter Leasing Corp.
Supreme Judicial Court of Massachusetts, 1982.
386 Mass. 425, 436 N.E.2d 387.

[Frost was injured in a motor vehicle accident. He and his wife sued the other driver for medical expenses incurred, pain and suffering, impaired earning capacity, and future expenses. His wife's claim was for loss of consortium. While this case was pending, Frost received medical expense benefits of $22,700 under a union health plan paid for by his employer. The insurer, Union Labor, intervened in the Frosts' tort action, claiming a right of subrogation as to damages plaintiff might recover for medical expenses. The insurer made no claim directly against the other driver. The Frosts then settled their tort claim for a lump sum of $250,000. In this phase of the case, the trial judge concluded that the insurer had a right of subrogation in the proceeds of the settlement to the extent it had paid Frost, less a share of the costs the Frosts had incurred in obtaining a settlement.]

Before HENNESSEY, C.J., and WILKINS, LIACOS, ABRAMS and O'CONNOR, JJ.

HENNESSEY, CHIEF JUSTICE.

A Superior Court judge has reported the question "[w]hether a group insurer which provides medical and hospital expenses benefits to an insured has a right of subrogation in a recovery by the insured against a tortfeasor for personal injuries even though the group insurance policy contains no express provision entitling the insurer to subrogation rights." We conclude that the insurer has no right, in the absence of a subrogation clause, to share in the insured's recovery against the tortfeasor.

.   .   .

Subrogation is an equitable adjustment of rights that operates when a creditor or victim of loss is entitled to recover from two sources, one of which bears a primary legal responsibility. If the secondary source (the subrogee) pays the obligation, it succeeds to the rights of the party it has paid (the creditor or loss victim, called the subrogor) against the third, primarily responsible party. [   ] The doctrine of subrogation applies, within limits to be discussed shortly, to payments under policies of insurance. Upon payment, the insurer is entitled to share the benefit of any rights of recovery the insured may have against a tortfeasor for the same loss covered by the insurance. [   ] If the insured recovers from the tortfeasor, the insurer's right becomes a right to the proceeds in the hands of the insured.[6] [   ]

An insurer's right of subrogation may be reserved in an agreement between the insurer and the insured, [   ] or may arise by implication, as a matter of general law [   ].[7] Here, Union Labor admits that Frost's insurance policy contained no provision for subrogation. Union Labor's claim is one of implied subrogation, and we express no opinion on the ability of parties to fix their rights by contract. [   ]

The reason for implied subrogation under contracts of insurance is to prevent an unwarranted windfall to the insured. [   ] If the insured recovers from both the insurer and the tortfeasor, his compensation may exceed his actual loss. Duplicative recovery is "a result which the law has never looked upon with favor." [   ] It is contrary to the indemnity purposes that underlie many insurance contracts, and produces a form of unjust enrichment. [   ] Further, duplicative recoveries by particular accident victims cause an inefficient distribution of the overall resources available for accident compensation. Subrogation returns any excess to the insurer, who can then recycle it in the form of lower insurance costs. See Fleming, The Collateral Source Rule and Loss Allocation in Tort Law, 54 Cal.L.Rev. 1478, 1481–1484 (1966).

Nevertheless, rights of subrogation do not arise automatically upon payment of benefits under any contract of insurance. The availability of

---

6. If the tortfeasor has settled with the insured, with knowledge of the insurer's claim, some courts have permitted the insurer to proceed against the tortfeasor. [   ]

7. In addition, statutes may provide for subrogation. [   ]

subrogation has generally depended on the type of coverage involved. Courts have readily implied rights of subrogation under policies covering property damage. [   ] The insurer's obligation under a policy of property insurance is viewed only as a duty to indemnify the insured for actual loss, and not as an absolute liability to pay a certain sum of money upon the happening of an event. [   ] Moreover, the insured's loss is generally liquidated, and tort recovery is comparable, if not identical, to insurance coverage. [   ] Therefore, the insured's actual loss, and the amount of any excess compensation from the combination of insurance proceeds and tort recovery, can be determined with certainty.

On the other hand, courts have not recognized implied rights of subrogation in the area of "personal insurance," a category that has included medical expense benefits as well as life insurance and other forms of accident insurance. [   ] Personal insurance is said to be less a contract of indemnity than a form of investment, imposing on the insurer an absolute duty to pay if the named condition occurs. [   ] Further the insured's receipt of both tort damages and insurance benefits may not produce a measurably duplicative recovery. The insured is likely to have suffered intangible losses that are insusceptible to precise measurement, and the two sources of his recovery may cover different ranges of loss and be differently affected by considerations such as fault. [   ]

Commentators have objected to the courts' classification of medical expense policies with other forms of personal insurance, and have argued that subrogation rights should be implied upon payment of benefits for medical and hospital expenses. They point out that medical coverage, like property insurance, is designed to indemnify the insured for quantifiable economic losses, and bears little similarity to an investment. [   ]

Although we recognize the indemnity character of medical and hospital expense benefits, we do not feel that the principles that support subrogation under policies of property insurance would be served by extending implied rights of subrogation into the field of insurance for personal injuries. Subrogation rights, as we have said, are implied to prevent unwarranted compensation and to facilitate sound distribution of compensation resources. If medical expenses are isolated from the other consequences of an accident, excess compensation of an insured accident victim may appear definite and quantifiable. However, when subrogation is based on broad principles of equity and efficiency, rather than on the contract of the parties, isolation of medical expenses is artificial, and the accident victim's position should be viewed as a whole. [   ] Subrogation played no part in the bargain between insurer and insured,[8] and in this circumstance, the courts should not intervene to adjust the rights of the parties unless all the adverse consequences of the accident have been offset. [   ]

---

8. Union Labor points out that the premiums for Frost's policy were paid by Frost's employer rather than by Frost himself. The fact that the benefits do not flow to the party who has paid premiums, however, should not detract from the force of legitimate expectations, both of the beneficiary and of the one who has paid. This is particularly true when, as here, the policy is an employment benefit, bargained for by the insured's union.

When the insured's losses are viewed in their entirety, duplicative compensation is both uncertain and unlikely. [   ] The insured may be faced with property damage, pain and suffering, and diminished earning capacity, in addition to medical bills. The costs of litigation, or the decision to settle, may reduce his overall recovery. Yet the insurer's implied right of subrogation must be limited to excessive recovery if it is to conform to the purposes that justify it. Further, when the insured has not agreed to subrogation, doubt should be resolved in his favor. [   ]

Perhaps a formula could be devised by which subrogation could be confined to recapture of duplicative compensation. The insurer might, for example, be permitted to recover if it could demonstrate that the insured's net recovery (insurance proceeds and tort recovery, less costs of collection) exceeded fair compensation for the insured's losses. [   ] However, the costs of implementing the formula could well undercut its justifications, particularly when, as here, the insured had reached a lump-sum settlement with the tortfeasor. [   ] If the inquiry covered the insured's overall loss from the accident—as in fairness it should—determination of the extent of excess recovery could be equally as complex as the personal injury trial the original parties sought to avoid by settlement. [   ] Thus, litigation over subrogation would impose additional burdens on the insured, and cut into his overall compensation for injury. Moreover, this added step in the adjustment of rights would detract from any generalized benefits that subrogation might bring to the sound use and distribution of resources available to compensate loss. Much of the "windfall" produced by overlapping coverage would be absorbed by the costs of dividing it, rather than recycled to reduce the costs of insurance. [   ]

For these reasons, we conclude that, in the absence of a subrogation agreement between the insurer and the insured, an insurer that has paid medical or hospital expense benefits has no right to share in the proceeds of the insured's recovery against a tortfeasor. Accordingly, we answer the reported question in the negative.

So ordered.

WILKINS, JUSTICE (concurring).

I agree with the conclusion of the court that, in the absence of a provision for subrogation in the applicable insurance policy, an insurer providing health insurance is not entitled to subrogation as to amounts paid or payable by a tortfeasor to the insured. I do not reach this result because of the asserted problems of administration of such a system of subrogation to which the court makes reference. The problems are manageable, and most are not substantial. I reach my conclusion on the ground that, in fairness to an insured, a policy should disclose the possibility of subrogation claims. A person or group purchasing coverage for medical costs should know the limitations of such coverage, and, as a realistic matter, a lay person cannot be expected to have knowledge of a common law right of subrogation.

I reject the implications of the opinion that subrogation presents substantial problems with respect to insurance payments made for medical expenses incurred as the result of injuries caused by a third party wrong-doer. The amount of the insured's loss, the insurer's payment, and the tort recovery are known with certainty. The subrogated insurer should acknowledge a proportionate reduction in its claim to reflect the services and expenses of the claimant's attorney in collecting on the tort claim. If the claim is settled, as most are, the subrogated insurer should accept a proportionate and reasonable reduction in its subrogation claim to reflect the discount that the claimant accepted in order to obtain a settlement. Assuming prompt assertion of the subrogation claim, the amount to be paid to the insurer on its subrogation claim can be readily determined in most cases as part of the settlement process.

Subrogation is a reasonable method of assisting in holding down the costs of health insurance. It prevents an undeserved windfall to the insured. It is appropriate to consider the matter of medical expenses apart from other aspects of the injured person's claim. Whatever uncertainty may exist with respect to other elements of damages, the amount paid under the medical insurance policy can be ascertained and dealt with independently. I see no justification for denying subrogation, as the court seems to suggest, because, in settling a case, the claimant may not have been made whole on all elements of his damages. The claimant can be and is made whole on his medical costs, to the extent of his coverage. A health insurer should not be obliged to forbear asserting subrogation rights in order to assist in making the claimant whole on some other aspect of his damages, such as lost wages and pain and suffering, for which the insured has not purchased coverage from the health insurer.

Notes and Questions

1. How does the majority distinguish between "property" insurance and "personal" insurance? What consequences flow from that distinction? Would the same result follow if plaintiff had obtained a judgment instead of having settled?

2. Under the concurrer's view, when would subrogation be allowed? How would legal expenses be allocated?

3. Consider the implications in terms of the collateral source rule and subrogation of the following independent fact situations:

a. P's mother renders gratuitous medical services for P, who was negligently hurt by D.

b. P's rich relative gives P money to pay his hospital bills for harm caused by D's negligence.

c. P's house is badly burned by a fire caused by P's careless smoking. The fire insurer pays P the agreed value of $90,000 for the damage done.

d. P's house is badly burned by D's negligence. P's insurer pays to P the $90,000 agreed value of the damage and proceeds against D. P has no other uncovered losses.

4. The concurrer suggests that when subrogation is allowed the amount should be reduced if the underlying tort claim is settled rather than litigated. Why?

5. How much of the $250,000 settlement in *Frost* should be allocated to medical expenses paid by Union Labor? In that connection, consider Smith v. Marzolf, 375 N.E.2d 995 (Ill.App.1978), in which P was injured by D's negligence. P was entitled to up to $50,000 of first-party benefits from Aetna for his medical bills and lost income. P sued D, and P's wife sued D for loss of consortium. The parties agreed to settle the case by allocating $10,000 to P's claim and $65,000 to his wife's. Aetna objected that it had already paid P almost $17,000 and future payments up to the $50,000 limit were likely. P and D then rewrote their settlement to give P $17,000 and his wife $58,000. Aetna still objected. The trial judge called the settlement "absolutely ridiculous" and a fraud on Aetna's subrogation rights. The refusal to permit the settlement was upheld on appeal because P had breached his duties to Aetna. Is it clear why Aetna should be involved in these settlement talks?

6. On the costs of subrogation, consider the following excerpt from Conard, The Economic Treatment of Automobile Injuries, 63 Mich.L.Rev. 279, 311 (1964):

> Consider the case of a one thousand dollar hospital bill incurred by a Blue Cross policyholder. When his bill is paid by Blue Cross, the cost to all Blue Cross policyholders combined is about 1,080 dollars. Assume further that Blue Cross obtains reimbursement by virtue of subrogation from Drivers' Liability Company, which has insured the tortfeasor. Blue Cross will presumably pay at least twenty-five per cent in collection expenses and will net about 750 dollars out of the one thousand dollars paid by Drivers' Liability. But the policyholders of Drivers' Liability will have incurred corresponding premium costs of sixteen hundred dollars, since liability insurers work at an expense rate equivalent to about sixty per cent of payouts. The net effect of the subrogation is to make liability insurance policyholders pay sixteen hundred dollars in order to save 750 dollars for health insurance policyholders. Probably a large majority of the health insurance policyholders are also liability insurance policyholders, who have their costs doubled by subrogation without any increase of their benefits. The principal beneficiaries of the shift are insurance companies and lawyers.

Professor Conard derived the cost figures used in his passage from other studies that he summarized as follows at pp. 290–91 of his article:

> The Michigan study also estimated total expenses of the damage system, adding to lawyers' fees the litigation expenses of claimants themselves, the costs of selling and administering insurance, and the

costs of keeping courts open for injury cases. This summation indicated that the operating costs of the damage system are about 120 percent of the net benefits that go to the injury victims themselves; the net amounts that the victims get are less than the total retained by insurance companies, law offices, and courts. Presumably, the cost ratio would be even higher in such states as New York and Illinois, where it appears that the legal expenses are substantially higher than in Michigan.

In contrast, private loss insurance systems (embracing principally life insurance and health insurance) showed average costs of about twenty-two percent of net benefits. In some Blue Cross systems the operating costs drop to less than five percent of the net benefits, and in Social Security programs they drop to about two percent.

Although the percentages have changed some since Conard wrote, the overall pattern persists. See O'Connell and Barker, Compensation for Injury and Illness: An Update of the Conard–Morgan Tabulations, 47 Ohio St. L.J. 913 (1986). See also Priest, The Current Insurance Crisis and Modern Tort Law, 96 Yale L.J. 1521, 1560 (1987):

The administrative costs of insurance delivered through tort law are vastly greater than the administrative costs of any first-party insurance regime. Blue Cross–Blue Shield first-party health insurance administration costs are 10% of benefits; SSI disability insurance administrative costs are 8% of benefits; Workers' Compensation disability insurance administration costs are (a much-criticized) 21% of benefits. In contrast, tort law administrative costs are estimated to be 53% of net plaintiff benefits.

The last figure is drawn from J. Kakalik & N. Pace, Costs and Compensation Paid in Tort Litigation (RAND 1986) and is broken down further there at p.70:

The legal fees and expenses paid by plaintiffs as a percent of total compensation were essentially the same for auto tort (31 percent) and other tort cases (30 percent). However, defendants' costs of litigation differ significantly. For auto tort cases, which are often straightforward, defense legal fees and expenses were an estimated 16 percent of total compensation. For other (nonauto) tort cases, which are often more complex, defense legal fees and expenses were much higher—28 percent of total compensation paid.

The plaintiffs' net compensation as a percentage of the total expenditures was 52 percent for auto torts and 43 percent for all other torts. This difference primarily reflects the higher defendants' litigation costs for nonauto torts.

Why might cost differences exist between first-party and third-party insurance? We return shortly to some possible implications of these cost differences.

7. In the Conard excerpt, is it likely that the insured will bring a tort action against the defendant? If so, how does this affect the costs of obtaining subrogation? How might Conard's example work in the case of property damage?

8. Is the justification for the collateral source rule dependent on the right of reimbursement or subrogation of insurers? Putting subrogation aside, why can't the "double recovery" of medical benefits or wage loss replacement benefits by an individual who has paid continuing premiums for such benefits be regarded as a return on an investment that has no bearing on the defendant's tort obligation? In response, can it be argued that the possibility of a tortious accident is only a secondary reason for acquiring these forms of insurance?

9. *Legal fees: subrogation v. liens.* Both opinions in *Frost* note that the insurer must share the legal costs incurred by the insured because of the nature of subrogation. Recall that in the Conard examples supra, it was assumed that the insurer would incur some legal costs.

But there is a crucial difference between subrogation and a lien. Most liens are created by statute to protect those who provide services to others but who are unlikely to have other ways to secure payments for the services that have been rendered. These include hospitals, garage mechanics, building contractors and others. If the money is owed for services rendered and without regard to future events, such as a successful tort suit or success in a lottery, should the lien holder share in any legal fees that must be paid to obtain a tort recovery? In Calvanese v. Calvanese, 710 N.E.2d 1079 (N.Y. 1999), a hospital had treated plaintiff patient and, under the Medicaid statute, had acquired a lien against the patient for the amount of the treatment. The patient sued defendant for the accident and settled—with all the money being called pain and suffering. The unanimous court held that the hospital's lien ran against the entire tort recovery—not only the part that might be (even fairly) attributable to medical expenses. Plaintiff argued that this approach would reduce Medicaid recoveries in the future because it would deter poor accident victims from bothering to sue or settle for a small amount if the entire lien must be satisfied. The court responded:

> That argument ignores the public welfare official's powers both to fix the amount of the lien and to release and discharge it [   ]. In order to facilitate settlement, the agency may agree to reduce the amount it will accept in satisfaction of its lien—whether to ensure that the value of the lien is not greater than defendants are willing to settle for, or simply to ensure that a settlement will yield a plaintiff additional compensation beyond having medical expenses paid by the State. This ability to settle, however, does not affect the agency's entitlement to full recovery when sufficient funds are made available by a responsible third party. To conclude otherwise would be to jeopardize Medicaid's status as a "payor of last resort," and to ignore limits on public resources available to fund the program.

The same result was reached in City & County of San Francisco v. Sweet, 906 P.2d 1196 (Cal.1995), on the ground that if the patient has independent means, the hospital can recover its full bill without depending on the tort claim. This might involve filing the lien on the patient's assets, such as a house or bank account or possibly on the patient's wages. Note that each of these steps involves its own expenses. But see In re Guardianship of Bloomquist, 523 N.W.2d 352 (Neb.1994), in which the hospital wanted to recover its $16,500 from a tort settlement of $100,000 without sharing in the legal fees. The court, recognizing that it was running against the weight of authority, accepted the "common fund" doctrine—an "equitable concept that an attorney who performs services in creating a fund should in equity and good conscience be allowed compensation out of the whole fund from all those who seek to benefit from it." The Nebraska court found it crucial that without the lawsuit the lien was worthless: "the claim or lien will only be paid if the injured party incurs the cost to effectuate a settlement or judgment."

10. Some implications of widespread first-party insurance are suggested in the following article.

The Collateral Source Rule and Loss Allocation in Tort Law

John Fleming.
54 Calif.L.Rev. 1478, 1546–49 (1966).

Two most perplexing features haunt the present state of American law. One arises directly from the last-mentioned fact that such reimbursement to the other fund cannot in general be technically accomplished without the aid of the collateral source rule, that is, precluding the tortfeasor from arguing that his liability has been reduced by the collateral subvention. Thus, whereas the collateral source rule is often enough invoked by courts wholly indifferent as to whether this will result in double recovery, there are others which at least condone it on the ground that, in the individual case, double recovery will be avoided by subrogation or some other like technique for passing the excess on to the collateral source. Finally, one also occasionally encounters a court purposefully insisting on the collateral source rule precisely in order to accomplish such a shifting of the loss.

Turning from double recovery to a consideration of other alternatives, we note that these differ from the former in posing a decision as to which of two sources of compensation to treat as the primary and which as the secondary. In contrast to cumulation of benefits, they force a confrontation with a basic policy orientation whether accident losses generally, or any particular accident loss, should be absorbed by the tortfeasor or by a collateral source, whether in accordance with the regime of tort law or the regime of private or social insurance. It calls for a fixing of priorities pursuant to relevant contemporary social and economic values as to loss allocation. In particular, the following criteria can be isolated as most important in their bearing on this assignment: (1) the reprehensiveness of the defendant's conduct, (2) the desirability of attributing the cost to the loss-causing enterprise for reasons of accident-prevention, proper cost allocation, etc., and (3) the function and, more important still, the economic base of the particular collateral compensation regime.

Not surprisingly, the predominant response has been to regard the tortfeasor as the primary source of compensation. Imbued with the philosophic values of a culture that has traditionally regarded tort law as the only and proper system for allocating accident losses, it is still widely considered as almost axiomatic that if an injurer's conduct justifies his being compelled to relieve the injured from the loss he has inflicted, it is also sufficient reason for his relieving anybody else who might otherwise have undertaken the job of reparation. This approach, dominated by lingering notions of promoting an individualistic morality against "wrongdoers," is reinforced by the impression that it would also reduce the cost to the community in general, and the plaintiff in particular, in maintaining the collateral fund. It is strongest in cases of private insurance, where to reduce the tortfeasor's liability would look like diverting the fruit of the plaintiff's own thrift into the pockets of one who least "deserves" it; but it has also found ardent advocates among social security organizations ever watchful to save the public purse.

These primarily moralistic postulates are gradually yielding in their appeal to an economic value system which places in the forefront the high collection costs of reshifting the loss from a collateral source to the tortfeasor, the attendant wastefulness of multiple insurance and, most important of all perhaps, an awareness that in these days, when tort liability qualifies as a significant source of compensation only in cases of defendants who can pass on the loss through liability insurance or pricing of their goods or services, the question is not so much whether a wrongdoer deserves to be relieved as which of several competing "risk communities" should bear the loss. Loss-bearing has become collectivized, whether it falls on the defendant or some other regime, like insurance or social security, to fill the role as conduit for distribution. While this focus does not provide ready-made solutions, still less generally valid answers, it stimulates a probe all along the line whether in any particular case there is sufficient justification for going to the trouble and expense of shifting the loss to the tortfeasor from some other regime that has already footed the bill and could as well or even better absorb it. Social security, for example, because of its broad base of contributors, has a strong claim for displacing *pro tanto* any "risk pool" represented by tort defendants. On the other hand, very special hazards presented by certain enterprises (for example, nuclear power stations) may make it advisable, for reasons of proper economic cost allocation as well as in the interest of maximizing accident prevention, to assign the ultimate loss to that enterprise rather than spread it on a broader base where these advantages would be lost. If deterrence in the old crude sense has any continuing appeal as a justification for tort liability, it will be confined to situations where it can realistically perform an admonitory function, namely, only against defendants guilty of serious misconduct. Somewhat paradoxically, tort law would shrink, at least in this respect, to its original starting-point as an adjunct of the criminal law in sanctioning immoral conduct. In several European countries, especially Scandinavia and Britain, vast encroachments on the erstwhile primacy of tort liability have already taken place along these lines. In the United States, this process of emancipation from the paralyzing legacy of largely obsolete folklore is still in its infancy, but is bound to gain increasing momentum as social security and other collateral regimes are assuming a greater role in the business of meeting accident costs.

In the upshot, there is thus emerging a second tier of principles of loss allocation; the first being concerned with the traditional problem of whether the person injured should be compensated at all, and the second with whether the tortfeasor rather than some other available fund should bear the ultimate burden of compensation. As a result, in many instances tort liability will become only an *excess* or a *guarantee* liability, its function being merely to allot responsibility for compensation to a person (labelled "tortfeasor") *to the extent that the cost of compensation has not been met by another source.*

In many ways this development represents a much more dramatic innovation than the sensational trend of recent years towards strict liability in the consumer protection area. It is more important by far because it adds an entirely new element to the grammar of loss allocation. Tort liability has ceased to be the sole point of reference in any inquiry, legislative or judicial, as to how particular accident losses should be absorbed.

Notes and Questions

1. What are the arguments in favor of Fleming's suggestion? Is the point limited to "social security?" What about cases in which the plaintiff has private medical and hospital coverage and private income-protection insurance?

2. Fleming suggests that cases involving "very special hazards" might well be treated differently. Why might this be? Why should this reasoning apply only to "very special hazards?"

3. What are the strongest general arguments against "displacing" tort law?

4. What view of Fleming's approach might be taken by those who emphasize the deterrent value of tort law?

5. Consider whether the legal resolutions of the following fact patterns support Fleming's argument.

Fire cases. Throughout the course, although we are primarily concerned with personal injuries, we have had occasion to consider cases involving property damage. For the most part, we have not drawn sharp distinctions between the results in the two types of cases. But might the role of first-party loss insurance in certain situations explain the outcomes of certain property damage cases? The 1866 *Ryan* case, p. 430, supra, creating the unique New York fire rule, may be an early example. Although the passage quoted earlier sought to explain the case in terms of proximate cause, another passage indicated that the availability of insurance had weighed heavily with the court:

> To sustain such a claim as the present, and to follow the same to its legitimate consequences, would subject to a liability against which no prudence could guard, and to meet which no private fortune would be adequate. Nearly all fires are caused by negligence, in its extended sense. In a country where wood, coal, gas and oils are universally used, where men are crowded into cities and villages, where servants are employed, and where children find their home in all houses, it is impossible that the most vigilant prudence should guard against the occurrence of accidental or negligent fires. A man may insure his own house or his own furniture, but he cannot insure his neighbor's building or furniture, for the reason that he has no interest in them. To hold that the owner must not only meet his own loss by fire, but that he must guarantee the security of his neighbors on both sides, and to an unlimited extent, would be to create a liability which would be the destruction of all civilized society. No community could long exist, under the operation of such a principle. In a commercial country, each man, to some extent, runs the hazard of his neighbor's conduct, and each, by insurance against such hazards, is enabled to obtain a reasonable security against loss. To neglect such precaution, and to call upon his neighbor, on whose premises a fire originated, to indemnify him instead, would be to award a punishment quite beyond the offense committed. It is to be considered, also, that if the negligent party is liable to the owner of a remote building thus consumed, he would also be liable to the insurance companies who should pay losses to such remote owners. The principle of subrogation would entitle the companies to the benefit of every claim held by the party to whom a loss should be paid.

A defendant at that time could not obtain insurance against liability. Does that justify the court's analysis? Recall the *Losee* case, p. 508, supra, decided in 1873, involving similar considerations about extended liability.

Even before *Ryan*, legislatures had addressed the relation between fire insurance and liability, as in Mass.Laws 1840, Ch. 85:

> When any injury is done to a building or other property, of any person or corporation, by fire communicated by a locomotive engine of any rail-road corporation, the said rail-road corporation shall be held responsible, in damages, to the person or corporation so injured; and any rail-road corporation shall have an insurable interest in the property for which it may be so held responsible in damages, along its route, and may procure insurance thereon in its own behalf.

What was the philosophy underlying the statute? What was the purpose of the "insurable interest" language? Must negligence be shown? In 1895 the statute was amended by Ch. 293, to provide that if held liable the railroad "shall be entitled to the benefit of any insurance effected upon such property by the owner thereof, less the cost of premium and expense of recovery." Why the change? How would the 1895 act work if the property is fully insured by the owner?

Water company cases. Although New York's fire rule may have been unique, the *Moch* case, p. 143, supra, which relied to some extent on *Ryan,* is followed in the overwhelming majority of states. Might the prevalence of fire insurance covering improved property explain the result? By the time of *Moch,* water companies could obtain liability insurance—and they could probably raise their rates without fear of competition or of losing customers. If they sustained losses due to tort liability for fires they could probably make those up by raising rates without bringing sanctions from the government rate regulators. But, what is the likely relationship between property owners and water users in a large city? Who are the likely winners if there is liability? If there is no liability? In *Moch,* it is difficult to support the catastrophe rationale because in those states permitting recovery against negligent water companies in fire cases, there is no showing that the rule adversely affected the economy. Should actual or available insurance play any part in judicial analysis?

In Weinberg v. Dinger, 524 A.2d 366 (N.J.1987), the court overruled earlier decisions that had refused to impose liability on water companies that negligently failed to supply water to fight fires. The water companies contended that "since property owners are invariably insured against loss from fire damage, a rule imposing liability on water companies would simply create a windfall for property-insurance carriers whose subrogated rights would permit them to recoup from water companies sums paid out pursuant to property insurance policies." The court observed that it was aware that increased water costs were "ultimately borne by the consumer [and that liability insurance] constitutes a less efficient method of insuring against fire loss than is afforded by property insurance." (Why is one method "less efficient" than the other?) The court was also aware that at the time of its decision there was a sudden difficulty in obtaining liability insurance. Nonetheless, relying on such earlier decisions, as *People Express,* p. 313, supra, the court overruled the earlier cases and imposed a duty of due care on water companies. Next, however, it concluded that the action should not lie for insured property losses:

> [W]e abrogate the water company's immunity for losses caused by the negligent failure to maintain adequate water pressure for fire fighting only to the extent of claims that are uninsured or underinsured [so as to avoid the carrier's subrogation claims against the water company]. This determination is made without prejudice to the right of a subrogation claimant, either in this or other litigation, to offer proof tending to demonstrate that any increase in water rates resulting from liability for subrogation claims would be substantially offset by reductions in fire-insurance premiums. If insurance rates were set on the basis of risk and experience, one would expect a high correlation between the increase in water company liability rates and the decrease in fire-insurance rates occasioned by the abrogation of water company immunity in cases like this. If that correlation were to be proven in

subsequent litigation, we would be prepared to reconsider our denial of the carrier's right to subrogation against a water company.

One justice dissented from the decision to retain immunity in subrogation cases. Another dissenter opposed any retreat from the preexisting immunity of water companies.

Is it likely that the demanded showing can be made? If the showing is made, why might that influence the majority to eliminate what remains of New Jersey's immunity of water companies? Is it relevant that the state's water companies are subject to the jurisdiction of the state's public utility commission?

The majority observed in passing that the argument for immunity did not address cases in which personal injury occurred during the fire. The case before the court involved only property damage—and there is apparently no reported case against a water company involving personal injury or death from fire. What is there about claims against water companies that might effectively limit them to property damage claims?

Suits against others for harm to property. In Eaves Brooks Costume Co. v. Y.B.H. Realty Corp., 556 N.E.2d 1093 (N.Y.1990), a commercial tenant sustained a large loss to its inventory when a water sprinkler system malfunctioned and an alarm system failed to warn of the failure. Plaintiff sued both the company that had contracted with the landlord to inspect sprinklers in the building and the installer of the alarm system that had contracted with the landlord to detect water flowing through the sprinklers and to inform the proper persons. Each contract provided a very small limit on liability unless a larger limit were written into the contract. The sprinkler inspection charge was $120 per year and did not include maintenance. The alarm company charged $660 per year. The unanimous court concluded that the defendants had not "assumed a duty to exercise reasonable care to prevent foreseeable harm to the plaintiff":

> If [the two defendants] were answerable for property damage sustained by one not in contractual privity with them, they would be forced to insure against a risk the amount of which they may not know and cannot control, and as to which contractual limitations of liability may be ineffective. The result would be higher insurance premiums passed along through higher rates to all those who require sprinkler system and alarm services. In effect, the cost of protection for those whose potential loss is the greatest would be subsidized by those with the least to lose. In this setting, we see no reason to distribute the risk of loss in such a manner.

> Furthermore, the prices paid for defendants' services, according to specific language in the contracts, were calculated on the understanding that the risk of loss remained with the building's owners. While plaintiff is not bound by the provisions of a contract to which it is not a party, the limited scope of defendants' undertaking is nonetheless relevant in determining whether a tort duty to others should arise from their performance of the contractual obligations. Moreover, it

suggests the need to contain liability within the limits envisioned in the contract in order to keep these services available at an affordable rate.

The court observed that plaintiff retained other remedies:

[N]othing in our decision precludes plaintiff from seeking damages from the building's owners, and the owners and plaintiff are both in a position to insure against losses such as those sustained here. The plaintiff and the owners know or are in a position to know the value of the goods stored and can negotiate the cost of the lease and limitations on liability accordingly.

Does this fact pattern resemble that of the water company cases?

The reference to the contract and to privity recalls the discussion in products cases where the product self-destructed or simply failed to work, p. 639, supra. The remedy there was in contract or there was no remedy. Here, again, the court is suggesting that the remedy, whether or not there is privity, is exclusively in contract. Are the reasons the same?

6. *Statutory change.* In recent years more than a dozen states have either abolished or sharply restricted the role of the collateral source rule and, with it, the role of subrogation. Again, California was the leader in the mid-1970s as part of its legislation to ease a perceived medical malpractice insurance crisis. Civil Code § 3333.1 provided that in a malpractice action if all or a part of the victim's medical bills had been paid by the victim's own insurance or some other source unrelated to the defendant, the jury should be told this—but not told what, if anything, to do with the information.

Other states have resolved the questions as matters of law. In New York, for example, money already received from most collateral insurance sources is to be deducted from the plaintiff's judgment, except that plaintiff is to receive credit for having paid premiums for up to two years. What should be done about future damages that may be covered by future insurance payments if those policies are still in effect some years from now? See N.Y. CPLR § 4545 (c) (reduce tort award by future insurance payments that "will, with reasonable certainty," be made in the future).

2.   LIABILITY INSURANCE

We now consider the development and impact of liability insurance. Virtually every private defendant who has been sued in the cases we have read in this course has probably been covered by insurance protecting, at least to some extent, against liability. Indeed, these cases were probably defended and litigated by the liability insurer and its attorneys. Some very large companies self-insure and would defend cases themselves with in-house counsel or would retain outside counsel. Large government defendants—states and the federal government—often self-insure as well, relying on the taxing power to make up any remaining uncovered liability losses. Smaller governments, such as towns and cities, often use private liability insurers to protect against crushing losses.

We will emphasize in this section the development of the institution of liability insurance, considering most extensively the development of automobile insurance because it has the longest history of involvement with accident law. (Liability insurance also made possible the development of workers' compensation legislation—a subject we consider in Chapter XI.)

The development of the automobile created an immediate awareness of the dangers of the product along with a concern about financial responsibility for accidents. Although courts continued to rely on substantive law that was developed during the days of the horse and buggy, the new problem was solvency of those who now had the power to do much more harm than previously. At first the courts tried to expand the group of responsible defendants by creating doctrines such as the "family purpose" doctrine (owner of a car held vicariously liable to strangers for torts of anyone using the car to carry out a family purpose) and "joint enterprise" (each member of a group venture vicariously liable for the torts of their driver). These doctrines have survived. See Nelson v. Johnson, 599 N.W.2d 246 (N.D. 1999), observing that the family purpose doctrine "is founded on the theory that the driver of a family car, in pursuit of recreation or pleasure, is engaged in the owner's business and is viewed as either the agent or servant of the owner. [ ] The respondeat superior theoretical basis for the doctrine is a fiction created in furtherance of the public policy of giving an injured party a cause of action against a financially responsible defendant. [ ] Under the family purpose doctrine, the owner of the vehicle is not liable for his own negligence, but is vicariously liable for the tortious acts of the driver."

These steps helped but did not assure financial responsibility because some car owners might not have the ability to respond in damages and also because of the gap left when the owner permitted a non-family member to drive the car. Under the traditional law of bailments the owner was not responsible for the negligence of the bailee unless there had been a negligent entrustment in the first instance. Recall *Vince,* p. 179, supra. Many states met this latter concern by adopting legislation making the owner liable for the negligence of *any* person operating the car with the express or implied permission of the owner—even if the owner used due care in selecting the permittee. Think about car rentals, such as *Kamman,* p. 438, supra. Some states limit this liability to a small dollar amount. See, e.g., Calif. Vehicle Code § 17151 (liability under this provision limited to $15,000/$30,000). What might justify such a limit?

Liability insurance began to emerge along with the automobile at the start of the twentieth century. Why might a person who bought a car decide to carry liability insurance? Which owners would be most likely to buy such insurance? At the outset, the insurance was known as "indemnity" insurance—the company agreed that if the insured was required to pay a victim for an accident, and actually did pay, the insurer would reimburse (indemnify) the insured for that amount. If the amount of the judgment was beyond the ability of the insured to pay, the victim was left unsatisfied and the insurer had to reimburse the insured only for whatever amount the victim had been able to wring from the insured. Apparently, insurers sometimes colluded with insureds to transfer the insured's assets to others so as to avoid all payments to victims. Soon, the policies were converted to "liability" policies, under which the insurer became obligated to pay the victim up to the policy's limits when the insured's liability was established.

Automobile policies had to take into account judicial impositions of liability that deviated from the paradigm case in which the owner and the driver were the same person. Two contract provisions emerged. One covered liability for the negligence of anyone driving the car with the owner's permission—the so-called "omnibus" clause. The other, the "drive-other-car" clause, provided that the insured was protected when driving not only the insured's own car but also any other car being driven with the permission of its owner. These provisions were necessary because, from the outset, automobile liability insurance was written for particular vehicles rather than for individual drivers.

Initially some thought that liability insurance would make the insured careless about the safety of others—the "moral hazard" problem. This was borne out occasionally in reported cases, as when, in Herschensohn v. Weisman, 119 A. 705 (N.H.1923), plaintiff passenger told defendant that he was driving carelessly and was assured, "Don't worry. I carry insurance for that." Despite such cases and the possibility of a diminished sense of responsibility, the advantages of liability insurance sustained it. What are those advantages? The disadvantages?

During this early period of liability insurance, the decision whether to acquire it was completely voluntary. But as early as the 1920s states became concerned about the insolvency of many negligent motorists. States began a series of legislative efforts to encourage motorists to carry liability insurance. Briefly, the steps were as follows. First, states passed financial responsibility laws requiring that after a judgment of liability in a first accident, a motorist had to give proof of adequate insurance or assets to be able to pay relatively small future judgments. Some states required this showing immediately after involvement in an accident rather than waiting until a first judgment of liability.

The problem with both forms of legislation was that there was no requirement that this level of solvency exist *before* the first negligently caused accident. The statutes came into play only after a first accident—for which the motorist might be unable to respond. A few states sought to fill this gap by denying driving privileges after a first accident unless the owner could show ability to pay for *that* accident if later found liable for it. The hope was that fear of this outcome would encourage the acquisition of insurance before any accident. Other states began to try to meet insolvency by creating "unsatisfied judgment funds" to which victims would have recourse up to limited maximum amounts, if they could not collect judgments from those liable for the injuries.

In 1927, Massachusetts required that motorists demonstrate a minimum amount of non-cancellable liability coverage before being permitted to register their cars. No state followed that route until New York and North

Carolina in the mid-1950s. (As this movement might have been gaining momentum, the "no-fault" movement was getting started and drew attention away from compulsory insurance, as we shall see in Chapter XI.) Among the problems of compulsory insurance, in addition to such gaps as hit-and-run accidents and out-of-state drivers, was what to do with a driver who was unable to obtain the required insurance from any private carrier. The answer has been to place such a person in an "assigned risk" pool—a group made up of the insurers in the state who write liability insurance—which must accept the coverage unless the applicant's driving record is badly flawed.

But what premium will the assigned-risk plan be able to charge? The state insurance commissioner is under political pressure to keep the rates down—so that motorists will not be forced off the road or forced to violate the vehicle-registration laws. There is also pressure to keep to a minimum the number of drivers rejected by the assigned risk plan. (These problems existed as well in states that had assigned risk plans without compulsory insurance except that in those states motorists could drive legally without insurance if they could not afford or did not want to pay the premiums.)

To counter the increasing regulation of the insurance field caused by increased legislative concern for uncompensated victims, insurers began offering, as part of their liability coverage, a clause that provided financial protection against being injured by negligent uninsured motorists. In effect, the insurer stood in the shoes of the uninsured motorist in a claim by the insured. (The complications of this situation are explored in the *Lalomia* case, p. 764, infra.) In addition, liability insurers added "med pay" provisions offering medical benefits to all persons injured in an accident without regard to fault.

By this point, the original justification for automobile liability insurance—protecting persons of means against having their funds diminished by their negligent harming of others—had given way to a highly regulated form of virtually compulsory insurance to assure that victims of negligent motorists would be compensated to some extent. (That extent, however, might be as low as $10,000/$20,000. Effective in 1996, New York increased its minimum liability coverage to $25,000/$50,000 for injuries other than death and double those limits in death cases—still far below the harm likely to be incurred in any serious auto accident.) Using the same framework as uninsured motorist coverage, insureds may now acquire "underinsured motorist" coverage. This coverage provides insureds additional protection in cases in which the person who negligently hurts them has lower, even if legally adequate, liability limits in his or her policy than those in the insured's policy. These policies are considered at length in Doyle v. Metropolitan Property & Casualty Insurance Co., 743 A.2d 156 (Conn.1999), Allstate Ins. Co. v. Remedios, 986 P.2d 823 (Wash.1999), and Prudential Property & Casualty Co. v. Szeli, 635 N.E.2d 282 (N.Y.1994).

Constitutional limits have restrained the states' efforts in this area. In Bell v. Burson, 402 U.S. 535 (1971), the Court held that where the question of fault was central to the regulatory policy of these statutes, it was a denial of due process of law for the state to suspend a motorist's license without a pre-suspension hearing at which the driver could show a lack of fault. A statute requiring liability insurance or the deposit of a bond as a precondition for all drivers would have avoided this constitutional problem.

In Perez v. Campbell, 402 U.S. 637 (1971), the Court held invalid under the Supremacy Clause a state statute providing that "discharge in bankruptcy following the rendering of [a judgment resulting from an automobile accident] shall not relieve the judgment debtor" from any "state obligations under its safety responsibility act, including payment of past judgments." A requirement that the insolvent motorist had to satisfy judgments arising from his or her negligence before being able to drive again, was held to conflict with the federal bankruptcy law's goal of giving debtors "a new opportunity in life and a clear field for future effort unhampered by the pressure and discouragement of preexisting debt."

Despite the blandishments and compulsion, perhaps 20% of all American motorists are uninsured. The figure is surely higher in some states. See, e.g., Uninsured Drivers: New Push for Law, S.F. Examiner, Feb. 19, 1995 at A–1, showing a statewide California figure of 31.5%. An accompanying chart indicated that in at least nine zip codes in the Bay Area, the figure exceeded 50%. Is this a sufficient concern to warrant further steps? If so, what might be done?

In 1996, California tried another way to encourage drivers to buy the legally required liability insurance. Proposition 213, an initiative, was adopted by over 75% of the electorate. Under Prop. 213, codified in Civil Code §§ 3333.3 and 3333.4, uninsured motorists (as well as drunk drivers) are barred from recovering non-economic damages in any action involving the use of a motor vehicle. In addition, felons are barred from recovering any damages at all for injuries caused by the commission of, or flight from, a felony. Several constitutional objections to the proposition have been rejected. See, e.g., Quackenbush v. Superior Court (Congress of California Seniors), 70 Cal.Rptr.2d 271 (App.1997), cert. denied, 525 U.S. 826 (1998). Many interpretation questions are arising. In Horwich v. Superior Court, 980 P.2d 927 (Cal.1999), for example, the fact that their decedent had been an uninsured motorist did not bar plaintiffs in a wrongful death action from recovering for their loss of care, comfort and society. In Hodges v. Superior Court, 980 P.2d 433 (Cal.1999), the court held that the initiative played no role in products claims because its goal was to protect those who contributed to auto liability insurance pools to a partial extent from those who had not contributed. Similarly, in Nakamura v. Superior Court, 100 Cal.Rptr.2d 97 (App. 2000), the initiative was held to have no impact on the punitive damages part of an auto claim.

We have been tracing common-law and legislative efforts to enhance the likelihood that negligent motorists will be able to respond in damages to their victims. Why was there no comparable concern during that period for victims of auto accidents in which fault could not be established?

Often the insurer accepts a risk in reliance upon the applicant's responses to questions. If the applicant is dishonest in an application for first-party insurance the insurer is often permitted to decline to pay for the loss if it occurs. But if an applicant for automobile liability coverage misrepresents his prior driving records, the situation may be different. In Barrera v. State Farm Mutual Automobile Ins. Co., 456 P.2d 674 (Cal. 1969), the court required the insurer to cover the liability in such a case. The basic policy of the state's Financial Responsibility Law (discussed infra) is "to make owners of motor vehicles financially responsible to those injured by them in the operation of such vehicles." Insurers who are held liable in such situations may be able to obtain indemnity from solvent insureds. See Reliance Ins. Cos. v. Daly, 363 N.E.2d 361 (N.Y.1977) (affirming an insurer's judgment entered on a jury verdict against an insured who failed to disclose, in response to a question, that he had had four moving violations in the preceding 39 months).

Non-auto liability insurance. The development of automobile liability insurance has been the subject of more legislation than has the development of liability insurance for medical malpractice, defective products, or liability for defective premises. Unless they self-insure, larger enterprises usually rely upon a standard form of commercial general liability (CGL) coverage to protect against liability for bodily injury. For specific risks, such as pollution or product liability, these companies may acquire in addition a special purpose coverage. Smaller companies often buy combined liability and property coverage called "commercial multi-peril" coverage. Physicians buy professional liability coverage—either from private insurers or, more recently, from "mutual" insurance companies formed by physicians' associations to compete with the commercial carriers.

The volume of non-auto liability insurance has grown dramatically. In 1958, medical malpractice premiums were $895 million. As of 1999, they were about $6 billion. Other premiums, for such things as products liability, environmental liability and other liability coverages, excluding auto and medical, totaled $784 million. By 1999, these totaled $28.2 billion. Best's Review Magazine, at www.bestreview.com/2000–08/pcstateresults.html.

Although there have been alleged "crises" in the pricing of these coverages, they have remained in the private sector with no legislative efforts to coerce the acquisition of coverage. Why, for example, not require some minimum liability coverage as a condition of practicing medicine? From time to time, in response to instability in the pricing and availability of these liability coverages, legislatures have changed substantive tort rules to make liability harder to establish which, in turn, has made the relevant insurance either cheaper or more readily available. Might some of the instability in liability markets be due to the voluntary nature of this insurance with the safer manufacturers (or physicians) opting out and choosing to self-insure, leaving the more dangerous and the untested newer entrants in the liability insurance markets? This thesis, based on the principle of "adverse selection," is developed in Priest, The Current Insurance Crisis in Modern Tort Law, 96 Yale L.J. 1521 (1987). For general discussion of the perceived insurance crisis of the mid-1980s, see Abraham, Making Sense of the Liability Insurance Crisis, 48 Ohio St.L.J. 399 (1987).

3. THE IMPACT OF INSURANCE ON TORT LITIGATION

a. The Impact on Substantive Rulings

Although judicial opinions in tort cases rarely spoke of loss or liability insurance, their impact was unmistakable. Recently, courts have been somewhat more explicit in referring to the prevalence of liability insurance—but not to whether the particular defendant was insured.

Judge Friendly was particularly explicit about the role of liability insurance in affecting attitudes toward the boundaries of tort liability. In *Kinsman I,* discussed at p. 431, supra, Judge Friendly observed that "[w]here the [liability] line will be drawn will vary from age to age; as society has come to rely increasingly on insurance and other methods of loss-sharing, the point may lie further off than a century ago." Also, in *Steinhauser,* p. 402, supra, after noting the broad acceptance of the "thin-skull" doctrine, he stated "[t]he seeming severity of this doctrine is mitigated by the prevalence of liability insurance which spreads the risks."

Judge Friendly's observations undoubtedly find support in the greater frequency with which juries are permitted to find negligence and product defect in the great mass of unspectacular cases. They undoubtedly also go far to explain such judicial developments as the family purpose doctrine, p. 762, supra, and the changes in family liability, p. 224, supra. Liability insurance also helps explain such cases as *Maloney v. Rath*, p. 8, supra, in which the car owner was held liable for the negligence of her service station mechanic.

Recall also the fire, water, and other property cases discussed in the notes after the Fleming excerpt, p. 755, supra.

b. The Impact of Insurance on Procedure and Settlement

Lalomia v. Bankers & Shippers Ins. Co.

Supreme Court of New York, Appellate Division, 1970.
35 App.Div.2d 114, 312 N.Y.S.2d 1018.

BENJAMIN, J. This action for a declaratory judgment calls upon us to determine which, if any, policies of insurance provide coverage for the plaintiffs, who were involved in a collision with a motorized bicycle.

The tragic accident out of which this litigation arose claimed the lives of 12-year-old Michael Maddock and of Jean Lalomia, a wife and the mother of four children. At the time of the collision Michael was operating a motorized bicycle, that is, a bicycle from which various operational parts, such as the pedals, had been removed and to which a 3-1/2 H.P. lawn mower gasoline engine had been added. The motorized bicycle collided with an automobile being operated by Jean Lalomia.

Defendant Bankers & Shippers Insurance Company (hereinafter called B & S) had issued two policies of automobile insurance to defendant Daniel Maddock, Michael's father, each of which covered a different specific automobile. Under their terms, these policies would only provide coverage for the motorized bicycle if it were held to be an after-acquired "private passenger automobile". Defendant Maddock had not been required to notify B & S of the acquisition of the motorized bicycle under the terms of the policies, as it had been acquired within 30 days before the accident.

The motorized bicycle, which is classified as a motor-driven cycle (Vehicle and Traffic Law, § 124), is a motor vehicle within the meaning of the Vehicle and Traffic Law [   ]. However, it is not a private passenger automobile either within the meaning of the B & S policies or of regulation 35–A promulgated by the Superintendent of Insurance (11 NYCRR 60.1). B & S is therefore not required to defend or indemnify defendant Maddock as a result of the accident.

To hold that the motor-driven cycle was not a motor vehicle would allow the indiscriminate use of such dangerous contraptions by youngsters on our public highways. It is only when such vehicles are registered and made to conform to minimum standards of safety (the vehicle involved herein had no brakes and could be made to stop only by "shorting" the sparkplug) that accidents of this type can be avoided.

The extension of coverage in policies insuring specific private passenger automobiles to after-acquired private passenger automobiles was not intended to alter the nature of the risk involved. It would be unfair to compel an insurer to automatically extend coverage to a motor-driven cycle, motorcycle or racing car by a strained construction of the words "private passenger automobile."

Defendant Insurance Company of North America had issued a homeowner's policy to defendant Maddock. The policy obligated the insurer to pay all sums which the insured would become legally obligated to pay as damages because of personal injury or property damage. However, the policy excluded from its coverage "the ownership, maintenance, operation, use, loading or unloading" of automobiles or midget automobiles while away from the insured premises. With certain exceptions, the policy defined "automobile" as a "land motor vehicle". As the accident herein took place some three or four blocks from the insured premises, and as the motor-driven cycle was a motor vehicle, this insurer is not liable to defend or indemnify defendant Maddock, either individually or as administrator of Michael Maddock's estate (Michael was also an insured as defined by the policy), insofar as the ownership, maintenance, operation or use of the motorized bicycle is concerned.

However, the complaint in the plaintiffs' negligence action alleges, in effect, that Daniel Maddock was guilty of negligence in placing a dangerous instrumentality in the possession of and at the disposal of a 12-year-old boy, knowing that it could be used in a dangerous manner likely to cause harm to others. These allegations set forth a valid cause of action grounded in common-law negligence [   ]. This theory of action is not directly related to the "ownership, maintenance, operation, use" of the vehicle and imposes an obligation upon the insurer within the terms of its policy [   ].

Defendant Liberty Mutual Insurance Company is liable under the terms of the uninsured motorist endorsement contained in the policy which it issued to plaintiff Laurence Lalomia, who was Jean Lalomia's husband. Although that endorsement, as it appears in the policy, refers to "uninsured automobiles," it is deemed to cover all uninsured motor vehicles (cf. Early v. MVAIC, 32 A.D.2d 1042, supra; Insurance Law, § 167, subd. 2–a.). The motor-driven cycle involved herein was an uninsured motor vehicle within the meaning of the endorsement.

The obligation imposed upon the Insurance Company of North America under its homeowner's policy is limited to the theory of negligently permitting the use and operation of a dangerous mechanism. As there is no other policy in force with respect to the use, maintenance or operation of the motor-driven cycle, the uninsured motorist endorsement contained in the Liberty policy is applicable. The judgment should be modified accordingly, on the law and the facts, without costs.

HOPKINS, ACTING P.J., MUNDER, MARTUSCELLO and KLEINFELD, JJ., concur.

Notes and Questions

1. *Lalomia* was affirmed on the opinion below. 291 N.E.2d 724 (N.Y. 1972).

2. Note that this was an action for a declaratory judgment. Many cases disputing insurance coverage follow the same route. How else might these disputes be resolved?

3. The duty to indemnify must be separated from the duty to defend. If the claims asserted by the plaintiff include at least one covered by the insurance policy, the insurer must defend. At the same time, the insured should obtain independent counsel because of the conflict of interest inherent in the insurer's willingness to let liability be found on the claim for which it is not responsible.

In Public Service Mut. Ins. Co. v. Goldfarb, 425 N.E.2d 810 (N.Y.1981), the insured was sued on a variety of claims. The insurer would be liable if certain claims were established but not if plaintiff prevailed on others. In view of the conflict, the court concluded that the insured was "entitled to defense by an attorney of his own choosing, whose reasonable fee is to be paid by the insurer."

4. The jury is not to be told whether the defendant is insured. Why? In cases in which the defendant has insurance, the plaintiff's attorney would like to ask if prospective jurors have any ties with insurance companies. Should such questions be permitted?

In Roman v. Mitchell, 413 A.2d 322 (N.J.1980), the court split 4–3 over the trial judge's action in excluding voir dire questions asking whether any prospective jurors held stock in, or were employed by, a casualty insurance company. The majority thought that the questions "tend to emphasize unduly the fact of insurance coverage. Absent some indication that a basis for asking them exists, they should ordinarily be rejected by the trial court." The majority feared that asking such questions, even in good faith, "can prejudice a defendant's right to a fair trial." One dissenter argued that modern jurors know about the existence of liability insurance and will not use the information to render excessive verdicts. He noted that insurance companies frequently advertised in national magazines to remind the public of the widespread incidence of liability insurance and to urge that jurors use restraint in awards. See also Taylor v. Republic Automotive Parts, Inc., 950 S.W.2d 318 (Mo.App.1997).

In Rodgers v. Pascagoula Public School District, 611 So.2d 942 (Miss. 1992), the verdict against the school district for a bus crash, in which it admitted liability, awarded nothing for pain and suffering or other noneconomic damages. The court ordered additur. Three concurring justices observed:

> I am compelled to question how a jury composed of taxpayers can be expected to render a fair award of damages when operating under the assumption that they, the taxpayers, would ultimately foot the bill.
>   . . . How can we continue [the policy of excluding mention of insurance] because of the presumed prejudice to an insurer when that same insurer can capitalize upon the gross prejudice that a jury of taxpayers will have toward assessing damages for the plaintiff? .   . .
> [In this type of case] I believe that evidence of liability coverage should be admitted to ensure a fair and adequate award, untainted by any misconceptions that it could lighten the pocketbooks of taxpaying jurors.

What is this "misconception?" How will the concurring opinion's position eliminate it?

Perhaps the most common approach to admissibility of evidence of insurance is found in Federal Rule of Evidence 411:

> Evidence that a person was or was not insured against liability is not admissible upon the issue whether he acted negligently or otherwise wrongfully. The rule does not require the exclusion of evidence of insurance against liability when offered for another purpose, such as proof of agency, ownership, or control, or bias or prejudice of a witness.

5. In *Lalomia,* Liberty Mutual was both liability insurer and the carrier for the uninsured motorist coverage. If an uninsured motorist in a two-car crash sues Lalomia, that involves the liability part of the policy. Lalomia's family may also sue Liberty Mutual on the uninsured motorist coverage. Note the potential conflict if both claims proceed, since it is to the insurer's interest to establish that both drivers were not negligent and try to defeat one or both drivers. Moreover, the liability limits may be different on the two coverages. The uninsured motorist coverage may thus make the insured and the insurer adversaries. How serious is this? How else might it have been handled?

6. Even though Mr. Maddock now has an insurer obligated to defend him in at least one phase of the case, do conflicts remain? For an extensive and critical view of insurers' practices in these areas, see Smith, The

Miscegenetic Union of Liability Insurance and Tort Process in the Personal Injury Claims System, 54 Cornell L.Rev. 645 (1969).

7. Industry efforts to keep the auto and the homeowner's policy from overlapping are collected in Aetna Cas. & Sur. Co. v. Safeco Ins. Co., 163 Cal.Rptr. 219 (App. 1980). See also State Farm Fire & Cas. Co. v. Kohl, 182 Cal.Rptr. 720 (App. 1982).

The reasoning of *Lalomia* was explicitly rejected in Barnstable County Mut. Fire Ins. Co. v. Lally, 373 N.E.2d 966 (Mass.1978), in which the homeowner's policy was held not to apply to a claim of negligent entrustment of a motor vehicle. The negligent entrustment theory "derived from the more general concepts of ownership, operation, and use of a motor vehicle" because it involved showing that the defendant owned or controlled the vehicle and permitted the driver to operate it. Compare Salem Group v. Oliver, 607 A.2d 138 (N.J.1992), requiring a homeowner's insurer to defend a claim brought by the insured's minor nephew who was hurt operating the insured's ATV off the premises after having been served alcohol by the insured.

Most courts have rejected *Lalomia*. See the dissent in Cone v. Nationwide Mut. Fire Ins. Co., 551 N.E.2d 92 (N.Y.1989), involving entrustment of an ATV. The court, 4–3, followed *Lalomia* and held that the parent's homeowners' insurer was obligated to defend. In the 18 years since *Lalomia* the language of the policy had not become sufficiently clear to deny coverage. The dissenters sought to distinguish *Lalomia* based on changes in the language brought about by the industry's reaction to *Lalomia*. If the attempted distinction failed, the dissenters wanted to overrule *Lalomia*.

In the *Mount Vernon* case, p. 742 supra, involving whether an insurer had to defend a nightclub over a criminal attack, the court, in passing, discussed *Lalomia,* in which the language was "based directly on" and *Cone*, in which the crucial term was "arising out of." The *Mount Vernon* court was doubtful about both cases: "Insofar as our decisions in [*Lalomia* and *Cone*] cannot be readily harmonized with *Val–Blue*, [p. 742, supra], those decisions should be limited to their facts."

8. *The settlement process.* It is one thing to consider the appellate law of damages. It is quite another to observe how liability and damages are handled by claimants, defendants, and their attorneys. Agreements not to sue that are made after the harm has occurred—usually at the time of a settlement—will be enforced in the absence of factors such as misrepresentation and duress that would also void any contract. The problem of the plaintiff who turns out to be more seriously hurt than anticipated is well discussed in Mangini v. McClurg, 249 N.E.2d 386 (N.Y.1969):

> [There are] many reasons, including doubtful liability, the willingness to take a calculated risk, the desire to obtain an earlier rather than a later settlement, and perhaps others, why releasors may wish to effect a settlement and intend to give the releasee a discharge of liability for any unknown injuries—in short to bargain for general peace. When general peace is the consideration, there can be no mutual mistake as to the extent of the injuries, known or unknown.

Some of these considerations, of course, also explain why some claims are settled for less than the damage sustained from known injuries. Citing authorities for the proposition that unknown injuries are not generally within the contemplation of the parties "despite the generality of standardized language in releases," the court concluded that the plaintiffs were entitled to try to prove, "directly or circumstantially, that there was no intention to release a claim for unknown injuries."

The "structured settlement" has been important in large cases. The defendant makes a payment now to cover past expenses and legal fees. The major part of the payment is used to buy an annuity that will provide, say, $50,000 in annual income for the life of the injured victim. The arrangement can be structured so that the annual income is tax free.

In 1982, the Stanford University Hospital settled with the parents of a child rendered quadriplegic and otherwise disabled at birth due to lack of sufficient oxygen, by paying for a series of three annuities that initially yielded $82,000 per year, rising to $275,000 per year in 2002. The money was for the child's medical costs and special treatment. If the child were to live her expected 76 more years, the payments would amount to $122 million. The package of annuities cost $2.3 million. An economist stated that the present cash value of the settlement was $8 million. N.Y. Times, Sept. 17, 1982 at 12. The payments are guaranteed for 20 years, with that guaranteed money to go to the child's heirs if she dies within 20 years. Cash payments at the outset included $150,000 to each parent, $650,000 to the plaintiff's lawyer, $41,000 for legal expenses, and $209,000 for current medical expenses. This $1.2 million was shared by the hospital and the physician. How does this approach compare to an award in court?

9. *The role of insurers.* The addition of insurers to the mix is treated in detail in H.L. Ross, Settled Out of Court: The Social Process of Insurance Claims Adjustments (1980 ed.). Consider the following excerpts from pp. 237–40:

> In order to process successfully vast numbers of cases, organizations tend to take on the characteristics of "bureaucracy" in the sociological sense of the term: operation on the basis of rules, government by a clear hierarchy, the maintenance of files, etc. Such an organizational form produces competence and efficiency in applying general rules to particular cases, but it is not well suited to making complex and individualized decisions. One form of response of bureaucracies to such demands involves a type of breakdown. There will be long delays, hewing to complicated and minute procedures, and a confusion of means with ends. A common and perhaps more constructive response is to simplify the task. This was the tack taken by the claims men I studied. Phone calls and letters replaced personal visits; only a few witnesses, rather than all possible, would be interviewed; and the law of negligence was made to lean heavily on the much simpler traffic law.
>
> Traffic laws are simple rules, deliberately so because their purpose is to provide a universal and comprehensible set of guidelines for safe

and efficient transportation. Negligence law is complex, its purpose being to decide after the fact whether a driver was unreasonably careless. However, all levels of the insurance company claims department will accept the former rules as generally adequate for the latter purpose. The underlying reason for this is the difficulty if not impossibility of investigating and defending a more complex decision concerning negligence in the context of a mass operation. In the routine case, the stakes are not high enough to warrant the effort, and the effort is not made. The information that a given insured violated a specific traffic law and was subsequently involved in an accident will suffice to allocate fault. No attempt is made to analyze why this took place or how. The legal concepts of negligence and fault in action contain no more substance than the simple and mechanical procedures noted here provide.

The law of damages is also simplified in action. Although the measurement of special damages appears rather straightforward even in formal doctrine, some further simplification occurs in action when, for instance, life table calculations are used to compute future earnings. More important, the measurement of pain, suffering, and inconvenience is thoroughly routinized in the ordinary claim. The adjuster generally pays little attention to the claimant's privately experienced discomforts and agonies; I do not recall ever having read recitals of these matters in the statements, which are the key documents in the settlement process and in which all matters considered relevant to the disposition of a claim are recorded. The calculation of general damages is for the most part a matter of multiplying the medical bills by a tacitly but generally accepted arbitrary constant. This practice is justified by claims men on the theory that pain and suffering are very likely to be a function of the amount of medical treatment experienced. There is of course a grain of truth in this theory, but it also contains several sources of error. Types of injury vary considerably in the degree of pain and suffering, the necessity for treatment, and the fees charged for treatment; and the correlations between these elements are low. I believe that the more important reason for the use of the formula is again that all levels of the claims department find it acceptable in justifying payment over and beyond special damages. The formula provides a conventional measurement for phenomena that are so difficult to evaluate as to be almost unmeasurable. It provides a rule by which a rule-oriented organization can proceed, though the rule is never formalized. This simplification also meets the comparable needs of plaintiffs' attorneys and is acceptable to them as well. Because of the mutual acceptability of the formula, attorneys will try to capitalize on it by adding to the use and cost of medical treatment, a procedure known as "building" the file, and adjusters will argue concerning the reasonableness of many items that purport to be medical expenses and thus part of the base to which the formula is applied.

Is this passage reassuring? Disillusioning?

Consent of the insured. The propriety of a settlement made by the insurer without the consent of the insured depends on the contract. In

Feliberty v. Damon, 527 N.E.2d 261 (N.Y.1988), a physician was sued for malpractice. After an adverse jury verdict setting plaintiff's liability at $743,000 (within the policy limits), the defendant insurer settled the patient's case for $700,000. The physician claimed that the insurer had settled without the physician's consent—and that he had wished to appeal. He alleged that the publicity following the verdict destroyed his practice.

The court recognized that the physician was undoubtedly troubled about the adverse verdict even though he had not had to pay any money. But the short answer was that the contract specified that the "company may make such investigation and such settlement of any claim or suit as it deems expedient." Unlike "bargained-for, and presumably costlier, policy provisions contemplating the insured's consent to settlement [ ], here the parties' contract unambiguously gave the insurer the unconditional right to settle any claim or suit without plaintiff's consent."

The strong reputational concerns of professionals are exhibited in a case in which a physician was sued for $75,000. The demand was finally reduced to $1. Still, the defendant refused to settle. The case went to trial and the jury returned a defense verdict. Kelley, Doctor Refuses to Settle Malpractice Suit for $1, L.A. Times, March 15, 1999 at B1; Doctor Cleared of Malpractice, San Diego Union–Tribune, April 7, 1999 at A3.

10. *Settlement strategies.* The variety of possible settlements is virtually unlimited. In the so-called "high-low" settlement, for example, each party wishes to avoid an extreme result. The most likely case is one in which the plaintiff is seriously injured but liability is seriously in doubt. The parties may agree before trial that if plaintiff recovers nothing or less than $100,000, the parties agree that the plaintiff is to receive $100,000. If the final outcome is an award of over $500,000, the parties agree to settle for $500,000. If the outcome is an award between $100,000 and $500,000 the parties agree to abide by that result or they agree on some other amount. For an argument that juries should be required to choose between the plaintiff's last demand and the defendant's last offer, see Note, "Baseball Litigation": A New Calculus for Awarding Damages in Tort Trials, 78 Tex. L. Rev. 439 (1999).

For a demonstration of uncertainty, see Ballard, 11th-Hour Deal Costs Company $6.9M, Natl. L.J., Aug, 24, 1998 at A6. While the jury was deliberating, the defendant company settled a toxic tort claim reportedly for $7 million. A few minutes later the jury returned a verdict worth $130,000.

c. Suing the Insurer

Pavia v. State Farm Mutual Automobile Ins. Co.

Court of Appeals of New York, 1993.
82 N.Y.2d 445, 626 N.E.2d 24, 605 N.Y.S.2d 208.

[One evening in April, 1985, Carmine Rosato, a 16-year-old, picked up the 19-year-old plaintiff and another youth in a car belonging to Rosato's mother. The car was insured by defendant with a $100,000 liability limit. Rosato, whose learner's permit did not authorize driving at night, turned a corner at apparently excessive speed and encountered a double-parked car. In his efforts to avoid that car he collided with a car driven by Amerosa. Plaintiff was seriously hurt. Further facts are set out in the opinion.]

TITONE, JUDGE.

. . .

In October 1985, Pavia commenced a personal injury action against the Rosatos and Mr. Amerosa. The record reveals that as early as March 1986 a line unit representative at State Farm responsible for a preliminary investigation of plaintiff's claim, concluded that the Rosatos were 100% liable for the accident. By August 1986, a State Farm claims representative responsible for handling the case on a daily basis was in receipt of medical reports attesting to the severity of plaintiff's injuries. A physical examination of plaintiff conducted by State Farm's physicians on April 27, 1987 confirmed those findings. New developments in the case against the Rosatos surfaced on June 9, 1987—the date that Carmine Rosato was deposed. Through Rosato's testimony, State Farm was led to believe that the double-parked car may have been backing up, suggesting that Rosato's quick maneuvering may have been justified under an "emergency defense"; that witnesses not previously identified could support this version of the incident; that Pavia failed to wear a seat belt; and that drugs were being used in the car that night, possibly supporting an assumption of the risk defense. By letter dated June 10, 1987, counsel retained for the Rosatos by State Farm acknowledged that the liability forecast was "extremely unfavorable," but recommended that a further inquiry be conducted in light of these new leads.

On June 26, 1987, admittedly without having read Rosato's deposition, plaintiff's counsel wrote to State Farm demanding the full $100,000 policy limit in settlement of the personal injury action and requiring acceptance of the offer within thirty days. The offer expired without response from State Farm. By this time, however, State Farm had embarked on a thorough investigation of the potential defenses illuminated by Rosato's deposition. In fact, State Farm had hired an investigator to locate the supposed witnesses who would corroborate Rosato's version of how the events leading to the accident unfolded. By November 1987, State Farm's efforts to locate those witnesses were abandoned because the search had proved fruitless. On December 1, 1987, State Farm's Claims Committee, whose members had the authority to offer payments in excess of $50,000, convened for the first time to discuss the reports generated by the claim representative assigned to the case. On December 16, 1987, the Committee authorized its counsel to offer plaintiff the full policy limits. This offer was conveyed to plaintiff's attorney by counsel retained by State Farm on the Rosatos' behalf on January 7, 1988 during a "settle or select" conference, but was rejected as "too late."

The trial of the underlying personal injury action commenced in March 1988. The jury returned a plaintiff's verdict in the amount of $6,322,000, attributing 85% of the fault to Carmine Rosato and 15% to co-defendant Amerosa. Supreme Court reduced the verdict upon State Farm's motion to $5,000,000 and the Appellate Division modified that judgment by further reducing the verdict to $3,880,000 upon plaintiff's stipulation.

The Rosatos subsequently assigned all causes of action they might have against State Farm to plaintiff by executing an assignment agreement, which included a covenant by plaintiff that he would not execute the excess portion of the judgment against the Rosatos. The Rosatos and plaintiff then commenced this action, alleging essentially that State Farm acted in bad faith by "failing to accept [plaintiff's] policy limits settlement offer within a reasonable time despite the clear liability and obvious damages exceeding the policy limits."

At the ensuing trial on the bad faith action, the jury was presented solely with the following question: "Did the defendant, State Farm, act in gross disregard of the interests of Carmine Rosato and Joanne Rosato, their insured, in that there was a deliberate or reckless decision to disregard the interest of their insured?" The jury answered affirmatively, and Supreme Court entered an "excess" judgment against State Farm in the amount of $4,688,030—the amount of the jury verdict in the underlying personal injury action as modified by the Appellate Division, less $110,000 already paid by State Farm and Amerosa's insurer, plus interest and costs.

The Appellate Division affirmed, holding that the trial court properly charged the jury that, in order to find bad faith, State Farm must have acted in "gross disregard" of the Rosatos' interests, and properly rejected the standard urged by State Farm—that bad faith required "an extraordinary showing of disingenuous or dishonest failure" to carry out the insurance contract (see Gordon v. Nationwide Mut. Ins. Co. (30 N.Y.2d 427, 437 [1972], cert. denied, 410 U.S. 931 [1973])). The court also rejected State Farm's contention that the evidence adduced at trial was insufficient as a matter of law to present a jury question on the "bad faith" issue, noting that State Farm "possessed the information necessary to accurately assess both the magnitude of Frank Pavia's injuries and the Rosatos' potential exposure well before the June 26, 1987 settlement offer was received" [ ]. Despite our conclusion that the courts below properly applied the "gross disregard" standard, as a matter of law the finding of bad faith is not supported by this record.

II.

The notion that an insurer may be held liable for the breach of its duty of "good faith" in defending and settling claims over which it exercises exclusive control on behalf of its insured is an enduring principle, well-settled in this State's jurisprudence [ ]. The duty of "good faith" settlement is an implied obligation derived from the insurance contract [ ]. Naturally, whenever an insurer is presented with a settlement offer within policy limits a conflict arises between, on the one hand, the insurer's interest in minimizing its payments and on the other hand, the insured's interest in avoiding liability beyond the policy limits [ ]. By refusing to settle within the policy limits, an insurer risks being charged with bad faith on the premise that it has "advanced its own interest by compromising those of its insured" [   ], or even those of an excess insurance carrier who "alone [may be] placed at further risk due to the defendant's intractable opposition to any settlement of the claim" [   ].

At the root of the "bad faith" doctrine is the fact that insurers typically exercise complete control over the settlement and defense of claims against their insureds, and, thus, under established agency principles may fairly be required to act in the insured's best interests [   ]. On the other hand, a countervailing policy consideration exists in the courts' understandable reluctance to expose insurance carriers to liability far beyond the bargained-for policy limits for conduct amounting to a mere mistake in judgment. Thus, established precedent clearly bars a "bad faith" prosecution for conduct amounting to ordinary negligence [   ]. Indeed, in *Gordon v Nationwide Mut. Ins. Co.* (supra), this Court held that even where an insurer had withdrawn from its insured's defense on the erroneous belief that the policy of insurance had lapsed, the error in judgment could not form the predicate for a bad faith action [   ].

Beyond that principle, the courts have had some difficulty selecting a standard for actionable "bad faith" because of the need to balance the insured's rightful expectations of "good faith" against the insurer's equally legitimate contract expectations. Consequently, a divergence of authority has arisen concerning whether a bad faith finding may be predicated on a showing of the insurer's recklessness or "gross disregard" for the insured's interests [   ], or whether a heightened showing of intentionally harmful, dishonest or disingenuous motive is required [   ].

Faced squarely with the question for the first time, we reject defendant's proposed requirement of a "sinister motive" on the part of the insurer [   ], and hold instead that, in order to establish a prima facie case of bad faith, the plaintiff must establish that the insurer's conduct constituted a "gross disregard" of the insured's interests—that is, a deliberate or reckless failure to place on equal footing the interests of its insured with its own interests when considering a settlement offer [   ]. In other words, a bad faith plaintiff must establish that the defendant insurer engaged in a pattern of behavior evincing a conscious or knowing indifference to the probability that an insured would be held personally accountable for a large judgment if a settlement offer within the policy limits were not accepted.

The gross disregard standard, which was utilized by the trial court here, strikes a fair balance between two extremes by requiring more than ordinary negligence and less than a showing of dishonest motives. The former would remove the latitude that insurers must be accorded in investigating and resisting unfounded claims, while the latter would be all but impossible to satisfy and would effectively insulate insurance carriers from conduct that, while not motivated by malice, has the potential to severely prejudice the rights of its insured. The intermediate standard accomplishes the two-fold goal of protecting both the insured's and the insurer's financial interests.

III.

Having established the proper legal standard, we necessarily shift to the sufficiency of plaintiff's proof in this case. Naturally, proof that a demand for settlement was made is a prerequisite to a bad faith action for failure to settle [   ]. However, evidence that a settlement offer was made and not accepted is not dispositive of the insurer's bad faith. It is settled that an insurer "cannot be compelled to concede liability and settle a questionable claim" [ ] simply "because an opportunity to do so is presented" [   ]. Rather, the plaintiff in a bad faith action must show that "the insured lost an actual opportunity to settle the claim" [   ] at a time when all serious doubts about the insured's liability were removed.

Bad faith is established only "where the liability is clear and the potential recovery far exceeds the insurance coverage" [   ]. However, it does not follow that whenever an injury is severe and the policy limits are significantly lower than a potential recovery the insurer is obliged to accept a settlement offer. The bad faith equation must include consideration of all of the facts and circumstances relating to whether the insurer's investigatory efforts prevented it from making an informed evaluation of the risks of refusing settlement. In making this determination, courts must assess the plaintiff's likelihood of success on the liability issue in the underlying action, the potential magnitude of damages and the financial burden each party may be exposed to as a result of a refusal to settle. Additional considerations include the insurer's failure to properly investigate the claim and any potential defenses thereto, the information available to the insurer at the time the demand for settlement is made, and any other evidence which tends to establish or negate the insurer's bad faith in refusing to settle. The insured's fault in delaying or ceasing settlement negotiations by misrepresenting the facts also factors into the analysis [   ].

Application of the aforementioned principles here leads us to the conclusion that plaintiffs have failed to establish a prima facie case of bad faith. Plaintiffs' allegations of bad faith stem principally from defendant State Farm's failure to abide by a settlement deadline unilaterally established by plaintiff Pavia's counsel and its delay in ultimately offering the policy limits in settlement.

However, defendant's failure to respond to the letter and overall delay under the circumstances of this case cannot serve as a basis for recovery. Permitting an injured plaintiff's chosen timetable for settlement to govern the bad faith inquiry would promote the customary manufacturing of bad faith claims, especially in cases where an insured of meager means is covered by a policy of insurance which could finance only a fraction of the damages in a serious personal injury case. Indeed, insurers would be bombarded with settlement offers imposing arbitrary deadlines and would be encouraged to prematurely settle their insureds' claims at the earliest possible opportunity in contravention of their contractual right and obligation of thorough investigation.

Here, plaintiff's time-limited settlement offer came at a relatively early point in the litigation. Moreover, at the time the 30-day settlement demand was made, there remained several significant questions about the insured's liability, which defendant was entitled to investigate and explore. That defendant could have acted more expeditiously does not convert inattention into a gross disregard for the insured's rights, particularly where, as here, there is no contention that the insurer failed to carry out an investigation, to evaluate the feasibility of settlement [   ], or to offer the policy limits before trial after the weakness of the insured's litigation position was clearly and fully assessed.

The facts that State Farm's preliminary liability forecasts were unfavorable and that the investigation ultimately proved those forecasts accurate certainly do not establish that the insurer was unjustified in engaging in further investigation and failing to effectuate an early settlement. On the contrary, State Farm's failure to conduct the continuing inquiry could have constituted a breach of its obligation to investigate and defend its insured. Moreover, State Farm should not be penalized for the delay in processing the claim and offering the full policy limits in settlement which resulted from its pursuit of an investigation prompted by its insured's representations which ultimately did not materialize [   ].

By any view of the evidence, State Farm's failure to promptly respond to the time-restricted demand did not amount to more than ordinary negligence—an insufficient predicate for a bad faith action. Evident as it may be with hindsight that State Farm should have responded to the settlement offer by at least requesting an extension, its failure to do so was not evidence of willful neglect of the insured's rights, but instead amounted to mistaken judgment or administrative delay in confirming what it had suspected it would do all along—settle for the policy limits. Thus, this record lacks any pattern or indicia of reckless or conscious disregard for the insured's rights upon which we could uphold a bad faith judgment.

.   .   . [The Appellate Division's order was reversed and the complaint dismissed.]

KAYE, C.J., and SIMONS, HANCOCK, BELLACOSA, SMITH and LEVINE, JJ., concur.

Notes and Questions

1. Is the court persuasive in arguing that a standard of "ordinary negligence" is inappropriate in this type of case?

2. How might settlements be affected by a system that made insurers strictly liable for any failure to settle within the policy limits if that failure results in a higher award than the one rejected?

3. The history of this action has produced a wide range of results. See Moradi–Shalal v. Fireman's Fund Ins. Cos., 758 P.2d 58 (Cal.1988), overruling Royal Globe Ins. Co. v. Superior Court, 592 P.2d 329 (Cal.1979), which had used the insurer's statutory obligation to act in good faith as the basis for implying a tort claim for bad faith refusal to settle a third party liability claim.

In 1999, the governor of California signed two bills restoring a modified form of *Royal Globe*. Although allowing bad faith suits against insurers, the laws limited these to claims arising from bodily injury (except in auto cases, where recovery for property damage was also permitted) and prevented consumers from suing if they had already accepted an insurance company's settlement offer. See Bridge, Davis Signs Legislation Restoring Bad Faith Suits, The Recorder, Oct. 11, 1999 at 1. The new laws were rendered moot, however, when California voters rejected Propositions 30 and 31—placed by insurers on the March 2000 ballot—by 2–1 and 3–1 margins respectively. (The propositions were phrased so that negative votes counted against the legislation.) The first would have established the *Royal Globe* principle within the California constitution, and the second would have modified it by saying that either party in a legal dispute could request binding arbitration in cases where the underlying claim was $50,000 or less. In their efforts to reject *Royal Globe*, insurers and others spent nearly $51 million, while supporters—including lawyers, labor and consumer groups—spent $5 million. See Howard, California Stops Bad–Faith Suits, National Underwriter Property and Casualty–Risk and Benefits Management (March 13, 2000).

4. Should an insurer be liable for not offering the insured the chance to pay something now in order to avoid a possibly greater liability later? In Parich v. State Farm Mut. Auto. Ins. Co., 919 F.2d 906 (5th Cir.1990), cert. denied 499 U.S. 976 (1991), the insurer refused a $37,000 settlement offer on a $25,000 policy limit without first asking the insured whether he would come up with the extra $12,000. The case went to trial, resulting in a verdict and judgment against the insured for some $400,000. The insurer was held liable for the entire judgment. What if the insurer in that case had asked the insured to come up with the extra $12,000 and the insured had refused? What if, instead of $12,000, the insurer asked the insured to contribute $17,000 to settle the case?

5. Should it matter in these cases whether the underlying dispute is over liability or over the extent of the damages suffered in a clear liability case? In Smith v. General Accident Insurance Co., 697 N.E.2d 168 (N.Y. 1998), the court held that a liability insurer's failure to keep the insured informed of ongoing settlement negotiations was admissible as some evidence of bad faith refusal to settle.

6. The *Pavia* court refused to extend its analysis to punitive damages. In Soto v. State Farm Ins. Co., 635 N.E.2d 1222 (N.Y.1994), defendant's insureds were adjudged liable for $420,000 in compensatory damages and $450,000 in punitive damages in connection with a fatal automobile accident. The insurer had defended the case on the ground that the driver did not have the insured's permission to drive the car. The jury found that the driver (the insured's live-in boyfriend) had permission—and was drunk at the time of the accident. After the judgment, defendant paid plaintiffs the full amount of the compensatory award (not just the $100,000 policy limits). The insureds assigned to the tort plaintiffs the insureds' claim that their insurer acted in bad faith when it refused a pretrial offer from plaintiffs to settle for the policy limits of $50,000 for each of two deaths. In this suit, plaintiff-assignees sought payment of the punitive award as well.

The court rejected the claim even though "for purposes of measuring the amounts recoverable in a bad-faith action against an insurer, [a punitive award] is no different in principle from an award of excess personal injury damages; both are unindemnified liabilities to which the insured would not have been exposed if the insurer had acted in good faith to reach a fair pretrial settlement." Nonetheless, the state's goal of "preserving the condemnatory and retributive character of punitive damage awards . . . cannot be reconciled with a conclusion that would allow the insured wrongdoer to divert the economic punishment to an insurer because of the insurer's unrelated, independent wrongful act in improperly refusing a settlement within policy limits:"

> Our system of civil justice may be organized so as to allow a wrongdoer to escape the punitive consequences of his own malfeasance in order that the injured plaintiff may enjoy the advantage of a swift and certain pretrial settlement. However, the benefit that a morally culpable wrongdoer obtains as a result of this system, i.e., being released from exposure to liability for punitive damages, is no more than a necessary incident of the process. It is certainly not a right whose loss need be made subject to compensation when a favorable pretrial settlement offer has been wasted by a reckless or faithless insurer.

California accepted *Soto* in PPG Industries, Inc. v. Transamerica Ins. Co., 975 P.2d 652 (Cal.1999). By a 4–3 vote, the court held that an insured's liability for punitive damages was not a recoverable item of damage in a suit for the insurer's negligent failure to settle. The insured was the proximate cause of its liability for punitive damages, and it was against public policy to allow indemnity for that liability. Moreover, passing along this liability would make all the other policy holders pay for these damages. The dissent feared that the result would encourage insurers to breach their duty to settle "when the claim of its insured's victim is deemed to expose the insured to a relatively small sum in compensatory damages and a relatively large sum in punitive damages." The dissent thought that the insurer should be liable for all the damages proximately caused by its negligent failure to settle.

7. What are the respective interests of the plaintiff, the insured, and the insurer in the *Pavia-Soto* situation? Has the court reached sound accommodations? If the insureds were independently wealthy would your answer change?

For a discussion of the various conflicts that may arise between insurers and insureds during settlement negotiations, and possible ways to resolve them, see Syverud, The Duty to Settle, 76 Va.L.Rev 1113 (1990).

8. *Excess coverage obligations.* "Excess insurance carriers" may face the same risks that insureds face. Since it has become common for persons and companies to purchase tiers of insurance ("primary" for the main coverage and "excess" or "umbrella" coverage for catastrophic losses beyond the limits of the primary policy), it is common for different companies to write each coverage. This creates questions analogous to those addressed earlier about the obligations of the primary insurer or the insured to settle the case so as to avoid exposing the excess carrier to severe losses. In Commercial Union Assurance Cos. v. Safeway Stores, Inc., 610 P.2d 1038 (Cal.1980), the court concluded that the insured owed no duty to the excess carrier to settle the underlying case if it could do so before reaching the amount at which the excess coverage began. Although an insured may have a "legitimate right to expect" the primary insurer to explore ways to protect the insured, no such expectation runs in favor of the excess carrier against the primary insurer. See also, Continental Casualty Co. v. Pacific Indemnity Co., 184 Cal.Rptr. 583 (App. 1982).

9. *Double coverage.* Since several insurance policies may cover the same liability, it has become important to determine the sequence in which the policies come into play. Sometimes this can be decided from the language of the policies—if one states that it is "primary" and the second states that it is only "excess" after others have been exhausted. Sometimes the policies all call for proration with other applicable policies. But if, for example, all the policies claim to be "excess," the language of the policies cannot control. For an introduction to this problem, see Note, Toward a More Equitable Method of Prorating Liability Insurance Policies, 51 S.Cal. L.Rev. 943 (1978). See also Carriers Ins. Co. v. American Policyholders' Ins. Co., 404 A.2d 216 (Me.1979).

10. *Contribution and indemnity.* The institution of insurance has also influenced attitudes toward contribution and indemnity. Although, in a world without insurance, these devices for sharing or shifting losses were thought to be just, some now argue that insurance has changed the situation. In James, Contribution Among Joint Tortfeasors: A Pragmatic Criticism, 54 Harv.L.Rev. 1156 (1941), Professor Fleming James argued that contribution was used in only two situations: (1) where an insurer or large self-insurer seeks it against an uninsured individual and (2) where an insurer or self-insurer seeks it against another such company. He would prefer barring contribution "even though it mars a theoretical symmetry in the law of negligence." For disagreement, see Gregory, Contribution Among Joint Tortfeasors: A Defense, 54 Harv.L.Rev. 1170 (1941). Does the introduction of comparative negligence among defendants change the arguments? What about deterrence?

Do the same considerations apply to subrogation? Consider these examples:

Landlord rented a home to defendant tenant who negligently caused fire damage to the house. The landlord's fire insurer paid the landlord and then sought subrogation against the tenant. The claim was upheld in Fire Insurance Exchange v. Hammond, 99 Cal.Rptr.2d 596 (App. 2000). There was no indication that the landlord's coverage was obtained for the mutual benefit of both landlord and tenant.

Fire district workers negligently started a fire that destroyed the home of rock star Grace Slick and her husband. Slick's insurer, Allstate, paid the couple $1.25 million and sought subrogation from the district. The district settled for $895,000, all but $220,000 of which went to Allstate. The payment "virtually wiped out [the district's] funds for acquiring lands to protect them from development." See Dougan, Slick Settlement Cleans Out Agency, S.F. Examiner, Nov. 24, 1994, at A–21.

CHAPTER XI

A Survey of Alternatives

In recent years, tort reform activity has been largely concentrated on efforts to adopt incremental changes in the existing system. We begin with a brief discussion of the principal types of initiatives in this category. There is a logical progression reflected in considering these strategies immediately after the chapter on damages and insurance. As will become evident, the dominant incremental reform measures in recent years have, in fact, been addressed to the remedial, or damages/insurance, side of the tort system, rather than aimed at altering substantive tort doctrine. Indeed, a number of these initiatives were noted in Chapter X, as we discussed non-pecuniary loss, punitive damages, collateral source recovery, and contingency fees (and earlier, in Chapters V and VI, when we discussed joint and several liability).

After examining incremental tort reform measures in greater detail, we will consider a wide variety of alternatives to the tort system. Some, such as workers' compensation and auto no-fault plans, are designed to replace all or a substantial part of tort law in major areas of injury activity. Others, such as vaccine and birth defect compensation schemes, focus on narrower areas of accidental harm. At the other extreme from these focused plans, we examine comprehensive no-fault and social insurance proposals that would replace much or all of tort law in injury and accident-related disease cases. The common theme in these diverse plans is that they are intended to serve as tort replacement measures. Their premise is that a better system than tort law can be designed to address the problem of accidental harm.

What are the dimensions of that problem? National Safety Council data indicate that in 1998 in a total U.S. population of more than 250 million, there were some 92,200 accidental deaths—the three major categories being 41,200 motor vehicle deaths, 28,200 deaths in the home, and 3,000 workplace deaths not involving motor vehicles. An estimated 19.4 million disabling injuries occurred (of which 2.6 million involved hospitalization), principally in the home (7.0 million), on the job (3.8 million), and in motor vehicles (2.2 million). In 1998, unintentional injuries were the fifth largest cause of death overall, and were the biggest killer of those aged 1 to 30 (except those in their mid-thirties), with motor vehicles leading in every age category up to 30.

The National Safety Council report also estimates the costs associated with accidental death and injury. The total of $480 billion for all accidents includes $246 billion in wage and productivity loss, $78 billion in medical expenses, and $82 billion in administrative costs (insurance, police and legal costs). The automobile looms large in these figures, with total cost of automobile accidents pegged at $191.6 billion, including $67.8 billion in wage and productivity losses. By comparison, worker injuries were estimated at $125 billion and home injuries at $113.5 billion. See National Safety Council, Injury Facts (1999 ed.).

How do these accident figures translate into tort claims? A Department of Justice study of state courts of general jurisdiction in the 75 largest counties in the U.S. by extrapolation estimated that in 1992 about 378,000 tort claims were filed involving 1.4 million plaintiffs and defendants—a claims figure that had held relatively steady for at least seven years. See Smith, et al., Tort Cases in Large Counties: Civil Justice Survey of State Courts, 1992 (Bureau of Justice Statistics Special Report (April 1995)). Since accidents in the home frequently do not give rise to lawsuits and those on the job are generally outside the tort system, the largest number of claims came from motor vehicle accidents. A sample of the overall claims indicated that 60% were auto cases, 17% involved premises liability (commercial as well as residential), 5% were in the medical malpractice area, and 3% involved products liability.

Only 3% of tort cases go to trial (7% in medical malpractice cases). Within one year, 44% of tort cases reach disposition; the mean processing time for all cases being 19.3 months. Auto cases again stand out—they have the shortest processing time among all categories. The most common type of tort case involved one individual suing another (47% of all tort cases—a large majority of auto cases fall in this category). Individuals sue businesses in 37% of the cases and about 5% involve suits by individuals against government agencies or hospitals.

To put tort cases in context, the 1995 Department of Justice study found that tort claims constituted about 10% of all civil filings—the largest category being domestic relations cases (41%). And from another perspective, recall the data from a 1991 RAND study, p. 1, supra, indicating that tort liability payments comprise only 11% of total compensation for loss from all sources in accidental harm cases. For comprehensive discussion of the interrelationship between tort and other sources of payment in accidental harm cases, see Abraham & Liebman, Private Insurance, Social Insurance, and Tort Reform: Toward a New Vision of Compensation for Illness and Injury, 93 Colum.L.Rev. 75 (1993).

Although it has been estimated that in 1985 injury victims obtained about 46% of the premiums paid by defendants in tort suits, that percentage varied from 52% of total expenditures received by plaintiffs in auto cases to an average of 43% in other accident cases. The study estimated that the legal fees and expenses of injury victims constitute about 30–31% of the total compensation paid to plaintiffs, and that defendants' legal fees and expenses average about 16% of the total compensation paid to plaintiffs in auto cases and 28% in non-auto cases. The study estimated that defendants' legal expenses had been growing annually at a rate of 6% in auto cases and 15% in non-auto cases during the past five years. Trend data were not available for plaintiffs' legal fees and expenses. See J. Kakalik & N. Pace, Costs and Compensation Paid in Tort Litigation (1986).

A system that pays one dollar in benefits for one dollar of premiums is not likely to be the goal. This point is made in Brandau, Compensating Highway Accident Victims–Who Pays the Insurance Cost?, 37 Ins.Counsel J. 598 (1970). Adverting to figures on the relative efficiency of various reparation systems, the author suggested (p. 605) that:

> . . . [T]he concept of efficiency often used in describing systems seems to imply that an absolutely efficient system would pay out $1.00 in benefits for every dollar it collected in payments. This is not the case. Such a system would ultimately prove to be very inefficient. Some expense is necessary to determine whether persons applying for benefits are qualified. Any system needs a control to determine eligibility for payments or else the system will be fraught with fraud. Of course, to the extent that there are extensive eligibility requirements, the expense of administering a program goes up. The justification of this expense is not a matter of efficiency, but rather a matter of judgment whether the eligibility requirements are worth the expense of administering the program.

Can the due care issue in negligence cases be regarded as an "eligibility requirement," in Brandau's terms? What about the causation issues in toxic tort cases? Assess the fault system and the tort system generally in Brandau's terms. Keep these considerations in mind as we consider other techniques for meeting the financial consequences of accidents.

A. INCREMENTAL TORT REFORM

Within the last 25 years, we can trace three periods of legislative activity related to aspects of tort reform. The first, in the mid-1970s, was centered on medical malpractice. Physicians complained of high malpractice insurance premiums: some left high-risk specialties; others "went bare"— dropped their liability coverage; some went on strike and marched to demand relief. Virtually all state legislatures responded—though with little uniformity. Among the common changes in malpractice cases were: placing caps on the amount that could be awarded for pain and suffering; regulating fees of plaintiffs' attorneys; shortening statutes of limitation; requiring periodic payments as to future awards; and altering or eliminating the collateral source rule.

One prominent example was California, which enacted the Medical Injury Compensation Reform Act (MICRA). The Act limited recovery for pain and suffering in medical malpractice cases to a maximum of $250,000. (Cal.Civ.Code § 3333.2). Also, in any case in which the award of future damages exceeded $50,000, the judge was required, at the request of either party, to direct that the money be paid periodically. If the victim died before the judgment was satisfied, the defendant might be relieved of paying for future medical expenses. The payments for future lost earnings would not be affected by death. (Cal.Code Civ.Pro. § 667.7). Maximum percentages for contingent fees were set (Cal.Bus. & Prof. Code § 6146). Lastly, the Act provided that if all or part of the victim's medical bills had been paid by the victim's own insurance or some other source unrelated to the defendant, the jury should be told this—but not told what to do with the information. Subrogation was eliminated. (Cal.Civ. Code § 3333.1).

The second wave of activity occurred in the mid-1980s, as the result of increasingly large damage awards, soaring insurance premiums, and, for a growing number of enterprises, the complete unavailability of liability insurance. The extent of this crisis was questioned by critics of the insurance industry (who blamed the industry's problems on the lowering of interest rates from their highs of the early 1980s). Whatever the truth, between 1985 and 1988, 48 state legislatures responded with some variety of tort reform legislation. These enactments addressed the concerns of tort defendants generally, unlike the physician-specific statutes of the mid-1970s.

The principal changes were in the damages and insurance areas. A large number of states enacted limitations in one form or another on recovery for non-economic loss (pain and suffering and/or punitive damages), on joint and several liability, and on the collateral source rule. In all, during this second wave 30 states changed their joint and several liability rules and 23 placed some type of ceiling on pain and suffering awards. Another 25 placed limits on punitive damage awards—either eliminating them, placing caps on them, requiring that they not exceed some fixed ratio to compensatory awards, or requiring that some percentage of the punitive award be paid to the state. Other areas of change involved limitations on attorneys' fees, adoption of special legislation covering dram shop and social host liability for drunken driving, and requirements of periodic payments in large-award cases. These developments are discussed in Sanders and Joyce, ''Off to the Races'': The 1980s Tort Crisis and the Law Reform Process, 27 Houst.L.Rev. 207 (1990). For an examination of the dramatic impact of these measures on some injury victims, as well as the perceived benefits to liability bearers, in one state that enacted an array of tort limitations during this period, see Geyelin, Tort Reform Test: Overhaul of Civil Law In Colorado Produces Quite Mixed Results, Wall St.J., March 3, 1992 at 1.

Generalization is difficult because each state took its own distinctive approach to tort reform. Even when states began with the same agenda, legislative compromise often produced quite disparate results. The Washington legislature, for example, limited the amount recoverable for all non-monetary losses in personal injury cases by a formula keyed to the state's average wage and the victim's life expectancy. On the other hand, some states enacted flat caps on non-economic damages, such as Maryland's $350,000.

New York adopted a comprehensive tort reform package that, among other things, altered the collateral source rule and provided for periodic payments. It also provided that most defendants who were held less than 50% at fault were liable to the plaintiff only for that percentage of the award for pain and suffering. California, by voter initiative, abolished all joint and several liability for non-economic damages, p. 370, supra.

In the same period when these across-the-board limitations were being enacted, several states adopted measures to protect defendants in products liability cases. The most common move was adoption of a statute of repose—a statute that protected sellers whose products caused harm more than a certain number of years after they put the product into the stream of commerce. Some states adopted similar legislation for architects and builders. A typical length of time was 10 or 12 years. This made it possible that the statute of repose would have run before the victim was hurt. See, e.g., Arsenault v. Pa–Ted Spring Co., 523 A.2d 1283 (Conn.1987)(claim involving 14-year-old product barred by 10-year statute of repose). Recall *Tanges*, p. 390, supra. A few states adopted "useful life" statutes in which the trier of fact must determine the average expected useful life of a generic product to determine if the injury in the case came from the normal aging of the product in question or from a "defect." See, Note, The Evolution of Useful Life Statutes in the Products Liability Reform Effort, 1989 Duke L.J. 1689. Note also that some states legislated to make the "open and obvious" nature of a danger relevant in products cases.

All of these reform efforts have been undertaken by state legislatures. The products area, however, raises unique problems in terms of the utility of seeking reform at the state level, as opposed to the federal level. It may well be that state courts developed and expanded tort liability doctrines in this area in part because they had little control over the common law's development and did not want their citizens to face barriers that citizens in other states did not face. The state focus has never been made clearer than in Blankenship v. General Motors Corp., 406 S.E.2d 781 (W.Va.1991). In response to questions certified by a federal district court, the court announced that it would adopt the doctrine of crashworthiness in an appropriate case. Although the court stated its doubts about much of existing products law, it also observed that:

> West Virginia is a small rural state with .66 percent of the population of the United States. Although some members of this Court have reservations about the wisdom of many aspects of tort law, as a court we are utterly powerless to make the *overall* tort system for cases arising in interstate commerce more rational: Nothing that we do will have any impact whatsoever on the set of economic trade-offs that occur in the *national* economy. And, ironically, trying unilaterally to make the American tort system more rational through being uniquely responsible in West Virginia will only punish our residents severely without, in any regard, improving the system for anyone else.

> . . .

> . . . . In light of the fact that all of our sister states have adopted a cause of action for lack of crashworthiness, General Motors is *already* collecting a product liability premium every time it sells a car anywhere in the world, including West Virginia. [   ] West Virginians,

then, are already paying the product liability insurance premium when they buy a General Motors car, so this Court would be both foolish and irresponsible if we held that while West Virginians must pay the premiums, West Virginians can't collect the insurance after they're injured.

The court announced further that if the federal courts were in doubt in any future crashworthiness case in which there was a real split of authority among the states, West Virginia would adopt the rule most favorable to plaintiffs.

How do you react to this position? Should a legislator in West Virginia react any differently if pressed to adopt legislation that would cut back on product liability rules that now favor plaintiffs?

After a brief hiatus, a third wave of tort reform activity arose in the early 1990s—once again featuring packages of reform targeted at some combinations of caps on non-economic loss and punitive damages, limitations on collateral source recovery, elimination of joint and several liability, and in some instances, restrictions on the contingency fee. In B. Franklin, Learning Curve: Lawyers Must Confront Impact of Changes on Litigation Strategies, 81 A.B.A.J. 62 (Aug. 1995), the author reports the following summary data on the cumulative status of incremental law reform efforts in the mid-1990s:

> While the American Tort Reform Association, a primary lobbying group, counts 18 states that impose caps on noneconomic damages, they do not apply the same ceilings or cover the same types of actions.

> Illinois, for example, caps noneconomic damages in all tort cases at $500,000, while adjacent Indiana caps noneconomic damages in medical malpractice cases at $750,000. In California, a $250,000 cap applies only to medical malpractice.

> Similar variations appear in caps on punitive damages in 29 states and product liability measures in 32 states, according to ATRA estimates.

> And, says ATRA, only Colorado, Florida, Montana, North Dakota and Oregon have acted in all five areas usually targeted by tort reform advocates: joint and several liability, product liability, punitive damages, noneconomic damages and the collateral source rule.

> Punitive damages are banned altogether in five states, and 21 have toughened standards for punitive damages, forcing plaintiff to show "clear and convincing" evidence of the defendant's conduct, according to ATRA. In 41 states, plaintiffs must confront the elimination or modification of joint and several liability.

> .   .   .

> According to ATLA [another primary lobbying group, on the plaintiffs' side, the American Trial Lawyers' Association], 17 states regulate attorney fees in medical malpractice or other tort cases, either through sliding scales like those in California or by allowing judges to review for reasonableness.

The series of articles in the same ABA Journal issue makes the overall point that for all the publicity given to expected federal tort reform action, it was in the states—as these figures indicate—that sweeping measures had been adopted. In fact, for many sessions Congress had been pressed, without success, to adopt a products liability bill that would cut back on some benefits now held by plaintiffs in products cases. In 1995, riding the wave of the campaign promises in the Contract with America, the House of Representatives passed a more comprehensive bill that would have capped punitive damages in all civil cases (and non-economic loss in medical malpractice cases), eliminated joint and several liability, and adopted a modified ''loser pays'' attorneys' fee rule in diversity cases brought in federal court. The Senate passed a more limited set of reforms targeted at punitive damages in products liability cases. After a conference committee agreed on a bill that was closer to the Senate version, President Clinton vetoed it.

Have the incremental tort reform measures been effective in addressing the tort law ''crisis?'' Patricia Danzon's research on the impact of the mid-1970s reforms in the medical malpractice area suggests some possible effects. Danzon analyzed data for the 1975–1984 period and concluded that damage caps, limits on the collateral source rule, and arbitration procedures had an appreciable effect on reducing the dollar amounts of tort claims and awards; shorter statutes of limitations, together with limits on the collateral source rule, had the greatest effect on reducing the frequency of tort claims. Danzon, The Frequency and Severity of Medical Malpractice Claims: New Evidence, 49 Law & Contemp.Probs. 57 (1986). See also Sloan, Mergenhagen & Bovbjerg, Effects of Tort Reforms on the Value of Closed Medical Malpractice Claims: A Microanalysis, 14 J. Health Politics, Policy and Law 663 (1989). For a comprehensive analysis of the empirical data on claims, award levels and costs in the tort system, concluding that we know very little about how the system in fact works, see Saks, Do We Really Know Anything about the Behavior of the Tort Litigation System—And Why Not?, 140 U.Pa.L.Rev. 1147 (1992).

Whatever the explanation, there seems to be a growing perception that the number of tort claims has levelled off in recent years after a period of sustained growth. For statistical evidence, see the Department of Justice study, p. 786, supra. This perception correlates with claims that tort doctrine has become less expansive in the same period. This thesis is explored, with an attempt at explanation, in Schwartz, The Beginning and Possible End of the Rise of Modern American Tort Law, 26 Ga. L.Rev. 601 (1992). See also Henderson & Eisenberg, The Quiet Revolution in Products Liability Law: An Empirical Study of Legal Change, 37 UCLA L.Rev. 479 (1990), locating the onset of stabilization in the products area in the mid-1980s.

Reconsider the discussions throughout the course of pain and suffering, punitive damages, joint and several liability, the collateral source rule and the contingency fee. What kinds of limitations, if any, seem especially warranted? A concise treatment of the pros and cons of adopting limitations in each of these areas, as well as an agenda for incremental reform, can be found in the American Bar Association Report of the Action Commission to Improve the Tort System (1987). Do the various legislative reforms serve the overall goals and objectives of the tort system, such as deterring unsafe behavior and compensating accident victims? Do particular reforms advance certain goals while retarding others? Did the discussion of products liability, medical malpractice and other doctrinal topics earlier in the course suggest the need for reform of these substantive rules of liability? For a discussion of the relationship of the joint and several liability limitations and the non-economic damages ceilings to the tort system's objectives, see Madden, Joint and Several Liability and Environmental Harm in the 1990's, 9 Fordham Envtl. Law J. 483 (1998) (criticizing the abolition of joint and several liability from the standpoints of corrective justice and economic efficiency and suggesting modified alternatives to the traditional approach).

An especially thorough discussion of the range of tort and insurance reforms considered by New York in the mid-1980s—most of which were adopted—is found in the two volume report of the Governor's Advisory Commission on Liability Insurance, Insuring Our Future (1986). On the waves of tort reform generally, see Apelbaum and Ryder, The Third Wave of Federal Tort Reform: Protecting the Public or Pushing the Constitutional Envelope? 8 Cornell J.L. & Pub. Pol'y 591 (1999); Peck, Marshall, and Kranz, Tort Reform 1999: A Building Without a Foundation, 27 Fla. St. U.L.Rev. 397 (2000).

The constitutionality of many of these reform efforts, particularly the enactment of caps on damages, has often been challenged—in some cases successfully—on state constitutional grounds, including right to jury trial, right to obtain damages, denial of equal protection, and right of access to courts. Indeed, the Illinois cap referred to in the summary above, was held unconstitutional in Best v. Taylor Machine Works, 689 N.E.2d 1057 (Ill. 1997) (invalidating cap on non-economic compensatory damages; modification of joint and several liability; and provision deeming plaintiff to have consented to unlimited disclosure of all medical records). For other recent examples, see McIntosh v. Melroe Co., 729 N.E.2d 972 (Ind.2000) (upholding ten-year statute of repose); Lakin v. Senco Products, Inc., 987 P.2d 463 (Or.1999) (invalidating cap on non-economic damages); State ex rel. Ohio Academy of Trial Lawyers v. Sheward, 715 N.E.2d 1062 (Ohio 1999) (invalidating entire act for violating the state's one-subject rule). For discussion of constitutional attacks on state legislative limits on punitive damages, most of which have been unsuccessful, see Hallahan, Social Interests versus Plaintiffs' Rights: The Constitutional Battle over Statutory Limitations on Punitive Damages, 26 Loy.U.Chi.L.J. 405 (1995).

B.   OCCUPATIONAL INJURIES—WORKERS' COMPENSATION

Occupational injuries emerged as a serious problem in this country after the Civil War. The rapid pace of industrialization brought a steadily increasing number of accidental injuries and deaths. Along with other accidental injury claims, workers' claims were handled in the tort system until the early years of the twentieth century. Within a decade, however, beginning in 1910, a majority of states enacted workers' compensation laws, replacing the tort remedy with a no-fault compensation scheme. The following excerpt describes these developments and discusses the basic features of the system.

Workers' Compensation: Strengthening the Social Compact

Orin Kramer & Richard Briffault.
13–27, 73–75 (1991).

A.   Basic Terms: No–Fault and Exclusive Remedy

At the heart of workers' compensation is a basic quid pro quo: employers must provide employees who suffer work-related injuries or disease with medical and income benefits regardless of whether the employee or the employer was at fault for the injury; employees, in turn, must treat workers' compensation benefits as their exclusive remedy against the employer and give up any common law tort claims against their employers. This no-fault principle embodies two fundamental concerns.

First, it is argued that fault should not be relevant because, as a matter of social justice, business should bear the financial burden of work-related accidents, much like any other cost of production. As Theodore Roosevelt put it, "Exactly as the working man is entitled to his wages, so should he be entitled to indemnity for the injuries sustained in the natural course of his labor." Moreover, making business bear the costs of industrial accidents maximizes employer interest in occupational safety and health and thus reduces the frequency and severity of injury.

Second, no-fault provides greater efficiency. By eliminating fault and making workers' compensation the employee's exclusive remedy, compensation can be provided on a swift, certain and self-executing basis, at minimal administrative cost and without the expense, delays, uncertainties, and adversarial confrontation of attorney involvement and common law litigation. The recent upsurge in attorney involvement due to external pressures and changes in the system now jeopardizes the goal of a low administrative cost, litigation-free, self-executing mechanism.

B.   Origins: Meeting the Challenge of the Industrial Revolution and Overcoming the Restrictions of the Common Law

The Industrial Revolution was accompanied by an enormous upsurge in work-related accidents. The rapid expansion and development of manufacturing, mining, steel mills, and railroads, the deployment of dangerous heavy machinery and high-speed industrial processes, and the employment of large numbers of new, relatively unskilled workers all resulted in unprecedented levels of workplace injuries.

1.   The "Unholy Trinity" of Employer Common Law Defenses

Under common law, the employer had a duty to provide a reasonably safe place in which to work and reasonably safe tools, appliances, and working materials. Therefore, in theory the employee who sustained a work-related injury, or his survivors, could bring a tort action for damages against the employer if the injury reflected a breach of the employer's duty of reasonable care. In practice, however, 19th century employers were largely immunized from liability for industrial accidents by three other common law doctrines.

First, under the "fellow servant" rule, an employee could not recover damages from the employer if another employee had contributed to the injury. Since in the large factories, mines and mills of an industrial economy the employer almost inevitably acts through other employees, the fellow servant rule was a nearly insuperable barrier to recovery.

Second, under the principle of "contributory negligence," the injured employee could not recover damages if he had in any way negligently contributed to his own injury.

Third, under the doctrine of "assumption of risk," employees were held to have assumed the risk of injury from the customary and observable dangers attendant upon their jobs.

Reformers, concerned about the plight of injured workers and their families, sought to overcome the harsh effects of this "unholy trinity" of employer common law defenses, and around the turn of the century courts and legislatures in several states modified or abandoned one or more of these three rules. However, this liberalization of the common law was of limited benefit to most injured workers since it still left in place the need to prove fault, and that often proved to be as high a hurdle to vault as the "unholy trinity" of defenses.

2.   The Burden of Fault

Under the fault system, an employee, or his survivors, needed to hire a lawyer, persuade fellow workers to testify against their employer, and attempt to survive without wages or money for medical bills until the litigation was resolved. Moreover, for many accidents it was difficult to prove that the employer had violated an established standard of care. As a result, although in some cases employees won generous awards, including damages for pain and suffering, in most cases they received little or nothing. One early 20th century study of workers killed on the job found that in 37% of the cases the families of the victims received no compensation, and that in another 42% of the cases the families received less than $500, or well under the average annual salary of $791.

Fault-based litigation, even without the "unholy trinity," was a costly and uncertain gamble for most workers. Employers, too, were troubled by rising levels of litigation and the prospect of serious damages in the few but increasing number of cases in which workers prevailed.

3.   The Adoption of Workers' Compensation

Workers' compensation was pioneered in Germany in the late 19th century. The first American workers' compensation measure was a federal statute adopted in 1908 that provided a limited program for federal workers and served as a forerunner of the current Federal Employees Compensation Act. In 1910, New York enacted the first state workers' compensation program, but the New York Court of Appeals found that the imposition of liability without fault was unconstitutional and invalidated the statute. The first effective state workers' compensation law was passed in Wisconsin in 1911. To avoid the constitutional issue, the state made workers' compensation elective. As an incentive to employer participation, the legislature provided for the waiver of the "unholy trinity" defenses for employers not participating in the program.

The Wisconsin model of "elective" workers' compensation was sustained in the courts and spread rapidly to other states. By the end of 1911, 10 states had adopted workers' compensation, and by 1917 it was on the books in 37 states. Since the enactment of legislation by Mississippi in 1949, there has been a workers' compensation program in every state.

By eliminating the requirement of proof of fault, workers' compensation laws enormously simplified the process of providing medical and disability compensation for injured workers. Employees no longer need plead and prove through costly litigation a standard of reasonable care for the operations of the workplace or of industrial equipment, or establish by a preponderance of the evidence that their employers had violated such a standard. The elimination of fault also removes the element of opprobrium from the employer as the duty to compensate is not based on misconduct but treated as a cost of production. Finally, the no-fault system was intended to eliminate the adversarial atmosphere that surrounds litigation and thus improve the quality of employer-employee relations.

C.   Evolution: The Expansion of Coverage, the Redefinition of Compensable Injury, and the Enhancement of Benefits

Although most states have had workers' compensation programs for more than 70 years, the system has undergone considerable change, particularly in recent decades. State legislatures have repeatedly amended their laws, modifying programs, and experimenting with new provisions. State courts have also played an important role in interpreting and often liberalizing the effects of state laws.

1.   The Pace and Direction of Change

The general direction of state legislatures and courts has been expansion: the inclusion of more workers and workplaces, the liberalization of the definition of compensable injury, the addition of new benefits, and the enhancement of existing benefits. The pace of change accelerated markedly following the publication of the Report of the National Commission on State Workmen's Compensation Laws in 1972 and the increased attention in the 1970s and early 1980s to the problems of occupational disease. Nor has the rate of change slackened significantly since the 1970s. Between 1982 and 1987, there were approximately 900 amendments to state workers' compensation laws, and an additional 155 changes were made in 1988 alone.

Many of these changes have advanced the societal goal of fair and adequate compensation for injured workers. But these changes have also added markedly to the costs of workers' compensation systems. In most states, the current workers' compensation system is, by design, more generous and thus considerably more costly than workers' compensation was in 1911 or 1972.

The expansion of workers' compensation coverage and the enhancement of benefits must be taken into account in assessing the costs of the system and the proper levels of premium for workers' compensation insurance. Indeed, a significant component of the current problems besetting workers' compensation is the failure of the regulatory system in some jurisdictions to respond to the real costs of an expanded compensation system.

2. Expansion of Coverage of Workers and Employers

Initially, workers' compensation was limited to large firms, firms engaged in "hazardous" or "ultra-hazardous" activities, and to limited categories of workers. Moreover, long after the constitutionality of no-fault had been revisited and sustained by most state courts, many states continued to make workers' compensation elective. In 1950, 77% of American workers were covered by workers' compensation laws. As late as 1968, 24 states had significant size-of-firm restrictions, and 23 states still permitted elective coverage.

Among the "essential recommendations" of the National Commission on State Workmen's Compensation Laws was universal workers' compensation coverage. The Commission called for the elimination of "elective" coverage, of the exemption of small employers, of the exemption of any class of employees, and for the extension of coverage to traditionally noncovered workers such as agricultural workers, household workers and government employees.

Although there has not been total state compliance with the National Commission's recommendations, and many states continue to exempt certain categories of workers and employees, the percentage of the work force covered by workers' compensation has grown to 87%. Only three states continue to make the program elective for covered workers. In only four states are fewer than 75% of employees under workers' compensation. In 23 states, more than 90% of all employees are covered by workers' compensation, and in four states and the District of Columbia coverage is universal.

3. Expansion of the Definition of Compensable Injury

a.   The Concept of Work–Relatedness

Workers' compensation did not and does not make the employer absolutely responsible for employee health care and disabilities. (For a description of the structure of workers' compensation benefits, see Appendix.) The employer's duty extends only to work-related injuries: injuries which, according to the language of virtually every state law, "arise out of and in the course of employment." In other words, although workers' compensation eliminates the requirement of employer fault, it continues to require proof of *work-related cause.*

i.   The Model of the Traumatic Accident

When workers' compensation was first adopted, it did not seem that proof of work-related causation would entail anything like the complexities and ambiguities implicit in fault-based compensation. The prevalent cause of work-related injury was the traumatic accident: a sudden, unexpected event which resulted in immediate injury. Since the place and physical cause of most injuries are readily apparent, it was assumed that employers and administrators could easily distinguish between work-related and non-work-related accidents, without resort to protracted dispute resolution processes, litigation or attorneys. And for the overwhelming majority of claims, that remains the case.

ii.   Traditional Gray Areas

There were, of course, always gray areas in determining the work-relatedness of even simple traumatic accidents. Injuries occurring on the employer's premises but outside the production process, such as during coffee breaks or lunch time; injuries involving employee violation of work rules or willful misconduct; and injuries occurring during commutation or off-premises have been a regular source of dispute. But these are a tiny fraction of compensation claims, and in most states these issues have been resolved by court decision or statutory amendment.

iii.   Soft Tissue Injuries and Aggravation of Existing Conditions

More numerically significant and more conceptually difficult than the traditional gray areas are soft tissue injuries that result from repeated activity, such as straining, bending, twisting or lifting, over a period of time. In these instances, it is more difficult to determine when the injury has occurred and whether the injury is the result of on-the-job or off-the-job activity. By one count, in 1988 approximately 48% of workplace injuries were the result of repetitive motion.

In aggravation of existing conditions cases, the injury may have occurred on the job, but its severity in terms of medical bills and time lost from work may be a result of a prior injury, unusual personal susceptibility or environmental factors unrelated to work. In this case the employer may seek to limit its liability to the work-related component of the injury. Today in many states the employer is responsible for the full extent of work-related injury, consistent with the well-established doctrine that the employer "takes the employee as he finds him."

Although soft tissue injuries and aggravation of existing conditions claims have added significant new costs to workers' compensation coverage, the real challenge to the work-relatedness requirement and to the system's ability to resolve the causation question without resort to extensive administrative or litigated proceedings has been occupational disease.

b.   The Challenge of Occupational Disease

i.   Initial Limitations on Coverage

Some occupational diseases do not fit within the national model of traumatic accidents. The onset of illness may not occur at the workplace or during the course of employment. Often illness will not result until years after exposure to the causative agent. The manifestations of occupational disease may not be distinctive and may be difficult to distinguish from those of non-occupational ailments or the aging process. The causation of disease may be complex and may involve the interaction of work, heredity, environment, personal lifestyle and other factors.

Most early workers' compensation laws did not provide compensation for disease or only provided coverage for specified, or "scheduled" diseases, like "black lung," silicosis or byssinosis ("brown lung"). These diseases were uniquely occupation-related in the sense that while many workers in an occupation eventually contracted the illness, few people not employed in that occupation ever suffered from the disease.

Moreover, recovery for occupational disease in some states was limited by procedural requirements. Statutes of limitations that ran from the time of last exposure to the disease-causing agent effectively blocked recovery in cases of long latency illnesses. Minimum exposure rules and recency of exposure requirements which had no scientific basis also restricted the availability of coverage, as did statutory provisions affecting the responsibilities of particular employers where the worker was exposed to the disease-causing hazard during a succession of jobs in an industry.

ii.   The Expansion of Coverage

In recent decades, the situation has changed dramatically. In the wake of liberalizing court decisions and the recommendation of the National Commission on State Workmen's Compensation Laws, all 50 states now provide workers' compensation for any work-caused illness. Moreover, many states have relaxed their procedural restrictions, for example, by starting statute of limitations requirements from the onset of the first manifestation of illness rather than from the last exposure to the causative agent. This makes it far easier for workers suffering from diseases with long latency periods to bring claims.

The workers' compensation system is now caught in a vise. On the one hand, expanding scientific and medical knowledge has suggested associations between certain workplace materials, conditions and processes and an increased risk of contracting many ordinary diseases, such as cancer, heart disease, lung diseases, dermatitis, hypertension, and degenerative diseases such as arthritis. Given the complex causation of these diseases, whether the risk actually results in illness may often turn on non-work-related factors.

On the other hand, state workers' compensation laws, although they have abandoned the "scheduled disease" approach, still continue to require that, to be compensable, a disease must result from factors "peculiar to the trade or occupation" and not be an "ordinary disease of life."

The result has been increased litigation over causation and the existence and scope of coverage in the area of occupational disease. In these cases, both claimants and employers or insurers make complex medical and legal arguments. These cases are marked by the claims of conflicting experts, the so-called "dueling doctors," with considerable litigation costs and uncertainty of outcome for all parties.

The overall trend has been to relax the claimant's burden of proof and permit recovery even where work-related factors are a contributing but not the sole cause of disease. In some cases, liability has been found even where work-related contributing causation was only "reasonably probable" in light of current medical knowledge. This means that the employer will have to pay the full costs of an illness which is at best only partially work-related.

It is critical to recognize that occupational diseases today represent only a modest cost in the workers' compensation system. In most states, only about 2% of claims involve work-related illness, and the majority of those claims involve conditions that can be handled easily by the system. However, these claims have a disproportionate impact on total workers' compensation costs. The special issues with respect to the proof of causation drive up administrative costs, while the average indemnity benefit for occupational disease is five times greater than for traumatic injuries.

Moreover, today's claims may be only the leading edge of future occupational disease filings. Scientific knowledge continues to expand our understanding of the relationship between work conditions and health and to provide new bases for claims for compensation. Most significantly, several observers have noted that "a new type of claim is on the horizon," one that portends steeply increased administrative and compensation burdens for the workers' compensation system in future years: mental stress.

iii. The Special Case of Mental Stress

Over the last decade, the number of mental stress claims has exploded, rising from virtually zero to more than 10% of all occupational disease claims. In California, the number of mental stress claims rose 511% from 1980 to 1987. Mental stress now accounts for approximately 25% of all occupational disease claims in California making it the leading source of occupational disease claims in the nation's largest state.

The earliest workers' compensation claims for mental injury grew out of cases based on some physical event, either a traumatic physical accident which resulted in subsequent psychiatric harm, or acute mental stress which led to a physical injury such as a heart attack. These "physical-mental" and "mental-physical" cases have been largely supplanted in notoriety by the so-called "mental-mental" cases in which a highly subjective mental or emotional injury results from a mental or emotional cause, without any physical accident or impairment.

Mental stress claims incorporate all the causation difficulties of some occupational disease claims, but taken to an extreme degree. Most mental stress claims have no single precipitating cause. A study of mental stress claims in California found that 90% are the result of cumulative events.

Few mental stress claims stem from conditions peculiar or unique to particular workplaces or occupations. Rather, a California study found that most such claims are due to non-specific "job pressures" or "harassment," features "pandemic to workplaces." Many mental stress claims involve the aggravation of pre-existing conditions and the interaction of workplace and non-workplace factors.

Mental stress claims are highly subjective, difficult to diagnose, assess, quantify or disprove. Medical knowledge with respect to the cause and treatment of mental stress is imprecise. Standards for determining when a mental or emotional problem rises to the level of illness are uncertain. And there is no uniform or agreed upon definition of what constitutes a compensable psychiatric injury.

The lack of determinate standards and the absence of physical symptoms make the resolution of mental stress claims particularly contentious. Employers and insurers are often skeptical of mental stress claims: a California Workers Compensation Institute study found that "antagonism and suspicion characterize claims management in mental stress cases." The subjectivity of the asserted injury makes mental stress claims especially litigable. In California 99% of mental stress cases are litigated.

Although nationwide there are still relatively few mental stress claims, this may only be the tip of the iceberg. The potential for claims growth is enormous. Virtually every employee is subject to some level of stress. The National Institute of Mental Health estimates that one person in five suffers from some psychiatric disorder. All told, 75% of corporate medical directors consider stress to be fairly pervasive.

A series of forces has contributed and will continue to contribute to the growth of workplace stress. The pace of work is accelerating and job security declining in a more competitive economic environment. Many employees have unfulfilled expectations about work and the quality of life. There has been an expansion of service sector jobs such as secretarial and office-manager, which some have suggested to be particularly stressful.

Social mores have changed so that acknowledgement of mental and emotional illness has become more acceptable, and the acceptance of psychiatric treatment has lost much of its former stigma. The broad and unlimited medical coverage under most state workers' compensation statutes, compared to the more limited coverage of psychiatric treatment under many private health plans, makes workers' compensation a particularly attractive target for mental stress claims.

Moreover, the rapid growth of mental stress claims has occurred despite the fact that in only eight states have appellate courts adopted an expansive definition of compensable mental stress claims. That broader definition provides coverage for stress that constitutes only a gradual increase over ordinary workplace stress and is not unusual in nature or degree. Courts in 21 other states permit compensation only if the mental stress is attributable to a sudden or frightening event, or if stress levels are in excess of ordinary employment conditions. Seven state appellate courts have ruled that "mental-mental" claims are not compensable, while courts in 14 states and the District of Columbia have yet to establish a legal standard for "mental-mental" claims. If more state courts adopt the expansive approach, the number of mental stress claims could soar.

On the other hand, several states have taken steps recently to adopt more objective standards and require that compensable stress derive from unusual workplace conditions. As of this year, Colorado will limit coverage to stress resulting from traumatic or extraordinary events. California's recent reforms require that mental stress claims be based on actual events and exclude compensability for injuries resulting from personnel actions of the employer. Oregon has required "clear and convincing evidence" to establish mental stress claims. But whether these measures are sufficient to check the potential magnitude of mental stress exposure remains to be seen.

4. The Expansion of Benefits

Workers' compensation provides medical benefits, indemnity benefits that compensate for lost wages during the period of recuperation and for permanent disability, and death benefits to the families of occupational injury victims. In the last two decades the levels of indemnity benefits have been very significantly enhanced. Moreover, a new benefit, mandatory vocational rehabilitation, is now provided in most states. Together, the enhancement in benefit levels and the addition of a new benefit have increased costs and contributed to the strains besetting the system.

a. The Enhancement of Benefit Levels

Indemnity benefits replace some specified percentage of lost wages, subject to a statutory ceiling on amount. Initially, benefits were relatively low, since the purpose of workers' compensation in its early years was, in part, not to make up for lost wages but to "prevent hardship." In 1920, only 20 states replaced as much as 60% of lost wages. By the 1960s, about two-thirds of the states had adopted the goal of replacing two-thirds of the injured worker's lost gross wages, but low statutory ceilings held down the amounts actually paid. In 46 states the benefit levels lagged so far below wage levels that a disabled worker earning the state average weekly wage could not receive a benefit that would produce the legislated wage replacement rate. Inevitably, there was a widespread sense that benefit levels were inadequate and that fair treatment of injured employees required a substantial increase in benefits.

i.   The Modernization of Benefit Levels

The 1972 Report of the National Commission on State Workmen's Compensation Laws precipitated a major modernization of benefit levels. The Report called on the states to adopt the goal of replacing two-thirds of pre-injury gross pay (or 80% of net wages) and to raise the statutory maximum to no lower than the state average weekly wage. Workers' compensation benefits are exempt from federal income taxation. Two-thirds of gross, or 80% of net, is designed to replace lost wages while maintaining a proper incentive to return to work. All states responded at least in part to the Report's recommendations. Currently, 48 states and the District of Columbia provide for replacement of two-thirds or more of gross wages, or 80% of net wages. In 31 states the statutory maximum for *temporary* disability is at or above the state average weekly wage, while in 29 states the statute maximum for *permanent* disability is at or above the state average weekly wage.

ii.   Continuing Increases

Approximately 40 states fix the statutory maximum in terms of the state average weekly wage itself, rather than as a specified dollar amount, so that benefit levels track inflation-driven wage increases. As a result of automatic adjustments and statutory amendments, benefit levels rose in 43 states and the District of Columbia in 1988 and in 42 states in 1989.

iii.   Benefit Levels and Benefit Utilization

Increasing benefit levels has two effects on workers' compensation claim costs. First, benefit increases directly raise costs when injured workers file for compensation. Second, benefit increases create incentives for greater utilization: More claims will be filed, and workers may stay out of work longer, thus extending the duration of the benefits period. Studies have found that a 20% increase in indemnity benefits is associated with a 7% increase in indemnity benefit filings and a 24% increase in the duration of indemnity claims. The impact on benefits utilization is particularly significant for less serious claims. In short, a 10% increase in benefit levels is associated with a 5% increase in utilization on top of the benefit increase, so that a 10% increase in benefits will raise aggregate payments by 15%. Most of that increased utilization is due to increased claim frequency, but some is attributable to increases in the duration of disability.

The enhancement of benefit levels in recent years has had a significant impact on the percentage of payroll devoted to workers' compensation and to mounting concerns among employers regarding the system's cost. For many years, workers' compensation amounted to an average of well under 1% of payroll, and there was little annual growth. In 1946 benefits were 0.54% of payroll, in 1960 they were 0.59% of payroll, and as late as 1972 they were still only 0.68%. But over the next decade and a half the percentage of payroll devoted to workers' compensation benefits doubled, to

1.39% in 1986. Today total average compensation costs are closer to 2% of payroll. And there is no sign that benefit growth is abating.

. . .

b. Vocational Rehabilitation: Growth of a New Benefit

Another area of change in the workers' compensation social contract has been vocational rehabilitation. Most state workers' compensation programs now make some provision for the costs of vocational rehabilitation services for eligible employees, although there is an enormous variance in the quality, extent and utilization of rehabilitation programs. Several states, including California and Florida, make vocational rehabilitation mandatory. In these states, rehabilitation has become a substantial and rising component of claim costs.

Vocational rehabilitation consists of the provision of services which attempt to maximize the ability of an injured worker to compete in the labor market. Rehabilitation is of great potential benefit to both employees and employers. It can serve to complete the employee's economic and psychological recovery from a disabling accident and improve employee morale, while mitigating the disability expenses attributable to injury and reducing the costs of hiring and training new workers to replace skilled but injured employees.

But vocational services can be quite expensive. Indeed, both utilization and claim costs have soared in the states with mandatory vocational rehabilitation, far outpacing increases in indemnity claims and costs generally. In California, the number of cases involving vocational rehabilitation rose from 5,236 in 1978 to 32,579 in 1987, a 440% increase. And vocational rehabilitation claims have risen at an even faster pace than utilization, with total claim costs escalating 775% in the same period. By contrast, over the same period personal disability claims rose only 33%, and personal disability claim costs 180%. When California first adopted mandatory rehabilitation in 1975, it was estimated that vocational rehabilitation would account for 2.7% of claim costs. Today vocational rehabilitation accounts for 13% of every benefit dollar. In Florida, 18% of all lost-time cases involve rehabilitation.

. . .

APPENDIX: WORKERS' COMPENSATION BENEFITS PROVIDED
Medical Benefits

In all U.S. jurisdictions, except for the Virgin Islands, there are no limits on medical coverage for conditions resulting from occupational disease or job-related injury. Medical coverage includes costs for physicians, hospitals, nursing service, physical therapy, dentists, chiropractors, and prosthetic devices.

Permanent Total Disability

Permanent total disability benefits are provided for those claimants whose job-related injury or occupational disease has rendered them permanently unable to engage in substantially remunerative employment. As in temporary total disability cases, claimants usually receive a wage-substitute benefit of 66 2/3% of their full or average weekly wage up to a statutory maximum rate. Permanent total disability claimants, however, are paid for a lifetime in most states and have higher total dollar amounts than temporary total disability claimants. Permanent total disability benefits continue until the claimant returns to substantially remunerative employment, dies, or exhausts the maximum dollar or time amount set by statute. For some statutorily defined severe injuries, such as total blindness, claimants are entitled to continued benefits in some states even if they successfully attain employment after being declared permanently and totally disabled.

Temporary Total Disability

Temporary inability to return to former employment constitutes a condition of temporary total disability, the most commonly awarded disability compensation. Claimants usually receive a wage-substitute benefit of 66 2/3% of the worker's pre-injury wage up to a statutory maximum rate. Temporary total disability payment often requires a waiting period of a few days to a few weeks before payment begins.

Waiting Period

Statutes provide that a waiting period must elapse during which income benefits are not available. The waiting period affects compensation only, since medical and hospital care are provided immediately. For most states the period is either three or seven days, while the remainder fall somewhere in between. If a worker's disability continues, most states provide for payment retroactive to the date of the injury. The retroactive period varies by state from five days to six weeks, with the norm being two to three weeks.

Temporary and Permanent Partial Disability

Partial disability compensation is payable to claimants who have suffered a negative effect on their earnings, earning capacity, or employability due to a job-related injury but are still able to engage in some remunerative employment. Some states calculate payment for earning capacity loss in the same manner as they calculate actual earnings losses, disregarding considerations of future earning capacity.

Vocational Rehabilitation

Vocational rehabilitation is designed to return injured workers to the labor market as rapidly as possible. All but two states (Indiana and South Carolina) have incorporated rehabilitation into their workers' compensation systems. The rehabilitation benefit usually provides an allowance for maintenance—board, lodging and travel, or as much as weekly compensation equivalent to temporary total disability—and payment for physical and vocational rehabilitation. Time limits of six-months to two years accompany the benefits. In some states continued payment of compensation is contingent upon a claimant attempting rehabilitation, while in others claimants are referred for rehabilitation review to determine whether they would be helped by rehabilitation. Compensation is payable until the claimant can return to remunerative employment or until it is determined that the injured worker failed to cooperate with vocational rehabilitation.

Medical Impairment—Permanent Partial Disability

Permanent partial disability awards are provided to give an injured worker an incentive to return to work, or simply to provide a cash award. Non-scheduled awards, or those not fixed by a statute, can be based strictly on medical impairment or the medical impairment's effect upon that individual's earning capacity.

Scheduled awards compensate injured workers through statutorily designated awards for injury. Schedules typically include payments for loss of arm, hand, leg, foot, eye, hearing in one or both ears, toes, and digits of the hand. Massachusetts only schedules benefits for the first six categories, and Georgia, Minnesota, and Nevada have no schedules at all.

Survivor Benefits

Weekly compensation benefits and burial allowances are paid to surviving dependents of workers killed in the course of employment or through occupational disease. Benefits are usually equivalent to 66 2/3% of the deceased worker's average weekly wage. About one-third of the states provide a limit on the total death award, and most states end death benefits to a surviving spouse upon remarriage. Surviving children lose benefits when they reach majority, or, if they are full-time students, at age 21, 23, or 25.

Notes and Questions

1. As the excerpt indicates, the first compulsory coverage plan adopted in the United States, enacted by New York early in this century, succumbed to constitutional attack in Ives v. South Buffalo Ry. Co., 94 N.E. 431 (N.Y.1911). After reviewing the possible reasons for the legislature's enactment of the law, the court concluded that the scheme violated the due process clauses of both the state and federal constitutions. The following excerpt from the opinion reflects its tone:

> If the argument in support of this statute is sound we do not see why it cannot logically be carried much further. Poverty and misfortune from every cause are detrimental to the state. It would probably conduce to the welfare of all concerned if there could be a more equal distribution of wealth. Many persons have much more property than they can use to advantage and many more find it impossible to get the means for a comfortable existence. If the legislature can say to an employer, "you must compensate your employee for an injury not caused by you or by your fault," why can it not go further and say to the man of wealth, "you have more property than you need and your neighbor is so poor that he can barely subsist; in the interest of natural justice you must

divide with your neighbor so that he and his dependents shall not become a charge upon the State?'' The argument that the risk to an employee should be borne by the employer because it is inherent in the employment, may be economically sound, but it is at war with the legal principle that no employer can be compelled to assume a risk which is inseparable from the work of the employee, and which may exist in spite of a degree of care by the employer far greater than may be exacted by the most drastic law. If it is competent to impose upon an employer, who has omitted no legal duty and has committed no wrong, a liability based solely upon a legislative fiat that his business is inherently dangerous, it is equally competent to visit upon him a special tax for the support of hospitals and other charitable institutions, upon the theory that they are devoted largely to the alleviation of ills primarily due to his business. In its final and simple analysis that is taking the property of A and giving it to B, and that cannot be done under our Constitutions.

New York promptly amended its state constitution to authorize the legislature to adopt a compensation system, and the Supreme Court held that a compulsory compensation system, at least as applied to ''hazardous employment,'' did not violate the federal constitution. New York Central R. Co. v. White, 243 U.S. 188 (1917). The most common reaction to the threat of judicial invalidation was to avoid the compulsory compensation approach and to allow employers to choose whether to participate in the system, but, as noted in the excerpt, to stack the tort rules against employers who opted against compensation.

2. Insurance arrangements under workers' compensation are summarized in Enterprise Responsibility for Personal Injury, Vol. I, The Institutional Framework, Report to the American Law Institute (1991) at 121:

> Rather than simply establish substantive rights and liabilities regarding workplace injuries, workers' compensation laws always require as well that funds be available to satisfy fully all potential claims that might be brought. Larger firms that can demonstrate the capacity to do so are permitted to self-insure (only about 1 percent of firms do so, but their companies comprise nearly 20 percent of payroll coverage). All other employers must purchase WC insurance through private carriers (about 60 percent of coverage) or state funds (about 20 percent).

3. In 1998, workers' compensation covered 121 million workers or about 92% of all wage and salary workers. The level of benefit disbursements totaled $41.7 billion. About 60% of the amount went to cash compensation to disabled workers or their survivors, with the remaining 40% going to medical care. The employers' costs in 1998 were $52.1 billion. See Mont, Burton & Reno, Workers' Compensation: Benefits, Coverage, and Costs, 1997–1998: New Estimates (National Academy of Social Insurance, 2000).

The trend towards expansion of coverage and enhancement of benefits that the Kramer & Briffault excerpt details was reversed for most of the

1990s. Spieler and Burton, Compensation for Disabled Workers: Workers' Compensation, in New Approaches to Disability in the Workplace 205 (Terry Thomason, John F. Burton, Jr., and Douglas E. Hyatt eds., 1998). Both the benefits and the costs of workers' compensation underwent an unprecedented decline from their respective peaks in 1992 and 1993. Spieler and Burton enumerate five causes for these reductions. First, the level of cash benefits provided was statutorily diminished—partially through cutting back on the maximum time-periods for temporary total disability payments, but most importantly through reforms in permanent partial disability payments. Second, rules governing compensability altered significantly; so-called mental-mental claims were restricted, claims based on the aggravation of a preexisting condition were limited, and threshold requirements for permanent total disability eligibility were raised. Furthermore, statutory changes tightened the standards of proof and evidentiary requirements for compensation. Third, reliance on traditional health care cost containment methods helped to reduce the costs of compensation. Fourth, principles of disability management—supported by the Americans with Disabilities Act—encouraged employers to provide workers with jobs to which they could return after they had been injured. Finally, employees have begun to resort to remedies outside workers' compensation—and within the common law tort system. How do these changes compare with those we have seen proposed in other areas? Spieler and Burton argue that workers' compensation must be conceived of according to the two—conflicting—principles of adequacy and affordability, and that, in the 1990s, adequacy was disregarded in favor of affordability. How should the two criteria be weighted?

According to statistics for 1997–98, the downward trend may have reached its nadir and be swinging back. Mont, Burton, and Reno, supra. In 1998, about 97% of the workforce as well as all federal employees, were covered by workers' compensation, with the employees of small farms and household workers earning less than a threshold amount representing the main exceptions. That year, the level of disbursements totaled $41.7 billion; this represented an increase in benefits of 2.7% from 1997, while employer costs rose little. Of the amount disbursed, 39.5% was supplied for medical care, and the rest took the form of cash compensation to disabled workers or their survivors. The premiums paid to insurers or self-insurance funds totaled over $52.1 billion.

4. The amount levied against each employer varies with the risks involved in the particular employment and is measured in terms of a percentage of the employer's payroll. In hazardous industries the rate may be 25%, but if clerical or office positions make up the bulk of an industry's payroll, the basic rates may be well below one percent of payroll. As the excerpt indicates, the overall national average in recent years has been about two percent. These basic rates may be altered for large employers on the basis of safety inspections or past safety experience. For a study of the injury prevention effects of workers' compensation, see M. Moore & W.K. Viscusi, Compensation Mechanisms for Job Risks: Wages, Workers' Compensation, and Product Liability (1990), concluding that the system has a substantial impact on job safety—reducing workplace fatalities alone by about 25% from the expected level without the system in effect.

5. The problems of "arising out of" and "in the course of" the employment cause occasional difficulty, as this sample of cases suggests.

a.   In Capizzi v. Southern Dist. Reporters, Inc., 459 N.E.2d 847 (N.Y.1984), plaintiff was on a business trip when she slipped and fell in the bathtub of her motel room. The court held that her injuries were compensable because she "was required to work and stay at a place distant from home, placed in a new environment thereby creating a greater risk of injury, and was engaged in a reasonable activity . . . attendant to, although not directly related to her employment duties.   . . ."

b.   In Richardson v. Fiedler Roofing, Inc., 493 N.E.2d 228 (N.Y.1986), the employee, a roofer, while waiting on a roof with no assigned work to do, moved to another part of the roof and removed some copper downspouts to sell as salvage. In the process, he slipped on a patch of ice and fell seven stories to his death. The court, 5–2, affirmed the Board's decision that his death was compensable even though he was engaged in theft at the time of the accident. The Board had found that "it was common practice in the industry for roofers to remove copper downspouts and sell them for scrap. It further found that this employer not only knew of the practice but also frequently had been required to pay for or replace downspouts stolen by its employees."

c.   In Rosen v. First Manhattan Bank, 641 N.E.2d 1073 (N.Y.1994), the court upheld a claim as "rooted in events started at or about the premises of the employer," where the claimant was killed in an assault by a co-worker that began with an argument in the lobby of the building and concluded in the stairwell one floor above the employer's premises.

d.   In Kish v. Nursing and Home Care, Inc., 727 A.2d 1253 (Conn. 1999), plaintiff nurse was delivering a commode to a patient when she saw a mail truck across the street and remembered that she had a card to mail. She stopped, crossed the street, gave the card to the mail carrier, and was killed recrossing the street. The court held that the trier of fact could find that her deviation was "so small as to be regarded as insubstantial." The court analogized the situation to one in which a worker was hurt while "pausing for a moment to converse with a colleague standing by the proverbial water cooler."

e.   In Guillory v. Interstate Gas Station, 653 So.2d 1152 (La.1995), the claimant was shot by her estranged husband while she was at work. The court held that the harm did not arise out of the employment and thus was not covered.

f.   In Dorosz v. Green & Seifter, 708 N.E.2d 162 (N.Y.1999), decedent, accountant for a private firm, suffered a fatal heart attack while bowling for a team sponsored by one of his firm's clients. The court upheld denial of recovery. A statute barred liability "where the injury was sustained in or caused by voluntary participation in an off-duty athletic activity not constituting part of the employee's work related duties" unless the employer

required the participation or compensated the participant or otherwise
"sponsors the activity." Although the participation here benefited the
employer, that was "a factor but is not alone the test." Compare Ezzy v.
W.C.A.B., 194 Cal.Rptr. 90 (App. 1983) (second-year law student who was
injured while playing on the softball team of the law firm for which she was
clerking was allowed recovery where one of the firm's partners, a rabid
member of the team, had continually reminded the student about upcoming
games and urged that she play so the mixed team would have the required
number of females for the game).

6. *Going and coming.* Suppose an employee is injured on the way to
or from work. When is the injury arising out of and in the course of the
employment? Compare the following illustrative cases.

a.   In Price v. W.C.A.B., 693 P.2d 254 (Cal.1984), a worker's injuries
were held within the scope of the statute when he arrived early at his place
of employment and was hit by a car while waiting for the premises to be
unlocked. The going and coming rule which would have barred compensation did not apply because the worker had finished his local commute at the
time of the injury. And even though he was pouring oil into his car when he
was injured, this personal act was within the course of employment under
the "dual purpose rule." Under that rule, where an employee is mixing his
own business with his employer's, " 'no nice inquiry will be made as to
which business he was actually engaged in at the time of injury, unless it
clearly appears that neither directly nor indirectly could he be serving his
employer.' [   ]." Here, the employee was "serving the interests of his
employer by waiting near the premises to begin work early."

b.   In Santa Rosa Junior College v. W.C.A.B., 708 P.2d 673 (Cal.1985),
a teacher was taking work home from campus when he was killed in a car
accident. If he had been required by his employer to work at home, his
home would have been considered a second jobsite and injuries sustained in
traveling from one jobsite to the other would have been within the scope of
the statute. Here, the decision to work at home was voluntary and the
teacher's death was not compensable.

c.   In Neacosia v. New York Power Authority, 649 N.E.2d 1188
(N.Y.1995), the claimant was involved in an auto accident while heading
home after dropping off his work uniforms at a dry cleaning establishment.
The court held that the determination of the workers' compensation board
that the injuries were compensable was entitled to "wide latitude," and
that the worker had been pursuing one of many options for complying with
the employer's requirement of clean uniforms.

7. *Smoking-related claims.* In Johannesen v. New York City Dept. of
Housing Preservation and Development, 638 N.E.2d 981 (N.Y.1994), the
employee claimed serious aggravation of her bronchial condition by exposure to heavy smoking by co-workers. The claim was upheld as a form of
occupational disease compensable under the act.

8.   Closely related to the "scope" question is a series of state defenses
excluding workers who are injured while engaging in "willful misconduct."

These are usually limited to deliberate exposure to danger and are construed narrowly to exclude instinctive behavior and bad judgment. Some violations of work rules are analyzed under this exclusion. Even if violation of such a rule falls short of being willful misconduct, it may bring disqualification under another statutory defense—unreasonable failure to observe safety rules or to use safety devices. This defense exists in almost half of the states. In some, violation will bar all compensation recovery; in others it will reduce compensation by 10 or 15%. Larson, 1A Law of Workmen's Compensation §§ 32.00–33.40 (1995 ed.).

Over half the states provide a statutory defense if the worker was intoxicated at the time of the injury. In most of these, intoxication can serve as a complete bar to compensation, but in a few it will serve only to reduce the award. The major difference among the statutes is the extent of causal connection required between the intoxication and the injury: this ranges from no requirement of causal connection to a requirement of demonstrating that intoxication was the "sole cause" of the injury. Larson, §§ 34.30–34.39. Is it consistent with the theory of the compensation acts to reduce the worker's benefits for misbehavior?

9. Several states increase the employee's compensation when injury results from the employer's violation of safety rules. In RTE Corp. v. Department of Industry, Labor & Human Relations, 276 N.W.2d 290 (Wis.1979), the court affirmed a 15% increase in the compensation award because the worker's death had resulted from the employer's violation of a safety regulation whose purpose was to prevent the kind of injury the worker sustained. Is it consistent with workers' compensation theory to increase an award if the employer has violated a safety order?

California Labor Code § 4553 requires that the compensation award be increased by one-half (together with costs and expenses not to exceed $250) if the worker's injury resulted from "serious and willful misconduct" of the employer. Such misconduct has been defined as "more than negligence, however gross. The type of conduct necessary to invoke the penalty . . . is that of a '*quasi* criminal nature, the intentional doing of something either with the knowledge that it is likely to result in serious injury, or with a wanton and reckless disregard of its possible consequences. . . .' " American Smelting & Ref. Co. v. W.C.A.B., 144 Cal. Rptr. 898 (App. 1978).

10. *Permanent partial disability.* The following statute from New York demonstrates the scheduling approach to permanent partial disability.

New York Workers' Compensation Law
Section 15 (1991).

. . .

3. Permanent partial disability. In case of disability partial in character but permanent in quality the compensation shall be sixty-six and two-

thirds per centrum of the average weekly wages and shall be paid to the employee for the period named in this subdivision, as follows:

Member lost	Number of weeks' compensation
a. Arm	312
b. Leg	288
c. Hand	244
d. Foot	205
e. Eye	160
f. Thumb	75
g. First finger	46
h. Great toe	38
i. Second finger	30
j. Third finger	25
k. Toe other than great toe	16
l. Fourth finger	15

m.   Loss of hearing. Compensation for the complete loss of the hearing of one ear, for sixty weeks, for the loss of hearing of both ears, for one hundred and fifty weeks.

. . .

r.   Total loss of use. Compensation for permanent total loss of use of a member shall be the same as for loss of the member.

s.   Partial loss or partial loss of use. Compensation for permanent partial loss or loss of use of a member may be for proportionate loss or loss of use of the member. . . .

t.   Disfigurement.

1.   The board may award proper and equitable compensation for serious facial or head disfigurement, not to exceed twenty thousand dollars, including a disfigurement continuous in length which is partially in the facial area and also extends into the neck region as described in paragraph two hereof.

2.   The board, if in its opinion the earning capacity of an employee has been or may in the future be impaired, may award compensation for any serious disfigurement in the region above the sterno clavicular articulations anterior to and including the region of the sterno cleido mastoid muscles on either side, but no award under subdivisions one and two shall, in the aggregate, exceed twenty thousand dollars.

3.   Notwithstanding any other provision hereof, two or more serious disfigurements, not continuous in length, resulting from the same injury, if partially in the facial area and partially in the neck region as described in paragraph two hereof, shall be deemed to be a facial disfigurement.

u.   Total or partial loss or loss of use of more than one member or parts of members. In any case in which there shall be a loss or loss of use of more than one member or parts of more than one member set forth in paragraphs a to t, both inclusive, of this subdivision, but not amounting to permanent total disability, the board shall award compensation for the loss or loss of use of each such member or part thereof, which awards shall run consecutively.

v. Additional compensation for impairment of wage earning capacity in certain permanent partial disabilities. Notwithstanding any other provision of this subdivision, additional compensation shall be payable for impairment of wage earning capacity for any period after the termination of an award under paragraph a, b, c, or d, of this subdivision for the loss or loss of use of fifty per centum or more of a member, provided such impairment of earning capacity shall be due solely thereto. . . .

w. Other cases. In all other cases in this class of disability, the compensation shall be sixty-six and two-thirds per centum of the difference between his average weekly wages and his wage-earning capacity thereafter in the same employment or otherwise, payable during the continuance of such partial disability, but subject to reconsideration of the degree of such impairment by the board on its own motion or upon application of any party in interest.

What are the strengths and weaknesses of this approach? Does it seem appropriate that both a construction worker and a law professor would receive the same benefits for loss of an arm—assuming both are above the average weekly wage ceiling—under the statute? Does it seem proper that the law professor would receive these benefits even if she suffered no loss of earning capacity? What justification might be offered for the scheduling of permanent partial disability benefits?

11. *Lump sums.* In death cases, most states provide lump sum payments to close out accounts when widows or widowers remarry. This raises the general question of lump sum payments in lieu of the periodic payments in some injury situations, too. In many states the lump sum has become common since it is at least superficially attractive to everyone concerned: the claimant, who gets one very large award; the attorney, who thus finds it easier to collect a fee; the employer, who can dispose of the matter once and for all and probably at a lower cost; and the court or administering agency, which avoids further litigation and supervision of the claim. Lump summing, however, does not meet one of the primary goals of the compensation system, provision of a regular benefit payment to take the place of lost wages. The objection is that the worker will find the lump sum soon spent, leaving him or her with no further recourse and in no better position than if there had been no compensation scheme at all. Are the lump sum problems of compensation systems different from those of the common law?

12. *Opting out.* Up to this point we have been dealing with cases in which the injured worker has sought coverage under a workers' compensation scheme. Sometimes, however, an injured worker may wish to avoid the rule that if an injury is compensable within the system, there may be no other remedy against the employer or co-workers. Though compensation plans originally provided the injured worker's only practical hope of recovery, the modern worker is much more likely to succeed in a tort action against the employer—if allowed to pursue it. In such a case, coverage may be a detriment to the worker.

a. In some cases the worker claims to be out of the scope of employment at the time of injury, while the employer argues for coverage. For example, in Scott v. Pacific Coast Borax Co., 294 P.2d 1039 (Cal.App.1956), the worker's hours had ended and he claimed that he was simply helping a co-worker and friend move a gas pump that exploded. The worker wanted to sue in tort but the court relied on the provision that said the compensation act "shall be liberally construed by the courts with the purpose of extending their benefits for the protection of persons injured in the course of their employment." Reasonable doubts were to be resolved in favor of coverage. However, in Peckham v. Peckham Materials Corp., 536 N.Y.S.2d 873 (App.Div. 1989), the court allowed the widow of a company president killed in the crash of a company helicopter to proceed with a tort suit against the employer. In finding that the death had not arisen out of and in the course of employment, the court noted that the decedent was returning from a golf outing with friends when the helicopter crashed; that there was no evidence that business was transacted or discussed while he was golfing; and that company funds were not used to pay for the outing.

b. Another way to escape the limits of compensation in many states is to prove that the employer committed an intentional tort. See the extended discussion in Magliulo v. Superior Court, 121 Cal.Rptr. 621 (App. 1975), allowing a tort action to a waitress whose employer allegedly hit her in anger and threw her down.

Some states provide by statute that the employer may be held liable for conduct short of intentional injury, but almost all states require that the employer must have acted with an actual intent to injure. Thus, in Bardere v. Zafir, 477 N.Y.S.2d 131 (App.Div.), affirmed on other grounds, 472 N.E.2d 37 (N.Y.1984), the court held that an employer's conduct in removing safety features from a machine to increase its speed, with knowledge that a worker might come in contact with the dangerous machine, was insufficient to establish an intentional tort and overcome the exclusive liability of workers' compensation.

In Cole v. Fair Oaks Fire Protection Dist., 729 P.2d 743 (Cal.1987), the court declined to allow an employee to sue an employer based on a claim of intentional infliction of emotional distress. As a result of a sustained campaign of harassment and humiliation, including an unjustified demotion by his employer in retaliation for his union activities, the plaintiff suffered a severe stroke that rendered him unable to move, care for himself, or communicate other than by blinking his eyes. The court refused to allow the lawsuit to proceed on the basis that the intent element of the tort could be satisfied by a showing that the defendant proceeded with reckless disregard to the possibility of causing emotional injury to the plaintiff. This, according to the majority opinion, could have the effect of transforming virtually every negative personnel decision into a tort claim. The dissent would have carved out an exception to the rule in cases where the employer acted deliberately with intent to cause emotional injuries to the employee. The majority rejected this approach on grounds that plaintiffs could get around the distinction simply by alleging an ulterior purpose behind the employer's actions. This would have the effect of forcing employers to pay the costs of mounting a legal defense which, even if successful, would not eliminate their responsibility to compensate the employee for the emotional injuries under the workers' compensation statute.

13. Sometimes, even though an injury falls within the scope of the statute, the particular harm suffered by the worker is not covered. "Non-disabling" injuries are often not compensable. The most obvious example is the refusal of compensation systems to pay anything for conventional pain and suffering. Other examples include injury to sexual organs; loss of taste, smell or sensation; disfigurement; and psychic damage.

The fact that a compensation scheme excludes these types of injury does not mean that tort law is available. Thus, in Fetterhoff v. Western Block Co., 373 N.Y.S.2d 920 (App.Div. 1975), a worker who alleged that his work-related injury had left him permanently unable to have sexual intercourse was barred from suing in tort even though his loss of sexual function was not compensable under workers' compensation. In Moss v. Southern Excavation, Inc., 611 S.W.2d 178 (Ark.1981), a worker who lost the non-compensable senses of taste and smell in an accident that was covered by workers' compensation was barred from suing in tort for these lost senses.

14. The exclusiveness of the workers' compensation remedy applies not only to the covered worker but also to plaintiffs who are not covered. Compensation schemes do not provide benefits to spouses or children of workers who are injured, or to the non-dependent relatives of workers who are killed. Generally, these family members are not permitted to bring tort actions for loss of consortium or wrongful death. Tort recovery may be allowed, though, where an independent injury has been inflicted on the family member, or where the worker was injured by the employer's intentional conduct. Recovery for loss of consortium is also allowed in some states that call it an independent rather than a derivative cause of action. Larson, Workmen's Compensation Law, § 66.30.

Note on Railroad and Maritime Workers

While the states were grappling with problems of workers' injuries, Congress confronted the special situation of persons employed in interstate commerce as that term was understood at the turn of the twentieth century. In 1908 Congress passed the Federal Employers' Liability Act (FELA), 45 U.S.C. §§ 51–60. The Act provided that common carriers by railroad while engaging in interstate commerce were liable to negligently injured employees and that any attempt by the employer to contract out of liability would be void. The original version of the Act barred assumption of risk in some situations; a 1939 amendment was held to have "obliterated" the doctrine. Tiller v. Atlantic Coast Line R. Co., 318 U.S. 54 (1943). Comparative negligence applies in all actions against the employer, unless the employer has violated a safety statute—in which case the worker's fault is not considered.

Several Supreme Court decisions in the 1940s and 1950s made the injured railroad worker's path much easier than that of a plaintiff in a common law negligence action. In addition to the elimination of the three major defenses, the task of establishing negligence has been simplified. See Rogers v. Missouri Pacific R. Co., 352 U.S. 500 (1957):

> Under this statute the test of a jury case is simply whether the proofs justify with reason the conclusion that employer negligence played any part, even the slightest, in producing the injury or death for which damages are sought. It does not matter that, from the evidence, the jury may also with reason, on grounds of probability, attribute the result to other causes, including the employee's contributory negligence. Judicial appraisal of the proofs to determine whether a jury question is presented is narrowly limited to the single inquiry whether, with reason, the conclusion may be drawn that negligence of the employer played any part at all in the injury or death. Judges are to fix their sights primarily to make that appraisal and, if that test is met, are bound to find that a case for the jury is made out whether or not the evidence allows the jury a choice of other probabilities. The statute expressly imposes liability upon the employer to pay damages for injury or death due "in whole or *in part*" to its negligence.

Railroad workers have steadfastly refused to give up FELA in favor of a compensation system. Recall *Buckley*, p. 270 supra, involving claims by railroad workers over exposure to asbestos.

A complex combination of fault, strict liability and compensation systems comes into play when maritime injuries occur.

Members of the crew. Those who are formal members of a ship's crew may sue under the Jones Act, 46 U.S.C. § 688, which makes the provisions of the FELA applicable to crew members. A second remedy is unseaworthiness, a doctrine that holds the shipowner strictly liable in tort whenever any aspect of the ship is not "reasonably fit." Finally, a crew member who falls ill or is hurt while serving on the ship is entitled to "maintenance and cure" until reaching the point of maximum recovery. There is no requirement that the condition be related to the employment. This item is bargained for in most union agreements. These remedies are discussed in historical perspective in Mitchell v. Trawler Racer, Inc., 362 U.S. 539 (1960).

Non-crew members. Many persons work around ships and piers but are not crew members. These workers, including longshoreworkers and carpenters, are entitled to compensation for job-related injuries under the Longshoremen's and Harbor Workers' Compensation Act, 33 U.S.C. §§ 901–950. In return for a substantial increase in compensation levels in 1972, Congress withdrew the right of these workers to sue shipowners for unseaworthiness. They do, however, retain their rights to sue shipowners for injuries resulting from negligence.

C. MOTOR VEHICLE INJURIES

Not long after the automobile became part of daily life the first doubts were raised about the adequacy of legal treatment of automobile accidents. We have already considered the legal theory underlying the fault system and the impact on it of the institution of insurance. Before considering current no-fault alternatives, we review briefly the history of proposed changes—both because they frame the basic issues and because they helped shape the legislation that followed.

1. THE PAST

The earliest thinking about extensions of the no-fault concept began shortly after the passage of the workers' compensation statutes. Writers saw that incongruities would occur: if a trolley car collided with an automobile, the employees on the trolley car would be eligible for compensation, but the trolley passengers and car occupants would have to prove fault. Professor Jeremiah Smith in his article, Sequel to Workmen's Compensation Acts, 27 Harv.L.Rev. 235, 363 (1914), concluded that the fault system and the compensation system could not live together in harmony: "In the end, one or the other of the two conflicting theories is likely to prevail. There is no probability, during the present generation, of a repeal of the Workmen's Compensation Acts." Smith then speculated on the creation of a state insurance law that would protect all, not only workers, against accident and disease. "It may include damage wholly due to a natural cause, such as a stroke of lightning. Whether legislation of the above description *ought* to be enacted is a question upon which no opinion is here intimated. Our immediate point is that the Workmen's Compensation legislation will inevitably give rise to a plausible agitation for such further legislation."* Reconsider the quote from Holmes, p. 6, supra.

Fifteen years after Professor Smith wrote, some lawyers and social scientists undertook an empirical analysis of automobile injuries in 8,849 cases across the United States. Their findings were remarkably similar to those of recent studies: "payments do not increase in proportion to the losses sustained; temporary disability cases with small losses are considerably overpaid, those with larger losses are slightly overpaid, while permanent disability cases of earners—the class with the largest losses and greatest need—receive just about enough to meet the losses incurred up to the time of our investigations and get nothing to apply against the

---

* Indeed, within two years plans began to appear. See Ballentine, A Compensation Plan for Railway Accident Claims, 29 Harv. L.Rev. 705 (1916), proposing a plan to cover injuries to passengers on railroads and street railways.

continued medical expense or wage loss resulting from their impaired earning ability." They were concerned about delay and uncompensated victims at a time when first-party insurance for injuries was unusual and tort law was the one available resource; workers' compensation was available only when a person was hurt on the job. The study is presented in Report by the Committee to Study Compensation for Automobile Accidents to the Columbia University Council for Research into the Social Sciences (1932).

The study suggested a workers' compensation model after considering its relevance to the automobile situation (134–36):

> In many respects there is a close analogy between the industrial situation where workmen's compensation has been developed and the motor vehicle situation where the application of a like principle is now being discussed. Accidents are inevitable, whether in industry or in the operation of motor vehicles. It has been accepted as sound policy that the major part of the cost of accidents to employees should be borne by the industry, and it is proposed that the major part of the cost of those caused by the operation of motor vehicles should be cast upon the persons for whose benefit the motor vehicles are being operated. The conditions calling for the application of the compensation plan are similar: The failure of the common law system to measure up to a fair estimate of social necessity.

Compensation was to be paid from compulsory insurance carried by every vehicle owner for the benefit of those harmed by the vehicle. The amount of compensation was to be scheduled much as with workers' compensation payments. The group recognized that the amounts of compensation would present different problems because of the greater diversity of potential automobile victims as compared to workers.

For an extended argument rejecting the analogy between the work accident and the auto accident, see W. Blum and H. Kalven, Jr., Public Law Perspectives on a Private Law Problem—Auto Compensation Plans 25–27 (1965). Their basic point was that the existence of the contractual relationship made the work accident a special case. Why might that be?

The developments between the Columbia Plan and the late 1960s can be summarized fairly readily. In 1946, the Canadian province of Saskatchewan enacted a plan under which all auto accident victims received modest no-fault benefits—and could still sue in tort as before. Part of any tort recovery would have to be used to reimburse the fund that had paid the no-fault benefits. The statute and its operation are discussed in R. Keeton and J. O'Connell, Basic Protection for the Traffic Victim 140–48 (1965).

In 1954, Professor Albert Ehrenzweig, in a book entitled "Full Aid" Insurance to the Traffic Victim, built upon the protection afforded accident victims under the no-fault medical payments provision, p. 739, supra, commonly found in auto liability insurance policies. If this were increased in amount and scope, it would be appropriate to free anyone carrying such protection from the burdens of liability for negligence.

In the early 1960s, Nationwide Insurance Company marketed a policy that embodied several of Ehrenzweig's ideas. Under this plan a person injured by the insured's vehicle could choose whether to proceed in tort as usual, or whether to take advantage of a package of modest no-fault benefits. Not surprisingly, victims with good legal claims tended to opt for tort and others opted for the no-fault package.

How much more than the usual liability insurance coverage would you have been willing to pay for the knowledge that, for example, a child darting into your car would receive some compensation even though you were not at fault? The Nationwide experience is discussed in King, The Insurance Industry and Compensation Plans, 43 N.Y.U.L.Rev. 1137 (1968).

During this period, Professors Blum and Kalven argued that if society wanted to compensate all victims of motoring accidents (something about which they were skeptical), motorists should not bear the burden. Their proposal, found in A Stopgap Plan for Compensating Auto Accident Victims, 1968 Ins.L.J. 661, argued that those hurt in cases not involving driver fault should receive money from "general tax revenues." The "widespread temptation" to put this burden on motorists was unsound. They cited accidents in which the victims are drunk, or in which pedestrians are hurt through nobody's fault. "In these instances, the injury in question is no more associated with motoring than it is with pedestrianism, drinking, or living in our society."

The major breakthrough occurred in 1965, with the publication of Basic Protection for the Traffic Victim, by Professors Robert E. Keeton and Jeffrey O'Connell. Not only did the authors attack the operation of the common law fault system in auto cases, they also proposed a new approach and presented a 37–page draft statute practically ready for introduction into state legislatures. Suddenly, no-fault legislation became a political possibility.

Briefly, they utilized a first-party structure building on the medical payments provision that would cover medical expenses and 85% of wages lost up to a total of $10,000, though lost wage payments would be limited to $750 per month. A deductible of $100 or 10% of the work loss, whichever was larger, was imposed to keep small claims from burdening the system. Those who wanted greater no-fault protection would be able to buy it. In any tort action against another driver, the judgment would exclude the first $10,000 of economic loss and the first $5,000 of pain and suffering. In suits against other defendants, such as railroads or car manufacturers, no deductions or exclusions would be made but the no-fault insurer would be reimbursed to prevent double recovery. For a short summary of the plan, see Keeton and O'Connell, Basic Protection Automobile Insurance, 1967 U.Ill.L.F. 400.

The impetus for change in Massachusetts was the great public outcry about high insurance rates. Its liability premiums were the highest in the country. Also, the state was the home of Professor Robert Keeton, who had co-authored the Keeton–O'Connell plan. In 1970, Massachusetts adopted a plan that was traceable to the Keeton–O'Connell plan.

The statute required compulsory no-fault coverage for all medical expenses and 75% of lost earnings incurred within two years up to a combined sum of $2,000. The act made no general provision for collateral sources but did require a worker to use up (subject to later reimbursement) any wage continuation protection before recovering for lost wages. Another provision correlated workers' compensation benefits with the no-fault benefits.

Tort actions for damages were permitted with an exclusion for the first $2,000 of the award. Pain and suffering was recoverable in a tort action if one of the following existed: medical and hospital expenses over $500, death, loss of body member, permanent disfigurement, loss of sight or hearing, or a "fracture." Compulsory liability insurance was continued at low limits to cover the tort action. Insureds could choose a deductible of up to $2,000 for their own losses. An assigned claims plan protected pedestrians and others who were hurt in the state by cars that didn't carry the no-fault coverage. The statute also regulated policy cancellations and renewals and provided explicitly for merit driving discounts, and surcharges for moving violations and involvement in accidents.

2.   THE NEW YORK EXPERIENCE

a.   *Background*

As soon as Massachusetts acted, the scene shifted to New York. In 1970, the state's Insurance Department had prepared a study of the operation of the tort system in auto cases. Automobile Insurance . . . for Whose Benefit?, A Report to Governor Nelson A. Rockefeller by the Insurance Department of the State of New York (1970). The study concluded that the system had failed. Among its points (pp. 17–44):

1.   One in four persons suffering bodily injury in auto accidents obtained "nothing whatever" from the fault system. Recall that New York did not adopt comparative negligence until 1973.

2.   Determinations "are made either by an overburdened judiciary on stale facts or else by insurance adjusters in a bargaining process. Part lottery and part bazaar, the fault insurance system is unreliable and unpredictable."

3.   Data showed, as in earlier studies, that benefits were malapportioned, with small claims being overcompensated to get rid of them with payments for pain and suffering far in excess of the economic loss sustained. Large claims, however, were being badly underpaid. "The seriously injured receive a sort of negative 'pain and suffering.' "

4.   Benefits were not coordinated with other support systems. Thus, 91% of workers in New York in 1970 were covered by health insurance and most were also covered by income continuation plans. The collateral source rule operated to provide double recoveries when these persons were hurt.

Workers with good fringe benefits got no reduction in their auto premiums. Instead, they got "a chance at redundant payment" if injured in the future.

5. Physical rehabilitation was delayed under the fault system because of the cost involved and the question of whether the victim would be able to pay for rehabilitation if no tort recovery were obtained.

6. The system was inefficient because 56 cents of each premium dollar went to operating expenses of the system. Of the 44 cents that reached victims 8 cents covered economic losses already covered by another source, 21.5 cents covered pain and suffering and only 14.5 cents was for net economic loss not otherwise covered.

7. Finally the litigation system bred overreaching and dishonesty. Insurers deal "with thousands of claimants who are adversaries the company never expects to see again, and is doing so in situations that afford no clear line between rigorous bargaining and downright dishonesty. . . . Too often, especially where injuries are serious, the insurer can simply wait out the injured victim to obtain a more favorable settlement." The highly abstract standard of "fault" and the indeterminate measure of damages "offer rich rewards to the claimant who will lie, the attorney who will inflame, the adjuster who will chisel and the insurance company which will stall or intimidate."

The study also discussed several problems of insurance administration. How many of the enumerated concerns are likely to be unique to auto accidents?

Consider the following discussion of how to evaluate an existing reparation system, taken from Conard, Morgan, Pratt, Voltz and Bombaugh, Automobile Accident Costs and Payments 106–07 (1964):

> No valid evaluation of reparation systems can be made which measures them by a single dimension. Some are better than others for procuring medical treatment, some for maintaining subsistence, some for compensating total loss, some for deterring negligence, some for raising the price of hazardous activities, some for spreading broadly the pain of loss, some for economy of operation. If any of the major elements in the scheme is knocked out, some important function will remain unperformed.
>
> This does not mean that nothing in the picture can be changed. In fact, a great many elements in the picture are quite recent. Workmen's compensation entered about fifty years ago; social security was added about twenty-five years ago for survivors' benefits and within the last ten years for disability benefits; hospital and medical insurance is largely a growth of the last fifteen years. It seems probable that further changes will be made in reparation systems, which might include the shifting of functions from one system to another, and altering the linkage between benefits and burdens. When such changes are made, they should be made with a clear perception of the plurality of functions to be performed, and of the plurality of systems now performing them.

For an extended discussion of the issues underlying the adoption of any no-fault proposal, see Blum & Kalven, Ceilings, Costs, and Compulsion in Auto Compensation Legislation, 1973 Utah L.Rev. 341. See also Epstein, Automobile No–Fault Plans: A Second Look at First Principles, 13 Creighton L.Rev. 769 (1980), comparing auto no-fault with systems of strict liability, negligence and no-liability from perspectives of equity, incentives and administrative costs.

b.   *The New York Statute*

The New York statute provides one of the most generous sets of no-fault benefits and one of the most significant limitations on tort actions of any of the 20–odd state statutes adopting some version of auto no-fault. The statute was adopted in 1973, and amended frequently to meet problems that appeared during its first years of operation. The statute that follows is the current version. The cross-references to articles six and eight of the Vehicle and Traffic Law are to provisions for compulsory insurance and other devices relating to financial security arrangements.

In reading the statute, keep in mind some general questions. Among those, who would get compensated under the statute if they were not compensated before? How does the amount of recovery compare with that currently available under tort? If the act is likely to be more expensive than the current system, where will the money come from? If there are savings, who will benefit? What about collateral sources and subrogation? Does the act internalize the costs of auto accidents so that the motoring activity pays for them? Is internalization important? What are the alternatives to internalizing the costs? Is the act conducive to fraudulent claims? More so than the existing system? What, if anything, remains of the tort action? What conception of justice does the statute reflect? How does that conception line up with your own? Is the act likely to have any effect on driving safety? Should safety be left to other parts of the legal system?

When reading a statute, lawyers and judges are usually looking for answers to specific questions. In reading this statute, assume a client who is asking about her rights under New York's current legislation. V is a 25-year-old commercial artist. Although she owns a car that is properly insured under the statute, she was hurt while walking home from a neighborhood movie house one evening. She was run over by a car owned and operated by D, who was probably negligent, and who possessed the proper insurance under the statute. V sustained a broken left arm (she is left-handed) and also sustained a four-inch-long permanent scar on her left forearm. The fracture healed perfectly. She had medical bills of $4,000, of which $2,500 was covered and paid by the group medical policy that she got as a fringe benefit at her office. She was out of work for a month and a half. Her salary was $3000 per month.

(a) What are V's rights?

(b) What if V owned no car?

(c) What if V had driven to and from the movie and collided with D's car?

(d) Some tests on D's new car have suggested that the crash might have been due to a defective steering column. Does it matter if the crash was due to the defect rather than D's negligence?

New York Insurance Law

Article 51, as amended through 1995.

§ 5101.   Title

This article shall be known and may be cited as the "Comprehensive Motor Vehicle Insurance Reparations Act".

§ 5102.   Definitions

In this chapter:

(a) "Basic economic loss" means, up to fifty thousand dollars per person of the following combined items, subject to the limitations of section five thousand one hundred eight of this article:

(1) All necessary expenses incurred for: (i) medical, hospital . . . , surgical, nursing, dental, ambulance, x-ray, prescription drug and prosthetic services; (ii) psychiatric, physical and occupational therapy and rehabilitation; (iii) any non-medical remedial care and treatment rendered in accordance with a religious method of healing recognized by the laws of this state; and (iv) any other professional health services; all without limitation as to time, provided that within one year after the date of the accident causing the injury it is ascertainable that further expenses may be incurred as a result of the injury. For the purpose of determining basic economic loss, the expenses incurred under this paragraph shall be in accordance with the limitations of section five thousand one hundred eight of this article.

(2) Loss of earnings from work which the person would have performed had he not been injured, and reasonable and necessary expenses incurred by such person in obtaining services in lieu of those that he would have performed for income, up to two thousand dollars per month for not more than three years from the date of the accident causing the injury. An employee who is entitled to receive monetary payments, pursuant to statute or contract with the employer, or who receives voluntary monetary benefits paid for by the employer, by reason of the employee's inability to work because of personal injury arising out of the use or operation of a motor vehicle, is not entitled to receive first party benefits for "loss of earnings from work" to the extent that such monetary payments or benefits from the employer do not result in the employee suffering a

reduction in income or a reduction in the employee's level of future benefits arising from a subsequent illness or injury.

(3) All other reasonable and necessary expenses incurred, up to twenty-five dollars per day for not more than one year from the date of the accident causing the injury.

(4) "Basic economic loss" shall not include any loss incurred on account of death; subject, however, to the provisions of paragraph four of subsection (a) of section five thousand one hundred three of this article.

(5) "Basic economic loss" shall also include an additional option to purchase, for an additional premium, an additional twenty-five thousand dollars of coverage, [which may be keyed to economic loss or medical bills as the buyer wishes and which comes into play after the first $50,000 is exhausted.] This optional coverage shall be made available and notice with explanation of such coverage [shall be provided by an insurer at the first policy renewal after the effective date of the statute].

(b) "First party benefits" means payments to reimburse a person for basic economic loss on account of personal injury arising out of the use or operation of a motor vehicle, less:

(1) Twenty percent of lost earnings computed pursuant to paragraph two of subsection (a) of this section.

(2) Amounts recovered or recoverable on account of such injury under state or federal laws providing social security disability benefits, or workers' compensation benefits, or disability benefits under article nine of the workers' compensation law, or medicare benefits, other than lifetime reserve days and provided further that the medicare benefits utilized herein do not result in a reduction of such person's medicare benefits for a subsequent illness or injury.

(3) Amounts deductible under the applicable insurance policy.

(c) "Non-economic loss" means pain and suffering and similar non-monetary detriment.

(d) "Serious injury" means a personal injury which results in death; dismemberment; significant disfigurement; a fracture; loss of a fetus; permanent loss of use of a body organ, member, function or system; permanent consequential limitation of use of a body organ or member; significant limitation of use of a body function or system; or a medically determined injury or impairment of a non-permanent nature which prevents the injured person from performing substantially all of the material acts which constitute such person's usual and customary daily activities for not less than ninety days during the one hundred eighty days immediately following the occurrence of the injury or impairment.

(e) "Owner" [is defined broadly].

(f) "Motor vehicle" [is very broadly defined by reference to include fire and police vehicles, but not to include motorcycles].

(g) "Insurer" means the insurance company or self-insurer, as the case may be, which provides the financial security required by article six or eight of the vehicle and traffic law.

(h) "Member of his household" means a spouse, child or relative of the named insured who regularly resides in his household.

(i) "Uninsured motor vehicle" means a motor vehicle, the owner of which is (i) a financially irresponsible motorist . . . or (ii) unknown and whose identity is unascertainable.

(j) "Covered person" means any pedestrian injured through the use or operation of, or any owner, operator or occupant of, a motor vehicle which has in effect the financial security required by . . . the vehicle and traffic law . . . or any other person entitled to first party benefits.

(k) "Bus" means both a bus and a school bus as defined in sections one hundred four and one hundred forty-two of the vehicle and traffic law.

(l) "Compensation provider" means the state insurance fund, or the person, association, corporation or insurance carrier or statutory fund liable under state or federal laws for the payment of workers' compensation benefits or disability benefits under article nine of the workers' compensation law.

(m) "Motorcycle" [is defined by reference to other statutes].

§ 5103. Entitlement to first party benefits; additional financial security required

(a) Every owner's policy of liability insurance issued on a motor vehicle in satisfaction of the requirements of article six or eight of the vehicle and traffic law shall also provide for . . . the payment of first party benefits to:

(1) Persons, other than occupants of another motor vehicle or a motorcycle, for loss arising out of the use or operation in this state of such motor vehicle. In the case of occupants of a bus other than operators, owners, and employees of the owner or operator of the bus, the coverage for first party benefits shall be afforded under the policy or policies, if any, providing first party benefits to the injured person and members of his household for loss arising out of the use or operation of any motor vehicle of such household. In the event there is no such policy, first party benefits shall be provided by the insurer of such bus.

(2) The named insured and members of his household, other than occupants of a motorcycle, for loss arising out of the use or operation of (i) an uninsured motor vehicle or motorcycle, within the United States, its territories or possessions, or Canada; and (ii) an insured motor vehicle or motorcycle outside of this state and within the United States, its territories or possessions, or Canada.

(3) Any New York resident who is neither the owner of a motor vehicle with respect to which coverage for first party benefits is required by this article nor, as a member of a household, is entitled to first party benefits

under paragraph two of this subsection, for loss arising out of the use or operation of the insured or self-insured motor vehicle outside of this state and within the United States, its territories or possessions, or Canada.

(4) The estate of any covered person, other than an occupant of another motor vehicle or a motorcycle, a death benefit in the amount of two thousand dollars for the death of such person arising out of the use or operation of such motor vehicle which is in addition to any first party benefits for basic economic loss.

(b) An insurer may exclude from coverage required by subsection (a) hereof a person who:

(1) Intentionally causes his own injury.

(2) Is injured as a result of operating a motor vehicle while in an intoxicated condition or while his ability to operate such vehicle is impaired by the use of a drug. . . .

(3) Is injured while he is: (i) committing an act which would constitute a felony, or seeking to avoid lawful apprehension or arrest by a law enforcement officer, or (ii) operating a motor vehicle in a race or speed test, or (iii) operating or occupying a motor vehicle known to him to be stolen, or (iv) operating or occupying any motor vehicle owned by such injured person with respect to which the coverage required by subsection (a) hereof is not in effect, or (v) a pedestrian, through being struck by any motor vehicle owned by such injured pedestrian with respect to which the coverage required by subsection (a) hereof is not in effect, or (vi) repairing, servicing or otherwise maintaining a motor vehicle if such conduct is within the course of a business of repairing, servicing or otherwise maintaining a motor vehicle and the injury occurs on the business premises.

(c) Insurance offered by any company to satisfy the requirements of subsection (a) hereof shall be offered (1) without a deductible and (2) with a family deductible of up to two hundred dollars (which deductible shall apply only to the loss of the named insured and members of his household). The superintendent may approve a higher deductible in the case of insurance policies providing additional benefits or pursuant to a plan designed and implemented to coordinate first party benefits with other benefits. . . .

. . .

(f) Every owner's policy of liability insurance issued on a motorcycle or an all terrain vehicle in satisfaction of the requirements of article six or eight of the vehicle and traffic law shall also provide for . . . the payment of first party benefits to persons, other than the occupants of such motorcycle or all terrain vehicle, another motorcycle or all terrain vehicle, or any motor vehicle, for loss arising out of the use or operation of the motorcycle or all terrain vehicle within this state. Every insurer and self-insurer may exclude from the coverage required by this subsection a person who intentionally causes his own injury or is injured while committing an act which would constitute a felony or while seeking to avoid lawful apprehension or arrest by a law enforcement officer.

(g) [A general health insurer may, with the consent of the superintendent of insurance] upon a showing that the company or corporation is qualified to provide for all of the items of basic economic loss specified in paragraph one of subsection (a) of section five thousand one hundred two of this article, provide coverage for such items of basic economic loss to the extent that an insurer would be required to provide under this article. Where a policyholder elects to be covered under such an arrangement the insurer providing coverage for the automobile shall be furnished with the names of all persons covered by the company or corporation under the arrangement and such persons shall not be entitled to benefits for any of the items of basic economic loss specified in such paragraph. The premium for the automobile insurance policy shall be appropriately reduced to reflect the elimination of coverage for such items of basic economic loss. Coverage by the automobile insurer of such eliminated items shall be effected or restored upon request by the insured and payment of the premium for such coverage. All companies and corporations providing coverage for items of basic economic loss pursuant to the authorization of this subsection shall have only those rights and obligations which are applicable to an insurer subject to this article.

.   .   .

§ 5104.   Causes of action for personal injury

(a) Notwithstanding any other law, in any action by or on behalf of a covered person against another covered person for personal injuries arising out of negligence in the use or operation of a motor vehicle in this state, there shall be no right of recovery for non-economic loss, except in the case of a serious injury, or for basic economic loss. The owner, operator or occupant of a motorcycle which has in effect the financial security required by article six or eight of the vehicle and traffic law .   .   . shall not be subject to an action by or on behalf of a covered person for recovery for non-economic loss, except in the case of a serious injury, or for basic economic loss.

(b) In any action by or on behalf of a covered person, against a non-covered person, where damages for personal injuries arising out of the use or operation of a motor vehicle or a motorcycle may be recovered, an insurer which paid or is liable for first party benefits on account of such injuries has a lien against any recovery to the extent of benefits paid or payable by it to the covered person. No such action may be compromised by the covered person except with the written consent of the insurer, or with the approval of the court, or where the amount of such settlement exceeds fifty thousand dollars. The failure of such person to commence such action within two years after accrual gives the insurer a cause of action for the amount of first party benefits paid or payable against any person who may be liable to the covered person for his personal injuries. The insurer's cause of action shall be in addition to the cause of action of the covered person except that in any action subsequently commenced by the covered person for such injuries, the amount of his basic economic loss shall not be recoverable.

(c) Where there is no right of recovery for basic economic loss, such loss may nevertheless be pleaded and proved to the extent that it is relevant to the proof of non-economic loss.

§ 5105. Settlement between insurers

(a) Any insurer liable for the payment of first party benefits to or on behalf of a covered person and any compensation provider paying benefits in lieu of first party benefits which another insurer would otherwise be obligated to pay pursuant to subsection (a) of section five thousand one hundred three of this article . . . has the right to recover the amount paid from the insurer of any other covered person to the extent that such other covered person would have been liable, but for the provisions of this article, to pay damages in an action at law. In any case, the right to recover exists only if at least one of the motor vehicles involved is a motor vehicle weighing more than six thousand five hundred pounds unloaded or is a motor vehicle used principally for the transportation of persons or property for hire. However, in the case of occupants of a bus other than operators, owners, and employees of the owner or operator of the bus, an insurer which, pursuant to paragraph one of subsection (a) of section five thousand one hundred three of this article, provides coverage for first party benefits for such occupants under a policy providing first party benefits to the injured person and members of his household for loss arising out of the use or operation of any vehicle of such household, shall have no right to recover the amount of such benefits from the insurer of such bus.

(b) The sole remedy of any insurer or compensation provider to recover on a claim arising pursuant to subsection (a) hereof, shall be the submission of the controversy to mandatory arbitration pursuant to procedures promulgated or approved by the superintendent. Such procedures shall also be utilized to resolve all disputes arising between insurers concerning their responsibility for the payment of first party benefits.

(c) The liability of an insurer imposed by this section shall not affect or diminish its obligations under any policy of bodily injury liability insurance.

§ 5106. Fair claims settlement

(a) Payments of first party benefits and additional first party benefits shall be made as the loss is incurred. Such benefits are overdue if not paid within thirty days after the claimant supplies proof of the fact and amount of loss sustained. If proof is not supplied as to the entire claim, the amount which is supported by proof is overdue if not paid within thirty days after such proof is supplied. All overdue payments shall bear interest at the rate of two percent per month. If a valid claim or portion was overdue, the claimant shall also be entitled to recover his attorney's reasonable fee, for services necessarily performed in connection with securing payment of the overdue claim, subject to limitations promulgated by the superintendent in regulations.

(b) Every insurer shall provide a claimant with the option of submitting any dispute involving the insurer's liability to pay first party benefits, or additional first party benefits, the amount thereof or any other matter which may arise pursuant to subsection (a) hereof to arbitration pursuant to simplified procedures to be promulgated or approved by the superintendent.

(c) An award by an arbitrator shall be binding except where vacated or modified by a master arbitrator in accordance with simplified procedures to be promulgated or approved by the superintendent. The grounds for vacating or modifying an arbitrator's award by a master arbitrator shall not be limited to those grounds for review set forth in article seventy-five of the civil practice law and rules. The award of a master arbitrator shall be binding except for the grounds for review set forth in article seventy-five of the civil practice law and rules, and provided further that where the amount of such master arbitrator's award is five thousand dollars or greater, exclusive of interest and attorney's fees, the insurer or the claimant may institute a court action to adjudicate the dispute de novo.

§ 5107.   Coverage for non-resident motorists

(a) Every insurer authorized to transact or transacting business in this state, or controlling or controlled by or under common control by or with such an insurer, which sells a policy providing motor vehicle liability insurance coverage or any similar coverage in any state or Canadian province, shall include in each such policy coverage to satisfy the financial security requirements of article six or eight of the vehicle and traffic law and to provide for the payment of first party benefits pursuant to subsection (a) of section five thousand one hundred three of this article when a motor vehicle covered by such policy is used or operated in this state.

(b) Every policy described in subsection (a) hereof shall be construed as having the coverage required by subsection (a) of section five thousand one hundred three of this article.

§ 5108.   Limit on charges by providers of health services

[Charges for health services specified in § 5102(a)(1) are not to exceed charges for those procedures set forth in schedules prepared for workers' compensation injuries. No provider of health services "may demand or request any payment in addition to" the authorized charges. Insurers are to report "any patterns of overcharging" within 30 days after they learn of them.]

Notes and Questions

1. *Is it constitutional?* A unanimous court rejected constitutional challenges to the statute in Montgomery v. Daniels, 340 N.E.2d 444 (N.Y.1975). The court observed that all line drawing raises questions of why the line was not drawn somewhere else; the test to be used was whether there is a reasonable connection between the perceived problem and the remedy adopted. Reviewing criticisms of the fault law of automobile accidents, the court found the statute responsive. The court also questioned the existence of a constitutional duty to provide a replacement for a remedy that is being abolished, citing the introduction of the guest statute and the abolition of actions for alienation of affections and for breach of promise to marry. It found it unnecessary, however, to decide that point here because the statute does provide a substitute remedy for victims of auto accidents. As for equal protection, the court found all the classifications to have a "reasonable basis."

Finally, the court held that abrogation of the right to recover entailed the abolition of any attaching right to a jury trial; the statute did not replace the jury with another fact finder but instead changed the substantive right. This point had been a problem in 1911 when the court held the then-new workers' compensation law unconstitutional in *Ives v. South Buffalo Ry. Co.*, p. 805, supra. But the *Montgomery* court observed that "Jurisprudence has marched many strides in the intervening years. Reliance on *Ives* is misplaced."

No-fault legislation has survived constitutional attack in most jurisdictions. See, e.g., Dimond v. District of Columbia, 792 F.2d 179 (D.C.Cir. 1986).

Death cases. The original statute provided that basic economic loss did not cover losses due to death. In 1977, § 5103(a)(4) was added to allow for $2,000 in death benefits in addition to basic economic loss. The drafters were concerned about a possible constitutional problem caused by Article I, § 16 of the New York Constitution: "The right of action now existing to recover damages for injuries resulting in death, shall never be abrogated; and the amount recoverable shall not be subject to any statutory limitation." The drafters of the statute left death claims out of the statute but allowed recovery for economic loss up to the death and, now, for a flat sum for death benefits, for funeral expenses. The wrongful death action is left intact with the first party insurer subrogated to any tort recovery. Note that § 5102(d) includes death within "serious injury."

Arbitration. Other provisions were challenged in Country–Wide Ins. Co. v. Harnett, 426 F.Supp. 1030 (S.D.N.Y.1977). The insurer challenged § 5106(b) permitting the claimant, but not the insurer, to demand binding arbitration of any dispute. A three-judge court rejected the challenge on the ground that the state could conclude rationally that the two parties were on different footings so far as the disputed claim was concerned and could treat them differently. Among the differences were the claimant's desire for speedy resolution of disputes and his lesser ability to bear the costs of litigation.

The court also rejected a challenge to the provisions that required insurers to renew policies existing at the time the act was adopted. The statutory goal was to prevent wholesale dumping of insureds from the voluntary markets, forcing them into the assigned risk plan. The court found that the need to protect the public and provide orderly transition justified the provisions. The Supreme Court affirmed without hearing argument. 431 U.S. 934 (1977). Justice White would have heard argument.

2. *First party benefits—Who is eligible?* Before considering the wisdom of the legislation, we must understand how it works. Review the questions posed just before the statute. Each is now presented in the context of specific situations. (In each assume that the person was hurt in a motor vehicle accident, unless that point is in doubt.)

a.   An inattentive driver crashes into a tree.

b.   An intoxicated driver crashes into a tree.

c.   A passenger is hurt when the driver of his car, who is intoxicated, drives off the road. May the passenger recover first party benefits?

In setting forth rules to be followed by insurers in settling claims for first party benefits, the Insurance Department has promulgated the following provisions (11 NYCRR 65.15(*m*)):

> (2) An insurer shall pay benefits to an applicant for losses arising out of an accident in the following situations:

>> (i) where coverage has been excluded for an applicant operating a vehicle while in an intoxicated condition or while the applicant's ability is impaired by the use of a drug, if such intoxicated or drugged condition was not a contributing cause of the accident causing the injuries;

>> (ii) where coverage has been excluded for an applicant operating or occupying a motor vehicle known to the applicant to be stolen, and the applicant is an involuntary operator or occupant of said vehicle;

>> (iii) where there is no physical contact between the applicant and a motor vehicle or motorcycle which is the proximate cause of the injury;

>> (iv) where the motor vehicle or motorcycle is used without the specific permission of the owner but is not a stolen vehicle; or

>> (v) where the accident arises out of repairing, servicing or otherwise maintaining a motor vehicle or a motorcycle, other than in the course of a business, and for which no charge or fee is contemplated.

Do these provisions appear consistent with the spirit of the legislation?

3. *When can insurers deny benefits?* Insurers have taken advantage of the opportunity afforded in § 5103(b) to write exclusions into their policies for certain types of behavior.

Claimant, "who was intoxicated at the time, climbed onto the hood of an automobile owned and operated by respondent's insured, and began to smash the car's windshield with his foot. It appears that the insured accelerated the car, causing the claimant to fall from the hood, and sustain injuries." The court upheld the arbitrator's award of no-fault benefits.

Claimant came within no permissible exclusion in § 5103(b). Nor was the award "contrary to strong public policy." The result was within "the letter and spirit of the no-fault law, which was designed to provide compensation to victims of motor vehicle accidents, regardless of fault." Bamond v. Nationwide Mut. Ins. Co., 427 N.Y.S.2d 642 (App.Div. 1980), affirmed 419 N.E.2d 872 (N.Y.1981).

Husband and wife were having a quarrel while they were driving home at 30 miles per hour. Husband "abruptly exited from the passenger side of the moving car." When the insurer denied benefits, husband sought arbitration. The arbitrator concluded that although the husband had "intentionally left the vehicle" there was "no evidence whatsoever that he intentionally caused his own personal injury." The master arbitrator vacated the arbitrator's award and concluded that there was "no rational basis upon which the arbitrator could have found" the injury to have been unintentional. The court held that the master arbitrator had not exceeded his powers of review in concluding that this behavior constituted "intentional self-caused injury" within the meaning of the statute and the policy. He had not reweighed evidence or credibility. Matter of Smith (Firemen's Ins. Co.), 433 N.E.2d 509 (N.Y. 1982).

An insurance company wrote a policy that excluded from coverage injury sustained by "any person as a result of operating a motor vehicle while in an intoxicated condition and while his ability to operate such vehicle is impaired by the use of a drug." Decedent's blood test results demonstrated a blood alcohol content of .21%, clearly indicating intoxication. Since there was no evidence that driver's ability was also impaired by the use of a drug, the exclusion could not apply. "The exclusionary language herein is clearly plain and unambiguous and, in the exercise of reason, susceptible to but one interpretation." Maxwell v. State Farm Mut. Auto. Ins. Co., 461 N.Y.S.2d 541 (App.Div. 1983).

4. *What constitutes "use or operation"?* Section 5102(b) defines "first party benefit" in terms of "injury arising out of the use or operation of a motor vehicle." "Use or operation," under insurance department regulations "includes the loading or unloading of such vehicle but does not include conduct within the course of a business of repairing, servicing, or otherwise maintaining motor vehicles, unless the conduct occurs off the business premises." Boundaries always cause litigation. In each case consider the consequences of a decision either way.

a. P, a pedestrian, was injured in a collision with a bicyclist. P sued the owner of a parked truck that had obstructed his view. The court held that the statute was inapplicable because the injuries did not arise out of the use or operation of a motor vehicle. Rather, the truck was "merely parked on a public street and was not, at that time, being used or otherwise engaged in some ongoing activity." Wooster v. Soriano, 561 N.Y.S.2d 731 (App.Div. 1990).

b. A bus driver was "stabbed by a passenger whom he refused to discharge from the bus at a location other than a designated bus stop." The driver's claim for no-fault benefits was denied. The injury, although occurring on a bus, did not arise from "the intrinsic nature of the bus, as such, nor did the bus, itself, produce the injury." Matter of Manhattan & Bronx Surface Transit Operating Authority (Gholson), 420 N.Y.S.2d 298 (App.Div. 1979).

P was shot by another driver after an accident involving their two cars. The other driver fled the scene and was never apprehended. The court, relying on *Gholson*, denied first-party benefits because the gunshot wound had not arisen from the use or operation of a vehicle. Locascio v. Atlantic Mutual Insurance Co., 511 N.Y.S.2d 934 (App.Div. 1987).

c.   Claimant fell three to six feet away from the waiting bus that she was going to board. Her heel caught in broken pavement. The arbitrator held claimant an "incipient passenger" who was hurt through the "use or operation" of the bus. Recognizing that judicial review of compulsory arbitration permitted wider judicial review than when voluntary arbitration was involved, the court concluded that the arbitrator's determination lacked a rational basis. "A pedestrian cannot be converted into a user [of a motor vehicle] by virtue of close proximity" to the vehicle. New York City Transit Authority v. Ambrosio, 428 N.Y.S.2d 131 (Sup.1980).

d.   P was injured while sailing over a frozen lake in a "parakite" that was tethered by a rope to the back of a Chevy pick-up truck. Her injuries occurred when she attempted to land the kite. The court upheld an arbitrator's award of benefits: "The operation of the vehicle caused the parakite to be airborne and, at the time of the landing, the parakite was still attached to the vehicle." Pierce v. Utica Mutual Insurance Co., 488 N.Y.S.2d 311 (App.Div. 1985). The court also held that the master arbitrator had abused his discretion in reviewing, de novo, the original arbitrator's decision where a rational basis existed for the original finding of coverage.

e.   A truck driver was hurt while unloading his truck at a supermarket when the supermarket's lift collapsed. Although the driver may have been "using" the truck at the time of the injury, his injury did not arise "out of the use or operation" of the vehicle. The use must be the "proximate cause of the injury" before the statute applies. The court approved an earlier case denying benefits to a victim hurt when the gas stove she was using in her "mini-motor home" exploded. Walton v. Lumbermens Mutual Casualty Co., 666 N.E.2d 1046 (N.Y.1996).

Note that the issue in *Walton* is different from the question whether a person injured while unloading a truck can recover damages from the owner for the operator's negligence. The plaintiff was hurt while unloading cargo that the owner's agent had put into the truck. In Argentina v. Emery World Wide Delivery Corp., 715 N.E.2d 495 (N.Y.1999), plaintiff claimed that the owner was liable for negligence committed during the permissive use or operation of the vehicle. The court held that loading and unloading could be "use or operation" of a vehicle and that the owner could be liable for the agent's careless loading. *Walton* was not controlling because the two laws "are distinct, with different purposes." *Walton* "created a needed limit to the benefits of no-fault insurance in line with that law's purposes." Not "all injuries in and among motor vehicles were meant to benefit" from the no-fault law. But the purpose of the financial responsibility laws is "to ensure recourse to the vehicle's owner, a financially responsible party." The "proximate cause limitation in *Walton* was necessary to avoid an overbroad application of the no-fault law. No similar concern arises regarding [the owner's liability statute] since it comes with built-in limitations. Negligence in the use of the vehicle must be shown, and that negligence must be a cause of the injury."

5.   *First party benefits—What is recoverable?* Once the question of eligibility is resolved, the next question becomes the amount of benefits that an eligible victim may recover.

a.   What is the relationship between "first party benefits" and "basic economic loss"?

b.   Are any major medical or other out-of-pocket expenses excluded from the victim's recovery?

c.   What is the maximum wage loss that a covered person may be paid after losing $4,000 in one month? The gross figure of $4,000 should be reduced by 20%. Since that amount exceeds $2,000, it should be reduced to the $2,000 maximum. (The $2,000 maximum in § 5102(a)(2) was raised from $1,000 in 1991.) See Kurcsics v. Merchants Mut. Ins. Co., 403 N.E.2d 159 (N.Y.1980), which overturned an insurance department regulation that had limited the benefits to 80% of the statutory maximum.

d.   What role do deductibles play in the scheme? Recall §§ 5103(c) and (g).

6.   *First party benefits—Special case of motorcycles.* The legislature originally excluded motorcyclists from having to provide coverage for themselves or their riders because of the high cost of such coverage. In 1977, the legislature added "or a motorcycle" to § 5103(a)(1) and added "other than occupants of a motorcycle" to § 5103(a)(2). At the same time the legislature added § 5103(f) providing that motorcycle liability policies must provide for payment of first party benefits to persons "other than occupants of such motorcycle, or any motor vehicle" for loss arising from the use of the motorcycle.

In Carbone v. Visco, 497 N.Y.S.2d 524 (App.Div. 1985), the court ruled that an injured motorcyclist is not entitled to first party benefits under the statute. Although a motorcyclist is required to maintain liability insurance under the financial security provisions of the Insurance Law, first-party benefits under the policy run only to pedestrians.

7.   *First party benefits—Whose insurer pays?* This problem is often phrased as whether the insurance "follows the car or follows the family." Consider which insurer pays if C, who owns a car and has a proper insurance policy:

a.   Drives off the road into a tree.

b.   Is a passenger in a friend's car when it goes into a tree.

c.   Is walking across the street and is run down by Y's car. Does it matter whether Y has insurance?

    d. Is hurt when C's car collides with Y's car. Is § 5105 relevant?

    e. The original version did not mention separate treatment for buses. What is the purpose of the provision in § 5103(a)(1)?

Does it matter whether the insurance follows the car or the family?

    Viruet was driving his uninsured car when he came upon a car in need. He pulled up in front of it, left his own car and had taken two steps to the rear when he was struck by the insured. The insurer rejected Viruet's claim for no-fault benefits, claiming that he was an occupant of his own car at the time. The court disagreed. Viruet testified that he was going to the disabled car and not to his own trunk. If that was accepted he was a pedestrian. But even if he was walking toward his own trunk with the intention of opening it and unloading equipment, "he clearly had not yet begun to do so and cannot be held to have been 'operating or occupying' his vehicle at the time he was struck." General Accident, Fire & Life Ins. Co. v. Viruet, 564 N.Y.S.2d 754 (App.Div. 1991). What if he had gone to the disabled car and then back to his own trunk to get a jack—and was hit as he was unlocking the trunk? Relocking it?

    Exclusion from coverage for an occupant of a motorcycle is different than for an occupant of a car. See General Accident Fire & Life Assur. Corp., Ltd. v. Avery, 452 N.Y.S.2d 125 (App.Div. 1982), where plaintiff, who had his "left leg on the ground, his right knee on the seat, his right hand on the right handle bar with his left arm and hand extending down to check his drive train," was deemed not to be an occupant of his motorcycle and thus was entitled to benefits. Compare the implications of calling P in the motorcycle case not an occupant to calling P in the automobile case not an occupant.

    8. *What is the role of arbitration?* As the statute and cases indicate, much of the work is handled by arbitrators. Resort to the courts is to be minimized—though when the decision of the master arbitrator awards at least $5,000, the disgruntled litigant may obtain a trial *de novo.* A master arbitrator "exceeds his statutory power by making his own factual determination, by reviewing factual and procedural errors committed during the course of the arbitration, by weighing the evidence, or by resolving issues such as the credibility of the witnesses." Richardson v. Prudential Property & Casualty Ins. Co., 646 N.Y.S.2d 850 (App.Div. 1996) (since there was a "rational basis for the original arbitrator's decision," the master arbitrator could not review the medical reports to determine whether the necessity of further medical treatment for the victim was ascertainable within one year).

    Judicial review of the master arbitrator's decision is generally limited to determining that the decision was not arbitrary and capricious and that it had a rational or plausible basis.

    9. *Serious injury—Is a tort action available?* The original version of the law contained a two-part definition of serious injury keyed to the nature of the injuries and the amount of the medical expenses. The monetary part provided that a serious injury would be established if reasonable medical costs exceeded $500. This part was repealed in 1977 because that level was attained too frequently, either because of inflation in medical costs or because victims obtained arguably needless medical treatment simply to exceed the $500 level.

Before a claim for pain and suffering can be pursued, the trial court must determine whether the plaintiff has established a prima facie case of serious injury. Licari v. Elliott, 441 N.E.2d 1088 (N.Y.1982). Determining what constitutes a "serious injury" under the statute has not been easy. In Miller v. Miller, 473 N.Y.S.2d 513 (App.Div. 1984), the "infant plaintiff" had suffered an injury in an automobile accident that resulted in the severing of the muscles circling the lips and the consequential inability to pucker. The court held that a "serious injury" had been established:

> [T]he "significant limitation of use of a body function'" does not require *permanence,* but instead requires a fact finding on the issue of whether the dysfunction is important enough to reach the level of *significance.* Similarly, the "permanent loss of . . . a body . . . function" does not involve in any fashion the element of *significance,* but only that of *permanence.* Indeed, if it did, there would be no need to list 'significant limitation of use of a body function' in a separate category.

Although the court found that a permanent loss need not be significant to constitute a serious injury, "[t]he fact that this function may not loom large when compared to other muscles and body functions may be relevant on the issue of damages."

The *Licari* court indicated that whether or not there has been serious injury is not always a jury question. In Scheer v. Koubek, 512 N.E.2d 309 (N.Y.1987), the court overturned a jury's finding of serious injury where the victim suffered severe, recurring back pain but had suffered no loss of mobility or any permanent disability. Pain alone could not form the basis for a serious injury under the statute. In Caruso v. Hall, 477 N.Y.S.2d 722 (App.Div. 1984), affirmed 476 N.E.2d 648 (N.Y.1985), the court overturned a jury award of $15,000 because a three-inch scar on the top of the victim's head did not constitute significant disfigurement; his hair grew over it within two weeks after the accident. In Savage v. Delacruz, 474 N.Y.S.2d 850 (App.Div. 1984), the court ruled that a material fact existed whether a sprained ankle and scars in the area of the knee constitute serious injury. The test for determining serious disfigurement is "whether a reasonable person viewing plaintiff's body in its altered state would regard the condition as unattractive, objectionable, or as the subject of pity or scorn." In Abdulai v. Roy, 647 N.Y.S.2d 778 (App.Div. 1996), the court upheld a jury determination of serious injury where plaintiff's physician "testified that a line-shaped scar under plaintiff's right eye was 'deeply discolored' and that a 1/3 inch scar on his nose was somewhat 'thickened.'" Both conditions were permanent.

What if P suffers a one month wage loss of $1,000 in wages and sues the motorist at fault for the $200 deducted under § 5102(b)(1)? Assume that P did not suffer "serious injury." What if P suffered a one month wage loss of $4,000?

In Duran v. Heller, 610 N.Y.S.2d 562 (App.Div. 1994), a victim who could not show serious injury was barred from recovering damages for pain and suffering from a drunk driver. Is this troublesome?

10. *What are the differences between suing a "covered person" and suing someone else?* Do these differences affect the plaintiff's recovery? Recall the problem your client presented, p. 821, supra.

When the insured may have a tort action against a non-covered person, the value of that claim depends upon whether the first party insurer is entitled to a lien under § 5104(b) and, if so, how large a lien. It is clear that "the insured and the tortfeasors cannot arbitrarily determine between themselves that any settlement is for pain and suffering rather than for items of basic economic loss." Firemen's Ins. Co. v. Bowley, 441 N.Y.S.2d 947 (Sup. 1981). In such cases, a hearing may be required to allocate the total award. If the parties agree that their settlement only relieves the tortfeasor of liability for pain and suffering (or if the suit claims only such harm), then the insurer is not prejudiced. Allocation issues also exist if the tort case results in a general jury verdict.

See Hyde v. North River Ins. Co., 461 N.Y.S.2d 468 (App.Div. 1983) (since recovery by insured against noncovered party was solely for pain, suffering, and future economic loss—carrier had already paid maximum amount—carrier had no lien against proceeds of judgment against tortfeasor). For a case on the risks of settlement with others without protecting the rights of the first party insurer, see Weinberg v. Transamerica Ins. Co., 465 N.E.2d 819 (N.Y.1984)("It is the burden of the insured to establish by virtue of an express limitation in the release or of a necessary implication arising from the circumstances of its execution that the release did not operate to prejudice the subrogation rights of the insurer").

In Biette v. Baxter, 440 N.E.2d 534 (N.Y.1982), a tort action was brought against the manufacturer of a defective metal plate put in plaintiff's leg as treatment after the auto accident. The court accorded the first party insurer a lien for the amounts it had paid out because of the defective prosthetic device. "Though not a joint tortfeasor, the manufacturer is a noncovered person whose product aggravated the personal injury for which the insurer was required to pay first-party benefits" and this gave rise to a lien under § 104(b).

11. *What happens to the uncovered victim?* Several lower court cases have struggled with the question of when, if ever, persons who do not qualify as "covered persons" may bring tort actions. Most commonly, these are uninsured drivers, or members of the family of an uninsured driver, who are hurt in a multi-vehicle collision. In each case, the victim has claimed the right to sue in tort under pre–1973 rules on the ground that the statute should not be read to change the common law more than it specifies—and it is silent on the tort rights of uncovered persons.

Several views are possible, including: tort law remains fully applicable; tort law is totally barred; and uncovered persons may sue in tort only if they sustain "serious injury." In Wilson v. E. & J. Trucking Corp., 462 N.Y.S.2d 660 (App.Div. 1983), a New York resident who registered his car in Connecticut was uninsured in either state. The court ruled that he did not qualify as a "covered person" and thus was not entitled to no-fault benefits for his basic economic loss. Although the trial court awarded him $23,000 from the third-party tortfeasor, the appellate court reduced the award by $2,000 "as the approximate total of medical expenses, loss of earnings and out-of-pocket expenses attributable to the accident."

What about passengers who are also injured? See Millan v. Yan Yee Lau, 420 N.Y.S.2d 529 (App.Term1979), concluding that the uninsured driver should "at the very least" be limited by the threshold requirement of serious injury of § 5102(d) but the "innocent" passengers in the uninsured vehicle should retain their common law tort action.

In Carbone v. Visco, note 6 supra, the court held that the injured motorcyclist, who was not covered by first party benefits, "is entitled to pursue his common law remedies in an action against defendants as owner and operator of a motor vehicle involved in the accident. Under these circumstances, he is not required to comply with the 'serious injury' provision of Insurance Law § 5104."

12. *Meshing auto no-fault, workers' compensation, and tort law.* The massive effort to draft no-fault legislation for the motor vehicle was so absorbing and complex that no one seemed to consider the problem of meshing the various systems as they are removed from the operation of tort law. Although § 5102(b)(2) provided that first party benefits do not include amounts recovered or recoverable under workers' compensation, the statute ignored the work-related motor vehicle accident. The courts were quickly engulfed by this problem.

After some uncertainty, the legislature amended the Workers' Compensation Law to provide that the compensation carrier shall have no lien on the proceeds of any recovery as to benefits it paid "which were in lieu of first party benefits which another insurer would have otherwise been obligated to pay" under the no-fault law. "The sole remedy" of the compensation carrier is the settlement process contained in § 5105, but only if at least one vehicle involved weighs more than 6,500 pounds unloaded or is a motor vehicle used principally for the transportation of persons or property for hire; except that as to occupants of a bus or school bus (other than operator or employee) a compensation carrier has no right to proceed under § 5105. For an extended discussion of the interplay of these regimes, see Johnson v. Buffalo & Erie County Private Industry Council, 636 N.E.2d 1394 (N.Y.1994) and Kesick v. Ulster County Self Insurance Plan, 665 N.Y.S.2d 454 (App.Div. 1997).

13. *Meshing no-fault benefits and uninsured motorist coverage.* When the covered person is the victim of a hit-and-run driver or an identified but uninsured motorist, the covered person's insurance policy is likely to provide for no-fault benefits and for tort damages, if fault can be established, under the uninsured motorist coverage. What happens when, after the insurer has paid no-fault benefits, the victim seeks recovery under the uninsured motorist coverage? The insurers have insisted on an offset to avoid double recovery for the same items. But the courts have held that to the extent the victim has suffered "serious injury," the tort recovery is for pain and suffering so there is no double recovery. Adams v. Government Employees Ins. Co., 383 N.Y.S.2d 319 (App.Div. 1976) and Sinicropi v. State Farm Ins. Co., 391 N.Y.S.2d 444 (App.Div. 1977)("The no-fault benefits are for basic economic loss and the uninsured motorist coverage is for pain and suffering and other expenses incurred which are not compensable by no-fault benefits. Neither the Insurance Law nor the insurance policy allows the insurer to set off those benefits.") Is there likely to be a case in which the entire recovery under the uninsured motorist coverage could not reasonably be allocated to items excluded under the no-fault system?

14. *First party pain and suffering?* Traditionally, we have thought about pain and suffering as an adjunct to a negligence action. Indeed, recall that Professor Jaffe, p. 690, supra, doubted that the award could be justified in the absence of fault. One of the stumbling blocks to the development of automobile no-fault plans has been the future of pain and suffering. In a thoroughgoing no-fault plan that abolished all tort recovery, would there be any place for pain and suffering?

To the extent that mixed no-fault plans have allowed tort actions for pain and suffering, how much of this is explained by the felt need to preserve the opportunity for injured victims to recover this item of damages? Has that need been perceived in terms of the desirability of the plaintiff getting the funds—or because of the sense that, in this civilized form of vengeance, the money must come from the defendant? Some have stressed the role of vengeance in personal injury law—particularly in something as personal as automobile driving. See Ehrenzweig, A Psychoanalysis of Negligence, 47 Nw.U.L.Rev. 855 (1953) and Linden, Faulty No Fault: A Critique of the Ontario Law Reform Commission Report on Motor Vehicle Accident Compensation, 13 Osgoode Hall L.J. 449 (1975): "It should be remembered that the tort suit was invented in order to try to assuage the thirst for vengeance in society by furnishing a peaceful substitute to the blood feud. If the right to sue were eliminated altogether, I would worry about people once again resorting to private vengeance upon those who do them wrong. In my view, it is preferable to pursue a wrongdoer with a writ rather than with a rifle." But see Hasson, Blood–Feuds, Writs and Rifles—A Reply to Professor Linden, 14 Osgoode Hall L.J. 445 (1976).

Despite this, it is not clear how much of the desire to retain access to the tort action for all, or at least serious, injuries has been based on the assumption that such a step is essential to preserve access to pain and suffering. For an extensive discussion of first-party insurance coverage for pain and suffering and of the market for such insurance, see Croley & Hanson, The Nonpecuniary Costs of Accidents: Pain-and-Suffering Damages in Tort Law, 108 Harv.L.Rev. 1785 (1995).

15. *Basic questions about the statute.*

a. Why make the first party benefits compulsory? Why not eliminate the tort action in the smaller cases (or all cases) and allow individuals to decide for themselves whether to obtain insurance?

b. Once the decision is made to compel substantial first party protection, why compel the purchase of liability insurance?

c. Is $50,000 an appropriate limit on first party benefits? Why might a state make the figure $5,000? $500,000? In addition to complaints about the tort system mentioned in the Report, some have objected to the tort system because it is regressive. See Hasson, Blood–Feuds, Writs and Rifles—A Reply to Professor Linden, supra, suggesting that no-fault systems are less regressive than negligence law: "Under the negligence system both a rich man and a poor man pay the same premium but there is no limit as to how much the rich person can recover under the negligence system." By way of contrast, he noted that as to lost income in no-fault systems, "a rich man would have to pay more than a person with a modest income to obtain adequate protection against future loss of income."

See also Lowenfeld and Mendelsohn, The United States and the Warsaw Convention, 80 Harv.L.Rev. 497, 565 (1967), reporting on debates over an international agreement for airplane crashes. The American delegates were arguing for a system with recovery limits higher than the then-ceiling of $8,300. (This was later achieved.) But other countries "asked why the poorer countries, the poorer airlines, and the poorer travelers should pay for the rich ones. Why, in the words of the Nigerian delegate, should the peasant be required to pay for the comfort of the king?" Is this an important concern? What factors should be most important in calculating premiums under the statute? The Warsaw Convention is discussed at p. 851, infra.

d. Should the first party benefits be primary as against private collateral sources such as hospital and accident insurance? Why not make the statutory benefits primary as against state workers' compensation payments? Is the deductible arrangement sound?

e. Is the statute likely to increase accidents?

f. If some limitation on tort law is desired, is the statute's approach to that limitation sound?

g. Might the goal of eliminating small cases have been achieved by excluding the first $10,000 of pain and suffering from the plaintiff's award?

16. *No-fault in the states.* As noted earlier, the Massachusetts version of no-fault provided minimal no-fault benefits but did bar the bringing of some tort actions. As the states began to adopt no-fault statutes in the 1970s, they tended to follow one of two paths. (No state adopted a "pure" no-fault plan that totally abolished tort—as had been proposed in 1968 by some insurers.) About half of the states that did act, adopted what are called "add-on" statutes because they do not change tort law in any way.

Instead, they provide for low first-party benefits to help meet medical expenses and lost wages. If the plaintiff does pursue an available tort action, the first-party insurer is entitled to have its no-fault payments reimbursed from the tort award.

Although it might seem that the combination of first-party benefits plus unaltered tort law should be more expensive than the existing system, there is some evidence that victims who gain quick and easy first-party benefits in small cases may not pursue the available tort remedy.

The other half of the states that have acted, have adopted what are called "mixed" plans. These plans provide some first-party benefits—in amounts varying from small to large—and also bar some plaintiffs from access to the traditional tort system. The generosity of the first-party benefits is usually commensurate with the difficulty of the tort barrier. Massachusetts, as we have seen, adopted a mixed plan with small benefits and a relatively minor barrier to tort actions. Consider how the Massachusetts plan would be changed if the no-fault benefits were raised from $2,000 to $20,000 and the tort exclusion were raised to $20,000. New York's approach is found only in Michigan, which provides even more generous no-fault benefits than New York and comparable restrictions on the tort action. (If a pedestrian who does not own a car is hit by an uninsured motorist, every no-fault state has some mechanism for providing no-fault benefits to the pedestrian.)

"Pure" no–fault? In 1995, the Hawaii legislature adopted a pure automobile no-fault scheme—the first in the United States. It was vetoed by the governor and did not become law. In March, 1996, California voters rejected an initiative creating a nearly-pure version of auto no-fault, in which the only lawsuits would be against drunk drivers.

See generally, Schwartz, Auto No–Fault and First–Party Insurance: Advantages and Problems, 73 S.Cal. L.Rev. 611 (2000), reviewing auto no-fault at length and concluding that hybrid plans that retain tort are so seriously compromised that proponents of auto no-fault plans should press for a pure version.

17. *No-fault and property damage.* Our concern has been primarily with the personal injury aspect of no-fault. If that can be handled to the satisfaction of the public, it is unlikely that property damage will cause an insoluble problem. Many motor vehicles on the road today are being bought on time payments. Financing companies insist that the vehicle be insured against damage and have comprehensive coverage to protect the lender's interest in the car in case the buyer defaults on the payments. Thus, when property damage occurs it is almost entirely covered by insurance and does not present serious dislocations. The amount of possible damage is readily ascertained and is unlikely to be great. It will be correlated with ability to bear the loss: the most expensive cars are usually owned by those who can most easily bear the loss—with or without insurance. But these people are also most likely to have their own insurance even if it is not required.

As matters now stand, property damage is generally excluded from coverage in no-fault states and tort law remains in effect. These cases are much easier to settle out of court than are personal injury actions—particularly since smaller sums are involved and most of the disputes are between insurance companies.

18. *Federal legislation?* Finally, we note that although the first steps in no-fault legislation have occurred at the state level, some would like to see the federal government enter the area. Congressional efforts failed by close votes in the 1980s and have not been seriously pushed since. The most seriously discussed legislation is a two-tier approach. Congress would set minimum requirements for the states to meet. The package would be more substantial than New York's and might include no-fault medical benefits in unlimited amount plus a very generous coverage for wage loss. A tort action would be possible along the lines of the New York statute—but excluding fractures. If a state did not "voluntarily" adopt such a plan by the deadline, the next tier—the direct federal plan—would become operative in that state. This plan would be the same as the first tier plan, plus a ban on limiting payments for economic loss and, perhaps, the abolition of all tort actions for pain and suffering.

Although some have argued that such a federal approach would be unconstitutional, the major attacks have been on the ground that the no-fault subject is a good one for state experimentation because there is little need for uniformity. Some states have no high premiums, court congestion, or dissatisfaction with current law. Also, urban states may find certain features more helpful than would rural states. Some have also opposed the federal plan on the merits—that it displaces an unduly large sector of tort law and that add-on plans are working well.

D.   FOCUSED NO-FAULT SCHEMES

Workers' compensation established a pattern for addressing perceived deficiencies in the common law tort system. Although it has not overridden the legislative impulse to adopt incremental changes such as those discussed at the beginning of this chapter, the workers' compensation approach—blocking out a category of accidental harm for no-fault treatment—has been a much-used strategy for effecting focused tort reform. In this section, we examine the principal areas other than workplace and motor vehicle injuries in which either the federal government or a state has decided to replace or to supplement the tort system with a no-fault scheme. At the same time, we will look at some of the major no-fault proposals that have been suggested but not yet adopted.

In analyzing the focused no-fault schemes discussed below, consider the rationale for developing alternatives to the tort system, the efficacy of the schemes presented, the nature of the trade-offs involved, and the wisdom of piecemeal revisions in the tort area. Are the programs that have been instituted special responses to egregious tort system performance? Could or should similar schemes be adopted more generally? What are the limits of this approach to reform? On these questions, see generally Rabin,

Some Reflections on the Process of Tort Reform, 25 San Diego L. Rev. 13 (1988).

The following excerpt describes some of the major no-fault legislation and proposals in the toxics area as part of a larger effort to evaluate the wisdom of adopting a broad-based toxics mass tort compensation scheme.

Some Thoughts on the Efficacy of a Mass Toxics Administrative Compensation Scheme

Robert L. Rabin.
52 Maryland Law Review 951, 955–62 (1993).

II. Toxics Compensation Schemes: Exploratory Models

A. Tort/No–Fault Hybrid: The Price–Anderson Act

The Price–Anderson Act[15] signaled one of the first legislative responses to perceived deficiencies of the common law tort model in dealing with potential mass tort liability. Congress passed the Act in 1957 with the express intent of encouraging investment in nuclear energy research and operations by a private sector daunted by the prospect of multimillion-dollar claims and a constrained insurance market. Overall the Act imposes a set of statutory constraints on possible catastrophic tort liability in the event of a nuclear accident, and has essentially established a hybrid system that combines components of both tort and no-fault compensation models.

The system is financed through a combination of private insurance and mandatory contributions to a common fund—contributions which, in the aggregate, set the limit on total liability for any nuclear incident. In accordance with recent amendments to the Act, each nuclear licensee is required to purchase $150 million of private liability insurance. In addition, each licensee must contribute $63 million to a common compensation fund in the event of a nuclear accident at any plant. The liability limit of the fund, with over 100 plants in operation, is approximately $7 billion at present.*

The Price–Anderson funding scheme closely resembles a no-fault model to the extent that it relies substantially on a pooling mechanism to compensate aggrieved parties, thus de-emphasizing the importance of individual responsibility. This pooling mechanism in conjunction with the lack of an experience or risk-rating provision in the statute, blunts the incentives for optimal safety investment by individual firms under Price–Anderson. But at the same time the non-tort sanctions on suboptimal safety that would result from a serious nuclear accident, including the destruction of the facility itself, are very powerful.

15. 42 U.S.C. § 2210 (1988).

* In 1995, the required amounts were $200 million of liability insurance and a $75 million maximum contribution in case of a nuclear accident. The liability limit of the fund was correspondingly higher.

The Act provides for the adjudication of claims as follows. In the event of an "extraordinary nuclear occurrence" (defined as a dispersal causing substantial radiation levels and damage to offsite victims), all claims are consolidated in the federal court for the district in which the incident occurred. The Act creates strict liability in tort for licensees involved in nuclear incidents and abrogates the defense of contributory fault. By consolidating all claims into one jurisdiction and applying a single body of law, Price–Anderson incorporates certain features of the public law tort model.[16]

With respect to establishing liability, however, Price–Anderson maintains some of the distinctive flavor of traditional tort law. The claims process retains a two-party character, with each individual claimant bearing the burden of establishing causation and particularizing proof of economic loss and intangible harm. In this sense the Price–Anderson approach, in practice, might prove to be almost as inefficient as the standard common law tort approach.

Allen v. United States,[17] a case filed under the Federal Tort Claims Act by alleged victims of the Nevada atomic bomb tests in the 1950's, provides a recent tort analogue that illustrates how causation and damage issues under Price–Anderson might be resolved in practice. After a three-month trial, the district court judge in *Allen* carefully distinguished among the variety of claims on the basis of medical literature on the etiology of various cancers, observational reports on the Nevada fallout, and testimony about victim exposure. Though the judge appears to have mastered the relevant scientific literature, *Allen* engenders deep pessimism about the efficacy of a Price–Anderson approach. The case took five years to dispose of at the trial court level, and, even if it had been affirmed, would still have left many types of claims open to dispute and further litigation.[18] The underlying problem in *Allen* arose from the court's retention of an individualized approach to damages and causation, which ensured a prolonged and costly process of decision. Similar problems would be virtually certain to arise in adjudication under Price–Anderson.[19]

Optimally, successful plaintiffs would collect from the fund the full extent of their proven economic and non-economic damages. However, Price–Anderson empowers the court to reduce the size of present claims proportionately when it appears that the ceiling on damages will be exceeded. In these situations the court is to establish a delayed injury fund,

16. For an articulation of the public law tort model, see Rosenberg, The Causal Connection in Mass Exposure Cases: A "Public Law" Vision of the Tort System, 97 Harvard Law Review 851 (1984).

17. 588 F.Supp. 247 (D.Utah 1984).

18. The case was, in fact, reversed on other grounds (the discretionary act exemption in the Federal Tort Claims act). See Allen v. United States, 816 F.2d 1417 (10th Cir.1987).

19. In recognition of these difficulties, a recent comprehensive review of Price–Anderson recommends generic determinations of causation and scheduled treatment of nonpecuniary loss as elements in a package of "administrative features designed to speed the resolution of claims." See Report to the Congress from the Presidential Commission on Catastrophic Nuclear Accidents 5–10 (1990).

setting aside part of the pooled contributions and insurance for claims arising within twenty years of the incident.[20]

B.   Narrowly–Focused No–Fault: The National Childhood Vaccine Injury Act of 1986

The National Childhood Vaccine Injury Act of 1986[21] is in essence a narrowly focused no-fault compensation package affording relief to a designated class of product users, namely, children injured by exposure to certain government-mandated vaccines. Congress passed the Act in response to concerns of the vaccine manufacturers, who had threatened to withdraw from the market in response to the possibility of crushing liability resulting from the infrequent but unavoidable injuries from exposure to vaccines. Like the Price–Anderson Act, the vaccine statute created an alternative to common law tort liability to induce the private sector to make available products deemed essential to the public interest.

The compensation fund is financed by an excise tax on each dose of vaccine disbursed. Since most vaccine manufacturers enjoy a near monopoly position, a rise in the excise tax to pay an increased number of claims would probably not affect any manufacturer's market share. However, a limited measure of non-tort deterrent pressure is probably assured by the political repercussions that might well accompany any significant rise in the price of vaccines.

The Act establishes a two-tier system: alleged victims first proceed under a no-fault approach but retain the back-up option of pursuing a tort claim. Plaintiffs initially file claims in federal district court, where a special master is appointed to gather evidence and determine the award. The

---

20.   In the mid-1970's a proposed federal no-fault scheme for commercial aviation accident victims was modeled on Price–Anderson, according to its author. See Kennedy, Accidents in Commercial Air Transportation—A Proposed Reform of the Liability and Compensation System, 41 Journal of Air Law & Commerce 247 (1975). Like Price–Anderson, the aviation scheme would establish activity-related liability, eliminating the fault inquiry (and, indeed, establishing a very expansive definition of causal responsibility, since the carrier would also be liable for damage resulting from sabotage). There would also be a governmental indemnity provision for liability in excess of privately available insurance—a key provision, now superseded, of the Price?Anderson approach. Finally, there would be consolidation of all cases in the federal court of the jurisdiction in which the accident occurred, as there is under the nuclear incident legislation.

Nevertheless, there are some critical differences in the approach. Kennedy would have federal indemnification financed from a surcharge on airline tickets, instead of the general revenue strategy originally adopted in Price–Anderson. Moreover, there is no provision for pooling of liability among the carriers above the insurance limits; rather, the government fund is an exclusive and unlimited source of indemnification. Also, the aviation plan eliminates pain and suffering liability except in cases of "permanent disfigurement or disability"—which, presumably, would be fairly common among survivors. (On the other hand, survival itself is quite uncommon.)

The proposal was never adopted. One can speculate that the capacity of the tort system to deal in a reasonably effective fashion with these "traditional" mass tort cases explains the relatively limited political appeal of the initiative.

21.   42 U.S.C. §§ 300aa–10 to 300aa–33 (West.Supp. 1990).

claimant must establish injury from a vaccine listed in the Vaccine Injury Table, demonstrate that the malady is on the list provided in the Table, and prove that the adverse reaction resulted within an exposure period designated in the Table. Claimants establishing these relatively straightforward conditions create a strong presumption of liability. By substantially eliminating contentious issues of causation, the Act is designed to settle claims in a more efficient manner than would the Price–Anderson Act.

Similarly, the vaccine statute provides a straightforward means of measuring damages. The statute covers all actual medical expenses as well as costs of rehabilitation. In addition, it provides compensation for lost earning power based on the average earnings of workers in the non-farm sector of the economy, determined annually on a prospective basis. The only indeterminate measure of damages is for pain and suffering, which may be awarded by the special master up to a limit of $250,000. Thus the Act strikes a balance between scheduled and individualized compensation, and, with the exception of retaining a scaled-down discretionary decision on pain and suffering, assesses damages in a simple and administratively efficient manner.

The claimant is entitled to reject the special master's award and seek tort relief instead. However, a number of disincentives are introduced to discourage this option. First, the Act adopts the principle of Restatement (Second) of Torts § 402A, comment *k*, which allows an appropriate warning to serve as an effective defense against [strict] liability [in prescription drug cases]. In addition, the Act adopts the "learned intermediary" doctrine, which requires adequate notice by the manufacturer only to the party administering the vaccination. Finally, the manufacturer is protected against punitive damage awards if it complies with the federal Food, Drug and Cosmetic Act and the Public Health Act. At least in its first few years of operation, this program design has had almost total success in inducing vaccine injury victims to accept the compensatory award and forgo their right to sue in tort.

In the final analysis, it must be emphasized that the compensation problem addressed by the vaccine statute is relatively narrow in scope. A determinate number of cases arise annually; litigation most often involves a single plaintiff alleging damages against an identifiable manufacturer after a relatively short latency period. The scientific information linking adverse reactions with a limited number of identified diseases is unusually reliable. So in most cases establishing liability under the Vaccine Injury Table is fairly simple. Consequently, the relevance of the vaccine statute to the most troublesome environmental or drug cases, with their mass tort, long-latency, identification, and causation problems, is far from clear.

C.   Expansive No–Fault for Toxic Harms: Superfund 301(e) Study Group Report and Environmental Law Institute Model Statute

The Superfund 301(e) Report[22] and the Environmental Law Institute (ELI) Model Statute[23] both propose no-fault compensation schemes for

22. A Report to Congress in Compliance with Section 301(e) of the Comprehensive Environmental Response, Compensation, and Liability Act of 1980, S. Comm. on Env't & Pub. Works, Serial No. 97–12, 97th Cong. 2d Sess. (Sept. 1982).

23. Trauberman, Statutory Reform of "Toxic Torts": Relieving Legal, Scientific, victims of toxic-related harms. Like the vaccine statute, both allow claimants the opportunity to pursue tort remedies if they are dissatisfied with the no-fault determinations. Unlike the Price–Anderson Act or the vaccine statute, however, neither proposal has been legislatively adopted. Since the Superfund and ELI proposals are relatively similar in scope, they will be considered together.

The Superfund proposal was developed as a by-product of the Superfund legislation of 1980. As such the scope of the proposal is limited to compensating harm that arises from exposure to a hazardous waste—defined by reference to a Toxic Substance Document prepared by a designated agency—released from a site that qualifies for cleanup under the Act. The ELI proposal is considerably broader, extending coverage to harms arising from exposure to a list of "hazardous chemical substances" that includes toxics presently designated under federal statutory schemes or subsequently listed under a petition process implemented by the Fund administrator. Consequently, the ELI proposal would cover harm resulting from exposure to a far wider array of actual or potential toxic agents, including asbestos, Agent Orange, and drugs.

The Superfund proposal would be financed in a manner analogous to the current Superfund design, relying on a tax levied on the production of toxic chemicals and crude oil and the disposal of hazardous waste. The ELI proposal would impose a tax on petroleum and chemical production as well, but would also phase in an annual hazard fee on such production which would reflect the risk-generating characteristics of the substances produced. To the extent that this variable fee is administratively feasible, the ELI financing scheme is superior to the Superfund scheme from a market deterrence perspective.

The adjudication of claims under the two proposals is very similar. The initial no-fault determination under the Superfund scheme addresses causation by a statutory rebuttable presumption, triggered when the claimant establishes that (1) a source was engaged at the time of exposure in the generation, transportation, or disposal of hazardous waste; (2) the claimant was exposed to the hazardous waste; and (3) the injury suffered by the claimant was of the kind known to result from such exposure. The Fund would use a Toxic Substance Document, analogous to the Vaccine Table, to assess the claimant's right to recovery.

Damages awarded under the Superfund proposal would include all medical expenses and two-thirds of lost income up to a high ceiling. Depending on the earning power of an individual claimant, the Superfund proposal would be either more or less generous than the vaccine statute in compensating for lost wages. However, the Superfund scheme would not allow any recovery for pain and suffering.

If a claimant were dissatisfied with the no-fault award, he would be allowed to initiate a tort claim. Like the vaccine statute, the Superfund scheme creates disincentives to make this mode of action unattractive. Among other provisions, if the tort award is less than 25 percent greater than the no-fault award, the plaintiff must pay the court costs and expert witness fees of the defendant. In addition, the Fund must be reimbursed for payments disbursed in all cases. The ELI proposal creates a far more substantial disincentive to sue by requiring that a claimant return any benefit payments to the Fund *before* initiating a tort suit.

Creating such disincentives, however, raises an important equity concern. To guarantee fairness to potential claimants, both proposals would need careful scrutiny to ensure that statutory award levels were sufficiently generous to avoid claimants' being coerced into accepting a dubious bargain under the no-fault scheme.

One other aspect of the ELI proposal deserves attention. Even though this proposal establishes wider coverage for addressing environmental and other mass toxic tort cases than does the vaccine statute or the Superfund proposal, it remains problematic. It is unclear whether the ELI version of the Toxic Substance Document would provide both a scientifically sound and an efficient basis for resolving the vexing problems of causation. In addition, the ELI proposal leaves unresolved the issue of how the system would shift claims initiated in the tort system to the no-fault scheme once the hazardous nature of the product was well documented. Finally, there is a threshold question of whether the tort system has been an indispensable institutional mechanism—through pretrial discovery and the litigation process—for identifying toxic health hazards in the first instance.[24]

Notes and Questions

1. Drawing on these models, the author cautiously concludes that a strong case could be made for adopting a mass toxics administrative compensation scheme if "there were a clear prospect of a significant number of discrete mass tort cases occurring in the future on the scale of asbestos or the Dalkon Shield." To place this comment in context, consider that the Dalkon Shield settlement trust eventually had to cover about 240,000 claims, and that in 1998, two years before it joined 25 other companies that once made asbestos in declaring bankruptcy, there were some 200,000 claims pending against Owens–Corning, which had by late 2000 paid compensation to about twice that number of claimants.

The main features of such a scheme were sketched out in Enterprise Responsibility for Personal Injury, Vol. II, Approaches to Legal and Institu-

24. See, e.g., P. Brodeur, *Outrageous* (1985). *Misconduct: The Asbestos Industry on Trial*

tional Change, Report to the American Law Institute (1991), at p. 481 and would include:

> . . . a broad definition of "toxic harm"—in other words the compensable event—that would include chemical substances for which an identifiable threshold of exposure has been linked with serious illness or disease by scientific consensus. Claimants would be required to establish exposure to a designated source of the substance in order to create a rebuttable presumption of harm. The requisite exposure/source/substance connection could be established either by reference to a Toxic Substance Document adopted by the administrative compensation board, or by judicial referral to the board following a court determination that filed claims indicated the likelihood of a significant number of related, long-latency toxic harm cases.

> Compensation would be for pecuniary loss, on the model of workers' compensation, with a modest allowance for scheduled nonpecuniary loss in serious cases. The tort system might be retained, but a claimant would be required to elect between no-fault benefits and a possible tort award. . . . The tort option would be scaled down by allowing only scheduled damages for nonpecuniary loss and by reversing the collateral source rule. The system would be financed, at least at the outset, by a flat tax on the gross revenues of toxics producers.

From this summary description, does a toxics no-fault scheme seem to have significant advantages over the tort system? Is it likely to have greater advantages in mass tort controversies than in "single incident" cases?

2. In thinking about alternatives to the tort system in mass toxics cases, no-fault is not the only possibility. In the article cited in footnote 16 of the Rabin article, David Rosenberg proposes a "public law tort model" that would significantly restructure the tort process in mass tort cases. The model would feature class action treatment of claims, probabilistic determination of causation, proportional liability among defendants, scheduled damages, and "insurance fund judgments" that would provide for later-arising cases. The Report to the American Law Institute, above, presents a later version of the model. See Report at pp. 412–39. For another perspective from an experienced mediator in mass tort cases, see McGovern, Resolving Mature Mass Torts, 69 B.U.L.Rev. 659 (1989). On the deficiencies of the traditional tort system in mass toxics cases, see Rabin, Tort System on Trial: The Burden of Mass Toxics Litigation, 98 Yale L. J. 813 (1989). What would be the key questions in deciding whether the public law tort model or an administrative no-fault scheme, if either, is a more desirable alternative to the traditional system in mass toxics cases?

3. Is the problem of creating well-defined boundaries as to what constitutes a "compensable event"—i.e. regarding scope of coverage under a scheme—likely to be surmountable? Recent experience suggests that even the narrowly focused Vaccine Act may be problematic on this score. In 1995, the Department of Health and Human Services promulgated new regulations reducing the number of potentially eligible recipients through narrower definitions of compensable events in the vaccine injury table, despite a 5–4 vote against the revisions by the Advisory Commission on Childhood Vaccines and the protests of parents' groups. By 2000, a total of 5236 cases had been adjudicated to date, with over $1 billion awarded for damages and attorney's fees. Out of all the claims filed, however, only 1601 claims were actually compensated, meaning that more than 60% of all claims filed by petitioners (3635 claims) had been dismissed. See Bureau of Health Professions, U.S. Dep't of Health & Human Servs., National Vaccine Injury Compensation Program: Monthly Statistics Report Through November 22, 2000 <http:// www.hrsa.dhhs.gov/bhpr/vicp/ monthly.htm>.

For overviews of the program, see Ridgway, No–Fault Vaccine Insurance: Lessons from the National Vaccine Injury Compensation Program, 24 J. Health Pol. Pol'y & L. 59 (1999); Note, A One Shot Deal: The National Childhood Vaccine Injury Act, 41 Wm. & Mary L. Rev. 309 (1999).

4. *Swine Flu Act.* In the summer of 1976, fearing the possibility of a Swine Flu epidemic of a proportion not encountered since 1918–19, when the flu claimed the lives of over 500,000 Americans, the federal government planned the largest mass-immunization program in the nation's history. Insurance companies, however, refused to underwrite the government's proposed immunization program in light of the potential liability that vaccine manufacturers might encounter, foreshadowed by Reyes v. Wyeth Laboratories, 498 F.2d 1264 (5th Cir.), cert. denied 419 U.S. 1096 (1974). Nor would the vaccine manufacturers provide the necessary vaccine without insurance. In response to the resulting stalemate, Congress passed the Swine Flu Act, 42 U.S.C. § 247b(j)–(1)(1976), which amended the Federal Tort Claims Act to allow those injured by the vaccine to bring suit against the federal government for their injuries.

Under the Swine Flu Act, the United States replaced the named defendant in any plaintiff's suit against a manufacturer or distributor of the vaccine or any public or private agency or medical or health personnel who provided no-cost inoculation. These suits were tried before judges in the appropriate federal district courts, and plaintiffs could proceed on any theory of liability provided by the law of the state in which the act or omission occurred, including negligence, strict liability in tort, and breach of warranty. See e.g., Unthank v. United States, 732 F.2d 1517 (10th Cir.1984)(interpreting the compensatory nature of the Act broadly and finding the government liable on three separate theories of liability). The Act gave the government an indemnification right against the named party defendants based on negligence or contract.

Within two months of the beginning of the immunization program, after 40 million Americans had been inoculated, the federal government stopped the mass vaccinations. The vaccinations had resulted in serious unexpected complications, including a twelve-fold increase in the incidence of Guillain–Barre syndrome, a sometimes severe generalized paralytic disease. At the same time, the fear of a swine flu epidemic had quieted as no new cases of the flu had come to light.

See L. Garrett, The Coming Plague: Newly Emerging Diseases in a World Out of Balance 182 (1994). For an interesting account of the 1918–19 pandemic, see G. Kolata, Flu: The Story of the Great Influenza Pandemic and the Search for the Virus that Caused It (1999).

5. *Black lung compensation.* Congress passed the Federal Coal Mine Health and Safety Act of 1969, Pub.L. No. 91–173, 83 Stat. 792 (1969), to aid those suffering from progressive coal mining-related respiratory disorders who were often prevented from recovering damages under state statutes of limitations and generally unable to recover from state workers' compensation plans because these plans did not compensate workers for occupational diseases. The Act has been amended three times since its original enactment. To receive compensation under the current federal black lung program, a miner (defined broadly to include all workers in mining-related work with a high degree of coal dust exposure) must prove the existence of black lung disease (known technically as pneumoconiosis), total disability from the disease, and that the disease was contracted from coal mining-related employment. Causation is presumed if the claimant can show ten years of coal mining-related work and contraction of black lung disease. Total disability is presumed upon proof of existence of a complicated black lung condition. For the current version, see 30 U.S.C. § 901 et seq.

Under the federal program, miners, or their survivors, file claims at a local Social Security Office, from which the claims are forwarded to the Department of Labor for processing. Compensatory payments are made by the last mine for which the miner worked for at least one year, and administrative expenses are paid by a Black Lung Disability Trust Fund, funded by an excise tax on coal.

The black lung program provides an interesting study of the problems associated with a federally coordinated, focused no-fault scheme because the availability of compensation under the program—determined chiefly by the number and strength of its presumptions—has been widened and narrowed substantially over its short life to respond to the need for compensation and subsequent charges of waste and overcompensation. The plan has been the subject of considerable controversy. In 1993, over 75,000 former miners were receiving black lung benefits at an annual cost of $1.3 billion.

For historical treatment, see P. Barth, The Tragedy of Black Lung: Federal Compensation for Occupational Disease (1987); A. Derickson, Black Lung: Anatomy of a Public Health Disaster (1998); for recent developments, see Mattingly, Black Lung Update: The Evolution of the Current Regulations and the Proposed Revolution, 100 W.Va. L.Rev. 601 (1998).

6. For a proposed no-fault scheme covering smoking-related harms, see Ausness, Compensation for Smoking–Related Injuries: An Alternative to Strict Liability in Tort, 36 Wayne L. Rev. 1085 (1990). The author states that the primary goal of the compensation scheme "would be to process claims for smoking-related injuries quickly and at minimal administrative cost. Compensation would be limited to economic losses and the program would be financed by an excise tax on cigarette manufacturing." Like many of the other toxic no-fault schemes, a smoking-related plan poses questions regarding causation and coverage limitations. In addition, it raises distinctive issues about no-fault and the "deserving" victim. How serious a consideration should this be?

Later proposals to extend no-fault to the tobacco area include, LeBel, Beginning the Endgame: The Search for an Injury Compensation System Alternative to Tort Liability for Tobacco–Related Harms, 24 N.Ky. L.Rev. 457 (1997); Hanson, Logue and Zamore, Smokers' Compensation: Toward a Blueprint for Federal Regulation of Cigarette Manufacturers, 22 S.Ill. U. L.J. 519 (1998). See generally, LeBel & Ausness, Toward Justice in Tobacco Policymaking: A Critique of Hanson and Logue and an Alternative Approach to the Costs of Cigarettes, 33 Ga. L.Rev. 693 (1999). A general product-related no-fault scheme is proposed and discussed in Ausness, An Insurance–Based Compensation Scheme for Product–Related Injuries, 58 U. of Pitt. L.Rev. 669 (1997).

7. *Note on liability of international air carriers.* The Warsaw Convention, Convention for the Unification of Certain Rules Relating to International Transportation by Air, Oct. 12, 1929, 49 Stat. 3000, T.S. No. 876 (1934), note following 49 U.S.C. § 1502, is a multilateral treaty that regulates the liability of international air carriers. The Convention was drafted in 1929 and the United States became a signatory in 1934. Its terms apply to the international carriage of persons, luggage, or goods, performed by aircraft, either for reward or gratuitously. The Supreme Court has noted that the Convention's principal purpose was to provide uniform liability limitations and foster the growth of commercial aviation. Trans World Airlines, Inc. v. Franklin Mint Corp., 466 U.S. 243, 256 (1984).

The Convention establishes a system of strict liability for personal injuries and cargo losses that occur on international flights and limits the damages that passengers may recover. As originally drafted, the Convention limited recovery for loss of life or injury to $8,300. The maximum recovery amount was subsequently increased to $75,000. The Convention's limitations on damages are not applicable in cases of willful misconduct by an international air carrier or its employees. However, even in cases involving willful misconduct, the Convention has been interpreted to preclude recovery of punitive damages. In re Korean Air Lines Disaster, 932 F.2d 1475 (D.C.Cir.), cert. denied 502 U.S. 994 (1991); In re Air Disaster at Lockerbie, Scotland, 928 F.2d 1267 (2d Cir.), cert. denied 502 U.S. 920 (1991).

In Eastern Airlines, Inc. v. Floyd, 499 U.S. 530 (1991), the Supreme Court determined that the Convention does not permit recovery for mental or psychic injuries unaccompanied by physical injury or physical manifestation of injury. Plaintiffs were passengers on defendant's flight from Miami to the Bahamas. Shortly after takeoff, the plane experienced mechanical difficulties. The flight crew attempted to return to Miami, but the malfunctions worsened; the plane began to lose altitude and the crew informed the passengers of an impending landing in the Atlantic Ocean. Before the plane crashed, the crew managed to restart the malfunctioning engine and safely returned the plane to Miami.

Plaintiffs brought an action against the airline for the mental distress they experienced as a result of the incident. A unanimous Court held that Article 17 of the Convention, which provides that a "carrier is liable for damages sustained in the event of the death or wounding of a passenger or any other bodily injury suffered by a passenger, if the accident which caused the damage so sustained took place on board the aircraft or in the course of any of the operations of embarking or disembarking[,]" is applicable only in cases that involve some form of physical injury. Since the Convention's authoritative text was in French, the Court's duty was to interpret "lesion corporelle" (the French term for "bodily injury") as of the time the Convention was drafted.

The Court held that since recovery for wholly psychic injuries "was unknown in many, if not most, jurisdictions in 1929, the drafters most likely would have felt compelled to make an unequivocal reference to purely mental injury if they had specifically intended to allow such recovery." The Court also determined that excluding recovery for mental and psychic injury was consistent with the contracting parties' overriding purpose of providing strict limits on air carrier liability. Reconsider the common-law approach to this issue in the emotional harm cases discussed at p. ___, supra. For a review of recent case law under the Warsaw Convention addressing the issue of recovery of psychological damages that are accompanied by some physical harm, see Chester, The Aftermath of the Airplane Accident: Recovery of Damages for Psychological Injuries Accompanied by Physical Injuries under the Warsaw Convention, 84 Marq. L. Rev. 227 (2000).

In El Al Israel Airlines, Ltd. v. Tsui Yuan Tseng, 525 U.S. 155 (1999), the Court held that the Warsaw Convention precludes an international air passenger from maintaining an action for personal injury damages under domestic law if the Convention does not allow for recovery for the injury. Plaintiff had sued El Al in state court, alleging that the airline caused her to suffer personal injuries when it subjected her to a security search prior to boarding a flight from New York to Tel Aviv. El Al removed the action to federal court on the ground that the airline was a "foreign state." Thereafter, the federal district court dismissed the passenger's claim on the ground that she failed to establish an injury cognizable under Article 17 of Warsaw Convention. On appeal of a remand by the second circuit court of appeals, the Supreme Court held that recovery for personal injury suffered "on board [an] aircraft or in the course of any of the operations of embarking or disembarking," if not allowed under Article 17 of the Warsaw Convention, is not available at all.

For a discussion of changes to the Warsaw agreement that have taken place through the years, see Pickelman, Draft Convention for the Unification of Certain Rules for International Carriage by Air: The Warsaw Convention Revisited for the Last Time?, 64 J. Air L. & Com. 273 (1998). For a comprehensive analysis of the Convention and its subsequent modification by various international agreements, see L.B. Goldhirsch, The Warsaw Convention Annotated: A Legal Handbook (1988). See also Lowenfeld

& Mendelsohn, The United States and the Warsaw Convention, 80 Harv. L.Rev. 497 (1967).

8. *Health care and No–fault.* In 1973 Professors Havighurst and Tancredi presented a model for applying no-fault insurance to medical malpractice claims. "Medical Adversity Insurance"—A No–Fault Approach to Medical Malpractice and Quality Assurance, 51 Milbank Memorial Fund Q. 125, reprinted in 1974 Ins.L.J. 69. That model was expanded two years later in Havighurst, "Medical Adversity Insurance"—Has Its Time Come?, 1975 Duke L.J. 1233. Medical Adversity Insurance (MAI) was designed to reduce the overall administrative cost of malpractice litigation by removing certain injuries from the fault system.

MAI policies would list "adverse outcomes," or "compensable events," for which a patient could recover without proof of fault. The lists would be created by medical experts who, on the basis of their experience, would identify adverse results that were probably avoidable: "An event would be added to the list if medical opinion indicated that the event was usually or frequently—though by no means invariably—avoidable under good-quality medical care and that the frequency of the event could be expected to diminish if providers' attention were directed more strongly to the quality of the outcomes being achieved."

In order to recover under the MAI system a patient would have to show that he or she had suffered a designated compensable event (DCE). Negligence would be irrelevant and, because the listed adverse outcomes would be highly specific, cause would not be a problem. The two most complex malpractice issues would thus be avoided. Case-by-case inquiries would ask only whether an adverse outcome had occurred, and what damages had resulted. The damages allowed under the system would depend on the policies issued, but Professor Havighurst suggested these would include at least all medical expenses, and wage losses subject to weekly limits.

The MAI scheme was not designed to replace the present fault system, but to remove a large number of cases from it. Not all victims of malpractice would suffer compensable events on MAI lists. If an unlisted event occurred, the patient would have to resort to the fault system, with whatever improvements could be brought to it.

Is the causation problem in medical cases manageable? Does a medical no-fault proposal based on the compensable event approach overcome the causation difficulties? Does it raise other problems?

In 1986, Professor Tancredi, conceding that a legislatively enacted DCE system was politically unlikely, turned his attention to the prospects for private adoption of the DCE system by insurance providers:

> . . . What is at stake is nothing less than the definition of the physician/patient relationship. The overriding issue is whether the terms of that intensely personal relationship ought to be prescribed exclusively by government through political and legal processes or whether the relationship should instead be shaped at least in part

through private negotiation of mutually satisfying arrangements. No-fault insurance offers an attractive opportunity to strengthen physician/patient bonds and to shore up the values of honesty and trust that are essential to a healthy, happy, and therapeutic relationship. Clinicians and others have observed that the current adversary system, which threatens to pit a patient against a health care professional in an acrimonious dispute, discourages the physician from revealing to the patient his doubts and the full truth about the outcomes of his management because such disclosures may trigger a malpractice suit. A no-fault scheme, by which a provider acknowledges risks and undertakes to protect patients against specific harms, should strengthen and improve both the subjective and the objective quality of care.

Tancredi, Designing a No–Fault Alternative, 49 Law & Contemp. Prob. 277, 280 (1986). Is there a reason to prefer a state-initiated remedy or does a system of private ordering have advantages over legislation? This question is discussed in a broader context in note 9, infra.

For a comprehensive analysis of the pros and cons of medical no-fault, see P. Weiler, Medical Malpractice on Trial 132–58 (1991). Prof. Weiler reviews the case for no-fault from a variety of perspectives—compensation, administration and prevention—and concludes that such a system, if it offered broad coverage of serious harms, has great appeal when compared to the present tort approach. Nonetheless, the problems of coverage/causation are sufficiently troublesome to lead him to propose as "an intermediate step" an elective no-fault system (for further discussion of this latter concept, see note 9, infra).

Assuming, however, that the present system is to be retained, Weiler offers another proposal, organizational liability. As he states it:

The technique I favor is to make the hospital or other health care organization primarily liable for all *accidental* (negligent, not intentional) injuries inflicted on patients due to malpractice committed by anyone affiliated with the institution, whether or not the actor is technically an employee of the hospital. In other words, for purposes of personal injury policy, the relationship of hospital and affiliated physicians should be deemed to be the functional equivalent of the relationship of an HMO to its staff physicians. In the HMO context, individual obstetricians or surgeons are not expected personally to pay the large malpractice premium required for their medical specialties, which are much riskier than those of the pediatrician or internist. Likewise, we do not expect that the pilots or mechanics working for an airline company should personally pay the substantial premiums that would be required for insurance against instances of careless behavior in these jobs, slipups that are far riskier than those which might be committed by a flight attendant or passenger agent working for the same airline. Instead, under this proposal each doctor in every specialty is treated as a member of a single firm engaged in the enterprise of health care, with the organization responsible for collecting revenues from the patients who receive the benefits of its services and for purchasing the insurance required to protect against the risk of serious injuries that occur. The analogy, again, is to pilots or mechanics, who are assumed as a matter of course to be parts of the larger enterprise of air travel, with the firm assuming immediate responsibility for injuries caused by the mistakes of its workers, and paying for those costs through revenues collected from all passengers on its flights.

Is the analogy to airline workers apt? From a deterrence perspective, would you expect organizational liability to be more or less effective than the existing tort system? Does it raise fairness concerns between large and small hospitals? High and low risk practitioners? For a summary version of Weiler's work in the area, which grew out of the Harvard Medical Practice Study, Patients, Doctors and Lawyers: Medical Injury, Malpractice Litigation and Patient Compensation in New York (1990), see Weiler, The Case for No–Fault Medical Liability, 52 Md.L.Rev. 908 (1993).

In a review of Weiler's 1991 volume, Sugarman, Doctor No, 58 U.Chi. L.Rev. 1499, 1500–01 (1991), the author summarizes the following data provided on the operations of the system:

> . . . of every 100,000 patients discharged from hospitals, nearly 4,000 suffered an "adverse event" from their medical treatment. About one-fourth of these are the result of medical malpractice. In short, hospital patients on average run about a four percent risk of an adverse event and about a one percent risk of medical malpractice. These 100,000 patient discharges and 1,000 malpractice-caused injuries generate about 125 claims. About sixty of the 125 claimants actually receive compensation. The rest of the claims lose at trial or are dropped. Of those sixty successful claimants, about twenty receive payment before they have filed a lawsuit, about thirty-five after a suit is filed but before (or during) trial, and only about five win at trial.

Sugarman goes on to indicate that Weiler's data also report that of every 125 claims that plaintiffs make, some 85 appear to expert evaluators to be cases in which no malpractice occurred—and perhaps 30% of these claimants receive some award. Do these data help evaluate the proposals discussed above?

Later studies by the Harvard Medical Practice group included a comparison of the Swedish approach to compensation of medical injuries—an elective no-fault system—with empirical data on the costs of medical malpractice in Utah and Colorado, two states that were contemplating implementation of a medical no-fault system; see Studdert, et al., Can the United States Afford a "No–Fault" System of Compensation for Medical Injury?, 60 Law & Contemp. Prob. 1 (1997). See also, Studdert, Brennan, and Thomas, Beyond Dead Reckoning: Measures of Medical Injury Burden, Malpractice Litigation, and Alternative Compensation Models from Utah and Colorado, 33 Ind. L.Rev. 1643 (2000), replicating the earlier Harvard study (which had been based on New York data) in Utah and Colorado, and concluding, once again, that "the link between no-fault and error reduction is quite compelling," and that "eliminating the specter of litigation would also remove the principal barrier to the free flow of information about medical errors."

Birth-related neurological injuries compensation acts. Fears that rising liability costs would deter insurers from covering necessary medical procedures led the states of Virginia and Florida to pass narrowly focused medical no-fault plans. By 1986, two of Virginia's big three malpractice insurance companies had declared a moratorium on new policies and the third refused to cover any obstetricians in practice groups of 10 or fewer because the burden of tort liability for birth-related neurological injuries was too great. In response, the Virginia state legislature passed the Birth–Related Neurological Injury Compensation Act (Injured Infant Act), Va. Code Ann. §§ 38.2–5000 to 5021 (Supp. 1987) over the heavy objections of the state plaintiffs' bar. Under the plan, there is no tort recovery for any severely brain-damaged infants whose injuries were "caused by the deprivation of oxygen or mechanical injury occurring in the course of labor, delivery, or resuscitation in the immediate post-delivery period in a hospital which renders the infant permanently motorically disabled and (i) developmentally disabled or (ii) for infants sufficiently developed to be cognitively evaluated, cognitively disabled." The disability must cause the infant to be "permanently in need of assistance in all activities of daily living." In addition, the delivery must have been performed by an obstetrician participating in the fund, or must have occurred in a participating hospital.

The compensation plan is principally funded by a flat annual fee on participating obstetricians—80% of whom signed on shortly after the Act was passed. The Act also provides that, if necessary, insurance companies can be taxed to maintain the fund. The fund pays for all medical expenses, but it has a collateral source rule that relieves it of any expenses that qualify for other private insurance or government coverage. It will also compensate for lost wages from the ages of 18 to 65 in the form of periodic installments equaling one-half of the average weekly wage in Virginia's private, nonfarm sector. Tort actions are excluded against participating physicians and hospitals except in cases of intentional or willful acts.

The establishment of the fund served its primary purpose, that of convincing one of the state's malpractice insurers to continue issuing policies. As of mid-1993, however, only five claims had been filed under the Act and four awards had been paid out. Critics contended that the scarcity of claims was due to the act's narrow definition of infants who qualified for compensation. Unlike most no-fault plans, whose goal is to compensate all accident victims within a broad activity category, Virginia's plan only gives compensation to a specific subset of birth-related injuries. The type of severe neurological damage covered by the act is relatively rare as opposed to the uncovered birth tragedies of severe mental retardation or cerebral palsy. See Duff, Compensation for Neurologically Impaired Infants: Medical No–Fault in Virginia, 27 Harv.J.Legis. 391 (1990).

As of 1996, 23 of 29 claims had been compensated under the Virginia act, and 96 of 196 claims had been compensated under the Florida Act, which has somewhat more generous qualifying provisions. For descriptions and empirical studies of both programs, see Sloan, et al., The Road from Medical Injury to Claims Resolution: How No–Fault and Tort Differ, 60 Law & Contemp. Prob. 35 (1997). The authors conclude that in light of the limited number of families compensated through these programs "no-fault is at best a partial substitute for tort." See also Bovbjerg and Sloan, No–Fault for Medical Injury: Theory and Evidence, 67 U. Cin. L.Rev. 53 (1998). On the Florida plan, with particular reference to the exclusivity provisions concerning tort and administrative compensation, see Studdert, Fritz and Brennan, The Jury is Still In: Florida's Birth–Related Neurological Injury Compensation Plan after a Decade, 25 J. Health Pol. Pol'y & L. 499 (2000).

   9. *Neo no-fault and early offers.* Professor Jeffrey O'Connell has been a leading advocate of a wide range of privately negotiated no-fault alternatives to the tort system for many years, in some instances backed by legislatively-imposed conditions. See J. O'Connell and C. Kelly, The Blame Game: Injuries, Insurance and Injustice (1986), in which he and a co-author advocate adoption of a universal "neo no-fault" scheme in which tort defendants would have the option within 180 days of offering a claimant periodic payment of the claimant's net economic losses. The claimant would be required to accept such an offer once tendered. For an illustration of one of his tailored schemes, see O'Connell, A Neo No–Fault Contract in Lieu of Tort: Pre-accident Guarantees of Post-accident Settlement Offers, 73 Calif.L.Rev. 898 (1985), describing the widely adopted Scholastic Lifetime Medical and Disability Policy, which provides for no-fault settlement offers for economic loss in cases of catastrophic injury to high school athletes. For his approach to the health care area, see O'Connell, Neo No–Fault Remedies for Medical Injuries: Coordinated Statutory and Contractual Alternatives, 49 Law & Contemporary Problems 125 (1986). O'Connell discusses his approach to the products liability area in O'Connell, Balanced Proposals for Product Liability Reform, 48 Ohio St.L.J. 317 (1987).

   More recently, he and a co-author have proposed an "early offer" plan that would once again operate across-the-board in accidental injury cases:

> The goal of the early offer proposal is to encourage prompt settlement of tort claims along insurance lines, paying promptly for economic (but not noneconomic) losses as they accrue, along with relatively low transaction costs. Its mechanics are relatively simple: a defendant may at its option offer an injured claimant within a defined period (e.g. within 120 days of a personal injury claim) a settlement of periodic payments sufficient to cover a claimant's wage loss and medical expenses, including rehabilitation plus a claimant's reasonable attorney's fee, but without any allowance for pain and suffering. Under one version, collateral sources paid or payable to the claimant are deducted in computing the amount of the early offer. The defendant is not forced to make an offer, and, if no offer is made, normal common-law principles apply. In extending an early offer, however, the defendant triggers strong incentive consequences. If the claimant accepts, that ends the matter. But a claimant who elects not to accept will face a higher burden of proof at trial (by either clear and convincing or even

beyond a reasonable doubt, depending on the terms of the legislation adopted), with the defendant judged by a lower standard of care on which liability is predicated (either wanton or intentional misconduct).

See O'Connell and Robinette, The Role of Compensation in Personal Injury Tort Law: A Response to the Opposite Concerns of Gary Schwartz and Patrick Atiyah, 32 Conn. L.Rev. 137 (1999). What are the pros and cons of such an approach?

E.   COMPREHENSIVE NO-FAULT AND BEYOND

As we have seen, the academic and political efforts in this country have been addressed primarily to piecemeal revision of tort law. Conceding that limited reform efforts may be politically expedient, however, it does not necessarily follow that considerations of either logic or fairness favor piecemeal revision over system-wide change. At the outset of the no-fault movement, Jeremiah Smith argued this point in his landmark article, Sequel to Workmen's Compensation, 27 Harv.L.Rev. 235 (1913):

> If the fundamental general principle of the modern common law of torts (that fault is requisite to liability) is intrinsically right or expedient, is there sufficient reason why the legislature should make the workmen's case an exception to this general principle? On the other hand, if this statutory rule as to workmen is intrinsically just or expedient, is there sufficient reason for refusing to make this statutory rule the test of the right of recovery on the part of persons other than workmen when they suffer hurt without the fault of either party?

In this section, we focus on comprehensive systems of compensation. We begin by examining the New Zealand experience. An interesting combination of factors led that country to assume a pioneering role in replacing its tort system with a comprehensive no-fault scheme covering all types of accidental injuries.

The New Zealand experience. In 1967, a Royal Commission headed by Justice Woodhouse, appointed to consider workers' compensation, concluded that employment injuries could not be separated from other injuries. It proposed abolition of the common law of accidental injuries and replacing it with a unified scheme based on five basic propositions: that all citizens must be protected against income loss and permanent disability; compensation should be related to the nature of the injury and not its cause; the scheme must stress physical and vocational recovery along with compensation; benefits should be paid for the duration of the incapacity; and the plan must be expeditious.

It should be stressed that the proposal of the Royal Commission was not a response to any public outcry against the existing tort system. No group, whether victims, physicians, manufacturers, motorists, or insurers had complained about the insurance premiums they were paying, the way their tort claims were being resolved in the courts, or any similar grievance. Rather, the Royal Commission perceived the common law to be a "lottery" in which some claimants received awards while others had to subsist on social welfare payments. There was also too little conscious attention to safety. The Royal Commission concluded that a new approach was needed. "If the scheme can be said to have a single purpose it is 24–hour insurance for every member of the work force, and for the housewives who sustain them." The emphasis was to be on accident prevention and rehabilitation, with compensation a third consideration.

The final version of the Accident Compensation Act became effective in 1974. Although the Act was amended several times, it remained essentially the same until the passage of the Accident Rehabilitation and Compensation Act of 1992, which substantially altered the original program. It may help in considering the discussion that follows to realize that New Zealand has a population of about three million persons and is about the size of Oregon or Colorado. For a comparison of demographic and accident data, see Franklin, Personal Injury Accidents in New Zealand and the United States: Some Striking Similarities, 27 Stan.L.Rev. 653 (1975).

The original Act abolished virtually all common law tort actions. In their place, the program provided for compensation to individuals who experienced a "personal injury by accident." This phrase was interpreted to include occupational disease and illness but to exclude ordinary sickness. Courts also found it difficult to distinguish between "medical, surgical, dental or first aid misadventure," which was covered by the statute, and "damage to the body or mind caused exclusively by disease, infection, or the aging process," which was excluded by the statute.

Compensation was and still is provided to accident victims out of one of three compensation schemes. Workers are protected against accidental injury under the earners' scheme, receiving 80% of lost earnings for the duration of a disability as well as all reasonable medical and rehabilitation expenses. Similar protection is afforded them under the scheme during off-hours. Those injured in motor vehicle accidents—other than earners who are protected under the earners' scheme—receive compensation for medical costs and lost earning capacity out of a fund supported by flat levies on motor vehicle owners. Non-workers, such as the elderly, homemakers, children and students, who are injured in accidents not involving motor vehicles, are compensated for medical costs out of the general treasury. In addition to payments for lost earnings and medical costs, the Act also used to provide for two different types of lump sum payments. The first provided for payments of up to $17,000 NZ (as of 1991) for loss of bodily part or function and the second provided for a payment of up to $10,000 NZ for pain and suffering, disfigurement and the loss of capacity for enjoying life if the loss was sufficiently serious in nature and duration.

The 1992 revisions significantly changed some of the Act's most important provisions. First, the 1992 revisions limited the types of injuries covered under the Act by restricting the definition of accident and by changing the phrase "personal injury by accident" to "personal injury by an accident" such that the accident must now be a separate cause of the injury in order for the injury to be compensable. Therefore, coverage no longer exists when only the result of an act is accidental, or when an injury cannot be attributed to any identifiable external event. Second, the new Act excludes coverage for mental distress not associated with physical injury to the person seeking compensation. Third, the revisions sharply changed the compensation system for "medical misadventure." Although the original Act provided for compensation for medical misadventures without defining the operative phrase, the new Act includes a comprehensive definition of the phrase which requires the injured party to prove something approaching negligence before he or she can receive compensation. Finally, the 1992 revisions eliminated the lump sum payments and replaced them with a much more modest "independence allowance" of up to $40 NZ per week.

In addition to these changes in the coverage and benefit provisions of the Act, the 1992 revisions significantly changed the Act's funding mechanisms. While employers continue to pay for employee injuries sustained on the job, employee injuries that occur off the job are compensated through insurance paid for by employees themselves. Flat levies on automobile owners continue to make up a large portion of the fund used to compensate motor vehicle injuries, but the 1992 revisions also provide for a $0.02/liter gasoline tax aimed at promoting a greater "user-pays" element within the Act. Finally, the 1992 revisions created a new account called the Medical Misadventure Account, funded through premiums paid by health professionals, for the purpose of compensating victims of medical misadventures. This change marked the first time since the passage of the Act that a risk-creating class has been directly held accountable to persons injured by the class. All of these changes arguably mark a distinct philosophical departure from the purposes of the original Act.

What are your reactions to the New Zealand approach? Do obvious practical, philosophical, or other problems occur to you? For a highly critical response to the 1992 amendments, arguing that the plan has lost much of the social insurance philosophy that once informed it, see Palmer, The Design of Compensation Systems: Tort Principles Rule, O.K.?, 29 Valp.L.Rev. 1115 (1995). For a detailed description and critique of the 1992 revisions, see Miller, An Analysis and Critique of the 1992 Changes to New Zealand's Accident Compensation Scheme, 52 Md.L.Rev. 1070 (1993). In 1998, a new version of the Act, entitled the Accident Insurance Act of 1998 was enacted, the major change being to partially privatize the system of insurance in the area of workers' compensation. This move was, in turn, reversed by still another reenactment of the scheme, the Accident Insurance (Transitional Provisions) Act 2000. For a comprehensive overview of the New Zealand program and its recent permutations, see Todd, Privatization of Accident Compensation: Policy and Politics in New Zealand, 39 Washburn L.J. 404 (2000).

The most extended discussion of the entire philosophy of the New Zealand development and its passage through the political process, is to be found in G. Palmer, Compensation for Incapacity: A Study of Law and Social Change in New Zealand and Australia (1979). As the title suggests, Australia seriously considered the New Zealand development, but lost interest after a change of national government.

Over the years, there was much discussion about adding sickness coverage to the existing act. An early chairman of the ACC suggested that the different treatment was an "anomaly" caused by the influence of the common law. Removing the anomaly would be "a matter of political philosophy and of economics. Political philosophy will determine the extent to which a country will devote a portion of its resources to the care of the disabled. Economics will dictate how far that philosophy can reasonably be applied." Might there be reasons for compensating disability from accident differently from disability due to sickness? The subject is discussed in P. Cane, Atiyah's Accidents, Compensation and the Law (6th ed. 1999), Chapter 16.

Social insurance proposals. For a detailed proposal that would go beyond New Zealand and compensate for all disability, whether accident-related or not, see S. Sugarman, Doing Away with Personal Injury Law (1989). As the title suggests, Sugarman would eliminate personal injury law virtually across-the-board, with the sole exception of a limited punitive damage action for intentional torts. His book surveys the literature on the workings of tort law and concludes that the system is a substantial failure from both the perspectives of compensation and deterrence.

Sugarman's comprehensive strategy would extend employment-based income replacement and health benefits to covered beneficiaries, whatever the source of their disability, in cases involving short-term needs (six months or less). In cases involving longer-term income replacement, as well as most cases of disability experienced by the various categories of non-employed persons, coverage would be provided by an expanded Social Security system. The tort system would be abandoned, along with pain and suffering damages, though in serious cases awards for pain and suffering on the original New Zealand model might be permitted. Accident prevention strategies would be left to the regulatory system. Anticipating the argument that his comprehensive plan is politically infeasible at present, Sugarman also outlines a first-step proposal that would concentrate on replacing the tort system in short-term injury cases and on limiting its applicability in longer-term cases through elimination of the collateral source rule and restrictions on pain and suffering recovery.

Does this outline of Sugarman's proposal suggest that the New Zealand approach may be, in fact, too modest in its coverage? See also P. Atiyah, The Damages Lottery (1997). Social insurance schemes currently in operation, including the Social Security Disability program, are discussed in Abraham & Liebman, Private Insurance, Social Insurance, and Tort Reform: Toward a New Vision of Compensation for Illness and Injury, 93 Colum.L.Rev. 75 (1993).

For an earlier effort to combine the benefits of social insurance for accidents and the advantages of internalized costs, see Franklin, Replacing the Negligence Lottery: Compensation and Selective Reimbursement, 53 Va.L.Rev. 774 (1967). This essay views the fault system as a lottery: Persons similarly injured may recover, if anything, very different amounts depending on the defendant's behavior and the origin of the injury, and persons committing the same wrongful act may be subject to very different liabilities depending upon the extent of the injury caused, if any, and to whom. Briefly, the goal was to separate the functions of compensation and deterrence, by having the former achieved through a social insurance fund and the latter through uninsurable fines and enterprise reimbursements of the fund for injury-creating activity. A somewhat similar proposal is offered in Pierce, Encouraging Safety: The Limits of Tort Law and Government Regulation, 33 Vand.L.Rev. 1281 (1980).

Professors Blum and Kalven argue that in large part "corrective justice is concerned not with deterring the wrongdoer, but with satisfying the victim's feeling of indignation. If the victim recovers only from the fund, he will not gain the satisfaction of seeing his wrong righted. Nor will it be much different if, after paying the victim, the fund later recovers from the tortfeasor." Blum and Kalven, The Empty Cabinet of Dr. Calabresi—Auto Accidents and General Deterrence, 34 U.Chi.L.Rev. 239, 268–69 (1967). Do you think most victims care about the source of their benefits? Under the current system does the victim see the wrong righted? The authors also urge that the law "not break sharply with the moral traditions of the society" and that the burden of satisfying indignation not be left solely to criminal law. What are these "moral traditions"?

The social insurance aspects of the Franklin, Pierce, Sugarman and New Zealand proposals may all be traced to the influential Beveridge Report of 1942 on Social Insurance and Allied Services in Great Britain. Cmd. 6404. Speaking of workers' compensation, Beveridge said (38–39):

> The pioneer system of social security in Britain was based on a wrong principle and has been dominated by a wrong outlook. It allows claims to be settled by bargaining between unequal parties, permits payment of socially wasteful lump sums instead of pensions in cases of serious incapacity, places the cost of medical care on the workman or charity or poor relief, and over part of the field, large in the numbers covered, though not in the proportion of the total compensation paid, it relies on expensive private insurance. There should be no hesitation in making provision for the results of industrial accident and disease in the future, not by a continuance of the present system of individual employer's liability, but as one branch of a unified Plan for Social Security. If the matter were now being considered in a clear field, it might well be argued that the general principle of a flat rate of compensation for interruption of earnings adopted for all other forms of interruption, should be applied also without reserve or qualification to the results of industrial accident and disease, leaving those who felt the need for greater security, by voluntary insurance, to provide an addition to the flat subsistence guaranteed by the State. If a workman loses his leg in an accident, his needs are the same whether the accident occurred in a factory or in the street; if he is killed, the needs of his widow and other dependents are the same, however the death occurred. Acceptance of this argument and adoption of a flat rate of compensation for disability, however caused, would avoid the anomaly

of treating equal needs differently and the administrative and legal difficulties of defining just what injuries were to be treated as arising out of and in the course of employment. Interpretation of these words has been a fruitful cause of disputes in the past; whatever words are chosen, difficulties and anomalies are bound to arise. A complete solution is to be found only in a completely unified scheme for disability without demarcation by the cause of disability.

Although Beveridge did not ultimately recommend a totally unified scheme, subsequent writers have adopted his theoretical exposition.

———

As early as 1955, Professor Kalven asserted that if poverty could be abolished, tort law could remain intact. "If the poor were not quite so poor, we could decently ask them to provide their own accident insurance." Book Review, 33 Texas L.Rev. 778, 782 (1955). How much criticism of the operation of tort law has been based on a concern for those at or below the poverty level? If one were to agree that poverty is an important problem, how should that affect one's attitude toward tort law?

CHAPTER XII

INTENTIONAL HARM

This chapter brings together personal injuries allegedly caused "intentionally." We focus on what the actor sought to achieve, or knew would occur, rather than on his or her motives for acting. Thus the definition of "intent" in the Restatement (Second) of Torts § 8A, requires "that the actor desires to cause consequences of his act, or that he believes that the consequences are substantially certain to result from it." Note that this definition is the final point on the Restatement's continuum from negligence through recklessness to intent. Negligence is defined as "conduct which falls below the standard established by law for the protection of others against unreasonable risk of harm" (§ 282). Recklessness involves a risk that is "substantially greater than that which is necessary to make his conduct negligent" (§ 500). Finally, in defining intent we no longer speak of risk but rather of "desire" to bring about consequences, or belief that such consequences are "substantially certain" to occur. Is that the same as saying that the consequences *are* "substantially certain" to occur? How can we prove what the actor "desires" or "believes"?

The long history of intentional torts has produced special rules for categories such as assault, battery, and false imprisonment. These rules reflect early procedure and the writ system but still have implications for questions of pleading and proof today, as we shall see. Beginning with false imprisonment and carrying through intentional infliction of emotional harm and government liability, we will also see how the courts have responded to distinctly contemporary injury claims by expanding the boundaries of intentional tort doctrine.

A plaintiff who can frame a case as an intentional tort may reap benefits beyond pleading and proof: contributory negligence and even contributory recklessness are not defenses to intentional misconduct, and punitive damages may be available.* Also, although liability for negligently inflicted harm may be discharged in bankruptcy, this does not apply to "willful and malicious injury." 11 U.S.C. § 523(6).**

* Recall *Clark v. Cantrell*, p. 724, supra, in which the court applied comparative fault in a case involving a reckless defendant—and reduced the compensatory but not the punitive award. Would that be appropriate for intentional torts? Traditionally, courts have not recognized comparative fault as a defense to intentional wrongdoing.

** The role of bankruptcy in tort law was clarified in Kawaauhau v. Geiger, 523 U.S. 57 (1998), in which malpractice plaintiffs sought to deny a discharge in bankruptcy to a physician who had been more than negligent in his conduct, which led to amputation of plaintiff's leg below the knee. Defendant was uninsured and, after the adverse judgment, sought protection under the bankruptcy laws.

A. BASIC DOCTRINE

1. INTENT

Garratt v. Dailey

Supreme Court of Washington, 1955.
46 Wash.2d 197, 279 P.2d 1091.

HILL, J.—The liability of an infant for an alleged battery is presented to this court for the first time. Brian Dailey (age five years, nine months) was visiting with Naomi Garratt, an adult and a sister of the plaintiff, Ruth Garratt, likewise an adult, in the backyard of the plaintiff's home, on July 16, 1951. It is plaintiff's contention that she came out into the backyard to talk with Naomi and that, as she started to sit down in a wood and canvas lawn chair, Brian deliberately pulled it out from under her. The only one of the three persons present so testifying was Naomi Garratt. (Ruth Garratt, the plaintiff, did not testify as to how or why she fell.) The trial court, unwilling to accept this testimony, adopted instead Brian Dailey's version of what happened, and made the following findings:

"III. . . . that while Naomi Garratt and Brian Dailey were in the back yard the plaintiff, Ruth Garratt, came out of her house into the back yard. Some time subsequent thereto defendant, Brian Dailey, picked up a lightly built wood and canvas lawn chair which was then and there located in the back yard of the above described premises, moved it sideways a few feet and seated himself therein, at which time he discovered the plaintiff, Ruth Garratt, about to sit down at the place where the lawn chair had formerly been, at which time he hurriedly got up from the chair and attempted to move it toward Ruth Garratt to aid her in sitting down in the chair; that due to the defendant's small size and lack of dexterity he was unable to get the lawn chair under the plaintiff in time to prevent her from falling to the ground. That plaintiff fell to the ground and sustained a fracture of her hip, and other injuries and damages as hereinafter set forth.

"IV. That the preponderance of the evidence in this case establishes that when the defendant, Brian Dailey, moved the chair in question *he did not have any wilful or unlawful purpose* in doing so; that *he did not have any intent to injure the plaintiff, or any intent to bring about any unauthorized or offensive contact with her person* or any objects appurtenant thereto; that the circumstances which immediately preceded the fall of the

---

The Supreme Court unanimously held that the statute allows discharge here since the underlying conduct was at most reckless. Given the narrow words used by Congress, the defendant must intend the consequences as well as the act that led to the harm. "The word 'willful' in (a)(6) modifies the word 'injury,' indicating that nondischargeability takes a deliberate or intentional injury, not merely a deliberate act that leads to injury."

The Court also noted that section 523(a)(9), added in 1984, bars discharge for liability incurred for "death or personal injury caused by the debtor's operation of a motor vehicle if such operation was unlawful because the debtor was intoxicated from using alcohol, a drug, or another substance." This addition would not have been needed if section 523(a)(6) covered cases of recklessness.

plaintiff established that the defendant, *Brian Dailey, did not have purpose, intent or design to perform a prank or to effect an assault and battery upon the person of the plaintiff.''* (Italics ours, for a purpose hereinafter indicated.)

It is conceded that Ruth Garratt's fall resulted in a fractured hip and other painful and serious injuries. To obviate the necessity of a retrial in the event this court determines that she was entitled to a judgment against Brian Dailey, the amount of her damage was found to be eleven thousand dollars. Plaintiff appeals from a judgment dismissing the action and asks for the entry of a judgment in that amount or a new trial.

The authorities generally, but with certain notable exceptions [   ], state that, when a minor has committed a tort with force, he is liable to be proceeded against as any other person would be. [   ]

In our analysis of the applicable law, we start with the basic premise that Brian, whether five or fifty-five, must have committed some wrongful act before he could be liable for appellant's injuries.

.   .   .

It is urged that Brian's action in moving the chair constituted a battery. A definition (not all-inclusive but sufficient for our purpose) of a battery is the intentional infliction of a harmful bodily contact upon another.   .   .   .

We have in this case no question of consent or privilege. We therefore proceed to an immediate consideration of intent and its place in the law of battery.   .   .   .

.   .   .

We have here the conceded volitional act of Brian, i.e., the moving of a chair. Had the plaintiff proved to the satisfaction of the trial court that Brian moved the chair while she was in the act of sitting down, Brian's action would patently have been for the purpose or with the intent of causing the plaintiff's bodily contact with the ground, and she would be entitled to a judgment against him for the resulting damages. Vosburg v. Putney [50 N.W. 403 (Wis.1891)].

The plaintiff based her case on that theory, and the trial court held that she failed in her proof and accepted Brian's version of the facts rather than that given by the eyewitness who testified for the plaintiff. After the trial court determined that the plaintiff had not established her theory of a battery (i.e., that Brian had pulled the chair out from under the plaintiff while she was in the act of sitting down), it then became concerned with whether a battery was established under the facts as it found them to be.

.   .   .

A battery would be established if, in addition to plaintiff's fall, it was proved that, when Brian moved the chair, he knew with substantial certainty that the plaintiff would attempt to sit down where the chair had been. If Brian had any of the intents which the trial court found, in the italicized portions of the findings of fact quoted above, that he did not have, he would of course have had the knowledge to which we have referred. The mere absence of any intent to injure the plaintiff or to play a prank on her or to embarrass her, or to commit an assault and battery on her would not absolve him from liability if in fact he had such knowledge. [   ] Without such knowledge, there would be nothing wrongful about Brian's act in moving the chair, and, there being no wrongful act, there would be no liability.

While a finding that Brian had no such knowledge can be inferred from the findings made, we believe that before the plaintiff's action in such a case should be dismissed there should be no question but that the trial court had passed upon that issue; hence, the case should be remanded for clarification of the findings to specifically cover the question of Brian's knowledge, because intent could be inferred therefrom. If the court finds that he had such knowledge, the necessary intent will be established and the plaintiff will be entitled to recover, even though there was no purpose to injure or embarrass the plaintiff. [   ] If Brian did not have such knowledge, there was no wrongful act by him, and the basic premise of liability on the theory of a battery was not established.

It will be noted that the law of battery as we have discussed it is the law applicable to adults, and no significance has been attached to the fact that Brian was a child less than six years of age when the alleged battery occurred. The only circumstance where Brian's age is of any consequence is in determining what he knew, and there his experience, capacity, and understanding are of course material.

. . .

Remanded for clarification.

SCHWELLENBACH, DONWORTH, and WEAVER, JJ., concur.

Notes and Questions

1. What is it precisely that the court says Brian must "intend" in order to be held liable for a battery? Suppose he wasn't thinking about plaintiff one way or the other—he simply grabbed the nearest chair, despite the fact that she was about to sit in it, because he was eager to sit down. Would he have had the requisite intent? Recall the discussion at p. 56 supra, of the relationship between negligence and age.

On remand, the trial court found that Brian did have the necessary intent, and entered judgment for the plaintiff for $11,000. The judgment was affirmed on appeal. 304 P.2d 681 (Wash.1956).

2. Suppose Brian did not believe to a "substantial certainty" that plaintiff was about to sit down. Might he still be liable on a negligence theory? Can you construct versions of the facts that clarify the distinctions between intentional, reckless and negligent misconduct? Might Brian's age make it more difficult to establish negligence than intentional wrongdoing here? Recall the discussion of the reasonable person standard as applied to minors, p. 56, supra. The issue is discussed at length in Weisbart v. Flohr,

67 Cal.Rptr. 114 (App. 1968), an action based on theories of negligence and battery by a five-year-old plaintiff against a seven-year-old defendant who put out her eye with a bow-and-arrow. The court upheld a judgment in favor of the defendant on the negligence count, but reversed a similar judgment on the battery claim.

3. Suppose Brian did know to a "substantial certainty" that plaintiff was about to sit in the chair. Does it make sense to have a separate tort category of "intentional torts" for such cases—distinguishing them from situations in which a manufacturer knows with similar certainty that one soda bottle out of 100,000 produced will explode during use?

4. D comes up behind a person he is quite certain is his friend, and offers the traditional greeting of a slap on the back. If the other person turns out to be a stranger, has D intended to hit him? Or suppose that D, hunting in a proper area, reasonably believes that the animal crossing in front of him some distance ahead is a deer. D shoots and kills the animal only to find that it is in fact P's slender cow. Did D intend to shoot the cow?

5. In the cited case of *Vosburg v. Putney*, the court held that one schoolboy who kicked another in the leg was liable for a battery despite the lack of any subjective intention to do harm. Moreover, the defendant was held liable for extraordinary harm that resulted because of the exacerbation of a pre-existing injury, the court tersely stating that "the wrongdoer is liable for all injuries resulting directly from the wrongful act, whether they could or could not have been foreseen by him." Recall the discussion of the thin-skulled plaintiff rule, p. 399, supra. Is it appropriate to apply a thin-skulled plaintiff rule to cases in which the defendant intended no actual harm to the plaintiff?

Vosburg has remained a great favorite of torts afficionados over the years. See its centennial celebration, including a sociolegal history of the case, Zile, *Vosburg v. Putney*: A Centennial Story, 1992 Wis.L.Rev. 877, and commentary by James A. Henderson (at 853), Robert L. Rabin (at 863), and J. Willard Hurst (at 875).

6. *Cause-in-fact.* On the relation of cause-in-fact problems to intentional torts, consider the following passage from Malone, Ruminations on Cause–In–Fact, 9 Stan.L.Rev. 60, 72–73 (1956):

> Some rules of law are tremendously exacting and rest upon time-honored moral considerations. They are safeguards for well-established interests of others, and their mantle of protection embraces a large variety of risks. He who violates such a rule will be held responsible for any harm that can be causally associated in any plausible way with his wrongdoing. The court, for instance, will seldom hesitate to allow the jury a free range of speculation on the cause issue at the expense of an intentional wrongdoer who is charged with having physically injured another person.

Malone also suggests that in fire cases "Sound judgment may dictate, for instance, that an arsonist be held responsible for a fire contribution that has a much smaller damaging potential than could be recognized in the case of a householder whose lamp was tipped over by the wind." Can these views be justified?

7. *Proximate cause.* In Baker v. Shymkiv, 451 N.E.2d 811 (Ohio 1983), the plaintiff and decedent, her husband, came home to find a trench being built across their driveway by defendant. An angry confrontation occurred. At this point plaintiff left to call the police. When she returned three minutes later she found her husband lying face down in a mud puddle while the defendants were driving away. He was pronounced dead of a heart attack shortly thereafter. The trial judge charged that although the defendants were trespassers they would not be liable for the death unless that harm could have been foreseen or reasonably anticipated by the wrongdoer. The Court of Appeals reversed a defense judgment and the Ohio Supreme Court unanimously affirmed. Quoting from an earlier case, the court reasoned that when confronted with an innocent victim and an intentional wrongdoer, it is not surprising that the interest of the victim in attaining full compensation "is placed above the interest of the wrongdoer in protecting himself against potentially speculative damage awards." That approach was supported by Restatement § 162, which provided that a trespasser was liable for any acts done or activity on the land that harms the possessor, others or property "irrespective of whether his conduct is such as would subject him to liability were he not a trespasser." Comment *f* provided that this rule applied "no matter how otherwise innocent such conduct may be." Accordingly, the court held that "damages caused by an intentional trespasser need not be foreseeable to be compensable." A new trial was ordered.

Should intentional wrongdoers be held to a higher standard of responsibility for extended consequences than negligent parties? See generally, Note, The Tie That Binds: Liability of Intentional Tort–Feasors for Extended Consequences, 14 Stan.L.Rev. 362 (1962). Compare Halberstam v. Welch, 705 F.2d 472 (D.C.Cir.1983), assigning tort liability to a woman whose live-in-companion killed someone who surprised him during a burglary. The woman had not been involved in the burglary, but was heavily involved in "laundering" activities connected with reaping profits from the burglar's stolen goods. The court discusses at length theories of civil conspiracy and aid-and-abetting in developing the concept of joint tort in the context of intentional harm.

8. *Punitive damages.* As we discussed earlier, in intentional tort cases defendant sometimes may be responsible not only for compensatory damages but for punitive damages as well. Reconsider the discussion of punitive damages for reckless conduct, p. 718, supra. Intentional tort situations have been considered the paradigm case for award of such damages. Should a distinction be drawn between cases involving intent to injure and cases like *Vosburg* in which defendant intended no serious harm?

Why should a plaintiff ever receive such a windfall? A handful of states wholly reject punitive damages in civil cases, and a few limit them in amount to the plaintiff's litigation expenses including attorneys' fees. See

Note, An Economic Analysis of the Plaintiff's Windfall from Punitive Damages, 105 Harv.L.Rev. 1900 (1992), analyzing the justifications for punitive damages and proposing that the portion of a punitive damages award in excess of litigation costs be allocated to the state. Punitive damages are not awarded as a matter of law but are discretionary with the trier of fact.

Is it consistent to argue that punitive damages should be permitted in minor intentional harm cases because criminal prosecutions are unlikely, and also in major tort cases such as raping a very young child? Is there less justification for punitive damages when the compensatory award will be high, as in the rape case, than when the compensatory award is likely to be small? Does a compensatory award "punish" the defendant? For comprehensive analysis of the justifications for punitive damages, see Trebilcock and Chapman, Punitive Damages: Divergence in Search of a Rationale, 40 Ala.L.Rev. 741 (1989).

9. *Insurance considerations.* What good is a judgment for $11,000 against Brian? Parents are not generally liable for the torts of their children. It is true that they have a duty of due care to prevent their children from causing intentional harm or unreasonable risks to others but this applies only when the parents are on notice of the child's tendencies and know or should know that an occasion has arisen calling for their exercise of control. See Restatement, Second, § 316. Alternatively, the parents may be liable for placing a dangerous instrumentality in the hands of one too young or inexperienced to know how to handle it. Compare *Weisbart v. Flohr*, note 2 supra (parents not liable for injury caused by their seven-year-old son's shooting arrow into girl's eye), with Reida v. Lund, 96 Cal.Rptr. 102 (App. 1971)(father liable to victims of 16-year-old sniper for father's failure to use due care to keep Swedish Mauser military rifle out of son's hands). In the absence of proof that the boy was a menace (and the lack of a claim by Ruth Garratt against the parents) parental liability cannot explain the suit.

This is another area in which liability insurance has been of considerable importance. Even if the parent's homeowners' policy covers family members, however, there is still a question whether intentional torts have been excluded. In Baldinger v. Consolidated Mutual Ins. Co., 222 N.Y.S.2d 736 (App.Div. 1961), affirmed without opinion 183 N.E.2d 908 (N.Y.1962), the policy excluded "bodily injury . . . caused intentionally." A six-year-old boy covered by the policy pushed the plaintiff to get her to move. She fell and broke her elbow. Relying on the maxim that an ambiguous provision should be construed against the insurer the court held that the exclusion did not apply because the "injury" was not "caused intentionally but was rather the unintended result of an intentional act." Recall *Lalomia*, p. 767, supra.

The issue is not limited to coverage of minors, of course. Can an insured who is legally insane commit an intentional act? In Economy Preferred Ins. Co. v. Mass, 497 N.W.2d 6 (Neb.1993), the insured, who had shot and killed his father, claimed that he was entitled to insurance coverage despite an intentional act exclusion clause because the trial court had found that he was legally insane at the time of the incident. The appellate court disagreed, holding that even if a mentally ill insured was unable to form the criminal intent necessary for criminal liability, he may nevertheless have still intended or expected the results of the injuries he caused. Therefore, the intentional act exclusion applied, and the insurance company was not obliged to cover its insured. But see Nationwide Insurance Company v. Estate of Kollstedt, 646 N.E.2d 816 (Ohio 1995), in which the court held that an intentional act exclusion clause does not apply when the insured was mentally incapable of committing an intentional act. Insurance considerations aside, the majority rule is that a defendant's insanity does not establish a defense to liability. See Williams v. Kearbey, 775 P.2d 670 (Kan.App.1989), in which defendant, a minor, shot and injured two people at his junior high school. The wounded individuals brought successful battery actions. The jury found that the defendant was insane at the time of the shootings and defendant argued that because of this fact, he should not be held civilly liable for his torts. The court followed the majority rule that a defendant's insanity does not establish a defense to liability. That rule reflected a policy decision "to impose liability on an insane person rather than leaving the loss on the innocent victim."

What if the insured is acting in self-defense? In Vermont Mutual Ins. Co. v. Singleton, 446 S.E.2d 417 (S.C.1994), the insured had acted in self-defense and had inflicted severe eye injuries upon his attacker. The court applied a two-prong analysis to determine if the intentional act exclusion clause would relieve the insurance company of having to cover the victim's costs under the insured's homeowners' policy. The court held that the first prong, whether the act causing the loss was intentional, was easily satisfied. The second prong, however—whether the results of the act were intended—was not satisfied. Since the insured intended only to protect himself and not to inflict a specific injury on the victim, the intentional act exclusion clause did not apply.

Finally, when if ever should public policy concerns persuade a court to hold that reckless conduct on the part of an insured should relieve an insurance company of coverage obligations under an intentional act exclusion clause? In R.W. v. T.F., 528 N.W.2d 869 (Minn.1995), a woman sued the insured for negligently transmitting genital herpes to her. The insurance company refused to defend, claiming that the insured's intentional act exclusion clause relieved it of its coverage obligations. The court held for the insurance company, arguing that the insured's actions were "intentional as a matter of law" because the insured knew the transmission of herpes was "substantially likely to occur." In reaching its decision, the court stated that it would be contrary to public policy to "promote the abdication of personal responsibility by providing insurance coverage when an insured engages in unprotected sexual intercourse despite having knowledge that he is infected with herpes, a highly contagious and serious sexually transmitted disease."

10. *Victim compensation statutes.* The vast majority of valid intentional tort cases founder on the insolvency of the perpetrator. Statutes may provide some aid to victims of crimes from the state or local treasury, an idea that originated in Great Britain. See Note, Compensation for Victims of Crime, 33 U.Chi.L.Rev. 531 (1966); Comment, Compensation for Victims of Violent Crimes, 26 Kan.L.Rev. 227 (1978). For comparison of the British approach and a variety of American statutory strategies, see Greer, A Transatlantic Perspective on the Compensation of Crime Victims in the United States, 85 J.Crim. & Criminology 333 (1994).

California, in 1965, was the first state to enact a comprehensive victim compensation statute. Since then, 35 states have enacted some form of victim compensation program. These programs differ from one another significantly both in scope and in level of reparations. For a detailed survey of the various state compensation programs, see D. Parent, B. Auerbach, & K. Carlson, Compensating Crime Victims: A Summary of Policies and Practices (National Institute of Justice 1992). The philosophical justifications for victim compensation programs are criticized in Henderson, The Wrongs of Victim's Rights, 37 Stan.L.Rev. 937 (1985).

At the turn of the century, several states enacted so-called mob violence statutes providing that persons whose property was damaged or destroyed in a riot might recover their losses from the city or county. The apparent goal was to encourage government officials to take steps to avert damage before it occurred. Governmental responsibility might be found more easily here than in the failure of government to prevent isolated acts of physical violence. Statutes in New York, Illinois, and California were repealed or suspended in the 1960s before any substantial harm occurred from the urban violence of that decade. See Note, Compensation for Victims of Urban Riots, 68 Colum.L.Rev. 57 (1968); Note, Municipal Liability for Riot Damage, 81 Harv.L.Rev. 653 (1968); and Note, Riot Insurance, 77 Yale L.J. 541 (1968).

11. In *Garratt,* the court offered two foundational observations before launching into its discussion of intent. First, the opinion defines the tort of battery, establishing the prima facie case as "the intentional infliction of a harmful bodily contact upon another." Next, the court observes that the most common defenses are not involved: "We have in this case no question of consent or privilege." The following cases discuss the related torts of assault and battery in greater detail. We then give independent consideration to false imprisonment and intentional infliction of emotional distress before turning to defenses and privileges.

2. ASSAULT AND BATTERY

Picard v. Barry Pontiac–Buick, Inc.
Supreme Court of Rhode Island, 1995.
654 A.2d 690.

[In the course of a brake inspection, plaintiff Picard became upset about the service work and contacted a local television news "troubleshooter" reporter. Shortly thereafter, when she returned for a reinspection, Picard took along a camera and photographed defendant service worker as he was inspecting the brakes. There was a dispute as to what happened next. Plaintiff testified that defendant lunged at her and spun her around; defendant denied touching her and testified that he "pointed at plaintiff and said, 'who gave you permission to take my picture?' then walked around the car to plaintiff, placed his index finger on the camera and again asked, 'who gave you permission to take my picture?'" The defendant denied grabbing plaintiff or threatening her in any way. In further testimony, which was less than entirely consistent, plaintiff and her doctor claimed permanent damage to her back as a consequence of the altercation.

At trial, plaintiff prevailed and was awarded $60,366 in compensatory damages and an additional $6,350 in punitive damages. Defendant appealed, arguing "1) that plaintiff failed to prove an assault and battery; 2) that plaintiff failed to prove that defendant's actions in fact caused the alleged harm to her; and 3) that the damage awards were grossly excessive and inappropriate as a matter of law." The supreme court vacated the award and remanded for a new trial on damages.]

LEDERBERG, JUSTICE.

. . .

The defendant contended that plaintiff failed to prove the occurrence of an assault because plaintiff was not placed in reasonable fear of imminent bodily harm. Further, defendant argued that plaintiff failed to prove a battery because the evidence failed to establish that defendant intended to inflict an unconsented touching of plaintiff. We disagree with both contentions.

Assault and battery are separate acts, usually arising from the same transaction, each having independent significance. [ ] "An assault is a physical act of a threatening nature or an offer of corporal injury which puts an individual in reasonable fear of imminent bodily harm." [ ] It is a plaintiff's apprehension of injury which renders a defendant's act compensable. [ ]; see also W. Page Keeton et al., Prosser and Keeton on the Law of Torts § 10, at 43 (5th ed. 1984)("[t]he damages recoverable for [assault] are those for the plaintiff's mental disturbance, including fright, humiliation and the like, as well as any physical illness which may result from them"). This apprehension must be the type of fear normally aroused in the mind of a reasonable person. [ ]

[margin note: Definition of assault]

The plaintiff testified that she was frightened by defendant's actions. A review of the attendant circumstances attests that such a reaction was reasonable. The defendant admitted approaching plaintiff, and the photograph taken that day clearly showed defendant pointing his finger at plaintiff as defendant approached her. Because plaintiff's apprehension of imminent bodily harm was reasonable at that point, plaintiff has established a prima facie case of assault.

[margin note: application]

We have defined battery as an act that was intended to cause, and in fact did cause, "an offensive contact with or unconsented touching of or

[margin note: definition of battery]

trauma upon the body of another, thereby generally resulting in the consummation of the assault. . . . An intent to injure plaintiff, however, is unnecessary in a situation in which a defendant willfully sets in motion a force that in its ordinary course causes the injury." [   ]

Application

In the instant case, defendant contended that a battery did not occur because defendant did not intend to touch or injure plaintiff. Rather, defendant argued, the evidence showed that he intended to touch plaintiff's camera, not plaintiff's person, and therefore the contact was insufficient to prove battery. With this contention we must disagree. Even if this court were to accept defendant's characterization of the incident, a battery had nonetheless occurred. The defendant failed to prove that his actions were accidental or involuntary. Therefore, defendant's offensive contact with an object attached to or identified with plaintiff's body was sufficient to constitute a battery. As noted in the comments to the Restatement (Second) Torts § 18, comment *c* at 31 (1965): "Unpermitted and intentional contacts with anything so connected with the body as to be customarily regarded as part of the other's person and therefore as partaking of its inviolability is actionable as an offensive contact with his person. There are some things such as clothing or a cane or, indeed, anything directly grasped by the hand which are so intimately connected with one's body as to be universally regarded as part of the person." The defendant's contact with the camera clutched in plaintiff's hand was thus sufficient to constitute a battery. We conclude, therefore, that plaintiff has proven the elements of assault and battery.

. . .

[The court next determined that the medical evidence in support of the claim for compensatory damages was inadequate and that the amount of damages awarded was excessive. In addition, the punitive damage award could not stand because "there was no proof of malice or bad faith."]

In conclusion, we deny in part and sustain in part the defendant's appeal. We affirm the judgment of the Superior Court in respect to the defendant's commission of assault and battery, but we vacate the awards of compensatory and punitive damages. We remand the case to the Superior Court for a new trial on the damages sustained by the plaintiff.

Notes and Questions

1. For an interesting early case illustrating an assault claim, see I. de S. v. W. de S., Y.B. Lib. Ass. folio 99, pl. 60 (1348), in which defendant, enraged at being told by plaintiff that the tavern was closed for the night, swung his hatchet at her as she stuck her head out of the window of the establishment. The court rejected the argument that no harm had been done, concluding that an actionable assault had occurred. The relationship between trespass claims and the later-developing action of trespass on the case is discussed at p. 29, supra, in the historical introduction to negligence in Chapter II.

2. Suppose defendant in *Picard* had gestured menacingly and threatened to harm plaintiff if she took a picture of him—but before she had actually done so. Would his actions have constituted an assault? Conditional threats, even if unjustifiable, were traditionally not considered assaults. An early common law case court held that the statement, "if it were not assize time, I would run this sword through you," was held not to amount to an assault because of its conditional nature. Tuberville v. Savage, 86 Eng.Rep. 684 (1669). How would the qualification for conditional statements apply here?

3. Note that the *Picard* court echoes *Garratt* in holding that an intent to injure is not required to establish a battery. What precisely was required to establish not just an assault but a battery as well in *Picard*?

4. Why should less than actual physical contact with plaintiff's body ever be sufficient to establish a battery? And, on the other hand, why should *any* physical contact suffice? In the leading case of Alcorn v. Mitchell, 63 Ill. 553 (1872), in which a disappointed litigant spat upon his adversary in the courthouse, the court allowed nominal compensatory and fairly substantial punitive damages in the subsequent action for the trespassory act. What justifications can be offered for extending battery actions beyond actual physical harm? Might a spit in the face warrant substantial compensatory damages?

5. Section 19 of the Second Restatement states that "A bodily contact is offensive if it offends a reasonable sense of personal dignity." Consider that section's application in Vitale v. Henchey, 24 S.W.3d 651 (Ky.2000). The patient's son, who held a medical power of attorney, consented by telephone that two surgeons operate on his 95-year-old mother. In fact, at the request of the first two surgeons, a third surgeon performed the surgery. From earlier conversations, the son had reason to think that the third surgeon was "too aggressive, not compassionate,"—and he testified that he would not have consented to surgery by the third surgeon. There was no showing that this substitution violated the accepted standard of care. The court, 5–2, held that such a showing was not required and upheld the battery claim against all three surgeons even though no harm from the substitution could be shown. As to damages, the court indicated that nominal damages were permissible in this situation. Beyond that, evidence that the patient was conscious would permit a recovery for the pain and suffering caused by the surgery. When defendants argued that there was no showing that this was greater than it would have been had another surgeon performed the operation, the court rejected the argument, noting simply that it found no authority to support it. The court concluded that plaintiff was entitled "to any damages resulting [from the battery]." Is that sound? Can this case be regarded as an "offensive" battery? Should the comparison be the pain and suffering from this surgery compared to the patient's condition without surgery? The dissenters observed that this "kind of lawsuit is sometimes referred to as a 'money hunt.'" Is that fair?

6. Once tortious conduct amounting to an assault and battery was established in *Picard*, is the court acting consistently when it reverses the punitive damage award because of the failure to establish "malice and bad faith?"

Wishnatsky v. Huey

Court of Appeals of North Dakota, 1998.
584 N.W.2d 859.

PER CURIAM.

Martin Wishnatsky appealed a summary judgment dismissing his battery action against David W. Huey, and an order denying his motion for an altered judgment. We conclude, as a matter of law, that no battery occurred, and we affirm the judgment and the order.

On January 10, 1996, Huey, an assistant attorney general, was engaged in a conversation with attorney Peter B. Crary in Crary's office. Without knocking or announcing his entry, Wishnatsky, who performs paralegal work for Crary, attempted to enter the office. Huey pushed the door closed, thereby pushing Wishnatsky back into the hall. Wishnatsky reentered the office and Huey left.

Wishnatsky brought an action against Huey, seeking damages for battery. Huey moved for summary judgment of dismissal. The trial court granted Huey's motion and a judgment of dismissal was entered. Wishnatsky moved to alter the judgment. The trial court denied Wishnatsky's motion.

Wishnatsky appealed, contending the evidence he submitted in response to Huey's motion for summary judgment satisfies the elements of a battery claim and the trial court erred in granting Huey's motion. Wishnatsky also contends Huey is not entitled to prosecutorial or statutory immunity.

. . . .

"In its original conception [battery] meant the infliction of physical injury." [ ] By the Eighteenth Century, the requirement of an actual physical injury had been eliminated:

At Nisi Prius, upon evidence in trespass for assault and battery, Holt, C.J. declared,

> 1. That the least touching of another in anger is a battery. 2. If two or more meet in a narrow passage, and without any violence or design of harm, the one touches the other gently, it is no battery. 3. If any of them use violence against the other, to force his way in a rude inordinate manner, it is a battery; or any struggle about the passage, to that degree as may do hurt, is a battery. [ ]

Cole v. Turner, Pasch. 3 Ann., 6 Mod. 149, 90 Eng.Rep. 958 (1704). Blackstone explained:

> The least touching of another's person willfully, or in anger, is a battery; for the law cannot draw the line between different degrees of

violence, and therefore totally prohibits the first and lowest stage of it: every man's person being sacred, and no other having a right to meddle with it, in any the slightest manner.

3 William Blackstone, Commentaries *120. On the other hand, "in a crowded world, a certain amount of personal contact is inevitable, and must be accepted." [Prosser & Keeton].

The American Law Institute has balanced the interest in unwanted contacts and the inevitable contacts in a crowded world in Restatement (Second) of Torts §§ 18, 19 (1965):

18. Battery: Offensive Contact

(1) An actor is subject to liability to another for battery if

(a) he acts intending to cause a harmful or offensive contact with the person of the other or a third person, or an imminent apprehension of such a contact, and

(b) an offensive contact with the person of the other directly or indirectly results.

(2) An act which is not done with the intention stated in Subsection (1,a) does not make the actor liable to the other for a mere offensive contact with the other's person although the act involves an unreasonable risk of inflicting it and, therefore, would be negligent or reckless if the risk threatened bodily harm.

.   .   .   .

19. What Constitutes Offensive Contact

A bodily contact is offensive if it offends a reasonable sense of personal dignity.

Comment *c* to § 18 notes that the contact need not be "directly caused by some act of the actor" and also notes that "the essence of the plaintiff's grievance consists in the offense to the dignity involved in the unpermitted and intentional invasion of the inviolability of his person and not in any physical harm done to his body." Comment *a* to § 19 explains what kind of conduct offends a reasonable sense of personal dignity:

In order that a contact be offensive to a reasonable sense of personal dignity, it must be one which would offend the ordinary person and as such one not unduly sensitive as to his personal dignity. It must, therefore, be a contact which is unwarranted by the social usages prevalent at the time and place at which it is inflicted.

Huey moved for summary judgment of dismissal, because, among other things, "as a matter of law, a battery did not occur on January 10, 1996." Huey supported the motion with his affidavit stating in part:

8. That Attorney Crary and I had settled into a serious discussion about the case and had established a good rapport when the door to his office suddenly swung open without a knock. An unidentified individual carrying some papers then strode in unannounced. I had not been told that anyone would be entering Attorney Crary's office during the

private meeting. . . . I subsequently learned that the individual's name is Martin Wishnatsky.

Wishnatsky responded to Huey's motion for summary judgment with an affidavit of Crary and with his own affidavit stating in part:

1. I am a born-again Christian and cultivate holiness in my life. [A]s a result I am very sensitive to evil spirits and am greatly disturbed by the demonic. However, in Christ there is victory.

2. On January 9, 1996, Mr. David Huey of the North Dakota Attorney General's office, visited the ministry where I was working at 16 Broadway in Fargo, North Dakota with an ex parte court order.

3. The following morning I entered the office of Peter Crary, an attorney for whom I do paralegal work, to give him certain papers that had been requested. Mr. Crary was speaking with Mr. David Huey at the time. As I began to enter the office Mr Huey threw his body weight against the door and forced me out into the hall. I had not said a word to him. At the same time, he snarled: "You get out of here." This was very shocking and frightening to me. In all the time I have been working as an aide to Mr. Crary, I have never been physically assaulted or spoken to in a harsh and brutal manner. My blood pressure began to rise, my heart beat accelerated and I felt waves of fear in the pit of my stomach. My hands began to shake and my body to tremble. Composing myself, I reentered the office, whereupon Mr. Huey began a half-demented tirade against me and stormed out into the hall. I looked at Mr. Crary in wonder.

We certainly agree with the Supreme Court's determination that when Wishnatsky attempted to enter the room in which Huey was conversing with Crary, "Huey apparently reacted in a rude and abrupt manner in attempting to exclude Wishnatsky from that conversation." Wishnatsky v. Huey, [560 N.W.2d 878 (N.D.1997)]. As a matter of law, however, Huey's "rude and abrupt" conduct did not rise to the level of battery.

The evidence presented to the trial court demonstrates Wishnatsky is "unduly sensitive as to his personal dignity." Restatement (Second) of Torts § 19 cmt. *a* (1965). Without knocking or otherwise announcing his intentions, Wishnatsky opened the door to the office in which Huey and Crary were having a private conversation and attempted to enter. Huey closed the door opened by Wishnatsky, thereby stopping Wishnatsky's forward progress and pushing him back into the hall. The bodily contact was momentary, indirect, and incidental. Viewing the evidence in the light most favorable to Wishnatsky, and giving him the benefit of all favorable inferences which can reasonably be drawn from the evidence, we conclude Huey's conduct in response to Wishnatsky's intrusion into his private conversation with Crary, while "rude and abrupt," would not "be offensive to a reasonable sense of personal dignity." In short, an "ordinary person . . . not unduly sensitive as to his personal dignity" intruding upon a private conversation in Wishnatsky's manner would not have been offended by Huey's response to the intrusion. We conclude that Huey's conduct did not constitute an offensive-contact-battery, as a matter of law, and the trial court did not err in granting Huey's motion for summary judgment dismissing Wishnatsky's action.

.   .   .

Affirmed.

HOBERG, C.J., WILLIAM F. HODNY, SURROGATE JUDGE, and DEBBIE G. KLEVEN, DISTRICT JUDGE, concur.

Notes and Questions

1. Can the court's affirmance of summary judgment be reconciled with the "balance" struck by sections 18 and 19 of the Second Restatement?

2. In *Vosburg v. Putney*, p. 868, supra, the court applied the thin-skulled plaintiff rule in holding defendant liable for damages exacerbated by a pre-existing injury. Is *Huey* a departure from the thin-skulled plaintiff rule?

3. Is there a role for implied consent here? We consider the consent defense shortly.

Alien Tort Claims Act

Recently, American courts have begun adjudicating civil liability for intentional torts and crimes under the Alien Tort Claims Act (ATCA), 28 U.S.C. § 1350. The development of this action is recounted in Wiwa v. Royal Dutch Petroleum Co., 226 F.3d 88 (2d Cir. 2000). That case involved civil suits brought against international Shell Oil defendants for the executions of several Nigerians, including prominent author Ken Saro Wiwa, arising out of disputes over the development of oil resources in the homeland of the Ogoni people. Plaintiffs alleged that, although the government of Nigeria tortured and executed the claimants and their decedents, these abuses were "instigated, orchestrated, planned, and facilitated by Shell Nigeria under the direction of the defendants," who were said to have "provided money, weapons, and logistical support to the Nigerian military . . ., participated in the fabrication of murder charges . . ., and bribed witnesses to give testimony." After finding personal jurisdiction, the court turned to the defendants' argument that the case should be pursued in England because of forum non conveniens. The plaintiffs asserted that in addition to the ATCA, the 1991 passage of the Torture Victim Prevention Act, 28 U.S.C. § 1350 App. argued for keeping their cases in the United States. In addressing that issue, the court extensively reviewed the scope of these statutes:

> The Alien Tort Claims Act was adopted in 1789 as part of the original Judiciary Act. In its original form, it made no assertion about legal rights; it simply asserted that "[t]he district courts shall have

original jurisdiction of any civil action by an alien for a tort only, committed in violation of the law of nations or a treaty of the United States." 28 U.S.C. § 1350. For almost two centuries, the statute lay relatively dormant, supporting jurisdiction in only a handful of cases. See, e.g., Filartiga v. Pena–Irala, 630 F.2d 876, 887 & n. 21 (2d Cir.1980) (identifying only two previous cases that had relied upon the ATCA for jurisdiction). As the result of increasing international concern with human rights issues, however, litigants have recently begun to seek redress more frequently under the ATCA. See, e.g., Abebe–Jira v. Negewo, 72 F.3d 844 (11th Cir.1996) (alleging torture of Ethiopian prisoners); Kadic v. Karadzic, 70 F.3d 232 (2d Cir.1995) (alleging torture, rape, and other abuses orchestrated by Serbian military leader); In re Estate of Ferdinand Marcos, 25 F.3d 1467 (9th Cir.1994) (alleging torture and other abuses by former President of Philippines); Tel–Oren v. Libyan Arab Republic, 726 F.2d 774 (D.C.Cir.1984) (alleging claims against Libya based on armed attack upon civilian bus in Israel); *Filartiga*, (alleging torture by Paraguayan officials); Xuncax v. Gramajo, 886 F.Supp. 162 (D.Mass.1995) (alleging abuses by Guatemalan military forces).

These suits produced several important decisions interpreting the meaning and scope of the 1789 Act. For example, in [*Filartiga v. Pena–Irala*], this court held that deliberate torture perpetrated under the color of official authority violates universally accepted norms of international human rights law, and that such a violation of international law constitutes a violation of the domestic law of the United States, giving rise to a claim under the ATCA whenever the perpetrator is properly served within the borders of the United States. More recently, we held in [*Kadic v. Karadzic*], that the ATCA reaches the conduct of private parties provided that their conduct is undertaken under the color of state authority or violates a norm of international law that is recognized as extending to the conduct of private parties.

In passing the Torture Victim Prevention Act [TVPA], Congress expressly ratified our holding in *Filartiga* that the United States courts have jurisdiction over suits by aliens alleging torture under color of law of a foreign nation, and carried it significantly further. While the 1789 Act expressed itself in terms of a grant of jurisdiction to the district courts, the 1991 Act (a) makes clear that it creates liability under U.S. law where under "color of law, of any foreign nation" an individual is subject to torture or "extra judicial killing," and (b) extends its remedy not only to aliens but to any "individual," thus covering citizens of the United States as well. [   ] The TVPA thus recognizes explicitly what was perhaps implicit in the Act of 1789—that the law of nations is incorporated into the law of the United States and that a violation of the international law of human rights is (at least with regard to torture) ipso facto a violation of U.S. domestic law. [   ]

Whatever may have been the case prior to passage of the TVPA, we believe plaintiffs make a strong argument in contending that the present law, in addition to merely permitting U.S. District Courts to entertain suits alleging violation of the law of nations, expresses a policy favoring receptivity by our courts to such suits. Two changes of statutory wording seem to indicate such an intention. First is the change from addressing the courts' "jurisdiction" to addressing substantive rights; second is the change from the ATCA's description of the claim as one for "tort . . . committed in violation of the law of nations . . ." to the new Act's assertion of the substantive right to damages under U.S. law. This evolution of statutory language seems to represent a more direct recognition that the interests of the United States are involved in the eradication of torture committed under color of law in foreign nations.

. . .

One of the difficulties that confront victims of torture under color of a nation's law is the enormous difficulty of bringing suits to vindicate such abuses. Most likely, the victims cannot sue in the place where the torture occurred. Indeed, in many instances, the victim would be endangered merely by returning to that place. It is not easy to bring such suits in the courts of another nation. Courts are often inhospitable. Such suits are generally time consuming, burdensome, and difficult to administer. In addition, because they assert outrageous conduct on the part of another nation, such suits may embarrass the government of the nation in whose courts they are brought. Finally, because characteristically neither the plaintiffs nor the defendants are ostensibly either protected or governed by the domestic law of the forum nation, courts often regard such suits as "not our business."

The new formulations of the Torture Victim Protection Act convey the message that torture committed under color of law of a foreign nation in violation of international law is "our business," as such conduct not only violates the standards of international law but also as a consequence violates our domestic law. In the legislative history of the TVPA, Congress noted that universal condemnation of human rights abuses "provide[s] scant comfort" to the numerous victims of gross violations if they are without a forum to remedy the wrong. [ ] This passage supports plaintiffs' contention that in passing the Torture Victim Prevention Act, Congress has expressed a policy of U.S. law favoring the adjudication of such suits in U.S. courts. If in cases of torture in violation of international law our courts exercise their jurisdiction conferred by the 1789 Act only for as long as it takes to dismiss the case for forum non conveniens, we will have done little to enforce the standards of the law of nations.

This is not to suggest that the TVPA has nullified, or even significantly diminished, the doctrine of forum non conveniens. The statute has, however, communicated a policy that such suits should not be facilely dismissed on the assumption that the ostensibly foreign controversy is not our business. The TVPA in our view expresses a policy favoring our courts' exercise of the jurisdiction conferred by the

ATCA in cases of torture unless the defendant has fully met the burden of showing that the [ ] factors "tilt [ ] strongly in favor of trial in the foreign forum." [ ]

The court held that defendants' showing was inadequate and rejected the defense of forum non conveniens.

3. FALSE IMPRISONMENT

Lopez v. Winchell's Donut House
Illinois Appellate Court, 1984.
126 Ill.App.3d 46, 466 N.E.2d 1309.

LORENZ, JUSTICE:

Plaintiff appeals from an order of the circuit court granting defendant corporation's motion for summary judgment. Plaintiff contends that the trial court erred in entering summary judgment against her because a genuine issue of material fact existed concerning her charge that she was falsely detained and imprisoned. For the reasons which follow, we affirm the trial court's decision.

Count I of plaintiff's unverified two-count complaint alleged that plaintiff was employed as a clerk in defendant's donut shop in Woodridge, Illinois, for approximately three years; that on or about April 8, 1981, defendant, through its agents and employees, Ralph Bell and James Cesario, accused her of selling donuts without registering sales and thereby pocketing defendant's monies; and that she was falsely detained and imprisoned against her will in a room located on defendant's premises, with force, and without probable and reasonable cause, by defendant's employees. Count I of her complaint also alleged that as a result of defendant's employees' wilful and wanton false imprisonment, she was exposed to public disgrace; greatly injured in her good name and reputation; suffered, and still suffers, great mental anguish, humiliation and shock; wrongfully terminated from her employment; required to seek medical attention; all of which prevented her from attending to her usual affairs.

[Defendant's answer consisted of an affirmative defense that it had reasonable grounds to believe that plaintiff had engaged in retail theft and that its inquiry as to whether she had failed to ring up certain retail sales was conducted "in a reasonable manner and for a reasonable length of time." Defendant then moved for summary judgment.]

The motion included portions of plaintiff's deposition which disclosed the following. James Cesario telephoned plaintiff at her home at 4:30 p.m. on April 9, 1981, and asked her to come down to the donut shop; he did not explain his reasons for wanting her to do so. As a result of this call, plaintiff walked to the store from her home, arriving ten minutes later. Upon her arrival at the store, Cesario asked her to accompany him into the baking room, which was located at the rear of the store; Ralph Bell was also present in the room. After Cesario asked plaintiff to sit down, she indicated that they (Cesario and Bell) closed the door and locked it by putting a "little latch on." She stated that the two men told her that they had proof that spotters going from store to store had purchased two dozen donuts from her, but that her register had not shown the sale. After refusing her request to view the "proof," plaintiff stated that she was "too upset" to respond to their questioning regarding the length of time that her alleged "shorting" of the cash drawer had been going on.

She further stated that defendant's employees never told her that she had to answer their questions or face the loss of her job; never directly threatened to fire her; and made no threats of any kind to her during the interrogation. She further testified that she at no time during the interrogation feared for her safety; that she at no time refused to answer any question put to her; that there was never a point in the interrogation that she said, "I want to leave" and was prevented from doing so; and that she got up, left the room and went home when she first decided to do so.

Plaintiff's written response to defendant's motion for summary judgment did not contradict the statements that she had made in her discovery deposition. In her affidavit filed in support of her response to defendant's motion for summary judgment, plaintiff averred that (1) she left the baking room after she began to shake, and when she felt that she was becoming ill; and (2) she was terminated from her employment by defendant.

The trial court entered summary judgment for defendant. Plaintiff appeals from that order. . . .

. . .

Plaintiff asserts that the trial court erred in granting defendant's motion for summary judgment as there exists a genuine issue of material fact. She posits that she felt compelled to remain in the baking room so that she could protect her reputation by protesting her innocence to the two men, and that she left the room once she began to shake and feel ill. Additionally, she attributes her "serious emotional upset" to her feelings of intimidation that she contends were caused by: James Cesario's sitting directly next to her during questioning, yellow pad and pencil in hand; Ralph Bell's repeated statement that his briefcase contained proof of her guilt; and his raised voice.

The common law tort of false imprisonment is defined as an unlawful restraint of an individual's personal liberty or freedom of locomotion. [ ] Imprisonment has been defined as "any unlawful exercise or show of force by which a person is compelled to remain where he does not wish to remain or to go where he does not wish to go." [ ] In order for a false imprisonment to be present, there must be actual or legal intent to restrain. [ ]

Unlawful restraint may be effected by words alone, by acts alone or both [ ]; actual force is unnecessary to an action in false imprisonment. [ ] The Restatement of Torts specifies ways in which an action may bring about the confinement required as an element of false imprisonment, including (1) actual or apparent physical barriers; (2) overpowering physical force, or by submission to physical force; (3) threats of physical force; (4) other duress; and (5) asserted legal authority. Restatement (Second) of Torts §§ 38–41 (1965).

It is essential, however, that the confinement be against the plaintiff's will and if a person voluntarily consents to the confinement, there can be no false imprisonment. [ ] "Moral pressure, as where the plaintiff remains with the defendant to clear himself of suspicion of theft, . . . , is not enough; nor, as in the case of assault, are threats for the future. . . . Any remedy for such wrongs must lie with the more modern tort of the intentional infliction of mental distress." [ ]

Plaintiff principally relies on the court's decision in *Marcus v. Liebman* (1978) [ ], for support of her position that summary judgment should not have been granted in the instant case. In *Marcus v. Liebman*, the court extensively examined the concept that threats of a future action are not enough to constitute confinement. [ ] There, the defendant psychiatrist threatened to have plaintiff committed to the Elgin State Hospital, and the *Marcus* court found that this was a present threat, constituting false imprisonment, as opposed to a threat of future action. The court in *Marcus* concluded that the lower court had incorrectly directed a verdict for the defendant, and reversed and remanded the case for trial on the question of imprisonment. The court noted that plaintiff was already voluntarily committed to the psychiatric wing of a private hospital when the defendant made the threat to commit her to a state mental hospital and reasoned, "[A]t the time the alleged threat was made plaintiff was already confined. It was certainly reasonable for the plaintiff to believe that before her release [from the private hospital], commitment procedures could have been concluded." [ ]

Our analysis of the *Marcus* decision, as well as the other cases cited by plaintiff, does not support plaintiff's position. All of these cases are easily distinguishable from the present case, as in each, either physical restraint or present threats of such were present.

In the case at bar, we are confronted with plaintiff's testimony, given under oath, that she voluntarily accompanied James Cesario to the baking room; that she stayed in the room in order to protect her reputation; that she was never threatened with the loss of her job; that she was never in fear of her safety; and that at no time was she prevented from exiting the baking room. Her affidavit, in which she averred that she left the baking room after she began to shake and when she felt that she was becoming ill, does not place into issue material facts which she had previously removed from contention. [ ] In her discovery deposition, given under oath, she stated that she "got up and left" when Ralph Bell asked her how long the cash register "shorting" had been going on.

In the tort of false imprisonment, it is not enough for the plaintiff to have felt "compelled" to remain in the baking room in order to protect her reputation (see Prosser, Torts, § 11); for the evidence must establish a restraint against the plaintiff's will, as where she yields to force, to the threat of force or the assertion of authority. (See Restatement (Second) of

Torts §§ 38–41 (1965).) In the present case, our search of the record reveals no evidence that plaintiff yielded to constraint of a threat, express or implied, or to physical force of any kind. Also, absent evidence that plaintiff accompanied Cesario against her will, we cannot say that she was imprisoned or unlawfully detained by defendant's employees. Finally, we find no merit to plaintiff's argument that defendant's affirmative defense constituted an admission of an unlawful restraint.

For the reasons stated above, we conclude that the trial court properly granted defendant's motion for summary judgment, as there exists no question of material fact in the present case.

AFFIRMED.

MEJDA, P.J., and SULLIVAN, J., concur.

Notes and Questions

1.   In *Lopez,* what appear to be the elements in the prima facie case of false imprisonment? What was the crux of the defendant's affirmative defense?

2.   Would summary judgment have been warranted if Bell and Cesario had told plaintiff that they weren't through questioning her when she decided to leave? What if they said that she was free to leave but if she did so she was fired?

3.   Suppose that plaintiff was one of three employees who were called in and subjected to the reported interrogation because defendants didn't know which of them had been stealing from the register. Would plaintiff's case remain as strong as in *Lopez*?

4.   The circumstances under which individuals have sought to restrain the freedom of movement of others defy generalization. For a bizarre case, involving the leader of a religious sect who imposed sanctions against the plaintiff straying too far from the yacht where she was domiciled, see Whittaker v. Sandford, 85 A. 399 (Me.1912). On the overambitious efforts of two "high-powered" car repossessors, see National Bond & Investment Co. v. Whithorn, 123 S.W.2d 263 (Ky.1938).

In Shen v. Leo A. Daly Co., 222 F.3d 472 (8th Cir. 2000), the Taiwanese government refused to permit plaintiff to leave the country until defendant, his former employer, satisfied certain obligations. The court held that confinement within a country did not amount to false imprisonment. The court observed that although "it is difficult to define exactly how close the level of restraint must be, in this case the country of Taiwan is clearly too great an area within which to be falsely imprisoned."

5.   False arrest cases constitute a special category. If the imprisonment resulted from an arrest, the defendant must have been legally entitled to make the arrest. Without a privilege, the defendant would be subject to liability for the particular form of false imprisonment known as false arrest. The rules governing false arrest are discussed, in the context of a survey of the historical development of the false imprisonment tort, in D. Dobbs, The Law of Torts 190–204 (2000).

6. *Malicious prosecution.* False arrest cases do not reach claims in which, although the warrant and legal forms were proper, no basis existed for the arrest in the first place. The defendant in the original case claims that the complainant began the prosecution without probable cause and for improper purposes. This claim, called an action for malicious prosecution, permits the original defendant, after exoneration, to bring an action for expenses and humiliation sustained in the first case. For an example of the interplay between false arrest and malicious prosecution in the shoplifting context, see Soares v. Ann & Hope of Rhode Island, Inc., 637 A.2d 339 (R.I.1994), upholding a claim that a store initiated criminal proceedings without probable cause.

One of the crucial and much-litigated elements is the showing of a favorable termination to the malicious prosecution plaintiff in the earlier proceeding. See Smith–Hunter v. Harvey, 734 N.E.2d 750 (N.Y.2000) (state no longer requires plaintiff to show innocence; any favorable termination "not inconsistent with innocence" will suffice).

A more restricted form of this action lies in many states against persons who wrongfully file civil actions. The history of these actions is traced in Note, Groundless Litigation and the Malicious Prosecution Debate: A Historical Analysis, 88 Yale L.J. 1218 (1979). For an interesting analysis of one state's development of the civil action, see Dupre, Case Comment, *Yost v. Torok* and Abusive Litigation: A New Tort to Solve an Old Problem, 21 Ga.L.Rev. 429 (1986).

Perhaps not surprisingly, some parties who have historically been disgruntled with the tort system are often plaintiffs in malicious prosecution cases. The medical community's experiences with such actions are discussed in Yardley, Malicious Prosecution: A Physician's Need for Reassessment, 60 Chi.-Kent L.Rev. 317 (1984). In City of Long Beach v. Bozek, 645 P.2d 137 (Cal.1982), vacated and remanded 459 U.S. 1095, on remand 661 P.2d 1072 (Cal.1983), the court held that the government could not bring a malicious prosecution action against an individual who had brought an unsuccessful action against the government. The court's decision is criticized in Faber, *City of Long Beach v. Bozek*: An Absolute Right to Sue the Government?, 71 Cal.L.Rev. 1258 (1983).

7. *Special problems of shoplifting.* The arrest of a suspected shoplifter presents special legal problems because a private citizen is usually the arrester. The problem is significant economically because retailers lost an estimated $17 billion to shoplifters in 1999, roughly 1% of annual sales. Coleman & Callahan, Detroit Death Raises Questions on Guard Attire, Wall St. J., Aug. 4, 2000 at B1. The losses are hard to itemize and are uninsurable.

Most shoplifting incidents are petty larcenies. In most states the misdemeanor of petty larceny covers theft of merchandise worth less than $50 or $100. Thus, the shopkeeper's suspicion is usually that someone has committed a misdemeanor. There is no time to get an officer or a warrant.

At common law, even a peace officer had no privilege to arrest for a misdemeanor committed in the officer's presence—unless the officer had a warrant—if the misdemeanor involved no breach of the peace.

Even states that have liberalized the common law misdemeanor arrest rules for police officers, may require that the offense have occurred in the officer's presence—an unlikely event in shoplifting cases unless the officer is not in uniform. For a "citizen's arrest," most states require that the misdemeanor have been committed in the citizen's presence and that the person arrested be guilty. In these states, even if a suspected theft occurs in the presence of a store employee, the shopkeeper still arrests at his or her peril: the arrested person must be proven guilty. Even in more lenient states the shopkeeper must establish that a misdemeanor has indeed occurred. Thus, if a suspect refuses to open packages or explain suspicious conduct, traditional law presents the shopkeeper with the choice of making a possibly unlawful citizen's arrest or letting the suspect go. A similar dilemma is presented if the shopkeeper seeks only to retrieve goods without making an arrest: if, in fact, the suspect has obtained the goods legally, the shopkeeper's reasonable belief that they were stolen will not protect against liability for battery if force is used to retrieve the goods.

Nor can the shopkeeper solve the problem by seeking the assistance of a police officer. The shopkeeper who detains the suspect against his or her will until a police officer arrives has in effect made an arrest. If, instead, the shopkeeper chases a suspect down the street shouting, "Stop that man; he is a thief!," and a police officer arrests him, the shopkeeper will be deemed to have instigated the arrest and will be subject to the standards of a citizen's arrest—though the police officer may be protected as having made the arrest on reasonable grounds.

In 1960, New York enacted General Business Law § 218:

> In any action for false arrest, false imprisonment, unlawful detention, defamation of character, assault, trespass, or invasion of civil rights, brought by any person by reason of having been detained on or in the immediate vicinity of the premises of a retail mercantile establishment for the purpose of investigation or questioning . . . as to the ownership of any merchandise, it shall be a defense to such action that the person was detained in a reasonable manner and for not more than a reasonable time to permit such investigation or questioning by a peace officer . . . or by the owner of the retail mercantile establishment, his authorized employee or agent, and that such officer, owner, employee or agent had reasonable grounds to believe that the person so detained . . . was committing or attempting to commit larceny on such premises of such merchandise. As used in this section, "reasonable grounds" shall include, but not be limited to, knowledge that a person has concealed possession of unpurchased merchandise of a retail mercantile establishment . . . and a "reasonable time" shall mean the time necessary to permit the person detained to make a statement or to refuse to make a statement, and the time necessary to

examine employees and records of the mercantile establishment relative to the ownership of the merchandise.   . . .

Similar statutes exist in other states. See, e.g., Calif.Penal Code § 490.5(f). Is this a sound approach? How does it compare with the common law approach in employee theft cases taken by the *Lopez* court? Are there better alternatives? The New York statute was amended slightly in 1994 to allow the owner of a movie theatre to detain someone reasonably believed to be using a recording device.

The New York statute's philosophy and operation are discussed in Jacques v. Sears, Roebuck & Co., 285 N.E.2d 871 (N.Y.1972)(protecting merchant who detained customer who had left store without paying for merchandise, but whose prosecution was dropped for lack of intent). See generally, Note, Merchants' Responses to Shoplifting: An Empirical Study, 28 Stan.L.Rev. 589 (1976).

In 1991, New York adopted legislation allowing merchants to impose civil penalties not exceeding $500 on shoplifters who make restitution of the value of the stolen goods; in return for agreeing to an informal settlement, the shoplifter gets no criminal record. See generally, Woo, Most States Now Have Laws Permitting Stores to Impose Civil Fines on Shoplifters, Wall St.J., Sept. 9, 1992 at B1. Is the statute likely to reduce the prospect of false imprisonment actions?

4. INTENTIONAL INFLICTION OF EMOTIONAL DISTRESS

An intentional tort of recent origin is the intentional infliction of emotional distress. Traditionally, courts were reluctant to recognize such an action for at least two reasons: the difficulties in assuring that actual harm had occurred—an issue that also applied to negligently inflicted emotional distress, p. 261, supra—and the belief that a certain amount of verbal abuse is a part of everyday life. This reluctance was still discernible in a 1948 case in which the defendant loudly and repeatedly on a crowded street called the pregnant plaintiff a "god-damned son of a bitch" and "a dirty crook." Plaintiff alleged general physical harm resulting from the shock. A split court refused relief on the ground that there is "no right to recover for bad manners" in the absence of an assault or defamation because of the "speculative" and "sentimental" nature of the injury and the difficulty of measuring damages. Bartow v. Smith, 78 N.E.2d 735 (Ohio 1948), overruled by Yeager v. Local Union 20, 453 N.E.2d 666 (Ohio 1983).

During this period other courts were granting relief not only for intentional infliction of emotional distress involving some physical injury, but also when it caused emotional distress alone—at least where the actor's behavior was particularly offensive. In State Rubbish Collectors Ass'n v. Siliznoff, 240 P.2d 282 (Cal.1952), the plaintiff sued for nonpayment of notes and the defendant's cross-complaint asked that the notes be cancelled because of duress. He also sought damages because plaintiff's members had coerced him to sign the notes to pay for a garbage collection contract he had signed with a customer—even though defendant did not belong to plaintiff association. He testified that the encounter was so distressing that he became ill and vomited several times. A jury award of both compensatory and punitive damages was upheld unanimously. For the court, Justice Traynor first concluded that "a cause of action is established when it is shown that one, in the absence of any privilege, intentionally subjects another to the mental suffering incident to serious threats to his physical well-being, whether or not the threats are made under such circumstances as to constitute a technical assault." Where mental suffering is a major element of the damages, it is anomalous to deny recovery on the ground that no physical injury followed:

> There are persuasive arguments and analogies that support the recognition of a right to be free from serious, intentional, and unprivileged invasions of mental and emotional tranquility. If a cause of action is otherwise established, it is settled that damages may be given for mental suffering naturally ensuing from the acts complained of [ ], and in the case of many torts, such as assault, battery, false imprisonment, and defamation, mental suffering will frequently constitute the principal element of damages. [ ] In cases where mental suffering constitutes a major element of damages it is anomalous to deny recovery because the defendant's intentional misconduct fell short of producing some physical injury.
>
> It may be contended that to allow recovery in the absence of physical injury will open the door to unfounded claims and a flood of litigation, and that the requirement that there be physical injury is necessary to insure that serious mental suffering actually occurred. The jury is ordinarily in a better position, however, to determine whether outrageous conduct results in mental distress than whether that distress in turn results in physical injury. From their own experience jurors are aware of the extent and character of the disagreeable emotions that may result from the defendant's conduct, but a difficult medical question is presented when it must be determined if emotional distress resulted in physical injury.   .   .   .

Does the rationale extend beyond threatening situations that don't quite measure up to assaults? Consider the following case.

Womack v. Eldridge

Supreme Court of Virginia, 1974.
215 Va. 338, 210 S.E.2d 145.

I'ANSON, CHIEF JUSTICE.

Plaintiff, Danny Lee Womack, instituted this action against the defendant, Rosalie Eldridge, to recover compensatory and punitive damages for mental shock and distress allegedly caused by the defendant's willful, wanton, malicious, fraudulent and deceitful acts and conduct toward him. The question of punitive damages was stricken by the trial court and the jury returned a verdict for the plaintiff in the amount of $45,000. The trial court set aside the verdict . . . on the ground that there could be no recovery for emotional distress in the absence of "physical damage or other bodily harm." We granted plaintiff a writ of error. . . .

Plaintiff assigned numerous errors, but the controlling question is whether one who by extreme and outrageous conduct intentionally or recklessly causes severe emotional distress to another is subject to liability for such emotional distress absent any bodily injury.

The evidence shows that defendant had been engaged in the business of investigating cases for attorneys for many years. She was employed by Richard E. Seifert and his attorney to obtain a photograph of the plaintiff to be used as evidence in the trial of Seifert, who was charged with sexually molesting two young boys. On May 27, 1970, about 8 a.m., defendant went to plaintiff's home and upon gaining admittance told him that she was a Mrs. Jackson from the newspaper and that she was writing an article on Skateland. Defendant asked plaintiff, who was a coach at Skateland, if she could take a picture of him for publication with the article, and he readily consented.

Shortly thereafter defendant delivered the photograph to Seifert's counsel while he was representing Seifert at his preliminary hearing. Seifert's counsel showed plaintiff's photograph to the two young boys and asked if he was the one who molested them. When they replied that he was not, counsel withdrew the photograph and put it in his briefcase. However, the Commonwealth's Attorney then asked to see the photograph and requested additional information about the person shown in it. Defendant was then called to the stand and she supplied the plaintiff's name and address. Plaintiff's photograph in no way resembled Seifert, and the only excuse given by defendant for taking plaintiff's picture was that he was at Skateland when Seifert was arrested. However, the offenses alleged against Seifert did not occur at Skateland.

The Commonwealth's Attorney then directed a detective to go to plaintiff's home and bring him to court. The detective told plaintiff that his photograph had been presented in court; that the Commonwealth's Attorney wanted him to appear at the proceedings; and that he could either appear voluntarily then or he would be summoned. Plaintiff agreed to go voluntarily. When called as a witness, plaintiff testified as to the circumstances under which defendant had obtained his photograph. He also said that he had not molested any children and that he knew nothing about the charges against Seifert.

A police officer questioned plaintiff several times thereafter. Plaintiff was also summoned to appear as a witness before the grand jury but he was not called. However, he was summoned to appear several times at Seifert's trial in the circuit court because of continuances of the cases.

Plaintiff testified that he suffered great shock, distress and nervousness because of defendant's fraud and deceit and her wanton, willful and malicious conduct in obtaining his photograph and turning it over to Seifert's attorney to be used in court. He suffered great anxiety as to what people would think of him and feared that he would be accused of molesting the boys. He had been unable to sleep while the matter was being investigated. While testifying in the instant case he became emotional and incoherent. Plaintiff's wife also testified that her husband experienced great shock and mental depression from the involvement.

.   .   .

The precise issue presented on this appeal has not been decided by this court.

Courts from other jurisdictions are not in accord on whether there can be a recovery for emotional distress unaccompanied by physical injury. However, most of the courts which have been presented with the question in recent years have held that there may be a recovery against one who by his extreme and outrageous conduct intentionally or recklessly causes another severe emotional distress.   .   .   .

The Restatement (Second) of Torts, § 46 at 71, provides: "(1) One who by extreme and outrageous conduct intentionally or recklessly causes severe emotional distress to another is subject to liability for such emotional distress, and if bodily harm to the other results from it, for such bodily harm." In comment (i) to the Restatement it is expressly stated that this rule also covers a situation where the actor knows that distress is certain, or substantially certain, to result from his conduct.

.   .   .

A great majority of cases allowing recovery for such a cause of action do so when the act was intentional and the wrongdoer desired the emotional distress or knew or should have known that it would likely result. [   ]

We adopt the view that a cause of action will lie for emotional distress, unaccompanied by physical injury, provided four elements are shown: One, the wrongdoer's conduct was intentional or reckless. This element is satisfied where the wrongdoer had the specific purpose of inflicting emotional distress or where he intended his specific conduct and knew or should have known that emotional distress would likely result. Two, the conduct was outrageous and intolerable in that it offends against the generally accepted standards of decency and morality. This requirement is aimed at limiting frivolous suits and avoiding litigation in situations where only bad manners and mere hurt feelings are involved. Three, there was a causal connection between the wrongdoer's conduct and the emotional distress. Four, the emotional distress was severe.

"It is for the court to determine, in the first instance, whether the defendant's conduct may reasonably be regarded as so extreme and outrageous as to permit recovery, or whether it is necessarily so. Where reasonable men may differ, it is for the jury, subject to the control of the court, to determine whether, in the particular case, the conduct has been sufficiently extreme and outrageous to result in liability." Restatement (Second) of Torts, *supra,* at 77.

In the case at bar, reasonable men may disagree as to whether defendant's conduct was extreme and outrageous and whether plaintiff's emotional distress was severe. Thus, the questions presented were for a jury to determine. A jury could conclude from the evidence presented that defendant willfully, recklessly, intentionally and deceitfully obtained plaintiff's photograph for the purpose of permitting her employers to use it as a defense in a criminal case without considering the effect it would have on the plaintiff. There is nothing in the evidence that even suggests that plaintiff may have been involved in the child molesting cases. The record shows that the only possible excuse for involving the plaintiff was that Seifert was arrested at the place where plaintiff was employed. A reasonable person would or should have recognized the likelihood of the serious mental distress that would be caused in involving an innocent person in child molesting cases. If the two boys had hesitated in answering that the man in the photograph was not the one who had molested them, it is evident that the finger of suspicion would have been pointed at the plaintiff.

Defendant contended in her brief, and in oral argument before us . . . that the action of the Commonwealth's Attorney in causing plaintiff's name to be revealed was an intervening cause which absolved her of any liability.

We will not consider those contentions because defendant did not assign cross-error. [   ]

For the reasons stated, the judgment of the court below is reversed, the jury verdict reinstated, and final judgment hereby entered for the plaintiff.

Notes and Questions

1. Suppose the evidence indicated that defendant had been hired without knowledge of the use to which the photograph would be put. Would the Restatement standard of liability, as interpreted by the court, be satisfied? Suppose, instead, defendant knew that it was to be used for purposes of identification in a criminal case—but nothing more. Would the standard be satisfied? Suppose she knew that the photo was to be used to incriminate plaintiff in a case in which he had no involvement—but she took the picture on the street. Would plaintiff have had a colorable claim?

2. If defendant had properly raised the claim that the Commonwealth Attorney was an "intervening cause which absolved her of any liability," should it have altered the disposition of the case?

3. What result if plaintiff had claimed intentional infliction of emotional distress against Seifert's attorney?

4. In Russo v. White, 400 S.E.2d 160 (Va.1991), the court affirmed dismissal of the plaintiff's claim in a case in which she alleged that the defendant had made 340 "hang-up" phone calls to her in a two month period after she refused to go out with him more than once. The court emphasized that plaintiff had not suffered any physical injury as a result of the stress and that defendant had not spoken during the calls. Asserting that the tort of intentional infliction, although recognized since *Womack,* is "not favored" in Virginia, the court quoted from Givelber, The Right to Minimum Social Decency and the Limits of Evenhandedness: Intentional Infliction of Emotional Distress by Outrageous Conduct, 82 Colum.L.Rev. 42, 42–43 (1982), in arguing:

> [Intentional infliction of emotional distress] "differs from traditional intentional torts in an important respect: it provides no clear definition of the prohibited conduct." . . . Assault, battery, and false imprisonment "describe specific forms of behavior," but the term "outrageous" "does not objectively describe an act or series of acts; rather, it represents an evaluation of behavior. The concept thus fails to provide clear guidance either to those whose conduct it purports to regulate, or to those who must evaluate that conduct."

Is the distinction drawn between the intentional infliction tort and other intentional torts persuasive? In any event, how serious is the problem? Is it addressed in the *Womack* opinion? Reconsider Justice Traynor's position in *Siliznoff,* p. 888, supra.

5. In an effort to make the standard of liability more concrete, Restatement (Second), § 46, comment *d* states "the case is one in which the recitation of the facts to an average member of the community would arouse his resentment against the actor, and lead him to exclaim, 'Outrageous!' " Givelber, in response, comments that "[t]o suggest, as the Restatement does, that civil liability should turn on the resentments of the average member of the community appears to turn the passions of the moment into law." He then notes that there would be serious constitutional difficulties in making "outrageous conduct" criminal. Do his concerns undermine the legitimacy of the intentional infliction tort?

6. Is there any room for the unusually sensitive plaintiff in these cases?

7. Courts have permitted intentional infliction of emotional distress claims to lie in cases of racial insults and harassment. See, e.g., Wiggs v. Courshon, 355 F.Supp. 206 (S.D.Fla.1973)(upholding verdict against waitress who hurled racial epithets at plaintiff when he inquired about his dinner order); Taylor v. Metzger, 706 A.2d 685 (N.J.1998) (single racial slur in employment context may suffice). But see, e.g., Bradshaw v. Swagerty, 563 P.2d 511 (Kan.App.1977)(plaintiff alleged that defendant, plaintiff's lawyer, hurled racial epithet during dispute over legal bill; court denied recovery on ground that such epithets are "mere insults of the kind which must be tolerated in our roughened society").

Section 46 claims are sometimes brought for cases of racial harassment in the workplace. See, e.g. Alcorn v. Anbro Eng'g Inc., 468 P.2d 216 (Cal.1970)(plaintiff, who was shop steward for the company's labor union, told his supervisor that a nonunion employee was not permitted to drive a truck from a job site; supervisor responded with a string of racial insults and fired plaintiff; court allowed plaintiff to proceed with his claim for intentional infliction of emotional distress). Some courts have denied relief for harassment in the workplace on the ground that the employer's words and actions, while offensive, do not constitute "extreme and outrageous" conduct. See, e.g., Patterson v. McLean Credit Union, 805 F.2d 1143 (4th Cir.1986), affirmed in part, vacated in part, and remanded on different grounds 491 U.S. 164 (1989) (plaintiff's allegations that her supervisor gave her too much work, required her to sweep and dust, and commented that blacks are slower than whites, did not rise to level of "extreme and outrageous" conduct). The tort system's response to verbal harassment in the workplace is discussed and criticized in Austin, Employer Abuse, Worker Resistance, and the Tort of Intentional Infliction of Emotional Distress, 41 Stan.L.Rev. 1 (1988).

The racial harassment issue has produced a good deal of commentary. See Delgado, Words That Wound: A Tort Action for Racial Insults, Epithets, and Name–Calling, 17 Harv. C.R.-C.L.L.Rev. 133 (1982); Love, Discriminatory Speech and the Tort of Intentional Infliction of Emotional Distress, 47 Wash. & Lee L.Rev. 123 (1990). The fine line between outrageous conduct and free expression has given rise to serious First Amendment concerns. For a constitutional defense of the state's ability to provide relief to victims of racial harassment, see Lawrence, If He Hollers Let Him Go: Regulating Racist Speech on Campus, 1990 Duke L.J. 431. For a contrary view, see Note, Dear Professor Lawrence, You Missed the School Bus; *Brown v. Board of Education* Supports Free Speech on Campus: A Reply, 72 B.U.L.Rev. 953 (1992).

For an argument that legislative developments have largely negated the need for common law protection, see Duffy, Intentional Infliction of Emotional Distress and Employment at Will: The Case against Tortification of Labor and Employment Law, 74 B.U.L.Rev. 387 (1994).

8. *Racial harassment—statutory claims.* Until recently, claims for workplace racial harassment were not actionable under 42 U.S.C. § 1981, an antidiscrimination statute passed during the Reconstruction era, which gives all persons equal rights "to make and enforce contracts." In *Patterson v. McLean Credit Union*, referred to in the preceding note, the United States Supreme Court held that § 1981's protections were limited to issues of contract formation, and thus provided no relief for harassment directed at a worker during the course of his or her employment. Plaintiffs retained the option of bringing an action under Title VII of the Civil Rights Act of 1964, 42 U.S.C. § 2000e et seq.; however, Title VII's framework for resolution imposes several procedural obstacles not present in a § 1981 action. Congress overruled the Court's interpretation of § 1981 in the Civil Rights Reform Act of 1991, Pub.L. 102—166, 105 Stat. 1071. Thus, claims for racial harassment on the job are now actionable under § 1981.

In Bolden v. PRC Inc., 43 F.3d 545 (10th Cir.1994), cert. denied 516 U.S. 826 (1995), plaintiff brought an action against his employer alleging racial discrimination under Title VII. The court found that plaintiff, an African–American, was "a sensitive and serious person working in a shop filled with boorish churls," and "was met with hostility by many of his co-workers." Nonetheless, though his co-workers made two racial remarks to plaintiff, those comments did not amount to the "steady barrage of opprobrious racial comments" that the court required before it found "harassment that was racial or stemmed from racial animus." See Oppenheimer, Negligent Discrimination, 141 U.Pa.L.Rev. 899 (1993), articulating a negligence-based theory of employer liability under Title VII.

Under Title VII, total monetary awards for both compensatory and punitive damages are capped according to the size of the employer—reaching a combined maximum of $300,000 for employers with more than 500 employees. By contrast, § 1981 permits unlimited punitive damages. In Deffenbaugh–Williams v. Wal–Mart Stores, 156 F.3d 581 (5th Cir.1998) rehearing en banc granted, opinion vacated by 169 F.3d 215 (5th Cir.1999), opinion reinstated on rehearing by 182 F.3d 333 (5th Cir.1999), the court addressed the issue of vicarious liability for punitive damages under § 1981. At the trial below, the jury found that a Wal–Mart supervisor discharged the plaintiff, a white female, because she was dating a black male in another department. On appeal, the court found that there was sufficient evidence for the jury to find that the supervisor discharged plaintiff with "malice" or "reckless indifference" to her right to be free of race discrimination by association. Relying on Faragher v. Boca Raton, 524 U.S. 775 (1998), and Burlington Industries, Inc. v. Ellerth, 524 U.S. 742 (1998), involving vicarious liability for sexual harassment, the court held that Wal–Mart was vicariously liable for the supervisor's malice or reckless indifference, and could be vicariously liable for punitive damages.

9. *Sexual harassment—statutory claims.* The law dealing with sexual harassment in the workplace has been dynamic in recent years. Courts have long held that employers violate Title VII if employment benefits are conditioned on sexual favors—so-called "quid pro quo" cases. In 1986, the Supreme Court broadened the Title VII standard to permit claims if discriminatory conduct created an "abusive working environment." Meritor Sav. Bank v. Vinson, 477 U.S. 57 (1986). Appeals courts then split on what type of conduct was necessary to state a claim. One court required serious injury to plaintiff's psychological well-being. Rabidue v. Osceola Refining Co., 805 F.2d 611 (6th Cir.1986), cert. denied 481 U.S. 1041 (1987). Applying a more expansive standard, another court held that the severity and pervasiveness of sexual harassment should be evaluated from the victim's perspective, Ellison v. Brady, 924 F.2d 872 (9th Cir.1991). Since "a sex-blind reasonable person standard tends to . . . systematically ignore the experiences of women," the court held that plaintiffs could state a prima facie case by alleging conduct that "a reasonable woman would consider sufficiently severe or pervasive" to create a hostile working environment.

The Supreme Court rejected both standards in Harris v. Forklift Sys. Inc., 510 U.S. 17 (1993). The male defendant had asked female plaintiff to remove coins from his pants pocket and repeatedly insulted her with comments such as "you're a dumb woman, what do you know?" and, during plaintiff's negotiation of a deal with a customer, "what did you do, promise the guy . . . [sex] Saturday night?" The Court denied that plaintiff had to show psychological injury to recover under Title VII but also declined to adopt a "reasonable woman" standard. Plaintiff had to show conduct "that is . . . severe or pervasive enough to create an objectively hostile or abusive work environment . . . [which] would reasonably be perceived, and is perceived, as hostile or abusive." The finder of fact was instructed to weigh all of the circumstances, including the frequency and severity of the harassment, whether the harassment involves humiliation or physical intimidation, and whether it interferes with the employee's work performance.

The Court's standard was subsequently interpreted to mean that, in proving a hostile work environment, plaintiff can rely only on harassing conduct of which she was aware while employed. Hirase–Doi v. U.S. West Communications, 61 F.3d 777 (10th Cir.1995).

In the wake of *Forklift's* caution that "merely offensive" conduct was not actionable, one court reversed a judgment against a defendant employer whose "sense of humor took final shape in adolescence," but who had neither threatened plaintiff nor solicited sex or a date with her. Baskerville v. Culligan International Co., 50 F.3d 428 (7th Cir.1995).

Plaintiffs may also state a cause of action under Title VII if they complain of sexual harassment and are subjected to retaliation. In Dunning v. Simmons Airlines Inc., 62 F.3d 863 (7th Cir.1995), plaintiff complained of sexual harassment and was subsequently assigned involuntarily to unpaid maternity leave. The court awarded plaintiff back pay and attorney fees for her retaliation claim though it made no finding on her sexual harassment claim.

The question of whether same-sex sexual harassment is actionable under Title VII was addressed in Oncale v. Sundowner Offshore Services Inc., 523 U.S. 75 (1998). In that case, plaintiff Oncale, a male employee, brought a Title VII action alleging sexual harassment against his former employer and against his male supervisors and co-workers. The alleged harassment occurred on an offshore oil platform in the Gulf of Mexico, where Oncale was employed as a roustabout on an eight-man crew. On several occasions, Oncale was forcibly subjected to sex-related humiliation in the presence of the crew. He was also physically assaulted in a sexual manner and threatened with rape. After getting no remedial response from his supervisors, Oncale quit. At his deposition, Oncale explained why he left his job: "I felt that if I didn't leave my job, that I would be raped or forced to have sex." Oncale then filed suit alleging employment discrimination because of his sex. The district court granted summary judgment for the defendants, holding that "Mr. Oncale, a male, has no cause of action under Title VII for harassment by male co-workers." On appeal, the Fifth Circuit affirmed. A unanimous Supreme Court reversed, holding that sex discrimination consisting of same-sex sexual harassment is actionable under Title VII.

During the same term that it decided *Oncale*, the Supreme Court also decided a pair of cases that dealt with the issue of an employer's vicarious liability under Title VII for sexual harassment engaged in by supervisory employees. In both *Ellerth* and *Faragher*, supra, the Court held that "[a]n employer is subject to vicarious liability to a victimized employee for an actionable hostile environment created by a supervisor with immediate (or successively higher) authority over the employee." In addition, if the supervisor's actions did not cause the employee any tangible job consequences, the employer could defend by showing that it had "exercised reasonable care to prevent and promptly correct any sexually harassing behavior" and that "the plaintiff employee unreasonably failed to take advantage of any preventive or corrective opportunities provided by the employer or to avoid harm otherwise."

The subject of sexual harassment has received extensive scholarly treatment. See C. MacKinnon, Sexual Harassment of Working Women (1979); Ehrenreich, Pluralist Myths and Powerless Men: The Ideology of Reasonableness in Sexual Harassment Law, 99 Yale L.J. 1177 (1990); Estrich, Sex at Work, 43 Stan.L.Rev. 813 (1991). For commentary after the Court's *Forklift* decision, see Vorwerk, The Forgotten Interest Group: Reforming Title VII to Address the Concerns of Workers While Eliminating Sexual Harassment, 48 Vand.L.Rev. 1019 (1995).

Violence Against Women Act. In 1994, Congress enacted the Violence Against Women Act (VAWA), creating a more direct route for suing for sexual harassment. Title III of the statute established a federal civil cause of action and remedy for victims of gender-motivated violence. 42 U.S.C. § 13981. In 1996, in the first lawsuit pursued under the act, a freshman at Virginia Polytechnic Institute sued two members of the university's football team after they allegedly raped her. In U.S. v. Morrison, 529 U.S. 598 (2000), the Supreme Court, 5–4, affirmed the en banc decision of the Fourth Circuit striking down the statute, and held that neither the commerce clause nor section five of the Fourteenth Amendment provided Congress with authority to enact the civil remedy provision of VAWA. For highly critical commentary, see MacKinnon, Disputing Male Sovereignty: On *U.S. v. Morrison*, 114 Harv. L.Rev. 135 (2000).

Harassment in schools. In Franklin v. Gwinnett County Pub. Sch., 503 U.S. 60 (1992), in which a high school student alleged sexual harassment by one of her teachers, the Court implied a private right of action under Title IX of the Education Amendments of 1972, and concluded—in terms that may have implications for other civil rights laws—that "we presume the availability of all appropriate remedies unless Congress has expressly indicated otherwise."

Building on *Franklin*, the Supreme Court articulated the standard governing such a private right of action under Title IX in Gebser v. Lago Vista Independent School Dist., 524 U.S. 274 (1998). In that case, which involved a Title IX teacher-student sexual harassment claim brought by a high school student and her parents against a school district, the Court rejected the student's claim and held that a school district may be liable for damages under Title IX only where it has actual notice of and is deliberately indifferent to acts of teacher-student sexual harassment.

A more difficult question is posed when a student (or parent) sues a school system for failing to protect her from harassment by other students. The Supreme Court addressed this issue of student-on-student harassment in Davis v. Monroe Country Board of Education, 526 U.S. 629 (1999). Plaintiff mother sued the school district and its officials under Title IX on the grounds that they failed to take action to stop a male student's verbal and physical sexual harassment of her fifth grade daughter. The district court dismissed the Title IX claim on the grounds that "student-on-student," or peer, harassment provided no basis for a private cause of action under the statute. Sitting en banc, the Eleventh Circuit affirmed. In a 5–4 decision, the Supreme Court reversed, holding that a school system may be sued for damages under Title IX in cases of student-on-student harassment as long as the "deliberate indifference" standard set forth in *Gebser* is met and the harassment is so severe that it effectively bars the victim's access to an educational opportunity or benefit. Writing for the dissent, Justice Kennedy claimed that the majority violated the principles of federalism by allowing for "federal control of the discipline of our Nation's schoolchildren [that] is contrary to our traditions and inconsistent with the sensible administration of our schools."

10. *Credit practices.* One type of situation that does recur frequently is the bill collector case. The extent to which a creditor may utilize self-help in attempting to collect a debt is debatable. Surely a creditor may write a letter warning the alleged debtor that unless the amount claimed to be due is paid within a certain number of days, a suit will be filed. Surely a creditor may not beat the alleged debtor to a pulp in efforts to collect money. Where should the line be drawn? Is it clear that some self-help should be encouraged so that not every creditor who wants to collect money need initiate a lawsuit? On the assumption that physical violence is never permissible, we may confine our speculation to the words used and the ways in which they are communicated. Consider the following acts allegedly committed by a collection agency seeking repayment of a loan in Sherman v. Field Clinic, 392 N.E.2d 154 (Ill.App.1979):

> . . . [t]elephoning plaintiffs' residence 10–20 times per day 3 days per week and 5–6 times per day 2 other days per week; sending numerous letters to plaintiffs' residence; making numerous telephone calls to Mr. Sherman at his place of business, though only Mrs. Sherman was responsible for any debts due the Clinic; threatening to "embarrass" Mr. Sherman by contacting his employers and co-workers; threatening to garnish half of Mr. Sherman's wages; frequently using profane and obscene language in calls to Mr. Sherman; calling and speaking to Mrs. Sherman's 15 year old daughter, plaintiff Deborah Billy, in connection with the debt, though only Mrs. Sherman was responsible for any debts due the Clinic; frequently making threats to the daughter that Mr. and Mrs. Sherman would be sent to jail for not paying the bill; and frequently using abusive language in calls to Mrs. Sherman.

In considering the propriety of each of the alleged acts if done alone, consider the following questions: (1) What is the basic purpose of the defendant's conduct? Does it "intend" to cause emotional harm? Physical harm? Should the courts focus on the harm that actually ensues, what the defendant intended to cause, or on what a reasonable defendant should have foreseen from its conduct? (2) Should the identity of the defendant matter? This case involves a finance company attempting to collect a loan it has made. Often a suit involves a retail merchant who has sold items on credit and is attempting to collect the debt himself or, more likely today, with the help of a credit collection agency. Larger retailers usually discount customer notes with a finance company that then becomes the creditor. Should each of these parties have the same self-help privilege? (3) If the alleged debtor denies owing the claimed amount, should that situation be treated differently from one in which the debtor admits the debt but claims financial difficulties and wants to delay repayment? (4) Should it matter if the creditor has had serious difficulties in locating the debtor? (5) Might other distinctions prove useful here?

Intentional Interference with Family Relationships

For centuries, courts have recognized two actions for intentional interference with the marital relation. The action for "criminal conversation" involved "sexual intercourse of an outsider with husband or wife," and is the tort action based on adultery. Historically, the action was available only to husbands because of the early property rights approach to the relationship between husband and wife. In recent times some states have extended the action to wives as well. But as some have expanded the action, about half the states have abolished the action entirely either legislatively or judicially. In Neal v. Neal, 873 P.2d 871 (Idaho 1994), the court, after rejecting the historical justification for the tort, explained its decision to abolish it:

> Revenge, which may be a motive for bringing the cause of action, has no place in determining the legal rights between two parties. Further, this type of suit may expose the defendant to the extortionate schemes of the plaintiff, since it could ruin the defendant's reputation. Deterrence is not achieved; the nature of the activities underlying criminal conversation, that is sexual activity, are not such that the risk of damages would likely be a deterrent. Finally, since the injuries suffered are intangible, damage awards are not governed by any true standards, making it more likely that they could result from passion or prejudice.

The second tort, for "alienation of affections," applies to behavior by which outsiders through any means drive a wedge between family members. See, e.g., Kirk v. Koch, 607 So.2d 1220 (Miss.1992) (jury could have found that defendant "directly and intentionally interfered" with plaintiff's marriage despite lack of showing of sexual relations or affectionate conduct between defendant and plaintiff's spouse). Again, many states have abolished this action, through judicial decision or by the enactment of "heart balm" statutes that prohibit suits based on alienation grounds. In many states, these statutes also preclude actions based upon breach of promise to marry and upon seduction.

In Veeder v. Kennedy, 589 N.W.2d 610 (S.D.1999), the court noted that 34 states had abandoned the alienation action by statute, but that only five had done so by judicial decision. In this case, the court again reviewed arguments against the action but retained it, affirming a judgment for compensatory and punitive damages totaling $265,000. The case involved a relationship between defendant bank manager and a married employee. The majority rejected arguments made by earlier judges that the "underlying rationale for alienation suits, that is, the preservation of the marriage, is ludicrous. And it is folly to hope any longer that a married person who has become inclined to philander can be preserved within an affectionate marriage by the threat of an alienation suit." The majority in *Veeder* declined to abolish the action, partly because it found legislative support for the action and thought that any abolition should come from the legislature, but also because it found value in the action, quoting a member of the court in a 1981 case:

> Finally, because we happen to be living in a period of loose morals and frequent extramarital involvements is no reason for a court to put its stamp of approval on this conduct; and I feel certain that a case will arise in the future where some party has so flagrantly broken up a stable marriage that we would rue the day that an alienation suit was not available to the injured party.

See also Bland v. Hill, 735 So.2d 414 (Miss.1999), in which a state that had already abolished criminal conversation retained the alienation action. The dissenters observed:

> Over the years, courts have increasingly been required to delve into matters which are not ideally suits for judicial intervention. . . . As it applies to two spouses, the judicial system cannot be called upon to make one spouse love another. When the marriage breaks down, it is usually the fault of both spouses.
>
> Hence, this Court is called upon under an archaic cause of action to put a price tag on the heart (love) by analyzing the love between two spouses . . . together with a third party and that party's role in allegedly breaking up the marriage that for all practical purposes was already heading for a divorce court.

The dissenters also noted that as early as 1935 states were abolishing this action "in response to a wide public sentiment . . . that such actions had been so abused, made the means of exploitation and blackmail, that the existence of such causes of action had become of greater injury than of benefit to society."

Intentional interference with custodial relationships. At the same time that actions for criminal conversation and alienation are finding favor in fewer courts, other actions are finding new support. In Stone v. Wall, 734 So.2d 1038 (Fla.1999), the court recognized an action for intentional interference with the parent-child relationship. The plaintiff father who had been given custody of his child sued members of the family of his deceased ex-wife for having failed to return the child from a visit and then concealing the child.

The court began by noting that an ancient action gave the "father an action for the abduction of his heir." Though the action was extended to the kidnapping of any child, it was not given to mothers because they had no property right in their children. In the modern day the court thought any parent or person with custodial rights should have such an action against those who interfere with such rights. The court noted that most states recognize the claim. The court observed that states widely recognized claims for "intentional interference with business relationships . . . because 'economic relations are entitled to freedom from unreasonable interference.' [   ] We find that the parental custody relationship should be entitled to no less legally recognized protection from unreasonable interference."

The following case explores the relationship between these torts and intentional infliction of emotional distress.

McDermott v. Reynolds

Supreme Court of Virginia, 2000.
530 S.E.2d 902.

KEENAN, JUSTICE.

In this appeal, we consider whether Code § 8.01–220 bars a plaintiff's action against his former wife's paramour for intentional infliction of emotional distress, when the conduct alleged would support an action for alienation of affection, a cause of action specifically prohibited by the statute.

Glenn R. McDermott [sued] William Reynolds for intentional infliction of emotional distress based on Reynolds' alleged conduct in maintaining an adulterous relationship with McDermott's wife. Reynolds [moved to dismiss], asserting that McDermott's action was "essentially one for alienation of affection" and, thus, was barred by Code § 8.01–220.

[The trial judge granted the motion to dismiss.]

On appeal, McDermott argues that his action for intentional infliction of emotional distress is separate and distinct from an action for alienation of affection. He contends that Code § 8.01–220 does not prohibit his action simply because the conduct on which his action is based has "overtones" of alienation of affection. McDermott also asserts that his damages arose from Reynolds' intentional infliction of emotional distress, not from Reynolds' alienation of the affection of McDermott's wife. We disagree with McDermott's arguments.

[Defendant's wife informed plaintiff that she had just followed defendant and plaintiff's wife, Flordeliza, to a motel.] McDermott had been married to Flordeliza for 18 years and they had three children. McDermott confronted Reynolds about his relationship with Flordeliza and demanded that Reynolds cease the adulterous relationship. Instead of ending the relationship, Reynolds "flaunted it outwardly."

Reynolds' conduct caused severe embarrassment and humiliation to McDermott and his three children. McDermott also alleged that by refusing his requests and continuing to "flaunt" the relationship, Reynolds acted maliciously and with the intent to cause McDermott severe emotional distress. As a result of his emotional distress, McDermott experienced sleeplessness, loss of weight, and interference with the performance of his duties as a physician. Further, Reynolds' conduct caused the "break up" of McDermott's family and required McDermott and his three children to seek counseling, resulting in financial losses to McDermott.

We first recognized the tort of intentional infliction of emotional distress in *Womack v. Eldridge*, [ ]. We held that a plaintiff may recover damages for emotional distress resulting from a non-tactile tort if he alleges and proves by clear and convincing evidence that: (1) the wrong-doer's conduct is intentional or reckless; (2) the conduct is outrageous and intolerable; (3) the wrongful conduct and the emotional distress are causally connected; and (4) the resulting distress is severe. [ ]

The statute at issue in this appeal, Code § 8.01–220, provides:

> A. Notwithstanding any other provision of law to the contrary, no civil action shall lie or be maintained in this Commonwealth for alienation of affection, breach of promise to marry, or criminal conversion upon which a cause of action arose or occurred on or after June 28, 1968.

> B. No civil action for seduction shall lie or be maintained where the cause of action arose or accrued on or after July 1, 1974.

The fact that Code § 8.01–220 does not contain a reference to the tort of intentional infliction of emotional distress does not affect our analysis, because that tort encompasses many types of conduct unrelated to the causes of action specified in the statute. We conclude that when the General Assembly enacted Code § 8.01–220, it manifested its intent to abolish common law actions seeking damages for a particular type of conduct, regardless of the name that a plaintiff assigns to that conduct. Therefore, in determining whether an action is barred by Code § 8.01–220, we consider the conduct alleged in the plaintiff's motion for judgment.

The essential basis of McDermott's claim is that the defendant had an adulterous relationship with McDermott's wife, which he continued in an open and notorious manner after being confronted by McDermott. This alleged conduct is precisely the type of conduct that the General Assembly intended to exclude from civil liability when it enacted Code § 8.01–220. Thus, the fact that McDermott labels his claim as intentional infliction of emotional distress and recites the elements of that tort in support of his action does not shield the action from the statutory bar. We must consider the nature of the cause of action pleaded, not merely its form, in determining whether a plaintiff has stated a cause of action that will permit recovery of damages for the conduct alleged. [   ]

We note that our conclusion is in accord with the decisions of a majority of jurisdictions that have considered claims for intentional infliction of emotional distress with reference to statutes substantially similar to Code § 8.01–220. The rationale underlying these decisions of our sister states, like our decision here, is based on the legislative intent manifested in these statutes to remove conduct of this nature from civil liability [citing cases from four states].

Our decision today reflects a disagreement with the analysis and result reached in Raftery v. Scott, 756 F.2d 335 (4th Cir.1985). There, the United States Court of Appeals for the Fourth Circuit [under Virginia law] considered an action in which a divorced spouse alleged that his former wife intentionally inflicted emotional distress on him by attempting to destroy his relationship with his son. The former wife sought dismissal of the action, contending that it essentially alleged that she caused an alienation of the child's affection for his father, and that such actions are barred by Code § 8.01–220. [   ]

The Court of Appeals held that the facts of the case independently supported a claim for intentional infliction of emotional distress, although the conduct alleged had "overtones of affection alienation." [   ] The Court stated that the two torts have different characteristics and require different proof, citing as an example the requirement for intentional infliction of emotional distress that the infliction be intentional and something more than a simple aggravation. [   ] Thus, the Court of Appeals focused its analysis on the elements of the two torts, rather than on the conduct asserted by the plaintiff.

In contrast, we have based our analysis on a defendant's alleged conduct because that methodology allows us to consider the legislative intent manifested in Code § 8.01–220. By using this analysis, we effectuate that intent and foreclose a revival of the abolished tort of alienation of affection asserted in the guise of an action for intentional infliction of emotional distress.

For these reasons, we will affirm the trial court's judgment.

[All the justices concurred.]

Notes and Questions

1. Do the allegations make out a claim for intentional infliction of emotional distress?

2. Is the court's approach to deciding whether the emotional distress action survives the statute superior to the approach taken by the *Raftery* court?

3. Does the outcome of the main case persuade you to rethink your initial reactions to the tort actions that have been abolished?

4. In C.M. v. J.M. v. W.P., 726 A.2d 998 (N.J.Ch. 1999), J.M. (plaintiff) had been led by his wife (C.M.) to believe that children born during their marriage were his own. When he found out that they were fathered by defendant (W.P.) during "an ongoing affair," he sued for intentional infliction of emotional distress. Defendant moved to dismiss on the ground that the claim was barred by the state's abolition of the actions for alienation of affections and criminal conversation. The court denied the motion because it understood the gist of the complaint to be "not being informed of the paternity of children that J.M. fathered as if his own. J.M., in opposition to W.P.s' motion to dismiss the third-party complaint, contends that the 'extreme and outrageous' conduct was not the extramarital affair between C.M. and W.P., but its ultimate effect upon the him and the children."

The court understood that J.M. was "not seeking recovery for the loss of C.M.'s 'bounty, love, and affection.' Quite differently, J.M. looks to recover for emotional distress resulting from the dissolution of his relationship with children he raised as his own. He seeks damages for his splintered relationship with his alleged children, not for his dissolved martial relationship. Therefore J.M.'s claim is not for 'alienation of affections,' and thus is not barred by the 'Heart Balm' Act.' " The court continued:

> Many of our sister states agree with [a case in New Jersey] that adultery alone, in the eyes of society, is not outrageous in and of itself. See, e.g., Strauss v. Cilek, 418 N.W.2d 378 (Iowa Ct.App.1987) (wife's tryst with husband's friend, although promiscuous, was not outrageous); Whittington v. Whittington, 766 S.W.2d 73 (Ky.Ct.App.1989) (fraud and adultery did not reach the status of outrageous); Poston v. Poston, 436 S.E.2d 854, 856 (N.C.App.1993) (wife who "repeatedly exposed her mind and spirit and body to the sexual advances" of a man other than her spouse was not outrageous).

> Some states do, however, find that an "outrage" does surface when an affair leads to the birth of a child held out to be another's.
> [   ]

>   .   .   .

> In the instant matter, it is conceded that the extra-marital affair started before, continued during, and transpired after the birth of both children. Much as in [   ], C.M. and W.P. behaved recklessly, in deliberate disregard of the high degree of probability that their affair would be uncovered after each birth, by maintaining their sexual relationship, and by concealing, from J.M., the true paternity of the children. [   ] Biologically speaking, so long as W.P. engaged in sexual intercourse with C.M., neither can deny that a very probable result of the copulation was child birth. It is illogical to argue that both W.P. and C.M. engaged in acts of sexual intercourse, prior to the conception of R.P. and K.E., yet are not both connected to the matter as a proximate cause of their births. But for W.P.s' sexual participation in this extramarital affair with C.M., these two children would not have been born. Furthermore, W.P. abandoned any obligation to the chil-

dren, while J.M. helped his wife feed, raise, fund, educate and nurture children that were not his own. This is indeed "outrageous" and, in the eyes of this court, W.P. is as accountable for these children as C.M., and thus should also bear responsibility for the consequences.

Keeping the duration of the affair a secret from J.M., as well as suppressing the true paternity of R.P. for almost three years, including four months after the paternity of K.E. had been disclosed, without regard to the high degree of probable harm to defendant, would indeed lead the average member of the community to exclaim "Outrageous!" Therefore, this court concludes that the allegations of the third-party complaint are severe enough to state a cause of action for emotional distress.

On the common law claim for intentional infliction of emotional distress, do the facts in J.M.'s case suffice?

————

Constitutional defense. In reading the next case it is important to know that in New York Times Co. v. Sullivan, 376 U.S. 254 (1964), the Court held that in libel cases public officials (later expanded to include public figures) who sue for false statements that harm their reputations must prove that the defendant made the statement knowing that it was false or recklessly uttered it without caring whether it was true or false. Proof of either prong constitutes "actual malice." The case is reprinted at p. 1000, infra.

Hustler Magazine, Inc. v. Falwell

Supreme Court of the United States, 1988.
485 U.S. 46, 108 S.Ct. 876, 99 L.Ed.2d 41.

CHIEF JUSTICE REHNQUIST delivered the opinion of the Court.

Petitioner Hustler Magazine, Inc., is a magazine of nationwide circulation. Respondent Jerry Falwell, a nationally known minister who has been active as a commentator on politics and public affairs, sued petitioner and its publisher, petitioner Larry Flynt.   .   .   .

The inside front cover of the November 1983 issue of Hustler Magazine featured a "parody" of an advertisement for Campari Liqueur that contained the name and picture of respondent and was entitled "Jerry Falwell talks about his first time." This parody was modeled after actual Campari ads that included interviews with various celebrities about their "first times." Although it was apparent by the end of each interview that this meant the first time they sampled Campari, the ads clearly played on the sexual double entendre of the general subject of "first times." Copying the form and layout of these Campari ads, Hustler's editors chose respondent as the featured celebrity and drafted an alleged "interview" with him in which he states that his "first time" was during a drunken incestuous rendezvous with his mother in an outhouse. The Hustler parody portrays respondent and his mother as drunk and immoral, and suggests that respondent is a hypocrite who preaches only when he is drunk. In small print at the bottom of the page, the ad contains the disclaimer, "ad parody—not to be taken seriously." The magazine's table of contents also lists the ad as "Fiction; Ad and Personality Parody."

Soon after the November issue of Hustler became available to the public, respondent brought this diversity action in the United States District Court for the Western District of Virginia against Hustler Magazine, Inc., Larry C. Flynt, and Flynt Distributing Co. Respondent stated in his complaint that publication of the ad parody in Hustler entitled him to recover damages for libel, invasion of privacy, and intentional infliction of emotional distress. The case proceeded to trial. At the close of the evidence, the District Court granted a directed verdict for petitioners on the invasion of privacy claim. The jury then found against respondent on the libel claim, specifically finding that the ad parody could not "reasonably be understood as describing actual facts about [respondent] or actual events in which [he] participated." [ ] The jury ruled for respondent on the intentional infliction of emotional distress claim, however, and stated that he should be awarded $100,000 in compensatory damages, as well as $50,000 each in punitive damages from petitioners [Hustler Magazine and Flynt]. Petitioners' motion for judgment notwithstanding the verdict was denied.

On appeal, the [Fourth Circuit] affirmed the judgment against petitioners. . . .[1] . . .

This case presents us with a novel question involving First Amendment limitations upon a State's authority to protect its citizens from the intentional infliction of emotional distress. We must decide whether a public figure may recover damages for emotional harm caused by the publication of an ad parody offensive to him, and doubtless gross and repugnant in the eyes of most. Respondent would have us find that a State's interest in protecting public figures from emotional distress is sufficient to deny First Amendment protection to speech that is patently offensive and is intended to inflict emotional injury, even when that speech could not reasonably have been interpreted as stating actual facts about the public figure involved. This we decline to do.

At the heart of the First Amendment is the recognition of the fundamental importance of the free flow of ideas and opinions on matters of public interest and concern. "[T]he freedom to speak one's mind is not only an aspect of individual liberty—and thus a good unto itself—but also is essential to the common quest for truth and the vitality of society as a whole." [ ] We have therefore been particularly vigilant to ensure that individual expressions of ideas remain free from governmentally imposed sanctions. The First Amendment recognizes no such thing as a "false" idea.

---

1. Under Virginia law, in an action for intentional infliction of emotional distress a plaintiff must show that the defendant's conduct (1) is intentional or reckless; (2) offends generally accepted standards of decency or morality; (3) is causally connected with the plaintiff's emotional distress; and (4) caused emotional distress that was severe. [ ]

[ ] As Justice Holmes wrote, "[W]hen men have realized that time has upset many fighting faiths, they may come to believe even more than they believe the very foundations of their own conduct that the ultimate good desired is better reached by free trade in ideas—that the best test of truth is the power of the thought to get itself accepted in the competition of the market. . . ." [ ]

The sort of robust political debate encouraged by the First Amendment is bound to produce speech that is critical of those who hold public office or those public figures who are "intimately involved in the resolution of important public questions or, by reason of their fame, shape events in areas of concern to society at large." [ ] Justice Frankfurter put it succinctly in Baumgartner v. United States, 322 U.S. 665, 673–674 (1944), when he said that "[o]ne of the prerogatives of American citizenship is the right to criticize public men and measures." Such criticism, inevitably, will not always be reasoned or moderate; public figures as well as public officials will be subject to "vehement, caustic, and sometimes unpleasantly sharp attacks," [*New York Times*]. "[T]he candidate who vaunts his spotless record and sterling integrity cannot convincingly cry 'Foul!' when an opponent or an industrious reporter attempts to demonstrate the contrary." [ ]

Of course, this does not mean that any speech about a public figure is immune from sanction in the form of damages. Since [*New York Times*] we have consistently ruled that a public figure may hold a speaker liable for the damage to reputation caused by publication of a defamatory falsehood, but only if the statement was made "with knowledge that it was false or with reckless disregard of whether it was false or not." [ ] False statements of fact are particularly valueless; they interfere with the truth-seeking function of the marketplace of ideas, and they cause damage to an individual's reputation that cannot easily be repaired by counter speech, however persuasive or effective. [ ] But even though falsehoods have little value in and of themselves, they are "nevertheless inevitable in free debate," [ ], and a rule that would impose strict liability on a publisher for false factual assertions would have an undoubted "chilling" effect on speech relating to public figures that does have constitutional value. "Freedoms of expression require 'breathing space.'" [ ] This breathing space is provided by a constitutional rule that allows public figures to recover for libel or defamation only when they can prove both that the statement was false and that the statement was made with the requisite level of culpability.

Respondent argues, however, that a different standard should apply in this case because here the State seeks to prevent not reputational damage, but the severe emotional distress suffered by the person who is the subject of an offensive publication. [ ] In respondent's view, and in the view of the Court of Appeals, so long as the utterance was intended to inflict emotional distress, was outrageous, and did in fact inflict serious emotional distress, it is of no constitutional import whether the statement was a fact or an opinion, or whether it was true or false. It is the intent to cause injury that is the gravamen of the tort, and the State's interest in preventing emotional harm simply outweighs whatever interest a speaker may have in speech of this type.

Generally speaking the law does not regard the intent to inflict emotional distress as one which should receive much solicitude, and it is quite understandable that most if not all jurisdictions have chosen to make it civilly culpable where the conduct in question is sufficiently "outrageous." But in the world of debate about public affairs, many things done with motives that are less than admirable are protected by the First Amendment. In [Garrison v. Louisiana, 379 U.S. 64 (1964)], we held that even when a speaker or writer is motivated by hatred or ill-will his expression was protected by the First Amendment:

> Debate on public issues will not be uninhibited if the speaker must run the risk that it will be proved in court that he spoke out of hatred; even if he did speak out of hatred, utterances honestly believed contribute to the free interchange of ideas and the ascertainment of truth. [   ]

Thus while such a bad motive may be deemed controlling for purposes of tort liability in other areas of the law, we think the First Amendment prohibits such a result in the area of public debate about public figures.

Were we to hold otherwise, there can be little doubt that political cartoonists and satirists would be subjected to damages awards without any showing that their work falsely defamed its subject. Webster's defines a caricature as "the deliberately distorted picturing or imitating of a person, literary style, etc. by exaggerating features or mannerisms for satirical effect." [   ] The appeal of the political cartoon or caricature is often based on exploration of unfortunate physical traits or politically embarrassing events—an exploration often calculated to injure the feelings of the subject of the portrayal. The art of the cartoonist is often not reasoned or evenhanded, but slashing and one-sided.   .   .   .

.   .   .

Despite their sometimes caustic nature, from the early cartoon portraying George Washington as an ass down to the present day, graphic depictions and satirical cartoons have played a prominent role in public and political debate. [Thomas] Nast's castigation of the Tweed Ring, Walt McDougall's characterization of presidential candidate James G. Blaine's banquet with the millionaires at Delmonico's as "The Royal Feast of Belshazzar," and numerous other efforts have undoubtedly had an effect on the course and outcome of contemporaneous debate. Lincoln's tall, gangling posture, Teddy Roosevelt's glasses and teeth, and Franklin D. Roosevelt's jutting jaw and cigarette holder have been memorialized by political cartoons with an effect that could not have been obtained by the photographer or the portrait artist. From the viewpoint of history it is clear that our political discourse would have been considerably poorer without them.

Respondent contends, however, that the caricature in question here was so "outrageous" as to distinguish it from more traditional political cartoons. There is no doubt that the caricature of respondent and his mother published in Hustler is at best a distant cousin of the political cartoons described above, and a rather poor relation at that. If it were possible by laying down a principled standard to separate the one from the other, public discourse would probably suffer little or no harm. But we doubt that there is any such standard, and we are quite sure that the pejorative description "outrageous" does not supply one. "Outrageousness" in the area of political and social discourse has an inherent subjectiveness about it which would allow a jury to impose liability on the basis of the jurors' tastes or views, or perhaps on the basis of their dislike of a particular expression. An "outrageousness" standard thus runs afoul of our longstanding refusal to allow damages to be awarded because the speech in question may have an adverse emotional impact on the audience.   .   .   .

.   .   .

Admittedly, these oft-repeated First Amendment principles, like other principles, are subject to limitations. We recognized in [FCC v. Pacifica Foundation, 438 U.S. 726 (1978)] that speech that is " 'vulgar,' 'offensive,' and 'shocking' " is "not entitled to absolute constitutional protection under all circumstances." [   ] In Chaplinsky v. New Hampshire, 315 U.S. 568 (1942), we held that a state could lawfully punish an individual for the use of insulting " 'fighting' words—those which by their very utterance inflict injury or tend to incite an immediate breach of the peace." [   ] These limitations are but recognition of the observation in [Dun & Bradstreet, Inc. v. Greenmoss Builders, 472 U.S. 749 (1985)] that this Court has "long recognized that not all speech is of equal First Amendment importance." But the sort of expression involved in this case does not seem to us to be governed by any exception to the general First Amendment principles stated above.

We conclude that public figures and public officials may not recover for the tort of intentional infliction of emotional distress by reason of publications such as the one here at issue without showing in addition that the publication contains a false statement of fact which was made with "actual malice," i.e., with knowledge that the statement was false or with reckless disregard as to whether or not it was true. This is not merely a "blind application" of the *New York Times* standard, [   ], it reflects our considered judgment that such a standard is necessary to give adequate "breathing space" to the freedoms protected by the First Amendment.

Here it is clear that respondent Falwell is a "public figure" for purposes of First Amendment law.[2] The jury found against respondent on his libel claim when it decided that the Hustler ad parody could not "reasonably be understood as describing actual facts about [respondent] or

---

2. Neither party disputes this conclusion. Respondent is the host of a nationally syndicated television show and was the founder and president of a political organization formerly known as the Moral Majority. He is also the founder of Liberty University in Lynchburg, Virginia, and is the author of several books and publications. [   ]

actual events in which [he] participated." [ ] The Court of Appeals interpreted the jury's finding to be that the ad parody "was not reasonably believable," [ ], and in accordance with our custom we accept this finding. Respondent is thus relegated to his claim for damages awarded by the jury for the intentional infliction of emotional distress by "outrageous" conduct. But for reasons heretofore stated this claim cannot, consistently with the First Amendment, form a basis for the award of damages when the conduct in question is the publication of a caricature such as the ad parody involved here. The judgment of the Court of Appeals is accordingly

Reversed.

JUSTICE KENNEDY took no part in the consideration or decision of this case.

JUSTICE WHITE, concurring in the judgment.

As I see it, the decision in [*New York Times*] has little to do with this case, for here the jury found that the ad contained no assertion of fact. But I agree with the Court that the judgment below, which penalized the publication of the parody, cannot be squared with the First Amendment.

Notes and Questions

1. Why wasn't the *New York Times* standard violated here? Wasn't the ad depiction a false statement of fact made with "actual malice"? If it wasn't a false statement of fact, as Justice White suggests in his concurring opinion, why does *New York Times* have any relevance to the case?

2. What is the strongest reason for protecting this kind of expression? Should it override the plaintiff's interest in recovery?

3. The court mentions a number of situations where expression is sometimes subject to limitation—obscenity, "fighting words," offensive material. Is the depiction here distinguishable?

4. Should the law protect some minimal level of "civility" in public discourse? See generally, R. Smolla, Jerry Falwell v. Larry Flynt: The First Amendment on Trial (1988); LeBel, Emotional Distress, the First Amendment, and "This Kind of Speech": A Heretical Perspective on *Hustler Magazine v. Falwell*, 60 Colo.L.Rev. 315 (1989); and Post, The Constitutional Concept of Public Discourse: Outrageous Opinion, Democratic Deliberation, and *Hustler Magazine v. Falwell*, 103 Harv.L.Rev. 601 (1990).

5. Would you expect the Court's holding to be limited to public figures? What if Hustler parodied, in similar fashion, an anonymous bank clerk? The distinction between public and private figures has received extensive treatment in defamation law. We return to it in the next chapter.

5. DEFENSES AND PRIVILEGES

We have seen that defenses play important roles in negligence and strict liability. So, too, with intentional torts.

a. Consent

Earlier, in the section on assumed risk as a defense to claims of negligence, we encountered the concept of "consent" as a recurring theme in the cases: Claims of express assumed risk by contractual disclosure in cases such as *Dalury*, p. 461, supra, and implied assumed risk in cases such as *Murphy*, p. 469, supra, required the courts to decide issues that could be taken as somewhat analogous to the claim, now to be considered in the context of intentional harms, that plaintiff consented to the defendant's invasive or offensive contact. Think about whether the defense claimed in the following case and notes rests on a rationale similar to that offered in the accidental harm situations previously considered (and in medical malpractice informed consent cases as well, p. 122, supra).

Hart v. Geysel

Supreme Court of Washington, 1930.
159 Wash. 632, 294 P. 570.

Main, J.

This action was brought by the administrator of the estate of Hamilton I. Cartwright, deceased, who died as the result of a blow received in a prize fight. [The complaint alleged that plaintiff's decedent and defendant engaged in a prize fight and that plaintiff died as a result of the encounter. A statute made the fight illegal. The complaint contained no allegations that the mutual combat was undertaken in anger, that there was malicious intent to seriously injure, or that there was excessive force. The trial court granted defendant's demurrer to the complaint.]

[T]he adjudicated cases, as well as the text-writers, are in conflict. One line supports what is known as the majority rule, and the other, the minority. The majority rule has been stated as follows:

Where the parties engage in mutual combat in anger, each is civilly liable to the other for any physical injury inflicted by him during the fight. The fact that the parties voluntarily engaged in the combat is no defense to an action by either of them to recover damages for personal injuries inflicted upon him by the other.

This rule is supported by the cases of [   ].

The minority rule has been stated as follows:

Where parties engage in a mutual combat in anger, the act of each is unlawful and relief will be denied them in a civil action; at least, in the absence of a showing of excessive force or malicious intent to do serious injury upon the part of the defendant.

The cases of [   ] support this rule.

.   .   .   .

The facts in the case now before us do not bring it within the authorities supporting the majority rule, because here there are no facts which show anger, malicious intent to injure, or excessive force. It may be stated that the facts of this case do not contain one element of the minority rule, that of anger. It is unnecessary, as we view it, in the present case to adopt either rule. It is sufficient to say that in our opinion one who engages in prize fighting, even though prohibited by positive law, and sustains an injury, should not have a right to recover any damages that he may sustain as the result of the combat, which he expressly consented to and engaged in as a matter of business or sport. To enforce the criminal statute against prize fighting, it is not necessary to reward the one that got the worst of the encounter at the expense of his more fortunate opponent. This view is supported by the rule tentatively adopted [in § 85 of draft Restatement of Torts. The court quoted from a draft comment to that section:]

> Notwithstanding the numerical weight of authority against the view that an assent to a breach of the peace is a legally effective consent to such invasions of interest of personality as are involved therein the minority view is preferred for the following reasons:

> The majority view is obviously an exception to the general principle that one who has sufficiently expressed his willingness to suffer a particular invasion has no right to complaint if another acts upon his consent so given. The very nature of rights of personality, which are in freedom to dispose of one's interests of personality as one pleases, fundamentally requires this to be so. There is a further principle, applicable not only in tort law but throughout the whole field of law, and perhaps more conspicuously in other subjects, to the effect that no man shall profit by his own wrongdoing.

> The majority view is an exception to both of these two fundamental principles. Clearly if a plaintiff has consented to being struck by another in the course of a brawl, his right to the control of his person and to determine by whom and how it shall be touched has not been invaded. And it is equally clear that if he has so expressed his consent to the blow that, were he not party to a breach of the peace, his assent would be an operative consent and so bar his liability, he is profiting by the illegality of his conduct if because he is party to the breach of the peace he gains a right of action which but for his criminal joinder therein he would not have had.

. . .

. . .

The judgment will be affirmed.

MITCHELL, C.J., and PARKER, TOLMAN, BEALS, MILLARD and BEELER, JJ., concur.

[Two dissenters favored the majority rule.]

Notes and Questions

1. Do the "two fundamental principles" that the Restatement draft cites to support the minority view—and which lead the *Geysel* court to recognize a consent defense—seem equally persuasive? If prize-fighting had been legal in the state would either or both principles still have equivalent persuasive force?

2. In *Vosburg v. Putney*, p. 868, supra, the court remarked that the case might have been different if the schoolboy kick had occurred in the playground instead of the classroom. Does the possibility that "consent" might have barred recovery in such a situation suggest still another rationale for the defense? Can a person jostled by others during rush hour on a subway bring battery actions against the offenders? Are these considerations relevant to *Huey*, p. 876, supra?

3. In a professional football game, plaintiff safety was near defendant fullback on pass coverage. When the pass was intercepted on the opposite side of the field, plaintiff tried to block defendant, and fell to the ground. "Acting out of anger and frustration, but without specific intent to injure, [defendant] stepped forward and struck a blow with his right forearm to the back of the kneeling plaintiff's head with sufficient force to cause both players to fall forward to the ground." The statute of limitations barred suit for an intentional tort, but plaintiff asserted claims of recklessness under § 500 of the Second Restatement, quoted at p. 437, supra, and negligence. The judge held, after trial, that plaintiff, who had 13 years of experience in professional football, "must have recognized and accepted the risk that he would be injured by such an act" as defendant committed, and the case went off on assumption of risk. On appeal, the court reversed and remanded for an assessment of plaintiff's rights in view of the official players' code and customs of the sport: "The general customs of football do not approve the intentional punching or striking of others." Hackbart v. Cincinnati Bengals, Inc., 601 F.2d 516 (10th Cir.), cert. denied 444 U.S. 931 (1979). See Nielsen, Controlling Sports Violence: Too Late for the Carrots—Bring on the Big Stick, 74 Iowa L.Rev. 681 (1989). Recall the discussion of sports participants at p. 472, supra. How might *Hackbart* be analyzed in battery-consent terms?

4. In O'Brien v. Cunard S.S. Co., 28 N.E. 266 (Mass.1891), plaintiff, a ship passenger, brought a battery action against defendant based on an alleged unconsented vaccination by the ship's surgeon, acting in anticipation of a quarantine order as the ship neared Boston. In determining whether she consented, the court observed:

> She was one of a large number of women who were vaccinated on that occasion, without, so far as appears, a word of objection from any of them. They all indicated by their conduct that they desired to avail themselves of the provisions made for their benefit. There was nothing in the conduct of the plaintiff to indicate to the surgeon that she did not wish to obtain a card which would save her from detention at quarantine, and to be vaccinated, if necessary, for that purpose. Viewing his conduct in the light of the surrounding circumstances, it was lawful; and there was no evidence tending to show that it was not.

Is the court suggesting that consent, as a protection of the plaintiff's interest in freedom from invasive conduct, is an objective inquiry, rather than a subjective determination of the individual plaintiff's expectations? Compare *Matthies*, p. 122, supra, on informed consent in the context of medical malpractice. Consider the following case on the issue of whether the inquiry is objective or subjective.

b. Self Defense

Courvoisier v. Raymond

Supreme Court of Colorado, 1896.
23 Colo. 113, 47 P. 284.

[Some rowdy men entered defendant's building after midnight without permission. With his gun drawn, he ejected them. Then they and other men gathered in the street outside as defendant stood at the steps in front of his building. Defendant claims that when plaintiff emerged from out of the crowd, defendant thought he was a member of the crowd, and shot him. Plaintiff obtained a judgment against defendant. Further facts are stated in the opinion.]

HAYT, C. J.

. . . . The parties expelled from the building, upon reaching the rear of the store, were joined by two or three others. In order to frighten these parties away, the defendant fired a shot in the air; but, instead of retreating, they passed around to the street in front, throwing stones and brickbats at the defendant, whereupon he fired a second, and perhaps a third, shot. The first shot fired attracted the attention of plaintiff, Raymond, and two deputy sheriffs, who were at the tramway depot across the street. These officers started towards Mr. Courvoisier, who still continued to shoot; but two of them stopped, when they reached the men in the street, for the purpose of arresting them, Mr. Raymond alone proceeding towards the defendant, calling out to him that he was an officer, and to stop shooting. Although the night was dark, the street was well lighted by electricity, and, when the officer approached him, defendant shaded his eyes, and, taking deliberate aim, fired, causing the injury complained of. The plaintiff's theory of the case is that he was a duly-authorized police officer, and in the discharge of his duties at the time; that the defendant was committing a breach of the peace; and that the defendant, knowing him to be a police officer, recklessly fired the shot in question. The defendant claims that the plaintiff was approaching him at the time in a threatening attitude, and that the surrounding circumstances were such as to cause a reasonable man to believe that his life was in danger, and that it was necessary to shoot in self-defense, and that defendant did so believe at the time of firing the shot.

. . . .

The next error assigned relates to the instructions given by the court to the jury, and to those requested by the defendant and refused by the court. The second instruction given by the court was clearly erroneous. The instruction is as follows: "The court instructs you that if you believe, from the evidence, that, at the time the defendant shot the plaintiff, the plaintiff was not assaulting the defendant, then your verdict should be for the plaintiff." The vice of this instruction is that it excluded from the jury a full consideration of the justification claimed by the defendant. The evidence for the plaintiff tends to show that the shooting, if not malicious, was wanton and reckless; but the evidence for the defendant tends to show that the circumstances surrounding him at the time of the shooting were such as to lead a reasonable man to believe that his life was in danger, or that he was in danger of receiving great bodily harm at the hands of the plaintiff, and the defendant testified that he did so believe. He swears that his house was invaded, shortly after midnight, by two men, whom he supposed to be burglars; that, when ejected, they were joined on the outside by three or four others; that the crowd so formed assaulted him with stones and other missiles, when, to frighten them away, he shot into the air; that, instead of going away, some one approached him from the direction of the crowd; that he supposed this person to be one of the rioters, and did not ascertain that it was the plaintiff until after the shooting. He says that he had had no previous acquaintance with plaintiff; that he did not know that he was a police officer, or that there were any police officers in the town of South Denver; that he heard nothing said at the time, by the plaintiff or any one else, that caused him to think the plaintiff was an officer; that his eyesight was greatly impaired, so that he was obliged to use glasses; and that he was without glasses at the time of the shooting, and for this reason could not see distinctly. He then adds: "I saw a man come away from the bunch of men, and come up towards me, and as I looked around I saw this man put his hand to his hip pocket. I didn't think I had time to jump aside, and therefore turned around and fired at him. I had no doubts but it was somebody that had come to rob me, because, some weeks before, Mr. Wilson's store was robbed. It is next door to mine."

By this evidence two phases of the transaction are presented for consideration: First. Was the plaintiff assaulting the defendant at the time plaintiff was shot? Second. If not, was there sufficient evidence of justification for the consideration of the jury? The first question was properly submitted, but the second was excluded by the instruction under review. The defendant's justification did not rest entirely upon the proof of assault by the plaintiff. A riot was in progress, and the defendant swears that he was attacked with missiles, hit with stones, brickbats, etc.; that he shot plaintiff, supposing him to be one of the rioters. We must assume these facts as established in reviewing the instruction, as we cannot say what the jury might have found had this evidence been submitted to them under a proper charge. By the second instruction, the conduct of those who started the fracas was eliminated from the consideration of the jury. If the jury believed, from the evidence, that the defendant would have been justified in shooting one of the rioters, had such person advanced towards him, as did the plaintiff, then it became important to determine whether the defendant mistook plaintiff for one of the rioters; and, if such a mistake was in fact made, was it excusable, in the light of all the circumstances leading up to and surrounding the commission of the act? If these issues had been resolved by the jury in favor of the defendant, he would have been entitled to a judgment. Morris v. Platt, 32 Conn. 75 [1864]; [   ]. The opinion in the first of the cases above cited contains an exhaustive review of the authorities, and is very instructive. The action was for damages resulting from a pistol-shot wound. The defendant justified under the plea of self-defense. The proof for the plaintiff tended to show that he was a mere bystander at a riot, when he received a shot aimed at another; and the court held that, if the defendant was justified in firing the shot at his antagonist, he was not liable to the plaintiff, for the reason that the act of shooting was lawful under the circumstances. Where a defendant, in a civil action like the one before us, attempts to justify on a plea of necessary self-defense, he must satisfy the jury, not only that he acted honestly in using force, but that his fears were reasonable under the circumstances, and also as to the reasonableness of the means made use of. In this case, perhaps, the verdict would not have been different, had the jury been properly instructed; but it might have been, and therefore the judgment must be reversed. Reversed.

Notes and Questions

1. Is the defendant's argument here that he did not "intend" to shoot plaintiff? If that is not his claim, why should the jury be allowed to find no liability? Can the case be reconciled with the *Garratt* court's holding that defendant Brian could be taken to have the requisite intent even if he did not "mean" to harm plaintiff? What is the interplay between the prima facie claim of battery and the counter of self-defense in these cases?

2. In Crabtree v. Dawson, 83 S.W. 557 (Ky.1904), defendant had just ejected from a party a man who then threatened to come back and attack him. Shortly thereafter, in a poorly lighted area, the plaintiff came running toward the doorway and the defendant, believing that this was the same man returning and that self-defense was called for, struck plaintiff. What if defendant's belief was reasonable though mistaken? What if he honestly but unreasonably believed self-defense was necessary? Could this case be subjected to conventional negligence analysis?

3. In a variation on *Crabtree*, assume instead that bouncer D tells his friend, F, about the incident and his concern that the evicted man will return. While D's back is turned and he is attending to another matter, P comes running toward D. F sees P running and, seeing that P fits the description of the man D had evicted, F uses reasonable force to keep P from reaching D. Should the question of F's liability to P be analyzed differently from that of D's liability in *Crabtree*? The Restatement Second § 76 states that one who defends a third person is entitled to use the same means as though defending himself if he "correctly or reasonably believes that (a) the circumstances are such as to give the third person a privilege of self-defense, and (b) his intervention is necessary for the protection of the third person." What other views might be taken of the problem?

4. Consider the following hypothetical from Morris on Torts 35 (2d ed. 1980):

> Suppose Bellicose advances on Quiet, saying, "Quiet, put up your fists; I'm going to knock the living daylights out of you." Quiet meets this threat with a quick blow on the point of Bellicose's chin, and Bellicose goes down. Bellicose then stands and staggers, obviously *hors de combat*. Nevertheless, the aroused Quiet delivers a second blow that breaks Bellicose's nose. Bellicose brings an assault and battery action claiming damages for the broken nose.

The authors explore whether by combining consent and self-defense it may be possible for Quiet to escape liability. Is *Hart v. Geysel* relevant?

5. In the cited *Morris v. Platt*, the innocent bystander was hit by an errant shot fired in legitimate self-defense. Does that case raise the same issue as in *Courvoisier*?

c. Protection of Property

Katko v. Briney

Supreme Court of Iowa, 1971.
183 N.W.2d 657.

[In 1957, defendant wife had inherited farmland on which her grandparents and parents had lived. No one occupied the house after the death of her parents. Defendant husband attempted to care for the land, but kept no machinery on it. Between 1957 and 1967 "there occurred a series of trespassing and housebreaking events with loss of some household items, the breaking of windows and 'messing up of the property in general.'" In July, 1967, the events that gave rise to this case occurred. A jury returned a verdict for plaintiff and against defendants husband and wife for $20,000 actual and $10,000 punitive damages. The trial judge rejected motions for judgment notwithstanding the verdict and for a new trial. Further facts appear in the opinion.]

MOORE, CHIEF JUSTICE.

The primary issue presented here is whether an owner may protect personal property in an unoccupied boarded-up farm house against trespassers and thieves by a spring gun capable of inflicting death or serious injury.

We are not here concerned with a man's right to protect his home and members of his family. Defendants' home was several miles from the scene of the incident to which we refer infra.

Plaintiff's action is for damages resulting from serious injury caused by a shot from a 20–gauge spring shotgun set by defendants in a bedroom of an old farm house which had been uninhabited for several years. Plaintiff and his companion, Marvin McDonough, had broken and entered the house to find and steal old bottles and dated fruit jars which they considered antiques.

. . .

Defendants through the years boarded up the windows and doors in an attempt to stop the intrusions. They had posted "no trespass" signs on the land several years before 1967. The nearest one was 35 feet from the house. On June 11, 1967 defendants set "a shotgun trap" in the north bedroom. After Mr. Briney cleaned and oiled his 20–gauge shotgun, the power of which he was well aware, defendants took it to the old house where they secured it to an iron bed with the barrel pointed at the bedroom door. It was rigged with wire from the doorknob to the gun's trigger so it would fire when the door was opened. Briney first pointed the gun so an intruder would be hit in the stomach but at Mrs. Briney's suggestion it was lowered to hit the legs. He admitted he did so "because I was mad and tired of being tormented" but "he did not intend to injure anyone". He gave no explanation of why he used a loaded shell and set it to hit a person already in the house. Tin was nailed over the bedroom window. The spring gun could not be seen from the outside. No warning of its presence was posted.

Plaintiff lived with his wife and worked regularly as a gasoline station attendant in Eddyville, seven miles from the old house. He had observed it for several years while hunting in the area and considered it as being abandoned. He knew it had long been uninhabited. In 1967 the area around the house was covered with high weeds. Prior to July 16, 1967 plaintiff and McDonough had been to the premises and found several old bottles and fruit jars which they took and added to their collection of antiques. On the latter date about 9:30 p.m. they made a second trip to the Briney property. They entered the old house by removing a board from a porch window which was without glass. While McDonough was looking around the kitchen area plaintiff went to another part of the house. As he started to open the north bedroom door the shotgun went off striking him in the right leg above the ankle bone. Much of his leg, including part of the tibia, was blown away. Only by McDonough's assistance was plaintiff able to get out of the house and after crawling some distance was put in his vehicle and rushed to a doctor and then to a hospital. He remained in the hospital 40 days.

[After some doubt, plaintiff's leg was saved but was permanently deformed and shortened. He wore a cast for one year and a brace for another year. His medical bills totaled about $3,600.]

III.   Plaintiff testified he knew he had no right to break and enter the house with intent to steal bottles and fruit jars therefrom. He further testified he had entered a plea of guilty to larceny in the nighttime of property of less than $20 value from a private building. He stated he had been fined $50 and costs and paroled during good behavior from a 60–day jail sentence. Other than minor traffic charges this was plaintiff's first brush with the law. On this civil case appeal it is not our prerogative to review the disposition made of the criminal charge against him.

IV. The main thrust of defendants' defense in the trial court and on this appeal is that "the law permits use of a spring gun in a dwelling or warehouse for the purpose of preventing the unlawful entry of a burglar or thief." They repeated this contention in their exceptions to the trial court's instructions 2, 5 and 6. They took no exception to the trial court's statement of the issues or to other instructions.

In the statement of issues the trial court stated plaintiff and his companion committed a felony when they broke and entered defendants' house. In instruction 2 the court referred to the early case history of the use of spring guns and stated under the law their use was prohibited except to prevent the commission of felonies of violence and where human life is in danger. The instruction included a statement that breaking and entering is not a felony of violence.

[Instruction 5 told the jury "that one may use reasonable force in the protection of his property, but such right is subject to the qualification that one may not use such means of force as will take human life or inflict great bodily injury. Such is the rule even though the injured party is a trespasser and is in violation of the law himself." Instruction 6 stated in part that "An owner of premises is prohibited from willfully or intentionally injuring a trespasser by means of force that either takes life or inflicts great bodily injury; and therefore a person owning a premise is prohibited from setting out 'spring guns' and like dangerous devices which will likely take life or inflict great bodily injury, for the purpose of harming trespassers. . . . The only time when such conduct of setting a 'spring gun' or a like dangerous device is justified would be when the trespasser was committing a felony of violence or a felony punishable by death, or where the trespasser was endangering human life by his act."]

The overwhelming weight of authority, both textbook and case law, supports the trial court's statement of the applicable principles of law.

Prosser on Torts, Third Edition, pages 116–118 [1964], states:

. . . the law has always placed a higher value upon human safety than upon mere rights in property, it is the accepted rule that there is no privilege to use any force calculated to cause death or serious bodily injury to repel the threat to land or chattels, unless there is also such a threat to the defendant's personal safety as to justify a self-defense. . . . spring guns and other man-killing devices are not justifiable against a mere trespasser, or even a petty thief. They are privileged only against those upon whom the landowner, if he were present in person would be free to inflict injury of the same kind.

[The court observed that Second Restatement § 85 and another treatise agreed with Prosser.]

In Hooker v. Miller, 37 Iowa 613 [1873], we held defendant vineyard owner liable for damages resulting from a spring gun shot although plaintiff was a trespasser and there to steal grapes. At pages 614–15, this statement is made:

This court has held that a mere trespass against property other than a dwelling is not a sufficient justification to authorize the use of a deadly weapon by the owner in its defense; and that if death results in such a case it will be murder, though the killing be actually necessary to prevent the trespass. [   ]

At page 617 this court said: "(T)respassers and other inconsiderable violators of the law are not to be visited by barbarous punishments or prevented by inhuman inflictions of bodily injuries."

[The court cited several cases from other states to the same effect.]

The legal principles stated by the trial court in instructions 2, 5 and 6 are well established and supported by the authorities cited and quoted supra. There is no merit in defendants' objections and exceptions thereto. Defendants' various motions based on the same reasons stated in exceptions to instructions were properly overruled.

V.   Plaintiff's claim and the jury's allowance of punitive damages, under the trial court's instructions relating thereto, were not at any time or in any manner challenged by defendants in the trial court as not allowable. We therefore are not presented with the problem of whether the $10,000 award should be allowed to stand.

We express no opinion as to whether punitive damages are allowable in this type of case. If defendants' attorneys wanted that issue decided it was their duty to raise it in the trial court.

. . .

Under our law punitive damages are not allowed as a matter of right. [   ] When malice is shown or when a defendant acted with wanton and reckless disregard of the rights of others, punitive damages may be allowed as punishment to the defendant and as a deterrent to others. Although not meant to compensate a plaintiff, the result is to increase his recovery. He is the fortuitous beneficiary of such an award simply because there is no one else to receive it.

. . .

Study and careful consideration of defendants' contentions on appeal reveal no reversible error.

Affirmed.

All Justices concur except LARSON, J., who dissents.

LARSON, JUSTICE (dissenting).

. . .

It is my feeling that the majority oversimplifies the impact of this case on the law, not only in this but other jurisdictions, and that it has not thought through all the ramifications of this holding.

. . .

[T]his appeal presents two vital questions which are as novel as they are difficult. They are, (1) is the owner of a building in which are kept household furniture, appliances, and valuables, but not occupied by a person or persons, liable in damages to an intruder who in the nighttime broke into and entered the building with the intent to steal and was shot and seriously injured by a spring gun allegedly set by the owner to frighten intruders from his property, and (2) if he is liable for compensatory damages, is this a proper case for the allowance of exemplary or punitive damages?

.   .   .

Although I am aware of the often-repeated statement that personal rights are more important than property rights, where the owner has stored his valuables representing his life's accumulations, his livelihood business, his tools and implements, and his treasured antiques as appears in the case at bar, and where the evidence is sufficient to sustain a finding that the installation was intended only as a warning to ward off thieves and criminals, I can see no compelling reason why the use of such a device alone would create liability as a matter of law.

[The dissent thought the jury instructions erroneous because they failed to recognize a defense to the intentional tort claims "if the defendant did not intend to cause serious harm or fatal injury." He also objected to allowing punitive damages to a plaintiff engaged in criminal activity.]

Being convinced that there was reversible error in the court's instructions, that the issue of intent in placing the spring gun was not clearly presented to the jury, and that the issue as to punitive damages should not have been presented to the jury, I would reverse and remand the matter for a new trial.

The majority seem to ignore the evident issue of punitive policy involved herein and uphold the punitive damage award on a mere technical rule of civil procedure.

Notes and Questions

1. Should the result have been different if defendant and his wife were occupying the house that evening? What if they occasionally occupied it, but were not there that night? What if plaintiff can establish that he was unarmed and interested solely in stealing more fruit jars?

2. Should the result be different if the defendant erected signs, "These premises protected by spring gun"? For sharply divergent comments on this problem, see Palmer, The Iowa Spring Gun Case: A Study in American Gothic, 56 Iowa L.Rev. 1219 (1971); Posner, Wounding or Killing to Protect a Property Interest, 14 J.L. & Econ. 201 (1971); Comment, Use of Mechanical Devices in the Defense of Property, 24 S.Cal.L.Rev. 133 (1972).

3. Posner argued that neither blanket permission nor blanket prohibition of the use of deadly force to protect property is likely to be the optimal rule. He proposed a "reasonableness test" to determine whether the use of deadly force is justified to protect property interests. The following considerations would be relevant:

(1) the value of the property at stake measured against the costs of human life and limb;

(2) the existence of an adequate legal remedy as an alternative to the use of force;

(3) the location of the property in terms of the difficulty of protecting it by other means;

(4) the kind of warning given;

(5) the deadliness of the device used;

(6) the character of the conflicting activities;

(7) the cost of avoiding interference by other means.

Posner maintained that "the dominant purpose of rules of liability is to channel people's conduct, and in such a way that the value of interfering activities is maximized." Is this an area in which the legal rule is likely to have a strong impact in shaping behavior? Is Posner's formulation likely to allow more, or less, use of force to protect property than a standard absolutely prohibiting the use of deadly force except to prevent felonies of violence, felonies punishable by death, and acts that threaten human injury? Is the role of the jury under Posner's test a factor that influences your assessment of it? If so, which way does it cut? For a wide-ranging economic analysis of intentional torts, see Landes and Posner, An Economic Theory of Intentional Torts, 1 Int'l Rev. of Law & Econ. 127 (1981).

d. Private Necessity

Suppose a private party uses, or in an extreme case, destroys the property of another in order to preserve his or her person or property of greater value. Is there a privilege to do so?

In the leading case of Ploof v. Putnam, 71 A. 188 (Vt.1908), plaintiff moored his sloop at a dock on defendant's private island in order to avoid the hazards of a storm. Defendant's servant cut loose the sloop which, as a result, was battered by the storm. The sloop and its contents were destroyed; plaintiff and his family were injured. In plaintiff's suit for damages, defendant argued that he was simply protecting his private property from use by plaintiff. The court awarded damages to plaintiff, recognizing a privilege, born of necessity, to use defendant's property.

Assuming a privilege exists, there is the further question whether the party exercising the privilege should nonetheless be liable for damages if in fact the "taking" of another's property results in damage. In *Ploof,* that issue would have been whether defendant had a claim for any damage done to the dock. The issue is raised by the famous case that follows. In reading this case, keep in mind, as well, the question that has been fundamental to our inquiry in this section: what are the essential characteristics of harm done to another that constitute an "intentional" tort?

Vincent v. Lake Erie Transportation Co.

Supreme Court of Minnesota, 1910.
109 Minn. 456, 124 N.W. 221.

O'BRIEN, J.

The steamship Reynolds, owned by the defendant, was for the purpose of discharging her cargo on November 27, 1905, moored to plaintiffs' dock in Duluth. While the unloading of the boat was taking place a storm from the northeast developed, which at about ten o'clock p.m., when the unloading was completed, had so grown in violence that the wind was then moving at fifty miles per hour and continued to increase during the night. There is some evidence that one, and perhaps two, boats were able to enter the harbor that night, but it is plain that navigation was practically suspended from the hour mentioned until the morning of the twenty ninth, when the storm abated, and during that time no master would have been justified in attempting to navigate his vessel, if he could avoid doing so. After the discharge of the cargo the Reynolds signaled for a tug to tow her from the dock, but none could be obtained because of the severity of the storm. If the lines holding the ship to the dock had been cast off, she would doubtless have drifted away; but, instead, the lines were kept fast, and as soon as one parted or chafed it was replaced, sometimes with a larger one. The vessel lay upon the outside of the dock, her bow to the east, the wind and waves striking her starboard quarter with such force that she was constantly being lifted and thrown against the dock, resulting in its damage, as found by the jury, to the amount of $500.

We are satisfied that the character of the storm was such that it would have been highly imprudent for the master of the Reynolds to have attempted to leave the dock or to have permitted his vessel to drift away from it. . . . Nothing more was demanded of them than ordinary prudence and care, and the record in this case fully sustains the contention of the appellant that, in holding the vessel fast to the dock, those in charge of her exercised good judgment and prudent seamanship.

It is claimed by the respondent that it was negligence to moor the boat at an exposed part of the wharf, and to continue in that position after it became apparent that the storm was to be more than usually severe. We do not agree with this position. The part of the wharf where the vessel was moored appears to have been commonly used for that purpose. It was situated within the harbor at Duluth, and must, we think, be considered a proper and safe place, and would undoubtedly have been such during what would be considered a very severe storm. The storm which made it unsafe was one which surpassed in violence any which might have reasonably been anticipated.

The appellant contends by ample assignments of error that, because its conduct during the storm was rendered necessary by prudence and good seamanship under conditions over which it had no control, it cannot be held liable for any injury resulting to the property of others, and claims that the jury should have been so instructed. An analysis of the charge given by the trial court is not necessary, as in our opinion the only question for the jury was the amount of damages which the plaintiffs were entitled to recover, and no complaint is made upon that score.

The situation was one in which the ordinary rules regulating property rights were suspended by forces beyond human control, and if, without the direct intervention of some act by the one sought to be held liable, the property of another was injured, such injury must be attributed to the act of God, and not to the wrongful act of the person sought to be charged. If during the storm the Reynolds had entered the harbor, and while there had become disabled and been thrown against the plaintiffs' dock, the plaintiffs could not have recovered. Again, if while attempting to hold fast to the dock the lines had parted, without any negligence, and the vessel carried against some other boat or dock in the harbor, there would be no liability upon her owner. But here those in charge of the vessel deliberately and by their direct efforts held her in such a position that the damage to the dock resulted, and, having thus preserved the ship at the expense of the dock, it seems to us that her owners are responsible to the dock owners to the extent of the injury inflicted.

. . .

Theologians hold that a starving man may, without moral guilt, take what is necessary to sustain life; but it could hardly be said that the obligation would not be upon such person to pay the value of the property so taken when he became able to do so. And so public necessity, in times of war or peace, may require the taking of private property for public purposes; but under our system of jurisprudence compensation must be made.

Let us imagine in this case that for the better mooring of the vessel those in charge of her had appropriated a valuable cable lying upon the dock. No matter how justifiable such appropriation might have been, it would not be claimed that, because of the overwhelming necessity of the situation, the owner of the cable could not recover its value.

This is not a case where life or property was menaced by any object or thing belonging to the plaintiffs, the destruction of which became necessary to prevent the threatened disaster. Nor is it a case where, because of the act of God, or unavoidable accident, the infliction of the injury was beyond the control of the defendant, but is one where the defendant prudently and advisedly availed itself of the plaintiffs' property for the purpose of preserving its own more valuable property, and the plaintiffs are entitled to compensation for the injury done.

Order affirmed.

Lewis, J. (dissenting).

I dissent. It was assumed on the trial before the lower court that appellant's liability depended on whether the master of the ship might, in the exercise of reasonable care, have sought a place of safety before the storm made it impossible to leave the dock. The majority opinion assumes that the evidence is conclusive that appellant moored its boat at respondents' dock pursuant to contract, and that the vessel was lawfully in position at the time the additional cables were fastened to the dock, and the reasoning of the opinion is that, because appellant made use of the stronger cables to hold the boat in position, it became liable under the rule that it had voluntarily made use of the property of another for the purpose of saving its own.

In my judgment, if the boat was lawfully in position at the time the storm broke, and the master could not, in the exercise of due care have left that position without subjecting his vessel to the hazards of the storm, then the damage to the dock, caused by the pounding of the boat, was the result of an inevitable accident. If the master was in the exercise of due care, he was not at fault. The reasoning of the opinion admits that if the ropes, or cables, first attached to the dock had not parted, or if, in the first instance, the master had used the stronger cables, there would be no liability. If the master could not, in the exercise of reasonable care, have anticipated the severity of the storm and sought a place of safety before it became impossible, why should he be required to anticipate the severity of the storm, and, in the first instance, use the stronger cables?

I am of the opinion that one who constructs a dock to the navigable line of waters, and enters into contractual relations with the owner of a vessel to moor the same, takes the risk of damage to his dock by a boat caught there by a storm, which event could not have been avoided in the exercise of due care, and further, that the legal status of the parties in such a case is not changed by renewal of cables to keep the boat from being cast adrift at the mercy of the tempest.

JAGGARD, J.

I concur with LEWIS, J.

Notes and Questions

1. Is it important to the majority that defendant continued to replace the fraying lines? Why does the dissent regard this behavior as inconsequential? Is one position more consistent with the act of God defense than the other?

2. Is *Vincent* an intentional tort case? Would the definition of intent utilized in *Garratt* and the Restatement apply here? Why does the majority think that the defendant should be held liable? Does the rationale bear any similarity to the basis for strict liability?

3. Suppose there had been only a one percent chance that securing the vessel would result in damage to the dock. Would the case then be one of unintended harm? If so, would defendant still have been liable—assuming the likelihood of harm to the dock was far less than the expected harm to the (unsecured) boat? Can the liability rules governing these two situations be reconciled? See Seavey, Negligence–Subjective or Objective?, 41 Harv.L.Rev. L, 8 (1927).

4. Is the pre-existing contractual relationship between the parties in *Vincent* of any relevance to the assignment of liability? On this score, do you agree with the assumed risk argument at the end of the dissenting opinion? Why does the majority make no reference to the contract? In a case like *Ploof,* where the parties had no contractual relationship, should the result be different?

5. Consider the following analysis from Morris on Torts 41–42 (2d ed. 1980):

> A justification for liability may possibly be brought to light by comparing the Vincent case to Cordas v. Peerless Transportation Co. [27 N.Y.S.2d 198 (N.Y.City Ct.1941)]. In the *Cordas* case, a pursued armed bandit jumped into a taxi-cab and ordered the driver to get going. The driver started the cab, shifted into neutral, suddenly slammed on his brakes to throw the bandit off-balance, and leaped out. The cab veered onto the sidewalk and injured a pedestrian. The court held the driver was not liable to the pedestrian in spite of the great likelihood that the driver's intentional act, done in a congested downtown locale, would cause injury and was done to save his own hide.

> The cab case differs from the dock case in several ways. The cab driver's conduct was fraught with only a possibility of injury; the ship captain's conduct was sure to injure the dock. The cab driver had much less time for deliberation than did the mariner. Another distinction may, however, have great significance. If the wharfinger could not hold the mariner responsible, he might have been tempted to cut the ship loose and risk liability for whatever harm might befall the ship or crew. That risk might not materialize; if the ship happened to weather the storm without damage, the dock owner would then incur no liability. He was sure that his dock would be harmed if the ship remained fast. But if he were assured of compensation for damage to the dock, he would have no incentive to cast the ship loose. In the cab case, however, the pedestrian could do nothing to impede the cab driver from executing his plan of escape. No promise of compensation is needed to affect the pedestrian's behavior; he need not be given assurance of compensation to encourage cooperation.

Do these considerations seem critical? In Fletcher, Corrective Justice for Moderns, 106 Harv.L.Rev. 1658, 1670–71 (1993), the author argues that the key to the case is "the inroad made by the emergency situation on the plaintiff's property rights. The plaintiff is forced, under the circumstances, to keep his dock open to someone who finds himself there when the storm comes up. Because his rights are compromised in the interests of another person, tort law makes up for what he loses under the law of property." Is this a convincing rationale? Compare the explanation of the case from a restitutionary perspective in E. Weinrib, The Idea of Private Law (1995) at 196–203.

In B. Fried, The Progressive Assault on Laissez Faire: Robert Hale and the First Law and Economics Movement 85 (1998), Professor Fried discussed Robert Hale's view of *Vincent*:

As Hale noted . . . this decision not only deprived plaintiff of the absolute right to exclude the defendant but also deprived plaintiff of the right to exact whatever defendant would have paid for the right not to be excluded. "The abrogation of the absolute power to exclude in view of the emergency abrogates likewise the power to take advantage of the shipowner's special needs, just as the power to appropriate property by eminent domain denies the owner the opportunity to take advantage of the taker's special needs."

Are these perspectives helpful ways to approach *Vincent*?

7. Is one party a superior risk-bearer to the other in *Vincent*? In what sense? Should that factor be given great weight? See R. Keeton, Conditional Fault in the Law of Torts, 72 Harv.L.Rev. 401 (1959).

8. Consider the following example from the Restatement (Second) of Torts § 73:

A, while driving B, a child of three, in a sleigh, is pursued by a pack of wolves which are rapidly closing upon him. To gain time A throws B to the wolves. The time consumed by the wolves in devouring B enables A to reach shelter a few seconds before the pack can reach him. A is subject to liability under a wrongful death statute for the death of B.

Do you agree that A should be held liable? What are the damages in the wolf case if there is liability? Is the situation distinguishable from *Vincent* and *Cordas*? Should the wolf example be decided differently if A's action were taken to save the lives of seven others as well as his own?

9. Is there any substance to the privilege of private necessity if the party exercising the privilege is obligated to pay damages for harm done?

10. *Public necessity.* Sometimes property is destroyed for the protection of the general public. In Harrison v. Wisdom, 7 Heisk. (55 Tenn.) 99 (1872), the defendants were residents of a town being approached by the Federal army. The defendants destroyed plaintiff's liquor supply to keep it from the troops. The court concluded that in cases of necessity involving protection of the public, "a private mischief is to be endured rather than a public inconvenience." Also, "Necessity, says Lord Coke, makes that lawful which would be otherwise unlawful: 8 Coke, 69." Should it matter whether the troops ever reached the town?

The same approach was adopted in Surocco v. Geary, 3 Cal. 69 (1853), in which the defendant, who was alcalde of San Francisco ordered the destruction of plaintiff's house to prevent the spread of a major fire. The suit was not for the damage to the house, which would clearly have been destroyed anyway, but rather for chattels that the plaintiff could have removed before the house caught fire, but were lost when the house was blown up. The court denied recovery, saying that in such situations "individual rights of property give way to the higher laws of impending necessity." Are these cases consistent with *Vincent*? As far as compensation is concerned, are there reasons to distinguish between private and public necessity? For an overview of this subject, see Christie, The Defense of

Necessity Considered from the Legal and Moral Points of View, 48 Duke L.J. 975 (1999).

The court in *Geary* denied that this was a "taking" of private property in the constitutional sense, a view that was sustained in United States v. Caltex (Philippines), Inc., 344 U.S. 149 (1952), in which the armed forces destroyed valuable property belonging to the plaintiff to keep it from falling into enemy hands. The Court, 7–2, held that there was no compensable taking. The majority noted that "The terse language of the Fifth Amendment is no comprehensive promise that the United States will make whole all who suffer from every ravage and burden of war. This Court has long recognized that in wartime many losses must be attributed solely to the fortunes of war, and not to the sovereign." Justices Black and Douglas dissented on the ground that the property was taken as clearly as are food and animals requisitioned for military use: "Whenever the Government determines that one person's property . . . is essential to the war effort and appropriates it for the common good, the public purse, rather than the individual, should bear the loss."

In Muskopf v. Corning Hospital Dist., 359 P.2d 457 (Cal.1961), Justice Traynor noted that abolishing governmental immunity "does not mean that the state is liable for all harms that result from its activities. . . . Thus the harm resulting from free competition among individuals is not actionable, nor is the harm resulting from the diversion of business by the state's relocation of a highway." Why must the state pay for property it takes to build a new highway but not for business losses caused to merchants along the old route? Should the state be able to claim reimbursement from those whose property values increase because of the new highway? What about paying dairy farmers when the state legalizes the sale of oleomargarine? In the same vein, should the government compensate those who are hurt by decreased government spending or emphasis in their fields? Those who lose their jobs may receive unemployment benefits but how about those harmed derivatively, like the restaurants and gas stations near a defense plant that is closed down?

There is a vast literature on compensable takings, a subject which is explored in the courses in Property and Constitutional Law.

B.   GOVERNMENT LIABILITY

In Chapter III, we considered the circumstances in which various governmental entities might retain a common law immunity from tort liability. In this section, we consider claims against government officials that usually involve deliberate interference with claimed legal rights of citizens. Our earlier focus was liability for miscalculation or negligence. Now we address cases that raise the issue of abuse of power by government officials.

1.   THE FEDERAL CIVIL RIGHTS ACTION

In the years following the end of the Civil War, widespread violence and lawlessness raged in the South. Murders, whippings and other atrocities were perpetrated by members of the Ku Klux Klan and other vigilante groups against blacks and Union sympathizers. Although virtually all of these acts of terrorism were violations of state and local law, law enforcement officials did little to intervene and, in some cases, they tacitly condoned the illegal acts and even conspired with the outlaws. In response to this situation, Congress, under its power to enforce the recently ratified Fourteenth Amendment, passed the Ku Klux Klan Act of 1871. Section 1 of the Act, now codified as 42 U.S.C. § 1983, provides:

> Every person who, under color of any statute, ordinance, regulation, custom, or usage, of any State or Territory, subjects, or causes to be subjected, any citizen of the United States or other person within the jurisdiction thereof to the deprivation of any rights, privileges, or immunities secured by the Constitution and laws, shall be liable to the party injured in an action at law, suit in equity, or other proper proceeding for redress.

The section lay dormant until Monroe v. Pape, 365 U.S. 167 (1961), in which plaintiffs alleged that "13 Chicago police officers broke into [their] home in the early morning, routed them from bed, made them stand naked in the living room, and ransacked every room, emptying drawers and ripping mattress covers." Further, Mr. Monroe was taken to the police station and held for ten hours without being arraigned or allowed to call his family or attorney. He was released without charges being filed. Plaintiffs alleged that the officers had no search or arrest warrants. They sued the officers and the City of Chicago under § 1983, claiming that defendants acted "under color of the statutes, ordinances, regulations, customs and usages" of the city and state.

The Court upheld the complaint. Although the original purposes of the statute were to "override certain kinds of state laws" and to "provide a remedy where state law was inadequate," the "purposes were much broader. The *third* aim was to provide a federal remedy where the state remedy, though adequate in theory, was not available in practice." The federal remedy was held "supplementary to the state remedy, and the latter need not be first sought and refused before the federal one is invoked." Thus, the fact that Illinois law outlawed unreasonable searches and seizures did not bar the present suit.

The Court then concluded that the officers had acted "under color of" state law, relying on an earlier case in which a plurality had concluded that "[m]isuse of power, possessed by virtue of state law and made possible only because the wrongdoer is clothed with the authority of state law, is action taken 'under color of' state law."

To state a claim under § 1983, a plaintiff must show that a "person" acting under color of state law, custom, or usage deprived him or her of a federally protected constitutional right. Each of the elements of the prima facie case discussed in *Monroe* has led to extensive litigation, but the principles established by *Monroe* have been generally followed. For an overview of the historical development of § 1983 doctrine, see Eisenberg, Section 1983: Doctrinal Foundations and An Empirical Study, 67 Cornell

L.Rev. 482 (1982). See also Weinberg, The *Monroe* Mystery Solved: Beyond the "Unhappy History" Theory of Civil Rights Litigation, 1991 B.Y.U.L.Rev. 737 (explaining the development of § 1983 litigation in terms of the Bill of Rights jurisprudence of the Warren Court).

"Every person." In Monell v. New York City Dept. of Social Services, 436 U.S. 658 (1978), the Court held that "every person" was broad enough to include municipal corporations as potential defendants. The Court went on to say that "a local government may not be sued under § 1983 for an injury inflicted solely by its employees or agents. Instead, it is when execution of a government's policy or custom, whether made by its lawmakers or by those whose edicts or acts may fairly be said to represent official policy, inflicts the injury that the government as an entity is responsible under § 1983."

Is this limitation likely to insulate governmental entities from liability very often? In Pembaur v. City of Cincinnati, 475 U.S. 469 (1986), the Court held that a single decision by a county prosecutor that deprived an individual of his Fourth and Fourteenth Amendment rights satisfied *Monell*'s "official policy" standard. The prosecutor had given local sheriffs the go-ahead to break down plaintiff's office door and conduct a search. The Supreme Court reinstated plaintiff's § 1983 action for the allegedly unlawful search. Because state law authorized sheriffs to obtain instructions to search from local prosecutors, and because the sheriffs in the case at bar had followed the prosecutor's directive, the prosecutor effectively acted as the county's "final decisionmaker," thereby exposing the county to § 1983 liability.

In Board of the County Commissioners of Bryan County, Oklahoma v. Brown, 520 U.S. 397 (1997), the Supreme Court held that in cases presenting difficult fault and causation questions, the plaintiff had to show more than that employee conduct is properly attributable to the municipality. Brown brought a § 1983 claim against the county based on a deputy's use of excessive force to remove her from her vehicle. The plaintiff claimed that the sheriff's decision to hire the deputy without performing an adequate background check on the new employee violated her federal rights. The deputy had a prior record of driving infractions, assault and battery, and other misdemeanors. The Court held that to establish a municipal policy necessary to give rise to liability, the plaintiff must show that deliberate conduct attributable to the municipality was the "moving force" behind the alleged injury. Specifically, the municipality must take the action with the requisite degree of culpability, and the plaintiff must establish a direct causal link between the municipal action and the deprivation of federal rights. The Court stated that a full review of the deputy's record would not necessarily have revealed that a reasonable policymaker should have concluded that the deputy's use of excessive force would be the "plainly obvious consequence" of the decision to hire the deputy.

A recurring issue before the Court has been whether a municipality's failure to provide adequate training to certain employees, most notably its police force, amounts to an official policy. In City of Canton v. Harris, 489

U.S. 378 (1989), plaintiff was arrested and brought to a police station where she twice slumped to the floor. The police left plaintiff on the floor so she wouldn't fall again, but they never summoned medical assistance for her. After the police released plaintiff, she was taken to a hospital and diagnosed as suffering from various emotional ailments. Plaintiff brought a § 1983 action against the city for its deprivation of her right to receive necessary medical care while in custody. She pointed to the city policy that gave station shift commanders the sole discretion to determine when an arrestee required medical care and the city's failure to train specially its officers to recognize when to summon such care. The Court, in remanding for further proceedings, held that "[t]he inadequacy of police training may serve as a basis for § 1983 liability only where the failure to train amounts to deliberate indifference to the rights of persons with whom the police come into contact." Furthermore, the Court required that the asserted training deficiency must actually have caused the officers' indifference to plaintiff's medical needs.

What constitutes "deliberate indifference?" In Farmer v. Brennan, 511 U.S. 825 (1994), a transsexual prison inmate claimed violation of Eighth Amendment rights by prison officials who placed him in the general prison population, allegedly subjecting him to special risks of harm, which came to fruition. In response to plaintiff's claim of deliberate indifference, the court held that its objective standard under *Canton* was not the appropriate test for cruel and unusual punishment under the Eighth Amendment. Rather, a subjective test was called for:

> We hold instead that a prison official cannot be found liable under the Eighth Amendment for denying an inmate humane conditions of confinement unless the official knows of and disregards an excessive risk to inmate health and safety.

The Court also refined *Canton* by concluding that not every failure to train government employees amounts to a constitutional violation. In Collins v. City of Harker Heights, 503 U.S. 115 (1992), the Court rejected a claim involving the death of a city sanitation worker who was asphyxiated in a manhole while attempting to unstop a sewer line. The Court held that the city's inadequate training of the employee did not amount to a violation of due process.

"Acting under color" of state law. In *Monroe,* the Court held that conduct under color of state law embraced conduct of a state official contrary to state law. This holding has been reaffirmed, and today the state action requirement under § 1983 is generally assumed to be identical to the threshold required by the Fourteenth Amendment. In Polk County v. Dodson, 454 U.S. 312 (1981), the court interpreted "under color of state law" narrowly by holding that a public defender was performing an essentially independent, private function in deciding how best to represent her client.

Even private action may be considered "state action" if made possible only because of state support or acquiescence, as where a shopkeeper detains a suspected shoplifter pursuant to an agreement with the police.

Adickes v. S.H. Kress & Co., 398 U.S. 144 (1970). In Richardson v. McKnight, 521 U.S. 399 (1997), the Court held that prison guards who are employed by a private prison management firm are subject to § 1983 liability. In addition, the Court held that the prison guards were not entitled to qualified immunity from § 1983 suits because it could not identify a history or purpose of granting immunity to privately employed prison guards.

See generally, Winter, The Meaning of "Under Color of" Law, 91 Mich.L.Rev. 323 (1992).

"Who subjects another or causes another to be subjected to." Section 1983 creates a cause of action only against a person who "subjects" another or "causes" another "to be subjected" to the deprivation of constitutional rights. A threshold issue was raised in DeShaney v. Winnebago County Dept. of Social Services, 489 U.S. 189 (1989), in which a child under the jurisdiction of defendant county department of social services was seriously injured by his father's sustained pattern of physical abuse. The § 1983 claim against defendant was for denial of a liberty interest in due process by failing to intervene and provide protection. In denying any affirmative obligation on the part of the governmental agency, the Court stated:

> . . . it is well to remember once again that the harm was inflicted not by the State of Wisconsin, but by [plaintiff's] father. The most that can be said of the state functionaries in this case is that they stood by and did nothing when suspicious circumstances dictated a more active role for them.

Recall the discussion of *Riss v. City of New York* and the notes that followed, at p. 226, supra. Are the considerations that were salient there the same as seem central in the § 1983 context?

The "subjects another or causes another to be subjected" language also raises problems when supervisory officials are sued. Occasionally, plaintiffs can show that the supervisory defendant directed, encouraged or participated in the unlawful conduct of the subordinate officials. Often, however, the supervisor may have been unaware of the conduct until after the harm occurred. In the latter situation, suits against supervisory officials under § 1983 are usually brought under a theory of failure to train subordinates adequately, lack of adequate supervision, or some form of vicarious liability.

Most courts construed this language in § 1983 to require some level of individual blameworthiness and held the doctrine of respondeat superior to be inapplicable. Williams v. Vincent, 508 F.2d 541 (2d Cir.1974). In Rizzo v. Goode, 423 U.S. 362 (1976), citizens brought a § 1983 action against superior officers of the Philadelphia Police Department seeking relief because of the officers' failure to correct unconstitutional conduct by subordinates. After finding a "pattern of frequent police violations" of the rights of minorities, the trial court granted injunctive relief. The Supreme Court reversed, finding insufficient evidence that the supervisory officials had implemented, or acquiesced in, an unconstitutional policy.

"Rights . . . secured by the constitution and laws." In 1980, the Court held that, since § 1983 speaks of rights "secured by the Constitution and laws" of the United States, an action lies under that section for purely statutory violations of federal law. Maine v. Thiboutot, 448 U.S. 1 (1980)(claim under § 1983 for deprivation of welfare benefits to which the plaintiffs claimed entitlement under the federal Social Security Act).

Section 1983 does not, however, provide a cause of action if (1) the statute in question does not create enforceable "rights" within the meaning of § 1983, or (2) Congress has foreclosed a § 1983 action in the enactment of the statute itself. Wright v. Roanoke Redevelopment & Hous. Auth., 479 U.S. 418 (1987).

In Golden State Transit Corp. v. City of Los Angeles, 493 U.S. 103 (1989), the Court laid out the basic three-part test for determining whether a particular statute or constitutional provision creates an enforceable "right" under § 1983. First, the provision must create obligations binding on the governmental unit; second, the plaintiff's interest must not be so vague and amorphous as to be beyond the judiciary's competence to enforce; and third, the provision at issue must have been intended to benefit the plaintiff. Applying this test, the Court held that the Supremacy Clause, which gives superior force to federal constitutional and statutory provisions whenever they conflict with state law, does not create rights that are enforceable under § 1983. In contrast, the Court has held that suits for alleged Commerce Clause violations may be brought under § 1983. Dennis v. Higgins, 498 U.S. 439 (1991).

With respect to a particular statutory enactment, Congress may foreclose a § 1983 action in one of two ways. First, Congress may include an express provision to that effect in the statute itself. Second, Congress may invest the statute with a remedial scheme that is sufficiently comprehensive to demonstrate an intent to preclude a judicial remedy via a § 1983 action. Wilder v. Virginia Hosp. Ass'n, 496 U.S. 498 (1990). In Middlesex County Sewerage Authority v. National Sea Clammers Ass'n, 453 U.S. 1 (1981), the Court found that the extensive enforcement mechanisms in several federal environmental statutes demonstrated a congressional intent to bar § 1983 actions for alleged state violations of those statutes. See Sunstein, Section 1983 and the Private Enforcement of Federal Law, 49 U.Chi.L.Rev. 394 (1982).

Issues may also arise in state criminal cases regarding the nature of the "rights" protected under § 1983. Heck v. Humphrey, 512 U.S. 477 (1994), held that no § 1983 action could be brought by a convicted defendant while his appeal from conviction was still pending. That must wait until the state conviction has been "reversed on direct appeal, expunged by executive order, declared invalid by a state tribunal authorized to make such determination, or called into question by a federal court's issuance of a writ of habeas corpus." In Albright v. Oliver, 510 U.S. 266 (1994), an earlier prosecution had been dismissed on the grounds that it failed to state an offense under Illinois law. The § 1983 claim against the state officials was based on denial of due process in groundlessly prosecuting the plaintiff. The Court held that any such claim, if actionable at all, must be based on the Fourth Amendment rather than on substantive due process—and no Fourth Amendment claim was before the court.

Immunity. A major problem confronting the Court has been the nature of defenses available under the statute. In reading the following case, keep in mind the discussion of governmental liability at p. 225, supra. Do any common considerations underlie the issues raised?

Wilson v. Layne

Supreme Court of the United States, 1999.
526 U.S. 603, 119 S.Ct. 1692, 143 L.Ed.2d 818.

CHIEF JUSTICE REHNQUIST delivered the opinion of the Court.

While executing an arrest warrant in a private home, police officers invited representatives of the media to accompany them. We hold that such a "media ride along" does violate the Fourth Amendment, but that because the state of the law was not clearly established at the time the search in this case took place, the officers are entitled to the defense of qualified immunity.

I

In early 1992, the Attorney General of the United States approved "Operation Gunsmoke," a special national fugitive apprehension program in which United States Marshals worked with state and local police to apprehend dangerous criminals. The "Operation Gunsmoke" policy statement explained that the operation was to concentrate on "armed individuals wanted on federal and/or state and local warrants for serious drug and other violent felonies." [ ] This effective program ultimately resulted in over 3,000 arrests in 40 metropolitan areas. [ ]

One of the dangerous fugitives identified as a target of "Operation Gunsmoke" was Dominic Wilson, the son of petitioners Charles and Geraldine Wilson. Dominic Wilson had violated his probation on previous felony charges of robbery, theft, and assault with intent to rob, and the police computer listed "caution indicators" that he was likely to be armed, to resist arrest, and to "assaul[t] police." [ ] The computer also listed his address as 909 North Stone Street Avenue in Rockville, Maryland. Unknown to the police, this was actually the home of petitioners, Dominic Wilson's parents. Thus, in April 1992, the Circuit Court for Montgomery County issued three arrest warrants for Dominic Wilson, one for each of his probation violations. The warrants were each addressed to "any duly authorized peace officer," and commanded such officers to arrest him and bring him "immediately" before the Circuit Court to answer an indictment as to his probation violation. The warrants made no mention of media presence or assistance.

In the early morning hours of April 16, 1992, a Gunsmoke team of Deputy United States Marshals and Montgomery County Police officers assembled to execute the Dominic Wilson warrants. The team was accompanied by a reporter and a photographer from the Washington Post, who had been invited by the Marshals to accompany them on their mission as part of a Marshal's Service ride-along policy.

At around 6:45 a.m., the officers, with media representatives in tow, entered the dwelling at 909 North Stone Street Avenue in the Lincoln Park neighborhood of Rockville. Petitioners Charles and Geraldine Wilson were still in bed when they heard the officers enter the home. Petitioner Charles Wilson, dressed only in a pair of briefs, ran into the living room to investigate. Discovering at least five men in street clothes with guns in his living room, he angrily demanded that they state their business, and repeatedly cursed the officers. Believing him to be an angry Dominic Wilson, the officers quickly subdued him on the floor. Geraldine Wilson next entered the living room to investigate, wearing only a nightgown. She observed her husband being restrained by the armed officers.

When their protective sweep was completed, the officers learned that Dominic Wilson was not in the house, and they departed. During the time that the officers were in the home, the Washington Post photographer took numerous pictures. The print reporter was also apparently in the living room observing the confrontation between the police and Charles Wilson. At no time, however, were the reporters involved in the execution of the arrest warrant. [   ] The Washington Post never published its photographs of the incident.

Petitioners sued the law enforcement officials in their personal capacities for money damages under Bivens v. Six Unknown Fed. Narcotics Agents, 403 U.S. 388 (1971) (the U.S. Marshals Service respondents) and, Rev. Stat. § 1979, 42 U.S.C. § 1983 (the Montgomery County Sheriff's Department respondents). They contended that the officers' actions in bringing members of the media to observe and record the attempted execution of the arrest warrant violated their Fourth Amendment rights. The District Court denied respondents' motion for summary judgment on the basis of qualified immunity.

[The court of appeals, upholding the defense of qualified immunity, declined to decide whether the actions of the police violated the Fourth Amendment.]

II

The petitioners sued the federal officials under *Bivens* and the state officials under § 1983. Both *Bivens* and § 1983 allow a plaintiff to seek money damages from government officials who have violated his Fourth Amendment rights. [   ] But government officials performing discretionary functions generally are granted a qualified immunity and are "shielded from liability for civil damages insofar as their conduct does not violate clearly established statutory or constitutional rights of which a reasonable person would have known." Harlow v. Fitzgerald, 457 U.S. 800, 818 (1982).

Although this case involves suits under both § 1983 and *Bivens*, the qualified immunity analysis is identical under either cause of action. [   ] A court evaluating a claim of qualified immunity "must first determine whether the plaintiff has alleged the deprivation of an actual constitutional right at all, and if so, proceed to determine whether that right was clearly established at the time of the alleged violation." [   ] This order of procedure is designed to "spare a defendant not only unwarranted liability, but unwarranted demands customarily imposed upon those defending a long drawn-out lawsuit." [   ] Deciding the constitutional question before addressing the qualified immunity question also promotes clarity in the legal standards for official conduct, to the benefit of both the officers and the general public. [   ] We now turn to the Fourth Amendment question.

[The Court reviewed the development of the Fourth Amendment.]

Here, of course, the officers had . . . a warrant, and they were undoubtedly entitled to enter the Wilson home in order to execute the arrest warrant for Dominic Wilson. But it does not necessarily follow that they were entitled to bring a newspaper reporter and a photographer with them. In Horton v. California, 496 U.S. 128, 140 (1990), we held "[i]f the scope of the search exceeds that permitted by the terms of a validly issued warrant or the character of the relevant exception from the warrant requirement, the subsequent seizure is unconstitutional without more." While this does not mean that every police action while inside a home must be explicitly authorized by the text of the warrant, [   ], the Fourth Amendment does require that police actions in execution of a warrant be related to the objectives of the authorized intrusion [   ].

Certainly the presence of reporters inside the home was not related to the objectives of the authorized intrusion. Respondents concede that the reporters did not engage in the execution of the warrant, and did not assist the police in their task. The reporters therefore were not present for any reason related to the justification for police entry into the home—the apprehension of Dominic Wilson.

This is not a case in which the presence of the third parties directly aided in the execution of the warrant. Where the police enter a home under the authority of a warrant to search for stolen property, the presence of third parties for the purpose of identifying the stolen property has long been approved by this Court and our common-law tradition. [   ]

Respondents argue that the presence of the Washington Post reporters in the Wilsons' home nonetheless served a number of legitimate law enforcement purposes. They first assert that officers should be able to exercise reasonable discretion about when it would "further their law enforcement mission to permit members of the news media to accompany them in executing a warrant." [   ] But this claim ignores the importance of the right of residential privacy at the core of the Fourth Amendment. It may well be that media ride-alongs further the law enforcement objectives of the police in a general sense, but that is not the same as furthering the purposes of the search. Were such generalized "law enforcement objectives" themselves sufficient to trump the Fourth Amendment, the protections guaranteed by that Amendment's text would be significantly watered down.

Respondents next argue that the presence of third parties could serve the law enforcement purpose of publicizing the government's efforts to combat crime, and facilitate accurate reporting on law enforcement activities. There is certainly language in our opinions interpreting the First Amendment which points to the importance of "the press" in informing the general public about the administration of criminal justice. . . . But the Fourth Amendment also protects a very important right, and in the present case it is in terms of that right that the media ride-alongs must be judged.

Surely the possibility of good public relations for the police is simply not enough, standing alone, to justify the ride-along intrusion into a private home. And even the need for accurate reporting on police issues in general bears no direct relation to the constitutional justification for the police intrusion into a home in order to execute a felony arrest warrant.

Finally, respondents argue that the presence of third parties could serve in some situations to minimize police abuses and protect suspects, and also to protect the safety of the officers. While it might be reasonable for police officers to themselves videotape home entries as part of a "quality control" effort to ensure that the rights of homeowners are being respected, or even to preserve evidence, [   ], such a situation is significantly different from the media presence in this case. The Washington Post reporters in the Wilsons' home were working on a story for their own purposes. They were not present for the purpose of protecting the officers, much less the Wilsons. A private photographer was acting for private purposes, as evidenced in part by the fact that the newspaper and not the police retained the photographs. Thus, although the presence of third parties during the execution of a warrant may in some circumstances be constitutionally permissible, [   ], the presence of these third parties was not.

The reasons advanced by respondents, taken in their entirety, fall short of justifying the presence of media inside a home. We hold that it is a violation of the Fourth Amendment for police to bring members of the media or other third parties into a home during the execution of a warrant when the presence of the third parties in the home was not in aid of the execution of the warrant.

III

Since the police action in this case violated the petitioners' Fourth Amendment right, we now must decide whether this right was clearly established at the time of the search. [   ] As noted above, Part–II supra, government officials performing discretionary functions generally are granted a qualified immunity and are "shielded from liability for civil damages insofar as their conduct does not violate clearly established statutory or constitutional rights of which a reasonable person would have known." [   ] What this means in practice is that "whether an official protected by qualified immunity may be held personally liable for an allegedly unlawful official action generally turns on the 'objective legal reasonableness' of the action, assessed in light of the legal rules that were 'clearly established' at the time it was taken." [   ]

In [   ], we explained that what "clearly established" means in this context depends largely "upon the level of generality at which the relevant 'legal rule' is to be established." "Clearly established" for purposes of qualified immunity means that "[t]he contours of the right must be sufficiently clear that a reasonable official would understand that what he is doing violates that right. This is not to say that an official action is protected by qualified immunity unless the very action in question has previously been held unlawful, but it is to say that in the light of pre-existing law the unlawfulness must be apparent." [   ]; see also United States v. Lanier, 520 U.S. 259, 270 (1997).

It could plausibly be asserted that any violation of the Fourth Amendment is "clearly established," since it is clearly established that the protections of the Fourth Amendment apply to the actions of police. Some variation of this theory of qualified immunity is urged upon us by the petitioners, [   ], and seems to have been at the core of the dissenting opinion in the Court of Appeals [   ]. However, as we explained in [   ], the right allegedly violated must be defined at the appropriate level of specificity before a court can determine if it was clearly established. [   ] In this case, the appropriate question is the objective inquiry of whether a reasonable officer could have believed that bringing members of the media into a home during the execution of an arrest warrant was lawful, in light of clearly established law and the information the officers possessed. Cf. [   ]

We hold that it was not unreasonable for a police officer in April 1992 to have believed that bringing media observers along during the execution of an arrest warrant (even in a home) was lawful. First, the constitutional question presented by this case is by no means open and shut. The Fourth Amendment protects the rights of homeowners from entry without a warrant, but there was a warrant here. The question is whether the invitation to the media exceeded the scope of the search authorized by the warrant. Accurate media coverage of police activities serves an important public purpose, and it is not obvious from the general principles of the Fourth Amendment that the conduct of the officers in this case violated the Amendment.

Second, although media ride-alongs of one sort or another had apparently become a common police practice, in 1992 there were no judicial opinions holding that this practice became unlawful when it entered a home. The only published decision directly on point was a state intermediate court decision which, though it did not engage in an extensive Fourth Amendment analysis, nonetheless held that such conduct was not unreasonable. [   ] From the federal courts, the parties have only identified two unpublished District Court decisions dealing with media entry into homes, each of which upheld the search on unorthodox non-Fourth Amendment right to privacy theories. [   ] These cases, of course, can not "clearly establish" that media entry into homes during a police ride-along violates the Fourth Amendment.

At a slightly higher level of generality, petitioners point to Bills v. Aseltine, 958 F.2d 697 (C.A.6 1992), in which the Court of Appeals for the Sixth Circuit held that there were material issues of fact precluding summary judgment on the question of whether police exceeded the scope of a search warrant by allowing a private security guard to participate in the search to identify stolen property other than that described in the warrant. [   ] *Bills*, which was decided a mere five weeks before the events of this case, did anticipate today's holding that police may not bring along third parties during an entry into a private home pursuant to a warrant for purposes unrelated to those justifying the warrant. [   ] However, we cannot say that even in light of *Bills*, the law on third-party entry into homes was clearly established in April 1992. Petitioners have not brought to our attention any cases of controlling authority in their jurisdiction at the time of the incident which clearly established the rule on which they seek to rely, nor have they identified a consensus of cases of persuasive authority such that a reasonable officer could not have believed that his actions were lawful.

Finally, important to our conclusion was the reliance by the United States marshals in this case on a Marshal's Service ride-along policy which explicitly contemplated that media who engaged in ride-alongs might enter private homes with their cameras as part of fugitive apprehension arrests. The Montgomery County Sheriff's Department also at this time had a ride-along program that did not expressly prohibit media entry into private homes. [   ] Such a policy, of course, could not make reasonable a belief that was contrary to a decided body of case law. But here the state of the law as to third parties accompanying police on home entries was at best undeveloped, and it was not unreasonable for law enforcement officers to look and rely on their formal ride-along policies.

Given such an undeveloped state of the law, the officers in this case cannot have been "expected to predict the future course of constitutional law." [   ] Between the time of the events of this case and today's decision, a split among the Federal Circuits in fact developed on the question whether media ride-alongs that enter homes subject the police to money damages. See [   ]. If judges thus disagree on a constitutional question, it is unfair to subject police to money damages for picking the losing side of the controversy.

For the foregoing reasons, the judgment of the Court of Appeals is affirmed.

It is so ordered.

[JUSTICE STEVENS concurred in finding the violation of the Fourth Amendment but dissented because he thought that "the homeowner's right to protection against this type of trespass was clearly established long before April 16, 1992"]:

The absence of judicial opinions expressly holding that police violate the Fourth Amendment if they bring media representatives into private homes provides scant support for the conclusion that in 1992 a competent officer could reasonably believe that it would be lawful to do so. Prior to our decision in United States v. Lanier, 520 U.S. 259 (1997), no judicial opinion specifically held that it was unconstitutional for a state judge to use his official power to extort sexual favors from a potential litigant. Yet, we unanimously concluded that the defendant had fair warning that he was violating his victim's constitutional rights. [ ] ("The easiest cases don't even arise" (citations and internal quotation marks omitted)).

. . .

Notes and Questions

1. Is the sequence for analyzing § 1983 actions recommended by the Court in *Wilson* the most efficient scheme for resolving these claims? Which of the Court's rationales is most persuasive for justifying the determination of whether a right has been deprived prior to initiating the qualified immunity analysis? See also County of Sacramento v. Lewis, 523 U.S. 833 (1998) (holding that a court should dismiss a § 1983 claim on qualified immunity grounds only if the court has first determined whether a constitutional right has been violated, because otherwise the "standards of official conduct would remain uncertain").

2. *Violation of constitutional or federal rights.* In *Wilson*, the Court held that the police's decision to take the media on a "ride along" during a seizure was a violation of the Fourth Amendment. The determination of whether a public actor's conduct has violated a plaintiff's constitutional or federal rights often entails a complicated and difficult analysis. In *County of Sacramento*, in the previous note, the Court determined that a police officer's decision to pursue a suspect in a high-speed chase did not violate the suspect's due process rights. To show a violation of due process in the context of a high-speed chase, the government actor's conduct must "shock the conscience." The Court also observed that conduct that may be a constitutional violation in one environment may be acceptable, lawful conduct in an alternative setting.

3. *Qualified immunity.* Are there persuasive reasons for granting immunities to government officials despite the lack of explicit mention in § 1983? Should government actors be liable only for the violation of "clearly established" statutory or constitutional rights? How does the Court define "clearly established" rights? Must the Supreme Court already have defined the scope of the right in question in a prior case? See *United States v. Lanier*, discussed in the principal case, holding that in a criminal action—for a judge's sexual harassment of a litigant—the "fair warning requirement" for immunity may be satisfied even though the right in question has not been previously identified in a Supreme Court decision.

4. *Absolute immunity.* Absolute immunities have traditionally been recognized for officials performing judicial and legislative functions. Can an absolute, as distinguished from a qualified, immunity be justified? Consider Mireles v. Waco, 502 U.S. 9 (1991), in which plaintiff attorney alleged that the defendant judge had ordered bailiffs to drag plaintiff from another courtroom in the building because he was late for the defendant's morning calendar call. The Court summarily decided that absolute immunity applied. The alleged act could not be a nonjudicial action because "a judge's direction to court officers to bring a person . . . before him is a function normally performed by a judge." The action was taken in the "very aid of the judge's jurisdiction over a matter before him" and thus could not be said to have been taken in the absence of jurisdiction. Is an absolute immunity warranted here?

What are the limits of the judicial function? In Forrester v. White, 484 U.S. 219 (1988), the Court limited the apparent rule of absolute immunity for judicial officers. The defendant, a state judge who was authorized to hire and fire probation officers, hired plaintiff to be an adult and juvenile probation officer. After promoting plaintiff to a supervisory position, defendant fired her. Plaintiff filed suit under § 1983 alleging sex discrimination in violation of the Fourteenth Amendment's equal protection clause. The Supreme Court rejected defendant's claim that as a judicial officer, he was entitled to absolute immunity from a civil damages suit. Applying a "functional" approach, the Court reasoned that immunity for "truly judicial" acts was needed to protect "judicial independence by insulating judges from vexatious actions prosecuted by disgruntled litigants." In the instant case, plaintiff's allegations went to defendant's administrative responsibilities. The threat of vexatious lawsuits brought by fired employees was not sufficiently grave to justify absolute immunity.

In Imbler v. Pachtman, 424 U.S. 409 (1976), the Court determined that state prosecutors enjoy absolute immunity from § 1983 for actions relating to their conduct "in initiating a prosecution and in presenting the State's case," insofar as that conduct is "intimately associated with the judicial phase of the criminal process[.]" In Kalina v. Fletcher, 522 U.S. 118 (1997), the Court held that absolute immunity shielded a prosecutor from § 1983 liability for allegedly making false statement in the preparation and filing of charging documents and an arrest warrant. The prosecutor, however, was protected by only qualified immunity for her conduct in executing a certification for determination of probable cause for the arrest. The Court reasoned that the absolute immunity of state prosecutors is limited to the performance of traditional functions of an advocate. The prosecutor's actions in serving as a complaining witness in support of the affidavit to establish probable cause for an arrest fell outside traditional advocate functions, and therefore, the prosecutor had only qualified immunity for such conduct.

In Buckley v. Fitzsimmons, 509 U.S. 259 (1993), the court held that a prosecutor is entitled only to qualified immunity when engaging in investigatory, rather than prosecutorial functions. Thus the prosecutor could claim only qualified immunity when he allegedly engaged in misconduct while attempting to determine if a bootprint at the crime scene had been left by the suspect.

5. *Immunity for government entities.* As noted above, government entities may be subject to § 1983 liability for employee conduct, resulting from a government's policy or custom that causes a violation of an individual's constitutional or statutory rights. Unlike public employees, the government is not granted the protection of qualified or absolute immunity. In Owen v. City of Independence, 445 U.S. 622 (1980), the city was held liable for a § 1983 violation when government officials dismissed the police chief without proper notice or hearing. The Court rejected the city's argument that municipalities should receive qualified immunity for their "good-faith constitutional violations."

The Court concluded that the traditional rationales for sovereign immunity were not sufficient to overcome the legislative purpose or considerations of public policy in enacting § 1983. First, government entities were historically granted immunity to protect governmental functions from the challenge or threat of liability, which could stifle decision-making and the execution of the law. The Court rejected this justification for immunity because the Congress enacted § 1983 with the purpose of making government entities amenable to suit. Second, government entities were granted immunity due to the discretionary nature of the legislative and executive processes. Sovereign immunity limited the ability of the courts to "substitut[e] their own judgment on matters within the lawful discretion of the municipality." In its rejection of this basis for immunity, the majority concluded that the violation of constitutional and statutory rights is not within the discretionary authority of the government, and therefore, § 1983 actions are necessary to prevent the misuse or abuse of government power.

In the absence of a right to qualified immunity, are government entities being held strictly liable for their employees' conduct? Is the underlying official misconduct in these cases likely to be "intentional" according to the traditional definition of intended harm? What are the strongest arguments for subjecting government entities to a type of vicarious liability in these cases?

Should it matter that the constitutional right relied on by plaintiff was declared after the contested dismissal occurred?

6. *State immunity.* In Quern v. Jordan, 440 U.S. 332 (1979), the Court, relying heavily on the Eleventh Amendment, held that states would be immune from liability under § 1983. The plaintiff, however, successfully circumvented state immunity in Kentucky v. Graham, 473 U.S. 159 (1985), by seeking prospective injunctive relief against a state officer in her official capacity. A range of Eleventh Amendment issues involving prospective versus retroactive relief and injunctive relief versus monetary damages remain unsettled.

7. What is the proper measure of damages for the deprivation of a constitutional right? In *Monroe,* Justice Harlan, concurring, had suggested that in enacting § 1983 Congress may have believed that:

A deprivation of a constitutional right is significantly different from and more serious than a violation of a state right . . . even though the same act may constitute both a state tort and the deprivation of a constitutional right.

In Carey v. Piphus, 435 U.S. 247 (1978), the plaintiffs had been denied procedural due process by being suspended from high school without a hearing. The court of appeals had held (1) that if the deprivation was in fact justified, the plaintiffs could recover no damages for the suspension but that (2) they could recover substantial presumed damages for the violation of the constitutional right itself. The Supreme Court agreed with the first ruling but reversed the second ruling and held that the plaintiffs would have to present proof of actual injury arising from the violation of the right, including mental and emotional distress. The Court drew on its recent decisions in defamation law, particularly the *Gertz* case, reprinted at p. 1025, infra. Finally, the court held that even if the plaintiffs could not show actual injury they were entitled to nominal damages of one dollar because their constitutional rights had been violated.

8. In City of Newport v. Fact Concerts, Inc., 453 U.S. 247 (1981), the Court held that a municipality could not be held liable for punitive damages. Nothing in the legislative history suggested that Congress sought such liability. Moreover, public policy would not permit such liability. Punitive damages were likely to be a windfall to the plaintiff and to cause an "increase in taxes or a reduction of public services for the citizens footing the bill." Although a public official who maliciously and knowingly deprives others of their civil rights may become the "appropriate object of the community's vindictive sentiments," a municipality "can have no malice independent of the malice of its officials. Damages awarded for *punitive* purposes, therefore, are not sensibly assessed against the governmental entity itself."

Nor did the deterrence rationale warrant a different result. Even compensatory damages imposed on a municipality may induce the public to vote the wrongdoers out of office. Also, a punitive award against the specific official is a more likely source of deterrence than the indirect deterrent of imposing punitive damages on the municipality.

9. *Section 1985(3).* Another section of the Ku Klux Klan Act—now 42 U.S.C. § 1985(3)—creates a damage remedy for citizens deprived of constitutional rights by persons acting in a conspiracy. In Griffin v. Breckenridge, 403 U.S. 88 (1971), the Supreme Court held that section 1985(3) could be invoked to redress injuries inflicted by purely private conspiracies though the participants lacked any state nexus. In *Griffin,* the four black Mississippi plaintiffs alleged that they were driving down the highway when the defendants, two white local residents, mistook the driver for a civil rights worker, stopped the car and clubbed the occupants.

The Court held that in order to state a cause of action under this section a plaintiff must allege the existence of a conspiracy for the purpose of depriving someone of equal protection or privileges and immunities, acts in furtherance of the conspiracy, and injury to the person or his property or deprivation of his constitutional rights. The Court stressed that a conspiratorial deprivation would not be redressable under § 1985(3) without proof of "invidiously discriminatory animus." This "animus" involved a "racial or otherwise class-based" attempt to discriminate against a certain group. Without proof of such class-based animus, the asserted constitutional deprivation would not rise above the level of an ordinary "tortious injury."

Section 1985(3) seems unlikely to provide many plaintiffs with an effective remedy. Plaintiffs have generally encountered great difficulty in attempting to demonstrate the requisite class-based animus. See Harrison v. Brooks, 519 F.2d 1358 (1st Cir.1975); McNally v. Pulitzer Pub. Co., 532 F.2d 69 (8th Cir.), cert. denied 429 U.S. 855 (1976). A second hurdle is that Congress may lack the power to bypass the "state action" requirement of the Fourteenth Amendment as to most civil rights. See Cohen v. Illinois Institute of Technology, 524 F.2d 818 (7th Cir.1975), cert. denied 425 U.S. 943 (1976). The Court in *Griffin* avoided this problem by finding Congressional authority to reach the defendant's behavior under the Congressional power to protect the right to travel and under the Thirteenth Amendment (relying here on Jones v. Alfred H. Mayer Co., 392 U.S. 409 (1968), which held that the Thirteenth Amendment authorized Congress to provide remedies for "racially discriminatory private action" aimed at depriving blacks "of the basic rights that the law secures to all free men").

Are the plaintiffs in *Griffin* better off than they would have been had they proceeded under state law?

2.   LIABILITY OF FEDERAL OFFICIALS

In Chapter III, we considered the availability of remedies against the United States under the Federal Tort Claims Act, p. 249, supra. As we have seen, liability for negligence may be available under the statute, though recovery on a strict liability basis is not permitted. Here, we consider the available remedies for citizens who sustain intentional injury at the hands of federal government employees.

The Federal Tort Claims Act addresses the problem of intentional torts in § 2680(h), which provides that the Act shall not apply to:

> (h) Any claim arising out of assault, battery, false imprisonment, false arrest, malicious prosecution, abuse of process, libel, slander, misrepresentation, deceit, or interference with contract rights: *Provided*, That, with regard to acts or omissions of investigative or law enforcement officers of the United States Government, the provisions of this chapter and section 1346(b) of this title shall apply to any claim arising, on or after the date of the enactment of this proviso, out of assault, battery, false imprisonment, false arrest, abuse of process, or malicious prosecution. For the purpose of this subsection, "investiga-

tive or law enforcement officer" means any officer of the United States who is empowered by law to execute searches, to seize evidence, or to make arrests for violations of Federal law.

The part before the proviso was in the original Act. The proviso was added in 1974 largely as the result of several "no-knock" raids carried out by federal narcotics agents. An action against the agents themselves became available only after Bivens v. Six Unknown Named Federal Narcotics Agents, 403 U.S. 388 (1971), which served as the basis for the claims against the federal officials in *Wilson v. Layne*. But Congress observed that the agents were unlikely to be solvent. On the 1974 amendment, see Boger, Gitenstein, and Verkuil, The Federal Tort Claims Act Intentional Torts Amendment: An Interpretative Analysis, 54 N.C.L.Rev. 497 (1976).

In *Bivens,* the plaintiff alleged that federal agents had ransacked his apartment during an illegal warrantless search. Though the only effective remedy was money damages, § 1983 was inapplicable because the wrongdoers were federal agents and therefore not acting under color of *state* law. Nevertheless, the Supreme Court recognized a federal claim for damages against the federal officials based directly upon the Fourth Amendment, despite the lack of a statutory remedy. Writing for the majority, Justice Brennan stated:

> "[I]t is . . . well settled that where legal rights have been invaded, and a federal statute provides for a general right to sue for such invasion, federal courts may use any available remedy to make good the wrong done." Bell v. Hood, 327 U.S. at 684 (footnote omitted). The present case involves no special factors counselling hesitation in the absence of affirmative action by Congress.

The court offered little guidance on when it would be proper to imply the damage remedy to vindicate constitutional interests. The Government had argued that the Court should create remedies based on the Constitution only when "essential" to the protection of the right, reasoning that Congress may displace or modify a Court-created remedy for statutory violations but is powerless to modify a remedy that the Court has determined is required by the Constitution. Justice Brennan rejected the "essentiality" standard but offered no alternative.

Once it is recognized that the Constitution creates federally protected interests, it seems clear that the *Bivens* rationale should apply to protect other rights guaranteed by the Constitution as well. Not surprisingly, therefore, claims have been recognized against federal officers for alleged deprivations of other Constitutional rights.

In Carlson v. Green, 446 U.S. 14 (1980), the Court decided that the fact that plaintiff could sue under the Federal Tort Claims Act did not bar a suit under the *Bivens* doctrine. The two actions were not equivalent. Under *Bivens,* deterrence might be stronger when the action is brought against the individual defendants, and punitive damages are available only under *Bivens.* Also, liability under the FTCA depends on whether a private person "would be liable to the claimant in accordance with the law of the place where the act or omission occurred." This creates a local focus in contrast to *Bivens,* which creates a unified system of substantive law.

A *Bivens* action is unavailable, however, where Congress has expressly created an alternative remedial scheme. See, e.g., Chappell v. Wallace, 462 U.S. 296 (1983)(redress against racial discrimination by a superior officer was available through the military justice system); Bush v. Lucas, 462 U.S. 367 (1983)(aerospace engineer allegedly fired in retaliation for exercise of his First Amendment rights had effective remedy through Civil Service System); Schweiker v. Chilicky, 487 U.S. 412 (1988)(individuals who alleged that their Social Security benefits were improperly terminated had effective remedy through congressionally provided administrative appeal system). For a critical discussion of the Court's rationales for barring certain *Bivens* actions, see Nichol, *Bivens, Chilicky,* and Constitutional Damages Claims, 75 Va.L.Rev. 1117 (1989).

In *Bivens* cases, as in cases under § 1983, the critical issues concern the role of defenses. In Butz v. Economou, 438 U.S. 478 (1978), plaintiff sued several officials in the Department of Agriculture after the Department brought an unsuccessful administrative proceeding against him. He sued under *Bivens* claiming that the officials (including the Secretary, Assistant Secretary, the administrative judge, the hearing examiner who recommended the proceeding, and the attorney who presented the case) had violated his constitutional rights in various ways. The Court, 5–4, held that when a plaintiff claims that officials of an executive department have violated constitutional rights, the defendants generally are entitled only to qualified immunity. These cases "have recognized that it is not unfair to hold liable the official who knows or should know he is acting outside the law, and that insisting on an awareness of clearly established constitutional limits will not unduly interfere with the exercise of official judgment." Federal officials "will not be liable for mere mistakes in judgment, whether the mistake is one of fact or one of law. But we see no substantial basis for holding, as the United States would have us do, that executive officers generally may with impunity discharge their duties in a way that is known to them to violate the United States Constitution or in a manner that they should know transgresses a clearly established constitutional rule." The majority believed that insubstantial suits "can be quickly terminated" at the pleading stage. (On this score, the Court later held that a plaintiff must "allege the violation of a clearly established constitutional right" to get beyond summary judgment on a defendant's qualified immunity claim. Siegert v. Gilley, 500 U.S. 226 (1991)).

The majority did recognize that there were "some officials whose special functions require a full exemption from liability." Specifically, the analogies to the judicial branch were so apt that they had to be followed. The reason for immunities in the judicial branch is not the officials' location within government, but the "special nature of their responsibilities." The case was remanded to determine how these principles should be applied to the various defendants before the court. Reconsider the discussion of judicial immunity under § 1983 at p. 940, supra.

When a former president was sued for improperly arranging to discharge a government employee who "blew the whistle" on military cost overruns, the Court, 5–4, accorded absolute immunity. Nixon v. Fitzgerald, 457 U.S. 731 (1982). The absolute immunity was "a functionally mandated incident of the President's unique office, rooted in the constitutional tradition of the separation of powers and supported by our history." The immunity extended to "damages liability predicated on his official acts."

Although absolute immunity accorded to other executive officials had been limited to the particular functions of the office, that limit would be inadequate here. The President "has discretionary responsibilities in a broad variety of areas, many of them highly sensitive. In many cases it would be difficult to determine which of the President's innumerable 'functions' encompassed a particular action." The absolute immunity would extend to acts within the "outer perimeter" of his official responsibility. The action alleged here fell within that broad sweep.

Such a result would not leave the country without sufficient protection against misconduct by its chief executive. Impeachment remained available as did "formal and informal checks" on Presidential action, including "constant scrutiny by the press," oversight by Congress, the desire for re-election, the need to maintain prestige as an element of Presidential influence, and the "President's traditional concern for his historical stature."

In Harlow v. Fitzgerald, 457 U.S. 800 (1982), the Court held that senior aides to the President did not automatically share his immunity for the firing of Fitzgerald. They would receive qualified or good faith immunity. If they claimed that absolute immunity was justified because they were entrusted with discretionary authority in a sensitive area like national security or foreign policy, the defendants had to establish the claim.

Empirical data on the frequency and success of both § 1983 and *Bivens* actions are discussed in Eisenberg & Schwab, The Reality of Constitutional Tort Litigation, 72 Cornell L.Rev. 641 (1987), and Schwab & Eisenberg, Explaining Constitutional Tort Litigation: The Influence of the Attorney Fees Statute and the Government as Defendant, 73 Cornell L.Rev. 719 (1988). See also Symposium on Section 1983, 15 Touro L.J. 1481–1650 (1999).

As to *Bivens* actions, see Pillard, Taking Fiction Seriously: The Strange Result of Public Officials' Individual Liability under *Bivens*, 88 Geo.L.J. 65 (1999), reporting that "out of approximately 12,000 *Bivens* claims filed between 1971 and 1985, *Bivens* plaintiffs actually obtained a judgment that was not reversed on appeal in only four cases." Although similar figures have not been kept since 1985, the author reports that "both settlements and litigated judgments continue to be extraordinarily rare." See generally Jeffries, The Right–Remedy Gap in Constitutional Law, 109 Yale L.J. 87 (1999).

CHAPTER XIII

DEFAMATION

A. COMMON LAW BACKGROUND

1. WHAT IS DEFAMATORY?

As with other torts, defamation has evolved through common-law developments as a matter of state law. Unlike the torts we have already considered, however, the law of defamation has been enormously influenced and reshaped by constitutional considerations of freedom of speech and press. Since 1964, the Supreme Court has become involved in continuing efforts to establish the boundaries between freedom of communication and protection of reputation.

In tracing the developments in this complex area, we must begin with the common law regime. The constitutional developments have not created a totally new legal area; rather, they have altered some of the pre-existing state rules and left others in place. As a result, despite the great impact of the Supreme Court, state law retains great significance in suits for defamation. It is often possible, for example, for a case to be decided under the traditional state rules without any invocation of the First Amendment.

Defamation has a venerable and still influential history. Early in the sixteenth century the common law courts began to recognize a claim for defamation that had previously been within the exclusive jurisdiction of the ecclesiastical courts. Since the common law remedy was framed as an action on the case, with its traditional focus on damages rather than ecclesiastical sanctions, the common law action became extremely popular. In another development during the same period, the Star Chamber assumed jurisdiction over all aspects of the press, and printed defamation came to be treated as a crime. Attacks on officials were seditious libels, and libels against private persons contributed to breaches of the peace. After the Restoration both concepts were preserved: the Star Chamber's view of libel as a crime, and the antecedent common law view of slander as a tort.

Although the English defamation law crossed the Atlantic, it seems never to have been enforced in the United States as vigorously as it was in England. This was true long before any constitutional questions were raised explicitly. In Government and Mass Communications 106–07 (1947), Professor Zechariah Chafee speculated:

> [The difference] is probably due to the fact that English jurymen and judges live in a different intellectual climate from the fluid and migratory society of the United States. The Englishman is born into a definite status where he tends to stick for life. What he *is* has at least

as much importance as what he *does* in an active career. A slur on his reputation, if not challenged, may cause him to drop several rungs down the social ladder. A man moves within a circle of friends and associates and feels bound to preserve his standing in their eyes. Consequently, *not* to sue for libel is taken as an admission of truth.

An able American has too much else to do to waste time on an expensive libel suit. Most strangers will not read the article, most of his friends will not believe it, and his enemies, who will believe it of course, were against him before. Anyway, it is just one more blow in the rough-and-tumble of politics or business. Even if his reputation is lowered for a while, he can make a fresh start at his home or in a new region and accomplish enough to overwhelm old scandals. A libeled American prefers to vindicate himself by steadily pushing forward his career and not by hiring a lawyer to talk in a courtroom.

Even in the United States, however, certain slurs cannot be ignored, and justify legal recourse. Since the notion of reputation is at the core of the defamation action, we will begin our consideration with a look at that concept. In our discussion of the common law, the fact that the defendant is a publisher or a broadcaster rather than an individual will not be central.

Romaine v. Kallinger
Supreme Court of New Jersey, 1988.
109 N.J. 282, 537 A.2d 284.

[This case arose out of a nonfiction book, "The Shoemaker," written about a man who went on a criminal rampage. One of the episodes involved events at the Romaine house. Part of that description included the following:

> A militant women's libber, Maria Fasching was famous among her friends for her battles on behalf of the weak and downtrodden. She would always try to rescue someone a bully had attacked, and she could not tolerate racists.
>
> Maria thought of herself as a "free spirit." She resisted anything that she considered a restriction on her freedom. She cared for cats that had been hit by cars and for birds with broken wings.
>
> Today, Maria Fasching was on the four-to-midnight shift at Hackensack Hospital, and she wore her nurse's uniform under her coat. In the morning Maria's friend Randi Romaine, who lived in the stucco house, had called Maria and asked her to drop over for coffee. The two women had not seen each other for a long time, for between hospital duties and preparations for her wedding, Maria's schedule was full.
>
> At first Maria said that she couldn't visit because she had to go to a wake. This wake, however, was only for an acquaintance. Randi and her twin sister, Retta, had been Maria's friends since they were all in the first grade. Besides, Maria was eager for news from Randi about a junkie they both knew who was doing time in prison. Finally, Maria

changed her mind. She didn't go to the wake, but drove her Volkswagen to the two-story tan stucco house at 124 Glenwood Avenue, the house of Mr. and Mrs. Dewitt Romaine.

During the ensuing episode Fasching was killed. Among the variety of claims pressed by several plaintiffs, we concern ourselves with Randi Romaine's libel claim against the publisher and author. The trial court granted defendants' motion for summary judgment and the Appellate Division affirmed.]

HANDLER, J.

. . .

According to plaintiffs, one sentence in the passage falsely depicts the reason for Ms. Fasching's visit: "Besides, Maria was eager for news from Randi about a junkie they both knew who was doing time in prison.". . .

Plaintiff Randi Romaine asserts that the particular sentence is defamatory as a matter of law, or alternatively, that the statement's defamatory content was at least a question for the jury. She claims this sentence falsely accuses her of criminality or associations with criminals. Plaintiff also contends that the false accusation was particularly damaging because it injured Ms. Romaine's professional reputation as a drug counsellor and a social worker, interfering with her ability to obtain future employment.

A defamatory statement is one that is false and "injurious to the reputation of another" or exposes another person to "hatred, contempt or ridicule" or subjects another person to "a loss of the good will and confidence" in which he or she is held by others. [ ]; see W. Keeton, D. Dobbs, R. Keeton & D. Owen, Prosser and Keeton on the Law of Torts, § 111 at 773–78 (5th ed. 1984); see also Restatement (Second) of Torts § 559 (1977)(a defamatory communication is one that "tends so to harm the reputation of another so as to lower him in the estimation of the community or to deter third persons from associating or dealing with him").

The threshold issue in any defamation case is whether the statement at issue is reasonably susceptible of a defamatory meaning. [ ] This question is one to be decided first by the court. [ ] In making this determination, the court must evaluate the language in question "according to the fair and natural meaning which will be given it by reasonable persons of ordinary intelligence." [ ] In assessing the language, the court must view the publication as a whole and consider particularly the context in which the statement appears. [ ]

If a published statement is susceptible of one meaning only, and that meaning is defamatory, the statement is libelous as a matter of law. [ ] Conversely, if the statement is susceptible of only a non-defamatory meaning, it cannot be considered libelous, justifying dismissal of the action. [ ] However, in cases where the statement is capable of being assigned more than one meaning, one of which is defamatory and another not, the question of whether its content is defamatory is one that must be resolved by the trier of fact. [   ]

Certain kinds of statements denote such defamatory meaning that they are considered defamatory as a matter of law. A prime example is the false attribution of criminality. [   ] *Lawrence v. Bauer Publishing & Printing Ltd.* [   ] (statement that plaintiff might be charged with criminal conduct defamatory as a matter of law). Relying essentially on this example of defamation, plaintiff Randi Romaine contends in this case that the published offending statement must be considered libelous per se. According to Ms. Romaine, the sentence has only a defamatory meaning, in that it accuses her of having engaged in criminal conduct or having associated with criminals relating to drugs.

The trial court concluded, and the Appellate Division agreed, that only the most contorted reading of the offending language could lead to the conclusion that it accuses plaintiff of illegal drug use or criminal associations. We concur in the determinations of the courts below. "[A]ccording to the fair and natural meaning which will be given [this statement] by reasonable persons of ordinary intelligence," *Herrmann v. Newark Morning Ledger Co.,* [   ] it does not attribute any kind of criminality to plaintiff. A reasonable and fair understanding of the statement simply does not yield an interpretation that the plaintiff was or had been in illegal possession of drugs or otherwise engaging in any illegal drug-related activity. See Valentine v. C.B.S., Inc., 698 F.2d 430, 432 (11th Cir.1983)("The Plaintiff's interpretation does not construe the words as the common mind would understand them but is tortured and extreme."); Forsher v. Bugliosi, 608 P.2d 716, 723 (Cal.1980)("the claimed defamatory nature of the book as it relates to appellant is so obscure and attenuated as to be beyond the realm of reasonableness").

At most, the sentence can be read to imply that plaintiff knew a junkie. Even if we assume that a commonly accepted and well-understood meaning of the term "junkie" is "a narcotics peddler or addict," Webster's Third New International Dictionary 1227 (1981), see also Dictionary of American Slang 300 (2d ed. 1975)(defining "junkie" as a "drug addict"), the statement still does not suggest either direct or indirect involvement by plaintiff herself in any criminal drug-related activities. Absent exceptional circumstances, the mere allegation that plaintiff knows a criminal is not defamatory as a matter of law. See, e.g., Gonzales v. Times Herald Printing Company, 513 S.W.2d 124 (Tex.Civ.App.1974)(statement that plaintiff's husband was engaged in the sale and importation of narcotics did not defame her); Rose v. Daily Mirror, Inc., 31 N.E.2d 182 (N.Y.1940) [   ] (plaintiff not defamed by being mistakenly described as the widow of a mobster); cf. Bufalino v. Associated Press, 692 F.2d 266 (2d Cir.1982)(mere imputation of family relationship with Mafia leader not defamatory; characterization of plaintiff as a political contributor with alleged mob ties found to have a potentially defamatory meaning), cert. den., 462 U.S. 1111 (1983).

Beyond the language itself, we are satisfied that the statement in its contextual setting cannot fairly and reasonably be invested with any defamatory meaning. Maria Fasching, we note, is described in the chapter as a person who had compassion for others and who would care for less fortunate persons. The reasonable meaning of the critical sentence that is implied from this context is that Ms. Fasching's interest in the "junkie" stemmed from sympathy and compassion, not from any predilection toward or involvement in criminal drug activity. As extended to Randi Romaine, the only fair inference to be drawn from the larger context is that Ms. Romaine shared her friend's feelings, attitudes and interests, and that her own interest in the junkie was similar to that of Ms. Fasching's.

We note the further contention that this statement had a defamatory meaning because it implied that the only reason for Ms. Fasching's visit to the Romaine home was her "interest" in news about a "junkie." A review of the full text, however, indicates that there were several reasons for the visit, only one of which was Ms. Fasching's interest in the "junkie." The lower courts soundly rejected this contention.

We conclude that the statement is not defamatory as a matter of law and accordingly uphold the ruling of the lower court on this point.

. . .

[JUSTICE O'HERN dissented on this point, contending that the passage was ambiguous and "reasonably susceptible of a defamatory meaning" and thus presented a jury question.]

Notes and Questions

1. *Publication.* Since harm to reputation is at the core of this tort, it is crucial that someone other than the plaintiff receive the statement. This element, called "publication," has nothing to do with mass circulation or with putting a statement into print. It simply means that the message must reach at least one third party who understands a defamatory thrust from the statement. Thus, making a statement over the telephone to someone other than the plaintiff is a "publication" of that statement. But at common law the plaintiff has to show that the publication was either intentional or negligent; no liability exists if a third person unexpectedly overhears a private conversation between plaintiff and defendant.

In Staples v. Bangor Hydro–Electric Co., 629 A.2d 601 (Me.1993), plaintiff's supervisor told superiors within the company that he had reason to believe that plaintiff had "sabotaged" a company computer. Among the defenses was one asserting that there had been no "publication" of the charge. The court recognized that some states hold that when one agent talks to another agent, the corporation "is simply communicating with itself." The court preferred the other view because "damage to one's reputation within the corporate community may be as devastating as that outside; and that the defense of qualified privilege [discussed at p. 976, infra] provides adequate protection." To hold otherwise "would be to ignore the nature of the right protected by the law of defamation."

Normally, sending a sealed letter that charges the addressee with a crime will not lead to a defamation action because the recipient will usually be responsible for showing the letter to others. Most states follow this approach even if the plaintiff is "compelled" to publish the defamation herself—as where she must show prospective future employers a termination letter from defendant when asked why she left that job. See Sullivan v. Baptist Memorial Hospital, 995 S.W.2d 569 (Tenn.1999). But see Overcast v. Billings Mutual Ins. Co., 11 S.W.3d 62 (Mo.2000) (allowing defamation action where recipient of letter accusing him of arson could be expected to have shown it to other insurers when they asked if he had ever had a claim denied or been denied insurance).

In unusual situations it may be possible to establish "publication" by showing that T posted a defamation and that D did not use due care to remove it promptly. See Tacket v. General Motors Corp., 836 F.2d 1042 (7th Cir.1987), finding a jury question of publication where an unknown person stenciled a 12″ x 48″ defamation of plaintiff employee on a wall of defendant's plant—which remained there for some seven months despite plaintiff's complaints.

2. *What is defamatory?* What is the core notion that makes a statement "defamatory"? Unless D says something as patent as "P murdered X," the determination of whether the statement is actionable usually involves two steps. The first is to determine whether the words can bear the "spin" that plaintiff is alleging. In *Romaine* this question is whether the words defendant actually used could reasonably be understood to accuse her of "criminality or associations with criminals." If the answer to that is negative, there is nothing further to do. If the answer is affirmative, the second question must be addressed: whether it is defamatory of someone to say that she engages in this sort of behavior or associates with criminals. Usually, the plaintiff will try to telescope these two questions into one by arguing that the words used by defendant can reasonably be understood to make a charge that reasonable recipients could consider defamatory.

The court notes that in determining the meaning of the passage in question the court must seek the "fair and natural meaning which will be given it by reasonable persons of ordinary intelligence." Why is that the standard—as opposed, say, to the "most impressionable" readers? Or the "most intelligent" readers?

3. *What do the words mean?* In interpreting statements, courts consider all of the accoutrements of language, such as punctuation and paragraphing. Thus, in Wildstein v. New York Post Corp., 243 N.Y.S.2d 386, affirmed without opinion 261 N.Y.S.2d 254 (App.Div. 1965), the defendant wrote that the plaintiff was one of "several women described as 'associated' with" a slain executive. The judge observed that if the word "associated" had not been in quotation marks the statement would not have been defamatory; the quotation marks implied a euphemistic use of the word, suggesting an illicit relationship between plaintiff and the deceased.

a. *Internal context.* The *Romaine* court also observes that it "must view the publication as a whole." Certainly, it would seem wrong to allow a libel to be based on one sentence of an article or book if the surrounding sentences make clear that the pinpointed sentence should be read innocently.

On the other hand, what if the first paragraph of a newspaper article is defamatory, but is totally explained away in the twentieth paragraph of the story? Should the court still view the article "as a whole"? What if a big headline conveys a defamatory meaning that is removed by the text? What if a caption under a photograph conveys a defamatory meaning but the text of the accompanying article removes it? In Gambuzza v. Time, Inc., 239 N.Y.S.2d 466 (App.Div. 1963), the court, 3–2, concluded that a defamatory caption accompanying a photo spread had to be read together with the text that removed the sting. Generally, courts require that headlines must be read in context with the story. Some courts have held that sensational headlines may be interpreted separately from the text: "a person passing a newsstand . . . may be able to catch a glimpse of a headline without the opportunity or desire to read the accompanying article or may skim through the paper jumping from headline to headline." In *Gambuzza,* however, the caption and text were so close to each other that they had to be read together. The dissenters argued that the critical words in the caption were in bold capital letters and thus should be considered separately.

See also Kunst v. New York World Telegram Corp., 280 N.Y.S.2d 798 (App.Div. 1967), in which the lead paragraph and a photo caption conveyed a defamatory implication. The majority upheld the complaint because the negation of the sting appeared only in a statement that a "persistent and careful reader would discover near the end of the reasonably lengthy article." A writing must be "construed, not with the high degree of precision expected of and used by lawyers and judges, but as it would be read and understood by an ordinary member of the public to whom it is directed." A dissenter responded that although the negating statement appeared near the end of the article, "the article is to be taken as a whole and read in its entirety."

b. *External context.* Although the point is not involved in this case, it is sometimes necessary for the plaintiff to allege facts beyond those asserted in the publication in order to show how the plaintiff was defamed by the publication. For example, suppose an article stated only that the plaintiff had often been seen at "123 Hay Road." What if some in the community knew that there was a brothel at that address? Plaintiff need not show that the defamation was contained solely in the published words. If the words alone do not clearly convey the defamatory thrust explicitly or by implication, the plaintiff must plead extrinsic facts that would explain how those who knew the unstated facts would take a defamatory meaning. Such an allegation—that neighbors and others know that 123 Hay Road is a brothel—is called the "inducement."

Where, after putting the explicit statement and added extrinsic facts together, the thrust of the defamation is still not obvious, the plaintiff must allege the "meaning" that plaintiff thinks flows from the combination. This is called the "innuendo." The innuendo is not a fact; it is the plaintiff's assertion of how the passage would be understood by those who received the explicit statement and knew the extrinsic facts (inducement). In our example, it would be that those who know about 123 Hay Road understood the newspaper article to imply that plaintiff frequents a brothel. In most cases, when the explicit statements and the extrinsic facts are combined the nature of the claimed defamation becomes clear.

c. *Roles of judge and jury.* The *Romaine* court observes that if the statement in question is clearly defamatory in its only reasonable reading (or in all its reasonable readings), the court will declare it so. On the other hand, if it is clearly not defamatory in any reasonable reading, the court will dismiss the case. But if there are two or more reasonable meanings that might be attached to the statement (on its face or as expanded upon by external context), with at least one being defamatory and at least one not, the trier of fact is to decide which meaning would be taken. How is the trier to make this determination? What evidence should be admissible on this question?

One simple example of the problem of ambiguity is Rovira v. Boget, 148 N.E. 534 (N.Y.1925), in which, while eating at the ship crew's mess, a member of the largely male French-speaking crew called plaintiff, a stewardess on the same ship, a "cocotte." A French interpreter testified at trial that to some men "cocotte" meant "prostitute." "In other associations it may mean a poached egg." How should the case proceed?

In the *Valentine* case, cited in *Romaine,* the claim arose from a song written by Bob Dylan and Jacques Levy questioning the fairness of a murder trial in which the plaintiff had testified as a witness for the prosecution. The theory of the song was that the criminal defendants had been convicted as the result of a conspiracy between Bello, Bradley and the police. Valentine argued that the fourth stanza asserted that Bello and Bradley lied and that the tenth stanza said that Valentine agreed with Bello's and Bradley's identification of the defendants. Plaintiff argued that putting the two together implied that Valentine had "acquiesced in the lie of the other two witnesses." The court concluded that a "review of the entire song makes it clear this interpretation is not reasonably possible."

At one point the *Romaine* court says that a particular allegation "is not defamatory as a matter of law." Is the court declaring as a matter of law that the statement is not defamatory, or indicating that the issue is one of fact rather than of law?

Illinois takes an unusual approach to ambiguous statements, called the "innocent construction rule." This requires the court to dismiss a defamation case if a reasonable nondefamatory meaning can be ascribed to the statement—even if plaintiff could prove that most readers would have taken the defamatory reading. The situation is summarized in Barter v. Wilson, 512 N.E.2d 816 (Ill.App.1987), in which the court held that saying "the fix is in" on plaintiff developer's permit application did not defame the developer. The court used a definition of "fix" from a law dictionary: "determine, settle, make permanent." Thus, the statement could have meant no more than that "a decision had already been made."

4. *Is the ascribed meaning defamatory?* Recall that the *Romaine* court quoted two approaches to determining whether a statement is defamatory—that of the Restatement and that of Prosser & Keeton. How do they differ? Some states, including New York, tend to list a series of more specific criteria. Consider, for example, that of Nichols v. Item Publishers, Inc., 132 N.E.2d 860 (N.Y.1956): a statement that "tends to expose a person to hatred, contempt or aversion, or to induce an evil or unsavory opinion of him in the minds of a substantial number in the community." Does this formulation differ significantly from the ones quoted in *Romaine*? Consider the following passage from 1 R. Sack, Sack on Defamation: Libel, Slander, and Related Problems 2–13 (3d ed. 2000):

> These variations among definitions of defamation have little apparent effect on the actual outcome of cases. If what is libelous in Mississippi is not libelous in New York, or vice versa, it is far more likely to reflect different social circumstances than the language adopted by particular courts to define the term "defamatory."

If that notion is correct, then what is the core that each of the differing formulations is trying to get at—if only for its own state? Apply these varying definitions in each of the following cases.

a.   A statement that the plaintiff has died. Decker v. Princeton Packet, Inc., 561 A.2d 1122 (N.J.1989)(an obituary "does not impugn reputation").

b.   An assertion that a lieutenant in the Marine Corps asked his father, a United States Senator, to intervene to prevent his being sent into combat in the Korean War. Defendant argued that this could not be defamatory because it was a "perfectly understandable and human reaction" and that the use of influence to achieve such a goal was not disgraceful or odious, but expectable. The court denied summary judgment: "While perhaps some might read [defendant's] statement in such a charitable light, a great many others would find it highly offensive that a Senator's son simply called home and used his father's political influence to escape combat duty at a time when many other Second Lieutenants and other members of the service were being wounded or killed." Robertson v. McCloskey, 666 F.Supp. 241 (D.D.C.1987).

c.   A false statement about incumbents' voting records that makes a group of voters less likely to vote to reelect them. In Tatur v. Solsrud, 498 N.W.2d 232 (Wis.1993), the court concluded that misrepresentations about votes on taxes and expenditures could not meet the Restatement's definition of defamatory. "None of the issues mentioned in the letter . . . are of the nature that a vote on one side or the other could harm the reputation of the voting official as to lower him in the estimation of the community or to deter third persons from associating or dealing with him." Even if the misstatements deterred voters from voting for the plaintiffs, that is not enough by itself to create defamation on these facts, though the court was unwilling to say that this could never be so as to any falsely reported vote.

d.   An assertion that plaintiff small town mayor was "manipulating" the press to keep it from reporting negative matters about the mayor. In West v. Thomson Newspapers, 872 P.2d 999 (Utah 1994), the court held that "Although a dictionary may define and give some content to allegedly defamatory words, it cannot be dispositive. A court simply cannot determine whether a statement is capable of sustaining a defamatory meaning by viewing individual words in isolation; rather it must carefully examine the context in which the statement was made, giving the words their most common and accepted meaning." Read this way, the use of "manipulating" was nothing more than a charge that a person in power, without running afoul of ethical or legal norms, was trying to use that power to get a favorable press. "While no politician would welcome such criticism—and indeed might find it personally offensive—this does not render it defamatory. 'A publication is not defamatory simply because it is nettlesome or embarrassing. . . .' [   ] West must establish that the statement is more than sharp criticism." The court said that no reasonable person could consider this charge damaging to reputation.

e.   A passage in the book "Den of Thieves" stated that plaintiff lawyer had drafted an affidavit for T to sign. T "read it over and had only one problem: the facts weren't true. He angrily refused to sign, and began looking for new lawyers." Armstrong v. Simon & Schuster, 649 N.E.2d 825 (N.Y.1995). The court concluded that the passage was "susceptible to a defamatory meaning: that Armstrong deliberately presented a false affidavit for one client (Cogut) to sign in order to exculpate another client (Lowell), resulting in Cogut's angry discharge of Armstrong and the retention of new counsel." The case involved "allegedly false statements of verifiable fact, with inferences flowing from those facts."

f.   Can a question be defamatory? During the Gulf War plaintiff began a project to send to soldiers overseas gift packages. Questions arose about the cost of the package compared to how much donors were being asked to pay. In an article about the controversy, defendant paper noted that one difficult question was "Who will benefit more from the project—GIs or [plaintiff]?" In Chapin v. Knight–Ridder, Inc., 993 F.2d 1087 (4th Cir. 1993), the court observed that a question "can conceivably be defamatory [if it must] be reasonably read as an *assertion* of a false *fact*; inquiry itself, however embarrassing or unpleasant to its subject, is not accusation." The question here cannot be read to charge "pocket-lining." Rather, "it simply provokes public scrutiny" of plaintiff's activities.

5.   *Insults and name-calling.* At a meeting of about 100 condominium owners, plaintiff wife stood up to make comments supporting those just made by her husband. At this point, defendant, sitting nearby, jumped up and shouted: "Don't listen to these people. They don't like [or hate] Jews. She's a bitch." The court held that neither expression was actionable. Ward v. Zelikovsky, 643 A.2d 972 (N.J.1994). The court used the standard of defamation stated in *Romaine*. Turning first to "content," the court relied largely on a passage from comment *e* to § 566 of the Restatement:

> There are some statements that . . . cannot reasonably be understood to be meant literally and seriously and are obviously mere vituperation and abuse. A certain amount of vulgar name-calling is frequently resorted to by angry people without any real intent to make a defamatory assertion, and it is properly understood by reasonable listeners to amount to nothing more. This is true particularly when it is obvious that the speaker has lost his temper and is merely giving vent to insult. Thus when, in the course of an altercation, the defendant loudly and angrily calls the plaintiff a bastard in the presence of others, he is ordinarily not reasonably to be understood as asserting the fact that plaintiff is of illegitimate birth but only to be abusing him to his face.

Can you think of a situation where the use of "bastard" would be actionable? As to "context," the court stressed the face-to-face confrontation distinguishing words uttered in that context from "words written after time for thought or published in a newspaper [that] may be taken to express the defamatory charge and to be intended to be taken seriously." (The court relied to some extent on a third criterion—"verifiability"—that is discussed in detail at p. 1061, infra, but was not central here.)

As to "bitch," as used here, a reasonable listener "would interpret the term to indicate merely that the speaker disliked Mrs. Ward and is otherwise inarticulate."

As to "dislikes [or hates] Jews," the court also found relevant a line of cases concluding that such political charges had become so common in recent years that they had lost content, citing Stevens v. Tillman, 855 F.2d 394 (7th Cir.1988), cert. denied 489 U.S. 1065 (1989)(charge of being a "racist" is not actionable because word has "been watered down by overuse, becoming common coin in political discourse"). A charge of bigotry might be defamatory if it alleged specific acts, such as making racist statements or denying employment to another because of race or religion, but there was no such charge or implication in these facts.

6. *Libel by implication.* What if each fact reported in an article is true but they are stated in such a way that the ordinary reader reaches a false, and defamatory, conclusion? In Healey v. New England Newspapers, Inc., 555 A.2d 321 (R.I.), cert. denied 493 U.S. 814 (1989), defendant reported that Lampinski had been involved in a personnel dispute with the local YMCA and had had a heart attack and died while demonstrating about 200 yards from a YMCA board meeting. The story continued that his family was angry because they felt he "should have been given early attention by either a doctor or a paramedic at the board meeting." The next paragraph began "Dr. Paul J. Healey is Y president and was at the meeting when Lampinski collapsed." How are these two sentences to be read?

The court upheld a jury verdict and judgment for $302,000. Looking at the evidence in the most favorable light to plaintiff, the court thought a reader could understand that "plaintiff was asked and refused to help Lampinski and that there was enough time for plaintiff to render aid to Lampinski."

The drawing of inferences may be essential to the analysis of many, if not most, defamation cases. Although this presented no special problems at common law, some constitutional questions have been raised. We review these at p. 1061, infra.

Remember that ambiguity must be distinguished from the situation in which readers may understand a statement differently because of different backgrounds they bring to the material. Is there a difference between bringing expertise to a subject and simply knowing more about the facts than most readers? In Ben–Oliel v. Press Publishing Co., 167 N.E. 432 (N.Y.1929), the plaintiff, an expert on Palestinian art and customs, was falsely stated to have written an article on that subject that appeared in the defendant's Sunday newspaper. The article would have impressed virtually all the newspaper's regular readers. Unfortunately, the article had several errors that would lead fellow experts to think the writer incompetent. The court held that a jury could find that plaintiff had been defamed in the eyes of the very small number of experts even though they were overwhelmed in number by the ordinary readers.

On this subject, the Second Restatement's section 559 comment *e* states that to be actionable the content of a statement must be of the sort that would hurt the plaintiff "in the eyes of a substantial and respectable minority" of the community. Was the minority substantial in the *Ben-Oliel* case? Should it have to be? The question of whether the minority is "respectable," or needs to be, is raised in the following case.

Matherson v. Marchello

New York Appellate Division, Second Department, 1984.
100 App.Div.2d 233, 473 N.Y.S.2d 998.

TITONE, J.P.

. . .

On October 28, 1980, radio station WBAB conducted an interview with the members of a singing group called "The Good Rats." Following a commercial which advertised a Halloween party at an establishment known as "OBI", a discussion ensued in which various members of the group explained that they are no longer permitted to play at OBI South because:

"Good Rat # 1:	Well, you know, we had that law suit with Mr. Matherson.
"A Good Rat:	And we used to fool around with his wife.
"Good Rat # 1:	And we won.
"A Good Rat:	One of us used to fool around with his wife. He wasn't into that too much.
"D.J.:	Oh yea.

"Good Rat # 1:   We used to start off our gigs over there with the
(interrupted and   National Anthem, and he was very upset about
joined by another   that, now all of a sudden he's very patriotic and
Good Rat)   he's using it in his commercials.
"A Good Rat: I don't think it was his wife that he got so upset
   about, I think it was when somebody started
   messing around with his boyfriend that he really
   freaked out. Really.
   (Laughter)
   That did it man."

Plaintiffs, who are husband and wife, subsequently commenced this action against "The Good Rats" (as individuals and against their record company), alleging that the words "we used to fool around with his wife" and "I don't think it was his wife that he got upset about, I think it was when somebody started messing around with his boyfriend that he really freaked out" were defamatory. They seek compensatory and punitive damages for humiliation, mental anguish, loss of reputation and injury to their marital relationship as well as for the loss of customers, business opportunities and good will allegedly suffered by Mr. Matherson. [The lower court] granted defendants' motion to dismiss. . . .

. . .

On the question of whether the allegedly defamatory statements are actionable, our scope of review is limited. . . . Unless we can say, as a matter of law, that the statements could not have had a defamatory connotation, it is for the jury to decide whether or not they did [ ].

Taken in the context of a rock and roll station's interview with musicians, and taking note of contemporary usage, we have no difficulty in concluding that the words "fooling around with his wife" could have been interpreted by listeners to mean that Mrs. Matherson was having an affair with one of the defendants. Such charges are clearly libelous. . . .

The second comment—"I don't think it was his wife that he got upset about, I think it was when somebody started messing around with his boyfriend that he really freaked out"—presents a far more subtle and difficult question (see Imputation of Homosexuality as Defamation, Ann., 3 A.L.R.4th 752). It is plaintiffs' contention that this statement constitutes an imputation of homosexuality which should be recognized as defamatory. Defendants, on the other hand, basically do not deny that such reading is plausible. Rather, they claim that many public officials have acknowledged their homosexuality and, therefore, no social stigma may be attached to such an allegation. We are constrained to reject defendants' position at this point in time.

It cannot be said that social opprobrium of homosexuality does not remain with us today. Rightly or wrongly, many individuals still view homosexuality as immoral (see Newsweek Aug. 8, 1983, p. 33, containing the results of a Gallup poll; [ ]). Legal sanctions imposed upon homosexuals in areas ranging from immigration (Matter of Longstaff, 716 F.2d 1439) to military service (Watkins v. United States Army, 721 F.2d 687) have recently been reaffirmed despite the concurring Judge's observation in *Watkins* (p. 691) that it "demonstrates a callous disregard for the progress

American law and society have made toward acknowledging that an individual's choice of life style is not the concern of government, but a fundamental aspect of personal liberty" [   ].

In short, despite the fact that an increasing number of homosexuals are publicly expressing satisfaction and even pride in their status, the potential and probable harm of a false charge of homosexuality, in terms of social and economic impact, cannot be ignored. Thus, on the facts of this case, where the plaintiffs are husband and wife, we find, given the narrow scope of review, that the imputation of homosexuality is "reasonably susceptible of a defamatory connotation". . . .

[The order of dismissal was reversed.]

THOMPSON, BRACKEN, and RUBIN, JJ., concur.

Notes and Questions

1. Applying the principles developed so far, is the first charge ("fooling around") defamatory as a matter of law—or is it a jury question?

2. The implication of homosexuality raises the question of what attributes we must ascribe to the "ordinary reader" or recipient of the message. It is one thing to ascribe certain reading abilities and certain intelligence. Now must we ask about the value systems of those who receive the message? The court looks to a survey that shows that "many" Americans "still view homosexuality as immoral." Is that the right question? What about those within the listening audience of WBAB? Or is it the views of those that plaintiff cares most about—those who learn about the statement who are in his social, business, or religious circle?

3. In Grant v. Reader's Digest Ass'n, 151 F.2d 733 (2d Cir.1945), cert. denied 326 U.S. 797 (1946), defendant published an article calling the plaintiff (a lawyer) "a legislative representative for the Massachusetts Communist Party." Judge L. Hand stated the question to be whether it was defamatory "to write of a lawyer that he has acted as agent of the Communist Party and is a believer in its aims and methods." Defendant argued that under New York law the question was whether "right thinking" persons would find the assertion defamatory. The court responded that a person "may value his reputation even among those who do not embrace the prevailing moral standards; and it would seem that the jury should be allowed to appraise how far he should be indemnified for the disesteem of such persons." It suffices "if there be some, as there certainly are," who would think ill of the plaintiff as the result of defendant's assertion "even though they would be 'wrong-thinking' people if they did."

4. Consider the following examples in terms of the nature of defamation and the role of minority attitudes:

a. A statement that the plaintiff was seduced by "the mad monk," Rasputin. Youssoupoff v. Metro–Goldwyn–Mayer Pictures, Ltd., 50 T.L.R. 581 (Eng.C.A.1934). A statement that Rasputin raped the plaintiff.

b. A statement that the plaintiff is of illegitimate birth. Shelby v. Sun Printing & Publishing Ass'n, 38 Hun 474 (1886), affirmed on the opinion below 15 N.E. 895 (N.Y.1888). Can it ever be defamatory to say that someone is of legitimate birth? Has the notion of "illegitimacy" lost its power to defame?

c. A letter from a woman with whom plaintiff had previously been "romantically involved" to a woman with whom plaintiff now had a "personal relationship" stating that plaintiff was "not divorced." Vereen v. Clayborne, 623 A.2d 1190 (D.C.App.1993).

d. A statement that a reputable physician illegally terminated life support services on a terminally ill patient who was in great pain and who had stated in writing several times that he wished to die. Might it be defamatory to say that the physician refused the patient's request to do so?

e. A statement that the plaintiff worked as a federal undercover agent. Agnant v. Shakur, 30 F.Supp.2d 420 (S.D.N.Y.1998).

f. A statement that erroneously accused a gunman of missing his target. See Note, The Community Segment in Defamation Actions: A Dissenting Essay, 58 Yale L.J. 1387 (1949).

For an extensive consideration of the nature of the tort and the interests it might vindicate, see Post, The Social Foundations of Defamation Law: Reputation and the Constitution, 74 Calif.L.Rev. 691 (1986).

5. *Parody.* Should a court accept a defendant's argument that a statement presented as fact is so preposterous it could not be taken seriously? A supermarket tabloid made that argument in Mitchell v. Globe International Publishing, Inc., 773 F.Supp. 1235 (W.D.Ark.1991). Under the headline "World's oldest newspaper carrier, 101, quits because she's pregnant!" the Sun published a story saying that a woman who had been delivering papers in Australia for 94 years became pregnant by a man she met on her paper route. The story was accompanied by a photo of plaintiff, a 96-year-old newsstand operator in Mountain Home, Arkansas.

The defendant moved for summary judgment on the ground the story could not be understood to describe actual facts about the plaintiff, in part because "every one is well aware that it is physically impossible for a 101- or 96-year-old woman to be pregnant." The court denied the motion, considering "the surrounding circumstances in which the statements were made, the medium by which they were published, and the audience for which they were intended." Even if the facts stated in the headline could not be believed, the implication of sexual promiscuity could, the judge said. "The articles are written in a purportedly factual manner. . . . The Sun apparently intends for the readers to determine which articles are fact and which are fiction or what percentage of a given article is fact or fiction." The case proceeded to trial and a jury returned a general verdict for the newspaper on the libel claim but awarded Mitchell substantial damages on the alternate theory of false light invasion of privacy, discussed in Chapter XIV.

Compare San Francisco Bay Guardian, Inc. v. Superior Court, 21 Cal.Rptr.2d 464 (App. 1993), in which the newspaper's April Fool's edition carried a purported letter from plaintiff landlord asserting such things as that his tenants behaved better after electroshock therapy. Plaintiff presented five readers—his accountant, his attorney, a fellow club member, an acquaintance, and a co-owner of several buildings—who said that they did not understand the parody and took the letter seriously.

The trial court's refusal to dismiss the complaint was reversed on appeal. The average reader, considering the entire newspaper, and the parody section, would understand the parody. The table of contents announced that the edition contained a "special parody section." That section appeared at the end of the regular paper and was printed upside down. It began with a picture of the publisher taking a position "at odds with the usual editorial stance of the Bay Guardian. The parody portion continued with mock articles and pictures, some of which are recognizable as jokes at first glance." Although the letters to the editor were not so obvious, the point was clear there too: the paper announced that it welcomed letters and that "Copies of all unsigned letters will be sent to the Federal Bureau of Investigation for cross-checking. In case of accident, we will notify next of kin."

Could this analysis have been applied to support the Sun's arguments in the *Mitchell* case?

2. "OF AND CONCERNING" PLAINTIFF

Identification. In addition to showing the defamatory nature of the publication, the plaintiff must show that the statement was understood to refer to, though not necessarily aimed at, the plaintiff. This is not difficult if the plaintiff is named or clearly identified in the publication, but sometimes the requirement can raise serious questions. This element is often called "colloquium" and establishes that the plaintiff is the person (or among the persons) defamed. In Taj Mahal Travel, Inc. v. Delta Airlines Inc., 164 F.3d 186 (3d Cir.1998), defendant wrote some customers of plaintiff (and other travel agencies) who held airline tickets that their tickets were reported stolen. The letter stated that Delta had not been paid for the tickets. The court held that a charge of criminality could be inferred. Although no travel agencies were named, a jury could conclude that those who paid money to plaintiff could have understood the charge to be "of and concerning" plaintiff.

A fairly common problem arises from the use of generic file photographs to illustrate a story in the print medium. See, e.g., Morrell v. Forbes, Inc., 603 F.Supp. 1305 (D.Mass.1985)(plaintiff fisherman's photo used to illustrate story about organized crime on the Boston waterfront). See also Clark v. American Broadcasting Cos., Inc., 684 F.2d 1208 (6th Cir.1982), cert. denied 460 U.S. 1040 (1983), involving a program about prostitution. The plaintiff, who had been photographed without her knowledge while walking on a city street, was shown on the screen while the narrator was describing the prevalence of prostitution in the neighborhood.

(For the special problems of identification of plaintiffs in works of fiction, see Symposium, Defamation in Fiction, 51 Brooklyn L.Rev. 223 (1985)).

Corporations. It is clear that corporations may be defamation plaintiffs. Section 561 of the Second Restatement states that a corporation for profit may sue if "the matter tends to prejudice it in the conduct of its business or to deter others from dealing with it." A corporation that is not for profit may sue if it "depends upon financial support from the public, and the matter tends to interfere with its activities by prejudicing it in public estimation."

A separate question involves the relationship between a corporation and its shareholders. If the corporation is large and its stock widely held, courts generally conclude that stockholders may not sue for the libel of the corporation. But in closely held corporations, courts have held that a libel of the corporation may be understood by the reasonable audience to be addressed as well to the controlling individuals, even if they are not mentioned in the story. This result is even clearer if the individual and the corporation have the same name. See discussion in Schiavone Construction Co. v. Time Inc., 619 F.Supp. 684 (D.N.J.1985).

These inquiries about corporate reputation focus on charges of misconduct that tend to lead others to think less of the management. Another type of charge relates only to the nature of the product that is produced—but does not suggest that management knew or even that it should have known about the problem. For example, in Auvil v. CBS "60 Minutes," 67 F.3d 816 (9th Cir.1995), discussed in Chapter XV, a guest on the Oprah Winfrey show asserted that American beef was unsafe. In this type of case the corporation's or the industry's sales may fall sharply, but the claim is not based on harm to reputation; it is harm to economic interests.

Group libel. Different problems arise when the statement is about one or more members of a group of individuals. In such cases might one member be able to claim that the statement hurt his or her personal reputation? At the extreme, an attack on all lawyers in the United States or on all clergymen would be held to be such a general broadside that no individual lawyer or clergyman could sue. The same would be true of broadside attacks on racial, religious, or ethnic groups.

At the other extreme, it is generally accepted that a charge made against a small group may defame all members of that group. For example, a newspaper article may assert that "the officers" of a corporation have embezzled funds. There are only four officers of the corporation. Each of them may be found to have been defamed even though the statement was that "one of the officers of the corporation" had embezzled funds. The group is small enough so that all four officials are put under a shadow, and most states would permit all four to sue.

As the group grows larger the impact of the statement may depend on the inclusiveness of the language as well as the size of the total group. In one case, a defamatory charge was made against one unidentified member of a 21-member police force. All 21 sued. The trial court's dismissal was affirmed. It was feared that allowing the action would permit a suit by an entire baseball team over a report that one member was disciplined for brawling. Such a result "would chill communication to the marrow." The court explained, "By no stretch of imagination can it be thought to suggest that the conduct of the one [described in the article] is typical of all. Noting the individual's membership in the group does not suggest a common determinant of character so much as simply a practical reference point." But suppose the charge had been against "all but one" of the members of that police force? Such a statement may reflect on each member of the force. Arcand v. Evening Call Publishing Co., 567 F.2d 1163 (1st Cir.1977).

One case presented three aspects of this problem. A book about Dallas stated that "some" Neiman–Marcus department store models were "call girls. . . . The salesgirls are good, too—pretty and often much cheaper. . . ." And "most of the [male] sales staff are fairies, too."

Suits were filed by all nine models, 30 of the 382 saleswomen, and 15 of the 25 salesmen. The defendants did not challenge the right of the nine models to sue. The other two groups were challenged as being too large.

The claim of "the salesgirls" was dismissed. The result would be the same even if the authors had explicitly referred to "all"—and even if all 382 had sued. The judge cited cases rejecting suits when the statements attacked all officials of a statewide union or all the taxicab drivers in Washington, D.C.

On the other hand, the salesmen's case was not dismissed. It was close to others involving members of a posse, or the 12 doctors on a hospital's residential staff. Would the result have been the same if the authors had referred to "some" or "a few" of the men? Neiman–Marcus v. Lait, 13 F.R.D. 311 (S.D.N.Y.1952).

Would the legal system find it administratively difficult to handle a damage action brought by 382 plaintiffs, even though they might deserve some compensation? Is the development of class actions relevant here?

One court has rejected the emphasis on the absolute size of the group in favor of the defined nature of the group, its prominence, and the role of the individual in the group. Using these criteria, the court concluded that 53 members of the 71-member police force of Newburgh, N.Y., in 1972 could sue for a statement in 1979 suggesting that, although they were not indicted for misdeeds along with 18 colleagues, the other 53 must have known what was going on. Brady v. Ottaway Newspapers, Inc., 445 N.Y.S.2d 786 (App.Div.1981).

Although defamation of large groups—ethnic, religious, professional— does not result in a cause of action in any state, some states have sought to develop criminal sanctions against such attacks. Even though these statutes were held constitutional, 5–4, in Beauharnais v. Illinois, 343 U.S. 250 (1952)(upholding statute barring portrayals of "depravity, criminality, unchastity, or lack of virtue of a class of citizens, of any race, color, creed, or religion" that subjected that group to "contempt, derision, or obloquy or which is productive of breach of the peace or riots"), they have been put in some doubt by R.A.V. v. City of St. Paul, 505 U.S. 377 (1992)(invalidating city ordinance punishing anyone who places on public or private property any "symbol, object, appellation, characterization or graffiti, including but not limited to, a burning cross or Nazi swastika, which one knows or has reasonable grounds to know arouses anger, alarm or resentment in others on the basis of race, color, creed, religions or gender").

3.   STRICT LIABILITY

The common law often held a publisher strictly liable for defamatory statements. Thus, the case was established even if the offending statement appeared to be either neutral or positive, but, when supplemented by other facts, unknown to defendant, turned out to be defamatory. For example, a newspaper might, based on reliable information, incorrectly report a baby's birth. If some readers knew that its parents had been married only three months, the newspaper would be held to have committed defamation because in the eyes of those readers who knew the additional fact the newspaper story suggested unchastity. If a magazine carries what it believes to be fiction but readers reasonably think the words refer to an identifiable plaintiff, a defamation may be found. These subjects are discussed at length in Smith, Jones v. Hulton: Three Conflicting Views as to Defamation, 60 U.Pa.L.Rev. 365, 461 (1912); Holdsworth, A Chapter of Accidents in the Law of Libel, 57 L.Q.Rev. 74 (1941).

In fact, the common law did not impose strict liability on what were viewed as disseminators of the finished product—newsstands, bookstores, and libraries. These institutions were held liable only if the plaintiff could establish that the defendant knew or had reason to know of the presence of the defamation in the work being sold or loaned. Although the common law might have evolved in cases involving computer bulletin boards, a Congressional enactment has been held to immunize Internet service providers (ISPs) for defamation uttered over their facilities. In Zeran v. America Online, Inc., 129 F.3d 327 (4th Cir.1997), cert. denied 524 U.S. 937 (1998), a few days after the bombing of the federal building in Oklahoma City, an AOL bulletin board carried what purported to be an advertisement for "Naughty Oklahoma T–Shirts" with offensive slogans. Interested buyers were given plaintiff's home phone number. P, who had no connection with the product, was bombarded with scurrilous and threatening letters. The court relied heavily on 47 U.S.C. § 2309(c)(1): "No provider or user of an interactive computer service shall be treated as the publisher or speaker of any information provided by another information content provider." According to the court, "lawsuits seeking to hold a service provider liable for its exercise of a publisher's traditional editorial functions—such as deciding whether to publish, withdraw, postpone or alter content—are barred." See Lidsky, Silencing John Doe: Defamation & Discourse in Cyberspace, 49 Duke L.J. 855 (2000).

Although, as we shall see shortly, the common law developed a few privileges that softened the rigors of strict liability on original publishers, strict liability has remained a fixture of the tort well. Most of the constitutional developments to be discussed are traceable to this feature.

4. DAMAGES: LIBEL AND SLANDER

Generally, in tort law, plaintiffs are entitled to recover damages for harm they can prove they sustained. Defamation generally—but not always—permits plaintiffs who can show that they have been defamed to recover proven damages. These may include lost wages and similar losses, as well as proven damages for broad reputational loss. The first type, called "special damages," includes specific identifiable pecuniary losses that the plaintiff can prove he or she sustained and can trace to the defendant's defamatory statement.

The second type, "general damages," includes damages to reputation that the plaintiff has suffered in ways that cannot be easily correlated with dollars and cents. This is usually a claim that the plaintiff has suffered general reputational harm in some community—whether it be a geographical community or one based on, say, religious, social, or professional relationships. Sometimes the plaintiff is able to prove that these losses have occurred—as, for example, by an opinion poll that reveals a massive loss of reputation—even though the damages sustained from that loss are not as obvious as a doctor's bill.

Defamation law has two aspects that are unlike tort law generally. One is that plaintiffs sometimes can recover "presumed" general damages—without proving that they have suffered any actual damage, whether special or general. In awarding damages for "presumed" general damages, the trier is to consider the words used, the medium used, and the predicted response of the community. The other unusual feature is that sometimes the plaintiff must prove the existence of special damages before being allowed to recover *any* general damages—even if plaintiff can prove that the general damages occurred.

Under these two unusual damage rules, some plaintiffs may receive a substantial recovery without proof of any damages, while others may recover nothing at all because they were required, but were unable, to prove special damages. In this latter situation, they are barred from recovering any general damages whether provable or presumed, in cases in which most people would recognize that the plaintiffs had been seriously harmed.

The determination of what damages plaintiffs must prove in defamation cases is largely rooted in history, and requires the introduction of the terms "libel" and "slander." When the relevant damage rules evolved, slanders, generally oral defamations, were sued upon in the common law courts. Libels, generally written defamations, had become a major concern of the English government because of the recent development of printing. Libels were addressed in the Court of Star Chamber. After the Star Chamber was abolished, oral and written defamations were both redressed by the common law courts. Those courts, however, preserved some damage distinctions between the two types of defamation that have survived to our day.

The following case explores the role of the libel-slander distinction.

Matherson v. Marchello

New York Appellate Division, Second Department, 1984.
100 App.Div.2d 233, 473 N.Y.S.2d 998.

[This is the same case reported earlier. In that excerpt, the court considered whether the passages were defamatory. Here the further question is whether the plaintiff must prove special damages in order to proceed with the case.]

TITONE, J.P.

. . .

Preliminarily, we observe that if special damages are a necessary ingredient of plaintiffs' cause of action, Special Term properly found the allegations of the complaint to be deficient.

Special damages consist of "the loss of something having economic or pecuniary value" (Restatement, Torts 2d, § 575, Comment b) which "must flow directly from the injury to reputation caused by the defamation; not from the [emotional] effects of defamation" [ ] and it is settled law that they must be fully and accurately identified "with sufficient particularity to identify actual losses" [ ]. When loss of business is claimed, the persons who ceased to be customers must be named and the losses itemized [ ]. "Round figures" or a general allegation of a dollar amount as special damages do not suffice [ ]. Consequently, plaintiffs' nonspecific conclusory allegations do not meet the stringent requirements imposed for pleading special damages [ ].

We must, therefore, determine whether an allegation of special damages is necessary. In large measure, this turns on which branch of the law of defamation is involved. As a result of historical accident, which, though not sensibly defensible today, is so well settled as to be beyond our ability to uproot it [ ], there is a schism between the law governing slander and the law governing libel [ ].[1]

A plaintiff suing in slander must plead special damages unless the defamation falls into any one of four per se categories [discussed in the next main case].

On the other hand, a plaintiff suing in libel need not plead or prove special damages. . . . Thus, unlike the law of slander, in the law of libel

---

1. . . . The distinction has . . . not gone unchallenged. As early as 1812, a defendant urged that a libel read by one person should not be treated more harshly than a slander spoken to hundreds in a crowd. While the Judge conceded the merits of the argument, he refused to overturn the firmly rooted contrary precedents. Thorley v. Lord Kerry [4 Taunt. 355, 128 Eng.Rep. 367 (1812)].

the existence of damage is conclusively presumed from the publication itself and a plaintiff may rely on general damages. . . .

. . .

Traditionally, the demarcation between libel and slander rested upon whether the words were written or spoken [ ]. Written defamations were considered far more serious because, at the time the distinction arose, few persons could read or write and, therefore, anything which was written would carry a louder ring of purported truth [ ]. In addition, a written defamation could be disseminated more widely and carried a degree of permanence.

With the advent of mass communication, the differential was blurred. Motion pictures were held to be libel [ ]. No set rule developed with respect to radio and television [ ]. In some cases, distinction was drawn between [extemporaneous] speech, which was classified as slander, and words read from a script, which were classified as libel [ ]. This distinction was the subject of considerable criticism.

We today hold that defamation which is broadcast by means of radio or television should be classified as libel. As we have noted, one of the primary reasons assigned to justify the imposition of broader liability for libel than for slander has been the greater capacity for harm that a writing is assumed to have because of the wide range of dissemination consequent upon its permanence in form. Given the vast and far-flung audiences reached by the broadcasting media today, it is self-evident that the potential harm to a defamed person is far greater than that involved in a single writing (see Hartmann v. Winchell, [73 N.E.2d 30 (N.Y.1947)], Fuld, J. concurring). Section 568A of the Restatement of Torts, Second, and the more recent decisions in sister States [ ] opt for holding such defamation to be libel and we perceive no basis for perpetuating a meaningless, outmoded, distinction.

[The court concluded that neither charge required special damages, and reversed the lower court's dismissal and reinstated the complaint.]

Notes and Questions

1. Which of the justifications offered for the differing treatment of written and oral defamation is strongest? In addition to those offered by the court, consider the notion that a writing still may be given more weight because it requires more thought and planning than a spontaneous oral utterance, which might simply be tossed off. (California, by statute, [Civil Code §§ 46 and 48.5(4)], treats defamations by radio and television as slander.)

2. Although most libels and slanders are conveyed by the use of words or writing, other actions may suffice. See, e.g., K–Mart Corp. v. Washington, 866 P.2d 274 (Nev.1993), concluding that marching the hand-cuffed plaintiff customer through defendant's store to the security office was an actionable pantomime that imputed shoplifting and thus was slander per se. But see Bolton v. Department of Human Services, 540

N.W.2d 523 (Minn.1995), in which the court refused to find a defamation when defendant's supervisor silently accompanied plaintiff to the exit door of defendant's facility immediately after plaintiff was discharged. The court observed that in this context "where there is no word spoken or conduct other than a simple escorting" there can be no defamation.

3. In some states, including New York, the answer to the special damages question is complete once the publication has been called libel because in those states libel never requires special damages. In a second group of states, however, even if the statement is called libel, special damages are required unless (1) the defamatory sting is clear on its face or (2) if not clear on its face, when fleshed out with extrinsic facts, the sting would be slander per se.

The terms "per se" and "per quod" have different meanings in libel and slander. Consider the following excerpt from 1 R. Sack, Sack on Defamation: Libel, Slander, and Related Problems 2–96 (3d ed. 2000):

> As a practical matter, words that, uttered orally, are slanderous per se, are *usually* also libelous per se when written. But the reason they are slanderous per se normally has little to do with the reason that they are libelous per se. To say of a woman that she is a whore or of a man that he robs his business associates blind is slanderous per se because it falls within one of the four categories. The same words when written are libelous per se, not because they fit within a slander category, but because they tend on their face to disgrace the person about whom they are written. Extrinsic facts are unnecessary to explain their defamatory meaning.

> But the converse is not true. Statements which are libelous per se when written often are not slanderous per se when spoken. However degrading a statement, however injurious to reputation, however outrageous, however plain the defamatory meaning on the face of the statement and therefore however clear that the statement when written is libelous per se, unless the defamatory charge falls within one of the four specific slander categories, it is not slanderous per se when merely spoken, and special damages must be pleaded and proved. To call someone a "coward," for example, is libelous per se but probably not slanderous per se.

Here a footnote states: "Unless the plaintiff is a policeman, professional soldier, or in a similar category, so that an imputation of cowardice tends to injure plaintiff in his or her trade, business, or profession."

Even if special damages must be proven, a plaintiff who is able to do so becomes eligible for general damages as well.

Liberman v. Gelstein

Court of Appeals of New York, 1992.
80 N.Y.2d 429, 605 N.E.2d 344, 590 N.Y.S.2d 857.

[Plaintiff landlord sued a member of the tenants' board of governors for slander. This case involves the second and fifth causes of action. In the second, defendant is alleged to have had the following exchange with Kohler, a fellow member of the board of directors:

> "Gelstein: Can you find out from your friend at the precinct which cop is on the take from Liberman?

> "Kohler: What are you talking about?

> "Gelstein: There is a cop on the take from Liberman. That's why none of the building's cars ever get tickets—they can park anywhere because Liberman's paid them off. He gives them a hundred or two hundred a week."

The fifth cause of action alleged that defendant made the following statement in the presence of employees of the building: "Liberman threw a punch at me. He screamed at my wife and daughter. He called my daughter a slut and threatened to kill me and my family."]

KAYE, JUDGE.

. . .

. . . . After discovery, defendant sought summary judgment dismissing the complaint. On the second cause of action, defendant invoked the "common interest" qualified privilege, characterizing his conversation with Kohler, a colleague on the board of governors, as an inquiry designed to uncover wrongdoing by the landlord affecting tenants. At his deposition, defendant testified that several vehicles operated by the building's management regularly parked in front of the building beyond the legal limit but never received parking summonses. He further testified that he was told by two building employees, whom he identified, that Liberman was bribing the police to avoid parking tickets. Defendant admitted that he did not know whether the allegations were true, but testified that they "sounded truthful" to him. Accordingly, defendant testified that he approached Kohler—whose friend was captain of the local police precinct—in an effort to discover whether the allegations were true.

. . .

[On the fifth cause of action, defendant argued that the statements were either true, not defamatory, or never made. The lower court dismissed the second cause of action on the ground that it was qualifiedly privileged and that plaintiff had failed to raise triable issues of malice. The fifth cause of action was dismissed on the ground that the words could only have been understood by those who were familiar with the parties' history of conflict as rhetorical hyperbole. The Appellate Division affirmed.]

II.

Slander as a rule is not actionable unless the plaintiff suffers special damage. [ ] Special damages contemplate "the loss of something having economic or pecuniary value" (Restatement § 575, comment *b*; [ ]). Plaintiff has not alleged special damages, and thus his slander claims are not sustainable unless they fall within one of the exceptions to the rule.

The four established exceptions (collectively "slander per se") consist of statements (i) charging plaintiff with a serious crime; (ii) that tend to injure another in his or her trade, business or profession; (iii) that plaintiff has a loathsome disease; or (iv) imputing unchastity to a woman [   ]. When statements fall within one of these categories, the law presumes that damages will result, and they need not be alleged or proven.

Plaintiff claims that both sets of statements were slanderous per se inasmuch as they charged him with criminal conduct. Not every imputation of unlawful behavior, however, is slanderous per se. "With the extension of criminal punishment to many minor offenses, it was obviously necessary to make some distinction as to the character of the crime, since a charge of a traffic violation, for example, would not exclude a person from society, and today would do little, if any, harm to his [or her] reputation at all" (Prosser [   ]). Thus, the law distinguishes between serious and relatively minor offenses, and only statements regarding the former are actionable without proof of damage (see, Restatement § 571, comment *g* [list of crimes actionable as per se slander includes murder, burglary, larceny, arson, rape, kidnapping]).

We agree with plaintiff that defendant's alleged statement that "[t]here is a cop on the take from Liberman" charges a serious crime—bribery (see, Penal Law § 200.00; [   ]). Accordingly, the statements constituting the second cause of action are actionable without the need to establish special harm, and absent any privilege would be sufficient to go to a jury.

We disagree, however, with plaintiff's contention that the statement "Liberman . . . threatened to kill me and my family" was slanderous per se. Plaintiff claims these words falsely attributed to him the commission of the crime of harassment (see, Penal Law § 240.25; [   ]). Harassment is a relatively minor offense in the New York Penal Law—not even a misdemeanor—and thus the harm to the reputation of a person falsely accused of committing harassment would be correspondingly insubstantial. Hence, even if we agreed with plaintiff that the statement would not have been construed by the listeners as rhetorical hyperbole, the cause of action must nevertheless be dismissed because it is not slanderous per se to claim that someone committed harassment.

Plaintiff alternatively argues that the statements in the fifth cause of action tended to harm him in his business as a property owner, and thus are actionable under the "trade, business or profession" exception. That exception, however, is "limited to defamation of a kind incompatible with the proper conduct of the business, trade, profession or office itself. The statement must be made with reference to a matter of significance and importance for that purpose, rather than a more general reflection upon the plaintiff's character or qualities" (Prosser [   ]). Thus, "charges against a clergyman of drunkenness and other moral misconduct affect his fitness for the performance of the duties of his profession, although the same charges against a business man or tradesman do not so affect him" (Restatement § 573, comment *c*). The statements at issue are unrelated to plaintiff's status as a landlord, and therefore do not fall into the "trade, business or profession" exception [   ].

In sum, the second cause of action is on its face sustainable without special damages because it involves charges of serious crime, and the fifth cause of action was correctly dismissed.

[The court concluded that the plaintiff had not presented enough to overcome defendant's privilege as to the bribery charge. The dismissal of the second cause of action was affirmed. We return to this issue at p. 978, infra.]

SIMONS, ACTING C.J., and TITONE, HANCOCK and BELLACOSA, JJ., concur with KAYE, J. [JUDGE SMITH dissented in part on an issue related to privilege, discussed infra].

Notes and Questions

1. Why does the second cause of action not require special damages? Why does the fifth cause of action require them? What kinds of special damages might a plaintiff in this situation be able to show?

2. What is so special about these four categories of words? In Nazeri v. Missouri Valley College, 860 S.W.2d 303 (Mo.1993), the court extended the fourth category to any "serious sexual misconduct" following the Second Restatement's gender-neutral approach in § 569, comment *f*.

In *Ward v. Zelikovsky*, p. 957 supra, involving the statement at a meeting of condominium owners, the lower court had found the charge of bigotry was actionable and then decided that it did not need special damages. The court reached that position by adding a fifth category to the slander per se list for imputations of racial or ethnic bigotry. In reversing on the ground that the statement was not actionable, the supreme court noted its refusal to add new categories to the four existing ones: the "trend of modern tort law is to focus on the injury not the wrong and the slander per se categories are a relic from tort law's previous age." It left for "another day" the question of whether to abolish the slander per se categories and require special damages for all slanders. See Anderson, Reputation, Compensation, and Proof, 25 Wm. & Mary L.Rev. 747 (1984).

3. In addition to general and special damages, two other classifications loom large in defamation law: nominal damages and punitive damages. Although nominal damages are unimportant in most tort actions, they may be central in defamation cases. The award of a symbolic amount such as six cents usually shows that the jury found the attack to be false but also found the words not to have hurt. But was that because the speaker was not credible or the plaintiff's strong reputation blunted the harm or his reputation was so low nothing could really hurt it? See Reynolds v. Pegler, 223 F.2d 429 (2d Cir.), cert. denied 350 U.S. 846 (1955)(upholding a jury award of $1 in compensatory damages and $175,000 in punitive damages against the various defendants).

4. Several states at common law have rejected the concept of punitive damages in all tort cases; others have sharply limited the amount of such damages. Recall p. 790, supra. Some states have decided to bar punitive damages only in defamation cases and other tort cases involving harm through speech. As we shall see shortly, recent federal and state constitutional developments may also restrict the availability of such damages in libel cases.

5. DEFENSES

In this section we consider the variety of state common law or statutory defenses to the basic defamation claim. Although traditional tort defenses such as consent apply, our focus here is on those defenses unique to defamation law. See Baker v. Bhajan, 871 P.2d 374 (N.M.1994), applying the consent bar to a plaintiff who, when applying for a job with the state, signed a contract that "agreed to release from liability those who provided information . . . under a guarantee of confidentiality" when responding to inquiries from the police.

a. Truth

The most obvious defense, but one little relied upon in litigation, is to prove the essential truth of the defamatory statement. During the period when the English government rigorously used the law of criminal libel, truth was not a defense because unfavorable truths about government or officials were more likely to stir up anti-government attitudes and actions than were falsehoods. But now truth is recognized as a complete defense to civil libel. Because the action is intended to compensate those whose reputations are damaged falsely, if the defendant has spoken the truth, the reputational harm is deemed to provide no basis for an action. (A minority of states purport to require the truth to have been spoken with "good motives" or for "justifiable ends" or both.)

The defendant need not prove literal truth but must establish the "sting" of the charge. Thus, if the defendant has charged the plaintiff with stealing $25,000 from a bank, truth will be established even if the actual amount was only $12,000. In Masson v. New Yorker Magazine, Inc., 501 U.S. 496 (1991), the Court captured the common law's spirit in observing that the common law of libel "overlooks minor inaccuracies and concentrates upon substantial truth." Thus, the test was whether what was published "would have had a different effect upon the mind of the reader from that which the pleaded truth would have produced." See also Haynes v. Alfred A. Knopf, Inc., 8 F.3d 1222 (7th Cir.1993)(the law protects false "details that, while not trivial, would not if corrected have altered the picture that the true facts paint"). Compare Posadas v. City of Reno, 851 P.2d 438 (Nev.1993), holding actionable a claim based on defendant's false charge that plaintiff police officer had "admitted he lied under oath" (the crime of perjury), when in fact he had admitted to lying (not under oath) to two other officers who questioned him about the charges against him— apparently not a crime.

On the other hand, the false accusation must be close to the true facts. "A sexual deviant might have a worse reputation than an embezzler, but it would not be a defense to a charge of falsely accusing a person of being an embezzler that while he is not an embezzler, he is a sexual deviant, which is worse." Desnick v. American Broadcasting Companies, Inc., 44 F.3d 1345 (7th Cir.1995). Nonetheless, it may help mitigate damages to show that the plaintiff's reputation was already in low esteem for other reasons and thus the plaintiff has suffered less harm than might otherwise have occurred.

In Rouch v. Enquirer & News of Battle Creek, 487 N.W.2d 205 (Mich.1992), cert. denied 507 U.S. 967 (1993), defendant newspaper asserted that plaintiff had been "arrested and charged" with sexual assault of a babysitter and that he had been identified by his children. In fact, plaintiff had never been arraigned and he had been identified by the children of his ex-wife. The court upheld the defense of truth. "Charge" has become an umbrella term for all the stages of the criminal process and may be used as synonymous with "accused." The second was a minor inaccuracy. If the article had been written as the plaintiff says it should have been, the court could not "agree that the gist or sting of the article is changed by these minor differences." Should the result have been different if the article had appeared in a legal newspaper read overwhelmingly by lawyers? See also Schwartz v. American College of Emergency Physicians, 215 F.3d 1140 (10th Cir.2000), holding, under New Mexico law, that a statement that plaintiff was being sued for "stock fraud," though technically inaccurate, was substantially true where plaintiff was being sued by a company for making negative statements about its treatment of its patients while he held a "short" position in that company's stock.

The role of headlines needs special attention because of the difficulty of capturing the story in a few words. In Gunduz v. New York Post Co., 590 N.Y.S.2d 494 (App.Div. 1992), the headline was "Public Enemy No.1" with a much smaller but adjacent sub-head, "City moves to yank license of Apple's 'worst taxi driver.'" The story, about New York City's efforts to revoke plaintiff's taxi license, reported that he had received more summonses and violations than any other cab driver in the city, and described incidents of overcharging and abusing customers. The court thought the big headline "was a fair index of the truthful matter contained in the related news article."

Expungement. In Bahr v. Statesman Journal Co., 624 P.2d 664 (Or. App.1981), a newspaper reported that plaintiff, a candidate for public office, in an interview had "refused to discuss a 1964 conviction on an embezzlement charge.   .   .   . 'I have no record of convictions. My record is clean. I have never been convicted of embezzlement.'" In fact, the conviction had occurred and had later been expunged under state law. The expungement statute gave plaintiff the right to deny that he had ever been convicted. But it also provided that the expungement itself could not be relied upon in a civil action in which the truth of the conviction was an element of the lawsuit. Thus, the newspaper's defense of truth succeeded. What result if the statute had not provided explicitly for the contingency of a libel suit?

———

Truth is little used as a defense, though it would enable a decisive confrontation, perhaps because most statements sued upon are false. Even where the defendant still thinks the statement true, it may be very expensive to establish that truth. A defendant relying on truth usually bears the legal costs of a full-dress trial as well as the sometimes major expense of investigating the matter and gathering enough evidence to ensure the outcome. Particularly when the charge involved is vague and does not allege specific events, the defense of truth may be quite expensive. It can also be risky, because a failed attempt to show truth may only impress the jury with the defendant's intransigence.

Recent constitutional developments have sharply altered the role of truth. See particularly p. 1063, infra.

b. *Privileges*

Not only are there disadvantages to the defense of truth, there are attractive alternatives. Over the centuries the law of defamation has developed several privileges to protect those who utter defamations.

Absolute privileges. Some privileges are "absolute" in the sense that if the occasion gives rise to an absolute privilege, there will be no liability even if the speaker deliberately lied about the plaintiff. The most significant example of this narrow group is the federal and state constitutional privilege afforded legislators, who may not be sued for defamation for any statement made during debate. High executive officials, judges, and participants in judicial proceedings also have an absolute privilege to speak freely on matters relevant to their obligations. No matter how such a speaker abuses the privilege by lying, no tort liability will flow. See Barr v. Matteo, 360 U.S. 564 (1959).

In Carradine v. State of Minnesota, 511 N.W.2d 733 (Minn.1994), the court considered immunity for an arresting officer's statements. The court noted that high-level executive officials—the state's commissioner of the department of public welfare, for example—had absolute privilege. But the test was not the defendant's level in the hierarchy; the rationale for extending such immunity was that "unless the officer in question is absolutely immune from suit, the officer will timorously, instead of fearlessly, perform the function in question and, as a result, government—that is, the public—will be the ultimate loser."

The court thought this standard justified extending such protection to the officer's arrest report. The report is an essential part of the officer's job; the report is also used by prosecutors in deciding whether to file charges and, if so, what charges; it plays a role in any trial in refreshing recollection and providing the basis for impeachment. The absence of immunity

> may well deter the honest officer from fearlessly and vigorously preparing a detailed, accurate report and increase the likelihood that the officer will hesitate to prepare anything more than a bland report that will be less useful within the department and in any subsequent prosecution and trial. To put it another way, instead of preparing a detailed report, the officer will be tempted to leave out certain details, saving those for trial, when any testimony by the officer is absolutely privileged under the judicial privilege.

This would lead to trial by surprise—something the state has been trying to avoid. On the other hand, statements by the arresting officer in response to press inquiries did not deserve such protection. It was not essential to the officer's duties to respond to the press. Such responses were "allowed" by the department but not required.

In Vultaggio v. Yasko, 572 N.W.2d 450 (Wis.1998), defendant attended a city council meeting at which she spoke about the changes in her neighborhood and, in the process, attacked the upkeep of several buildings belonging to plaintiff. In his suit, the court held, 4–3, that defendant should not be absolutely privileged. The majority cited other cases denying such a privilege to those "who supply voluntary testimony to a legislative body." What are the arguments each way?

In another important area, the courts split on whether a litigant has an absolute privilege to announce publicly and to the press that he has just filed a civil complaint. The act of filing the complaint is absolutely privileged in all states—the split is over the public announcement that summarizes the contents of the complaint. See the discussion in Shahvar v. Superior Court, 30 Cal.Rptr.2d 597 (App. 1994), noting that the statutory privilege in California speaks of statements made "in" judicial proceedings—not statements "about" such proceedings. (The statute was then amended to abrogate *Shahvar*. See Rothman v. Jackson, 57 Cal.Rptr.2d 284 (App. 1996), denying attorney a litigation privilege at a press conference.) Attorneys who are privileged to speak freely in judicial proceedings may not claim that same level of protection when responding to reporters' questions. Kennedy v. Zimmermann, 601 N.W.2d 61 (Iowa 1999).

The broadcast media are given an absolute privilege when they are required to grant candidates access to the airwaves. If a candidate commits defamation, the broadcaster is not liable. See Farmers Educational & Cooperative Union of America v. WDAY, Inc., 360 U.S. 525 (1959). The *Medico* case, p. 985, infra, provides another privilege that resembles in some important ways an absolute privilege.

Qualified or conditional privileges. The much more common type of privilege is "qualified" or "conditional," and is considered in the following case. (The terms "qualified" and "conditional" are synonymous.)

Liberman v. Gelstein

Court of Appeals of New York, 1992.
80 N.Y.2d 429, 605 N.E.2d 344, 590 N.Y.S.2d 857.

KAYE J.

[The facts are reprinted at p. 970, supra. After finding that the charge concerning the parked cars was actionable, the court turned to the next issue.]

We next consider whether the courts below properly concluded that defendant's conversation with Kohler was conditionally privileged and that plaintiff failed to raise an issue of fact on malice.

Courts have long recognized that the public interest is served by shielding certain communications, though possibly defamatory, from litigation, rather than risk stifling them altogether [ ]. When compelling public policy requires that the speaker be immune from suit, the law affords an absolute privilege, while statements fostering a lesser public interest are only conditionally privileged [ ].

One such conditional, or qualified, privilege extends to a "communication made by one person to another upon a subject in which both have an interest" [ ]. This "common interest" privilege (see, Restatement § 596) has been applied, for example, to employees of an organization [ ], members of a faculty tenure committee [ ], and constituent physicians of a health insurance plan [ ]. The rationale for applying the privilege in these circumstances is that so long as the privilege is not abused, the flow of information between persons sharing a common interest should not be impeded.

We thus agree . . . that defendant's conversation with Kohler was conditionally privileged (see, Restatement § 596, comment d ["Tenants in common . . . are included within the rule stated in this Section as being conditionally privileged to communicate among themselves matter defamatory of others which concerns their common interests"]). Gelstein and Kohler were members of the governing body of an association formed to protect the tenants' interests. If Liberman was in fact bribing the police so that his cars could occupy spaces in front of the building, that would be inimical to those interests. Thus, Gelstein had a qualified right to communicate his suspicions—though defamatory of Liberman—to Kohler.

The shield provided by a qualified privilege may be dissolved if plaintiff can demonstrate that defendant spoke with "malice" [ ]. Under common law, malice meant spite or ill will [ ]. In New York Times Co. v. Sullivan, 376 U.S. 254 (1964), however, the Supreme Court established an "actual malice" standard for certain cases governed by the First Amendment: "knowledge that [the statement] was false or . . . reckless disregard of whether it was false or not" [ ]. Consequently, the term "malice" has become somewhat confused [ ]. Indeed, as the Supreme Court itself recently acknowledged [Masson v. New Yorker Mag., 501 U.S. 496 (1991)]:

Actual malice under the *New York Times* standard should not be confused with the concept of malice as an evil intent or a motive arising from spite or ill will. . . . We have used the term actual malice as a shorthand to describe the First Amendment protections for speech injurious to reputation and we continue to do so here. But the term can confuse as well as enlighten. In this respect, the phrase may be an unfortunate one.

Nevertheless, malice has now assumed a dual meaning, and we have recognized that the constitutional as well as the common-law standard will suffice to defeat a conditional privilege [   ].

Under the *Times* malice standard, the plaintiff must demonstrate that the "statements [were] made with [a] high degree of awareness of their probable falsity" [   ] In other words, there "must be sufficient evidence to permit the conclusion that the defendant in fact entertained serious doubts as to the truth of [the] publication" [   ]; see also, Restatement § 600, comment *b*.

Applying these principles, we conclude that there is no triable malice issue under the *Times* standard. Although the dissenter below suggested that Gelstein's admission that he did not know whether the bribery charge was true raised a triable issue on malice, there is a critical difference between not knowing whether something is true and being highly aware that it is probably false. Only the latter establishes reckless disregard in a defamation action. Moreover, as the motion court correctly observed, plaintiff's mere characterization of Gelstein's informants as "disgruntled" is insufficient to raise a triable issue. Although plaintiff criticizes defendant for not producing affidavits from the informants—arguing that "it has never been factually established that Gelstein had any source"—it was plaintiff's burden to raise a factual issue on malice, and he did not seek to depose the employees either. In sum, this record is insufficient to raise a triable issue of fact under the *Times* standard of malice.

Similarly, there is insufficient evidence of malice under the common-law definition. A jury could undoubtedly find that, at the time Gelstein discussed his bribery suspicions with Kohler, Gelstein harbored ill will toward Liberman. In this context, however, spite or ill will refers not to defendant's general feelings about plaintiff, but to the speaker's motivation for making the defamatory statements, [   ]. If the defendant's statements were made to further the interest protected by the privilege, it matters not that defendant also despised plaintiff. Thus, a triable issue is raised only if a jury could reasonably conclude that "malice was the one and only cause for the publication" [   ].

Plaintiff has not sustained that burden. Significantly, Gelstein did not make a public announcement of his suspicions—from which an inference could be drawn that his motive was to defame Liberman—but relayed them to a colleague who was in a position to investigate. As noted, the conversation was within the common interest of Gelstein and Kohler, and there is nothing in this record from which a reasonable jury could find that Gelstein was not seeking to advance that common interest.

Thus, the courts below properly concluded that defendant's conversation with Kohler was qualifiedly privileged, and plaintiff failed to raise a fact issue on malice.

Accordingly, the order of the Appellate Division should be affirmed, with costs.

SIMONS, ACTING C.J., and TITONE, HANCOCK and BELLACOSA, JJ., concur with KAYE, J.

[Judge Smith dissented in part and would have reinstated the second cause of action. He thought the record indicated that plaintiff might be able to prove either kind of malice and thus overcome the privilege.]

Notes and Questions

1. Why does this situation not deserve an absolute privilege? Why does it deserve a qualified privilege? What if defendant had told his suspicions to a tenant who was not on the board? To a social friend in a nearby building who has a friend on the police force?

2. Consider the introductory note to Restatement § 592A, stating that a qualified privilege is based on the view "that it is essential that true information be given whenever it is reasonably necessary for the protection of one's own interests, the interests of third persons or certain interests of the public." Would that formulation apply to the tenant in *Liberman*?

3. *Employer references.* One important area for qualified privilege protects responses from employers or former employers to inquiries from prospective employers about how an employee performed on the job. See Erickson v. Marsh & McLennan Co., Inc., 569 A.2d 793 (N.J.1990), using three criteria to determine that a qualified privilege was appropriate: "the appropriateness of the occasion on which the defamatory information is published, the legitimacy of the interest thereby sought to be protected or promoted, and the pertinence of the receipt of that information by the recipient."

The immediate concern is to encourage this exchange of information without opening the door to dishonest attacks on the employee. Traditionally, most states have accorded a qualified privilege based on the "common interest" of the inquirer and the responder—a protection that may not apply when the former employer volunteers information. See Coclin v. Lane Press, Inc., 620 N.Y.S.2d 41 (App.Div. 1994), finding a qualified privilege when an employer sent information on an employee to an outsider. The court quoted an earlier decision of the court of appeals:

> A communication made bona fide upon any subject matter in which the party communicating has an interest, or in reference to which he has a duty, is privileged if made to a person having a corresponding interest or duty, although it contained criminating matter which, without this privilege, would be slanderous and actionable, and this though the duty be not a legal one, but only a moral or social duty of imperfect obligation.

Employers assert that the law is inducing them to refuse to respond to such inquiries or to stating only the dates of employment. Initially, one might have thought that this terse reply itself might carry implied defamation. Today, however, it is such a common technique that it does not carry pejorative meaning. Rather, the concern is that the flow of information has been retarded by employer fears of lawsuits or vengeance. See Rovella, Laws May Ease the Risky Business of Job References, Nat'l L.J., Oct. 23, 1995 at B1, reporting that in a study by a consulting firm 63% of 1,331 managers said that they had refused to provide information for fear of lawsuits and nearly 40% said it was a good idea not to provide information. On the other hand, 73% said "that reference checking is more important now" than before.

See also Wald, Board Blames Pilot for Commuter Crash, N.Y. Times, Oct. 25, 1995 at A10, reporting that a pilot suspected of causing a crash had been on the verge of being fired by one airline when he applied for work at a commuter line. The prospective employer had not asked prior employers about the pilot's work—but it would not have mattered because the former employer's policy was not to provide such information. The article reports crash investigators as saying that "few airlines will tell another about a former employee's performance, for fear of being sued by the applicant if the information is used to deny the person a job."

Is this a problem? Should it be handled by changing the qualified privilege to an absolute privilege? By creating a duty to respond when asked about a former employee's record? Note that if the former employer writes a dishonest report that praises the worker as a way of easing the worker's departure that may come back to haunt the employer. In one case, since settled, Rovella reports that several co-employees were killed by a violent colleague who had recently been hired after his former employer allegedly "in an effort to eliminate an unpleasant and potentially danger-ous" situation gave the killer "a neutral reference signed by a company vice president, allegedly omitting the real reasons" for the termination. Is there a duty to disclose an observed potential for violence in a former worker? Recall *Randi W.*, p. 170, supra. The issue of making a partial disclosure that may be a misleading half-truth is discussed in the context of deceit in Chapter XV.

Some statutes may prevent employers from informing prospective employers about disciplinary actions taken against the worker—including true statements. See the discussion of the Illinois statute in Delloma v. Consolidation Coal Co., 996 F.2d 168 (7th Cir.1993). What might motivate this type of legislation?

4. Another important issue here is raised by credit reports. Most states agree that a qualified privilege protects reporting services. E.g., Weir v. Equifax Services, Inc., 620 N.Y.S.2d 675 (App.Div. 1994); Stationers Corp. v. Dun & Bradstreet, Inc. 398 P.2d 785 (Cal.1965). The common law in this area has, however, been largely replaced by litigation under the federal Fair Credit Reporting Act, 15 U.S.C.A. § 1681a(f), granting subjects of credit reports certain protections. See, e.g., Guimond v. Trans Union

Credit Information Co., 45 F.3d 1329 (9th Cir.1995); Henson v. CSC Credit Services, 29 F.3d 280 (7th Cir.1994).

5. Efforts to invoke a qualified privilege for general news reporting of matters important to the community have generally failed. In California, for example, Civil Code section 47(c) provides a privilege for "a communication, without malice, to a person interested therein, (1) by one who is also interested, or (2) by one who stands in such a relation to the person interested as to afford a reasonable ground for supposing the motive for the communication innocent, or (3) who is requested by the person interested to give the information."

Although some lower courts had applied this section to media reports of events of public interest in the community, that view was rejected in Brown v. Kelly Broadcasting Co., 771 P.2d 406 (Cal.1989). A consumer affairs segment of a daily television news show incorrectly attributed poor workmanship to plaintiff contractor. The court concluded that the legislature had not intended this section to apply to such media reports and that to find such coverage would mean that it "would apply to virtually every defamatory communication. Presumably, the news media generally publish and broadcast only matters that the media believe are of public interest, and the media defendant in every defamation action would therefore argue that the communication was a matter of public interest." Such a privilege would swallow the basic rule. (The court also noted that qualified privileges had developed during a period when strict liability was the rule in libel cases. Since, as we soon discuss, that is no longer the case, the court saw less need for extending them today.)

6. *Abuse.* After a situation warranting a qualified privilege is found, the next question is whether the privilege has been "abused." The criterion for abuse under common law was malice—which meant, as the court indicates, spite or ill will toward the plaintiff. This might be shown by evidence about the relationship, and sometimes might be inferred from defendant's behavior in making the statement to those who had no interest in learning it or not believing what was said. Recall the *Liberman* court's statement that defendant "did not make public announcement of his suspicions—from which an inference could be drawn that his motive was to defame Liberman," rather than to accomplish what he was seeking to accomplish. See Boyd v. Nationwide Mutual Ins. Co., 208 F.3d 406 (2d Cir.2000) (allowing plaintiff to proceed to discovery where his employer had attributed theft to plaintiff without having first checked its own records).

7. The arrival of constitutional law has confused the question of abuse under common law. As the court notes, "actual malice" has now taken on the meaning of "knowledge that [the statement] was false or . . . reckless disregard of whether it was false or not." Although we will consider this phrase at length, beginning at p. 1000, infra, it is already clear that "actual" (or "constitutional" or "Times") malice focuses on the defendant's attitude toward the truth of the statement—not defendant's attitude toward the person attacked in the statement.

In light of the emergence of the constitutional standards, the courts have adopted various stances. Some have adhered to the idea that abuse is shown by the defendant's ill will or spite toward the plaintiff. Others, such as New York in *Liberman*, and Maine in *Staples,* p. 952, supra, have concluded that a plaintiff can overcome a qualified privilege by showing either type of malice. Still others, including New Jersey in *Erickson*, note 3, supra, have decided that to show abuse the plaintiff must establish "actual malice" in the constitutional sense. Although the intricacies of "actual malice" will be addressed later, it is important to realize here that the focus in "abuse" cases appears to be shifting from the defendant's attitude toward the plaintiff to defendant's attitude toward the truth.

8. *Fair comment.* Although most common law privileges primarily benefit non-media individuals, one is of special use to the media—fair comment.

Apparently this privilege entered English law in 1808 in Carr v. Hood, 1 Camp. 355, 170 Eng.Rep. 983. The defendant was charged with ridiculing the plaintiff author's talent so severely that sales of his book were discouraged and his reputation was destroyed. The plaintiff's attorney conceded that his client had exposed himself to literary criticism by making the book public, but insisted that the criticism should be "fair and liberal" and seek to enlighten the public about the book rather than to injure the author. The judge noted that ridicule may be an appropriate tool of criticism, but that criticism unrelated to the author as such would not be privileged. He urged that any "attempt against free and liberal criticism" should be resisted "at the threshold." The result was a rule that criticism, regardless of its merit, was privileged if it was made honestly, with honesty being measured by the accuracy of the critic's descriptive observations. If a critic describing a literary, musical, or artistic endeavor gave the "facts" accurately and fairly, the critic's honest conclusions would be privileged as "fair comment."

American law recognized this privilege, and as long as it was applied in cases of literary and artistic criticism it caused little confusion. Classic cases discussing the privilege are Triggs v. Sun Printing & Pub. Ass'n, 71 N.E. 739 (N.Y.1904), Adolf Philipp Co. v. New Yorker Staats–Zeitung, 150 N.Y.Supp. 1044 (App.Div. 1914), and Cherry v. Des Moines Leader, 86 N.W. 323 (Iowa 1901).

But at the end of the nineteenth century, cases arose in which the privilege of fair comment was claimed with regard to other matters of public interest, including the conduct of politicians. The privilege claimed would permit citizens to criticize and argue about the conduct of their officials, and these cases presented the problem of distinguishing between facts and opinion. In literary criticism the application of the privilege could depend upon the accuracy of the "facts" because they were usually readily apparent—in the book, on the stage, or in the restaurant. When dealing with politics, however, the "facts" were often elusive. This new problem created a judicial split.

In Post Publishing Co. v. Hallam, 59 Fed. 530 (6th Cir.1893), Judge Taft ruled that in order for criticism of officials to be privileged, it must be based upon true underlying facts. The newspaper asserted that it should be judged under the accepted rule that a former master responding to a request for information about a former servant would be privileged if the master stated some "facts" about the servant honestly but mistakenly. Judge Taft refused to apply this rule because in the servant case only the prospective master learned of the defamation, while here the entire public would hear of it. He continued:

> The existence and extent of privilege in communications are determined by balancing the needs and good of society against the right of an individual to enjoy a good reputation when he has done nothing which ought to injure it. The privilege should always cease where the sacrifice of the individual right becomes so great that the public good to be derived from it is outweighed.   .   .   . But, if the privilege is to extend to cases like that at bar, then a man who offers himself as a candidate must submit uncomplainingly to the loss of his reputation, not with a single person or a small class of persons, but with every member of the public, whenever an untrue charge of disgraceful conduct is made against him, if only his accuser honestly believes the charge upon reasonable ground. We think that not only is such a sacrifice not required of everyone who consents to become a candidate for office, but that to sanction such a doctrine would do the public more harm than good.
>
> We are aware that public officers and candidates for public office are often corrupt, when it is impossible to make legal proof thereof, and of course it would be well if the public could be given to know, in such a case, what lies hidden by concealment and perjury from judicial investigation. But the danger that honorable and worthy men may be driven from politics and public service by allowing too great latitude in attacks upon their characters outweighs any benefit that might occasionally accrue to the public from charges of corruption that are true in fact, but are incapable of legal proof. The freedom of the press is not in danger from the enforcement of the rule we uphold. No one reading the newspaper of the present day can be impressed with the idea that statements of fact concerning public men, and charges against them, are unduly guarded or restricted; and yet the rule complained of is the law in many of the states of the Union and in England.

The privilege became more narrow as those courts following the *Hallam* view came to treat questions of motive—why the politician or official acted as he or she did—as "facts" that had to be true in order for subsequent comment to be privileged.

A contrasting position was taken in Coleman v. MacLennan, 98 P. 281 (Kan.1908), in which the court noted that "men of unimpeachable character from all political parties continually present themselves as candidates in sufficient numbers to fill the public offices and manage the public institutions" even though Kansas had long held that facts relating to matters of public interest are themselves privileged if they are honestly believed to be true; and, if the facts are privileged even if wrong, the comments based upon those facts are also privileged if they are honestly believed. *Coleman* adhered to the state's rejection of the *Hallam* distinction between fact and comment or opinion.

The common law majority view is that a statement is privileged as fair comment only if it is based on true or privileged facts about a matter of public interest. Privileged facts will be discussed below, but it is important to keep in mind that the fair comment privilege applies only where the comment expressed is honestly believed.

The fair comment privilege has become intertwined with constitutional developments that we discuss at p. 1061, infra.

c.   *Fair and Accurate Report*

Medico v. Time, Inc.

United States Court of Appeals, Third Circuit, 1981.
643 F.2d 134.
Certiorari denied, 454 U.S. 836 (1981).

Before ADAMS, GARTH and SLOVITER, CIRCUIT JUDGES.

ADAMS, CIRCUIT JUDGE.

This appeal from a summary judgment in favor of the defendant presents an important question concerning the law of defamation. We must review the district court's determination that a news magazine enjoys a privilege, under the common law of Pennsylvania, to publish a summary of FBI documents identifying the plaintiff as a member of an organized crime "family." We affirm.

I.

In its March 6, 1978 issue, Time magazine published an article describing suspected criminal activities of then-Congressman Daniel J. Flood. . . .

As an example of suspected misconduct, the Time article listed the following:

> Among the matters under scrutiny: Ties between Flood and Pennsylvania Rackets Boss Russell Bufalino. The suspected link: the Wilkes–Barre firm of Medico Industries, controlled by President Philip Medico and his brothers. The FBI discovered more than a decade ago that Flood steered Government business to the Medicos and traveled often on their company jet. Investigators say Bufalino frequently visited the Medico offices; agents tape-recorded Bufalino's description of Philip as a capo (chief) in his Mafia family. [Testimony by a former Flood aide] has sparked new investigative interest in the Flood–Medico–Bufalino triangle.

. . .

In January 1980, Time again moved for summary judgment based on the substantial truth of its publication. Time resubmitted the two FBI documents it had proffered to support its initial motion, supplemented with affidavits of two FBI agents. . . .

On this occasion the district court granted Time's motion for summary judgment, but not on the basis of the truth defense. . . .

After declining to hold for Time on the truth theory, the district court considered whether the Time article fell within the common law privilege accorded the press to report on official proceedings. The judge seemed troubled because Pennsylvania courts apparently had so far extended the privilege only to reports of proceedings open to the public, whereas Time had summarized reports which the FBI had kept secret and whose release to Time evidently had been unauthorized. But after an exhaustive analysis of Pennsylvania precedents, the court concluded that Pennsylvania courts, if presented with the question, would find summaries of non-public government reports within the privilege. The district judge then ascertained that the Time article represented a fair and accurate account of the FBI documents. Accordingly he held that the publication was privileged, and awarded summary judgment in favor of Time.

On appeal, Medico argues that the district court incorrectly determined that Time's publication was privileged under Pennsylvania law. Time counters that the district judge accurately construed the applicable state law on privilege, and contends further that the defense of truth applies and affords an alternate basis for affirming the district court. . . .

II.

The fair report privilege on which the district court relied developed as an exception to the common law rule that the republisher of a defamation was subject to liability similar to that risked by the original defamer. . . . The common law regime created special problems for the press. When a newspaper published a newsworthy account of one person's defamation of another, it was, by virtue of the republication rule, charged with publication of the underlying defamation. Thus, although the common law exonerated one who published a defamation as long as the statement was true, a newspaper in these circumstances traditionally could avail itself of the truth defense only if the truth of the underlying defamation were established.

To ameliorate the chilling effect on the reporting of newsworthy events occasioned by the combined effect of the republication rule and the truth defense, the law has long recognized a privilege for the press[9] to publish accounts of official proceedings or reports even when these contain defamatory statements. So long as the account presents a fair and accurate

---

9. There is some dispute whether the privilege is available to non-press defendants. The *Restatement* [covers] "any person who makes an oral, written or printed report" on an official proceeding should have access to the defense. . . .

summary of the proceedings, the law abandons the assumption that the reporter adopts the defamatory remarks as his own.[11] The privilege thus permits a newspaper or other press defendant to relieve itself of liability without establishing the truth of the substance of the statement reported. The fair report privilege has a somewhat more limited scope than the truth defense, however. So long as the speaker establishes the truth of his statement, he is shielded from liability, regardless of his motives; the fair report privilege, on the other hand, can be defeated in most jurisdictions by a showing that the publisher acted for the sole purpose of harming the person defamed.

Unlike many states, Pennsylvania has never codified the fair report privilege. . . . We believe it appropriate to accept as the law of Pennsylvania the version of the fair report privilege embodied in the current *Restatement*.

Section 611 of Restatement (Second) provides:

Report of Official Proceeding or Public Meeting

The publication of defamatory matter concerning another in a report of an official action or proceeding or of a meeting open to the public that deals with a matter of public concern is privileged if the report is accurate and complete or a fair abridgement of the occurrence reported.

With respect to the present controversy, the basic inquiry is whether Time's summary of FBI documents concerning Philip Medico is "a report of an official action or proceeding."[17]

The district court examined and rejected the possibility that the FBI reports in question are not "official" because they are not generally available to the public. Medico does not challenge this reasoning on appeal, and we perceive no need to rehearse arguments that the district court has already canvassed. Medico contends before this Court that the FBI documents should not be deemed "official" because they express only tentative and preliminary conclusions that the FBI has never adopted as accurate. He points out that the title page to the FBI report on La Cosa Nostra bears the following legend: "This document contains neither recommendations nor conclusions of the FBI. It is the property of the FBI and is loaned to your agency; it and its contents are not to be distributed outside your agency."

Neither the text of Section 611 nor the accompanying comments dispose of the issue Medico raises. Section 611 itself speaks only of

---

11. [ ]. Analytically, the fair report privilege is similar to the truth defense. Both make verity the issue, although requiring that a report be fair and accurate may allow the press a somewhat greater margin of error than requiring that its report be true.
. . .

17. Although the Time article did not explicitly credit the FBI Report on La Cosa Nostra or the FBI personal file card on Medico as the Magazine's sources of information, the statements about Medico, taken in context, may reasonably be understood to inform the reader that the story was based on FBI materials. . . .

"official" action or proceedings, without elaborating on when a statement is made in an official capacity. [The court notes that two comments to that section point in different ways on whether the report is within the scope of the privilege. Nor did case law resolve it. The closest case protected a news report that summarized a defamatory civil complaint that had formed the basis for a temporary restraining order. Hanish v. Westinghouse Broadcasting Co., 487 F.Supp. 397 (E.D.Pa.1980)].[21]

Assuming the court in *Hanish* correctly predicted Pennsylvania law, we think that decision supports application of the Section 611 privilege to the present case. FBI files seem at least as "official" as the pleadings in civil cases. Although civil complaints are instituted, for the most part, by private parties, the FBI documents concerning Medico were compiled by government agents acting in their official capacities. Moreover, the danger that a civil litigant will willfully insert defamatory assertions in his complaint generally would appear at least as great as the risk that a criminal investigatory agency will knowingly include false or malicious statements in its files. If Pennsylvania courts would grant the privilege to newspaper accounts of civil complaints on which a court has acted ex parte, we think it likely that they would grant the privilege to republication of defamatory items from the FBI materials on Medico.

III.

Three policies underlie the fair report privilege, and an examination of them provides further guidance for our decision today. Initially, an agency theory was offered to rationalize a privilege of fair report: one who reports what happens in a public, official proceeding acts as an agent for persons who had a right to attend, and informs them of what they might have seen for themselves. The agency rationale, however, cannot explain application of the privilege to proceedings or reports not open to public inspection.

A theory of public supervision also informs the fair report privilege. Justice Holmes, applying the privilege to accounts of courtroom proceedings, gave the classic formulation of this principle:

> [The privilege is justified by] the security which publicity gives for the proper administration of justice. . . . It is desirable that the trial of causes should take place under the public eye, not because the controversies of one citizen with another are of public concern, but because it is of the highest moment that those who administer justice should always act under the sense of public responsibility and that every citizen should be able to satisfy himself with his own eyes as to the mode in which a public duty is performed.

Cowley v. Pulsifer, 137 Mass. 392, 394 (1884). The supervisory rationale has been invoked in the context of executive action as well.

We believe the public supervision rationale applies to the present case. As public inspection of courtroom proceedings may further the just admin-

---

21. Considerable controversy surrounds republication of defamations contained in pleadings on which no official action has been taken. . . .

istration of the laws, public scrutiny of the proceedings and records of criminal investigatory agencies may often have the equally salutary effect of fostering among those who enforce the laws "the sense of public responsibility." For example, exposing the content of agency records may, in some cases, help ensure impartial enforcement of the laws.

[We need not] decide, however, whether the supervisory rationale is relevant to every republication of documents found in FBI files. For any general supervisory concern with respect to the FBI is heightened in the present case by the public's interest in examining the conduct of individuals it elects to positions of civic trust. Elected officials derive their authority from, and are answerable to, the public. If the citizenry is effectively and responsibly to discharge its obligation to monitor the conduct of its government, there can be no penalty for exposing to general view the possible wrongdoing of government officials. Because the alleged defamation of Medico occurred in an article analyzing the conduct of former Congressman Flood, we believe it implicates this aspect of the supervisory rationale. Moreover, even though Time's publication arguably may have tarnished the reputation of Medico, a private individual, as well as that of Representative Flood, the public has a lively interest in considering the relationships formed by elected officials.

A third rationale for the fair report privilege rests, somewhat tautologically, on the public's interest in learning of important matters.[27] While "mere curiosity in the private affairs of others is of insufficient importance to warrant granting the privilege," the present case does not involve such idle probing. The Time article discussed two topics of legitimate public interest. First, for the same reasons that support the supervisory rationale, examination of the affairs of elected officials is obviously a matter of legitimate public concern. In addition, as various federal courts have already recognized, there is significant public importance to reports on investigations of organized criminal activities, whether or not these implicate government officials.

Because the Time article focused on organized crime, we think the informational rationale is especially relevant. The district court in the case at hand commented on the difficulty of gathering information pertaining to organized criminal activity: "Due to the size, sophistication and secrecy of most organized criminal endeavors, only the largest and most sophisticated intelligence-gathering entities can monitor them effectively. In practice this task has been taken up primarily by the Justice Department of the federal government and, in particular, by the FBI." Indeed, the documents that Time summarized had been compiled by a government agency. In light of the difficulty in obtaining independent corroboration of FBI information, the press may often have to rely on materials the government acquires if it is to report on organized crime at all. We believe Time's publication of FBI

---

27. . . .

Some jurisdictions rely on the informational rationale to extend the privilege to accounts of the proceedings of public meet-ings of private, nongovernmental organizations, as long as the meeting deals with matters of concern to the public.

materials mentioning Medico served a legitimate public interest in learning about organized crime.

Care must be taken, of course, to ensure that the supervisory and informational rationales not expand into justifications for reporting any defamatory matter maintained in any government file. Personal interests in privacy are not to be taken lightly, and are not to be overborne by mere invocation of a public need to know.[30] But we believe that the public interest is involved when, as here, information compiled by an enforcement agency may help shed light on a Congressman's alleged criminal or unethical behavior.

. . .

V.

Once the libel defendant establishes the existence of a "privileged occasion" for the publication of a defamatory article, the burden returns to the plaintiff to prove that the defendant abused its privilege. [ ] Pennsylvania recognizes two forms of "abuse": the account of an official report may fail to be fair and accurate,[40] as when the publisher overly embellishes the account, [ ] or the defamatory material may be published for the sole purpose of causing harm to the person defamed. [ ]. Inasmuch as Medico does not allege that Time published its article for the purpose of harming him, the sole issue with respect to abuse of privilege is whether the district court erred in concluding that there was no genuine question whether Time's publication fairly and accurately summarized the FBI materials concerning Medico.

We agree with the district court that nothing in the record suggests that the Time article unfairly or inaccurately reported on the FBI materials. . . .

. . . Time has accurately portrayed the FBI records as indicating that Medico has been identified as part of the Bufalino crime family.

VI.

Medico further contends that Time can avail itself of the fair report privilege only if it actually based its article on the FBI materials; if the report reflects the contents of the official materials merely by coincidence, the privilege does not attach. Medico maintains there is a genuine issue of fact whether Time employees worked with the FBI materials in preparing the article.

Pennsylvania law squarely contradicts this argument. . . .

30. The excesses of the McCarthy era, for example, prompted some commentators to point out the reputational injury the republication of official defamation can cause, and to advocate restricting the fair report privilege. [ ]

40. Placement on the plaintiff of the burden of demonstrating that a privileged report was not fair and accurate traditionally distinguished the fair report privilege from the truth defense, in which defendant bore the burden of proving truth. . . .

VII.

. . .[42]

The judgment of the district court granting Time's motion for summary judgment will be affirmed.

Notes and Questions

1. The court discusses three theories that have been asserted to support the fair report privilege. Which one appears most persuasive? Will one generally support a broader protective net than the others?

2. *Coverage of the privilege.* The court understands state law not to require actual reliance on the official report or proceeding. Do the three theories differ on this? The Second Circuit disagreed with the *Medico* court on its reading of Pennsylvania law on the ground that the privilege could not be "divorced from its underlying policy of encouraging the broad dissemination of public records." Protecting a defendant who did not actually rely on an official report "does nothing to encourage the initial reporting of public records and proceedings. Certainly, § 611 should not be interpreted to protect unattributed, defamatory statements supported only after-the-fact through a frantic search of official records." Bufalino v. Associated Press, 692 F.2d 266 (2d Cir.1982), cert. denied 462 U.S. 1111 (1983).

3. In a footnote, the *Bufalino* court observed that "even where the reporter has actually relied on official records, the privilege can be lost through failure to make proper attribution." Would the *Medico* court agree? What do the theories have to say on this point?

4. The coverage varies greatly state by state. In some states, for example, as suggested in *Medico,* the privilege extends to the fact of an arrest and the charges but not to details of the alleged crime that an arresting officer provides.

5. In Rouch v. Enquirer & News of Battle Creek, Mich., 398 N.W.2d 245 (Mich. 1986), (a later stage of this case is discussed at p. 975, supra), the newspaper reported oral statements made by the police in connection with the plaintiff's arrest for rape. After plaintiff, who was never charged,

---

42. The possible interpretations of Time's publication about Medico may be used to illustrate the different approaches to the truth defense. The Time article is subject to at least three constructions:

A. Medico is a Mafia *capo.*

B. Government agents overheard Bufalino describe Medico as a Mafia *capo.*

C. FBI records indicate that government agents overheard Bufalino describe Medico as a Mafia *capo.*

Under the fair report privilege, the accuracy of C relieves Time of liability. If the privilege did not apply, however, we would have to ascertain whether Pennsylvania law would exonerate Time on the basis of the truth defense if Time established the truth of B, or whether Time would have to prove A. In light of our holding that Time's publication comes under the fair report privilege, we need not dispose of this question. In addition, we need not review the district court's determination that Time has failed to demonstrate the truth of either A or B.

was exonerated, he sued the newspaper. The paper's reliance on the state's privilege for fair and accurate report of "any public and official proceeding" was rejected on the ground that an "arrest that amounts to no more than an apprehension" was not a "proceeding." The statute was not intended to create a "government action," "arrest record," or "public records" privilege.

The legislature reacted by amending the privilege statute, Mich.Comp. Laws § 600.2911, which extended protection to "a fair and true report of matters of public record, a public and official proceeding, or of a governmental notice, announcement, written or recorded report or record generally available to the public, or act or action of a public body." Should such a statute extend to open meetings of a local political party or the state bar association?

6. Should the fair report privilege cover a report of a proceeding that is not open to the public? Dorsey v. National Enquirer, Inc., 973 F.2d 1431 (9th Cir.1992), involved the singer Arnold Dorsey, whose stage name is Engelbert Humperdinck. The National Enquirer ran a story headlined "Mom of Superstar Singer's Love Child Claims in Court . . . Engelbert has AIDS Virus." The story was based on an affidavit filed by the mother in family court in New York seeking to force Dorsey to buy life insurance naming the child as beneficiary. It stated the mother's "information and belief" that Dorsey "has AIDS related syndrome."

The Enquirer conceded the falsity of the allegation but won summary judgment on the basis of the California statute which recognizes a privilege for a fair and true report "of (1) a judicial, (2) a legislative, or (3) other public official proceeding, or (4) anything said in the course thereof. . . ." Dorsey argued that the wording of subsection (3) implied that subsection (1) covered only public judicial proceedings. But the court construed the statute as applicable to closed judicial proceedings, citing previous decisions applying the privilege to an internal agency report, an FBI "rap sheet," and grand jury proceedings. The court then held that in the absence of disputed facts and where all reasonable inferences from the evidence pointed in the same direction, summary judgment should be granted to the defendant. The addition to the article of some out-of-court remarks did not go beyond the gist or sting of the affidavit.

7. On the question of whether the privilege should extend to reports of actions of foreign governments, see Lee v. The Dong–A Ilbo, 849 F.2d 876 (4th Cir.1988), cert. denied 489 U.S. 1067 (1989)(concluding, 2–1, that Virginia would not extend its privilege to a newspaper's accurate report of a press release issued by South Korean intelligence agencies that identified plaintiff as a North Korean agent). *Lee* is rejected in Friedman v. Israel Labor Party, 957 F.Supp. 701 (E.D.Pa.1997) (finding privilege under Pennsylvania law for fair republication of official acts of foreign governments).

8. *Codification.* As noted in *Medico* and in the discussion of several cases in these notes, many states have adopted legislation to codify this privilege. One typical version is New York's Civil Rights Law § 74, which provides:

A civil action cannot be maintained against [any defendant] for the publication of a fair and true report of any judicial proceeding, legislative proceeding or other official proceeding.   .   .   .

This section does not apply to a libel contained in any other matter added by any person concerned in the publication; or in the report of anything said or done at the time and place of such a proceeding which was not a part thereof.

Notice that this does not protect reports of public meetings held by nongovernmental organizations, such as medical associations or publicly held corporations, or remarks made by political, sports, or entertainment figures outside of official proceedings. Should it? Does it protect a report of remarks made by an audience member at a meeting of a city council?

If a New York court should be confronted with the *Medico* situation and conclude that the statute does not cover the case, could it nonetheless create a common law fair report privilege to cover the situation? Should it? In Wright v. Grove Sun Newspaper Co., 873 P.2d 983 (Okla.1994), the court concluded that the state statute did not extend protection to the report of a press conference held by a district attorney, but that the common law privilege had not been abrogated by the statute, and it could be used to provide that protection. Recall that in *Rouch*, note 5, supra, the court refused to expand the statute.

9. *Losing the privilege.* Although the defendant must establish the conditions showing that the privilege applies to the situation in the first instance, the plaintiff may be able to establish that the privilege has been lost.

Courts have not required precise use of legal language in testing the accuracy of these reports. How accurate must the report be? See Holy Spirit Ass'n for the Unification of World Christianity v. New York Times Co., 399 N.E.2d 1185 (N.Y.1979):

[N]ewspaper accounts of legislative or other official proceedings must be accorded some degree of liberality. When determining whether an article constitutes a "fair and true" report, the language used herein should not be dissected and analyzed with a lexicographer's precision. This is so because a newspaper article is, by its very nature, a condensed report of events which must, of necessity, reflect to some degree the subjective view of its author. Nor should a fair report which is not misleading, composed and phrased in good faith under the exigencies of a publication deadline, be thereafter parsed and dissected on the basis of precise denotative meanings which may literally, although not contextually, be ascribed to the words used.

Most courts adopt a view similar to that in the discussion earlier of "substantial truth." Thus, in Koniak v. Heritage Newspapers, Inc., 499 N.W.2d 346 (Mich.App.1993), the defendant reported that plaintiff had been charged with assaulting someone 30 to 55 times when in fact he had been charged with eight assaults. The court observed that "whether plaintiff assaulted his stepdaughter once, eight times or thirty times would have little effect on the reader."

Although specific decisions may depend on the statutory language involved, in general the courts appear to be quite generous in applying this privilege so long as the defendant appeared to be trying to comply with the provisions. Even so, there are limits. In Crane v. The Arizona Republic, 972 F.2d 1511 (9th Cir.1992), the California privilege covered a report of a Congressional investigation into corruption within the Justice Department. But the article as written, by not giving the dates on which the reporter conducted two interviews, gave the impression that one of the two interviewees must have been lying. For this reason, the court refused to rule as a matter of law that the report was fair and accurate. The case was remanded for trial.

Questions of fairness usually arise in connection with the condensation or summary of a report. Comment *f* to § 611 states that "although it is unnecessary that the report be exhaustive and complete, it is necessary that nothing be omitted or misplaced in such a manner as to convey an erroneous impression to those who hear or read it, as for example a report of the discreditable testimony in a judicial proceeding and a failure to publish the exculpatory evidence." The matter is discussed in Schiavone Construction Co. v. Time, Inc., 735 F.2d 94 (3d Cir.1984), in which defendant magazine reported that an individual's name appeared several times in FBI reports concerning the disappearance of Jimmy Hoffa, but did not cite the part of the report that said that none of the references "suggested any criminality or organized crime associations" on plaintiff's part. This raised a fact question about fairness that barred summary judgment.

If the incriminating evidence in a trial emerged on the first day of the trial and the exculpatory evidence on the second day is the newspaper obligated to report the second day's events in order to be protected for the first day's events? What if a newspaper reports that defendant was convicted yesterday after a trial—but reversal of the conviction a year later is not reported?

Courts disagree over whether the question of fairness and accuracy are for the court in all cases or whether the jury should resolve close questions. The states are split over whether "malice" in the sense of spite or ill will deprives the defendant of the privilege. Why might the defendant's desire to harm the subject of the article be relevant here?

What if the defendant "knows" or "believes" that the report being published is false? In Rosenberg v. Helinski, 616 A.2d 866 (Md.1992), cert. denied 509 U.S. 924 (1993), the court stated:

> Under the modern view, the privilege exists even if the reporter of defamatory statements made in court believes or knows them to be false; the privilege is abused only if the report fails the test of fairness and accuracy.

Is this consistent with the rationale for the privilege? This privilege is extensively discussed in D. Elder, The Fair Report Privilege (1988).

d. *Retraction and Other Defenses*

In this section we consider a variety of defenses that do not go directly to the merits of the claim. Some, if successful, are complete defenses to the libel claim. Others, even if successful, are at most partial defenses.

Burnett v. National Enquirer, Inc.

Court of Appeal of California, 1983.
114 Cal.App.3d 991, 193 Cal.Rptr. 206.
Appeal dismissed for want of jurisdiction, 465 U.S. 1014 (1984).

Before ROTH, P.J., GATES and BEACH, JJ.

ROTH, P.J.

On March 2, 1976, appellant caused to appear in its weekly publication, the National Enquirer, a "gossip column" headlined "Carol Burnett and Henry K. in Row," wherein a four-sentence item specified in its entirety that:

> In a Washington restaurant, a boisterous Carol Burnett had a loud argument with another diner, Henry Kissinger. Then she traipsed around the place offering everyone a bite of her dessert. But Carol really raised eyebrows when she accidentally knocked a glass of wine over one diner and started giggling instead of apologizing. The guy wasn't amused and "accidentally" spilled a glass of water over Carol's dress.

Maintaining the item was entirely false and libelous, an attorney for Ms. Burnett, by telegram the same day and by letter one week later, demanded its correction or retraction "within the time and in the manner provided for in Section 48(a) of the Civil Code of the State of California," failing which suit would be brought by his client [respondent herein], a well known actress, comedienne and show-business personality.

In response to the demand, appellant on April 6, 1976, published the following retraction, again in the National Enquirer's gossip column:

> An item in this column on March 2 erroneously reported that Carol Burnett had an argument with Henry Kissinger at a Washington restaurant and became boisterous, disturbing other guests. We understand these events did not occur and we are sorry for any embarrassment our report may have caused Miss Burnett.

On April 8, 1976, respondent, dissatisfied with this effort in mitigation, filed her complaint for libel in the Los Angeles Superior Court. [A jury trial resulted in an award of $300,000 compensatory damages and $1.3 million punitive damages. The trial judge reduced these to $50,000 and $750,000 respectively.] This appeal followed.

 . . . [T]he principal issues here are whether the National Enquirer is excluded from the protection afforded by Civil Code section 48a, and whether the damage award and penalty specified in the judgment can stand.

[The court quoted the entire section 48a at this point. The major provisions are that in any action for libel against a "newspaper" or slander in a broadcast, the "plaintiff shall recover no more than special damages unless a correction be demanded and be not published or broadcast, as hereinafter provided." The demand must be written, specifying the "statements claimed to be libelous and demanding that the same be corrected. Said notice and demand must be served within 20 days after knowledge of the publication or broadcast of the statements claimed to be libelous." If the correction be demanded and "be not published or broadcast in substantially as conspicuous a manner in said newspaper or on said broadcasting station as were the statements claimed to be libelous, in a regular issue thereof published or broadcast within three weeks after such service, plaintiff . . . may recover general, special, and exemplary damages." The statute defines each type of damages in conventional terms. Exemplary (punitive) damages were recoverable only if plaintiff proved "actual malice" and then only at the discretion of the trier of fact. "Actual malice" was defined as "that state of mind arising from hatred or ill will toward the plaintiff; provided, however, that such a state of mind occasioned by a good faith belief on the part of the defendant in the truth of the libelous publication or broadcast shall not constitute actual malice."]

. . .

The National Enquirer is a publication whose masthead claims the "Largest Circulation Of Any Paper in America." It is a member of the American Newspaper Publishers Association. It subscribes to the Reuters News Service. Its staff call themselves newspaper reporters. It describes its business as "newspaper" in its filings with the Los Angeles County Assessor and in its applications for insurance. A State Revenue Department has ruled it qualifies as a newspaper and is thus exempt from sales and use tax. The United States Department of Labor describes it as "belonging to establishments primarily engaged in publishing or printing and publishing newspapers."

By the same token the National Enquirer is designated as a magazine or periodical in eight mass media directories and upon the request and written representation of its general manager in 1960 that "In view of the feature content and general appearance [of the publication], which differ markedly from those of a newspaper . . .," its classification as a newspaper was changed to that of magazine by the Audit Bureau of Circulation. It does not subscribe to the Associated Press or United Press International news services. According to statements by its Senior Editor it is not a newspaper and its content is based on a consistent formula of "how to" stories, celebrity or medical or personal improvement stories, gossip items and TV column items, together with material from certain other subjects. It provides little or no current coverage of subjects such as politics, sports or crime, does not attribute content to wire services, and in general does not make reference to time. Normal "lead time" for its subject matter is one to three weeks. Its owner allowed it did not generate stories "day to day as a daily newspaper does."

[In addressing the issue whether the trial court erred in denying the Enquirer the benefits of section 48a, the court treated the question as one of law. The trial court had concluded that the statute's major rationale was to protect publications that are "not generally in a position adequately to guard against the publication of material which is untrue." This led the trial court to focus on the element of time and to conclude that the Enquirer's mode of operation did not come within the rationale for the protection.]

Appellant . . . maintains that the special classification approved in Werner v. Southern Cal. etc. Newspapers, [216 P.2d 825 (Cal. 1950)], depended on the public's interest in the "free dissemination of news," without reference to questions of timeliness; [and that several cases constituted an "unbroken line" of authority consistent with that view. The court explored several earlier cases, including a few that applied the statute to magazines without ever addressing the question.]

[The court concluded that the question was still open.] We nevertheless are of the opinion that what emerges as the better view from the authorities discussed is the proposition that the protection afforded by the statute is limited "to those who engage in the immediate dissemination of news on the ground that the Legislature could reasonably conclude that such enterprises . . . cannot always check their sources for accuracy and their stories for inadvertent publication errors. . . . [ ]"

Seen in this light, the essential question is not then whether any publication is properly denominated a magazine or by some other designation, but simply whether it ought to be characterized as a newspaper or not within the contemplation of § 48a, a question which must be answered, as the trial court supposed, in terms which justify an expanded barrier against damages for libel in those instances, and those only, where the constraints of time as a function of the requirements associated with production of the publication dictate the result.

[The trial court, using the proper rationale,] correctly determined the National Enquirer should not be deemed a newspaper for the purposes of the instant litigation.

[The court then upheld liability but reduced the punitive damages to $150,000. A dissenter would have affirmed the full award.]

Notes and Questions

1. Since special damages are hard to show, p. 967, supra, what is the justification behind the retraction statute? Why do retraction statutes focus on damages rather than liability?

2. Under the court's analysis what result where the defamation appears in a regular edition of a weekly news magazine? In the weekly news section of a Sunday "newspaper"? In a special edition of a weekly news magazine that is produced in response to a major news event?

3. If the court had found the Enquirer eligible to invoke the statute, it would then have had to face the question of whether the defendant had in fact published a "correction." Could it be argued that the correction was inadequate? (In the damages part of the opinion, the court found the correction "evasive" and "incomplete," and considered this relevant in the award of punitive damages.)

4. If the correction is adequate there is the further question whether it was published in substantially as conspicuous a manner as the original story. If the story is published in the same place, as apparently occurred in *Burnett,* there is little problem on this score. What if the correction is published in a regular box on page 2 of the publication that is devoted to corrections but whose headline "Day's Corrections" is smaller than the headline that accompanied the original story that appeared on page 5? Page 1?

Some retraction statutes state simply that the retraction may be taken into account in measuring damages. Even in states without retraction statutes it is generally held that an early correction may be relevant at trial to reduce the plaintiff's damages.

5. Some statutes have been interpreted to apply even though the original defamation is found to have been intentional. The California statute was so interpreted and upheld in the *Werner* case (cited in *Burnett*), which was later settled.

Oregon's statute, which applied unless plaintiff could prove that the defendant "actually intended to defame the plaintiff," was upheld in Holden v. Pioneer Broadcasting Co., 365 P.2d 845 (Or.1961), appeal dismissed and cert. denied 370 U.S. 157 (1962).

About half the states have retraction statutes of some sort. A few states have declared such statutes unconstitutional. See Boswell v. Phoenix Newspapers, Inc., 730 P.2d 186 (Ariz.1986), cert. denied 481 U.S. 1029 (1987)(statute violated state constitutional provision that right of action "to recover damages for injuries shall never be abrogated") and Madison v. Yunker, 589 P.2d 126 (Mont.1978)(statute violated state constitutional provision that courts be "open to every person, and speedy remedy afforded for every injury to person, property, or character").

6. Injunctions have never been available to prevent personal defamation. See Pound, Equitable Relief against Defamation and Injuries to Personality, 29 Harv.L.Rev. 640 (1916); Leflar, Legal Remedies for Defamation, 6 Ark.L.Rev. 423 (1952); Sedler, Injunctive Relief and Personal Integrity, 9 St. Louis L.J. 147 (1964).

7. *The libel-proof plaintiff.* It has been traditional common law that defendant may show that the plaintiff's reputation was already low either because of earlier publications of the charge in question or for other reasons. This might induce the jury to lower its estimate of the compensatory damage that defendant's defamation had caused plaintiff.

A few courts have moved beyond this mitigation defense and have begun to dismiss libel cases on the ground that the plaintiff's reputation is already so bad that there is no chance that plaintiff can obtain and keep any damage award. In Jackson v. Longcope, 476 N.E.2d 617 (Mass.1985), a convicted multiple murderer sued over a statement that he had raped and strangled all of his victims. The court dismissed the case after concluding that plaintiff's reputation was so poor that he could have suffered no harm from any error in defendant's article: "A libel-proof plaintiff is not entitled to burden a defendant with a trial in which the most favorable result the plaintiff could achieve is an award of nominal damages."

Judge (now Justice) Scalia expressed great skepticism about the doctrine in Liberty Lobby v. Anderson, 746 F.2d 1563 (D.C.Cir.1984), vacated on other grounds 477 U.S. 242 (1986). For the majority, he observed that reputation is not monolithic. The law "proceeds upon the optimistic assumption that there is a little good in all of us—or perhaps the pessimistic assumption that no matter how bad someone is, he can always be worse." He offered this analogy: "It is shameful that Benedict Arnold was a traitor; but he was not a shoplifter to boot, and one should not have been able to make that charge while knowing its falsity with impunity."

See also Simmons Ford, Inc. v. Consumers Union, 516 F.Supp. 742 (S.D.N.Y.1981), in which a plaintiff with a previously good reputation was found to have been rendered libel-proof by the unchallenged or true parts of the same article that was the basis for the defamation: "Given the abysmal performance and safety evaluations [of plaintiff's electrically powered car] detailed in the article, plaintiffs could not expect to gain more than nominal damages based on the addition to the article of the misstatement relating to federal safety standards." This issue is also addressed in Jewell v. NYP Holdings, Inc., 23 F.Supp.2d 348 (S.D.N.Y.1998) (refusing to apply Simmons Ford approach to articles discussing the past of a former Olympic guard in Atlanta who was suspected in a bombing).

Is there an analytical difference between (a) concluding that a reputable person has not been hurt in this instance because true statements have already badly hurt this aspect of plaintiff's reputation, and (b) denying an action to the plaintiff in Jackson? Can the Simmons Ford situation, which is often referred to as involving "incremental harm," be justified on the same basis as the "libel-proof plaintiff" doctrine? See Note, Libel–Proof Plaintiffs and the Question of Injury, 71 Texas L.Rev. 401 (1992).

Single publication rule. At common law, the sale of each individual copy of a publication could be considered a separate cause of action. Most states, either by case law or by adoption of the Uniform Single Publication Act, 13 U.L.A. 517, have developed the rule that the entire edition of a printed work is to be treated as a single publication and that all damages for this publication must be recovered in a single action. At first this was limited to one action in each state, but now it is recognized that all damages for the nationwide single publication may, and in some cases must, be resolved in a single action. If a new edition of the work is published, however, such as a new edition of a book or a soft-cover version of a hardback book, it is considered a new and separate publication for which a separate cause of action arises.

Jurisdiction. The Supreme Court has twice unanimously denied media defendants special jurisdictional protections over and above those available to other defendants who conduct interstate business. Calder v. Jones, 465 U.S. 783 (1984); Keeton v. Hustler Magazine, Inc., 465 U.S. 770 (1984).

B. PUBLIC PLAINTIFFS AND THE CONSTITUTION

The First Amendment provides:

> Congress shall make no law respecting an establishment of religion, or prohibiting the free exercise thereof; or abridging the freedom of speech, or of the press; or the right of the people peaceably to assemble, and to petition the Government for a redress of grievances.

In Near v. Minnesota, 283 U.S. 697 (1931), in the process of invalidating what it saw as a prior restraint, the majority observed,

> But it is recognized that punishment for the abuse of the liberty accorded to the press is essential to the protection of the public, and that the common-law rules that subject the libeler to responsibility for the public offense, as well as for the private injury, are not abolished by the protection extended in our Constitution.

In the late 1930s a syndicated columnist asserted that Congressman Sweeney was blocking the appointment of a federal judge because the prospective appointee was Jewish. Sweeney sued several newspapers, with varying results. Compare Sweeney v. Patterson, 128 F.2d 457 (D.C.App.), cert. denied 317 U.S. 678 (1942), holding the column privileged, with Sweeney v. Schenectady Union Pub. Co., 122 F.2d 288 (2d Cir.1941), affirmed by an equally divided court 316 U.S. 642 (1942), in which the lower court had found no privilege. This Supreme Court split vote suggested the presence of a difficult constitutional question.

In Chaplinsky v. New Hampshire, 315 U.S. 568 (1942), however, libelous words, along with "fighting words" and obscenity, were said to be among the "well-defined and narrowly limited classes of speech, the prevention and punishment of which have never been thought to raise any Constitutional problem." The proposition that libelous utterances were not "within the area of constitutionally protected speech" was relied upon by Justice Frankfurter, writing for a 5–4 majority in *Beauharnais v. Illinois,* p. 965, supra, to sustain a state criminal libel law.

This sequence set the stage for the following case from Alabama, a state that had long followed the narrow *Hallam* view, p. 984, supra, for criticism of public officials.

1. PUBLIC OFFICIALS

New York Times Co. v. Sullivan

Supreme Court of the United States, 1964.
376 U.S. 254, 84 S.Ct. 710, 11 L.Ed.2d 686.

[This action was based on a full-page advertisement in the New York Times on behalf of several individuals and groups protesting a "wave of terror" against blacks involved in non-violent demonstrations in the South. Plaintiff, one of three elected commissioners of Montgomery, the capital of Alabama, was in charge of the police department. When he demanded a retraction, as state law required, the Times instead responded that it failed to see how he was defamed, even though it did subsequently publish a retraction at the request of the Alabama governor, whose complaint was similar to Sullivan's. Plaintiff then filed suit against the Times and four clergymen whose names appeared—although they denied having authorized this—in the ad. Plaintiff alleged that the third and the sixth paragraphs of the advertisement libelled him:

> "In Montgomery, Alabama, after students sang 'My Country, 'Tis of Thee' on the State Capitol steps, their leaders were expelled from school, and truckloads of police armed with shotguns and tear-gas ringed the Alabama State College Campus. When the entire student body protested to state authorities by refusing to re-register, their dining hall was padlocked in an attempt to starve them into submission."

> . . .

> "Again and again the Southern violators have answered Dr. King's peaceful protests with intimidation and violence. They have bombed his home almost killing his wife and child. They have assaulted his person. They have arrested him seven times—for 'speeding,' 'loitering' and similar 'offenses.' And now they have charged him with 'perjury'— a *felony* under which they could imprison him for *ten years*. . . ."

Plaintiff claimed that he was libelled in the third paragraph by the reference to the police, since his responsibilities included supervision of the Montgomery police. He asserted that the paragraph could be read as charging the police with ringing the campus and seeking to starve the students by padlocking the dining hall. As to the sixth paragraph, he contended that the word "they" referred to his department since arrests are usually made by the police and the paragraph could be read as accusing him of committing the acts charged. Several witnesses testified that they read the statements as referring to plaintiff in his capacity as commissioner.

The defendants admitted several inaccuracies in these two paragraphs: the students sang The Star Spangled Banner, not My Country, 'Tis of Thee; nine students were expelled, not for leading the demonstration, but for demanding service at a lunch counter in the county courthouse; the dining hall was never padlocked; police at no time ringed the campus though they were deployed nearby in large numbers; they were not called to the campus in connection with the demonstration; Dr. King had been arrested only four times; and officers disputed his account of the alleged assault. Plaintiff proved that he had not been commissioner when three of the four arrests occurred and that he had nothing to do with procuring the perjury indictment.

The trial judge charged that the statements were libel per se, that the jury should decide whether they were made "of and concerning" the plaintiff and, if so, general damages were to be presumed. Although noting that punitive damages required more than carelessness, he refused to charge that they required a finding of actual intent to harm or "gross negligence and recklessness." He also refused to order the jury to separate its award of general and punitive damages. The jury returned a verdict for $500,000—the full amount demanded. The Alabama Supreme Court affirmed, holding that malice could be found in several aspects of the Times's conduct.]

Mr. Justice Brennan delivered the opinion of the Court.

.   .   .

I.

We may dispose at the outset of two grounds asserted to insulate the judgment of the Alabama courts from constitutional scrutiny. The first is the proposition relied on by the State Supreme Court—that "The Fourteenth Amendment is directed against State action and not private action." That proposition has no application to this case. Although this is a civil lawsuit between private parties, the Alabama courts have applied a state rule of law which petitioners claim to impose invalid restrictions on their constitutional freedoms of speech and press. It matters not that that law has been applied in a civil action and that it is common law only, though supplemented by statute. [   ] The test is not the form in which state power has been applied but, whatever the form, whether such power has in fact been exercised. [   ]

The second contention is that the constitutional guarantees of freedom of speech and of the press are inapplicable here, at least so far as the Times is concerned, because the allegedly libelous statements were published as part of a paid, "commercial" advertisement. [The argument was rejected.]

II.

Under Alabama law as applied in this case, a publication is "libelous per se" if the words "tend to injure a person .   .   . in his reputation" or to "bring [him] into public contempt"; the trial court stated that the standard was met if the words are such as to "injure him in his public office, or impute misconduct to him in his office, or want of official integrity, or want of fidelity to a public trust.   .   .   ." The jury must find that the words were published "of and concerning" the plaintiff, but where the plaintiff is a public official his place in the governmental hierarchy is sufficient evidence to support a finding that his reputation has been affected by statements that reflect upon the agency of which he is in charge. Once "libel per se" has been established, the defendant has no defense as to stated facts unless he can persuade the jury that they were true in all their particulars. [   ] His privilege of "fair comment" for expressions of opinion depends on the truth of the facts upon which the comment is based. [   ] Unless he can discharge the burden of proving truth, general damages are presumed, and may be awarded without proof of pecuniary injury. A showing of actual malice is apparently a prerequisite to recovery of punitive damages, and the defendant may in any event forestall a punitive award by a retraction meeting the statutory requirements. Good motives and belief in truth do not negate an inference of malice, but are relevant only in mitigation of punitive damages if the jury chooses to accord them weight. [ ]

The question before us is whether this rule of liability, as applied to an action brought by a public official against critics of his official conduct, abridges the freedom of speech and of the press that is guaranteed by the First and Fourteenth Amendments.

Respondent relies heavily, as did the Alabama courts, on statements of this Court to the effect that the Constitution does not protect libelous publications. Those statements do not foreclose our inquiry here. None of the cases sustained the use of libel laws to impose sanctions upon expression critical of the official conduct of public officials. . . . In deciding the question now, we are compelled by neither precedent nor policy to give any more weight to the epithet "libel" than we have to other "mere labels" of state law. NAACP v. Button, 371 U.S. 415, 429 (1963). Like insurrection, contempt, advocacy of unlawful acts, breach of the peace, obscenity, solicitation of legal business, and the various other formulae for the repression of expression that have been challenged in this Court, libel can claim no talismanic immunity from constitutional limitations. It must be measured by standards that satisfy the First Amendment.

The general proposition that freedom of expression upon public questions is secured by the First Amendment has long been settled by our decisions. . . . Mr. Justice Brandeis, in his concurring opinion in Whitney v. California, 274 U.S. 357, 375–376 (1927), gave the principle its classic formulation:

> Those who won our independence believed . . . that public discussion is a political duty; and that this should be a fundamental principle of the American government. . . . Believing in the power of reason as applied through public discussion, they eschewed silence coerced by law—the argument of force in its worst form. Recognizing the occasional tyrannies of governing majorities, they amended the Constitution so that free speech and assembly should be guaranteed.

Thus we consider this case against the background of a profound national commitment to the principle that debate on public issues should be uninhibited, robust, and wide-open, and that it may well include vehement, caustic, and sometimes unpleasantly sharp attacks on government and public officials. See Terminiello v. Chicago, 337 U.S. 1, 4 (1949); De Jonge v. Oregon, 299 U.S. 353, 365 (1937). The present advertisement, as an expression of grievance and protest on one of the major public issues of our time, would seem clearly to qualify for the constitutional protection. The question is whether it forfeits that protection by the falsity of some of its factual statements and by its alleged defamation of respondent.

Authoritative interpretations of the First Amendment guarantees have consistently refused to recognize an exception for any test of truth—whether administered by judges, juries, or administrative officials—and especially one that puts the burden of proving truth on the speaker. Cf. Speiser v. Randall, 357 U.S. 513, 525–526 (1958). The constitutional protection does not turn upon "the truth, popularity, or social utility of the ideas and beliefs which are offered." NAACP v. Button, 371 U.S. 415, 445 (1963). As Madison said, "Some degree of abuse is inseparable from the proper use of every thing; and in no instance is this more true than in that of the press." 4 Elliot's Debates on the Federal Constitution (1876), p. 571. In Cantwell v. Connecticut, 310 U.S. 296, 310 (1940), the Court declared:

> In the realm of religious faith, and in that of political belief, sharp differences arise. In both fields the tenets of one man may seem the rankest error to his neighbor. To persuade others to his own point of view, the pleader, as we know, at times, resorts to exaggeration, to vilification of men who have been, or are, prominent in church or state, and even to false statement. But the people of this nation have ordained in the light of history, that, in spite of the probability of excesses and abuses, these liberties are, in the long view, essential to enlightened opinion and right conduct on the part of the citizens of a democracy.

That erroneous statement is inevitable in free debate, and that it must be protected if the freedoms of expression are to have the "breathing space" that they "need . . . to survive," NAACP v. Button, 371 U.S. 415, 433 (1963), was also recognized by the Court of Appeals for the District of Columbia Circuit in Sweeney v. Patterson, 128 F.2d 457, 458, cert. denied 317 U.S. 678 (1942). Judge Edgerton spoke for a unanimous court which affirmed the dismissal of a Congressman's libel suit based upon a newspaper article charging him with anti-Semitism in opposing a judicial appointment. He said:

> Cases which impose liability for erroneous reports of the political conduct of officials reflect the obsolete doctrine that the governed must not criticize their governors. . . . The interest of the public here outweighs the interest of appellant or any other individual. The protection of the public requires not merely discussion, but information. Political conduct and views which some respectable people approve, and others condemn, are constantly imputed to Congressmen. Errors of fact, particularly in regard to a man's mental states and processes, are inevitable. . . . Whatever is added to the field of libel is taken from the field of free debate.[13]

13. See also Mill, On Liberty (Oxford: Blackwell, 1947), at 47:

". . . [T]o argue sophistically, to suppress facts or arguments, to misstate the elements of the case, or misrepresent the opposite opinion . . . . all this, even to the most aggravated degree, is so continually done in perfect good faith, by persons who are not considered, and in many other respects may not deserve to be considered, ignorant or incompetent, that it is rarely possible, on adequate grounds, conscientiously to stamp the misrepresentation as morally culpable; and still less could law presume to

Injury to official reputation affords no more warrant for repressing speech that would otherwise be free than does factual error. Where judicial officers are involved, this Court has held that concern for the dignity and reputation of the courts does not justify the punishment as criminal contempt of criticism of the judge or his decision. Bridges v. California, 314 U.S. 252 (1941). This is true even though the utterance contains "half-truths" and "misinformation." Pennekamp v. Florida, 328 U.S. 331, 342, 343, n. 5, 345 (1946). . . . Criticism of their official conduct does not lose its constitutional protection merely because it is effective criticism and hence diminishes their official reputations.

If neither factual error nor defamatory content suffices to remove the constitutional shield from criticism of official conduct, the combination of the two elements is no less inadequate. This is the lesson to be drawn from the great controversy over the Sedition Act of 1798, 1 Stat. § 596, which first crystallized a national awareness of the central meaning of the First Amendment. . . .

Although the Sedition Act was never tested in this Court,[16] the attack upon its validity has carried the day in the court of history. Fines levied in its prosecution were repaid by Act of Congress on the ground that it was unconstitutional. . . . The invalidity of the Act has also been assumed by Justices of this Court. [ ] These views reflect a broad consensus that the Act, because of the restraint it imposed upon criticism of government and public officials, was inconsistent with the First Amendment.

There is no force in respondent's argument that the constitutional limitations implicit in the history of the Sedition Act apply only to Congress and not to the States. It is true that the First Amendment was originally addressed only to action by the Federal Government, and that Jefferson, for one, while denying the power of Congress "to controul the freedom of the press," recognized such a power in the States. [ ] But this distinction was eliminated with the adoption of the Fourteenth Amendment and the application to the States of the First Amendment's restrictions. [ ]

What a State may not constitutionally bring about by means of a criminal statute is likewise beyond the reach of its civil law of libel. The fear of damage awards under a rule such as that invoked by the Alabama courts here may be markedly more inhibiting than the fear of prosecution under a criminal statute. [ ] Alabama, for example, has a criminal libel law which subjects to prosecution "any person who speaks, writes, or prints of and concerning another any accusation falsely and maliciously importing the commission by such person of a felony, or any other indictable offense involving moral turpitude," and which allows as punishment upon conviction a fine not exceeding $500 and a prison sentence of six months. [ ] Presumably a person charged with violation of this statute enjoys ordinary criminal-law safeguards such as the requirements of an indictment and of proof beyond a reasonable doubt. These safeguards are not available to the

interfere with this kind of controversial misconduct."

16. The Act expired by its terms in 1801.

defendant in a civil action. . . . And since there is no double-jeopardy limitation applicable to civil lawsuits, this is not the only judgment that may be awarded against petitioners for the same publication.[18] Whether or not a newspaper can survive a succession of such judgments, the pall of fear and timidity imposed upon those who would give voice to public criticism is an atmosphere in which the First Amendment freedoms cannot survive. Plainly the Alabama law of civil libel is "a form of regulation that creates hazards to protected freedoms markedly greater than those that attend reliance upon the criminal law." Bantam Books, Inc. v. Sullivan, 372 U.S. 58, 70 (1963).

The state rule of law is not saved by its allowance of the defense of truth. . . . Allowance of the defense of truth, with the burden of proving it on the defendant, does not mean that only false speech will be deterred.[19] Even courts accepting this defense as an adequate safeguard have recognized the difficulties of adducing legal proofs that the alleged libel was true in all its factual particulars. See, e.g., Post Publishing Co. v. Hallam, 59 F. 530, 540 (C.A.6th Cir.1893); see also Noel, Defamation of Public Officers and Candidates, 49 Col.L.Rev. 875, 892 (1949). Under such a rule, would-be critics of official conduct may be deterred from voicing their criticism, even though it is believed to be true and even though it is in fact true, because of doubt whether it can be proved in court or fear of the expense of having to do so. They tend to make only statements which "steer far wider of the unlawful zone." [*Speiser v. Randall*]. The rule thus dampens the vigor and limits the variety of public debate. It is inconsistent with the First and Fourteenth Amendments.

The constitutional guarantees require, we think, a federal rule that prohibits a public official from recovering damages for a defamatory falsehood relating to his official conduct unless he proves that the statement was made with "actual malice"—that is, with knowledge that it was false or with reckless disregard of whether it was false or not. An oft-cited statement of a like rule, which has been adopted by a number of state courts, is found in the Kansas case of Coleman v. MacLennan, 98 P. 281 (Kan.1908). . . .

Such a privilege for criticism of official conduct is appropriately analogous to the protection accorded a public official when *he* is sued for libel by a private citizen. In Barr v. Matteo, 360 U.S. 564, 575 (1959), this Court held the utterance of a federal official to be absolutely privileged if made "within the outer perimeter" of his duties. The States accord the same immunity to statements of their highest officers, although some differenti-

---

18. The Times states that four other libel suits based on the advertisement have been filed against it by others who have served as Montgomery City Commissioners and by the Governor of Alabama; that another $500,000 verdict has been awarded in the only one of these cases that has yet gone to trial; and that the damages sought in the other three total $2,000,000.

19. Even a false statement may be deemed to make a valuable contribution to public debate, since it brings about "the clearer perception and livelier impression of truth, produced by its collision with error." Mill, On Liberty (Oxford: Blackwell, 1947), at 15; see also Milton, Areopagitica, in Prose Works (Yale, 1959), Vol. II, at 561.

ate their lesser officials and qualify the privilege they enjoy. But all hold that all officials are protected unless actual malice can be proved. The reason for the official privilege is said to be that the threat of damage suits would otherwise "inhibit the fearless, vigorous, and effective administration of policies of government" and "dampen the ardor of all but the most resolute, or the most irresponsible, in the unflinching discharge of their duties." [*Barr v. Matteo*]. Analogous considerations support the privilege for the citizen-critic of government. It is as much his duty to criticize as it is the official's duty to administer. . . . As Madison said, [ ], "the censorial power is in the people over the Government, and not in the Government over the people." It would give public servants an unjustified preference over the public they serve, if critics of official conduct did not have a fair equivalent of the immunity granted to the officials themselves.

We conclude that such a privilege is required by the First and Fourteenth Amendments.

III.

We hold today that the Constitution delimits a State's power to award damages for libel in actions brought by public officials against critics of their official conduct. Since this is such an action, the rule requiring proof of actual malice is applicable. While Alabama law apparently requires proof of actual malice for an award of punitive damages, where general damages are concerned malice is "presumed." Such a presumption is inconsistent with the federal rule. . . . Since the trial judge did not instruct the jury to differentiate between general and punitive damages, it may be that the verdict was wholly an award of one or the other. But it is impossible to know, in view of the general verdict returned. Because of this uncertainty, the judgment must be reversed and the case remanded.

Since respondent may seek a new trial, we deem that considerations of effective judicial administration require us to review the evidence in the present record to determine whether it could constitutionally support a judgment for respondent. . . .

Applying these standards, we consider that the proof presented to show actual malice lacks the convincing clarity which the constitutional standard demands, and hence that it would not constitutionally sustain the judgment for respondent under the proper rule of law. The case of the individual petitioners requires little discussion. Even assuming that they could constitutionally be found to have authorized the use of their names on the advertisement, there was no evidence whatever that they were aware of any erroneous statements or were in any way reckless in that regard. The judgment against them is thus without constitutional support.

As to the Times, we similarly conclude that the facts do not support a finding of actual malice. [The testimony of the Secretary of the Times that he believed the advertisement to be "substantially correct" was "at least a reasonable [belief], and there was no evidence to impeach the witness' good faith in holding it." Nor was the later retraction for the governor evidence of actual malice toward plaintiff. Leaving open the question of whether failure to retract "may ever constitute such evidence," it could not suffice here because the letter showed reasonable doubt whether the ad referred to plaintiff at all, and also because the letter was not a final refusal. The Court responded to the claim that the Times published the ad without first checking news stories in its own files, by noting that the "mere presence" of such stories "does not, of course, establish that the Times' knew 'the advertisement was false', since the state of mind required for actual malice would have to be brought home to the persons in the Times' organization having responsibility for the publication of the advertisement." Those persons relied on the "good reputation of many of those whose names were listed as sponsors of the advertisement, and upon the letter from A. Philip Randolph, known to them as a responsible individual, certifying that the use of the names was authorized."]

We also think the evidence was constitutionally defective in another respect: it was incapable of supporting the jury's finding that the allegedly libelous statements were made "of and concerning" respondent. Respondent relies on the words of the advertisement and the testimony of six witnesses to establish a connection between it and himself. . . . There was no reference to respondent in the advertisement, either by name or official position. A number of the allegedly libelous statements—the charges that the dining hall was padlocked and that Dr. King's home was bombed, his person assaulted, and a perjury prosecution instituted against him—did not even concern the police; despite the ingenuity of the arguments which would attach this significance to the word "They," it is plain that these statements could not reasonably be read as accusing respondent of personal involvement in the acts in question. The statements upon which respondent principally relies as referring to him are the two allegations that did concern the police or police functions: that "truckloads of police . . . ringed the Alabama State College Campus" after the demonstration on the State Capitol steps, and that Dr. King had been "arrested . . . seven times." These statements were false only in that the police had been "deployed near" the campus but had not actually "ringed" it and had not gone there in connection with the State Capitol demonstration, and in that Dr. King had been arrested only four times. The ruling that these discrepancies between what was true and what was asserted were sufficient to injure respondent's reputation may itself raise constitutional problems, but we need not consider them here. Although the statements may be taken as referring to the police, they did not on their face make even an oblique reference to respondent as an individual. Support for the asserted reference must, therefore, be sought in the testimony of respondent's witnesses. But none of them suggested any basis for the belief that respondent himself was attacked in the advertisement beyond the bare fact that he was in overall charge of the Police Department and thus bore official responsibility for police conduct; to the extent that some of the witnesses thought respondent to have been charged with ordering or approving the conduct or otherwise being personally involved in it, they based this notion not on any statements in the advertisement, and not on any evidence that he had in fact been so involved, but solely on the unsupported assumption that, because of his official position, he must have been. This reliance on the bare fact of respondent's official position was made explicit by the Supreme Court of Alabama.   .   .   .

This proposition has disquieting implications for criticism of governmental conduct. For good reason, "no court of last resort in this country has ever held, or even suggested, that prosecutions for libel on government have any place in the American system of jurisprudence." City of Chicago v. Tribune Co., [139 N.E. 86, 88 (Ill.1923)]. The present proposition would sidestep this obstacle by transmuting criticism of government, however impersonal it may seem on its face, into personal criticism, and hence potential libel, of the officials of whom the government is composed. There is no legal alchemy by which a State may thus create the cause of action that would otherwise be denied for a publication which, as respondent himself said of the advertisement, "reflects not only on me but on the other Commissioners and the community." Raising as it does the possibility that a good-faith critic of government will be penalized for his criticism, the proposition relied on by the Alabama courts strikes at the very center of the constitutionally protected area of free expression.[30] We hold that such a proposition may not constitutionally be utilized to establish that an otherwise impersonal attack on governmental operations was a libel of an official responsible for those operations. Since it was relied on exclusively here, and there was no other evidence to connect the statements with respondent, the evidence was constitutionally insufficient to support a finding that the statements referred to respondent.

The judgment of the Supreme Court of Alabama is reversed and the case is remanded to that court for further proceedings not inconsistent with this opinion.

Reversed and remanded.

MR. JUSTICE BLACK, with whom MR. JUSTICE DOUGLAS joins, concurring.

I concur in reversing this half-million-dollar judgment against the New York Times Company and the four individual defendants. In reversing the Court holds that "the Constitution delimits a State's power to award damages for libel in actions brought by public officials against critics of their official conduct." I base my vote to reverse on the belief that the First and Fourteenth Amendments not merely "delimit" a State's power to award damages to "public officials against critics of their official conduct" but completely prohibit a State from exercising such a power. The Court goes on to hold that a State can subject such critics to damages if "actual malice" can be proved against them. "Malice," even as defined by the

---

30. Insofar as the proposition means only that the statements about police conduct libeled respondent by implicitly criticizing his ability to run the Police Department, recovery is also precluded in this case by the doctrine of fair comment. See American Law Institute, Restatement of Torts (1938), § 607. Since the Fourteenth Amendment requires recognition of the conditional privilege for honest misstatements of fact, it follows that a defense of fair comment must be afforded for honest expression of opinion based upon privileged, as well as true, statements of fact. Both defenses are of course defeasible if the public official proves actual malice, as was not done here.

Court, is an elusive, abstract concept, hard to prove and hard to disprove. The requirement that malice be proved provides at best an evanescent protection for the right critically to discuss public affairs and certainly does not measure up to the sturdy safeguard embodied in the First Amendment. Unlike the Court, therefore, I vote to reverse exclusively on the ground that the Times and the individual defendants had an absolute unconditional constitutional right to publish in the Times advertisement their criticisms of the Montgomery agencies and officials. . . .

The half-million-dollar verdict does give dramatic proof, however, that state libel laws threaten the very existence of an American press virile enough to publish unpopular views on public affairs and bold enough to criticize the conduct of public officials. . . . In fact, briefs before us show that in Alabama there are now pending eleven libel suits by local and state officials against the Times seeking $5,600,000 and five such suits against the Columbia Broadcasting System seeking $1,700,000. Moreover, this technique for harassing and punishing a free press—now that it has been shown to be possible—is by no means limited to cases with racial overtones; it can be used in other fields where public feelings may make local as well as out-of-state newspapers easy prey for libel verdict seekers. . . . This record certainly does not indicate that any different verdict would have been rendered here whatever the Court had charged the jury about "malice," "truth," "good motives," "justifiable ends," or any other legal formulas which in theory would protect the press. Nor does the record indicate that any of these legalistic words would have caused the courts below to set aside or to reduce the half-million-dollar verdict in any amount.

. . .

. . . An unconditional right to say what one pleases about public affairs is what I consider to be the minimum guarantee of the First Amendment.[6]

I regret that the Court has stopped short of this holding indispensable to preserve our free press from destruction.

Mr. Justice Goldberg, with whom Mr. Justice Douglas joins, concurring in the result.

. . .

In my view, the First and Fourteenth Amendments to the Constitution afford to the citizen and to the press an absolute, unconditional privilege to criticize official conduct despite the harm which may flow from excesses and abuses. . . .

. . .

. . . It may be urged that deliberately and maliciously false statements have no conceivable value as free speech. That argument, however, is not responsive to the real issue presented by this case, which is whether

---

6. Cf. Meiklejohn, Free Speech and Its Relation to Self–Government (1948).

that freedom of speech which all agree is constitutionally protected can be effectively safeguarded by a rule allowing the imposition of liability upon a jury's evaluation of the speaker's state of mind. If individual citizens may be held liable in damages for strong words, which a jury finds false and maliciously motivated, there can be little doubt that public debate and advocacy will be constrained. And if newspapers, publishing advertisements dealing with public issues, thereby risk liability, there can also be little doubt that the ability of minority groups to secure publication of their views on public affairs and to seek support for their causes will be greatly diminished. . . .

. . .

This is not to say that the Constitution protects defamatory statements directed against the private conduct of a public official or private citizen. Freedom of press and of speech insures that government will respond to the will of the people and that changes may be obtained by peaceful means. Purely private defamation has little to do with the political ends of a self-governing society. The imposition of liability for private defamation does not abridge the freedom of public speech or any other freedom protected by the First Amendment.[4] . . .

. . .

Notes and Questions

1. What is the problem with strict liability? Would a negligence standard raise the same problems? Would absolute privilege be objectionable? How does the "actual malice" standard appear to differ from the *Hallam* standard, p. 984, supra? The *Coleman* standard?

Do you consider either of the concurring opinions preferable to the majority approach?

2. Justice Brennan's concern lest speakers have to "steer far wider of the unlawful zone" than legally necessary has been articulated by others as the concern that fear of liability has the potential to "chill" speech. In the cited case of *Speiser v. Randall* the Court invalidated a procedure under which veterans seeking a California tax exemption bore the burden of proving that they had not advocated the overthrow of the government. Justice Brennan, writing in that case, noted that where speech is close to the line between lawful and unlawful,

> the possibility of mistaken factfinding—inherent in all litigation—will create the danger that the legitimate utterance will be penalized. The man who knows that he must bring forth proof and persuade another

---

4. In most cases, as in the case at bar, there will be little difficulty in distinguishing defamatory speech relating to private conduct from that relating to official conduct. I recognize, of course, that there will be a gray area. The difficulties of applying a public-private standard are, however, certainly of a different genre from those attending the differentiation between a malicious and nonmalicious state of mind. . . . .

of the lawfulness of his conduct necessarily must steer far wider of the unlawful zone than if the state must bear these burdens.

How is this concern relevant to the problems raised by libel law?

3. Which single step seems more likely to prevent the "chilling" of speech: shifting the burden of proving falsity to plaintiffs or introducing "actual malice"? Although the Court might have made only one of these changes, lower courts took the Court's definition of the "actual malice" to have subsumed the showing of falsity as well: proof that the statement was made with "knowledge that it was false or with reckless disregard of whether it was false or not." This is discussed further at p. 1063, infra.

4. Toward the end of the opinion the Court discusses whether the libel was of and concerning the plaintiff. Why isn't that a jury question? For a discussion of how the Times's argument that the article was not about the plaintiff expanded during the oral argument, see Miller and Barron, The Supreme Court, The Adversary System, and the Flow of Information to the Justices: A Preliminary Inquiry, 61 Va.L.Rev. 1187 (1975). For a discussion of the opinion drafting process, see B. Schwartz, Super Chief: Earl Warren and His Supreme Court—A Judicial Biography 531–41 (1983). The story of the Supreme Court's deliberation in the *Sullivan* case is told in intriguing detail in A. Lewis, "Make No Law" (1991).

5. Commenting after the *Times* case, Professor Kalven speculated on the case's future:

> The closing question, of course, is whether the treatment of seditious libel as the key concept for development of appropriate constitutional doctrine will prove germinal. It is not easy to predict what the Court will see in the *Times* opinion as the years roll by. It may regard the opinion as covering simply one pocket of cases, those dealing with libel of public officials, and not destructive of the earlier notions that are inconsistent only with the larger reading of the Court's action. But the invitation to follow a dialectic progression from public official to government policy to public policy to matters in the public domain, like art, seems to me to be overwhelming. If the Court accepts the invitation, it will slowly work out for itself the theory of free speech that Alexander Meiklejohn has been offering us for some fifteen years now.

Kalven, The *New York Times* Case: A Note on "The Central Meaning of the First Amendment," 1964 Sup.Ct.Rev. 191, 221. Does his prediction seem sound? Keep it in mind as we proceed.

6. The majority in the *New York Times* case did not explicitly condemn the concurring approaches. A few months later, in Garrison v. Louisiana, 379 U.S. 64 (1964), the Court, in an opinion by Justice Brennan, extended the *Times* rule to cases of criminal libel and also held that truth must be a defense in cases brought by public officials. The majority explained its refusal to protect deliberate falsity:

Although honest utterance, even if inaccurate, may further the fruitful exercise of the right of free speech, it does not follow that the lie, knowingly and deliberately published about a public official, should enjoy a like immunity. At the time the First Amendment was adopted, as today, there were those unscrupulous enough and skillful enough to use the deliberate or reckless falsehood as an effective political tool to unseat the public servant or even topple an administration. [   ] That speech is used as a tool for political ends does not automatically bring it under the protective mantle of the Constitution. For the use of the known lie as a tool is at once at odds with the premises of democratic government and with the orderly manner in which economic, social, or political change is to be effected. Calculated falsehood falls into that class of utterances which "are no essential part of any exposition of ideas, and are of such slight social value as a step to truth that any benefit that may be derived from them is clearly outweighed by the social interest in order and morality.   .   .   ." [*Chaplinsky*]. Hence the knowingly false statement and the false statement made with reckless disregard of the truth, do not enjoy constitutional protection.

In an explicit, but not entirely successful, effort to avoid confusion between common-law malice and "actual malice," the Court observed that:

Debate on public issues will not be uninhibited if the speaker must run the risk that it will be proved in court that he spoke out of hatred; even if he did speak out of hatred, utterances honestly believed contribute to the free interchange of ideas and the ascertainment of the truth.

2.   PUBLIC FIGURES

Shortly after *New York Times*, the Court considered two cases together: Curtis Publishing Co. v. Butts, and Associated Press v. Walker, 388 U.S. 130 (1967).

In *Butts* the defendant magazine had accused the plaintiff athletic director of disclosing his game plan to an opposing coach before their game. Although he was on the staff of a state university, Butts was paid by a private alumni organization. In *Walker*, the defendant news service reported that the plaintiff, a former United States Army general who resigned to engage in political activity, had personally led students in an attack on federal marshals who were enforcing a desegregation order at the University of Mississippi.

In both cases, lower courts affirmed substantial jury awards against the defendants and refused to apply the *Times* doctrine on the ground that public officials were not involved. The Supreme Court divided several ways, affirming *Butts*, 5–4, and reversing *Walker*, 9–0. Chief Justice Warren wrote the pivotal opinion in which he concluded that both men were "public figures" and that the standard developed in *New York Times* should apply to "public figures" as well:

To me, differentiation between "public figures" and "public officials" and adoption of separate standards of proof for each has no basis in law, logic, or First Amendment policy. Increasingly in this country, the distinctions between governmental and private sectors are blurred. Since the depression of the 1930's and World War II there has been a rapid fusion of economic and political power, a merging of science, industry, and government, and a high degree of interaction between the intellectual, governmental, and business worlds. Depression, war, international tensions, national and international markets, and the surging growth of science and technology have precipitated national and international problems that demand national and international solutions. While these trends and events have occasioned a consolidation of governmental power, power has also become much more organized in what we have commonly considered to be the private sector. In many situations, policy determinations which traditionally were channeled through formal political institutions are now originated and implemented through a complex array of boards, committees, commissions, corporations, and associations, some only loosely connected with the Government. This blending of positions and power has also occurred in the case of individuals so that many who do not hold public office at the moment are nevertheless intimately involved in the resolution of important public questions or, by reason of their fame, shape events in areas of concern to society at large.

Viewed in this context then, it is plain that although they are not subject to the restraints of the political process, "public figures," like "public officials," often play an influential role in ordering society. And surely as a class these "public figures" have as ready access as "public officials" to mass media of communication, both to influence policy and to counter criticism of their views and activities. Our citizenry has a legitimate and substantial interest in the conduct of such persons, and freedom of the press to engage in uninhibited debate about their involvement in public issues and events is as crucial as it is in the case of "public officials." The fact that they are not amenable to the restraints of the political process only underscores the legitimate and substantial nature of the interest, since it means that public opinion may be the only instrument by which society can attempt to influence their conduct.

He found that on the merits malice had not been shown in *Walker*. In *Butts* he found that defendant's counsel had deliberately waived the *Times* doctrine and he also found evidence establishing reckless behavior. He thus voted to reverse *Walker* and affirm *Butts*.

Justice Harlan, joined by three others, argued that something less than the *Times* standard should apply to public figures because criticism of government was not involved:

We consider and would hold that a "public figure" who is not a public official may also recover damages for a defamatory falsehood whose substance makes substantial danger to reputation apparent, on a showing of highly unreasonable conduct constituting an extreme departure from the standards of investigation and reporting ordinarily adhered to by responsible publishers.

Applying that standard, Justice Harlan concluded that Walker had failed to establish a case, but that Butts had shown that the Saturday Evening Post ignored elementary precautions in preparing a potentially damaging story. Together with the Chief Justice's vote, there were five votes to affirm *Butts*.

Justices Brennan and White agreed with the Chief Justice in *Walker* but found no waiver in *Butts* and would have reversed both cases. They agreed with the Chief Justice that Butts had presented enough evidence to come within the *Times* standard but thought that errors in the charge required a new trial.

Justices Black and Douglas adhered to their position, urged that the *Times* rule be abandoned, and voted to reverse both cases.

Although some courts seemed to regard Justice Harlan's opinion as the prevailing opinion, in part because it came first in the reports, it should have been clear that the same "actual malice" standard that applied in "public official" cases also applied in "public figure" cases. Should it? For an extended argument against identical standards for the two categories, see Schauer, Public Figures, 25 Wm. & Mary L.Rev. 905 (1984).

Later in this chapter we will attempt to identify the critical features of the "public figure." For now, however, the important point is to recognize that the identical "actual malice" rules apply to plaintiffs called "public officials" and to those called "public figures"—and to consider how those rules work.

3.   THE "ACTUAL MALICE" STANDARD

The Court's choice of the phrase "actual malice" in 1964 was the source of much confusion that would not have occurred if the Court had created some new term that had no link with the traditions of common law libel. The phrase "actual malice" did not clearly convey the shift in focus from the common law's attention to hatred, ill will, or spite toward the plaintiff to the new notion of looking at the defendant's attitude toward the truth of the defamatory statement. The Court has had several occasions to consider "actual malice" in detail. After considering substantive aspects of the doctrine, we turn to procedural issues.

a.   *Substantive issues*

In St. Amant v. Thompson, 390 U.S. 727 (1968), the defendant repeated false charges against plaintiff without having checked the charges or investigating the source's reputation for veracity. The Supreme Court concluded that "reckless disregard" had not been shown. It recognized that the term could receive no single "infallible definition" and that its outer limits would have to be developed in "case-to-case adjudication." The record must provide "sufficient evidence to permit the conclusion that the defendant in fact entertained serious doubts as to the truth of his publication" in order for recklessness to be found. Anticipating the argument that this position would encourage publishers not to verify their assertions, Justice White, for the Court, stated:

> The defendant in a defamation action brought by a public official cannot, however, automatically insure a favorable verdict by testifying that he published with a belief that the statements were true. The finder of fact must determine whether the publication was indeed made in good faith. Professions of good faith will be unlikely to prove persuasive, for example, where a story is fabricated by the defendant, is a product of his imagination, or is based wholly on an unverified anonymous telephone call. Nor will they be likely to prevail when the publisher's allegations are so inherently improbable that only a reckless man would have put them in circulation. Likewise, recklessness may be found where there are obvious reasons to doubt the veracity of the informant or the accuracy of his reports.

Justice Fortas dissented on the ground that the failure to make "a good-faith check" of the statement was sufficient to establish "reckless disregard." How would the Court's test apply to an extreme partisan who would readily believe anything derogatory about his opponent?

In the second case, Herbert v. Lando, 441 U.S. 153 (1979), the plaintiff, Colonel Anthony Herbert, an admitted public figure, sued the producer and reporter of the television program "60 Minutes" and the CBS network for remarks on the program about his behavior while in military service in Vietnam. During his deposition, Lando, the producer, was generally responsive, but he refused to answer some questions about why he made certain investigations and not others; what he concluded about the honesty of certain people he interviewed for the program; and about conversations he had with Mike Wallace, the reporter, in the preparation of the program segment. Lando contended that these thought processes and internal editorial discussions were protected from disclosure by the First Amendment. The Supreme Court disagreed.

Justice White, for the Court, understood the defendants to be arguing that "the defendant's reckless disregard of truth, a critical element, could not be shown by direct evidence through inquiry into the thoughts, opinions and conclusions of the publisher but could be proved only by objective evidence from which the ultimate fact could be inferred." This was a barrier of some substance, "particularly when defendants themselves are prone to assert their good-faith belief in the truth of their publications, and libel plaintiffs are required to prove knowing or reckless falsehood with 'convincing clarity.'"

Although pretrial discovery techniques had led to "mushrooming litigation costs," this was happening in all areas of litigation. Until major changes in pretrial procedures were developed for all cases, the Court would rely on "what in fact and in law are ample powers of the district judge to prevent abuse."

Plaintiff also sued the Atlantic Monthly for a story written by Lando. The magazine "conducted no independent inquiry into the facts because that is not its practice. It maintains no research department." Since Lando, a freelance author, was "an apparently reasonable journalist" and the article was not "inherently implausible," the magazine had no obligation to investigate the facts and was not vicariously liable for Lando's statements. Herbert v. Lando, 596 F.Supp. 1178 (S.D.N.Y.1984), affirmed on other grounds 781 F.2d 298 (2d Cir.), cert. denied 476 U.S. 1182 (1986).

Would it raise First Amendment problems if a state were to conclude that "actual malice" on the part of an employee in the print shop or a dishonest reporter could subject the publisher to damages?

In Harte–Hanks Communications, Inc. v. Connaughton, 491 U.S. 657 (1989), the newspaper accused a judicial candidate of having used "dirty tricks" to smear his opponent, the incumbent. A unanimous Court upheld an award of $5,000 compensatory and $195,000 punitive damages.

The evidence of "dirty tricks" relied heavily on a source whose credibility had been seriously impugned by other witnesses and whose version of the episode was essentially unconfirmed. Reviewing the record extensively, the Court concluded that actual malice could be found from several uncontroverted findings: (1) the newspaper's failure to interview "the one witness that both [the plaintiff and the source] claimed would verify their conflicting accounts of the relevant events" was "utterly bewildering"; (2) the paper's failure to listen to a tape that the paper had been told exonerated plaintiff, which plaintiff had delivered to the paper at the paper's request; (3) an earlier article on the election that "could be taken to indicate that [the editor] had already decided to publish [the source's] allegations, regardless of how the evidence developed and regardless of whether or not [the source's] story was credible upon ultimate reflection"; and (4) that a crucial witness was not interviewed—or a variety of arguably inconsistent reasons offered by defendant's employees.

Accepting the jury's implicit determination that the newspaper's explanations for not interviewing the crucial witness and for not listening to the tape "were not credible, it is likely that the newspaper's inaction was a product of a deliberate decision not to acquire knowledge of facts that might confirm the probable falsity of [the source's] charges. Although failure to investigate will not alone support a finding of actual malice [*St. Amant*], the purposeful avoidance of the truth is in a different category."

In a footnote at that point, the Court noted that it was not suggesting that a newspaper must accept, or be shaken by, vehement "denials." These are "so commonplace in the world of polemical charge and countercharge that, in themselves, they hardly alert the conscientious reporter to the likelihood of error."

In passing, the Court observed that a "newspaper's motive in publishing the story—whether to promote an opponent's candidacy or to increase its circulation—cannot provide a sufficient basis for finding actual malice."

The Masson case. In Masson v. New Yorker Magazine, Inc., 501 U.S. 496 (1991), plaintiff alleged that an article in defendant magazine written by Janet Malcolm had attributed to plaintiff fabricated quotations that hurt his reputation. The lower courts had upheld summary judgment for the defendants. The Supreme Court reversed. First, the Court concluded that readers of non-fiction in a magazine that "at the relevant time seemed to enjoy a reputation for scrupulous factual accuracy," could take the accuracy of quotations "at face value. A defendant may be able to argue to the jury that quotations should be viewed by the reader as nonliteral or reconstructions, but we conclude that a trier of fact in this case could find that the reasonable reader would understand the quotations to be nearly verbatim reports of statements made by the subject."

The plaintiff then argued that "excepting corrections of grammar or syntax, publication of a quotation with knowledge that it does not contain the words the public figure used demonstrates actual malice." The Court was unwilling to go that far. Interviewers often must reconstruct interviews from notes. Use of language that the subject did not use does not amount to actual malice in that situation. Even if an interview is tape recorded, the "full and exact statement will be reported in only rare circumstances:"

> We conclude that a deliberate alteration of the words uttered by a plaintiff does not equate with knowledge of falsity for purposes of [*Times*] unless the alteration results in a material change in the meaning conveyed by the statement. The use of quotation to attribute words not in fact spoken bears in a most important way on that inquiry, but it is not dispositive in every case.

In this case readers may have found the article "especially damning because so much of it appeared to be a self-portrait, told by the [plaintiff] in his own words." The Court doubted that "readers will assume that direct quotations are but a rational interpretation of the speaker's words, and we decline to adopt any such presumption in determining the permissible interpretations of the quotations in question here."

Applying these principles to the case, the Court reversed the summary judgment. It concluded that several passages could be read as more damning in the article than what the plaintiff alleges he in fact said and the record contained evidence that would support a jury determination that Malcolm "deliberately or recklessly altered the quotations."

On remand in the *Masson* case, the court concluded that although a publisher who has no "obvious reasons to doubt" the accuracy of a story "is not required to initiate an investigation that might plant such doubt," once "doubt exists, the publisher must act reasonably in dispelling it." Although this approach puts publishers who fact-check stories "at somewhat of a disadvantage compared to other publishers such as newspapers and supermarket tabloids that cannot or will not engage in thorough fact-checking," the different treatment "makes considerable sense":

Readers of reputable magazines such as the New Yorker are far more likely to trust the verbatim accuracy of the stories they read than are the readers of supermarket tabloids or even daily newspapers, where they understand the inherent limitations in the fact-finding process. The harm inflicted by a misstatement in a publication known for scrupulously investigating the accuracy of its stories can be far more serious than a similar misstatement in a publication known not to do so.

Masson v. New Yorker Magazine, Inc., 960 F.2d 896 (9th Cir.1992). The court did, however, dismiss the case against the publisher of the book into which the New Yorker articles were converted. The publisher was entitled to rely on the New Yorker's reputation for accuracy and on its rejection of the plaintiff's complaints about the series. The book publisher had no "obvious reasons to doubt" the story's accuracy and thus no obligation to investigate.

At the ensuing trial, the jury found actual malice as to two of the five remaining quotations but hung on the question of damages. Impasse Over Damages in New Yorker Libel Case, N.Y. Times, June 4, 1993, at A1. The jury did find that Malcolm was an independent contractor and that the New Yorker did not act with "actual malice." This pair of findings led to the New Yorker's dismissal from the case.

On retrial, the jury found that two of the five passages were false and that one of them defamed Masson. But the jury found no actual malice and returned a defense verdict. Motions for a new trial were denied and the defense judgment was affirmed on appeal. 85 F.3d 1394 (9th Cir.1996).

Actual malice in the lower courts. Some important questions about actual malice have been addressed by lower courts. A few follow.

1. Can bits of evidence, each insufficient to show malice, be cumulated? In Tavoulareas v. Piro, 817 F.2d 762 (D.C.Cir.) (en banc), cert. denied 484 U.S. 870 (1987), the court answered with a cautious "yes"—but stated that evidence of the reporter's "ill will or bad motives will support a finding of actual malice only when combined with other, more substantial evidence of a defendant's bad faith."

2. Is lack of fairness in the article probative? In Westmoreland v. CBS, Inc., 601 F.Supp. 66 (S.D.N.Y.1984), the court said no:

The fairness of the broadcast is not at issue in the libel suit. Publishers and reporters do not commit a libel in a public figure case by publishing unfair one-sided attacks. . . . The fact that a commentary is one sided and sets forth categorical accusations has no tendency to prove that the publisher believed it to be false. The libel law does not require the publisher to grant his accused equal time or fair reply. . . . A publisher who honestly believes in the truth of his accusations . . . is under no obligation under the libel law to treat the subject of his accusations fairly or evenhandedly.

In Costello v. Ocean County Observer, 643 A.2d 1012 (N.J.1994), the court held that a "highly unfair" story did not show actual malice. The fact that the reporter was young and had been a reporter for only seven months was relevant in trying to determine whether his work was the result of actual malice or negligence. The defendants "narrowly escape liability, but they do not escape the loss of credibility that results from slipshod journalism."

3. Is haste alone enough to show malice? In Meisler v. Gannett Co., 12 F.3d 1026 (11th Cir.) cert. denied 512 U.S. 1222 (1994), the defendant carried an article based on an Associated Press wire service story marked "URGENT" even though AP indicated that "MORE" would be coming on this story. Although the second version arrived before the deadline, the author of the first version never saw it. Since the writer had no serious doubt about the article's accuracy at the time of publication, actual malice was not established.

4. Can a journalist avoid trial by asserting that he honestly thought he saw something that did not in fact exist? The court said no in Currier v. Western Newspapers, Inc., 855 P.2d 1351 (Ariz.1993), in which plaintiff presented evidence that defendant repeated a defamatory statement after plaintiff had informed the newspapers of the falsity—a columnist's claim that he "believed [he] saw" a crucial signature on a document when it was not in fact there. The court denied summary judgment on the actual malice question: the columnist "either did not look at the public records at all or was careless in reading and recording what he saw."

5. Is failure to investigate enough? In Sweeney v. Prisoners' Legal Services of New York, Inc., 647 N.E.2d 101 (N.Y.1995), the court reversed the determination of two lower courts that actual malice had been shown. Failure to investigate standing alone was not enough to establish actual malice. Evidence that defendants purposefully avoided the truth may support a finding of actual malice if supported by evidence that the inaction sprang from a desire not to know, citing *Harte-Hanks, Inc.* In the absence of "some direct evidence that defendants in this case were aware that [the quoted source's charge] was probably false, they cannot be found to have harbored an intent to avoid the truth."

Libel by implication. We have already seen that it is possible to publish a series of statements that are each literally true but which, when put together, lead the average reader to draw a conclusion that is both defamatory and false. Recall p. 958, supra.

We also noted that some courts appeared unwilling to permit such an inference to be drawn by the jury. This unwillingness might have been based on the view that average readers in the specific cases did not and could not reasonably draw the implication that the plaintiff is relying upon. In fact, however, it appears that the courts were relying on a legal proposition drawn from their reading of the *New York Times* case.

In Mihalik v. Duprey, 417 N.E.2d 1238 (Mass.App.1981), the defendants sought to convey to the readership the impression that the plaintiff school board member had behaved improperly by taking his materials to the local trade school to have the students make furniture from them. The defendants left unstated the (apparently not widely known) fact that any local resident could do the same.

In Schaefer v. Lynch, 406 So.2d 185 (La.1981), the plaintiff was director of the state retirement system. The defendant reporter wrote a story that permitted readers to draw the conclusion that plaintiff had used his office to influence commercial lenders so as to further a personal investment. The court reasoned that because statements about public officials are privileged in the absence of actual malice, it "surely follows that all truthful statements are also constitutionally protected. Even though a false implication may be drawn by the public, there is no redress for its servant."

Some courts have gone the other way. In Saenz v. Playboy Enterprises, Inc., 841 F.2d 1309 (7th Cir.1988), a public official was written about in a way that permitted the reader to conclude that while in Uruguay on official government business, the official either knew that Uruguayans were torturing prisoners and did nothing about it or that he participated in the torture.

The court noted that a person may be "disadvantaged greatly in responding to the varying inferences that may be gleaned from inexact accusations." To bar liability in such cases "goes too far; it invokes the spectre of heinous abuse by crafty and mischievous authors whose subtle art of insinuation is honed for destruction." It was for the jury to decide which meaning to take from the piece:

> We are extremely mindful of the importance and value the people and laws of this country place on a free and independent press. . . . A legal fiction denying the existence of clearly discernible, though not explicit, charges exposes public officials to baseless accusations and public mistrust while promoting an undisciplined brand of journalism both unproductive to society and, as we see it, unprotected by constitutional considerations.

The court required the plaintiff to show with "clear and convincing evidence that the defendants intended or knew of the implications that the plaintiff is attempting to draw from the allegedly defamatory material." The case was dismissed for failure to show this element: "Not only must the plaintiff establish that the statement is susceptible of a defamatory meaning which the defendant knew to be false or which the defendants published with reckless disregard for its potential falsity, but also that the defendants intended to imply or were reckless toward the implications. Evidence of defamatory meaning and recklessness regarding potential falsity does not alone establish the defendant's intent."

Even if libel actions based on "impressions" are not precluded by federal constitutional law, should they be barred as a matter of state law? For a general discussion of implied libel, see Dienes and Levine, Implied Libel, Defamatory Meanings, and State of Mind: The Promise of *New York Times Co. v. Sullivan*, 78 Iowa L.Rev. 2337 (1992).

b. Procedural Issues

1. *Convincing clarity.* Although the "actual malice" rule is the major substantive protection available to defendants being sued by public plaintiffs, an important procedural protection developed in *New York Times* requires public plaintiffs to prove their actual malice cases with "convincing clarity."

In Long v. Arcell, 618 F.2d 1145 (5th Cir.1980), cert. denied 449 U.S. 1083 (1981), after a jury finding for the public-figure plaintiff, the trial court granted the defendant newspaper a judgment notwithstanding the verdict. The trial court's ruling was affirmed on appeal. The only evidence for the jury involved conflicting accounts of conversations:

> If the applicable burden of proof had been a preponderance of the evidence, a jury verdict either way would have to stand. Similarly, if liability could be imposed on a clear and convincing showing of negligence, we would be hard pressed to disregard the jury's verdict. We repeat, however, that the plaintiff's burden was to prove actual malice by clear and convincing evidence. This record simply does not contain clear and convincing evidence that the defendants knew that their information was incorrect or had a "high degree of awareness of . . . [its] probable falsity." [*Garrison*].

Although not required to do so, some states have adopted this heightened burden of proof for some aspects of the state libel action. See, e.g., *Erickson*, p. 980, supra, in which the court gave a qualified privilege to an employer responding to an inquiry about an employee's work. The court then demanded that plaintiff show abuse of the privilege by "clear and convincing evidence." But see *Staples*, p. 952, supra, using a preponderance standard to conclude that plaintiff had shown abuse of a qualified privilege for intra-company communication.

2. *Independent appellate review.* The requirement of clear and convincing evidence has been bolstered by a further explicit requirement that appellate courts must exercise "independent review" to assure that the required proof has been presented with the required clarity. In Bose Corp. v. Consumers Union, 466 U.S. 485 (1984), a federal judge sitting as trier found actual malice and entered judgment against defendant magazine. The court of appeals understood its obligation to be to "independently examin[e] the record to ensure that the district court has applied properly the governing constitutional law and that the plaintiff has indeed satisfied its burden of proof." Using that standard the court of appeals reversed.

The Court, 6–3, upheld the court of appeals. It analogized libel cases to those others in which the unprotected character of particular communications depends upon "judicial evaluation of special facts that have been deemed to have constitutional significance:"

> The rule of independent appellate review . . . emerged from the exigency of deciding concrete cases; it is law in its purest form under our common law heritage. It reflects a deeply held conviction that judges—and particularly members of this Court—must exercise such

review in order to preserve the precious liberties established and ordained by the Constitution. The question whether the evidence in the record in a defamation case is of the convincing clarity required to strip the utterance of First Amendment protection is not merely a question for the trier of fact. Judges, as expositors of the Constitution, must independently decide whether the evidence in the record is sufficient to cross the constitutional threshold that bars the entry of any judgment that is not supported by clear and convincing proof of "actual malice."

For extended discussion, see the Court's discussion in the *Connaughton* case, p. 1017, supra, upholding a determination of actual malice.

Bose is criticized in Monaghan, Constitutional Fact Review, 85 Colum.L.Rev. 229 (1985). See also, Bezanson, Fault, Falsity and Reputation in Public Defamation Law: An Essay on *Bose Corporation v. Consumers Union*, 8 Hamline L.Rev. 105 (1985).

3. *The summary judgment standard.* In Anderson v. Liberty Lobby, Inc., 477 U.S. 242 (1986), the Court held, 6–3, that the standard for considering summary judgment motions under Federal Rule 56 must take into account the burden plaintiff will have to meet at trial. For public plaintiffs, then, on a summary judgment motion the judge must decide "whether the evidence in the record could support a reasonable jury finding either that the plaintiff has shown actual malice by clear and convincing evidence or that the plaintiff has not." Using a "preponderance" standard was rejected because it "makes no sense to say that a jury could reasonably find for either party without some benchmark as to what standards govern its deliberations and within what boundaries its ultimate decision must fall, and these standards and boundaries are in fact provided by the applicable evidentiary standards."

The Court denied that its holding denigrated the role of the jury. "Credibility determinations, the weighing of the evidence, and the drawing of legitimate inferences from the facts are jury functions, not those of a judge, whether he is ruling on a motion for summary judgment or for a directed verdict."

Several states, noting that the *Liberty Lobby* case was decided on nonconstitutional grounds, have declined to follow it.

4. *Confidential sources and proof of actual malice.* How can the plaintiff prove actual malice if the defendant journalist asserts reliance on a "confidential source" who is not identified? This important question, beyond the scope of this book, is explored in M. Franklin, D. Anderson, F. Cate, Cases and Materials on Mass Media Law 337 (6th ed. 2000).

5. *SLAPP suits.* In recent years, much concern has been expressed about defamation suits brought against persons making public statements in an apparent effort to dissuade them from participating in public discourse. Much of this involved suits against tenants' associations, environmental groups, and persons testifying at city council meetings. See Pring, SLAPPs: Strategic Lawsuits Against Public Participation, 7 Pace Envtl.

L.Rev. 3 (1989). The concern led to what have been called anti-SLAPP statutes, which do not alter the substantive law applicable to the case. Rather, they offer procedural devices by which to identify and dismiss at an early stage nonmeritorious suits that interfere with free speech rights. Those who believe that they are the victims of such a suit, may prevail on an early "motion to strike, unless the court determines that the plaintiff has established that there is a probability that the plaintiff will prevail on the claim."

For the California version of the statute, see Cal.Code Civ.Proc. § 425.16. For a discussion of the philosophy behind the statute and how it operates, see Wilcox v. Superior Court, 33 Cal.Rptr.2d 446 (App. 1994). See also, Dixon v. Superior Court, 36 Cal.Rptr.2d 687 (App. 1994)(applying statute to dismiss suit brought against professor who wrote letters critical of work of surveyor during public review period in environmental impact dispute involving university land) and Lafayette Morehouse, Inc. v. Chronicle Pub.Co., 44 Cal.Rptr.2d 46 (App. 1995)(holding statute broad enough to protect a newspaper defendant sued by a university that the paper had criticized).

C. PRIVATE PLAINTIFFS AND THE CONSTITUTION

Soon after deciding its first "public figure" cases, the Court confronted Rosenbloom v. Metromedia, Inc., 403 U.S. 29 (1971), involving a broadcaster's report that a magazine distributor sold obscene material and was arrested in a police raid. For a plurality, Justice Brennan, joined by Chief Justice Burger and Justice Blackmun, concluded that the *Times* standards should be extended to "all discussion and communication involving matters of public or general concern, without regard to whether the persons involved are famous or anonymous." The arrest and the distributor's subsequent claims against the police were thought to fit this category and the *Times* standard was applied. In reaching that position Justice Brennan concluded that the focus on the plaintiff's status begun in the *Times* case bore "little relationship either to the values protected by the First Amendment or to the nature of our society. . . . Thus, the idea that certain 'public' figures have voluntarily exposed their entire lives to public inspection, while private individuals have kept theirs carefully shrouded from public view is, at best, a legal fiction." Discussion of a matter of public concern must be protected even when it involves an unknown person. If the states fear that private citizens will be unable to respond to adverse publicity, "the solution lies in the direction of ensuring their ability to respond, rather than in stifling public discussion of matters of public concern," a reference to possible use of the right of reply.

Justice White concurred on the narrow ground that the press is privileged to report "upon the official actions of public servants in full detail." Justice Black provided the fifth vote against liability, for the reasons stated in his earlier opinions. Justice Douglas did not participate in the case. Justices Harlan, Stewart and Marshall dissented on various grounds but they agreed that the private plaintiff should be required to prove no more than negligence in this case. The dissenters also agreed that some limitations on damages should exist. Yet the dissenters disagreed with each other as well as with the plurality on major points. The area was ripe for rethinking.

Gertz v. Robert Welch, Inc.

Supreme Court of the United States, 1974.
418 U.S. 323, 94 S.Ct. 2997, 41 L.Ed.2d 789.

[Plaintiff, an attorney, was retained to represent the family of a youth killed by Nuccio, a Chicago policeman. In that capacity, plaintiff attended the coroner's inquest and filed an action for damages but played no part in a criminal proceeding in which Nuccio was convicted of second degree murder. Respondent published American Opinion, a monthly outlet for the views of the John Birch Society. As part of its efforts to alert the public to an alleged nationwide conspiracy to discredit local police, the magazine's editor engaged a regular contributor to write about the Nuccio episode. The article that appeared charged a frame-up against Nuccio and portrayed plaintiff as a "major architect" of the plot. It also falsely asserted that he had a long police record, was an official of the Marxist League for Industrial Democracy, and was a "Leninist" and a "Communist-fronter." The editor said he had no reason to doubt the charges and made no effort to verify them.

Gertz filed an action for libel in District Court because of diversity of citizenship. The trial judge first ruled that Gertz was not a public official or public figure and that under Illinois law there was no defense. The jury awarded $50,000. On further reflection, the judge decided that since a matter of public concern was being discussed, the *Times* rule should apply and he granted the defendant judgment notwithstanding the jury's verdict. He thus anticipated the plurality's approach in *Rosenbloom v. Metromedia, Inc.* The court of appeals, relying on the intervening decision in *Rosenbloom,* affirmed because of the absence of clear and convincing evidence of actual malice. According to *St. Amant v. Thompson*, p. 1015, supra, failure to investigate, without more, could not establish reckless disregard for truth. Gertz appealed.]

MR. JUSTICE POWELL delivered the opinion of the Court.

.   .   .

III.

We begin with the common ground. Under the First Amendment there is no such thing as a false idea. However pernicious an opinion may seem, we depend for its correction not on the conscience of judges and juries but on the competition of other ideas. But there is no constitutional value in false statements of fact. Neither the intentional lie nor the careless error materially advances society's interest in "uninhibited, robust, and wide-open" debate on public issues.   .   .   .

Although the erroneous statement of fact is not worthy of constitutional protection, it is nevertheless inevitable in free debate. . . . And punishment of error runs the risk of inducing a cautious and restrictive exercise of the constitutionally guaranteed freedoms of speech and press. Our decisions recognize that a rule of strict liability that compels a publisher or broadcaster to guarantee the accuracy of his factual assertions may lead to intolerable self-censorship. Allowing the media to avoid liability only by proving the truth of all injurious statements does not accord adequate protection to First Amendment liberties. . . . The First Amendment requires that we protect some falsehood in order to protect speech that matters.

The need to avoid self-censorship by the news media is, however, not the only societal value at issue. If it were, this Court would have embraced long ago the view that publishers and broadcasters enjoy an unconditional and indefeasible immunity from liability for defamation. . . .

The legitimate state interest underlying the law of libel is the compensation of individuals for the harm inflicted on them by defamatory falsehood. We would not lightly require the State to abandon this purpose, for, as Mr. Justice Stewart has reminded us, the individual's right to the protection of his own good name

"reflects no more than our basic concept of the essential dignity and worth of every human being—a concept at the root of any decent system of ordered liberty. The protection of private personality, like the protection of life itself, is left primarily to the individual States under the Ninth and Tenth Amendments. But this does not mean that the right is entitled to any less recognition by this Court as a basic of our constitutional system." Rosenblatt v. Baer [ ] (concurring opinion).

Some tension necessarily exists between the need for a vigorous and uninhibited press and the legitimate interest in redressing wrongful injury. . . .

The *New York Times* standard defines the level of constitutional protection appropriate to the context of defamation of a public person. Those who, by reason of the notoriety of their achievements or the vigor and success with which they seek the public's attention, are properly classed as public figures and those who hold governmental office may recover for injury to reputation only on clear and convincing proof that the defamatory falsehood was made with knowledge of its falsity or with reckless disregard for the truth. This standard administers an extremely powerful antidote to the inducement to media self-censorship of the common-law rule of strict liability for libel and slander. And it exacts a correspondingly high price from the victims of defamatory falsehood. Plainly many deserving plaintiffs, including some intentionally subjected to injury, will be unable to surmount the barrier of the *New York Times* test. Despite this substantial abridgment of the state law right to compensation for wrongful hurt to one's reputation, the Court has concluded that the protection of the *New York Times* privilege should be available to publishers and broadcasters of defamatory falsehood concerning public officials and public figures. [ ] We think that these decisions are correct, but we do not find their holdings justified solely by reference to the interest of the press and broadcast media in immunity from liability. Rather, we believe that the *New York Times* rule states an accommodation between this concern and the limited state interest present in the context of libel actions brought by public persons. For the reasons stated below, we conclude that the state interest in compensating injury to the reputation of private individuals requires that a different rule should obtain with respect to them.

Theoretically, of course, the balance between the needs of the press and the individual's claim to compensation for wrongful injury might be struck on a case-by-case basis. As Mr. Justice Harlan hypothesized, "it might seem, purely as an abstract matter, that the most utilitarian approach would be to scrutinize carefully every jury verdict in every libel case, in order to ascertain whether the final judgment leaves fully protected whatever First Amendment values transcend the legitimate state interest in protecting the particular plaintiff who prevailed." [*Rosenbloom*]. But this approach would lead to unpredictable results and uncertain expectations, and it could render our duty to supervise the lower courts unmanageable. Because an *ad hoc* resolution of the competing interests at stake in each particular case is not feasible, we must lay down broad rules of general application. Such rules necessarily treat alike various cases involving differences as well as similarities. Thus it is often true that not all of the considerations which justify adoption of a given rule will obtain in each particular case decided under its authority.

With that caveat we have no difficulty in distinguishing among defamation plaintiffs. The first remedy of any victim of defamation is self-help—using available opportunities to contradict the lie or correct the error and thereby to minimize its adverse impact on reputation. Public officials and public figures usually enjoy significantly greater access to the channels of effective communication and hence have a more realistic opportunity to counteract false statements than private individuals normally enjoy.[9] Private individuals are therefore more vulnerable to injury, and the state interest in protecting them is correspondingly greater.

More important than the likelihood that private individuals will lack effective opportunities for rebuttal, there is a compelling normative consideration underlying the distinction between public and private defamation plaintiffs. An individual who decides to seek governmental office must accept certain necessary consequences of that involvement in public affairs. He runs the risk of closer public scrutiny than might otherwise be the case. And society's interest in the officers of government is not strictly limited to the formal discharge of official duties. As the Court pointed out in [*Garri-*

---

9. Of course, an opportunity for rebuttal seldom suffices to undo harm of defamatory falsehood. Indeed, the law of defamation is rooted in our experience that the truth rarely catches up with a lie. But the fact that the self-help remedy of rebuttal, standing alone, is inadequate to its task does not mean that it is irrelevant to our inquiry.

son v. Louisiana], the public's interest extends to "anything which might touch on an official's fitness for office. . . . Few personal attributes are more germane to fitness for office than dishonesty, malfeasance, or improper motivation, even though these characteristics may also affect the official's private character."

Those classed as public figures stand in a similar position. Hypothetically, it may be possible for someone to become a public figure through no purposeful action of his own, but the instances of truly involuntary public figures must be exceedingly rare. For the most part those who attain this status have assumed roles of especial prominence in the affairs of society. Some occupy positions of such persuasive power and influence that they are deemed public figures for all purposes. More commonly, those classed as public figures have thrust themselves to the forefront of particular public controversies in order to influence the resolution of the issues involved. In either event, they invite attention and comment.

Even if the foregoing generalities do not obtain in every instance, the communications media are entitled to act on the assumption that public officials and public figures have voluntarily exposed themselves to increased risk of injury from defamatory falsehood concerning them. No such assumption is justified with respect to a private individual. He has not accepted public office or assumed an "influential role in ordering society." *Curtis Publishing Co. v. Butts*, [   ], (Warren, C.J., concurring in result). He has relinquished no part of his interest in the protection of his own good name, and consequently he has a more compelling call on the courts for redress of injury inflicted by defamatory falsehood. Thus, private individuals are not only more vulnerable to injury than public officials and public figures; they are also more deserving of recovery.

For these reasons we conclude that the States should retain substantial latitude in their efforts to enforce a legal remedy for defamatory falsehood injurious to the reputation of a private individual. The extension of the *New York Times* test proposed by the *Rosenbloom* plurality would abridge this legitimate state interest to a degree that we find unacceptable. And it would occasion the additional difficulty of forcing state and federal judges to decide on an *ad hoc* basis which publications address issues of "general or public interest" and which do not—to determine, in the words of Mr. Justice Marshall, "what information is relevant to self-government." [*Rosenbloom*]. We doubt the wisdom of committing this task to the conscience of judges. Nor does the Constitution require us to draw so thin a line between the drastic alternatives of the *New York Times* privilege and the common law of strict liability for defamatory error. The "public or general interest" test for determining the applicability of the *New York Times* standard to private defamation actions inadequately serves both of the competing values at stake. On the one hand, a private individual whose reputation is injured by defamatory falsehood that does concern an issue of public or general interest has no recourse unless he can meet the rigorous requirements of *New York Times*. This is true despite the factors that distinguish the state interest in compensating private individuals from the analogous interest involved in the context of public persons. On the other hand, a publisher or broadcaster of a defamatory error which a court deems unrelated to an issue of public or general interest may be held liable in damages even if it took every reasonable precaution to ensure the accuracy of its assertions. And liability may far exceed compensation for any actual injury to the plaintiff, for the jury may be permitted to presume damages without proof of loss and even to award punitive damages.

We hold that, so long as they do not impose liability without fault, the States may define for themselves the appropriate standard of liability for a publisher or broadcaster of defamatory falsehood injurious to a private individual. This approach provides a more equitable boundary between the competing concerns involved here. It recognizes the strength of the legitimate state interest in compensating private individuals for wrongful injury to reputation, yet shields the press and broadcast media from the rigors of strict liability for defamation. At least this conclusion obtains where, as here, the substance of the defamatory statement "makes substantial danger to reputation apparent." [*Butts*] This phrase places in perspective the conclusion we announce today. Our inquiry would involve considerations somewhat different from those discussed above if a State purported to condition civil liability on a factual misstatement whose content did not warn a reasonably prudent editor or broadcaster of its defamatory potential. Cf. Time, Inc. v. Hill, 385 U.S. 374 (1967). Such a case is not now before us, and we intimate no view as to its proper resolution.

IV.

Our accommodation of the competing values at stake in defamation suits by private individuals allows the States to impose liability on the publisher or broadcaster of defamatory falsehood on a less demanding showing than that required by *New York Times*. This conclusion is not based on a belief that the considerations which prompted the adoption of the *New York Times* privilege for defamation of public officials and its extension to public figures are wholly inapplicable to the context of private individuals. Rather, we endorse this approach in recognition of the strong and legitimate state interest in compensating private individuals for injury to reputation. But this countervailing state interest extends no further than compensation for actual injury. For the reasons stated below, we hold that the States may not permit recovery of presumed or punitive damages, at least when liability is not based on a showing of knowledge of falsity or reckless disregard for the truth.

The common law of defamation is an oddity of tort law, for it allows recovery of purportedly compensatory damages without evidence of actual loss. Under the traditional rules pertaining to actions for libel, the existence of injury is presumed from the fact of publication. Juries may award substantial sums as compensation for supposed damage to reputation without any proof that such harm actually occurred. The largely uncontrolled discretion of juries to award damages where there is no loss unnecessarily compounds the potential of any system of liability for defamatory falsehood to inhibit the vigorous exercise of First Amendment freedoms. Additionally, the doctrine of presumed damages invites juries to punish unpopular opinion rather than to compensate individuals for injury sustained by the publication of a false fact. More to the point, the States have no substantial interest in securing for plaintiffs such as this petitioner gratuitous awards of money damages far in excess of any actual injury.

We would not, of course, invalidate state law simply because we doubt its wisdom, but here we are attempting to reconcile state law with a competing interest grounded in the constitutional command of the First Amendment. It is therefore appropriate to require that state remedies for defamatory falsehood reach no farther than is necessary to protect the legitimate interest involved. It is necessary to restrict defamation plaintiffs who do not prove knowledge of falsity or reckless disregard for the truth to compensation for actual injury. We need not define "actual injury," as trial courts have wide experience in framing appropriate jury instructions in tort actions. Suffice it to say that actual injury is not limited to out-of-pocket loss. Indeed, the more customary types of actual harm inflicted by defamatory falsehood include impairment of reputation and standing in the community, personal humiliation, and mental anguish and suffering. Of course, juries must be limited by appropriate instructions, and all awards must be supported by competent evidence concerning the injury, although there need be no evidence which assigns an actual dollar value to the injury.

We also find no justification for allowing awards of punitive damages against publishers and broadcasters held liable under state-defined standards of liability for defamation. In most jurisdictions jury discretion over the amounts awarded is limited only by the gentle rule that they not be excessive. Consequently, juries assess punitive damages in wholly unpredictable amounts bearing no necessary relation to the actual harm caused. And they remain free to use their discretion selectively to punish expressions of unpopular views. Like the doctrine of presumed damages, jury discretion to award punitive damages unnecessarily exacerbates the danger of media self-censorship, but, unlike the former rule, punitive damages are wholly irrelevant to the state interest that justifies a negligence standard for private defamation actions. They are not compensation for injury. Instead, they are private fines levied by civil juries to punish reprehensible conduct and to deter its future occurrence. In short, the private defamation plaintiff who establishes liability under a less demanding standard than that stated by *New York Times* may recover only such damages as are sufficient to compensate him for actual injury.

V.

Notwithstanding our refusal to extend the *New York Times* privilege to defamation of private individuals, respondent contends that we should affirm the judgment below on the ground that petitioner is either a public official or a public figure. There is little basis for the former assertion. Several years prior to the present incident, petitioner had served briefly on housing committees appointed by the mayor of Chicago, but at the time of publication he had never held any remunerative governmental position. Respondent admits this but argues that petitioner's appearance at the coroner's inquest rendered him a "de facto public official." Our cases recognize no such concept. Respondent's suggestion would sweep all lawyers under the *New York Times* rule as officers of the court and distort the plain meaning of the "public official" category beyond all recognition. We decline to follow it.

Respondent's characterization of petitioner as a public figure raises a different question. That designation may rest on either of two alternative bases. In some instances an individual may achieve such pervasive fame or notoriety that he becomes a public figure for all purposes and in all contexts. More commonly, an individual voluntarily injects himself or is drawn into a particular public controversy and thereby becomes a public figure for a limited range of issues. In either case such persons assume special prominence in the resolution of public questions.

Petitioner has long been active in community and professional affairs. He has served as an officer of local civic groups and of various professional organizations, and he has published several books and articles on legal subjects. Although petitioner was consequently well known in some circles, he had achieved no general fame or notoriety in the community. None of the prospective jurors called at the trial had ever heard of petitioner prior to this litigation, and respondent offered no proof that this response was atypical of the local population. We would not lightly assume that a citizen's participation in community and professional affairs rendered him a public figure for all purposes. Absent clear evidence of general fame or notoriety in the community, and pervasive involvement in the affairs of society, an individual should not be deemed a public personality for all aspects of his life. It is preferable to reduce the public-figure question to a more meaningful context by looking to the nature and extent of an individual's participation in the particular controversy giving rise to the defamation.

In this context it is plain that petitioner was not a public figure. He played a minimal role at the coroner's inquest, and his participation related solely to his representation of a private client. He took no part in the criminal prosecution of Officer Nuccio. Moreover, he never discussed either the criminal or civil litigation with the press and was never quoted as having done so. He plainly did not thrust himself into the vortex of this public issue, nor did he engage the public's attention in an attempt to influence its outcome. We are persuaded that the trial court did not err in refusing to characterize petitioner as a public figure for the purpose of this litigation.

We therefore conclude that the *New York Times* standard is inapplicable to this case and that the trial court erred in entering judgment for respondent. Because the jury was allowed to impose liability without fault and was permitted to presume damages without proof of injury, a new trial is necessary. We reverse and remand for further proceedings in accord with this opinion.

It is so ordered.

MR. JUSTICE BLACKMUN, concurring.

[Although I joined the *Rosenbloom* plurality opinion,] I am willing to join, and do join, the Court's opinion and its judgment for two reasons:

1. By removing the specters of presumed and punitive damages in the absence of *New York Times* malice, the Court eliminates significant and powerful motives for self-censorship that otherwise are present in the traditional libel action. By so doing, the Court leaves what should prove to be sufficient and adequate breathing space for a vigorous press. What the Court has done, I believe, will have little, if any, practical effect on the functioning of responsible journalism.

2. The Court was sadly fractionated in *Rosenbloom*. A result of that kind inevitably leads to uncertainty. I feel that it is of profound importance for the Court to come to rest in the defamation area and to have a clearly defined majority position that eliminates the unsureness engendered by *Rosenbloom's* diversity. If my vote were not needed to create a majority, I would adhere to my prior view. A definitive ruling, however, is paramount.
[ ]

For these reasons, I join the opinion and the judgment of the Court.

MR. CHIEF JUSTICE BURGER, dissenting.

. . .

Agreement or disagreement with the law as it has evolved to this time does not alter the fact that it has been orderly development with a consistent basic rationale. . . . I would prefer to allow this area of law to continue to evolve as it has up to now with respect to private citizens rather than embark on a new doctrinal theory which has no jurisprudential ancestry.

The petitioner here was performing a professional representative role as an advocate in the highest tradition of the law, and under that tradition the advocate is not to be invidiously identified with his client. The important public policy which underlies this tradition—the right to counsel— would be gravely jeopardized if every lawyer who takes an "unpopular" case, civil or criminal, would automatically become fair game for irresponsible reporters and editors who might, for example, describe the lawyer as a "mob mouthpiece" for representing a client with a serious prior criminal record, or as an "ambulance chaser" for representing a claimant in a personal injury action.

I would reverse the judgment of the Court of Appeals and remand for reinstatement of the verdict of the jury and the entry of an appropriate judgment on that verdict.

MR. JUSTICE DOUGLAS, dissenting.

. . .

. . . The standard announced today leaves the States free to "define for themselves the appropriate standard of liability for a publisher or broadcaster" in the circumstances of this case. This of course leaves the simple negligence standard as an option with the jury free to impose damages upon a finding that the publisher failed to act as "a reasonable man." With such continued erosion of First Amendment protection, I fear that it may well be the reasonable man who refrains from speaking.

Since in my view the First and Fourteenth Amendments prohibit the imposition of damages upon respondent for this discussion of public affairs, I would affirm the judgment below.

MR. JUSTICE BRENNAN, dissenting.

I agree with the conclusion, expressed in Part V of the Court's opinion, that, at the time of publication of respondent's article, petitioner could not properly have been viewed as either a "public official" or "public figure"; instead, respondent's article, dealing with an alleged conspiracy to discredit local police forces, concerned petitioner's purported involvement in "an event of public or general interest." . . .

. . .

Although acknowledging that First Amendment values are of no less significance when media reports concern private persons' involvement in matters of public concern, the Court refuses to provide, in such cases, the same level of constitutional protection that has been afforded the media in the context of defamation of public persons. The accommodation that this Court has established between free speech and libel laws in cases involving public officials and public figures—that defamatory falsehood be shown by clear and convincing evidence to have been published with knowledge of falsity or with reckless disregard of truth—is not apt, the Court holds, because the private individual does not have the same degree of access to the media to rebut defamatory comments as does the public person and he has not voluntarily exposed himself to public scrutiny.

While these arguments are forcefully and eloquently presented, I cannot accept them, for the reasons I stated in *Rosenbloom:*

> The *New York Times* standard was applied to libel of a public official or public figure to give effect to the [First] Amendment's function to encourage ventilation of public issues, not because the public official has any less interest in protecting his reputation than an individual in private life. While the argument that public figures need less protection because they can command media attention to counter criticism may be true for some very prominent people, even then it is the rare case where the denial overtakes the original charge. Denials, retractions, and corrections are not "hot" news, and rarely receive the prominence of the original story. When the public official or public figure is a minor functionary, or has left the position that put him in the public eye . . ., the argument loses all of its force. In the vast majority of libels involving public officials or public figures, the ability to respond through the media will depend on the same complex factor

on which the ability of a private individual depends: the unpredictable event of the media's continuing interest in the story. Thus the unproved, and highly improbable, generalization that an as yet [not fully defined] class of "public figures" involved in matters of public concern will be better able to respond through the media than private individuals also involved in such matters seems too insubstantial a reed on which to rest a constitutional distinction. [   ]

.   .   .

.   .   . Under a reasonable-care regime, publishers and broadcasters will have to make pre-publication judgments about juror assessment of such diverse considerations as the size, operating procedures, and financial condition of the newsgathering system, as well as the relative costs and benefits of instituting less frequent and more costly reporting at a higher level of accuracy. [   ] Moreover, in contrast to proof by clear and convincing evidence required under the *Times* test, the burden of proof for reasonable care will doubtless be the preponderance of the evidence.   .   .   .

The Court does not discount altogether the danger that jurors will punish for the expression of unpopular opinions. This probability accounts for the Court's limitation that "the States may not permit recovery of presumed or punitive damages, at least when liability is not based on a showing of knowledge of falsity or reckless disregard for the truth." [   ] But plainly a jury's latitude to impose liability for want of due care poses a far greater threat of suppressing unpopular views than does a possible recovery of presumed or punitive damages. Moreover, the Court's broadranging examples of "actual injury," including impairment of reputation and standing in the community, as well as personal humiliation, and mental anguish and suffering, inevitably allow a jury bent on punishing expression of unpopular views a formidable weapon for doing so. Finally, even a limitation of recovery to "actual injury"—however much it reduces the size or frequency of recoveries—will not provide the necessary elbowroom for First Amendment expression.   .   .   .

On the other hand, the uncertainties which the media face under today's decision are largely avoided by the *Times* standard. I reject the argument that my *Rosenbloom* view improperly commits to judges the task of determining what is and what is not an issue of "general or public interest." [A footnote here asserted that states might enact statutes under which plaintiffs unable to prove fault could bring action "for retraction or for publication of a court's determination of falsity"—eds.] I noted in *Rosenbloom* that performance of this task would not always be easy. [   ] But surely the courts, the ultimate arbiters of all disputes concerning clashes of constitutional values, would only be performing one of their traditional functions in undertaking this duty.   .   .   .

MR. JUSTICE WHITE, dissenting.

.   .   .

The impact of today's decision on the traditional law of libel is immediately obvious and indisputable. No longer will the plaintiff be able to rest his case with proof of a libel defamatory on its face or proof of a slander historically actionable *per se.* In addition, he must prove some further degree of culpable conduct on the part of the publisher . . . And if he succeeds in this respect, he faces still another obstacle: [denial of recovery for presumed damages]. The Court rejects the judgment of experience that some publications are so inherently capable of injury, and actual injury so difficult to prove, that the risk of falsehood should be borne by the publisher, not the victim. . . .

So too, the requirement of proving special injury to reputation before general damages may be awarded will clearly eliminate the prevailing rule, worked out over a very long period of time, that, in the case of defamations not actionable *per se,* the recovery of general damages for injury to reputation may also be had if some form of material or pecuniary loss is proved. Finally, an inflexible federal standard is imposed for the award of punitive damages. No longer will it be enough to prove ill will and an attempt to injure.

These are radical changes in the law and severe invasions of the prerogatives of the States. . . .

. . .

The Court evinces a deep-seated antipathy to "liability without fault." But this catch-phrase has no talismanic significance and is almost meaningless in this context where the Court appears to be addressing those libels and slanders that are defamatory on their face and where the publisher is no doubt aware from the nature of the material that it would be inherently damaging to reputation. He publishes notwithstanding, knowing that he will inflict injury. With this knowledge, he must intend to inflict that injury, his excuse being that he is privileged to do so—that he has published the truth. But as it turns out, what he has circulated to the public is a very damaging falsehood. Is he nevertheless "faultless"? Perhaps it can be said that the mistake about his defense was made in good faith, but the fact remains that it is he who launched the publication knowing that it could ruin a reputation.

In these circumstances, the law has heretofore put the risk of falsehood on the publisher where the victim is a private citizen and no grounds of special privilege are invoked. The Court would now shift this risk to the victim, even though he has done nothing to invite the calumny, is wholly innocent of fault, and is helpless to avoid his injury. . . . The press today is vigorous and robust. To me, it is quite incredible to suggest that threats of libel suits from private citizens are causing the press to refrain from publishing the truth. I know of no hard facts to support that proposition, and the Court furnishes none.

The communications industry has increasingly become concentrated in a few powerful hands operating very lucrative businesses reaching across the Nation and into almost every home. Neither the industry as a whole nor its individual components are easily intimidated, and we are fortunate that they are not. Requiring them to pay for the occasional damage they do to private reputation will play no substantial part in their future performance or their existence.

In any event, if the Court's principal concern is to protect the communications industry from large libel judgments, it would appear that its new requirements with respect to general and punitive damages would be ample protection.   .   .   .

It is difficult for me to understand why the ordinary citizen should himself carry the risk of damage and suffer the injury in order to vindicate First Amendment values by protecting the press and others from liability for circulating false information. This is particularly true because such statements serve no purpose whatsoever in furthering the public interest or the search for truth but, on the contrary, may frustrate that search and at the same time inflict great injury on the defenseless individual. The owners of the press and the stockholders of the communications enterprises can much better bear the burden. And if they cannot, the public at large should somehow pay for what is essentially a public benefit derived at private expense.

.   .   .

For the foregoing reasons, I would reverse the judgment of the Court of Appeals and reinstate the jury's verdict.

Notes and Questions

1. Why did the majority adhere to the *Times* rule for public officials? For public figures?

2. Why does the majority in *Gertz* prefer its approach to the plurality's approach in *Rosenbloom*?

3. The *Gertz* retrial, which did not occur for several years, produced a jury verdict for plaintiff for $100,000 compensatory damages and $300,000 punitive damages. On appeal, the court affirmed. It concluded that the jury could find "actual malice" on the editor of the magazine, who solicited a person with a "known and unreasonable propensity to label persons or organizations as Communist, to write the article; and after the article was submitted, made virtually no effort to check the validity of statements that were defamatory *per se* of Gertz, and in fact added further defamatory material based on [the writer's] 'facts.' " It also held that, contrary to most cases involving freelance writers, the conduct of the writer could be imputed to the magazine because of the "significant control" exercised by the editor over the content and focus of the article. An agency relationship had been created. Gertz v. Robert Welch, Inc., 680 F.2d 527 (7th Cir.1982), cert. denied 459 U.S. 1226 (1983).

4. Even if the constitutional law does not bar punitive damages in cases in which actual malice is shown, state law may impose a variety of impediments, such as barring punitive damages in all tort cases, or in cases involving speech. Many of the state tort reform statutes that limit punitive damages to a maximum or to a multiple of compensatory damages, though written primarily with personal injury in mind, apply also to defamation actions. Also, some states require a showing of some further element, such as animosity toward plaintiff, in addition to actual malice. Moreover, some states have demanded that the state law requirements for punitive damages be shown with convincing clarity.

5. *State privileges.* Even if the plaintiff is private for constitutional purposes, the state may develop a state law privilege on the same facts. New Jersey has been active in this development. In Dairy Stores, Inc. v. Sentinel Publishing Co., 516 A.2d 220 (N.J.1986), defendant newspapers, during a drought, reported that the water being bottled and sold at plaintiff's local store was not the pure spring water it purported to be. Although the lower court had denied defendants' motions for summary judgment on the ground that plaintiff was private and did not need to prove actual malice, the state's highest court thought that "the more appropriate principle is the common-law privilege of fair comment."

Although "constitutional considerations have dominated defamation law in recent years, the common law provides an alternative, and potentially more stable, framework for analyzing statements about matters of public interest." The safety of drinking water was a "paradigm of legitimate public concern." To overcome the state privilege, plaintiff would have to prove "actual malice" in the constitutional sense. In Turf Lawnmower Repair, Inc. v. Bergen Record Corp., 655 A.2d 417 (N.J.1995), the court, using the negligence standard in a case about a report on the conduct of a lawnmower repair company, limited *Dairy Stores* to "activities that intrinsically implicated important public interests."

See also Rocci v. Ecole Secondaire MacDonald–Cartier, 755 A.2d 583 (N.J.2000), holding that a school teacher suing over a critical letter written to her superiors, must prove, beyond actual malice, "pecuniary or reputational harm" since the case involved an issue of public concern.

6. Before we explore the nature of negligence and related operational aspects of the *Gertz* case, it is important to note how few cases truly present these questions. The vast majority of reported cases against media (and we would expect unreported cases as well) are litigated as "actual malice" cases and not as negligence cases.

First, plaintiffs mentioned in the media are likely to be either admittedly public or found to be public. Second, even a plaintiff called "private" who wants to recover presumed or punitive damages must go the "actual malice" route from the start. If the jury finds that the plaintiff has succeeded in that effort, there is no occasion to focus on the meaning of "actual injury" damages. Similarly, in cases in which the plaintiff cannot establish "actual injury" damages—no matter what they are held to encompass—the litigation will likely go off on an attempt to prove "actual malice." (There is the further limitation that the Court's language in *Gertz* referred to "publishers" and "broadcasters," leaving doubt about what parts of the case might apply to nonmedia defendants.)

7. Justice White is particularly concerned about having private citizens bear the burden of defamation. If the media cannot bear the expense of the harm they do, the public should "somehow pay for what is essentially a public benefit derived at private expense." It has been widely observed that defamation law has been running counter to the trends in other areas of tort law. Thus, personal injury law has been moving toward greater imposition of liability, through techniques that increase chances of recovery in negligence cases and through development of new doctrines that increase the imposition of strict liability, as in aspects of the law of defective products. Meanwhile, defamation law had been moving the other way— from strict liability to denying liability in many cases unless something substantially greater than negligence can be shown. Is this an even more appropriate occasion for strict liability than the defective products area?

For an extensive discussion of the cross currents in strict liability see Weiler, Defamation, Enterprise Liability, and Freedom of Speech, 17 U.Toronto L.J. 278 (1967). See also Kalven, The Reasonable Man and the First Amendment: *Hill, Butts,* and *Walker,* 1967 Sup.Ct.Rev. 267. But see Anderson, Libel and Press Self–Censorship, 53 Texas L.Rev. 422, 432 n. 52 (1975), arguing that the analogy is flawed because the other enterprises "have no choice but to accept the additional risk of liability if they are to continue their profit-making activities, while most broadcasters and publishers can avoid liability, without discontinuing their activities or reducing their profits, by ceasing to carry material that creates the risk of liability— i.e., by increasing their self-censorship." Can a sound argument be made for strict liability in this area? Note the lack of a first-party insurance device for potential libel victims that would operate along the lines of medical and income-protection insurance available to potential personal injury victims.

8. *The role of negligence.* Justice Powell phrased the permissible standard in private citizen cases negatively: states may use whatever standard they wish "so long as they do not impose liability without fault." It may be theoretically possible to develop a standard more protective than strict liability but less rigorous than negligence, but states have not made the attempt. Note that at the end of part IV, Justice Powell himself used "negligence" in a way that suggests that he thinks that it is the next level above strict liability: " . . . punitive damages are wholly irrelevant to the state interest that justifies a negligence standard for private defamation actions."

Almost all the states that have ruled on this question have set the state standard of care at negligence. The California Supreme Court found 33 states clearly adopting the negligence standard, six applying negligence without discussion, and a few more in which federal courts have interpreted the states as having adopted negligence law. The court found only three or four states that had explicitly refused to adopt the negligence standard. *Brown v. Kelly Broadcasting Co.,* p. 982, supra, (aligning California with the negligence group).

A very few states have adopted some version of the *Rosenbloom* plurality's approach. But by far the most important aberration has been New York, which has developed its own standard for private figure cases: "where the content of the article is arguably within the sphere of legitimate public concern, which is reasonably related to matters warranting public exposition, the party may recover; however, to warrant such recovery he must first establish, by a preponderance of the evidence, that the publisher acted in a grossly irresponsible manner without due consideration for the standards of information gathering and dissemination ordinarily followed by responsible parties." Chapadeau v. Utica Observer–Dispatch, Inc., 341 N.E.2d 569 (N.Y.1975). Is this closer to *Gertz* or to *Rosenbloom?*

Much litigation has addressed the scope and effect of *Chapadeau.* In Huggins v. Moore, 726 N.E.2d 456 (N.Y.1999), defendant newspaper ran articles reporting charges by plaintiff's ex-wife that he had committed "economic spousal abuse" by cheating her out of her interest in an entertainment company they had built together. Holding the articles entitled to protection under *Chapadeau* the court reviewed the situation:

> To make the determination of whether content is arguably within the sphere of legitimate public concern, allegedly defamatory statements "can only be viewed in the context of the writing as a whole, and not as disembodied words, phrases or sentences" [   ]. Courts must examine their " 'content, form, and context' " [   ].

> A publication's subject is not a matter of public concern when it falls "into the realm of mere gossip and prurient interest" [   ]. In addition, publications directed only to a limited, private audience are "matters of purely private concern" [   ]. Moreover, the fact that the article has been published in a newspaper is not conclusive that its subject matter warrants public exposition [   ].

> Yet we have stated repeatedly that the *Chapadeau* standard is deferential to professional journalistic judgments. Absent clear abuse, the courts will not second-guess editorial decisions as to what constitutes matters of genuine public concern [   ]. This applies equally to the determination whether any particular portion of the text is "reasonably related" to the subject of public concern in the article [   ]. There is no "abuse of editorial discretion" [   ] so long as a published report can be "fairly considered as relating to any matter of political, social, or other concern of the community" [   ].

> In applying this standard, our cases establish that a matter may be of public concern even though it is a "human interest" portrayal of events in the lives of persons who are not themselves public figures, so long as some theme of legitimate public concern can reasonably be drawn from their experience. . . . Thus, the *Chapadeau* standard applies to statements about a "private legal dispute," so long as those statements, in the context of the entire publication, are illustrative of a larger subject of legitimate concern to the public at large.

In the case before it, the court rejected the lower court's emphasis on the fact that the case involved an acrimonious divorce:

> That the "core" of the dispute between Moore and plaintiff was a divorce is not conclusive. The articles also portrayed Moore's alleged victimization by her financial as well as marital partner to the point of economic and career ruination. It is this episode of human interest that reflected a matter of genuine social concern.

What are the merits and demerits of the New York approach?

9. *How negligence operates.* Justice Powell spoke of the "reasonably prudent editor or broadcaster." The phrase "reasonably prudent" makes sense when applied to automobile drivers or airplane pilots or physicians. But how is that phrase to be applied to a field in which the media vary from sedate, if not stodgy, journals at one extreme to racy tabloids and scandal sheets at the other; from those that treat public relations releases as news to those that disbelieve every statement made by government officials and engage in extensive investigative reporting? What about differences between editors at very well financed and profitable publications or broadcast stations and those at marginal media with small, or nonexistent, research staffs and budgets too tight to keep a libel lawyer on retainer?

The Restatement (Second) of Torts § 580B, comment *h*, suggests that the reasonableness of the investigation varies with the following factors: 1. The "time element"—investigations may be shorter for topical news than for a story that has no time pressure. 2. The "nature of the interest promoted by publication"—a story informing the public of matters important in a democracy may warrant quicker publication than a story involving "mere gossip." 3. "Potential damage to plaintiff if the communication proves to be false"—whether the statement is defamatory on its face; how many readers will understand the defamation; how harmful is the charge. Do these factors take into account "social harm" from publication of a false story?

One court has stated two other factors: the nature and reliability of the source of the information and the "reasonableness in checking the veracity of the information, considering its cost in terms of money, time, personnel, urgency of the publication, nature of the news and any other pertinent element." Torres–Silva v. El Mundo, 3 Med.L.Rptr. 1508 (P.R.1977). See generally Bloom, Proof of Fault in Media Defamation Litigation, 38 Vand. L.Rev. 247 (1985).

Some have questioned the emphasis on time pressure. In Schaefer, Defamation and the First Amendment, 52 Colo.L.Rev. 1 (1980), the former Chief Justice of Illinois said:

> It has been suggested that the press, television, and radio all operate under severe time constraints and that this consideration should excuse or justify defamatory statements. It should not be forgotten, however, that these time constraints are entirely self-imposed. Apparently the media people believe that for competitive reasons it is desirable to be first with a particular news story. My own

impression is that the public is massively unconcerned about that question. But if my impression is wrong, deadline pressures afford no more justification for harm caused by negligent attacks upon reputation than for harm caused by a reporter's negligent driving in his haste to cover a story. Both negligent acts are and have been insurable.

Do you agree?

How different is the New York requirement in *Chapadeau* cases of proof that the defendant acted in a "grossly irresponsible manner"? In Robare v. Plattsburgh Publishing Co., 685 N.Y.S.2d 129 (App.Div. 1999), the reporter relied on erroneous information from a court clerk in a story about plaintiff's prior convictions. The reporter presented evidence that the clerk had "consistently provided her with reliable, accurate information relating to similar matters for over 15 years" and that she "was aware of no other means of verifying the accuracy of the information he provided." In the absence of counter evidence defendant was entitled to summary judgment. Would the same result be reached in a negligence case?

10. *The role of experts.* Another question is whether the standard should be stated in terms of professional negligence or ordinary due care. This may be significant both in formulating the standard and in requiring expert testimony to show the standard and the deviation. The few states that have addressed this question have split. In Gobin v. Globe Pub. Co., 531 P.2d 76 (Kan.1975), the court stated the standard to be "the conduct of the reasonably careful publisher or broadcaster in the community or in similar communities under the existing circumstances." Troman v. Wood, 340 N.E.2d 292 (Ill.1975), rejected the professional negligence approach because "it would make the prevailing newspaper practices in a community controlling. In a community having only a single newspaper, the approach suggested would permit that paper to establish its own standards. And in any community it might tend, in 'Gresham's law' fashion, toward a progressive depreciation of the standard of care."

The Second Restatement's § 580B, comment *g*, states that a professional disseminator of news "is held to the skill and experience normally possessed by members of that profession. Customs and practices within the profession are relevant in applying the negligence standard, which is, to a substantial degree, set by the profession itself, though a custom is not controlling." How have courts handled medical malpractice cases involving a single physician in a small community?

11. *Plaintiffs must prove falsity—The Hepps case.* Although the Court's focus has been on the fault requirement, the role of falsity has also raised questions. In Philadelphia Newspapers, Inc. v. Hepps, 475 U.S. 767 (1986), the Court, 5–4, held that the plaintiff had the burden of proving falsity in cases brought by private plaintiffs, at least where the speech was of public concern. For the majority, Justice O'Connor concluded that to "ensure that true speech on matters of public concern is not deterred, we hold that the common-law presumption that defamatory speech is false cannot stand when a plaintiff seeks damages against a media defendant for speech of public concern." (Two of the five joining the majority opinion rejected the limitation to "media" defendants.) Even though this burden would "insulate from liability some speech that is false, but unprovably so," that result was essential to avoid the "chilling" effect that would otherwise accompany true speech on matters of public concern.

The majority asserted that its conclusion added "only marginally to the burdens" on libel plaintiffs because a jury is more likely to accept a "contention that the defendant was at fault in publishing the statements at issue if convinced that the relevant statements were false. As a practical matter, then, evidence offered by plaintiffs on the publisher's fault . . . will generally encompass evidence of the falsity of the matters asserted."

Justice Stevens, for the dissenters, thought the majority result "pernicious," positing a situation in which a defendant, knowing that the plaintiff could not prove the statement false, deliberately lied about the plaintiff. This situation might occur due to the passage of time, the loss of critical records, or the absence of an eyewitness. The majority's analysis was an "obvious blueprint for character assassination."

12. *Procedural issues.* Most courts refuse to apply independent appellate review in cases in which the negligence standard controls. See Levine v. CMP Publications, Inc., 738 F.2d 660 (5th Cir.1984) rehearing and rehearing en banc denied, 753 F.2d 1341 (5th Cir.1985). Most courts also refuse to require "clear and convincing" evidence of negligence. See Lansdowne v. Beacon Journal Publishing Co., 512 N.E.2d 979 (Ohio 1987).

13. *Actual injury.* As we have already seen, the subject of damages in defamation cases was complicated enough at common law. Whether a plaintiff needed to show "special" damages and, if so, what constituted "special" damages produced much litigation. The Supreme Court's introduction, in *Gertz*, of "actual injury damages" did not purport to track any pre-existing concept of damages. Indeed, the Court went out of its way to use examples that showed that the new term did not track "special" damages. The problem has fallen to the lower courts to give content to this term, drawing solely from the few sentences in *Gertz* that address the problem—and from the *Firestone* case.

In Time Inc. v. Firestone, 424 U.S. 448 (1976), discussed in detail p. 1048, infra, plaintiff withdrew her claim for reputational harm on the eve of trial. Defendant argued that this barred her from recovering under *Gertz*. The Court disagreed. If Florida permitted recoveries in defamation actions that did not claim harm to reputation, *Gertz* did not forbid it:

> In [*Gertz*] we made it clear that States could base awards on elements other than injury to reputation, specifically listing "personal humiliation, and mental anguish and suffering" as examples of injuries which might be compensated consistently with the Constitution upon a showing of fault.

In *Firestone*, the plaintiff had presented evidence from her minister, her attorney in the divorce proceedings, and several friends and neighbors. One of the latter was a physician who testified to "having to administer a sedative to respondent in an attempt to reduce discomfort wrought by her worrying about the article." Plaintiff also testified that she feared the effect that the false report of her adultery might have on her young son when he grew older. "The jury decided these injuries should be compensated by an award of $100,000. We have no warrant for re-examining this determination."

In addition to the reasons discussed earlier, fewer cases discuss actual injury than might be expected because of (1) the cases in New York and the few other states that have higher standards of liability produce fewer discussions of any damage issues than would occur under a negligence standard; and (2) the cases that go off on state issues—as when the defendant argues that plaintiff's proof does not satisfy a state rule requiring "special" damages or requiring certain types of proof for compensatory damages, or when defendant asserts that the damages are excessive under state law. The result of all these is that relatively few courts have been forced to decide the content of *Gertz* "actual injury" damages.

Hearst Corporation v. Hughes, 466 A.2d 486 (Md.1983), chose to follow Florida's path in *Firestone* by permitting recovery of proven "personal humiliation and mental anguish" in the absence of reputational harm, though it noted that other state courts had disagreed. E.g., Gobin v. Globe Publishing Co., 649 P.2d 1239 (Kan.1982). The Maryland court asserted that the Kansas view failed to "respect the centuries of human experience which led to a presumption of harm flowing from words actionable per se. One reason for that common law position was the difficulty a defamation plaintiff has in proving harm to reputation." Since victims of defamation "can reasonably become genuinely upset as a result of the publication," the court saw "no social purpose to be served by requiring the plaintiff additionally to prove actual impairment of reputation."

D. THE PUBLIC-PRIVATE DISTINCTION

Now that we have considered the two categories developed by the Supreme Court, we turn to the crucial issue of deciding how to classify plaintiffs. We begin with the determination of whether plaintiff is a public official. We then turn to the more complex question of classifying non-governmental plaintiffs.

1. IDENTIFYING A "PUBLIC OFFICIAL"

In Rosenblatt v. Baer, 383 U.S. 75 (1966), plaintiff Baer had been hired by the three elected county commissioners to supervise a public recreation facility owned by the county. When he sued over a newspaper attack on the management of the facility, Justice Brennan's majority opinion held that Baer might be a "public official" under the *Times* rule:

> Criticism of government is at the very center of the constitutionally protected area of free discussion. . . . It is clear . . . that the "public official" designation applies at the very least to those among the hierarchy of government employees who have, or appear to the

public to have, substantial responsibility for or control over the conduct of government affairs.

> . . . Where a position in government has such apparent importance that the public has an independent interest in the qualifications and performance of the person who holds it, beyond the general public interest in the qualifications and performance of all government employees, both elements we identified in *New York Times* are present and the *New York Times* malice standards apply.[13]

Justice Stewart's separate concurrence in *Rosenblatt* sought to express the affirmative values to be found in a libel action:

> The right of a man to the protection of his own reputation from unjustified invasion and wrongful hurt reflects no more than our basic concept of the essential dignity and worth of every human being—a concept at the root of any decent system of ordered liberty.

From the social perspective, he warned of dangers associated with Senator Joseph McCarthy:

> Moreover, the preventive effect of liability for defamation serves an important public purpose. For the rights and values of private personality far transcend mere personal interests. Surely if the 1950's taught us anything, they taught us that the poisonous atmosphere of the easy lie can infect and degrade a whole society.

Candidates. In a pair of cases involving false charges made about a candidate for office, the Court unanimously extended the *Times* rationale to candidates because "it can hardly be doubted that the constitutional guarantee has its fullest and most urgent application precisely to the conduct of campaigns for political office." Monitor Patriot Co. v. Roy, 401 U.S. 265 (1971), and Ocala Star–Banner Co. v. Damron, 401 U.S. 295 (1971). In *Roy,* a newspaper column published three days before the election falsely accused a candidate for the United States Senate of criminal activity that allegedly took place many years earlier. The Court decided that the *Times* rule should include "anything which might touch on an official's fitness for office" when a candidate's behavior is being discussed:

> A candidate who, for example, seeks to further his cause through the prominent display of his wife and children can hardly argue that his qualities as a husband or father remain of "purely private" concern. And the candidate who vaunts his spotless record and sterling integrity cannot convincingly cry "Foul!" when an opponent or an industrious reporter attempts to demonstrate the contrary. Any test adequate to

---

13. It is suggested that this test might apply to a night watchman accused of stealing state secrets. But a conclusion that the *New York Times* malice standards apply could not be reached merely because a statement defamatory of some person in government employ catches the public's interest: that conclusion would virtually disregard society's interest in protecting reputation. The employee's position must be one which would invite public scrutiny and discussion of the person holding it, entirely apart from the scrutiny and discussion occasioned by the particular charges in controversy.

safeguard First Amendment guarantees in this area must go far beyond the customary meaning of the phrase "official conduct."

Given the realities of our political life, it is by no means easy to see what statements about a candidate might be altogether without relevance to his fitness for the office he seeks. The clash of reputations is the staple of election campaigns, and damage to reputation is, of course, the essence of libel. But whether there remains some exiguous area of defamation against which a candidate may have full recourse is a question we need not decide in this case.

The Court concluded that a "charge of criminal conduct, no matter how remote in time or place, can never be irrelevant to an official's or a candidate's fitness for office" for purposes of applying the *Times* rule.

In *Damron*, a newspaper reported two weeks before a local election that a candidate had been charged with perjury, when in fact his brother was the one charged. Again, the *Times* rule applied.

Since these early cases, the Supreme Court has given lower courts no guidance except for a dictum in Hutchinson v. Proxmire, 443 U.S. 111 (1979)(discussed p. 1049, infra), noting that the Court had not "provided precise boundaries for the category of 'public official'; it cannot be thought to include all public employees, however."

The three-legged stool. Perhaps the most extensive effort to grapple with the "public official" category occurred in Kassel v. Gannett Co., Inc., 875 F.2d 935 (1st Cir.1989), in which plaintiff staff psychologist for the Veterans Administration claimed that he was defamed by an article in defendant's newspaper mistakenly attributing to him a statement about the Vietnam war. The district court ruled that plaintiff was not a public official, and the jury found for the plaintiff. The court of appeals affirmed on the issue of plaintiff's status.

The court thought that the test rested on a "tripodal base." The first leg recognizes that discussion of issues of public importance must be "uninhibited, robust, and wide-open." Thus, "[p]olicymakers, upper-level administrators, and supervisors" are public officials because they "occupy niches of 'apparent importance' sufficient to give the public an independent interest in the qualifications and performances of the persons who hold them." If, as stated in the *Rosenblatt* footnote, "a night watchman accused of stealing state secrets" is not a public official, then the "inherent attributes of the position, not the occurrence of random events, must signify the line of demarcation."

The second leg entails the plaintiff's access to media to counteract the impact of false and injurious statements (building on *Gertz*). The court explained that "government workers who, by virtue of their employment, may easily defuse erroneous or misleading reports without judicial assistance should more likely be ranked as 'public officials' for libel law purposes. Conversely, those who work for the sovereign, but who enjoy little or no sway over, or 'special' access to, the news media are less likely to be trapped within the seine" of public officialdom.

The final leg, again drawing on *Gertz*, involves the degree to which the plaintiff has assumed the risk of exposure to criticism by the media: "[p]ersons who actively seek positions of influence in public life do so with the knowledge that, if successful in attaining their goals, diminished privacy will result." On the other hand, there are public employees who have not assumed an influential role in government and cannot be said to have "exposed themselves to increasing risk of injury from defamatory falsehood concerning them."

The court then applied its analysis to the facts of the case: (1) plaintiff held a lower level position at the VA that did not invite scrutiny independent of the controversy caused by the defendant's story and did not "govern" in any sense of the word. His job was "seeing patients and administering tests." (2) He did not have access to channels of communication that would enable him to counteract false and injurious statements. The plaintiff's position as staff psychologist "commanded no extraordinary media exposure" and his "duties did not involve answering press inquiries." To focus on the attention he attracted *after* the story was "bootstrapping of the most flagrant sort." (3) There was "no evidence that, by accepting employment as a staff psychologist in a VA hospital, Kassel assumed the risk of sensationalist media coverage."

Is *Kassel* consistent with the two alternative approaches suggested in *Rosenblatt*? Do the self-help and assumed-risk analyses make sense in the context of public officials? Consider *Rosenblatt* and *Kassel* in the context of each of the following occupations.

Police officers and firefighters. There is virtual unanimity that police officers are public officials for defamation purposes. See Rotkiewicz v. Sadowsky, 730 N.E.2d 282 (Mass.2000):

> Law enforcement officials, from a chief of police to a patrol officer, necessarily exercise State power in the performance of their duties. All police officers are empowered to further the preservation of law and order in the community, including the investigation of wrongdoing and the arrest of suspected criminals. Even patrol-level police officers are "vested with substantial responsibility for the safety and welfare of the citizenry in areas impinging most directly and intimately on daily living; the home, the place of work and of recreation, the sidewalks and streets." [   ] Further, although a patrol officer such as the plaintiff is "low on the totem pole" and does not set policy for the department, abuse of the office "can result in significant deprivation of constitutional rights and personal freedoms, not to mention bodily injury and financial loss." [   ] All police officers have the ability and authority to exercise force. [   ] We conclude, in line with the vast majority of other jurisdictions, that "[t]he abuse of a patrolman's office can have great potentiality for social harm; hence, public discussion and public criticism directed toward the performance of that office cannot constitutionally be inhibited by threat of prosecution under State libel laws."

Firefighters have been treated differently. When one sued over a newscast about his termination for inability to pass the EMT examination, the court thought it "strain[ed] credibility to say that [plaintiff], as a low-ranking fire fighter, had substantial responsibility over the conduct of governmental affairs." The plaintiff here "did not have responsibility or influence comparable to that of a captain of a police force [who had been held public in an earlier case]." Jones v. Palmer Communications, Inc., 440 N.W.2d 884 (Iowa 1989).

Public school personnel. The courts are split over whether public school teachers are public officials. Kelley v. Bonney, 606 A.2d 693 (Conn.1992) concluded that they are public officials because they hold a position that "if abused, potentially might cause serious psychological or physical injury to school aged children. Unquestionably, members of society are profoundly interested in the qualifications and performance of the teachers who are responsible for educating and caring for the children in their classrooms." The court cited several cases on both sides of the question. Courts disagree about public school principals. Compare Palmer v. Bennington School Dist., 615 A.2d 498 (Vt.1992)(public official) with Ellerbee v. Mills, 422 S.E.2d 539 (Ga.1992), cert. denied 507 U.S. 1025 (1993) (not public official).

Social workers. In the relatively few cases presenting the issue, social workers have been held to be public officials. In Kahn v. Bower, 284 Cal.Rptr. 244 (App. 1991), a social worker accused of incompetence was held to be public:

> Nothing in the record before us indicates plaintiff had any significant control over government *policy*. The same may be said, however, of a patrolman. Nonetheless, the power exercised by police officers, and their public visibility, naturally subject them to public scrutiny and make them public officials for purposes of defamation law. Plaintiff too possessed considerable power over the lives affected by her work as a child welfare worker. Her assessments and decisions directly and often immediately determined whether the educational, social, medical and economic needs of developmentally disabled children in her care would adequately be met. She exercised far more control over the lives she touched than does a classroom teacher.

For a similar result, see Villarreal v. Harte–Hanks Communications, Inc., 787 S.W.2d 131 (Tex.App.1990), cert. denied 499 U.S. 923 (1991), in which the court observed that a "child protective services specialist . . . certainly had greater control over governmental affairs than a court reporter, school teacher, attorney or justice of the peace."

Former public officials. Former officials remain public officials for purposes of commentary on their past performance. In Milgroom v. News Group Boston, Inc., 586 N.E.2d 985 (Mass.1992), a former judge criticized for conduct during her tenure on the bench was held to remain a public official for commentary on that performance since the "administration of justice" is a "subject of continuing public interest." See also Zerangue v. TSP Newspapers, Inc., 814 F.2d 1066 (5th Cir.1987)(former public officials remained in category at least six years after losing their jobs for purposes of coverage of their activities while in office).

A former head of the Justice Department's organized crime strike force was a public official when charged with having "avoided prosecuting certain organized crime figures." But he was a private person as to charges that after leaving office, as an attorney he exploited personal contacts in the department to seek favorable treatment for his clients. Crane v. The Arizona Republic, 972 F.2d 1511 (9th Cir.1992).

For an extended examination of public official case law, see Elder, Defamation, Public Officialdom, and the *Rosenblatt v. Baer* Criteria—A Proposal for Revivification Two Decades after *New York Times Co. v. Sullivan,* 33 Buffalo L.Rev. 572 (1984), arguing that lower courts have misconstrued Supreme Court public official cases and that courts should restrict the scope of public officialdom through "thoughtful application of [*Rosenblatt's*] two-part alternative test for 'public official,' infused with the *Gertz* substratal 'assumption of risk' [and] 'compelling normative consideration' " points.

2.   IDENTIFYING A "PUBLIC FIGURE"

After *Gertz* it became critically important to be able to distinguish between public and private plaintiffs. The Court addressed that topic in a series of cases that we now briefly summarize, and which are discussed again in the principal case that follows.

The Firestone case. In *Time Inc. v. Firestone,* p. 1042, supra, a magazine incorrectly reported that a member of "one of America's wealthier industrial families" had received a divorce because of his wife's adultery. A five-member majority held plaintiff to be private: "Respondent did not assume any role of especial prominence in the affairs of society, other than perhaps Palm Beach society, and she did not thrust herself to the forefront of any particular public controversy in order to influence the resolution of the issues involved in it." The fact that the case may have been of great public interest, did not make plaintiff a public figure. Moreover, the Court observed, plaintiff was compelled to go to court to seek relief in a marital dispute and her involvement was not voluntary. The fact that she held "a few" press conferences during the case did not change her otherwise private status. She did not attempt to use them to influence the outcome of the trial or to thrust herself into an unrelated dispute. (Defendant's added argument that reporting of judicial proceedings should never give rise to recovery for negligence, was rejected as an attempt to resurrect the subject matter criterion, which *Gertz* had rejected.)

The Wolston case. In Wolston v. Reader's Digest Ass'n, 443 U.S. 157 (1979), defendant's 1974 book incorrectly listed plaintiff as one of a group "who were convicted of espionage or falsifying information or perjury and/or contempt charges following espionage indictments or who fled to the Soviet bloc to avoid prosecution." In fact, he had been indicted for and convicted of contempt of court for failing to appear before a grand jury.

During the six weeks in 1958 between his failure to appear and his sentencing, plaintiff's case was the subject of 15 stories in Washington and

New York newspapers. "This flurry of publicity subsided" following the sentencing, and plaintiff "succeeded for the most part in returning to the private life he had led" prior to the subpoena. A six-member majority held plaintiff private because he had neither "voluntarily thrust" nor "injected" himself into the forefront of the controversy surrounding the investigation of Soviet espionage in the United States. Wolston had not "engaged the attention of the public in an attempt to influence the resolution of the issues involved. . . . He did not in any way seek to arouse public sentiment in his favor and against the investigation. Thus, this is not a case where a defendant invites a citation for contempt in order to use the contempt citation as a fulcrum to create public discussion about the methods being used in connection with an investigation or prosecution."

The Hutchinson case. In Hutchinson v. Proxmire, 443 U.S. 111 (1979), decided the same day as *Wolston,* defendant, a United States Senator, had criticized government grants to certain scientists, including plaintiff, on the grounds that the grants were examples of wasteful government spending on unjustifiable scientific research. (Absolute privilege did not apply because the claimed defamations were in press releases and newsletters.)

The eight-member majority held plaintiff to be private. Neither the fact that plaintiff had successfully applied for federal funds nor that he had access to media to respond to Senator Proxmire's charges, "demonstrates that Hutchinson was a public figure prior to the controversy." Rather, his "activities and public profile are much like those of countless members of his profession. His published writings reach a relatively small category of professionals concerned with research in human behavior." Those charged with defamation "cannot, by their own conduct, create their own defense by making the claimant a public figure. See [*Wolston*]." Nor had plaintiff "assumed any role of public prominence in the broad question of concern about expenditures."

The Court then left the lower courts to work out the distinction. The following case suggests the kind of inquiry that is required.

Wells v. Liddy

United States Court of Appeals, Fourth Circuit, 1999.
186 F.3d 505.

[This case grew out of the Watergate break-in at the Democratic National Committee in June, 1972. The "majority or conventional" theory has been that the burglars were attempting to replace a malfunctioning listening device that had been installed in an earlier break-in. During the break-in period plaintiff Ida Maxine ("Maxie") Wells had worked as secretary to Spencer Oliver, who was Executive Director of the Association of State Democratic Chairmen, whose phone was tapped. Wells often used Oliver's phone when he was not there and her calls were also intercepted. A key to her desk was found in the burglars' possession when they were arrested. Wells was subpoenaed to testify before the grand jury and also (though not on television) before the Senate Select Committee that investigated the break-in.

Defendant Liddy at the time was counsel to the Committee to Reelect the President (Nixon). As a result of the break-in he was convicted on multiple counts, including burglary, conspiracy, and interception of wire and oral communications, and served 52 months in jail.

In 1984, the book *Secret Agenda* by Jim Hougan, mentions the possibility that the break-in was tied in some way to the arrest of an attorney named Phillip Mackin Bailley for Mann Act charges. Wells is identified as the person whose desk key was found on one of the burglars, but Wells is not mentioned in connection with prostitution. In 1991, Len Colodny and Robert Gettlin wrote a book called "Silent Coup: The Removal of a President," which relied heavily on Bailley, and asserted that the break-in had been ordered by John Dean, legal counsel to President Nixon, to see whether the DNC was arranging call girls for visiting dignitaries. The book asserted that Dean wanted to learn whether Maureen Biner's name appeared on the list or in photographs that were said to be locked in a drawer in Wells's desk. Alfred Baldwin, who was operating the listening post and other surveillance, was said to have posed as a friend of Oliver's and obtained a visit to the DNC office to "case" it, during which he "somehow obtained a key from Wells or stole one."

By 1991, Liddy had concluded that the book's theory was correct and began repeating it in various forms in various contexts. This case involves suits over four such appearances: (1) a speech at James Madison University in Virginia; (2) during his talk on a cruise ship in the Mediterranean; (3) over a radio show heard nationwide; and (4) the web site of an organization, Accuracy in Media.

The trial judge granted summary judgment on all four episodes. The court of appeals concluded that the statement in the JMU speech was defamatory under Virginia law because listeners could well have taken it to mean that "Wells was a participant in a scheme to procure prostitutes." The same analysis applied to the cruise ship. After reviewing the transcript of the radio show the court concluded that it could not be found defamatory. Nor could the court find any proof that Liddy had ever authorized Accuracy in Media to state his theory. The court then turned to the constitutional questions that remained in the two actions that survived state law requirements.]

Before WILKINS and WILLIAMS, CIRCUIT JUDGES, and LEE, UNITED STATES DISTRICT JUDGE for the Eastern District of Virginia, sitting by designation.

WILLIAMS, CIRCUIT JUDGE [after considering the foregoing issues]:

IV.

Wells next appeals the district court's conclusion that for purposes of the public debate on Watergate she is an involuntary public figure, and therefore required to prove that Liddy acted with actual malice before she can recover compensatory damages for actual injury. Liddy argues that the district court's conclusion that Wells is an involuntary public figure is correct and asserts in the alternative that Wells's participation in Watergate-related dialogue is sufficient to qualify her as a voluntary limited-purpose public figure. Because the level of culpability the plaintiff must prove to recover compensatory damages under state law is dependent upon the plaintiff's public or private figure status, we must address this issue, which is a matter of law. [   ]

A.

[The court reviewed the constitutional developments from *New York Times* to *Gertz*—and noted that there was no claim that Wells was an "all-purpose public figure."], [W]e have interpreted *Gertz* as creating three distinct types of public figures:

> (1) "involuntary public figures," who become public figures through no purposeful action of their own; (2) "all-purpose public figures," who achieve such pervasive fame or notoriety that they become public figures for all purposes and in all contexts; and (3) "limited-purpose public figures," who voluntarily inject themselves into a particular public controversy and thereby become public figures for a limited range of issues.

Foretich v. Capital Cities/ABC, Inc., 37 F.3d 1541, 1551–52 (4th Cir.1994).

Since *Gertz*, it has been clear that the First Amendment sets limits on a public figure's ability to recover for defamation. A public figure "may recover for injury to reputation only on clear and convincing proof that the defamatory falsehood was made with knowledge of its falsity or with reckless disregard for the truth." [   ] After *Gertz*, however, the level of defendant's fault that must be proved by private figures to recover compensatory damages in defamation actions is left to the states even when the defamatory communication touches on matters of public concern, with the caveat that strict liability schemes run afoul of the First Amendment. [   ]

B.

The Court has revisited public figure status three times since it handed down its decision in *Gertz*. [The Court reviewed *Firestone, Wolston* and *Proxmire*.]

C.

Applying the foregoing Supreme Court precedents, this Circuit has developed a five-factor test to determine whether a plaintiff is a limited-purpose public figure. Liddy has asserted that Wells meets the test for limited-purpose public figure status. Because the jurisprudence regarding limited-purpose public figures is well-established in this Circuit, we address Liddy's contentions regarding the voluntary nature of Wells's participation in the Watergate controversy first, before weighing-in on the district court's ultimate conclusion that Wells qualifies as an involuntary public figure.

Before a plaintiff can be classified, as a matter of law, as a limited-purpose public figure, the defendant must prove that:

(1) the plaintiff has access to channels of effective communication;

(2) the plaintiff voluntarily assumed a role of special prominence in the public controversy;

(3) the plaintiff sought to influence the resolution or outcome of the controversy;

(4) the controversy existed prior to the publication of the defamatory statement; and

(5) the plaintiff retained public-figure status at the time of the alleged defamation.

See Reuber v. Food Chemical News, Inc., 925 F.2d 703, 708–10 (4th Cir.1991) (en banc). In *Foretich*, we added an additional consideration to the limited-purpose public figure inquiry when we held that if the content of a defamatory statement touches upon an area that state law has traditionally considered to be defamatory per se, then the plaintiff cannot be categorized as a limited-purpose public figure solely because he makes reasonable public replies to the statement. [   ] In evaluating an individual's limited-purpose public figure status we look at "the nature and extent of an individual's participation in the particular controversy giving rise to the defamation." [*Gertz*]

In order to prevail on his assertion that Wells's participation in the Watergate controversy merits her classification as a limited-purpose public figure Liddy must establish each of the five elements recited above. See *Foretich*, [   ] (noting that the defendant bears the burden on all five elements). According to Liddy, Wells's voluntary injection into the Watergate controversy, an event of unprecedented historical interest and importance, is sufficient to satisfy the five-part test because she was interviewed by the FBI, mentioned in the newspaper, subpoenaed to testify before the grand jury, and called before the Senate in the early 1970s. Additionally, Liddy points to several media exposures Wells has had since the prostitution-oriented theory of the Watergate break-in emerged in 1984. Specifically, Liddy points out that Wells published a letter to the editor in the *New York Times* in 1985, spoke to a reporter on the twentieth anniversary of the Watergate break-in for an article that appeared in the *Washington Post* in 1992, spoke to the BBC in 1993, was named in an Arts & Entertainment Network broadcast entitled "The Key to Watergate" and a Geraldo Rivera documentary "Now it Can be Told," and spoke to historian James Rosen. Although Liddy has amply demonstrated that Wells has "access to channels of effective communication," we conclude that Liddy has failed to show that Wells has "voluntarily assumed [a role] of special prominence in the . . . public controversy." [In a footnote the court noted that Watergate was "perhaps the quintessential public controversy."] Therefore, we cannot conclude that Wells is a limited-purpose public figure.

[The court concluded that *Gertz, Firestone*, and *Wolston* supported the view that limited purpose public figure status requires that the plaintiff play an active role in a controversy.]

In light of the foregoing, viewing Wells's public exposures during and after the Watergate break-in collectively, we conclude that Wells has not "voluntarily assumed [a role] of special prominence in the . . . public controversy." *Foretich* [   ]. *Gertz, Firestone*, and *Wolston* establish conclusively that Wells was not a public figure during the immediate aftermath of the Watergate break-in in the 1970s. Like Wolston, Wells's involvement in the Watergate investigation was wholly involuntarily; she was "dragged unwillingly into the controversy," [   ], initially by the commission of a crime at her workplace and later by the governmental investigation that ensued. Wells's discussions with the FBI, response to the grand jury subpoena, and appearance before the Senate committee simply were not voluntary actions but rather were compelled by the force of law. [   ] Even if we assume *arguendo* that Wells was involved in criminal activity during her employment at the DNC, precedent counsels that activity likely to engender publicity, even criminal activity, does not equate to taking on a role of special prominence in a public controversy. See *Wolston*, [   ] ("reject[ing] the further contention . . . that any person who engages in criminal conduct automatically becomes a public figure for purposes of comment on a limited range of issues relating to his conviction."); *Gertz*, [   ] (holding that an attorney who took on a case linked to a public controversy but who did not speak to the press was not a public figure).

The question then arises whether Wells voluntarily has attained special prominence in the Watergate controversy as a result of the revelation of the prostitution-related theory of the break-in. For the most part, Wells's reported role in Watergate has remained unchanged after *Secret Agenda* [an earlier book on Watergate] and *Silent Coup*—Wells is named as Spencer Oliver's secretary and a woman whose phone calls were overheard on illegal wire taps. To the extent that Wells's role has expanded, it has done so because *Secret Agenda* and *Silent Coup* revealed that Watergate burglar Martinez possessed a key to her desk, exposed prostitution activities that purportedly were occurring at the DNC, and implied that Wells may have had some connection to those illicit activities. There is no proof that any of these disclosures were the result of Wells's voluntary interaction with the authors. Instead, it is clear, as the district court concluded, that the story was divulged by a sole source, Bailley. [   ] Because the disclosures of *Secret Agenda* and *Silent Coup* cannot be fairly attributed to Wells's voluntary participation, we cannot conclude that she sought a prominent role in the Watergate controversy as a result of being named therein.

Therefore, the question of whether Wells has "voluntarily assumed [a role] of special prominence in the . . . public controversy," *Foretich*, [   ], ultimately, on this record, revolves around four media contacts: (1) her letter-to-the-editor of the *New York Times*, published in 1985; (2) her 1992 interview with a *Washington Post* reporter on the twentieth anniversary of the Watergate break-in; (3) her interview with the BBC in 1993; and (4) her discussions with historian James Rosen. The letter-to-the-editor, made in response to a book review of *Secret Agenda* that named her as a figure involved in arranging dates with prostitutes, clearly falls within the category of self-help and reasonable response to reputation-injuring statements of the type that we approved in Foretich. [   ] Therefore, Wells's letter-to-the-editor should not contribute to the public figure analysis.

Regarding Wells's three other media contacts, *Firestone* makes clear that voluntary discussion of events with the press does not per se indicate that a defamation plaintiff has "thrust herself to the forefront of [a public] controversy." [   ] Rather, when an individual has had contact with the press, the proper questions are whether he has attempted to influence the merits of a controversy, or has "draw[n] attention to himself in order to invite public comment," *Wolston*, [   ], or "invited that degree of public attention and comment . . . essential to meet the public figure level," [*Hutchinson v. Proxmire*]. . . .

Twenty-seven years after the event, the still-controversial aspects of Watergate revolve around bigger issues such as why the break-in occurred, who was responsible, whether our Constitutional checks and balances are adequate, whether the American populace lost confidence in politicians as a result of the scandal, etc. Liddy has failed to point to evidence demonstrating that Wells has made any attempt to become a spokesperson on any of these types of matters. Therefore, we cannot conclude that Wells has voluntarily undertaken a position at the forefront of the Watergate controversy. The record establishes that Wells has conducted only a handful of interviews over the course of twenty-seven years and each one has been in response to inquiries from reporters requesting her eye-witness account. As a result, we conclude that Liddy has not met his burden of proving each of the five elements of this circuit's limited-purpose public figure test, and we must determine that Wells is not a limited-purpose public figure under our jurisprudence.

D.

The district court also concluded that Wells did not meet the five-part test governing limited-purpose public figure status. Rather, the district court concluded that Wells was an involuntary public figure. [   ] Wells appeals this ruling. We conclude that Wells was not an involuntary public figure and reverse.

The concept of an involuntary public figure has its origins in one sentence from *Gertz*: "Hypothetically, it may be possible for someone to become a public figure through no purposeful action of his own, but the instances of truly involuntary public figures must be exceedingly rare." [   ] So rarely have courts determined that an individual was an involuntary public figure that commentators have questioned the continuing existence of that category. [   ] Although we have acknowledged that involuntary public figures constitute one of the three classes of public figures categorized in *Gertz*, we have never explored the parameters of the involuntary branch of the public figure typography. [   ] Thus, Wells's challenge to the district court's conclusion that she is an involuntary public figure presents a novel question of law.

The district court ruled, applying Dameron v. Washington Magazine, Inc., 779 F.2d 736 (D.C.Cir.1985), that Wells was an involuntary public figure because she had the "misfortune" of being "drawn by a series of events into the Watergate controversy." [   ] Because we conclude that "misfortune" is but one aspect of the considerations that should be weighed before concluding that an individual is an involuntary public figure, we are not persuaded by the district court's analysis.

The *Dameron* case, the leading case on involuntary public figure status, involved an air-traffic controller who had been the sole controller on duty during a 1974 airline crash near Dulles Airport in Northern Virginia. [   ] In 1982, following the crash of Air Florida Flight 90 into the Potomac River on takeoff from National Airport in Washington, D.C., *Washingtonian* magazine published a story that listed, *inter alia*, plane crashes that had occurred in the Washington, D.C. metropolitan area and were attributable to controller error. [   ] The magazine article stated that controller error was partially to blame for the 1974 Dulles crash. [   ] As a result, the air traffic controller filed a defamation action. [   ]

The D.C. Circuit, recognizing that the air traffic controller had not voluntarily injected himself into a public controversy, and therefore could not satisfy the court's definition of a limited-purpose public figure, concluded that the air traffic controller could nevertheless be considered a public figure. [   ] The court applied two of the three parts of its *Waldbaum* test for limited-purpose public figures and evaluated whether there was a public controversy and whether the allegedly defamatory statements concerned the public controversy. [   ] (citing Waldbaum v. Fairchild Publications, Inc., 627 F.2d 1287, 1296–98 (D.C.Cir.1980)). Instead of inquiring whether the air traffic controller had voluntarily entered the fray, however, the D.C. Circuit concluded that "[b]y sheer bad luck" the air traffic controller had become a prominent figure, central to the resolution of a public question. [   ] On that basis, the D.C. Circuit held that the air traffic controller was an involuntary public figure. [   ]

We are hesitant to rest involuntary public figure status upon "sheer bad luck." *Gertz* tells us that involuntary public figures "must be exceedingly rare," [   ], and, unfortunately, bad luck is relatively common. The *Dameron* definition of an involuntary public figure, someone who by bad luck is an important figure in a public controversy, runs the risk of returning us to the *Rosenbloom* plurality's conception of defamation law. Under *Rosenbloom*, all defamation plaintiffs were required to prove actual malice when the allegedly defamatory statements occurred during "discussion and communication involving matters of public or general concern, without regard to whether the persons involved are famous or anonymous." [   ] The Supreme Court expressly repudiated the "public interest" test in *Gertz*, [   ], and further disavowed it in *Wolston*, [   ] ("To accept such reasoning would in effect reestablish the doctrine advanced by the plurality opinion in *Rosenbloom* . . . which concluded that the *New York*

Times standard should extend to defamatory falsehoods relating to private persons if the statements involved matters of public or general concern. We repudiated this approach in *Gertz* and in *Firestone*, however, and we reject it again today."). Because *Dameron* has not narrowly tailored the class of possible involuntary public figures, it has created a class of individuals who must prove actual malice that is equivalent to the class in *Rosenbloom*. Under either *Dameron* or *Rosenbloom* all individuals defamed during discourse on a matter of public concern must prove actual malice. In light of the Supreme Court's repeated rejection of *Rosenbloom*, we are unwilling to adopt an approach that returns us to an analysis that is indistinguishable. [ ]

In order to flesh out the boundaries of who may constitute an involuntary public figure, a return to *Gertz*, the only Supreme Court case to mention the concept, is in order. In *Gertz*, Justice Powell iterated two rationales for concluding that public figure status must be the determinative inquiry in the balance of interests between the plaintiff and the First Amendment in a defamation case. First, the public figure can take better advantage of the free press and has an easier time resorting to self-help because notoriety guarantees better access to the media and channels of communication. [ ] Second, the public figure has taken actions through which he has voluntarily assumed the risk of publicity. [ ] We conclude that in order to ensure that the balance between states' and individuals' interests in protection of reputation and First Amendment freedoms at the heart of Constitutional defamation law is maintained, any standard for determining who is an involuntary public figure must be mindful of both of these underpinnings. See Khawar v. Globe Int'l, Inc., [965 P.2d 696, 702 (Cal.1998), reprinted infra] (holding that the characterization of involuntary public figure must be reserved for those individuals who satisfy both of *Gertz*'s supporting grounds), cert. denied, 526 U.S. 1114 (1999). Yet, because the usual and natural conception of a public figure encompasses a sense of voluntary participation in public debate, and because to do otherwise would threaten a return to *Rosenbloom*, the class of involuntary public figures must be a narrow one, so as to encompass only "exceedingly rare" cases. [ ]

With *Gertz*'s two supporting rationales and the need for a narrow class of involuntary public figures in mind, we believe that the following considerations are warranted. First, to prove that a plaintiff is an involuntary public figure the defendant must demonstrate to the court that the plaintiff has become a central figure in a significant public controversy and that the allegedly defamatory statement has arisen in the course of discourse regarding the public matter. To prove that the plaintiff is a central figure in the controversy, the defendant must put forth evidence that the plaintiff has been the regular focus of media reports[26] on the controversy. A

---

26. The extent of media coverage required to prove that the plaintiff is a central figure will vary greatly depending upon the scope of the public controversy. For a controversy that is localized in a specific community, the defendant may rely on local media outlets such as the local newspaper and the local television news. In contrast, when the significant public controversy is one that touches upon serious issues relating to, for example, community values, historical events, governmental or political activity, arts, education, or public safety. Second, although an involuntary public figure need not have sought to publicize her views on the relevant controversy, she must have nonetheless assumed the risk of publicity. Therefore, the defendant must demonstrate that the plaintiff has taken some action, or failed to act when action was required, in circumstances in which a reasonable person would understand that publicity would likely inhere. See Reuber v. Food Chemical News, Inc., 925 F.2d 703, 709 (4th Cir.1991) (en banc) ("[E]ven involuntary participants can be public figures when they choose a course of conduct which invites public attention."). Unlike the limited-purpose public figure, an involuntary public figure need not have specifically taken action through which he has voluntarily sought a primary role in the controversy to influence the outcome of debate on the matter.

To summarize, an involuntary public figure has pursued a course of conduct from which it was reasonably foreseeable, at the time of the conduct, that public interest would arise. A public controversy must have actually arisen that is related to, although not necessarily causally linked, to the action. The involuntary public figure must be recognized as a central figure during debate over that matter. Further, we retain two elements of the five-part *Reuber* test, specifically: (1) the controversy existed prior to the publication of the defamatory statement; and (2) the plaintiff retained public-figure status at the time of the alleged defamation. [   ] Additionally, to the extent that an involuntary public figure attempts self-help, the *Foretich* rule must apply with equal strength. [   ]

We believe that the foregoing test captures that "exceedingly rare" individual who, although remaining mute during public discussion of the results of her action, nevertheless has become a principal in an important public matter. Further, this test excludes from the category of involuntary public figures those individuals who by happenstance have been mentioned peripherally in a matter of public interest or have merely been named in a press account. Also, the foregoing analysis avoids resurrecting *Rosenbloom* because this conception of the involuntary public figure does not cast too broad a net and encompass all individuals who become linked in the media to a matter of public concern. Every plaintiff who is allegedly defamed during discussion of a public controversy will not necessarily be required to prove actual malice to recover compensatory damages under this test.

Applying this formulation to Wells, we determine that she is not an involuntary public figure. Wells simply has not been a central figure in media reports on Watergate. Liddy has been able to point to very few published reports on Watergate even mentioning Wells by name. Prior to the revelation of the call-girl ring theory, Liddy has shown that Wells was mentioned by name only in an *International Herald Tribune* article noting that her conversations, and those of her boss Spencer Oliver, had been

defendant seeks to show that the plaintiff is a central figure in a national or international controversy, the scope of media coverage must be significantly broader.

overheard on a listening device. Since the emergence of the call-girl ring theory, in those instances where the media has mentioned Wells, she has been a very minor figure in the discussion of the primary actors in the Watergate affair—the burglars, Dean, [E. Howard] Hunt, Liddy, and, of course, President Nixon. We cannot say that in any of the reports contained in the record Wells is portrayed as a central figure in the Watergate controversy. The focus has always been on the roles of other people.

. . .

E.

Based upon the preceding analysis, we must conclude that Wells is a private figure. She need not prove actual malice to recover compensatory damages under the applicable law. Therefore, this case must be remanded for the district court to reconsider Wells's claims under the lesser standard. Because, however, punitive and presumed damages hinge on a finding of actual malice, we proceed below to consider Wells's final assignment of error.

V.

[After an extended review of the record, the court concluded that Wells might be able to show actual malice by clear and convincing evidence.]

VI.

In sum, two statements identified by Wells as potentially defamatory are capable of defamatory meaning: the JMU speech, governed by the substantive law of Virginia, and the cruise ship speech, governed by the maritime common law. Because Wells is a private figure, these two claims must be remanded for trial under the applicable negligence standards for Liddy's culpability. Finally, Wells has succeeded in raising a genuine issue of material fact on the issue of Liddy's actual malice. For these reasons we remand this case for further proceedings consistent with this opinion.

Notes and Questions

1. What element to make plaintiff a public figure was missing?

2. Who should have the burden of proof on these facts?

3. The court notes how important it is to judge these matters by general standards so that others will know where they stand. What kind of guidance can be drawn from this case to advise others?

4. It is clear under federal law that the question of whether plaintiff is public or private is a question for the court. The court in *Kassel v. Gannett Co.*, p. 1045, supra, concluded that the issue "must be decided by the trial judge even where disputed fact questions prevent the resolution of the issue on a motion for summary judgment." Most state cases agree.

5. *General public figures.* General public figures have been few and far between since *Gertz*. According to *Waldbaum*, cited in the principal case:

> [A] general public figure is a well-known "celebrity," his name a "household word." The public recognizes him and follows his words and deeds, either because it regards his ideas, conduct, or judgment as worthy of the attention or because he actively pursues that consideration.

Is that consistent with *Gertz*? Is it a useful way to approach the question? See also Buckley v. Littell, 539 F.2d 882 (2d Cir.1976), cert. denied 429 U.S. 1062 (1977)(William F. Buckley, Jr.); Carson v. Allied News Co., 529 F.2d 206 (7th Cir.1976)(Johnny Carson); Chuy v. Philadelphia Eagles Football Club, 595 F.2d 1265 (3d Cir.1979) (en banc) (a professional football player who is alleged to have a career-ending disease is a public figure). All except *Waldbaum* were decided before *Hutchinson* and *Wolston*. Which of the following might meet the *Waldbaum* standard: The Rev. Jesse Jackson? Michael Jordan? David Letterman? Dan Rather? Robert Redford? John Updike? Oprah Winfrey? Is law-student familiarity or unfamiliarity with a name probative? Conclusive?

6. *Involuntary public figures.* Involuntary public figures have been very rare. For cases other than *Dameron* finding such figures, see Meeropol v. Nizer, 560 F.2d 1061 (2d Cir.1977), cert. denied 434 U.S. 1013 (1978)(children of convicted spies Julius and Ethel Rosenberg); Carson v. Allied News Co., 529 F.2d 206 (7th Cir.1976)(Johnny Carson's wife—unless she is "voluntary" because she married a famous person); Street v. National Broadcasting Co., 645 F.2d 1227 (6th Cir.), cert. granted and then dismissed after settlement, 454 U.S. 1095 (1981)(main prosecution witness in famous Scottsboro case of 1931, in which nine black youths in Alabama were accused of raping plaintiff and another white woman; alleged defamation occurred 40 years after trial). Are these cases consistent with *Gertz* and *Wolston?* Is *Dameron?*

May a person's job produce at least limited-purpose public figure status by virtue of the associations it entails? In Clyburn v. News World Communications, Inc., 903 F.2d 29 (D.C.Cir.1990), plaintiff's job brought him into constant contact, socially and officially, with a group of people that included the mayor of the District of Columbia. Several members of the group were involved in drugs. When a woman in the group died of an overdose the media paid much attention to the group and the drug issue. The court observed that plaintiff's behavior "before any controversy arose put him at [the controversy's] center" when it did arise:

> One may hobnob with high officials without becoming a public figure, but one who does so runs the risk that personal tragedies that for less well-connected people would pass unnoticed may place him at the heart of a public controversy. Clyburn engaged in conduct that he knew markedly raised the chances that he would become embroiled in a public controversy.

7. *Limited purpose public figures.* Consider the following capsule descriptions of a selection of cases raising the issue.

a. A surgeon who was championing a new technique on local radio and television programming. The court concluded that plaintiff had stepped out of the realm of his practice by seeking access to media. Park v. Capital Cities Communications Inc., 585 N.Y.S.2d 902 (App.Div. 1992).

Compare Georgia Society of Plastic Surgeons v. Anderson, 363 S.E.2d 140 (Ga.1987), holding that an otolaryngologist who wrote an article in the Journal of the Medical Association of Georgia arguing that ear, nose and throat specialists, rather than plastic surgeons, should do certain surgery, was a private person when he sued over a sharp response in the same journal.

b. A person who had filed over 24 lawsuits in a decade and was accused of " 'working a scam' by filing numerous lawsuits to extract monetary settlements on a full-time basis." The court held that plaintiff was not a public figure because he was not pervasively well known and had not voluntarily placed himself in a public controversy. Kumaran v. Brotman, 617 N.E.2d 191 (Ill.App.1993).

c. An attorney asserted to have overcharged a client. He was not a public official or a public figure despite serving as an acting municipal judge, being an appointed member of the state Racing Commission, and having been elected by fellow lawyers to be second vice-president of the state bar (which was solely advisory to the state supreme court) because these roles did not relate to this controversy. The court found him to be private. Hinerman v. The Daily Gazette Co., 423 S.E.2d 560 (W.Va.1992), cert. denied 507 U.S. 960 (1993). What if the claim had appeared in the state bar journal?

d. An operator of a jai alai fronton who had been accused by defendant broadcaster of arson and other crimes in connection with the burning of his fronton. Defendant's program discussed the problems of gambling and arson in the jai alai world. In Silvester v. American Broadcasting Companies, Inc., 839 F.2d 1491 (11th Cir.1988), the court relied on *Waldbaum* to hold plaintiff a limited purpose public figure. First, there was a major public controversy over "corruption in the jai alai industry." Plaintiff's argument that "he had been pushed into the limelight through a press-created controversy" was rejected in part because ABC had not previously covered jai alai at all. (Might this lack of prior coverage help plaintiff?) Second, the plaintiffs were in a position to "invite attention and comment" with respect to their participation in the controversy. They were prominent in the industry and "because they were the primary or sole focus of certain aspects of the controversy, they were in a position to influence its outcome." Certain public announcements, such as offering a reward for the arsonists, indicated that plaintiff had "voluntarily thrust himself forward in an attempt to influence the public's view on the issue and to arouse their sympathy to his position." Third, the broadcast was germane to the plaintiff's participation in the controversy.

8. *Corporations as public figures.* The overwhelming majority of courts have concluded that the fact of incorporation alone does not make the plaintiff a public figure. See Schiavone Construction Co. v. Time, Inc., 619 F.Supp. 684 (D.N.J.1985); Bank of Oregon v. Independent News, Inc., 693 P.2d 35 (Or.), cert. denied 474 U.S. 826 (1985). Contra, Jadwin v. Minneapolis Star and Tribune Co., 367 N.W.2d 476 (Minn.1985):

> We hold . . . that corporate plaintiffs in defamation actions must prove actual malice by media defendants when the defendants establish that the defamatory material concerns matters of legitimate public interest in the geographic area in which the defamatory material is published, either because of the nature of the business conducted or because the public has an especially strong interest in the investigation or disclosure of the commercial information at issue. Such a rule will encourage the media to probe the business world to the depth which is necessary to permit the kind of business reporting vital to an informed public.

For other discussions of the issue see Steaks Unlimited, Inc. v. Deaner, 623 F.2d 264 (3d Cir.1980)(seller of inspected but ungraded frozen beef who advertised extensively is limited-purpose public figure for broadcast report questioning the quality of the meat and plaintiff's sales practices); Arctic Co., Ltd. v. Loudoun Times Mirror, 624 F.2d 518 (4th Cir.1980), cert. denied 449 U.S. 1102 (1981)(private firm contracting to provide county with environmental report is not a public figure for article in local paper criticizing quality of plaintiff's work because it is "not generally known in the community" and was performing "narrowly-defined professional service in a highly technical field"); Bruno & Stillman, Inc. v. Globe Newspaper Co., 633 F.2d 583 (1st Cir.1980)(largest regional manufacturer and seller of fishing boats, "the paradigm middle echelon, successful manufacturer-merchant," is private person in suit over newspaper stories listing defects in its boats—success or size alone does not make plaintiff public); Saro Corp. v. Waterman Broadcasting Corp., 595 So.2d 87 (Fla.App.1992)(transmission shop said to have recommended unneeded repair work and charged for work not done is private person because it engaged in no effort to gain attention in controversy and was "dragged into a limelight it least desired"). Would any of these be decided differently if the plaintiff were a private entrepreneur?

E.   THE DEFENDANT AS COMMENTATOR

Dictum in Justice Powell's *Gertz* opinion denying the concept of a "false idea" was once thought to suggest another constitutional defense. Many lower courts understood this to create a means by which defendants were able to win cases on "constitutional" grounds as early as the motion to dismiss the complaint. The Court had already decided a case involving a citizen's charge at a city council meeting that plaintiff was "blackmailing" the city in connection with pending real estate negotiations. Greenbelt Cooperative Publishing Ass'n v. Bresler, 398 U.S. 6 (1970). Although in some contexts a charge of "blackmail" might be understood as charging a specific crime, that was not true in this case. The word was "no more than rhetorical hyperbole, a vigorous epithet used by those who considered Bresler's vigorous negotiating position extremely unreasonable." Since no reasonable reader could have taken the report to charge a crime in context, the words were not actionable.

In Letter Carriers v. Austin, 418 U.S. 264 (1974), decided at the same time as *Gertz,* the union had published Jack London's famous definition of a "scab" as a "traitor to his God, his country, his family and his class." The Court held that no one could reasonably understand this to be a charge of the crime of treason. The words were being used "in a loose, figurative sense . . . merely rhetorical hyperbole, a lusty and imaginative expression of the contempt felt by union members toward those who refuse to join them."

Lower courts extended the analysis to claims based on vague language, such as calling plaintiff a "fellow traveler" of the fascists or describing a magazine as an "openly fascist journal." One court called these "loosely definable, variously interpretable statements of opinion . . . made inextricably in the contest of political, social, or philosophical debate." But the same court declared actionable the following charge:

> Like Westbrook Pegler, who lied day after day in his column about Quentin Reynolds and goaded him into a lawsuit, Buckley could be taken to court by any one of several people who had enough money to hire competent legal counsel and nothing else to do.

Buckley v. Littell, 539 F.2d 882 (2d Cir.1976), cert. denied 429 U.S. 1062 (1977). Why the different treatments?

The "epithet" or "rhetorical hyperbole" analysis had been part of the common law long before the libel area began being constitutionalized. As one court summarized the reasons in rejecting an action by someone referred to as one of "those bastards:"

> [I]t is perfectly apparent that [the words] were used as mere epithets, as terms of abuse and opprobrium. As such they had no real meaning except to indicate that the individual who used them was under a strong emotional feeling of dislike toward those about whom he used them. Not being intended or understood as statements of fact they are impossible of proof or disproof. Indeed such words of vituperation and abuse reflect more on the character of the user than they do on that of the individual to whom they are intended to refer.

Curtis Publishing Co. v. Birdsong, 360 F.2d 344 (5th Cir.1966). Do these reasons justify the common law rule? What if the speaker "intended" the words to be understood as statements of fact?

In the 1980s a number of courts recognized a constitutional defense for "opinion." A good example is Ollman v. Evans, 750 F.2d 970 (D.C.Cir.1984) (en banc), cert. denied 471 U.S. 1127 (1985). Briefly, syndicated columnists Evans and Novak argued against the proposed appointment of a Marxist political science professor to head the Department of Government and Politics at the University of Maryland. Among other statements, the column quoted a political scientist who, refusing to be identified, was said to have asserted that "Ollman has no status within the profession, but is a pure and simple activist." The president of the University of Maryland rejected the appointment.

The trial judge's dismissal was affirmed by a split court that produced seven opinions. The lead opinion emphasized four factors for analysis: (1) "the common usage or meaning of the specific language of the challenged statements itself;" (2) "the statement's verifiability—is the statement capable of being objectively characterized as true or false?;" (3) "the full context of the statement—the entire article or column;" and (4) "the broader context or setting in which the statement appears. Different types of writing have . . . widely varying social conventions which signal to the reader the likelihood of a statement's being either fact or opinion."

After lower courts spent some years arguing over the *Ollman* approach, the Supreme Court addressed the issue.

Milkovich v. Lorain Journal Co.

Supreme Court of the United States, 1990.
497 U.S. 1, 110 S.Ct. 2695, 111 L.Ed.2d 1.

[Milkovich was coach of the Maple Heights High School wrestling team, which was involved in a brawl with a competing team. After a hearing, the Ohio High School Athletic Association (OHSAA) censured Milkovich and placed his team on probation. Parents of some of the team members sued to enjoin OHSAA from enforcing the probation, contending OHSAA's investigation and hearing violated due process. Milkovich and Scott, the superintendent, testifying at a judicial hearing on the suit, both denied that Milkovich had incited the brawl through his behavior toward the crowd and a meet official. The judge granted the restraining order sought by the parents. A sports columnist who had attended the meet, but not the judicial hearing, wrote about the hearing in a column published the next day in the defendant newspaper. The headline was "Maple beat the law with the 'big lie.' " The theme of the column was that at the judicial hearing Milkovich and Scott misrepresented Milkovich's role in the altercation and thereby prevented the team from receiving the punishment it deserved. The concluding paragraphs of the column were as follows:

> Anyone who attended the meet, whether he be from Maple Heights, Mentor [the opposing school] or impartial observer, knows in his heart that Milkovich and Scott lied at the hearing after each having given his solemn oath to tell the truth.

> But they got away with it.

> Is that the kind of lesson we want our young people learning from their high school administrators and coaches?

> I think not.

Milkovich and Scott both sued the newspaper, alleging that the column accused them of perjury and thus was libelous per se. After 15 years of litigation and several appeals, the Ohio Court of Appeals held in Milkovich's case that the column was constitutionally protected opinion and granted the newspaper's motion for summary judgment. The Supreme Court reversed.]

CHIEF JUSTICE REHNQUIST delivered the opinion of the Court.

[The opinion reviewed the various constitutional limitations imposed on state libel law in the series of cases beginning with *New York Times v. Sullivan.* The Court also mentioned *Hepps,* p. 1041, supra, and its holding in *Hustler Magazine, Inc. v. Falwell,* p. 905, supra, that an ad parody "could not reasonably have been interpreted as stating actual facts about the public figure involved."]

Respondents would have us recognize, in addition to the established safeguards discussed above, still another First Amendment-based protection for defamatory statements which are categorized as "opinion" as opposed to "fact." For this proposition they rely principally on the following dictum from our opinion in *Gertz:*

"Under the First Amendment there is no such thing as a false idea. However pernicious an opinion may seem, we depend for its correction not on the conscience of judges and juries but on the competition of other ideas. But there is no constitutional value in false statements of fact." [   ]

Judge Friendly appropriately observed that this passage "has become the opening salvo in all arguments for protection from defamation actions on the ground of opinion, even though the case did not remotely concern the question." [Cianci v. New Times Publishing Co., 639 F.2d 54 (2d Cir.1980)]. Read in context, though, the fair meaning of the passage is to equate the word "opinion" in the second sentence with the word "idea" in the first sentence. Under this view, the language was merely a reiteration of Justice Holmes' classic "marketplace of ideas" concept. [   ]

Thus we do not think this passage from *Gertz* was intended to create a wholesale defamation exemption for anything that might be labeled "opinion." Not only would such an interpretation be contrary to the tenor and the context of the passage, but it would also ignore the fact that expressions of "opinion" may often imply an assertion of objective fact.

If a speaker says, "In my opinion John Jones is a liar," he implies a knowledge of facts which lead to the conclusion that Jones told an untruth. Even if the speaker states the facts upon which he bases his opinion, if those facts are either incorrect or incomplete, or if his assessment of them is erroneous, the statement may still imply a false assertion of fact. Simply couching such statements in terms of opinion does not dispel these implications; and the statement, "In my opinion Jones is a liar," can cause as much damage to reputation as the statement, "Jones is a liar." As Judge Friendly aptly stated: "[It] would be destructive of the law of libel if a writer could escape liability for accusations of [defamatory conduct] simply by using, explicitly or implicitly, the words 'I think,' " see *Cianci* [   ]. It is worthy of note that at common law, even the privilege of fair comment did not extend to a "false statement of fact, whether it was expressly stated or implied from an expression of opinion." Restatement (Second) of Torts, *supra*, § 566 Comment *a*.

Apart from their reliance on the *Gertz* dictum, respondents do not really contend that a statement such as, "In my opinion John Jones is a liar," should be protected by a separate privilege for "opinion" under the First Amendment. But they do contend that in every defamation case the First Amendment mandates an inquiry into whether a statement is "opinion" or "fact," and that only the latter statements may be actionable. They propose that a number of factors developed by the lower courts (in what we hold was a mistaken reliance on the *Gertz* dictum) be considered in deciding which is which. But we think the " 'breathing space' " which " 'freedoms of expression require to survive' " [   ] is adequately secured by existing constitutional doctrine without the creation of an artificial dichotomy between "opinion" and fact.

Foremost, we think *Hepps* stands for the proposition that a statement on matters of public concern must be provable as false before there can be liability under state defamation law, at least in situations, like the present, where a media defendant is involved.[6] Thus, unlike the statement, "In my opinion Mayor Jones is a liar," the statement, "In my opinion Mayor Jones shows his abysmal ignorance by accepting the teachings of Marx and Lenin," would not be actionable. *Hepps* ensures that a statement of opinion relating to matters of public concern which does not contain a provably false factual connotation will receive full constitutional protection.

Next, the *Bresler-Letter Carriers–Falwell* line of cases provide protection for statements that cannot "reasonably [be] interpreted as stating actual facts" about an individual. [   ] This provides assurance that public debate will not suffer for lack of "imaginative expression" or the "rhetorical hyperbole" which has traditionally added much to the discourse of our nation. [   ]

The *New York Times–Butts* and *Gertz* culpability requirements further ensure that debate on public issues remains "uninhibited, robust, and wide-open." [   ] Thus, where a statement of "opinion" on a matter of public concern reasonably implies false and defamatory facts regarding public figures or officials, those individuals must show that such statements were made with knowledge of their false implications or with reckless disregard of their truth. Similarly, where such a statement involves a private figure on a matter of public concern, a plaintiff must show that the false connotations were made with some level of fault as required by *Gertz*. Finally, the enhanced appellate review required by *Bose Corp.*, provides

---

6. In *Hepps* the Court reserved judgment on cases involving nonmedia defendants, [   ] and accordingly we do the same. Prior to *Hepps*, of course, where public-official or public-figure plaintiffs were involved, the *New York Times* rule already required a showing of falsity before liability could result. [   ]

assurance that the foregoing determinations will be made in a manner so as not to "constitute a forbidden intrusion of the field of free expression." [   ]

We are not persuaded that, in addition to these protections, an additional separate constitutional privilege for "opinion" is required to ensure the freedom of expression guaranteed by the First Amendment. The dispositive question in the present case then becomes whether or not a reasonable factfinder could conclude that the statements [in the column] imply an assertion that petitioner Milkovich perjured himself in a judicial proceeding. We think this question must be answered in the affirmative.   .   .   . This is not the sort of loose, figurative or hyperbolic language which would negate the impression that the writer was seriously maintaining petitioner committed the crime of perjury. Nor does the general tenor of the article negate this impression.

We also think the connotation that petitioner committed perjury is sufficiently factual to be susceptible of being proved true or false. A determination of whether petitioner lied in this instance can be made on a core of objective evidence by comparing, inter alia, petitioner's testimony before the trial court. As the [Ohio Supreme Court noted in the case of the superintendent] "[w]hether or not H. Don Scott did indeed perjure himself is certainly verifiable by a perjury action with evidence adduced from the transcripts and witnesses present at the hearing. Unlike a subjective assertion the averred defamatory language is an articulation of an objectively verifiable event." [   ] So too with petitioner Milkovich.

The numerous decisions discussed above establishing First Amendment protection for defendants in defamation actions surely demonstrate the Court's recognition of the Amendment's vital guarantee of free and uninhibited discussion of public issues. But there is also another side to the equation; we have regularly acknowledged the "important social values which underlie the law of defamation,".   .   .   .

We believe our decision in the present case holds the balance true. The judgment of the Ohio Court of Appeals is reversed and the case remanded for further proceedings not inconsistent with this opinion.

[JUSTICE BRENNAN, joined by JUSTICE MARSHALL, dissented. He said the Court addressed the opinion issue "cogently and almost entirely correctly," and agreed that the lower courts had been under a "misimpression that there is a so-called opinion privilege wholly in addition to the protections we have already found to be guaranteed by the First Amendment." But he disagreed with the application of agreed principles to the facts: "I find that the challenged statements cannot reasonably be interpreted as either stating or implying defamatory facts about petitioner. Under the rule articulated in the majority opinion, therefore, the statements are due 'full constitutional protection.' "

He characterized the columnist's assumption that Milkovich lied as "patently conjecture" and asserted that conjecture is as important to the free flow of ideas and opinions as "imaginative expression" and "rhetorical hyperbole," which the majority agreed are protected. He offered several examples:

> Did NASA officials ignore sound warnings that the Challenger Space Shuttle would explode? Did Cuban–American leaders arrange for John Fitzgerald Kennedy's assassination? Was Kurt Waldheim a Nazi officer? Such questions are matters of public concern long before all the facts are unearthed, if they ever are. Conjecture is a means of fueling a national discourse on such questions and stimulating public pressure for answers from those who know more.

The dissent argued that the language of the column itself made clear to readers that the columnist was engaging in speculation, personal judgment, emotional rhetoric, and moral outrage. "No reasonable reader could understand [the columnist] to be impliedly asserting—as fact—that Milkovich had perjured himself."]

Notes and Questions

1. Why does the constitution require protection of rhetorical hyperbole but not opinion? Is rhetorical hyperbole less likely to damage reputation? Is it a more valuable form of speech?

2. The majority says "the statement, 'In my opinion Mayor Jones shows his abysmal ignorance by accepting the teachings of Marx and Lenin,' would not be actionable." If the mayor does not accept the teachings of Marx and Lenin, might the statement be actionable? Does the Court mean only that the statement that the mayor is abysmally ignorant is not actionable if the rest of the statement is true?

3. What should the trial judge do if persuaded that the lay readers of a mass-circulation publication took a statement as one of fact but that there is simply no way in which to try the truth or falsity of the statement? For example, what result if a survey showed that virtually all who read that statement concluded that it asserted a "fact." Does that affect the verifiability issue?

4. The procedural history of the *Milkovich* case, described at length in omitted portions of the majority opinion, illustrates the persistence and endurance that libel litigation sometimes demands of its participants. The column was published in 1974. The case settled shortly after this opinion. See generally, Sack, Protection of Opinion under the First Amendment: Reflections on Alfred Hill, "Defamation and Privacy under the First Amendment," 100 Colum.L.Rev. 294 (2000).

5. The state and lower federal courts have struggled with the approach announced in *Milkovich*, as the following suggests.

Flamm v. American Association of University Women

United States Court of Appeals, Second Circuit, 2000.
201 F.3d 144.

Before: MESKILL, MINER and PARKER, CIRCUIT JUDGES.

MESKILL, CIRCUIT JUDGE:

. . .

Appellees American Association of University Women and the AAUW Legal Advocacy Fund (collectively "AAUW") are non-profit corporations dedicated to improving educational opportunities for women and girls. Among its other programs and services, the AAUW maintains a referral service of attorneys and other professionals who are willing to consult with women involved in higher education who have brought or are considering bringing gender discrimination actions. As part of this service, the AAUW compiles a directory of the participating attorneys and other professionals, listing names, contact information, and a short blurb about each person. In October 1997 the AAUW distributed copies of the directory, together with a cover letter, to the people listed in it, to members of the AAUW, and to any others requesting a copy.

Neither the cover letter nor the directory explained how the directory was compiled, although two of the directory entries included the notation "not reached in survey." Some of the entries appear to include statements made by the person listed. For example, Mr. K stated: "If they [cases] cannot be resolved early on, then I plan on being there for the long run, since these cases can take 5+ years to work up, try and handle appeals." However, of the approximately 275 entries in the directory, only Flamm's contained a negative comment. His directory entry appeared as follows:

Leonard N. Flamm
880 Third Ave.
New York, N.Y. 10022
B–212/752–3380
H–212/755–7867
Mr. Flamm handles sex discrimination cases in the area of pay equity, harassment, and promotion. *Note: At least one plaintiff has described Flamm as an "ambulance chaser" with interest only in "slam dunk cases."*

Flamm filed suit in state court, alleging that the description "an 'ambulance chaser' with interest only in 'slam dunk cases'" constitutes libel *per se*. He sought both compensatory and punitive damages. The AAUW removed the action to federal court and filed a motion to dismiss. The district court granted the motion because it determined that the statement challenged by Flamm could not reasonably be construed as a statement of objective fact. [   ]

We disagree. In light of the inclusion of the statement in an otherwise fact-laden directory, the description of Flamm as an "ambulance chaser" might imply to the reader of the directory that Flamm engages in the unethical solicitation of clients. Consequently, dismissal at this stage of the proceedings was improper.

DISCUSSION

The central issue on appeal is whether the statement challenged by Flamm is protected by either the United States Constitution or the New

York Constitution. . . . The Court's opinion in *Gertz* was widely understood to extend an "absolute constitutional protection" to expressions of opinions. See, e.g., Steinhilber v. Alphonse, [501 N.E.2d 550, 553 (N.Y. 1986)].

Subsequently, however, the Supreme Court disclaimed "an additional separate constitutional privilege for 'opinion'" under the First Amendment. [*Milkovich*]. . . .

In response, the Court of Appeals of New York grounded its pre-*Milkovich* protection for expressions of opinion in the New York Constitution. See Immuno AG. v. Moor–Jankowski, [567 N.E.2d 1270 (N.Y.1991)]. In its decision, the court reaffirmed that "the standard articulated and applied in *Steinhilber* furnishes the operative standard in this State for separating actionable fact from protected opinion." [ ] To resolve this appeal we must test the statement challenged by Flamm against the standards set by both the First Amendment and the New York Constitution. Although the analysis "does and is intended to differ," the dispositive inquiry here is the same: whether the challenged statement can reasonably be construed to be stating or implying facts about the defamation plaintiff. [ ]

I. *The Federal Standard*

In defamation suits against media defendants, a statement that involves a matter of public concern must be provable as false before liability can be established. [ ] This follows directly from [*Hepps*], which requires defamation plaintiffs to bear the burden of proving falsity in suits against media defendants that involve matters of public concern. [ ] The *Milkovich* Court did not decide, however, whether the same rules apply in suits against nonmedia defendants. . . .

The distinctions found in the law of defamation—between matters of public and private concern, between media and nonmedia defendants, and between public officials or public figures and private plaintiffs—were enunciated in an attempt to balance "the State's interest in compensating private individuals for injury to their reputation against the First Amendment interest in protecting . . . expression." See, e. g., Dun & Bradstreet v. Greenmoss Builders, 472 U.S. 749, 757–61 (1985); [The court reviewed the *Rosenbloom-Gertz* sequence.]

The Court re-examined *Gertz* in *Dun & Bradstreet*. In *Dun & Bradstreet*, a defamation action against a credit-reporting agency, the jury awarded plaintiff presumed and punitive damages. The state trial court granted a new trial after the defendant challenged the award under *Gertz*. On appeal, the Vermont Supreme Court reversed. The court acknowledged that a distinction between media defendants and nonmedia defendants would not always be easy to draw, but nonetheless concluded that the constitutional protection of *New York Times* did not extend to nonmedia defendants such as Dun & Bradstreet.

The Supreme Court affirmed on different grounds. Although there was no opinion for the Court, a majority of justices agreed that the *Gertz* rule requiring a showing of actual malice to support recovery of presumed or punitive damages does not apply to cases involving matters of only private concern. The plurality opinion explained: "It is speech on 'matters of public concern' that is 'at the heart of the First Amendment's protection.' . . . In contrast, speech on matters of purely private concern is of less First Amendment concern." [   ]

Significantly, the plurality opinion and the concurring opinions declined to adopt the media/nonmedia distinction drawn by the state court, and that distinction was expressly rejected by the four dissenting justices and by Justice White [who concurred]: "Such a distinction is irreconcilable with the fundamental First Amendment principle that '[t]he inherent worth of . . . speech in terms of its capacity for informing the public does not depend upon the identity of its source, whether corporation, association, union, or individual.' First Amendment difficulties lurk in the definitional questions such an approach would generate. And the distinction would likely be born an anachronism." [   ]

We agree that a distinction drawn according to whether the defendant is a member of the media or not is untenable. However, we need not extend the constitutional safeguards of *Hepps* and *Milkovich*, which involved media defendants, to every defamation action involving a matter of public concern. Rather, in a suit by a private plaintiff involving a matter of public concern, we hold that allegedly defamatory statements must be provably false, and the plaintiff must bear the burden of proving falsity, at least in cases where the statements were directed towards a public audience with an interest in that concern. [   ]

This approach, akin to a "common interest" privilege for matters of public concern, balances the competing values at stake. On the one hand, the state interest in compensating private individuals for wrongful injury to reputation is significantly weaker "when the factfinding process [is] unable to resolve conclusively whether the speech is true or false; it is in those cases that the burden of proof is dispositive." [*Hepps*] On the other hand, the First Amendment interest in protecting free expression is advanced by requiring private plaintiffs to prove the falsity of allegedly defamatory statements involving matters of public concern, especially when the challenged statements are directed towards a public audience with an interest in that concern.

Turning to the case at bar, whether a publication addresses a matter of public concern "must be determined by the content, form, and context of a given statement, as revealed by the whole record." Connick v. Myers, 461 U.S. 138, 147–48, (1983); see also [*Dun & Bradstreet*]. Gender discrimination is a problem of constitutional dimension, and the efforts of the AAUW to combat it clearly relate to a matter of public concern. The purported allegation that Flamm, an attorney specializing in the field, engages in the unethical solicitation of victims of gender discrimination is also a matter for public concern, especially when brought to the public's attention by way of a publication with the imprimatur of the AAUW. See [Unelko Corp. v. Rooney, 912 F.2d 1049, 1056 (9th Cir.1990)] (holding statements about product effectiveness aired on "60 Minutes" to be matter of public concern). Indeed, the common law recognizes that publications commenting on "persons who present [ ] themselves or their services or goods to the public" are matters of public concern. [ ] The directory was also distributed to a public audience with an interest in issues of gender discrimination. It was mailed, at a minimum, to hundreds of Flamm's peers and fellow professionals nationwide. This mailing was clearly intended to, and can reasonably be viewed as an attempt to, influence public discourse and affect the public response to incidents of gender discrimination.

For the foregoing reasons we conclude that, to survive this motion to dismiss, Flamm must have shown that a reasonable person could find that the challenged statement alleges or implies a provably false fact. We conclude that he has.

[The court reviewed *Milkovich* at length.]

Flamm alleges in his complaint that his description in the AAUW directory as an "ambulance chaser" states that he "has engaged in improper activities to solicit and obtain clients." Following *Milkovich*, we must decide whether the description of Flamm as an "ambulance chaser" reasonably implies that he has engaged in unethical solicitation, and if so, whether the accusation of unethical solicitation is capable of being proven false. The second question, however, is conceded by the defendants. They admit that the term "ambulance chaser" is provable as true or false when understood literally to accuse a lawyer of the unethical or criminal behavior of solicitation.

We conclude that the statement challenged by Flamm reasonably implies that he has engaged in unethical solicitation. The directory in all other respects states facts: names, addresses and phone numbers; a note that Ms. R "will not be able to consult with anyone affiliated with the Florida State University system because of a conflict of interest"; the warning that Mr. A "charges a $50.00 initial consultation fee and does not discuss potential cases over the phone"; and so on. Furthermore, the directory has the stated purpose of providing referrals to qualified attorneys and professionals to assist victims of gender discrimination. A reader of the directory, seeing the only negative comment among several hundred entries, would likely turn elsewhere for assistance. Indeed, the note about Flamm is highlighted in italics, suggesting that it warrants special attention and consideration.

[The court held that *Letter Carriers*, p. 1062 supra, did not apply here because "scab" was used in a "loose, figurative sense." The "use of the word 'traitor' could not reasonably imply that the plaintiffs were, in fact, being accused of treason."] See also Greenbelt Coop. Publ'g Ass'n v. Bresler, 398 U.S. 6, 14 (1970) (finding it "impossible to believe" that readers of a newspaper article reporting statements made at public hearings would understand "blackmail" to be charging plaintiff with a crime). Here, however, we do not think it would be "impossible to believe" that the description of Flamm as an "ambulance chaser" implies that he engages in unethical solicitation. More to the point, it would not be unreasonable to think so, even if "ambulance chaser" is a figurative way to describe it. Exaggerated rhetoric may be commonplace in labor disputes, but a reasonable reader would not expect similar hyperbole in a straightforward directory of attorneys and other professionals. Indeed, the opposite is true. A reasonable reader is more likely to treat as fact the description of Flamm as an "ambulance chaser" because there is nothing in the otherwise fact-laden directory to suggest otherwise.

Next, the AAUW contends that the phrase "with interest only in 'slam dunk cases'" indicates that the challenged statement cannot be read literally, because "slam dunk" is an imprecise term of slang suggesting that the entire statement amounts to a purely subjective judgment. There is little merit to this argument. Even if the "slam dunk" language might cause a reasonable reader to consider whether the entire statement was merely an informal complaint, we cannot say that it would be unreasonable to conclude otherwise. The description "an 'ambulance chaser' with interest only in 'slam dunk cases'" can reasonably be interpreted to mean an attorney who improperly solicits clients and then takes only easy cases. This reading, which separates to a degree the "ambulance chaser" characterization from the "slam dunk cases" language, is especially plausible because, in the challenged statement as printed, each of those phrases was separately enclosed in quotation marks. It would not be unreasonable to read the "ambulance chaser" excerpt literally, because it could have been unrelated to the "slam dunk cases" reference in whatever passage the AAUW was quoting.

· · ·

The AAUW also argues that "ambulance chaser" cannot be read in the literal sense of a lawyer who "has engaged in improper activities to solicit and obtain clients" because dictionary definitions of "ambulance chaser" typically refer to solicitation of negligence or accident victims. [   ] This peculiar argument, challenging the alleged meaning of "ambulance chaser" as overly literal because not literal enough, is without merit. Although "rhetorical hyperbole" and "lusty and imaginative expression" may not be actionable, [*Letter Carriers*], there is at the same time no requirement that the defamatory meaning of a challenged statement correspond to its literal dictionary definition. It is sufficient, for the purpose of defeating this motion to dismiss, that the challenged statement reasonably implies the alleged defamatory meaning.

We therefore hold that the challenged statement is "reasonably susceptible to the defamatory meaning imputed to it." [   ] However, it remains for the jury to decide whether the challenged statement was likely to be understood by the reader in a defamatory sense. [   ]

In sum, the AAUW's contention that the term "ambulance chaser" was mere hyperbole falls short. Considering the "general tenor" of the publication—a directory for referrals put out by a national professional organization—it would not be unreasonable to think that the description of

Flamm conveyed an assertion of fact. Thus, the challenged statement reasonably implies a defamatory fact capable of being proven false, and the AAUW is not entitled to dismissal under the First Amendment.

II. *The New York Standard*

In New York, the courts employ a flexible approach in distinguishing actionable fact from non-actionable opinion. Three factors are generally considered: "(1) whether the specific language in issue has a precise meaning which is readily understood; (2) whether the statements are capable of being proven true or false; and (3) whether either the full context of the communication in which the statement appears or the broader social context and surrounding circumstances are such as to 'signal . . . readers or listeners that what is being read or heard is likely to be opinion, not fact.'" [ ] (quoting *Steinhilber*]. These criteria apply whether the defendant is a member of the media or not. [ ]

The Court of Appeals of New York has made clear, however, that a proper analysis should not consist of a mechanical enumeration of each factor adopted in *Steinhilber*. Instead, "the court should look to the over-all context in which the assertions were made and determine on that basis 'whether the reasonable reader would have believed that the challenged statements were conveying facts about the libel plaintiff.'" [ ]

Since *Steinhilber*, the Court of Appeals of New York has consistently focused its analysis on the overall context in which the complained-of assertions were made. See [ ] (statements published on op-ed page of newspaper); [ ] (accusation made in the course of a lengthy, copiously documented newspaper series); [*Immuno AG*] (letter to the editor of a scientific journal); see also [*Steinhilber*] (examining first "the content of the whole communication as well as its tone and its apparent purpose"). The *Immuno AG* court only subsequently analyzed the presence of specific language, e.g., the use of "appeared to be," "might well be," "could well happen," and "should be" to signal presumptions and predictions rather than facts. [ ]

In the present case, the challenged language appears in a national directory nearly seventy pages in length, compiled and distributed by a reputable professional organization with a 100 year history of supporting education. The directory purports to list "attorneys and other specialists" willing to consult with women involved in higher education who are seeking redress for sex-based discrimination. The directory provides names, addresses, phone numbers and, generally, a short statement of the person's area of interest or expertise. In such a fact-laden context, the reasonable reader would be "less skeptical and more willing to conclude that [the directory] stated or implied facts." [ ]

The cases cited by the AAUW are unavailing, involving situations (unlike the situation here) that suggest that the alleged defamations should not be understood to be stating facts. . . .

Finally, the district court held that the phrase "with interest only in 'slam dunk cases' " rendered the entire statement so informal as to lack a precise and readily understood meaning. Although acknowledging that " 'ambulance chaser' standing alone may have a precise meaning," and indeed, "does have a specific meaning, particularly among lawyers and professionals," the court focused on the "slam dunk" language. [   ] The court reasoned that "an 'ambulance chaser' is not someone who is interested only in 'slam dunk cases,' but rather, he is someone who is much less selective and who must 'chase' after cases." [   ] We do not agree. There is nothing inherently inconsistent about an "ambulance chaser" interested only in "slam dunk" cases. To accuse Flamm of improper solicitation—but only of easy cases—is still to accuse him of improper solicitation.

The AAUW's other arguments were considered previously and rejected in our discussion of First Amendment privilege. Consequently, the AAUW is not entitled to dismissal at this stage of the litigation.

. . .

Notes and Questions

1. What should happen on remand of this case? Will the jury have a role?

2. Why does the court conclude that the defendant is entitled to the protections accorded to the press? Is this conclusion consistent with *Dun & Bradstreet*?

3. Why does the plaintiff have the burden of proof on the issue of falsity?

4. How does the federal standard for determining whether a statement is actionable differ from the New York standard? Why is New York permitted to adopt a different standard? Is the court's analysis of the statement sound under both standards?

5. Is the court's analysis consistent with *Letter Carriers*? With *Greenbelt*?

6. All courts have been struggling to identify what words are actionable. Some examples follow.

a.   Moldea v. New York Times Co., 22 F.3d 310 (D.C.Cir.), cert. denied 513 U.S. 875 (1994), holding that a book reviewer's assertion that the plaintiff's book on professional football contained "too much sloppy journalism to trust the bulk" of the book, was not actionable.

b.   Phantom Touring, Inc. v. Affiliated Publications, 953 F.2d 724 (1st Cir.), cert. denied 504 U.S. 974 (1992), holding that a critic's treatment of one of two competing stage versions of "Phantom of the Opera," both derived from a public domain novel, was not actionable. The court relied in large part on the ground that the critic explicitly stated the bases for his reaction. One article quoted a Washington Post critic to the effect that plaintiff's version "bears as much resemblance to its celebrated counterpart as Jell–O does to Baked Alaska," and described it as "a rip-off, a fraud, a scandal, a snake-oil job."

The most serious issue involved passages that could be read on their face to assert that the confusion was intentional, even though the advertising stated that there was no connection between the two shows. Arguably a charge of "deliberate deception" could be proven false by showing, for example, long-standing plans to tour the plaintiff's show before the other version rose to prominence. But the "sum effect of the format, tone and entire content of the articles is to make it unmistakably clear that Kelly was expressing a point of view only." The language appeared in a column generally understood to be more opinionated than a typical news report. (Although this was given no weight in *Milkovich*, the *Phantom* court thought that was only because of the facts of that case—not because context was never relevant):

> Thus, the article in *Milkovich*, unlike Kelly's "Phantom" columns, was not based on facts accessible to everyone. Indeed, a reader reasonably could have understood the reporter in *Milkovich* to be suggesting that he was singularly capable of evaluating the plaintiffs' conduct. In contrast, neither of Kelly's columns indicated that he, or anyone else, had more information about Phantom Touring's marketing practices than was reported in the articles.

Is the court's approach compromised if the plaintiff can present ten witnesses who say they read the column and understood that the author "must have had more facts" than he stated?

c. Sullivan v. Conway, 157 F.3d 1092 (7th Cir.1998), involving a statement to a group at a meeting of union officials that their lawyer "was a very poor lawyer." The statement was not actionable:

> It is one thing to say that a lawyer is dishonest, or has falsified his credentials, or has lost every case he has tried, or can never file suit within the statute of limitations. These are all readily verifiable statements of fact. But to say that he is a very poor lawyer is to express an opinion that is so difficult to verify or refute that it cannot feasibly be made a subject of inquiry by a jury. . . . It would be unmanageable to ask a court, in order to determine the validity of the defendants' defense of truth, to determine whether "in fact" Sullivan is a poor lawyer.
>
> . . . If Conway had said that Sullivan had been or should be disbarred, this would be actionable (if false) because it would imply that Conway knew things about Sullivan that could be shown to be either true or false, since the grounds for disbarment are factual and not mere matters of subjective opinion or surmise. That was not the character of his statement.

d. In Stevens v. Tillman, 855 F.2d 394 (7th Cir.1988), cert. denied 489 U.S. 1065 (1989), defendant called plaintiff a "racist." The court dismissed the claim on the ground that "racist" has lost its core meaning and is no longer actionable when used by itself. Courts cannot insist that speakers cling to older core meanings of words. "In daily life 'racist' is hurled about so indiscriminately that it is no more than a verbal slap in the face." Is this pre-*Milkovich* analysis still valid? The court in *Ward v. Zelikovsky*, p. 957, supra, relied heavily on *Stevens v. Tillman* in its discussion of the charge of "disliking" or "hating Jews." Does *Milkovich* require the results in these cases?

e. In *Staples v. Bangor Hydro–Electric Co.*, p. 952, supra, involving a supervisor's statement that plaintiff had "sabotaged" computers, the court held that "the jury could rationally find that [the supervisor's] statement that he had reason to believe that [plaintiff] had sabotaged the computers implied the existence of undisclosed defamatory facts."

State law. As *Flamm* indicates, some states have asserted that the state's constitutional law applicable to comments may provide broader protection than *Milkovich* offers. New York has been the leader in this move.

See also *West v. Thomson Newspapers*, p. 957, supra, in which defendant charged a public official with "trying to manipulate the press." In dismissing the claims, the court held that Utah's constitution was more protective of speech than the First Amendment as interpreted in *Milkovich*. The court relied on the wide-open nineteenth-century history of the state's press at the time the state's constitution was adopted.

Private Plaintiffs and Matters of Public Interest

As noted in *Flamm*, in the cited *Greenmoss* case, the Supreme Court has addressed the category of private plaintiffs who are swept up in discussions of matters of public interest. In *Greenmoss*, D & B, the credit reporting agency, whose business involves providing confidential information to subscribers about the credit ratings of businesses and others, sent a report to five subscribers stating that Greenmoss Builders, Inc. had filed a voluntary petition for bankruptcy. The report, prepared by a high school student employed by the defendant to review state bankruptcy proceedings, had incorrectly attributed to Greenmoss a bankruptcy petition filed by one of its former employees.

The trial judge permitted the jury to award presumed and punitive damages without finding actual malice. The jury awarded $50,000 in compensatory damages and $300,000 in punitive damages. The Vermont Supreme Court upheld the award on the ground that as a "matter of federal constitutional law, the media protections outlined in *Gertz* are inapplicable to nonmedia defamation actions." The Supreme Court affirmed, 5–4, but on grounds that did not involve the distinction between media and non-media defendants.

For a plurality of three, Justice Powell interpreted *Gertz* to apply only to cases in which the expression involved (variously) "a public issue," "public speech," or "an issue of public concern." Although no passages in *Gertz* drew this distinction, the "context of *Gertz*" was such that the opinion could have applied only to "cases involving public speech." Justice

Powell asserted that in this case the First Amendment interest differed from that in *Gertz*:

> We have long recognized that not all speech is of equal First Amendment importance. It is speech on "matters of public concern" that is "at the heart of the First Amendment's protection. . . ." In contrast, speech on matters of purely private concern is of less First Amendment concern. . . .
>
> While such speech is not totally unprotected by the First Amendment, [ ], its protections are less stringent. In *Gertz*, we found that the state interest in awarding presumed and punitive damages was not "substantial" in view of their effect on speech at the core of First Amendment concern. [ ] This interest, however, *is* "substantial" relative to the incidental effect these remedies may have on speech of significantly less constitutional interest. The rationale of the common law rules has been the experience and judgment of history that "proof of actual damage will be impossible in a great many cases where, from the character of the defamatory words and the circumstances of publication, it is all but certain that serious harm has resulted in fact." [ ] As a result, courts for centuries have allowed juries to presume that some damage occurred from many defamatory utterances and publications. [ ] This rule furthers the state interest in providing remedies for defamation by ensuring that those remedies are effective. In light of the reduced constitutional value of speech involving no matters of public concern, we hold that the state interest adequately supports awards of presumed and punitive damages—even absent a showing of "actual malice."

Justice Powell also replied to the dissenters:

> If the dissent were the law, a woman of impeccable character who was branded a "whore" by a jealous neighbor would have no effective recourse unless she could prove "actual malice" by clear and convincing evidence. This is not malice in the ordinary sense, but in the more demanding sense of *New York Times*. The dissent, would, in effect, constitutionalize the entire common law of libel.

Finally, Justice Powell briefly explained why the speech in the case did not "involve a matter of public concern":

> In a related context, we have held that "[w]hether . . . speech addressed a matter of public concern must be determined by [the expression's] content, form, and context . . . as revealed by the whole record." Connick v. Myers, 461 U.S. at 147–148 [district attorney's power to discipline an assistant depends in part on whether the assistant's speech that provoked the discipline involved a "matter of public interest"-eds.]. These factors indicate that petitioner's credit report concerns no public issue. It was speech solely in the individual interest of the speaker and its specific business audience. [ ] This particular interest warrants no special protection when—as in this case—the speech is wholly false and clearly damaging to the victim's

business reputation. [   ] Moreover, since the credit report was made available only to five subscribers, who, under the terms of the subscription agreement, could not disseminate it further, it cannot be said that the report involves any "strong interest in the free flow of commercial information." [   ] There is simply no credible argument that this type of credit reporting requires special protection to ensure that "debate on public issues [will] be uninhibited, robust and wide-open."

In addition, the speech here, like advertising, is hardy and unlikely to be deterred by incidental state regulation. [   ] It is solely motivated by the desire for profit, which, we have noted, is a force less likely to be deterred than others. [   ] Arguably, the reporting here was also more objectively verifiable than speech deserving of greater protection. [   ] In any case, the market provides a powerful incentive to a credit reporting agency to be accurate, since false credit reporting is of no use to creditors. Thus, any incremental "chilling" effect of libel suits would be of decreased significance.

Chief Justice Burger concurred in the judgment only because he felt bound by *Gertz* until it was overruled. He thought *Gertz* was limited to expressions that concern "a matter of general public importance, and that the expression in question here related to a matter of essentially private concern."

Justice White also concurred only in the judgment. He thought both *Times* and *Gertz* had been wrongly decided: He asserted that Justice Powell "declines to follow the *Gertz* approach," which Justice White thought "was intended to reach cases that involve any false statements of fact injurious to reputation, whether the statement is made privately or publicly and whether or not it implicates a matter of public importance."

Justice White agreed with the result in *Greenmoss* because (1) he was still unreconciled to *Gertz* and (2) strict liability should be used for publications that do not deal with matters of public importance. (He also suggested alternative approaches that the Court might take in these cases—alternatives that we consider p. 1094, infra, as part of a more general look at possible "reform".)

There were thus five votes for the recovery of presumed and punitive damages without a showing of actual malice.

Justice Brennan, joined by Justices Marshall, Blackmun and Stevens, dissented. Although protecting the speech in this case is admittedly not the "central meaning of the First Amendment," *Gertz* "makes clear that the First Amendment nonetheless requires restraints on presumed and punitive damages awards for this expression." Apart from unhappiness that the majority justices were "cut[ting] away the protective mantle of *Gertz*," Justice Brennan objected that "[w]ithout explaining what *is* a 'matter of public concern,' the plurality opinion proceeds to serve up a smorgasbord of reasons why the speech at issue here is not, [   ], and on this basis affirms" the award. Any standard that can be gleaned from the opinions is "impoverished" and "irreconcilable with First Amendment principles. The credit reporting at issue here surely involves a subject matter of sufficient public concern to require the comprehensive protections of *Gertz*."

Speech about "economic matters . . . is an important part of our public discourse." An "announcement of the bankruptcy of a local company is information of potentially great concern to residents of the community where the company is located; like the labor dispute at issue in *Thornhill*, such a bankruptcy 'in a single factory may have economic repercussions for a whole region.' "

Justice Brennan asserted in a footnote that, since the subject matter "would clearly receive the comprehensive protections of *Gertz* were the speech publicly disseminated, [the] factor of confidential circulation to a limited number of subscribers is perhaps properly understood as the linchpin" of Justice Powell's analysis.

The possibility that *Greenmoss* might lead to a distinction between media and nonmedia defendants has not been borne out. In this and other cases, a majority of the justices have rejected that distinction. Nonmedia defendants have not been stripped of *Gertz* protection solely because of their nonmedia status. See, e.g., Underwager v. Salter, 22 F.3d 730 (7th Cir.), cert. denied 513 U.S. 943 (1994) (holding that Wisconsin law would require public figure to prove actual malice in suit against nonmedia defendant).

If the media-nonmedia distinction is not at work, why did the defendant lose *Greenmoss*? Why was this information not a matter of public concern? Was it that only five persons received the information? Was it that the five could not disseminate it further? Most observers have thought that this limited circulation explained the case because it seems unlikely that news of a commercial bankruptcy would not qualify as a matter of public interest. Indeed it seems certain that *Gertz* would have applied if the erroneous report had appeared in the local newspaper.

Nor has *Greenmoss* been read as allowing public plaintiffs to recover without having to show "actual malice" See, e.g., Dworkin v. Hustler Magazine Inc., 867 F.2d 1188 (9th Cir.), cert. denied 493 U.S. 812 (1989) ("we doubt that it is possible to have speech about a public figure but not of public concern"). Why should that be?

In Snead v. Redland Aggregates, Ltd., 998 F.2d 1325 (5th Cir.1993), cert. dismissed 511 U.S. 1050 (1994), one party sued over a press release issued (in connection with the filing of a complaint) by the other party after failed negotiations between the two. The court treated the case as one involving a private plaintiff and private content so as to come within the framework of *Greenmoss*. The court, concluding that five justices there supported the use of "common law standards" for what it called "private-private" cases, held that presumed and punitive damages could be awarded without a showing of fault.

In Johnson v. Johnson, 654 A.2d 1212 (R.I.1995), in a restaurant, defendant ex-husband called his ex-wife a "whore." Although the trial judge concluded that the statement was true, he upheld a jury award of

$5,000 compensatory and $20,000 punitive damages. Under the state's constitution, in civil and criminal actions for libel or slander "the truth, unless published or uttered from malicious motives, shall be sufficient defense to the person charged." The court upheld the finding that the words had been uttered with ill will sufficient to sustain the compensatory award. But the provocation of the situation was such that punitive damages were not permissible under state law. Although the court noted that the defendant had not preserved "federal constitutional issues," it nonetheless concluded that no federal rule prevented the recovery here. *Greenmoss* showed that *Gertz* did not apply since the statement was not of public concern. Nor did the *Garrison* case, p. 1012, supra, which "absolutely prohibits punishment of truthful criticisms of public officials," apply to *Johnson* "because we are not dealing with public officials, public figures, or even matters of public concern."

In Nadel v. Regents of the University of California, 34 Cal.Rptr.2d 188 (App. 1994), cert. denied 516 U.S. 1028 (1995), the court of appeal held that government officials were entitled to the protection of the *New York Times* doctrine in comments made about public figures. In a case of first impression the court was sensitive to the need to add a third consideration to the two ("unfettered interchange of ideas" and "protection of vulnerable citizens from defamation") already used in the development of the *Times* line. That third was framed as "the overarching constitutional interest in protecting people from abuses of governmental power." The court approved a passage from Shiffrin, Governmental Speech, 27 UCLA L.Rev. 565 (1980):

> Government has legitimate interests in informing, in educating, and in persuading. If government is to secure cooperation in implementing its programs, if it is to be able to maintain a dialogue with its citizens about their needs and the extent to which government can or should meet those needs, government must be able to communicate. An approach that would invalidate all controversial government speech would seriously impair the democratic process.

The court recognized that government had unique power in the war of words with citizens—and that "[e]vents of the past few decades have demonstrated that government is quite capable of misleading the public and defaming its citizens." But the extent of this concern had become "debatable in light of general post-Watergate skepticism about anything government has to say." Moreover, this "claim of plaintiff vulnerability could be made as to any 'big media' defendant." The court concluded that holding government officials to liability under the *New York Times* doctrine would reduce potential abuse of power since officials would know they could be held liable under *Times* or *Gertz*. Common law strict liability was thought inconsistent with the role government had to play in the public debate.

As a separate ground for its result, the court noted that in *New York Times*, the Court had suggested that since government officials were often protected for their speech, giving citizens a comparable protection would balance the power. That view suggested that in this case constitutional protection was needed to put the officials not otherwise protected in balance with the citizens.

———

Recall that the AAUW did not make the statements on its own. Rather, it purported to quote an unidentified respondent. Should the analysis in the case have been different if the source of the statement had been identified in the directory? The following case addresses the issue of repeating the defamations of others.

F. THE PRESS AS REPEATER

As noted earlier, the common law developed the fair report privilege to protect those who repeated certain kinds of statements. A situation not traditionally covered by that privilege is addressed in the following case.

Khawar v. Globe International, Inc.

Supreme Court of California, 1998.
19 Cal.4th 254, 965 P.2d 696, 79 Cal.Rptr.2d 178.
Certiorari denied, 526 U.S. 1114 (1999).

KENNARD, JUSTICE.

We granted review to decide certain issues concerning the federal Constitution's guarantees of freedom of speech and of the press insofar as they restrict a state's ability to impose tort liability for the publication of defamatory falsehoods. More specifically, we address the definition of a "public figure" for purposes of tort and First Amendment law, the existence in this state of a privilege for "neutral reportage," and the showings required to support awards of compensatory and punitive damages for the republication of a defamatory falsehood.

On these issues, we conclude: (1) A young journalist who was photographed near a nationally prominent politician moments before the politician's assassination, but who was never a suspect in the government's investigation of the assassination, whose views on the assassination were never publicized, and who never sought to influence public discussion about the assassination, was not a public figure in relation to a tabloid newspaper's article reporting a book's false accusation that the journalist assassinated the politician; (2) this state does not recognize a neutral reportage privilege for republication of a libel concerning a private figure (and we need not and do not decide here whether this state recognizes a neutral reportage privilege for republication of a libel concerning a public official or public figure); and (3) the evidence produced at the trial in this case supports the jury's findings of negligence and actual malice, which in turn support the awards of compensatory and punitive damages.

[In June, 1968, when Senator Robert F. Kennedy was assassinated in Los Angeles, plaintiff was a free-lance photographer working on assignment. He was photographed near Kennedy by a friend. Plaintiff did not follow Kennedy into the hall where he was shot. In 1988, a publisher brought out a book by Robert Morrow entitled *The Senator Must Die: The Murder of Robert Kennedy* (the Morrow book), alleging that the Iranian Shah's secret police (SAVAK), working together with the Mafia, carried out the 1968 assassination. The book contended that Kennedy's assassin was not Sirhan Sirhan, who had been convicted of the murder, but a man named Ali Ahmand, whom the Morrow book described as a young Pakistani who, on the evening of the Kennedy assassination, wore a gold-colored sweater and carried what appeared to be a camera but was actually the gun with which Ahmand killed Kennedy. The Morrow book contained four photographs of a young man the book identified as Ali Ahmand standing in a group of people around Kennedy at the Ambassador Hotel in Los Angeles shortly before Kennedy was assassinated.]

Globe International, Inc., (Globe) publishes a weekly tabloid newspaper called Globe. Its issue of April 4, 1989, contained an article on page 9 under the headline: *Former CIA Agent Claims*: IRANIANS KILLED BOBBY KENNEDY FOR THE MAFIA (the Globe article). Another headline, appearing on the front page of the same issue, stated: *Iranian secret police killed Bobby Kennedy*. The Globe article, written by John Blackburn (a freelance reporter and former Globe staff reporter), gave an abbreviated, uncritical summary of the Morrow book's allegations. The Globe article included a photograph from the Morrow book showing a group of men standing near Kennedy; Globe enlarged the image of these individuals and added an arrow pointing to one of these men and identifying him as the assassin Ali Ahmand. [In fact, the arrow pointed to plaintiff.]

[Plaintiff and his father (Ali Ahmad—not Ahmand) sued for defamation.] Morrow defaulted, and Roundtable settled with both Khawar and Ahmad before trial. As part of the settlement, Roundtable executed a retraction disavowing "any and all statements, intimations, or references that Khalid Iqbal Khawar or Ali Ahmad were in any way associated with or committed the assassination of United States Senator Robert F. Kennedy." A jury trial ensued on the claims against Globe.

. . . . After Khawar read the Globe article, he became very frightened for his own safety and that of his family. He received accusatory and threatening telephone calls about the article from as far away as Thailand, he and his children received death threats, and his home and his son's car were vandalized. A Bakersfield television station interviewed Khawar about the Globe article.

. . . . As to Khawar, the jury returned, among others, these special verdicts: (1) the Globe article contained statements about Khawar that were false and defamatory; (2) Globe published the article negligently and with malice or oppression; (3) with respect to Kennedy's assassination, Khawar was a private rather than a public figure; and (4) the Globe article was a neutral and accurate report of the Morrow book. The parties had previously agreed that the jury's findings on the last two issues would be advisory only. The jury awarded Khawar $100,000 for injury to his reputation, $400,000 for emotional distress, $175,000 in presumed damages, and, after a separate punitive damages phase, $500,000 in punitive damages.

After the return of these special verdicts, the trial court reviewed those that were deemed advisory and determined as a matter of law that (1) the Globe article was *not* an accurate and neutral report of the statements and charges made in the Morrow book (thus disagreeing with and rejecting the jury's advisory special verdict); and (2) with respect to the events in question, Khawar was a private and not a public figure (thus agreeing with and adopting the jury's advisory special verdict). The trial court's finding that the Globe article was not an accurate and neutral report of the Morrow book was apparently based on the court's subsidiary finding that although Khawar could be identified from the photograph of him that appeared in the Globe article, which included an arrow pointing directly at Khawar, it was impossible to identify Khawar from the smaller, darker, and less distinct image of him, without an arrow, that appeared in the Morrow book. Based upon its findings that Khawar was not named in and could not be identified from the photographs in the Morrow book, the trial court vacated Morrow's default and ultimately entered judgment in his favor. The court granted judgment on the special verdicts for Khawar and against Globe in the amount of $1,175,000.

Globe appealed from the judgment. The Court of Appeal reached these conclusions: (1) Khawar was not a public figure; (2) California has not adopted a neutral reportage privilege for private figures; (3) in light of these conclusions, it was unnecessary to decide whether California has adopted a neutral reportage privilege for public figures or whether the Globe article was a neutral and accurate report of the Morrow book; and (4) the evidence supported the trial court's findings of negligence and actual malice. The Court of Appeal affirmed the judgment.

We granted Globe's petition for review raising these issues: (1) When a published book places a person at the center of a public controversy, is that person an involuntary public figure for the limited purpose of a media report about that book and that controversy? (2) Does the First Amendment to the federal Constitution mandate a privilege for a media defendant's publication of a neutral and accurate report about a controversial book's allegations regarding matters of public concern? (3) Does the evidence support the jury's special verdict finding of actual malice? (4) Does the evidence support the jury's special verdict finding of negligence? (5) Did the trial court usurp the jury's role and violate Globe's right to due process of law when it determined the Globe article to be an "original libel" without giving Globe the opportunity to be heard or present evidence on that issue?

II. PUBLIC FIGURE

We consider first Globe's contention that the trial court and the Court of Appeal erred in concluding that Khawar is a private rather than a public figure for purposes of this defamation action.

[The court first rejected the argument that plaintiff was an involuntary public figure. "[A]ssuming a person may ever be accurately characterized as an involuntary public figure, we infer from the logic of Gertz that the high court would reserve this characterization for an individual who, despite never having voluntarily engaged the public's attention in an attempt to influence the outcome of a public controversy, nonetheless has acquired such public prominence in relation to the controversy as to permit media access sufficient to effectively counter media-published defamatory statements." No evidence supported such a finding here. Recall that the court in *Wells v. Liddy*, p. 1049, supra, cited *Khawar* on the involuntariness question.

The court also rejected arguments that plaintiff was a public figure based on his actions in having his photograph taken with Senator Kennedy before his speech. First the conduct occurred before the controversy arose. Second, any role in the political campaign was "trivial at best."]

III.   NEUTRAL REPORTAGE PRIVILEGE

Globe contends that the trial court and the Court of Appeal erred in holding that the neutral reportage privilege does not apply to insulate from defamation liability its republication of the Morrow book's defamatory falsehoods.

A.   Background

At common law, one who republishes a defamatory statement is deemed thereby to have adopted it and so may be held liable, together with the person who originated the statement, for resulting injury to the reputation of the defamation victim. [ ] California has adopted the common law in this regard [ ], although by statute the republication of defamatory statements is privileged in certain defined situations (see, e.g., Civ.Code, § 47).

In a 1977 decision, a federal appellate court held that, under certain circumstances, as an exception to the common law republication rule, the federal Constitution's First Amendment mandates an absolute privilege for the republication of defamatory statements. (Edwards v. National Audubon Society, Inc. (2d Cir.1977) 556 F.2d 113, cert. den. 434 U.S. 1002 (*Edwards*).) This privilege has since come to be known as the neutral reportage privilege. The *Edwards* court defined the privilege this way: "[W]hen a *responsible, prominent organization . . . makes serious charges against a public figure*, the First Amendment protects the *accurate and disinterested reporting* of those charges, regardless of the reporter's private views regarding their validity." ([ ], italics added.)[1]

---

1. The neutral reportage privilege to some extent resembles and overlaps the common law privilege of "fair report," which California has codified in Civil Code section 47, subdivisions (d) and (e) [ ] and also the "wire service defense," which has been adopted by some courts in other jurisdictions [ ] but has yet to be considered by any published decision of a court of this state. Globe does not argue that either the statutory fair report privilege or the wire service defense immunizes it from liability to Kha-

The theory underlying the privilege is that the reporting of defamatory allegations relating to an existing public controversy has significant informational value for the public regardless of the truth of the allegations: If the allegations are true, their reporting provides valuable information about the target of the accusation; if the allegations are false, their reporting reflects in a significant way on the character of the accuser. In either event, according to the theory, the very making of the defamatory allegations sheds valuable light on the character of the controversy (its intensity and perhaps viciousness). As we understand it, the theory also rests on a distinction between publication and republication. Applying this distinction, proponents of the neutral reportage privilege urge that the reporting of a false and defamatory accusation should be deemed neither defamatory nor false if the report accurately relates the accusation, makes it clear that the republisher does not espouse or concur in the accusation, and provides enough additional information (including, where practical, the response of the defamed person) to allow the readers to draw their own conclusions about the truth of the accusation.

The United States Supreme Court has not stated whether it agrees with this theory, and it has never held that the First Amendment mandates a neutral reportage privilege [   ]. Nor have we ever addressed the question whether the neutral reportage privilege will be recognized in this state.

In other jurisdictions, some state and federal appellate courts have rejected the privilege entirely [   ], while courts that have adopted it have disagreed as to its elements (compare, e.g., Martin v. Wilson Pub. Co. (R.I.1985) 497 A.2d 322, 330 [stating that privilege applies "only in the extremely limited situation in which the publication accurately attributes such statements to an identified and responsible source"] with Barry v. Time, Inc. (1984) 584 F.Supp. 1110, 1125–1127 [applying privilege to report of accusations made by other than a "responsible" person or organization]).

Commentators are similarly divided, with some arguing that the privilege is inconsistent with the United States Supreme Court's First Amendment jurisprudence and therefore should be rejected [   ], and others endorsing the privilege in concept but taking differing positions about how it should be defined (compare [   ] [would require that the target be a public figure or official, that the report relate to a preexisting public controversy, that the report not concur in or endorse the defamation, and that the report be fair and accurate], with [   ] [would not require that report be neutral or that source be responsible and would recognize privilege if either source or target is a public figure]).

---

war for damages occasioned by publication of the Globe article. Accordingly, we have no occasion to consider application of Civil Code section 47 to the circumstances of this case.

Also, because Globe conceded at trial that the Globe article was not a book review,

we have no occasion here to consider whether republication of a defamatory statement in the context of a book review would require a different analysis or result.

B. Analysis

Without deciding whether some form of the neutral reportage privilege should be recognized in this state, the Court of Appeal in this case declined to apply the neutral reportage privilege on the ground that Khawar is a private figure. Globe argues that this conclusion is erroneous either because Khawar is a public figure or because the neutral reportage privilege extends to defamatory falsehoods about private figures. In concluding that Khawar is a private figure, we have already rejected the first of these grounds. We now consider the second.

. . .

Some commentators have argued that the privilege should apply to a published report of an accusation that a public figure has made against a private figure because "the public has a greater interest in knowing what its public figures are saying than it does in protecting private figures from accusations by public figures." [ ] They reason like this: "Through an understanding of who is saying what, public figures may be analyzed more insightfully, their statements reflecting as much about themselves as they do about the target. Inevitably, the conflicting interests are considered in a balancing test. It is more important to refrain from chilling republication of speech made by public figures, often the political speech at the core of the first amendment, than to protect the reputations of private figure targets." Under this view, the neutral reportage privilege would protect the Globe article, even though it reported a false and defamatory accusation against a private figure (that is, Khawar), if the person who made the original accusation (that is, Morrow) was a public figure.

Because we do not accept this view of the neutral reportage privilege, we do not decide whether Morrow was a public figure. We find more persuasive the arguments of other commentators that republication of accusations made against private figures is never protected by the neutral reportage privilege, whether or not the person who made the original accusation was a public figure. These commentators explain that although the public has a legitimate interest in knowing that prominent individuals have made charges, perhaps unfounded, against a private figure, recognition of an absolute privilege for the republication of those charges would be inconsistent with the United States Supreme Court's insistence on the need for balancing the First Amendment interest in promoting the broad dissemination of information relevant to public controversies against the reputation interests of private figures: "If the scope of the privilege were to include defamations of private figures, a neutral reportage route out of liability could emasculate the *Gertz* distinction between private and public figure plaintiffs." [ ]

We agree. Only rarely will the report of false and defamatory accusations against a person who is neither a public official nor a public figure provide information of value in the resolution of a controversy over a matter of public concern. On the other hand, the report of such accusations can have a devastating effect on the reputation of the accused individual, who has not voluntarily elected to encounter an increased risk of defamation and who may lack sufficient media access to counter the accusations. As this court has remarked, "[a] reasonable degree of protection for a private individual's reputation is essential to our system of ordered liberty." [   ] The availability of a defamation action against the source of the falsehood may be an inadequate remedy if the source is insolvent or otherwise unable to respond in damages. Moreover, it is questionable whether money damages are ever a completely adequate compensation for injury to reputation.

.   .   .

Because in this defamation action Khawar is a private figure plaintiff, he was required to prove only negligence, and not actual malice, to recover damages for actual injury to his reputation. But Khawar was required to prove actual malice to recover punitive or presumed damages for defamation involving the Kennedy assassination. Because Khawar sought punitive and presumed damages as well as damages for actual injury, the issues of both actual malice and negligence were submitted to the jury. The jury found that in publishing the Globe article Globe acted both negligently and with actual malice. Globe challenged both findings on appeal. In this court, Globe contends that the Court of Appeal erred in rejecting its challenges to these two findings.

We consider first the issue of actual malice. In doing so, we consider only actual malice as defined in decisions of the United States Supreme Court imposing constitutional restrictions on the right to recover damages for defamation. Because Globe has raised no issue concerning proof of malice as defined under state law (see, e.g., Civ.Code, § 48a, subd. 4(d)), we do not address what additional proof requirements, if any, state law may impose.

.   .   .

.   .   . When, as in this case, a finding of actual malice is based on the republication of a third party's defamatory falsehoods, "failure to investigate before publishing, even when a reasonably prudent person would have done so, is not sufficient." [   ] Nonetheless, the actual malice finding may be upheld " 'where there are obvious reasons to doubt the veracity of the informant or the accuracy of his reports' " [   ], and the republisher failed to interview obvious witnesses who could have confirmed or disproved the allegations [   ] or to consult relevant documentary sources ([*Harte-Hanks*] [failure to listen to tape]).

There were, to say the least, obvious reasons to doubt the accuracy of the Morrow book's accusation that Khawar killed Kennedy. The assassination of a nationally prominent politician, in the midst of his campaign for his party's nomination for the presidency, had been painstakingly and exhaustively investigated by both the FBI and state prosecutorial agencies. During this massive investigation, these agencies accumulated a vast quantity of evidence pointing to the guilt of Sirhan as the lone assassin. As a result, Sirhan alone was charged with Kennedy's murder. At Sirhan's trial, "it was undisputed that [Sirhan] fired the shot that killed Senator Kennedy" and "[t]he evidence also established conclusively that he shot the victims of the assault counts." (*People v. Sirhan*, [   ]) The jury returned a verdict finding beyond a reasonable doubt that Sirhan was guilty of first degree murder. On Sirhan's appeal from the resulting judgment of death, this court carefully reviewed the evidence and found it sufficient to sustain the first degree murder conviction. [   ] In asserting that Khawar, and not Sirhan, had killed Kennedy, the Morrow book was making the highly improbable claim that results of the official investigation, Sirhan's trial, and this court's decision on Sirhan's appeal, were all fundamentally mistaken.

Because there were obvious reasons to doubt the accuracy of the Morrow book's central claim, and because that claim was an inherently defamatory accusation against Khawar, the jury could properly conclude that Globe acted with actual malice in republishing that claim if it found also, as it impliedly did, that Globe failed to use readily available means to verify the accuracy of the claim by interviewing obvious witnesses who could have confirmed or disproved the allegations or by inspecting relevant documents or other evidence. [   ] The evidence at trial supports the jury's implied finding that neither Blackburn (who wrote the Globe article) nor Globe's editors made any such effort. [The court detailed the sources that could have been asked but were not. The court upheld the trial judge's rejection of the jury's finding that the report was neutral and accurate. The court found "no substantial evidence that either Blackburn or Globe's editors were aware of facts about Morrow that would justify unquestioning reliance on Morrow's highly improbable accusations."]

Having independently reviewed the record, we agree with the Court of Appeal that the evidence at trial strongly supports an inference that Globe purposefully avoided the truth and published the Globe article despite serious doubts regarding the truth of the accusation against Khawar. In short, we conclude that clear and convincing evidence supports the jury's finding that in republishing the Morrow book's false accusation against Khawar, Globe acted with actual malice—that is, with reckless disregard of whether the accusation was false or not.

.   .   .

The judgment of the Court of Appeal is affirmed.

GEORGE, C.J., and MOSK, BAXTER, WERDEGAR, CHIN and BROWN, JJ., concur.

Notes and Questions

1. How does the "neutral report" privilege discussed here differ from the common law privilege of fair and accurate report that we explored p. 985, supra? How often are the two likely to overlap?

2. Is the court's determination that plaintiff is not a public figure sound? For neutral report purposes why should it matter whether the plaintiff is a public figure? Does a privilege exist for a newspaper to report accurately that a senator has claimed that his otherwise anonymous hometown neighbor is threatening the senator's family?

3. What are the justifications offered for the privilege? What are the arguments against it? Is the proposed privilege inconsistent with *Gertz*? The court suggests that the source's insolvency is one argument against the privilege. Is that problem unique to this aspect of libel law? To libel law generally?

4. Context was relevant in the previous section. In a footnote here the court suggests that if the discussion had occurred in a book review a different result might be warranted. Why might that be?

5. *Edwards* summarized its privilege as follows: "Succinctly stated, when a responsible, prominent organization . . . makes serious charges against a public figure, the First Amendment protects the accurate and disinterested reporting of those charges, regardless of the reporter's private views of their validity." Consider each element in more detail.

"Responsible, prominent organization." What is there in the nature of this privilege that should require that the charge come from this type of source? For example, consider an even-handed story that reported a youth's charges that plaintiff police officer had coerced the youth to confess to a murder that he had not committed. The article carried the officer's denial and his suggestion that the youth, a "slow-spoken young man who has a speech impediment" (according to the reporter) with "the mind of a 9-year-old" (according to his mother) confessed to get attention. See Stockton Newspapers, Inc. v. San Joaquin Superior Court, 254 Cal.Rptr. 389 (App. 1988) (article protected).

What if the source of the defamation is a rumor? In *Martin v. Wilson Publishing Co.*, discussed in *Khawar*, the defendant paper reported on the reactions of a very small community whose residents were concerned that plaintiff was acquiring a vast percentage of the property in the community. Despite his announced good intentions for the community, plaintiff's actions made many residents apprehensive. The article stated that "[s]ome residents stretch available facts when they imagine Mr. Martin is connected with the 1974 rash of fires in the village." The court rejected any analogy to the common law fair report because the source was not identified: "To attempt to defend against a rumor is not unlike attempting to joust with a cloud. Publication of a rumor further fuels the continued repetition and does so in an especially egregious way by enshrining it in print." Nor would it adopt *Edwards* in this situation.

What if time is of the essence? Assume that there is a rumor in the community that a candidate in a forthcoming election is under investigation for having engaged in a massive fraud. The local paper runs an article before the election truthfully announcing that the rumor—which it repeats—is being widely discussed and then reporting that despite extensive efforts the paper found nothing to support the rumor. Might the candidate have an action? What if, in the above example, the newspaper in the course of normal election coverage truthfully reports the existence and content of the rumor but makes no effort to check its accuracy? See Frederick Schauer, Slightly Guilty, 1993 U.Chi.L.Forum 83.

Outside the election context, consider the example from 1 R. Sack, Sack on Defamation: Libel, Slander, and Related Problems 7–51 (3d ed. 2000): "Suppose a rumor surfaces that the chairman of a large publicly held brokerage firm is about to be indicted for securities fraud and, as a result, the stock of the company falls precipitously." Can a story explaining why the stock fell be reported without running the risk of liability for libel? Is this a stronger, or weaker, case for legal protection than the election situation? In a footnote to this example, Sack states: "The republisher may be expected to report that a rumor is no more than that and to state that the rumor is false if it is known to be." What does "known" mean here? Was the falsity "known" in *Martin*? Is this requirement consistent with the rationale of the privilege?

"Makes serious charges." Why must the charges be serious? Why is it not enough that charges are flying between two persons or groups? Beyond that, must the charges be "made" in public before the newspaper writes its story? *Edwards* arose in large part because the Audubon Society had its own media outlets and had published its own charges in the first instance.

Suppose there is no accusation in circulation until the reporter elicits it? In McManus v. Doubleday & Co., Inc., 513 F.Supp. 1383 (S.D.N.Y.1981), defendant's book asserted about the plaintiff priest, who was national coordinator for some Irish–American groups, that his "Irish Embassy file bears the mention 'homicidal tendencies.'" The information was said to have come from an interview with an Embassy official that the author initiated. The court rejected the neutral report defense. The judge first quoted *Edwards* for the view that the privilege was to keep the public "fully informed about controversies that often rage around sensitive issues." Unlike the reporter in *Edwards,* "who simply reported an autonomous news event, albeit with certain factual embellishments, [the author here] was engaged in purely investigative reporting. Unlike *Edwards,* no controversy raged around the libelous statements before the reporter entered the scene. . . . Since there is no indication in the *Edwards* opinion that the neutral reportage privilege was meant to cover investigative reporting, and since including reports of such journalist-induced charges within the protection of the privilege is unnecessary for promoting the purposes of *Edwards,* the freer reporting of raging controversies," the court denied the privilege. Would the analysis differ if the official had come to the author and volunteered the information?

"Against a public figure." This element has already been considered.

"Accurate and disinterested reporting of those charges." It seems agreed (except possibly in the rumor situation) that the publication must take no position on where the truth lies in the dispute. For an extended analysis of a case rejecting the privilege on the ground that the publication in fact took sides, see *Cianci,* p. 1064, supra.

What if, after one side attacks publicly, the other side refuses to comment? How, if at all, is the local newspaper to report this situation? Can the newspaper preserve the privilege by including in the story the accurate statement that "repeated phone calls to [the plaintiff or an attorney] were not returned"?

What if the article is indeed written with scrupulous fairness by a writer who does not honestly believe one side? In the *Stockton Newspapers* case, for example, the reporter admitted having doubts about the truth of the youth's story. Some have argued that a neutral report is of little use to the public because in most situations readers cannot judge the credibility of the sources being quoted. "Where the reporter has knowledge of falsity or serious doubts about the truth of a charge, meeting the 'actual malice' test, the reporter should be under a duty to report that information. Where there is reason to know the falsity of a statement, the reporter must do more than merely print a refutation." Note, The Privilege of Neutral Reportage, 1978 Utah L.Rev. 347.

As noted, virtually every element of *Edwards* has been interpreted narrowly by some courts. These disagreements may induce courts to expand the common law privilege to avoid entering the *Edwards* controversy. In Chapin v. Knight–Ridder, Inc., 993 F.2d 1087 (4th Cir.1993), for example, the court concluded that the state's fair report privilege would cover a report of the unofficial remarks of a congressman, and noted that until "we face a case with a 'prominent, responsible' but nongovernmental speaker, we need not cast our lot one way or the other on the full *Edwards* fair reportage privilege."

Broadcasting. In print journalism, the editor is able to make a considered judgment about what outside submissions warrant publication, as with letters to the editor or syndicated material. See Franklin, Libel and Letters to the Editor: Toward an Open Forum, 57 Colo.L.Rev. 651 (1986). In broadcasting, with live call-in shows, that element of reflection and the ability to identify the persons submitting views are missing. So far as defamation is concerned it will be difficult to establish actual malice or negligence if the broadcaster has no opportunity to review the material for libel or falsity before it is broadcast. Could a court properly conclude that using a live call-in format was itself actionable because it gave irresponsible callers the opportunity to defame others over the airwaves? (The much-publicized delay buttons are much more suited to preventing vulgarity than to allowing the person in charge to prevent subtle defamations.) See, e.g., Pacella v. Milford Radio Corp., 462 N.E.2d 355 (Mass.App.1984), affirmed by an equally divided court 476 N.E.2d 595 (Mass.), cert. denied 474 U.S. 844 (1985) (radio talk show host not liable for failing to cut off anonymous speaker).

G.   REFORM PROPOSALS

1.   NEED FOR REFORM?

Plaintiffs, defendants and the public have had occasion to rethink the current state of the law of defamation.

Plaintiffs. As the sections on doctrine suggest, plaintiffs have had a most difficult time winning cases under the "actual malice" rule. Their success rate, leaving aside a relatively small number of settlements, runs under 10%. Plaintiffs whose primary interest was in showing the falsity of the story rather than in obtaining dollars, might have been satisfied if the system had offered them a chance to prove that falsity. But with over 75% of the cases resulting in summary judgments for the defendant, the issue of truth or falsity is rarely decided. A case that produces a jury verdict of falsity but without actual malice, is a rarity.

Plaintiffs who can get past summary judgment succeed with juries well over 50% of the time. But defendants appeal virtually all jury losses and obtain reversals or partial relief in some 70% of the cases. Most of these lead to dismissals; a few lead to new trials or reduced awards.

Private plaintiffs who seek to recover only for actual injury fare somewhat better because they get to juries more often, win before juries at least as often, and are not likely to lose their awards on appeal for failure to prove negligence.

Defendants. As a group, defendants obviously cannot complain about their overall success rate in these cases. But they do contend that the constitutional protections should operate earlier in the litigation process; that pretrial discovery is expensive; and that appeals are necessary to obtain reversals of so many plaintiffs' trial judgments.

Larger media stress the high costs of successful defense and suggest that they are being diverted from the investigative reporting that they should be doing by the demands of litigation. The largest judgment upheld on appeal has been $24 million in Sprague v. Walter, 656 A.2d 890 (Pa.Super.1995). The court upheld awards against Philadelphia Newspapers, Inc. of $2.5 million in compensatory damages but reduced a punitive award from $31.5 million to $21.5 million. After a failed effort to appeal to the state supreme court, the newspaper filed a petition for certiorari. The case was settled at that stage for an undisclosed sum. An award of $10 million was upheld in Prozeralik v. Capital Cities Communications, Inc., 635 N.Y.S.2d 913 (App.Div. 1995).

The trial median award in all libel cases tried over two decades was $210,000, and more than half of these awards were overturned on appeal. The median sum actually paid during this period was $70,000. (The averages were $2.8 million and $271,000, respectively.) See Libel Defense Research Center, Report of Trials and Damages, Jan. 31, 1999 (covering 1980–98).

Smaller media claim concern about the very fact of being sued and having to spend money for legal defense. They assert that a judgment of tens of thousands of dollars, much less millions, might bankrupt them— and that insurance is expensive because of the large defense costs (but that may account for the low payouts). Smaller media, in particular, claim that insurance is not much protection for several reasons. First, libel insurance is frequently written with a "deductible" or retained exposure under which the insured bears the first several thousand dollars of expenses in the case. This amount is intended to cause the management to consider carefully the material it is about to run and whether it wants to engage in investigative reporting at all. Second, one of the few major libel insurers now requires that in addition to the "deductible," insureds bear 20% of the legal expenses throughout the case, whatever the outcome. Smaller media claim the problem with both these limits on coverage is that the publication may suffer uncovered losses whenever it is sued, even if it ultimately wins the case. Thus, smaller media say that they are more likely to stop doing investigative reporting or to avoid running stories that may antagonize litigious persons or groups in the community. One counter-pressure is the increased willingness of courts to award legal fees to defendants who win baseless suits.

Public. If the defendants are likely to perceive the situation as "chilling" and to respond by reducing their coverage of important activities, the public may lose by learning less true information about how our government and society are functioning. Although occasional stories purport to document the "chilling effect," it is something that major media figures do not like to talk about and often deny. Smaller media, on the other hand, do assert that this is affecting their coverage.

But note that, to the extent the public now benefits from the constitutional protections we have been considering, these benefits are being financed by the victims of the defamations who cannot recover for the harm they have suffered. Should the public be paying in some way for the harms individual victims are suffering so that the public can get its "uninhibited, robust, and wide-open" debate? Recall Justice White's comments, p. 1034, supra. For a discussion of this line of thought with explorations of various funding mechanisms, see Schauer, Uncoupling Free Speech, 92 Colum.L.Rev. 1321 (1992).

Data. The amount of litigation is tiny compared to the physical harm area. According to the study cited at p. 1092, supra, in the decade of the 1980s, 213 libel cases were tried by jury to a verdict. Another 22 jury trials were ended by directed verdicts. Data suggest that about 3 in 4 cases that are started do not get to the trial stage because motions to dismiss (generally state law privileges) or summary judgments (constitutional privileges) derail them. This would suggest that some 1,000 cases were commenced against media during the decade based on 254 trials begun (including here 19 bench trials).

Of the 213 jury trials that reached verdict, plaintiffs got verdicts in 158 or 74% of the cases. The plaintiffs in all the trials begun were public in 144 cases and private in 97 of the cases in which that information was available. Note that this is probably not the ratio in which suits are brought. Far more suits brought by public plaintiffs are dismissed in pretrial stages than are suits brought by private plaintiffs—at least if the private plaintiffs are not seeking presumed or punitive damages. Plaintiffs prevailed at trial in 64% of the actual malice cases and 73% of the negligence cases.

Recall that not all plaintiffs who prove actual malice will recover punitive damages. Some states bar punitive damages in all cases; a few bar them in cases involving communications. In others, including the important state of New York, plaintiffs seeking punitive damages must prove, in addition to actual malice, some further element, such as spite or ill will—something difficult to show in media cases.

In post-trial motions, the plaintiff's verdict was changed in 45 of the 158 cases: 16 judgments n.o.v.; 26 remittiturs; and 3 new trials. Of a total of 147 appeals, 78 (53%) were reversed (and either dismissed or remanded for new trials) and 25 (17%) had damages reduced. This 70 percent reversal rate is substantially higher than for civil litigation generally. Plaintiffs either obtained outright affirmance or had a reduced award affirmed in approximately 60 jury cases.

Taking the broad picture, it seems clear that if the defendant cannot prevail before trial, at least one appeal lies ahead for the vast majority. It is also clear that the awards of jury (and judge as well) are very unlikely to survive that appeal. Much expensive legal effort has been exerted by all concerned to reach a result that often produces no award or requires a retrial. The vast bulk of libel insurance is not paid to plaintiffs but is absorbed in defense and legal expenses. And reputations have not been retrieved, even in cases of clear falsity.

From the standpoint of the individual newspaper or broadcaster, one might focus on the variance in the awards between the medians and the averages. The award need bear no relationship to any obvious anchors, such as the medical bills and lost earnings found in physical injury cases. It is thus no surprise that once a case is begun, little expense is spared in defending it. It is little solace that "most" awards are reduced or overturned on appeal. In an individual case an award may be affirmed on appeal that may seriously impede the defendant's continued viability.

2.   PROPOSED REFORMS

By and large, the proposals for change have focused on two main avenues: constitutional change at the doctrinal level and statutory or common law changes that seek to work within the existing constitutional framework. (A third approach is already in existence with some courts trying interstitial changes such as channeling discovery to a single issue that might be dispositive or assessing legal fees against parties who are not proceeding in good faith.)

Changes in case law. In the first category are the suggestions of either overruling *New York Times* and/or *Gertz* or cutting back on their scope or level of protection. This is usually tied to some proposed change in damage rules. In the *Greenmoss* case, p. 1076, supra, Justice White observed that the law had evolved in an unsatisfactory way:

> The *New York Times* rule thus countenances two evils: first, the stream of information about public officials and public affairs is polluted and often remains polluted by false information; and second, the

reputation and professional life of the defeated plaintiff may be destroyed by falsehoods that might have been avoided with a reasonable effort to investigate the facts. In terms of the First Amendment and reputational interest at stake, these seem grossly perverse results.

He noted that there was "much talk" about "liability without fault and the unfairness of presuming damages." But if the goal was to protect the press "from intimidating damages liability that might lead to excessive timidity, . . . it is evident that the Court engaged in severe overkill" in both *New York Times* and *Gertz.*

Justice White then suggested that the Court might better have (1) barred or limited punitive damages; or (2) barred or limited presumed damages. In such a situation strict liability could have been retained and the defamed public official "upon proving falsity, could at least have had a judgment to that effect. . . . He might have also recovered a modest amount, enough perhaps to pay his litigation expenses."

He doubted that defendants would be "unduly chilled by having to pay for the actual damages caused to those they defame." Other "commercial enterprises in this country not in the business of disseminating information must pay for the damage they cause as a cost of doing business, and it is difficult to argue that the United States did not have a free and vigorous press before the rule in *New York Times* was announced. In any event, the *New York Times* standard was formulated to protect the press from the chilling danger of numerous large damage awards. Nothing in the central rationale behind *New York Times* demands an absolute immunity from suits to establish the falsity of a defamatory misstatement about a public figure where the plaintiff cannot make out a jury case of actual malice."

As for *Gertz,* Justice White observed:

. . . I doubt that the decision in that case has made any measurable contribution to First Amendment or reputational values since its announcement. Nor am I sure that it has saved the press a great deal of money. . . . I suspect the press would be no worse off financially if the common-law rules were to apply and if the judiciary were careful to insist that damages awards be kept within bounds. A legislative solution to the damages problem would also be appropriate. Moreover, since libel plaintiffs are very likely more interested in clearing their names than in damages, I doubt that limiting recoveries would deter or be unfair to them. In any event, I cannot assume that the press, as successful and powerful as it is, will be intimidated into withholding news that by decent journalistic standards it believes to be true.

Is there any reason why judicial control over damages should be more difficult here than in tort law generally?

For other suggestions that the focus be on control of damages rather than changing the rules of liability, see, e.g., Epstein, Was *New York Times v. Sullivan* Wrong? 53 U.Chi.L.Rev. 782 (1986); Anderson, Reputation, Compensation and Proof, 25 Wm. & Mary L.Rev. 747 (1984).

Proposals within existing law. The second type of change is the statutory approach within existing constitutional lines. Aside from damage limitation plans, these have tended to fall into one of two groups. One centers on a type of declaratory judgment action that permits an adjudication of the truth or falsity of the defamatory charge without addressing questions of fault. In this first group, critics have disagreed over whether the shift from a damage action to a declaratory judgment action should occur at the plaintiff's behest or whether the defendant should control the choice. Compare Franklin, A Declaratory Judgment Alternative to Current Libel Law, 74 Calif.L.Rev. 809 (1986) (proposing that plaintiff control that decision) with Barrett, Declaratory Judgment for Libel: A Better Alternative, 74 Calif.L.Rev. 847 (1986) (proposing that the choice be given to defendants).

Judge Pierre Leval, who presided over the famous libel case brought by General William Westmoreland against CBS, argued afterwards that a plaintiff could get around the constitutional strictures of the *New York Times* case by bringing an action for declaratory judgment and explicitly stating that no damages were being sought. Of course, that alone would not suffice unless state law permitted such an action. Leval, The No–Money, No–Fault Libel Suit: Keeping *Sullivan* in Its Proper Place, 101 Harv.L.Rev. 1287 (1988). The article also discusses negotiated agreements in which the parties might agree to dispense with the actual malice rule but litigate falsity.

The second approach centers on retraction and reply as ways to reduce or eliminate the harm done, working with the common law remedies discussed at 995, supra. See Ackerman, Bringing Coherence to Defamation Law through Uniform Legislation: The Search for an Elegant Solution, 72 N.C.L.Rev. 291 (1994). For an elaborate empirical study of libel litigation and a proposal that libel cases be removed from the damage context and placed in the setting of some alternative mode of dispute resolution, see R. Bezanson, G. Cranberg, and J. Soloski, Libel Law and the Press: Myth and Reality (1987). Professor, later Dean, Bezanson was the reporter and drafter of the proposals developed by the Uniform Commissioners.

Proposals introduced in several state legislatures to implement libel reform have rarely gotten out of committee. See generally, Bezanson, The Libel Tort Today, 45 Wash. & Lee L.Rev. 535 (1988) and LeBel, Reforming the Tort of Defamation: An Accommodation of the Competing Interests within the Current Constitutional Framework, 66 Nebr.L.Rev. 249 (1987).

Most commentators and critics have concluded that reform must come from the legislative branch. For a differing view, see Anderson, Is Libel Law Worth Reforming?, 140 U.Pa.L.Rev. 487 (1991), agreeing that the "present law of libel is a failure," and then suggesting that the Supreme Court itself should be "the principal reformer of libel law:"

> The Court would prescribe new accommodations of speech and reputational interests as a matter of constitutional law. It might decree, for example, that the Constitution requires no showing of fault if the remedy sought is only a declaration of falsity. It might announce new

limitations of damages, with corresponding reductions in plaintiff's burdens. The Court might devise a more sophisticated accommodation, one that addresses the dynamics and costs of libel litigation as well as questions of fault and remedies. It might explicitly authorize trial judges to decide at the outset whether the challenged statement was sufficiently factual, harmful, and remote from truth to be justifiably burdened by further litigation. Acknowledging that effective protection of speech requires a diminished role for juries, it might authorize even more aggressive use of summary judgment and judicial review. The Court might even take the assessment of damages out of the jury's hands.

Comprehensive law reform is not a familiar task for the Supreme Court. It is not accustomed to reviewing systems of law rather than specific rules. Case-by-case adjudication of specific constitutional issues does not invite advocacy on the redesign of an entire branch of tort law. Those are weighty objections, but they come too late. Over the past quarter century, case by case and bit by bit, the Court has thoroughly revised the common law of libel. It has created not merely a few constitutional limitations on state tort rules, but a matrix of substantive principles, evidentiary rules, and de facto innovations in judge-jury roles and other procedural matters. These are all constitutionally based and can only be changed by those who have the power to change constitutional rules. Having created the system that is the source of so much dissatisfaction, the Court cannot now demur on the ground that law reform is not its business.

Are you convinced that wholesale re-working of *New York Times* and its progeny is warranted?

CHAPTER XIV

PROTECTING PRIVACY

Privacy is a relatively new legal concept with many facets. We focus first on disclosure of true statements that an individual would rather not have publicly disseminated. This is sometimes called the tort of "public disclosure of private facts." We then turn to statements that present the plaintiff in a "false light," a tort that recalls defamation. We turn next to the "intrusion" aspect of privacy to ask how far others may go either to obtain information from unwilling sources or to impart information to unwilling recipients. We conclude with a section in which, although the word "privacy" is used, it appears that the plaintiffs are relying more upon a notion of controlling "publicity" than of privacy.

The idea that privacy should be legally protected is traceable to a law review article by Louis D. Brandeis and his law partner, Samuel D. Warren, entitled The Right to Privacy, 4 Harv.L.Rev. 193 (1890). The authors, reacting to the editorial practices of Boston newspapers, particularly a report about a family gathering that the Warrens had thought was private, made clear their concerns:

> The press is overstepping in every direction the obvious bounds of propriety and of decency. Gossip is no longer the resource of the idle and of the vicious, but has become a trade, which is pursued with industry as well as effrontery. To satisfy a prurient taste the details of sexual relations are spread broadcast in the columns of the daily papers. To occupy the indolent, column upon column is filled with idle gossip, which can only be procured by intrusion upon the domestic circle. . . . When personal gossip attains the dignity of print, and crowds the space available for matters of real interest to the community, what wonder that the ignorant and thoughtless mistake its relative importance. Easy of comprehension, appealing to that weak side of human nature which is never wholly cast down by the misfortunes and frailties of our neighbors, no one can be surprised that it usurps the place of interest in brains capable of other things. Triviality destroys at once robustness of thought and delicacy of feelings. No enthusiasm can flourish, no generous impulse can survive under its blighting influence.

Working with a variety of rather remote precedents from other areas of law, the authors developed an argument that courts should recognize an action for invasion of privacy by media publication.

The theory was rejected in the first major case to consider it. In Roberson v. Rochester Folding Box Co., 64 N.E. 442 (N.Y.1902), the defendants, a flour company and a box company, obtained a good likeness of the plaintiff, a very pretty girl, and reproduced it on their advertising posters. Plaintiff said she was humiliated and suffered great distress. The court, 4–3, rejected a common law privacy action on grounds that suggested concern about innovating after so many centuries; an inability to see how the doctrine, once accepted, could be judicially limited to appropriate situations; and skepticism about finding liability for an action that might actually please some potential "victims." The Warren and Brandeis article was discussed at length, but the court concluded that the precedents relied upon were too remote to sustain the proposed right.

The outcry was immediate. At its next session, the New York legislature created a statutory right of privacy (New York Civil Rights Law, §§ 50 and 51). The basic provision was that "a person, firm or corporation that uses for advertising purposes, or the purposes of trade, the name, portrait or picture of any living person without having first obtained the written consent of such person, or if a minor of his or her parent or guardian, is guilty of a misdemeanor." The other section provided for an injunction and created an action for compensatory and punitive damages.

The unique New York development. Since New York is such an important state in law generally and in tort law in particular, it is important to note at the outset that the New York experience has been substantially different from that of the vast majority of states, which developed a common law jurisprudence. New York's highest court still adheres to positions that deny the opportunity for common law development in the privacy area—and look almost exclusively to the statute to resolve most of the tort claims that we explore in this chapter. For example, in Freihofer v. Hearst Corp., 480 N.E.2d 349 (N.Y.1985), plaintiff husband in a divorce action sued defendant newspaper for stories relating to the action. The stories were based upon the reporter's having read some court documents that, by statute, were to be kept confidential by court officials. Since the reporter did not violate the confidentiality statute, the court held that the only basis for liability would be the privacy statute. The articles were not published for "advertising purposes" and were not for "purposes of trade" even though they were published to help the paper make a profit. The critical factor under the controlling statute "is the content of the published article in terms of whether it is newsworthy, which is a question of law, and not the defendant's motive to increase circulation."

In Stephano v. News Group Publications, Inc., 474 N.E.2d 580 (N.Y. 1984), the court held that the newsworthiness exception in the statute "applies not only to reports of political happenings and social trends [ ], but also to news stories and articles of consumer interest including developments in the fashion world." The court rejected an action by a male model whose photograph in a "bomber jacket" was used in a magazine's "Best Bets" column. The text included the approximate price of the jacket, the name of the designer, and the names of three stores at which the jacket could be bought. The court concluded that the use was not an advertisement in disguise. Similar information was used in reviews and in news announcements of new products or new books or movies. "In short, the plaintiff has not presented any facts which would set this particular article apart from the numerous other legitimate news items concerning new products.''

In Messenger ex rel. Messenger v. Gruner & Jahr Printing and Publishing, 727 N.E.2d 549 (N.Y.), cert. denied 121 S.Ct. 57 (2000), a 14-year-old aspiring model brought suit after the magazine YM (Young and Modern) used pictures it had taken of her on a photo shoot to illustrate its ''Love Crisis'' column. The pictures of plaintiff were captioned so as to correspond to events recounted in a letter from another 14-year-old, identified only as ''Mortified,'' who claimed that she had sex with two of her boyfriend's friends as well as her boyfriend after getting drunk at a party. Although plaintiff had allowed her picture to be taken, no consent form had been signed by a parent or guardian.

The court explained that, even if an article or other piece is newsworthy, liability may be found for a photograph accompanying it if either there is no real relationship between the picture and the article, or if the article is an advertisement in disguise. Distinguishing older cases involving largely fictitious biographies of the famous that held that ''substantially fictionalized'' accounts could also produce liability, the majority instead analogized the model's situation to more recent cases in which a real relationship had been found between a photo and the article it was used to illustrate. Messenger ''may not recover under the Civil Rights Law, regardless of any false implication that might be reasonably drawn from the use of her photographs to illustrate the article.'' Otherwise liability under Civil Rights Law § 51 would ''become indistinguishable from the common-law tort of false light invasion of privacy,'' a tort not recognized in New York because of the statute.

To avoid the complications of the New York statute, this chapter will focus on common law cases. We turn now to the type of privacy invasion that lay at the core of the Warren and Brandeis article.

A. PUBLIC DISCLOSURE OF PRIVATE FACTS

1. STATE TORT ANALYSIS

In the early twentieth century, other states, perhaps learning from the New York experience, slowly began to develop a common law right to privacy that was not influenced by statutory language and not limited to advertising invasions. In addition to an action for commercial use of one's name (discussed later in this chapter), the courts also developed an action for truthful use of plaintiff's name in situations that were thought to be outside the areas of legitimate public concern. The action for invasion of privacy by publication of true editorial material began to take hold during the 1920s and early 1930s.

Beginning in the late 1930s, however, courts became more attentive to the Supreme Court's expanding protection of expression through the First Amendment. Operating on a common law level, the state courts tended to broaden protection for the media by taking a narrow view of what were legitimately private areas. This "newsworthiness" defense expanded because courts were reluctant to impose normative standards of what should be newsworthy. Instead, they leaned toward a descriptive definition that protected whatever an editor had decided would interest his or her readers. See, Comment, The Right of Privacy: Normative–Descriptive Confusion in the Defense of Newsworthiness, 30 U.Chi.L.Rev. 722 (1963). By the 1960s, it was unclear whether this branch of the action for invasion of privacy had any remaining vitality. See, Kalven, Privacy in Tort Law—Were Warren and Brandeis Wrong?, 31 Law and Contemporary Problems 326 (1966); Bloustein, Privacy, Tort Law, and the Constitution: Is Warren and Brandeis' Tort Petty and Unconstitutional As Well?, 46 Texas L.Rev. 611 (1968). Also, by the 1960s, the Supreme court was beginning to apply First Amendment protection in tort cases, beginning with *New York Times Co. v. Sullivan*, p. 1000, supra.

Yet, also during the late 1960s and early 1970s, society began sensing that privacy as a general social value was being threatened in different ways by the encroachment of computers, data banks, and electronic devices, as well as the media. Other aspects of privacy were also protected in Supreme Court cases dealing with birth control, abortion, and other personal issues—though these involved claims seeking to protect areas of privacy from government interference.

We begin our consideration with an exploration of state law that is developing in the so-called "public disclosure" tort. We will then turn to the constitutional developments in this area.

Haynes v. Alfred A. Knopf, Inc.
United States Court of Appeals, Seventh Circuit, 1993.
8 F.3d 1222.

[The book, The Promised Land: The Great Black Migration and How It Changed America, by Nicholas Lemann, used the life of Ruby Lee Daniels to illustrate its themes about the social, political, and economic effects of the movement of blacks from the rural South to the cities of the North between 1940 and 1970. The author switched between general discussion of that migration and discussion of the migration's personal dimensions as reflected in Daniels's descriptions of her life and experiences, beginning when she was a sharecropper in Mississippi and progressing through her move to Chicago and her life there over the next 40 years. Among the things she discussed was her relationship with her ex-husband, Luther Haynes. She depicted him as a man who drank heavily, who neglected his children, could not keep a job, was unfaithful, and eventually left her for another woman. The court quoted one excerpt:

> It got to the point where [Luther] would go out on Friday evenings after picking up his paycheck and Ruby would hope he wouldn't come home, because she knew he would be drunk. On the Friday evenings when he did come home—over the years Ruby developed a devastating

imitation of Luther, and could re-create the scene quite vividly—he would walk into the apartment, put on a record and turn up the volume, and saunter into their bedroom, a bottle in one hand and a cigarette in the other, in the mood for love. On one such night, Ruby's last child, Kevin, was conceived. Kevin always had something wrong with him—he was very moody, he was scrawny, and he had a severe speech impediment. Ruby was never able to find out exactly what the problem was, but she blamed it on Luther; all that alcohol must have gotten into his sperm, she said.

Haynes admitted many of the incidents in the book, but alleged that they had all occurred 25 years earlier, and that since then he had reformed, remarried, and lived an exemplary life. He and his present wife, Dorothy, sued the author and publisher for libel and invasion of privacy. The trial court granted summary judgment for the defendants. The court first held that the plaintiffs had no libel claim because the defamatory statements about them were substantially true. It then turned to the privacy claim.]

Before POSNER, CHIEF JUDGE, and MANION and WOOD, CIRCUIT JUDGES.

POSNER, CHIEF JUDGE.

. . .

The major claim in the complaint, and the focus of the appeal, is . . . invasion of the right of privacy. In tort law the term "right of privacy" covers several distinct wrongs. Using a celebrity's (or other person's) name or picture in advertising without his consent. [ ] Tapping someone's phone, or otherwise invading a person's private space. [ ] Harassing a celebrity by following her too closely, albeit on a public street. [ ] Casting a person in a false light by publicizing details of the person's life that while true are so selected or highlighted as to convey a misleading impression of the person's character. [ ] Publicizing personal facts that while true and not misleading are so intimate that their disclosure to the public is deeply embarrassing to the person thus exposed and is perceived as gratuitous by the community. [ ] The last, the publicizing of personal facts, is the aspect of the invasion of privacy charged by the Hayneses.

Even people who have nothing rationally to be ashamed of can be mortified by the publication of intimate details of their life. Most people in no way deformed or disfigured would nevertheless be deeply upset if nude photographs of themselves were published in a newspaper or a book. They feel the same way about photographs of their sexual activities, however "normal," or about a narrative of those activities, or about having their medical records publicized. Although it is well known that every human being defecates, no adult human being in our society wants a newspaper to show a picture of him defecating. The desire for privacy illustrated by these examples is a mysterious but deep fact about human personality. It deserves and in our society receives legal protection. The nature of the injury shows, by the way, that the defendants are wrong to argue that this branch of the right of privacy requires proof of special damages. [ ]

But this is not the character of the depictions of the Hayneses in *The Promised Land*. Although the plaintiffs claim that the book depicts their "sex life" and "ridicules" Luther Haynes's lovemaking (the reference is to the passage we quoted in which the author refers to Ruby's "devastating imitation" of Luther's manner when he would come home Friday nights in an amorous mood), these characterizations are misleading. No sexual act is described in the book. No intimate details are revealed. Entering one's bedroom with a bottle in one hand and a cigarette in the other is not foreplay. Ruby's speculation that Kevin's problems may have been due to Luther's having been a heavy drinker is not the narration of a sexual act.

. . .

[The branch of privacy law in this case] is concerned with the propriety of stripping away the veil of privacy with which we cover the embarrassing, the shameful, the tabooed, truths about us. [   ] The revelations in the book are not about the intimate details of the Hayneses' life. They are about misconduct, in particular Luther's. (There is very little about Dorothy in the book, apart from the fact that she had an affair with Luther while he was still married to Ruby and that they eventually became and have remained lawfully married.) The revelations are about his heavy drinking, his unstable employment, his adultery, his irresponsible and neglectful behavior toward his wife and children. So we must consider cases in which the right of privacy has been invoked as a shield against the revelation of previous misconduct.

Two early cases illustrate the range of judicial thinking. In Melvin v. Reid, 297 Pac. 91 (Cal.App.1931), the plaintiff was a former prostitute, who had been prosecuted but acquitted of murder. She later had married and (she alleged) for seven years had lived a blameless respectable life in a community in which her lurid past was unknown—when all was revealed in a movie about the murder case which used her maiden name. The court held that these allegations stated a claim for invasion of privacy. The Hayneses' claim is similar although less dramatic. They have been a respectable married couple for two decades. Luther's alcohol problem is behind him. He has steady employment as a doorman. His wife is a nurse, and in 1990 he told Lemann that the couple's combined income was $60,000 a year. He is not in trouble with the domestic relations court. He is a deacon of his church. He has come a long way from sharecropping in Mississippi and public housing in Chicago and he and his wife want to bury their past just as Mrs. Melvin wanted to do and in *Melvin v. Reid* was held entitled to do. [   ] In Luther Haynes's own words, from his deposition, "I know I haven't been no angel, but since almost 30 years ago I have turned my life completely around. I stopped the drinking and all this bad habits and stuff like that, which I deny, some of [it] I didn't deny, because I have changed my life. It take me almost 30 years to change it and I am deeply in my church. I look good in the eyes of my church members and my community. Now, what is going to happen now when this public reads this garbage which I didn't tell Mr. Lemann to write? Then all this is going to go down the drain. And I worked like a son of a gun to build myself up in a good reputation and he has torn it down."

But with *Melvin v. Reid* compare *Sidis v. F–R Publishing Corp.*, 113 F.2d 806 (2d Cir.1940), another old case but one more consonant with modern thinking about the proper balance between the right of privacy and the freedom of the press. A child prodigy had flamed out; he was now an eccentric recluse. The New Yorker ran a "where is he now" article about him. The article, entitled "April Fool," did not reveal any misconduct by Sidis but it depicted him in mocking tones as a comical failure, in much the same way that the report of Ruby's "devastating imitation" of the amorous Luther Haynes could be thought to have depicted him as a comical failure, albeit with sinister consequences absent from Sidis's case. The invasion of Sidis's privacy was palpable. But the publisher won. No intimate physical details of Sidis's life had been revealed; and on the other side was the undoubted newsworthiness of a child prodigy, as of a woman prosecuted for murder. Sidis, unlike Mrs. Melvin, was not permitted to bury his past.

. . .

. . . People who do not desire the limelight and do not deliberately choose a way of life or course of conduct calculated to thrust them into it nevertheless have no legal right to extinguish it if the experiences that have befallen them are newsworthy, even if they would prefer that those experiences be kept private. The possibility of an involuntary loss of privacy is recognized in the modern formulations of this branch of the privacy tort, which require not only that the private facts publicized be such as would make a reasonable person deeply offended by such publicity but also that they be facts in which the public has no legitimate interest. [　]

The two criteria, offensiveness and newsworthiness, are related. An individual, and more pertinently perhaps the community, is most offended by the publication of intimate personal facts when the community has no interest in them beyond the voyeuristic thrill of penetrating the wall of privacy that surrounds a stranger. The reader of a book about the black migration to the North would have no legitimate interest in the details of Luther Haynes's sex life; but no such details are disclosed. Such a reader does have a legitimate interest in the aspects of Luther's conduct that the book reveals. For one of Lemann's major themes is the transposition virtually intact of a sharecropper morality characterized by a family structure "matriarchal and elastic" and by an "extremely unstable" marriage bond to the slums of the northern cities, and the interaction, largely random and sometimes perverse, of that morality with governmental programs to alleviate poverty. Public aid policies discouraged Ruby and Luther from living together, public housing policies precipitated a marriage doomed to fail. No detail in the book claimed to invade the Hayneses' privacy is not germane to the story that the author wanted to tell, a story not only of legitimate but of transcendent public interest.

The Hayneses question whether the linkage between the author's theme and their private life really is organic. They point out that many social histories do not mention individuals at all, let alone by name. That is true. Much of social science, including social history, proceeds by abstraction, aggregation, and quantification rather than by case studies.   .   .   . But it would be absurd to suggest that cliometric or other aggregative, impersonal methods of doing social history are the only proper way to go about it and presumptuous to claim even that they are the best way. Lemann's book has been praised to the skies by distinguished scholars, among them black scholars covering a large portion of the ideological spectrum—Henry Louis Gates, Jr., William Julius Wilson, and Patricia Williams. Lemann's methodology places the individual case history at center stage. If he cannot tell the story of Ruby Daniels without waivers from every person who she thinks did her wrong, he cannot write this book.

Well, argue the Hayneses, at least Lemann could have changed their names. But the use of pseudonyms would not have gotten Lemann and Knopf off the legal hook. The details of the Hayneses' lives recounted in the book would identify them unmistakably to anyone who has known the Hayneses well for a long time (members of their families, for example), or who knew them before they got married; and no more is required.   .   .   . Lemann would have had to change some, perhaps many, of the details. But then he would no longer have been writing history. He would have been writing fiction. The nonquantitative study of living persons would be abolished as a category of scholarship, to be replaced by the sociological novel. That is a genre with a distinguished history punctuated by famous names, such as Dickens, Zola, Stowe, Dreiser, Sinclair, Steinbeck, and Wolfe, but we do not think that the law of privacy makes it (or that the First Amendment would permit the law of privacy to make it) the exclusive format for a social history of living persons that tells their story rather than treating them as data points in a statistical study. Reporting the true facts about real people is necessary to "obviate any impression that the problems raised in the [book] are remote or hypothetical." [ ] And surely a composite portrait of ghetto residents would be attacked as racial stereotyping.

The Promised Land does not afford the reader a titillating glimpse of tabooed activities. The tone is decorous and restrained. Painful though it is for the Hayneses to see a past they would rather forget brought into the public view, the public needs the information conveyed by the book, including the information about Luther and Dorothy Haynes, in order to evaluate the profound social and political questions that the book raises. Given the *Cox* decision [discussed below], moreover, all the discreditable facts about the Hayneses that are contained in judicial records are beyond the power of tort law to conceal; and the disclosure of those facts alone would strip away the Hayneses' privacy as effectively as *The Promised Land* has done. (This case, it could be argued, has stripped them of their privacy, since their story is now part of a judicial record—the record of this case.) We do not think it is an answer that Lemann got his facts from Ruby Daniels rather than from judicial records. The courts got the facts from Ruby. We cannot see what difference it makes that Lemann went to the source.

Ordinarily the evaluation and comparison of offensiveness and newsworthiness would be, like other questions of the application of a legal standard to the facts of a particular case, matters for a jury, not for a judge on a motion for summary judgment. But summary judgment is properly granted to a defendant when on the basis of the evidence obtained in pretrial discovery no reasonable jury could render a verdict for the plaintiff, [   ], and that is the situation here.   .   .   .

Illinois has been a follower rather than a leader in recognizing claims of invasion of privacy. [   ] The plaintiffs are asking us to innovate boldly in the name of the Illinois courts, and such a request is better addressed to those courts than to a federal court.   .   .   .

Does it follow, as the Hayneses' lawyer asked us rhetorically at oral argument, that a journalist who wanted to write a book about contemporary sexual practices could include the intimate details of named living persons' sexual acts without the persons' consent? Not necessarily, although the revelation of such details in the memoirs of former spouses and lovers is common enough and rarely provokes a lawsuit even when the former spouse or lover is still alive. The core of the branch of privacy law with which we deal in this case is the protection of those intimate physical details the publicizing of which would be not merely embarrassing and painful but deeply shocking to the average person subjected to such exposure. The public has a legitimate interest in sexuality, but that interest may be outweighed in such a case by the injury to the sensibilities of the person made use of by the author in such a way. [   ] At least the balance would be sufficiently close to preclude summary judgment for the author and publisher. [   ]

The judgment for the defendants is affirmed.

Notes and Questions

1. Compare *Melvin v. Reid* and *Sidis*. Are the cases distinguishable or are they in conflict?

2. Does the plaintiff in *Haynes* lose because the material was not sufficiently offensive? Because although it was offensive it was nonetheless "newsworthy" or "of legitimate concern to the public"? Are the two factors related? Compare the approach of the Second Restatement in § 652D:

> One who gives publicity to a matter concerning the private life of another is subject to liability to the other for invasion of his privacy, if the matter publicized is of a kind that
>
> (a) would be highly offensive to a reasonable person, and
>
> (b) is not of legitimate concern to the public.

Does this formulation suggest any interaction between the two elements?

3. It should not be surprising that those who seek the public limelight should be thought to have a lesser claim to privacy protection than those brought into the glare of publicity simply because they are either the unfortunate victims of an accident or crime or are otherwise swept up in an event. But involuntary subjects may not be that much different. As comment *f* to § 652D puts it:

> These persons are regarded as properly subject to the public interest, and publishers are permitted to satisfy the curiosity of the public as to its heroes, leaders, villains and victims, and those who are closely associated with them. As in the case of the voluntary public figure, the authorized publicity is not limited to the event that itself arouses the public interest, and to some extent includes publicity given to facts about the individual that would otherwise be purely private.

As comment *h* adds:

> Permissible publicity to information concerning either voluntary or involuntary public figures is not limited to the particular events that arouse the interest of the public. That interest, once aroused by the event, may legitimately extend, to some reasonable degree, to further information concerning the individual and to facts about him, which are not public and which, in the case of one who had not become a public figure, would be regarded as an invasion of his purely private life. Thus the life history of one accused of murder, together with such heretofore private facts as may throw some light upon what kind of person he is, his possible guilt or innocence, or his reasons for committing the crime, are a matter of legitimate public interest. . . . On the same basis the home life and daily habits of a motion picture actress may be of legitimate and reasonable interest to the public that sees her on the screen.
>
> The extent of the authority to make public private facts is not, however, unlimited. There may be some intimate details of her life, such as sexual relations, which even the actress is entitled to keep to herself. In determining what is a matter of legitimate public interest, account must be taken of the customs and conventions of the community; and in the last analysis what is proper becomes a matter of the community mores. The line is to be drawn when the publicity ceases to be the giving of information to which the public is entitled, and becomes a morbid and sensational prying into private lives for its own sake, with which a reasonable member of the public, with decent standards, would say that he had no concern.

4. What is the justification for using plaintiff's name? In some privacy cases, the event is important, and the question is whether to name some participant in the event who happened to have something embarrassing happen to him or her. Should a rape victim who is not independently newsworthy be identified? Should a local resident on whom a load of manure was accidentally dumped be named?

On the other hand, some stories are newsworthy because they involve newsworthy people. Of all the people each day who get parking citations, the newspapers are likely to be interested in very few—but probably would be eager to learn that the mayor's spouse picked up ten parking violations in three days. Or the paper might find irony if a recently released felon assaulted the daughter of a parent who has been active in urging early release for violent felons.

How different are these two types of situations? What fact pattern is involved in *Knopf*?

Ross v. Midwest Communications, Inc., 870 F.2d 271 (5th Cir.), cert. denied 493 U.S. 935 (1989), involved the identification of a rape victim. Defendant's investigative reporting team came to the conclusion that a man convicted in two rape cases had been wrongfully accused. In its program to that effect it presented facts about the two rapes, including the identities of the victims and a photograph of the house in which plaintiff had lived at the time.

The court of appeals affirmed a summary judgment for the defendant. Although plaintiff claimed that all the facts about the rape were private, her major claim was that defendant should not have identified her as the victim. The court, relying on an earlier case, stated that the name and the photograph "strengthen the impact and credibility of the article. They obviate any impression that the problems raised in the article are remote or hypothetical." The court noted that the "infamous Janet Cooke controversy (about the fabricated, Pulitzer–Prize-winning Washington Post series on the child-addict, Jimmy) suggests the legitimate ground for doubts that may arise about the accuracy of a documentary that uses only pseudonyms." Since the program sought to persuade the public and the authorities that an innocent man had been convicted, it was especially important to use real names.

The court did leave open the possibility of recovery where "the details of the rape victim's experience are not so uniquely crucial to the story as they are in this case, or when the publisher's 'public concern' goes to a general, sociological issue."

In Doe v. Berkeley Publishers, 496 S.E.2d 636 (S.C.1998), plaintiff brought an action against the publishers of The Berkeley Independent after the newspaper—truthfully—reported that he had been the victim of sexual assault while incarcerated. The court held that "the commission of a violent crime between inmates of a county jail is a matter of public significance as a matter of law." Do the considerations articulated by the court in *Ross* apply here as well?

In Gilbert v. Medical Economics Co., 665 F.2d 305 (10th Cir.1981), an article about malpractice identified plaintiff anesthesiologist as one who had negligently caused two serious injuries. To establish its thesis that this type of situation resulted from a "collapse" of self-policing and hospital disciplinary action, the article reported plaintiff's "history of psychiatric and related personal problems." Plaintiff conceded that the topic was newsworthy but asserted that her name and accompanying private facts about her personal and marital life added nothing to the article. Any relationship was "purely speculative."

The court disagreed. The name and photograph obviated any impression that the article lacked solid foundation. The facts were connected to the article by "the rational inference that plaintiff's personal problems were the underlying cause of the acts of alleged malpractice." Editors must be permitted leeway in drawing inferences that one event is connected with another. The connection was "not so purely conjectural that no reasonable editor could draw them other than through guesswork and speculation."

5. In Virgil v. Time Inc., 527 F.2d 1122 (9th Cir.1975), cert. denied, 425 U.S. 998 (1976), a prominent surfer sued about a report that he dove head first down a flight of stairs, ate "spiders and other insects," had never learned to read, and was thought "abnormal" by other surfers. All these were thought to have some bearing on plaintiff's "reckless disregard for his own safety" in body surfing. Nonetheless, summary judgment was inappropriate. The court thought an issue remained as to whether the revelations were of "legitimate public concern" and the trial court was to consider whether the article might be found to be "morbid and sensational prying."

On remand, the trial judge granted the magazine summary judgment. Although the facts were "generally unflattering and perhaps embarrassing," they did not approach being highly offensive. "Even if" offensiveness were found, the magazine was entitled to summary judgment because the parties "agree that body surfing at the Wedge is a matter of legitimate public interest, and it cannot be doubted that Mike Virgil's unique prowess at the same is also of legitimate public interest. Any reasonable person . . . would have to conclude that the personal facts concerning Mike Virgil were included as a legitimate journalistic attempt to explain Virgil's extremely daring and dangerous style of body surfing at the Wedge. There is no possibility that a juror could conclude that the personal facts were included for any inherent morbid, sensational, or curiosity appeal they might have." Virgil v. Sports Illustrated, 424 F.Supp. 1286 (S.D.Cal.1976).

In Peckham v. Boston Herald, Inc., 719 N.E.2d 888 (Mass.App.1999), plaintiff was a prominent businessman in the Boston community. In 1989, Gendron, a woman whom he had hired as a real estate broker for one of his companies, told him she was pregnant with his child. When he refused to acknowledge paternity, she commenced a suit. Peckham told only his daughter and two close friends about these developments, but a gossip columnist somehow found out about Gendron's claim and, after interviewing her attorney, published the information in the Boston Herald.

The court first stated that there might be a fact question whether Peckham, in disseminating the news to others, "due to the particular circumstances and manner of disclosure, has relinquished an expectation of privacy." It did not resolve this issue, however, and instead focused on whether or not the information "was a matter of 'legitimate public concern' that could not be the subject of an invasion of privacy action." Discussing the advisability of deciding the question of newsworthiness on summary judgment, the court explained that important interests in this type of case weigh against protracted litigation.

In this case, the gossip column was held newsworthy, "if only marginal[ly]," for several reasons. First, Peckham "was noteworthy both as a prominent real estate professional and as a recognized civic leader, and the circumstances of the paternity suit had a nexus to both of these roles in the community." Second, the article concerned topics of interest to the public. These included "a workplace liaison between an employee and her superior, the subsequent disavowal of paternity and layoff of the employee, and the possibility that a mother would be forced to seek public assistance because the putative father refused to give support." Third, the subject of the column was a judicial proceeding.

In Shulman v. Group W Productions, Inc., 955 P.2d 469 (Cal.1998), part of which is reprinted at p. 1174, infra, plaintiff was badly hurt in an auto accident. A medical evacuation helicopter was called—on which there was a nurse and a video cameraman filming for a news segment on rescue operations. The segment included use of plaintiff's first name, brief shots of her torso or a limb, and some of her statements, such as "I just want to die." In the public disclosure part, the court concluded, 5–2, that the "disputed material was newsworthy as a matter of law." The focus was seen as being on the medical crew's demanding work at some personal risk.

6. Must the editor's judgment concerning the relationship of the plaintiff's name or photograph to a story be reasonable as well as honest? What does "reasonable" mean in this context? What if the court thinks that the editor honestly saw a connection between two events but that most people would not see it the same way? Most editors?

7. Might the nature of the publication be relevant? Could a daily newspaper in plaintiff's hometown identify a rape victim—while a distant paper could not? Vice versa?

What if the disclosure in *Haynes* had been made in a tabloid newspaper or on a television talk show? What missing element might that context supply?

8. In defamation, the source of the statement was relevant and often crucial to the decision. Here, the court says that the source is not important. What is the difference?

9. Although "public disclosure" claims usually arise within a media context, they also emerge in other settings as well. One of the questions that must be answered in the absence of mass publication is what constitutes public disclosure. In Ozer v. Borquez, 940 P.2d 371 (Colo.1997), the court explored the nature of "publicity." During his employment with the law firm Ozer & Mullin, plaintiff associate, who had not disclosed his homosexuality to his colleagues, discovered that his partner had AIDS. Plaintiff concluded that because of his distress at this situation and his anxiety about his own future, he should find substitutes for, or reschedule, a deposition and arbitration hearing. He decided to disclose the situation, requesting confidentiality, to Robert Ozer, president of the firm. Ozer, however, disseminated the information to several others, and soon everyone in the firm knew. Borquez was subsequently fired, and brought a claim of wrongful discharge and of publication of private facts. (We explore at p. 1131, infra, a distinct claim for breach of confidence.) A judgment for plaintiff was reversed on appeal for instructional error.

In analyzing the "public disclosure" element, the court observed that the "requirement of public disclosure connotes publicity, which requires communication to the public in general or to a large number of persons, as distinguished from one individual or a few." Yet, even if "the disclosure must be made to the general public or to a large number of persons, there is no threshold number." Each case was fact-specific. Furthermore, the defendant may "merely initiate the process whereby the information is eventually disclosed to a large number of persons." The trial judge had instructed the jury that the disclosure requirement would be met if Ozer had revealed the information to one other person. This instruction misstated the law, since defendant's publication to a single other person would be insufficient, and a new trial was ordered. Would disclosure to two people be considered "public"? Three? What if those three people were known to gossip assiduously? If they were the only three partners of the firm?

Rejecting the privacy action. A few states have rejected the "true-facts" privacy action. In Anderson v. Fisher Broadcasting Companies, Inc., 712 P.2d 803 (Or.1986), the court on state law grounds rejected the privacy action brought by an accident victim against a television station that used film of him, bleeding and in pain, in promotional spots for a forthcoming special news report on emergency medical treatment. In so doing, the court observed:

> What is "private" so as to make its publication offensive likely differs among communities, between generations, and among ethnic, religious, or other social groups, as well as among individuals. Likewise, one reader's or viewer's "news" is another's tedium or trivia. The editorial judgment of what is "newsworthy" is not so readily submitted to the ad hoc review of a jury as [the lower court] believed. It is not properly a community standard. Even when some editors themselves vie to tailor "news" to satisfy popular tastes, others may believe that the community should see or hear facts or ideas that the majority finds uninteresting or offensive.

See also Hall v. Post, 372 S.E.2d 711 (N.C.1988), rejecting the action largely because it will generally duplicate the action for intentional infliction of emotional distress.

Before becoming a judge, Professor Richard Posner suggested that a person who seeks to withhold some part of his or her past is himself trying to present a misrepresentation to the public. Although the individual was free to try to hide this information, Posner argued that the law should not impose sanctions on those who tell the public the truth about such a person. Posner, The Right of Privacy, 12 Ga.L.Rev. 393 (1978). Five comments on the article immediately follow it.

Is it relevant to the question of creating this type of action that, even when the law permits publication, the press often decides against publication because of ethical concerns? These issues are frequently discussed among journalists.

———

Against the backdrop of the common law tort, consider the following array of cases.

Some Illustrations

Sexual Matters

1. During an assassination attempt on President Ford in San Francisco, Oliver Sipple knocked the arm of the assailant, Sara Jane Moore, as she sought to aim a second shot at the President. Sipple was the object of extensive media attention, including stories that disclosed his homosexuality. Sipple, asserting that relatives who lived in the Midwest did not know of his sexual preference, sued the San Francisco Chronicle. The newspaper defended in part on the argument that privacy was not involved because Sipple had marched in gay parades and had acknowledged that at least 100 to 500 people in San Francisco knew he was a homosexual.

Summary judgment was affirmed on appeal. First, the facts were not private. Second, they were newsworthy. The article was prompted by "legitimate political considerations, i.e., to dispel the false public opinion that gays were timid, weak and unheroic figures and to raise the equally important political question whether the President of the United States entertained a discriminatory attitude or bias against a minority group such as homosexuals." Sipple v. Chronicle Publishing Co., 201 Cal.Rptr. 665 (App. 1984).

2. A group of Pittsburgh Steelers fans urged a photographer from Sports Illustrated to take pictures of them. The photographer did so. From among many photographs available for use, the editors chose one that showed the plaintiff with his fly open. Neff v. Time, Inc., 406 F.Supp. 858 (W.D.Pa.1976)(case dismissed).

Criminal Behavior

3. A magazine article, to prove that truck hijacking was a chancy venture, reported that 11 years earlier the plaintiff and another had hijacked a truck in Kentucky, only to find that it contained four bowling pin spotting machines. The article was published in 1967, by which time plaintiff alleged that he had served his time, had become rehabilitated, and was living in California with family and friends who did not know about his past. Briscoe v. Reader's Digest Ass'n, 483 P.2d 34 (Cal.1971)(case remanded to determine whether the defendant published with "reckless disregard" for the article's offensiveness).

4. Plaintiff was arrested for drunk driving. At the police station, he was "hitting and banging on his cell door, hollering and cursing from the time of his arrest" until five hours later. A local broadcaster taped some of

the noise and played excerpts on the radio. Holman v. Central Arkansas Broadcasting Co., 610 F.2d 542 (8th Cir.1979)(case dismissed).

Embarrassment or Ridicule

5.   Regardie's, a monthly magazine, ran an article in September 1986, that purported to be a list with short biographies of Washington's 100 wealthiest individuals. It also carried a list of those included in previous years but omitted this year because the minimum net worth had risen from $20 million to $30 million. In this "Gone But Not Forgotten" group was plaintiff, a lawyer, who was said to have made his fortune in real estate. Plaintiff explained his failure to sue the prior year on the ground that it seemed best to refrain from pursuing the matter to avoid further publicity. The data had been collected from court files, tax ledgers, and federal and city agency records. The case was dismissed for lack of any private facts. Wolf v. Regardie, 553 A.2d 1213 (D.C.App.1989).

6.   Plaintiff was a janitor who found $240,000 that had fallen from an armored car. He returned it (and received a reward of $10,000) to the scorn of his neighbors and his children's friends. When their hostile reaction was reported, he received many congratulatory letters and messages, including one from President Kennedy. The full story was reported in a periodical and reprinted in a college English textbook. Johnson v. Harcourt, Brace, Jovanovich, Inc., 118 Cal.Rptr. 370 (App. 1974)(case dismissed.)

7.   Defendants searched the trash bin at an abortion clinic and obtained the names of two women who were scheduled to have abortions the following day. When the women arrived defendants raised "large signs" listing the plaintiffs' real names that implored them, among other things, not to "kill their babies." Doe v. Mills, 536 N.W.2d 824 (Mich.App.1995)(summary judgment reversed; the court also upheld an action for intentional infliction of emotional distress).

Private information. Which of the foregoing cases seemed strongest in this regard? Which weakest? Courts have uniformly rejected the claim that information about one person can invade another's privacy. E.g., Hendrickson v. California Newspapers, Inc., 121 Cal.Rptr. 429 (App. 1975)(obituary of deceased reported that he had a criminal record and also named his survivors); Fry v. Ionia Sentinel–Standard, 300 N.W.2d 687 (Mich.App. 1980)(news story reported that plaintiff's husband and a woman had been killed in accidental fire, and identified dead man's wife and children as his survivors).

Highly offensive to a reasonable person. Which of the foregoing cases seemed strongest in this regard? Which seemed weakest? Although the article in the *Sidis* case was "merciless in its dissection of intimate details," that did not mean it would be highly offensive to reasonable persons. That some people may wish to keep private some of their quirks does not mean that reasonable people would find the revelation of that information highly offensive.

"Newsworthiness" or "legitimate concern." Which of the cases presented the weakest claim to being newsworthy? The strongest?

————

In the *Haynes* excerpt, Judge Posner observed that facts contained in "judicial records are beyond the power of tort law to conceal." He also mentioned that in certain situations the First Amendment would not permit privacy law to recognize a tort. We turn now to cases that explore the range of constitutional limits on the privacy tort.

2.   CONSTITUTIONAL PRIVILEGE

In 1975, the Supreme Court decided its first "true-facts" privacy case. In Cox Broadcasting Corp. v. Cohn, 420 U.S. 469 (1975), a 17-year-old had been raped in Georgia and did not survive. A Georgia criminal statute made it a misdemeanor for "any news media or any other person to print and publish, broadcast, televise or disseminate through any other medium of public discussion . . . the name or identity of any female who may have been raped." During a recess in a criminal hearing in the case, a television reporter was allowed to inspect the indictment, which named the victim. Cox Broadcasting used the victim's name in reporting on the case that night.

The victim's father brought a tort action for revelation of his daughter's name. The state supreme court held that the complaint stated a common law action for damages. A First Amendment defense was rejected on the ground that the statute was an authoritative declaration that Georgia considered a rape victim's name not to be a matter of public concern. The court could discern "no public interest or general concern about the identity of the victim of such a crime as will make the right to disclose the identity of the victim rise to the level of First Amendment protection."

The Supreme Court reversed. Cox Broadcasting argued for a "broad holding that the press may not be made criminally or civilly liable for publishing information that is neither false nor misleading but absolutely accurate, however damaging it may be to reputation or individual sensibilities." Justice White's majority opinion avoided the broad ground by addressing the narrower question of "whether the State may impose sanctions on the accurate publication of the name of a rape victim obtained from public records—more specifically, from judicial records which are maintained in connection with a public prosecution and which themselves are open to public inspection. We are convinced that the State may not do so."

Justice White noted that the public relies on the press to provide in convenient form the facts about the operation of government. Without such information "most of us and many of our representatives would be unable to vote intelligently or to register opinions on the administration of government generally." The "commission of crime, prosecutions resulting from it, and judicial proceedings arising from the prosecutions . . . are without question events of legitimate concern to the public and consequently fall within the responsibility of the press to report the operations of government."

Justice White noted that the developing law of privacy afforded the press a privilege to report the events of judicial proceedings. "By placing the information in the public domain on official court records, the State must be presumed to have concluded that the public interest was thereby being served. Public records by their very nature are of interest to those concerned with the administration of government, and a public benefit is performed by the reporting of the true contents of the records by the media." Freedom to publish material released by government is of "critical importance to our type of government in which the citizenry is the final judge of the proper conduct of public business." In such situations, "the States may not impose sanctions on the publication of truthful information contained in official court records open to public inspection."

The Court was "reluctant to embark on a course that would make public records generally available to the media but forbid their publication if offensive to the sensibilities of the supposed reasonable man. Such a rule would make it very difficult for the media to inform citizens about the public business and yet stay within the law. The rule would invite timidity and self-censorship and very likely lead to the suppression of many items that would otherwise be published and that should be made available to the public."

To appreciate fully the significance of the following case it is necessary to be familiar with the major features of a few Supreme Court cases in which the press disclosed information despite a judge's order or a statute to the contrary. Oklahoma Publishing Co. v. District Court, 430 U.S. 308 (1977), struck down a judge's order barring the identification of juveniles when the judge had held an open proceeding that allowed those present to learn the identity by observation. Landmark Communications, Inc. v. Virginia, 435 U.S. 829 (1978), struck down a state bar against the publication of truthful news reports that a sitting judge was under investigation by a state commission. Smith v. Daily Mail Publishing Co., 443 U.S. 97 (1979), barred criminal prosecution against a newspaper that, in violation of a statute against such conduct, had identified a juvenile suspect based on interviews with eyewitnesses to the event.

These three cases, decided after *Cox Broadcasting*, came into play as the Court decided another case involving the identification of rape victims. At the time, Florida was one of a handful of states that sought to prevent such publications by criminal statute.

The Florida Star v. B.J.F.

Supreme Court of the United States, 1989.
491 U.S. 524, 109 S.Ct. 2603, 105 L.Ed.2d 443.

JUSTICE MARSHALL delivered the opinion of the Court.

Florida Stat. section 794.03 (1987) makes it unlawful to "print, publish, or broadcast . . . in any instrument of mass communication" the name of the victim of a sexual offense. Pursuant to this statute, appellant The Florida Star was found civilly liable for publishing the name of a rape victim which it had obtained from a publicly released police report. The issue presented here is whether this result comports with the First Amendment. We hold that it does not.

I

The Florida Star is a weekly newspaper which serves the community of Jacksonville, Florida, and which has an average circulation of approximately 18,000 copies. A regular feature of the newspaper is its "Police Reports" section. The section, typically two to three pages in length, contains brief articles describing local criminal incidents under police investigation. On October 20, 1983, appellee B.J.F. reported to the Duval County, Florida, Sheriff's Department (the Department) that she had been robbed and sexually assaulted by an unknown assailant. The Department prepared a report on the incident which identified B.J.F. by her full name. The Department then placed the report in its press room. The Department does not restrict access either to the press room or to the reports made available therein.

A Florida Star reporter-trainee sent to the press room copied the police report verbatim, including B.J.F.'s full name, on a blank duplicate of the Department's forms. A Florida Star reporter then prepared a one-paragraph article about the crime, derived entirely from the trainee's copy of the police report. The article included B.J.F.'s full name. It appeared in the "Robberies" subsection of the "Police Reports" section on October 29, 1983, one of fifty-four police blotter stories in that day's edition. The article read: "[B.J.F.] reported on Thursday, October 20, she was crossing Brentwood Park, which is in the 500 block of Golfair Boulevard, enroute to her bus stop, when an unknown black man ran up behind the lady and placed a knife to her neck and told her not to yell. The suspect then undressed the lady and had sexual intercourse with her before fleeing the scene with her 60 cents, Timex watch and gold necklace. Patrol efforts have been suspended concerning this incident because of lack of evidence."

In printing B.J.F.'s full name, The Florida Star violated its internal policy of not publishing the names of sexual offense victims.

[B.J.F. sued both the newspaper and the Sheriff's Department. The latter settled for $2,500. The Star's motion to dismiss was denied.]

At the ensuing day-long trial, B.J.F. testified that she had suffered emotional distress from the publication of her name. She stated that she had heard about the article from fellow workers and acquaintances; that her mother had received several threatening phone calls from a man who stated that he would rape B.J.F. again; and that these events had forced B.J.F. to change her phone number and residence, to seek police protection, and to obtain mental health counseling. In defense, The Florida Star put forth evidence indicating that the newspaper had learned B.J.F.'s name from the incident report released by the Department, and that the newspaper's violation of its internal rule against publishing the names of sexual offense victims was inadvertent.

At the close of B.J.F.'s case, and again at the close of its defense, The Florida Star moved for a directed verdict. On both occasions, the trial judge denied these motions. He ruled from the bench that section 794.03 was constitutional because it reflected a proper balance between the First Amendment and privacy rights, as it applied only to a narrow set of "rather sensitive . . . criminal offenses." [   ] At the close of the newspaper's defense, the judge granted B.J.F.'s motion for a directed verdict on the issue of negligence, finding the newspaper per se negligent based upon its violation of section 794.03. [   ] This ruling left the jury to consider only the questions of causation and damages. The judge instructed the jury that it could award B.J.F. punitive damages if it found that the newspaper had "acted with reckless indifference to the rights of others." [   ] The jury awarded B.J.F. $75,000 in compensatory damages and $25,000 in punitive damages. Against the actual damage award, the judge set off B.J.F.'s settlement with the Department.

The First District Court of Appeal affirmed in a three-paragraph per curiam opinion. . . . The Supreme Court of Florida denied discretionary review.

The Florida Star appealed to this Court. We noted probable jurisdiction, [   ], and now reverse.

II

The tension between the right which the First Amendment accords to a free press, on the one hand, and the protections which various statutes and common-law doctrines accord to personal privacy against the publication of truthful information, on the other, is a subject we have addressed several times in recent years. Our decisions in cases involving government attempts to sanction the accurate dissemination of information as invasive of privacy, have not, however, exhaustively considered this conflict. On the contrary, although our decisions have without exception upheld the press' right to publish, we have emphasized each time that we were resolving this conflict only as it arose in a discrete factual context.

The parties to this case frame their contentions in light of a trilogy of cases which have presented, in different contexts, the conflict between truthful reporting and state-protected privacy interests. [The Court briefly reviewed *Cox Broadcasting, Oklahoma Publishing,* and *Daily Mail.*]

Appellant takes the position that this case is indistinguishable from *Cox Broadcasting.* [   ] Alternatively, it urges that our decisions in the above trilogy, and in other cases in which we have held that the right of the press to publish truth overcame asserted interests other than personal privacy, can be distilled to yield a broader First Amendment principle that the press may never be punished, civilly or criminally, for publishing the truth. [ ] Appellee counters that the privacy trilogy is inapposite, because in each case the private information already appeared on a "public record," [ ] and because the privacy interests at stake were far less profound than in the present case. [ ] In the alternative, appellee urges that *Cox Broadcasting* be overruled and replaced with a categorical rule that publication of the name of a rape victim never enjoys constitutional protection. [ ]

We conclude that imposing damages on appellant for publishing B.J.F.'s name violates the First Amendment, although not for either of the reasons appellant urges. Despite the strong resemblance this case bears to *Cox Broadcasting*, that case cannot fairly be read as controlling here. The name of the rape victim in that case was obtained from courthouse records that were open to public inspection, a fact which Justice White's opinion for the Court repeatedly noted, [ ] (noting "special protected nature of accurate reports of *judicial* proceedings")(emphasis added); [ ]. Significantly, one of the reasons we gave in *Cox Broadcasting* for invalidating the challenged damages award was the important role the press plays in subjecting trials to public scrutiny and thereby helping guarantee their fairness. [ ] That role is not directly compromised where, as here, the information in question comes from a police report prepared and disseminated at a time at which not only had no adversarial criminal proceedings begun, but no suspect had been identified.

Nor need we accept appellant's invitation to hold broadly that truthful publication may never be punished consistent with the First Amendment. Our cases have carefully eschewed reaching this ultimate question, mindful that the future may bring scenarios which prudence counsels our not resolving anticipatorily. See, e.g., *Near v. Minnesota* [ ] (hypothesizing "publication of the sailing dates of transports or the number and location of troops"); see also *Garrison v. Louisiana*, [ ] (endorsing absolute defense of truth "where discussion of public affairs is concerned," but leaving unsettled the constitutional implications of truthfulness "in the discrete area of purely private libels"); Landmark Communications, Inc. v. Virginia, 435 U.S. 829, 838 (1978); Time, Inc. v. Hill, 385 U.S. 374, 383, n. 7 (1967). Indeed, in *Cox Broadcasting*, we pointedly refused to answer even the less sweeping question "whether truthful publications may ever be subjected to civil or criminal liability" for invading "an area of privacy" defined by the State. [ ] Respecting the fact that press freedom and privacy rights are both "plainly rooted in the traditions and significant concerns of our society," we instead focused on the less sweeping issue of "whether the State may impose sanctions on the accurate publication of the name of a rape victim obtained from public records—more specifically, from judicial records which are maintained in connection with a public prosecution and which themselves are open to public inspection." [ ] We continue to believe that the sensitivity and significance of the interests presented in clashes between First Amendment and privacy rights counsel relying on limited principles that sweep no more broadly than the appropriate context of the instant case.

In our view, this case is appropriately analyzed with reference to such a limited First Amendment principle. It is the one, in fact, which we articulated in *Daily Mail* in our synthesis of prior cases involving attempts to punish truthful publication: "[I]f a newspaper lawfully obtains truthful information about a matter of public significance then state officials may not constitutionally punish publication of the information, absent a need to further a state interest of the highest order." [ ] According the press the ample protection provided by that principle is supported by at least three separate considerations, in addition to, of course, the overarching "public interest, secured by the Constitution, in the dissemination of truth." [ ] The cases on which the *Daily Mail* synthesis relied demonstrate these considerations.

First, because the *Daily Mail* formulation only protects the publication of information which a newspaper has "lawfully obtain[ed]," [ ], the government retains ample means of safeguarding significant interests upon which publication may impinge, including protecting a rape victim's anonymity. To the extent sensitive information rests in private hands, the government may under some circumstances forbid its nonconsensual acquisition, thereby bringing outside of the *Daily Mail* principle the publication of any information so acquired. To the extent sensitive information is in the government's custody, it has even greater power to forestall or mitigate the injury caused by its release. The government may classify certain information, establish and enforce procedures ensuring its redacted release, and extend a damages remedy against the government or its officials where the government's mishandling of sensitive information leads to its dissemination. Where information is entrusted to the government, a less drastic means than punishing truthful publication almost always exists for guarding against the dissemination of private facts. See, e.g., [*Landmark Communications*] ("much of the risk [from disclosure of sensitive information regarding judicial disciplinary proceedings] can be eliminated through careful internal procedures to protect the confidentiality of Commission proceedings"); [*Oklahoma Publishing*] (noting trial judge's failure to avail himself of the opportunity, provided by a state statute, to close juvenile hearing to the public, including members of the press, who later broadcast juvenile defendant's name); [*Cox Broadcasting*] ("If there are privacy interests to be protected in judicial proceedings, the States must respond by means which avoid public documentation or other exposure of private information").[1]

---

1. The *Daily Mail* principle does not settle the issue of whether, in cases where information has been acquired *unlawfully* by a newspaper or by a source, government may ever punish not only the unlawful acquisition, but the ensuing publication as well. This issue was raised but not definitively resolved in New York Times Co. v. United States, 403 U.S. 713 (1971), and reserved in [*Landmark Communications*]. We have no occasion to address it here.

A second consideration undergirding the *Daily Mail* principle is the fact that punishing the press for its dissemination of information which is already publicly available is relatively unlikely to advance the interests in the service of which the State seeks to act. It is not, of course, always the case that information lawfully acquired by the press is known, or accessible, to others. But where the government has made certain information publicly available, it is highly anomalous to sanction persons other than the source of its release. We noted this anomaly in *Cox Broadcasting:* "By placing the information in the public domain on official court records, the State must be presumed to have concluded that the public interest was thereby being served." [   ] The *Daily Mail* formulation reflects the fact that it is a limited set of cases indeed where, despite the accessibility of the public to certain information, a meaningful public interest is served by restricting its further release by other entities, like the press. As *Daily Mail* observed in its summary of *Oklahoma Publishing*, "once the truthful information was 'publicly revealed' or 'in the public domain' the court could not constitutionally restrain its dissemination." [   ]

A third and final consideration is the "timidity and self-censorship" which may result from allowing the media to be punished for publishing certain truthful information. [   ] *Cox Broadcasting* noted this concern with overdeterrence in the context of information made public through official court records, but the fear of excessive media self-suppression is applicable as well to other information released without qualification, by the government. A contrary rule, [denying] protection to those who rely on the government's implied representations of the lawfulness of dissemination, would force upon the media the onerous obligation of sifting through government press releases, reports, and pronouncements to prune out material arguably unlawful for publication. This situation could inhere even where the newspaper's sole object was to reproduce, with no substantial change, the government's rendition of the event in question.

Applied to the instant case, the *Daily Mail* principle clearly commands reversal. The first inquiry is whether the newspaper "lawfully obtain[ed] truthful information about a matter of public significance." [   ] It is undisputed that the news article describing the assault on B.J.F. was accurate. In addition, appellant lawfully obtained B.J.F.'s name. Appellee's argument to the contrary is based on the fact that under Florida law, police reports which reveal the identity of the victim of a sexual offense are not among the matters of "public record" which the public, by law, is entitled to inspect. [   ] But the fact that the state officials are not required to disclose such reports does not make it unlawful for a newspaper to receive them when furnished by the government. Nor does the fact that the Department apparently failed to fulfill its obligation under section 794.03 not to "cause or allow to be . . . published" the name of a sexual offense victim make the newspaper's ensuing receipt of this information unlawful. Even assuming the Constitution permitted a State to proscribe *receipt* of information, Florida has not taken this step. It is clear, furthermore, that the news article concerned "a matter of public significance," [   ] in the sense in which the *Daily Mail* synthesis of prior cases used that term. That is, the article generally, as opposed to the specific identity contained within it, involved a matter of paramount public import: the commission, and investigation, of a violent crime which had been reported to authorities. See *Cox Broadcasting* (article identifying victim of rape-murder); [*Oklahoma Publishing*] (article identifying juvenile alleged to have committed murder); [*Daily Mail*] (same); cf. [*Landmark Communications*] (article identifying judges whose conduct was being investigated).

The second inquiry is whether imposing liability on appellant pursuant to section 794.03 serves "a need to further a state interest of the highest order." [*Daily Mail*] Appellee argues that a rule punishing publication furthers three closely related interests: the privacy of victims of sexual offenses; the physical safety of such victims, who may be targeted for retaliation if their names become known to their assailants; and the goal of encouraging victims of such crimes to report these offenses without fear of exposure. [   ]

At a time in which we are daily reminded of the tragic reality of rape, it is undeniable that these are highly significant interests, a fact underscored by the Florida Legislature's explicit attempt to protect these interests by enacting a criminal statute prohibiting such dissemination of victim identities. We accordingly do not rule out the possibility that, in a proper case, imposing civil sanctions for publication of the name of a rape victim might be so overwhelmingly necessary to advance these interests as to satisfy the *Daily Mail* standard. For three independent reasons, however, imposing liability for publication under the circumstances of this case is too precipitous a means of advancing these interests to convince us that there is a "need" within the meaning of the *Daily Mail* formulation for Florida to take this extreme step. Cf. *Landmark Communications* (invalidating penalty on publication despite State's expressed interest in nondissemination, reflected in statute prohibiting unauthorized divulging of names of judges under investigation).

First is the manner in which appellant obtained the identifying information in question. As we have noted, where the government itself provides information to the media, it is most appropriate to assume that the government had, but failed to utilize, far more limited means of guarding against dissemination than the extreme step of punishing truthful speech. That assumption is richly borne out in this case. B.J.F.'s identity would never have come to light were it not for the erroneous, if inadvertent, inclusion by the Department of her full name in an accident report made available in a press room open to the public. Florida's policy against disclosure of rape victims' identities, reflected in section 794.03, was undercut by the Department's failure to abide by this policy. Where, as here, the government has failed to police itself in disseminating information, it is clear under *Cox Broadcasting, Oklahoma Publishing,* and *Landmark Communications* that the imposition of damages against the press for its subsequent publication can hardly be said to be a narrowly tailored means of safeguarding anonymity. [   ] Once the government has placed such information in the public domain, "reliance must rest upon the judgment of those who decide what to publish or broadcast," [*Cox Broadcasting*] and hopes for restitution must rest upon the willingness of the government to compensate victims for their loss of privacy, and to protect them from the other consequences of its mishandling of the information which these victims provided in confidence.

That appellant gained access to the information in question through a government news release makes it especially likely that, if liability were to be imposed, self-censorship would result. Reliance on a news release is a paradigmatically "routine newspaper reporting techniqu[e]." [*Daily Mail*] The government's issuance of such a release, without qualification, can only convey to recipients that the government considered dissemination lawful, and indeed expected the recipients to disseminate the information further. Had appellant merely reproduced the news release prepared and released by the Department, imposing civil damages would surely violate the First Amendment. The fact that appellant converted the police report into a news story by adding the linguistic connecting tissue necessary to transform the report's facts into full sentences cannot change this result.

A second problem with Florida's imposition of liability for publication is the broad sweep of the negligence per se standard applied under the civil cause of action implied from section 794.03. Unlike claims based on the common law tort of invasion of privacy, [ ], civil actions based on section 794.03 require no case-by-case findings that the disclosure of a fact about a person's private life was one that a reasonable person would find highly offensive. On the contrary, under the per se theory of negligence adopted by the courts below, liability follows automatically from publication. This is so regardless of whether the identity of the victim is already known throughout the community; whether the victim has voluntarily called public attention to the offense; or whether the identity of the victim has otherwise become a reasonable subject of public concern—because, perhaps, questions have arisen whether the victim fabricated an assault by a particular person. Nor is there a scienter requirement of any kind under section 794.03, engendering the perverse result that truthful publications challenged pursuant to this cause of action are less protected by the First Amendment than even the least protected defamatory falsehoods: those involving purely private figures, where liability is evaluated under a standard, usually applied by a jury, of ordinary negligence. See *Gertz v. Robert Welch, Inc.*, [ ]. We have previously noted the impermissibility of categorical prohibitions upon media access where important First Amendment interests are at stake. See Globe Newspaper Co. v. Superior Court, 457 U.S. 596, 608 (1982)(invalidating state statute providing for the categorical exclusion of the public from trials of sexual offenses involving juvenile victims.) More individualized adjudication is no less indispensable where the State, seeking to safeguard the anonymity of crime victims, sets its face against publication of their names.

Third, and finally, the facial under-inclusiveness of section 794.03 raises serious doubts about whether Florida is, in fact, serving, with this statute, the significant interests which appellee invokes in support of affirmance. Section 794.03 prohibits the publication of identifying information only if this information appears in an "instrument of mass communication," a term the statute does not define. Section 794.03 does not prohibit the spread by other means of the identities of victims of sexual offenses. An individual who maliciously spreads word of the identity of a rape victim is thus not covered, despite the fact that the communication of such information to persons who live near, or work with, the victim may have consequences equally devastating as the exposure of her name to large numbers of strangers. [   ]

When a State attempts the extraordinary measure of punishing truthful publication in the name of privacy, it must demonstrate its commitment to advancing this interest by applying its prohibition evenhandedly, to the small time disseminator as well as the media giant. Where important First Amendment interests are at stake, the mass scope of disclosure is not an acceptable surrogate for injury. A ban on disclosures effected by "instrument[s] of mass communication" simply cannot be defended on the ground that partial prohibitions may effect partial relief. See [*Daily Mail*] (statute is insufficiently tailored to interest in protecting anonymity where it restricted only newspapers, not the electronic media or other forms of publication, from identifying juvenile defendants); *id.*, at 110 (Rehnquist, J., concurring in judgment)(same); cf. Arkansas Writers' Project, Inc. v. Ragland, 481 U.S. 221, 229 (1987); Minneapolis Star & Tribune Co. v. Minnesota Comm'r of Revenue, 460 U.S. 575, 585 (1983). Without more careful and inclusive precautions against alternative forms of dissemination, we cannot conclude that Florida's selective ban on publication by the mass media satisfactorily accomplishes its stated purpose.

III

Our holding today is limited. We do not hold that truthful publication is automatically constitutionally protected, or that there is no zone of personal privacy within which the State may protect the individual from intrusion by the press, or even that a State may never punish publication of the name of a victim of a sexual offense. We hold only that where a newspaper publishes truthful information which it has lawfully obtained, punishment may lawfully be imposed, if at all, only when narrowly tailored to a state interest of the highest order, and that no such interest is satisfactorily served by imposing liability .   .   . under the facts of this case. The decision below is therefore reversed.

JUSTICE SCALIA, concurring in part and concurring in the judgment.

I think it sufficient to decide this case to rely upon the third ground set forth in the Court's opinion [   ]: that a law cannot be regarded as protecting an interest "of the highest order" [   ], and thus as justifying a restriction upon truthful speech, when it leaves appreciable damage to that supposedly vital interest unprohibited. I would anticipate that the rape victim's discomfort at the dissemination of news of her misfortune among friends and acquaintances would be at least as great as her discomfort at its publication by the media to people to whom she is only a name. Yet the law in question does not prohibit the former in either oral or written form. Nor is it clear, as I think it must be to validate this statute, that Florida's general privacy law would prohibit such gossip. Nor, finally, is it credible that the interest meant to be served by the statute is the protection of the victim against a rapist still at large—an interest that arguably would extend only to mass publication. There would be little reason to limit a statute with that objective to rape alone; or to extend it to all rapes, whether or not the felon has been apprehended and confined. In any case, the instructions here did not require the jury to find that the rapist was at large.

This law has every appearance of a prohibition that society is prepared to impose upon the press but not upon itself. Such a prohibition does not protect an interest "of the highest order." For that reason, I agree that the judgment of the court below must be reversed.

[JUSTICE WHITE, joined by CHIEF JUSTICE REHNQUIST and JUSTICE O'CONNOR, dissented. He distinguished the three cases on which the Court relied (but noted that *Oklahoma Publishing* was much less relied upon than the other two). The "State-law scheme [in *Cox Broadcasting*] made public disclosure of the victim's name almost inevitable; here, Florida law forbids such disclosure." "By amending its public records statute to exempt rape victims' names from disclosure [   ], and forbidding its officials from releasing such information, [   ], the State has taken virtually every step imaginable to prevent what happened here." *Cox Broadcasting* bars the state only from making the press "its first line of defense in withholding private information from the public—it cannot ask the press to secrete private facts that the State makes no effort to safeguard in the first place."

Justice White distinguished *Daily Mail* on the ground that it involved revelation of the name of the perpetrator of a murder and this case involved a victim: "whatever rights alleged criminals have to maintain their anonymity pending an adjudication of guilt—the rights of crime victims must be infinitely more substantial." Also, *Daily Mail* noted that the case involved "no issue of privacy." "But in this case, there is an issue of privacy—indeed, this is the principal issue—and therefore, this case falls outside of [*Daily Mail*]."

Justice White then turned to the Court's "independent" reasons for deciding *Florida Star*. First, the government's release of the information was "inadvertent." When the state makes a mistake in its efforts to protect privacy "it is not too much to ask the press, in instances such as this, to respect simple standards of decency and refrain from publishing a victim's name, address, and/or phone number." In a footnote at this point, Justice White noted that the Court's proper concern for a free press should "be balanced against rival interests in a civilized and humane society. An absolutist view of the former leads to insensitivity as to the latter."

Second, the Court's concern about strict liability was unavailable on this record because the jury found the Star reckless. In any event, it was permissible for the standard of care to be set by the legislature rather than the courts.

As to the third point—under-inclusiveness—Justice White was willing to accept the apparent legislative conclusion that "neighborhood gossips do not pose the danger and intrusion to rape victims that 'instrument[s] of mass communication' do. Simply put: Florida wanted to prevent the widespread distribution of rape victims' names, and therefore enacted a statute tailored almost as precisely as possible to achieving that end." Moreover, it was entirely possible that Florida's common law of privacy might apply against neighborhood gossips in an appropriate case.

Justice White then turned to "more general principles at issue here to see if they recommend the Court's result." He feared that the result would "obliterate one of the most noteworthy legal inventions of the 20th century: the tort of the publication of private facts." If the plaintiff here could not prevail it was hard to imagine who could win such a case. There was no public interest in identifying the plaintiff here and "no public interest in immunizing the press from liability in the rare cases where a State's efforts to protect a victim's privacy have failed."]

Notes and Questions

1. Why is the Star's case not precisely covered by *Cox Broadcasting?*

2. Why is the Star's case not precisely covered by *Daily Mail?*

3. How might the Star's case have been analyzed in a state in which there was no statute?

4. How might the Star's case have been analyzed if the Star had learned about the name from an eyewitness rather than as the result of a mistake in the sheriff's office?

5. What might change if it turned out that the Star got the name from a sheriff's deputy who violated a statute in revealing the name?

6. In *Briscoe v. Reader's Digest Ass'n*, p. 1112, supra, involving the allegedly rehabilitated hijacker, the court stated that "Ideally, his neighbors should recognize his present worth and forget his past life of shame. But men are not so divine as to forgive the past trespasses of others, and plaintiff therefore endeavored to reveal as little as possible of his past life." The court concluded that it was for the trier of fact to decide whether plaintiff had been rehabilitated, whether "identifying him as a former criminal would be highly offensive and injurious to the reasonable man," whether defendant published the information "with a reckless disregard for its offensiveness," and whether any independent justification existed for printing plaintiff's identity. How is each determination to be made? How much of *Briscoe* remains after *Cox* and *Florida Star?*

7. Recent cases have expressed serious doubt about *Briscoe's* viability. In *Romaine v. Kallinger,* reprinted at p. 949, supra, for its discussion of defamation, the court also addressed a claim that the book had invaded the plaintiff's privacy. The court concluded that the claim failed because "the facts revealed are not private, and even if they were private, they are of legitimate concern to the public and so privileged under the 'newsworthiness' exception to the 'unreasonable publication of private facts' claim.'' The facts were not private because they were contained in nonconfidential official court records of the trial. Plaintiff argued that *Cox Broadcasting* did not apply because eight years had passed between the crime and the book. The court refused to read *Cox Broadcasting* to limit the protection accorded to reports of official records ''if the events are not contemporaneous or recent.'' It also cited courts that had applied the *Cox Broadcasting* rationale to cases in which 19 and 23 years had passed. ''The news value and public interest in criminal events are not abated by the passage of time. [ ] Most courts that have addressed the effect of the passage of time on the public interest have concluded that a lapse of time does not dilute newsworthiness or lessen the legitimacy of the public's concern.'' The *Romaine* court thought *Briscoe*'s viability had been ended by *Cox Broadcasting*'s holding on public records.

An even more drastic situation was presented in Uranga v. Federated Publications, Inc., 2000 WL 1056095 (Idaho App. 2000) petition for review filed. In 1955, three men were arrested by the police in Boise, Idaho for participating in sexual acts involving boys, an event that began what came to be called the ''Boys of Boise'' investigations, which involved 1,500 witness interrogations and led to 16 arrests. In his statement, Melvin Dir, one of the men ultimately convicted, described a sexual encounter between himself and someone named F.J. (who, when Dir's allegations surfaced, was expelled from West Point, and subsequently committed suicide). He also recounted a conversation in which F.J. mentioned an affair with his cousin, plaintiff Uranga. Almost 40 years later, The Idaho Statesman, a Boise daily newspaper, published an account—which it described as ''a cautionary tale''—of the Boys of Boise episode and the havoc it had wreaked on F.J.'s life. In doing so, it published Dir's handwritten statement, which included his allegations about Uranga. Uranga filed suit with several privacy claims—including public disclosure, false light, and intrusion—but the court held that the Statesman was protected under the First Amendment. Even though Dir's statement had never been introduced in evidence at a trial, the fact that it could be found in a court file that was available for public inspection was enough for protection under *Cox Broadcasting*.

The lapse of 40 years between the statement and its publication in the Statesman did not remove the information from the public domain. The court ''questioned the continued viability'' of the *Briscoe* line of cases on which plaintiff relied, and stated that ''allowing liability for the publication of a court record, based solely upon the passage of time, would not be consistent with *Cox Broadcasting*. . . .'' Although the court had ''sympathy for Uranga's position,'' and found the idea of a staleness test ''appealing,'' it thought that the ''flaw'' in the approach was the need to use a case-by-case approach ''with outcome uncertainty.'' That would create the ''sort of self-censorship by the press that *Cox Broadcasting* sought to prevent.''

Does there seem to be any room under *Cox Broadcasting* for claims of staleness? Is a history book that uses such documents to discuss an episode half a century earlier less newsworthy than a media report?

Is the privilege of *Cox Broadcasting* and *Florida Star* so broad that it bars exceptions such as one that would facilitate the rehabilitation of criminals? Do these cases suggest that the use of expungement may be legally suspect? Why?

The *Shulman* majority, p. 1110, supra, in the case involving the medical helicopter, avoided confronting *Briscoe*. A concurring justice expressed doubt about *Briscoe*:

> Certainly, a widespread application of *Briscoe* could significantly alter the practice of biography and history, for even in the case of notable figures much of what occurs in their private lives may have faded from the public mind and, under the plurality opinion's test, may no longer be newsworthy by the time the biographer or historian arrives on the scene.

> I do not doubt the need to protect individual privacy against the ever-increasing intrusions upon it. I do question whether the publication of private facts can be prohibited on the basis of the perceived newsworthiness of the facts without creating a conflict with current First Amendment doctrine.   .   .   .

8. In *Haynes*, p. 1101, supra, although basing his decision on state law grounds, Judge Posner also discussed the implications of constitutional developments for his analysis. Noting that states had divided along the *Melvin-Sidis* line until *Cox Broadcasting*, he observed that *Cox* "may have consigned the entire *Melvin* line to the outer darkness." He noted that *Cox* protected the publication of information contained in public records "even if publication would offend the sensibilities of a reasonable person." In both *Cox* and *Florida Star*, the Court had been "careful not to hold that states can never provide a tort remedy to a person about whom truthful, but intensely private, information of some interest to the public is published:"

> We do not think the Court was being coy in *Cox* or *Florida Star* in declining to declare the tort of publicizing intensely personal facts totally defunct. (Indeed, the author of *Cox* dissented in *Florida Star*.) The publication of facts in a public record or other official document, such as the police report in the *Florida Star*, is not to be equated to publishing a photo of a couple making love or of a person undergoing some intimate medical procedure; we even doubt that it would make a difference in such a case if the photograph had been printed in a government document (say the patient's file in a Veterans Administration hospital).

> Yet despite the limited scope of the holdings of *Cox* and *Florida Star*, the implications of those decisions for the branch of the right of privacy that limits the publication of private facts are profound, even for a case such as this in which, unlike *Melvin v. Reid*, the primary source of the allegedly humiliating personal facts is not a public record.

(The primary source is Ruby Daniels.) The Court must believe that the First Amendment greatly circumscribes the right even of a private figure to obtain damages for the publication of newsworthy facts about him, even when they are facts of a kind that people want very much to conceal. To be identified in the newspaper as a rape victim is intensely embarrassing. And it is not invited embarrassment. . . .

. . .

. . . No modern cases decided after *Cox*, and precious few before, go as far as the plaintiffs would have us go in this case. Almost all the recent cases on which they rely, [   ], involve the vindication of paramount social interests, such as the protection of children, patients, and witnesses—interests not involved in this case. The plaintiffs' best post-*Cox* cases are Vassiliades v. Garfinckel's, [492 A.2d 580 (D.C.App. 1985)] and Huskey v. National Broadcasting Co., 632 F.Supp. 1282, 1290–92 (N.D.Ill.1986), the former involving before-and-after photos of a face lift, the latter involving television pictures of a prisoner dressed only in gym shorts. Photographic invasions of privacy usually are more painful than narrative ones, and even partial nudity is a considerable aggravating factor. *Vassiliades* also involved the special issue of patient rights, though it was not emphasized by the court.

The court decided that Illinois would not follow these two cases. Does Judge Posner suggest a distinction between names and photographs? What kind of privacy action might pass Supreme Court muster?

9. In State v. Globe Communications Corp., 648 So.2d 110 (Fla.1994), the Globe was prosecuted for violating the Florida statute involved in *Florida Star* by identifying the complainant in the rape trial of William Kennedy Smith. The state eventually conceded that the statute could not be constitutionally applied against the Globe, but argued that it was not facially invalid. The court, relying heavily on *Florida Star*, disagreed. Nonetheless it observed that "Although we decline to rewrite section 794.03 to correct the defects outlined in *Florida Star*, we do not rule out the possibility that the legislature could fashion a statute that would pass constitutional muster." Is it likely to be easier to frame a constitutional statute in this area or to find a fact situation that will give rise to a permissible common law tort action?

10. *Shulman reprise.* The *Shulman* majority concluded that *Cox Broadcasting* and *Florida Star* did not "enunciate a general test of newsworthiness applicable to other factual circumstances or provide a broad theoretical basis for discovery of such a general constitutional standard." Newsworthiness—"constitutional or common law—is also difficult to define because it may be used as either a descriptive or a normative term. . . . If 'newsworthiness' is completely descriptive—if all coverage that sells papers or boosts ratings is deemed newsworthy—it would seem to swallow the publication of private facts tort, for 'it would be difficult to suppose that publishers were in the habit of reporting occurrences of little interest.' [   ] At the other extreme, if newsworthiness is viewed as a purely normative concept, the courts could become to an unacceptable degree editors of the news and self-appointed guardians of public taste:''

An analysis measuring newsworthiness of facts about an otherwise private person involuntarily involved in an event of public interest by their relevance to a newsworthy subject matter incorporates considerable deference to reporters and editors, avoiding the likelihood of unconstitutional interference with the freedom of the press to report truthfully on matters of legitimate public interest. In general, it is not for a court or jury to say how a particular story is best covered.

The Problem for Editors. In *Virgil,* p. 1109, supra, the publisher argued that the First Amendment protected all true statements from liability. The court disagreed:

To hold that privilege extends to all true statements would seem to deny the existence of ''private'' facts, for if facts be facts—that is, if they be true—they would not (at least to the press) be private, and the press would be free to publicize them to the extent it sees fit. The extent to which areas of privacy continue to exist, then, would appear to be based not on rights bestowed by law but on the taste and discretion of the press. We cannot accept this result.

Defendant then made a different argument:

A press which must depend upon a governmental determination as to what facts are of ''public interest'' in order to avoid liability for their truthful publication is not free at all. . . . A constitutional rule can be fashioned which protects all the interests involved. This goal is achieved by providing a privilege for truthful publications which is defeasible only when the court concludes as a matter of law that the truthful publication complained of constitutes a clear abuse of the editor's constitutional discretion to publish and discuss subjects and facts which in his judgment are matters of public interest.

Again the court disagreed. In libel and obscenity cases juries utilize community standards, and the court thought they should do so here, too, ''subject to close judicial scrutiny to ensure that the jury resolutions comport with First Amendment principles.'' What is the difference between Time's position and that adopted by the court?

The courts have tended to take this area case by case, and editors complain that such an approach breeds intolerable uncertainty. An editor must decide today what might happen in court in several years—and the standards are said to be vague. Who can predict what will be found ''highly offensive to a reasonable person'' or to violate ''community standards and mores''? Juries given these questions may punish unpopular publishers or broadcasters.

Compare this situation with that confronting an editor in the defamation area. There the editor, with advice from lawyers, must decide whether the *Times* or *Gertz* rule applies and then determine whether the publication's conduct meets that standard. And truth is always a defense. Do you see a sharp difference between the editor's position in defamation and in privacy? See Ingber, Rethinking Intangible Injuries: A Focus on Remedy, 73 Calif.L.Rev. 772, 849–56 (1985).

Successful plaintiffs. During the 1960s and 1970s it began to look as though the public disclosure tort was interesting academically but was not working in the courts. The 1980s began to show signs of change.

In Diaz v. Oakland Tribune, Inc., 188 Cal.Rptr. 762 (App. 1983), a columnist wrote of plaintiff:

> More education stuff: The students at the College of Alameda will be surprised to learn that their student body president, Toni Diaz, is no lady, but is in fact a man whose real name is Antonio.
>
> Now I realize that in these times, such a matter is no big deal, but I suspect his female classmates in P.E. 97 may wish to make other showering arrangements.

The plaintiff had had transsexual surgery. A judgment for $775,000 (of which $250,000 was compensatory) was reversed on appeal for trial errors but the court went out of its way to say that recovery was permitted on these facts and that the size of the recovery might not be a problem. The author knew the result would be "devastating" but never sought to contact plaintiff beforehand. His attempt to be "flip" and what the jury could find to be his "callous and conscious disregard for Diaz's privacy interests" justified the punitive award. The case was then settled.

A plaintiff won—and kept—a privacy award of $1,500 actual and $25,000 punitive damages in Hawkins v. Multimedia, Inc., 344 S.E.2d 145 (S.C.), cert. denied 479 U.S. 1012 (1986)(Brennan, J., dissenting). In a sidebar article to a story on teenage pregnancies, defendant's newspaper identified plaintiff as the teenage father of an illegitimate child. Most of the article focused on the teenage mother. After the mother identified plaintiff as the father, the reporter called plaintiff twice to obtain comments. The reporter first spoke with plaintiff's mother. The second time she spoke with the reluctant plaintiff for three or four minutes. "In neither call did the reporter request permission to identify or quote [plaintiff]."

Over defendant's objection, the trial judge charged that a minor cannot consent to an invasion of privacy. The appellate court did not reach the issue because it found that defendant had failed to establish consent in the first place. Although plaintiff did not hang up immediately, he was "very shy." He never agreed to the use of his name.

The court rejected defense arguments that the article was of "general interest" because that defense requires "legitimate" public interest. "Public or general interest does not mean mere curiosity, and newsworthiness is not necessarily the test." This issue was properly submitted to the jury.

Finally, the trial judge refused the defendant's charge that "malice must be shown by clear and convincing evidence." The appellate court concluded that malice "need not be shown to recover for invasion of privacy." It is relevant only for punitive damages. The proper burden for punitive damages was not argued at trial and could not be raised on appeal.

Enjoining invasions of privacy. As *Haynes* noted, even successful plaintiffs sacrifice, rather than protect, the sought-after privacy. This has led plaintiffs who obtain advance notice of an impending invasion to seek injunctive relief. Although injunctions in defamation cases have long been impermissible for nonconstitutional reasons, see p. 998, supra, the situation in privacy is not so clear.

Twice, the Supreme Court has been prepared to address the issue. The first case involved an unauthorized biography of a sports star. The Supreme Court asked the parties specifically to address the propriety of injunctive relief. Julian Messner, Inc. v. Spahn, 393 U.S. 818 (1968). Then the parties settled the case. 393 U.S. 1046 (1969). The second time the Court heard argument in a case in which a patient was trying to prevent her analyst from publishing a book about the therapy. Plaintiff claimed that the disguises used in the book were too thin to protect her privacy and that an implied covenant barred such a book. The state courts had enjoined publication of the book pending the outcome of the litigation. The Supreme Court granted certiorari, Roe v. Doe, 417 U.S. 907 (1974), heard arguments and then dismissed the writ as having been "improvidently granted." 420 U.S. 307 (1975). On remand, the state court found liability and ordered all of the books, except for 220 that had been distributed early, destroyed. Doe v. Roe, 400 N.Y.S.2d 668 (Sup.1977).

In a case involving the movie "Titticut Follies," the state courts had enjoined the general distribution of the movie because it invaded the privacy of inmates of a state institution for the criminally insane. The Supreme Court denied certiorari over a long dissent by Justice Harlan, joined by Justice Brennan. Justice Douglas also dissented. Wiseman v. Massachusetts, 398 U.S. 960 (1970). A petition for rehearing was denied over the dissents of Justices Harlan, Brennan, and Blackmun. "Mr. Justice Douglas took no part in the consideration or decision of this motion and petition." 400 U.S. 954 (1970). In the summer of 1991, a judge lifted the injunction and the film was shown publicly.

Breach of confidence?

Several cases to this point have suggested behavior that might not rise to the level of the privacy tort being pursued, but may still warrant some tort sanction. Recall, for example, *Ozer v. Borquez*, p. 1110, supra, involving the law firm partner who revealed to the firm that plaintiff was homosexual and that his partner had AIDS. We explore here a claim that in some respects is easier to establish than the public disclosure tort and in other respects is more difficult.

Humphers v. First Interstate Bank of Oregon

Supreme Court of Oregon, 1985.
298 Or. 706, 696 P.2d 527.

LINDE, JUSTICE.

[The complaint alleged that, in 1959, plaintiff, referred to as Ramona, who was unmarried at the time, gave birth to a daughter named Dawn, whom she immediately gave up for adoption. Ramona, who had been admitted to the hospital under an alias, later remarried. Her mother, her new husband and Dr. Mackey, who delivered the baby, were the only ones who knew of the birth and adoption. In 1980, Dawn wanted to meet her birth mother. Unable to gain access to the confidential court file, she located Dr. Mackey and asked for his help. He gave Dawn a letter that falsely stated that Ramona had taken DES during pregnancy and it was thus important for Dawn to learn about her mother's medical history. Hospital personnel, relying on the letter, identified the mother.]

Ramona Humphers was not pleased. The unexpected development upset her and caused her emotional distress, worry, sleeplessness, humiliation, embarrassment, and inability to function normally. She sought damages from the estate of Dr. Mackey, who had died, by this action against defendant as the personal representative. After alleging the facts recounted above, her complaint pleads for relief on five different theories: First, that Dr. Mackey incurred liability for "outrageous conduct"; second, that his disclosure of a professional secret fell short of the care, skill and diligence employed by other physicians in the community and commanded by statute; third, that his disclosure wrongfully breached a confidential or privileged relationship; fourth, that his disclosure of confidential information was an "invasion of privacy" in the form of an "unauthorized intrusion upon plaintiff's seclusion, solitude, and private affairs;" and fifth, that his disclosures to Dawn Kastning breached a contractual obligation of secrecy. The circuit court granted defendant's motion to dismiss the complaint on the grounds that the facts fell short of each theory of relief and ordered entry of judgment for defendant. On appeal, the Court of Appeals affirmed the dismissal of the first, second, and fifth counts but reversed on the third, breach of a confidential relationship, and the fourth, invasion of privacy. [   ] We allowed review. We hold that if plaintiff has a claim, it arose from a breach by Dr. Mackey of a professional duty to keep plaintiff's secret rather than from a violation of plaintiff's privacy.

A physician's liability for disclosing confidential information about a patient is not a new problem. In common law jurisdictions it has been more discussed than litigated throughout much of this century. There are precedents for damage actions for unauthorized disclosure of facts conveyed in confidence, although we know of none involving the disclosure of an adoption. Because such claims are made against a variety of defendants besides physicians or other professional counselors, for instance against banks, see, e.g., [   ]. and because plaintiffs understandably plead alternative theories of recovery, the decisions do not always rest on a single theory.

[The court noted that a claim based on outrageous conduct might fail for inability to show that the physician had the requisite intent; a malpractice claim might fail in light of the professional standards in this situation; and a contract claim might fail for lack of financial loss—though arguably emotional concerns were at the core of any contract in this case. In any event, the court noted that these claims were not involved because the plaintiff was no longer pursuing the first, second and fifth claims.]

PRIVACY

Although claims of a breach of privacy and of wrongful disclosure of confidential information may seem very similar in a case like the present, which involves the disclosure of an intimate personal secret, the two claims depend on different premises and cover different ground. Their common denominator is that both assert a right to control information, but they differ in important respects. Not every secret concerns personal or private information; commercial secrets are not personal, and governmental secrets are neither personal nor private. Secrecy involves intentional concealment. "But privacy need not hide; and secrecy hides far more than what is private." Bok, Secrets 11 (1983).

For our immediate purpose, the most important distinction is that only one who holds information in confidence can be charged with a breach of confidence. If an act qualifies as a tortious invasion of privacy, it theoretically could be committed by anyone. In the present case, Dr. Mackey's professional role is relevant to a claim that he breached a duty of confidentiality, but he could be charged with an invasion of plaintiff's privacy only if anyone else who told Dawn Kastning the facts of her birth without a special privilege to do so would be liable in tort for invading the privacy of her mother.

    · · ·

Doubtless plaintiff's interest qualifies as a "privacy" interest. That does not require the judgment of a court or a jury; it is established by the statutes that close adoption records to inspection without a court order. ORS 7.211, 432.420. The statutes are designed to protect privacy interests of the natural parents, the adoptive parents, or the child. But as already stated, to identify an interest deserving protection does not suffice to collect damages from anyone who causes injury to that interest. Dr. Mackey helped Dawn Kastning find her biological mother, but we are not prepared to assume that Ms. Kastning became liable for invasion of privacy in seeking her out.[13] Nor, we think, would anyone who knew the facts without an obligation of secrecy commit a tort simply by telling them to Ms. Kastning.

---

13. The use of a false medical document to gain access to the records of St. Charles Medical Center resembles Illustration 4 to Restatement (Second) Torts § 652B (based on Brex v. Smith, 386, 146 A. 34 (N.J.Eq. 1929)), in which defendant obtains bank records by displaying a forged court order. But Dawn Kastning is not a defendant here, and the complaint does not allege that she asked Dr. Mackey to prepare a false letter or knew that it was false.

Plaintiff's interest in nondisclosure would have been just as much invaded if the letter had been true and if Ms. Kastning had obtained a court order upon showing medical necessity, but the intrusive conduct would lack the wrongfulness required for liability.

Dr. Mackey himself did not approach plaintiff or pry into any personal facts that he did not know; indeed, if he had written or spoken to his former patient to tell her that her daughter was eager to find her, it would be hard to describe such a communication alone as an invasion of privacy. The point of the claim against Dr. Mackey is not that he pried into a confidence but that he failed to keep one. If Dr. Mackey incurred liability for that, it must result from an obligation of confidentiality beyond any general duty of people at large not to invade one another's privacy. We therefore turn to plaintiff's claim that Dr. Mackey was liable for a breach of confidence, the third count of the complaint.

BREACH OF CONFIDENCE

It takes less judicial innovation to recognize this claim than the Court of Appeals thought. A number of decisions have held that unauthorized and unprivileged disclosure of confidential information obtained in a confidential relationship can give rise to tort damages. [ ] The theory that a wrongful breach of confidence would be actionable goes back at least to Simonsen v. Swenson, [177 N.W. 831 (Neb.1920)], though the physician's disclosure in that case was found to be privileged. [ ]

One commentator, upon analyzing the cases allowing or denying recovery on a variety of theories, concluded that the tort consists in a breach of confidence in a "nonpersonal" confidential relationship, using the word "nonpersonal" to exclude liability for failing to keep secrets among members of a family or close friends. Note, Breach of Confidence: An Emerging Tort, 82 Colum.L.Rev. 1426 (1982). The problem with this formulation of civil liability lies in identifying the confidential relationships that carry a duty of keeping secrets. The writer suggests that the duty arises in all nonpersonal relationships "customarily understood" to carry such an obligation. [ ] In any such relationship, a person who discloses personal information conveyed in confidence would have the burden of showing that the disclosure was justified or privileged.

We do not think the law casts so wide a net. It requires more than custom to impose legal restraints on "the right to speak, write, or print freely on any subject whatever." Or. Const., Art. I, § 8. Tort liability, of course, may be a remedy for "injury to person, property, or reputation," Or. Const., Art. I, § 10, even by speech. See [ ] (liability for abusive accusations in employment relationship). But a legal duty not to speak, unless voluntarily assumed in entering the relationship, will not be imposed by courts or jurors in the name of custom or reasonable expectations. Tort liability is the consequence of a nonconsensual duty of silence, not its source.

In the case of the medical profession, courts in fact have found sources of a nonconsensual duty of confidentiality. Some have thought such a duty toward the patient implicit in the patient's statutory privilege to exclude the doctor's testimony in litigation, enacted in this state in OEC 504–1(2). [ ] More directly in point are legal duties imposed as a condition of engaging in the professional practice of medicine or other occupations.

As early as 1920, the Supreme Court of Nebraska, where a medical licensing statute defined professional misconduct to include "betrayal of a professional secret to the detriment of the patient," wrote in [*Simonsen v. Swenson*]:

> By this statute, it appears to us, a positive duty is imposed upon the physician, both for the benefit and advantage of the patient as well as in the interest of general public policy. The relation of physician and patient is necessarily a highly confidential one. It is often necessary for the patient to give information about himself which would be most embarrassing or harmful to him if given general circulation. This information the physician is bound, not only upon his own professional honor and the ethics of his high profession, to keep secret, but by reason of the affirmative mandate of the statute itself. A wrongful breach of such confidence, and a betrayal of such trust, would give rise to a civil action for the damages naturally flowing from such wrong.

Professional regulations were similarly cited in [   ].

This strikes us as the right approach to a claim of liability outside obligations undertaken expressly or implied in fact in entering a contractual relationship. [   ] The contours of the asserted duty of confidentiality are determined by a legal source external to the tort claim itself. A plaintiff asserting a breach of such a nonconsensual duty must identify its source and terms. If the tort claim asserts violation of a statute or regulation, the rule must validly apply to the facts, whether or not it actually is applied by those responsible for enforcement. When the asserted rule is one administered by a specialized agency, such as a professional board, and its scope is disputed, this may on occasion require reference to the agency's primary jurisdiction if the court does not find application of the rule to the facts clear as a matter of law.   .   .   .

Because the duty of confidentiality is determined by standards outside the tort claim for its breach, so are the defenses of privilege or justification. Physicians, like members of many ordinarily confidential professions and occupations, also may be legally obliged to report medical information to others for the protection of the patient, of other individuals, or of the public. See, e.g., ORS 418.750 (physician's duty to report child abuse); ORS 433.003, 434.020 (duty to report certain diseases). That was true of the defendant in *Simonsen v. Swenson*, supra, who reported a guest's contagious disease to a hotel. The court noted that this disclosure was legally required and affirmed a directed verdict for the defendant. Even without such a legal obligation, there may be a privilege to disclose information for the safety of individuals or important to the public in matters of public interest. [   ] Some cases have found a physician privileged in disclosing information to a patient's spouse, [   ] or perhaps an intended spouse, [   ]. In any event, defenses to a duty of confidentiality are determined in the same manner as the existence and scope of the duty itself. They necessarily will differ from one occupation to another and from time to time. A physician or other member of a regulated occupation is not to be held to a noncontractual duty of secrecy in a tort action when disclosure would not be a breach or would be privileged in direct enforcement of the underlying duty.

A physician's duty to keep medical and related information about a patient in confidence is beyond question. It is imposed by statute. ORS 677.190(5) provides for disqualifying or otherwise disciplining a physician for "wilfully or negligently divulging a professional secret." The Court of Appeals thought that breach of this statutory provision could not lead to civil liability when such liability would be quite inappropriate to provisions of ORS 677.190, but that misses the point. The actionable wrong is the breach of duty in a confidential relationship; ORS 677.190(5) only establishes the duty of secrecy in the medical relationship.

It is less obvious whether Dr. Mackey violated ORS 677.190(5) when he told Dawn Kastning what he knew of her birth. She was not, after all, a stranger to that proceeding.   .   .   . If Ms. Kastning needed information about her natural mother for medical reasons, as Dr. Mackey pretended, the State Board of Medical Examiners likely would find the disclosure privileged against a charge under ORS 677.190(5); but the statement is alleged to have been a pretext designed to give her access to the hospital records. If only ORS 677.190(5) were involved, we do not know how the Board would judge a physician who assists at the birth of a child and decades later reveals to that person his or her parentage. But as already noted, other statutes specifically mandate the secrecy of adoption records. ORS 7.211 provides that court records in adoption cases may not be inspected or disclosed except upon court order, and ORS 432.420 requires a court order before sealed adoption records may be opened by the state registrar. Given these clear legal constraints, there is no privilege to disregard the professional duty imposed by ORS 677.190(5) solely in order to satisfy the curiosity of the person who was given up for adoption.

For these reasons, we agree with the Court of Appeals that plaintiff may proceed under her claim of breach of confidentiality in a confidential relationship. The decision of the Court of Appeals is reversed with respect to plaintiff's claim of invasion of privacy and affirmed with respect to her claim of breach of confidence in a confidential relationship, and the case is remanded to the circuit court for further proceedings on that claim.

Notes and Questions

1. How might a court analyze a privacy claim based on publication of private facts? Why does the court assert that it would not hold Dawn Kastning liable for invading her birth mother's privacy? How is the tort of wrongful disclosure of confidential information—or breach of confidence, as it is sometimes called—distinguishable from public disclosure? Can it circumvent the (sometimes constitutional) problems that the public disclosure tort has encountered?

In McCormick v. England, 494 S.E.2d 431 (S.C.App.1997), the court recognized a cause of action against a physician who breached his duty of confidentiality by revealing his diagnosis of plaintiff's depression and alcoholism in a letter to the court during her divorce proceeding. The court distinguished between publication of private facts and breach of confidence. First, the standard applied in the former type of case—that the conduct must be "highly offensive" and "likely to cause serious mental injury"—is inappropriate for a breach of confidence case "because it focuses on the content, rather than the source of the information." Likewise, whereas "[p]ublicity involves disclosure to the public, not just an individual or a small group," breach of confidence may occur even in the case of disclosure to one person—for example, a spouse. How does this reasoning compare with that of the *Humphers* court?

2. What is the source of the duty that the court recognized in *Humphers*? The court denominates the duty in this case "nonconsensual." Why is "custom" not sufficient to establish the claim? Is the existence of a confidentiality statute essential to the court's analysis in *Humphers*? Recall *Uhr*, supra, p. 151.

In Wynne v. Orcutt Union School District, 95 Cal.Rptr. 458 (App. 1971), a five-year-old child's parents, apparently to explain the child's expected absences, informed his teacher that the boy was suffering from a progressive and, ultimately, fatal disease. They implored his teacher to keep this information confidential. She did not respond, but a few months later revealed the information to the rest of the class—who promptly told the child himself, who asked his parents whether he would soon die. In a claim for damages for emotional distress, the court determined that there was no pre-existing duty and that, although "one may arise from a voluntary undertaking," the teacher did not fulfill the requirements of this criterion here. According to the court, "no such undertaking is alleged here," and "Betty Wynne merely informed Martin's teacher 'in strict confidence' of Martin's disease, and the complaint says nothing about the teacher's request for information or about any promise of hers not to reveal it to others. Subsequent characterization of a conversation as confidential cannot create a retrospective duty of concealment not assumed at the time. . . . The illness of a child, the child's discovery that death may come sooner rather than later, the bruiting of this eventuality in the community, these events bring pain and sorrow to those affected. Yet this pain and sorrow, part of the human condition, remain outside the sphere of injury for which courts provide relief through monetary compensation."

4. Why is a new tort needed? What are the grounds for recognizing it? The Columbia Law Review note, seen in *Humphers* as formulating the tort too broadly, has been widely cited and may explain some of the interest that has been displayed in this cause of action during the past two decades. In Vickrey, Breach of Confidence: An Emerging Tort, 82 Colum.L.Rev. 1426 (1982), the author attempted to justify and define the relatively new claim, which, at the time, was recognized predominantly in physician-patient and bank-depositor cases. After surveying the case law, he argued that:

> [A] strong case can be made for recognizing a distinct tort to cover broken confidences. First, the duty of confidentiality, where it exists, generally arises out of broadly applicable societal norms and public

policy concerning the kind of relationship at issue. It does not arise out of specific agreement or particularized circumstances. Moreover, the object of the law when this duty is violated is compensation for the resulting injuries, not fulfillment of expectation. Therefore, liability should be grounded in tort law. Second, a separate tort focused directly on the broken confidence should be recognized because it would address squarely the individual and societal interests at stake in a confidential relationship.

Trying to encapsulate the tort, he then asserted that it "can be defined in general terms as the unconsented, unprivileged disclosure to a third party of nonpublic information that the defendant has learned within a confidential relationship," and then delineated the nature of both a "confidential relationship" and an "unprivileged disclosure."

According to *McCormick*, note 1 supra, most states faced with the issue, as of 1997, had "recognized a cause of action against a physician for the unauthorized disclosure of confidential information unless the disclosure is compelled by law or is in the patient's interest or the public interest" [citing cases from 13 states]. Courts' primary difficulties with the tort, however, continue to be the question of what kinds of confidential relationships should be recognized and the issue of what would constitute a privileged disclosure. For more recent scholarship on this area, see Gilles, Promises Betrayed: Breach of Confidence as Remedy for Invasions of Privacy, 43 Buff.L.Rev. 1 (1995) and Comment, Confidentiality: A Measured Response to the Failure of Privacy, 140 U.Pa.L.Rev. 2385 (1992).

5. In *Humphers*, the court mentioned that Dr. Mackey had falsely concocted the story that Ramona had taken DES during pregnancy. How might the court's analysis have differed if this allegation had been true? Within what limits should the breach of confidence tort be confined? Recall *Tarasoff*, p. 158, supra. Do you foresee any First Amendment problems arising in this area, as with the public disclosure tort?

6. Could Dawn Kastning have been held liable for inducing Dr. Mackey to breach his duty of confidentiality? Biddle v. Warren General Hospital, 715 N.E.2d 518 (Ohio 1999), arose after the hospital, at a lawyer's suggestion, disclosed patient medical information to that lawyer. The lawyer was to use the information to determine whether these patients could recover Supplemental Security Income and thus be in a better position to pay their hospital bills. The court held that "a third party [the lawyer] can be held liable for inducing the unauthorized, unprivileged disclosure of nonpublic medical information that a physician or hospital has learned within a physician-patient relationship." One dissenter argued that the law firm should be considered an agent of the hospital, not a third party.

7. The type of protections accorded to privacy and the nature of the interests privileged differ in the constitutional and tort law contexts. A constitutional right of privacy has been found in the due process clause of the Fourteenth Amendment. That jurisprudence has developed primarily in the area of family law, in which a woman's right to make decisions about contraception and abortion has been deemed fundamental. See, e.g., Planned Parenthood v. Casey, 510 U.S. 1309 (1994)), and a parent's capacity to make decisions about the care, custody, and control of her children has also been protected (see, e.g., Troxel v. Granville, 530 U.S. 57 (2000). Tort liability for invasion of privacy may be imposed, as we have seen, in a much broader range of cases. Likewise, although the constitutional right of privacy can be enforced only as against government action, privacy claims can be pursued under tort law wherever a duty is found. Furthermore, tort law gives damages to the plaintiff whose privacy has been invaded, while statutes or other measures that unconstitutionally burden individuals' privacy can be generally invalidated.

8. *Adoption.* The adoption area is one of the few in which the constitutional and tort contexts may converge. Complications plague the breach of confidence tort in the adoption area. The state of the law today in Oregon—and in other states—differs substantially from that described in *Humphers.* Although adoption was not recognized at common law, state statutes governing adoption have been passed since the mid-nineteenth century. These did not initially provide for confidentiality, and the first legislation restricting access to adoption records occurred in 1917 in Minnesota; by the end of the 1940s, most states ensured the confidentiality of adoption proceedings. However, in the 1960s, adoption agencies began collecting—and selectively releasing—information about birth parents that adoptees and their adoptive parents might have a need to know. Then in the 1970s, some adoptees commenced legal actions—based on their Constitutional right to privacy—attempting to force disclosures. These plaintiffs were largely unsuccessful.

In the 1980s, however, states began to move towards more open statutes. Some created registries in which birth parents and adoptees could voluntarily disclose their identities; others set up state-provided "confidential intermediaries" who would seek out an adoptee or birth mother at the other's request. A few have begun to allow complete disclosure, without even a hearing, to adoptees over the age of 21. In 1998, voters in Oregon adopted a ballot proposition allowing adults who had been adopted to receive their original birth certificates. For the history and current state of adoption law, see Cahn & Singer, Adoption, Identity, and the Constitution, 2 U.Pa.J.Const.L. 150 (1999) (arguing for more openness in the adoption process) and Comment, The Fear of Opening Pandora's Box: The Need to Restore Birth Parents' Privacy Rights in the Adoption Process, 28 Sw. U.L.Rev. 133 (1998) (insisting on the parents' Constitutional privacy claims)

The Oregon proposition was challenged by plaintiff birth parents who invoked both federal and state constitutions in support of their contractual and privacy rights. See Does 1, 2, 3, 4, 5, 6, and 7 v. State, 993 P.2d 822 (Or.App.1999). After denying that there had ever been a statutory contract with birth mothers guaranteeing that their identities would be kept confidential, the court considered the state privacy claims. It concluded that "[n]othing in *Humphers* . . . suggests that the Oregon Constitution recognizes a privacy interest, much less guarantees a constitutional privacy interest that is coextensive with, or indeed greater than, privacy interests that may be protected by tort law." It also rejected plaintiffs' federal constitutional privacy claims, distinguishing the setting of adoption from others in which an individual may have a fundamental right:

> A decision to prevent pregnancy, or to terminate pregnancy at an early stage, is a decision that may be made unilaterally by individuals seeking to prevent conception or by a woman who wishes to terminate a pregnancy. A decision to relinquish a child for adoption, however, is not a decision that may be made unilaterally by a birth mother or by any other party. Given that reality, it cannot be said that a birth mother has a fundamental right to give birth to a child and then have someone else assume legal responsibility for that child.

Furthermore, adoption "involves a child that already has been born, and a birth is, and historically has been, essentially a public event." A similar result was reached in state and federal constitutional challenges to a Tennessee law allowing disclosure of sealed adoption records to adult adoptees. See Doe v. Sundquist, 2 S.W.3d 919 (Tenn.1999) and Doe v. Sundquist, 106 F.3d 702 (6th Cir.), cert. denied, 522 U.S. 810 (1997).

9. What kinds of damages should be recoverable for breach of a duty of confidentiality?

B.   FALSE-LIGHT PRIVACY

The conventional idea of invasion of privacy as conceived by Warren and Brandeis involved true statements about aspects of plaintiff's life that others had no business knowing. But along the way, a few cases surfaced that placed the plaintiff in a false light but did not do harm to "reputation" so as to permit an action for defamation. For example, a group used plaintiff's name without authorization on a petition to the governor to veto a bill. Although falsely stating that plaintiff had signed the petition would not have been defamatory, the court found the situation actionable because it cast plaintiff in a false light. Hinish v. Meier & Frank Co., 113 P.2d 438 (Or.1941).

This type of case obviously tested the line between defamation and privacy. The distinction between the false light cause of action and the "true" privacy case, however, also became blurred after Time, Inc. v. Hill, 385 U.S. 374 (1967). In 1952, James Hill and his family were held hostage in their home for 19 hours by three escaped convicts who apparently treated them decently. The incident received extensive nationwide coverage. Thereafter the Hills moved to another state, sought seclusion and refused to make public appearances. A novel modeled in general on the event was published the following year. In 1955, Life magazine, in a very short article, announced that a play and a motion picture were being made from the novel, which they said was "inspired" by the Hill episode. The play, "a heart-stopping account of how a family rose to heroism in a crisis," would enable the public to see the Hill story "re-enacted." Photographs in the magazine showed actors performing scenes from the play at the house at which the original events had occurred. The Hills claimed that the story was inaccurate because the novel and the play showed the convicts committing violence on the father and uttering a "verbal sexual insult" at the daughter.

Suit was brought under the New York statute that required plaintiff to show that the article was being used for advertising purposes or for purposes of trade. A claim based on a truthful article, no matter how offensive and unpleasant for the Hills, would have failed. On the other hand, a few state courts had previously indicated that falsity would show that the article was really for purposes of trade and not for public enlightenment. (Recall that this hint has since been rejected in *Messenger*, p. 1110, supra.) The state courts allowed the Hills a recovery after lengthy litigation.

The Supreme Court, by a very fragile majority, decided that the privilege to comment on matters of public interest had constitutional protection and could not be lost by the introduction of falsity unless the falsity was either deliberate or reckless. The Court used the defamation analogy that was then being developed in the wake of *New York Times* and applied it to this privacy case that involved falsity, ignoring the fact that the falsity was relatively trivial. Was the false report any more harmful than an absolutely true one would have been? If not, why does the falsity matter? The Court had not yet considered defamation actions by private citizens. (The preliminary vote of the Court in *Time, Inc. v. Hill* favored the Hills. For the story and the opinions in that first stage, see B. Schwartz, The Unpublished Opinions of the Warren Court 240–303 (1985). For an account of the case from the vantage point of the attorney for the Hill family, Richard M. Nixon, see L. Garment, Annals of Law: The *Hill* Case, The New Yorker, Apr. 17, 1989 at 90.)

For contemporaneous comment, see Kalven, The Reasonable Man and the First Amendment: *Hill, Butts,* and *Walker,* 1967 Sup.Ct.Rev. 267.

Cantrell v. Forest City Publishing Co.

Supreme Court of the United States, 1974.
419 U.S. 245, 95 S.Ct. 465, 42 L.Ed.2d 419.

Mr. Justice Stewart delivered the opinion of the Court.

Margaret Cantrell and four of her minor children brought this diversity action in a Federal District Court for invasion of privacy against the Forest City Publishing Co., publisher of a Cleveland newspaper, the Plain Dealer, and against Joseph Eszterhas, a reporter formerly employed by the Plain Dealer, and Richard Conway, a Plain Dealer photographer. The Cantrells alleged that an article published in the Plain Dealer Sunday Magazine unreasonably placed their family in a false light before the public through its many inaccuracies and untruths. The District Judge struck the claims relating to punitive damages as to all the plaintiffs and dismissed the actions of three of the Cantrell children in their entirety, but allowed the case to go to the jury as to Mrs. Cantrell and her oldest son, William. The jury returned a verdict* against all three of the respondents for compensatory money damages in favor of these two plaintiffs.

The Court of Appeals for the Sixth Circuit reversed, holding that, in the light of the First and Fourteenth Amendments, the District Judge should have granted the respondents' motion for a directed verdict as to all the Cantrells' claims. . . .

I.

On December 1967, Margaret Cantrell's husband Melvin was killed along with 43 other people when the Silver Bridge across the Ohio River at Point Pleasant, West Virginia, collapsed. The respondent Eszterhas was assigned by the Plain Dealer to cover the story of the disaster. He wrote a "news feature" story focusing on the funeral of Melvin Cantrell and the impact of his death on the Cantrell family.

Five months later, after conferring with the Sunday Magazine editor of the Plain Dealer, Eszterhas and photographer Conway returned to the Point Pleasant area to write a follow-up feature. The two men went to the Cantrell residence, where Eszterhas talked with the children and Conway took 50 pictures. Mrs. Cantrell was not at home at any time during the 60 to 90 minutes that the men were at the Cantrell residence.

Eszterhas' story appeared as the lead feature in the August 4, 1968, edition of the Plain Dealer Sunday Magazine. The article stressed the family's abject poverty; the children's old, ill-fitting clothes and the deteriorating condition of their home were detailed in both the text and accompanying photographs. As he had done in his original, prize-winning article on the Silver Bridge disaster, Eszterhas used the Cantrell family to illustrate the impact of the bridge collapse on the lives of the people in the Point Pleasant area.

It is conceded that the story contained a number of inaccuracies and false statements. Most conspicuously, although Mrs. Cantrell was not present at any time during the reporter's visit to her home, Eszterhas wrote, "Margaret Cantrell will talk neither about what happened nor about how they are doing. She wears the same mask of non-expression she wore at the funeral. She is a proud woman. Her world has changed. She says that after it happened, the people in town offered to help them out with money and they refused to take it." Other significant misrepresentations were contained in details of Eszterhas' descriptions of the poverty in which the Cantrells were living and the dirty and dilapidated conditions of the Cantrell home.

The case went to the jury on a so-called "false light" theory of invasion of privacy. In essence, the theory of the case was that by publishing the false feature story about the Cantrells and thereby making them the objects of pity and ridicule, the respondents damaged Mrs. Cantrell and her

---

* The verdict was for $60,000—ed.

son William by causing them to suffer outrage, mental distress, shame, and humiliation.[2]

II.

In [*Hill*], the Court considered a similar false-light, invasion-of-privacy action. The New York Court of Appeals had interpreted New York Civil Rights Law §§ 50–51 to give a "newsworthy person" a right of action when his or her name, picture or portrait was the subject of a "fictitious" report or article. Material and substantial falsification was the test for recovery. [ ] Under this doctrine the New York courts awarded the plaintiff James Hill compensatory damages based on his complaint that Life Magazine had falsely reported that a new Broadway play portrayed the Hill family's experience in being held hostage by three escaped convicts. This Court, guided by its decision in *New York Times Co. v. Sullivan,* [ ], which recognized constitutional limits on a State's power to award damages for libel in actions brought by public officials, held that the constitutional protections for speech and press precluded the application of the New York statute to allow recovery for "false reports of matters of public interest in the absence of proof that the defendant published the report with knowledge of its falsity or in reckless disregard of the truth." [ ] Although the jury could have reasonably concluded from the evidence in the *Hill* case that Life had engaged in knowing falsehood or had recklessly disregarded the truth in stating in the article that "the story re-enacted" the Hill family's experience, the Court concluded that the trial judge's instructions had not confined the jury to such a finding as a predicate for liability as required by the Constitution. [ ]

The District Judge in the case before us, in contrast to the trial judge in *Time Inc. v. Hill,* did instruct the jury that liability could be imposed only if it concluded that the false statements in the Sunday Magazine feature article on the Cantrells had been made with knowledge of their falsity or in reckless disregard of the truth. No objection was made by any of the parties to this knowing-or-reckless-falsehood instruction. Consequently, this case presents no occasion to consider whether a State may constitutionally apply a more relaxed standard of liability for a publisher or broadcaster of false statements injurious to a private individual under a false-light theory of invasion of privacy, or whether the constitutional standard announced in *Time Inc. v. Hill* applies to all false-light cases. Cf. [*Gertz*]. Rather, the sole question that we need decide is whether the Court of Appeals erred in setting aside the jury's verdict.

III.

At the close of the petitioners' case-in-chief, the District Judge struck the demand for punitive damages. He found that Mrs. Cantrell had failed to

---

2. Although this is a diversity action based on state tort law, there is remarkably little discussion of the relevant Ohio or West Virginia law by the District Court, the Court of Appeals, and counsel for the parties. It is clear, however, that both Ohio and West Vir- ginia recognize a legally protected interest in privacy. [ ] Publicity that places the plaintiff in a false light in the public eye is generally recognized as one of the several distinct kinds of invasions actionable under the privacy rubric. [ ]

present any evidence to support the charges that the invasion of privacy "was done maliciously within the legal definition of that term." The Court of Appeals interpreted this finding to be a determination by the District Judge that there was no evidence of knowing falsity or reckless disregard of the truth introduced at the trial. Having made such a determination, the Court of Appeals held that the District Judge should have granted the motion for a directed verdict for respondents as to all the Cantrells' claims. [ ]

.   .   .

Although the verbal record of the District Court proceedings is not entirely unambiguous, the conclusion is inescapable that the District Judge was referring to the common-law standard of malice rather than to the *New York Times* "actual malice" standard when he dismissed the punitive damages claims.   .   .   .

Moreover, the District Judge was clearly correct in believing that the evidence introduced at trial was sufficient to support a jury finding that the respondents Joseph Eszterhas and Forest City Publishing Co. had published knowing or reckless falsehoods about the Cantrells.[5] There was no dispute during the trial that Eszterhas, who did not testify, must have known that a number of the statements in the feature story were untrue. In particular, his article plainly implied that Mrs. Cantrell had been present during his visit to her home and that Eszterhas had observed her "wear[ing] the same mask of non-expression she wore [at her husband's] funeral." These were "calculated falsehoods," and the jury was plainly justified in finding that Eszterhas had portrayed the Cantrells in a false light through knowing or reckless untruth.

The Court of Appeals concluded that there was no evidence that Forest City Publishing Co. had knowledge of any of the inaccuracies contained in Eszterhas' article. However, there was sufficient evidence for the jury to find that Eszterhas' writing of the feature was within the scope of his employment at the Plain Dealer and that Forest City Publishing Co. was therefore liable under traditional doctrines of *respondeat superior*.   .   .   .

For the foregoing reasons, the judgment of the Court of Appeals is reversed and the case is remanded to that court with directions to enter a judgment affirming the judgment of the District Court as to the respondents Forest City Publishing Co. and Joseph Eszterhas.

It is so ordered.

MR. JUSTICE DOUGLAS, dissenting.

.   .   .

A bridge accident catapulted the Cantrells into the public eye and their disaster became newsworthy. To make the First Amendment freedom to

---

5. Although we conclude that the jury verdicts should have been sustained as to Eszterhas and Forest City Publishing Co., we agree with the Court of Appeals' conclusion that there was insufficient evidence to support the jury's verdict against the photographer Conway.   .   .   .

report the news turn on subtle differences between common-law malice and actual malice is to stand the Amendment on its head. Those who write the current news seldom have the objective, dispassionate point of view—or the time—of scientific analysts. They deal in fast-moving events and the need for "spot" reporting. The jury under today's formula sits as a censor with broad powers—not to impose a prior restraint, but to lay heavy damages on the press. The press is "free" only if the jury is sufficiently disenchanted with the Cantrells to let the press be free of this damages claim. That regime is thought by some to be a way of supervising the press which is better than not supervising it at all. But the installation of the Court's regime would require a constitutional amendment. Whatever might be the ultimate reach of the doctrine Mr. Justice Black and I have embraced, it seems clear that in matters of public import such as the present news reporting, there must be freedom from damages lest the press be frightened into playing a more ignoble role than the Framers visualized.

I would affirm the judgment of the Court of Appeals.

Notes and Questions

1. How would you analyze a defamation action brought by the Cantrells? How would you analyze a public disclosure privacy action brought by the Cantrells?

2. Justice Stewart readily analyzes this case as involving the "false light" category of privacy. Might it also be analyzed as a public disclosure privacy case in which the media claimed the defense of newsworthiness but lost because the defense is not available when the material reported is deliberately or recklessly false? What are the differences between the two analyses?

A few years after *Cantrell,* in *Zacchini v. Scripps–Howard Broadcasting Co.,* p. 1187, infra, the Court approvingly quoted Dean Prosser's statement that the interest protected in false light actions "is clearly that of reputation, with the same overtones of mental distress as in defamation." Under this view, why might a state permit liability for errors that do not harm reputation?

3. What is this tort getting at? A few states have doubted its utility and have rejected it. See, e.g., Renwick v. The News and Observer Publishing Co., 312 S.E.2d 405 (N.C.), cert. denied 469 U.S. 858 (1984), in which the court noted that in states that recognize the action "the false light need not necessarily be a defamatory light. [ ] In many if not most cases, however, the false light is defamatory and an action for libel or slander will also lie." The court stated that it would "create a grave risk of serious impairment of the indispensable service of a free press in a free society if we [were to] saddle the press with the impossible burden of verifying to a certainty the facts associated in news articles with a person's name, picture or portrait, particularly as related to nondefamatory matter." The court thought the action "constitutionally suspect" and thought it "would not differ significantly" from the existing defamation action. See also Cain v.

Hearst Corp., 878 S.W.2d 577 (Tex.1994)(rejecting false light action because it "substantially duplicates the tort of defamation while lacking many of its procedural limitations.")

In Lake v. Wal–Mart Stores, Inc., 582 N.W.2d 231 (Minn.1998), nude photos of two plaintiff women showering together were developed at defendant's store and disseminated by defendant's employee. The court announced that it would recognize the other types of invasion of privacy torts—but in dictum declined to recognize false light publicity. Observing that "False light is the most widely criticized of the four privacy torts and has been rejected by several jurisdictions," the court relied most heavily on the observation that the false light tort overlaps significantly with defamation, and, thus, there are hardly any pure false light claims: "The primary difference between defamation and false light is that defamation addresses harm to reputation in the external world, while false light protects harm to one's inner self. . . . [B]ecause of the overlap . . . a case has rarely succeeded squarely on a false light claim."

4. States that have adopted the action must determine the relation between false light and defamation, including whether the array of common-law and statutory limitations on defamation, such as retraction statutes, special damage requirements, and statutes of limitations, apply as well to false light privacy.

In Fellows v. National Enquirer, Inc., 721 P.2d 97 (Cal.1986), defendant's article asserted that "Gorgeous Angie Dickinson's all smiles about the new man in her life—TV producer Arthur Fellows. Angie's steady-dating Fellows all over TinselTown, and happily posed for photographers with him as they exited the swanky Spago restaurant in Beverly Hills." Accompanying the article was a photograph of Dickinson and Fellows over the caption stating that Dickinson was "Dating a Producer."

Fellows demanded a retraction under Calif.Civil Code § 48a, asserting that plaintiff "has never dated Miss Dickinson, is not 'the new man in her life,' and has been married to Phyllis Fellows for the last 18 years." Defendant refused retraction and plaintiff sued for libel and false light privacy. Plaintiff withdrew his libel claim and proceeded solely on a false light claim with no allegation of special damages.

Under California law, libel that relies on extrinsic facts has to be supported by special damages. Civil Code § 45a. Plaintiff's privacy claim asserted that he had been falsely portrayed as the "new man" in Dickinson's life and as "steady-dating" her. The trial judge dismissed the privacy claim for lack of special damages and was affirmed on appeal.

The clear purpose of section 45a was to provide additional protection to libel defendants. Since "virtually every published defamation would support an action for false light invasion of privacy, exempting such actions from the requirement of proving special damages would render the statute a nullity." Under this rationale, is there any state requirement that protects libel defendants that would not also be applied to plaintiffs who sue on a false light theory? What should happen if a false light claim is based on language that does not rise to the level of being defamatory? The court went out of its way to announce that its ruling did not apply to false light claims "that would be actionable as a public disclosure of private facts had the representation made in the publication been true."

5. In Peoples Bank & Trust Co. v. Globe International Pub., Inc., 978 F.2d 1065 (8th Cir.1992), defendant's supermarket tabloid (Sun) ran a story about a 101-year-old Australian newspaper carrier who became pregnant by one of her customers. The story included a photo of plaintiff, a 96-year-old woman. The jury rejected her libel claim but awarded damages on her false-light claim. Is this consistent? The court rejected defendant's argument that the entire tabloid was fiction and could only be understood that way on the ground that the magazine combined true stories and fiction so thoroughly that even its writers could not tell which were which. The readers could reasonably have believed that this story portrayed actual facts and that the defendant had "recklessly failed to anticipate that result." After remand, plaintiff was awarded $150,000 compensatory damages and $850,000 in punitive damages. See 817 F.Supp. 72 (W.D.Ark.), appeal dismissed 14 F.3d 607 (8th Cir.), cert. denied 510 U.S. 931 (1993).

6. What is the nature of the *respondeat superior* problem in *Cantrell*? Might this point be significant in defamation cases in determining whose behavior to evaluate in considering liability? Recall the second appeal in *Gertz*, p. 1025, supra.

7. How are compensatory damages to be measured in *Cantrell*? Is the falsity relevant in that calculation?

8. In Machleder v. Diaz, 618 F.Supp. 1367 (S.D.N.Y.1985), the jury found a television station and its reporter liable for presenting the plaintiff in a false light as the result of an "ambush" interview. The crew caught the 71-year-old plaintiff off guard and began questioning him on camera. He was shown saying such things as "get that damn camera out of here" and generally not responding effectively to claims that his small company had polluted a nearby area.

P: I don't want to be involved with you people . . .

D: Just tell me why—why are those chemicals dumped in the back . . .

P: I don't want . . . I don't need . . . I don't need any publicity . . .

D: Why are those chemicals dumped in the back?

P: We don't . . . we didn't dump 'em.

In fact, plaintiff had reported the presence of the chemicals to the authorities two years earlier, as the program noted.

The jury rejected plaintiff's claims for libel, slander, trespass, and assault, but awarded plaintiff $250,000 in compensatory damages and $1,000,000 in punitive damages on the false light claim that the program made him appear "intemperate and evasive." The court of appeals reversed. Machleder v. Diaz, 801 F.2d 46 (2d Cir.1986), cert. denied 479 U.S.

1088 (1987). "Any portrayal of plaintiff as intemperate and evasive could not be false since it was based on his own conduct which was accurately captured by the cameras." Even if falsity had been found, the case should still have been dismissed because as a matter of law the portrayal was not "highly offensive."

9. In Dempsey v. National Enquirer, 702 F.Supp. 934 (D.Me.1989), plaintiff, an experienced pilot, had fallen out of a small airplane in flight but clung to the open boarding ladder on the side and survived his co-pilot's emergency landing with only a few scratches. Defendant Star magazine carried a story about the episode. The article was prefaced by a short third person narrative that concluded: "Here, Dempsey . . . tells in his own words how he found himself suddenly thrust into the ultimate daredevil stunt." The by-line said "by Henry Dempsey" and the article was a dramatic first person narrative that included quoted statements purporting to be Dempsey's reactions. Plaintiff alleged that he had never been interviewed by Star, had not given them information, and had not written the article in question. Defendant moved to dismiss plaintiff's false light claim.

The court denied the motion. Although the article was essentially a true account of what had happened to plaintiff, this article "unequivocally attributed authorship to the plaintiff." This falsity could be found by a jury to portray plaintiff as "otherwise than as he is," and to be highly offensive to a reasonable person.

Recall the *Masson* case, p. 1018, supra, involving the claim of fabricated quotations. Might plaintiff have relied also on a false light theory?

10. *False light by association?* A few cases have permitted a false light recovery to persons whose photographs have appeared in certain magazines without their consent. One involved a model whose nude photographs appeared in Hustler magazine. Douglass v. Hustler Magazine, Inc., 769 F.2d 1128 (7th Cir.1985), cert. denied 475 U.S. 1094 (1986). After the court described the magazine's contents, it concluded that a jury could reasonably find that the magazine was offensive and that "to be depicted as voluntarily associated with [Hustler] . . . is unquestionably degrading to a normal person, especially if the depiction is erotic." For other reasons, plaintiff's judgment was reversed and a new trial ordered.

In Braun v. Flynt, 726 F.2d 245 (5th Cir.), cert. denied 469 U.S. 883 (1984), plaintiff was employed at an amusement park. Part of her job included working in a novelty act with "Ralph, the Diving Pig." "Treading water in a pool, plaintiff would hold out a bottle of milk with a nipple on it. Ralph would dive into the pool and feed from the bottle." Publicity photographs of the act were used without authorization in Chic Magazine in a section entitled "Chic Thrills," a collection of vignettes, most of which "either concerned sex overtly or were accompanied by a photograph or cartoon of an overtly sexual nature." According to the court, the "particular issue of the magazine with which the case is involved contained numerous explicit photographs of female genitalia. Suffice it to say that *Chic* is a glossy, oversized, hard-core men's magazine."

From that base, the court concluded that the jury had implicitly found that "the ordinary reader automatically will form an unfavorable opinion about the character of a woman whose picture appears in *Chic* magazine." Even if no reader thought plaintiff unchaste, the jury "might have found that the publication implied Mrs. Braun's approval of the opinions expressed in *Chic* or that it implied Mrs. Braun had consented to having her picture in *Chic*. Either of these findings would support the jury verdict that the publication placed Mrs. Braun in a false light highly offensive to a reasonable person." A reduced judgment was upheld.

In Faloona v. Hustler Magazine, Inc., 799 F.2d 1000 (5th Cir.1986), cert. denied 479 U.S. 1088 (1987), plaintiffs had consented to be photographed nude for two books on human sexuality. Hustler published an excerpt from one book and a review of the other. Photographs of plaintiffs accompanied both publications. Their false light theory was rejected on the ground that "no reasonable person could consider the photographs as indicating plaintiffs' approval of *Hustler,* or that they were willing to pose nude for *Hustler.* It is obvious that the photographs were reproductions from the books being reviewed or excerpted. No tie to *Hustler* is claimed or suggested. It is this sharp definition of context which distinguishes this case from" *Douglass* and *Braun*.

In the absence of the clear context in *Faloona,* why might readers in the *Douglass* and *Braun* cases think that persons whose names and photographs appear in a publication have had any control over that use?

In a second case involving the pilot who fell from his plane, Dempsey v. National Enquirer, 702 F.Supp. 927 (D.Me.1988), the court refused to apply the *Douglass* and *Braun* cases to an article that appeared in the Enquirer. The text of the Enquirer article about the episode quoted statements given to the magazine by "friends" or by "an airport official" or a "neighbor." These negated the idea that plaintiff had cooperated or associated with the magazine itself. Moreover, "even if the article could imply that the plaintiff consented to the publication," the complaint failed to show that "association per se with the [National Enquirer] would be highly objectionable to a reasonable person." *Douglass* and *Braun* did not apply because there was no allegation here that the Enquirer was a magazine like the ones involved in those cases.

11. *Actual malice or negligence?* In a footnote to his concurring opinion in *Cox Broadcasting,* p. 1114, supra, Justice Powell observed:

> . . . The Court's abandonment of the "matter of general or public interest" standard as the determinative factor for deciding whether to apply the *New York Times* malice standard to defamation litigation brought by private individuals, [ ], calls into question the conceptual basis of *Time, Inc. v. Hill.* In neither *Gertz* nor our more recent decision in [*Cantrell*], however, have we been called upon to determine whether a State may constitutionally apply a more relaxed standard of liability under a false-light theory of invasion of privacy.
> [ ]

How might *Hill* have been compromised?

The question of actual malice or negligence in false light cases has persisted. The situation is summarized in Lovgren v. Citizens First National Bank of Princeton, 534 N.E.2d 987 (Ill.1989), in which the court upheld such a claim in favor of a plaintiff whose property was advertised without his consent as being up for sale at a forthcoming public auction. After summarizing the *Hill-Cantrell* sequence, the court concluded that it would, as a matter of state law, insist on "actual malice." It quoted from the Prosser & Keeton treatise:

> It is suggested that virtually all actionable invasions of privacy have been intentional invasions or invasions of a kind that defendant knew or had reason to know would not only be offensive but rightly so and are therefore examples of outrageous conduct that was committed with knowledge or with reason to know that it would cause severe mental stress. Recovery for an invasion of privacy on the ground that the plaintiff was depicted in a false light makes sense only when the account, if true, would not have been actionable as an invasion of privacy. In other words, the outrageous character of the publicity comes about in part by virtue of the fact that some part of the matter reported was false and deliberately so.

Is it that most cases fit this pattern or is it that this should be the minimum for this type of tort for some other reason? If the falsity is the key notion then why shouldn't the state use the same standards that it has developed for libel? Is there something "weaker" or "less important" about the false light action than about libel? (In the *Lovgren* case the "highly offensive" element was satisfied by "the allegation that the unauthorized advertisement made it practically impossible for plaintiff to obtain refinancing of his mortgage loan. A trier of fact could conclude that the defendants knew that the publication of this false fact would prove highly offensive to the plaintiff.")

In discussing the requirement that the publication be "highly offensive to a reasonable person" the *Lovgren* court cautioned that "minor mistakes in reporting, even if made deliberately, or false facts that offend a hypersensitive individual will not satisfy this element." What might motivate the court to protect deliberately false reporting?

The same point was made in one of the *Dempsey* cases involving the pilot who fell out of his plane. In his suit for an article that he alleged was replete with quotations falsely ascribed to him, the court held that, even if the alleged falsehoods existed, the publication was "not so offensive as to be 'highly objectionable to a reasonable person.'" Even if they were deliberate?

Do these cases suggest that the combination of serious fault and highly offensive falsity is essential to persuade states to adopt this tort? Even if states would adopt the tort on lesser grounds does the combination meet the constitutional minimum? For differing perspectives on the need for a false-light tort, compare Schwartz, Explaining and Justifying a Limited

Tort of False Light Invasion of Privacy, 41 Case W.Res.L.Rev. 885 (1991), with Zimmerman, False Light Invasion of Privacy: The Light That Failed, 64 N.Y.U.L.Rev. 364 (1989).

When prominent plaintiffs complain about false assertions that they endorse a particular publication or other enterprise, courts have developed an analysis that we consider at p. 1186, infra.

C. INTRUSION

In this section we consider efforts to gather information about or from an unwilling source. Intrusion may also involve efforts to impart information or "noise" to an unwilling recipient. We begin with cases that do not involve consent. We then turn to cases in which the defendant asserts the defense of consent.

Nader v. General Motors Corp.

Court of Appeals of New York, 1970.
25 N.Y.2d 560, 255 N.E.2d 765, 307 N.Y.S.2d 647.

[Plaintiff Ralph Nader, at the time a famous author and lecturer on consumer safety, had been a severe critic of defendant for several years. Nader alleged that the defendant, learning that he was about to publish a book, "Unsafe at Any Speed," initiated a series of efforts to intimidate him and suppress his criticism. These included inquiries into his political, social, racial, and religious views, his integrity, and his sexual behavior; casting aspersions on his character; keeping him under lengthy surveillance in public places; having "girls" accost him to entrap him into illicit relationships; making threatening, harassing and obnoxious telephone calls to him; tapping his telephone and eavesdropping mechanically and electronically on his private conversations; conducting a continuing and harassing investigation of him. The parties agreed that the law of the District of Columbia controlled the litigation. The trial court denied defendant's motion to dismiss the privacy claims in the case and the appellate division affirmed.]

CHIEF JUDGE FULD.

. . .

Turning, then, to the law of the District of Columbia, it appears that its courts have not only recognized a common-law action for invasion of privacy but have broadened the scope of that tort beyond its traditional limits. (See Pearson v. Dodd, 410 F.2d 701 [1969]; Afro–American Pub. Co. v. Jaffe, 366 F.2d 649 [1966]; [   ].) Thus, in the most recent of its cases on the subject, [*Pearson*], the Federal Court of Appeals for the District of Columbia declared:

"We approve the extension of the tort of invasion of privacy to instances of *intrusion,* whether by physical trespass or not, into spheres from which an ordinary man in a plaintiff's position could reasonably expect that the particular defendant should be excluded." (Italics supplied.)

It is this form of invasion of privacy—initially termed "intrusion" by Dean Prosser in 1960 (Privacy, 48 Cal.L.Rev. 383, 389 et seq.; Torts, § 112)—on which the two challenged causes of action are predicated.

Quite obviously, some intrusions into one's private sphere are inevitable concomitants of life in an industrial and densely populated society, which the law does not seek to proscribe even if it were possible to do so. "The law does not provide a remedy for every annoyance that occurs in everyday life." [   ] However, the District of Columbia courts have held that the law should and does protect against certain types of intrusive conduct, and we must, therefore, determine whether the plaintiff's allegations are actionable as violations of the right to privacy under the law of that jurisdiction. To do so, we must, in effect, predict what the judges of that jurisdiction's highest court would hold if this case were presented to them. [   ] In other words, what would the Court of Appeals for the District of Columbia hold is the character of the "privacy" sought to be protected? More specifically, would that court accord an individual a right, as the plaintiff before us insists, to be protected against any interference whatsoever with his personal seclusion and solitude? Or would it adopt a more restrictive view of the right as the appellant urges, merely protecting the individual from intrusion into "something secret," from snooping and prying into his private affairs?

The classic article by Warren and Brandeis [   ]—to which [*Pearson*] referred as the source of the District's common-law action for invasion of privacy [   ]—was premised, to a large extent, on principles originally developed in the field of copyright law. The authors thus based their thesis on a right granted by the common law to "each individual . . . of determining, ordinarily, to what extent his thoughts, sentiments and emotions shall be communicated to others" [   ]. Their principal concern appeared to be not with a broad "right to be let alone" (Cooley, Torts [2d ed.], p. 29) but, rather, with the right to protect oneself from having one's private affairs known to others and to keep secret or intimate facts about oneself from the prying eyes or ears of others.

In recognizing the existence of a common-law cause of action for invasion of privacy in the District of Columbia, the Court of Appeals has expressly adopted this latter formulation of the nature of the right. [   ] Quoting from the Restatement, Torts (§ 867), the court in the *Jaffe* case [   ] has declared that "[l]iability attaches to a person who 'unreasonably and seriously interferes with another's interest in *not having his affairs known to others.*'" (Emphasis supplied.) And, in *Pearson*, where the court extended the tort of invasion of privacy to instances of "intrusion," it again indicated, contrary to the plaintiff's submission, that the interest protected was one's right to keep knowledge about oneself from exposure to others, the right to prevent *the obtaining of the information* by improperly intrusive means" ([   ]; emphasis supplied). In other jurisdictions, too, the cases which have recognized a remedy for invasion of privacy founded upon intrusive conduct have generally involved the gathering of private facts or information through improper means. [   ]

It should be emphasized that the mere gathering of information about a particular individual does not give rise to a cause of action under this theory. Privacy is invaded only if the information sought is of a confidential nature and the defendant's conduct was unreasonably intrusive. Just as a common-law copyright is lost when material is published, so, too, there can be no invasion of privacy where the information sought is open to public view or has been voluntarily revealed to others. [ ] In order to sustain a cause of action for invasion of privacy, therefore, the plaintiff must show that the appellant's conduct was truly "intrusive" and that it was designed to elicit information which would not be available through normal inquiry or observation.

The majority of the Appellate Division in the present case stated that *all of "[t]he activities complained of"* in the first two counts constituted actionable invasions of privacy under the law of the District of Columbia [ ]. We do not agree with that sweeping determination. At most, only two of the activities charged to the appellant are, in our view, actionable as invasions of privacy under the law of the District of Columbia. However, since the first two counts include allegations which are sufficient to state a cause of action, we could—as the concurring opinion notes—merely affirm the order before us without further elaboration. To do so, though, would be a disservice both to the judge who will be called upon to try this case and to the litigants themselves. In other words, we deem it desirable, nay essential, that we go further and, for the guidance of the trial court and counsel, indicate the extent to which the plaintiff is entitled to rely on the various allegations in support of his privacy claim.

. . .

Turning, then, to the particular acts charged in the complaint, we cannot find any basis for a claim of invasion of privacy, under District of Columbia law, in the allegations that the appellant, through its agents or employees, interviewed many persons who knew the plaintiff, asking questions about him and casting aspersions on his character. Although those inquiries may have uncovered information of a personal nature, it is difficult to see how they may be said to have invaded the plaintiff's privacy. Information about the plaintiff which was already known to others could hardly be regarded as private to the plaintiff. Presumably, the plaintiff had previously revealed the information to such other persons, and he would necessarily assume the risk that a friend or acquaintance in whom he had confided might breach the confidence. If, as alleged, the question tended to disparage the plaintiff's character, his remedy would seem to be by way of an action for defamation not for breach of his right to privacy. [ ]

Nor can we find any actionable invasion of privacy in the allegations that the appellant caused the plaintiff to be accosted by girls with illicit proposals, or that it was responsible for the making of a large number of threatening and harassing telephone calls to the plaintiff's home at odd hours. Neither of these activities, howsoever offensive and disturbing, involved intrusion for the purpose of gathering information of a private and confidential nature.

As already indicated, it is manifestly neither practical nor desirable for the law to provide a remedy against any and all activity which an individual might find annoying. On the other hand, where severe mental pain or anguish is inflicted through a deliberate and malicious campaign of harassment or intimidation, a remedy is available in the form of an action for the intentional infliction of emotional distress—the theory underlying the plaintiff's third cause of action. But the elements of such an action are decidedly different from those governing the tort of invasion of privacy, and just as we have carefully guarded against the use of the prima facie tort doctrine to circumvent the limitations relating to other established tort remedies [ ], we should be wary of any attempt to rely on the tort of invasion of privacy as a means of avoiding the more stringent pleading and proof requirements for an action for infliction of emotional distress. (See, e.g., Clark v. Associated Retail Credit Men, 105 F.2d 62, 65 [D.C.Cir. 1939].)

Apart, however, from the foregoing allegations which we find inadequate to spell out a cause of action for invasion of privacy under District of Columbia law, the complaint contains allegations concerning other activities by the appellant or its agents which do satisfy the requirements for such a cause of action. The one which most clearly meets those requirements is the charge that the appellant and its codefendants engaged in unauthorized wiretapping and eavesdropping by mechanical and electronic means. [*Pearson*] expressly recognized that such conduct constitutes a tortious intrusion [ ], and other jurisdictions have reached a similar conclusion. [ ] In point of fact, the appellant does not dispute this, acknowledging that, to the extent the two challenged counts charge it with wiretapping and eavesdropping, an actionable invasion of privacy has been stated.

There are additional allegations that the appellant hired people to shadow the plaintiff and keep him under surveillance. In particular, he claims that, on one occasion, one of its agents followed him into a bank, getting sufficiently close to him to see the denomination of the bills he was withdrawing from his account. From what we have already said, it is manifest that the mere observation of the plaintiff in a public place does not amount to an invasion of his privacy. But, under certain circumstances, surveillance may be so "overzealous" as to render it actionable. (See [*Pearson*]; Pinkerton Nat. Detective Agency v. Stevens, 108 Ga.App. 159 [1963].) Whether or not the surveillance in the present case falls into this latter category will depend on the nature of the proof. A person does not automatically make public everything he does merely by being in a public place, and the mere fact that Nader was in a bank did not give anyone the right to try to discover the amount of money he was withdrawing. On the other hand, if the plaintiff acted in such a way as to reveal that fact to any casual observer, then, it may not be said that the appellant intruded into his private sphere. In any event, though, it is enough for present purposes to say that the surveillance allegation is not insufficient as a matter of law.

Since, then, the first two causes of action do contain allegations which are adequate to state a cause of action for invasion of privacy under District of Columbia law, the courts below properly denied the appellant's motion to dismiss those causes of action. It is settled that, so long as a pleading sets forth allegations which suffice to spell out a claim for relief, it is not subject to dismissal by reason of the inclusion therein of additional nonactionable allegations. [ ]

We would but add that the allegations concerning the interviewing of third persons, the accosting by girls and the annoying and threatening telephone calls, though insufficient to support a cause of action for invasion of privacy, are pertinent to the plaintiff's third cause of action—in which those allegations are reiterated—charging the intentional infliction of emotional distress. However, as already noted, it will be necessary for the plaintiff to meet the additional requirements prescribed by the law of the District of Columbia for the maintenance of a cause of action under that theory.

The order appealed from should be affirmed, with costs. . . .

BREITEL, J. (concurring in result). There is no doubt that the first and second causes of action are sufficient in alleging an invasion of privacy under what appears to be the applicable law in the District of Columbia [ ]. This should be the end of this court's proper concern with the pleadings, the only matter before the court being a motion to dismiss specified causes of action for insufficiency.

Thus it is not proper, it is submitted, for the court directly or indirectly to analyze particular allegations in the pleadings, once the causes of action are found sufficient, in order to determine whether they would alternatively sustain one cause of action or another, or whether evidence offered in support of the allegations is relevant only as to one rather than to another cause of action. Particularly, it is inappropriate to decide that several of the allegations as they now appear are referable only to the more restricted tort of intentional infliction of mental distress rather than to the common-law right of privacy upon which the first and second causes of action depend. The third cause of action is quite restricted. Thus many of the quite offensive acts charged will not be actionable unless plaintiff succeeds in the very difficult, if not impossible, task of showing that defendants' activities were designed, actually or virtually, to make plaintiff unhappy and not to uncover disgraceful information about him. The real issue in the volatile and developing law of privacy is whether a private person is entitled to be free of certain grave offensive intrusions unsupported by palpable social or economic excuse or justification.

True, scholars, in trying to define the elusive concept of the right of privacy, have, as of the present, subdivided the common law right into separate classifications, most significantly distinguishing between unreasonable intrusion and unreasonable publicity. [ ] This does not mean, however, that the classifications are either frozen or exhausted or that several of the classifications may not overlap.

Concretely applied to this case, it is suggested, for example, that it is premature to hold that the attempted entrapment of plaintiff in a public place by seemingly promiscuous ladies is no invasion of any of the categories of the right to privacy and is restricted to a much more limited cause of action for intentional infliction of mental distress. Moreover, it does not strain credulity or imagination to conceive of the systematic "public" surveillance of another as being the implementation of a plan to intrude on the privacy of another. Although acts performed in "public," especially if taken singly or in small numbers, may not be confidential, at least arguably a right to privacy may nevertheless be invaded through extensive or exhaustive monitoring and cataloguing of acts normally disconnected and anonymous.

These are but illustrations of the problems raised in attempting to determine issues of relevancy and allocability of evidence in advance of a trial record. The other allegations so treated involve harassing telephone calls, and investigatory interviews. It is just as important that while allegations treated singly may not constitute a cause of action, they may do so in combination, or serve to enhance other violations of the right to privacy.

It is not unimportant that plaintiff contends that a giant corporation had allegedly sought by surreptitious and unusual methods to silence an unusually effective critic. If there was such a plan, and only a trial would show that, it is unduly restrictive of the future trial to allocate the evidence beforehand based only on a pleader's specification of overt acts on the bold assumption that they are not connected causally or do not bear on intent and motive.

It should be observed, too, that the right to privacy, even as thus far developed, does not always refer to that which is not known to the public or is confidential. Indeed, the statutory right of privacy in this State and perhaps the most traditional right of privacy in the "common law sense" relates to the commercialized publicity of one's face or name, perhaps the two most public aspects of an individual. [   ]

There is still further difficulty. In this State thus far there has been no recognition of a common law right of privacy, but only that which derives from a statute of rather limited scope (Civil Rights Law, §§ 50, 51; Flores v. Mosler Safe Co., 7 N.Y.2d 276, 280 [1959]; Roberson v. Rochester Folding Box Co., 171 N.Y. 538, 556–557 [1902]). Consequently, this court must undertake the hazardous task of applying what is at present the quite different law of the District of Columbia. True, this may be the court's burden eventually, if the case were to return to it for review after trial, especially if the plaintiff were to prevail upon such a trial. However, there is no occasion to advance, now, into a complicated, subtle and still-changing field of law of another jurisdiction, solely to determine before trial the relevancy and allocability among pleaded causes of action of projected but not yet offered items of evidence. It is not overstatement to say that in the District of Columbia the law of the right of privacy is still inchoate in its development, perhaps more so than in many other jurisdictions that accept this newly coined common-law cause of action, despite unequivocal acceptance as a doctrine and extension by dictum to cases of intrusion [*Pearson*]. In the absence of a trial record, the court should avoid any unnecessary extrapolation of what the District of Columbia Court of Appeals has characterized as "an untried and developing area of tort law" [*Pearson*].

. . .

The broad statements in the opinion of the Appellate Division can be met, as this court has done so often, by declaring that they are not necessarily adopted in concluding that a cause or causes of action have been stated.

Accordingly, because of the prematurity of ruling on any other question but the sufficiency of the causes of action, I concur in result only.

JUDGES SCILEPPI, BERGAN and GIBSON concur with CHIEF JUDGE FULD; JUDGE BREITEL concurs in result in an opinion in which JUDGES BURKE and JASEN concur.

Notes and Questions

1. As a matter of judicial strategy, who has the better of the argument about how far the appellate opinion should go at this time? Is your view affected by the fact that a few months later General Motors, denying any wrongdoing, paid Nader $425,000 to settle his claims for $2 million in compensatory damages and $7 million in punitive damages? Actions against two detective agencies were also dropped as part of the settlement. N.Y. Times, Aug. 14, 1970, at 1.

2. This case, in addition to presenting a range of asserted invasions by means of intrusion into plaintiff's privacy, also indicates the close relationship between the tort aspects of privacy law and other tort areas. The alleged surveillance provides a good example. Can you suggest facts that would make surveillance an invasion of privacy? An intentional infliction of emotional distress? A defamation? Are these categories mutually exclusive or might the same surveillance situation be actionable under two or more categories?

3. Is there a given degree of surveillance that must be shown before there can be any action at all? Under any theory what is the minimum that Nader must show about the bank episode? Might you be liable for looking over the shoulder of the person in line ahead of you at the bank?

4. Even if such surveillance is shown, what justifications might be available to the defense? Perhaps the most common instances are insurance companies' efforts to ascertain whether claimants are hurt as seriously as they allege. Should this behavior be permitted at all? If so, what limits should be placed upon it? In Pinkerton National Detective Agency, Inc., v. Stevens, 132 S.E.2d 119 (Ga.App.1963), cited in *Nader,* plaintiff alleged that detectives spied on her home intermittently for five months; that they followed her when she left the house; cut a hole in her hedge to peek through and came up to the windows to peep and to eavesdrop day and night. The plaintiff became upset, developed nervous spasms, sleeplessness, nightmares and a bad rash, and needed medical and psychiatric aid. The court said that "[b]y making a claim for personal injury appellant must expect reasonable inquiry and investigation to be made of her claim and to this extent her interest in privacy is circumscribed. . . . This petition does not limit the defendant's acts to that reasonable and unobtrusive observation which would ordinarily be used to catch one in normal activities unaware, but sets out a course of conduct which would disturb an ordinary person without hypersensitive reactions." The court held that the petition stated a cause of action for invasion of privacy.

Likewise, in I.C.U. Investigations v. Jones, 2000 WL 869595 (Ala. 2000), a workers' compensation claimant brought an intrusion claim against a private investigation firm hired by his employer. Jones had suffered an electric shock and fallen from a truck bed, thereby dislocating and fracturing his shoulder. Since he and his employer disputed the amount of the compensation claim, they prepared for a hearing. As part of that preparation, the employer hired an investigation firm to monitor plaintiff's daily activities. During the surreptitious videotaping, the I.C.U. Investigations employee taped four occasions in which Jones urinated in his front yard. When Jones learned what was on the tape, he filed the instant action.

The court reversed a judgment for plaintiff, stating that the "key issue in Jones's workers' compensation case was the extent of his injury. Jones, therefore, should have expected a reasonable investigation regarding his physical capacity." Nor were the means used in the investigation "offensive or objectionable;" during all the tapings, Jones was always in public view and the investigator was on public land.

One dissenter argued that the tape of Jones urinating could not have served any legitimate purpose in the investigation. Another dissenter, emphasizing the deference that should be accorded to jury verdicts, explained that, in determining whether an intrusion into seclusion is actionable, both the purpose and the means must be evaluated. He insisted that "filming activity inside the home or even in the backyard can be an invasion of privacy. Although ICU filmed Jones urinating in his front yard, Jones's act of urinating was a private act, one not usually exposed to the public gaze."

Similarly, creditors are given leeway to attempt to reach the debtor and to recover what is claimed to be owing. See Montgomery Ward v. Shope, 286 N.W.2d 806 (S.D.1979).

Surveillance may also be employed during the course of an action for divorce or a custody battle. Plaxico v. Michael, 735 So.2d 1036 (Miss.1999), arose after a mother's former husband, Michael, took photographs of the mother's lesbian partner sitting in bed nude from the waist up during the course of investigations he undertook to obtain custody of their child. He showed the pictures only to his lawyer, who then disclosed them to the former wife during pre-trial discovery. Plaxico, the wife's companion, brought a suit against the husband for intrusion after he was awarded custody of the daughter. On appeal, a divided court affirmed a judgment against plaintiff, stating that, although "Plaxico was in a state of solitude or seclusion in the privacy of her bedroom where she had an expectation of privacy," "a reasonable person would not feel Michael's interference with Plaxico's seclusion was a substantial one that would rise to the level of gross offensiveness as required to prove . . . intentional intrusion upon seclusion or solitude." According to the majority, the husband's attempt to obtain verification of the rumors he had heard about his ex-wife's relationship was justifiable. Since Michael was concerned about the welfare of his daughter, and "believed that he took these pictures for the sole purpose to protect his minor child," his actions could not be construed as highly offensive to a reasonable person. If the rumors had been groundless, would the court's result have been the same? What if they had been disseminated by someone that the husband knew held a grudge against the wife?

The dissenters protested that Michael's goal of ensuring the best interest of his child should not justify the means he took to obtain it. "Neither rumors concerning an ex-wife's lifestyle nor a parent's justifiable concern over the best interests of his child . . . gave Michael a license to spy on a person's bedroom, take photographs of her in a semi-nude state and have those photographs developed by third parties and delivered to his attorney thereby exposing them to others." The publication of the photographs to others was significant only in demonstrating the offensiveness of Michael's act.

Contrast Fischer v. Hooper, 732 A.2d 396 (N.H.1999). Plaintiff wife had been divorced from her husband, and the two had joint custody of their daughter, who divided her time between them. A guardian ad litem and a therapist were also appointed for the daughter. When friction arose about the visitation agreement, the guardian ad litem advised that all telephone calls between the parties, and between each parent and their daughter, be recorded to resolve the problem—with, of course, the parties' permission. Defendant husband, however, initiated such taping without plaintiff's consent. In addition to suing under wiretapping and eavesdropping statutes, plaintiff initiated a common law action for intrusion. The supreme court affirmed the trial court's denial of summary judgment, rejecting his argument that "because the therapist and guardian ad litem were charged with supervising the plaintiff's relationship with her daughter, the plaintiff could not reasonably expect her conversations with her daughter to remain private." Although the daughter might "divulge the content of the conversation to the therapist or others," this did not prevent the jury from finding an expectation of privacy.

Are the divorced parent and the injured employee situations comparable?

5. In *Pearson v. Dodd,* discussed in *Nader,* two employees of Senator Thomas Dodd and two former employees secretly removed papers from the Senator's file overnight, photocopied them, replaced the originals, and gave the copies to defendant newspaper columnists who knew the manner in which they had been obtained. The court refused to hold the defendants liable for the actions of those who actually invaded the files:

> If we were to hold appellants liable for invasion of privacy on these facts, we would establish the proposition that one who receives information from an intruder, knowing it has been obtained by improper intrusion, is guilty of a tort. In an untried and developing area of tort law, we are not prepared to go so far. A person approached by an eavesdropper with an offer to share in the information gathered through the eavesdropping would perhaps play the nobler part should he spurn the offer and shut his ears. However, it seems to us that at this point it would place too great a strain on human weakness to hold one liable in damages who merely succumbs to temptation and listens.

What is the significance of the court's conclusion that this is a developing area of law? Is the same analysis applicable to those who look over shoulders at the bank?

6. *Conversion.* In *Pearson v. Dodd*, the plaintiff also alleged that his papers had been converted. The court rejected the contention in an extended passage that set out the nature of conversion and related actions:

> Conversion is the substantive tort theory which underlay the ancient common law form of action for trover. A plaintiff in trover alleged that he had lost a chattel which he rightfully possessed, and that the defendant had found it and converted it to his own use. With time, the allegations of losing and finding became fictional, leaving the question of whether the defendant had "converted" the property the only operative one.

> The most distinctive feature of conversion is its measure of damages, which is the value of the goods converted. The theory is that the "converting" defendant has in some way treated the goods as if they were his own, so that the plaintiff can properly ask the court to decree a forced sale of the property from the rightful possessor to the converter.

> Because of this stringent measure of damages, it has long been recognized that not every wrongful interference with the personal property of another is a conversion. Where the intermeddling falls short of the complete or very substantial deprivation of possessory rights in the property, the tort committed is not conversion, but the lesser wrong of trespass to chattels.

> The Restatement, Second, Torts has marked the distinction by defining conversion as:

>> ". . . [A]n intentional exercise of dominion or control over a chattel which so seriously interferes with the right of another to control it that the actor may justly be required to pay the other the full value of the chattel."

> Less serious interferences fall under the Restatement's definition of trespass.

The difference is more than a semantic one. The measure of damages in trespass is not the whole value of the property interfered with, but rather the actual diminution in its value caused by the interference. More important for this case, a judgment for conversion can be obtained with only nominal damages whereas liability for trespass to chattels exists only on a showing of actual damage to the property interfered with. . . .

It is clear that on the agreed facts appellants committed no conversion of the physical documents taken from appellee's files. Those documents were removed from the files at night, photocopied, and returned to the files undamaged before office operations resumed in the morning. Insofar as the documents' value to appellee resided in their usefulness as records of the business of his office, appellee was clearly not substantially deprived of his use of them.

The court then considered whether the documents had some derivative value beyond physical possession, and concluded:

The question here is not whether appellee had a right to keep his files from prying eyes, but whether the information taken from those files falls under the protection of the law of property, enforceable by a suit for conversion. In our view, it does not. The information included the contents of letters to appellee from supplicants, and office records of other kinds, the nature of which is not fully revealed by the record. Insofar as we can tell, none of it amounts to literary property, to scientific invention, or to secret plans formulated by appellee for the conduct of commerce. Nor does it appear to be information held in any way for sale by appellee, analogous to the fresh news copy produced by a wire service.

Appellee complains, not of the misappropriation of property bought or created by him, but of the exposure of information either (1) injurious to his reputation or (2) revelatory of matters which he believes he has a right to keep to himself. Injuries of this type are redressed at law by suit for libel and invasion of privacy respectively, where defendants' liability for those torts can be established under the limitations created by common law and by the Constitution.

A concurring judge observed that "Conduct for which a law enforcement officer would be soundly castigated is, by the phraseology of the majority opinion, found tolerable; conduct which, if engaged in by government agents would lead to the suppression of evidence obtained by these means, is approved when used for the profit of the press." Since the court's review was confined to the amended complaint as restricted by certain stipulations, he also concluded that Dodd would hardly be without legal remedy "if the entire factual situation herein were before us on pleadings encompassing all possible legal aspects suggested by the facts."

7. The *Nader* majority emphasizes that not every annoyance in life has a legal remedy. Compare Vernars v. Young, 539 F.2d 966 (3d Cir.1976), in which the court upheld a complaint alleging that the principal officer of a small corporation opened and, without consent, read mail that was addressed to plaintiff. Plaintiff was another officer of the corporation, but the mail was "addressed to her and marked personal." The court relied on the Restatement (Second) § 652B, providing that "One who intentionally intrudes . . . upon the solitude or seclusion of another, or his private affairs or concerns, is subject to liability . . . if the intrusion would be highly offensive to a reasonable person." Is it relevant that plaintiff might have avoided this situation by having personal mail sent to her home or a postal box rather than her office?

8. Should it be an invasion of privacy to ask neighbors about Nader's views, interests, and sexual habits? Can you add facts that might convert this inquiry into an intentional infliction of emotional distress? A defamation? If you find an action under any of these theories, would you permit the defendant the same justifications allowed for surveillance?

9. Nader alleged that the invasions were all intentional. Should that be a necessary element in this type of invasion of privacy?

What does intent mean in the intrusion context? In Mauri v. Smith, 929 P.2d 307 (Or.1996), defendant police officers were called to the scene of an altercation between a civil process server and Mauri (the parent of the person who was being served). The officers then entered their apartment uninvited, with the process server in tow. The court, reversing a directed verdict for defendants, followed the basic definition of "intent" in the Second Restatement, p. 864, supra:

> A person intrudes by thrusting himself or herself in without invitation, permission, or welcome. A person acts intentionally when he or she either desires to cause the consequence of an act or believes that the consequence is substantially certain to result from the act. By definition, then, an actor commits an intentional intrusion if the actor either desires to cause an unauthorized intrusion or believes that an unauthorized intrusion is substantially certain to result from committing the invasive act in question.

Would this differ from the approach to intent taken in *Nader*? In *Mauri*, the evidence, viewed most favorably to plaintiffs, could be read "to establish (a) that the officers lacked plaintiffs' consent to enter their apartment or had consent to enter, but only for a particular purpose, and (b) that the officers either desired to cause an unauthorized intrusion or believed that an unauthorized intrusion was substantially certain to result from their entry."

10. For another example of intrusion by photography, see Estate of Berthiaume v. Pratt, M.D., 365 A.2d 792 (Me.1976) in which the deceased, a patient of a physician other than the defendant, objected to defendant physician's efforts to photograph him as he lay dying in a hospital bed. A jury could have found that the patient had objected as strongly as he could by raising a clenched fist and moving his head. The court held that even in the absence of publication of the photographs, a jury could find that an actionable intrusion had occurred. The court rejected defendant's argument that these photographs would allow better evaluation of the progress of malignancy of the face in other patients. No matter how valuable the photographs would be to medical science, the plaintiff still had control over whether his "facial characteristics should be recorded for another's benefit."

Would that analysis hold even if the photographs might save the lives of 50 patients now in the hospital with the same condition? Is this like sacrificing one victim to save the lives of 50 other members of the community from the wrath of an approaching army? Recall, p. 927, supra.

11. In Melvin v. Burling, 490 N.E.2d 1011 (Ill.App.1986), plaintiffs brought an action for invasion of privacy based on the intentional ordering of merchandise in their name, without their consent. The court first determined that a cause of action based on intrusion does exist in Illinois. To support the action, the court indicated that the following facts must be shown: (1) an unauthorized intrusion or prying into plaintiff's seclusion; (2) the intrusion must be offensive or objectionable to a reasonable person; (3) the matter upon which the intrusion occurs must be private; and (4) the intrusion must cause anguish and suffering. The court held that sufficient facts to sustain the elements were present, and reversed the lower court's dismissal of the case.

Galella v. Onassis

United States Court of Appeals, Second Circuit, 1973.
487 F.2d 986.

[Photographer Ron Galella sued Jacqueline Kennedy Onassis for false arrest and malicious prosecution after he had been arrested by Secret Service agents who were protecting Mrs. Onassis's children, John and Caroline. Mrs. Onassis denied the charges and counterclaimed for injunctive relief against Galella's continuous efforts to photograph her and her children. The court of appeals affirmed the dismissal of Galella's claim. The portion of the opinion that follows deals with the propriety of the District Court's grant of injunctive relief to Mrs. Onassis and to the government, which had intervened in its capacity as protector of the children's safety.]

Before SMITH, HAYS and TIMBERS, CIRCUIT JUDGES.

J. JOSEPH SMITH, CIRCUIT JUDGE.

. . .

Galella fancies himself as a "paparazzo" (literally a kind of annoying insect, perhaps roughly equivalent to the English "gadfly"). Paparazzi make themselves as visible to the public and obnoxious to their photographic subjects as possible to aid in the advertisement and wide sale of their works.

Some examples of Galella's conduct brought out at trial are illustrative. Galella took pictures of John Kennedy riding his bicycle in Central Park across the way from his home. He jumped out into the boy's path, causing the agents concern for John's safety. The agents' reaction and interrogation of Galella led to Galella's arrest and his action against the agents; Galella on other occasions interrupted Caroline at tennis, and invaded the children's private schools. At one time he came uncomfortably close in a power boat to Mrs. Onassis swimming. He often jumped and postured around while taking pictures of her party notably at a theater opening but also on numerous other occasions. He followed a practice of bribing apartment house, restaurant and nightclub doormen as well as romancing a family servant to keep him advised of the movements of the family.

.   .   .

After a six-week trial the court dismissed Galella's claim and granted relief to both the defendant and the intervenor. Galella was enjoined from (1) keeping the defendant and her children under surveillance or following any of them; (2) approaching within 100 yards of the home of defendant or her children, or within 100 yards of either child's school or within 75 yards of either child or 50 yards of defendant; (3) using the name, portrait or picture of defendant or her children for advertising; (4) attempting to communicate with defendant or her children except through her attorney.

.   .   .

Discrediting all of Galella's testimony[10] the court found the photographer guilty of harassment, intentional infliction of emotional distress, assault and battery, commercial exploitation of defendant's personality, and invasion of privacy. Fully crediting defendant's testimony, the court found no liability on Galella's claim. Evidence offered by the defense showed that Galella had on occasion intentionally physically touched Mrs. Onassis and her daughter, caused fear of physical contact in his frenzied attempts to get their pictures, followed defendant and her children too closely in an automobile, endangered the safety of the children while they were swimming, water skiing and horseback riding. Galella cannot successfully challenge the court's finding of tortious conduct.[11]

Finding that Galella had "insinuated himself into the very fabric of Mrs. Onassis' life . . .." the court framed its relief in part on the need to prevent further invasion of the defendant's privacy. Whether or not this accords with present New York law, there is no doubt that it is sustainable under New York's proscription of harassment.

10. The court's findings on credibility are indeed broad, but they are supported in the record. Galella demonstrated a galling lack of respect for the truth and gave no indication of any consciousness of the meaning of the oath he had taken. Not only did he admit blatantly lying in his testimony, he admitted attempting to have other witnesses lie for him.

11. Harassment is a criminal offense [in New York] when with intent to harass a person follows another in a public place, inflicts physical contact or engages in any annoying conduct without legitimate cause. Galella was found to have engaged in this proscribed conduct. Conduct sufficient to invoke criminal liability for harassment may be the basis for private action. [   ]

Of course legitimate countervailing social needs may warrant some intrusion despite an individual's reasonable expectation of privacy and freedom from harassment. However the interference allowed may be no greater than that necessary to protect the overriding public interest. Mrs. Onassis was properly found to be a public figure and thus subject to news coverage. [   ] Nonetheless, Galella's action went far beyond the reasonable bounds of news gathering. When weighed against the *de minimis* public importance of the daily activities of the defendant, Galella's constant surveillance, his obtrusive and intruding presence, was unwarranted and unreasonable. If there were any doubt in our minds, Galella's inexcusable conduct toward defendant's minor children would resolve it.

Galella does not seriously dispute the court's finding of tortious conduct. Rather, he sets up the First Amendment as a wall of immunity protecting newsmen from any liability for their conduct while gathering news. There is no such scope to the First Amendment right. Crimes and torts committed in news gathering are not protected. [   ] There is no threat to a free press in requiring its agents to act within the law.

.   .   .

Injunctive relief is appropriate. Galella has stated his intention to continue his coverage of defendant so long as she is newsworthy, and his continued harassment even while the temporary restraining orders were in effect indicate that no voluntary change in this technique can be expected. New York courts have found similar conduct sufficient to support a claim for injunctive relief. [   ]

The injunction, however, is broader than is required to protect the defendant. Relief must be tailored to protect Mrs. Onassis from the "paparazzo" attack which distinguishes Galella's behavior from that of other photographers; it should not unnecessarily infringe on reasonable efforts to "cover" defendant. Therefore, we modify the court's order to prohibit only (1) any approach within twenty-five (25) feet of defendant or any touching of the person of the defendant Jacqueline Onassis; (2) any blocking of her movement in public places and thoroughfares; (3) any act foreseeably or reasonably calculated to place the life and safety of defendant in jeopardy; and (4) any conduct which would reasonably be foreseen to harass, alarm, or frighten the defendant.

Any further restriction on Galella's taking and selling pictures of defendant for news coverage is, however, improper and unwarranted by the evidence. [   ]

Likewise, we affirm the grant of injunctive relief to the government modified to prohibit any action interfering with Secret Service agents' protective duties. Galella thus may be enjoined from (a) entering the children's schools or play areas; (b) engaging in action calculated or reasonably foreseen to place the children's safety or well being in jeopardy, or which would threaten or create physical injury; (c) taking any action which could reasonably be foreseen to harass, alarm, or frighten the children; and (d) from approaching within thirty (30) feet of the children.

As modified, the relief granted fully allows Galella the opportunity to photograph and report on Mrs. Onassis' public activities. Any prior restraint on news gathering is minuscule and fully supported by the findings.

.   .   .

TIMBERS, CIRCUIT JUDGE [dissented from the reduction of the distance limits imposed by the trial judge].

.   .   .

Notes and Questions

1. In 1982, Galella was found guilty of 12 violations of the earlier order for taking photographs within 25 feet of Mrs. Onassis. The judge suspended a fine of $120,000 when Galella agreed to pay the $10,000 in legal fees incurred by Onassis and agreed never again to photograph her. Galella was told that if he should renege, the judge would revive the fine or impose a six-month jail sentence for each violation. N.Y.L.J., Mar. 25, 1982 at 1. See Galella v. Onassis, 533 F.Supp. 1076 (S.D.N.Y. 1982).

2. The court's analysis was affected by the fact that New York law controlled and the New York statute made it difficult to press a direct privacy claim. But the court in an omitted footnote suggested that the New York courts would not read the statute to preclude the judicial development of an action that treated unjustified intrusion into one's solitude as an actionable tort. The court thought the statute was directed only to liability for publishing as opposed to gathering activities. Nonetheless, the court did not need to reach the question since it found liability on clearer grounds.

3. Might § 652B of the Second Restatement, p. 1162, supra, apply to Galella's actions?

4. The court observed that Onassis was a "public figure." What is the significance of that fact in this type of case? What if Onassis had been an ordinary citizen whose appearance attracted Galella—and the publications that purchased his photographs?

5. In 1975, it was disclosed that a reporter had been sifting through the contents of garbage cans outside the home of Secretary of State Henry Kissinger. If the cans were on the public sidewalk waiting to be emptied by the garbage collectors, has the reporter committed any tort? A very short editorial attacked the practice: "Pawing through someone else's garbage is a revolting exercise and doing it in the name of journalism makes it none the less so." Editor & Publisher, July 19, 1975, at 6.

In California v. Greenwood, 486 U.S. 35 (1988), the Court rejected a claim that criminal defendants had a reasonable expectation of privacy with respect to trash that was searched by police after the defendants had placed it on the street for collection. Writing for a six-member majority, Justice White said, "It is common knowledge that plastic garbage bags left on or at the side of a public street are readily accessible to animals, children, scavengers, snoops, and other members of the public.   .   .   . Accordingly, having deposited their garbage in an area particularly suited for public inspection and . . . for the express purpose of having strangers take it, [ ] respondents could have had no reasonable expectation of privacy in the inculpatory items that they discarded."

6. *Stalking.* Courts and legislatures have begun developing sanctions against "stalking." In addition to criminal sanctions, some states have developed civil remedies. Calif.Civ.Code § 1708.7 requires the plaintiff to show that the defendant (1) engaged in a "pattern of conduct the intent of which was to follow, alarm, or harass" the plaintiff, (2) as a result of which the plaintiff "reasonably feared for his or her safety, or the safety of an immediate family member," and (3) that the defendant either violated a restraining order, or made a "credible threat with the intent to place the plaintiff in reasonable fear for his or her safety, or the safety of an immediate family member and, on at least one occasion, the plaintiff clearly and definitively demanded that the defendant cease and abate the pattern of conduct and that the defendant persisted in his or pattern of conduct." Damages and an injunction are available. Would this have been useful to the plaintiff in *Galella v. Onassis*? For common law liability for stalking, see Summers v. Bailey, 55 F.3d 1564 (11th Cir.1995)(seller of store liable under Florida law for stalking buyer in an attempt to regain the store).

Desnick v. American Broadcasting Companies, Inc.

United States Court of Appeals, Seventh Circuit, 1995.
44 F.3d 1345.

[The plaintiffs, two doctors and the ophthalmic clinic known as the "Desnick Eye Center" at which they worked, appeal from the dismissal of their suit against the ABC television network, a producer of the ABC program PrimeTime Live named Entine, and the program's main reporter, Donaldson. The complaint alleged that Entine told Dr. Desnick, the clinic's owner—who is not a plaintiff in this case—that he wanted to do a segment on cataract practice; that it would not involve "ambush" interviews or "undercover" surveillance, and that it would be "fair and balanced." Plaintiff permitted an ABC crew to film a "live" operation and to interview personnel in the Chicago office. Plaintiff clinic alleged that unbeknownst to it, Entine dispatched persons who posed as patients with concealed cameras to other Desnick eye centers in Indiana and Wisconsin where the individual doctors worked.]

Before POSNER, CHIEF JUDGE, and COFFEY and MANION, CIRCUIT JUDGES.

POSNER, CHIEF JUDGE.

. . .

The program aired on June 10. Donaldson introduces the segment by saying, "We begin tonight with the story of a so called 'big cutter,' Dr. James Desnick. . . . [I]n our undercover investigation of the big cutter you'll meet tonight, we turned up evidence that he may also be a big charger, doing unnecessary cataract surgery for the money." . . . . Donaldson tells the viewer that PrimeTime Live has hired a professor of ophthalmology to examine the test patients who had been told they needed cataract surgery, and the professor tells the viewer that they didn't need it. With regard to one, he says, "I think it would be near malpractice to do surgery on him." Later in the segment he denies that this could just be an honest difference of opinion between professionals.

[The court detailed other parts of the program including interviews with former staff members; interviews with some patients who reported bad results; reports that records were changed and that machines were tampered with so that patients would think that they had cataracts; and a report of an administrative proceeding charging Dr. Desnick with malpractice and deception. Also, in an "ambush" interview, Donaldson is shown accosting Desnick at O'Hare Airport: "Is it true, Doctor, that you changed medical records to show less vision than your patients actually have? We've been told, Doctor, that you've changed the glare machine so we have a different reading. Is that correct? Doctor, why won't you respond to the questions?" The court refused to dismiss the defamation claim.]

The second class of claims in this case concerns, as we said, the methods that the defendants used to create the broadcast segment. There are four such claims: that the defendants committed a trespass in insinuating the test patients into the Wisconsin and Indiana offices of the Desnick Eye Center, that they invaded the right of privacy of the Center and its doctors at those offices (specifically Glazer and Simon), that they violated federal and state statutes regulating electronic surveillance, and that they committed fraud by gaining access to the Chicago office by means of a false promise that they would present a "fair and balanced" picture of the Center's operations and would not use "ambush" interviews or undercover surveillance.

To enter upon another's land without consent is a trespass. The force of this rule has, it is true, been diluted somewhat by concepts of privilege and of implied consent. But there is no journalists' privilege to trespass. [ ]; Le Mistral, Inc. v. Columbia Broadcasting System, 402 N.Y.S.2d 815 (App.Div. 1978). And there can be no implied consent in any nonfictitious sense of the term when express consent is procured by a misrepresentation or a misleading omission. The Desnick Eye Center would not have agreed to the entry of the test patients into its offices had it known they wanted eye examinations only in order to gather material for a television expose of the Center and that they were going to make secret videotapes of the examinations. Yet some cases, illustrated by Martin v. Fidelity & Casualty Co., 421 So.2d 109, 111 (Ala.1982), deem consent effective even though it was procured by fraud. There must be something to this surprising result. Without it a restaurant critic could not conceal his identity when he ordered a meal, or a browser pretend to be interested in merchandise that he could not afford to buy. Dinner guests would be trespassers if they were false friends who never would have been invited had the host known their true character, and a consumer who in an effort to bargain down an automobile dealer falsely claimed to be able to buy the same car elsewhere at a lower price would be a trespasser in the dealer's showroom. Some of these might be classified as privileged trespasses, designed to promote competition. Others might be thought justified by some kind of implied consent—the restaurant critic for example might point by way of analogy to the use of the "fair use" defense by book reviewers charged with copyright infringement and argue that the restaurant industry as a whole would be injured if restaurants could exclude critics. But most such efforts at rationalization would be little better than evasions. The fact is that consent to an entry is often given legal effect even though the entrant has intentions that if known to the owner of the property would cause him for perfectly understandable and generally ethical or at least lawful reasons to revoke his consent.

The law's willingness to give effect to consent procured by fraud is not limited to the tort of trespass. The Restatement gives the example of a man who obtains consent to sexual intercourse by promising a woman $100, yet (unbeknownst to her, of course) he pays her with a counterfeit bill and intended to do so from the start. The man is not guilty of battery, even though unconsented to sexual intercourse is a battery. Restatement (Second) of Torts § 892B, illustration 9, pp. 373–74 (1979). Yet we know that to conceal the fact that one has a venereal disease transforms "consensual" intercourse into battery. [ ] Seduction, standardly effected by false promises of love, is not rape, [ ]; intercourse under the pretense of rendering medical or psychiatric treatment is, at least in most states. [ ] It certainly is battery. [ ] Trespass presents close parallels. If a homeowner opens his door to a purported meter reader who is in fact nothing of the sort—just a busybody curious about the interior of the home—the homeowner's consent to his entry is not a defense to a suit for trespass. [ ] And likewise if a competitor gained entry to a business firm's premises posing as a customer but in fact hoping to steal the firm's trade secrets. [ ]

How to distinguish the two classes of cases—the seducer from the medical impersonator, the restaurant critic from the meter reader impersonator? The answer can have nothing to do with fraud; there is fraud in all the cases. It has to do with the interest that the torts in question, battery and trespass, protect. The one protects the inviolability of the person, the other the inviolability of the person's property. The woman who is seduced wants to have sex with her seducer, and the restaurant owner wants to have customers. The woman who is victimized by the medical impersonator has no desire to have sex with her doctor; she wants medical treatment. And the homeowner victimized by the phony meter reader does not want strangers in his house unless they have authorized service functions. The dealer's objection to the customer who claims falsely to have a lower price from a competing dealer is not to the physical presence of the customer, but to the fraud that he is trying to perpetuate. The lines are not bright—they are not even inevitable. They are the traces of the old forms of action, which have resulted in a multitude of artificial distinctions in modern law. But that is nothing new.

There was no invasion in the present case of any of the specific interests that the tort of trespass seeks to protect. The test patients entered offices that were open to anyone expressing a desire for ophthalmic services and videotaped physicians engaged in professional, not personal, communications with strangers (the testers themselves). The activities of the offices were not disrupted, as in [ ], another case of gaining entry by false pretenses. See also *Le Mistral, Inc. v. Columbia Broadcasting System*, [ ]. Nor was there any "inva[sion of] a person's private space," [ ], as in our hypothetical meter reader case, as in the famous case of De May v. Roberts, 9 N.W. 146 (Mich.1881)(where a doctor, called to the plaintiff's home to deliver her baby, brought along with him a friend who was curious to see a birth but was not a medical doctor, and represented the friend to be his medical assistant), as in one of its numerous modern counterparts, Miller v. National Broadcasting Co., 232 Cal.Rptr. 668, 679 (App.1986), and as in Dietemann v. Time, Inc., 449 F.2d 245 (9th Cir.1971), on which the plaintiffs in our case rely. *Dietemann* involved a home. True, the portion invaded was an office, where the plaintiff performed quack healing of nonexistent ailments. The parallel to this case is plain enough, but there is a difference. Dietemann was not in business, and did not advertise his services or charge for them. His quackery was private.

No embarrassingly intimate details of anybody's life were publicized in the present case. There was no eavesdropping on a private conversation; the testers recorded their own conversations with the Desnick Eye Center's physicians. There was no violation of the doctor patient privilege. There was no theft, or intent to steal, trade secrets; no disruption of decorum, of peace and quiet; no noisy or distracting demonstrations. Had the testers been undercover FBI agents, there would have been no violation of the Fourth Amendment, because there would have been no invasion of a legally protected interest in property or privacy. [ ] "Testers" who pose as prospective home buyers in order to gather evidence of housing discrimination are not trespassers even if they are private persons not acting under color of law. [ ] The situation of the defendants' "testers" is analogous. Like testers seeking evidence of violation of antidiscrimination laws, the defendants' test patients gained entry into the plaintiffs' premises by misrepresenting their purposes (more precisely by a misleading omission to disclose those purposes). But the entry was not invasive in the sense of infringing the kind of interest of the plaintiffs that the law of trespass protects; it was not an interference with the ownership or possession of land. We need not consider what if any difference it would make if the plaintiffs had festooned the premises with signs forbidding the entry of testers or other snoops. Perhaps none, [ ], but that is an issue for another day.

What we have said largely disposes of two other claims: infringement of the right of privacy, and illegal wiretapping. The right of privacy embraces several distinct interests, but the only ones conceivably involved here are the closely related interests in concealing intimate personal facts and in preventing intrusion into legitimately private activities, such as phone conversations. [ ] As we have said already, no intimate personal facts concerning the two individual plaintiffs (remember that Dr. Desnick himself is not a plaintiff) were revealed; and the only conversations that were recorded were conversations with the testers themselves. [   ]

The federal and state wiretapping statutes that the plaintiffs invoke allow one party to a conversation to record the conversation unless his purpose in doing so is to commit a crime or a tort or (in the case of the state, but not the federal, law) to do "other injurious acts." 18 U.S.C. § 2511(2)(d); [   ]. The defendants did not order the camera armed testers into the Desnick Eye Center's premises in order to commit a crime or tort. Maybe the program as it was eventually broadcast was tortious, for we have said that the defamation count was dismissed prematurely. But there is no suggestion that the defendants sent the testers into the Wisconsin and Indiana offices for the purpose of defaming the plaintiffs by charging tampering with the glare machine. The purpose, by the plaintiffs' own account, was to see whether the Center's physicians would recommend cataract surgery on the testers. By the same token it was not to injure the Desnick Eye Center, unless the public exposure of misconduct is an "injurious act" within the meaning of the Wisconsin statute. Telling the world the truth about a Medicare fraud is hardly what the framers of the statute could have had in mind in forbidding a person to record his own conversations if he was trying to commit an "injurious act." [   ]

Last is the charge of fraud in the defendants' gaining entry to the Chicago office and being permitted while there to interview staff and film a cataract operation, and in their obtaining the Desnick Eye Center's informational videotape. [The court held that under the unusual law of Illinois, promissory fraud was not actionable unless it was part of a scheme to defraud. Since that did not exist here there was no basis for liability. Nor did harm flow from the alleged fraud.]

One further point about the claims concerning the making of the program segment, as distinct from the content of the segment itself, needs to be made. The Supreme Court in the name of the First Amendment has hedged about defamation suits, even when not brought by public figures, with many safeguards designed to protect a vigorous market in ideas and opinions. Today's "tabloid" style investigative television reportage, conducted by networks desperate for viewers in an increasingly competitive television market [   ], constitutes—although it is often shrill, one sided, and offensive, and sometimes defamatory—an important part of that market. It is entitled to all the safeguards with which the Supreme Court has surrounded liability for defamation. And it is entitled to them regardless of the name of the tort, see, e.g., Hustler Magazine, Inc. v. Falwell, 485 U.S. 46 (1988), and, we add, regardless of whether the tort suit is aimed at the content of the broadcast or the production of the broadcast. If the broadcast itself does not contain actionable defamation, and no established rights are invaded in the process of creating it (for the media have no general immunity from tort or contract liability, [   ]), then the target has no legal remedy even if the investigatory tactics used by the network are surreptitious, confrontational, unscrupulous, and ungentlemanly. In this case, there may have been—it is too early to tell—an actionable defamation, and if so the plaintiffs have a remedy. But none of their established rights under either state law or the federal wiretapping law was infringed by the making, as opposed to the dissemination, of the broadcast segment of which they complain, with the possible and possibly abandoned exception of contract law.

Affirmed in Part, Reversed in Part, and Remanded.

Notes and Questions

1. *Trespass.* We have explored the notion of trespass twice already. In the first instance, p. 190, supra, we considered actions for personal injury brought by entrants on land. In the second instance, p. 652, supra, we considered actions brought by land owners for invasions of their possessory interests. How does the trespass action in this case differ?

2. In the cited *Le Mistral* case, employees of WCBS–TV were ordered to take a camera crew to visit restaurants that had been cited for health code violations. Defendants entered plaintiff's restaurant at lunch time "with cameras rolling" and used bright lights that were necessary to get the pictures. The jury could find that the crew entered "in a noisy and obtrusive fashion and following the loud commands of the reporter, Rich, to photograph the patrons dining." Some patrons left without paying their bills. Others "hid their faces behind napkins or table cloths or hid themselves beneath tables." This was held an actionable trespass. When Rich claimed that the restaurant was a place of public accommodation, the court responded that defendants admitted that the crew "did not seek to avail themselves of the plaintiff's 'accommodation'; they had no intention of purchasing food or drink."

How does this case fit into the *Desnick* court's analysis?

3. In the cited *Dietemann* case, a reporter and photographer went to the entrance of plaintiff's home and falsely stated that one of them needed advice and that they had been referred by someone. After being admitted to plaintiff's home and taken into his den, the defendants secretly taped and photographed as the plaintiff waved a wand over the "patient" and advised her that she had a lump in her breast because she had eaten rancid butter 11 years, 9 months and 7 days earlier. Photos and a story appeared in defendant's magazine.

The court stated that the initial entry was not actionable because "one who invites another to his home or office takes a risk that the visitor may not be what he seems, and that the visitor may repeat all he hears and observes when he leaves." (Why is that?) But the surreptitious use of tape recorders and cameras was actionable. One "does not and should not be required to take the risk that what is heard and seen will be transmitted by photograph or recording, or in our modern world, in full living color and hi-fi to the public at large or to any segment of it that the visitor may select. A different rule could have a most pernicious effect upon the dignity of man and it would surely lead to guarded conversations and conduct where candor is most valued, e.g., in the case of doctors and lawyers.''

How does this case fit into the *Desnick* court's analysis? Is there a difference between a tape recorder, which preserves the words actually spoken, and a camera, which creates and preserves visual images that the reporters could have described afterward only verbally and only from memory?

4. Should it be relevant that *Le Mistral* was brought on a trespass theory and that *Dietemann* was brought on a privacy theory?

5. In *Desnick* why did the court's disposition of the trespass claim also dispose of the privacy claim?

6. Restatement (Second) of Torts § 892B provides that consent to the conduct of another is effective ''for all consequences of the conduct and for the invasion of any interests resulting from it'' unless within the limitation of subsection (2):

> If the person consenting to the conduct of another is induced to consent by a substantial mistake concerning the nature of the invasion of his interests or the extent of the harm to be expected from it and the mistake is known to the other or is induced by the other's misrepresentation, the consent is not effective for the unexpected invasion or harm.

Is this relevant in *Desnick*? To Dietemann's misunderstanding about who sent the visitors and why they were there?

7. *Wiretapping.* Why does the wiretapping claim fail in *Desnick*? The federal statute is less protective than some state provisions because it exempts from the ban any conversation in which one party records the contents or in which one party authorizes a third party to record it.

Florida made it criminal for any ''person not acting under color of law'' to intercept a wire or oral communication unless all parties to the communication had given prior consent. Reporters and others challenged the statute, claiming that the use of concealed recording equipment was essential to investigative reporting for three reasons: it aided accuracy of reporting; persons being interviewed would not be candid if they knew they were being recorded; and the recording provided corroboration in case of suit for defamation.

The Florida Supreme Court upheld the statute's constitutionality. The statute allows ''each party to a conversation to have an expectation of privacy from interception by another party to the conversation. It does not exclude any source from the press, intrude upon the activities of the news media in contacting sources, prevent the parties to the communication from consenting to the recording, or restrict the publication of any information gained from the communication. First Amendment rights do not include a constitutional right to corroborate news gathering activities when the legislature has statutorily recognized the private rights of individuals.''

The court quoted *Dietemann*'s concern about the effect on the "dignity of man." In response to the argument that secret recording may be the only way to get credible information about crime, the court stated that protection against intrusion might extend even to a person "reasonably suspected of committing a crime." Shevin v. Sunbeam Television Corp., 351 So.2d 723 (Fla.1977).

The Supreme Court dismissed the appeal by the press for want of a substantial federal question, 435 U.S. 920 (1978). Justices Brennan, White and Blackmun would have noted probable jurisdiction and set the case for oral argument.

8. In Ribas v. Clark, 696 P.2d 637 (Cal.1985), a wife asked the defendant to listen in on an extension phone as she talked to her estranged husband. The husband learned about the episode when the defendant testified in an arbitration hearing about matters she overheard. He then sued for violation of Calif.Penal Code § 631(a), which provides in relevant part for punishment of any person "who . . . intentionally taps, or makes any unauthorized connection . . . with any . . . telephone wire, line, cable or instrument, . . . or who willfully and without the consent of all parties to the communication, or in any unauthorized manner, reads, or attempts to read, or to learn the contents or meaning of any message . . . while the same is in transit . . ., or is being sent from, or received at any place within this state. . . ."

Section 637.2 provided a civil action against violators for the greater of $3,000 or trebled actual damages. The court upheld the complaint. The statute was read broadly to bar "far more than illicit wiretapping," including the recording of a conversation without the other's consent:

> While one who imparts private information risks the betrayal of his confidence by the other party, a substantial distinction has been recognized between the secondhand repetition of the contents of a conversation and its simultaneous dissemination to an unannounced second auditor, whether that auditor be a person or mechanical device. [ ]
>
> As one commentator has noted, such secret monitoring denies the speaker an important aspect of privacy of communication—the right to control the nature and extent of the firsthand dissemination of his statement. [   ] Partly because of this factor, the Privacy Act has been read to require the assent of all parties to a communication before another may listen.

Shulman v. Group W Productions, Inc., et al.

Supreme Court of California, 1998.
18 Cal.4th 200, 955 P.2d 469, 74 Cal.Rptr.2d 843.

WERDEGAR, JUSTICE.

[Plaintiffs, mother and son, were injured when a car in which they and other family members were riding, overturned, tumbled down an embankment and came to rest upside down in a ditch on state-owned property. Ruth, the mother, was pinned in the wreckage. A Mercy Air rescue helicopter was dispatched to the scene by county officials. On board were nurse Carnahan, the pilot, a medic, and Joel Cooke. A video cameraman employed by defendant Group W., Cooke was recording the events for later broadcast. Carnahan was wearing a wireless microphone that picked up conversations with the victims and other rescue personnel. A nine-minute tape was broadcast on a segment on rescue operations. After Carnahan steps from the helicopter, she can be seen and heard speaking about the situation with various rescue workers. A firefighter assures her they will hose down the area to prevent any fire from the wrecked car. Only a glimpse is shown of the son, Wayne, and his voice is never heard. "Ruth is shown several times, either by brief shots of a limb or her torso, or with her features blocked by others or obscured by an oxygen mask. She is also heard speaking several times. Carnahan calls her 'Ruth' and her last name is not mentioned on the broadcast."]

While Ruth is still trapped under the car, Carnahan asks Ruth's age. Ruth responds, "I'm old." On further questioning, Ruth reveals she is 47, and Carnahan observes that "it's all relative. You're not that old." During her extrication from the car, Ruth asks at least twice if she is dreaming. At one point she asks Carnahan, who has told her she will be taken to the hospital in a helicopter: "Are you teasing?" At another point she says: "This is terrible. Am I dreaming?" She also asks what happened and where the rest of her family is, repeating the questions even after being told she was in an accident and the other family members are being cared for. While being loaded into the helicopter on a stretcher, Ruth says: "I just want to die." Carnahan reassures her that she is "going to do real well," but Ruth repeats: "I just want to die. I don't want to go through this."

Ruth and Wayne are placed in the helicopter, and its door is closed. The narrator states: "Once airborne, Laura and [the flight medic] will update their patients' vital signs and establish communications with the waiting trauma teams at Loma Linda." Carnahan, speaking into what appears to be a radio microphone, transmits some of Ruth's vital signs and states that Ruth cannot move her feet and has no sensation. The video footage during the helicopter ride includes a few seconds of Ruth's face, covered by an oxygen mask. Wayne is neither shown nor heard.

The helicopter lands on the hospital roof. With the door open, Ruth states while being taken out: "My upper back hurts." Carnahan replies: "Your upper back hurts." "That's what you were saying up there." Ruth states: "I don't feel that great." Carnahan responds: "You probably don't."

Finally, Ruth is shown being moved from the helicopter into the hospital. The narrator concludes by stating: "Once inside both patients will be further evaluated and moved into emergency surgery if need be. Thanks to the efforts of the crew of Mercy Air, the firefighters, medics and police who responded, patients' lives were saved." As the segment ends, a brief, written epilogue appears on the screen, stating: "Laura's patient spent months in the hospital. She suffered severe back injuries. The others were all released much sooner.''

[Ruth, who was left paraplegic, saw the program in her hospital room when her son called to tell her it was on. She testified that she was "shocked, so to speak, that this would be run and I would be exploited, have my privacy invaded, which is what I felt had happened."] She did not know her rescue had been recorded in this manner and had never consented to the recording or broadcast. Ruth had the impression from the broadcast "that I was kind of talking non-stop, and I remember hearing some of the things I said, which were not very pleasant." Asked at deposition what part of the broadcast material she considered private, Ruth explained: "I think the whole scene was pretty private. It was pretty gruesome, the parts that I saw, my knee sticking out of the car. I certainly did not look my best, and I don't feel it's for the public to see. I was not at my best in what I was thinking and what I was saying and what was being shown, and it's not for the public to see this trauma that I was going through."

[The plaintiff sued for both intrusion and public disclosure of private facts. Plaintiffs stipulated that Mercy Air was sent based on an agreement with the county, and "that auto accidents on public highways and publicly provided emergency rescue and medical services were both matters of public interest that constituted public affairs." The trial court granted defendants summary judgment.]

[The court, 5–2, affirmed the dismissal of the private facts part of both claims. Recall the discussion at pp. 1110, 1127–28, supra. The court then turned to the intrusion claims.]

As to intrusion, the Court of Appeal correctly found triable issues exist as to whether defendants invaded plaintiffs privacy by accompanying plaintiffs in the helicopter. Contrary to the holding below, we also hold triable issues exist as to whether defendants tortiously intruded by listening to Ruth's confidential conversations with Nurse Carnahan at the rescue scene without Ruth's consent. Moreover, we hold defendants had no constitutional privilege so as to intrude on plaintiffs' seclusion and private communications.

.   .   .

II. Intrusion

Of the four privacy torts identified by Prosser, the tort of intrusion into private places, conversations or matter is perhaps the one that best captures the common understanding of an "invasion of privacy." It encompasses unconsented-to physical intrusion into the home, hospital room or other place the privacy of which is legally recognized, as well as unwarranted sensory intrusions such as eavesdropping, wiretapping, and visual or photographic spying. [ ] It is in the intrusion cases that invasion of privacy is most clearly seen as an affront to individual dignity. "[A] measure of personal isolation and personal control over the conditions of its abandonment is of the very essence of personal freedom and dignity, is part of what our culture means by these concepts. A man whose home may be entered at the will of another, whose conversations may be overheard at the will of another, whose marital and familial intimacies may be overseen at the will of another, is less of a man, has less human dignity, on that account. He who may intrude upon another at will is the master of the other and, in fact, intrusion is a primary weapon of the tyrant." [   ]

Despite its conceptual centrality, the intrusion tort has received less judicial attention than the private facts tort, and its parameters are less clearly defined. The leading California decision is Miller v. National Broadcasting Co., [232 Cal.Rptr. 668 (App. 1986)] (*Miller*). *Miller*, which like the present case involved a news organization's videotaping the work of emergency medical personnel, adopted the Restatement's formulation of the cause of action: "One who intentionally intrudes, physically or otherwise, upon the solitude or seclusion of another or his private affairs or concerns, is subject to liability to the other for invasion of his privacy, if the intrusion would be highly offensive to a reasonable person." [   ]

As stated in *Miller* and the Restatement, therefore, the action for intrusion has two elements: (1) intrusion into a private place, conversation or matter, (2) in a manner highly offensive to a reasonable person. We consider the elements in that order.

We ask first whether defendants "intentionally intrude[d], physically or otherwise, upon the solitude or seclusion of another," that is, into a place or conversation private to Wayne or Ruth. [   ] "[T]here is no liability for the examination of a public record concerning the plaintiff. . . . [Or] for observing him or even taking his photograph while he is walking on the public highway. . . ." (Rest.2d Torts, § 652B, com. *c*.); see, e.g., Aisenson v. American Broadcasting Co. [269 Cal.Rptr. 379 (App. 1990)][where judge who was subject of news story was filmed from public street as he walked from his home to his car, any invasion of privacy was "extremely de minimis"]; [   ]. To prove actionable intrusion, the plaintiff must show the defendant penetrated some zone of physical or sensory privacy surrounding, or obtained unwanted access to data about, the plaintiff. The tort is proven only if the plaintiff had an objectively reasonable expectation of seclusion or solitude in the place, conversation or data source. [   ]

Cameraman Cooke's mere presence at the accident scene and filming of the events occurring there cannot be deemed either a physical or sensory intrusion on plaintiffs' seclusion. Plaintiffs had no right of ownership or possession of the property where the rescue took place, nor any actual control of the premises. Nor could they have had a reasonable expectation that members of the media would be excluded or prevented from photographing the scene; for journalists to attend and record the scenes of accidents and rescues is in no way unusual or unexpected. (Cf. Pen.Code, §§ 409.5, subd. (d), 409.6, subd. (d) [exempting press representatives from certain emergency closure orders].)

Two aspects of defendants' conduct, however, raise triable issues of intrusion on seclusion. First, a triable issue exists as to whether both plaintiffs had an objectively reasonable expectation of privacy in the interior of the rescue helicopter, which served as an ambulance. Although the attendance of reporters and photographers at the scene of an accident is to be expected, we are aware of no law or custom permitting the press to ride in ambulances or enter hospital rooms during treatment without the patient's consent. [   ] Other than the two patients and Cooke, only three people were present in the helicopter, all Mercy Air staff. As the Court of Appeal observed, "[i]t is neither the custom nor the habit of our society that any member of the public at large or its media representatives may hitch a ride in an ambulance and ogle as paramedics care for an injured stranger." [   ]

Second, Ruth was entitled to a degree of privacy in her conversations with Carnahan and other medical rescuers at the accident scene, and in Carnahan's conversations conveying medical information regarding Ruth to the hospital base. Cooke, perhaps, did not intrude into that zone of privacy merely by being present at a place where he could hear such conversations with unaided ears. But by placing a microphone on Carnahan's person, amplifying and recording what she said and heard, defendants may have listened in on conversations the parties could reasonably have expected to be private.

The Court of Appeal held plaintiffs had no reasonable expectation of privacy at the accident scene itself because the scene was within the sight and hearing of members of the public. The summary judgment record, however, does not support the Court of Appeal's conclusion; instead, it reflects, at the least, the existence of triable issues as to the privacy of certain conversations at the accident scene, as in the helicopter. The videotapes (broadcast and raw footage) show the rescue did not take place "on a heavily traveled highway," as the Court of Appeal stated, but in a ditch many yards from and below the rural superhighway, which is raised somewhat at that point to bridge a nearby crossroad. From the tapes it appears unlikely the plaintiffs' extrication from their car and medical treatment at the scene could have been observed by any persons who, in the lower court's words, "passed by" on the roadway. Even more unlikely is that any passersby on the road could have heard Ruth's conversation with Nurse Carnahan or the other rescuers.

Whether Ruth expected her conversations with Nurse Carnahan or the other rescuers to remain private and whether any such expectation was reasonable are, on the state of the record before us, questions for the jury. We note, however, that several existing legal protections for communications could support the conclusion that Ruth possessed a reasonable expectation of privacy in her conversations with Nurse Carnahan and the other rescuers. A patient's conversation with a provider of medical care in the course of treatment including emergency treatment, carries a traditional and legally well-established expectation of privacy.   .   .   .

.   .   .

We turn to the second element of the intrusion tort, offensiveness of the intrusion. In a widely followed passage, the *Miller* court explained that determining offensiveness requires consideration of all the circumstances of the intrusion, including its degree and setting and the intruder's "motives and objectives." [ ] The *Miller* court concluded that reasonable people could regard the camera crew's conduct in filming a man's emergency medical treatment in his home, without seeking or obtaining his or his wife's consent, as showing "a cavalier disregard for ordinary citizens' rights of privacy" and, hence, as highly offensive. [ ]

We agree with the *Miller* court that all the circumstances of an intrusion, including the motives or justification of the intruder, are pertinent to the offensiveness element. Motivation or justification becomes particularly important when the intrusion is by a member of the print or broadcast press in the pursuit of news material. Although, as will be discussed more fully later, the First Amendment does not immunize the press from liability for torts or crimes committed in an effort to gather news [ ], the constitutional protection of the press does reflect the strong societal interest in effective and complete reporting of events, an interest that may—as a matter of tort law—justify an intrusion that would otherwise be considered offensive. . . .

In deciding, therefore, whether a reporter's alleged intrusion into private matters (i.e., physical space, conversation or data) is "offensive" and hence actionable as an invasion of privacy, courts must consider the extent to which the intrusion was, under the circumstances, justified by the legitimate motive of gathering the news. Information collecting techniques that may be highly offensive when done for socially unprotected reasons— for purposes of harassment, blackmail or prurient curiosity, for example— may not be offensive to a reasonable person when employed by journalists in pursuit of a socially or politically important story. Thus, for example, "a continuous surveillance which is tortious when practiced by a creditor upon a debtor may not be tortious when practiced by media representatives in a situation where there is significant public interest [in discovery of the information sought]." [ ]

The mere fact the intruder was in pursuit of a "story" does not, however, generally justify an otherwise offensive intrusion; offensiveness depends as well on the particular method of investigation used. At one extreme, " 'routine . . . reporting techniques,' " such as asking questions of people with information ("including those with confidential or restricted information") could rarely, if ever, be deemed an actionable intrusion. [ ] At the other extreme, violation of well-established legal areas of physical or sensory privacy—trespass into a home or tapping a personal telephone line, for example—could rarely, if ever, be justified by a reporter's need to get the story. Such acts would be deemed highly offensive even if the information sought was of weighty public concern; they would also be outside any protection the Constitution provides to newsgathering. [ ]

Between these extremes lie difficult cases, many involving the use of photographic and electronic recording equipment. Equipment such as hidden cameras and miniature cordless and directional microphones are powerful investigative tools for newsgathering, but may also be used in ways that severely threaten personal privacy. California tort law provides no bright line on this question; each case must be taken on its facts.

On this summary judgment record, we believe a jury could find defendants' recording of Ruth's communications to Carnahan and other rescuers, and filming in the air ambulance, to be "highly offensive to a reasonable person." [   ] With regard to the depth of the intrusion [   ], a reasonable jury could find highly offensive the placement of a microphone on a medical rescuer in order to intercept what would otherwise be private conversations with an injured patient. In that setting, as defendants could and should have foreseen, the patient would not know her words were being recorded and would not have occasion to ask about, and object or consent to, recording. Defendants, it could reasonably be said, took calculated advantage of the patient's "vulnerability and confusion." [   ] Arguably, the last thing an injured accident victim should have to worry about while being pried from her wrecked car is that a television producer may be recording everything she says to medical personnel for the possible edification and entertainment of casual television viewers.

For much the same reason, a jury could reasonably regard entering and riding in an ambulance—whether on the ground or in the air—with two seriously injured patients to be an egregious intrusion on a place of expected seclusion. Again, the patients, at least in this case, were hardly in a position to keep careful watch on who was riding with them, or to inquire as to everyone's business and consent or object to their presence. A jury could reasonably believe that fundamental respect for human dignity requires the patients' anxious journey be taken only with those whose care is solely for them and out of sight of the prying eyes (or cameras) of others.

Nor can we say as a matter of law that defendants' motive—to gather usable material for a potentially newsworthy story—necessarily privileged their intrusive conduct as a matter of common law tort liability. A reasonable jury could conclude the producers' desire to get footage that would convey the "feel" of the event—the real sights and sounds of a difficult rescue—did not justify either placing a microphone on Nurse Carnahan or filming inside the rescue helicopter. Although defendants' purposes could scarcely be regarded as evil or malicious (in the colloquial sense), their behavior could, even in light of their motives, be thought to show a highly offensive lack of sensitivity and respect for plaintiffs' privacy. [   ] A reasonable jury could find that defendants, in placing a microphone on an emergency treatment nurse and recording her conversation with a distressed, disoriented and severely injured patient, without the patient's knowledge or consent, acted with highly offensive disrespect for the patient's personal privacy comparable to, if not quite as extreme as, the disrespect and insensitivity demonstrated in *Miller*.

Turning to the question of constitutional protection for newsgathering, one finds the decisional law reflects a general rule of *nonprotection*: the press in its newsgathering activities enjoys no immunity or exemption from generally applicable laws. [The court, after reviewing several Supreme Court decisions, concluded that] defendants enjoyed no constitutional privilege, merely by virtue of their status as members of the news media, to eavesdrop in violation of section 632 [the state's wiretapping and eavesdropping statute—ed.] or otherwise to intrude tortiously on private places, conversations or information.

Courts have impliedly recognized that a generally applicable law might, under some circumstances, impose an "impermissible burden" on newsgathering [   ]; such a burden might be found in a law that, as applied to the press, would result in "a significant constriction of the flow of news to the public" and thus "eviscerate[   ]" the freedom of the press. [   ] No basis exists, however, for concluding that either section 632 or the intrusion tort places such a burden on the press, either in general or under the circumstances of this case. The conduct of journalism does not depend, as a general matter, on the use of secret devices to record private conversations. (Accord, [*Dietemann*]; [   ]). More specifically, nothing in the record or briefing here suggests that reporting on automobile accidents and medical rescue activities depends on secretly recording accident victims' conversations with rescue personnel or on filming inside an occupied ambulance. Thus, if any exception exists to the general rule that "the First Amendment does not guarantee the press a constitutional right of special access to information not available to the public generally" [   ], such exception is inapplicable here.[18]

As should be apparent from the above discussion, the constitutional protection accorded newsgathering, if any, is far narrower than the protection surrounding the publication of truthful material; consequently, the fact that a reporter may be seeking "newsworthy" material does not in itself privilege the investigatory activity. The reason for the difference is simple: the intrusion tort, unlike that for publication of private facts, does not subject the press to liability for the contents of its publications. Newsworthiness, as we stated earlier, is a complete bar to liability for publication of private facts and is evaluated with a high degree of deference to editorial judgment. The same deference is not due, however, when the issue is not the media's right to publish or broadcast what they choose, but their right to intrude into secluded areas or conversations in pursuit of publishable material.   .   .   .

Defendants urge a rule more protective of press investigative activity. Specifically, they seek a holding that "when intrusion claims are brought in the context of newsgathering conduct, that conduct be deemed protected so long as (1) the information being gathered is about a matter of legitimate concern to the public and (2) the underlying conduct is lawful (i.e., was undertaken without fraud, trespass, etc.)." Neither tort law nor constitutional precedent and policy supports such a broad privilege. [*Miller, Diete-*

---

18. Defendants urge us to hold that any damages for intrusion do not include compensation for injury resulting from the publication of material gathered through intrusion. The only intrusion case defendants cite on this point is against them. [*Diete-* *mann*] [allowing publication damages in intrusion case]; [   ] We do not reach the question, as the measure of plaintiffs' damages is not before us on this appeal from summary judgment in favor of the defense.

mann] and [   ] were all cases in which the reporters and photographers were acting in pursuit of newsworthy material, but were held to have tortiously intruded on the plaintiffs' privacy because their conduct was highly offensive to a reasonable person, not because they had committed any independent crime or tort.[19] [   ]

. . .

. . . [N]o constitutional precedent or principle of which we are aware gives a reporter general license to intrude in an objectively offensive manner into private places, conversations or matters merely because the reporter thinks he or she may thereby find something that will warrant publication or broadcast.

. . .

In short, the state may not intrude into the proper sphere of the news media to dictate what they should publish and broadcast, but neither may the media play tyrant to the people by unlawfully spying on them in the name of newsgathering. Summary judgment for the defense was . . . improper as to the cause of action for invasion of privacy by intrusion. . . .

The judgment of the Court of Appeal is affirmed except insofar as the Court of Appeal reversed and remanded for further proceedings on Ruth Shulman's cause of action for publication of private facts.

G EORGE, C.J., and K ENNARD, J., concur.

K ENNARD, J USTICE, concurring.

[This concurrence, joined by Justice Mosk, focused on the private facts part of the case.]

C HIN, J USTICE, concurring [in the private facts part of the case] and dissenting [on the intrusion part].

. . .

Although I agree with the plurality's premises, I disagree with the conclusion it draws from those premises. The plurality concludes that a reasonable person in Ruth's position might well have assumed that her conversation with the nurses and doctors assisting her rescue would be kept private. Likewise, the plurality believes, a reasonable person in Ruth's position might not expect to find media personnel aboard a rescue helicopter. A jury might well decide that defendants' desire for complete footage did not justify these privacy intrusions. [   ]

---

19. In *Miller* the camera crew's entry into the Miller home was also deemed a trespass [   ], but the court's discussion of the intrusion tort does not depend on this fact. [   ]

In *Dietemann* [   ], reporters for Life Magazine gained consensual access to the home office of a quack doctor, where they secretly photographed him and recorded his remarks as he purportedly diagnosed a medical condition of one of the reporters. [   ] The federal court, applying California law, concluded the facts showed an invasion of privacy. [   ] Presumably because a peaceable entry by consent does not constitute trespass under California law [   ], no question of liability for trespass arose in *Dietemann*.

Ruth's expectations notwithstanding, I do not believe that a reasonable trier of fact could find that defendants' conduct in this case was "highly offensive to a reasonable person," the test adopted by the plurality. Plaintiffs do not allege that defendants, though present at the accident rescue scene and in the helicopter, interfered with either the rescue or medical efforts, elicited embarrassing or offensive information from plaintiffs, or even tried to interrogate or interview them. Defendants' news team evidently merely recorded newsworthy events "of legitimate public concern" [ ] as they transpired. Defendants' apparent motive in undertaking the supposed privacy invasion was a reasonable and nonmalicious one: to obtain an accurate depiction of the rescue efforts from start to finish. The event was newsworthy, and the ultimate broadcast was both dramatic and educational, rather than tawdry or embarrassing.

No illegal trespass on private property occurred, and any technical illegality arising from defendants' recording Ruth's conversations with medical personnel was not so "highly offensive" as to justify liability. Recording the innocuous, inoffensive conversations that occurred between Ruth and the nurse assisting her [ ] and filming the seemingly routine, though certainly newsworthy, helicopter ride [ ] may have technically invaded plaintiffs' private "space," but in my view no "highly offensive" invasion of their privacy occurred.

We should bear in mind we are not dealing here with a true "interception"—e.g., a surreptitious wiretap by a third party—of words spoken in a truly private place—e.g., in a psychiatrist's examining room, an attorney's office, or a priest's confessional. Rather, here the broadcast showed Ruth speaking in settings where others could hear her, and the fact that she did not realize she was being recorded does not ipso facto transform defendants' newsgathering procedures into *highly* offensive conduct within the meaning of the law of intrusion.

In short, to turn a jury loose on the defendants in this case is itself "highly offensive" to me. I would reverse the judgment of the Court of Appeal with directions to affirm the summary judgment for defendants on all causes of action.

MOSK, J., concurs.

[Justice Brown, joined by Justice Baxter, agreed with the resolution of the intrusion part of the case but dissented from the dismissal of the private facts part.]

Notes and Questions

1. Why does Justice Werdegar conclude that the helicopter episode might amount to actionable intrusion? The events at the accident scene?

2. Note that the opinion suggests that asking questions of one with confidential or restricted information is not actionable intrusion. Is that consistent with *Nader*?

3. Does the court suggest that the weight to be given to newsworthiness should be different in public disclosure cases from what it is in intrusion cases? Would that make sense?

4. Does the opinion suggest that some actions might be so intrusive that they could not be justified no matter how important the story? Would that be sound? What if the story were as important as the burglary at the Watergate? Consider Boehner v. McDermott, 191 F.3d 463 (D.C.Cir.1999), cert. petition pending, involving a suit by Republican Congressman John Boehner against Democratic Congressman James McDermott. McDermott had received the tape of a conference call among a group of Republican representatives including then-speaker Newt Gingrich, Boehner, and others—a tape obtained by private parties eavesdropping over a radio scanner. During their conversation, the participants discussed their strategy for an upcoming Ethics Subcommittee meeting about Gingrich. After listening to the recording, McDermott disseminated transcripts to the media. Boehner alleged that, in doing so, McDermott had violated the Electronic Communications Privacy Act, and sought damages under its civil liability provisions.

The Act, 18 U.S.C. § 2511(1)(c), rendered potentially liable anyone who "intentionally discloses, or endeavors to disclose, to any other person the contents of any wire, oral, or electronic communication, knowing or having reason to know that the information was obtained through the interception of a wire, oral, or electronic communication in violation of this subsection." McDermott moved to dismiss, claiming that applying the statute to him would be unconstitutional because the First Amendment "prohibits . . . punishment . . . for the disclosure of truthful and lawfully obtained information on a matter of substantial public concern."

Two judges rejected McDermott's argument, although they disagreed on the reasons. One, assuming rather than deciding that the First Amendment protected McDermott from suit on the basis of his delivery of the tape to the newspapers, maintained that the holding of *Florida Star*, p. 1116, supra, did not apply to him since he had not, in fact, lawfully obtained the tape. The other judge believed that McDermott had engaged in conduct, not speech, when he delivered the tape, and also argued that, under *Florida Star*, there might not be a "First Amendment right to publish illegally acquired information."

Both did agree, however, that, because the statute involved both speech and non-speech elements, intermediate rather than strict scrutiny applied. Since the statute expressed the substantial government interest in protecting the privacy of communications, it should be upheld:

> [A]lthough the "essential thrust of the First Amendment is to prohibit improper restraints on the voluntary public expression of ideas," there is "a concomitant freedom not to speak publicly, which serves the same ultimate end as freedom of speech in its affirmative aspect." . . .
>
> The freedom not to speak publicly, to speak only privately, is violated whenever an illegally intercepted conversation is revealed, and it is violated even if the person who does the revealing is not the person who did the intercepting.

The dissenter argued that the statute was subject to strict scrutiny because it burdened the freedom of speech. Furthermore, he stated: "I do not see how we can draw a line today that would punish McDermott and not hold liable for sanctions every newspaper, every radio station, every broadcasting network that obtained the same information from McDermott's releases and published it again." Would you agree? Might it matter whether the media got the tape from those who recorded or from McDermott?

Contrast the result in Bartnicki v. Vopper, 200 F.3d 109 (3d Cir. 1999), certiorari granted 120 S.Ct. 2716 (2000), a suit brought under the same federal statute—as well as an analogous state law. A cell phone conversation between two representatives of the Wyoming Valley West School District Teacher's Union—which was involved in contentious negotiations with the school district—was recorded by an unknown party and given to Yocum, a union opponent who passed the tape to local radio stations. The two individuals sued both Yocum and the radio stations. Among the question on appeal was the validity of those provisions of the Electronic Communications Privacy Act imposing damages and counsel fees for the use and disclosure of intercepted material on those who knew of the illegality but played no part in the interception.

The *Bartnicki* court refused to read First Amendment precedents to suggest that a distinction between legally and illegally obtained information should be applied in evaluating what level of scrutiny to use in analyzing the protection to be given speech. It concluded that the federal statute was a content-neutral restriction and, thus, held that intermediate scrutiny was appropriate. Applying the intermediate scrutiny approach, the court held that the relevant provisions could not be applied to the *Bartnicki* defendants. Although the government's two objectives—"denying the wrongdoer the fruits of his labor" and "eliminating the demand for those fruits by third parties"—were legitimate, the wrongdoer was unaffected by the provisions at issue, and the relationship between the goal of deterrence and the statute was too indirect. The court distinguished *Boehner* on the ground of the presence of a media defendant in *Bartnicki* and the lesser culpability of Yocum as compared with McDermott. Are they in conflict? *Bartnicki*, was argued in the Supreme Court in December, 2000.

5. Note that the *Shulman* dissent on this point suggests that the conduct was less intrusive than wiretapping. Why might that be so? Why is it that the entry in *Dietemann* and Cooke's presence here are not themselves actionable?

Does the use of technology contribute to the offensiveness of an intrusion? In Sanders v. American Broadcasting Companies, Inc., 978 P.2d 67 (Cal.1999), a newsgatherer obtained employment with a telepsychic marketing company and covertly obtained videotaped statements from plaintiff employee during discussions in the office. The unanimous court decided that the plaintiff, although having limited privacy rights against coworkers who might repeat his statements, had a privacy right against covert photography, recalling the *Dietemann* case, discussed p. 1172, supra.

After this decision, the *Sanders* case was settled for $900,000. New Media and the Law, Summer 2000.

6. Does the court respond soundly to the media request for a collecting privilege in this case? How would the proposed two-prong test have applied to the facts here? Are damages relevant to this proposed privilege?

7. Should publication of private facts and intrusion be considered one tort or two? In *Shulman*, *Dietemann*, and other cases, the issue of the connection between the two arises and may be critical on the issue of damages. In footnote 18, the *Shulman* court raises the question of whether damages for an actionable intrusion can include those from a publication that would itself not be actionable under the public disclosure doctrine. How should this be resolved? Is *Dietemann* helpful? Would restricting damages recoverable for intrusion provide an alternative way of protecting the First Amendment issues that concerned the *Shulman* court?

In Food Lion, Inc. v. Capital Cities/ABC, Inc., 194 F.3d 505 (4th Cir.1999), the Food Lion chain sued ABC and two ABC television employees who had used false resumes to procure jobs at Food Lion stores and secretly videotape "unwholesome" food handling practices—including re-packaging and re-dating meat that had passed its expiration date, grinding old beef with new, and applying barbeque sauce to chicken to mask its rancid odor. On appeal, the court considered whether the employees of ABC had breached their duty of loyalty and committed a trespass, and whether Food Lion should, on First Amendment grounds, be prevented from proving publication damages as the result of the intrusion.

On the trespass claim, the court held—citing *Desnick*—that the two employees could not be considered liable on the basis of their resume misrepresentations, since these did not completely negate the fact that Food Lion had consented to their employment; " 'Consent to an entry is often given legal effect' even though it was obtained by misrepresentation or concealed intentions." The ABC reporters were, however, liable for breach of their duty of loyalty to Food Lion. Since "[t]he interests of the employer (ABC) to whom Dale and Barnett gave complete loyalty were adverse to the interests of Food Lion, the employer to whom they were unfaithful," the two had committed "a wrongful act in excess of Dale and Barnett's authority to enter Food Lion's premises as employees."

Despite this fact, Food Lion could not recover damages for publication. Although the district court had denied these damages on the basis of proximate cause, the Fourth Circuit determined instead that First Amendment concerns would prohibit Food Lion from recovering them. According to the court, "What Food Lion sought to do . . . was to recover defamation-type damages under non-reputational tort claims, without satisfying the stricter (First Amendment) standards of a defamation claim." Does this limitation on damages seem justified?

D. APPROPRIATION

"Appropriation" claims involve the attempts of celebrities to control the exploitation of their names, likenesses, and fame and any pecuniary value resulting therefrom. The claim was explicitly recognized for the first time in Haelan Laboratories v. Topps Chewing Gum, Inc., 202 F.2d 866 (2d Cir.), cert. denied 346 U.S. 816 (1953), in which the court spoke of the need to protect the proprietary interest of celebrities in their names and likenesses. *Haelan* involved a famous baseball player who had assigned the right to the use of his name and likeness to a bubblegum manufacturer for the promotion of its products. A competing manufacturer subsequently induced the ballplayer to enter into a similar contract with full knowledge of the preexisting agreement. The court recognized the ballplayer's right to control commercial use of his name and likeness as a method through which such misappropriation could be prevented.

Since *Haelan,* similar claims have been widely recognized. Although some states have adopted the action as a separate common law remedy, most have developed it as an offshoot of either the common law right of privacy or of a privacy statute.

Is the claim a type of privacy, or should it properly be conceptualized as a distinct tort? One inherent difference between it and the more traditional privacy rights is that privacy protects against undesired public intrusion into one's personal life, while the right of publicity is usually invoked to protect against persons who would profit by taking, without compensation, something the celebrity would prefer to sell. For example, a famous person may not generally object to commercial exploitation of his or her name or other feature but may want to be compensated for it. But some cases appear to go beyond the desire for compensation. See, e.g., Martin Luther King, Jr., Center for Social Change, Inc. v. American Heritage Products, Inc., 296 S.E.2d 697 (Ga.1982), in which plaintiff successfully stopped defendant from making plastic busts of the late Dr. King. Could plaintiff have stopped a ''recognized'' painter from painting a portrait of Dr. King?

Whether or not the claim for appropriation is considered as a subset of privacy rights has important implications for its judicial development. For example, it is unclear whether it survives the death of the celebrity in whom the right is based; that is, whether a celebrity's heirs or assigns can profit from any such right after the famous person has died. Courts that have held the right to be descendible have analogized it to an ordinary property right or a copyright, both of which are inheritable. Courts that have rejected a descendible right have emphasized the personal nature of the claim, the analogy to rights of privacy, which are not inheritable, and the line-drawing difficulties inherent in any development of a right that survives the death of the celebrity.

Zacchini v. Scripps–Howard Broadcasting Co.

Supreme Court of the United States, 1977.
433 U.S. 562, 97 S.Ct. 2849, 53 L.Ed.2d 965.

MR. JUSTICE WHITE delivered the opinion of the Court.

Petitioner, Hugo Zacchini, is an entertainer. He performs a ''human cannonball'' act in which he is shot from a cannon into a net some 200 feet away. Each performance occupies some 15 seconds. In August and September 1972, petitioner was engaged to perform his act on a regular basis at the Geauga County Fair in Burton, Ohio. He performed in a fenced area, surrounded by grandstands, at the fair grounds. Members of the public attending the fair were not charged a separate admission fee to observe his act.

On August 30, a freelance reporter for Scripps–Howard Broadcasting Co., the operator of a television broadcasting station and respondent in this case, attended the fair. He carried a small movie camera. Petitioner noticed the reporter and asked him not to film the performance. The reporter did not do so on that day; but on the instructions of the producer of respondent's daily newscast, he returned the following day and videotaped the entire act. This film clip, approximately 15 seconds in length, was shown on the 11 o'clock news program that night, together with favorable commentary.[1]

Petitioner then brought this action for damages, alleging that he is "engaged in the entertainment business," that the act he performs is one "invented by his father and . . . performed only by his family for the last fifty years," that respondent "showed and commercialized the film of his act without his consent," and that such conduct was an "unlawful appropriation of plaintiff's professional property." [ ] Respondent answered and moved for summary judgment, which was granted by the trial court.

. . .

. . . Insofar as the Ohio Supreme Court held that the First and Fourteenth Amendments of the United States Constitution required judgment for respondent, we reverse the judgment of that court.

. . .

Even if the judgment in favor of respondent must nevertheless be understood as ultimately resting on Ohio law, it appears that at the very least the Ohio court felt compelled by what it understood to be federal constitutional considerations to construe and apply its own law in the manner it did. In this event, we have jurisdiction and should decide the federal issue; for if the state court erred in its understanding of our cases and of the First and Fourteenth Amendments we should so declare, leaving the state court free to decide the privilege issue solely as a matter of Ohio law. [ ] If the Supreme Court of Ohio "held as it did because it felt under compulsion of federal law as enunciated by this Court so to hold, it should

---

1. The script of the commentary accompanying the film clip read as follows:

"This . . . now . . . is the story of a *true spectator* sport . . . the sport of human cannonballing . . . in fact, the great *Zacchini* is about the only human cannonball around, these days . . . just happens that,

where he is, is the Great Geauga County Fair, in Burton . . . and believe me, although it's not a *long* act, it's a thriller . . . and you really need to see it *in person* . . . to appreciate it. . . ." (Emphasis in original.)

be relieved of that compulsion. It should be freed to decide . . . these suits according to its own local law." [   ]

The Ohio Supreme Court relied heavily on *Time, Inc. v. Hill*, [   ], but that case does not mandate a media privilege to televise a performer's entire act without his consent. Involved in *Time, Inc. v. Hill* was a claim under the New York "Right of Privacy" statute that Life Magazine, in the course of reviewing a new play, had connected the play with a long-past incident involving petitioner and his family and had falsely described their experience and conduct at that time. The complaint sought damages for humiliation and suffering flowing from these nondefamatory falsehoods that allegedly invaded Hill's privacy. The Court held, however, that the opening of a new play linked to an actual incident was a matter of public interest and that Hill could not recover without showing that the Life report was knowingly false or was published with reckless disregard for the truth—the same rigorous standard that had been applied in [*New York Times Co. v. Sullivan*].

Time, Inc. v. Hill, which was hotly contested and decided by a divided Court, involved an entirely different tort from the "right of publicity" recognized by the Ohio Supreme Court.   .   .   .

The differences between these two torts are important. First, the State's interests in providing a cause of action in each instance are different. "The interest protected" in permitting recovery for placing the plaintiff in a false light "is clearly that of reputation, with the same overtones of mental distress as in defamation." Prosser, [Privacy, 48 Calif.L.Rev. 383, 400 (1960)]. By contrast, the State's interest in permitting a "right of publicity" is in protecting the proprietary interest of the individual in his act in part to encourage such entertainment. As we later note, the State's interest is closely analogous to the goals of patent and copyright law, focusing on the right of the individual to reap the reward of his endeavors and having little to do with protecting feelings or reputation. Second, the two torts differ in the degree to which they intrude on dissemination of information to the public. In "false light" cases the only way to protect the interests involved is to attempt to minimize publication of the damaging matter, while in "right of publicity" cases the only question is who gets to do the publishing. An entertainer such as petitioner usually has no objection to the widespread publication of his act as long as he gets the commercial benefit of such publication. Indeed, in the present case petitioner did not seek to enjoin the broadcast of his act; he simply sought compensation for the broadcast in the form of damages.

Nor does it appear that our later cases such as [*Rosenbloom; Gertz;* and *Firestone*] require or furnish substantial support for the Ohio court's privilege ruling. These cases, like *New York Times*, emphasize the protection extended to the press by the First Amendment in defamation cases, particularly when suit is brought by a public official or a public figure. None of them involve an alleged appropriation by the press of a right of publicity existing under state law.

Moreover, *Time, Inc. v. Hill, New York Times,* [*Rosenbloom*], *Gertz,* and *Firestone* all involved the reporting of events; in none of them was there an attempt to broadcast or publish an entire act for which the performer ordinarily gets paid. It is evident, and there is no claim here to the contrary, that petitioner's state-law right of publicity would not serve to prevent respondent from reporting the newsworthy facts about petitioner's act. Wherever the line in particular situations is to be drawn between media reports that are protected and those that are not, we are quite sure that the First and Fourteenth Amendments do not immunize the media when they broadcast a performer's entire act without his consent. The Constitution no more prevents a State from requiring respondent to compensate petitioner for broadcasting his act on television than it would privilege respondent to film and broadcast a copyrighted dramatic work without liability to the copyright owner, [ ], or to film and broadcast a prize fight, [ ], or a baseball game, [ ], where the promoters or the participants had other plans for publicizing the event. There are ample reasons for reaching this conclusion.

The broadcast of a film of petitioner's entire act poses a substantial threat to the economic value of that performance. As the Ohio court recognized, this act is the product of petitioner's own talents and energy, the end result of much time, effort, and expense. Much of its economic value lies in the "right of exclusive control over the publicity given to his performance"; if the public can see the act free on television, it will be less willing to pay to see it at the fair.[12] The effect of a public broadcast of the performance is similar to preventing petitioner from charging an admission fee. . . . Moreover, the broadcast of petitioner's entire performance, unlike the unauthorized use of another's name for purposes of trade or the incidental use of a name or picture by the press, goes to the heart of petitioner's ability to earn a living as an entertainer. Thus, in this case, Ohio has recognized what may be the strongest case for a "right of publicity"—involving, not the appropriation of an entertainer's reputation to enhance the attractiveness of a commercial product, but the appropriation of the very activity by which the entertainer acquired his reputation in the first place.

Of course, Ohio's decision to protect petitioner's right of publicity here rests on more than a desire to compensate the performer for the time and effort invested in his act; the protection provides an economic incentive for him to make the investment required to produce a performance of interest to the public. This same consideration underlies the patent and copyright laws long enforced by this Court. . . .

---

12. It is possible, of course, that respondent's news broadcast increased the value of petitioner's performance by stimulating the public's interest in seeing the act live. In these circumstances, petitioner would not be able to prove damages and thus would not recover. But petitioner has alleged that the broadcast injured him to the extent of $25,-000. App. 5, and we think the State should be allowed to authorize compensation of this injury if proved.

There is no doubt that entertainment, as well as news, enjoys First Amendment protection. It is also true that entertainment itself can be important news. *Time, Inc. v. Hill*. But it is important to note that neither the public nor respondent will be deprived of the benefit of petitioner's performance as long as his commercial stake in his act is appropriately recognized. Petitioner does not seek to enjoin the broadcast of his performance; he simply wants to be paid for it. Nor do we think that a state-law damages remedy against respondent would represent a species of liability without fault contrary to the letter or spirit of [*Gertz v. Robert Welch, Inc.*]. Respondent knew exactly that petitioner objected to televising his act but nevertheless displayed the entire film.

We conclude that although the State of Ohio may as a matter of its own law privilege the press in the circumstances of this case, the First and Fourteenth Amendments do not require it to do so.

Reversed.

Mr. Justice Powell, with whom Mr. Justice Brennan and Mr. Justice Marshall join, dissenting.

Disclaiming any attempt to do more than decide the narrow case before us, the Court reverses the decision of the Supreme Court of Ohio based on repeated incantation of a single formula: "a performer's entire act." The holding today is summed up in one sentence:

> "Wherever the line in particular situations is to be drawn between media reports that are protected and those that are not, we are quite sure that the First and Fourteenth Amendments do not immunize the media when they broadcast a performer's entire act without his consent."

I doubt that this formula provides a standard clear enough even for resolution of this case.[1] In any event, I am not persuaded that the Court's opinion is appropriately sensitive to the First Amendment values at stake, and I therefore dissent.

Although the Court would draw no distinction, [ ] I do not view respondent's action as comparable to unauthorized commercial broadcasts of sporting events, theatrical performances, and the like where the broadcaster keeps the profits. There is no suggestion here that respondent made any such use of the film. Instead, it simply reported on what petitioner concedes to be a newsworthy event, in a way hardly surprising for a

---

1. Although the record is not explicit, it is unlikely that the "act" commenced abruptly with the explosion that launched petitioner on his way, ending with the landing in the net a few seconds later. One may assume that the actual firing was preceded by some fanfare, possibly stretching over several minutes, to heighten the audience's anticipation: introduction of the performer, description of the uniqueness and danger, last-minute checking of the apparatus, and entry into the cannon, all accompanied by suitably ominous commentary from the master of ceremonies. If this is found to be the case on remand, then respondent could not be said to have appropriated the "entire act" in its 15-second newsclip—and the Court's opinion then would afford no guidance for resolution of the case. Moreover, in future cases involving different performances, similar difficulties in determining just what constitutes the "entire act" are inevitable.

television station—by means of film coverage. The report was part of an ordinary daily news program, consuming a total of 15 seconds. It is a routine example of the press fulfilling the informing function so vital to our system.

The Court's holding that the station's ordinary news report may give rise to substantial liability has disturbing implications, for the decision could lead to a degree of media self-censorship. [ ] Hereafter whenever a television news editor is unsure whether certain film footage received from a camera crew might be held to portray an "entire act," he may decline coverage—even of clearly newsworthy events—or confine the broadcast to watered-down verbal reporting, perhaps with an occasional still picture. The public is then the loser. This is hardly the kind of news reportage that the First Amendment is meant to foster. [ ]

In my view the First Amendment commands a different analytical starting point from the one selected by the Court. Rather than begin with a quantitative analysis of the performer's behavior—is this or is this not his entire act?—we should direct initial attention to the actions of the news media: what use did the station make of the film footage? When a film is used, as here, for a routine portion of a regular news program, I would hold that the First Amendment protects the station from a "right of publicity" or "appropriation" suit, absent a strong showing by the plaintiff that the news broadcast was a subterfuge or cover for private or commercial exploitation.[4]

.   .   . In a suit like the one before us, however, the plaintiff does not complain about the fact of exposure to the public, but rather about its timing or manner. He welcomes some publicity, but seeks to retain control over means and manner as a way to maximize for himself the monetary benefits that flow from such publication. But having made the matter public—having chosen, in essence, to make it newsworthy—he cannot, consistent with the First Amendment, complain of routine news reportage. Cf. *Gertz v. Robert Welch, Inc.*, [ ] (clarifying the different liability standards appropriate in defamation suits, depending on whether or not the plaintiff is a public figure).

Since the film clip here was undeniably treated as news and since there is no claim that the use was subterfuge, respondent's actions were constitutionally privileged. I would affirm.

[Mr. Justice Stevens dissented on the ground that he could not tell whether the Ohio Supreme Court had relied on federal constitutional issues in deciding the case. He would have remanded the case to that court "for clarification of its holding before deciding the federal constitutional issue."]

---

4. This case requires no detailed specification of the standards for identifying a subterfuge, since there is no claim here that respondent's news use was anything but bona fide. [ ] I would point out, however, that selling time during a news broadcast to advertisers in the customary fashion does not make for "commercial exploitation" in the sense intended here. [ ]

On remand, the Ohio Supreme Court took advantage of the opportunity afforded by the majority opinion and decided that nothing in the Ohio Constitution protected the behavior of the media defendant. The case was remanded for trial and for assessment of damages if liability was established. Zacchini v. Scripps–Howard Broadcasting Co., 376 N.E.2d 582 (Ohio 1978).

Notes and Questions

1. How important is it that the majority treats the 15 seconds as the "entire act"? In a case involving the televising of a figure skating championship, a telecaster argued that a short newscast drawn from hours of film would not be an "entire" act under *Zacchini*. The judge, however, said it was "conceivable that a two-minute broadcast, focused solely on the top performer of the day, would embody the essence of the commercially valuable performance, and thus could possibly be a broadcast of the 'entire' act." The case went off on other issues. Post Newsweek Stations–Connecticut, Inc. v. Travelers Insurance Co., 510 F.Supp. 81 (D.Conn.1981).

2. Does *Zacchini* involve an aspect of "privacy"? Of "publicity"? Why did the defendant in *Cox Broadcasting* not have to pay for using the name of the rape victim, or the defendant in *Haynes* not have to pay anyone who appeared in the book though the defendant in *Zacchini* may have to pay for what it did?

3. After *Zacchini,* what would happen in a case in which a street artist who survives on contributions from passersby—a mime, an accordionist, a dancer—is taped by the local television station and shown in a story about summer diversions on the streets of the city? Is the street artist's claim as strong as Zacchini's?

4. Promoters of entertainment and sports events normally protect their rights by controlling access to the event. Terms of admission often prohibit use of cameras or tape recorders. Broadcasting rights are protected by allowing only those who have contracted with the promoters to set up their broadcasting equipment. Performers, in turn, protect their interests through their contracts with the promoters; whether the promoter has a right to authorize a live broadcast of a concert, for example, is usually determined by the terms of the contract between the performer and the promoter.

If Zacchini did not protect his rights contractually, why should the courts provide him a remedy through tort law? The television station was permitted—probably even encouraged—by the fair officials to broadcast film of various events at the fair. Should the station be entitled to rely on that invitation without inquiring into the officials' authority to extend it?

5. Plaintiffs generally have been unsuccessful when they have tried to invoke *Zacchini* to create a cause of action not otherwise provided by the law of copyright or the tort of commercial exploitation of name or likeness. Ginger Rogers, who often performed with dancer Fred Astaire, relied on

Zacchini in an attempt to prevent Federico Fellini from using the title "Ginger and Fred" for his 1986 movie about an Italian dancing couple. The district court characterized *Zacchini* as a "narrowly drawn opinion effectively limited to its facts," and distinguished it on the ground that "Ginger and Fred" did not threaten Rogers's economic viability. Rogers v. Grimaldi, 695 F.Supp. 112 (S.D.N.Y.1988), affirmed 875 F.2d 994 (2d Cir.1989).

Cardtoons, L.C. v. Major League Baseball Players Association

United States Court of Appeals, Tenth Circuit, 1996.
95 F.3d 959.

Before TACHA, LOGAN, and REAVLEY, CIRCUIT JUDGES.

TACHA, CIRCUIT JUDGE.

Cardtoons, L.C., ("Cardtoons") brought this action to obtain a declaratory judgment that its parody trading cards featuring active major league baseball players do not infringe on the publicity rights of members of the Major League Baseball Players Association ("MLBPA"). The district court held that the trading cards constitute expression protected by the First Amendment and therefore read a parody exception into Oklahoma's statutory right of publicity. MLBPA appeals, arguing that (1) the district court lacked jurisdiction to issue a declaratory judgment and (2) Cardtoons does not have a First Amendment right to market its trading cards. We exercise jurisdiction pursuant to 28 U.S.C. § 1291. Because Cardtoons' First Amendment right to free expression outweighs MLBPA's proprietary right of publicity, we affirm.

I. Background

Cardtoons formed in late 1992 to produce parody trading cards featuring caricatures of major league baseball players. Cardtoons contracted with a political cartoonist, a sports artist, and a sports author and journalist, who designed a set of 130 cards. The majority of the cards, 71, have caricatures of active major league baseball players on the front and humorous commentary about their careers on the back. The balance of the set is comprised of 20 "Big Bang Bucks" cards (cartoon drawings of currency with caricatures of the most highly paid players on the front, yearly salary statistics on the back), 10 "Spectra" cards (caricatures of active players on the front, nothing on the back), 10 retired player cards (caricatures of retired players on the front, humorous commentary about their careers on the back), 11 "Politics in Baseball" cards (cartoons featuring caricatures of political and sports figures on the front, humorous text on the back), 7 standing cards (caricatures of team logos on the front, humorous text on the back), and 1 checklist card. Except for the Spectra cards, the back of each card bears the Cardtoons logo and the following statement: "Cardtoons baseball is a parody and is NOT licensed by Major League Baseball Properties or Major League Baseball Players Association."

A person reasonably familiar with baseball can readily identify the players lampooned on the parody trading cards. The cards use similar names, recognizable caricatures, distinctive team colors, and commentary about individual players. For example, the card parodying San Francisco Giants' outfielder Barry Bonds calls him "Treasury Bonds," and features a recognizable caricature of Bonds, complete with earring, tipping a bat boy for a 24 carat gold "Fort Knoxville Slugger." The back of the card has a team logo (the "Gents"), and the following text:

Redemption qualities and why Treasury Bonds is the league's most valuable player:

1. Having Bonds on your team is like having money in the bank.

2. He plays so hard he gives 110 percent, compounded daily.

3. He turned down the chance to play other sports because he has a high interest rate in baseball.

4. He deposits the ball in the bleachers.

5. He is into male bonding.

6. He is a money player.

7. He has a 24–karat Gold Glove.

8. He always cashes in on the payoff pitch.

NOTICE: Bonds is not tax-free in all states but is double exempt.

At the end of the 1992 season, Barry Bonds was a two-time winner of the National League's Most Valuable Player award, a three-time winner of a Gold Glove award, and had just signed a six-year contract for $43.75 million, making him the highest-paid player in baseball. Richard Hoffer, The Importance of Being Barry: The Giants' Barry Bonds is the Best Player in the Game Today—Just Ask Him, Sports Illustrated, May 24, 1993, at 13. No one the least bit familiar with the game of baseball would mistake Cardtoons' "Treasury Bonds" for anyone other than the Giants' Barry Bonds. Other caricatures, such as "Ken Spiffy, Jr." of the "Mari–Nerds" (Ken Griffey, Jr., of the Seattle Mariners), are equally identifiable.

The trading cards ridicule the players using a variety of themes. A number of the cards, including the "Treasury Bonds" card and all of the Big Bang Bucks cards, humorously criticize players for their substantial salaries. (The irony of MLBPA's counterclaim for profits from the cards is not lost on this panel.) Other trading cards mock the players' narcissism, as exemplified by the card featuring "Egotisticky Henderson" of the "Pathet-ics," parodying Ricky Henderson, then of the Oakland Athletics. The card features a caricature of Henderson raising his finger in a "number one" sign while patting himself on the back, with the following text:

Egotisticky Henderson, accepting the "Me–Me Award" from himself at the annual "Egotisticky Henderson Fan Club" banquet, sponsored by Egotisticky Henderson:

"I would just like to thank myself for all I have done. (Pause for cheers.) I am the greatest of all time. (Raise arms triumphantly.) I love myself. (Pause for more cheers.) I am honored to know me. (Pause for louder cheers.) I wish there were two of me so I could spend more time with myself. (Wipe tears from eyes.) I couldn't have done it without me. (Remove cap and hold it aloft.) It's friends like me that keep me going. (Wave to crowd and acknowledge standing ovation.)

The remainder of the cards poke fun at things such as the players' names ("Chili Dog Davis" who "plays the game with relish," a parody of designated hitter Chili Davis), physical characteristics ("Cloud Johnson," a parody of six-foot-ten-inch pitcher Randy Johnson), and onfield behavior (a back-flipping "Ozzie Myth," a parody of shortstop Ozzie Smith).

The format of the parody trading cards is similar to that of traditional baseball cards. The cards, printed on cardboard stock measuring 2 1/2 by 3 1/2 inches, have images of players on the front and player information on the back. Like traditional cards, the parody cards use a variety of special effects, including foil embossing, stamping, spectra etching, and U–V coating. Cardtoons also takes advantage of a number of trading card industry techniques to enhance the value of its cards, such as limiting production, serially numbering cases of the cards, and randomly inserting subsets and "chase cards" (special trading cards) into the sets.

After designing its trading cards, Cardtoons contracted with a printer (Champs Marketing, Inc.) and distributor (TCM Associates) and implemented a marketing plan. As part of that plan, Cardtoons placed an advertisement in the May 14, 1993, issue of Sports Collectors Digest. That advertisement tipped off MLBPA, the defendant in this action, and prompted its attorney to write cease and desist letters to both Cardtoons and Champs.

MLBPA is the exclusive collective bargaining agent for all active major league baseball players, and operates a group licensing program in which it acts as the assignee of the individual publicity rights of all active players. Since 1966, MLBPA has entered into group licensing arrangements for a variety of products, such as candy bars, cookies, cereals, and, most importantly, baseball trading cards, which generate over seventy percent of its licensing revenue. MLBPA receives royalties from these sales and distributes the money to individual players.

After receiving the cease and desist letter from MLBPA, Champs advised Cardtoons that it would not print the parody cards until a court of competent jurisdiction had determined that the cards did not violate MLBPA's rights. Cardtoons then filed this suit seeking a declaratory judgment that its cards do not violate the publicity or other property rights of MLBPA or its members. Cardtoons also sought damages for tortious interference with its contractual relationship with Champs, as well as an injunction to prevent MLBPA from threatening legal action against Champs or other third parties with whom Cardtoons had contracted concerning the cards. MLBPA moved to dismiss for lack of subject matter jurisdiction, and counterclaimed for a declaratory judgment, injunction, and damages for violation of its members' rights of publicity under Oklahoma law.

The district court referred the case to a magistrate, who issued his Report and Recommendation in favor of MLBPA. The magistrate stated that the parody cards infringed on MLBPA's right of publicity and that, under either a trademark balancing test or a copyright fair use test, Cardtoons did not have a First Amendment right to market its cards without a license from MLBPA. The district court initially adopted the magistrate's Report and Recommendation, Cardtoons, L.C. v. Major League Baseball Players Association, 838 F.Supp. 1501 (N.D.Okla.1993), but subsequently vacated that decision and issued Cardtoons, L.C. v. Major League Baseball Players Association, 868 F.Supp. 1266 (N.D.Okla.1994). In its second opinion, the court wholly rejected application of a trademark balancing test to the right of publicity, and instead applied a copyright fair use analysis. Unlike the magistrate, however, the court held that a fair use analysis requires recognition of a parody exception to the Oklahoma publicity rights statute, and issued a declaratory judgment in favor of Cardtoons. This appeal followed.

[The court concluded that it had federal question jurisdiction and that there was a case or controversy.]

III.   The Merits

Cardtoons asks for a declaration that it can distribute its parody trading cards without the consent of MLBPA. There are three steps to our analysis of this issue. First, we determine whether the cards infringe upon MLBPA's property rights as established by either the Lanham Act or Oklahoma's right of publicity statute. If so, we then ascertain whether the cards are protected by the First Amendment. Finally, if both parties have cognizable rights at stake, we proceed to a final determination of the relative importance of those rights in the context of this case.

A.   MLBPA's Property Rights

1.   The Lanham Act

We begin by determining whether the cards violate MLBPA's property rights under the Lanham Act. Section 43(a)(1) of the Lanham Act, 15 U.S.C. § 1125(a)(1), creates a federal remedy for false representations or false designations of origin used in connection with the sale of a product. The statute provides civil liability for:

(a)(1) Any person who, on or in connection with any goods or services, or any container for goods, uses in commerce any word, term, name, symbol, or device, or any combination thereof, or any false designation of origin, false or misleading description of fact, or false or misleading representation of fact, which—

(A) is likely to cause confusion, or to cause mistake, or to deceive as to the affiliation, connection, or association of such person with another person, or as to the origin, sponsorship, or approval of his or her goods, services, or commercial activities by another person,.   .   .   .

The hallmark of a Lanham Act suit is proof of the likelihood of confusion, which occurs "when consumers make an incorrect mental association between the involved commercial products or their producers." [   ]

[The court affirmed the trial court's ruling that there was no likelihood of confusion.]

2.   The Right of Publicity

The right of publicity is the right of a person to control the commercial use of his or her identity. [   ] While the right was originally intertwined with the right of privacy, courts soon came to recognize a distinction between the personal right to be left alone and the business right to control use of one's identity in commerce. [   ]; Michael Madow, Private Ownership of Public Image: Popular Culture and Publicity Rights, 81 Cal.L.Rev. 127, 167–78 (1993). The latter was first acknowledged as a distinct privilege and termed the "right of publicity" in Haelan Laboratories, Inc. v. Topps Chewing Gum, Inc., 202 F.2d 866 (2d Cir.), cert. denied, 346 U.S. 816 (1953). *Haelan Laboratories*, appropriately enough, involved two rival chewing gum manufacturers who were arguing over exclusive rights to use the image of a professional baseball player to promote their product. In resolving the dispute, the court concluded that "a man has a right in the publicity value of his photograph." [   ] The court explained:

> This right might be called a "right of publicity." For it is common knowledge that many prominent persons (especially actors and ball-players), far from having their feelings bruised through public exposure of their likenesses, would feel sorely deprived if they no longer received money for authorizing advertisements, popularizing their countenances, displayed in newspapers, magazines, busses, trains and subways. This right of publicity would usually yield them no money unless it could be made the subject of an exclusive grant which barred any other advertiser from using their pictures.

[   ]. The development of this new intellectual property right was further cultivated by Melville Nimmer in his seminal article The Right of Publicity, 19 Law & Contemp. Probs. 203 (1954). Nimmer, who was counsel for Paramount Pictures at the time, [   ], referred to "the needs of Broadway and Hollywood" in describing the foundations and parameters of the right, [   ]. The right of publicity is now recognized by common law or statute in twenty-five states. [   ]

Like trademark and copyright, the right of publicity involves a cognizable property interest. [*Zacchini*; [   ]] Most formulations of the right protect against the unauthorized use of certain features of a person's identity—such as name, likeness, or voice—for commercial purposes. [   ] Although publicity rights are related to laws preventing false endorsement, they offer substantially broader protection. Suppose, for example, that a company, Mitchell Fruit, wanted to use pop singer Madonna in an advertising campaign to sell bananas, but Madonna never ate its fruit and would not agree to endorse its products. If Mitchell Fruit posted a billboard featuring a picture of Madonna and the phrase, "Madonna may have ten platinum albums, but she's never had a Mitchell banana," Madonna would not have a claim for false endorsement. She would, however, have a publicity rights claim, because Mitchell Fruit misappropriated her name and likeness for commercial purposes. Publicity rights, then, are a form of property protection that allows people to profit from the full commercial value of their identities.

Oklahoma first recognized the right of publicity as early as 1965, but expanded the right in a 1985 statute that is virtually identical to California's right of publicity statute, Cal.Civ.Code §§ 990 and 3344. The heart of the Oklahoma statute provides that:

> Any person who knowingly uses another's name, voice, signature, photograph, or likeness, in any manner, on or in products, merchandise, or goods, or for purposes of advertising or selling, or soliciting purchases of, products, merchandise, goods, or services, without such persons prior consent, . . . shall be liable for any damages sustained by the person or persons injured as a result thereof, and any profits from the unauthorized use that are attributable to the use shall be taken into account in computing the actual damages.

Okla. Stat. tit. 12, § 1449(A). Thus, a civil suit for infringement of MLBPA's publicity right under § 1449(A) requires proof of three elements: (1) knowing use of player names or likenesses (2) on products, merchandise, or goods (3) without MLBPA's prior consent. If MLBPA proves these three elements, then the burden shifts to Cardtoons to raise a valid defense.

There is little question that Cardtoons knowingly uses the names and likenesses of major league baseball players. This is evident from an examination of the cards and the testimony of the president of Cardtoons, who conceded that the cards borrow the likenesses of active players. Indeed, the caricatures are only humorous because they, along with the parodied name, team, and commentary, are accurate enough to allow identification of the players being parodied. The second and third elements of the statute are also satisfied. The cards are clearly a product, designed to be widely marketed and sold for profit. In addition, the parties have stipulated that MLBPA has not consented to Cardtoons' use of player likenesses. Cardtoons' parody cards, then, do infringe upon MLBPA's publicity right as defined in § 1449(A).

The Oklahoma publicity statute contains two exceptions designed to accommodate the First Amendment. The first, a "news" exception, exempts use of a person's identity in connection with any news, public affairs, or sports broadcast or account, or any political campaign, from the dictates of the statute. Okla. Stat. tit. 12, § 1449(D). The second exception, roughly analogous to the First Amendment concept of "incidental use," exempts use in a commercial medium that is not directly connected with commercial sponsorship or paid advertising. Okla. Stat. tit. 12, § 1449(F). The news and incidental use exceptions, however, provide no haven for Cardtoons. Cardtoons' commercial venture is not in connection with any news account. Moreover, the company's use of player likenesses is directly connected with a proposed commercial endeavor; indeed, the players were specifically selected for their wide market appeal. Thus, notwithstanding any First Amendment defense, Cardtoons' use of player likenesses on its cards violates the Oklahoma statute and infringes upon the property rights of MLBPA.

B.   Cardtoons' First Amendment Right

Because the parody trading cards infringe upon MLBPA's property rights, we must consider whether Cardtoons has a countervailing First Amendment right to publish the cards. The First Amendment only protects speech from regulation by the government. Although this is a civil action between private parties, it involves application of a state statute that Cardtoons claims imposes restrictions on its right of free expression. Application of that statute thus satisfies the state action requirement of Cardtoons' First Amendment claim. [*New York Times v. Sullivan*]

Cardtoons' parody trading cards receive full protection under the First Amendment. The cards provide social commentary on public figures, major league baseball players, who are involved in a significant commercial enterprise, major league baseball. While not core political speech (the cards do not, for example, adopt a position on the Ken Griffey, Jr., for President campaign), this type of commentary on an important social institution constitutes protected expression.

The cards are no less protected because they provide humorous rather than serious commentary. Speech that entertains, like speech that informs, is protected by the First Amendment because "[t]he line between the informing and the entertaining is too elusive for the protection of that basic right." Winters v. New York, 333 U.S. 507, 510 (1948); [   ]. Moreover, Cardtoons makes use of artistic and literary devices with distinguished traditions. Parody, for example, is a humorous form of social commentary that dates to Greek antiquity, and has since made regular appearances in English literature. [   ] In addition, cartoons and caricatures, such as those in the trading cards, have played a prominent role in public and political debate throughout our nation's history. See [*Hustler Magazine v. Falwell*]. Thus, the trading cards' commentary on these public figures and the major commercial enterprise in which they work receives no less protection because the cards are amusing.

[The court rejected MLBPA claims that Cardtoons' speech should receive less protection because (1) it fails to use a traditional medium of expression and (2) it was "commercial merchandise rather than protected speech."]

MLBPA further argues that the parody cards are commercial speech and should therefore receive less protection under the First Amendment. . . . Thus, commercial speech is best understood as speech that merely advertises a product or service for business purposes, [   ]. As such, commercial speech may receive something less than the strict review afforded other types of speech. [   ]

Cardtoons' trading cards, however, are not commercial speech—they do not merely advertise another unrelated product. Although the cards are sold in the marketplace, they are not transformed into commercial speech merely because they are sold for profit. [ ] Contrary to MLBPA's argument, therefore, the cards are unlike the parody in the only other circuit court decision addressing the constitutional tensions inherent in a celebrity parody, White v. Samsung Electronics America, Inc., 971 F.2d 1395 (9th Cir.), cert. denied, 508 U.S. 951 (1993). In that case, defendant Samsung published an advertisement featuring a costumed robot that parodied Vanna White, the letter-turner on television's Wheel of Fortune, and White sued for violation of her right of publicity. The court noted that in cases of noncommercial parodies, "the first amendment hurdle will bar most right of publicity actions against those activities." [ ] However, without engaging in a methodical commercial speech analysis of Samsung's First Amendment defense, the court ruled that White's claim was sufficient to withstand Samsung's motion for summary judgment. We disagree with the result in that case for reasons discussed in the two dissents that it engendered. Id. at 1407–08 (Alarcon, J., concurring in part and dissenting in part); White v. Samsung Elecs. Am., Inc., 989 F.2d 1512, 1512–23 (9th Cir.1993) (denial of rehearing en banc) (Kozinski, J., dissenting). Moreover, our case is distinguished by the fact that the speech involved is not commercial, but rather speech subject to full First Amendment protection. White, therefore, is inapposite, and we must directly confront the central problem in this case: whether Cardtoons' First Amendment right trumps MLBPA's property right.

C.   Balancing Free Speech Rights with Property Rights

In resolving the tension between the First Amendment and publicity rights in this case, we find little guidance in cases involving parodies of other forms of intellectual property. Trademark and copyright, for example, have built-in mechanisms that serve to avoid First Amendment concerns of this kind. As discussed above, proof of trademark infringement under the Lanham Act requires proof of a likelihood of confusion, but, in the case of a good trademark parody, there is little likelihood of confusion, since the humor lies in the difference between the original and the parody. The Copyright Act of 1976 contains a similar mechanism, the fair use exception, which permits the use of copyrighted materials for purposes such as criticism and comment. 17 U.S.C. § 107; see Campbell v. Acuff–Rose Music, Inc., 510 U.S. 569 (1994) (applying the fair use exception to parody). Oklahoma's right of publicity statute, however, does not provide a similar accommodation for parody, and we must therefore confront the First Amendment issue directly.

MLBPA urges us to adopt the framework established in Lloyd Corp. v. Tanner, 407 U.S. 551 (1972), in order to reconcile the free speech and property rights at stake in this case. The issue in *Lloyd* was whether a private shopping center could prevent the distribution of handbills on its premises. The Court focused on the availability of "adequate alternative avenues of communication . . ." [The court concluded that "in the context of intellectual property," *Lloyd*'s "no adequate alternative avenues" test does not sufficiently accommodate the public's interest in free expression. . . . Restrictions on the words or images that may be used by a speaker, therefore, are quite different than restrictions on the time, place, or manner of speech."]

This case instead requires us to directly balance the magnitude of the speech restriction against the asserted governmental interest in protecting the intellectual property right. We thus begin our analysis by examining the importance of Cardtoons' right to free expression and the consequences of limiting that right. We then weigh those consequences against the effect of infringing on MLBPA's right of publicity.

1.   The Effect of Infringing Upon Cardtoons' Right to Free Speech

Cardtoons' interest in publishing its parody trading cards implicates some of the core concerns of the First Amendment. "Parodies and caricatures," noted Aldous Huxley, "are the most penetrating of criticisms." Point Counter Point, ch. 13 (1928); see *Hustler Magazine*, [   ]. A parodist can, with deft and wit, readily expose the foolish and absurd in society. Parody is also a valuable form of self-expression that allows artists to shed light on earlier works and, at the same time, create new ones. Thus, parody, both as social criticism and a means of self-expression, is a vital commodity in the marketplace of ideas.

Parodies of celebrities are an especially valuable means of expression because of the role celebrities play in modern society. . . . Through their pervasive presence in the media, sports and entertainment celebrities come to symbolize certain ideas and values. Commentator Michael Madow gives the following example:

> In December 1990, . . . shortly before the outbreak of the Gulf War, a story circulated in Washington that President Bush had boasted to a congressional delegation that Saddam Hussein was "going to get his ass kicked." When reporters pressed Bush to confirm the statement, he did not answer directly. Instead, he hitched up his pants in the manner of John Wayne. Everyone got the point.

Madow, [   ]. Celebrities, then, are an important element of the shared communicative resources of our cultural domain.

Because celebrities are an important part of our public vocabulary, a parody of a celebrity does not merely lampoon the celebrity, but exposes the weakness of the idea or value that the celebrity symbolizes in society. Cardtoons' trading cards, for example, comment on the state of major league baseball by turning images of our sports heroes into modern-day personifications of avarice. In order to effectively criticize society, parodists need access to images that mean something to people, and thus celebrity parodies are a valuable communicative resource. Restricting the use of celebrity identities restricts the communication of ideas.

Without First Amendment protection, Cardtoons' trading cards and their irreverent commentary on the national pastime cannot be freely distributed to the public. Instead, as required by Oklahoma law, the production and distribution of the cards would be subject to MLBPA's consent. The problem with this scheme, as the Supreme Court noted in the context of copyright parody, is that "the unlikelihood that creators of imaginative works will license critical reviews or lampoons of their own productions removes such uses from the very notion of a potential licensing market." [*Campbell*]. The potential for suppression is even greater in the context of publicity rights because the product involved is the celebrity's own persona. Indeed, the director of licensing for MLBPA testified that MLBPA would never license a parody which poked fun at the players. Thus, elevating the right of publicity above the right to free expression would likely prevent distribution of the parody trading cards. This would not only allow MLBPA to censor criticism of its members, but would also have a chilling effect upon future celebrity parodies. Such a result is clearly undesirable, for "[t]he last thing we need, the last thing the First Amendment will tolerate, is a law that lets public figures keep people from mocking them." *White*, 989 F.2d at 1519 (Kozinski, J., dissenting).

2.   The Effect of Infringing Upon MLBPA's Right of Publicity

We now turn to an evaluation of society's interest in protecting MLBPA's publicity right. The justifications offered for the right of publicity fall into two categories, economic and noneconomic. The right is thought to further economic goals such as stimulating athletic and artistic achievement, promoting the efficient allocation of resources, and protecting consumers. In addition, the right of publicity is said to protect various noneconomic interests, such as safeguarding natural rights, securing the fruits of celebrity labors, preventing unjust enrichment, and averting emotional harm. We examine the applicability of each of these justifications to the facts of this case.

The principal economic argument made in support of the right of publicity is that it provides an incentive for creativity and achievement. See, e.g., [*Zacchini*]; [   ]. Under this view, publicity rights induce people to expend the time, effort, and resources to develop the talents prerequisite to public recognition. While those talents provide immediate benefit to those with commercially valuable identities, the products of their enterprise— such as movies, songs, and sporting events—ultimately benefit society as a whole. Thus, it is argued, society has an interest in a right of publicity that is closely analogous to its interest in other intellectual property protections such as copyright and patent law. [   ]

This incentives argument is certainly a compelling justification for other forms of intellectual property. Copyright law, for example, protects the primary, if not only, source of a writer's income, and thus provides a significant incentive for creativity and achievement. The incentive effect of publicity rights, however, has been overstated. Most sports and entertainment celebrities with commercially valuable identities engage in activities that themselves generate a significant amount of income; the commercial value of their identities is merely a by-product of their performance values.

[   ] Although no one pays to watch Cormac McCarthy write a novel, many people pay a lot of money to watch Demi Moore "act" and Michael Jordan play basketball. Thus, the analogy to the incentive effect of other intellectual property protections is strained because "[a]bolition of the right of publicity would leave entirely unimpaired a celebrity's ability to earn a living from the activities that have generated his commercially marketable fame." Madow [   ]

This distinction between the value of a person's identity and the value of his performance explains why [*Zacchini*] is a red herring. . . . The Court's incentive rationale is obviously more compelling in a right of performance case than in a more typical right of publicity case involving the appropriation of a celebrity's identity. [   ]

Moreover, the additional inducement for achievement produced by publicity rights are often inconsequential because most celebrities with valuable commercial identities are already handsomely compensated. . . . In addition, even in the absence of publicity rights, celebrities would still be able to reap financial reward from authorized appearances and endorsements. The extra income generated by licensing one's identity does not provide a necessary inducement to enter and achieve in the realm of sports and entertainment. Thus, while publicity rights may provide some incentive for creativity and achievement, the magnitude and importance of that incentive has been exaggerated.

The argument that publicity rights provide valuable incentives is even less compelling in the context of celebrity parodies. Since celebrities will seldom give permission for their identities to be parodied, granting them control over the parodic use of their identities would not directly provide them with any additional income. It would, instead, only allow them to shield themselves from ridicule and criticism. The only economic incentive gained by having control over the use of one's identity in parody is control over the potential effect the parody would have on the market for nonparodic use of one's identity. MLBPA claims, for example, that publication of the parody cards will decrease demand for traditional baseball cards because Cardtoons and other makers of parody trading cards would compete with manufacturers of licensed cards in the same limited trading card market. Parody, however, rarely acts as a market substitute for the original, [*Campbell*], and there is no evidence in this record that convinces us otherwise. Even if there is some substitutive effect, and card collectors with limited resources decide to buy parody cards instead of traditional, licensed cards, the small amount of additional income generated by suppressing parody cards will have little, if any, effect on the incentive to become a major league baseball player.

The incentives argument would be even more tenuous, indeed perverse, if good-humored celebrities were to license use of their identities for parody. The right of publicity would then provide an incentive to engage in the socially undesirable behavior that might give rise to a reason to parody. Although part of any parody's market appeal depends upon the prominence of the celebrity, the critical element of the parody's value hinges on the accuracy of the caricature or criticism. Society does not have a significant interest in allowing a celebrity to protect the type of reputation that gives rise to parody.

We recognize that publicity rights do provide some incentive to achieve in the fields of sports and entertainment. However, the inducements generated by publicity rights are not nearly as important as those created by copyright and patent law, and the small incentive effect of publicity rights is reduced or eliminated in the context of celebrity parodies. In sum, it is unlikely that little leaguers will stop dreaming of the big leagues or major leaguers will start "dogging it" to first base if MLBPA is denied the right to control the use of its members' identities in parody.

The second economic justification for the right of publicity is that it promotes the efficient allocation of resources, a version of the familiar tragedy of the commons argument used to prove the superiority of private property over common property. [ ] Without the artificial scarcity created by publicity rights, identities would be commercially exploited until the marginal value of each use is zero. [ ] "Creating artificial scarcity preserves the value to [the celebrity], to advertisers who contract for the use of his likeness, and in the end, to consumers, who receive information from the knowledge that he is being paid to endorse the product." [ ] Giving people control of the commercial use of their identities, according to this analysis, maximizes the economic and informational value of those identities.

This efficiency argument is most persuasive in the context of advertising, where repeated use of a celebrity's likeness to sell products may eventually diminish its commercial value. The argument is not as persuasive, however, when applied to nonadvertising uses. It is not clear, for example, that the frequent appearance of a celebrity's likeness on t-shirts and coffee mugs will reduce its value; indeed, the value of the likeness may increase precisely because "everybody's got one." [ ] Further, celebrities with control over the parodic use of their identities would not use the power to "ration the use of their names in order to maximize their value over time," [ ]. They would instead use that power to suppress criticism, and thus permanently remove a valuable source of information about their identity from the marketplace.

The final economic argument offered for rights of publicity is that they protect against consumer deception. [ ] The Lanham Act, however, already provides nationwide protection against false or misleading representations in connection with the sale of products. Moreover, as discussed above, the use of celebrity names or likenesses in parodies in general, and in Cardtoons' trading cards in particular, are not likely to confuse or deceive consumers. Thus, this final economic justification has little merit.

There are also several noneconomic reasons advanced for the right of publicity. First, some believe that publicity rights stem from some notion of natural rights. . . . [B]lind appeals to first principles carry no weight in our balancing analysis.

The second noneconomic justification is that publicity rights allow celebrities to enjoy the fruits of their labors. [ ] According to this argument, "[a] celebrity must be considered to have invested his years of practice and competition in a public personality which eventually may reach marketable status." [ ] People deserve the right to control and profit from the commercial value of their identities because, quite simply, they've earned it. Thus, in this view, the right of publicity is similar to the right of a commercial enterprise to profit from the goodwill it has built up in its name. [ ]

Celebrities, however, are often not fully responsible for their fame. Indeed, in the entertainment industry, a celebrity's fame may largely be the creation of the media or the audience. [ ] As one actor put it, "Only that audience out there makes a star. It's up to them. You can't do anything about it. . . . Stars would all be Louis B. Mayer's cousins if you could make 'em up." Jack Nicholson, quoted in Jib Fowles, Starstruck: Celebrity Performers and the American Public 84 (1992). Professional athletes may be more responsible for their celebrity status, however, because athletic success is fairly straightforwardly the result of an athlete's natural talent and dedication. Thus, baseball players may deserve to profit from the commercial value of their identities more than movie stars. Once again, however, the force of this justification is diminished in the case of parody, because there is little right to enjoy the fruits of socially undesirable behavior.

The third, related justification for publicity rights is the prevention of unjust enrichment. [ ] In this view, whether the commercial value of an identity is the result of a celebrity's hard work, media creation, or just pure dumb luck, no social purpose is served by allowing others to freely appropriate it. Cardtoons, however, is not merely hitching its wagon to a star. As in all celebrity parodies, Cardtoons added a significant creative component of its own to the celebrity identity and created an entirely new product. Indeed, allowing MLBPA to control or profit from the parody trading cards would actually sanction the theft of Cardtoons' creative enterprise.

A final justification offered for the right of publicity is that it prevents emotional injuries. For example, commercial misappropriation may greatly distress a celebrity who finds all commercial exploitation to be offensive. Lugosi v. Universal Pictures, 603 P.2d 425, 439 n. 11 (Cal.1979) (Bird, C.J., dissenting). Even celebrities who crave public attention might find particular uses of their identities to be distressing. See, e.g., O'Brien v. Pabst Sales Co., 124 F.2d 167, 170 (5th Cir.1941) (professional football player, active in an organization devoted to discouraging alcohol use among young people, sued to stop the use of his image in a Pabst Blue Ribbon beer advertising calendar). The right of publicity allows celebrities to avoid the emotional distress caused by unwanted commercial use of their identities. Publicity rights, however, are meant to protect against the loss of financial gain, not mental anguish. Zacchini, 433 U.S. at 573; Lugosi, 603 P.2d at 438–39 (Bird, C.J., dissenting). Laws preventing unfair competition, such as the Lanham Act, and laws prohibiting the intentional infliction of emotional distress adequately cover that ground. Moreover, fame is a double-edged sword—the law cannot allow those who enjoy the public limelight to so easily avoid the ridicule and criticism that sometimes accompany public prominence.

Thus, the noneconomic justifications for the right of publicity are no more compelling than the economic arguments. Those justifications further break down in the context of parody, where the right to profit from one's persona is reduced to the power to suppress criticism. In sum, the effect of limiting MLBPA's right of publicity in this case is negligible.

IV. Conclusion

One of the primary goals of intellectual property law is to maximize creative expression. The law attempts to achieve this goal by striking a proper balance between the right of a creator to the fruits of his labor and the right of future creators to free expression. Underprotection of intellectual property reduces the incentive to create; overprotection creates a monopoly over the raw material of creative expression. The application of the Oklahoma publicity rights statute to Cardtoons' trading cards presents a classic case of overprotection. Little is to be gained, and much lost, by protecting MLBPA's right to control the use of its members' identities in parody trading cards. The justifications for the right of publicity are not nearly as compelling as those offered for other forms of intellectual property, and are particularly unpersuasive in the case of celebrity parodies. The cards, on the other hand, are an important form of entertainment and social commentary that deserve First Amendment protection. Accordingly, we AFFIRM.

Notes and Questions

1. What are the strongest economic arguments for each side? The strongest non-economic arguments?

2. Is the court suggesting that celebrities have no interest in emotional tranquility? Does the First Amendment override that interest? In the *O'Brien* case, cited near the end of the opinion, might the plaintiff have succeeded in an action for intentional infliction of emotional distress? For defamation? Recall *Burnett v. National Enquirer, Inc.*, p. 995, supra.

3. Why is *Zacchini* a "red herring" for the court?

4. Is the court correct in its example about Mitchell Fruit Co. and Madonna?

5. *White v. Samsung.* Also in connection with the Madonna example, consider White v. Samsung Electronics America, Inc., 971 F.2d 1395 (9th Cir.1992), rehearing denied 989 F.2d 1512 (en banc), cert. denied 508 U.S. 951 (1993). Defendant's television commercial—one of a series promoting the idea that its product will still be popular in the next century—used a robot that suggested TV personality Vanna White in her role of turning letters on the program "Wheel of Fortune." After holding that White had no action under the California publicity statute because the robot was not a "likeness" within the statute, the majority held that her common-law right of publicity had been violated. It was "not important how the defendant has appropriated the plaintiff's identity, but whether the defendant has done so:"

> Viewed separately, the individual aspects of the advertisement in the present case say little. Viewed together, they leave little doubt about the celebrity the ad is meant to depict. The female-shaped robot is wearing a long gown, blond wig, and large jewelry. Vanna White dresses exactly like this at times, but so do many other women. The robot is in the process of turning a block letter on a game-board. Vanna White dresses like this while turning letters on a game-board but perhaps similarly attired Scrabble-playing women do this as well. The robot is standing on what looks to be the Wheel of Fortune game show set. Vanna White dresses like this, turns letters, and does this on the Wheel of Fortune game show. She is the only one. Indeed, defendants themselves referred to their ad as the "Vanna White" ad. We are not surprised.

> Television and other media create marketable celebrity identity value. Considerable energy and ingenuity are expended by those who have achieved celebrity value to exploit it for profit. The law protects the celebrity's sole right to exploit this value whether the celebrity has achieved her fame out of rare ability, dumb luck, or a combination thereof. We decline [defendants'] invitation to permit the evisceration of the common law right of publicity through means as facile as those in this case. Because White has alleged facts showing that [defendants] had appropriated her identity, the district court erred by rejecting, on summary judgment, White's common law right of publicity claim.

When defendant argued that the ad was constitutionally protected, the majority responded:

> In defense, defendants cite a number of cases for the proposition that their robot ad constituted protected speech. The only cases they cite which are even remotely relevant to this case are [*Hustler Magazine v. Falwell*] and L.L. Bean, Inc. v. Drake Publishers, Inc., 811 F.2d 26 (1st Cir.1987). Those cases involved parodies of advertisements run for the purpose of poking fun at Jerry Falwell and L.L. Bean, respectively. This case involves a true advertisement run for the purpose of selling Samsung VCRs. The ad's spoof of Vanna White and Wheel of Fortune is subservient and only tangentially related to the ad's primary message: "buy Samsung VCRs." Defendants' parody arguments are better addressed to non-commercial parodies. The difference between a "parody" and a "knock-off" is the difference between fun and profit.

One judge dissented. An effort to obtain rehearing en banc was rejected over three dissents. The flavor of that extended dissent—finding incompatibility with the Copyright Act, the Copyright Clause, and the First Amendment—may be gauged from the following excerpts:

KOZINSKI, CIRCUIT JUDGE, with whom CIRCUIT JUDGES O'SCANNLAIN and KLEINFELD join, dissenting from the order rejecting the suggestion for rehearing en banc.

I

Saddam Hussein wants to keep advertisers from using his picture in unflattering contexts. Clint Eastwood doesn't want tabloids to write about him. Rudolf Valentino's heirs want to control his film biography. The Girl Scouts don't want their image soiled by association with certain activities. George Lucas wants to keep Strategic Defense Initiative fans from calling it "Star Wars." Pepsico doesn't want singers to use the word "Pepsi" in their songs. Guy Lombardo wants an exclusive property right to ads that show big bands playing on New Year's Eve. Uri Geller thinks he should be paid for ads showing psychics bending metal through telekinesis. Paul Prud-homme, that household name, thinks the same about ads featuring corpulent bearded chefs. And scads of copyright holders see purple when their creations are made fun of. [The opinion cites references for each example.]

Something very dangerous is going on here. Private property, including intellectual property, is essential to our way of life. It provides an incentive for investment and innovation; it stimulates the flourishing of our culture; it protects the moral entitlements of people to the fruits of their labors. But reducing too much to private property can be bad medicine. Private land, for instance, is far more useful if separated from other private land by public streets, roads and highways. Public parks, utility rights-of-way and sewers reduce the amount of land in private hands, but vastly enhance the value of the property that remains.

So too it is with intellectual property. Overprotecting intellectual property is as harmful as underprotecting it. Creativity is impossible without a rich public domain. Nothing today, likely nothing since we tamed fire, is genuinely new: Culture, like science and technology, grows by accretion, each new creator building on the works of those who came before. Overprotection stifles the very creative forces it's supposed to nurture. [   ]

The panel's opinion is a classic case of overprotection. Concerned about what it sees as a wrong done to Vanna White, the panel majority erects a property right of remarkable and dangerous breadth: Under the majority's opinion, it's now a tort for advertisers to remind the public of a celebrity. Not to use a celebrity's name, voice, signature or likeness; not to imply the celebrity endorses a product; but simply to evoke the celebrity's image in the public's mind. This Orwellian notion withdraws far more from the public domain than prudence and common sense allow. It conflicts with the Copyright Act and the Copyright Clause. It raises serious First Amendment problems. It's bad law, and it deserves a long, hard second look.

II

. . .

The ad that spawned this litigation starred a robot dressed in a wig, gown and jewelry reminiscent of Vanna White's hair and dress; the robot was posed next to a Wheel-of-Fortune-like game board. [ ] The caption read "Longest-running game show. 2012 A.D." The gag here, I take it, was that Samsung would still be around when White had been replaced by a robot.

Perhaps failing to see the humor, White sued, alleging Samsung infringed her right of publicity by "appropriating" her "identity." Under California law, White has the exclusive right to use her name, likeness, signature and voice for commercial purposes. [ ] But Samsung didn't use her name, voice or signature, and it certainly didn't use her likeness. The ad just wouldn't have been funny had it depicted White or someone who resembled her—the whole joke was that the game show host(ess) was a robot, not a real person. No one seeing the ad could have thought this was supposed to be White in 2012.

.   .   .

VI

.   .   .

The majority dismisses the First Amendment issue out of hand because Samsung's ad was commercial speech. [ ] So what? Commercial speech may be less protected by the First Amendment than noncommercial speech, but less protected means protected nonetheless.   .   .   .

In our pop culture, where salesmanship must be entertaining and entertainment must sell, the line between the commercial and noncommercial has not merely blurred; it has disappeared. Is the Samsung parody any different from a parody on Saturday Night Live or in Spy Magazine? Both are equally profit-motivated. Both use a celebrity's identity to sell things—one to sell VCRs, the other to sell advertising. Both mock their subjects. Both try to make people laugh. Both add something, perhaps something worthwhile and memorable, perhaps not, to our culture. Both are things that the people being portrayed might dearly want to suppress. [ ]

.   .   .

VII

For better or worse, we are the Court of Appeals for the Hollywood Circuit. Millions of people toil in the shadow of the law we make, and much of their livelihood is made possible by the existence of intellectual property rights. But much of their livelihood—and much of the vibrancy of our culture—also depends on the existence of other intangible rights: The right to draw ideas from a rich and varied public domain, and the right to mock, for profit as well as fun, the cultural icons of our time.

In the name of avoiding the "evisceration" of a celebrity's rights in her image, the majority diminishes the rights of copyright holders and the public at large. In the name of fostering creativity, the majority suppresses it. Vanna White and those like her have been given something they never had before, and they've been given it at our expense. I cannot agree.

————

Does the panel majority or the Kozinski opinion reach the Madonna example?

6. *Identities.* In Wendt v. Host International, Inc., 125 F.3d 806 (9th Cir.1997), rehearing and rehearing en banc denied, 197 F.3d 1284 (9th Cir.1999) cert. denied 121 S.Ct. 33 (2000), the defendant created animatronic robots allegedly based on the likenesses of two actors from the television show "Cheers," and placed the robots in airport bars modeled after the bar in the television program. The district court granted summary judgment to the defendant. The court of appeals reversed, holding that fact issues existed concerning whether the robots violated the actors' rights of publicity and whether use of the robots created a likelihood of confusion regarding the actors' endorsement of the bars. The majority relied on the circuit's earlier ruling in *White v. Samsung.* Judge Kozinksi, joined by two other judges, dissented with opinion from the denial of rehearing en banc.

7. *The Eastwood case.* In Eastwood v. Superior Court, 198 Cal.Rptr. 342 (App. 1983), relied upon by the majority in *White v. Samsung,* Clint Eastwood sued the National Enquirer for the unauthorized use of his likeness on the cover and in related television advertisements about a false nondefamatory story inside the issue. The story involved allegations that Eastwood was romantically involved with two female celebrities. The court concluded that the use was commercial exploitation and was not privileged under state or federal law. The trial court had improperly sustained a demurrer to the complaint. The court of appeal saw no reason why Eastwood should have to show that he was being falsely said to be endorsing the National Enquirer. This was one way to impose liability but it was not essential. The court also concluded that the article was not necessarily protected as a news account because of an allegation that the story was a calculated falsehood. The court discussed at length the emerging right of publicity.

In a subsequent episode a federal jury awarded Eastwood $150,000 against the National Enquirer for a "bogus interview with him published in December 1993." The theory was that although the alleged interview was not necessarily defamatory, "Clint didn't want to be associated with the National Enquirer." The defendant asserted that it was unaware that the interview that it had purchased from a freelancer was bogus. See Nat'l L.J., Nov. 13, 1995 at A22.

At the time of *Eastwood,* the statute required a showing of unauthorized use in a product advertisement or endorsement. In 1984, § 3344 was amended to "encompass any unauthorized use 'on or in products, merchandise or goods.' " In KNB Enterprises v. Matthews, 92 Cal.Rptr.2d 713 (App. 2000), the court observed that plaintiffs like Eastwood no longer had to try to force their cases into the narrower setting.

Might each of these claims have been analyzed as false-light cases?

8. *Cher's case.* In Cher v. Forum International, Ltd., 7 Med.L.Rptr. 2593 (C.D.Cal.1982), the judge, after a nonjury trial, awarded the plaintiff entertainer $663,000 for loss of her right of publicity. Cher had agreed to give an interview to Us Magazine, reserving the right to bar publication if she did not like the results. She exercised that right. The interviewer, however, then sold the interview to the two defendant magazines, each of which published excerpts. One defendant's cover asserted that it was an exclusive interview. Cher alleged that she would not have given either of the defendants an interview because she did not approve of them.

On the appeal in Cher's case, the court reversed as to one magazine but affirmed as to the other. Cher v. Forum International, Ltd., 692 F.2d 634 (9th Cir.1982), cert. denied 462 U.S. 1120 (1983). Star had put on its cover "Exclusive Series" followed by "Cher: My life, my husbands and my many, many men." The court concluded that Star "was entitled to inform its readers that the issue contained an article about Cher, that the article was based on an interview with Cher herself, and that the article had not previously appeared elsewhere." The words used to convey that information "cannot support a finding of the knowing or reckless falsity required under *Time, Inc. v. Hill.*" Nor did the words convey the false claim that Cher endorsed the magazine. The then-existing version of the California "right of publicity" statute had an express exception for news accounts that was held to cover this case.

Forum magazine changed the text to make it appear that Forum was posing the questions to Cher in an interview—"apparently a common practice in the industry." The cover said "Exclusive: Cher Talks Straight." Forum also used Cher's name on a subscription pullout card that asserted that things Cher would not tell US Magazine she was telling Forum. The card also stated "So join Cher and Forum's hundreds of thousands of other adventurous readers today." The claim that Cher was telling Forum readers things she would not tell US was "patently false. This kind of mendacity is not protected by the First Amendment. . . ." The falsity was particularly clear here because US was a magazine to which Cher *was* willing to give an interview.

The trial court had also found liability for the "join Cher" language on the card. Although the court of appeals thought the language somewhat ambiguous, it was willing to accept the trial court's reading that this was an implied endorsement of Forum and its conclusion that the falsity of that reading showed a reckless disregard for the truth. The court of appeals concluded that "no matter how carefully the editorial staff of Forum may have trod the border between the actionable and the protected, the advertising staff engaged in the kind of knowing falsity that strips away the protection of the First Amendment."

9. *Advertising prior work.* New York has decided that a medium's use of an earlier story to advertise its own product does not come within "advertising purposes" under the statute. In Booth v. Curtis Publishing Co., 223 N.Y.S.2d 737 (App.Div.), affirmed without opinion 182 N.E.2d 812

(N.Y.1962), Holiday magazine published a photograph of actress Shirley Booth in a story about a prominent resort. The color photograph was "a very striking one, show[ing] Miss Booth in the water up to her neck, but wearing a brimmed, high-crowned, street hat of straw." Several months after the story appeared, Holiday took out full-page advertisements in the New Yorker and Advertising Age magazines. Both reprinted the Booth photograph as a sample of the content of Holiday magazine. "Because of the photograph's striking qualities it would be quite effective in drawing attention to the advertisements; but it was also a sample of magazine content."

The court found the use of the photograph to be an "incidental" mentioning of plaintiff in the course of advertising itself. "It stands to reason that a publication can best prove its worth and illustrate its content by submission of complete copies of or extraction from past editions. . . . And, of course, it is true that the publisher must advertise in other public media, just as it must by poster, circular, cover, or soliciting letter. This is a practical necessity which the law may not ignore in giving effect to the purposes of the statute."

Although the court recognized that "realistically" the use of the photograph attracted the attention of the reader, that use was outweighed by the magazine's need to demonstrate its content. Finally, nothing in the advertisement suggested that plaintiff endorsed defendant's magazine.

This was followed in Namath v. Sports Illustrated, 371 N.Y.S.2d 10 (App.Div. 1975), affirmed 352 N.E.2d 584 (N.Y.1976). See also Montana v. San Jose Mercury News, Inc., 40 Cal.Rptr.2d 639 (App. 1995)(denying claim by former football star for defendant newspaper's sale of poster reproductions of its newspaper pages that showed plaintiff's photograph).

10. *The Riggins case.* In Town & Country Properties, Inc. v. Riggins, 457 S.E.2d 356 (Va.1995), defendant realtor distributed some 1,600 one-page flyers inviting real estate brokers to an open house to view "John Riggins' Former Home." Riggins was "formerly a prominent professional football player" who still made his living in the area by working as a part-time commentator on a radio sports program and by making appearances for which he charged between $5,000 and $90,000—unless it was for a charitable cause. When he learned of the flyer he claimed to have been " 'angry,' 'humiliated,' and felt a loss of 'integrity and dignity.' Plaintiff said he felt 'violated' and that his 'livelihood' had been threatened by this flyer.' " His suit was under a statute almost identical to New York's, for having had his "name" used without his consent "for advertising purposes or for purposes of trade."

A judgment for $25,000 compensatory and similar amount for punitive damages was upheld on appeal. That the flyer was truthful was no defense because it was used for both of the barred purposes. The name was not relevant to information about the house such as its physical condition, architectural features or quality. "Simply, this is not the type of commercial speech accorded constitutional protection." The amount of the award was supported by expert testimony and fell within the range of his prior fees. Punitive damages were justified under the statute where the name is "knowingly used."

How might this case be analyzed in a state without legislation in this area?

11. What if the product asserts that it is a fictional account of a celebrity's life? In Hicks v. Casablanca Records, 464 F.Supp. 426 (S.D.N.Y. 1978), defendants based a novel on a fictionalized explanation of Agatha Christie's mysterious 11-day disappearance in 1926.

The court engrafted upon the right of publicity a protection for "matters of news, history, biography, and other factual subjects of public interest despite the necessary references to" the names of living persons. That protection did not apply here, however, because the 11-day episode discussed in the book was fictional and did not purport to be biographical.

The book was accorded constitutional protection. Although fiction, it did not contain deliberate falsehood and did not falsely purport to be biographical. The reader would know by the word "novel" that the work was fictitious. The "protection usually accorded novels and movies outweighs whatever publicity rights plaintiffs may possess."

Docudramas. How should one analyze the relatively new technique of the "docudrama," in which the program mixes truth and fiction? When ABC announced in 1982 that it was planning a docudrama on the life of Elizabeth Taylor, the actress responded by seeking an injunction. Her first theory was that "I am my own commodity. I am my own industry." Someday "I will write my autobiography, and perhaps film it, but that will be my choice. By doing this, ABC is taking away from my income." What if she had tried to block an unauthorized biography?

Taylor's second theory was false light invasion of privacy. "They plan to use my name throughout the show, to hire an actress who supposedly resembles me and to have her speak lines which they want the public to believe I used in numerous personal and private conversations."

Taylor's lawyer contended: "The docudrama is a fairly new form of expression. It's not biography, it's not a documentary and its not her story. It's a drama. We're talking about a live actress who is entitled not to have lies told about her. When you mix fact and fiction and say this is a life story, no matter how flattering you are, you're showing the subject in a false light, and creating a wrong image."

Later, ABC announced that it had dropped its plans, for "creative reasons." This account of the dispute is taken mainly from Lewin, Whose Life Is It Anyway? Legally, It's Hard to Tell, N.Y. Times, Nov. 21, 1982, § II, at 1. See Manson, The Television Docudrama and the Right of Publicity, in Comm. & the Law, Feb. 1985, at 41, concluding that since the docudrama is "neither fiction nor straight documentary" it does not fall within the protection accorded "biographies and documentaries; it does not provide a dissemination of information. Furthermore, the docudrama does not come under the first amendment protection of drama; it is not evident to the public that the events depicted in the docudrama are fictitious." By its "very nature, the docudrama tends to confuse the viewer, making it difficult to discern when true events in the life of the public figure portrayed merge and blend with purely fanciful fabrications. To confuse the viewer is a disservice to the public—to society. Further, confusion also diminishes and thereby damages the value of the public figure's 'name, likeness and persona.' "

NBC also pursued the development of a miniseries based on Taylor's life story. She was unsuccessful in attempting to enjoin production of the miniseries, which was eventually completed in 1996. Taylor v. National Broadcasting Co., 1994 WL 780690 (Cal. Super. 1994).

In a more recent case, Ruffin–Steinback v. dePasse, 82 F.Supp.2d 723 (E.D.Mich.2000), former members of the Motown group the "Temptations" sued several defendants involved in producing a mini-series docudrama based on the group's story. The court granted summary judgment for the defendants, holding that the depiction of one's life story, "particularly where some of the events are fictionalized," does not violate the right of publicity under Michigan law. It further observed that, "Plaintiffs have failed to cite caselaw from any jurisdiction supporting their claim that the right of publicity may be extended to preclude depiction of one's life-story."

Which is the easier case for the plaintiff—complaining about a work that is called fiction or a docudrama?

Nonfamous plaintiffs. A teenager was filmed at an accident site by a TV news crew. She had gone to the site of a car accident in the mistaken belief that her boyfriend's sister might have been killed. The news photographer sold the footage to a film producer. That footage later found its way into a movie called *Faces of Death*, which has been banned in 46 countries because of its grisly content. In the movie, the footage of the teenager was edited to make it appear that she was reacting to seeing the bloody body of a bicyclist killed by a semitrailer truck. What harm, if any, has the teenager suffered? Should she have an action for false light privacy? For commercial appropriation of her face? Recall the *Shulman* case, p. 1174, supra. The teenager sued the photographer, the film's producer, and its distributor, seeking royalties, damages, and an injunction barring exhibition until deletion of the scene. Editor & Publisher, Jan. 28, 1989, at 26. How would you measure her damages on each claim?

In Staruski v. Continental Tel. Co., 581 A.2d 266 (Vt.1990), plaintiff's employer, without consent, ran her name, photo, and a purported statement about what work she did and how she enjoyed her work. Although plaintiff was not a famous person she was entitled to sue for the appropriation of her name and likeness for commercial purposes. Although there may be "incidental" uses, as in crowd scenes in commercials, there was "nothing incidental about plaintiff's appearance in the ad."

Recall that the *Roberson* case itself involved a nonfamous person whose face was used for an advertisement.

CHAPTER XV

INTENTIONAL ECONOMIC HARM

We turn now to a group of claims based on economic loss. These subjects are not being raised for the first time. Recall, for example, that we have already considered questions of the duty owed by attorneys and accountants to non-clients, p. 302, supra. The question there was one of the scope of liability for negligence. Here we begin by considering the scope of liability for intentional misrepresentation. We continue with an examination of intentional efforts to interfere with the contract rights or expected economic advantage of others. Again, recall that we considered the scope of liability for negligent interference with these interests at p. 313, supra.

A. MISREPRESENTATION

1. INTRODUCTION

Although we have been concerned primarily with physical acts that have caused harm, we have also had occasion to consider situations in which words have caused harm. Recall the misleading recommendations that may have led to assault, p. 170, supra, problems of product labels and instructions, p. 581, supra, and the incorrect accounting reports and legal advice that caused harm to others, p. 302, supra. In this section we explore the problem of misrepresentation, emphasizing the cases in which the parties are dealing directly with one another. The fear of unlimited liability, which played such a large role earlier, recedes—to be replaced by problems of determining the boundary between contract and tort, and the role of negotiations preliminary to entering into contracts. Although we have addressed the tort-contract line earlier, e.g., in connection with the line between the Uniform Commercial Code and tort law, p. 639, supra, our focus here is on the use of words that mislead and cause economic harm to the relying party.

Sometimes it is clear that only one form of remedy, if any, is available. Thus, when the only problem is a failure to fulfill a contractual obligation, usually no tort remedy is available. But consider Channel Master Corp. v. Aluminum Ltd. Sales, Inc., 151 N.E.2d 833 (N.Y.1958), in which defendant orally expressed willingness to supply 400,000 pounds of aluminum ingot per month to plaintiff for five months. After the defendant failed to supply the ingots, any contract action would have been barred by the statute of frauds. But the court held that a tort action might still lie:

> The present action is in tort, not contract, depending not upon agreement between the parties, but rather upon deliberate misrepre-

sentation of fact, relied on by the plaintiff to his detriment. . . . If the proof of a promise or contract, void under the statute of frauds, is essential to maintain the action, there may be no recovery, but, on the other hand, one who fraudulently misrepresents himself as intending to perform an agreement is subject to liability *in tort* whether the agreement is enforceable or not. [ ] The policy of the statute of frauds is "not directed at cases of dishonesty in making" a promise [ ]; never intended as an instrument to immunize fraudulent conduct, the statute may not be so employed.

In The Common Law Tradition–Deciding Appeals 473 (1960), Professor Karl Llewellyn attacked the statute of frauds holding in *Channel Master:*

The situation is one in which the torts theorists (Restatement, Harper and James, Prosser, all gathered and cited) have launched as unconsidered a jamboree as ever has been suggested in the books: in the instant "application" of the idea, word-of-mouth negotiations for a contract which have led to no acceptance, which need not have led even to an offer, and which would in an action on an actually completed contract be incapable of submission to the jury for lack of a signed writing— these become admissible in the teeth of the statute against frauds and perjuries, admissible moreover, in such fashion as to allow damages of a range and extent which would be dubious of procurement in any action based on an agreement fully closed, formally authenticated, and unambiguously relied on. All of this by virtue of merely adjusting the pleadings and the evidence to run down an alley which is rather easier to travel with persuasiveness than is the alley of contract-closing. . . .

Later courts have recognized the tension between the two views and have reconciled it "through a rule, widely adopted by the state and federal courts, pursuant to which a false promise can support a claim of fraud only where that promise was 'collateral or extraneous' to the terms of an enforceable agreement in place between the parties." GBJ Corp. v. Eastern Ohio Paving Co., 139 F.3d 1080 (6th Cir.1998).

Questions about allowing tort remedies in these cases may arise when consideration fails, when the statute of limitations differs, or when the contract itself asserts that neither party is relying on oral statements that are not reflected in the written contract. States disagree about the viability of tort in each situation. If both tort and contract actions are available, the plaintiff's preference will depend upon such factors as the applicable measure of compensatory damages, the availability of punitive damages, and the impact of the statute of limitations. Of course, proof of fault is more likely to play a role in tort law. Although the remedy of rescission does not require a showing of fault, Seneca Wire and Mfg. Co. v. A. B. Leach & Co., 159 N.E. 700 (N.Y.1928), the plaintiff may not be in a position to undo the transaction after learning about the misrepresentation. The parties may have engaged in further deals or actions that make it impossible to rescind. See, e.g., Mertens v. Wolfeboro National Bank, 402 A.2d 1335 (N.H.1979).

2. DECEIT

The tort actions arising from misrepresentations first became clearly identified in cases involving deliberate misstatements. Actions for this type of misrepresentation became known as actions for "deceit" or "fraud."

Scienter. In the leading English case, Derry v. Peek, 14 A.C. 337 (H.L. 1889), Lord Herschell stated that:

> [F]raud is proved when it is shown that a false representation has been made (1) knowingly, or (2) without belief in its truth, or (3) recklessly, careless whether it be true or false. Although I have treated the second and third as distinct cases, I think the third is but an instance of the second, for one who makes a statement under such circumstances can have no real belief in the truth of what he states. To prevent a false statement being fraudulent, there must, I think, always be an honest belief in its truth.

As a corollary he noted that "making a false statement through want of care falls far short of, and is a very different thing from fraud, and the same may be said of a false representation honestly believed though on insufficient grounds." On the matter of belief he stated:

> I quite admit that the statements of witnesses as to their belief are by no means to be accepted blindfolded. The probabilities must be considered. Whenever it is necessary to arrive at a conclusion as to the state of mind of another person, and to determine whether his belief under given circumstances was such as he alleges, we can only do so by applying the standard of conduct which our own experience of the ways of men has enabled us to form; by asking ourselves whether a reasonable man situated as the defendants were, with their knowledge and means of knowledge, might well believe what they state they did believe, and consider that the representations made were substantially true.

How does this compare with the notion of "actual malice" developed in libel cases? What is the apparent role of honest, but unreasonable, belief?

In Chatham Furnace Co. v. Moffatt, 18 N.E. 168 (Mass.1888), the court stated:

> [T]he charge of fraudulent intent, in an action for deceit, may be maintained by proof of a statement made as of the party's own knowledge, which is false; provided the thing stated is not merely a matter of opinion, estimate or judgment, but is susceptible of actual knowledge; and in such case it is not necessary to make any further proof of an actual intent to deceive. The fraud consists in stating that the party knows the thing to exist when he does not know it to exist; and, if he does not know it to exist, he must ordinarily be deemed to know that he does not. Forgetfulness of its existence after a former knowledge, or a mere belief of its existence, will not warrant or excuse a statement of actual knowledge.

The types of conduct discussed in *Derry v. Peek* come to be grouped under the Latin term "scienter." The elements of the action for deceit were stated by the court in *Channel Master* to be "[mis]representation of a material existing fact, falsity, *scienter,* deception and injury."

In Greycas, Inc. v. Proud, 826 F.2d 1560 (7th Cir.1987), cert. denied 484 U.S. 1043 (1988), an attorney incorrectly asserted that no liens existed on a client's property. The court noted that although the plaintiff was suing for negligent misrepresentation, the case appeared to be one of fraud:

> No doubt Proud was negligent in failing to conduct a search, but we are not clear why the misrepresentation is alleged to be negligent rather than deliberate and hence fraudulent. . . . Proud did not merely say, "There are no liens"; he said, "I have conducted a U.C.C., tax, and judgment search"; and not only is this statement, too, a false one, but its falsehood cannot have been inadvertent, for Proud knew he had not conducted such a search.

The court then speculated about the plaintiff's choice of theory:

> It may have feared that Proud's insurance policy for professional malpractice excluded deliberate wrongdoing from its coverage, or may not have wanted to bear the higher burden of proving fraud, or may have feared that an accusation of fraud would make it harder to settle the case—for most cases, of course, are settled, though this one has not been.

The passage about the "the higher burden of proving fraud" refers to the fact that in civil fraud cases, most state courts have stated that plaintiffs must prove their cases with "clear and convincing evidence." The explanation has generally been based on the close relationship between civil and criminal fraud or on the ease with which plaintiff may claim that the defendant has made a specific statement at a time when no one else was present. This position has been rejected in a few states on the ground that there is no reason to reject the usual "preponderance of the evidence" standard in civil cases involving fraud. See the discussion in Liodas v. Sahadi, 562 P.2d 316 (Cal.1977).

Ambit. Even when courts found the requisite scienter to justify a deceit action, they generally restricted the persons eligible to recover damages by permitting recovery only by those to whom the misrepresentations were made. If a prospective victim declined to go ahead but told a friend about the opportunity, early courts denied the friend an action.

The ambit has been expanding. See, e.g., Geernaert v. Mitchell, 37 Cal.Rptr.2d 483 (App. 1995), extending a fraudulent seller's liability to a buyer several steps down the chain where each successive seller (perhaps innocently) repeated the misrepresentation. Nonetheless, it still appears that the ambits of liability for misrepresentation are narrower for both intentional and negligent tortfeasors than they are for those who commit intentional or negligent acts resulting in physical injury or damage to property. This, of course, recalls the reservations courts expressed about extending liability for economic harm caused by negligence, in Chapter IV.

Material existing fact. Problems of scienter aside, the greatest difficulty has surrounded the efforts to identify a "material existing fact." Why should a fact have to be "material" if it is deliberately false and achieves its purpose of deceiving the plaintiff to his detriment? Does the requirement help in determining whether the defendant should have foreseen or did foresee the plaintiff's reliance on the misrepresentation? Restatement (Second) of Torts § 538(2) provides that a fact is material if "(a) a reasonable man would attach importance to its existence or nonexistence in determining his choice of action in the transaction in question, or (b) the maker of the representation knows or has reason to know that its recipient regards or is likely to regard the matter as important in determining his choice of action although a reasonable man would not so regard it." What kinds of situations are excluded? Should they be?

The term "existing fact" has a broad sweep. Courts generally consider a statement of intention to be a statement of "existing fact" because a "person's intent, his state of mind . . . is capable of ascertainment." Moreover, according to the Second Restatement's § 525, comment *f*, a statement in the form of a "prediction or promise as to the future course of events may justifiably be interpreted as a statement that the maker knows of nothing which will make the fulfillment of his prediction or promise impossible or improbable."

In California Conserving Co. v. D'Avanzo, 62 F.2d 528 (2d Cir.1933), defendant, when he was in dire financial straits, bought goods from the plaintiff on credit. He went bankrupt and the plaintiff sought to reclaim the goods for fraud. If successful, he need not have shared pro rata with other creditors. In discussing the alleged fraud Judge Learned Hand observed:

> He may mean to pay if he survives, though he knows that he is extremely unlikely to do so. If his promise declares only that he intends to pay, it would be hard in such a case to say that he has deceived the seller; and the doctrine presupposes some deceit. But promises, like other utterances, must be read with their usual implications. True, they are predictions and no one can foretell the future; the seller knows this as well as the buyer. However, a man's affairs may reach such a pass that ordinarily honest persons would no longer buy, if they had no greater chance to pay; and the seller is entitled to rely upon that implication. He may assume that the buyer would not promise if the odds were so heavy against him. He may read the promise as more than the declaration of a conditional intent, as affirming that that intent had reasonable hope of fruition. In that event, if the buyer knows that it has no such hope, he deceives the seller, as much as though he intended not to pay at all. This duty does not indeed depend upon what reasonable persons would think of his chances.

Another aspect of defining "fact" involves the distinction between "fact" and "opinion." Consider the statement of Judge Learned Hand in Vulcan Metals Co. v. Simmons Mfg. Co., 248 Fed. 853 (2d Cir.1918), involving claims made concerning a vacuum cleaner. To induce the buyer to take over its vacuum cleaner manufacturing business, Simmons made a number of representations about the product. These included commendations of the cleanliness, economy, and efficiency of the machine; that it was absolutely perfect in even the smallest detail; that water power, by which it worked, marked the most economical means of operating a vacuum cleaner with the greatest efficiency; that the cleaning was more thoroughly done than by beating or brushing; that, having been perfected, it was a necessity which every one could afford; that it was so simple that a child of six could use it; that it worked completely and thoroughly; that it was simple, long-lived, easily operated, and effective; that it was the only sanitary portable cleaner on the market; that perfect satisfaction would result from its use; that it would last a lifetime; that it was the only practical jet machine on the market; and that perfect satisfaction would result from its use, if properly adjusted. Speaking of these general claims, Judge Hand observed:

> An opinion is a fact, and it may be a very relevant fact; the expression of an opinion is the assertion of a belief, and any rule which condones the expression of a consciously false opinion condones a consciously false statement of fact. When the parties are so situated that the buyer may reasonably rely upon the expression of the seller's opinion, it is no excuse to give a false one. [ ] And so it makes much difference whether the parties stand "on an equality." For example, we should treat very differently the expressed opinion of a chemist to a layman about the properties of a composition from the same opinion between chemist and chemist, when the buyer had full opportunity to examine. The reason of the rule lies, we think, in this: There are some kinds of talk which no sensible man takes seriously, and if he does he suffers from his credulity. If we were all scrupulously honest, it would not be so; but, as it is, neither party usually believes what the seller says about his own opinions, and each knows it. Such statements, like the claims of campaign managers before election, are rather designed to allay the suspicion which would attend their absence than to be understood as having any relation to objective truth. It is quite true that they induce a compliant temper in the buyer, but it is by a much more subtle process than through the acceptance of his claims for his wares.

> . . .

> In the case at bar, since the buyer was allowed full opportunity to examine the cleaner and to test it out, we put the parties upon an equality. It seems to us that general statements as to what the cleaner would do, even though consciously false, were not of a kind to be taken literally by the buyer. As between manufacturer and customer, it may not be so; but this was the case of taking over a business, after ample chance to investigate. Such a buyer, who the seller rightly expects will undertake an independent and adequate inquiry into the actual merits of what he gets, has no right to treat as material in his determination statements like these. The standard of honesty permitted by the rule may not be the best; but, as Holmes, J., says in Deming v. Darling, 20

N.E. 107 [Mass. 1889], the chance that the higgling preparatory to a bargain may be afterwards translated into assurances of quality may perhaps be a set-off to the actual wrong allowed by the rule as it stands. We therefore think that the District Court was right in disregarding all these misrepresentations.

Why should "consciously false" statements ever be protected? What element of the misrepresentation action is missing?

Compare Powell v. Flechter, 18 N.Y.S. 451 (N.Y.Com.Pl.1892), in which defendant vendor knowingly misrepresented to plaintiff purchaser, "a woman utterly ignorant of violins and their value," that a violin was made by Gaspard di Dniffoprugear and was worth at least $1,000. The trial record showed that plaintiff did not rely on the representation of make but did rely on the representation of value. On defendant's appeal from a judgment for plaintiff, the court stated that an intentionally false statement as to value is actionable "where one in purchasing goods, the value of which can only be known to experts, relies upon the vendor, who is a dealer in such goods, to give him accurate information concerning them."

Do consumers generally expect honesty in all types of transactions? Do merchants expect honesty from each other? Should the law here be trying to tailor the rules to what typical parties actually expect, or should it attempt to mold expectations?

In Banner v. Lyon & Healy, Inc., 293 N.Y.S. 236 (App.Div. 1937), affirmed without opinion 13 N.E.2d 774 (N.Y.1938), defendant sold plaintiff a violin represented as having been made by Stradivarius. There was evidence that it was made by another violin maker. The court considered the statement to be one of opinion:

> When the sale took place in 1919, Stradivarius had been dead for some 200 years, a fact known to the whole world and to the parties concerned. Plaintiff himself was a noted violinist, generally familiar with violins and of those made by Stradivarius. In these circumstances, he must have understood that the defendant Freeman, in any representations made, was but expressing his opinion and honest belief that the instrument was in all respects genuine.

Would a different result follow if the purchaser were the plaintiff in *Powell*?

The line between fact and opinion is continually changing. For current applications, see Meade v. Cedarapids, Inc., 164 F.3d 1218 (9th Cir.1999) (action available against employer who induced recruits to relocate to new job by falsely asserting that it had no intention of moving or closing its plant) and Voilas v. General Motors Corp., 170 F.3d 367 (3d Cir.1999) (action available to employees induced to take early retirement by false statement that company intended to close plant).

Although "fact" is usually contrasted with "opinion," it is also contrasted with "law." In National Conversion Corp. v. Cedar Bldg. Corp., 246 N.E.2d 351 (N.Y.1969), the defendant lessor stated that the land plaintiff proposed to lease had no zoning restraints and could be used for garbage conversion. The land was in fact zoned for light manufacturing, which permitted garbage conversion only if odors were not readily detectable at the lot lines. On appeal from a plaintiff's judgment the defendant argued that the representation was not actionable. The unanimous court disagreed:

> Landlords also contend that only a misrepresentation of law rather than of fact is involved and, therefore, that fraud will not lie. There is no longer any doubt that the law has recognized, even in this State, a sharp distinction between a pure opinion of law which may not, except in unusual circumstances, base an action in tort, and a mixed statement of fact as to what the law is or whether it is applicable. . . .
>
> Most important it is that the law has outgrown the over-simple dichotomy between law and fact in the resolution of issues in deceit. It has been said that "a statement as to the law, like a statement as to anything else, may be intended and understood either as one of fact or one of opinion only, according to the circumstances of the case." [   ] The statements in this case, both before the execution of the lease, and in the body of the lease, exemplify ideally an instance in which the statements are not intended or understood merely as an expression of opinion. Landlords said they knew the premises were in an unrestricted district. This meant that they knew, as a fact, that the zoning resolution did not restrict the use of the particular premises, and tenant so understood it. . . .

A curious case of misrepresentation of law was raised by the Watergate break-in, when a burglar claimed that his superiors had told him that the break-in would be legal. The court held that even if the representation were actionable, the burglar's reliance was unreasonable. Democratic National Committee v. McCord, 416 F.Supp. 505 (D.D.C.1976).

Not all misrepresentations are made with words. One important cluster of cases involves acts of active concealment—cases in which defendants paint over leaking surfaces to hide them from a prospective buyer. These cases have presented no problems for the courts and have been analyzed as though the defendant had made a deliberate misrepresentation. See Herzog v. Capital Co., 164 P.2d 8 (Cal.1945). A situation that still presents serious problems is that of nondisclosure, discussed in the following case.

Ollerman v. O'Rourke Co., Inc.

Supreme Court of Wisconsin, 1980.
94 Wis.2d 17, 288 N.W.2d 95.

ABRAHAMSON, JUSTICE.

This appeal is from an order overruling the motion of O'Rourke Co., Inc., the seller, . . . to dismiss Roy Ollerman's, the buyer's, amended complaint for failing to state a claim upon which relief can be granted. We conclude that the complaint states a claim, and we affirm the order of the circuit court.

[The buyer alleged that he bought a vacant lot in order to build a house; and that while excavating for the house a well was uncapped and water was released.]

The complaint further alleges that the seller is a corporation engaged in the business of developing and selling real estate; that it is experienced in matters of real estate; that it had owned and subdivided the area of real estate in which the subject lot is located; that it was offering the subject lot and other lots in the same area for public sale; that it is familiar with the particular area of real estate in which the lot is located; that the area is zoned residential and that the seller knew it was zoned residential.

The complaint further states that the buyer "was a stranger to the area"; that he was inexperienced in matters of real estate transactions; that he purchased the lot to construct a house; that he did not know of the existence of a well under the land surface hidden from view; that if he had known of the well, he either would not have purchased the property or would have purchased it at a lower price; that the well constituted a defective condition of the lot; that the well made the property worth less for residential purposes than he had been led to believe; that the well made the property unsuitable for building without added expense; and that the seller's failure to disclose the existence of the well was relied upon by the buyer and he was thereby induced to buy this lot in ignorance of the well.

. . .

Additional allegations applicable to what is labeled in the complaint as the "first cause of action" are that the seller, through its agents, knew of the existence of the underground well and, in order to induce buyer to buy the land, "falsely and with intent to defraud," failed to disclose this fact which it had a duty to disclose and which would have had a material bearing on the construction of a residence on the property.

[A "second cause of action" alleged that defendant knew or should have known about the well, and had a duty to ascertain and disclose such information.]

. . .

This court has recognized that misrepresentation is a generic concept separable into the three familiar tort classifications: intent (sometimes called fraudulent misrepresentation, deceit or intentional deceit), negligence and strict responsibility.

. . .

II.

We discuss first whether the complaint states a claim for intentional misrepresentation. Initially we observe, as did the seller, that the complaint does not allege the first two elements of the tort of intentional misrepresentation, namely that the seller made a representation of fact and that the representation was untrue. The gravamen of the wrong is the nature of the false words used and the reliance which they may reasonably induce. In lieu of these allegations of false words, the complaint recites that the seller failed to disclose a fact, the existence of the well. The general rule is that silence, a failure to disclose a fact, is not an intentional misrepresentation unless the seller has a duty to disclose.[7] If there is a duty to disclose a fact, failure to disclose that fact is treated in the law as equivalent to a representation of the non existence of the fact. . . .

The question thus presented in the case at bar is whether the seller had a duty to disclose to the buyer the existence of the well. If there is a duty to disclose, the seller incurs tort liability for intentional misrepresentation (i.e., the representation of the non-existence of the fact), if the elements of the tort of intentional misrepresentation are proved. [ ]

The question of legal duty presents an issue of law. . . .

We recognize that the traditional rule in Wisconsin is that in an action for intentional misrepresentation the seller of real estate, dealing at arm's length with the buyer, has no duty to disclose information to the buyer and therefore has no liability in an action for intentional misrepresentation for failure to disclose.

The traditional legal rule that there is no duty to disclose in an arm's-length transaction is part of the common law doctrine of caveat emptor which is traced to the attitude of rugged individualism reflected in the business economy and the law of the 19th century. The law of misrepresentation has traditionally been closely aligned with mores of the commercial world because the type of interest protected by the law of misrepresentation in business transactions is the interest in formulating business judgments without being misled by others that is, an interest in not being cheated.

Under the doctrine of caveat emptor no person was required to tell all that he or she knew in a business transaction, for in a free market the diligent should not be deprived of the fruits of superior skill and knowledge lawfully acquired. The business world, and the law reflecting business mores and morals, required the parties to a transaction to use their faculties and exercise ordinary business sense, and not to call on the law to stand in loco parentis to protect them in their ordinary dealings with other business people.

> The picture in sales and in land deals is, in the beginning, that of a community whose trade is simple and face to face and whose traders are neighbors. The goods and the land were there to be seen during the negotiation and particularly in the case of land, everybody knew everybody's land; if not, trade was an arm's length proposition with wits matched against skill. Of course caveat emptor would be the rule in such a society. But caveat emptor was more than a rule of no liability; it was a philosophy that left each individual to his own devices

---

7. 3 Restatement (Second) of Torts, sec. 551, Comment *b* (1977) states: ". . . In the absence of a duty of disclosure . . . one who is negotiating a business transaction is not liable in deceit because of his failure to disclose a fact that he knows his adversary would regard as material. . . ." [ ]

with a minimum of public imposition of standards of fair practice. In the beginning the common law did grant relief from fraud and did recognize that if the seller made an express promise as to his product at the time of the sale he remained liable after the sale on this "collateral" promise. Indeed covenants for title in the deed were such collateral promises which survived the sale. [   ]

Over the years society's attitudes toward good faith and fair dealing in business transactions have undergone significant change, and this change has been reflected in the law. Courts have departed from or relaxed the "no duty to disclose" rule by carving out exceptions to the rule and by refusing to adhere to the rule when it works an injustice. Thus courts have held that the rule does not apply where the seller actively conceals a defect or where he prevents investigation;[13] where the seller has told a half-truth or has made an ambiguous statement if the seller's intent is to create a false impression and he does so; where there is a fiduciary relationship between the parties; or where the facts are peculiarly and exclusively within the knowledge of one party to the transaction and the other party is not in a position to discover the facts for himself.

On the basis of the complaint, the case at bar does not appear to fall into one of these well-recognized exceptions to the "no duty to disclose" rule. However, Dean Prosser has found a "rather amorphous tendency on the part of most courts toward finding a duty of disclosure in cases where the defendant has special knowledge or means of knowledge not open to the plaintiff and is aware that the plaintiff is acting under a misapprehension as to facts which could be of importance to him, and would probably affect his decision."

Dean Keeton [in Fraud Concealment and Nondisclosure, 15 Tex.L.Rev. 1, 31 (1936)], described these cases abandoning the "no duty to disclose" rule as follows:

> In the present stage of the law, the decisions show a drawing away from this idea (that nondisclosure is not actionable), and there can be seen an attempt by many courts to reach a just result in so far as possible, but yet maintaining the degree of certainty which the law must have. The statement may often be found that if either party to a contract of sale conceals or suppresses a material fact which he is in good faith bound to disclose then his silence is fraudulent.

> The attitude of the courts toward nondisclosure is undergoing a change and . . . it would seem that the object of the law in these cases should be to impose on parties to the transaction a duty to speak whenever justice, equity, and fair dealing demand it. This statement is made only with reference to instances where the party to be charged is

---

13. 3 Restatement (Second) of Torts, sec. 550 (1977) states: "One party to a transaction who by concealment or other action intentionally prevents the other from acquiring material information is subject to the same liability to the other, for pecuniary loss as though he had stated the nonexistence of the matter that the other was thus prevented from discovering." [   ]

an actor in the transaction. This duty to speak does not result from an implied representation by silence, but exists because a refusal to speak constitutes unfair conduct.

The test Dean Keeton derives from the cases to determine when the rule of nondisclosure should be abandoned—that is "whenever justice, equity and fair dealing demand it"—presents, as one writer states, "a somewhat nebulous standard, praiseworthy as looking toward more stringent business ethics, but possibly difficult of practical application." [ ]

. . .

The draftsmen of the most recent Restatement of Torts (Second)(1977) have attempted to formulate a rule embodying this trend in the cases toward a more frequent recognition of a duty to disclose. Sec. 551(1) of the Restatement sets forth the traditional rule that one who fails to disclose a fact that he knows may induce reliance in a business transaction is subject to the same liability as if he had represented the nonexistence of the matter that he failed to disclose if, and only if, he is under a duty to exercise reasonable care to disclose the matter in question.[17] Subsection (2) of sec. 551 then sets forth the conditions under which the seller has a duty to use reasonable care to disclose certain information.[18] Sec. 551(2)(e) is the "catch-all" provision setting forth conditions under which a duty to disclose exists; it states that a party to a transaction is under a duty to exercise reasonable care to disclose to the other "facts basic to the transaction, if he knows that the other is about to enter into it under a mistake as to them, and that the other, because of the relationship between them, the customs of the trade or other objective circumstances, would reasonably expect a disclosure of those facts." Comment *l* to sec. 551 recognizes the difficulty of specifying the factors that give rise to a reasonable expectation of disclosure:

l. The continuing development of modern business ethics has, however, limited to some extent this privilege to take advantage of ignorance. There are situations in which the defendant not only knows

17. Sec. 551 Liability for Nondisclosure "(1) One who fails to disclose to another a fact that he knows may justifiably induce the other to act or refrain from acting in a business transaction is subject to the same liability to the other as though he had represented the nonexistence of the matter that he has failed to disclose, if, but only if, he is under a duty to the other to exercise reasonable care to disclose the matter in question."

18. Sec. 551 "(2) One party to a business transaction is under a duty to exercise reasonable care to disclose to the other before the transaction is consummated, (a) matters known to him that the other is entitled to know because of a fiduciary or other similar relation of trust and confidence between them; and (b) matters known to him that he knows to be necessary to prevent his partial or ambiguous statement of the facts from being misleading; and (c) subsequently acquired information that he knows will make untrue or misleading a previous representation that when made was true or believed to be so; and (d) the falsity of a representation not made with the expectation that it would be acted upon, if he subsequently learns that the other is about to act in reliance upon it in a transaction with him; and (e) facts basic to the transaction, if he knows that the other is about to enter into it under a mistake as to them, and that the other, because of the relationship between them, the customs of the trade or other objective circumstances, would reasonably expect a disclosure of those facts."

that his bargaining adversary is acting under a mistake basic to the transaction, but also knows that the adversary, by reason of the relation between them, the customs of the trade or other objective circumstances, is reasonably relying upon a disclosure of the unrevealed fact if it exists. In this type of case good faith and fair dealing may require a disclosure.

It is extremely difficult to be specific as to the factors that give rise to this known, and reasonable, expectation of disclosure. In general, the cases in which the rule stated in Clause (e) has been applied have been those in which the advantage taken of the plaintiff's ignorance is so shocking to the ethical sense of the community, and is so extreme and unfair, as to amount to a form of swindling, in which the plaintiff is led by appearances into a bargain that is a trap, of whose essence and substance he is unaware. In such a case, even in a tort action for deceit, the plaintiff is entitled to be compensated for the loss that he has sustained.

Section 551(2)(e) of the Restatement (Second) of Torts limits the duty to disclose to disclosure of those "facts basic" to the transaction. Comment *j* to sec. 551 differentiates between basic facts and material facts as follows: "A basic fact is a fact that is assumed by the parties as a basis for the transaction itself. It is a fact that goes to the basis, or essence, of the transaction, and is an important part of the substance of what is bargained for or dealt with. Other facts may serve as important and persuasive inducements to enter into the transaction, but not go to its essence. These facts may be material, but they are not basic."

However, the draftsmen of the Restatement recognized that the law was developing to expand the duty to disclosure beyond the duty described in [comment *l* to] sec. 551:

There are indications, also, that with changing ethical attitudes in many fields of modern business, the concept of facts basic to the transaction may be expanding and the duty to use reasonable care to disclose the facts may be increasing somewhat. This Subsection is not intended to impede that development.

This court has moved away from the rule of caveat emptor in real estate transactions, as have courts in other states.

. . . .

An analysis of the cases of this jurisdiction and others indicates that the presence of the following elements is significant to persuade a court of the fairness and equity of imposing a duty on a vendor of real estate to disclose known facts: the condition is "latent" and not readily observable by the purchaser; the purchaser acts upon the reasonable assumption that the condition does (or does not) exist; the vendor has special knowledge or means of knowledge not available to the purchaser; and the existence of the condition is material to the transaction, that is, it influences whether the transaction is concluded at all or at the same price.

The seller argues that public policy demands that we not abandon the traditional rule that no action lies against the seller of real estate for failure to disclose in an arm's-length transaction. The seller contends, in its brief, that if this court affirms the circuit court's order overruling the motion to dismiss and allows the buyer to proceed to trial, the court is adopting "what really amounts to a strict policy of 'let the seller beware.'" The seller goes on to state, "Woe indeed to anyone who sells a home, a vacant lot or other piece of real estate and fails to itemize with particularity or give written notice to each prospective buyer of every conceivable condition in and around the property, regardless of whether such a condition is dangerous, defective or could become so by the negligence or recklessness of others. A seller of real estate is not and should not be made an insurer or guarantor of the competence of those with whom the purchaser may later contract."

The seller's position is that imposing a duty to disclose on a vendor of real estate dealing at arm's length with a purchaser would result in an element of uncertainty pervading real estate transactions; that there would be chaos if a vendor were subject to liability after parting with ownership and control of the property; that a rash of litigation would ensue; and that a purchaser could protect himself or herself by inspection and inquiry and by demanding warranties.

The seller's arguments are not persuasive in light of the facts alleged in the complaint and our narrow holding in this case.

Where the vendor is in the real estate business and is skilled and knowledgeable and the purchaser is not, the purchaser is in a poor position to discover a condition which is not readily discernible, and the purchaser may justifiably rely on the knowledge and skill of the vendor. Thus, in this instant case a strong argument for imposing a duty on the seller to disclose material facts is this "reliance factor." The buyer portrayed in this complaint had a reasonable expectation of honesty in the marketplace, that is, that the vendor would disclose material facts which it knew and which were not readily discernible. Under these circumstances the law should impose a duty of honesty on the seller.

In order to determine whether the complaint states a claim for intentional misrepresentation we hold that a subdivider-vendor of a residential lot has a duty to a "non-commercial" purchaser to disclose facts which are known to the vendor, which are material to the transaction, and which are not readily discernible to the purchaser. A fact is known to the vendor if the vendor has actual knowledge of the fact or if the vendor acted in reckless disregard as to the existence of the fact. This usage of the word "know" is the same as in an action for intentional misrepresentation based on a false statement. [   ] A fact is material if a reasonable purchaser would attach importance to its existence or nonexistence in determining the choice of action in the transaction in question; or if the vendor knows or has reason to know that the purchaser regards or is likely to regard the matter as important in determining the choice of action, although a reasonable purchaser would not so regard it. See 3 Restatement (Second) of

Torts, sec. 538 (1977). Whether the fact is or is not readily discernible will depend on the nature of the fact, the relation of the vendor and purchaser and the nature of the transaction.

The seller's brief asserts that the well is not a material fact because it does not constitute a defective condition; that the existence of the well was well known in the community; and that the buyer should have made inquiry about the lot. These are matters to be raised at trial, not on a motion to dismiss. The buyer must prove at trial that the existence of the well was a material fact and that his reliance was justifiable.[26]

III.

We turn now to the second cause of action, an action in negligence based on misrepresentation. [The court observed that this was a more difficult duty to establish and deferred a ruling on its validity until the case had been tried.]

We have enumerated several public policy reasons for not imposing liability despite a finding of negligence as a causal factor producing injury:

(1) The injury is too remote from the negligence; or (2) the injury is too wholly out of proportion to the culpability of the negligent tortfea-

---

26. We previously discussed the purchaser's reliance on the seller in determining whether to impose a duty on the seller to disclose material facts which are not readily discernible. "Reliance" is thus an important factor in determining the existence of the duty to disclose, but it is also an element of the tort of intentional misrepresentation. The buyer in the case at bar has to prove the elements of intentional misrepresentation which this court has frequently set forth: " 'To be actionable the false representation must consist, first, of a statement of fact which is untrue; second, that it was made with intent to defraud and for the purpose of inducing the other party to act upon it; third, that he did in fact rely on it and was induced thereby to act, to his injury or damage.' " [   ]

As we noted previously, the failure to disclose (silence), if there is a duty to speak, is typically treated as the equivalent of a representation of the nonexistence of the fact. [   ]

Goldfarb, in his article entitled Fraud & Nondisclosure in the Vendor–Purchaser Relation, 8 Western R.L.Rev. 5, 6–9 (1956), points up some of the difficulties of treating a "nondisclosure" as if it were fraudulent misrepresentation especially as to the element of reliance:

"The courts and commentators treat actionable silence or, as it is more often denominated, 'actionable nondisclosure' as a variety of misrepresentation. It is one of the implied theses of the present inquiry that it is not logical, or even helpful, to do so. True, under some circumstances, a failure to speak may amount to the equivalent of an actual, verbal representation of fact. Silence is, after all, a type of conduct, or at least of forbearance. If the representation thus implied is, in fact, false, and if the other elements of fraud are present, the plaintiff ought to be entitled to a remedy. But, under many circumstances, silence is merely silence. It says nothing. The silent party may fail to deny or assert a given fact. But it may be unfair and unreasonable to label his behavior as a representation, much less a misrepresentation. And yet, even under such circumstances, the silence may be tortious." "The courts' insistence on relating such nondisclosure to misrepresentation seems to stem from a tradition of labeling and categorizing. It will avail us little to fight this tendency. It is enough to be aware of it. This awareness alone can help prevent us from falling prey to that most treacherous of semantic traps: the tyranny of labels." . . .

sor; or (3) in retrospect it appears too highly extraordinary that the negligence should have brought about the harm; or (4) because allowance of recovery would place too unreasonable a burden on the negligent tortfeasor; or (5) because allowance of recovery would be too likely to open the way for fraudulent claims; or (6) allowance of recovery would enter a field that has no sensible or just stopping point. [ ]

Courts have imposed liability in negligence actions for personal injury or property damage caused by false statements or caused by nondisclosure. However, courts have been more reluctant to impose liability in negligence actions for misrepresentations causing pecuniary loss (not resulting from bodily harm or physical damage to property). . . .

. . .

Similarly, the draftsmen of the Restatement of Torts (Second), in discussing liability for information negligently supplied for the guidance of others in their business transactions, caution that the scope of liability for failing to exercise reasonable care in supplying correct information is not determined by the rules that govern liability for the negligent supplying of chattels that imperil the security of persons or property or other negligent misrepresentation that results in physical harm. When there is no intent to deceive, but only negligence, the fault of the maker of the misrepresentation is sufficiently less to justify a narrower responsibility for its consequences.

The reason a narrower scope of liability is fixed for negligent misrepresentation than for deceit is to be found in the difference between the obligations of honesty and of care, and in the significance of this difference to the reasonable expectations of the users of information that is supplied in connection with commercial transactions. Honesty requires only that the maker of a representation speak in good faith and without consciousness of a lack of any basis for belief in the truth or accuracy of what he says. The standard of honesty is unequivocal and ascertainable without regard to the character of the transaction in which the information will ultimately be relied upon or the situation of the party relying upon it. Any user of commercial information may reasonably expect the observance of this standard by a supplier of information to whom his use is reasonably foreseeable.

On the other hand, it does not follow that every user of commercial information may hold every maker to a duty of care.

By limiting the liability for negligence of a supplier of information to be used in commercial transactions to cases in which he manifests an intent to supply the information for the sort of use in which the plaintiff's loss occurs, the law promotes the important social policy of encouraging the flow of commercial information upon which the operation of the economy rests. The limitation applies, however, only in the case of information supplied in good faith, for no interest of society is served by promoting the flow of information not genuinely believed by its maker to be true. Restatement (Second) of Torts, sec. 552, Comment *a* (1977). [   ]

. . .

We conclude that at the complaint and motion-to-dismiss stage in the case at bar we cannot resolve the public policy issues involved; a full trial must precede the trial court's and appellate court's determination of the issue as to what liability, if any, attaches to the seller for its failure to exercise ordinary care in ascertaining or disclosing the existence of the well. A trial court or jury finding as to negligence, damage and the causal relation between them would be material and helpful in evaluating the public policy considerations. [   ]

. . .

For the reasons set forth, we hold that the allegations of the complaint state a claim upon which relief can be granted and that the motion to dismiss the complaint was properly overruled.

[Three concurring justices agreed that the complaint set forth a claim on which relief could be granted. They disagreed with the majority's extended discussion of the law when only an amended complaint was before it. "There is no necessity for expounding on various legal principles relating to the theories of recovery advanced by the plaintiff at the pleading stage. In most instances, attempting to decide the law of the case when the case has not been tried and the facts are not before the court is an appellate practice to be avoided."]

Notes and Questions

1. The complaint asserts that the seller "falsely and with intent to defraud" failed to disclose the well's existence. How can silence ever be "false"? How might it be found false in this case?

2. The court lists several categories of cases in which courts had already decided that silence was actionable, but notes that plaintiff's case "does not appear to fall into" any of them. Why not? What is the basis on which this complaint is upheld?

3. When the court lists the elements that it finds working toward a duty to disclose in this case, one of them is that "the vendor has special knowledge or means of knowledge not available to the purchaser." Can the purchaser ever have such knowledge?

4. What is the role of "reliance" in this case? Reliance is considered extensively after these notes.

5. Why does the court defer decision on a duty to use due care to ascertain and reveal important information?

6. The trend away from caveat emptor continues. In Strawn v. Canuso, 657 A.2d 420 (N.J.1995), the court held that if conditions are known to the developer or broker and "unknown and not readily observable by the buyer" and their existence "is of sufficient materiality to affect the habitability, use, or enjoyment of the property and, therefore, render the property substantially less desirable or valuable to the objectively reasonable buyer," the conditions must be disclosed. Here the issue was the existence nearby of an off-site closed landfill. See also Stambovsky v. Ackley, 572 N.Y.S.2d 672 (App.Div. 1991)(duty to disclose that house had been "haunted"—the so-called "poltergeist case"); Reed v. King, 193 Cal.Rptr. 130 (App. 1983)(duty on brokers to disclose that multiple murders had occurred in the house); Silva v. Stevens, 589 A.2d 852 (Vt. 1991)(duty to disclose may arise in arm's-length transaction from the relations of the parties, such as that of trust or confidence, or superior knowledge or means of knowledge"—here historical facts that were not readily accessible to the buyer).

But see Nelson v. Wiggs, 699 So.2d 258 (Fla.App.1997), holding, 2–1, that defendant seller had no duty to warn plaintiffs that the land they were buying for a home and to keep animals was uninhabitable, due to flooding that was ankle to knee deep, and kept smaller vehicles from entering the area. The buyer had not asked specifically about flooding, there was nothing concealed, and the information was available to the buyers through diligent attention. The dissenter observed that having failed to obtain judicial relief, the buyers would do to another what the seller had done to them: put up a sign "for sale by owner" and wait "for another naïve buyer to come along. When that buyer comes along they will do unto him or her as was done unto them, and the vicious cycle of fraud by silence will continue."

7. *Duty of due care.* So far as the duty of due care is concerned, a few cases reject any such duty in arm's length cases. E.g., South County, Inc. v. First Western Loan Co., 871 S.W.2d 325 (Ark.1994)(no action where developer claimed that a lender had negligently misrepresented intent to make a loan, thus inducing the developer to continue spending on the proposed development; deceit action was adequate protection).

In Onita Pacific Corp. v. Trustees of Bronson, 843 P.2d 890 (Or.1992), purchasers sued their vendors for harm arising when they relied on the vendors' allegedly negligent misrepresentations about when certain lots would be released to the plaintiffs. The court held, 5–2, that such claims are not actionable in arm's length transactions. Plaintiffs could have avoided the problem by "insisting that the [crucial] provision [ ] be included in the written agreements" rather than relying on an alleged representation.

A dissenter observed that "Oregon's future commercial interests, including its prospect for international trade growth, are not likely to be served by an outmoded rule that one party in a business transaction may not rely on what she, he, or it is told by the other party. Oregon will be best served by requiring care to not mislead your business 'partners.' I think Oregonians believe and expect that the best business is where both sides to a transaction make a profit and are able to invest in new activities." The majority approach was "based on an urban savagery where all are divided by the 'limiting notion' of 'us versus them.' "

Oregon adhered to its position in Conway v. Pacific University, 924 P.2d 818 (Or.1996) (during recruiting process dean owed no duty of due care when telling faculty recruit that poor student evaluations "would be no problem" in obtaining tenure).

Although the no-duty approach was once the dominant view, most courts reject it today. In Williams Ford, Inc. v. Hartford Courant Co., 657 A.2d 212 (Conn.1995), a newspaper allegedly misrepresented terms to prospective advertisers. Defendant argued that "between two sophisticated commercial parties with full access to information concerning a business transaction" there was no duty of due care. The court disagreed. It found Onita "unpersuasive" and found "very little justification for not extending liability to all parties and agents to a bargaining transaction for making misrepresentations negligently."

Section 552 (1) of the Second Restatement has been quite influential in leading to a duty in this type of case:

> (1) One who, in the course of his business, profession or employment, or in any other transaction in which he has a pecuniary interest, supplies false information for the guidance of others in their business transactions, is subject to liability for pecuniary loss caused to them by their justifiable reliance upon the information, if he fails to exercise reasonable care or competence in obtaining or communicating the information.

The range of persons owing a duty of the type set forth in § 552(1) stretches well beyond accountants and attorneys. Consider the following cases:

a. In Aesoph v. Kusser, 498 N.W.2d 654 (S.D.1993), plaintiff farmers alleged that they asked defendant insurance agent about getting federal crop insurance and that he incorrectly responded that they were not eligible. To determine eligibility apparently required reading and understanding seven single spaced pages of a manual. The court asserted that a duty existed if "the relationship of the parties, arising out of contract or otherwise, [is] such that in morals and good conscience the one has the right to rely upon the other for information, and the other giving the information owes a duty to give it with care." When asked, defendant "had no obligation to provide any answer. However, when he chose to provide an answer he changed the relationship and undertook a duty to exercise care in providing the answer" on the subject of "the complex matter of eligibility for federal crop insurance." Is "morals and good conscience" comparable to the language of section 552?

b. In Mohr v. Commonwealth, 653 N.E.2d 1104 (Mass.1995), adoptive parents alleged that the defendant social service agency, after learning that the child's mother had suffered from schizophrenia and that the child had cerebral atrophy, made negligent misrepresentations to plaintiffs regarding the child's emotional and medical history. The court, after tracing the development of this type of claim, upheld a "wrongful adoption" action for the adoptive parents. An adoption agency, whether public or private, has "an affirmative duty to disclose to adoptive parents information about a child that will enable them to make a knowledgeable decision about whether to accept the child for adoption." The award was for economic harm that would be sustained in providing "the structured, residential placement that Elizabeth will need throughout her lifetime." Should damages for emotional distress be recoverable in this type of case? See also Gibbs v. Ernst, 647 A.2d 882 (Pa.1994), imposing a duty of disclosure in adoption cases but rejecting an affirmative duty on the agency to investigate the child's background.

8. *Partial disclosure.* In Junius Constr. Corp. v. Cohen, 178 N.E. 672 (N.Y.1931), plaintiff was to buy some land from defendant, who informed plaintiff that the final maps of the local governing body showed two roads that, if opened, would modify the plot's boundaries to minor extents. Defendant did not tell plaintiff about a third street that, if opened, would cut the plot in half. Judge Cardozo stated:

> Misrepresentation, if there was any, as to a risk so vital was something that went to the very essence of the bargain. We do not say that the seller was under a duty to mention the projected streets at all. That question is not here. What we say is merely this, that having undertaken or professed to mention them, he could not fairly stop half way, listing those that were unimportant and keeping silent as to the other. The enumeration of two streets, described as unopened but projected, was a tacit representation that the land to be conveyed was subject to no others, and certainly subject to no others materially affecting the value of the purchase.

Does the rationale apply only to other roads or would it extend to sewer lines? How about a forthcoming tax increase? Are there any limits?

In *Silva v. Stevens*, note 6 supra, the court held that after a partial disclosure—noting that leaks had been present but had been fixed—actionable fraud could be found as to other leaks even if there had been no duty to say anything in the first place. See also Gibb v. Citicorp Mortgage, Inc., 518 N.W.2d 910 (Neb.1994), in which buyer was shown visible termite damage that had been fixed and assured that this was the only such damage in the house—although defendants knew that there was unfixed termite damage that was not visible.

9. *Falsity.* Although the element of "falsity" has presented little legal difficulty, it produces many questions of fact. The courts earlier concluded that although statements might literally be accurate, they might be found to be false if they would mislead recipients. In Remeikis v. Boss & Phelps, Inc., 419 A.2d 986 (D.C.App.1980), a termite report stated that there was "no visible evidence of present termite activity." Although literally true, it might be actionable if "made to create a false impression" as with extensive "invisible" damage or visible evidence of "past" activity. The court relied on an earlier case in which the seller of a rooming house was held liable for a statement that accurately told the level of present rentals but that left the incorrect impression that those rental charges were legally permissible.

10. *Reliance.* The element of reliance is really a composite of several different ideas. The first is "actual" reliance, which corresponds to the actual-cause requirement in other torts. If the plaintiff has not relied on the defendant's misrepresentation, then the critical connection between misconduct and damages is missing. In Nader v. Allegheny Airlines, Inc., 626 F.2d 1031 (D.C.Cir.1980), the plaintiff was "bumped" from a plane because by the time he arrived other confirmed passengers on the over-booked flight had already been seated. As a result he missed a rally at which he was to deliver a speech. He asserted that the airline had misrepresented its policy concerning "confirmed" reservations by not informing passengers that it engaged in overbooking. Among the reasons for dismissing the case, the court noted that Nader "was an extraordinarily knowledgeable passenger, an able lawyer and a famous and distinguished advocate of consumer rights, including the rights of airline passengers." In fact, he had been bumped twice before in similar situations, the second time only two days before he reserved his seat for the Allegheny flight. It "cannot be said that Nader relied on his confirmed reservation with Allegheny as a guarantee of passage."

A proximate-cause aspect of reliance requires that plaintiff's harm must come from reliance on the misrepresented fact. Assume that D misrepresents several facts about a company's financial health in order to induce P to buy that company's stock. D is not liable if the stock suddenly falls in value solely because of the unexpected death of the company's chief operating officer—even though P would not have bought the stock had D not misrepresented. See Restatement (Second) § 548A.

The reliance must also be "justifiable." Restatement (Second) § 545A, comment *b*, addresses the matter as follows:

> Although the plaintiff's reliance on the misrepresentation must be justifiable, . . . this does not mean that his conduct must conform to the standard of the reasonable man. Justification is a matter of the qualities and characteristics of the particular plaintiff, and the circumstances of the particular case, rather than of the application of a community standard of conduct to all cases. Negligent reliance and action sometimes will not be justifiable, and the recovery will be barred accordingly; but this is not always the case. There will be cases in which a plaintiff may be justified in relying upon the representation, even though his conduct in doing so does not conform to the community standard of knowledge, intelligence, judgment or care. Thus, under the rule stated in § 540, the recipient of a fraudulent misrepresentation is not required to investigate its truth, even when a reasonable man of ordinary caution would do so before taking action; and it is only when he knows of the falsity or it is obvious to him that his reliance is not justified. (See § 541). . . .

> Cases frequently arise in which negligent reliance is justified, when the defendant knows of the plaintiff's incapacity to conform to the standard of conduct of a reasonable man, or of his credulity,

gullibility or other tendency to depart from it, and deliberately practices upon the deficiencies of the plaintiff in order to deceive him.
 . . . Thus one who presents a document to an illiterate man, misrepresenting its contents, and invites him to sign it, knowing that he cannot read it, cannot be heard to say that he is negligent in doing so. The same may be true when there is a relation of trust and confidence between the parties or the defendant has made successful efforts to win the confidence of the plaintiff and then takes advantage of it to deceive him.

Does this discussion of reliance clarify its role on remand in *Ollerman*?

Can reliance be found in inaction? See Greenfield v. Fritz Companies, Inc., 98 Cal.Rptr.2d 530 (App.), hearing granted 12 P.3d 1068 (Cal.2000), allowing a misrepresentation action to shareholders who, relying on alleged misrepresentations, held their stock instead of selling it. Another complex aspect of reliance that applies to the securities world involves whether a plaintiff can recover for what is called "fraud on the market." This theory excuses class action plaintiffs from showing individual reliance where a misrepresentation has been spread widely. See the extended discussion in Kaufman v. i-Stat Corp., 754 A.2d 1188 (N.J. 2000).

11. *Defenses.* The courts generally agree that contributory negligence is no defense whatever to intentional misrepresentation. See Florenzano v. Olson, 387 N.W.2d 168 (Minn.1986). There is some disagreement, though, over whether comparative negligence should be used when the defendant has negligently misrepresented. The court in *Florenzano* concluded that the reasons that warranted using comparative negligence in personal injury cases applied as well to cases of economic harm. See also *Greycas, Inc. v. Proud*, p. 1219, supra, asserting that plaintiff's negligence "is as much a defense to negligent misrepresentation as to any other tort of negligence." See also Gilchrist Timber Co. v. ITT Rayonier, Inc., 696 So.2d 334 (Fla. 1997), construing the state's general comparative fault statute to apply to negligent misrepresentations. The leading contra case is Carroll v. Gava, 159 Cal.Rptr. 778 (App. 1979), in which the court said that in business deals it is important for the information to be accurate. Denying the defense of comparative negligence will encourage those who provide information to make it accurate. Is the element of justifiable reliance adequately distinguished from a defense of contributory negligence?

12. *Merger and "as is" clauses.* Courts increasingly conclude that the existence of an "as is" provision in the contract or a statement that the buyer is relying only on a personal inspection will not prevent the plaintiff from showing that fraud occurred. See, e.g., Ron Greenspan Volkswagen, Inc. v. Ford Motor Land Devel.Corp., 38 Cal.Rptr.2d 783 (App. 1997) ("when the agreement itself is procured by fraud, none of its provisions have any legal or binding effect"). The *Gibb* and *Silva* cases, supra, involving partial disclosures, both involved clauses that unsuccessfully attempted to negate any claim that the plaintiff had relied on disclosures. Whether reliance is justifiable when the contract contains such a disclaimer is generally a question of fact. Beyond that, courts require that plaintiffs, even in claims of fraudulent concealment, show that they exercised "diligent attention, observation and judgment," though they may rely upon a representation in all cases if it is a positive statement of fact and if an investigation would be required to discover the truth. See also Dunbar Medical Systems Inc. v. Gammex Inc., 216 F.3d 441 (5th Cir.2000) (rejecting "as is" and merger clauses as defenses against fraudulent inducement action).

13. *Damages.* A plaintiff who surmounts these difficulties is entitled to damages. There is disagreement over the proper way to measure the compensatory award. The tort standard would appear to be the cost of the property plaintiff bought less the actual value of that property. This is the usual out-of-pocket rule. But some states use the difference between what the value would have been if the representations had been true and the actual value—the usual contract measure, often called the benefit-of-the-bargain rule. Some states follow one or the other exclusively. Others use one or the other depending on the specific facts. See, e.g., American Family Service Corp. v. Michelfelder, 968 F.2d 667 (8th Cir.1992)(prospective buyer entitled to benefit-of-the-bargain damages where seller misrepresented intent to sell).

The choice of the compensatory rule may affect the state's attitude toward punitive damages in deceit cases. In Walker v. Sheldon, 179 N.E.2d 497 (N.Y.1961), plaintiff alleged that defendants' misrepresentations were made "in the regular course of" their business "and as the basis of their business knowing that plaintiff would, as others similarly situated had in the past, act upon said representations." The complaint asked compensatory damages of $1,380 and punitive damages of $75,000. Defendants moved to strike the request for punitive damages as irrelevant and prejudicial. The court of appeals, 4–3, affirmed denial of the motion. The majority recognized that in "ordinary" fraud and deceit cases it did not allow punitive damages, but held that where defendant's conduct "evinced a high degree of moral turpitude and demonstrated such wanton dishonesty as to imply a criminal indifference to civil obligations" punitive damages might lie. It noted that punitive damages often induce the victim to take action against a wrongdoer that he might not otherwise take:

> Exemplary damages are more likely to serve their desired purpose of deterring similar conduct in a fraud case, such as that before us, than in any other area of tort. One who acts out of anger or hate, for instance, in committing assault or libel, is not likely to be deterred by the fear of punitive damages. On the other hand, those who deliberately and coolly engage in a far-flung fraudulent scheme, systematically conducted for profit, are very much more likely to pause and consider the consequences if they have to pay more than the actual loss suffered by an individual plaintiff. An occasional award of compensatory damages against such parties would have little deterrent effect. A judgment simply for compensatory damages would require the offender to do no more than return the money which he had taken from the plaintiff.

The dissent condemned the use of tort law for punishment and urged that the criminal law be used for that purpose, with tort law used only for compensation. It viewed the recovery of punitive damages by the plaintiff as an unjust windfall. If hesitant plaintiffs had to be encouraged to sue, the dissent preferred that they be permitted to recover court costs or some other finite amount, rather than having access to the broad discretion of a jury. Does this debate add anything to the battle over the general propriety of punitive damages in tort law? Recall the discussion at p. 718, supra.

Might the majority in *Walker* have been influenced by the fact that New York follows the out-of-pocket rule? Note also that, depending on their language, some legislative changes in the law of punitive damages discussed at p. 738, supra, may well limit such recoveries even for fraud. For a discussion of the role of punitive damages in fraud cases, including their justification in light of the difficulty of discovering fraud, see Perez v. Z Frank Oldsmobile, Inc., 223 F.3d 617 (7th Cir.2000) cert.pet.filed Jan. 16, 2001 (falsified odometer).

3. STRICT LIABILITY

Because the law allows rescission of contracts on grounds of innocent, negligent, or fraudulent misrepresentations, there has been a recent movement away from the scienter requirement. The focal point of the debate has been Restatement (Second) of Torts § 552C, providing in part: "One who, in a sale, rental or exchange transaction with another, makes a misrepresentation . . . is subject to liability to the other for pecuniary loss caused to him . . . even though it is not made fraudulently or negligently." Subsection (2) provides that the amount recoverable is "limited to the difference between the value of what the other has parted with and the value of what he has received in the transaction." A caveat expresses no opinion whether strict liability might apply to other types of business transactions.

Comment *b* observes that "it is difficult to say with certainty whether this rule should be regarded as one of strict liability in the law of torts, eliminating the requirement of intent or negligence in making the representation, or one of the law of restitution, eliminating the requirement of rescinding and restoring the status quo."

Although the Restatement expresses no view on extensions to other types of transactions, most courts have declined to extend strict liability. A few courts have imposed strict liability on agents selling for their principals. See, e.g., Bortz v. Noon, 729 A.2d 555 (Pa.1999), recognizing the availability of rescission for an innocent misrepresentation by a broker but rejecting any tort action under those facts. See also Hoffman v. Connall, 736 P.2d 242 (Wash.1987), holding that a negligence standard adequately protected buyers who had been harmed by a misrepresentation of boundary lines. Brokers had no duty to verify a seller's representations unless they had reason to doubt them. Moreover, the buyers could have protected themselves by purchasing title insurance. An effort in Alaska to create a tort action on agents for innocent misrepresentation was soon overturned by statute. Amyot v. Luchini, 932 P.2d 244 (Alaska 1997).

B.   INTERFERENCE WITH CONTRACT

Earlier we had occasion to consider questions arising when the defendant's negligence interfered with the contractual relations of others. Recall the negligence that injured the hockey club's goalie, p. 323, supra. Those defendants had no desire to interfere with anyone's contracts, and the cases tested how far courts thought it appropriate to extend liability for this type of harm.

Now we consider cases in which defendants, knowing of the existence of a contract between the plaintiff and a third party, deliberately undertake to interfere with that contractual relationship.

Imperial Ice Co. v. Rossier

Supreme Court of California, 1941.
18 Cal.2d 33, 112 P.2d 631.

TRAYNOR, J. The California Consumers Company purchased from S.L. Coker an ice distributing business, inclusive of good will, located in territory comprising the city of Santa Monica and the former city of Sawtelle. In the purchase agreement Coker contracted as follows: "I do further agree in consideration of said purchase and in connection therewith, that I will not engage in the business of selling and or distributing ice, either directly or indirectly, in the above described territory so long as the purchasers, or anyone deriving title to the good will of said business from said purchasers, shall be engaged in a like business therein." Plaintiff, the Imperial Ice Company, acquired from the successor in interest of the California Consumers Company full title to this ice distributing business, including the right to enforce the covenant not to compete. Coker subsequently began selling in the same territory, in violation of the contract, ice supplied to him by a company owned by W. Rossier, J.A. Matheson, and Fred Matheson. Plaintiff thereupon brought this action in the superior court for an injunction to restrain Coker from violating the contract and to restrain Rossier and the Mathesons from inducing Coker to violate the contract. The complaint alleges that Rossier and the Mathesons induced Coker to violate his contract so that they might sell ice to him at a profit. The trial court sustained without leave to amend a demurrer to the complaint of the defendants Rossier and the Mathesons and gave judgment for those defendants. Plaintiff has appealed from the judgment on the sole ground that the complaint stated a cause of action against the defendants Rossier and the Mathesons for inducing the breach of contract.

The question thus presented to this court is under what circumstances may an action be maintained against a defendant who has induced a third party to violate a contract with the plaintiff.

It is universally recognized that an action will lie for inducing breach of contract by a resort to means in themselves unlawful such as libel, slander, fraud, physical violence, or threats of such action. [ ] Most jurisdictions also hold that an action will lie for inducing a breach of contract by the use of moral, social, or economic pressures, in themselves lawful, unless there is sufficient justification for such inducement. [   ]

Such justification exists when a person induces a breach of contract to protect an interest that has greater social value than insuring the stability of the contract. (Rest., Torts, sec. 767.) Thus, a person is justified in inducing the breach of a contract the enforcement of which would be injurious to health, safety, or good morals. (Brimelow v. Casson, (1924) 1 Ch. 302; [   ].) The interest of labor in improving working conditions is of sufficient social importance to justify peaceful labor tactics otherwise lawful, though they have the effect of inducing breaches of contracts between employer and employee or employer and customer. [   ] In numerous other situations justification exists (see Rest., Torts, secs. 766 to 774) depending upon the importance of the interest protected. The presence or absence of ill-will, sometimes referred to as "malice," is immaterial, except as it indicates whether or not an interest is actually being protected. (Boyson v. Thorn, 98 Cal. 578 [1893].)

It is well established, however, that a person is not justified in inducing a breach of contract simply because he is in competition with one of the parties to the contract and seeks to further his own economic advantage at the expense of the other. [   ] Whatever interest society has in encouraging free and open competition by means not in themselves unlawful, contractual stability is generally accepted as of greater importance than competitive freedom. Competitive freedom, however, is of sufficient importance to justify one competitor in inducing a third party to forsake another competitor if no contractual relationship exists between the latter two. [   ] A person is likewise free to carry on his business, including reduction of prices, advertising, and solicitation in the usual lawful manner although some third party may be induced thereby to breach his contract with a competitor in favor of dealing with the advertiser. [   ] Again, if two parties have separate contracts with a third, each may resort to any legitimate means at his disposal to secure performance of his contract even though the necessary result will be to cause a breach of the other contract. [   ] A party may not, however, under the guise of competition actively and affirmatively induce the breach of a competitor's contract in order to secure an economic advantage over that competitor. The act of inducing the breach must be an intentional one. If the actor had no knowledge of the existence of the contract or his actions were not intended to induce a breach, he cannot be held liable though an actual breach results from his lawful and proper acts. [   ]

In California the case of *Boyson v. Thorn*, supra, has been considered by many as establishing the proposition that no action will lie in this state for inducing breach of contract by means which are not otherwise unlawful. In that case the manager of a hotel induced the owner of the hotel to evict plaintiffs in violation of a contract. The complaint expressly alleged the existence of malicious motives on the part of the manager. This court affirmed a judgment entered on an order which sustained a demurrer without leave to amend, stating that an act otherwise lawful was not rendered unlawful by the existence of "malice." It is clear that the confidential relationship that existed between the manager of the hotel and the owner justified the manager in advising the owner to violate his contract with plaintiffs. His conduct thus being justified, it was lawful despite the existence of ill-will or malice on his part. The statements to the effect that no interference with contractual relations is actionable if the means employed are otherwise lawful were not necessary to the decision and should be disregarded. .   .   .

The complaint in the present case alleges that defendants actively induced Coker to violate his contract with plaintiffs so that they might sell ice to him. The contract gave to plaintiff the right to sell ice in the stated territory free from the competition of Coker. The defendants, by virtue of their interest in the sale of ice in that territory, were in effect competing with plaintiff. By inducing Coker to violate his contract, as alleged in the complaint, they sought to further their own economic advantage at plaintiff's expense. Such conduct is not justified. Had defendants merely sold ice to Coker without actively inducing him to violate his contract, his distribution of the ice in the forbidden territory in violation of his contract would not then have rendered defendants liable. They may carry on their business of selling ice as usual without incurring liability for breaches of contract by their customers. It is necessary to prove that they intentionally and actively induced the breach. Since the complaint alleges that they did so and asks for an injunction on the grounds that damages would be inadequate, it states a cause of action, and the demurrer should therefore have been overruled.

The judgment is reversed.

EDMONDS, J., SHENK, J., and GIBSON, C.J., concurred. CURTIS, J., concurred in the judgment.

Notes and Questions

1.   This action originated in Lumley v. Gye, 118 Eng.Rep. 749 (Q.B. 1853), involving Lumley, who was lessee and manager of Queen's Theatre, Johanna Wagner, a world-famous singer, and Gye, who was Lumley's competitor. Gye, by offering more money, apparently induced Wagner to breach her contract to perform for a stated period in Lumley's theatre. Lumley then brought an action to enforce a negative covenant in his contract with Wagner that prohibited her from performing for anyone else during the term of her contract without Lumley's consent. That injunction was granted in Lumley v. Wagner, 42 Eng.Rep. 687 (Ch. 1852), but apparently Wagner decided to sing for no one and did not return to the plaintiff's theatre. (Why didn't Lumley seek specific performance of his contract? Is enforcement of the negative covenant uncomfortably close to ordering performance?) When the first action did not bring Wagner back, Lumley brought his second action—against Gye for inducing breach of contract. Although a statute had been passed in 1349, in the wake of the Black Death, designed to deter scarce workers from changing their jobs, it had been limited to master-servant relations. In *Lumley v. Gye*, such meddling was barred in personal service contracts as well. The doctrine has since been extended to protect contracts generally from intentional interference. Do Lumley and Imperial Ice Co. need tort actions in addition to their contract actions?

2. Assuming that the elements of the tort action have been satisfied, what should determine whether the plaintiff receives damages, an injunction, or both? How do these remedies against inducing breach of contract relate to the plaintiff's possible action against the party who has been induced to breach?

3. For a discussion of whether plaintiff must prove "improper" motives or the defendant has the burden of justifying the behavior, see United Truck Leasing Corp. v. Geltman, 551 N.E.2d 20 (Mass.1990). The action was recognized in Kenty v. Transamerica Premium Ins. Co., 650 N.E.2d 863 (Mass.1995).

4. *Mixed motive.* Generally, if the defendant has a legitimate economic justification for interfering with the plaintiff's contract, additional improper motives will not defeat the privilege. E.g., Trepanier v. Getting Organized, Inc., 583 A.2d 583 (Vt.1990). Some courts, however, when confronted with both proper and improper motives, have sought the "dominant" one. In such cases the defendant has the burden of proving that the predominant motive justified the interference. See also Crandall Corp. v. Navistar Int'l Trans. Corp., 395 S.E.2d 179 (S.C.1990). Since evidence in cases involving multiple motives is usually conflicting, virtually all of these cases go to a jury. See Hatten v. Union Oil Co., 778 P.2d 1150 (Alaska 1989)(reversing defendant's summary judgment where the question was whether defendant had interfered with plaintiff's employment contract with a third party because defendant had been concerned about safety on its premises or because it was angry with plaintiff for another reason).

5. Why does *Imperial Ice* say that contractual stability is "generally accepted as of greater importance than competitive freedom"? In Perlman, Interference with Contract and Other Economic Expectancies: A Clash of Tort and Contract Theory, 49 U.Chi.L.Rev. 61 (1982), the author suggests that the notion of "efficient breach" in contract law should lead to the encouragement of breaches that serve the social interest in putting limited resources to higher-valued uses unless the means are unlawful: "In [the] case of other lawful acts, tort liability works at cross-purposes with contract policies. Contract remedies seem to promote efficiency, whereas the addition of inducer liability inhibits efficient outcomes."

6. As *Imperial Ice* indicates, a defendant may justify an otherwise unpermitted interference with the contract relations of others. It is clear that one cannot interfere with a contract for a finite term on the ground of economic self-interest. Bank of New York v. Berisford, Int'l, 594 N.Y.S.2d 152 (App.Div. 1993). Beyond that, deciding whether the interest that the defendant is seeking to protect has greater social value than that of insuring the stability of contract is a difficult and often unpredictable task.

In the cited *Brimelow v. Casson*, the producer of a touring company of dancers sued an actors' association for inducing theatre owners to breach their contracts that permitted plaintiff to perform in their theatres. The defendants had told the owners that since the plaintiff refused to pay his dancers a living wage, several of them had to resort to immorality to support themselves. The owners responded by canceling the leases. The court held that the association was privileged to tell this to the owners and to ask them to breach the contract. Apparently the charges were true. What if the defendants had honestly believed the charges but had been misled by some of the dancers? What result if the defendants had been unable to persuade the owners by their true stories but did succeed by threatening physical violence unless the owners agreed to cancel plaintiff's troupe? As Perlman indicates, some acceptable justifications have become crystallized, such as giving advice in family relationships and seeking to enforce conflicting claims against the same promisor.

It is permissible to interfere in order to protect your own contract rights. In Personal Preference Video, Inc. v. Home Box Office, Inc., 986 F.2d 110 (5th Cir.1993), plaintiff understood that it had certain exclusive telecast rights to a boxing match. When it appeared that the contracting party had subsequently given a second party conflicting rights, plaintiff took steps that interfered with that second contract. The privilege was held to apply "if (1) the interference was done in a bona fide exercise of the defendant's own rights or (2) the defendant had an equal or superior right in the subject matter to that of the plaintiff. [   ] This privilege extends to good faith assertions of colorable legal rights."

It is generally permissible to talk with plaintiff's dissatisfied customers but not to attempt to enlist satisfied customers who are under contract with the plaintiff. See Kendall/Hunt Publishing Co. v. Rowe, 424 N.W.2d 235 (Iowa 1988).

One of the most important justifications has been the claim of labor organizations referred to in *Imperial Ice*. So long as violent and other tortious means are not involved, the states' power to impose liability for such action has been preempted by federal legislation regulating labor-management relations. United Auto., Aircraft and Agr. Implement Workers v. Russell, 356 U.S. 634 (1958). To the extent traditional torts are involved, state law is still applicable. Concerted refusals to deal that seek to gain competitive advantage are now regulated extensively by antitrust legislation at both the federal and state levels. This is explored in courses on Antitrust Law, Labor Law and Unfair Competition.

7. Courts disagree over how far these doctrines extend to contracts that are voidable or terminable at will. See Guard–Life Corp. v. S. Parker Hardware Manufacturing Corp., 406 N.E.2d 445 (N.Y.1980), concluding that liability may flow from interference with a contract that was voidable for lack of mutuality. Sterner v. Marathon Oil Co., 767 S.W.2d 686 (Tex.1989), permitted an interference action when the contract was terminable at will. But see ACS Investors, Inc. v. McLaughlin, 943 S.W.2d 426

(Tex.1997), rejecting the part of *Sterner* that required the defendant to plead and prove legal justification for its actions.

Courts appear to be tending toward treating interference with these contracts as closer to interference with prospective economic advantage, p. 1246, infra, in which improper means are essential to the imposition of liability. See, e.g., NBT Bancorp Inc. v. Fleet/Norstar Financial Group, Inc., 664 N.E.2d 492 (N.Y.1996), holding that a disappointed bidder could not proceed under a theory of interference with contract relations. *Guard-Life*, supra, did not apply to the negotiations preliminary to the creation of a contract. The plaintiff argued that the conduct engaged in by defendant in this case was the same as that engaged in by the defendant in *Guard-Life*. The court responded that the defendant's conduct is not the determinative factor in "striking the balance and fixing the rule. Rather, the determinative factor is the nature of the relationship that suffered the interference, with greater protection accorded enforceable contact rights and greater deference accorded free competition where the contract rights are only prospective." The nature of that latter protection is explored in the next section.

See also Bed, Bath & Beyond of La Jolla, Inc. v. La Jolla Village Square Venture Partners, 60 Cal.Rptr.2d 830 (App. 1997) (claims based on unenforceable contracts should be analyzed as interference with opportunities and not contracts). In any event, the fact that either party can void the contract or terminate at will may well affect the measure of damages or the scope of privilege to interfere.

8. On occasion, the defendant's interference does not take the form of inducing the promisor to breach, but rather involves efforts to make it more difficult for the promisor to perform. For example, in McNary v. Chamberlain, 34 Conn. 384 (1867), plaintiff alleged that the defendant, knowing that the town was paying plaintiff a flat rate to keep a particular road in good repair, dumped stones and rubbish on the road and clogged a drain to flood the road. The court held that a claim had been stated because defendant "knew that the plaintiff had made such a contract, and took advantage of its existence to injure him in the manner described. He made use of the contract as an instrument to accomplish his purpose. As well may it be claimed that where one beats another with a bludgeon, the injury is too remote because the damage was done by the bludgeon."

By analogy, a party whose act renders the performance of a contract of less or no value to the person entitled to its benefits, may be liable in tort for interfering with the contract. In DEP Corp. v. Interstate Cigar Co., 622 F.2d 621 (2d Cir.1980), a British corporation, which had the world-wide distribution rights to Pears Soap, entered into a contract that gave plaintiff the exclusive right to distribute the product in the United States and Puerto Rico. Defendants bought Pears Soap through European middlemen and sold the soap in the United States, despite plaintiff's exclusive distribution rights. The district court's dismissal was reversed. Defendants had knowingly interfered with plaintiff's exclusive distribution contract.

9. *Consultants.* Consultants hired by a business to advise it cannot be liable when they suggest that the business breach its contract with the plaintiff so long as the consultant was asked for advice and gave it honestly and in good faith. See *Trepanier*, supra. See also Pacific Gas & Elec. Co. v. Bear Stearns & Co., 791 P.2d 587 (Cal.1990), protecting a consultant that advised its client to sue to terminate its contract with plaintiff. To allow an action against the consultant "when the only interference alleged is that defendant induced the bringing of potentially meritorious litigation would be an unwarranted expansion of the scope of these torts and a pernicious barrier to free access to the courts."

10. Although courts have not extended this action beyond intentional interference, Union Camp Corp. v. Southern Bulk Indus., Inc., 388 S.E.2d 524 (Ga.1990), non-intentional harm may be actionable as negligent infliction of economic harm, discussed in Chapter IV.

11. *The Pennzoil–Texaco case.* The biggest civil judgment in American history involved a suit for interference with contract. In 1983, Pennzoil entered into negotiations with major shareholders of Getty Oil Co., that would have given Pennzoil 43 percent of Getty's shares with the understanding that Pennzoil would acquire control of Getty if it could work out a restructuring agreement acceptable to Getty's board. A month later, Pennzoil and Getty began drafting a definitive merger agreement. As this agreement was being reached, Getty representatives entered into negotiations to sell Getty shares to Texaco. When the share sale was announced Pennzoil informed the Getty board that it expected Getty to honor its arrangement with Pennzoil. Nonetheless, Texaco and Getty eventually signed a formal merger agreement that gave Texaco control over Getty.

Pennzoil's suit against Texaco in Texas alleged interference with Pennzoil's contractual relations with Getty. The jury returned a verdict for $10.53 billion, including $7.53 in compensatory damages and $3 billion in punitive damages. On appeal, liability was affirmed but the punitive award was reduced to $1 billion. Texaco, Inc. v. Pennzoil, Co., 729 S.W.2d 768 (Tex.App.1987), cert. dismissed 485 U.S. 994 (1988). Efforts to set the judgment aside failed and the parties ultimately settled for $3 billion. The episode is noted in 33 N.Y.L.Sch.L.Rev. 111 (1988).

C.   INTERFERENCE WITH PROSPECTIVE ECONOMIC ADVANTAGE

We have just examined instances in which defendants were found liable for damages resulting from intentional interference with existing contractual relationships. The question of how far that action might extend beyond contracts has been the subject of much discussion and confusion. The following case addresses the issue—and at the same time reappraises *Imperial Ice v. Rossier*.

Della Penna v. Toyota Motor Sales, U.S.A., Inc.
Supreme Court of California, 1995.
11 Cal.4th 376, 902 P.2d 740, 45 Cal.Rptr.2d 436.

ARABIAN, J.

We granted review to reexamine, in light of divergent rulings from the Court of Appeal and a doctrinal evolution among other state high courts, the elements of the tort variously known as interference with "prospective economic advantage," "prospective contractual relations," or "prospective economic relations," and the allocation of the burdens of proof between the parties to such an action.   .   .   .

[Toyota was trying to prevent imported Lexus autos from being re-exported to Japan and took several steps to prevent that from happening. When it became apparent that this was in fact happening, defendant compiled a list of "offenders" and warned its dealers that those who did business with such offenders faced possible sanctions. Plaintiff did a profitable business as a wholesaler buying Lexus cars from retailers at near retail prices and exporting them to Japan for resale. As a result of defendant's efforts, plaintiff's supply of cars dried up.

When its tort claim for interference with prospective economic advantage was tried to a jury, the judge decided, over objection, to charge that the plaintiff had the burden of showing that the defendant's interference was "wrongful." After losing that objection, plaintiff framed a definition of "wrongful" that the judge read to the jury that included conduct "outside the realm of legitimate business transactions.   .   .   . Wrongfulness may lie in the method used or by virtue of an improper motive." The jury returned a defense verdict. The court of appeal reversed on the ground that the judge erred by putting the burden of proof on the plaintiff.]

II

A

[The court began by noting that *Lumley v. Gye*, p. 1242, supra, was generally thought to be the origin of the "two torts—interference with contract and its sibling, interference with prospective economic relations— in the form in which they have come down to us."]

The opinion in *Lumley* dealt, of course, with conduct intended to induce the breach of an existing contract, not conduct intended to prevent or persuade others not to contract with the plaintiff. That such an interference with prospective economic relations might itself be tortious was confirmed by the Queen's Bench over the next 40 years. [The court discussed Temperton v. Russell (1893) 1 Q.B. 715, in which a labor union in a dispute with builders demanded that the builders' suppliers cease furnishing materials to the builder. If a supplier failed to comply the union would bring pressure on those who supplied that supplier to cease doing so. In a suit by one supplier against the union, the court recognized a tort action on the ground that "in the words of Lord Esher, the Master of the Rolls, 'the distinction   .   .   . between the claim for inducing persons to break contracts already entered into   .   .   . and   .   .   . inducing persons not to enter into contracts   .   .   . can [not] prevail.' "]

"There was the same wrongful intent in both cases, wrongful because malicious," Lord Esher wrote. "There was the same kind of injury to the plaintiff. It seems rather a fine distinction to say that, where a defendant maliciously induces a person not to carry out a contract already made with the plaintiff and so injures the plaintiff, it is actionable, but where he injures the plaintiff by maliciously preventing a person from entering into a contract with the plaintiff, which he otherwise would have entered into, it is not actionable." [*Temperton*].

As a number of courts and commentators have observed, the keystone of the liability imposed in [*Lumley* and *Temperton*] to judge from the opinions of the justices, appears to have been the "malicious" intent of a defendant in enticing an employee to breach her contract with the plaintiff, and damaging the business of one who refused to cooperate with the union in achieving its bargaining aims. While some have doubted whether the use of the word "malicious" amounted to anything more than an intent to commit an act, knowing it would harm the plaintiff (see, e.g., Dobbs, Tortious Interference with Contractual Relationships (1980) 34 Ark. L.Rev. 335, 347, fn. 37). Dean Keeton, assessing the state of the tort as late as 1984, remarked that "[w]ith intent to interfere as the usual basis of the action, the cases have turned almost entirely upon the defendant's motive or purpose and the means by which he has sought to accomplish it. As in the cases of interference with contract, any manner of intentional invasion of the plaintiff's interests may be sufficient if the purpose is not a proper one." [ ]

.   .   .

[Historically] the plaintiff need only allege a so-called "prima facie tort" by showing the defendant's awareness of the economic relation, a deliberate interference with it, and the plaintiff's resulting injury. [ ] By this account of the matter—the traditional view of the torts and the one adopted by the first Restatement of Torts—the burden then passed to the defendant to demonstrate that its conduct was privileged, that is, "justified" by a recognized defense such as the protection of others or, more likely in this context, the defendant's own competitive business interests. [ ]

These and related features of the economic relations tort and the requirements surrounding its proof and defense led, however, to calls for a reexamination and reform as early as the 1920's. .   .   . The nature of the wrong itself seemed to many unduly vague, inviting suit and hampering the presentation of coherent defenses. More critically in the view of others, the procedural effects of applying the prima facie tort principle to what is essentially a business context led to even more untoward consequences.

.   .   .

Calls for a reformulation of both the elements and the means of establishing the economic relations tort reached a height around the time the Restatement Second of Torts was being prepared for publication and are reflected in its departures from its predecessor's version. Acknowledging criticism, the American Law Institute discarded the prima facie tort requirement of the first Restatement. A new provision, section 766B, required that the defendant's conduct be "improper," and adopted a multifactor "balancing" approach, identifying seven factors for the trier of fact to weigh in determining a defendant's liability. The Restatement Second of Torts, however, declined to take a position on the issue of which of the parties bore the burden of proof, relying on the "considerable disagreement on who has the burden of pleading and proving certain matters" and the observation that "the law in this area has not fully congealed but is still in a formative stage" [ ]. In addition, the Restatement Second provided that a defendant might escape liability by showing that his conduct was justifiable and did not include the use of "wrongful means." [ ]

B

In the meantime, however, an increasing number of state high courts had traveled well beyond the Second Restatement's reforms by redefining and otherwise recasting the elements of the economic relations tort and the burdens surrounding its proof and defenses. In Top Service Body Shop, Inc. v. Allstate Ins. Co. (Ore.1978) 582 P.2d 1365 (*Top Service*), the Oregon Supreme Court, assessing this "most fluid and rapidly growing tort," noted that "efforts to consolidate both recognized and unsettled lines of development into a general theory of 'tortious interference' have brought to the surface the difficulties of defining the elements of so general a tort without sweeping within its terms a wide variety of socially very different conduct." [ ]

Recognizing the force of these criticisms, the court went on to hold in *Top Service* [ ], that a claim of interference with economic relations "is made out when interference resulting in injury to another *is wrongful by some measure beyond the fact of the interference itself.* Defendant's liability may arise from improper motives or from the use of improper means. They may be wrongful by reason of a statute or other regulation, or a recognized rule of common law, or perhaps an established standard of a trade or profession. No question of privilege arises unless the interference would be wrongful but for the privilege; it becomes an issue only if the acts charged would be tortious on the part of an unprivileged defendant." [ ]; (italics added).

[The court then traced similar developments in other courts, concluding that "[o]ver the past decade or so, close to a majority of the high courts of American jurisdictions have imported into the economic relations tort variations on the *Top Service* line of reasoning, explicitly approving a rule that requires the plaintiff in such a suit to plead and prove the alleged interference was either 'wrongful,' 'improper,' 'illegal,' 'independently tortious' or some variant on these formulations."]

III

In California, the development of the economic relations tort has paralleled its evolution in other jurisdictions. For many years this court declined to adopt the holding of [*Lumley*] on the ground that, as we reasoned in Boyson v. Thorn (1893) 98 Cal. 578, "[i]t is a truism of the law that an act which does not amount to a legal injury cannot be actionable because it is done with a bad intent. . . . If it is right, and the means used to procure the breach are right, the motive cannot make it a wrong. . . ." [ ]. In [*Imperial Ice Co.*], however, a unanimous court, speaking through Justice Traynor, pronounced these statements in *Boyson* "not necessary to the decision" and directed that they be "disregarded." [ ] California thus joined the majority of jurisdictions in adopting the view of the first Restatement of Torts by stating that "an action will lie for *unjustifiably* inducing a breach of contract." [ ]; (italics added).

[The court then traced its own thinking in this area at length. It then noted that developments in the court of appeal had "if anything, outdistanced our own formulations of the elements of the tort and the allocation of the burden of proof in at least two respects." The first was that plaintiff was being given the burden of proving "wrongful" conduct. The second was that defendant could "defeat liability by showing that its conduct was not independently 'wrongful.' "]

IV

In searching for a means to recast the elements of the economic relations tort and allocate the associated burdens of proof, we are guided by an overmastering concern articulated by high courts of other jurisdictions and legal commentators: The need to draw and enforce a sharpened distinction between claims for the tortious disruption of an existing contract and claims that a prospective contractual or economic relationship has been interfered with by the defendant. Many of the cases do in fact acknowledge a greater array of justificatory defenses against claims of interference with prospective relations. Still, in our view and that of several other courts and commentators, the notion that the two torts are analytically unitary and derive from a common principle sacrifices practical wisdom to theoretical insight, promoting the idea that the interests invaded are of nearly equal dignity. They are not.

The courts provide a damage remedy against third party conduct intended to disrupt an existing contract precisely because the exchange of promises resulting in such a formally cemented economic relationship is deemed worthy of protection from interference by a stranger to the agreement. Economic relationships short of contractual, however, should stand on a different legal footing as far as the potential for tort liability is reckoned. Because ours is a culture firmly wedded to the social rewards of commercial contests, the law usually takes care to draw lines of legal liability in a way that maximizes areas of competition free of legal penalties.

. . . . Our courts should, in short, firmly distinguish the two kinds of business contexts, bringing a greater solicitude to those relationships that have ripened into agreements, while recognizing that relationships short of that subsist in a zone where the rewards and risks of competition are dominant.

Beyond that, we need not tread today. It is sufficient to dispose of the issue before us in this case by holding that a plaintiff seeking to recover for alleged interference with prospective economic relations has the burden of pleading and proving that the defendant's interference was wrongful "by some measure beyond the fact of the interference itself." [ ] It follows that the trial court did not commit error when it [required] the jury to find that defendant's interference was "wrongful." And because the instruction defining "wrongful conduct" given the jury by the trial court was offered by plaintiff himself, we have no occasion to review its sufficiency in this case. The question of whether additional refinements to the plaintiff's pleading and proof burdens merit adoption by California courts—questions embracing the precise scope of "wrongfulness," or whether a "disinterested malevolence," in Justice Holmes's words (American Bank & Trust Co. v. Federal Reserve Bank (1921) 256 U.S. 350, 358) is an actionable interference in itself, or whether the underlying policy justification for the tort, the efficient allocation of social resources, justifies including as actionable conduct that is recognized as anticompetitive under established state and federal positive law [ ]—are matters that can await another day and a more appropriate case.

    . . . The judgment of the Court of Appeal is reversed and the cause is remanded with directions to affirm the judgment of the trial court.

LUCAS, C.J., and KENNARD, BAXTER, GEORGE and WERDEGAR, JJ., concur.

Concurring opinion by MOSK, J.

    . . .

Like the majority, I would reverse the Court of Appeal's judgment in this regard. As I shall explain, I believe that any instructional error was not prejudicial.

I

With the dissonance caused by such terms as "malice," "justification," and "privilege" [ ], the common law on the tort of intentional interference with prospective economic advantage, both in American jurisdictions generally and in California specifically, is fast approaching incoherence. [ ]

    . . .

A

One reason for the common law's near-incoherence on the tort of intentional interference with prospective economic advantage may be discovered in its doctrinal basis.

During the second half of the 19th century and the first half of the 20th, as the times pressed hard on both law and society, common law courts, first in England and then in the United States, developed what has become known as the "prima facie tort doctrine." [ ] The traditional source was the old action on the case. [ ] The analytical object was a framework "capable of assisting comprehension and guiding an internal systematic development of the subject matter" [   ] to the end that "principle rather than precedent" might govern [   ].

In Mogul Steamship Company v. McGregor, Gow, & Co. (1889) 23 Q.B.D. 598, 613, affirmed [1891] A.C. 25, Lord Justice Bowen in the Court of Appeal made the famous statement of the prima facie tort doctrine: "[I]ntentionally to do that which is calculated in the ordinary course of events to damage, and which does, in fact, damage another in that person's property or trade, is actionable if done without just cause or excuse."

In Aikens v. Wisconsin (1904) 195 U.S. 194, 204, Justice Holmes, who "was in large measure responsible for the introduction of the [prima facie tort] doctrine in this country" [   ], made the equally famous statement: "It has been considered that, prima facie, the intentional infliction of temporal damage is a cause of action, which, as a matter of substantive law, whatever may be the form of pleading, requires a justification if the defendant is to escape."

In the middle of this century, Dean Pound made the following restatement: "One who intentionally does anything which on its face is injurious to another is liable to repair the resulting damage unless he can establish a liberty or privilege by identifying his claim to act as he did with some recognized public or social interest." (3 Pound, Jurisprudence (1959) p. 9.)

.   .   .

The prima facie tort doctrine exhibits a general deficiency. Perhaps it has resulted in a kind of "internal systematic development of the subject matter." [   ] But if it has, it has done so by sacrificing an external connection to society. "The idea is that 'intentional infliction of harm' is, prima facie, a tort. The problem is that almost any legitimate act can cause 'intentional' harm.   .   .   ." [Dobbs]. Therefore, "[i]t must be understood that intentional infliction of harm   .   .   . covers a multitude of desirable acts as well as a multitude of sins". [   ] "The prima facie tort rule, then, is not a rule about wrongdoing at all. It seems to be a philosophical effort to state all"—or at least much—of "tort law in a single sentence rather than an effort to state a meaningful principle." [Dobbs]: "[P]rinciple rather than precedent" may indeed govern. [   ] But it is a principle that is peculiarly empty.

.   .   .

B

A second reason for the common law's near-incoherence on the tort of intentional interference with prospective economic advantage may be discovered within the law itself.

To borrow words from Brennan v. United Hatters [65 A. 165 (N.J.L. 1906)], the premise of the tort seems to be that, "[i]n a civilized community which recognizes the right of private property among its institutions, the notion is intolerable that a man should be protected by the law in the enjoyment of property once it is acquired, but left unprotected by the law in his efforts to acquire it."

The tort's "protectionist" premise, however, is at war with itself. For the person who deserves protection in the acquisition of property is not only the interfered-with party but also the interfering party. . . .

Further, liability under the tort may threaten values of greater breadth and higher dignity than those of the tort itself.

One is the common law's policy of freedom of competition. "The policy of the common law has always been in favor of free competition, which proverbially is the life of trade. So long as the plaintiff's contractual relations are merely contemplated or potential, it is considered to be in the interest of the public that any competitor should be free to divert them to himself by all fair and reasonable means. . . . In short, it is no tort to beat a business rival to prospective customers. Thus, in the absence of prohibition by statute, illegitimate means, or some other unlawful element, a defendant seeking to increase his own business may cut rates or prices, allow discounts or rebates, enter into secret negotiations behind the plaintiff's back, refuse to deal with him or threaten to discharge employees who do, or even refuse to deal with third parties unless they cease dealing with the plaintiff, all without incurring liability." [ ]

.   .   .

C

A third reason for the common law's near-incoherence on the tort of intentional interference with prospective economic advantage may be discovered in its focus on the interfering party's motive, that is, why he seeks whatever it is that he seeks through his interference, and on his moral character as revealed thereby.

[In an extended discussion of *Boyson v. Thorn,* Justice Mosk approvingly quoted its language that "the existence of a bad motive, in the case of an act which is not in itself illegal, will not convert that act into a civil wrong for which reparation is due." He concluded that *Imperial Ice* had erred when it rejected *Boyson*'s assertion that motive was irrelevant.]

The untoward results of the focus on the interfering party's motive may present themselves in individual cases in the form of arbitrary and capricious outcomes. [ ] In matters in which the trier of fact believes it has discerned good motive or at least persuades itself it has, an interfering party who has both engaged in objectively bad conduct and produced objectively bad consequences may evade liability for injury. By contrast, in matters in which it adopts a contrary view, an interfering party who has neither engaged in such conduct nor produced such consequences may be made to pay for what is simply damnum absque injuria. In a word, much may depend on mere appearances and perceptions and on nothing more.

.   .   .

II

With all this said, we are put to the question: What are we to do about the tort of intentional interference with prospective economic advantage?

It would be unreasonable to choose to do nothing. As stated, in this regard the common law is approaching incoherence. It is not about to turn to consistency of its own accord.

It would also be unreasonable to choose abolition. Such a course commands little support among courts or commentators. That is unsurprising. Most agree that the interfering party should not be granted general immunity, but should be exposed to liability under at least some circumstances. [   ] For just as "[i]t cannot be . . . a theorem of justice that liability is always just" [   ], neither can it be a principle of law that immunity is invariably proper.

In view of the foregoing, the only reasonable choice is reformulation. . . .

It follows that the tort may be satisfied by intentional interference with prospective economic advantage by independently tortious means. [   ]

[In an extended discussion, Justice Mosk develops bases for recovery in this situation. Although the harm is generally directed at the plaintiff, that is not required—as in cases in which the defendant makes misrepresentations to third parties to persuade them not to deal with plaintiff. The tort also may be satisfied by a showing of "restraint of trade, including monopolization." The common "independently tortious means" including "assault and battery, defamation, and fraud and deceit, are well defined and long settled." Such an approach would remove the tort's "protectionist" premise, leaving plaintiffs subject only to defendant's use of "independently tortious means or restraints of trade." He then turned to the case at bar.]

Under the tort as reformulated, it is plain that the Court of Appeal erred. To be sure, the instructions appear erroneous. They did not expressly require objective, and unlawful, conduct or consequences. Neither, it seems, did they do so impliedly. Any error, however, was not prejudicial. The reason is manifest. To the extent that they were satisfied by mere "wrongfulness"—which, at Della Penna's request, was defined under a kind of " 'business ethics' standard" as behavior "outside the realm of legitimate business transactions" because of "method" or "motive"—they were satisfied by far too little. For to that extent they did not demand the use of independently tortious means or restraints of trade. It is true that their focus on motive—"[w]rongfulness may lie . . . by virtue of an improper motive"—might threaten an arbitrary and capricious outcome in a given case. The same is true of their use of the term "wrongful" and its cognates, which are inherently ambiguous [   ]. But, in spite of the foregoing, there is simply no basis to conclude that the outcome here was either arbitrary or capricious.

IV

It is evident in the analysis presented above that, on many points, I agree with the majority's discussion of the tort of intentional interference with prospective economic advantage and Della Penna's claim against Toyota asserting such a cause of action.

On two major points, however, I am compelled to state my disagreement.

First, I would not adopt the "standard" of "wrongfulness." As I have noted, the term and its cognates are inherently ambiguous. They should probably be avoided. They should surely not be embraced. . . .

Second, if I were to adopt such a "standard," I would not allow it to remain undefined. Otherwise, our effort . . . to rationalize the governing principles would be undermined. Formerly, the interfering party as defendant was left "knowing he was entitled to some defense, but not knowing what defenses would be accounted sufficient." . . . Any definition of the "standard," of course, should avoid suggesting that the interfering party's motive might be material for present purposes. As I have explained, the focus on this issue is inappropriate. [ ] A position of this sort, one must acknowledge, would result in the imposition of no liability on a person who is purely, but merely, "malicious"—who acts, to quote Justice Holmes, with "disinterested malevolence" (Amer. Bank & Trust Co. v. Federal Bank (1921) 256 U.S. 350, 358). Although such a person might be held responsible in conscience, he should not be made answerable in tort. To reiterate: "The law has no roving commission to root out bad people or people whose minds may harbor bad thoughts." . . .

. . .

Notes and Questions

1. What error did the court of appeal find in the trial judge's conduct in this case? Why did the supreme court reject that determination?

2. What are the consequences of the majority's decision? Should plaintiff's case ever have gone to trial?

3. How did the first and second Restatements differ? Did the court adopt the approach of either one? Section 767 lists the seven factors referred to by the court that are to be considered in determining whether or not an intentional interference with either a contractual or prospective contractual relation is improper:

(a) the nature of the actor's conduct,

(b) the actor's motive,

(c) the interests of the other with which the actor's conduct interferes,

(d) the interests sought to be advanced by the actor,

(e) the social interests in protecting the freedom of action of the actor and the contractual interests of the other,

(f) the proximity or remoteness of the actor's conduct to the interference, and

(g) the relations between the parties.

How might these factors have affected *Imperial Ice*? *Della Penna*? How might the majority react to these factors? How might Justice Mosk?

4. Does the majority reject the result of *Imperial Ice*? The analysis? What is the concurring opinion's stance concerning that case? What differences between interference with contract and interference with prospective economic advantage can be justified?

5. *Unlawful means.* Justice Mosk identifies several independently tortious means of inflicting harm. In the business context, other types of conduct have also been important. We briefly review a few of these, which are covered more extensively in courses on Unfair Competition and Copyright.

a. False statements about a competitor's product. The action of "slander of title" or "trade libel" or "disparagement" has evolved to cover false statements concerning ownership of goods and was further extended to untrue statements dealing with the quality of goods as well as the title to them. See, e.g., System Operations, Inc. v. Scientific Games Development Corp., 555 F.2d 1131 (3d Cir.1977) listing the elements of disparagement as the "(1) publication (2) with malice (3) of false allegations concerning plaintiff's property or product (4) causing special damages, i.e., pecuniary harm." As might be expected, "malice" is a subject of confusion. Some attacks on product quality may impugn management and be actionable as defamations. See Harwood Pharmacal Co. v. National Broadcasting Co., 174 N.E.2d 602 (N.Y.1961).

State law has flatly barred injunctions in defamation cases. Since disparagement occurs in the context of competition, some courts have been willing to view the disparagement as the basis of a tort for unfair competition or intentional interference with economic advantage and have permitted injunctive relief on those bases. Now that the Supreme Court has accorded "commercial speech" at least some First Amendment protection (Virginia State Bd. of Pharmacy v. Virginia Citizens Consumer Council, Inc., 425 U.S. 748 (1976)), courts may become increasingly reluctant to enjoin speech in commercial contexts.

In Proctor & Gamble Co. v. Haugen, 222 F.3d 1262 (10th Cir.2000), competitors of plaintiff and their distributors spread a rumor that plaintiff's president had told a television show that a "large portion of the profits from [P & G] products go to support his satanic church." When asked whether announcing this would hurt his business he was said to have responded "[t]here are not enough Christians in the United States to make a difference." In addition to reinstating a statutory action, the court held that a state tort claim lay for interference with prospective economic advantage. A jury could find that the defendants were intending to interfere with plaintiff's business relationships with "anti-satanic consumers and distributors."

b. False statements about a firm's own product. Tort actions may be harder to ground where the falsity is in the puffing of the speaker's own product rather than the disparagement of a competitor's product. It has been harder to show that plaintiff suffered from the statement—and how much.

In Mosler Safe Co. v. Ely–Norris Safe Company, 273 U.S. 132 (1927), Mosler falsely advertised that its safes had explosion-proof chambers. The Supreme Court refused to allow a suit by a company whose safes did have such a device. What if Ely–Norris Safe Company were the only manufacturer of explosion-proof safes? What about a class action? The inaccessibility of a tort action led to the creation of statutory remedies to deter false advertising.

c. Conscious imitation of a product's appearance. A statutory or common law action for trademark infringement or an action for unfair competition will lie when a competitor "passes off" its own product as that of another competitor by the use of intentionally similar and potentially confusing trademarks or trade dress. See Harold F. Ritchie, Inc. v. Chesebrough–Pond's, Inc., 281 F.2d 755 (2d Cir.1960), in which defendant was found liable for infringement of plaintiff's registered trademark "Brylcreem" by the marketing of its hair care product, "Valcream."

In Harlequin Enterprises Ltd. v. Gulf & Western Corp., 644 F.2d 946 (2d Cir.1981), the court held that defendant's deliberate imitation of the cover format of Harlequin Romances for its own series titled "Silhouette Romances" was properly enjoined since the covers were so "startlingly" similar that "[a]n ordinary buyer of romance fiction would not recognize the disparities without setting out to find them [and a] buyer who did notice the difference between the names and the colophons would be reasonably justified in believing both products came from the same publisher." But see Best Cellars Inc. v. Grape Finds at Dupont, Inc., 90 F.Supp.2d 431 (S.D.N.Y.2000), doubting whether the second circuit still adhered to *Harlequin.*

For other developments in the trademark area, see Qualitex Co. v. Jacobson Products Co., Inc., 514 U.S. 159 (1995) (single color may be trademark if it has come to identify the product to consumers); Pebble Beach Co. v. Tour 18 I Ltd., 155 F.3d 526 (5th Cir.1998) (functional feature cannot be trademark); Nora Beverages, Inc., v. Perrier Group of America, Inc., 164 F.3d 736 (2d Cir.1998) (shape and texture of a bottle could be trademark).

d. Misappropriation of patents, copyrights and trade secrets. Patents and copyrights provide specific protection for products and writings that meet certain statutory requirements. Infringement of a patent or copyright gives rise to an action for damages and injunction under federal statutes.

Trade secrets do not enjoy the same type or level of protection accorded to patents. Whereas an inventor has a monopoly on a patented invention for a statutory period of time, competitors can make use of a company's trade secret so long as the information was obtained in a legitimate manner—reverse engineering, independent research, or disclosure by the firm itself, for example. But improper methods used by a competitor to acquire another's trade secrets will lead to a common law tort action.

The tortious methods may be unlawful in themselves, such as fraud, theft, wiretapping or other acts of industrial espionage. Liability may also be based on inducing others to divulge secret business information told them in confidence. Kewanee Oil v. Bicron Corp., 416 U.S. 470 (1974). See also Note, A Balanced Approach to Employer–Employee Trade Secrets Disputes in California, 31 Hastings L.J. 671 (1980).

e. Misappropriation of other commercial "quasi–property." In International News Service v. Associated Press, 248 U.S. 215 (1918), the Supreme Court went beyond the traditional protections of copyright, patent, trademark and trade secret, and extended protection to material that was not copyrightable. INS and AP were rivals in gathering news and supplying newspapers with that information. When INS was found to have been copying the facts from AP, the Court permitted INS to be enjoined from such behavior. Justice Brandeis, in a famous dissent, attacked the majority's finding of a new private right and considered the problem one best left to the legislature:

> Plaintiff further contended that defendant's practice constitutes unfair competition, because there is "appropriation without cost to itself of values created by" the plaintiff; and it is upon this ground that the decision of this court appears to be based. To appropriate and use for profit, knowledge and ideas produced by other men, without making compensation or even acknowledgment, may be inconsistent with a finer sense of propriety; but, with the exceptions indicated above [copyright and patent], the law has heretofore sanctioned the practice.
>
> . . .
>
> Courts are ill-equipped to make the investigations which should precede a determination of the limitations which should be set upon any property right in news or of the circumstances under which news gathered by a private agency should be deemed affected with a public interest.

See Baird, Common Law Intellectual Property and the Legacy of International News Service v. Associated Press, 50 U.Chi.L.Rev. 411 (1983).

The issue was further clouded by the Supreme Court's decisions in Sears, Roebuck & Co. v. Stiffel, 376 U.S. 225 (1964) and Compco Corp. v. Day–Brite Lighting, Inc., 376 U.S. 234 (1964), in which the Court overturned lower courts' findings of liability for unfair competition for copying the designs of unpatented lighting fixtures. In discussing the federal preemption of certain state unfair competition laws, Justice Black observed in Sears:

> To allow a State by use of its law of unfair competition to prevent the copying of an article which represents too slight an advance to be patented would be to permit the State to block off from the public something which federal law has said belongs to the public. The result would be that while federal law grants only 14 to 17 years' protection

to genuine inventions, see 35 U.S.C. §§ 154, 173, States could allow perpetual protection to articles too lacking in novelty to merit any patent at all under federal constitutional standards. This would be too great an encroachment on the federal patent system to be tolerated.

Sears and *Compco* did not refer to the *INS* decision.

6. *Beyond competition.* Some important cases of economic harm arise from situations in which the parties are not in competition. For example, in Auvil v. CBS "60 Minutes," 67 F.3d 816 (9th Cir.1995), defendant in 1989 reported that "[t]he most potent cancer-causing agent in our food supply is a substance sprayed on apples to keep them on the trees longer and make them look better" and that those most at risk were children. Following the broadcast, "consumer demand for apples and apple products decreased dramatically." A disparagement action was allowed to proceed and then dismissed for failure to prove falsity. As a result of the broadcast, several states adopted statutes creating civil actions in behalf of producers of perishable products against anyone who "wilfully or maliciously" dissemi-nates "false information" that a food product is not safe for human consumption. "False information" is defined as "not based on reliable, scientific facts and reliable scientific data which the disseminator knows or should have known to be false." See Fla.Stat.Ann. § 865.065 (1994).

For an action involving both common law disparagement and a dispar-agement statute, see Texas Beef Group v. Winfrey, 201 F.3d 680 (5th Cir.2000), in which plaintiff cattle ranchers alleged that defendant televi-sion personality falsely stated that American beef was unsafe because of the existence in Great Britain of "mad cow disease." The trial judge dismissed all counts except common law disparagement, which the jury rejected after trial. The court of appeal affirmed.

When boycotts or other concerted actions do not involve labor disputes or economic conflicts, they tend to have political, social, or religious ramifications. Some examples follow:

a. In Watch Tower Bible & Tract Society v. Dougherty, 11 A.2d 147 (Pa.1940), the defendants Roman Catholic Archbishop of Philadelphia and a priest were sued by the plaintiff religious society. For ten years the plaintiff had conducted a series of radio programs on a Philadelphia station owned indirectly by a department store. The priest objected that the plaintiff "attacks the Catholic Church, misrepresents her teachings and foments religious hatred and bigotry," and threatened to cancel his charge account at the store if it renewed the plaintiff's contract to broadcast. The plaintiff also alleged that the defendants urged their parishioners to inun-date the store with similar messages. The store refused to renew plaintiff's contract. The trial court's dismissal of the complaint was affirmed in one paragraph:

> The order of the court below was proper. No valid cause of action was pleaded. The defendants are leaders of their church. They cannot be mulcted in damages for protesting against the utterances of one who they believe attacks their church and misrepresents its teachings nor

for inducing their adherents to make similar protests. A right of action does not arise merely because a group withdraws its patronage or threatens to do so and induces others to do likewise where the objects sought to be obtained are legitimate.

What if defendants' threat to withdraw patronage had been made during the term of plaintiff's contract?

b. In Missouri v. National Organization of Women, Inc., 620 F.2d 1301 (8th Cir.), cert. denied 449 U.S. 842 (1980), the State of Missouri brought a suit to enjoin NOW's campaign discouraging groups from scheduling conventions in states that had not ratified the proposed Equal Rights Amendment. The district court's denial of relief was affirmed. Because NOW's concerted action was an effort to exercise its First Amendment right to petition the government and to seek to influence the legislature's actions, the Sherman Antitrust Act did not apply and liability for tortious interference with an advantageous relationship did not lie. "[T]he right to petition is of such importance that it is not an improper interference even when exercised by way of a boycott."

Would the case be different if NOW sought to persuade groups that had already signed agreements to hold their conventions in Missouri to cancel those plans?

c. In National Ass'n for the Advancement of Colored People v. Claiborne Hardware Co., 458 U.S. 886 (1982), the NAACP organized a boycott of white merchants in Claiborne County, Mississippi, to gain acceptance of "a lengthy list of demands for equality and racial justice." Some violence occurred during the boycott. Merchants who had suffered economic losses during the extended boycott sued the NAACP for damages for the concerted conduct. The state courts found that violence and the fear of reprisal had been influential in causing some blacks to withhold patronage from the white merchants. This led to the conclusion that the NAACP was liable for all the damages resulting from the boycott, a total of more than one million dollars.

The Supreme Court unanimously reversed. The boycott "clearly involved constitutionally protected activity":

. . . Through speech, assembly, and petition—rather than through riot or revolution—petitioners sought to change a social order that had consistently treated them as second-class citizens.

The presence of protected activity, however, does not end the relevant constitutional inquiry. Governmental regulation that has an incidental effect on First Amendment freedoms may be justified in certain narrowly defined instances. [   ] A nonviolent and totally voluntary boycott may have a disruptive effect on local economic conditions. This Court has recognized the strong governmental interest in certain forms of economic regulation, even though such regulation may have an incidental effect on rights of speech and association. [   ] The right of business entities to "associate" to suppress competition may be curtailed. [   ] Unfair trade practices may be restricted. Secondary boycotts and picketing by labor unions may be prohibited, as part of "Congress' striking of the delicate balance between union freedom of expression and the ability of neutral employers, employees, and consumers to remain free from coerced participation in industrial strife." [ ]

While states have broad power to regulate economic activity, we do not find a comparable right to prohibit peaceful political activity such as that found in the boycott in this case.   .   .   .

.   .   .

The First Amendment does not protect violence. "Certainly violence has no sanctuary in the First Amendment, and the use of weapons, gunpowder, and gasoline may not constitutionally masquerade under the guise of 'advocacy.' " [ ] Although the extent and significance of the violence in this case is vigorously disputed by the parties, there is no question that acts of violence occurred. No federal rule of law restricts a State from imposing tort liability for business losses that are caused by violence and by threats of violence. When such conduct occurs in the context of constitutionally protected activity, however, "precision of regulation" is demanded. [ ] Specifically, the presence of activity protected by the First Amendment imposes restraints on the grounds that may give rise to damages liability and on the persons who may be held accountable for those damages.   .   .   .

.   .   . While the State legitimately may impose damages for the consequences of violent conduct, it may not award compensation for the consequences of nonviolent, protected activity. Only those losses proximately caused by unlawful conduct may be recovered.

.   .   .

The taint of violence colored the conduct of some of the petitioners. They, of course, may be held liable for the consequences of their violent deeds. The burden of demonstrating that it colored the entire collective effort, however, is not satisfied by evidence that violence occurred or even that violence contributed to the success of the boycott. A massive and prolonged effort to change the social, political, and economic structure of a local environment cannot be characterized as a violent conspiracy simply by reference to the ephemeral consequences of relatively few violent acts.

Questions about the legality of various "means" have not been common.

7. *"Disinterested malevolence."* How does Justice Mosk's position differ from that of the majority on the question of "disinterested malevolence"? Consider some of the classic cases that raise this issue.

a. In Tuttle v. Buck, 119 N.W. 946 (Minn.1909), plaintiff, a village barber, alleged that the local banker was trying to destroy plaintiff's business by, among other things, employing a series of barbers to operate a competing shop rent-free when he could not find a barber to rent it.

Although plaintiff also alleged that the defendant's sole purpose was to destroy the plaintiff's business and not to serve "any legitimate interest of his own," there was apparently no explicit allegation that the defendant was planning to close his own shop after he succeeded in eliminating plaintiff. The trial judge denied a motion to dismiss the complaint and the supreme court affirmed. On appeal, the court in *Tuttle* stated:

> To divert to one's self the customers of a business rival by the offer of goods at lower prices is in general a legitimate mode of serving one's own interest, and justifiable as fair competition. But when a man starts an opposition place of business, not for the sake of profit to himself, but regardless of loss to himself, and for the sole purpose of driving his competitor out of business, and with the intention of himself retiring upon the accomplishment of his malevolent purpose, he is guilty of a wanton wrong and an actionable tort. In such a case he would not be exercising his legal right, or doing an act which can be judged separately from the motive which actuated him. To call such conduct competition is a perversion of terms. It is simply the application of force without legal justification, which in its moral quality may be no better than highway robbery.

Why is it a "perversion" to speak of this behavior as competition? What if the defendant can establish that after driving plaintiff out of business he plans to continue his barbershop, which will then become profitable, at least until another competitor appears?

b. In Beardsley v. Kilmer, 140 N.E. 203 (N.Y.1923), defendants manufactured a patent medicine called "Swamp Root" in the city of Binghamton. The plaintiff was managing editor and a major stockholder of the Binghamton Herald, which, under his direction, frequently ridiculed the defendants' product. The defendants, provoked by plaintiff's attacks, started their own newspaper. The plaintiff's paper was forced out of business. The evidence at trial showed that the defendants had mixed motives in starting their paper: to force the plaintiff's paper out of business, to defend themselves against what the defendants thought were unfair charges, and to "give Binghamton the best paper in the state." There was no evidence that the defendants' paper was "not an enterprising, creditable and reputable paper, or that it was unsuccessful or unprofitable." The lower court dismissed the complaint. On appeal, the court said:

> [I]f our interpretation of the evidence is correct we have a case where the plaintiff is complaining of and seeking redress for injuries caused by an act which is the product of mixed motives some of which are perfectly legitimate. The question is whether his cause of action can successfully rest upon such a foundation. We feel sure it cannot. . . .
>
> [This view finds] recent support in one of Mr. Justice Holmes' epigrammatic phrases which, in a discussion of this general subject, speaks of "disinterested malevolence" and which is supposed to mean that the genesis which will make a lawful act unlawful must be a malicious one unmixed with any other and exclusively directed to

injury and damage of another. (American Bank & Trust Co. v. Fed. Reserve Bank of Atlanta, 256 U.S. 350 [1921].)

. . . We cannot afford to move the law to a stage where any person who, for his own advantage, starts a new business, will be compelled to submit to the decision of a jury the question whether also there was not a malicious purpose to injure some person who is thus brought under a new and disadvantageous competition.

Would it be useful to try to weigh each motive? What would happen in *Beardsley* if the court concluded that the defendants were mainly eager to destroy the plaintiff but also that they thought it might be fun to run a newspaper and that the city would benefit from their doing so?

Compare section 870 of the Restatement (Second) of Torts (1977):

One who intentionally causes injury to another is subject to liability to the other for that injury, if his conduct is generally culpable and not justifiable under the circumstances. This liability may be imposed although the actor's conduct does not come within a traditional category of tort liability.

Does section 870 appear to require "disinterested malevolence"? Should it?

Even courts that might otherwise impose tort liability for disinterested malevolence may find it not possible because of overriding concerns. Those who claim that they have been harmed by perjured testimony given in judicial proceedings have tried to recover their damages from the alleged perjurer. These have failed virtually everywhere. See Niedert v. Rieger, 200 F.3d 522 (7th Cir.1999), holding that under Wisconsin law a witness at a hearing who lies under oath and damages plaintiff cannot be held liable. See also Cooper v. Parker–Hughey, 894 P.2d 1096 (Okla.1995)(following general rule that grants witnesses absolute immunity from civil liability and recognizing that Maine, by statute, is the only state contra). What is the policy behind protecting alleged perjurers?

D. CONTRACT AND TORT IN THE ECONOMIC SPHERE

We have considered the interrelationship between contract and tort at several points in the course. Some, as in the section on the economic loss, p. 301, supra, and the discussion of economic loss caused by defective products, p. 639, supra, have been explicit. Others, as when we considered medical malpractice, have been implicit. We take a last look at the relationship between the two in the important context of economic harms.

All–Tech Telecom, Inc. v. Amway Corporation

United States Court of Appeals, Seventh Circuit, 1999.
174 F.3d 862.

Before POSNER, CHIEF JUDGE, and BAUER and MANION, CIRCUIT JUDGES.

POSNER, CIRCUIT JUDGE.

A disappointed plaintiff, All–Tech Telecom, appeals from the district court's grant of summary judgment to the defendant, Amway, on All–

Tech's claims of intentional and negligent misrepresentation and promissory estoppel. All–Tech was allowed to get to the jury on claims of breach of warranty, and the jury found a breach but awarded no damages. There is no challenge to the jury's verdict, only to the grant of summary judgment on the other claims. The basis of federal jurisdiction is diversity of citizenship, and the parties agree that the substantive issues are governed by Wisconsin law.

In 1987, Amway had offered distributors a new product (really a product plus a service), the "TeleCharge" phone. The phone was intended for the use of customers of hotels and restaurants. The customer would use a credit card or telephone calling card to pay for a long-distance call. The hotel or restaurant, along with the distributor, Amway, and the long-distance phone companies involved in the calls, would divide the line charges. Beginning in 1988, All–Tech, which was created for the very purpose of being an Amway distributor of TeleCharge phones and the associated telephone service, bought a large number of the phones. For a variety of reasons beyond All–Tech's control, including equipment problems, regulatory impediments to the provision of the TeleCharge program, and finally the obsolescence of the phones, which caused Amway to withdraw the product from the market in 1992, TeleCharge was a flop. All–Tech claims to have been lured into and kept in this losing venture by a series of misrepresentations, such as that Amway had done extensive research before offering the service, that the service would be the "best" in the nation, that any business telephone line could be used with the Tele–Charge phone, that the service had been approved in all 50 states and did not require the approval of any telephone company, that each phone could be expected to generate an annual revenue for the distributor of $750, that the carrier retained by Amway to handle the calls and billings for the TeleCharge phones (International Tele–Charge, Inc. (ITI)) was the largest company of its kind in the nation, and that the purchaser of a TeleCharge phone would have to deal with ITI—the phone could not be reprogrammed to work with any other carrier.

The district court threw out All–Tech's claims of misrepresentation on the basis of the "economic loss" doctrine of the common law. Originally this doctrine was merely a limitation on who could bring a tort suit for the consequences of a personal injury or damage to property: only the injured person himself, or the owner of the damaged property himself, and not also persons having commercial links to the owner, such as employees or suppliers of a merchant whose store was burned down as a result of the negligence of a third party, the tort defendant. [ ] Since damage to property and even to person is a real cost and hence "economic," the doctrine would be better named the "commercial loss" doctrine. [ ]

One explanation for it is that a tort may have indirect consequences that are beneficial—in the example just given, to competitors of the burned-down store—as well as harmful, and since the tortfeasor is not entitled to sue for the benefits, neither should he have to pay for the losses. [ ] Another and less esoteric explanation is the desirability of confining remedies for contract-type losses to contract law. Suppliers injured in their pocketbook because of a fire at the shop of a retailer who buys and distributes their goods sustain the kind of purely business loss familiarly encountered in contract law, rather than the physical harm, whether to person or to property, with which tort law is centrally concerned. These suppliers can protect themselves from the loss caused them by the fire by buying business-loss insurance, by charging a higher price, or by including in their contract with the retailer a requirement that he buy a minimum quantity of goods from the supplier, regardless. The suppliers thus don't need a tort remedy. [ ]

This point has implications for commercial fraud as well as for business losses that are secondary to physical harms to person or property. Where there are well-developed contractual remedies, such as the remedies that the Uniform Commercial Code (in force in all U.S. states) provides for breach of warranty of the quality, fitness, or specifications of goods, there is no need to provide tort remedies for misrepresentation. The tort remedies would duplicate the contract remedies, adding unnecessary complexity to the law. Worse, the provision of these duplicative tort remedies would undermine contract law. That law has been shaped by a tension between a policy of making the jury the normal body for resolving factual disputes and the desire of parties to contracts to be able to rely on the written word and not be exposed to the unpredictable reactions of lay factfinders to witnesses who testify that the contract means something different from what it says. Many doctrines of contract law, such as the parol evidence and "four corners" rules, are designed to limit the scope of jury trial of contract disputes (another example is the statute of frauds). Tort law does not have these screens against the vagaries of the jury. In recognition of this omission, the "economic loss" doctrine in the form invoked by the district judge in this case on the authority of a growing body of case law illustrated by [ ], forbids commercial contracting parties (as distinct from consumers, and other individuals not engaged in business) to escalate their contract dispute into a charge of tortious misrepresentation if they could easily have protected themselves from the misrepresentation of which they now complain. The principle is well illustrated by Tatge v. Chambers & Owen, Inc., [579 N.W.2d 217 (Wis.1998)], a suit by a former employee claiming that the employer had misrepresented the employment contract to be terminable only for cause, rather than at will. The bearing of those representations could be fully considered in a suit for breach of contract.

The function of the economic-loss doctrine in confining contract parties to their contractual remedies is particularly well illustrated by cases involving product warranties, [ ]. If the seller makes an oral representation that is important to the buyer, the latter has only to insist that the seller embody that representation in a written warranty. The warranty will protect the buyer, who will have an adequate remedy under the Uniform Commercial Code if the seller reneges. To allow him to use tort law in effect to enforce an oral warranty would unsettle contracts by exposing sellers to the risk of being held liable by a jury on the basis of self-interested oral testimony and perhaps made to pay punitive as well as compensatory damages. This menace is averted by channeling disputes into warranty (contract) law, where oral warranties can be expressly disclaimed, or extinguished by operation of the parol evidence rule. UCC §§ 2–202, 2–316(1) and comment 2; 1 James J. White & Robert S. Summers, Uniform Commercial Code, § 12–4 (3d ed. 1988). It is true that, in principle, the cheapest way to prevent fraud is to punish the fraudfeasor; but in practice, owing to the ever-present possibility of legal error, the really cheapest way in some cases may be to place a burden of taking precautions on the potential victim. Cf. Alon Harel, "Efficiency and Fairness in Criminal Law: The Case for a Criminal Law Principle of Comparative Fault," 82 Calif. L. Rev. 1181 (1994).

Some of our cases describe the economic-loss doctrine in words that might seem to imply the abolition of the tort of misrepresentation (including deliberate fraud) in all cases in which the plaintiff and the defendant are business firms having a preexisting contractual relationship that had given rise to the fraud or other misrepresentation. [   ] But it is a disservice to courts, as well as a common source of erroneous predictions concerning the scope and direction of the law, to treat a judicial opinion as if it were a statute, every clause of which was Law. It is difficult to write a judicial opinion without making some general statements by way of background and explanation. But in a system of case law such statements can be misleading if carelessly lifted from the case-specific contexts in which they were originally uttered. That is why courts in assessing the binding effect of previous decisions distinguish between the dicta, which are the inessential parts of the opinion, and the holding.

If commercial fraud is to go completely by the boards, as a literal reading of some of the economic-loss cases might suggest, then prospective parties to contracts will be able to obtain legal protection against fraud only by insisting that the other party to the contract reduce all representations to writing, and so there will be additional contractual negotiations, contracts will be longer, and, in short, transaction costs will be higher. And the additional costs will be incurred in the making of every commercial contract, not just the tiny fraction that end up in litigation. Granted, there are costs of uncertainty from the possibility of falsely charging fraud when a contractual relationship sours, as it did in this case. But the fraud tort comes with safeguards against false claims, such as the requirement of pleading fraud with particularity and (in many though not all jurisdictions) a heightened burden of proof—clear and convincing evidence versus a bare preponderance of the evidence, the standard civil burden. [   ]

But the representations challenged in this case do not press against the boundaries of the economic-loss doctrine. For they are in the nature of warranties (remember that the plaintiff made warranty claims, which the judge sent to the jury), and we cannot think of a reason why the fact that the "product" warranted was a hybrid of a product and a service should affect the application of the doctrine. A genuine stumbling block to affirming on its basis, however, is the fact that its application to cases of intentional misrepresentation [in Wisconsin] is uncertain. . . . We need not choose. Amway has a solid alternative ground for affirmance: All–Tech failed to present any evidence of actionable misrepresentation. Some of the alleged misrepresentations were corrected before All–Tech bought its first TeleCharge phone, such as the misrepresentations that the phone could be installed on any business line and that regulatory approval of the service had been obtained in all 50 states. The victim of a misrepresentation about a product who learns the truth before he buys, but decides to buy the product anyway, cannot complain about the misrepresentation. [ ] Whatever he has relied on, it is not that.

Some of the representations were made not by Amway but by one of its distributors, at a trade meeting attended by All–Tech's principals. Amway distributors are independent contractors, [ ], rather than employees whose representations might bind their employer by force of the doctrine of respondeat superior. The distributor in question was describing his own experience in selling TeleCharge phones, and there is no evidence that he was speaking with Amway's actual or apparent authority or that Amway ratified and by ratifying adopted his remarks. In these circumstances, Amway was not legally responsible for them. [ ] An agent "cannot just bootstrap himself into a position where he can bind his principal." [ ] It would be absurd to hold a supplier to every representation made by distributors or dealers in its products—distributors or dealers who in the case of some suppliers, such as Amway, number in the thousands.

Many of Amway's alleged misrepresentations were either pure puffing (such as TeleCharge is "the best")—which is to say, empty superlatives on which no reasonable person would rely, [ ]—or meaningless sales patter, such as that Amway had put the same effort into developing this product as it did with its other products. Amway sells a vast array of products, and obviously doesn't expend the same absolute or proportional amount of money on the development of each one; no one could believe such a thing, as pointed out in [ ]. "There are some kinds of talk which no sensible man takes seriously, and if he does he suffers from his credulity." Vulcan Metals Co. v. Simmons Mfg. Co., 248 F. 853, 856 (2d Cir.1918) (L. Hand, J.). All–Tech doesn't claim to be run by the sort of naifs who got suckered into raising Chinchillas in the 1950s.

The TeleCharge service was new, and like many new services it ran into unexpected, and ultimately fatal, problems. As these problems surfaced, Amway would notify its distributors, including All–Tech. Despite a barrage of bad news, All–Tech continued buying TeleCharge phones. It could not have been relying on the alleged misrepresentations. All of them had either been corrected before All–Tech bought the phones or would not have misled a commercial purchaser. Or were not material, such as ITI's size—whether or not it was the largest company of its kind, the kind the parties call "alternative operator service," it was not a fly-by-night outfit incapable of providing the service for which Amway had contracted with it. Or were hypothetical: "If you charge the one dollar maximum access fee, with an average of only three billable long-distance calls a day, five days per week, 50 weeks per year, you may generate up to $750 a year from just one phone"—impeccable arithmetic, given the premises, which Amway did not warrant. Or were predictions that either were too vague to ground reasonable reliance or were not falsified. Or were not made at all, such as the representation that the phone could not be reprogrammed to work with another operator service besides ITI. There were, in short, no actionable misrepresentations.

All–Tech's alternative claim is promissory estoppel. The doctrine of promissory estoppel provides an alternative basis to consideration for treating a promise as a contractual undertaking. When applicable, which to say when the promise is definite enough to induce a reasonable person to rely, [   ], the doctrine makes the promise enforceable.

Promises are usually forward-looking; one promises to do something, necessarily in the future. The promise that All–Tech stresses as the basis for its claim of promissory estoppel—that Amway had thoroughly researched the TeleCharge program before offering it to distributors—is not of that character. It warrants a past or existing condition rather than committing to some future action and is thus more precisely described as a warranty than as a promise. [   ] But a warranty is a type of promise—in this case a promise by Amway to pay for the consequences should the research that went into the development of TeleCharge not have been thorough after all. Metropolitan Coal Co. v. Howard, 155 F.2d 780, 784 (2d Cir.1946) (L. Hand, J.) (a warranty "amounts to a promise to indemnify the promisee for any loss if the fact warranted proves untrue, for obviously the promisor cannot control what is already in the past"); [   ].

Since a warranty can induce reasonable reliance, its breach can be the basis for a claim of promissory estoppel. [   ] But only in limited circumstances. A promisee cannot be permitted to use the doctrine to do an end run around the rule that puffing is not actionable as misrepresentation or around the parol evidence rule. [   ] That rule is as applicable to a suit on an oral warranty as to a suit on any other oral promise. The Uniform Commercial Code is explicit about this. UCC § 2–316(1) and comment 2; [   ].

The objections to All–Tech's claim of promissory estoppel are related to our earlier point that the economic-loss doctrine serves to protect contract doctrines and to prevent the piling on of duplicative remedies. Promissory estoppel is meant for cases in which a promise, not being supported by consideration, would be unenforceable under conventional principles of contract law. When there is an express contract governing the relationship out of which the promise emerged, and no issue of consideration, there is no gap in the remedial system for promissory estoppel to fill. [   ] To allow it to be invoked becomes in those circumstances gratuitous duplication or, worse, circumvention of carefully designed rules of contract law. In our case the parties had a contract covering the relationship in the course and within the scope of which the alleged warranty of thorough research was made. This either was one of the warranties of the contract or it was not (by virtue of disclaimer, the puffing exemption, or the parol evidence rule). If it was not (and it was not), we cannot think of any reason for using the doctrine of promissory estoppel to resuscitate it. "Promissory estoppel is not a doctrine designed to give a party . . . a second bite at the apple in the event it fails to prove a breach of contract." [   ]

Affirmed.

Notes and Questions

1.   Does the distinction between "economic loss" and "commercial loss" help clarify the nature of the underlying "doctrine?" Recall the discussion of the *Rardin* case, p. 649, supra. Which of the justifications for the doctrine presented here seem the strongest?

2.   Should the doctrine apply as well to cases of "commercial fraud" as to the area of secondary harms? Recall *Channel Master*, p. 1216, supra.

3.   At one point the opinion suggests that contract law has many more "screens" than tort law. Do you agree? Later, the opinion observes that the tort law surrounding "fraud" claims has more screens than other tort claims. Is that sound?

4.   Is the limitation of the court's discussion to cases involving "commercial contracting parties (as distinct from consumers, and other individuals not engaged in business)" an important limitation? The extent of the uncertainty in privity situations is seen in such cases as Douglas–Hanson Co. v. BF Goodrich Co., 607 N.W.2d 621 (Wis.2000), in which the appellate court upheld an award of compensatory and punitive damages. It concluded that the economic loss doctrine does not bar a claim for tort damages "when an intentional misrepresentation fraudulently induces a plaintiff to enter a contract." On further appeal, the supreme court affirmed by an equally divided court.

5.   Are cases like *Delta Airlines*, p. 646, supra, involving claims for damage to planes explained by the approach in *All–Tech?*

6.   The court expresses concern about the role of "legal error" in adjudication. How does that apply in this case? Might that type of concern explain some cases of misrepresentation, such as those concerning the entry onto premises by false pretenses in *Dietemann*, p. 1172, supra?

7.   How are the distinctions between promises and warranties relevant to the discussion? Is the distinction between statements of past or existing conditions and those relating to future conditions important?

8.   Toward the end of the opinion the court suggests that a dispute over whether a contract was at will or for a term can be resolved in an action for breach of contract. There are still, however, several contract areas in which tort claims are at least plausible.

a.   The commercial contract. The leading case on the tort of bad faith breach was Seaman's Direct Buying Service, Inc. v. Standard Oil Co., 686 P.2d 1158 (Cal.1984). The court suggested that the tort action be available when the contractual relationship in question was analogous to that between insurer and insured—and the defendant in bad faith denied that the contract existed. After a period of confusion and criticism, the court overruled *Seaman's* but announced that "nothing in this opinion should be read as affecting the existing precedent governing enforcement of the implied covenant in insurance cases." See Freeman & Mills, Inc. v. Belcher Oil Co., 900 P.2d 669 (Cal.1995)("[I]t seems anomalous to characterize as 'tortious' the bad faith denial of the existence of a contract, while treating as 'contractual' the bad faith denial of liability or responsibility under an acknowledged contract"). See also *Erlich v. Menezes*, p. 296, supra, rejecting an emotional distress claim over a poorly built home, in which the court observed that it would generally enforce contract breaches exclusively through contract law unless the breach violated a social policy that merited the imposition of tort remedies.

In K.M.C. Co., Inc. v. Irving Trust Co., 757 F.2d 752 (6th Cir.1985), the court, applying New York law, upheld a magistrate's decision imposing $7.5 million in compensatory damages on the Irving Trust Company for refusing to honor plaintiff's request to draw funds on its line of credit. The court recognized that the contract between the parties did not require the lender to extend the loan in question. Nonetheless, the court held that a lender violates the implied duty of good faith and fair dealing when, in the context of an ongoing business relationship, its refusal to extend a requested loan is objectively unreasonable. Liability for such a refusal is not conditioned upon proof of any actual bad faith. But see Flagship Nat. Bank v. Gray Distribution Systems, Inc., 485 So.2d 1336 (Fla.App.1986), holding that, absent an explicit contractual agreement, a lender is under no duty to supply an existing customer with a line of credit. The state's statutory good faith requirement could not be imposed to override the express terms in a contract. The court, as have others, criticized the *K.M.C.* approach.

b. Refusal to contract. In Schimmel v. Norcal Mut. Ins. Co., 46 Cal.Rptr.2d 401 (App. 1995), the plaintiff physician alleged that when his malpractice policy expired, defendant insurer refused to renew it for reasons, including the ethnicity of his patients, that allegedly violated public policy. The court held that there was no tort duty to renew a fixed term policy whatever the reason or for no reason whatever. The only exception in the state is automobile insurance which, as the result of a ballot initiative, must be renewed. Employment cases were inapposite; even if apposite, there was the crucial difference that the employment cases involved firing employees who were under at-will arrangements—not term contracts.

c. The employment context. A few courts have applied the tort of breach of the implied covenant of good faith and fair dealing in the employment context. At the outset, it is crucial to distinguish the tort of bad faith breach from the tort of wrongful discharge. The latter is an action that an employee may bring if he or she has been dismissed for refusing to participate in an immoral or illegal act or for asserting constitutional or statutory rights, as in Nees v. Hocks, 536 P.2d 512 (Or.1975)(employee fired for refusing to seek exemption from jury duty has action); Tameny v. Atlantic Richfield Co., 610 P.2d 1330 (Cal.1980)(firing an employee who refused to commit illegal price fixing was actionable); Kraus v. New Rochelle Hosp. Med. Center, 628 N.Y.S.2d 360 (App.Div.1995)(recognizing action under statute for retaliatory firing where plaintiff reported on unsafe medical practice of hospital personnel); Shick v. Shirey, 716 A.2d 1231 (Pa.1998) (action for discharge in retaliation for filing workers' compensation claim). Is there a distinction between a discharge and a failure to rehire a former employee who pursued workers' compensation benefits? See Warnek v. ABB Combustion Engineering Services, Inc., 972 P.2d 453 (Wash.1999) (distinguishing the two situations: plaintiffs had "not been 'fired' or 'discharged.' They are merely former employees who were not rehired").

Some states have adopted legislation to protect the jobs of "whistle-blowers" and others. E.g., Fleming v. Correctional Healthcare Solutions, Inc., 751 A.2d 1035 (N.J.2000), protecting an employee under the state's Conscientious Employee Protective Act. Others have become more restrictive about tort remedies in this situation. See, e.g., Green v. Ralee Engineering Co., 960 P.2d 1046 (Cal.1998), in which the court limited *Tameny*, supra, to cases in which the public policy can be discerned from constitutional or legislative provision or from administrative regulation. After finding relevant federal safety regulations, the court allowed a tort action for the retaliatory discharge of an employee who complained about defendant's airplane inspection practices.

In most states, as these cases suggest, the issue is not the reason for the firing but rather whether the action should be recognized at all. Underlying that concern may be the unease created by difficult cases like Gardner v. Loomis Armored Inc., 913 P.2d 377 (Wash.1996). Gardner was the driver of one of defendant's armored cars. One of the company's "fundamental" rules was that the driver must not leave the truck unattended. The rule was so strong that even if a police officer pulled the truck over, the driver was to show a sign saying that he would not exit the vehicle but would follow the officer to a police station. On the day in question, plaintiff's partner left the vehicle to make a scheduled stop at a bank. While alone, plaintiff observed a man with a knife chasing a woman he knew. The plaintiff left the truck, saved the woman, helped apprehend the man—and was fired for violating the company's rule. The court held that, although the rule was defensible and quite important, the discharge violated the state's policy. That policy was based on encouraging citizens to render aid to those facing life-threatening situations. (The policy of encouraging cooperation with law enforcement was not thought sufficient.) Defendant argued that plaintiff could have used his radio or his horn to help. The court responded that the reasons for leaving the truck must be considered—such as a fire. By focusing on "the narrow public policy encouraging citizens to save human lives from life-threatening situations, we continue to protect employers from frivolous lawsuits."

Three concurrers observed that although the rule was normally sensible and reasonable for plaintiff's own safety and that of his partner, it "defies what I believe is true about human nature that anyone would be willing to watch a person die in order to comply with a company safety rule." A dissenter accepted the defendant's argument that its rule "actually serves the interests of society, is consistent with public policy and therefore cannot be the basis of a claim for wrongful termination in violation of public policy." He also observed that the rule will now be drawn into question in all future cases: what if the driver leaves the truck in the reasonable, but mistaken, belief that another is in mortal danger or if there is a danger but it is not life-threatening. What if the belief is honest but not reasonable? Do the dissenter's concerns suggest doubt about the majority's analysis?

INDEX

References are to Pages

ACCOUNTANTS
Liability of, 302

ACTUAL CAUSE
See Cause in Fact

"ACTUAL MALICE"
Defamation, 929, 943

ADMIRALTY LAW
See Maritime Injuries

AIRPLANES
Ground damage, liability for, 518
No fault, 851
Passengers, liability to, 64

ALIENATION OF AFFECTIONS
Described, 899

ALTERNATIVES TO TORT
See, also, Automobiles, Compensation Plans,
    New Zealand, Workers' Compensation
    Generally, 785
Auto no-fault, 816
Comprehensive no fault, 858
Medical malpractice no-fault, 853
Social insurance, 861
Toxic compensation plans, 842
Vaccinations, 844, 849
Workers' compensation, 793

AMERICAN LAW INSTITUTE
Excerpts,
    On role of tort system, 1
    On specific no-fault plans, 848
    On workers' compensation, 629, 806

ARREST
Malicious prosecution compared, 886
Shoplifting, 886

ASSAULT
Defined, 872

ASSUMPTION OF RISK
Comparative negligence, relation to, 476
Duty, relation to, 469
Employment context, 37, 483
Express, 460
Firefighter's rule, 484
Negligence, relation to, 469

ASSUMPTION OF RISK—Cont'd
Implied, 469
Sports participants,
    Express assumption, 461
    Implied assumption, 472
    Spectators, 475
Strict liability, 519

ATTORNEYS
Duties to third persons, 310
Fees, 15, 697
Standard of care, 308

AUTOMOBILES
Drunk driving, 182, 185, 718
Financial responsibility laws, 762
Key in ignition, 82, 183
Liability insurance, 761
Licensing statute, violation of, 83
No-fault legislation,
    Constitutionality, 828
    Federal legislation, 841
    History, 816
    Motorcycles, 833
    Pain and suffering, 838
    Property damage, 840
    "Pure" no-fault, 840
    "Serious injury," 834
    Tort system, meshed with, 837
    Uninsured motorist coverage, meshed
        with, 837
    Workers' compensation, meshed with, 837
Plans,
    Blum & Kalven, 818
    Columbia, 817
    Ehrenzweig, 817
    Keeton & O'Connell, 818
Res ipsa loquitur, 91
Rockefeller report, 819
Statutes,
    Massachusetts, 818
    New York, 821
    Saskatchewan, 817
Underinsured motorist coverage, 764
Uninsured motorist coverage, 764, 837
Use or operation of vehicle, 831
Vicarious liability, 762
Workers' compensation analogy, 816

AVOIDABLE CONSEQUENCES
Comparative negligence and, 457
Defective products and, 611
Seat belts, 458

BATTERY
Defined, 865

BIRTH DEFECTS
See Family Relationships, Wrongful Birth, Wrongful Life

BRANDEIS, LOUIS
Excerpt on privacy, 1098

BREACH OF CONFIDENCE
Relation to privacy, 1131

BREACH OF WARRANTY
See Contracts, Products Liability, Strict Liability

BRIFFAULT, RICHARD
Excerpt on workers' compensation, 793

CALABRESI, GUIDO
Entitlements and Nuisance, 674
Excerpts on economic theory, 524, 531

CAUSATION
See Cause in Fact; Proximate Cause

CAUSE IN FACT
Generally, 341
Burden of proof, 342
Enhanced risk, 346
Expert testimony, 355
Intentional harm, 868
Joint & several liability, 368
Lost opportunity, 359
Market share liability, 378
Multiple defendants, 374
Products liability cases, 556
Proximate cause contrasted, 399
Statistics, use of, 342
Toxic harm, 391
Violation of statute, 359

CIVIL RIGHTS ACTIONS
Bivens action, 945
Federal officials, liability of, 249
Immunity, 934
Section 1983 actions, 929
State officials, liability of, 929
Title VII actions, race, 894
Title VII actions, sex, 895
Title IX actions, 897
Violence Against Women Act, 897

COASE, RONALD
Economic theorem described, 531
Excerpt on nuisance, 676

COLLATERAL SOURCES
Rule described, 710, 747

COMPARATIVE NEGLIGENCE
See, also, Contributory Negligence

COMPARATIVE NEGLIGENCE—Cont'd
Generally, 435
Assumption of risk, role of, 476
Avoidable, consequences, 457
Causation, relation to, 444
Conduct to be compared, 444
Contribution and indemnity, 373
Contributory negligence compared, 439
Imputed negligence and, 438, 448
Insolvency and, 447
Joint and several liability, 446
Judgments, set-off, 447
Jury instructions, 450
Last clear chance, 437, 451
Modified version, 440, 444
Multiple defendants, 446
Punitive damages, effect on, 724
Pure version, 440, 444
Recklessness, role of, 445
Res ipsa and, 451
Rescue and, 451
Settlements and, 447
Seat belts, 458
Strict liability, role in, 520, 605
Uniform Comparative Fault Act, 441

COMPENSATION PLANS
See, also, Automobiles, Workers' Compensation
Automobile accidents, 816
Black lung disease, 850
Constitutional questions, 792
International airlines, 851
Malpractice, 853
New York automobile statute, 821
New Zealand, 858
Nuclear accidents, 842
Social insurance approach, 861
Smoking, 850
Toxics, 842
Vaccine-related injuries, 844, 849
Victims of violent crime, 872
Workers, 793

COMPETITION
False statements, 1256
Imitation, 1257
Misappropriation, 1257

CONARD, ALFRED
Excerpt on reparation systems, 820
Excerpt on subrogation, 752

CONSENT
Defamation, role in, 974
Duty to disclose, 122
Informed, 122
Intentional torts, 911

CONSORTIUM, LOSS OF
See Family Relationships

CONSTITUTIONAL LAW
Compensation plans and, 792
Defamation and falsity, 1040
Defamation and free speech, 1000

CONSTITUTIONAL LAW—Cont'd
Legislators' privilege, 976
Neutral reportage, 1081
No-fault insurance, 828
Privacy, application to, 1114, 1141
Punitive damages, 726
Publicity, right of, 1187, 1194
Workers' compensation, 805

CONSTITUTIONAL TORTS
Bivens actions, 942

CONTINGENT FEES
In general, 15, 697

CONTRACTS
See also Economic Harm
Agreements not to sue, 460
Breach of warranty, 545, 639
Disclaimers, 643, 646
Inducement to breach as tort, 1240
Intentional interference with, 1240
Negligent interference with, 282
Privileges to interfere, 1246
Relationship to tort law, generally, 301, 649, 1263
Releases, 460

CONTRIBUTION
Defined, 373
Settling and, 447

CONTRIBUTORY NEGLIGENCE
See, also, Defenses
Avoidable consequences distinguished, 457
Comparative negligence compared, 439
Defense,
 Negligence, 435
 Recklessness, 437
 Statutory violation, 436
 Strict liability cases, 520, 605
Imputation of, 438
Judge and jury, 439
Last clear chance, 437
Rescuers, application to, 436

CONVERSION
Explained, 1160

CRIMES
See, Intentional Harm, Land Occupiers

CRIMINAL CONVERSATION
Described, 899

CUSTOM
Generally, 67
Medical malpractice, role in, 109

DAMAGES
See, also, Compensation Plans
Attorney's fees, relation to, 15, 697
Avoidable consequences, 457
Collateral sources, 710, 747
Compensatory, 679
Defamation, 967, 995, 1024
Discounting to present value, 689

DAMAGES—Cont'd
Future earnings, 687
Inflation, effect of, 687
Introduction to, 14
Loss of consortium, 697
Negligence, generally, 679
Pain and suffering, 680, 690, 697
Pecuniary losses,
 Future, 687
 In general, 680
 Past, 687
Proportional recovery, 346
Punitive,
 Comparative negligence, 724
 Constitutionality, 726
 Defamation, 967, 973, 1092
 Defective products, 726
 Drunk driving, 718
 In general, 717
 Insurability, 740, 744
 Mass-victim cases, 726, 737
 Statutory change, 738
Seat belt, failure to use, 458
Size of awards, 695
Wrongful birth, 326
Wrongful death, 707
Wrongful life, 326

DEFAMATION
"Actual malice," 1000, 1015
Broadcasters, 1091
Colloquium, 963
Commentary, press, 1061
Constitutional aspects, 1000
Context of words, 954
Convincing clarity, 1000, 1022
Corporation as plaintiff, 964, 1061
Criminal charges, 968
Damages,
 Actual injury, 1025, 1042
 General, 967
 Nominal, 973
 Punitive, 967, 973, 1092
 Special, 967
Declaratory judgment, 1096
Defamatory meaning, 949
Defenses,
 See, also, Privilege, infra
 Fair and accurate report, 985
 Fair comment, 983
 Opinion rejected, 1062
 Retraction, 995
 Truth, 974
English and American attitudes, 948
Experts, role of, 1041
Group libel, 964
Identification, 963
Inducement, 954
Innocent construction rule, 955
Innuendo, 955
Insults compared, 957, 1074
Judge & jury, 955
Jurisdiction, 1000
Libel and slander distinguished, 967

DEFAMATION—Cont'd
Libel by implication, 958, 1020
"Libel-proof" plaintiffs, 998
Media v. non-media defendants, 1079
Negligence, role of, 1025, 1038
Neutral reportage, 1081
New York Times rule, 1000
"Of and concerning," 963
Opinion-fact distinction, rejected, 1063
Private plaintiff, 1024, 1048
Privilege,
    Absolute, 976
    Abuse of, 982
    Common interest, 978
    Conditional privilege, 977
    Constitutional, 1000
    Credit reports, 981
    Employers, 980
    Fair and accurate report, 985
    Fair comment, 983
    Governmental proceedings, report of, 985
    Judicial officer, 976
    Legislators, 976
    Losing fair report privilege, 9993
    Protecting one's interest, 1049
    Protecting public interest, 982
Proof,
    Actual malice, 1015
    Burden of, 1041
    Falsity, 1041
"Public Concern," 1076
Public figures,
    All-purpose, 1059
    Candidates for office, 1044
    Corporations, 1061
    In general, 1013
    Involuntary, 1049, 1059
    Limited purpose, 1060
Public officials,
    Candidates, 1044
    Criticism of, 1000
    Identification of, 1046
    In general, 1000
    Police officers, 1046
    Teachers, 1047
    "Three-legged stool," 1045
Public-private distinction, 1000, 1024, 1043
Publication requirement, 952
Quotations, falsification of, 1018
Record libel, 985
Reform proposals, 1091
Repeaters, 985, 1081
Reputation, nature of, 949
Retraction, 995
Single publication rule, 999
Slander per se, 967
Strict liability, 966
Summary judgment standard, 1023
Truth, 974

DEFECT
See Products Liability

DEFENSES
Agreements not to sue, 460
Assumption of risk, 460
Comparative negligence, 440
Consent, 122, 911
Contributory negligence, 435
Government contractors, 554
Intentional harm generally, 910
Private Necessity, 922
Protection of property, 917, 921
Self-defense, 914
Products liability, 605
Public Necessity, 927
Strict liability, 519

DERIVATIVE ACTIONS
See Family Relationships

DETERRENCE
As goal of tort law, 7, 526, 535

DISCLAIMERS
Assumption of risk, 460
Validity in products cases, 643, 645

DUTY
    See, also, Duty to Act, Duty to Warn,
      Emotional Harm, Land Occupiers,
      Products Liability, Proximate Cause
Accountants, 302
Affirmative, 131
Assumption of risk, relation to, 469
Attorneys, 308
Bartenders, 185
Broadcasters, 190
Contractual relationships limiting duty, 143,
    144
Controlling conduct of others, 158
Crime, prevention of, 158, 205, 226
Custodial relationships, 214, 233
Criminal statutes as creating, 136, 155
Doctors, 158, 312, 325
Economic harm, 301
Emotional distress, negligently inflicted, 261
Governmental entities,
    Federal, 249
    In general, 225
    Military, 259
    Municipal, 226, 232
    Police, 226, 232
    State, 244
Hospitals, 158
Insurer to insured, 709
Introduction to, 130
Land occupiers generally, 190
Landlords, 144, 204, 205
Lenders, 179
Loss of consortium, 297
Manufacturers, 540, 546, 556, 558, 581
Misfeasance and nonfeasance, 131
Municipalities, 226
Non-delegable, 18
Non-physical harm, 261
Physical harm, 130
Police officers, 226, 232

DUTY—Cont'd
Rescuers, 137, 141, 155
Retailers, 206
Road maintenance, 244
Schools, 233
Social hosts, 185
Statutes, relation to, 136, 151, 155
Suppliers of products, 540

DUTY TO ACT
Nonfeasance and misfeasance, 131
Physicians, 164
Required rescue, 155
Voluntary undertaking, 137

ECONOMIC ANALYSIS
Cheapest cost avoiders, 535
Efficient level of accidents, 7, 45
In general, 520
Risk spreading, 6
Subsidizing industrial development, 37

ECONOMIC HARM
Accountants, 302
Attorneys, 308
Deceit, 1218
False statements, 1216, 1256
Foreseeability standard, 313
Imitation of product, 1257
Intentional infliction, 1218, 1246
Interference with contract,
    Negligent, 313
    Intentional, 1240
Intellectual property, 1257
Misrepresentation, 1216
Negligent infliction, 301
Physicians, 325
Privity of contract, 301
Prospective economic advantage, loss of, 313,
    1246
Relationship between contract and tort, 1263
Strict liability, and, 1239

EDUCATION
Failure to educate, 234
Inadequate testing, 236
Negligent supervision, 233

EMOTIONAL HARM
    See, also, Family Relationships, Intention-
    al Harm
Before death, 268
Bystanders, 282
Caused by harm to property, 282
Contemporaneous observation requirement,
    282
Debt collection, 820, 828
Dillon test, 282, 287
Illness, risk of, 347
Impact rule, 261
Intentional infliction,
    Alienation of affection, 899
    Credit practices, 888, 898
    Custodial relationships, interference with,
    900

EMOTIONAL HARM—Cont'd
Intentional infliction—Cont'd
    Criminal conversation, 899
    In general, 888
    Media, by, 905
    Physical injury requirement, 889
    Racial harassment, 894
    Sexual harassment, 895
Loss of consortium, 297
Negligent infliction, 261
Physical injury requirement 278, 889
Presence at scene of injury to another, 282
Racial harassment, 894
Reasonable foreseeability test, 287
Relationship requirement, 282
Risk of future illness, 347
Unmarried couples, 289, 299
Workers' compensation, 814
Zone of danger rule, 261, 282

ENTERPRISE LIABILITY
Discussed, 387, 520
Market share liability, 378

ENVIRONMENTAL HARM
Cause in fact, 347, 391
No-fault and, 845
Nuisance, as, 658
Pollution, 653, 663
Strict liability and, 498, 511, 520, 525
Toxic releases, 845
Trespass, as, 652

EPSTEIN, RICHARD A.
Excerpts,
    On duty to act, 134
    On strict liability theory, 534

FALSE IMPRISONMENT
Elements, 814

FAMILY RELATIONSHIPS
Alienation of affections, 899
Duties within, 214
Loss of consortium, 297
Negligent interference, 282
Parental liability, 56, 870
Wrongful birth, 326
Wrongful death, 282
Wrongful life, 326

FEDERAL CIVIL RIGHTS ACTION
Against federal officials, 944
Against state officials, 928

**FEDERAL EMPLOYERS' LIABILITY
    ACT**
Discussed, 814

FEDERAL TORT CLAIMS ACT
    Generally, 249
Exemptions, 249, 944
Strict liability, 519
Text, 249

FELLOW SERVANT DOCTRINE
See Vicarious Liability

FIREFIGHTER'S RULE
Discussed, 484

FLEMING, JOHN
Excerpt on liability theory, 755

FLETCHER, GEORGE
Excerpt on liability theory, 533

FRAUD
See Misrepresentation

FRIEDMAN, LAWRENCE
Excerpt on industrial revolution, 29

GOVERNMENTAL ENTITIES
See Duty; Federal Civil Rights Actions; Federal Employers' Liability Act; Federal Tort Claims Act

GREGORY, CHARLES
Excerpt on negligence history, 37

HARPER, JAMES & GRAY ON TORTS
Excerpts on reasonable person, 50

HOLMES, OLIVER WENDELL
Excerpts,
    On critique of strict liability, 6
    On nature of responsibility, 51
    On negligence per se, 59

IMMUNITIES
Charitable, 226
Family units, 214
Governmental units, 225

IMPUTED NEGLIGENCE
    See, also, Vicarious Liability
Comparative, 448
Contributory, 438

INDEMNITY
    See, also, Insurance
Generally, 739
Servant, liability of, 17

INJUNCTION
Nuisance, 663
Privacy, 1131

INSURANCE
    See, also, Automobiles, No–Fault Legislation
Generally, 739
Automobile plans, 816
Automobile policy terms, 739
Collateral source Rule, 710, 747
Compulsory, 763
Exclusion from coverage, 740
Financial responsibility laws, 763
Homeowners' coverage, 740, 767
"Insurable interest," 744
Insurer's liability to insured, 774
Intentional torts, 870
Liability,
    Compulsory, 763
    Duty to defend, 767

INSURANCE—Cont'd
Liability—Cont'd
    Effect on liability rules, 757, 767
    Excess coverage, 781
    In general, 761
    Overlapping coverage, 782
    Refusal to settle, 774
    Settlement, 771
Litigation, effect on, 767
Loss,
    Collateral sources, 747
    Effect on liability, 767
    In general, 747
    Subrogation, 747
"Moral hazard," 744
Multiple policies, 782
Property, 740, 757, 767
Punitive damages, 744
Settlement, 771
Social, 858
Subrogation, 747
Underinsured motorist coverage, 764
Uninsured motorist coverage, 764
Workers' compensation, 793

INTENTIONAL HARM
    See, also, Economic Harm, Emotional Harm
Alien Tort Claims Act, 879
Arrest, 882
Assault, 872
Bankruptcy, effect of, 864
Battery, 868, 872
Cause in fact, 868
Children, liability for, 56, 179, 865
Civil rights actions, 928
Constitutional torts, 944
Contract, interference with, 1240
Credit practices, 898
Defenses and privileges
    Consent, 911
    Constitutional defense, 905
    Private necessity, 922
    Protection of property, 917
    Public necessity, 927
    Self-defense, 914
Duty to disclose, 1223
Economic harm, 1216
Emotional distress, 888
False imprisonment, 882
Government liability, 928
Hate speech, 894
Insurance, 870
Intent, 865
Malicious prosecution, 886
Misrepresentation, 1216
Nuisance, 661
Privileges, see Defenses and privileges, supra
Prospective economic advantage, 1246
Proximate cause, 869
Punitive damages, 869
Racial harassment, 894
Restatement analysis, 864
Riot damage, liability for, 872

INTENTIONAL HARM—Cont'd
Robbery, 206, 212
Sexual harassment, 895
Shoplifting, 886
Trespass, 652
Victim compensation statutes, 872

INVITEE
Explained, 190

JAFFE, LOUIS
Excerpt on pain and suffering, 690

JOINT AND SEVERAL LIABILITY
Cause in fact, 368
Comparative negligence and, 446
Statutory changes, 369

JONES ACT
Discussed, 815

JURY
Role of,
    Negligence cases, 58
    Tort cases generally, 11

KING, JOSEPH H., Jr.
Excerpt on strict liability, 525

KRAMER, ORIN
Excerpt on workers' compensation, 726

LAND OCCUPIERS
    See, also, Trespass
Ice and snow, 197
Invitees, 190
Landlord and tenant, 204
    Protection against violence, 205
Licensees, 190
Open dangers, 195
Recreational land, 197
Store proprietors during robberies, 205
Trespassers, 194
Trespassing children, 196
Violence, protection against, 205, 206

LAST CLEAR CHANCE
Contributory fault and, 437
Explained, 437

LIBEL
See Defamation

LICENSEE
Explained, 190

LLEWELLYN, KARL
Excerpt on statute of frauds, 1217

MAINTENANCE AND CURE
For seamen, 753

MALPRACTICE
See Attorneys, Education, Medical Malpractice, Negligence

MARITIME INJURIES
Discussed, 815

MARKETSHARE LIABILITY
See Cause in Fact

MEDICAL MALPRACTICE
Cause in fact, 359
Compensation plans, 791
Consent to treatment, 122
Custom, role of, 109
Duty to warn of risks, 122
Economic harm, 312
Elective surgery, 122
Expert testimony, 109, 117
Legislative developments, 787
Lost opportunity, 359
No-fault, 853
Proposed changes, 853
Res ipsa loquitur, 117
Standard of care, 109
Strict liability, relation to, 632
Unconscious patient, 101

MISAPPROPRIATION
See Competition

MISREPRESENTATION
    Generally, 1216
Accountants' liability, 302
Contributory negligence as defense, 1237
Damages, measure of, 1238
Deceit, 1218
Defenses, 1237
Duty to disclose, 1223
Fact and law compared, 1222
Fact and opinion, 1220
Innocent, 1239
Negligence and fraud distinguished, 1218
Partial disclosure, 1235
Reliance, 1236
Rescission, basis for, 1217, 1239
Scienter, 1218
Statute of frauds, 1217
Strict liability and, 1239

MORRIS ON TORTS
Excerpts on intentional harm, 926

MOTOR VEHICLES
See Automobiles

MUNICIPALITIES
See Duty, Immunities

NEGLIGENCE
    See, also, Assumption of Risk, Comparative Negligence, Contributory Negligence, Duty, Medical Malpractice, Proximate Cause, Res Ipsa Loquitur, Vicarious Liability
Attorneys' fees, 15
Attorneys' standard of care, 308
Cause in fact, 341
Children, standards for, 56
Comparative negligence, 440
Custom, role of, 67
Defective products, 540
Defenses,

NEGLIGENCE—Cont'd
Defenses—Cont'd
  Assumption of risk, 460
  Comparative negligence, 440
  Contributory negligence, 345
Degrees of care, 49, 64
Duty, 130
Economic harm, 301
Emergency doctrine, 58
Emotional harm, 261
Entrustment to others, 179
FELA compared, 814
Historical development, 29
Jury, role of, 58
Learned Hand calculus, 41
Licensing statutes, 83
Medical malpractice, 109
Misrepresentation, 1233
Proof,
  Direct, 85
  Res ipsa loquitur, 91
  Spoliation of evidence, 99
Proximate cause, 399
Reasonable person,
  Children, 56
  Elderly, 54
  In general, 47
  Mental incompetence, 53
  Possessing unusual skill, 56
Risk calculus, 41
Standard of care, generally, 37
Statutes,
  Compliance, effect of, 83
  Purpose, role of, 80
  Validity, effect of, 75
  Violation, effect of, 73

NEW ZEALAND
Accident compensation statute, 858

NO–FAULT LEGISLATION
  See, also, Automobiles, Products Liability,
    Medical Malpractice, New Zealand
Air carriers, 851
Automobiles, 816
Black lung, 850
Focused, generally, 841
Health care and, 853
Nuclear accidents, 842
Social insurance proposals, 858
Toxic releases, 842
Vaccines, 844, 848, 849

NUISANCE
  Generally, 658
Intentional, defined, 661
Land use and, 663
Pollution as, 663, 673
Private, 661
Public, 659
Reasonableness, role of, 661, 669
Remedies, 663, 673
Social costs, 676
Zoning, relation to, 671

OCCUPATIONAL INJURIES
  See Federal Employers' Liability Act,
    Maritime Injuries, Workers' Compen-
    sation

PATENT
See Competition

PHYSICIANS
See Medical Malpractice

POLICE
See Duty
POSNER, RICHARD A.
Excerpts,
  On Hand formula, 43
  On negligence liability, 7
  On strict liability theory, 535

PRIVACY
  Generally, 1098
Appropriation,
  Docudramas, 1214
  In general, 1186
  Publicity, right of, 1187, 1194
Breach of confidence, 1131
Constitutional problems, 1114, 1141, 1167,
  1194
Conversion compared, 1160
False light,
  By association, 1148
  Defamation compared, 1145, 1149
  In general, 1140
  New York Times rule, application of, 1141
  Television interviews, 1147
Injunctions, 1131, 1163
Intrusion,
  Harassment compared, 1163
  In general, 1151
  Photography, 1163, 1167
  Stalking, 1167
  Surveillance, 1151
  Wiretapping, 1173
Pictorial representation, 1187, 1194
Public disclosure of private facts,
  Constitutional aspects, 1114
  Criminal behavior, 1101
  Embarrassment or ridicule, 1101, 1113
  History of, 1098
  Idiosyncracies, 1109
  Newsworthiness, 1101
  Official records, 1114, 1125
  Public interest, 1101
Publicity, right of, compared, 1186
Rejection of action, 1098, 1111
Sexual matters, disclosure of, 1101, 1112
Successful suits, 1130

PRIVILEGE
See Defamation; Intentional Harm

PRIVITY
Breach of warranty, 545
Duty of care, 143, 144, 540
Suppliers of chattels, 540

PROCEDURE
Introduction to, 9

PRODUCTS LIABILITY
See, also, Privity, Strict Liability, Warnings
Alteration of product, 582
Alternative designs, availability of, 555, 567, 572
Bulk suppliers, 625
Burden of proof, 559
Bystanders, liability to, 552
Causation, 556, 572
Consumer expectations, 559, 579
Contractors,
    Government, 554
Crashworthiness, 572
Defect,
    Design, 558
    Labeling, 581
    Manufacturing, 556
Defenses,
    Apportionment, 610
    Comparative fault, 605
    Contributory negligence, 605
    In general, 605
    Preemption, 614
    Statute of limitations, 647
    Warranty defenses, 648
Design defects,
    In general, 558
    Restatement, 555
    Types, 559
Duty,
    Of care, 540
    To warn, 581, 602
Employment setting, 614
Government contractor defense, 554
Intended use, rejected, 554
Learned intermediary, 592
Misuse, 591
Negligence, compared, 546
Preemption by federal regulation, 614
Prescription drugs, 596
Professional services and, 632
Proof, 556
Risk-benefit analysis, applied, 559, 572
Safety instructions, 581
Safety devices, removal, 582
Sale and service, 632
Successor liability, 553
UCC and tort compared,
    Economic harm, 639
    Personal injury, 648
Unavoidably unsafe product, 570
Undiscovered danger, 600
Unexpected danger, 600
Unreasonable danger, defined, 558
Warnings, 581
Warranty compared, 545, 546, 550, 648
Work-related injuries, 614

PROPERTY
Conversion, 1160

PROPERTY—Cont'd
Force to protect, 917
Real,
    Nuisance, 658
    Trespass, 652

PROXIMATE CAUSE
See, also, Negligence, Rescuers
Cause in fact compared, 399
Direct cause, 404
Distance, 430
Economic harm, 433
Fire rule, 430
Foreseeability of harm, 405
Foreseeable plaintiff, 419
Intervening time, 430
Liability and damage, 404
Manner of occurrence, 412
Medical aggravation, 403
Negligence, relation to, 405
Rescue, 428
Suicide, 403
"Thin skull" cases, 399
Victim's sensitivity, 399

PSYCHOTHERAPIST
See Duty to Warn

PUBLIC FIGURES
See Defamation

PUBLIC OFFICIALS
See Defamation

PUNITIVE DAMAGES
See Damages

RABIN, ROBERT L.
Excerpts,
    On risks of employment, 483
    On toxic harm, 391
    On toxics compensation schemes, 842

REASONABLE CARE
See Negligence

RECKLESSNESS
Basis of liability, 437
Comparative fault, effect on, 445
Defamation, 1000
Defenses to, 437, 445
Fraud, 1218
Punitive damages, 718

RELEASES
See Disclaimers

RES IPSA LOQUITUR
Automobiles, 100
Comparative negligence and, 451
Discovery, relation to, 99
Elements, 91, 94
Inference or presumption, 98
Medical malpractice, 101, 117
Multiple defendants, 101
Origin of, 91
Specific evidence and, 98

RES IPSA LOQUITUR—Cont'd
Unconscious victim, 101

RESCUERS
Comparative negligence and, 451
Contributory negligence of, 436
Duty owed to, 428
Professional rescuers, duty to, 484

RESPONDEAT SUPERIOR
See Vicarious Liability

RETRACTION
See Defamation

RISK
See Assumption of Risk, Insurance, Negligence

ROBINSON, GLEN
Excerpt on environmental liability, 389

ROSS, H. LAURENCE
Excerpt on insurance practices, 772

SCHAEFER, WALTER V.
Excerpt on libel, 969

SCHOOLS
See Duty, Education

SCHWARTZ, GARY
Excerpt on negligence history, 30

SEAT BELTS
Use of, 458

SLANDER
See Defamation

SOCIAL HOST LIABILITY
See Duty

SOCIAL INSURANCE
Accident proposals, 858

SOVEREIGN IMMUNITY
See Immunities

STATUTES
Accident compensation, New Zealand, 858
Alien Tort Claims Act, 879
"Black lung," 850
Civil, violation of, 151, 155
Civil Rights Act, 928
Civil Rights Law, New York, 1099
Comparative negligence, 441
Compliance, effect of, 83
Creating new duties, 151, 155
Criminal, violation of, 73, 156
Duty to rescue, Vermont, 155
False arrest, New York, 887
Federal Employers' Liability Act, 814
Federal Tort Claims Act, 249, 519
Jones Act, 815
Licensing statutes, effect of, 83
Longshoremen & Harbor Workers' Compensation Act, 815
National Childhood Vaccine Act, 844

STATUTES—Cont'd
Negligence, relation to, 73
New York Workers' Compensation Schedule, 810
No-fault acts,
    Massachusetts, 818
    New York, 821
Price–Anderson Act, 842
Privacy, New York, 1099
Products liability law, New Jersey, 600
Purpose of statute, 80
Superfund law, 845
Survival, 17
Swine Flu Act, 849
Uniform Comparative Fault Act, 441
Victim compensation, 872
Violence Against Women Act, 897
Wrongful death, 17

STRICT LIABILITY
See, also, Products Liability
Abnormally dangerous activity, generally, 510
Absolute liability distinguished, 9, 510
Airplanes, application to, 518
Common carriers, 511
Common law, role at, 30
Defamation, 966
Defenses, 519
Doctrinal development, 498
Economic theory, 531, 535
Environmental harm, 498, 511
Explosives, use of, 506
Federal Tort Claims Act and, 519
Independent contractors and, 501
Landowners, 498
Moral theories of, 532
Negligence, compared, 3
Restatement analysis, 510
Sale and service, 632
Theoretical perspectives, 520
Traditional, 498
Trespass, relation to, 502
Ultrahazardous activity, generally, 510

SUBROGATION
See, also, Insurance
Explained, 680

SURVIVAL ACTION
Origin of, 17

THIN SKULL PLAINTIFF
See Proximate Cause

TOXIC TORTS
See Environmental Harm

TRADE SECRET
See Competition

TANCREDI, LAURENCE R.,
Excerpt on medical malpractice no-fault, 853

TRESPASS
Generally, 652

TRESPASS—Cont'd
By children, 196
Liability of occupier to, 190
Nuisance compared, 653
On the case, 29, 33
Writ of, 29, 33

ULTRAHAZARDOUS ACTIVITY
See Strict Liability

UNFAIR COMPETITION
See Competition

VICARIOUS LIABILITY
See, also, Indemnity
Independent contractors, 24
Introduction to, 17
Justifications for, 17, 22
Liability for negligence of contractors, 27
Master and servant, 17
Fellow servant doctrine, 37
Parent and child, 56

WARNINGS
See, also, Medical Malpractice, Products
Liability
Adequacy of, 581, 585
Duty, 581
Intrinsic risk, 582
Physicians, by, 122
Preemption, 614
Safety Instructions, 581
Types, 581
Unexpected manner of use, 591

WARREN, SAMUEL D.
Excerpt on privacy, 1098

WEILER, PAUL
Excerpt on medical malpractice, 854

WORKERS' COMPENSATION
Administration of, 793
Benefits, 801
Compensable injuries, 797
Constitutionality of, 805
Coverage, conditions of, 795, 807
Disability defined, 803
Emotional distress, 799
Employers, suits against, 812
FELA distinguished, 814
Firefighters, 484
History of, 793, 805
Injury and disease, 798
Insurance arrangements, 806
Maritime workers, 815
New York statute, 810
Opting out of coverage, 812
Other remedies, relation to, 629
Railroad workers, 814
Third-party law suits, 629
Tort, meshed with, 629
Willful misconduct, 810

WRONGFUL BIRTH
Damages, 326

WRONGFUL DEATH
Emotional distress and, 282
Measurement of damages, 707
Origin of action for, 17

WRONGFUL LIFE
Damages, 326